Finding Your Way Around the Windows XP Start Menu

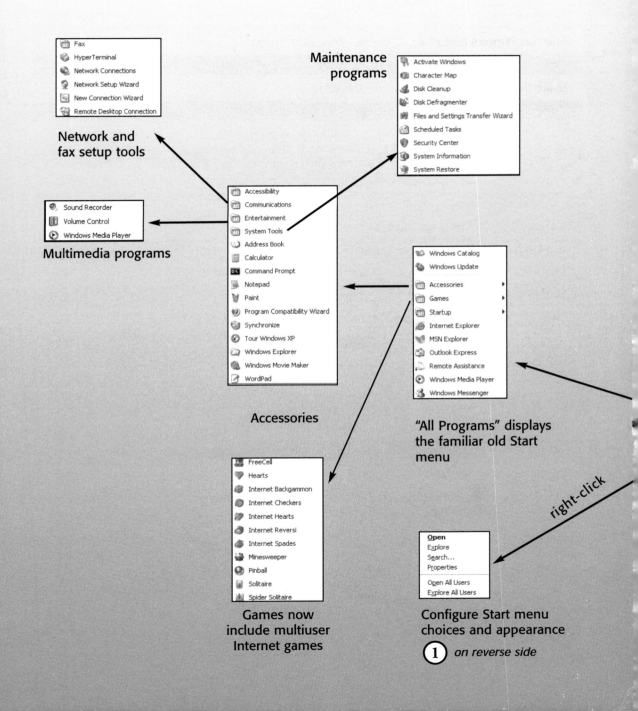

Fax
HyperTerminal
Network Connections
Network Setup Wizard
New Connection Wizard
Remote Desktop Connection

Network and fax setup tools

Maintenance programs

Activate Windows
Character Map
Disk Cleanup
Disk Defragmenter
Files and Settings Transfer Wizard
Scheduled Tasks
Security Center
System Information
System Restore

Sound Recorder
Volume Control
Windows Media Player

Multimedia programs

Accessibility
Communications
Entertainment
System Tools
Address Book
Calculator
Command Prompt
Notepad
Paint
Program Compatibility Wizard
Synchronize
Tour Windows XP
Windows Explorer
Windows Movie Maker
WordPad

Accessories

Windows Catalog
Windows Update
Accessories ▶
Games ▶
Startup ▶
Internet Explorer
MSN Explorer
Outlook Express
Remote Assistance
Windows Media Player
Windows Messenger

"All Programs" displays the familiar old Start menu

FreeCell
Hearts
Internet Backgammon
Internet Checkers
Internet Hearts
Internet Reversi
Internet Spades
Minesweeper
Pinball
Solitaire
Spider Solitaire

Games now include multiuser Internet games

right-click

Open
Explore
Search...
Properties
Open All Users
Explore All Users

Configure Start menu choices and appearance

(1) *on reverse side*

Set up users and passwords

Helpful wizards

Internet access

⑤ Control Panel

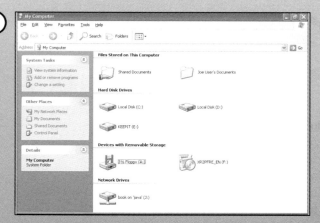

Network setup

Enable remote assistance

Windows and applications setup

Disk and computer management

Security Center is new!

Control Panel

The revamped Control Panel breaks operations into related categories. Switch to Classic View reverts to the old-style Control Panel, in case you're lost. Network and Internet Connections replaces the old Dial-up Networking window. Performance and Maintenance leads to many disk and system maintenance tools.

Bootup and crash recovery options

④ My Computer

My Computer

Lets you view drives, folders, and files on your computer. *Tip: Choose Folders, View, Details to easily check how much free space you have on each disk drive.* Click the Folders button in the toolbar to see a handy tree-view of your computer's contents in the left pane.

n of your XP sys-
. The Computer
etwork workgroup
ections to your
ce.

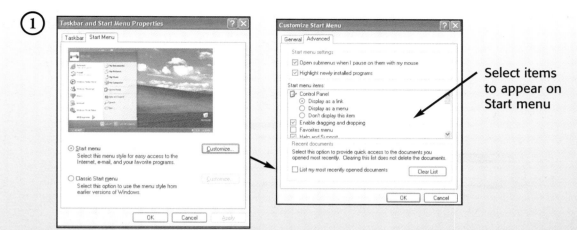

① **Taskbar and Start Menu Properties**

Select items to appear on Start menu

Taskbar and Start Menu Properties

Sets the look of Windows XP (to classic or XP) and selects which items appear on the Start menu. The Taskbar tabs control the behavior of the taskbar and notification area, such as "autohide." Click the Customize button and then the Advanced tab to add items to the Start menu, such as My Network Places.

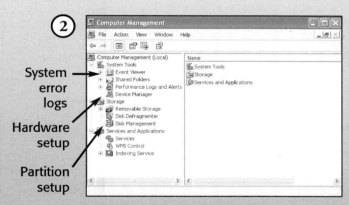

②

System error logs

Hardware setup

Partition setup

Computer Management

Powerful interface to investigate and manage system details. Device Manager lets you check inventory on your hardware installation and change settings; Event Viewer shows system and application errors; Disk Management is useful for partitioning and error-checking drive volumes.

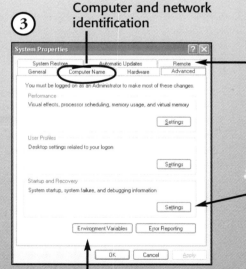

③ Computer and network identification

Set environment variables

System Properties

Seven tabs here control the global operatio[n] tem, startup, shutdown, and crash recover[y] Name tab sets your computer's name and [...] membership. The Remote tab enables con[...] computer from afar using Remote Assistan[ce]

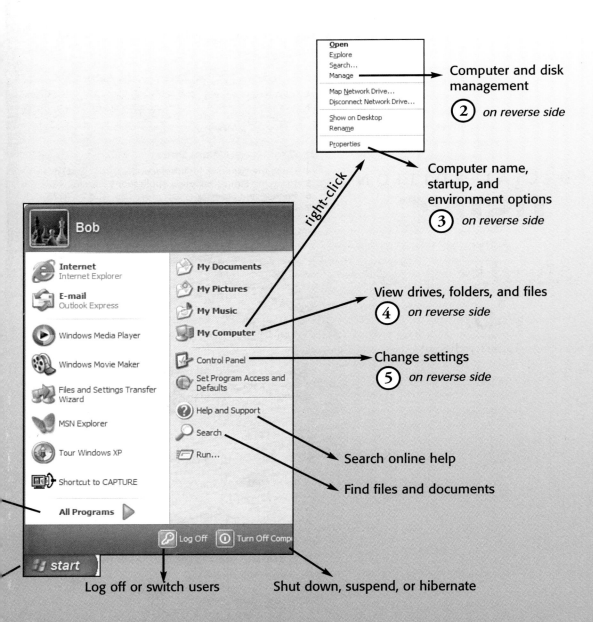

The Windows XP Start menu is the starting point for using and configuring your computer. If you are moving to Windows XP from Windows 95, 98, Me, NT, or 2000, you'll find that many of the important dialog boxes, programs, and maintenance tools have been moved, and many are difficult to find. You'll find this map a useful reference for quickly finding your way around XP.

This map shows you how to get from the Start menu to various control panels, configuration dialog boxes, and menus. Items that are marked with circled numbers lead to more detailed descriptions on the reverse side of this tear-out card.

SPECIAL EDITION

USING

Microsoft®

Windows XP Home

Third Edition

Robert Cowart

Brian Knittel

800 East 96th Street
Indianapolis, Indiana 46240

SPECIAL EDITION USING MICROSOFT® WINDOWS XP HOME, THIRD EDITION

Copyright © 2005 by Que Publishing

International Standard Book Number: 0-7897-3279-3

Library of Congress Catalog Card Number: 2004111336

Printed in the United States of America

First printing: November 2004

07   06   05   04   4   3   2   1

Trademarks

Warning and Disclaimer

Bulk Sales

Que Publishing offers excellent discounts on this book when ordered in quantity for bulk purchases or special sales. For more information, please contact

U.S. Corporate and Government Sales
1-800-382-3419
corpsales@pearsontechgroup.com

For sales outside of the United States, please contact

International Sales
international@pearsoned.com

Publisher
Paul Boger

Associate Publisher
Greg Wiegand

Executive Editor
Rick Kughen

Development Editor
Todd Brakke

Managing Editor
Charlotte Clapp

Project Editor
Andy Beaster

Indexer
John Sleeva

Proofreader
Susan Eldridge

Technical Editor
Mark Reddin

Publishing Coordinator
Sharry Lee Gregory

Multimedia Developer
Dan Scherf

Book Designer
Anne Jones

CONTENTS

IV Networking

VI System Administration and Maintenance

VII Appendixes

About the Authors

Robert Cowart has written more than 40 books on computer programming and applications, with more than a dozen on Windows. His titles include *Windows NT Unleashed*, *Mastering Windows 98*, *Windows NT Server Administrator's Bible*, and *Windows NT Server 4.0: No Experience Required*. Several of his books have been best-sellers in their category and have been translated into more than 20 languages. He has written on a wide range of computer-related topics for such magazines as *PC Week*, *PC World*, *PC Magazine*, *PC Tech Journal*, *Mac World*, and *Microsoft Systems Journal*. In addition to working as a freelance consultant specializing in small businesses, he has taught programming classes at the University of California Extension in San Francisco. He has also appeared as a special guest on the PBS TV series *Computer Chronicles*, CNN's Headline News, ZD-TV's *The Screen Savers*, and ABC's *World News Tonight with Peter Jennings*. He is president and co-founder of Brainsville.com, a company specializing in creating multimedia training materials. Robert resides in Berkeley, California.

In his spare time he is involved in the music world, presenting chamber music concerts and playing classical piano. He also is a teacher of the Transcendental Meditation technique and meditates regularly in hopes of rewiring his inner computer.

Brian Knittel has been a software developer for more than 25 years. After doing graduate work in medical imaging technologies, he began a career as an independent consultant. An eclectic mix of clients has led to long-term projects in medical documentation; workflow management; real-time industrial system control; and, most importantly, more than 15 years of real-world experience with MS-DOS, Windows, and computer networking in the business world. He has written *Windows XP Under the Hood: Hardcore Scripting and Command Line Power*, coauthored *Special Edition Using Microsoft Windows XP Professional* and *Special Edition Using Microsoft Windows 2000 Professional*, and contributed to several of Bob Cowart's other Windows books. Brian lives in Albany, California, halfway between the tidal wave zone and the earthquake fault. He spends his free time restoring antique computers (check out www.ibm1130.org) and trying to perfect his wood-fired pizza recipes.

About the Contributors

Elaine Kreston has a natural affinity for helping others solve computer problems. This talent was discovered while procrastinating from her real job, that of a professional cellist.

Mark Edward Soper has been a PC user for 18 years and has been a computer trainer and technical writer since 1988. Author of more than 150 magazine articles and several books, including *The Complete Idiot's Guide to High-Speed Internet Connections* and *TechTV's Upgrading Your PC*, he also has written frequently about Windows from version 3.1 to Windows XP. He lives in Evansville, Indiana, where he enjoys researching the history of transportation.

James Michael Stewart has been writing about Microsoft, the Internet, and certification for nearly 7 years. Michael has contributed to more than 75 books in this area. His technical interests include IT certification, Windows, security, and the Internet. Michael also is an instructor at Networld+Interop. He spends his spare time learning to do everything, one hobby at a time.

Will Schmied (BSET, MCSE 2000, MCSA, CWNA, Server+, Network+, A+) is a freelance consultant and technical writer. Will has contributed works to several of the Internet's largest IT Web sites, including MCPMag.com, TCPMag.com, TechRepublic.com, CertCities.com, Cramsession.com, ISAServer.org, and MSExchange.org. Will has also worked on books for several publishers, including Que, Osborne/McGraw-Hill, and Syngress, in addition to writing several print magazine articles.

Will earned a bachelor's degree in engineering technology from Old Dominion University. He currently resides in Newport News, Virginia, with his wife Allison, their children Christopher, Austin, Andrea, and Hannah, and their pets Peanut and Squeaky. When he is not busy playing with the latest in technologies, you can usually find Will trying to improve his bowling average or logging some serious time on Dungeon Siege.

You can visit Will at www.netserverworld.com or www.soitslikethat.com.

DEDICATION

To my teacher and friend, Adyashanti, for his tireless dedication to those who are intent on discovering who they are. —Bob

To my friend Frank Banks, who has taught me so much about courage, growth, compassion, and snowboarding. —Brian

ACKNOWLEDGMENTS

This book, as much as the product it covers, is the result of a team effort. We couldn't have produced this without the great team at Que, the assistance of contributing writers, the patience and support of our friends, and so on....

We feel privileged to be part of the consistently professional *Special Edition Using* family. Producing these highly technical, state-of-the art books requires a dedicated and knowledgeable staff, and once again the staff at Que did an amazing job. Executive Editor Rick Kughen has provided unflagging, cheerful support and guidance through our three *SE Using* volumes and three editions. Our development editor, Todd Brakke, pored over every word on every page of this volume and our equally weighty Windows XP Professional book and offered invaluable direction and tuning. This is a much better book than it would have been without him.

We'd like to acknowledge the efforts of our technical editor: Mark Reddin. We also would like to thank the editorial, indexing, layout, art, proofing, and other production staff at Que—Andy Beaster, John Sleeva, Susan Eldridge, and Tim Osborn. These folks labor away largely unseen and often unthanked. You did a marvelous job.

No book could make it to market without the real-world personal relationships developed between booksellers on the one hand and the sales and marketing personnel back at the publishers. We've had the opportunity to meet sales and marketing folks in the computer publishing world and know what a difficult job selling and keeping up with the thousands of computer titles can be. Thanks to all of you for your pivotal role in helping us pay our mortgages!

Finally, we should acknowledge those who made it possible for us to get through the months of writing. Bob first thanks his agents, Chris Van Buren and Danielle Jatlow, for standing by him with encouragement on down days and sharing his excitement after his successes. Many thanks for fighting for better contracts, keeping things in perspective, and phoning in long distance (even from Brazil!) for conference calls. And, as always, thanks to friends and family who, even though they're used to seeing him disappear for months on end, let him back in the fold when it's over. Also thanks to Homer the cat for his companionship.

Brian adds special thanks to Bryce Carter for guidance, and his friends and family for patience and support.

WE WANT TO HEAR FROM YOU!

As the reader of this book, *you* are our most important critic and commentator. We value your opinion and want to know what we're doing right, what we could do better, what areas you'd like to see us publish in, and any other words of wisdom you're willing to pass our way.

As an associate publisher for Que Publishing, I welcome your comments. You can email or write me directly to let me know what you did or didn't like about this book—as well as what we can do to make our books better.

Please note that I cannot help you with technical problems related to the topic of this book. We do have a User Services group, however, where I will forward specific technical questions related to the book.

When you write, please be sure to include this book's title and authors as well as your name, email address, and phone number. I will carefully review your comments and share them with the authors and editors who worked on the book.

Email: feedback@quepublishing.com

Mail: Greg Wiegand
         Associate Publisher
         Que Publishing
         800 East 96th Street
         Indianapolis, IN 46240 USA

For more information about this book or another Que Publishing title, visit our Web site at www.quepublishing.com. Type the ISBN (excluding hyphens) or the title of a book in the Search field to find the page you're looking for.

INTRODUCTION

In this introduction

WELCOME

Thank you for purchasing or considering the purchase of *Special Edition Using Microsoft®
Windows XP Home, Third Edition*. It's amazing the changes that nearly 20 years can bring to
a computer product such as Windows. When we wrote our first Windows book back in the
mid-1980s, our publisher didn't even think the book would sell well enough to print more
than 5,000 copies. Microsoft stock wasn't even a blip on most investors' radar screens. Boy,
were they wrong! Who could have imagined that a little more than a decade later, anyone
who hoped to get hired for even a temp job in a small office would need to know how to
use Microsoft Windows, Office, and a PC. Eighteen or so Windows books later, we're still
finding new and exciting stuff to tell our readers.

Some people (including the U.S. Department of Justice) claim Microsoft's predominance on
the PC operating system arena was won unethically through monopolistic practices.
Whether this is true (we're going to stay out of the politics in this book), we believe
Windows has earned its position today through reasons other than having a stranglehold on
the market. Consider that Windows NT 3.1 had 5 million lines of code. Windows XP
weighs in with more than 30 million. This represents a lot of work, by anyone's accounting.
Who could have imagined in 1985 that any decent operating system two decades later must
have support for so many technologies that didn't even exist at the time: CD-ROM, DVD,
CD-R and CD-RW, Internet and intranet, MP3, MPEG, DV, USB, FireWire, PPoE,
802.11g, Bluetooth, APM, ACPI, RAID, email and newsgroup clients, UPS, fault tolerance,
disk encryption and compression…? The list goes on. And could we have imagined that a
Microsoft Certified System Engineer certificate (MCSE) would prove as lucrative as a medical or law degree?

Although rarely on the bleeding edge of technology, and often taking the role of the dicta-
tor, Bill Gates has at least been benevolent from the users' point of view. In 1981, when we
were building our first computers, the operating system (CP/M) had to be modified in
assembly language and recompiled and hardware parts had to be soldered together to make
almost any new addition (such as a video display terminal) work. Virtually nothing was standardized, with the end result being that computers remained out of reach for average citizens.

Together, Microsoft and IBM changed all that. Today, you can purchase a computer,
printer, scanner, Zip drive, keyboard, modem, monitor, and video card over the Internet;
plug them in; and install Windows, and they'll probably all work together. The creation and
adoption (and sometimes forcing) of hardware and software standards that have made the
PC a household appliance the world over can largely be credited to Microsoft, like it or not.
The unifying glue of this PC revolution has been Windows.

Yes, we all love to hate Windows, but it's here to stay. Linux is on the rise, but for most of
us—at least for some time—Windows and Windows applications are where it's at. And
Windows XP ushers in truly significant changes to the landscape. That's why we were
excited to write this book.

This book covers Windows XP Home Edition as well as the latest upgrade to XP, which is called Service Pack 2 (SP2). SP2 adds significant new security features to Windows XP and its accessory programs such as Internet Explorer and Outlook Express.

WHY THIS BOOK?

We all know this book will make a hefty doorstop in a few years. You probably have a few already. (We've even written a few!) If you think it contains more information than you need, just remember that it can serve as a reference that will be there as you grow into this product. And we all know that computer technology changes so fast that it's sometimes easier just to blink and ignore a phase than to study up on it. Windows XP Home Edition is definitely a significant upgrade in Windows technology and one you'll need to understand. Microsoft has folded all its operating systems into the Windows XP product line, so rest assured it will be around for some time.

On the surface, Windows XP might look like Windows 98 and Windows Me, but it's a completely different animal. From the way users sign on, to the new Start menu, to its day-to-day management tools, XP bears little resemblance to its predecessors. Don't let that worry you: In all ways, it's superior to any operating system Microsoft has ever produced.

Is Windows XP so easy to use that books are unnecessary? Unfortunately, no. True, as with other releases of Windows, online help is available. As has been the case ever since Windows 95, however, no printed documentation is available (to save Microsoft the cost), and the Help files are written by the Microsoft cronies. You won't find criticisms, complaints, workarounds, or talk of third-party programs there.

You might know that Windows XP comes in two versions: Home Edition and Professional. These are very similar versions of the same fundamental operating system, and all the same applications and utilities are present in both. The Home Edition, though, has a simpler management scheme and omits advanced networking features that are used only in corporate networks. Following suit, we've produced two books. This one was written to address you, a user of XP Home Edition, specifically. Other publishers have produced combined volumes to cover both operating systems, but we think that will only confuse readers. We wanted you to have a book that discusses only the Windows version you'll be working with and focuses on the needs of the home and small home-office user. We assume you are not a corporate techno-geek, and we'll do our best to speak in plain English and not snow you with jargon.

In this book's many pages, we focus not just on the gee-whiz side of the technology, but why you should care, what you can get from it, and what you can forget about. The lead author on this book has previously written 18 books about Windows, all in plain English (several best-sellers), designed for everyone from rank beginners to full-on system administrators deploying NT Server domains. The coauthor has designed software and networks for more than 25 years. We work with and write about various versions of Windows year in and year out. We have a clear understanding of what confuses users and system administrators about installing, configuring, and using Windows, as well as (we hope) how to best convey the solutions to our readers.

This book is now in its third edition and builds on the experience we've gained over the years since XP's initial release. We spent many months adding coverage of new Windows features, testing Windows XP service pack betas through numerous builds, participating in the Microsoft beta newsgroups, documenting and working through bugs, and installing and reinstalling Windows XP on a variety of networks and computers. The result is what you hold in your hands.

While writing this book, we tried to stay vigilant of four cardinal rules:

- Keep it practical.
- Keep it accurate.
- Keep it concise.
- Keep it interesting, and even crack a joke or two.

We believe that you will find this to be the best book available on Windows XP Home Edition for the intermediate to advanced user. While writing it, we targeted an audience ranging from the power user in the small home office to the support guru in a major corporation. Whether you use a Windows XP PC at home or work, or support others who do, this book covers it all.

We're also willing to tell you what we don't cover. No book can do it all. As the title implies, this book is about Windows XP *Home Edition*. We don't cover the advanced networking features of Windows XP Professional, nor the various Server versions of this operating system called Windows Server 2003, Advanced Server, and Datacenter. However, we do tell you how to connect to and interact with other operating systems, including MacOS, Linux, and older variants of Windows over a local area network. And, due to space limitations, there is only passing coverage of Windows XP's command-line utilities, batch file language, and Windows Script Host. For that (in spades!), pick up a copy of Brian's book *Windows XP Under the Hood: Hardcore Scripting and Command Line Power*, also published by Que. Finally, if you feel you've earned a graduation from the knowledge found in this book, be sure to check out our *Platinum Edition Using Microsoft Windows XP* (published by Que, of course).

We worked hard not to assume too much knowledge on your part, yet we didn't want to assume you aren't already experienced with Windows. The working assumption here is that you are already conversant at least with some form of Windows. However, we provide a primer on the Windows XP interface because the look and feel of Windows XP is significantly different from its predecessors. Even when you've become a Windows XP pro, we think you'll find this book to be a valuable source of reference information in the future. Both the table of contents and the very complete index will provide easy means for locating information when you need it quickly.

How Our Book Is Organized

Although this book advances logically from beginning to end, it's written so you can jump in at any location, get the information you need quickly, and get out. You don't have to read it from start to finish, nor do you need to work through complex tutorials.

This book is broken down into six major parts. Here's the skinny on each one:

Part I, "Introducing Windows XP Home Edition," introduces Windows XP and explains its features, new screen elements (GUI), and the design and architecture behind Windows XP. It then explains how to ready your hardware and software for installation of XP and describes the installation process itself.

Part II, "Getting Your Work Done," is, well, about getting your work done. Perhaps the bulk of readers will want to study and keep on hand this part as a reference guide. Here, we cover using the interface, running programs, organizing documents, sharing data between applications, printing and faxing documents, and managing fonts. We also cover how to best work with the increasingly popular plethora of digital imaging tools and formats encountered with digital photography and nonlinear video editing in your PC.

Part III, "Windows XP and the Internet," introduces you to Windows XP networking, Internet style. We start with Internet connection options and then move on to the supplied Internet tools. We provide in-depth coverage of Outlook Express for mail and newsgroups, Internet Explorer for Web surfing, Windows Messenger for audio and videoconferencing, and the new security features these program gained in Service Pack 2. We also have included sections on Internet diagnostic utilities such as ping and ipconfig.

Part IV, "Networking," deals with networking on the LAN. Here, we explain the fundamentals of networking and walk you through planning and installing a functional LAN in your home or office. We cover the use of a Windows XP network; give you a chapter on dial-up, remote, and portable networking; and finish up with crucial security tips and troubleshooting advice that the Windows Help files don't cover. This section also covers the updated Windows Firewall and Windows XP's Remote Desktop and Remote Assistance features, and it shows you how to set up a secure, shared Internet connection for your home LAN.

Part V, "System Configuration and Customization," covers system configuration and maintenance. We tell you how to work with Control Panel applets, provide tips and tricks for customizing the graphical user interface to maximize efficiency, and describe a variety of ways to upgrade your hardware and system software (including third-party programs) for maximum performance.

Part VI, "System Administration and Maintenance," dives even deeper into system administration and configuration, with coverage of supplied system administration tools such as the Microsoft Management Console (MMC) and its plug-ins. We also provide techniques for managing multiple users; means for managing the hard disk, including multiple file system formats such as FAT32 and NTFS; and details on setting up multiboot machines with

Windows 9x, DOS, Linux, and Windows 2000. We cap off this part with coverage of the Windows Registry and a chapter on troubleshooting and repairing problems with your Windows XP installation.

Finally in the book's last chapter, we decided to briefly introduce and cover another flavor of Windows that is garnering a lot of attention: Windows Media Center Edition (MCE). Even if you don't have an MCE-based computer, you'll want to check out this chapter to learn what MCE is and what it can do. If you *do* have an MCE computer, you'll find some tips on how to take control of the digital video recorder to watch TV on your large-screen projector without commercials, how to run captivating slideshows of your digital pictures, how to burn DVDs of movies and TV shows you record, and how to organize your MP3 files. You'll even learn how to build an MCE computer.

Appendix A, "Installing Service Pack 2," covers installation of Service Pack 2, and Appendix B, "New Features in Service Pack 2," describes the changes SP2 brings, with cross references to coverage of its new features throughout the book.

What's on the CD?

We've made a 45-minute CD-ROM–based video presentation, so not only can we tell you how to use and manage Windows XP, but we can actually demonstrate specific skills so you can learn more quickly. We show you how to get around the new XP interface as well as how to set up a simple network—one of XP Home's strengths. You'll want to be sure to check this out and meet the authors.

Conventions Used in This Book

Special conventions are used throughout this book to help you get the most from the book and from Windows XP Home Edition.

Text Conventions

Various typefaces in this book identify terms and other special objects. These special typefaces include the following:

Type	Meaning
Italic	New terms or phrases when initially defined
Monospace	Information that appears in code or onscreen
Bold monospace	Information you type

Words Separated by Commas

All Windows book publishers struggle with how to represent command sequences when menus and dialog boxes are involved. In this book, we separate commands using a comma. Yeah, we know it's confusing, but this is traditionally how the *Special Edition Using* book series does it, and traditions die hard. So, for example, the instruction "select Edit, Cut" means you should open the Edit menu and select Cut. Another, more complex example would be "click Start, Settings, Control Panel, System, Hardware, Device Manager."

Key combinations are represented with a plus sign. For example, if the text calls for you to press Ctrl+Alt+Delete, you would press the Ctrl, Alt, and Delete keys at the same time.

TIPS FROM THE WINDOWS PROS

Ever wonder how the experts get their work done better and faster than anyone else? Ever wonder how they became experts in the first place? You'll find out in these special sections throughout the book. We've spent a lot of time under the Windows hood, so to speak, getting dirty and learning what makes Windows XP tick. So, with the information we provide in these sections, you can roll up your shirt sleeves and dig in.

SPECIAL ELEMENTS

Throughout this book, you'll find notes, cautions, sidebars, cross-references, and troubleshooting tips. Often, you'll find just the tidbit you need to get through a rough day at the office or the one whiz-bang trick that will make you the office hero. You'll also find little nuggets of wisdom, humor, and lingo you can use to amaze your friends and family—not to mention making you cocktail-party literate.

TIPS

TIP

> We specially designed these tips to showcase the best of the best. Just because you get your work done doesn't mean you're doing it in the fastest, easiest way possible. We'll show you how to maximize your Windows experience. Don't miss these tips!

NOTES

NOTE

> Notes point out items you should be aware of, but you can skip them if you're in a hurry. Generally, we've added notes as a way to give you some extra information on a topic without weighing you down.

CAUTIONS

CAUTION

> Pay attention to cautions! They could save you precious hours in lost work. Don't say we didn't warn you.

TROUBLESHOOTING NOTES

 We designed these elements to call attention to common pitfalls you're likely to encounter. When you see a troubleshooting note, you can flip to the end of the chapter to learn how to solve or avoid a problem.

CROSS-REFERENCES

Cross-references are designed to point you to other locations in this book (or other books in the Que family) that will provide supplemental or supporting information. Cross-references appear as follows:

→ For information on updating offline Web pages, see "Browsing Offline," **p. 295**.

SIDEBARS

Sidebars
Sidebars are designed to provide information that is ancillary to the topic being discussed. Read this information if you want to learn more details about an application or a task.

INTRODUCING WINDOWS XP HOME EDITION

INTRODUCING WINDOWS XP HOME EDITION

In this chapter

1

AN OVERVIEW OF WINDOWS XP HOME EDITION

Windows XP Home Edition is the first home-oriented version of Windows that is no longer built on the creaky foundation of Windows 9x (and thus no longer contains any native MS-DOS code!). As the name suggests, Windows XP Home Edition is the home-oriented member of the Windows XP family, the first Windows family to combine home-oriented and business-oriented releases of Windows into a single product family.

The goal that Microsoft had in mind for Windows XP Home Edition was an ambitious one: to create an easy-to-use, reliable operating system whose features would appeal to home users with the latest PCs, while providing application and hardware compatibility with products made for older versions of Windows, and even MS-DOS game and graphics applications. And, to stop the wasteful and confusing development of two distinctly different versions of Windows, which required different device drivers (the software that makes your hardware work) and utilities (the software that fixes problems), Windows XP Home Edition had to share the same underlying software instructions as the rest of the Windows XP family.

It's a tough job, but Windows XP Home Edition meets these requirements quite well. Windows XP Home Edition combines improved versions of the multimedia and crash-recovery features pioneered by Windows 98 and Windows Me with the reliability of Windows 2000. Because you're likely to be using a mixture of older and newer hardware and software, Windows XP Home Edition is designed to work much better than Windows 2000 did with older Windows (and even DOS-based) software, while still supporting the latest games and educational, recreational, and productivity programs from Microsoft and other publishers.

A LITTLE WINDOWS HISTORY

As you surely know, Windows is a *graphical user interface (GUI)* and *operating system (OS)* that is the heart and soul of your computer. While Windows was once a toy (I remember when people bought Windows mainly because of the graphical word processor and paint program it included), it's now an essential element in your computing experience.

When Windows first hit the market in 1985, it was actually a shell that sat upon the increasingly shaky foundations of MS-DOS (see Figure 1.1). Early versions were frequently used as menuing systems for launching MS-DOS programs, as programs that required Windows were quite scarce for several years.

As you can see, Windows 1.0 left a lot to be desired. Or, put another way, there was a lot of room for growth. Most PC screens didn't show color at the time, so it's in black and white. In Figure 1.1, you see the Windows Executive, which was the central (and only) place from which you ran programs and managed your files.

Figure 1.1
Notice that there were scary, non-user–friendly error messages, even back in the old days.

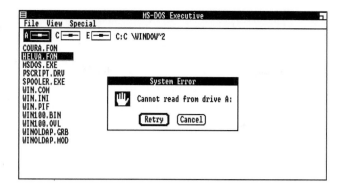

Windows didn't really take off until the introduction of Windows 3.0 in 1990 (it could multitask both DOS and Windows programs if you used a 386 or 486 processor) and Windows 3.1 in 1992, which introduced TrueType scalable fonts. Windows for Workgroups 3.1 (1992) and 3.11 (1994) pioneered the built-in networking features that would typify all subsequent versions of Windows up to the present. Windows for Workgroups 3.11 was the last version of Windows to require that MS-DOS or a comparable text-based operating system be present at installation time.

Although Windows 95, Windows 98, and Windows Me no longer required MS-DOS, they still used an improved form of DOS for some operations. This dependence upon MS-DOS made for an increasingly unstable operating system because the management tricks necessary to keep MS-DOS, old 16-bit Windows applications, and new 32-bit Windows programs running on the same hardware at the same time led to frequent reboots and system lockups. Although many of the features pioneered by Windows 9x and Windows Me have been retained and enhanced in Windows XP, Windows XP is not a true descendent of DOS-based Windows.

Instead, the Windows XP family is the latest descendent of the "other" Windows family: a family of Windows products which do not use MS-DOS as a foundation. Microsoft's development of a non–DOS-based operating system goes back to 1987 and the joint development (with IBM) of a Windows replacement called OS/2. OS/2 was aimed squarely at the emerging corporate network world then dominated by Novell and its NetWare network operating system.

Unlike NetWare, Microsoft and IBM's OS/2 was designed to handle both the server and the desktop side of network computing. Unfortunately for OS/2, the IBM-Microsoft partnership broke up in 1991 after a series of disagreements about the direction of OS/2. IBM kept OS/2, while Microsoft stuck with Windows. Microsoft had already begun the development of Windows NT in October 1988 with the hiring of Dave Cutler, who had developed the VMS (Virtual Memory System) operating system for Digital Equipment (DEC)'s line of VAX multitasking and multiuser computers.

The development of Windows NT took several years: the first version to reach retail shelves, Windows NT 3.1, was introduced in mid-1993. Windows NT introduced several features common to all its successors, including Windows 2000 and Windows XP:

- **Preemptive multitasking**—The user doesn't need to wait for one task to finish before starting another one.

- **Client/server model for computing**—The operating system is divided up into two parts, just as with mainframe systems.

- **Dynamic disk caching/virtual memory**—The operating system can use more than one drive as virtual memory (using disk space in place of RAM); desktop Windows versions up through Windows Me can use only one drive for virtual memory.

- **Fault tolerance features**—The ability to handle power outages and disk crashes.

- **Capability to start and stop network services without rebooting**.

- **Fully 32-bit architecture**—Windows NT and its successors are free from the limitations of 16-bit Windows (and MS-DOS!) instructions.

Windows NT 4.0, introduced in mid-1996, was modeled after the Windows 95 user interface (instead of the Windows 3.1 user interface used by earlier Windows NT versions), and provided crash protection superior to that of Windows 95. However, it lacked support for Plug and Play, the easy hardware installation feature introduced by Windows 95, and many Windows 95-compatible hardware devices wouldn't work with Windows NT 4.0.

Windows 2000, introduced in early 2000, was originally called NT 5.0 during its prerelease period, and began the NT family's move toward becoming more user-friendly. Many of Windows 2000's features have become part of Windows XP Home Edition, including *Plug-and-Play* hardware support, *ACPI* power management, support for *USB* and *IEEE-1394* ports and devices, *AGP* video, *Internet Connection Sharing*, and enhanced system management.

Windows XP Home Edition can be fairly described as a combination of the security and stability of Windows 2000 and the multimedia and entertainment features of Windows Me.

WHAT'S NEW IN WINDOWS XP?

Now that you know Windows XP's family history, you're ready to find out what new features Windows XP brings to the Windows family. One of the questions people ask me as I write books about each new version of Windows is whether the new version is different enough to justify upgrading. The Windows XP family is a major upgrade from any previous version of Windows, and the jump from Windows 98 or Windows Me to Windows XP Home Edition is as massive a jump as the one from Windows 3.1 to Windows 95 was a few years ago. Windows XP Home Edition isn't just a much-improved version of the Windows 2000 family with new features added for home users (and corporate-only features pruned away), but is also a full replacement for the long-lived Windows 9x/Me family.

How big a change is Windows XP? Estimates are that by the time it was released, it contained about 40 million lines of code (see Table 1.1). That's over one-third more code than its immediate predecessor, Windows 2000, and plenty of room for its new and enhanced features.

TABLE 1.1 LINES OF CODE COMPARISON

Operating System	Lines of Programming Code
Windows NT 3.1	6.5 million
Windows NT 3.5	10 million
Windows 95	10 million
Windows 98	13 million
NT 4	16.5 million
Windows 2000	~29 million
Windows 2000 Advanced Server	~33 million
Windows 2000 Datacenter	>40 million
Windows XP	~40 million

Windows XP is much bigger than Windows 2000 because it adds new multimedia and entertainment features absent from Windows 2000 Professional. It also contains improvements to features carried over from Windows 2000.

Because Windows XP Home Edition offers so many improvements and new features when compared to Windows 98 and Windows Me, in this section we'll highlight some of the new and improved features and what each feature does. Table 1.2 highlights some of the key improvements found in Windows XP Home Edition and points you to the chapter in which it is covered.

TABLE 1.2 COVERAGE OF NEW AND IMPROVED WINDOWS XP HOME EDITION FEATURES

Feature	Covered in Chapter
New setup process	3
New interface: My Documents, My Pictures, My Music, custom toolbars, intelligent Menus, new help system, search function	4
Multimedia improvements: DVD, DirectX 8.1, image color management, scanner and digital camera support, Windows Movie Maker 2, Windows Media Player 9, CD burning, Web Publishing	4, 6, 7, 21
Wizard Hardware support: Plug and Play, multiple monitors, FireWire	27

continues

TABLE 1.2   CONTINUED

Feature	Covered in Chapter
Active Directory	14, 16
Enhanced Web browsing and security with IE 6	9
Safer email and news reader with Outlook Express 6	11
Security Center	19
Change default "middleware" programs	22
Improved mobile support and power management	17
New Microsoft Management Console (MMC)	22
Improved Installer/Remover	21
Internet Connection sharing	18
Fast User Switching	25
NetMeeting	12
Windows Messenger	12
Remote Assistance	30
Files and Settings Transfer Wizard	25
System Restore	30
Network Setup Wizard	15
System File Protection	30
Windows Firewall	19
Credential Manager	19
Task Manager	23
Personalized Welcome Screen	25
Taskbar Grouping	21
File Management	4
Compatibility Mode	23
Dual View	27
ClearType	4
Windows Help	30
Device Driver Rollback	30
Home Networking Wizard	15
Network Bridging	18
Internet gaming	5

INTERFACE IMPROVEMENTS

Windows XP definitely is the best-looking version of Windows ever, but the improvements are more than just skin-deep. Windows XP takes full advantage of today's widespread support for high-resolution, 24-bit (16.8 million color) displays to provide subtle shading and animation effects to make working easier, but it also provides a more intelligent and customizable interface compared to previous Windows versions.

STARTUP AND START MENU IMPROVEMENTS

After you get to the splash screen, Windows XP Home Edition looks like no other Windows version. Before the splash screen loads, pressing F8 brings up a troubleshooting options menu that most closely resembles the one provided for Windows 2000, although Windows 9x/Me users will also find it familiar. This Advanced Options menu lets you boot into alternative modes such as "safe mode" to do troubleshooting (see Figure 1.2). Normal boot processes display a splash screen that is more compact than the previous full-screen one used by Windows 9x/Me and has an easy-to-see progress bar in the middle of the screen.

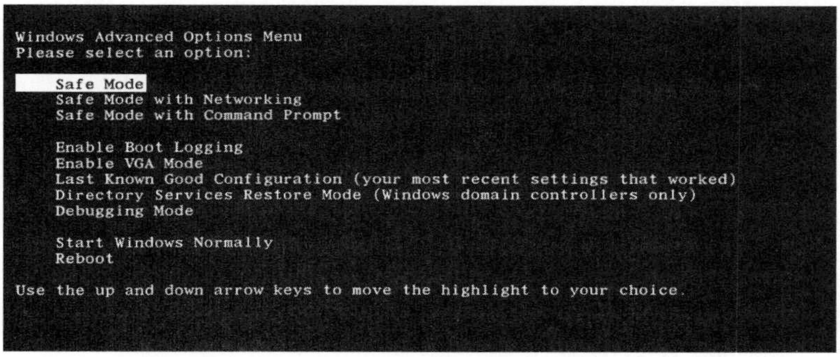

Figure 1.2
New startup options in Windows XP Home Edition offer various troubleshooting options if you simply press F8 at boot time.

```
Windows Advanced Options Menu
Please select an option:

    Safe Mode
    Safe Mode with Networking
    Safe Mode with Command Prompt

    Enable Boot Logging
    Enable VGA Mode
    Last Known Good Configuration (your most recent settings that worked)
    Directory Services Restore Mode (Windows domain controllers only)
    Debugging Mode

    Start Windows Normally
    Reboot

Use the up and down arrow keys to move the highlight to your choice.
```

The Windows XP Home Edition Start menu makes it easier to use the most popular programs. It shows you the major new features, and a link called All Programs displays the rest of the programs ready for your use.

If you need help through the Internet or email, or with your system's configuration, the Start menu items Control Panel, Help and Support, Internet Explorer, and Outlook Express are all available as soon as you click the Start button.

Right-click on the taskbar, select Properties, Start Menu, Customize, and you can control the appearance of the Start menu and the programs and features that will be displayed (see Figure 1.3).

Figure 1.3
Customize your Start menu by selecting the number of popular program shortcuts, icon sizes, and default Web browser and email programs.

Select large icons for better visibility, or small icons to show more programs at a time. By default, the Start menu displays the six programs you use most often, but you can set the number or clear the list of programs. By default, Internet Explorer is displayed as the standard Web browser, and Outlook Express is the standard email program, but you can remove them from the Start menu or choose alternatives you've installed.

Click Advanced to specify other Start menu features (see Figure 1.4), including

■ Disabling such features as submenus opening when you pause over them

Figure 1.4
The Advanced dialog box lets you choose which Windows XP folders and tools to display on the Start menu, which display options to use, and other customizations.

- Disabling the highlighting of newly installed programs until you run them for the first time
- Whether to display the Control Panel, Favorites menu, Help and Support, My Computer, My Documents, My Music, My Network Places, My Pictures, Network Connections, Printers and Faxes, Run command, Search, and System Administration tools

You also can select whether to scroll the programs menu, select how to display some menu items, and whether to display recently opened documents. Figure 1.5 shows a typical menu on a Windows XP Home Edition system.

As you can see in Figure 1.5, the menu also adapts to your recent selections, placing shortcuts to the last six programs into the blank space at the left side of the Start menu, as discussed earlier in this section.

The following is the rundown of a few other interface niceties which are new or improved, especially if you previously used Windows 9x or Windows Me:

- **My Music**—A new My Music folder has been added for MP3 and WMA digital music files you download or create. You can play the music in this folder by clicking the Play All button, and shop for more music online. This complements the My Documents and My Pictures folders for unified storage of all types of media files.

Figure 1.5
The Windows XP main menu on a typical system. As you use different programs, the contents of the lower-left side of the menu will vary.

- **Customizable toolbars**—You can drag toolbars, such as the Web address toolbar, around on the desktop or add them to the taskbar at the bottom of the screen.

Additional personalized Start menu and taskbar settings are available from the Taskbar Properties dialog box shown in Figure 1.6 (right-click the Taskbar and choose Properties).

Figure 1.6
In this dialog box, you can choose new options for taskbar properties.

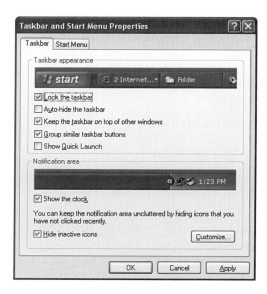

- **Media toolbar**—In all Explorer windows, you can add a Media toolbar. From this toolbar, you can easily choose music or radio stations to listen to while you work and you can view current movie previews.

- **Smarter Open dialog boxes**—Many dialog boxes, such as the ones you use to open and save files, now remember the most recently entered filenames. Open dialog boxes also sport an iconic representation of the common locations in a new left pane, called the *Places Bar* (see Figure 1.7). Not all applications support the Places Bar, but those that do make it easier to save files to different local or network drives.

- **Customizable Explorer toolbars**—The toolbars are customizable, just like in IE or Office.

- **Improved topic-based help system in enhanced HTML**—The Windows XP Help and Support Center most closely resembles the hugely remodeled help system introduced in Windows Me. To save search time, major topics are displayed on the left side, and common tasks are listed on the right side. The index is a click away on the top of the screen, and a Favorites button makes it easy to collect help pages you use frequently, and display them instantly. Click the Home button to return to the main Help and Support Center menu at any time.

- **New balloon help tips**—Novice users will appreciate the new balloon help tips that pop up, such as when you let your mouse pointer hover over certain icons, when network connections are made, reporting the connection speed, or to report immediate problems which require quick action (see Figure 1.8).

Figure 1.7
New Open dialog boxes include the Places Bar at the left side of the window.

ENHANCED SEARCH FEATURE AND HISTORY

The Windows XP Search option replaces Find in Windows 9x; you can search from any and all Windows Explorer windows. When you search the Internet, the LAN, or your local hard disk, you use the same dialog box now. You can search for a file, folder, network computer, person, Web topic, help topic, or map. You can display a thumbnail view of search results to see what files or other items have been found. If the network you're on is using the new MS Index Server, the discovered items are also ranked according to closeness of match, just like search engines do. A friendly animated dog provides minimal levels of entertainment during Search, but you can banish the dog off-screen by changing your search preferences.

Pressing the Windows key + F or choosing Search from the Start menu brings up the box you see in Figure 1.9. This integrated, easier-to-use search feature helps you find information on your computer, your network, or on the Web. Select the type of search you want to perform, enter all or part of the name, and start the search.

Figure 1.8
The Windows XP Help system makes it easy to move within the current topic or to switch to related topics, and balloon help pops up to provide immediate warnings.

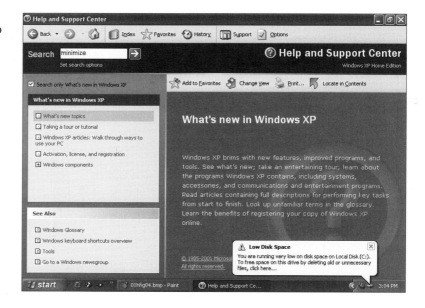

Figure 1.9
The Windows XP search tool works within Explorer and supports file, media, computer, Internet, and Help searches.

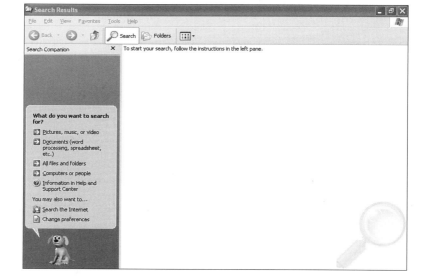

ENHANCED ACCESSIBILITY SUPPORT

Using computers is hard enough for those of us who have full mobility and physical abilities, considering how cryptic and idiosyncratic Windows is. For many folks, just the physical act of using a computer poses an additional challenge. Windows XP Home Edition provides the following accessibility features via the Accessibility Options icon in Control Panel:

- **Onscreen keyboard**—Allows text entry via the mouse
- **StickyKeys**—Allows keyboard combinations to be entered one keystroke at a time
- **FilterKeys**—Adjusts repeat rate and helps Windows ignore brief or repeated keystrokes
- **ToggleKeys**—Plays tones when keys such as Caps Lock are pressed
- **SoundSentry**—Displays your choice of visual alerts when your computer plays a sound
- **ShowSounds**—Provides captions for programs' speech and sounds
- **High-Contrast displays**—Choice of a variety of extra-large text sizes and high-contrast Windows desktops
- **Adjustable cursor blink rate and cursor width**—Makes it easier to find the text cursor onscreen
- **MouseKeys**—Enables the numeric keypad to run the mouse pointer
- **Serial keys**—Enables alternative keyboard and pointing devices to be attached via serial ports

The following accessibility features can be started from the Accessibility folder (Start, All Programs, Accessories, Accessibility) or by pressing the Windows key + U:

- **Magnifier**—Provides an enlarged view of the area under and near the mouse cursor
- **Narrator**—A simple text-to-speech program (English only) for onscreen events and typed characters
- **Onscreen keyboard**

INTERNET AND NETWORK CONNECTIONS AND SOFTWARE

Windows XP Home Edition makes Internet and network use easier than ever. Its New Connection Wizard provides a one-stop interface for setting up Internet, home networking, direct serial/parallel/infrared connections (Direct Cable Connection for you Windows 9x fans), and remote office network connections via either dial-up or virtual private networking (VPN) connections.

Windows XP Home Edition also supports Internet Connection Sharing, using either a conventional modem (for the Internet) and a network card (for the rest of the network) or two network cards (the second one is for use with broadband connections) in the host system. And, if you're already running ICS on a Windows 9x/Me/2000 system, you can connect your Windows XP computer to it easily.

Internet Explorer 6.0, an improved version of the browser Microsoft has used to take over the browser market from one-time leader Netscape, is standard in retail and upgrade versions of Windows XP; hardware vendors who preinstall Windows XP on new computers can choose to omit it, although it's unlikely that most will. It now offers 128-bit encryption straight out of the box, meaning that you no longer need a strong encryption upgrade before you can go to some online banking, stock brokerage, or shopping sites.

Internet Explorer 6.0 is visually different than IE 5.5 in its icon display. For example, the Stop icon is now a red X in a page, rather than in a circle. The Favorites icon is a star instead of a folder. Beneath the surface, more significant differences include

- Integrated MSN Messenger support
- New Privacy tab in Internet Options to control cookies and personal data
- New Clear SSL State option on the Content tab to flush SSL (Secure Sockets Layer) certificates from the SSL cache for security
- Automatic resizing of images too large to be displayed in the browser window without scrolling
- Enhanced Internet setup options
- New Reset Web Settings option on the Programs tab

As of Service Pack 2, IE includes

- A configurable tool that prevents pop-up ads from appearing (pop-up blocking)
- An add-in manager to help you see and control any plug-ins, toolbars, and other extra features that have been added to your IE browser with or without your consent.

IE 6.0 also retains the integrated search tool used in previous versions of IE, integrates it with the Explorer Search tool, and offers a much wider variety of search engines from which to choose. IE's Search acts as a front end to popular search tools. Initially, it searches using the default search tool (MSN) or your preferred replacement (I like Google.com). After completing that search, you can send the search to other major search engines, one at a time. Type in two or more words, and the Search tool treats it as a phrase to get you more accurate results in most cases and fewer non-relevant hits.

Windows XP Home Edition provides these brand-new enhancements to its networking and Internet feature set:

- **An integrated Internet Connection Firewall**—This feature (as of SP-2 renamed Windows Firewall), which is controlled from the network connection properties sheet, helps protect your connection from hacking by outside users, and is especially useful for full-time, always-on broadband connections such as cable modem and DSL. Service Pack 2 increased the effectiveness of the firewall by monitoring both incoming and outgoing messages for suspicious activity. Monitoring outgoing activity can expose 'spyware', 'trojan horses', and other such nefarious programs.
- **Network bridging**—One computer can run two different types of networks (such as Fast Ethernet and IEEE 802.11b [Wi-Fi] wireless Ethernet) and act as a connection between them. You need a network card for each network type you're bridging.
- **Auto-configuration of Wi-Fi networks**—Wi-Fi (wireless Ethernet) networks are harder to configure than wired networks such as Fast Ethernet, because you must synchronize the card to the wireless access point that allows your PC to talk to others. Windows XP Home Edition detects the correct settings automatically.

- **Program Access and Defaults**—A tool for easily choosing which company's programs you want to use for Web browsing, email, media playing, instant messaging, and running programs in Java (via the Java "virtual machine"). The inclusion of this tool is a concession Microsoft made to the US Department of Justice as part of its antitrust settlement (see Figure 1.10).

Figure 1.10
The Program Access Defaults tool lets you easily choose third-party 'middleware' programs to replace Microsoft's own applications such as Media Player and Internet Explorer.

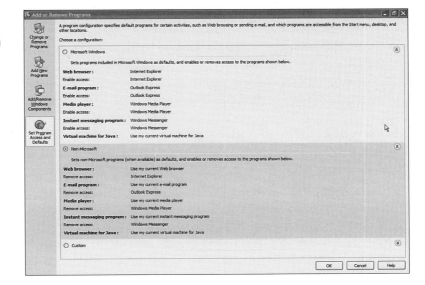

- **Outlook Express protection**—Outlook Express now has the ability to block images in HTML emails and thus isolate potentially dangerous email attachments (such as those with the .exe extension).

- **Security Center**—Due to the increased importance of security when systems are connected to LANs and the Internet, Microsoft has now provided a one-stop shop for displaying and altering the system's security settings. Now up front and center, the Security Center provides even the most inexperienced newcomer with the information they need to get their system secure when it's not. The Security Center interface shows settings for your firewall, Automatic Updates, and virus protection, as well as giving you quick access to Internet Options and System control panel.

All in all, Windows XP Home Edition makes Internet access, local area networking, and system security features more powerful and easier to adjust.

HARDWARE IMPROVEMENTS

Although Windows XP Home Edition is built upon the foundation of the "all-business" Windows NT 4.0 and Windows 2000 versions, it is still designed to be a replacement for the consumer operating systems (Windows 9x/Me). So Microsoft is determined to support a much broader range of hardware in Windows XP than in previous versions.

Drivers for many popular devices are supplied on the Windows XP Home Edition CD-ROM or are available from the vendor; Windows XP Home Edition will check Microsoft's Windows Update Web site for new drivers if it doesn't locate the right driver for your hardware. Windows XP uses the same Windows driver model (WDM) technology originally developed for hardware drivers in Windows 98/Me/2000, but, thanks to the widespread pre-installation of Windows XP Home Edition on new PC's, users should have a wider assortment of drivers to choose from initially than Windows 2000 users did. If you can't get a Windows XP-specific driver for your hardware, most Windows 2000 device drivers will work with Windows XP Home Edition.

In the meantime, if you have rare, discontinued, or otherwise nonstandard hardware, be sure to check Microsoft's Hardware Compatibility List at `http://www.microsoft.com/whdc/hcl/default.mspx` before upgrading.

→ To learn more about hardware support issues, **see** Chapter 2, "Getting Your Hardware and Software Ready for Windows XP."

The following is the lowdown on the newly added hardware support, help, and troubleshooting:

- **Device Manager**—It is launched as a part of the Microsoft Management Console (MMC) and offers online help, more ways to view devices, and easier driver updates.

- **Add Hardware Wizard**—It has been enhanced to make installing drivers for new hardware easier and more reliable, and to make it harder to install drivers for "phantom" devices not already installed in or connected to your system.

- **Scanner and Camera Wizard**—Was introduced in Windows Me. It has been included and now supports flash memory card readers used by digital cameras.

- **Windows XP Home Edition**—Includes DirectX 9.x for full support of the newest 3D games and multimedia programs. It supports USB, digital joysticks, more realistic 3D graphics effects and better sound.

- **Windows XP**—Provides full support for DVD playback via the Windows Media Player; you will need to install a third-party DVD decoder first.

- **Windows XP**—Supports CD-R and CD-RW drives without the need to install third-party software.

PLUG AND PLAY AND OTHER GOODIES

Windows XP Home Edition supports *Plug and Play (PnP)*, meaning you can add new stuff to your computer, such as a printer, video card, USB port, and so on, and Windows will attempt to automatically assign it resources and add drivers. It does so, assuming the add-on hardware is Plug and Play compatible and the computer's BIOS is Plug and Play compliant. Windows XP Home Edition's version of Plug and Play works better than the Windows 9x/Me flavor, locating new hardware faster and mapping more PCI-based hardware to the same IRQ than Windows 9x/Me could do. This reduces hardware conflicts considerably.

Windows XP Home Edition also supports ACPI's enhancements to Plug and Play, USB devices, IEEE-1394 (FireWire / i.Link) devices, AGP video cards, DVD, and CD-ROM drives on a par with Windows 98/Me and Windows 2000.

New hardware supported in Windows XP Home Edition includes:

- Portable audio players
- CD-R and CD-RW drives

Windows XP Home Edition offers wizards to make copying files to these devices very easy.

FILE SYSTEM IMPROVEMENTS

Realizing the inherent security and efficiency limitations in the old DOS (FAT 16) file system, Microsoft has developed two improved file systems over the last several years—FAT32 and NTFS. NTFS was introduced with NT 3.1; FAT32, with Windows 98. Each has its strengths and weaknesses. FAT32's big advantage is that it's highly compatible with FAT16 yet supports larger disk drive partitions and divides the drive into smaller clusters than FAT16, thus economizing on disk space. However, it's not nearly as secure as NTFS.

Microsoft's updates and tweaks to NTFS in NT 4 service packs pushed NTFS's security even further, and Windows XP Home Edition uses the same enhanced NTFS 5.0 version originally introduced with Windows 2000. Now file caching for networked and shared drives is an option, and 128-bit file and folder encryption is built in. Caching speeds up access to the files as well and allows users to work with them offline.

NOTE
> You still can use FAT16 and FAT32 file systems with Windows XP Home Edition, but you might want to convert to NTFS either during the installation process or later for more efficient and secure file storage. You can convert either FAT file system to NTFS, but you cannot convert FAT16 to FAT32 with Windows XP.

MORE STABILITY

Windows XP Home Edition inherits its stability in performance from Windows NT and Windows 2000. What makes the Windows NT/2000/XP family more stable than consumer Windows (3.x/9x/Me)?

Windows XP Home Edition is more stable than Windows 9x/Me (not to mention old Windows 3.1!) because its internal design protects the system kernel, which is the core of the operating system. Windows XP Home Edition's system kernel never interfaces directly with applications or hardware, which could corrupt the kernel and crash the system. Instead, applications and hardware make requests to subsystems, which then request attention from the kernel.

Windows XP Home Edition's stability also comes from its use of *preemptive multitasking*, which uses a scheduler to tell each program running how much CPU time it can use.

Windows XP Home Edition divides tasks into four priority rankings and provides the most CPU time to real-time processes, followed by high-priority processes, normal priority tasks, and, finally, idle tasks.

To make multitasking work even better, Windows XP Home Edition also uses *multithreading*, which enables a single program to be divided up into separate *threads* (or subprocesses) which can be managed and run separately for greater efficiency.

When Windows XP Home Edition runs a program, it automatically assigns that program to an exclusive area of your system's memory. No other programs can touch that area of memory. Nor can that program or other programs gain access to the area of memory in which the basics of the operating system are running. This prevents the kinds of crashing well-known to Windows 9x/Me users.

IMPROVED SYSTEM MANAGEMENT

Windows XP Home Edition's Windows 2000 roots are very visible when it comes time to manage your system. It includes Computer Management (better known to Windows 2000 users as the Microsoft Management Console or MMC). Computer Management provides a single interface for managing hardware (System Tools), drives (storage), and services such as indexing.

You can use Computer Management to prepare new hard drives (replacing Windows 9x's fdisk and Format with a single integrated wizard), view error records, check system performance, start disk defragmentation, and check hardware configuration. It replaces the hodge-podge of programs and features found in earlier versions of Windows with a single interface (see Figure 1.11). It's also extensible with new "snap-in" modules provided by Microsoft or other companies.

Figure 1.11
Windows XP Home Edition's Computer Management tool offers many different system services under one roof.

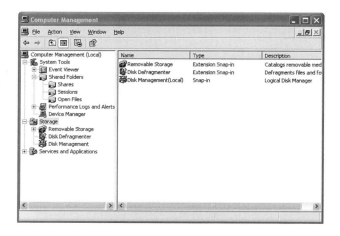

EASILY VIEWING AND REMOVING WINDOWS UPDATES

New as of SP-2, the Add/Remove Programs applet in the Control Panel now lets you easily view or hide XP system updates. This is a useful and thoughtful feature because it separates the arcanely named system software additions from user-recognizable applications such as Microsoft Office. A single check box on the Add/Remove Programs dialog box turns on or off the system updates, service packs, and hotfixes from the list, for potential removal.

NEW AND IMPROVED WIZARDS

Windows XP Home Edition features improved versions of wizards originally found in Windows 9x, Windows Me, or Windows 2000, including

- **Network Connection Wizard**—This wizard lets you start up network connections on-the-fly, whether in the office or at home (phoning into the Internet via your ISP), creating a Virtual Private Networking (VPN) connection to a LAN in another location, or whatever. The Network Connection Wizard is also used to set up direct connections to other computers, directly through infrared, parallel, or serial connections (see Figure 1.12). Note that infrared connections between computers are now supported for an ad hoc instant (slow-speed) cable-less LAN.

Figure 1.12
You can use the Network Connection Wizard to create several different types of connections.

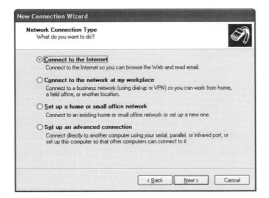

- **Add Printer Wizard**—This wizard makes it easy to set up and connect to local and network printers, even from an application, right from the Print dialog box (see Figure 1.13). No more fishing around for the Printers folder. The wizard automatically tries to determine the make and model of your printer without forcing you to scroll through a list of options.

EASIER USER MANAGEMENT

Windows XP Home Edition departs from its Windows NT and Windows 2000 predecessors in one important area: the balance between system security and user management.

Figure 1.13
You can choose or create a new printer without opening the Printers Control Panel.

Windows NT and Windows 2000 were designed almost exclusively for corporate networking, and thus supported high security settings. On the other hand, a home computer is designed to be shared, and often has a line of family members and friends waiting for their turn (especially if you're the first one on the block with a broadband Internet connection!).

To serve this growing need, XP introduces a brilliant feature: multiple simultaneous users on a single computer. Just as with older versions of Windows, each user has his or her own apps, desktop items, personal settings, and so on. But here's the twist. Suppose you're working on a major project when a housemate comes along and needs to check email. He or she can log in and check mail without you logging out. All your docs and applications stay running. After the email session, the other user can log out (or not), and you just switch back to your work as you left it. Your applications and documents are protected from view of the other users, too.

Windows XP Home Edition is designed to be friendly, but not too friendly. You can set up user accounts at one of two levels:

- **Administrator**—Administrators can do everything (and I mean everything!) with—or to—the computer. Make sure that people with Administrator privileges can be trusted, and note that Windows XP Home Edition defaults to the Computer Administrator mode when you create new accounts.

- **Limited**—A user with a limited account can change the parts of the system that affect them directly, such as their own password, their desktop, and their own files. They may not be able to install some programs or use some software designed before Windows XP was introduced (see Figure 1.14).

Figure 1.14
A limited account prevents users from disturbing other users' settings, but may not work with older software.

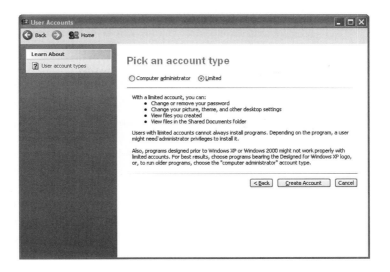

TIP

If you occasionally have visitors who sit down at your PC for a bit of Web surfing or email, enable the Guest account feature, which prevents Guests from accessing password-protected files, folders, and settings.

WHAT IS NOT IN WINDOWS XP HOME EDITION

Although all versions of Windows XP share common program code (also called the *code base*) beneath the surface and a common user interface (the "Luna" interface), Windows XP Home Edition represents the most basic form of Windows XP. The features missing from Windows XP Home Edition are features that Microsoft believes you, as a home computer user, just don't need or wouldn't use. They include

- **No support for advanced management features**—Windows XP Home Edition doesn't support Remote Desktop (which allows remote access to a corporate desktop computer and remote administration of client computers on a network), Active Directory domains, group policies, IntelliMirror configuration and change management, and roaming user profiles.

- **No support for connections to a domain controller**—Domain controllers make many remote management features possible, but Windows XP Home Edition doesn't support logons to domains.

- **No multiprocessor support**—Windows XP Home Edition is designed for single-processor systems.

- **No dynamic disk support**—Windows XP Home Edition supports only basic hard disk partition types (primary, extended, and logical drive letters within an extended partition).

- **No Web server**—While Web developers using Windows 98 have been able to test their Web pages with the integrated IIS Personal Web Server, this feature is not present in Windows XP Home Edition.

- **No support for encryption or file-level access management**—You can use share-level controls (a password for each shared folder or drive), but you cannot create groups of users with different levels of access to drives or devices.

- **No support for multiple-language installations**—Wanting to install Windows so you can support a foreign exchange student's native language or make it easier for your kids to write their non-English term papers and still be able to switch back to English? Forget using Windows XP Home Edition, since it supports only one language per installation.

- **No support for advanced network features**—If you need IPSec (IP Security), SNMP network management, simple TCP/IP, SAP Agent, Client Services for NetWare, Network Monitor or roving features, you need Windows XP Professional.

Most of these missing features can be summed up thus: Home Edition is for home users with no network or a small peer-to-peer network. Professional is for network and corporate users who need system management features. The limitations of Windows Me for networking and system management have been largely carried over into Windows XP Home Edition.

DIFFERENCES BETWEEN WINDOWS XP HOME EDITION, WINDOWS XP PROFESSIONAL, AND 64-BIT WINDOWS XP VERSIONS

Windows XP comes in two distinct varieties for 32-bit processors:

- Home Edition
- Professional

Although both versions contain the same integrated applications and multimedia features, Windows XP Professional also includes corporate network support, backup and security features similar to those found in Windows 2000 Professional.

The now-available 64-bit CPUs, such as Intel Itanium and AMD's Athlon 64 and Opteron, can run advanced versions of XP designed to take advantage of their speed and other enhancements. Windows XP 64-bit Edition is the Intel-based workstation version. It supports up to 16GB of physical RAM and up to 16TB of virtual memory, and it takes full advantage of the superior floating-point performance of the Itanium processor. One or two Itanium processors can be used. Windows XP 64-bit Edition runs 32-bit Windows programs in a subsystem. The user interface is similar to Windows XP Professional, but the features vary. Another 64-bit version has been developed for the AMD Athlon 64 and Opteron chips, dubbed Windows XP 64-Bit Edition for 64-Bit Extended Systems.

Both 64-bit versions use an emulation layer called WOW64 to run Win32-based applications. When running on the Intel 64-bit processor, complaints are that the 32-bit programs run a bit too slowly. Claims are that the AMDs run 32-bit applications faster than the Itaniums do.

NOTE

64-bit versions are supplied preinstalled on computer hardware.

What about 32-bit server versions of Windows XP? Microsoft has multiple server editions of Windows XP, generally dubbed Microsoft Windows 2003 Server. The editions differ based on variations in the total amount of memory used by each version, the number of processors supported, and the number of domains that can be controlled. As of this writing, I counted 16 specialized servers for areas such as storage servers, SQL servers, speech servers, commerce servers, and so on.

Table 1.3 compares Windows XP Home Edition and Windows XP Professional to other versions of Windows.

TABLE 1.3 VARIOUS CAPABILITIES OF WINDOWS XP HOME EDITION AS COMPARED TO EARLIER VERSIONS OF WINDOWS

Feature	Windows 9x/Me	Windows NT 3.xx	Windows NT 4 Workstation	Windows NT 4 Server	Windows 2000 Professional	Windows 2000 Server	Windows 2000 Advanced Server	Windows 2000 Datacenter Server	Win XP Home	Win XP Pro
Virtual memory management (paging file on hard disk)	Yes	Yes	Yes	Yes	Yes	Yes	Yes	Yes	Yes	Yes
Multitasking type	Preemptive	Preemptive	Preemptive	Preemptive	Preemptive	Preemptive	Preemptive	Preemptive	Preemptive	Preemptive
Multithreading	Yes	Yes	Yes	Yes	No	Yes	Yes	Yes	Yes	Yes
Number of CPUs (maximum)	1	2 native, 4 with OEM modified HAL	2	4	2	4	8	32	1	2
Maximum RAM supported					4GB	4GB	64GB	64GB	64GB	64GB
Access security	No	Yes	Yes	Yes	Yes	Yes	Yes	Yes	No	Yes
Kerberos security	No	No	No	No	No	Yes	Yes	Yes	No	Yes
Runs real-mode device drivers	Yes	No	No	No	No	No	No	No	No	Yes
Runs 16-bit DOS and Windows applications	Yes	Yes	Yes	Yes	Yes	Yes	Yes	Yes	Yes	Yes
Runs 32-bit Windows applications	Yes	Yes	Yes	Yes	Yes	Yes	Yes	Yes	Yes	Yes

Feature	Windows 9x/Me	Windows NT 3.xx	Windows NT 4 Workstation	Windows NT 4 Server	Windows 2000 Professional	Windows 2000 Server	Windows 2000 Advanced Server	Windows 2000 Datacenter Server	Win XP Home	Win XP Pro
Runs OS/2 applications	No	Yes	Yes	Yes	Yes	Yes	Yes	Yes	Yes	Yes
Runs POSIX applications	No	Yes	Yes	Yes	Yes	Yes	Yes	Yes	Yes	Yes
Supports DOS FAT16	Yes	Yes	Yes	Yes	Yes	Yes	Yes	Yes	Yes	Yes
Support DOS FAT32	95 OSR2 and 98/Me only	No	No	No	Yes	Yes	Yes	Yes	Yes	Yes
Supports OS/2 HPFS	No	Yes	No	No	No	No	No	No	No	No
Supports NTFS	No	Yes	Yes	Yes	Yes	Yes	Yes	Yes	Yes	Yes
Supports disk compression	Yes	No	Yes	Yes	Yes	Yes	Yes	Yes	Yes	Yes
File encryption	No	No	No	No	Yes	Yes	Yes	Yes	Yes	Yes
RAID support/ levels	No	Yes	No	Yes	No	Yes	Yes	Yes	No	Yes
Built-in networking	Yes	Yes	Yes	Yes	Yes	Yes	Yes	Yes	Yes	Yes
Built-in email	Yes	Yes	Yes	Yes	Yes	Yes	Yes	Yes	Yes	Yes
Minimum Intel CPU required	386	386	Pentium	Pentium	Pentium	Pentium	Pentium	Pentium	Pentium	Pentium

continues

1

TABLE 1.3 CONTINUED

Feature	Windows 9x/Me	Windows NT 3.xx	Windows NT 4 Workstation	Windows NT 4 Server	Windows 2000 Professional	Windows 2000 Server	Windows 2000 Advanced Server	Windows 2000 Datacenter Server	Win XP Home	Win XP Pro
Supports RISC chips	No	Yes/MIPS R4000 Alpha	Yes/ R4000 Alpha	Yes/ R4000 Alpha	Yes/DEC Alpha	Yes/DEC Alpha	Yes/DEC Alpha	Yes/DEC Alpha	No	No
Supports Active Directory	Planned	No	No	No	Yes	Yes	Yes	Yes	No	Yes
Supports clustering	No	No	No	Yes, only in Enterprise Edition	No			Yes	No	No
Supports load balancing	No	No	No	No	No	No	Yes	Yes	No	No
Supports Novell NDS	No	No	Yes	Yes	Yes	Yes	Yes	Yes	No	Yes
Includes Web server/maximum number of connections	Yes/10	No/unlim	Yes/10	Yes/unlim	Yes/10	Yes/unlim	Yes/unlim	Yes/unlim	No	Yes/10

CHAPTER 2

GETTING YOUR HARDWARE AND SOFTWARE READY FOR WINDOWS XP

In this chapter

General Considerations

So much for the hype about Windows XP, all its new features, and some of the details of its design and architecture you learned about in Chapter 1, "Introducing Windows XP Home Edition." So, the question at this point is, "Are you really going to install it?" If you are, you should go ahead and read this chapter and the next one. In this chapter, I'll coach you on preparing for the installation and checking your hardware and software requirements; then I'll discuss some compatibility issues that might affect your product-purchasing decisions. The next chapter covers more specific installation issues, such as choosing disk formats, upgrading versus installing fresh, and dual-booting. I'll also walk you through the setup procedure.

Of course, if Windows XP Home Edition is already installed on your PC, you can probably skip Chapter 3, "Installing Windows XP Home Edition." You should, however, at least take a brief look at this one because it includes some discussion that might affect software and hardware installation decisions you might make when using Windows XP Home Edition in the future. Understanding what you can do with, and shouldn't expect from, an operating system is always good background material when you use as complex a tool as a computer on a regular basis. Pay particular attention to the section about RAM and hard disk upgrades and how to research hardware compatibility, and check out the Windows XP-approved applications list on the Windows Catalog site.

As you'll learn in the next chapter, the Windows XP Setup program automatically checks your hardware and software and reports any potential conflicts. Using it is one way to find out whether your system is ready for prime time. It can be annoying, however, to find out something is amiss at midnight when you're doing an installation, especially when you could have purchased RAM or some other installation prerequisite the previous day when you were out at the computer store. Likewise, you don't want to be technically capable of running Windows XP Home Edition only to experience disappointing performance. To help you prevent such calamity or surprise, the first part of this chapter will cover hardware compatibility issues.

In general, I'll say this about Windows XP hardware compatibility. Microsoft's goal was for 90 percent of systems sold since January 2000 to have a "positive upgrade experience." Microsoft defines a positive upgrade experience as everything working without any issues at all. This is a significantly high figure. The remaining ten percent may have a speed bump along the way, not necessarily a computer that doesn't boot. Generally, these speed bumps are devices in, or attached to, your PC that might not have a driver that tells Windows XP how to use it; or maybe there's an application or two on your system that doesn't run.

Hardware Requirements

Let's start with the basics. The principal (and minimal) hardware requirements for running Windows XP Home Edition are as follows:

Windows XP Home Minimum

PC with 300MHz or higher processor clock speed recommended; 233MHz minimum required (single or dual processor system); Intel Pentium/Celeron family, or AMD K6/Athlon/Duron family, or compatible processor recommended

64MB RAM (128MB recommended for all features to work); 4GB of RAM (maximum)

At least 1.5GB of free disk space

Super VGA (800 × 600 resolution) or higher video adapter and monitor with 16-bit or higher color depth

Keyboard

Mouse or compatible pointing device

CD-ROM (12x minimum speed) or DVD drive

These are Microsoft's suggested minimums, and not necessarily what will provide satisfactory or exceptional performance. Some users have reported that they have installed on lesser machines. Microsoft tries to quote minimum requirements that will provide performance the average user can live with. I have installed XP on a little Sony VAIO n505VE which has an Intel Celeron 333MHz processor, and it works like a champ.

Table 2.1 compares system requirements for popular operating systems.

TABLE 2.1   HARDWARE REQUIREMENTS BY OPERATING SYSTEM

Operating System	CPU (Minimum Required/ Recommended)	Memory (Minimum Required/ Recommended)	Disk Space (Minimum Required/ Recommended)
Windows 98	P133 MMX/ PII-300	16MB/64MB	300MB
Windows NT 4.0 Workstation	P133/P166	16MB/32MB	110MB
Windows NT 4.0 Server	P133/P166	32MB/64MB	200MB
Windows 2000 Professional	P133/PII-300	64MB/128MB	650MB/500MB
Windows 2000 Server	P133/PII-300	64MB/128MB	850MB/1GB
Novell NetWare 5	386	64MB/256MB	500MB/1GB

continues

TABLE 2.1 CONTINUED

Operating System	CPU (Minimum Required/ Recommended)	Memory (Minimum Required/ Recommended)	Disk Space (Minimum Required/ Recommended)
Red Hat Linux 9 Desktop	P200	64MB	1.6GB
Windows XP Professional	P233/P300+	64/128MB	1.5GB
Windows XP Home Edition	P233/P300+	64/128MB	1.5GB

Surprised that you can run this operating system on a machine that's only a 233MHz Pentium? By today's standards, that's a pokey old processor. I've actually heard of people running Windows NT on 33MHz machines with decent performance, assuming the system had enough RAM. But with over 30 million lines of programming code in Windows XP, (NT had only 5 million) additional horsepower is clearly a good idea for XP.

TIP

> With the plummeting prices of CPUs these days, there's scant disincentive to upgrading your CPU and motherboard or just getting a whole new system for Windows XP. The price wars between Intel and AMD might be brutal on the corporate battlefield, but the consumer is clearly the winner. 1GHz–2GHz-class desktop clone computers with 40GB or larger hard disks and 128MB of RAM are easily available for around $500 as of this writing. (Of course, this statement will be out of date in a week or two, so forgive us!).

Anyway, based on what you can get for a song these days, you shouldn't have any difficulty hustling up the bucks to buy a machine that will run Windows XP adequately. Almost a decade ago when I was writing about Windows NT 3.1, the cost of admission was significantly higher; you had to be on the bleeding edge of computing to build a quality NT-style workstation.

As a consultant, I get more phone calls and emails asking what kind of computer to buy than on any other topic. Despite the rapid de-escalation in prices and apparent exponential increase in computing speed, putting together a machine to run Windows XP Home Edition successfully for your needs might not be as easy as you think. Whenever I build a new system, I'm surprised by twists I hadn't considered, new hardware standards I didn't know even existed, and so on. You probably know the story.

If you're a power-user type or hardware jock running the PCs at your company, you probably spend your coffee breaks poring over magazines like *Killer PC* or belong to the Captain Number Crunch fan club. You can find some blindingly fast stuff, such as accelerated 3D AGP video cards, serial ATA drive arrays, PCI Express busses, new kinds of high-speed RAM (such as DDR2), and so on. As much fun as it is for speed freaks, a screamer PC that will take the computing Grand Prix doesn't necessarily a good XP box make. And as much as everyone is hoping that Windows XP will broaden hardware and application compatibility over the annoying confines that Windows NT and Windows 2000 suffered, it's still a protected and somewhat picky system. Hardware that purrs away happily under Windows 9x might not necessarily operate under Windows XP. Before you go cutting purchase orders or checks for your personal PC or 20 for the office, look a little further by at least skimming through this chapter.

OPTION 1: USING WHAT YOU'VE GOT: ENSURING COMPATIBILITY

You can take three basic approaches to ensure hardware compatibility. The first is relatively simple and may prevent your having to purchase anything new. Microsoft has done most of the compatibility testing for you already and posted that information in its XP catalog (see Figure 2.1). (It used to have an online Hardware Compatibility List [HCL] for XP but no longer.) To get to the catalog, browse to this address:

```
http://www.microsoft.com/windows/catalog/
```

Figure 2.1
Use the online Microsoft XP Catalog to check on your hardware before you purchase or when you decide to upgrade to Windows XP.

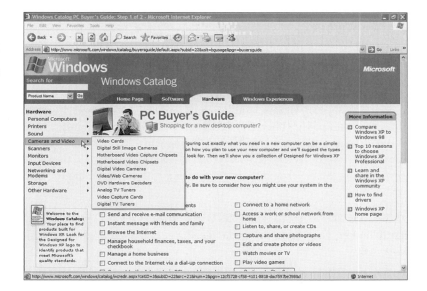

Then click Shopping for a new PC? (At least that was the link as of this writing.) Otherwise, poke around until you find links for various types of hardware. Typically, it is a navigation bar on the left side of the Web page with drop-down lists for classes of hardware. If the Designed for Windows XP logo is listed next to the product, you know it will work. Some products have a clickable link under them. Clicking such a product's link opens another page that might offer additional compatibility information.

If your hardware isn't listed, that doesn't mean setup on your PC won't be successful, but there is a chance you'll encounter problems. XP has been around long enough that many XP drivers are now available that aren't necessarily Microsoft-certified.

TIP

> To find general information about Windows XP Home Edition, including compatibility, check out the following:
>
>   http://www.microsoft.com/WindowsXP/
>
> Although the Hardware Compatibility List doesn't list XP compatibility, it does show Windows 2000 compatibility. As a general rule, these operating systems are similar enough under the hood and use much the same standards for device drivers (unlike Windows 9x drivers, which are very different from XP or 2000). So, you can get a sense of the likelihood of XP compatibility by checking the HCL at `http://www.microsoft.com/whdc/hcl/default.mspx` and doing a search for your specific hardware. If a device has Windows 2000 compatibility, it will work with XP.

 For a list of URLs related to upgrading to Windows XP, see "Compatibility and Upgrade Help," in the "Troubleshooting" section at the end of this chapter.

Don't know what's in your system or not sure if you thought of everything that might conflict with Windows XP Home Edition? No problem. You can run the Windows XP Compatibility Tool (testing program) from the CD. This program detects your hardware and verifies compatibility. Insert the CD (you'll have to borrow one from someone who has it, if you don't want to purchase it just to find out), and choose Perform Additional Tasks from the main menu. Then choose Check System Compatibility. During a system upgrade, you will see the option for this on the introductory screen. (You can also run the tool from the command line by typing `<CDROM DRIVE>:\i386\winnt32 /checkupgradeonly`. You can perform just the check and then exit the tool without installing the operating system, if you wish.)

When you run the program, a report is generated telling you whether your computer cuts the mustard.

NOTE

> If you forget to run the test in advance, don't worry, you'll still get the report. Why? It's run automatically when you activate the Setup program to install XP. It's just nice to do it in advance so you are aware of contingency problems well ahead of time. (The Setup program and some examples of reports are covered in Chapter 3.)

What do you do if some component of your system (or your entire computer) doesn't rank high enough to appear and isn't listed in the compatibility list? Well, you can wing it and see how things work out. Just install XP onto the computer in a separate directory or disk partition (dual-boot); then see what happens. If this approach doesn't work, you can revert to using your old operating system, having only lost an hour's time. You should also approach the hardware manufacturer and ask whether a Windows XP driver is available for the component. (How to set up a Dual-booting arrangement is discussed in Chapter 3.)

TIP

> Some people say that you don't need to ensure availability of drivers for Plug and Play devices. Although the idea was that all officially sanctioned Plug and Play devices (bearing the PnP logo) are automatically supported by Windows, this isn't always true. Check carefully to see that any new PnP device you're considering comes with drivers for, or has been tested with, Windows 2000 Professional or XP. If the box says "Designed for Microsoft Windows 2000" or "Designed for Microsoft Windows XP" and bears the Windows 2000 and/or XP logo, you're probably home free. Since Windows 2000 and XP are built on the same base code, drivers for one should in most cases work with the other.

OPTION 2: CHOOSING A WINDOWS XP-READY PC

It isn't a bad idea to just bite the bullet and shell out for a new machine once every two years or so. I'm a holdout myself, even though I'm a techno-junkie who often has to be an early adopter of new hardware. The bottom line is that I'm cheap, so I try to squeeze out every last CPU cycle from my computers and keep them running for a very long time. I'm still using an old machine based on Intel's 386 processor (which is two generations removed from the original Pentium) running DOS as my path to the Internet. Clearly, I don't like to participate in the "throw-away society's" idea of planned obsolescence. But every time I upgrade to a new computer, I notice a significant number of niceties across the board. For example, quicker response, more inclusive power management so my system uses less power when it's idle (and cuts my utility bills!), reduced energy consumption due to lower chip count (which also cuts my utility bills), more hardware setting options, a faster DVD drive with support for CD-ROM media, high-speed ports such as USB 2 and FireWire (also known as i.Link and IEEE 1394b) that work with the newest scanners, printers, and drives, faster video display, and so on.

If you have decided to start fresh and purchase new PCs for your personal or corporate arsenal, let me suggest an easier way to research each piece of gear separately. On the Windows Catalog site, just click on the "Hardware" tab, then Personal Computers and choose a system style (desktop, laptop, and so on) to find one in the list. Microsoft's testing lab awards the "Windows XP-Ready PC" merit badge to computers that meet their requirements.

There's no shortage of systems there, so get ready to do a little head scratching.

TIP

> If you have a PC guaranteed to run Windows 2000, it will probably run XP. An HP laptop I bought a few years ago emblazed with the Designed for Windows Me logo even installed XP just fine.

WHAT YOU GET WITH A WINDOWS XP-READY PC

When you purchase a Microsoft-sanctioned Windows XP computer, you get more than you asked for, but I guess that's capitalism and, besides, with "bloatware" being so prevalent these days, it's better to prepare for the coming need for bigger and faster everything.

A Windows XP-ready PC will meet or more often than not exceed the requirements listed in Table 2.2.

TABLE 2.2 WINDOWS XP-READY PC REQUIREMENTS[1]

Feature	Requirements
Operating system	It comes preinstalled with Windows XP.
RAM	Includes at least 128MB of RAM.
Logo rating	It bears the "Designed for Windows XP" logo.
Power Management	Supports Advanced Configuration and Power Interface (ACPI) for laptops to increase battery life, among other benefits.
CPU	Desktop and laptop machines come with at least a 500MHz Pentium III processor or equivalent.
Other	USB ("FireWire") ports, DVD, DVD-RW, CD-R, or CD-RW drive, Wake-On LAN network interface card. Possibly no parallel or serial ports. Possibly a microphone and Web camera, and an IEEE-1394 (FireWire) port.

1 The requirements listed in Table 2.2 are preferred. They exceed the minimum requirements to run Windows XP. See the beginning of this chapter for the minimum requirements.

OPTION 3: UPGRADING YOUR COMPUTER

Don't want to purchase a whole new computer, but your hardware isn't all on the Catalog or HCL? Or do you have some old, stodgy CD-ROM drive, SCSI controller, video adapter, motherboard, or some other piece of gear that you want to upgrade anyway? You're not alone. The PC upgrade business is booming, as evidenced by the pages and pages of ads in the backs of computer rags and the popularity of computer "swap meets," where precious little swapping is going on except that of hardware components for the hard-earned green stuff. If only my coauthor and I had written Scott Mueller's book, *Upgrading and Repairing PCs*, we would be very happy authors. It's perennially one of the best-selling computer books.

Buy It or Build It?

I have a word of caution about the "building your own" mindset. I started in PCs back before IBM got into the fray, and in those days, you had no choice but to build your own microcomputer. Lots of the building required using a soldering iron, too (and close proximity to the freezer to thrust burned fingers into).

The notion of a completely packaged PC ready to go was sort of disgusting to hobbyists, of course, at least at first. I've been through about 20 PCs so far. After my first few fully integrated (packaged) systems, it started to dawn on me that I didn't have to spend half my time under the hood, and I could really get some work done. I was pretty much hooked, even though I get stung by the upgrade bug once in a while, adding peripherals, hard drives, scanners, CD-RW drives, video cameras, and backup devices.

Overall, though, my advice is this: If you think you're going to save a lot of time and money while building yourself a better mousetrap than you can get from some serious vendor or systems integration house, "forget about it!" as Crazy Eddie says. Any company worth its salt has engineers and testers whose job is to iron out the software and hardware incompatibilities that you don't want to lose sleep over. And of course, for many, having technical support and a warranty have their distinct advantages.

If you want to upgrade what you have, that's not necessarily terrible, but if you want to build a new system from the ground up, I advise against it. Save yourself some agony, and buy a computer from a reputable dealer, preferably someone who will guarantee it to work with the operating system you have in mind. Especially when you're dealing with local clone builders, you should get that guarantee in writing. Get as much in the box as you can, including video, audio, modem, network card, CD-ROM/DVD/CD-R/CD-RW, hard disk, floppy drive, USB, and serial and parallel ports. The basic system with keyboard, mouse, and drives should all work and boot.

2

The next few sections describe upgrading your PC for operation under Windows XP Home Edition in case you're the incurable upgrader type and want to take that route.

PREPARING YOUR HARDWARE FOR WINDOWS XP

The amount of hardware upgrading you might need to make to prepare your system for Windows XP depends in great measure on how close your system is to the minimum hardware requirements discussed earlier in the chapter. Because Windows XP's user-friendly multimedia and system protection features demand more computer power than previous versions of Windows, a system that barely exceeds the minimum hardware requirements for CPU, memory, video, and hard disk space can make running Windows XP an ordeal instead of a pleasure. I've had slow machines with small hard drives and fast machines with large hard drives; faster and larger is better, both for you and for Windows XP.

THE MOTHERBOARD AND CPU

So, you want a general upgrade to the performance of your system? The cheapest upgrade you can make is probably to add more RAM (see below). But if your wallet allows, and you want to get to the core of your system for a serious upgrade, start with the motherboard. Don't bother upgrading just your CPU without upgrading the motherboard too. Although CPU upgrade kits are available to allow some older systems to use newer processors, recent changes in CPU speeds, physical packaging, and electrical requirements mean you're much better off upgrading both the motherboard and the CPU if you need a speed boost. Even if you're considering a RAM upgrade, do the motherboard/CPU upgrade first because a new motherboard often uses a better, faster type of RAM than your current system. Motherboard improvements roll down the pike every few months, and adding a new CPU to an old design isn't going to net you much.

Motherboards are pretty cheap—typically around $100–$150 even for a good one, such as an Intel, Supermicro, Abit, or ASUS. (This price is sans CPU; figure anywhere from $75 to $200 more for the CPU, depending on how close to the "bleeding edge" you want to go.) Don't get a motherboard from a company that doesn't put its name on the board, doesn't have a good Web site for technical support, or doesn't have a phone number. It's not worth saving a few bucks. Also, check the Microsoft catalog, of course, to see whether it has been tested (look under Other Hardware on the catalog page).

Ideally, you'll want a modern motherboard with a snappy CPU. So, get your hands on a motherboard that supports the ACPI power management scheme (not just APM) *and* a reasonably quick processor (in the 1GHz–3GHz range or faster), such as an Intel Pentium 4 or AMD Athlon 64 (or the older Athlon XP). If performance is your game, check out the hyper-threading Intel Pentium 4s. (This technology enables a single CPU to process information similar to how a dual-processor system does.) Also, your mobo (motherboard) should have a fast internal bus (called the *front-side bus [FSB]*), support for ATA-100 hard drives (or better, such as serial ATA drives) and AGP or PCI Express graphics, a flashable (upgradable) BIOS, and be designed around the processor you have in mind. In fact, it should come with the CPU installed. Installing a CPU isn't that difficult, but if you don't do it right, the CPU can overheat and croak.

This goes without saying for anyone who has built a PC recently, but virtually all new motherboards are of the "ATX" format (though a few newer form factors are available, notably microBTX). These motherboards don't fit in the older AT-style cases and don't work with the AT power supplies, either. ATX power supplies work hand-in-hand with the ACPI chipset and operating system, allowing the software to control the power states of the PC, including sleep, suspend, soft power down and up, and so on. Some AT-style boards are still available, but I suggest getting a new case and power supply and opting for the ATX version of whatever motherboard you're considering. A new case and power supply shouldn't cost you more than $60 (though better cases/power supply combos can cost upwards of $100).

NOTE

Check the Web site www.motherboards.org for in-depth information about the latest motherboards, chipsets, types of RAM, 64-bit CPUs, dual CPUs, and much more. You can even find information on building your own computer. It's a pretty amazing site. Note that Windows XP Home doesn't support dual CPUs, so unless you want to upgrade to XP Pro, don't attempt this. Also, most of the time, only a 10%–50% performance increase can be achieved with a second CPU. Unless you do a great deal of graphics design (using 3D Studio Max, Lightwave, Adobe PhotoShop, and so on) and you continuously have many CPU-taxing applications running simultaneously, it won't net you much speed gain.

If you really want to delve into the research, check the Usenet newsgroups. Point your newsreader to

    alt.comp.periphs.mainboard

You can find many other motherboard groups as well, addressing specific brands, but this is the place to start. You'll have your reading cut out for you. If you prefer to use a Web browser to search newsgroups, send your browser to groups.google.com.

SLOTS

When you're scoping out a motherboard, think about how many slots you will need for plug-in boards (which can include cards for your sound, video, modem, and so on). More and more hardware is built onto the main boards now because very large-scale integration chips (VLSI) make it possible; therefore, you'll tend to need fewer slots than in the past. Often network support, audio, and even AGP video are built into the motherboard. If you want to use your own sound card and high-end video adapter, you can save a few bucks by getting the "bare-bones" version of the same motherboard that does not include sound or video on it. However, if you want to avoid the hassle and keep more slots available for your other boards, buy the motherboard with this stuff integrated on it (such as on-board audio, which provides lower-cost—and lower-performance—audio capability that should suit your needs, unless you're a hard-core gamer or audiophile). For one thing, all the parts are guaranteed to work together. If you think you'll want to add your own boards for the motherboard-included functions, make sure you can turn them off (usually with jumpers or software settings in the BIOS).

As of this writing, most motherboards were strong in PCI slots and have phased out ISA slots. Few have even one ISA slot these days. And most motherboards now have an accelerated graphics port (AGP) for plugging in a fast video card. AGP is based on the PCI bus but fine-tuned for the needs of high-performance 3D graphics. I recently opted for five PCI slots, one AGP, and one ISA, which seem to be enough for my needs. High-end performance machines will use a new standard called PCI Express starting in late 2004, so keep an eye out for that. This is a revved-up version of PCI.

RAM

Like other versions of Windows NT, Windows XP Home Edition uses the memory it finds in the system intelligently. And it loves memory! The cheapest and easiest upgrade you can make to your PC is to add RAM. If your computer seems to "hit the hard disk" (that is, you have a delay in activity and you hear some clickity-click sounds in the computer and see the disk access light on the front of your system flash annoyingly) every time you click something or move the mouse around, Windows is doing way too much disk swapping. You should be able to quickly switch among 5 to 10 programs without a lot of wait or noise from your PC. Go get some new memory that matches the kind of board you have (read the motherboard or your PC's manual), and *carefully* install the memory. Unplug the computer. Open the case, and find the RAM slots. Touch the metal case with your other hand before inserting the RAM. (RAM chips are very susceptible to damage by static electricity.) Get the fastest kind of memory that your motherboard can take advantage of.

Modern motherboards automatically detect memory you install (no switch setting is necessary), and Windows XP reads this setting and uses it as necessary. In general, the more memory you have installed, the better. As mentioned earlier, Microsoft suggests 128MB for decent system performance. If you're running lots and lots of programs at once, I suggest more on the order of 256MB–1GB. For the record, I've found 128MB adequate for even running 10 or more programs, while many folder windows were open, along with a couple of browser windows.

 If you can't seem to get your newly installed RAM to be detected, see "RAM Not Recognized" in the "Troubleshooting" section at the end of this chapter.

HARD DISK

You need approximately 1.5GB of free hard disk space just to install Windows XP. This amount is just a little indication of Windows XP's storage hunger. With bloatware on the rise (programmers figure why bother making programs fast and tight with storage being so cheap, I guess), it behooves you to have lots of storage space. Like upgrading RAM, upgrading the hard disk is easy these days—even on the pocket book. Get down to Costco, or check www.buy.com for the latest prices on hard disks. They continue to plummet. For less than $100, you can get a huge disk. I hesitate to even quote sizes. It seems that every year sees an increase of a factor of 10 in hard disk storage. In any case, the 1.5GB you need for the installation will look like nothing.

As with RAM, modern motherboards autodetect and configure hard disks when you insert them. Installing the current crop of ATA drives has become very easy. The biggest nuisances with drive upgrades are figuring out whether to ditch the old one or keep it, deciding which will be the boot drive, and figuring how to back up and restore. The EIDE spec allows for four drives, one of which is probably your CD-ROM. That typically leaves room for three, unless you have a CD-RW or another type of removable-media drive (such as a Zip or SuperDisk drive) in the box. There are too many options to cover here, but the easiest upgrade path is to make the new drive a "slave" on the primary IDE channel. Make sure to set jumpers on the drives' circuit as necessary, and ensure that you have the necessary cables to hook up the drives. Jumper your boot drive as *master* and the secondary drive as *slave*.

TIP

If you want to install another hard disk rather than remove the one you already have, and both of your IDE cables already have two drives connected, you can add additional ATA/IDE ports with an Ultra ATA/133 adapter card from Maxtor (www.maxtor.com), SIIG (www.siig.com), or Promise Technologies (www.promise.com). All you need is an empty PCI slot to add support for up to four more IDE/ATA drives.

If you have no more 3.5-inch drive bays for your hard disk, but you have an empty 5.25-inch drive bay (the drive bay size used by CD-ROM drives), use the adapter kit packaged with most retail-boxed drives, or purchase a separate kit from a computer store. The kit has spacers and screws to allow your small drive to fit into the larger bay.

A newer type of ATA drive, called Serial ATA, uses smaller, simpler-to-connect cables and transfers data much faster than ATA or UltraATA drives. The cables on normal (parallel) ATA drives are bulky, inflexible, fragile, and too short. This causes hard disks and optical drives to be placed in strange positions and results in many frustrated system builders. The width of those cables also blocks airflow within the computer's box, and with modern CPUs and video cards generating so much heat, good airflow is essential to a stable system. Serial

ATA (S-ATA as opposed to P-ATA) drives also can transfer data at a slightly faster rate than typical P-ATA drives. First-generation S-ATA drives run at a bandwidth of 150MBps. This is a seemingly disappointing 13% improvement over the popular P-ATA standard called Ultra/ATA 133 (133MBps). However, today's hard drives rarely use that much bandwidth, so 150MBps is more than enough. In later incarnations, S-ATA will run even faster.

→ To learn more details about multibooting schemes, **see** Chapter 28, "Multibooting Windows XP with Other Operating Systems."

MONITOR/VIDEO CARD SUPPORT

Because a doggy, older video card can bring even a snappy system to a crawl when you scroll the screen or move a window around, you'll want to find yourself a fast AGP card if your motherboard has an AGP slot. Microsoft has made the move to support video nicely in Windows XP Home Edition. You have the option of connecting up to ten monitors, for example, if you can imagine that. You should check your video cards' specs and the Windows Catalog site to see whether they will work in multimonitor arrangements before purchasing, though.

Generally speaking, most popular SuperVGA-compatible video cards work with Windows XP, but if you're thinking about upgrading for more speed or features, research the latest AGP boards that have the bells and whistles you want—TV support, video capture, a fast 3D chipset for games, whatever; any recent motherboard which doesn't have on-board video will have an AGP slot. Decide the resolution you want to use, and make sure the card supports the number of colors you'll need at that resolution; if you choose a video card with at least 16MB of RAM, you can handle resolutions up to 1,600x1,280 with 24-bit (16.8 million) color. If you have a 17-inch CRT or 15-inch LCD monitor, you'll want to be running at 1024x768 resolution. Make sure the board can run at 72Hz refresh rate at the color depth and resolution you desire, too, so you won't see flicker on your CRT screen (LCD monitors don't require a high refresh rate). (P.S. Your monitor needs to be able to do it, too. Check the monitor specs. Some older monitors can't run at, say, 1024x768 while refreshing at 72Hz.)

The speed of AGP boards (and connectors on the motherboard) is continually increasing. As of this writing, the fastest AGP hardware ran at AGP 8X speed, which means eight times faster than the speed of the original AGP boards introduced in 1996. Keep in mind that your motherboard *and* video card have to support the same speed (4X, 8X, and so on) to gain the benefits of a fast card. The new PCI Express standard is an alternative.

If you're looking for a new monitor for use with Windows XP, keep in mind that 15-inch LED panels have about the same usable screen space as 17-inch conventional monitors (CRT), a 17-inch LCD is equivalent to a 19-inch CRT, and so on.

TIP

> Many users who are in the market for a new monitor are buying LCD panels instead of conventional glass-tube CRTs. If you're shopping for a new monitor, keep these differences between LCD and CRT monitors in mind.
>
> Laptop and other flat-panel screens look very good at only one resolution—the so-called "native resolution." Other resolutions can be displayed, but they tend to look blocky. Some LCDs look better than others in nonnative resolutions due to built-in antialiasing firmware. If you plan to switch resolutions (as with older DOS-based games or for previewing Web pages you're building), check the quality of the LCD panel at different resolutions. And, unlike standard CRT monitors, LCD monitors look best at low refresh rates. If you buy an LCD monitor, be sure to set the refresh rate to 60Hz. It will probably look clearer that way. You don't have to worry about flicker on an LCD monitor; it's not an issue, and any advertising about high refresh capabilities of an LCD monitor is bogus and misleading. The pixels are transistors and simply don't flicker because they don't have to be refreshed to stay on.
>
> You'll still pay 2–3 times more for an LCD panel than for a CRT, but if you're crowded for space on your desk, they're great.

Windows XP comes with a large complement of 32-bit driver support for many devices, including a wide variety of video cards. It's quite likely that your card is going to be recognized, but you should check with the online Windows Catalog just to make sure, as mentioned earlier in this chapter.

PLUG AND PLAY ITEMS

Plug and Play (or *PnP*, as it is commonly abbreviated) has brought a new level of sophistication to the PC. Much of the headache of PC upgrades stemmed from internal conflicts between plug-in boards and peripheral devices that were not easily detected by the operating system and too difficult for users to configure. Installing even a simple modem was often an exercise in failure for many users as they struggled to determine and set the board's jumpers, dip switches, or software settings to use an available IRQ (Interrupt Request). With PnP, you just plug in a board, screen, printer, scanner, or other peripheral, and reboot.

PnP doesn't always work as advertised, but most of the time it does, and it's a big step in the right direction. NT-based platforms began supporting PnP with Windows 2000. Now with XP, PnP installations are easier than ever. If XP can't find a driver when you install a device, the Windows Update site will be queried if you have an Internet connection available. There are currently thousands of drivers on the Windows update site. Chances are good the system will automatically find a driver for you somewhere.

NOTE

The pivotal question to ask when wondering whether your hardware is XP-compatible is whether the manufacturer or Microsoft supplies a Windows 2000 driver for it. Windows 2000 and XP rely on what is called the Windows Driver Model (WDM). (In addition to WDM, Windows 98 also supported older 16-bit drivers, but Windows 2000 and Windows XP don't.) As mentioned earlier in this chapter, the bottom line is that if there is a Windows 2000 driver for a piece of your hardware, it will probably work okay in XP.

In cases where a driver won't work with XP, rather than causing a system crash, XP utilizes a trick called *defective driver blocking (DDB)*. DDB prevents problem drivers from ruining a user's system. When an acceptable driver for a detected hardware device can't be found, you'll see a window that lets you offer feedback to Microsoft, such as "Hey, the driver for my _____ didn't work." If and when a driver for that device is developed, an AutoUpdate notification will pop up and offer it to you. If by fluke a bad driver is actually loaded, it shouldn't cause your system not to boot. Instead, the system should boot into "Safe Mode," and use System Restore or otherwise remove the driver so that the system will boot normally.

→ For more information about Safe Mode, **see** Chapter 30, "Troubleshooting and Repairing Windows XP."

→ For more information about removing devices and drivers, **see** Chapter 27, "Installing and Replacing Hardware."

→ For more information about System Restore, **see** Chapter 30, "Troubleshooting and Repairing XP."

TIP

To be permitted to display the "Windows 2000 compatible," "Windows Me compatible," or "Windows XP compatible" logo, hardware and software must be PnP capable. Look for this logo or the Plug and Play moniker when buying.

Preparing Your Software for Windows XP

In preparation for upgrading to, or installing Windows XP fresh, you need to consider software compatibility issues. Chapter 1, "Introducing Windows XP Home Edition," described how Windows XP is largely backward compatible with DOS, Windows 3.x, Windows 9x, and Windows 2000 applications. Windows 2000's support for older programs, was, well, not so great. In fact, during the development of Windows 2000, application compatibility (especially for consumer end-users) was almost an afterthought. The focus for Windows 2000 was the corporate user. As a result, numerous consumer-oriented applications, such as games, failed to run on Windows 2000, leaving many power users and home consumers in the lurch.

Windows XP focuses much more on consumers. To ensure expanded software compatibility, Microsoft set up an Application Compatibility Experience group shortly after the XP project began in December 1999. This group consisted of more than 200 testers, developers, and program managers who tested applications in a variety of scenarios (clean installs, migrations, upgrades) using various hardware configurations.

The result is that your existing software, whether Windows 98, Windows NT, Windows 2000, or even DOS and Windows 3.x, will likely run under XP. Even some older DOS games will run (although it's a little hit and miss). As an example, SoundBlaster-compatible sound works in DOS boxes under Windows XP. This means you can spend your lunch hour playing games like *Doom* and *Castle Wolfenstein* in Windows XP—in a window or in full-screen mode.

TIP

> Heavy gamers report that games that predate dedicated sound cards tend to work better than those that don't. More "modern" DOS games such as *Duke Nukem*, can hang. However, some utilities such as DOS Box can mitigate these problems. (`http://dosbox.sourceforge.net/`).

TIP

> Although discussed more in Chapter 3, it is worth mentioning that XP Home Edition will support upgrades from Windows 98, 98 SE, and Me, but not from Windows 95, NT 4.0 Workstation, or Windows 2000 Professional. Users of Windows XP Professional can also upgrade from Windows 95, NT 4.0 Workstation, and Windows 2000 Professional. The moral is that if you want to upgrade rather than to dual-boot, and you're running Windows 95, NT 4.0 Workstation, or Windows 2000 Professional, you'll need to purchase Windows XP Professional.

The good news is that Windows XP (both Home Edition and Professional) will be highly compatible with many DOS and Windows 3.x applications, and with virtually all 32-bit Windows programs that were designed for Windows 9x, Me, NT, and 2000. In addition, all your software (especially 3.x software) will benefit from having a face-lift—nicer borders, more options in the dialog boxes, smoother functioning, an increased capability to work with larger files, and so forth.

For programs that are quirky, you may have to resort to the new Windows XP compatibility modes. Windows XP's programmers have supposedly pinpointed more than 150 areas where apps from earlier versions of Windows might fail. They've created fixes for these problems and supplied XP with "compatibility modes" that let you fake out the offending application, running it in such a way that it believes it's running under Windows 95, or Windows 98, Me, NT 4, or 2000. The fixes can be applied to an application shortcut so that it always works properly when executed. This was mentioned in Chapter 1. For some apps, you may be alerted that there's a downloadable patch for the application (this may happen also when installing Windows XP, as described in Chapter 3).

Although Windows XP is designed to run most older applications and games, this backward compatibility doesn't apply to utility programs, which must work at a very deep level with the operating system and hardware. Programs such as older versions of disk-repair utilities like Norton Utilities, antivirus programs, such as Norton Antivirus and McAfee Virus Scan, and system-management utilities, such as Norton System Works and Ontrack System Suite and others, might not be compatible with Windows XP because of differences in how Windows XP handles internal programs, memory, and drives compared to earlier Windows versions. If you're wondering whether a particular disk, antivirus, or system utility works with Windows XP, contact the vendor before you run the program.

To avoid problems that can be caused by running programs which are not designed with Windows XP in mind (and can't be tamed by the compatibility options built into Windows XP), Windows XP will block programs from running if they won't work. Windows XP also features a new technology called AppsHelp, which is triggered when problematic programs try to run. Thus, Windows XP is designed to achieve the twin goals of making your older software work while protecting your system from any problems that some older programs can cause.

In general, if you have your arsenal of programs and utilities chugging away under Windows 9x, Me, NT or 2000 successfully, your applications will upgrade to Windows XP with only minor incident. Setup's compatibility testing program will alert you about any needs or incompatibilities.

WHY SHOULD YOU CARE?

Enough theory. What does this mean to you and to your application choices? Most of your older software will probably run fine after the upgrade. But if you're upgrading from Windows 3.x or 9x and you've been running older 16-bit programs, especially hard disk utilities, you might run into trouble.

CAUTION

Even though you might be able to run some of your older programs such as disk utilities that interact directly with your computer's hard disk by forcing the issue with the XP compatibility modes, it doesn't mean that it's advisable. Windows 3.x programs, for example, don't know about long filenames and can truncate long filenames or at least not display them or accept them in dialog boxes, which can be annoying. Running such programs is not recommended, and I suggest you put them in cryogenic suspension. With XP, the upgrade might be significantly easier than Windows 2000 was (or might have been), but that doesn't mean you should necessarily be cheap and not upgrade to the XP versions of your favorite apps when you get the chance.

As mentioned, Setup examines the applications you have installed and attempts to warn you of incompatibilities. In some cases, you'll just be told to bag the program. In other cases, you'll be prompted to contact the maker for updates, called *upgrade packs*, or to insert the disks with upgrade packs on them at the appropriate time.

WINDOWS XP-APPROVED APPLICATIONS

So, which programs are really ready for Windows XP? The logo requirements for "Windows XP-Ready Software" are similar to those discussed previously for hardware. Just check the product's packaging or the Web page description of the product you're thinking of purchasing. If it's Windows 2000-compatible, chances are good that it will run under Windows XP, but that's not guaranteed. I suggest you contact the maker or check a few sites on the Web first.

TROUBLESHOOTING

RAM NOT RECOGNIZED

I've added RAM to my computer, and it doesn't seem to show up.

You must check several things when adding RAM to ensure that it shows up correctly in Windows. If the BIOS detects the RAM, you can be assured that it will be detected in Windows, so don't worry about any settings within Windows per se. Just do what is necessary for the computer to report the correct amount of total RAM when it is booting within the BIOS. Older machines used to require switch settings or BIOS setting adjustments when you added RAM, but virtually all new computers do not. Of course, you can and should always consult the manual supplied with your computer when performing a RAM upgrade. Follow this checklist:

- Be sure you purchased the correct type, form factors, and capacity of RAM.
- Be sure the RAM is the correct speed for the computer.
- Double-check that the RAM is inserted correctly and firmly seated in the computer. With the power off, try removing and reinserting it.
- Be sure you inserted the RAM in the correct slot. Most computers have a few slots for RAM. Many motherboards require that RAM slots be filled in a specific order, or autodetection of RAM will not work.
- If it's still a no-go, remove the RAM (turn off the power first, of course), carefully package the RAM in an antistatic bag, and return it to the dealer to be tested.

COMPATIBILITY AND UPGRADE HELP

Where can I learn more about compatibility and upgrade options for my Windows XP computer?

Microsoft maintains several resources for Windows XP. You can check the following:

- The Microsoft Technical Articles Web site includes operating system migration guides, pointers to training resources, strategic upgrades, and more. Although this is technically a page for Windows XP Pro, it includes links for XP in general and is located at this address: http://www.microsoft.com/technet/prodtechnol/winxppro/default.mspx.
- The Windows Hardware Compatibility List provides quick access to compatibility information for a variety of equipment vendors, computer systems, and specific peripherals by name and type. Typically, Windows 2000 compatibility will mean Windows XP compatibility. It's located at this address: http://www.microsoft.com/hcl.

- An updated list of Windows 2000 device drivers is available at this address:
  `http://www.microsoft.com/technet/itsolutions/drivers/default.mspx`
- The Windows XP Home Edition site is located at this address:
  `http://www.microsoft.com/windowsxp/home/default.mspx`
- Microsoft's "Windows XP Ready" program can help you find workstations and servers that are 100 percent Windows XP-compatible. Check with your PC vendor to see whether existing products can be retrofitted to comply with Microsoft's specifications. Go to the following address:
  `http://www.microsoft.com/windows/catalog/`
- Information about the 64-bit Editions of XP is located at this address:
  `http://www.microsoft.com/windowsxp/64bit/default.mspx`

SPECIAL NOTE REGARDING XP MEDIA CENTER EDITION PCs

Several variants of Windows XP are not as visible in the marketplace as are the Home and Professional versions. There are server products for corporate settings; a version for use with tablet PCs; and 64-bit Editions (one for Intel Itanium processors, and one for AMD 64-bit chips such as the Opteron). There's also an increasingly-popular Media Center version for use with computers with specialized parts for recording and manipulating multiple kinds of digital media such as photographs, music, and video.

Although this book isn't aimed at MCE users and doesn't discuss in great detail the multimedia aspects of MCE, it's interesting to note that Media Center Edition is built on a Windows XP Home operating system platform and therefore the material in this book is relevant to an MCE computer. Most XP-MCE books devote the preponderance of their pages to multimedia topics and cater to beginner users, glossing over the nuts and bolts of using the operating system. If you have an MCE computer, this book will provide a good reference to it, assuming that you use that PC for more than an entertainment system. XP Media Center Edition is available only on new computers—officially, that is. This is because it can run only on computers with special tech specs, such as having fast video cards, a built-in TV tuner, DVD-RW drives, and so on. You can read Microsoft's pitch about Media Center PCs at `http://www.microsoft.com/windowsxp/mediacenter/`.

TIPS FROM THE WINDOWS PROS: SHOPPING FOR THE RIGHT HARDWARE AND SOFTWARE

Many people ask how I decide what hardware and software to purchase or discard when preparing for an operating system upgrade such as Windows XP. Here are some personal notes.

When I want to use one of my old utilities or applications for my Windows XP machine, I first check to see whether what I want to do is already covered by some other program. A better mousetrap is always around. Consider zip utilities, for example. I used to use DOS-based zip programs; then I moved on to WinZip. Under Windows 98, I used Windows 98 Plus! which includes native support for zip in the GUI, so I could zip and unzip right in the Explorer interface. When I upgraded to Windows 2000 Professional and I was wondering what to use, I popped onto the Web and did a search or two and came across Turbo Zip. I think the link said something about working with NT, so I gave it a shot. Now I'm using Power Archiver. It's excellent and adds a bunch of right-click options to Windows Explorer for easily compressing and decompressing individual files or groups of files. Although Windows XP has native compression included, like Windows 98 Plus! and Windows Me, you might want to use WinZip, Turbo Zip, or Power Archiver if you are familiar with them and like them.

As for productivity applications, I'm game to try anything I was using under Windows 98 and Me: Photoshop, Adaptec Easy CD Creator, CoolEdit 96, Excel 97, Word 97, Ulead Media Studio Pro, RealJukebox MP3 player, FrontPage Express, CuteFTP, ThumbsPlus, even some 3.x applications such as Collage Image Capture (for capturing screen shots for this book). I trust that Windows XP will alert me if the application isn't safe to use.

If I hear that a 32-bit version of a previously 16-bit application is available and will run faster (I usually assume it will at least have some nifty new features, such as better Save As and Open dialog boxes, support for more file formats, or something) then I'll spring for it if the price isn't too outrageous or if an upgrade option is available. Many programs check online to see whether a newer version is available and alert me if there is, often doing an effortless download. I typically don't complain, unless they want more money from me or there are rumors about spyware or annoying pop-up ads associated with the upgrade. Newer isn't always better.

I used to hang with Netscape Navigator, but frankly I like Internet Explorer better mostly because I've become accustomed to hitting the F11 key that increases the browser size to the full screen so that I can see the maximum amount of text at one time. In the interest of full disclosure, I'm using an extension to IE called NetCaptor for my browser. It has very cool program that uses IE under its hood but adds a feature called tabbed pages at the top of the window, letting you have a zillion Web pages open a once and easily switch between them. It's much better than having tons of separate IE windows open. You can also create groups of related Web sites (or your favorite group of sites) and open them all at the same time, with a single click.

Because I have a PocketPC as my PDA, Microsoft got me hooked on Outlook because that's really the only program that thoroughly integrates with PocketPC PDAs. (Microsoft got me on this one, sorry to say.)

About a decade ago, after first starting to use Windows 95, it took me several months to get used to using the desktop and the taskbar. But soon I was converted. Anyone upgrading from Windows 3.x will probably go through the same confusion at first. Whereas my home base had been the 3.x Program Manager and File Manager, I quickly became addicted to dropping folders and documents right on the desktop, dragging files to a floppy drive on the desktop, and so forth. The Windows XP interface is better-looking and has more features than the Windows 9x interface also familiar to Windows Me, NT, and 2000 users, and it offers even more file-management features. It's getting easier and easier to copy files around, drop them in email, or view a slide show of images from my digital camera using thumbnails in an Explorer window. The need for many of the shell add-ons that I once used in earlier Windows has vaporized.

When it comes to hardware, although I'm an experimenter and always want to try out the latest gizmos, I'm hard-core practical. Got that from my parents, I guess. Trying out new hardware and returning it aren't nearly as easy as deciding not to purchase software after trying the demo for free. As the saying goes, "Learn from other people's mistakes because you won't live long enough to make them all yourself." Too bad you can't try hardware for free; shipping charges, restocking fees, and hassles with sales people are too much for me to worry about. I don't buy new hardware unless it's on the Microsoft Catalog or HCL for the operating system that I'll be using with the system. It's that easy. I have too much weird off-brand hardware sitting in closets around my office or that I've donated to local community groups just because it didn't work with my operating system. Before I purchase, I also look around to see what the most popular item in a niche is, even if it's not the coolest or most powerful. Buying mainstream means I'll have more add-on products, supplies, cables, media, drivers, and online support from users. That support is worth the extra few dollars or loss of bleeding-edge features any day.

And finally, I usually go for version 2.0. If a product catches on and has industry-wide support, I'll go for it, but not until then. I never bought a Sony Beta VCR, an eight-track tape player, or an Atari or Timex-Sinclair computer.

CHAPTER **3**

INSTALLING WINDOWS XP HOME

In this chapter

NOTE

> If you're only upgrading to SP-2 and have already installed XP, be sure to check Appendixes A and B, which cover SP-2 upgrades.

CHOOSING AN UPGRADE PATH

This chapter describes the variety of installation options available for Windows XP Home. Even if your system is already installed, you might be interested in reading through this chapter for some helpful information about dual-booting various operating systems and working with multiple formats of disk partitions (FAT, FAT32, and NTFS). For information on partitions, see the "Disk Partitioning Tips" section later in this chapter. A file system is a logical structure applied to a partition which enables the computer to read and write data onto a hard drive. For more information on file systems, see the "Choosing a File System: FAT, FAT32, or NTFS?" section later in this chapter.

Due to improvements and standardization in user interfaces and to Microsoft-imposed installation procedures for Windows programs, setup of application programs nowadays is typically a piece of cake and self-explanatory. Likewise, installation of all newer Windows versions has grown increasingly automated. Installing Windows XP is usually a fairly simple process, but it takes an hour or more to complete.

This chapter covers the installation issues you will need to ponder under differing scenarios. I walk you through a typical installation, but if you've installed any Windows product since Windows 98 you shouldn't be surprised by anything. I also describe the basic decision tree you need to mull over before committing to Windows XP and the path you follow to get it up and running. Along the way, I discuss why you might make one choice over another and what to do when the process goes awry.

There are two primary installation scenarios: clean installation or upgrade installation. A clean installation is performed onto a new/formatted empty hard drive or to overwrite an existing OS. An upgrade installation retains existing settings and applications. In addition to the type of installation to perform, you must also address the issues of multi-booting and selecting a file system.

In this chapter, you learn what to expect when upgrading. Look for the section that applies to your upgrade situation. Also, check the general discussions about dual-booting and upgrading your file system because they apply in all cases. A more in-depth discussion of multi-booting can be found in Chapter 28, "Multibooting Windows XP with Other Operating Systems."

NOTE

> In addition to this chapter, you should also read two informative text files found on the Windows XP CD. The first is the file Read1st.txt, which is on the root directory of the CD. This file contains last-minute installation information Microsoft didn't publish until it released the final version of Windows XP. The second file is PERS1.txt, found in the SETUPTXT folder of the CD. This file contains detailed release notes covering topics such as installation, customization, and startup.

As mentioned in Chapter 1, "Introducing Windows XP Home Edition," Windows XP also supports installation capabilities attractive to the IS professional, such as *push* installations and automated installations that require no user intervention. For more information about these kinds of sophisticated deployment processes and automated installation tools, you should seek the aid of Microsoft's Windows XP Resource Kit. There, you'll find instructions for creating automated installation scripts. I provide a short overview of automated installations at the end of this chapter.

CLEAN INSTALLATION VERSUS UPGRADE

Let's talk about installing Windows XP Home. The next major question you must ask is whether to upgrade from an existing operating system or install fresh. Windows XP Home supports upgrading from Windows 98, OSR2, Second Edition (SE), and Millennium Edition (Me).

If your system is running any OS not included in this list (such as Windows 95, Windows NT, Windows 2000, or even Windows 3.x), you must perform a clean install. Clean installs do not retain any settings or applications. All settings must be reconfigured and all applications must be reinstalled after the clean installation of Windows XP is complete.

NOTE

> Windows XP Home edition can be upgraded to Windows XP Professional edition. Windows XP Home cannot be used to upgrade Windows NT 4.0 Workstation or Windows 2000 Professional. If you need to upgrade one of these two OSes, you must use Windows XP Professional.

Most Windows veterans know by now that doing a fresh installation is usually the most beneficial approach in the long run, even though it means more work up front installing applications and reentering personal settings, remote access and networking details, and so forth. You probably have some seat-of-the-pants experiences with Windows operating systems becoming polluted over time by wacko applications that mysteriously trash the Registry or erase or overwrite important files, like .DLL files, that Windows needs to operate properly.

With a clean installation, such worries are forgotten. It's like selling off that lemon of a car you've been wrestling with for the last five years. And yes, you lose lots of settings that are annoying to input again, such as Internet dial-up and TCP/IP settings, email accounts, address books, and so forth. You should attempt to back up as much important data as you can, such as your address books, email, personal documents, and so on before performing a clean installation over an existing OS. Windows XP is somewhat self-healing. Because system files and DLLs are protected against trampling, you're going to have a more sturdy system in the long run anyway. If your system is acting a little unpredictable (unexpected crashes, for example), it's better to do a clean installation. A clean installation can optionally reformat your boot partition (that's the one where Windows lives) and will just edit your system partition (that's the one that boots the system and displays the boot menu). In those cases where the boot and system partitions are the same, that partition can optionally be reformatted, too. You don't have to format the target partition when doing a clean installation. You simply choose a new system folder to install your operating system into. You should choose a partition that doesn't have another operating system on it.

When you choose to upgrade an existing operating system, you also run the possibility that some applications won't work properly afterward because they aren't fully compatible with Windows XP. Fortunately, Windows XP is even more backward-compatible than Windows 2000, especially with its Windows Compatibility mode.

NOTE

> Windows Compatibility mode is a nifty feature than enables Windows XP to support a wider range of software products than Windows 95 and Windows NT combined. A compatibility mode is simply a designation for a software platform emulation environment. In other words, when an application is launched with compatibility mode enabled, a virtual machine representing that application's native environment (DOS, Windows 95, Windows 98, Windows NT, or Windows 2000) is created in such a way that the application is fooled into thinking that it is the only application present on the computer system running its preferred OS. More details on working with applications is discussed in Chapter 21, "Tweaking the GUI."

Table 3.1 compares performing a clean installation versus upgrading your existing Windows installation.

TABLE 3.1   CLEAN INSTALLATION VERSUS UPGRADING

Perform a new installation answer "yes" to any of the following:	Consider upgrading when you can when you can answer "yes" to all the following:
You've just purchased a new hard disk or reformatted it.	Your current operating system supports upgrading.
The operating system you have on your computer isn't among those on the upgrade list.	You want to fully replace your previous Windows operating system with Windows XP.

Perform a new installation answer "yes" to any of the following:	Consider upgrading when you can when you can answer "yes" to all the following:
Your computer has an operating system already, but you're ready to kill it and start fresh with Windows XP.	You want to keep your existing files and preferences.
You want to create a dual-boot configuration with Windows XP and your current system. (Note that Microsoft recommends using two partitions to do so.)	You're ready to chance that in some rare cases, applications or hardware won't immediately work as they do under the present operating system.

DUAL-BOOTING VERSUS SINGLE BOOTING

In addition to the upgrade/fresh installation issue, you also must consider the dual- or multi-boot issue. Dual-booting is a scheme that lets you keep your old operating system and install Windows XP as a clean installation. Windows XP can be installed onto any hard disk volume or partition within a computer, it is not limited or restricted to drive C as is Windows 9x. Thus, by adding a new hard drive and installing Windows XP onto it, you retain your original OS. When you boot up, you are given a choice of operating system to start, as shown in Figure 3.1.

NOTE

> Notice that in this book the term *dual-booting* is used often. This usually refers to having only two OSes on the same system. We use this term because in most multiple OS scenarios only two OSes are installed. But the term *multi-booting* could just as easily have been substituted to include those systems with two or more OSes. So, when you see dual-booting, don't limit your thinking to only two OSes.

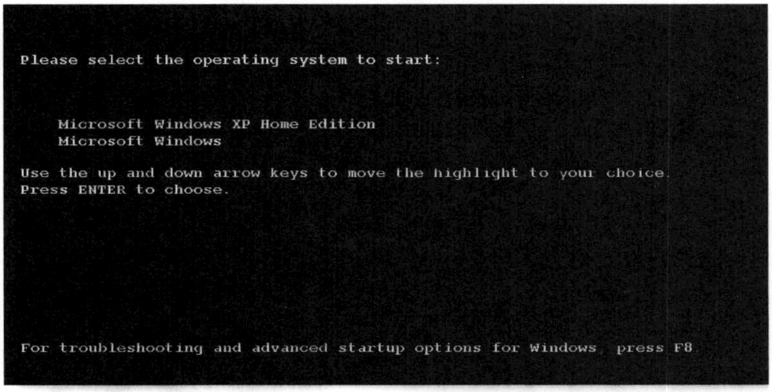

Figure 3.1
When a system is set up for dual-booting, a menu like this appears at boot time.

```
Please select the operating system to start:


    Microsoft Windows XP Home Edition
    Microsoft Windows

Use the up and down arrow keys to move the highlight to your choice.
Press ENTER to choose.




For troubleshooting and advanced startup options for Windows, press F8
```

Windows XP officially supports dual-booting with any Microsoft Windows operating systems as well as MS-DOS and OS/2. You can multi-boot almost any OS that uses FAT or NTFS file systems on the boot drive. We'll talk more about the different kinds of file systems and what they offer you. Basically, file system refers to the format of the hard drive and the way the OS stores your data files on the drive.

> **NOTE**
>
> Third-party partition or multi-boot managers include Partition Magic from Power Quest (`http://www.symantec.com/partitionmagic/`and System Commander from V Communications (`www.v-com.com`).

PROS OF DUAL-BOOTING

There are lots of reasons for setting up a dual- or multi-booting computer, especially if you are in the business of testing computers, or you run a wide variety of software and hardware on your computers. Personally, of the five computers in my office, four of them are dual-booting. Below are a few thoughts about dual-booting that you might want to consider before making the decision:

- I multi-boot on a couple of my machines because I run lots of Windows tools, hardware-specific programs like video editing programs, CD-writers or rewriters, and so on. Also, I'm always testing new programs. No matter how much I would prefer to run a single operating system, sometimes I need to run other versions of Windows to get a driver or some application to work. So, it makes sense for me to multi-boot.

- If you're regularly testing or running lots of different kinds of software and own an abundance of hardware, or you're a new hardware junkie like me, being stuck with just a single operating system is like being in jail. Choose to multi-boot, even though this choice can cause some headaches, as described in the following section.

- If you have doubts about compatibility with your hardware or software and don't want to jeopardize your existing operating system, use a dual-boot arrangement for a while and see what you think. If you become confident that XP is going to work for you, you can either perform an upgrade installation over your existing operating system, or move over into using XP only. (That is, you can migrate your data and applications into your XP setup.) If you decide to upgrade over your old OS, rather than migrate into the clean XP, you can then remove the clean XP "test" system to free up disk space. If you decide XP doesn't cut the mustard, you can remove it. Regardless of how you do the eventual upgrade, this kind of approach gives you the time to test things out. You'll eventually end up with a single OS in the long run, one you're happy with.

TIP

> There is an alternative to dual- or multi-booting that makes installing multiple OSes on your computer easier, although not quite as quick or responsive. A program called Virtual PC lets you install and run multiple operating systems at the same time. One "host" operating system runs the secondary operating systems within it. For example, you could have Windows Me be the host to run Windows XP. You boot up Windows Me, run the Virtual PC program, and then tell Virtual PC to boot up Windows XP. You end up having Windows Me and Windows XP running at the same time. It's pretty impressive. Use of virtual computers is covered in Chapter 28.

CONS OF DUAL-BOOTING

Dual or multi-booting isn't always as simple or attractive as it might seem at first. You have to take care that you understand the limitations and requirements of making your computer a home for more than one operating system. Operating systems are, for the most part, egotistical and stingy. They don't always coexist on the same computer peaceably. Therefore, you should be aware of a few points before deciding to dual-boot your machine:

- You must reinstall many applications, particularly ones that make Registry entries, such as Office, or ones that put portions of themselves (for example, DLL files) in the operating system directory. You must run the Setup routines for each such program once for each operating system. Your applications still work in both environments, and contrary to what you might think, you don't have to duplicate all the files on disk—if you install them into the same directories under each operating system. Still, you must go through the process of installation again.

- Some applications that run in both environments just don't behave properly or cooperate as you would hope. This is especially true of ones that share the same data files or futz with the Registry. If a program tweaks the Registry or alerts your data files to what operating system has been working with it, and then you reboot in the other operating system (each operating system has its own Registry files, remember), unexpected incompatibilities can crop up.

NOTE

> Some programs are, obviously, less picky because they are not as integrated into the operating system. Netscape seems to live quite peaceably in a multi-boot arrangement, mail and all.

- Any application that relies on the operating systems' rights settings, user identities, or multiple profiles will likely not interrelate properly between the operating systems. As you probably know, Windows XP, Windows 98/SE/Me, Windows NT, and Windows 2000 can be set up with multiple-user settings stored on the same machine. Applications that take advantage of these settings often store individual settings in the Registry and in folders such as Windows\profiles or C:\windows\application data or, in the case of Windows 2000 and Windows XP, C:\documents and settings. In any

3

case, because applications sometimes look to the operating system for information about a user's individual settings (whether it's gleaned from the Registry or user-specific folders such as the Desktop folder), things can go awry if you're hoping to run certain applications under either operating system, and you're not a bit crafty. One way to live with this situation is to focus on using one operating system and use the other only when some application or hardware refuses to run in the first operating system.

- Upgrading to Windows XP pulls in all (or as many as possible) of the preexisting settings, such as email accounts, LAN settings and dial-up connections, machine user accounts, and so on. If you dual-boot, you have to create these settings from scratch for the new operating system.

- Security is a biggie. Is security an issue for you? Do you need to keep prying eyes at bay? Unless you're going to set up a separate partition or drive with NTFS and encryption on it, you're increasing the chances of security breaches by dual-booting. Drive, volume, partition, and file security are minimal under any OS using FAT16 or FAT32 partitions (including Windows 9x/Me), because these can be altered by anyone who can boot the system in DOS or a DOS-based operating system. If you want to dual-boot and maintain decent security, then you should install Windows XP on a second drive, formatted in NTFS. Alternatively, you can create an NTFS partition on your main drive and install into it. Use the NTFS partition for your Windows XP files and encrypt sensitive data files. When installing, you are given the option of converting to NTFS. (Encryption can be performed after Windows XP is installed.)

- The only Microsoft operating systems that read NTFS partitions are Windows NT, Windows 2000, and Windows XP. If you want to multi-boot and gain the advantages of NTFS, remember that you can't access any data files on the NTFS partitions when you're running DOS, Windows 3.x, or Windows 9x/SE/Me. (Linux, however, can read and write to NTFS partitions.)

PRECAUTIONS WHEN DUAL-BOOTING

If, after reading the pros and cons, you think you want to set up a dual-boot system, consider the following precautions in addition to those listed previously. This part takes a little studying, so put on your thinking cap.

- Though it is technically possible to install multiple OSes into the same partition on your hard drive, don't do it. Many of the Windows operating systems, specifically Windows 95 and 98/SE/Me as well as Windows 2000 and Windows XP, share similar common directory names (such as \Windows, \Program Files, and \Documents and Settings). Installing a new OS into the same partition as an existing OS runs the risk of overwriting important files. This is true, even if you select to use a different primary folder name. I highly recommend installing each OS into its own partition (with the possible exception of DOS). You make this choice when installing Windows XP through the advanced options during the initial phase of setup. Most other OSes (especially Windows NT and Windows 2000) offer similar options.

- Microsoft doesn't suggest mixing file systems in dual-boot arrangements because it complicates matters. Microsoft says "such a configuration introduces additional complexity into the choice of file systems." Microsoft's warning is probably just an admonition against burdening the operating system and your applications with multiple file systems *and* multiple operating systems on the same machine. Admittedly, mixing them does complicate things. If you want to play it safe, go with the lowest common denominator of file systems for the operating systems you're installing. Typically, it is FAT or FAT32. (See "Choosing a File System: FAT, FAT32, or NTFS?" later in this chapter.)

- Installation order is important in some cases. To set up a dual-boot configuration between MS-DOS/Windows 3.x or Windows 95 with Windows XP, you should install Windows XP last. Otherwise, important files needed to start Windows XP could be overwritten by the other operating systems. For dual-booting between Windows 98/SE/Me, Windows NT, Windows 2000, and Windows XP, installation order is irrelevant.

- To set up a dual-boot configuration between MS-DOS/Windows 3.x or Windows 95 with Windows XP, the primary partition (that is, the one from which you boot) must be formatted as FAT. If you're dual-booting Windows 95 OSR2, Windows 98, Windows NT, or Windows 2000 with Windows XP, the primary partition must be FAT or FAT32, not NTFS. These two rules make sense because, without third-party drivers, Windows 9x/SE/Me can't read or exist with NTFS, and Windows 95 can't read either NTFS or FAT32.

- There is more than one version of NTFS. Windows XP and Windows 2000 both use NTFS v5. Windows NT 4.0 right out of the box uses NTFS v4. But Windows NT 4.0 can be upgraded to use NTFS v5 by installing Service Pack 4. This becomes important when you attempt to dual-boot with Windows NT 4.0 (without Service Pack 4) and Window XP. The NT OS will be unable to access files on the Windows XP NTFS formatted partitions. Your only options are to apply SP4 to NT or use FAT.

- You can install Windows XP on a compressed drive if that drive was compressed using the NTFS disk compression utility, but not if it was made with DoubleSpace or DriveSpace or some other disk compressor such as Stacker. If you're going to dual-boot with Windows 9x, remember that Windows XP won't see the compressed DoubleSpace and DriveSpace partitions; and any NTFS partitions, compressed or not, are invisible to Windows 9x without third-party drivers.

- Sometimes an operating system reconfigures your hardware through soft settings. Suppose you install some new hardware and run Windows 98. That operating system detects it and might do some software setting on the hardware that works with Windows 98 but which conflicts with Windows XP. This problem should be rare because most hardware these days is Plug and Play-compatible and should be configurable on-the-fly as the operating system boots up. But be aware of the possibility. A good example is that two operating systems might have different video display drivers for the same video adapter, causing you to have to manually adjust the screen size and orientation when you switch between them.

3

PRECAUTIONS WHEN DUAL-BOOTING WINDOWS NT AND WINDOWS XP

You must follow some weird rules when dual-booting Windows NT (3 or 4) and Windows XP. Mostly, they have bearing on which file systems you can use. For folks testing Windows XP while keeping the tried and true Windows NT 4 around, they can pose a bit of an annoyance. Here's the list:

- You should upgrade to at least NT 4.0 Service Pack 4 if you want to dual-boot with Windows XP sharing NTFS partitions. Upgrade first and then install Windows XP; otherwise, your NT 4 system will not boot.

- If your hard disk is formatted with only NTFS partitions, Microsoft recommends against dual-booting Windows XP and Windows NT. It makes this recommendation because Windows NT and Windows XP use different versions of the NTFS specification, and they bump into one another. Either use FAT32 or, when you're installing Windows XP, opt *not* to upgrade to NTFS 5.

- Computers dual-booting Windows NT and Windows XP in a networked environment must have different computer names under each boot configuration if the computers are connected to an NT domain. Otherwise, the domain controller is given conflicting information about the workstation, and it deals with these two types of workstations in slightly different ways.

NOTE

> Dual-booting with Windows 2000 does not encounter these issues because it shares the same version of NTFS that Windows XP uses. For more detailed information about configuring your computer to dual-boot, see Chapter 28, "Multibooting Windows XP with Other Operating Systems," which is devoted to this topic.

CHOOSING A FILE SYSTEM: FAT, FAT32, OR NTFS?

The next major consideration on the pre-installation agenda is determining what type of file system you intend to use. The rules and regulations discussed in the preceding section might have narrowed down this choice for you. Still, you might want to read about the pros and cons of the various file-keeping schemes in use on Windows XP machines and consider a few details on how they influence your installation.

NOTE

> Windows XP doesn't know about compressed drives such as those created with DriveSpace or DoubleSpace. You have to decompress them before installing to Windows XP. Decompressing is a real pain if your disk space is totally packed (because this process causes your files to take up more space). You might have to decompress in stages, moving data off the hard disk to backup media or another drive.

As mentioned in the previous sections on dual-booting Windows XP and a second operating system, it's a good idea to think about what file system you're going to use, preferably before installing Windows XP. Although you can use utilities in Windows XP and external utilities such as Partition Magic to convert partitions between file systems after the fact, forethought and advance partition preparation are the better path. Let's do a little review of file systems you can use and advantages of each.

A file system is a scheme by which data files and directories (folders) are stored and retrieved on a floppy disk or hard disk. Tape and other media have file systems as well, but here I'm talking only about hard disks. Windows XP supports several file systems: the NT File System (NTFS) or one of the file allocation table file systems (FAT or FAT32).

A BRIEF HISTORY OF FILE SYSTEMS

In the beginning (of PCs, that is), there was FAT, and it was good. FAT is the system that DOS uses; it's been around for a long time, since the early eighties. FAT stands for File Allocation Table. A file allocation table is basically a table of contents of the disk that the operating system uses to look up the location of a file, even if the file is broken up in pieces (sectors) scattered across the disk's surface. The FAT scheme brought relatively simple, reliable, and efficient floppy and small hard disk storage to the PC. It's also the scheme that, unlike the Macintosh file system, brought the confining 8.3 file-naming convention that many of us learned to live with and hate. The 8.3 file-naming convention simply means that a file can have a maximum of 8 characters for its filename and up to three characters for its extension (after the period). For example, myletter.doc is an example of the longest-possible 8.3 file name.

When NT 3.x appeared, it included NTFS as an acknowledgment of the shortcomings of the FAT system, including support for a much-larger hard drive partition size limit of 2 gigabytes (GB). NTFS also provided long-awaited long filenames, more security and fault tolerance, better disk compression, support for hard disks up to 2 terabytes (that's big), and support for advanced multiple-disk arrangements (RAID). Also, as drives become larger, efficiency of disk storage didn't fall off under NTFS as it did with FAT.

Windows 95 brought long filenames to FAT through some sleight of hand, but still the system was not good at dealing with the newer larger drives and wasted a bunch of space on them when it stored tiny files. So, to both provide good backward compatibility with FAT disks and still offer support for large drives, Windows 95 OSR2 and Windows 98 both included a new file system called FAT32. Essentially a beefed up FAT file system, FAT32 isn't as robust as NTFS, and it's not compatible with NTFS. But the FAT32 system eliminated the 2GB upper limit on partition size support (it also can run as high as 2TB) and increased effective storage capacity by lowering the cluster size on large drives. NT 4 can't read or work with FAT32, nor can DOS and Windows 3.x. However, both Windows 2000 and Windows XP support FAT32.

NOTE

> Clusters are the smallest amount of space that can be used to store information on a hard disk. On smallish drives, the cluster size is also pretty small, so storing dinky files that are only, say, 1K in size is pretty efficient (there is little wasted space). But on today's huge drives, under the FAT scheme, the cluster would necessarily be much larger (this is a limitation of the FAT system, not the drive). You end up donating serious amounts of space to no good cause. The bottom line is that FAT32 and NTFS get you more bang for your hard disk buck, because lowering the cluster size allows for more efficient use of space, especially on larger drives.

The bottom line? As with Windows NT and Windows 2000, NTFS is the recommended file system for use with Windows XP. NTFS has all the basic capabilities of FAT as well as all the advantages of FAT32 file systems. The weird thing is that now you have to think about three different file systems when considering dual-booting. When you consider that you have at least nine Microsoft operating systems to choose from, and three file systems, the combinations get complex. Therefore, understanding the limitations of each is important.

TIP

> You can convert an existing partition to NTFS during Setup, but if you want to do it after you install XP, no problem. You can convert it at any time by using a command-line utility called convert.exe (see the "Convert" section in Chapter 26). Another approach is to use a third-party tool like PartitionMagic.

One of the prime points to remember is that if you're dual-booting, only Windows NT, Windows 2000, and Windows XP systems can read NTFS partitions. If you don't care about accessing the NTFS partition from, say, Windows 98, this is not a big deal. It simply does not appear in Windows Explorer or is not available from your applications. This is the main reason Microsoft doesn't want you to mix file systems; it simply confuses people.

When you're running partitions larger than 32GB, you should really format them as NTFS. If you choose to use FAT, anything over 2GB should be formatted FAT32.

NOTE

> File systems are terribly complex and a subject far beyond what I can cover in a Windows book. For the most part, you don't need to know more than what is presented here, unless you are naturally inclined to learn everything you can about complex topics (don't worry, you are not alone). In that case, I recommend that you pick up a copy of *Upgrading and Repairing PCs, 16th Edition*, by Scott Mueller (also published by Que).

Disk Partitioning Tips

Disk partitioning is a scheme by which you can have a single hard disk look like multiple hard disks to the operating system. If you partition a disk into, say, two partitions, the operating system displays disks C and D rather than just C. You split up the space on the drive between the partitions based on your needs.

One of the most notable needs for disk partitioning was to accommodate operating systems that imposed limitations on the size of partitions. As hard disks grew in size, partitioning was required in order to use the entire disk. Because FAT had a limitation of 2GB, users relied on partitioning or other software driver schemes to get around this imposed top end. Another common reason for partitioning is for running dissimilar operating systems, ones that cannot read from or write to a common file system. Because each partition can have its own disk format, this could often circumambulate such requirements. One partition could be FAT, another NTFS, and another HPFS (for OS/2), and so on. Any hard disk can contain up to four primary partitions.

Only primary partitions can be marked active. An active primary partition is where the computer's BIOS looks for a bootable operating system when powered on. In addition to primary partitions, there are extended partitions. A system can have up to four primary partitions or a maximum of three primary partitions and a single extended partition. The extended partition is a bit different than a primary partition. First, extended partitions cannot be marked active. Second, extended partitions must be divided into logical drives. Only primary partitions and logical drives can be formatted and assigned a drive letter. The total number of primary partitions plus logical drives cannot exceed 32 for a single hard drive.

For examples of these issues, see Figure 3.2. Disk 0 has a single primary partition (C), and an extended partition. The extended partition contains two logical drives (D and G) and 1.86 GB of free space. The extended partition is highlighted with a thick border, that's how you distinguish it from primary partitions. This extended partition could contain another 29 logical drives before reaching the 32 division maximum per drive. Disk 1 consists of a single primary partition (F) and 15.11 GB of free space. This free space could be used to create up to 3 additional primary partitions, or up to 2 additional primary partitions and an extended partition containing logical drives. Drive 2 consists of a single primary partition (E).

In most cases, you rarely need to divide a drive into more than 4 sections. And then, that might only occur when you need to divide a large drive into FAT partitions (because each partition cannot be larger than 2GB). The tools you use to create partitions manage the division classification for you. If you use FDISK, you're a bit more aware of the presence of extended partitions and logical drives. If you use the Windows NT, Windows 2000, or Windows XP drive tools (such as the Disk Management tool) you see extended partitions and logical drives labeled, but the OS manages when these need to be created.

Some people use partitions for dividing up their data rather than for accommodating different file systems. You might want a partition to organize information—for example, one for backup data, one for documents and data files, one for applications only, or for the operating system only. Then you can more easily design your backup strategy.

Figure 3.2
Disk Management
viewed through
Computer
Management, showing
drive partitioning.

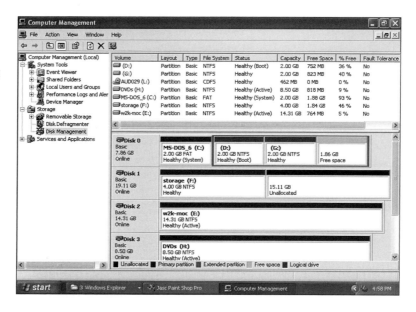

NOTE

When you do a new installation of Windows XP, the Setup program looks around and automatically selects an appropriate disk partition as the destination based on size and format. You can override the choice by clicking the Advanced Options button during Setup, though.

If you're going to dual-boot, you should install on a separate partition. Either create one or use one that is already present. The reason for using a separate partition for each operating system is to prevent Setup from overwriting important files belonging to the other operating system. If you have unpartitioned (different from unused) space on your disk, Setup can create a partition during installation.

If you intend to dual-boot Windows 9x and Windows XP, Windows 9x should be on the first partition. In general computer terms, this means the boot drive. In Windows NT speak, this is the system partition.

→ If you're considering creating a system that is bootable in more than one operating system, **see** "Dual-Booting Versus Single Booting," **p. 63**.

The exact options you have during Setup change depending on your existing hard disk configuration. You might have as many as four options when partitioning your hard disk:

■ If you have adequate unpartitioned space, you can create a new Windows XP partition in that space and install Windows XP in it.

■ If the hard disk is unpartitioned (no partitions at all—freshly formatted) you can create and size the Windows XP partition.

■ If the disk has an existing partition, but you don't care what's in it, Setup lets you delete the partition and create a new one of your chosen format for installing Windows XP. Beware, though; deleting an existing partition destroys *every file* on the partition.

> **TIP**
>
> Don't even try to install Windows XP on a partition that is less than 3GB. Although Windows XP only requires 1.5GB (only!), I think creating a 3GB partition is more reasonable. If you are upgrading you need an extra 300MB to store the recovery files, and setup doesn't allow you to start the process with less than 1.5GB of free space. You'll want (and need) the additional free space later for future additions and modifications to the operating system.

FILE SYSTEM CONVERSION LIMITATIONS

This section lists a few ridiculous warnings and limitations—ridiculous because these steps are not required if you use an intelligent program such as PartitionMagic to prepare your drive partitions before you begin installing XP. Due to limitations of Setup and Microsoft's supplied disk tools (FDISK, for example), you should be aware of these issues. First, most conversions between file systems are multi-step processes involving backing up and then restoring the partitions after reformatting.

For example, although converting *to* NTFS during installation is easy, if you change your mind and want to revert to FAT, you have to back up all your files on the NTFS partition, reformat the partition as FAT (which erases all the files), and then restore the files from backup. The same is true of converting a FAT partition to FAT32. One workaround is to use the FAT32 converter in Windows 98 or 95 OSR2. Each of these operating systems has a tool that performs such a conversion quite easily.

Second, you can't restore an NTFS v4 (file system from NT 4) partition after you convert it to NTFS v5 (file system from Windows XP, Windows 2000, and Windows NT 4.0 SP4+). There's no easy way out on that score. There is support for NTFS v5 file formats via tools like Partition Magic, though.

GETTING YOUR NETWORK INFORMATION TOGETHER

Windows XP Home is designed mostly for standalone (non-networked) PCs. However, it does support basic networking functions because more and more folks are setting up little networks in their homes or home offices. If a network interface is detected during the installation, the basic networking components are installed. The basic components are the Microsoft Networking Client and the TCP/IP protocol. You're able to configure networking components during installation, but you aren't offered the chance to manage workgroup or domain membership during installation.

If networking components are installed, Windows XP Home is automatically a member of the MSHOME workgroup. You can change the workgroup membership, but Windows XP

3

Home cannot be a domain client. You must use Windows XP Professional if you need a domain client. A domain client is a system which is a member of a centrally controlled and secured network environment.

You should leave the network component configuration set to its defaults and change the settings after the installation is complete. They are set by default to seek out a DHCP server to obtain the necessary (and tedious) IP configuration details that earlier operating systems made you enter manually. (Details about post-installation manual configuration of network components are discussed in Part IV, "Networking.")

If you are upgrading a system that already has network connectivity, Windows XP Home retains that connectivity, but only if that connectivity is centered around a workgroup. Otherwise, it becomes a member of the MSHOME workgroup by default.

IT'S BACKUP TIME!

Okay, so you're ready to do the installation. Need I say it? If you're upgrading from a previous version, Setup is supposed to let you back out and restore your system to its previous state if you panic in the middle. I've actually backed out of Setup a few times successfully, but that doesn't mean it always works. Setup does lots of stuff to your operating system and hard disk files, and things could get particularly sticky if it bombs halfway through the process. So ask yourself, "Do I have important data on my computer?" If so, back it up before you start your installation. Can you afford the downtime incurred should you need to reinstall your applications and operating system? If not, back them up, too.

Windows XP brings a thoughtful feature to the table when you upgrade from Windows 9x/SE/Me. This new feature is the ability to uninstall Windows XP and return to the previous OS. During the initial stages of the upgrade installation, a complete backup of the existing 9x OS is created (about 300MB of stuff). This backup is performed automatically to protect users. There are advanced command line startup options that can be used to disable this activity, but if you are smart enough to figure out how to do that, you are smart enough to make your own backup. Plus, this backup feature not only allows you to roll back but it protects you during installation. If the upgrade install fails, the system returns to the previous OS automatically. After about 60 days or so, you are prompted whether to retain or delete this backup archive of the previous OS. This backup procedure consumes about 300MB of space, so if your destination partition does not have around 1GB of free space the Setup routine terminates before even getting started. This backup protection is used only for Windows 9x/SE/Me; it is not available for upgrades over Windows NT or Windows 2000.

Backing Up to a Disk Image

One technique I like for doing serious backups is to make a disk image of my main hard drive. With a disk image, if the drive dies or some other catastrophe occurs—such as a new operating system installation goes south—I can just restore the drive to its previous state, boot tracks, operating system, data, applications, all in one fell swoop. I use a program called DriveImage from Symantec for this task, though some people swear by a competing product called Norton Ghost (oddly enough, also from Symantec). Both are powerful tools for making backups and recovering from a dead operating system. These programs work by copying your hard disk sector by sector and storing the whole image in a huge, single file on another drive. The large file they create contains all the necessary information to replace the data in the original tracks and sectors.

If you have a CD-writer, you can use a CD-R as the backup medium. If you have a CD-RW drive (RW = rewritable), it can provide a very cost efficient (though slow) means of backing up and restoring. It also works with a second hard disk in the computer, a second partition on a hard disk, and removable media such as or Zip or Jazz drives. Another approach is to store an image on a hard disk across a network on another workstation, though recovering from the remote station is a little more complex than recovering from a local drive.

If you must back up data only and don't care about reinstalling your applications or operating system (this backup approach is easier, of course), you can use a backup program or you can simply copy the files onto other drives using Windows Explorer or another utility. How you back up your files depends on your current operating system. If you're running Windows 9x/SE/Me/NT/2000, one obvious approach is to employ the Windows Backup program (by choosing Start, Programs, Accessories, System Tools, Backup). You might have to install it if it's not there. To do so, open the Control Panel, choose Add/Remove Programs, and then select Windows Setup. Remember, in Windows NT, you need a tape drive installed for the Backup tool to work. All other Windows OSes versions of Backup can store the backup files to any writable media. If you're in doubt about the use of the Backup program, check the Windows Help system.

→ To learn more details about backup strategies, **see** "Backup Tools and Strategies," **p. 923**.

Okay, enough of the safety speech. You are old enough to know to put on your parachute before you jump out of the plane.

CLEAN INSTALLATION PROCEDURE

The three basic types of clean installation procedures are as follows:

- Install on a brand new disk or computer system
- Erase the disk, format it, and install
- Install into a new directory for dual-booting (see the multi-boot discussion earlier in this chapter)

If you intend to use either of the first two methods, make sure you are equipped to boot your computer from the CD-ROM. Most of today's computers support booting from the CD-ROM drive. Doing so might require changing the drive boot order in the BIOS or CMOS, but try it first without the change. With no floppy disk inserted and a clean hard disk, the CD-ROM drive should be tried next. The Windows XP CD-ROM is bootable and should run the Setup program automatically.

The Windows XP setup procedure can also be launched using the five setup boot floppies. On an older computer, you might have to ensure you can boot into DOS from a floppy.

People preparing to set up Windows on older computers often overlook this point. They wipe the hard disk and then boot up with a floppy only to find the CD-ROM drive isn't recognized, so they can't run the Setup program on the CD. If you have the boot floppy for Windows XP, your CD-ROM drive should be recognized upon booting, assuming your CD-ROM drive is among those supported. If you have misplaced your floppies or they were not included with your Windows XP CD, then check out the "Making Replacement Startup Floppies" section later this chapter.

 If you can't get DOS to recognize your CD-ROM drive, see "DOS Won't Recognize the CD-ROM Drive" in the "Troubleshooting" section at the end of this chapter.

NOTE

> Remember to check Chapter 2, "Getting Your Hardware and Software Ready for Windows XP," to ensure your hardware components meet the minimum requirements to run Windows XP.

Installation takes 60–90 minutes depending on the speed of your machine. Refer to the following sections if you have questions about the steps of the process. The process is fairly similar for each category of installation, with the addition of the software compatibility report when you're upgrading from an older operating system.

TYPICAL CLEAN SETUP PROCEDURE

If you're installing into an empty partition, and you can boot an operating system that is supported for the purpose of Setup (Windows 9x/SE/Me/NT/2000), just boot up, insert the CD, and choose Install Windows XP from the resulting dialog box. Then, you can follow the installation step-by-step procedure below.

If Windows doesn't automatically detect the CD when you insert it, you must run the Setup program, setup.exe, manually from the Start, Run dialog box. After the Setup routine has started, you can follow the installation step-by-step procedure below.

Another method of kick-starting the installation of Windows XP can be performed from any OS that has access to the CD. If the existing OS is a non-Windows non-32-bit OS, then execute \i386\winnt.exe. If the OS is a 32-bit Windows OS, then execute \i386\winnt32.exe. If you are able to use the winnt32 launch tool, you can follow the typical installation step-by-step procedure below.

If your computer has a blank hard disk, or your current operating system isn't supported, the process is different. You will need to start the installation by using Setup floppy disks or by booting from the Windows XP CD (this approach works only if your computer is newer, and you can boot from the CD-ROM drive). Setup automatically runs if you boot from the CD-ROM.

→ If you need to create Setup floppy disks, **see** "Making Startup Floppies," **p. 84**.

If you used the winnt launch tool, used the boot floppies to initiate setup, or were able to start from a bootable CD, your installation varies from the typical installation step-by-step procedure as follows:

1. A text-only step wizard is launched.

2. Verify that the displayed path is the correct location of the Windows XP source files. Press Enter.

3. Setup copies numerous files to the hard drive of the computer; this might take a few minutes. After the copying process is complete, the system reboots.

4. After the system reboots, the setup wizard continues.

5. Jump to step 15 of the following typical clean installation step-by-step procedure to continue.

The typical clean installation step-by-step procedure is as follows:

1. The Windows Setup wizard appears. Using the Installation Type pull-down list, select New Installation. (Note: Upgrading is discussed later in this chapter.)

2. Click Next. The License Agreement page appears.

NOTE

> Corporate attorneys know that people don't read these software agreements. I've even heard reports of software in which the agreements make you promise not to write a review of the software without alerting the manufacturer first. I'm sure some interesting, precedent-setting cases will occur in upcoming years.

3. Read the agreement then select the "I accept this agreement" radio button.

4. Click Next. The Your Product Key page appears.

5. Type in your 25-digit Product Key.

6. Click Next. The Setup Options page appears.

7. Click the Advanced Options button.

8. Verify that the path for the location of the source files is correct (it should be <cd-rom drive letter>:\i386 or if you are installing over a network this would be \\<servername>\<sharename>\i386).

9. If you wish, change the name of the main Windows directory.

10. To force setup to duplicate all necessary files to the hard drive before initiating the installation procedure, mark the Copy all installation files from the Setup CD check box.

NOTE

> Copying all the Setup files to the hard disk has two advantages. First, you can save yourself some time because the file copying and decompressing process is faster from the hard disk than from a CD-ROM drive. Second, the next time Windows XP needs access to Setup files (when you add new hardware, for example), you don't have to insert the CD-ROM. Just browse to the correct directory. Copying the over 6,000 files (yes, that's thousand, amounting to about 450MB) from the CD takes about 15 minutes on a reasonably fast system.

11. To be able to select the partition into which to install Windows XP (other than drive C), mark the I want to choose the install drive letter and partition during Setup check box.

12. Click OK. Click Next. The Performing Dynamic Update page appears.

13. If your system has Internet access from the pre-existing OS, you can optionally select to download the latest setup files for Windows XP at this time. Mark the Yes radio button. If your system does not currently have Internet access, select No, click Next, then skip to step 15.

14. Click Next. The setup routine attempts to contact the Microsoft download site and retrieve any new Setup files. After this is completed, the setup routine reboots the system automatically.

15. After the system reboots, the Welcome to Setup text-only screen prompts you to install Windows XP, repair an existing installation, or exit setup. Press Enter to continue with setup.

16. Your drives are examined and the partition manager is displayed. This tool is used to select the installation partition for Windows XP. If the partition already exists, use the arrow keys to select it, then skip to step 25.

TIP

> If you want to install Windows XP into a separate partition, make sure the partition is preexisting or that you have some unpartitioned space on your hard drive. Sorry to state the obvious, but Setup doesn't let you change the *size* of existing partitions on-the-fly, even though it does convert from FAT to NTFS and does create NTFS partitions from an unpartitioned space.
>
> If you have a large hard disk all in one partition (typical with today's cheap drives when they come from the factory) and want to split it, use a utility program such as FDISK, NT's Disk Administrator tool, 2000's Computer Management tool, or PartitionMagic (I recommend the latter highly). If you want to install into an NTFS partition, remember that FDISK can't create NTFS partitions. As a workaround, you either have to convert the target partition to NTFS during or after Setup or use a utility such as PartitionMagic that can make or convert FAT partitions to NTFS. Note that the NTFS partition does not have to be formatted in advance of your running Setup; as long as it exists as a partition, Setup offers to format it for you.
>
> The main advantage of having multiple partitions on a hard disk these days is to support different file system formats for use with multiple operating systems. You can use FAT or FAT32 on one partition to run DOS or Windows 9x, for example, and use an NTFS partition for Windows XP.

17. If an existing partition must be deleted to create unpartitioned space where you want to install Windows XP, go on to step 18. Otherwise, skip to step 21.

18. Use the arrow keys to select the partition to delete, then press D.

19. If the selected partition is a system partition, you must press Enter to confirm the deletion of a system partition.

20. Press L to confirm deletion of the partition. (Yes, this is a valid extra step to make sure you are aware that you are deleting a partition.)

21. To create a new partition out of unpartitioned space, use the arrow keys to select the unpartitioned space, then press C.

22. Type in the size of the partition you want to create out of the unpartitioned space. The default size listed is the maximum size that can be created. After you have typed in a number, press Enter.

23. Use the arrow keys to select the newly created partition.

24. Press Enter to install Windows XP into the selected partition.

25. Select the file system to format the partition. If the partition is already properly formatted with NTFS v5, another option of "Leave the current file system intact (no changes)" is available. If this option is available, select it and press Enter. Then skip to step 28.

26. Use the arrow keys to select the NTFS file system (not the option with (Quick) next to it).

NOTE

> The Quick options for both NTFS and FAT are only there when you are converting or over-formatting a partition that has already been formatted. It's a way to save time, especially if you are formatting a 2GB or larger drive. I recommend staying away from the Quick format and let the setup wizard perform a full format on the destination partition. It takes a little longer, but it ensures a properly formatted drive.

→ If you want to know more information about deciding whether you should change file systems, **see** "Choosing a File System: FAT, FAT32, or NTFS?" **p. 68**. Also, Chapters 26 and 28 contain additional information about file systems and formats.

27. Press Enter to initiate formatting. A progress of the formatting action is displayed.

28. After formatting is complete, files are copied to the destination partition. This might take 10 minutes.

29. After the file copy procedure completes, the system automatically reboots.

30. After it's rebooted, Setup launches a basic Windows GUI environment. After performing numerous operations (these could take 10 minutes or more), the Setup Wizard appears displaying the Regional and Language Options page. The defaults are for

English and a US keyboard; if you require other settings, click the Customize of Details buttons to change them.

 If the Windows installer crashes during the installation, see "Windows Crashes During Installation" in the "Troubleshooting" section at the end of this chapter.

31. Click Next. The Personalize Your Software page appears.

32. Type in your name and a company name if appropriate.

33. Click Next. The What's your computer's name page appears.

34. Type in a meaningful computer name for this system in the Computer name field, such as wxp-den or Bob's-PC.

> **NOTE**
>
> Choose a computer name that is unique. It must differ from any other computer or workgroup on the network. You'll probably want to enter your name or a name of your own choosing, though Setup supplies some cryptic name for you.

35. Click Next.

36. If you have a modem present on your system, the Modem Dialing Information page appears. Type in your area code, then click Next.

37. The Data and Time Settings page appears. Set the date and time and select a time zone.

38. Click Next. If a network interface is detected, the system installs networking components, then the Networking Settings page appears. If no network interface is installed in your system, skip to step 40.

39. The default network configuration is set to connect to a Microsoft local area network (LAN) using DHCP to obtain TCP/IP address configuration settings. I think you should wait until later to configure networking for Windows XP Home systems, so, select the Typical settings radio button, and click Next. DHCP or Dynamic Host Configuration Protocol is a networking service operating from a Windows Server system which can provide clients with IP configuration upon bootup. As mentioned earlier, DHCP takes the pain out of setting up network (and Internet) connections because it means you don't have to enter lots of cryptic numbers into little dialog boxes just to get connected. The DHCP server and your Windows XP computer negotiate those numbers between themselves.

40. Setup proceeds with installing the OS using the settings you've just provided. This takes 20 minutes or more.

41. If any issues or problems were encountered during the installation, a pop-up dialog box appears. If you want to view the log file of errors now, click Yes. If not, click No. You can always view this information by reading the setuperr.log file later with any text editor, such as Notepad or WordPad.

42. At this point, the Setup process is complete and the system needs to be rebooted. This might occur automatically or you might be prompted to confirm the reboot.

43. Windows XP is booted, but there are still several steps remaining before you can gain access.

44. The Welcome to Microsoft Windows XP screen appears, accompanied with an animated wizard. You must wait until it is through "talking" to you. Then, click Next.

45. Setup checks your system for Internet connectivity. No matter what setup determines, you must indicate whether the system gains Internet access through a local network (the Yes radio button) or must establish a dial-up connection (the No radio button). If you have a cable modem or a connection over a network, select Yes. If you use a dial-up connection, you'll be prompted for the connection specifics (such as phone number, username, and password).

46. Click Next. The Ready to activate Windows screen appears.

47. Unless you have a specific reason not to, select the Yes, activate Windows over the Internet now radio button.

NOTE

In an effort to curb software piracy, Microsoft has implemented a new scheme to prevent unauthorized installations of Windows XP. After installing Windows XP, you must activate it within 30 days. When you activate Windows XP, your product key is filed into a database along with hardware identifiers from your computer. Activation prevents the same product key from being used numerous times. Microsoft claims the hardware identifiers cannot be used to trace a specific computer and that the activation process is fully anonymous. If you fail to activate within the time limit, the system fails to function until activation is completed.

Activation can occur over the telephone if you do not have an Internet connection. The phone numbers to call are listed on the activation screen and in the readme file on the distribution CD.

If you choose to skip activation during setup, an activation command is added to the top of the All Programs section of the Start menu.

48. Click Next. The Ready to register with Microsoft screen appears.

49. Unless you want to offer private information to Microsoft, select the No, Not At This Time radio button.

NOTE

Registration is a separate and distinct process from activation. Activation is mandatory for a functioning OS past the 30-day grace period. Registration is voluntary. You should register if you want to get junk snail mail and email from Microsoft, since Microsoft uses this information to focus product marketing.

50. Click Next. The "Will you be sharing this computer with other users?" screen appears.

51. If you want to maintain unique user accounts for each person who uses this system, select Yes. If you select no, Windows XP is configured to log in automatically with the administrator account each time the computer boots. If you select No, skip to step 54.

> **NOTE**
>
> Selecting not to create unique user accounts for each person does not mean you cannot switch to this in the future. However, if you select No, you must initially log into the system with the administrator account. After you've logged on, you can create other local user accounts. See Chapter 25, "Managing Users," for details on creating user accounts.

52. Click Next. The Who Will Use This Computer? screen appears.

53. Type in the names of up to six users for this system, one in each field.

54. Click Next. The Thank you! page appears; click Finish.

55. The Windows XP Welcome screen appears with the names of the user accounts created in step 53 listed in a column on the right ready for logon. If you selected No in step 51, you'll be automatically logged on as the administrator and presented the Windows XP desktop.

The final step necessary to complete the installation of Windows XP is to log in.

→ If you don't already know how to log into Windows XP, **see** "Logging In to Windows XP," **p. 93**.

 If Windows refuses to boot after the installation is complete, see "Windows XP Fails to Boot After Installation" in the "Troubleshooting" section at the end of this chapter.

> **NOTE**
>
> It is likely that after the final reboot, you will see a Help Protect your PC dialog box announcing the Windows XP Security Center settings. This dialog box is triggered for three reasons: Windows Firewall isn't turned on, Automatic Updates are not turned on, or no antivirus software is installed.
>
> The dialog box encourages you to set up automatic updates and install an antivirus program if it doesn't detect one. Presumably, you just did a clean install; therefore, it wouldn't find antivirus software because no such program comes built in to XP. But if you were doing an upgrade to SP-2 (See Appendix A, "Installing Service Pack 2," for coverage of that issue) or an upgrade from another operating system and you already had antivirus software installed (and one that XP recognizes), you wouldn't be prompted to act on that score. (See Chapter 24, "System Utilities," for coverage of the Security Center.)

Upgrading Over an Existing Operating System

If you're upgrading rather than performing a clean installation, the process is a bit different. Setup checks on the advisability of upgrading and asks a few more questions. This section provides a few points concerning the upgrade or dual-boot with preexisting operating systems.

The process of performing an upgrade install is much simpler than the clean installation process. Just be sure to select Upgrade instead of New Installation on the initial Windows Setup wizard. After accepting the License Agreement and providing the Product Key, you have little to do (refer to the previous section and perform the steps for doing a clean installation). You won't see all of the steps listed in the clean install, but you'll easily be able to follow your way through it catching the steps the setup wizard prompts you to respond to.

Just before the setup routine begins copying Windows XP over your previous OS, it inspects your system. This inspection produces an upgrade report (see next section). After the upgrade report, you just need to wait until you are prompted by the Welcome to Microsoft Windows XP screen where you activate the system. You can jump into step 44 of the typical clean installation step-by-step to complete the process.

UPGRADE REPORT

After you supply your product key, Setup creates an upgrade report summarizing everything that might not work with Windows XP and giving you a chance to access updated files that hardware or software vendors might have available (check their Web sites). If you don't have upgrade files for the listed items, you might skate by their Web sites anyway.

The upgrade report is a pretty spiffy HTML-based dialog box that details what might not work if you go ahead with the installation. It has a link to the Windows XP Hardware Compatibility List (HCL) for easily checking to see whether the Brand X video card you just bought really won't work or if the compatibility test was just out of date. Do check the list, assuming your computer is connected to the Internet.

Although your list might be long, it might not be catastrophic news. Most of the stuff my systems showed didn't end up causing problems. For example, I know that the video card I have is supported, as is the Epson printer. Both were listed as potentially problematic. Most of the other things such as shares, Recycle Bin, backup files, and DOS startup file issues were no big deal. The new operating system takes care of most of these issues, mostly due to Plug and Play and good hardware detection during Setup. Plus, I probably had some old junk in my AUTOEXEC.BAT and CONFIG.SYS files (holdover configuration files used in the days of DOS) that's no longer valuable. The DOS exceptions were Sound Blaster drivers that DOS-based games used—the kinds of things that most Windows XP users are not going to worry about.

If you see anything listed about your video card, disk controller, sound card, or tape backup, you might want to check on those items a little more closely and download a driver update pack from the manufacturer before you update. Basically, you should take seriously anything that might suggest incompatibility that prevents basic operation or bootability of the system, and you can acknowledge but not sweat the rest.

TIP

> If you just want to run the upgrade report and not execute the complete Setup program, insert the installation CD in the CD-ROM drive, or connect over the LAN to the CD. If the Welcome to Microsoft Windows XP splash screen appears, click Check System Compatibility, and then Check my system automatically. Follow the wizard's prompts to perform an upgrade or XP compatibility test. If the splash screen does not appear or you are working from DOS, then issue the following command:
>
> ```
> winnt32 /checkupgradeonly
> ```
>
> This command generates just the report.

Just follow the rest of the instructions as they come up on the screen. Your computer might have to restart several times in the process. If the computer seems to be stuck, wait several minutes to ensure it's really stopped functioning properly. Then reboot it. Windows XP uses an "intelligent" Setup feature that should restart where it left off. Eventually, after much spinning of the hard disks, the system boots up into Windows XP. But before you are granted access to the new system, there are the issues of activation, registration, and user accounts to deal with. Jump to step 51 in the typical clean installation step-by-step, to complete the installation procedure.

 If Windows refuses to boot after the installation is complete, see "Windows XP Fails to Boot After Installation" in the "Troubleshooting" section at the end of this chapter.

MAKING STARTUP FLOPPIES

Windows XP Setup can be launched from floppy disks if necessary. However, the Setup CD-ROM does not contain the utility program needed to create setup floppy disks. You can download the utility, makeboot.exe, from the Microsoft Web site at http:// support.microsoft.com/default.aspx?scid=kb;EN-US;q310994. Or perhaps more simply, searching the www.support.microsoft.com knowledge base for 310994 yields the same result in case that URL isn't available.

After you've downloaded the appropriate file for your version and language of Windows XP, simply double-click it to begin the diskette creation process. You will need to have six 3 1/2–inch empty, formatted floppy disks ready. You might want to label the first disk Windows XP Setup Boot Disk and the remaining disks Windows XP Setup Disk #2 through #6.

After you have created your Windows XP Setup disks, you can use them to perform a clean installation of Windows XP only; you cannot use them for performing upgrade installations.

TROUBLESHOOTING

Windows XP and the setup process itself is very resilient. I've performed dozens of installations while writing this book and I've yet to have a failed install. In general, as each new generation of Microsoft OS hits the streets, there are fewer installation problems. I remember the days of installing Windows NT 4.0, which had problems more often than not. I probably spent upwards of two days on a single system once just to get the main OS installed! Anyway, just because it is much improved over previous OSes, doesn't mean that the Windows XP installation procedure can't experience problems when you perform the install. There are several common causes of problems and several common problems. In the next sections I tackle each of these and provide you with realistic solutions.

WINDOWS CRASHES DURING INSTALLATION

I tried to install Windows XP, but it crashes while installing.

The trick with any Windows Setup is to get it to complete without crashing or freaking out about some setting you try to make during the process. Hold off on doing anything fancy— stuff like network settings, screen savers, video display settings, and so on—until well after you have finished the installation. Just get through the installation as simply as possible, and then poke around and tweak up your settings later.

→ To learn more details about recovering a trashed installation of Windows XP, **see** "Recovery Console," **p. 1043**.

Windows Setup is intelligent. It keeps tabs on where in the process things are stalled. Simply restarting Setup should result in its picking up where it left off. This, at least, is some consolation. Next time around, keep it simple, and get by with as few settings as possible. Just make the necessary ones. A machine might hang when you're playing with the Regional settings, language, or something you can easily change later. Also, avoid the Advanced settings if you don't need them.

At a certain stage, Setup switches from character-based screens to graphical screens (GUI mode). If, at this point, Setup crashes, your video display card might not be compatible with Windows XP. Make sure you checked your system's innards against the Hardware Compatibility List. Also, ensure that you meet the minimum requirements in terms of RAM and hard disk space. Most of the causes of installation problems are directly related to non-HCL compliant hardware.

MY EXISTING OS WON'T RECOGNIZE THE CD-ROM DRIVE

I can't get my existing OS to recognize my CD-ROM drive, so I can't install Windows XP.

The following are a few other workarounds for those weird occasions when you just can't get DOS to recognize your CD-ROM drive:

- Create the Setup floppy disks needed to start the installation. See the section "Making Startup Floppies," earlier in this chapter.

- Create an Emergency Startup Disk (ESD) from Windows 98. As of Windows 98, popular CD-ROM drivers are dumped on the ESDs when you create them by choosing Control Panel, Add/Remove Programs, Startup Disk.

- Use an old DOS startup disk with installable device drivers for the CD-ROM drive on it as stipulated in the AUTOEXEC.BAT and CONFIG.SYS files on the floppy. Creating such a disk typically takes a little knowledge of MSCDEX command-line arguments, and you need the driver supplied with the CD-ROM drive.

- Using your existing operating system or a floppy disk with network client software on it, connect to the network and run Setup from a remote CD-ROM drive. This process can take some work if you have to boot in DOS, however. You must know lots of network settings and use the command line to get them going. Your network administrator might have to tell you the exact path of the setup command. You're looking for the file winnt.exe or winnt32.exe from the i386 directory of the distribution files.

- Another solution is to copy all the appropriate CD-ROM files to your hard disk one way or another (even lap-linking between two computers is an approach I've used successfully). You need all the files in the root directory of the CD and everything in the I386 folder. When files are on the hard disk, switch to the folder in which you stored the file, and run winnt.exe or winnt32.exe.

WINDOWS XP FAILS TO BOOT AFTER INSTALLATION

I got through the installation, but Windows XP won't boot now.

You can take several steps when an installation doesn't seem to have worked out. As I mentioned in the first troubleshooting tip, you can try to determine when Setup failed. If, by observation, you can determine the point at which it failed, you might be able to avoid whatever it was you did the first time around. Restart Setup, and see whether reinstalling helps.

While you're installing again, note that Setup asks whether you want to load any SCSI drivers at a certain point. At about this point, you can opt not to install support for power management. Try opting out of the power management. You can install it later by choosing Control Panel, Add New Hardware. Sometimes power management can cause problems on a machine that doesn't support it correctly, or doesn't support it at all.

Another tip has to do with the hard drive not being detected after installation. This is a pretty obscure problem, but it can happen. How it appears and the solution are thus: You successfully run the initial phase of the XP install process, but the system can't boot the drive. You might even have noticed that it took a long time to detect it during XP installation. The solution is to jumper the drive as Cable Select (instead of Master). Then you should be able to boot properly from the drive.

TIPS FROM THE WINDOWS PROS: AUTOMATING SETUP

If you intend to install Windows XP on a bevy of computers, answering all of its installation questions repeatedly can prove an exercise in inefficiency. Instead, you can create a special script to automate the process. The Setup Manager Wizard helps you design the script, or you can base yours on the example supplied on the Windows XP CD.

The script you create is called an *answer file*, and it is used to install Windows XP in so-called *unattended mode*. In this mode, nobody needs to interact with the computer during installation. The script simply supplies the answers that you would normally have to enter from the keyboard, such as acceptance of the license agreement, workgroup and computer name, network details, and so on. The script can fully automate or only partially automate the Setup process. For example, you might want to supply defaults for the user but let him or her change them. A script can additionally stipulate the creation of special folders, execution of programs upon completion of Setup, location of Setup files, and more.

Of course, creating answer files makes sense only when you're installing Windows XP on multiple computers with a hardware complement that you know will install Windows XP properly; otherwise, you can waste more time trying to troubleshoot what happened in your absence that caused a failed or broken installation. As you know, sometimes unexpected developments occur during Setup that might require intervention. The Setup routine is fairly successful at detecting hardware when doing installations, so it's worth a try if you're deploying a large number of machines. In most cases, the time spent creating an answer file for automated unattended setup becomes cost effective when you must install three or more systems.

Performing unattended setups is a fairly advanced topic. I would need to devote several chapters to it in order to give it reasonable coverage. Instead of listing step-by-step information here, I prefer to point you to the best reference available on the subject: Microsoft itself. The Windows XP Resource Kit has complete and exhaustive information about automating installation. Plus, check out the text, HTML, and Word document files on the distribution CD (don't forget to check the support subdirectory); a fairly useful description is there, too.

PART II

GETTING YOUR WORK DONE

CHAPTER 4

USING THE WINDOWS XP INTERFACE

In this chapter

WHO SHOULD READ THIS CHAPTER?

Before going on in this book, make sure you've read the introduction and installed Windows XP correctly onto your computer. (Installation is explained in Chapter 3, "Installing Windows XP Home.") When those hurdles are completed, return here to learn about the user interface.

Many wonder why a book geared toward past Windows users such as this would include coverage of something as basic as the user interface. This is a decision that was primarily driven by the knowledge that many users of Windows XP Home are upgrading from Windows 9x/Me, NT, and even 2000. For those users, savvy as they might be with Windows concepts, the Windows XP interface is different enough that they need a roadmap to get started.

NOTE

> We've also included a video introduction to the XP interface on the CD-ROM accompanying this book.

After you become familiar with Windows XP Home, you'll wonder how you ever got around in those old clunky environments. In addition to the new look of Windows XP, many new functions are woven into the fabric of the new user interface (UI). And you don't want to miss out on them! Some UI tips and tricks you might not have known about are also included in this chapter. So, even if you consider yourself a Windows veteran, at least take the time to skim through this chapter before you move on.

NOTE

> Microsoft stopped offering support for MS-DOS, Windows 1.0–3.x, Windows for Workgroups, and Windows 95 on December 31, 2001; support for Windows 98 (OSR2, SE, and Me) and Windows NT 4 Workstation was dropped on June 30, 2003. Support for Windows 2000 Professional is slated to end June 30, 2005. When Microsoft says it's dropping support, that means the Microsoft technical support system won't respond to calls or email with questions regarding these operating systems. So, upgrade or be left in the dust all alone.

Don't just take our word for it. Experiment with the new UI as you read this chapter. We've found that nothing can substitute for direct hands-on operation to get an understanding and a feel for the new user environment. Most of the information presented in this chapter is not of a level or type that can damage your system, but whenever caution is needed you're warned about it in clear language.

This chapter doesn't cover everything about the new environment, but it does a good job of covering the important aspects of interest to most readers. If you run across a button or command that you don't recognize, don't be afraid to explore the Windows Help service for details and instructions. The XP help system is much improved over its predecessors and includes much meaningful content.

→ If you're looking for ways to tweak and customize the new GUI, **see** Chapter 21, "Tweaking the GUI," **p. 707**.

At any time you desire to put this book down and walk away from your system, jump to the "Exiting Windows XP Gracefully" section near the end of this chapter to find out how to log off with aplomb.

Logging In to Windows XP

At this point, you should have Windows XP Home installed. But before you explore the OS, you have to log on. There are often several steps required before you gain access to your system. First, obviously, you must power up the system if it is not already. Be sure that all bootable CDs are removed from the CD drives and that no floppies or Zip/Jaz disks are present in their respective drives (this is necessary only if your BIOS is set to attempt a boot first from media other than your hard drive).

After the system is fully booted, you need to log on. Depending on which logon mode the system is using, you need to either use the Welcome screen to click on a user name/icon or press Ctrl+Alt+Del twice to provide logon credentials to gain access to the system. If your system was a part of a network before an upgrade install, or you altered the default settings of the network components during a manual or unattended installation, you need to use the secure logon, which is covered in the section titled, "Using the Classic Logon" later in the chapter. Otherwise, Windows XP presents you with the Welcome screen for one-click access to the desktop.

NOTE

> Shortly after installing, or upon booting the first time and logging in, you might see a balloon notification at the bottom of your screen warning you that your computer might be at risk because you don't have an antivirus program installed. Clicking the balloon brings up the Security Center (new as of SP-2). Please see the section "Security Center" in Chapter 22 for more about the Security Center.

Logging In from the Welcome Screen

The Welcome screen that appears when your PC boots presents a list of available user accounts that can be employed to access this system. Just click a user to log on. If a password is associated with a selected account, you will be prompted to provide it. If you need a hint (and a hint is defined for that account), click the question mark. If your system is not set up for multiple users or password access, Windows XP logs you in automatically.

Every time you boot your system, you must log on. Also, any time you return to your system after another user has logged off, you must log on. The Welcome screen is the default logon mode for Windows XP. In this mode, the screen lists all local user accounts available for accessing this system. This mode offers no real logon security; it is simply a means by which the system maintains unique user environments (that is, profiles) between which it can easily switch. (As mentioned in Chapter 1, "Introducing Windows XP Home Edition," even running applications are maintained in memory as users sign in and out.)

USING THE CLASSIC LOGON

You can log on using the more "classic logon" screen you might have seen in other Windows versions by pressing Ctrl+Alt+Del twice while the Welcome screen is showing. This is a secure logon method for accessing the machine you're using. However, for the Classic logon to be used as a default, the system has to be configured through the User Accounts applet (see "Changing the Default Logon Mode" later this chapter).

Keep in mind that the logon credentials required for a secure logon are *username and password*. The logon location on a Windows XP Home system is always local only. Windows XP Home does not support what's called "domain" logon (domains are used in large networks, typically in corporations). Even if your system is a member of a workgroup, you log on locally. More about the issues of networking and workgroups is discussed in later chapters (see Part IV, "Networking").

If you don't have a user account with which to log on, go to the secure logon screen and log on using the administrator account (if you know the password). Keep in mind that, to log on as the system administrator, you must use the secure logon screen. If you want to create other user accounts (either for yourself or others), see the section, "Working with User Accounts."

The classic logon method is labeled as secure for two specific reasons. First, you must always provide a password. Even though a blank password can be assigned, thus making an insecure account, the password field must be addressed at logon. Second, you must provide a valid username. By default, the last username to successfully log on will be displayed, but that's the only user account name you get to see. This is unlike the Welcome logon screen, which openly displays the names of all defined user accounts.

If you see a Press Ctrl+Alt+Del to Log On message, follow these steps:

1. Press Ctrl+Alt+Del. The Log On to Windows dialog box appears.
2. In the User Name field, type your user account name.
3. If your computer is not part of a network and you did not upgrade a system that had local user accounts with passwords, you can ignore the Password field. If you are using an account upgraded from a previous system, you need to provide the password you used to log in before you upgraded to Windows XP. If you've forgotten your password, talk with your network administrator or jump to Chapter 25, "Managing Users," or Chapter 30, "Troubleshooting and Repairing Windows XP."
4. Click the green arrow next to the Password field to continue.

Changing the Default Logon Mode

Changing the default logon mode requires the following steps:

1. Click the Start button, and then click Control Panel. The Control Panel appears.

2. Click User Accounts to open the User Accounts interface.

NOTE

> If you're unfamiliar with processes involved in using a networked OS (like Windows XP) are no doubt finding much of this material—such as managing accounts or having to log on to your computer using an account—is new to you. All you need to know for now is the following:
>
> - A domain is a logical collection of computers that are members of the same network. A domain is *centrally controlled*, which means one (or a few) server defines the domain, controls access to resources, and verifies your identity at logon (also known as credential authorization). Windows XP Home does not support domain membership or domain logon.
>
> - The administrator is a default user account on every Windows NT, 2000, and XP system that has full and unrestricted access to the system. The administrator account typically is used to configure hardware and software, install new applications, and define user access to resources.
>
> If you'd like to know more about domains, please see Part IV; and if you'd like to know more about the administrator account, look at Chapter 25, "Managing Users."
>
> The layout and presentation of many aspects of Windows XP is different from any previous Microsoft OS. If you prefer the more familiar look and feel of previous versions of Windows, look for options that let you display windows and dialog boxes like the Control Panel in Classic mode. This most often means returning to a Windows 2000 or Windows Me layout.
>
> The main difference between the two is that the Category mode displays links only to common actions that it has grouped into categories, whereas (in the case of the Control Panel) Classic mode displays *all* the individual Control Panel applets.

3. Click Change the Way User Logs On or Off. The Select Logon and Logoff Options page appears as shown in Figure 4.1.

4. If you leave the Use the Welcome Screen box checked, the system continues to use the Welcome log on screen in which you choose an account by selecting it from the list of accounts available to that machine. If you uncheck the box, the system requires a secured logon using Ctrl+Alt+Del, in which you must type in the user account name and password to which you want to log on.

5. If you leave the Use the Welcome Screen check box checked, an additional check box of Use Fast User Switching becomes available. This lets users quickly log on and off while keeping their programs actively running and operating in the background. It's an easy and efficient way for people to share a computer.

Figure 4.1
The Select logon and logoff options page of the User Accounts interface.

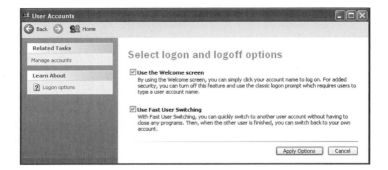

6. Click OK to save your changes and close the Select logon and logoff options.

7. Click the red X button on the title bar to close the User Accounts interface and then do the same to close the Control Panel.

Your changes take affect the next time you log out and log back on.

After you've logged on, you can explore the user interface, or as Microsoft likes to say, have the user experience.

WORKING WITH USER ACCOUNTS

During the installation of Windows XP Home, you defined a password for the administrator account. If you also defined additional user accounts during that process, Windows considers these accounts to be equal to the administrator account. If you performed an upgrade install on a system with pre-existing user accounts, any pre-existing accounts are retained, and their access levels are converted into an XP equivalent. Two types of local accounts are available on Windows XP Home:

- **Computer administrator**—This type of user can create, change, and delete user accounts; make system level changes; install programs; and access all files.

- **Limited**—This type of user is restricted to only minimal system access and has no ability to alter system configuration.

> **NOTE**
>
> If you purchase a system with XP pre-installed, the system will prompt you for a few specifics, such as a computer name and an administrator password, during the first bootup.

There is always at least one user account on Windows XP—namely, the administrator account. This account is always protected by a password. There is also another default account, the Guest account. This account has restricted system access and by default is disabled, so it might not always be available for use as a logon. Plus, even if it is enabled, you aren't able to make any system changes or even create other user accounts under its security restrictions.

When performing normal tasks on your system, you should always log on with a limited user account instead of the administrator account or any account with computer administrator level access. Why? Because it's very easy to make a system level change that damages or significantly alters your system. By removing your ability to make sweeping changes you limit your exposure to this risk.

CREATING NEW USER ACCOUNTS

User account management is performed by the administrator or any other user account with computer administrator-level access. This includes creating new users and altering the settings on existing users. Let's explore new user creation first:

1. Open the Control Panel by clicking the Start menu, then clicking Control Panel. The Control Panel appears.

2. Click User Accounts. The User Accounts interface appears as shown in Figure 4.2.

Figure 4.2
The User Accounts interface enables you to change, create, and modify user accounts.

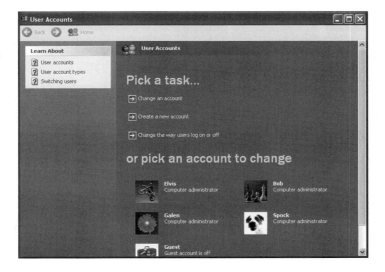

3. Click Create a New Account.

4. The first prompt is for the name of the user account. Type a name into the field (for example, Joe or lab1user), and then click Next. Your account name may consist of upper- and lowercase letters, numbers, and symbols except for /\[]":;|<>+=,?*. The account name can be up to 20 characters long.

5. The second prompt is to select the access level for the account. Select the Limited radio button, and then click Create Account.

6. You're returned to the User Accounts interface. The newly created user account appears in the list of user accounts at the bottom of this window.

MODIFYING AN EXISTING ACCOUNT

After you create an account, there are several changes you can make to it that tailor it to that user's needs. To alter the settings on an existing account from the User Accounts interface perform the following steps:

1. With the User Accounts window open (as described in the previous section), click Change an Account.

2. Click the name/icon of the account to alter.

3. A menu of options for this account are displayed (Figure 4.3).

Figure 4.3
The alter user account menu.

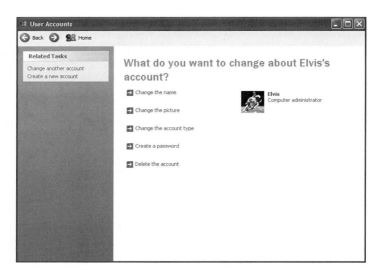

For a limited account, these include

- Change the name
- Create a password
- Change the picture
- Change the account type
- Delete the account

Click on one of these selections, and follow the prompts to make the desired change to the selected account.

4. After you complete altering the current account, click the Back button. This returns you to the account to change selection list. If you wish to alter a different account, go back to step 2.

5. If you are finished altering accounts, click the Back button again to return to the User Accounts interface.

6. Go ahead and click the X button to close the User Accounts windows, and then do the same for the Control Panel.

USING PASSWORDS

By default, new accounts do not have passwords. After you define a password for an account, you are prompted for that password whenever you attempt to log on with that user account, whether through the Welcome screen or Ctrl+Alt+Del. Through the Welcome screen, if you forget your password, click the ? button to obtain a hint (if you defined one when you created the password). The password hint is not accessible through the Ctrl+Alt+Del logon mode.

Create a unique user account for every user of this system. Also, be sure to grant computer administrator access only to those users who actually need it. In other words, give access only to those users who install a lot of hardware and software and perform systemwide configuration changes.

If anyone is concerned about other users snooping into their stuff, define passwords for each user account. Password-protected user accounts are a necessity in office environments, but they can also be a blessing at home.

→ There is a lot more to working with user accounts than what is described here. For more exhaustive coverage of user account management, **see** Chapter 25, "Managing Users."

When you first log on to Windows XP, you are deposited directly into your so-called Windows XP *user experience*. This consists of a desktop with a recycle bin and a taskbar with a Start menu and a clock/icon tray. Microsoft has finally provided a clean, elegant first logon screen. It's up to you to populate your desktop and customize your environment to fit your needs, habits, and desires.

This new look might be a little disconcerting at first if you are a veteran Windows user. You might wonder where the icons, such as My Computer, Internet Explorer, and Network Neighborhood, are. Don't worry, there are other ways to get to these, and you can add them to the desktop later. But for now, you can access them through the Start menu.

USING WINDOWS XP—THE USER EXPERIENCE

Windows XP has a familiar, yet different, user interface. Most of the visual aspects of the desktop environment have been updated, but most of the tools and applications you remember from Windows 9x and Windows 2000 are right where you expect. The new interface or user experience is called Luna. Luna includes visual updates and improvements to all native dialog boxes, displays, windows, and interfaces. Most notably, these changes are seen on the Start menu, the taskbar, the Explorer, and the Control Panel. If you want the older styling of previous Windows versions (mainly Windows 2000 visual styling), revert to the Classic style. However, I highly recommend giving the new look and feel a try for a week or so before ditching it.

Microsoft's visual palette has moved from a flat gray to include brilliant blues and subtle off-whites. In addition, Microsoft has rounded the corners of windows, added 3-D icons, and added *action centers* (that is, tasks and commands focused on content) everywhere. The result is not only eye pleasing, but elegantly simple to work with. Even with all the enhancements, everything still seems to have a similar function or placement to that of Windows 2000, 9x, and Me. Thus, you can easily leverage your existing experience and expertise in navigating and operating Windows XP. After a few days, you might forget how you got by without all these useful improvements.

WINDOWS IN BRIEF

At its most basic, the Windows operating platforms are based around using windows to contain, control, and display information. A window is nothing more than a defined rectangular area on your display, that usually has a title bar, menu bar, and border. The real beauty of the Windows interface concept is the ability to switch back and forth between windows and even to layer windows on top of one another. Most Windows systems with reasonable hardware support 20 or more windows open simultaneously. Switching between open windows is accomplished by clicking the window you want to move to (if it is visible), or by clicking its button on the taskbar. In addition to using the mouse to navigate, there are also keyboard commands and issue commands to help you move around. For example, holding down the Alt button while pressing Tab is used as a shortcut to easily switch between the various windows you might have open. Or, holding down Shift+Alt while pressing Tab moves you backward through the open windows in the reverse order that they opened.

NOTE

> For a nearly exhaustive list of keyboard shortcuts for navigating and controlling aspects of Windows XP, check out the "Windows keyboard shortcuts overview" document through the Help and Support Center. Just click Start, Help and then click the Information in Help and Support Center Option. In the window that appears, type the title in the Search field, then click the green arrow. Links to this overview will appear in the Suggested Topics and Full-Text Search Matches sections of the Search Results area.

To facilitate the exchange of information between windows, especially those hosting documents or text fields, the Windows operating systems include an internal facility called the Clipboard. If you've used any version of Windows in the last 10 years, you are already familiar with this utility. Using the "cut and paste" method, multiple applications can share data, pictures, video, sounds, and text among similar, or even dissimilar, document types. For example, you can copy a section of a photograph from a PhotoShop window into a company report or a Web page design window you're working in. You can also take some spreadsheet numbers and dump them into an email you're writing about how fast your Internet stocks are growing (or plummeting)! Essentially, Windows is the glue that lets dissimilar programs work together. Due to the common interface between all Windows programs, after you learn to use one Windows program, learning subsequent ones is fairly easy. This is because similar techniques (menus, buttons, icons, and so on) are used to control most all Windows applications.

However, Windows is more than just an operating system and graphical user interface. Like other versions of Windows, Windows XP includes a broad collection of useful programs, from a simple arithmetic calculator to fancy system and network management tools. This list also includes a word-processing program called WordPad, a drawing program called Paint, Internet Explorer for cruising the Web, Outlook Express for email, MovieMaker for creating digital movies, NetMeeting for video and telephone conferencing over the Internet, CD-burning software to create your own CDs (if you have a CD-RW drive), a DVD playback tool (for those with a DVD-ROM drive), and utilities for keeping your hard disk in good working order, to name just a few.

PARTS OF THE WINDOWS XP SCREEN

At this point, you should be booted and signed in. After you've logged on, Windows XP deposits you in its basic environment (called the *desktop*). You'll probably notice two things almost immediately: the taskbar at the bottom of the screen and an empty (or nearly so) desktop (see Figure 4.4).

The taskbar is the central control mechanism for the Windows XP user experience. It hosts the Start menu, quick launch bar, active program buttons, system tray, and clock. The only item that is present on your desktop is the Recycle Bin. If you purchased a computer system with XP pre-installed, you might see other icons on the desktop. Notice that it's located by default in the bottom right corner. (That's awfully Macintosh-ish, don't you think?)

NOTE

> If you or someone else has used your Windows XP setup already, it's possible that some open windows might come up on the screen automatically when Windows boots (starts up). It's also possible that more icons show up on the Desktop than are shown in Figure 4.4. This depends on the options chosen when Windows XP was installed, whether other applications were loaded before upgrading, and whether custom shortcuts to the desktop have been defined.

There are three primary areas of the screen to explore: the desktop, icons, and the taskbar. After you're familiar with these essential building blocks and how to manipulate a window and its commands, you're able to use Windows XP's interface. If you've been using Windows 3.*x*, 9x, NT, or 2000, then you already know how to manipulate a window and its commands. You just need to be brought up to speed on the advanced XP interface specifics. As mentioned in the introduction, for the purposes of this book, it is assumed that you have basic Windows proficiency with either Windows 9x, NT, or 2000. Therefore, subjects such as how to click the mouse, what double-clicking is, and how to scroll a window are not covered. (If you need this level of hand-holding, you might want to find a beginner's book, such as *Easy Windows XP*, published by Que, instead.)

Start menu   Desktop   Taskbar   Icon

Figure 4.4
The default Windows XP desktop is much less cluttered than in previous versions of Windows.

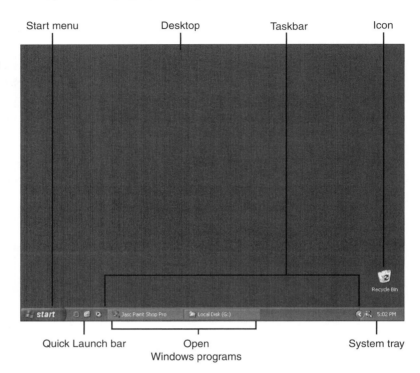

Quick Launch bar   Open Windows programs   System tray

THE DESKTOP

Let's start with the desktop. This is your home base while doing your work in Windows. It is always on the screen as the backdrop (whether you see it or not) and you can deposit files and folders right on it for storage. It's analogous to a real desktop in this way. It also serves as a handy, temporary holding area for files you might be copying from, say, a floppy disk to a hard disk folder. The *Recycle Bin* holds deleted work objects such as files and folders until you empty it (with caveats). Just as in previous versions of Windows (or the Mac for that matter, if you're coming from that background), you do all your work in Windows XP using graphical representations of your files and applications (called *icons*).

The desktop analogy is a bit corny, but it's a very easy medium for organizing your various activities. For example, you can put your most-used folders, documents, and application shortcuts right on the desktop so that you don't have to fish around in your hard disk directories to get to them. Every time you boot up, they're waiting for you on the desktop.

All the desktop icons you are familiar with from Windows 9x and 2000 have been moved to the Start menu. You can gain access to My Computer, My Documents, and My Network

Places with a simple click of the Start button. If you revert to the previous Windows 2000 Start menu (called Classic), then these items re-appear on the desktop (see Chapter 21's section titled "Start Menu Pizzazz"). In either case, you control which icons or shortcuts appear on your desktop.

You can add icons and shortcuts to your desktop to you heart's content. However, Windows XP doesn't want to let things stay cluttered. So, if you fail to use any of the items on your desktop for more than 60 days, the Desktop Cleanup Wizard is launched automatically to prod you into removing unused items or moving them into a special folder.

A folder labeled Unused Desktop Shortcuts appears on the desktop automatically after the Desktop Cleanup wizard is used to remove unused shortcuts. When the Desktop Cleanup Wizard launches, just follow the wizard's prompts to select which icons to remove (or more specifically move into the Unused Desktop Shortcuts folder).

THE RECYCLE BIN

The Recycle Bin acts a bit like the waste paper basket at the side of your desk. After you throw something into it, it's basically trash to be thrown out; however, you still can retrieve items from it if you get there before the cleaning staff empties it and throws it away for good. Within Windows XP, the Recycle Bin holds those files you've deleted using either Windows Explorer, My Computer, or the Open/Save as dialog boxes. It does not capture files deleted by third-party tools, files deleted from floppies, network drives, or by uninstalling a program.

The Recycle Bin has a limited storage capacity. By default, it retains deleted files that total up to 10% of the total capacity of each hard drive on your computer. After the maximum size of the Recycle Bin is reached, the oldest files are permanently removed from the hard drive to make room for newly deleted files. The size of the Recycle Bin can be customized as a percentage across all drives or a unique size on each individual drive. The Recycle Bin is customized through its Properties dialog box. The configuration options are discussed in Chapter 21, but if you want to get there now, just right-click the Recycle Bin icon and select Properties from the pop-up menu (see Figure 4.5).

After a file is removed from the Recycle Bin, it cannot be recovered using native tools. You must either restore the files from a backup, use a third-party recover tool (often needed to be in place before the file is deleted), or live without the lost files. If you don't want your excess trashing sitting around, you can also configure the system to bypass the Recycle Bin entirely so that it permanently deletes files immediately instead of granting you a recovery period.

To restore a file still retained in the Recycle Bin, double-click the desktop icon to open the Recycle Bin, locate and select the file to restore, then issue the Restore command from the File menu or the Recycle Bin Tasks list (see Figure 4.6). The file or folder will be returned to its original location.

4

Figure 4.5
The Recycle Bin
Properties dialog box.

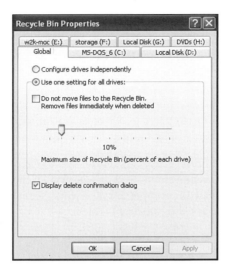

Figure 4.6
Restoring a file from
the Recycle Bin.

You also can manually empty the Recycle Bin. This often is a useful activity before defragmenting your hard drive or just wanting to permanently delete files and folders. The Empty Recycle Bin command, found in the right-click pop-up menu for the icon and the File menu (be sure no items are selected, otherwise the File menu's context changes to file/folder restore operations) and Recycle Bin Tasks list of the Recycle Bin interface, is used to clear out all files being retained.

ICONS

As you probably know, the small graphical representations of your programs and files are called *icons*. Windows XP uses icons to represent folders, documents, programs, and groups of settings (such as dial-up connections). For example, Recycle Bin and My Computer are icons. Graphically, icons got a 3D facelift in Windows XP, even when compared to their Windows 2000 counterparts. In most cases, the default icon displayed for an object represents the function of that object. For example, a folder object's icon is a folder, a text document icon is a pad of paper with writing on it, and the Recycle Bin is a stylish, translucent, plastic trash can.

NOTE

In recent versions of Windows, Microsoft has begun using the term folder instead of directory. The designers want to focus your thoughts toward the idea of your files being stored on the hard drive in a manner similar to that of a filing cabinet for manila folders. Although this analogy is helpful, this book doesn't always stick to Microsoft-speak. So, when you see "folder" or "directory" anywhere in this book, keep in mind they are considered to be the same thing.

Icons are either objects or shortcuts. A shortcut is a means to gain access to an object from multiple locations throughout the environment. Shortcuts are the preferred mechanism by which access to the same object is achieved from multiple locations rather than making duplicate copies of the original object or application. Duplicating the object often causes version problems, such as never knowing which one has your most recent changes, and difficulties in upgrading or replacing applications. Shortcuts eliminate these issues and take up less space. You could have thousands of shortcuts pointing to the same application or document and still save drive space!

Additionally, a shortcut can define alternate launching parameters, such as default directories, command line parameters, compatibility mode, and so on. To alter the settings of a shortcut, just right-click and select Properties from the pop-up menu.

Another kind of icon is called a *taskbar button*. These buttons appear on the taskbar at the bottom of the screen when you minimize the program or window to get it off the screen for the moment. Technically, it's called a *minimized window*. This kind of icon is covered later, along with the taskbar and running your programs (see "The Taskbar, Start Menu, and Other Tools" section later in this chapter).

NOTE

Compatibility mode is a nifty new feature that enables Windows XP to support a wider range of software products than Windows 95 and Windows NT combined. A compatibility mode is simply a designation for a software platform emulation environment. In other words, when an application is launched with compatibility mode enabled, a virtual machine representing that application's native environment (Windows 95, Windows 98,

continues

continued

Windows NT, or Windows 2000) is created in such a way that the application is fooled into thinking that it is the only application present on the computer system running its preferred OS.

Don't fret that I didn't include MS-DOS or Windows 16-bit (Windows 3.x) applications in that list of environments. Those are already automatically launched into their own virtual machine. That is discussed in Chapter 21.

Just as in Windows 9x, NT, and 2000, when it is minimized, a program is still running and a document is still open—they're just removed from display on the screen. For example, a program can render a video effect, fetch your email, or calculate a spreadsheet while minimized.

WINDOW CONTROLS

On most Windows XP windows and dialog boxes, there are three buttons in the upper-right corner. These buttons are minimize, maximize, and close, from left to right. The maximize button also serves as the Restore Down (i.e. return the window to its pre-maximized size and location) button when a window is already maximized. The close button, the red box with a white X symbol, is used to close a window. If you have unsaved documents or settings within the window, you're prompted for confirmation (and whether to save the document or settings) before the close action is executed.

The usual mouse techniques for resizing a window are as follows:

1. Grab the edge of a window (the cursor turns to a double-headed arrow when you're positioned appropriately) and drag it.

2. Release when it reaches the size you want. Some windows in the new interface have a serrated tab in the lower-right corner, thus making it a little easier to grab them for resizing.

3. With Windows XP's full window drag effect, you see the contents of the window resize as you drag the window edge, or when you drag the whole window. To drag the whole window, grab its title bar (it must be sized smaller than the screen).

   The following are two much-overlooked tricks:

   - Double-click the title bar of the window to toggle it from full screen to restored size.

   - Right-click over an application button on the taskbar to gain quick access to restore, move, size, minimize, maximize, and close commands.

DIALOG BOX CHANGES

The Open and Save dialog boxes (a.k.a. file or browse dialog boxes) for most applications still offer the same shortcuts and controls as those of Windows 9x, Me, and 2000. This typically includes a shortcut menu to History, Desktop, My Documents, My Computer, and My Network Places. You'll also still find the Look In pull-down list with quick selections to local drives, user home directories, shared folders, and more. Not all applications that function on Windows XP offer a fully enhanced file dialog box.

Many dialog boxes have tabs that often appear at the top of a dialog box, as shown in Figure 4.7, with the tabs for General and Sharing. Tabs are used to offer multiple pages or displays of controls within a single smaller window. Many of the configuration settings dialog boxes have tabs, so watch for them. To select another tab, just click on it. In some cases, tabs are easy to miss. The new color scheme and display enhancements don't always direct your eyes to tabs.

Figure 4.7
A properties dialog box contains tabs you can click to see additional settings.

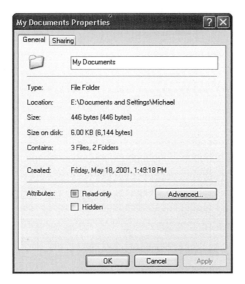

MY COMPUTER AND WINDOWS EXPLORER

My Computer and Windows Explorer are still present with much of the same functions and features as in previous versions of Windows, but a few interesting enhancements have been made. Yes, Windows Explorer is still hidden away in the Accessories area of the Start menu. Microsoft wants to draw your attention away from how files are managed on the hard drive and direct your attention to how documents are arranged within your personal folders (i.e., My Documents, My Pictures, and so on). My Computer and Windows Explorer are used to access the folder structure of your hard drives to locate files. With these tools, you can move, copy, delete, rename, create new, and more.

T I P

> Surprisingly, Windows XP still includes a Program Manager from the days of Windows 3.x. It's there for full backward compatibility for applications. If you want to work with it, just execute `Progman.exe` in the Start, Run box. Keep in mind that File Manager doesn't work with long filenames. Second, it doesn't have the capability to exploit the advancements in the interface, such as links to the Web. Third, it lacks the flexibility in cutting, copying, and pasting objects between locations, including networked workstations.

WEBVIEW

WebView is Microsoft's attempt to make your local content integrate as seamlessly as possible with Internet-based content. This integration offers benefits of more information displayed within the interface by default and quick access to common activities. For example, a single click can initiate a file or folder rename, or move, copy, or even delete a selected item (or items).

N O T E

> Part III, "Windows XP and the Internet," covers the ins and outs of getting connected, browsing the Web, using search engines, creating and serving Web pages, and using email, newsgroups, and so forth. However, what's relevant here is how the Windows XP WebView affects how you work with files and folders.

The WebView display option for Windows Explorer and My Computer have been greatly improved. No longer a direct annoyance, WebView finally offers useful information, true content-directed capabilities, and easier data object manipulation. Basically, WebView transforms the interfaces of your file and folder utilities into more Web-like mechanisms. They offer graphical representations of objects, they display more details about the selected objects, and most of the functions or commands are single-click activated.

Figure 4.8 shows the Windows Explorer in WebView. WebView gives you access to common tasks related to files and folders. In addition to the list of quick access tasks, WebView displays a quick access panel of Other Places that enables you to jump quickly to other resource locations. The Details section displays basic information about a selected item, such as

- The selected item's name and type (includes document, folder, application, and so on)
- The date at which it was most recently modified
- Its size, author, and other item-specific information

Much of this information also appears in a tool tip when the mouse cursor is placed over an object.

Figure 4.8
Windows Explorer in
WebView.

The following are some of the key WebView effects integrated into Windows XP:

- Your desktop is active; it can display Web page information (such as your home page) or streaming data gathered from the Internet, such as news, weather reports, traffic reports, stock tickers, and so on.

- My Computer and Windows Explorer have Back, Forward, Search, and History buttons, just like a Web browser.

- The toolbars in Folder and Explorer windows are customizable and have address lines, just like a browser. You can type in a Web address, hit Enter (or click Go), and the window will adjust appropriately to display the content. If you enter a Web address, that page displays. If you enter a drive letter (c:, for example), it's contents is displayed.

- Every folder on your system can be customized with a background color, picture, hot links, instructions, and so forth. Basic customizations are made without knowledge of HTML coding, through a wizard.

- Many of the Windows preset folders already have hot links to relevant sites, help files, and troubleshooting tools.

- WebView can be fully customized with unique icons for each folder and file, different display layouts for each folder, and thumbnails of album art on music files.

- Windows XP can navigate the contents of compressed archives, such as zip files, without a third-party utility. Archive files act as compressed folders.

There are many more features and options in the interface, and they're covered in the sections on customizing with the Control Panel as well as in the Windows Explorer and My Computer coverage. Chapter 21 also covers even more ways to change the interface.

WebView is enabled by default on Windows XP. But, if you decide you would rather live without WebView, it is not difficult to return to the Classic style of Windows 2000's interfaces. WebView is enabled and disabled through the Folder Options Control Panel applet, by choosing Tools, Folder Options from any My Computer or Windows Explorer window. As shown in Figure 4.9, WebView is enabled or disabled on the General tab of the Folder Options Control Panel applet by selecting either Show Common Tasks in Folders or Use Windows Classic Folders. This is a system-wide change. After WebView is disabled, it is disabled on all Windows Explorer and My Computer windows.

Figure 4.9
The General tab of the Folder Options Control Panel applet.

If you're the controlling type, you might want to fine-tune other aspects of your folders' behavior. Go back to the Folder Options applet, then select the View tab. A bevy of options that affect how folders and their contents are displayed appear. Change any settings you like. (Some of these are pretty technical, though. If you don't understand a setting, don't touch it.) We'll check out most of these in Chapter 21.

SELECTING SEVERAL ITEMS

On most lists, especially within My Computer and Windows Explorer not to mention the File and Browser dialog boxes, you can select multiple items at once to save time. The normal rules of selection apply:

- Draw a box around the files you want to select by clicking and holding over empty space near the first item then drag across and over the desired selections until all are highlighted and/or contained within the selection box, then release the mouse button.

- Select the first of the items, hold down the Ctrl key, and click to select each additional object you want to work with. Use this technique to select a bunch of noncontiguous items.

- Select the first of the items, hold down the Shift key, and click the last item. This selects the entire *range* of objects between the starting and ending points.

After several items are selected (they show onscreen as being highlighted), right-clicking any one of the objects brings up the Cut, Copy, Paste menu. The option you choose applies to *all* the selected items. Also, clicking anywhere outside of the selected items deselects them all, and pressing Ctrl and then clicking one selected object deselects it.

TIP

> Take a look at the Edit menu in any folder window. There are two commands at the bottom of the menu: Select All and Invert Selection. These are also useful when you want to select a group of files. Suppose you want to select all but two files; select the two you don't want and then choose Edit, Invert Selection.

Drag-and-drop support is implemented uniformly across the Windows XP interface. In general, if you want something placed somewhere else, drag it from the source to the destination. For example, drag items from the Search box into a folder or onto the Desktop, or add a picture attachment to an email you're composing by dragging the picture file into the new email's window. Also, the destination folder does not have to be open in a window. Items dropped onto a closed folder icon are added to that folder. You can also drag-and-drop items via the taskbar by dragging an item over an application button and waiting a second for that application to be brought to the forefront. You can also drop items into the Start menu to add them to the listings, as well as drop items over desktop icons to open them with the application to which you drop the item (assuming the application supports the object's file type).

Arranging your screen to see both the source and destination is graphically and intuitively reassuring, because you can see the results of the process. However, it's not always the easiest. After you get familiar with the interface, try the Cut, Copy, and Paste methods of moving files and folders.

Without making the source and destination windows or folders visible at the same time, copy or cut an item (or group of items) and copy or paste it into the new folder location, using the familiar Edit menu choices or shortcut keys. The right-click menu works, too. Here are the steps:

1. Select the item or items to be moved.

2. Choose Edit, Cut (or press Ctrl+X).

3. At this point, failing to paste the file into a destination or pressing Esc aborts the cutting and copying process. Nothing is lost and the file remains in its original location.

4

However, if you open the destination folder and either right-click in it and choose Paste or open its Edit menu and choose Paste (or press Ctrl+V), it magically shows up in the new location. If, when you try to paste, the Paste command is grayed out, it means you didn't properly cut or copy the object. Try again. Remember, you must use the Cut or Copy command on a file or other object immediately before using the Paste command.

Note that if you want to make a copy of the file rather than move the original, you choose Copy (or Ctrl+C) rather than Cut from the menu. Then, when you use the paste command, a copy of the file appears in the destination location.

Finally, to delete items, don't use Cut. Cutting is reserved for moving. If you cut a folder or file and then don't paste it, the GUI assumes you changed your mind—it won't be altered. Therefore, you might be surprised to find a cut item that's still right where you last saw it. This is not standard Windows behavior, because in a program such as a text editor, cutting deletes the selection even if you don't bother to paste it elsewhere. If you want to delete a folder, file, or other object, highlight it and choose File. Then select Delete, press Del, or click the X in the toolbar. The icon should fully disappear and not leave a ghost behind, as is the case when cutting.

As an alternative to this method, delete almost anything in Windows by dragging it into the Recycle Bin. You're always asked to confirm the deletion. There's no easy way to turn off this sometimes-annoying confirmation query. If you throw something away, you can get it back until you empty the trash.

4

C A U T I O N

Deleting a folder deletes all it contents, too. That content could include additional subfolders. Use the Delete command with forethought when nixing folders.

MOVING VERSUS COPYING

Windows XP usually assumes you are *moving* an object rather than making a copy of it during a drag-and-drop procedure within the same drive. When you're moving items between folders, this is the logical assumption. However, it's not always what you want. The general rule about moving versus copying is simple; when you *move* something by dragging, the mouse pointer keeps the shape of the moved object. However, when you *copy*, the cursor takes on a plus sign.

When using drag-and-drop methods, you can easily switch between copying and moving by pressing the Ctrl key as you drag. In general, holding down the Ctrl key makes a copy. The plus sign shows up in the icon so you know you're making a copy. Pressing Shift as you drag ensures that the object is moved, not copied.

This trick isn't always reliable, however. Therefore, when I'm in doubt about whether the GUI is going to copy or move an item, and it's a critical item, I ensure the correct operation. Here's the trick: The easiest way to fully control what's going to happen when you drag an item around is to *right-click and drag*. Place the pointer on the object you want to move, copy, or make a shortcut for and then press the right mouse button and drag the item to the destination. When you drop the object, you're asked what you want to do with it.

Choose your desired option. Being able to create a shortcut this way is pretty nifty, too. Often, rather than dragging a document file (and certainly a program) out of its home folder just to put it on the desktop for convenience, you want to make a shortcut out of it. Clicking the shortcut then runs the application, opens the document, or does whatever it's programmed to do when you double-click it.

CAUTION

Don't try moving program files unless you know they have not registered themselves with the operating system and they can harmlessly be moved around between folders.

TIP

It's not uncommon that, due to a slip of the wrist (or a finger on a touchpad), you might realize you've accidentally dragged an item, such as an entire folder, from one location to another. Sometimes you won't even know what you've done—a folder just suddenly disappears. All you can assume is that it has been dragged and dropped into a destination folder somewhere. Instead of going hunting, you should just check the Edit menu to see whether there's an option at the top of the menu called Undo Move. If there is, choose it to reverse the action. You can also try pressing Ctrl+Z, but keep in mind this undo action takes place within the context of the currently active application and not the last action performed anywhere within the OS.

4

Putting Items on the Desktop

The desktop is a convenient location for either permanent or temporary storage of items. Many folks use the desktop as a home for often-used documents and program shortcuts. I'm quite fond of using the desktop as an intermediary holding tank when moving items between drives, computers, or to and from floppy disks. It's particularly good for pulling found items out of a Search window or other folder while they're awaiting final relocation elsewhere.

Here are some quick notes about using the desktop that you should know about. For starters, you can send a shortcut of an object to the Desktop very easily by right-clicking it and choosing Send To, Desktop (thus creating shortcut) from the menu that appears.

Second, remember that the desktop is nothing magical. Actually, it's just another folder with a few additional properties. Prime among them is the option to have live active Internet-based information, such as stock tickers, weather, and the like. Also, each user on the machine can have his/her own desktop setup, with icons, background colors, screen saver, and such.

The major feature of the desktop is that whatever you put on it is always available by minimizing or closing open windows or, more easily, by clicking the Show Desktop button on the Quick Launch bar. Keep in mind that some items cannot be moved onto the desktop—only their shortcuts can. For example, if you try dragging a Control Panel applet to the desktop, you see a message stating that you cannot copy or move the item to this location.

If you must be able to access a Control Panel applet from the desktop, the answer is clear in this case because you don't really have a choice. Just create a shortcut to the applet and place it on the Desktop. However, in other cases when you're copying and moving items around, particularly when using the right-click method, you're presented with the options of copying, moving, or creating a shortcut to the item. What's the best choice?

Here are a few reminders about shortcuts. Remember that they work just as well as the objects they point to (for example, the program or document file), yet take up much less space on the hard disk. For this reason, they're generally a good idea. What's more, you can have as many shortcuts scattered about for a given object as you want. Therefore, put the shortcut for programs or folders you use a lot wherever you need them—put one on the desktop, one on the Quick Launch bar, one on the Start menu, and another in a folder of your favorite programs on the Desktop. Plus, deleting a shortcut will not affect the original program.

Make up shortcuts for other objects you use a lot, such as folders, disk drives, network drives and printers, and Web links. From Internet Explorer, for example, drag the little blue e icon that precedes a URL in the address bar out to the Desktop to save it as a shortcut. Clicking it brings up the Web page.

CAUTION

> Remember that shortcuts are not the item they point to. They're aliases only. Therefore, copying a document's shortcut to a floppy or a network drive or adding it as an attachment to an email doesn't copy the document itself. If you want to send a document to some colleagues, don't make the mistake of sending them the shortcut unless it's something they have access to over a network or the World Wide Web. If it's a shortcut to, say, a word-processing document or folder, they're left with nothing to open. Remember, if the icon has a little curved arrow on it, it's a shortcut, not the real thing.

The link between shortcuts and the objects they point to can be broken. This happens typically when the true object is erased or moved. If this is the case, clicking the shortcut can result in an error message. In Windows 2000 and in Windows XP, this problem is addressed in an ingenious way. Shortcuts are automatically adjusted when linked objects are moved. The operating system keeps track of all shortcuts and attempts to prevent breakage. Shortcut "healing" is built into Windows XP for those situations where the automated recover mechanism fails.

NOTE

> The automated recovery mechanism is a function that enables Windows to search for a similarly named program required by a shortcut in the event the specified location fails.

If you're in doubt about the nature of a given shortcut, try looking at its properties. You might find them telling, or at least interesting. Right-click the shortcut and choose Properties. Clicking on Find Target locates the object to which the shortcut links and displays it in a folder window.

TIP

To quickly bring up the Properties dialog box for most objects in the Windows GUI, you can highlight the object and press Alt+Enter.

SAVING FILES ON THE DESKTOP FROM A PROGRAM

Because the desktop is a convenient place to plop files and folders, modern applications' Save As boxes list desktop as a major option (see Figure 4.10). Even if the app's dialog box doesn't have the desktop icon in the left pane, the drop-down list at the top of the box has it.

Figure 4.10
A typical Save As dialog box.

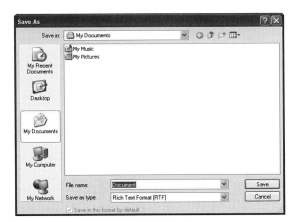

NOTE

Locating the desktop in a Windows 3.x program's Save As box is a pain, because long filenames are truncated to 8.3-style names and have ~ marks imposed on them. Here's how that works: For 16-bit programs, Windows removes spaces, shortens long names to six characters, and inserts a ~ character and then a number. If two files have the same first six characters (for example, Bob's resume and Bob's resume revised), the number is incremented for the second file. Therefore, those files appear as bobres~1 and bobres~2.

PROPERTIES AND THE RIGHT-CLICK

Ever since Windows 95, a common theme that unites items within Windows is the aspect called *properties*. Properties are pervasive through Windows 9x, Windows NT 4, Windows

2000, and now Windows XP. The Properties dialog boxes provide a means for making changes to the behavior, appearance, security level, ownership, and other aspects of objects through the operating system. Object properties apply to everything from individual files to folders, printers, peripherals, screen appearance, even to the computer, itself, or a network or workgroup. All these items have property sheets that enable you to easily change various settings that apply to these objects. For example, you might want to alter whether a printer is the default printer or whether a folder on your hard disk is shared for use by coworkers on the LAN.

A typical set of properties is shown in Figure 4.11, which displays the properties for the G: drive (hard disk) on a computer. Notice that there are several tab pages on this sheet. Some property sheets only have a single page, whereas others might have many.

Figure 4.11
A typical property sheet for a hard disk.

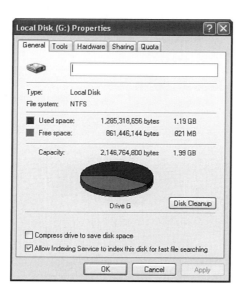

Property sheets are very useful and often serve as shortcuts for modifying settings that otherwise would take you into the Control Panel or through some other circuitous route. With some document files (for example, Word files), you can examine many settings that apply to the file, such as the creation date, author, editing history, and so forth. A typical printer's property sheet contains security, color management, location, name, and share status information. You can even change your screen colors, display resolution, screen savers, and more by right-clicking over the desktop and clicking Properties from the pop-up menu. This opens the Display applet without having to traverse the Control Panel.

Although everyday users might not have need for property sheets, power users certainly do. As you use property sheets, you also become familiar with and accustomed to another aspect of the Windows XP interface: the right-click. Until Windows 9x, the left (primary) mouse button was the one you did all your work with, unless you were using a program that specifically utilized the other buttons, such as some art programs. However, Windows 9x instituted the use of the right-click to bring up various context-sensitive menus in programs and throughout the interface. These have been incorporated into Windows XP.

Here are some typical uses of right-click context menus:

- Sharing a folder on the network
- Changing the name of your hard disk and checking its free space
- Changing a program's icon
- Creating a new folder
- Setting the desktop's colors, background, screen saver, and so on
- Adjusting the date and time of the clock quickly
- Closing an application by right-clicking on its icon in the taskbar and choosing Close
- Displaying a font's technical details
- Renaming an object
- Accessing an object's Properties dialog box

As an example of the right-click, simply get to an empty place on the desktop and right-click it. Right by the cursor, you should see a menu that looks like the one shown in Figure 4.12.

Figure 4.12
This is an example of a right-click menu from an empty location on the desktop. Notice how it contains fly-open menus.

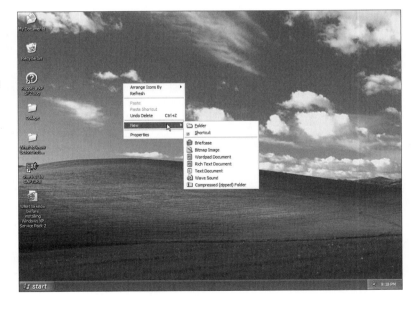

Notice that you can slide up and down the menu to make choices. Notice that some of the options in these menus have commands with a small arrow to one side. If you highlight one of these commands, a submenu will fly open, hence the term "fly-open menu."

Here are some other examples of useful right-click activities:

- Right-clicking any window's title bar produces a menu containing the Restore, Move, Size, Minimize, Maximize, and Close commands.

- Right-clicking and dragging an icon from the Explorer or a Folder onto the desktop reveals a pop-up menu with the selections of Copy Here, Move Here, Create Shortcuts Here, and Cancel.

- In many applications, selecting text and then right-clicking produces an edit menu at the cursor location that lets you choose Cut, Copy, or Paste.

- Right-clicking an empty area of the taskbar gives you a menu that lets you manage the display of all the windows you have open. For example, you can tile all open windows or set the properties of the taskbar. (The taskbar is discussed in more detail later in this chapter in the section "The Taskbar, Start Menu, and other Tools.")

- In the Explorer, right-clicking a file lets you work with it in various ways, depending on the file type. You can open the document, send it to an email recipient, run a program, install or set up a utility such as a screen saver, play a sound file, and so forth.

If you want to use Windows most efficiently, make a habit of right-clicking on objects to see what pops up. You might be surprised to see how much time you save with the resulting shortcuts.

4

NOTE

> Starting with this chapter, it is assumed that you understand the choice between single-click mode (that is, WebView) and double-click mode. Some of the figures in the book might have icons, files, or other object names underlined, whereas other might not, based on the mode the computer was set in when the screen shots were grabbed. Don't let it throw you. Also, to "double-click something," means to run it or open it by whatever technique is applicable based on your click setting. Also, "click it," means select it. Remember that if you have single-clicking turned on, that means just hovering the pointer over (that is, pointing to) the item selects it. Generally, this book works with and discusses issues using the defaults set by Microsoft.

USING THE FOLDERS BAR (A.K.A. WINDOWS EXPLORER)

For a bird's-eye view of your computer, turning on the Folders bar is the way to go. It makes copying, moving, and examining all the contents of your computer easier than navigating up and down the directory tree through folders. If you're doing housekeeping, copying and moving items around from one folder to another or across the network, or hopping back and forth between viewing Web pages and your local hard disk, mastering this view will serve you well.

Introduced with Windows 95, the folder view idea was given the name Windows Explorer, and although it's still in XP under that name, it's not featured as much as it used to be. The functionality of Windows Explorer is added to all folder windows (such as My Computer) by simply clicking on the Folders button in the toolbar. It's a very capable tool, and the one that most power users prefer over the usual folder system, which can clutter your screen with a bunch of overlapping windows if you have lots of them open. Instead, with folder view (call it Windows Explorer, if you wish) whether you want to examine the Control Panel, the local area network, the Internet, your hard disk, or the Recycle Bin, it can all be done with a minimum of effort from the Explorer. Folder View also makes copying and moving files between far-flung folders and drives a snap.

To recap, you can get to the Windows Explorer in two ways.

- Open My Computer (or any folder) and choose View, Explorer Bar, Folders (or easier yet, click on the Folders button in the toolbar).
- Click Start, All Programs, Accessories, Windows Explorer.

Figure 4.13 shows the folders that appear on my own computer in folder view.

Figure 4.13
The basic Windows Explorer screen, showing the computer's major components on the left and the contents on the right.

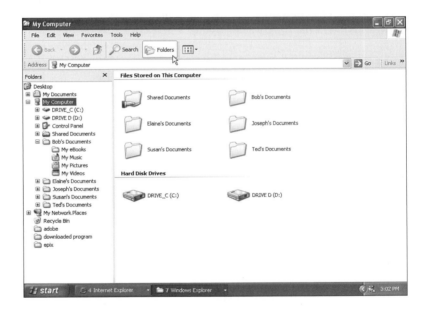

TIP

As an easy way into Windows Explorer, I always keep a shortcut to it on the Quick Launch bar or on the Desktop (see Chapter 21 for how to use the Quick Launch bar). Another trick is to right-click the Start button and choose Explore. This brings up the Windows Explorer, too.

DISPLAYING THE CONTENTS OF YOUR COMPUTER

When you run Windows Explorer, all the objects constituting your computer appear in the list on the left. Some of those objects have a plus sign (+) next to them, which means the object is collapsed; it contains subitems that aren't currently showing.

Click an item in the left pane to see its contents in the right pane. If the item has a plus sign, click it to open up the sublevels in the left pane, showing you the relationship of the folders and other items in a tree arrangement. In the figure, you can see that the Bob's Documents folder has been opened in this way. Notice that the + is replaced with a minus (-) sign, indicating that the object's display has been expanded. Clicking the minus sign causes that branch to collapse. This interface should be nothing new, because it's well integrated into many Web pages and programs nowadays.

Click the Desktop icon at the top of the tree. Notice that all the objects on your Desktop appear in the right pane.

If you open a local disk drive or disk across the network, you can quickly get a graphical representation of the disk's folder layout. Then, click a folder to see its contents. By right-clicking on disks, folders, or files, you can examine and set properties for them. The straight lines connecting folders indicate how they're related. If you have more folders than can be seen at one time, the window will have a scrollbar that you can use to scroll the tree up and down.

Notice that there are two scrollbars—one for the left pane and one for the right. These scroll independently of one another—a feature that can be very useful when you're copying items from one folder or drive to another.

WORKING WITH FILE AND FOLDERS IN EXPLORER

Working with folders and files in this view is simple. As explained previously, you just click an item in the left pane, and its contents appear in the right pane. Choose the view (Large Icons, Small Icons, List, or Details) for the right pane using either the toolbar's View button or the View menu. In Details view, you can sort the items by clicking the column headings.

Now here's the good part: After you select the source item in the left pane and its contents are displayed in the right pane, you can manipulate them. You can drag items to other destinations, such as a local hard disk, a floppy drive, or a networked drive. You can drag and drop files, run programs, open documents that have a program association, and use right-click menu options for various objects. For example, you can right-click files or folders and choose Send To, 3 1/2 Floppy to copy items to a floppy disk.

With a typical hard disk containing many files, when its folders are all listed in the left pane, some will be offscreen. Because the two panes have independent scrollbars, dragging items between distant folders is not a problem. Here's the game plan:

1. Be sure the source and destination folders are open and visible in the left pane, even if you have to scroll the pane up and down. For example, a network drive should be

expanded, with its folders showing (using and mapping network drives are covered in Chapter 16, "Using a Windows XP Network.")

2. Click the source folder in the left pane. Now its contents appear to the right.

3. Scroll the left pane up or down to expose the destination folder. (Only click the scroll-bar, not a folder in the left pane; if you do, it will change the displayed items on the right side.)

4. In the right pane, locate and drag the items over to the left, landing on the destination folder. The folder must be highlighted; otherwise, you've aimed wrong.

This technique will suffice most of the time. Sometimes it's too much of a nuisance to align everything for dragging. In that case, use the cut/copy-and-paste technique discussed earlier in the chapter. Remember, you can copy and paste across your home LAN as well as between your local drives.

Here are a few tips when selecting folders:

- Only one folder can be selected at a time in the left pane. If you want to select multiple folders, click the parent folder (such as the drive icon) and select the folders in the right pane. Use the same techniques described earlier for making multiple selections.

- When a folder is selected in the left pane, its name become highlighted. This is a reminder of which folder's contents are showing in the right pane.

- You can jump quickly to a folder's name by typing its first letter on the keyboard. If there's more than one folder with the same first letter, each press of the key will advance to the next choice.

- The fastest way to collapse all the branches of a given drive is to click that drive's plus sign.

- You can quickly rearrange a drive's folder structure in the left pane by dragging folders around. You can't drag disk drives, but you can create shortcuts for them (for example, a network drive) by dragging them to, say, the desktop.

- If a folder has subfolders, those will appear in the right pane as folder icons. Clicking one of those will open it as though you had clicked that subfolder in the left pane.

- When dragging items to collapsed folders (ones with a plus sign), hovering the pointer over the folder for a seconds will cause it to open.

- You can use the right-click-drag technique when dragging items if you want the option of clearly choosing Copy, Move, or Create Shortcut when you drop the item on the target.

- To create a new folder, in the left pane, click the folder under which you want to create the new folder. Right-click in the right pane and choose New, Folder.

- Delete a folder by right-clicking on it and choosing Delete. You'll be asked to confirm.

4

CAUTION

> Although powerful, the folder view is also dangerous. It makes accidental rearrangement of your hard disk's folders extremely easy. When selecting folders, be careful not to accidentally drag them! The icons are small, and this is easy to do accidentally, especially over in the left pane. A little flick of the wrist and a click of the mouse, and you've dragged one folder on top of another folder. This makes it a subfolder of the target. Remember, the left pane is "live" too. Rearranging the directory tree could make programs and files hard to find, and some programs might not even work. If you think you've accidentally dragged a folder (its subfolders will go, too) into the wrong place, open the Edit menu. The first choice probably will read Undo Move. Choose it, and the folders or files you dragged are returned to their previous locations.

THE TASKBAR, START MENU, AND OTHER TOOLS

The taskbar is the command center for your user environment under Windows XP. With few or no desktop icons after initial setup, everything you do within Windows XP has to start with the taskbar. The taskbar (refer to Figure 4.9) is host to several other highly useful tools, such as the Start menu, the quick launch bar, the open application buttons, and the system tray.

The Start menu is the control center for Windows XP. Most native applications and installed applications have an icon within the Start menu used to launch or access them. The Start menu has two columns of access elements. The left column includes Internet and email access on top and a list of most recently used applications on the bottom. By default, it displays the last six accessed applications.

A fresh installation of Windows XP will include pre-stocked items in this list, such as Windows Media Player, MSN Explorer, Windows Movie Maker, Tour Windows XP, and Files and Settings Transfer Wizard—leaving room for only a single recently accessed application. These pre-stocked items will eventually disappear, but can take up to 60 days. You can forcibly remove them one at a time by issuing the Remove from This List command from the right-click pop-up menu.

At the bottom of the left column is All Programs, which is an access point to the rest of the Start menu. Those of you from Windows 9x/Me/NT/2000 might recognize this as the Programs section of your Start menus. The Start menu's right column lists My Documents, My Pictures, My Music, My Computer, (optionally) My Network Places, Control Panel, Set Program Access and Defaults, Help and Support, Search, and Run. Below both columns are the Log Off and Turn Off Computer buttons. Log Off is used to either fully log off the system or switch user contexts. The Turn Off Computer command replaces Shutdown and is used to power down (turn off), restart, or hibernate the computer.

 TIP

> Pressing Ctrl+Esc or the Windows key opens the Start menu as though you clicked the Start button. After it's open, you can navigate in it using the arrow keys. The Enter key is used to launch or access the selected item.

The top level of the Start menu is managed by the system itself; you don't get to change what is displayed there, other than launching applications so they show up in the most-recently used (MRU) list.

It should be obvious that clicking on any of the items listed on the Start menu either launches an application or opens a new dialog box or menu.

The organization of the All Programs section of the Start menu can be altered as you see fit. This is done through a series of drag-and-drop operations. New items are added to the Start menu by dragging the item from My Computer or Windows Explorer over the Start menu button, then over All Programs, and then to the location where you wish to drop it.

The area immediately to the right of the Start menu is the Quick Launch Bar. Microsoft sticks the Show Desktop tool, which minimizes all open windows, as well as links to Internet Explorer and Windows Media Player here by default. You can add your own just by dragging and dropping an application icon over this area. The Quick Launch Bar is not enabled by default. To enable this handy tool, open Taskbar and Start Menu Properties, select the Taskbar tab, and then mark the Show Quick Launch check box.

To the far right on the taskbar is the *system tray*. Some services, OS functions, and applications place icons into this area. These icons provide instant access to functions and settings as well as status displays. For example, when you're working from a portable system, a battery appears in the system tray that indicates how much juice is left. The clock is also located in the system tray.

Between the Quick Launch Bar and the system tray are the active application buttons. These are grouped by similarity, not by order of launch. If the taskbar becomes crowded, multiple instances of similar applications are cascaded into a single button.

> **NOTE**
>
> You can reposition the taskbar on the right, left, or top of the screen. Just click any part of the taskbar other than a button and drag it to the edge of your choice. The Taskbar and Start Menu Properties dialog box includes a locking option to prevent the taskbar from being moved accidentally. To deselect this option, right-click the taskbar and select the Lock The Taskbar option. This removes the check mark next to it and allows you to manipulate the size and position of the taskbar.

You can further control and modify the taskbar and Start menu through their Properties dialog boxes.

→ For more information on customizing the taskbar and Start menu, **see** Chapter 21.

RUNNING YOUR APPLICATIONS

If you're upgrading from Windows 9*x*, you already know how to run applications, how to switch between them, and how to manage them. But, if you are new to Windows OSes, here is a quick how-to guide.

HOW TO LAUNCH YOUR APPS

Applications are launched under Windows XP in a number of different ways. You'll probably end up employing the technique that best fits the occasion. To run an application, perform one of the following tasks (ranked in order of ease of use):

- Use the Start button to find the desired application from the resulting menus.
- Drag an application shortcut to the Quick Launch bar at the bottom of the screen and click it to run.
- Open My Computer or Windows Explorer, browse through your folders to find the application's icon, and double-click it.
- Find the application with the Start, Search command and double-click it. (see "Running Applications with the Search Command" later in this chapter)
- Enter command names from the command prompt (click Start, All Programs, Accessories, Command Prompt to open the command prompt window). You must know the exact name and the folder in which it's most likely to be stored.
- Press Ctrl-Alt-Del to launch the Task Manager. Click New Task and then type in the executable filename for the program (for example, word.exe).

An alternative approach is to open a document that's associated with a given application. This is a tricky way to open the application:

- Locate a document that was created with the application in question and double-click it. This runs the application and loads the document into it. With some applications, you can then close the document and open a new one if you need to.
- Right-click the desktop or in a folder and choose New. Then choose a document type from the resulting menu. This creates a new document of the type you desire, which, when double-clicked, runs the application.

Here's how to open an existing document in an application (ranked in order of ease of use):

- Click Start, Documents, and look among the most recently edited documents. Clicking one opens the document in the appropriate application.
- Use the Start, Search command to locate the document.
- Run the application that created the document and check the document's MRU (most recently used) list on the File menu. It might be there. If so, click it.

In the name of expediency, this book doesn't cover all these options. After you get the hang of the most common approaches, you'll understand how to use the others. Notice that some of the approaches are "application-centric," whereas others are "document-centric." An application-centric person thinks, "I'll run Word so I can write up that trip expense report." A document-centric person thinks, "I have to work on that company manual. I'll look for it and double-click it."

RUNNING PROGRAMS FROM THE START BUTTON

The most popular way to run applications is with the Start button, which is located in the lower-left corner of your screen. When you install a new program, the program's name is usually added somewhere to the Start button's More Program menu lists. If you've recently used an application, Windows XP might list it in the recently used list on the top-level Start menu area. Sometimes you'll have to "drill down" a level or two to find a certain program, because software makers sometimes like to store their applications under their company names (for example, Real Networks creates a group called Real, which you have to open to run the Real Player). Then you just find your way to the program's name, choose it, and the program runs. Suppose you want to run the calculator. Here are the steps to follow:

1. Click the Start button.
2. Point to All Programs.
3. Point to Accessories, and then choose Calculator.

Note that all selections with an arrow pointing to the right of the name have submenus—meaning that they open when you click them or hover the pointer over them. There might be several levels of submenus. For example, to see the System Tools submenu, you have to go through All Programs, Accessories, System Tools.

> **TIP**
>
> Sometimes, spotting a program in a list is a visual hassle. Press the first letter of the program you're looking for and the cursor jumps to it. If multiple items start with that letter, each key press advances one item in the list. Also, pressing the right-arrow key opens a submenu. The Enter key executes the highlighted program. Items in the lists are ordered alphabetically, although folders appear first, in order, with programs after that.

You might accidentally open a list that you don't want to look at (say, the Games submenu). Just move the pointer to the one you want and wait a second, or press the Esc key. Each press of Esc closes one level of any open lists. To close down all open lists, just click anywhere else on the screen, such as on the desktop or another window. All open Start button lists go away.

 If a shortcut on your Start menu doesn't work, see "Shortcut Doesn't Work" in the "Troubleshooting" section at the end of this chapter.

RUNNING A PROGRAM FROM MY COMPUTER OR WINDOWS EXPLORER

If you're a power user, chances are good you're sleuthing around on your hard disk using either the My Computer approach or the Windows Explorer. I certainly have programs floating around on my hard disk that do not appear in my Start button program menus, and I have to execute them directly. In general, the rule for running programs without the Start menu is this: If you can find and display the program's icon, just double-click it to make it run.

TIP

> Just as in Windows 2000 and Windows Me, the differences between My Computer and Windows Explorer within Windows XP are more cosmetic than functional. In fact, simply by changing the defaults of the display mode (WebView or Classic), the same view (for example, the same layout, panes, and details) is obtainable using either interface. To alter the views, use the View menu (or the toolbar buttons).
>
> Right-clicking My Computer and choosing Manage launches a powerful computer manager program called Computer Management. This is covered in Chapter 24, "System Utilities."
>
> My Network Places is a version of the My Computer interface that is used to gain access to network resources. Overall, it's used in the same manner as My Computer. The only key is that you must be on a network and someone must grant you access to shared resources on other systems for this tool to be of any use. Thus, we've left the discussion of this tool to Part IV, "Networking."

Getting to a program you want is often a little convoluted, but it's not too difficult to grasp. Plus, if you understand the DOS directory tree structure or you've used a Mac, you already know more about XP than you think. Double-click a drive to open it, and then double-click a directory to open it. Then, double-click the program you want to run. Figure 4.14 shows a typical directory listing for My Computer.

Figure 4.14
A typical directory as shown in My Computer.

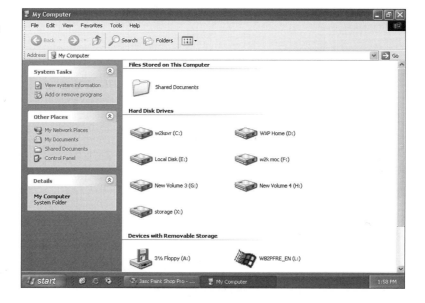

Here are some notes to remember:

■ Get to the Desktop quickly by clicking the Show Desktop icon in the Quick Launch bar (just to the right of the Start Button).

- Folders are listed first, followed by files. Clicking a folder reveals its contents.

- If you want to see more folders on the screen at once to help in your search, you have several options. The View menu or the View button on the toolbar can be used to change view options. The Titles view shows large icons with titles and other descriptors. The Icons view uses small icons with only the object name. The Thumbnails view displays images extracted from the file objects themselves; this view is most useful for graphic files. The List view displays everything in a column by its object name only. The Details view offers the most comprehensive information about file system objects in a multi-column display with object names, object type, size, modified date, comments, and so on.

TIP

Pressing Backspace while in any folder window moves you up one level in the directory tree. Also, the Back and Forward buttons work just like they do in a Web browser; they move you forward and back through folders you've already visited.

Of course, many of the files in your folders are *not* programs. They're documents or support files. To easily find the applications, choose the Details view and then click the column head for Type. This sorts the listing by type, making it easy to find applications in the list (which carry an Application label).

NOTE

Applications, registered file types, and certain system files do not have their file extensions (a period and three-letter label that follows the file name) displayed by default. Hidden system files and directories are invisible, too. This choice was made to prevent cluttering the display with files that perform duties for the operating system but not directly for users. It also prevents meddling with files that could cripple applications and documents, or even the system at large. Personally, I like seeing as many details about files as possible, so when I install a system, I change the default settings to show me every file on my system. This is done through the View tab of the Folder Options applet accessed through the My Computer or Windows Explorer Tools menu or the Control Panel.

4

RUNNING APPLICATIONS WITH THE SEARCH COMMAND

One of the first rules of organization is to know where things are, and how to keep them in their proper places. The Search command from the Start menu is a tool often used in this mission. It is invaluable for those of us who are too lazy to get organized. Just let Windows XP do a search for that file you know you stored *somewhere* but can't remember to save your life. Yes, indeed, it's a wonderful tool for the absent minded. If you're interested in organizing your "stuff" (the lexicon's term *du jour* for anything in your computer), you must find it first. The Search command offers a major assist in the sleuth.

The Search tool found at the top level of the Start menu is a powerful tool for locating files, folders, computers, people, and even Internet resources. (Press F3 or Windows+F on your keyboard as shortcuts to the Search tool.) The first page of the search tool prompts you to select the type of search to perform. The options include Pictures, music, or video; Documents; All files and folders; and Printers, computers, and people.

You can limit your search to the local system or include anywhere within your reach over the network. It always helps to know the exact name of the object you are looking for, but even if you only know part of it, the Search tool quickly locates all the possibilities. You can use standard DOS-style wildcards in your searches for files. For example, the * character substitutes for a character string of any length, and ? replaces one character. For example, searching for "*.txt" returns all files with the .txt extension, while searching for "blue??.doc" returns all files that have "blue" as the first four letters of a six-letter filename. After a list of possible suspects is returned, click one to open it in its respective application (see Figure 4.15).

Figure 4.15
The Search tool window with results from a "*.txt" search.

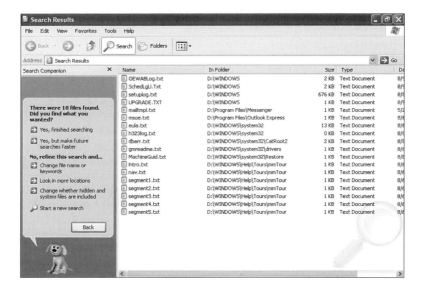

After an item is listed in the search results, it is accessed by double-clicking it. If it is an application, it is launched. If it is a data file, it is opened within its associated application. If it is a Web URL, your Web browser launches to view it. If it is a media file, the correct player launches to play it or display it. The Search tool can be used to execute a program that you can't seem to find in the Start menu, can't find anywhere on the system using My Computer, and won't execute from the Run command. Also keep in mind that applications that don't execute from the Run command are outside of the paths known to Windows XP. *Paths* is an environmental variable (see Chapter 22, "Configuration via Control Panel Applets") that defines all common locations that Windows searches for executables or other necessary files. If the application lies outside the path, then Windows XP can't find it without help.

When using Search's All files and folders, be sure to pay attention to the Look In selection. By default, Search looks on all local hard drives. If you want to limit the search to a single drive or want to search over the network, you need to alter this setting. Fortunately, there is a pull-down list with all the common options, plus the Browse option. The Browse option is used to select any folder or drive within your reach over the network or locally.

USING MY DOCUMENTS, MY PICTURES, AND MY MUSIC

Windows XP is designed to help you focus on your creative tasks rather than the underlying OS, which supports the tools and files. Part of this includes the My Documents, My Pictures, and My Music Start menu items. These links also appear on most File or Browse Windows as well as within My Computer and Windows Explorer. These three "My" labeled elements link you back to a standard location where your personal data files are stored.

The My Documents folder is the master folder for all of your personal data files. This is the default storage location whenever you save a new document or data file. This is also where the My Music and My Pictures sub-folders reside. These folders are provided to you to simplify the storage and retrieval of your most intimate file-stored creations. Clicking one of these Start menu links opens a My Computer window.

TIP

> My Documents is not the same as the Documents item seen on the top-level of the Windows 2000 Start menu. Documents is a quick-access list of the 15 most recently accessed resources. This included documents, music files, image files, archive files, and even (sometimes) programs. Microsoft discovered that the Documents feature of the Start menu was under-used because most Windows-enabled applications have their own most recently used lists located within their File menu. So, Microsoft opted to disable this feature on Windows XP, which is now called My Recent Documents. To re-enabled it, right-click the Start menu, select Properties, click Customize, select the Advanced tab, mark the List My Most Recently Opened Documents check box, and then click OK twice. If you ever want to clear out the list of recently accessed documents, the Clear List button beside the check box does just that.

4

USING THE HELP SYSTEM

We've yet to advance our computing systems to the level displayed in Star Trek where officers command an action and it takes place. When you want your computer to do something, you need to tell it what to do. Often, you have to explain in great detail at every step exactly what actions to take or not to take. The Windows XP Help system is designed to aid you in finding out what everything within the environment can and cannot do as well as teach you how to perform the activity you need for work or play.

The help system is accessed by clicking the Help and Support item on the top-level of the Start menu. The Help system offers a wide range of options from a search routine to topic organized texts to task assisting walk-throughs to Internet updated dynamic content help.

The Help system also includes access to a full index, a history list, and a favorites list. It operates in much the same way as a Web browser—using hyperlinks, back and forward buttons, and the ability to return to the start of the system using the Home button. When searching for material, you can use Boolean rules to fine-tune your keyword search phrases (AND, OR, NOT, and NEAR). This is definitely a tool that is worth your effort to explore and to consult in times of trouble or confusion.

EXITING WINDOWS GRACEFULLY

When you've finished a Windows XP session, you should properly shut down or log off to ensure that your work is saved and that no damage is done to the operating system. Shall I reiterate? Shutting down properly is very important. You can lose your work or otherwise foul up Windows settings if you don't shut down before turning off your computer. If multiple people share the computer, you should at least log off when you're finished so that others can log on. Logging off protects your work and settings from prying eyes. When you shut down, Windows does some housekeeping, closes all open files, prompts you to save any unsaved work files, and alerts the network that you and your shared resources are no longer available for consultation.

There are several ways to shut down the computer, all or only some of which might apply to your machine. Newer machines have more shutdown features because they're likely to have advanced power management built into them via ACPI.

Here are the steps for correctly exiting Windows:

1. Close any programs that you have running. (This can almost always be done from each program's File, Exit menu or by clicking the program's close button.) If you forget to close programs before issuing the Logout or Shut Down command, Windows attempts to close them for you. If you haven't saved your work, you're typically prompted to do so. Windows alerts you if it can't automatically close an open program. If you are just switching user context, your open application's status is saved so you can quickly return to it later.

2. Click Start, Turn Off Computer. The dialog box shown in Figure 4.16 come onscreen.

3. Click the desired option.

Figure 4.16
The Turn Off Computer selection dialog box.

Here are some points to consider:

- The Hibernate option records the current state of the system to disk, then shuts down the computer. When the power is turned back on, the system reboots. If you log back in as the same user who initiated the hibernation, the system returns to its exact state at the moment of hibernation.

- If your computer has Advanced Power Manager (APM) or ACPI built in, you see the Standby option instead of Hibernate. (Standby is explained later in this section.) This is certainly the case with PCs fitted with ATX motherboards (as opposed to the older AT-style PC) and power supplies. The ATX motherboards have standby capability that Windows XP can recognize and utilize. If your system isn't ACPI enabled, you won't see the Standby option.

- If you have an APM or ACPI system and want to Hibernate your system rather than put it on Standby, you can access this option by pressing and holding Shift. This action changes the Standby button to Hibernate (it acts like a toggle when it is pressed). Be sure to hold the Shift key down while you click the Hibernate button.

- If you want to log off, use the Log Off command button from the Start menu instead of the Turn Off Computer command button (first click Cancel on the Turn Off Computer dialog box). There are no log off options offered in the Turn Off Computer dialog box.

- If you attempt to shutdown the computer while another user's desktop is still active (for example, if Switch User was employed and at least one other user is still logged on), a warning message stating that performing a shutdown could result in data loss along with the options to continue with shutdown (Yes) or abort (No).

TIP

> Logging off clears personal settings from memory and puts the computer in a neutral state, waiting for another user to log on. However, it doesn't bring the system to its knees. Logging off does not stop running services, which can include some applications, such as Web services, file sharing, print sharing, UPS support, and scheduled tasks, to name a few. When the Log Off command button is pressed on the Start menu, you are offered two options: Switch User or Log Off. The latter exits you from the system and closes all applications. The former retains your environment while allowing another user to gain access to his or her desktop.

Standby puts the computer in a suspended state, letting you quickly come right back to where you were working before you suspended the PC. This means you don't have to exit all your applications before turning off your computer. You only have to choose Standby. This also saves energy, because the hard drives, CPU, CPU fan, some internal electronics, and possibly the power supply and fan go into a low-power state. Your monitor, if Energy Star compliant, should also go into a frugal state of energy consumption. When you want to start up again, a quick press of the power switch (on some computers a key press on the keyboard or a jiggle of the mouse does the trick) starts up the system right where you left off. Make sure to press the power button for just a second or so. Anything over four seconds on most modern computers in a standby state causes the computer to completely power down.

Be aware that Standby holds your system state only as long as the computer has power. If the power fails, everything stored in the computer's RAM is lost. You'll end up doing a cold boot when the power is restored or, if it's a laptop with a dead battery, when you hook your AC adapter up to your laptop again. The moral is to be cautious when using Standby. You should save your work before going into standby mode, if not close important documents.

One of the most welcome features of recent versions of Windows, including Windows XP, is *hibernation*. Like standby mode, hibernation lets you pause your work, and resume later, without laboriously shutting down and reopening all your applications and files. But unlike Standby, Hibernate isn't volatile. If the AC power fails or batteries run flat, it doesn't matter because Hibernate stores the "system state" on a portion of the hard disk rather than keeping the system RAM alive in a low-power state. After storing the system state to the hard disk, the computer fully shuts down. When restarted, a little internal flag tells the boot loader that the system has been stored on disk, and it's reloaded into memory.

Hibernation requires as much free hard disk as you have RAM in your PC. If you have 128MB of RAM, you need 128MB of free disk space for hibernation to work. If Hibernate is not an option on your shutdown menu, enable it through the Power Options in Control Panel. The dialog box reports the amount of disk space needed for your system in case you're unaware of the amount of RAM in your system.

When you choose Hibernate from the shutdown menu, Windows XP has to create a fairly large file on disk. In my case, for example, it's 2GB in size. On a 3GHz Intel Pentium 4, the entire process takes about 15 seconds. Restarting takes about the same amount of time. Remember, if you're going to put a laptop running on batteries to sleep for more than a few hours, use Hibernate or just do a complete shut down, closing your applications and documents. That way, if the batteries run out, you don't lose your work.

DEALING WITH A CRASHED APPLICATION OR OPERATING SYSTEM

Even though Windows XP is fairly immune to crashing, the applications that run on it are not necessarily so robust. Not to be cynical, but many IS professionals don't consider any version of Windows worth their trouble until at least a service pack or two hit the streets, because they know bugs tend to be prevalent in first-release software. As of SP-2, XP has made that milestone. Still, with an operating system as complex as Windows XP, we bet there are a few gotchas lurking.

 If your system is really still stuck but you can get the Task Manager up, see "Forcing Your Computer to Shut Down" in the "Troubleshooting" section at the end of this chapter.

 If your laptop computer won't shut down no matter what you do, see "Ctrl+Alt+Delete Doesn't Work" in the "Troubleshooting" section at the end of this chapter.

My point here is that you're going to bump into some unstable behavior from time to time. If you notice that a program is not responding, you might have a crash on your hands. To gracefully survive a crash, possibly even without losing any of your data, try the following steps:

1. Try pressing Esc. Some a program gets stuck in the middle of a process and Esc gets it back on track. For example, if you accidentally pressed Alt, this activates the menus. A press of Esc gets you out of that loop. If you've opened a menu, two presses of Esc or a click within the application's window might be required to return to normal operation.

2. Windows XP has greatly improved application-management facilities. In most cases, even after an application has crashed, you should still be able to minimize, maximize, move, resize, and close its window.

3. Can you switch to the app to bring its window up front? First try clicking any portion of the window. If that doesn't work, click its button in the taskbar. Still no luck? Try using successive presses of Alt+Tab. If you get the window open and responding, try to save any unfinished work in the app and then try to close it by clicking the close button or selecting the File, Exit.

4. If that doesn't work, try right-clicking the program's button in the taskbar and choosing Close from the pop-up menu.

5. If that doesn't work, press Ctrl+Shift+Esc to launch the Task Manager. Notice the list of running applications. Does the one in question display Not Responding next to it? If so, click it, and then click End Task.

6. If Task Manager reports that you don't have sufficient access to terminate the task, you must reboot the system. First, attempt a graceful shutdown using the Turn Off Computer command. However, if that fails (for example, it hangs on the hung application or it never seems to complete the shutdown process), you need to resort to power cycling (shutting off your PC with the power button on the case). After the system reboots you should be back to normal. To do a hard-restart of the PC, you have to push and hold down the power button for at least four seconds. This signals the power supply to completely shut down.

TROUBLESHOOTING

SHORTCUT DOESN'T WORK

I click a shortcut key somewhere in my Start menus and nothing happens or I get an error message.

Windows isn't smart enough, or to put another way, it's too much software overhead for the OS to keep track of all the shortcuts and update them, as necessary, when the files they point to are moved or deleted. A system that's been in use for some time certainly has "dead" shortcuts, just as Web pages have broken links floating around. When you click a shortcut icon anywhere in the system—be it the Start menus, the Desktop, or in a folder— and you get an error message about the program file, click OK and let Windows take a stab at solving the problem by searching for the application. If it's found, Windows XP "heals" the shortcut so that it works the next time you try to use it.

If that doesn't work, try searching yourself using Start, Search. See whether you can track down the runaway application. If you're successful, you'll probably be best off erasing the bad shortcut and creating a new one that points to the correct location. You can create a new shortcut by right-clicking the app's icon and choosing Create Shortcut. Then drag, copy, or move the shortcut to wherever you want, such as onto the Start button.

Another good trick to help you sort out a bad shortcut or to follow where its trail is leading is to right-click the icon and choose Properties, Find Target.

TIP

> Remember, moving folders containing applications (for example, Office might be in C:\Program Files\MSOffice) is a *really* bad idea. After they're installed, it's best to leave them where they are.

FORCING YOUR COMPUTER TO SHUT DOWN

The system is acting sluggish, nonresponsive, or otherwise weird.

If your system is acting erratically or stuck in some serious way and you've already killed any unresponsive programs, press Ctrl+Alt+Delete. This should bring up the Task Manager (Ctrl+Shift+Esc does too). Click the Shut Down menu, then select Turn Off. If you get this far, there's hope for a graceful exit. You might have to wait a minute or so for the Turn Off command to take effect. If you're prompted to shut some programs or save documents, do so. Hope for a speedy shutdown. Then reboot.

CTRL+ALT+DELETE DOESN'T WORK

Even Ctrl+Alt+Delete doesn't do anything.

If Turn Off doesn't work, it's time to power-cycle the computer. Press the power switch to turn off the machine. On a machine with APM or ACPI support (one that can perform a soft power down), this might require holding the power button in for more than four seconds. You could lose some work, but what else are you going to do? Sometimes it happens. This is one good reason for saving your work regularly, and looking for options in your programs that perform autosaving. Writers often set their AutoSave function in MS Word to save every five minutes. That way, we can recover from a system crash and only lose up to 5 minutes of work instead of everything.

Incidentally, although it's extremely rare, I've known laptops to not respond to any form of command or power button when the operating system was fully hung. I've even had to remove the AC connection, fully remove the main battery, wait a few seconds, and then reinsert the battery and reboot. Removal of the battery is important; otherwise, the battery keeps the computer in the same stuck state, thinking it's just in standby mode.

TIPS FROM THE WINDOWS PROS: WORKING EFFICIENTLY

The interface is your portal into the operating system and therefore into your computer. You're likely to be using it every day, so it behooves you to "work the system" as effectively and efficiently as possible. As a writer and programmer on deadlines, I use my computer at breakneck speed most of the time. Cutting corners on how you control the system interface saves you literally hundreds of miles of mousing around your desktop over the course of a few years. Here are our top timesaving and motion-saving tips for using Windows XP:

- To get to the desktop (minimize all open windows), press the Windows key and M at the same time. To reverse the effect, press Shift+Windows+M. This is a real timesaver. If you prefer the mouse, use the Desktop button in the Quick Launch bar. It does the same thing.

- Change between apps with Alt+Tab. Aiming for an application's little button on the taskbar is a hassle. You'll get tendonitis doing that all day.

- Buy an ergonomic keyboard, split in the middle. Try not to rest your wrists on a hard surface. Cut a mouse pad in half and use Velcro, tape, or glue to affix it to the palm rest in front of the keys, if you're a "leaner."

- Double-click a window's title bar to make it go full screen. Editing in little windows on the screen is a hassle and requires unnecessary scrolling.

- To close the foreground program or window, press Alt+F4. It's that easy. Alternatively, right-click its button on the taskbar and choose Close. Aiming for that little X in the upper-right corner takes too much mouse movement.

- Put all your favorite applications, dialup connections, folders, and documents on the Quick Launch bar. Forget about the Start button. You can put about 20 things down there on the Quick Launch bar, for easy, one-click access. Use it. When an item falls out of use, erase it. They're only shortcuts, so it doesn't matter if you erase them.

NOTE

> On Windows XP Home, the Quick Launch bar is disabled by default. To turn it on, right-click over an empty area on the taskbar, then from the pop-up menu that appears select Toolbars, Quick Launch.

- If there are too many items within the Quick Launch bar to be displayed within the current area, two little arrows (>>) are displayed. This indicates that other Quick Launch icons are present but are currently hidden from view. To see the hidden icons, click on the double arrow to see a pop-up menu or click and drag the edge of the main toolbar area (just to the right of the Quick Launch bar) to expand the space available for the Quick Launch bar.

- Those little double arrows appear in many locations throughout the user experience. They're on the Quick Launch bar, the system tray, the WebView details pane, ends of toolbars, and more. They simply indicate that more data is available but it's currently hidden from view. Or they can mean that all data is currently displayed but it can be hidden or reduced in size. In some cases, the double arrows are a toggle between minimum and expanded views. At other times, the double arrows display the hidden items when clicked but return to their previous display when you make a selection or click somewhere else.

- Use Standby and Hibernate! Don't boot up every time you turn on your computer. It's a waste of valuable time. Keep you favorite programs open: email, word processor, picture viewer, Web browser, spreadsheet, whatever. Do save your work, maybe even close your document, but leave the apps open and keep the machine in standby or hibernate mode.

- If you use a laptop in the office, get a good external keyboard to work with it. Your hands will probably be happier, and you'll type faster. Also, get a pointing device that works best for you. Those "pointing stick" mouse devices found on many laptops are not for everyone. Try a few different pointing devices and come up with one that works best for you.

- Discover and use right-click shortcuts whenever possible. For example, in Outlook Express, you can easily copy the name and email address of someone from the Address Book and paste them into an email. People are always asking me for email addresses of mutual friends or colleagues. I click on a person's entry in the Address Book and press Ctrl+C (for copy); then I switch back to the email I'm writing and press Ctrl+V (paste). Then I just press Ctrl+Enter, and the email is sent.

- Also in Outlook Express, you can reply to an email with Ctrl+R. Forward one with Ctrl+F. Send a message you've just written by pressing Ctrl+Enter. Send and Receive all mail with Ctrl+M.

- In Internet Explorer, use the F11 toggle to go full screen. This gets all the other junk off the screen. Also, use the Search panel to do your Web searches (opened by clicking the magnifying glass search toolbar button). You can easily check search results without having to use the Back button. And speaking of the Back button, don't bother moving the mouse up there to click Back. Just press Alt+left arrow. The left- and right-arrow buttons with Alt are the same as the Back and Forward buttons.

- In most Microsoft applications, including Outlook Express and Internet Explorer, F5 is the "refresh" key. In OE, for example, pressing F5 sends and receives all your mail, as long as the Inbox is highlighted. In IE, it refreshes the page. In Windows Explorer, it updates the listing in a window (to reflect the results of a file move, for example). Remember F5!

- In Word, Excel, and many other apps, Ctrl+F6 is the key that switches between open windows within the same app. No need to click on the Window menu in the app and choose the document in question. Just cycle through them with Ctrl+F6.

■ In the apps you use most, look for shortcut keys or macros you can use or create to avoid unnecessary repetitive work. Most of us type the same words again and again. (See, there I go.) As a writer, for example, I have macros programmed in MS Word for common words such as *Windows XP Home*, *Control Panel*, *Desktop*, *Folders*, and so on. Bob has created a slew of editing macros that perform tasks such as "delete to the end of line" (Ctrl+P), "delete line" (Ctrl+Y), and so on. In Word, press Alt+T+A and check out the AutoCorrect and AutoText features.

→ **See** Chapter 21 to add more timesaving tricks to your arsenal.

USING THE SIMPLE SUPPLIED APPLICATIONS

In this chapter

A SEA OF FREEBIES

Although you no doubt have collected your own arsenal of workhorse programs to assist you in your daily chores, Windows XP Home, like past versions of Windows, comes replete with numerous freebie utility programs to handle common, everyday tasks. These utility programs range from the bizarre to the useful—from pinball and solitaire to audio CD and DVD movie players, word processing programs, and a calculator, to name but a few. Whether they are intended for entertainment or as daily helpmates for such tasks as jotting down simple notes or making quick calculations, none of these programs requires a degree in rocket science to figure out. They are fairly self-explanatory, and it's possible you've used them before in their previous versions. Therefore, this chapter covers them only briefly, suggests a few tips, and leaves the rest to you and the Windows Help file.

Because many of the accessory programs fall into discrete categories, such as communications, multimedia entertainment, or system tools, look to relevant sections of this book to find coverage of such tools. This chapter covers the more basic, yet still quite useful, tools that don't fit neatly into a pigeonhole.

TIP

Windows XP comes with a bunch of games (FreeCell, Minesweeper, Pinball, Solitaire, Hearts, Internet Backgammon, Internet Checkers, Internet Hearts, Internet Reversi, Internet Spades, and Spider Solitaire). You can get to these from Start, All Programs, Games. If there are some of these missing, you can load them in by using Add or Remove Programs in Control Panel. (Control Panel is covered in Chapter 22, "Configuration via Control Panel Applets"). Once you are in Add or Remove Programs, choose Windows Components (on the left side of the dialog box), then highlight Accessories and Utilities and click Details. Then click Games and click Details. Then checkmark the games you want.

This book doesn't cover the specifics of each of these games because you can probably figure them out yourself. Click Help in each game for game rules and guidance. If you like games, you might check them out.

NOTEPAD

Notepad has been around since Windows 3.0. It's a simple, no-frills text editor that does no fancy formatting (though it does enable you to change the display font) and is popular for composing "clean" ASCII files. I use Notepad for jotting down quick notes. You could say Notepad is a *text editor*, whereas WordPad (see the "WordPad" section later in this chapter) is a *word processor*. Unlike WordPad, Notepad cannot view or edit Microsoft Word (.doc) or Rich Text Format (.rtf) files. It's a perfect tool to call up whenever you need to view a simple README.TXT file or fine-tune some program code (programmers like this tool).

TIP

> Here's a quick way to create a Notepad file. Just right-click the desktop or a folder, choose New, Text document. Then type in the name for your document and press Enter. Now press Enter or double-click the icon, and the new Notepad file opens. This is a good technique for taking down a quick memo, making notes about a phone call, or keeping a to-do list on your desktop.

Text-only files contain text characters and nothing else—no character formatting such as italics, bold, underlining, or paragraph formatting information such as line spacing. Sometimes such files are called ASCII files, plain ASCII files, or simply *text files*. As of Notepad 5.x (in Windows 2000), the Save As dialog box allows you to save in several text-only file formats: ANSI, Unicode, UTF-8, and Unicode big endian. These formats provide you with greater flexibility when you're working with documents that use different character sets. The default is ANSI, and unless you are inserting non-U.S. characters, you should use this format when you save files.

ASCII, ANSI, and Unicode—Alphabet Soup Anyone?

ASCII stands for American Standard Code for Information Interchange. Standard ASCII is a 7-bit character-encoding scheme used to represent 128 characters (upper- and lowercase letters, the numbers 0 through 9, punctuation marks, and special control characters) used in U.S. English. Most current Intel-based systems support the use of extended (or "high") ASCII, which is an 8-bit system. The 8th bit allows an additional 128 special symbol characters, foreign-language letters, and graphic symbols to be represented. Even with 8 bits, ASCII is not capable of representing all the combinations of letters and diacritical marks that are used in the Roman alphabet. DOS uses a superset of ASCII called *extended ASCII* or *high ASCII*. A more universal standard is the ISO Latin-1 set of characters, which is used by many operating systems, as well as Web browsers.

ANSI stands for the American National Standards Institute. Windows uses the ANSI character set, which is similar to ASCII. Windows 3.x and Windows 95 support the ANSI character set, which includes 256 characters, numbered 0 to 255. Values 0 to 127 are the same as in the ASCII character set. Values 128 to 255 are similar to the ISO Latin-1 character set but naturally have extensions and incompatibilities.

Unicode, which uses 16 bits, goes beyond ASCII and ANSI. Developed by the Unicode Consortium between 1988 and 1991, Unicode enables almost all the written languages of the world to be represented using a single character set. Using Unicode, 65,536 possible characters can be represented, approximately 39,000 of which have now been assigned, 21,000 of them being used for Chinese ideographs.

Although they're visually boring and lackluster, text files do have some important advantages over formatted text documents. Most importantly, they are the lowest common denominator for exchanging text between different programs and even between different types of computers. Literally any kind of word processor and many other types of programs, from email tools to databases, can share textual information using simple text files, regardless of computer type or operating system. To be sure your recipients using other kinds of computers can read a text email attachment or a text file on a disk, stick with the simple text files such as the ones Notepad creates.

Source code used to generate computer programs is often stored as text files, too. Because files are clean, without extraneous codes for formatting, program *compilers* (software that converts the source code into a working program) are not confused. Good examples of simple ASCII program code or configuration file code are found in the WIN.INI, SYS.INI, -PROTOCOL.INI, BOOT.INI, CONFIG.SYS, and AUTOEXEC.BAT files. These files, found in many Windows computers, control various aspects of Windows, all of which can be edited with Notepad. HTML code for Web pages is another example. You can safely edit HTML in Notepad.

Windows recognizes any file with a .txt extension as a text file and opens it in Notepad when you click it. For this reason, README files supplied with programs—even some supplied with Windows—are stored as .txt files. Take a look around on the Windows XP Home CD, and you'll find some pithy files about setup, networking, and so on. After you open them in Notepad, turn on the word wrap feature (by choosing Format, Word Wrap) to view the document correctly.

NOTEPAD'S LIMITATIONS

As I mentioned previously, Notepad does no formatting. In fact, it doesn't even wrap lines of text to fill the window unless you tell it to. Notepad can't properly render or print formatted documents created with WordPad, Microsoft Word for Windows, WordPerfect, or any other fancy word processor. You can open these document types, but they look like gibberish. Also, it doesn't have any fancy pagination options, though it does print with headers and footers via the Page Setup dialog box. Although you can change the font in Notepad 5, font information isn't stored in the file. Font choice is a personal preference for viewing and printing, and applies to all files you open in Notepad.

TIP

> Be careful about opening formatted text files with Notepad. Typically this will take a little doing, because when you use the File, Open command, the box defaults to .txt files. But you could enter the entire name of a preexisting file that you wanted to examine, such as mydocument.doc or mydocument.rtf. A formatted file probably will appear as gibberish in Notepad. Nonetheless, if you accidentally save the file, the formatting is stripped out of it, and the file can become useless. If you want to examine executable files or initialization or control files used by programs, I suggest a file viewer intended for this purpose, such as FVIEW. Many utility programs for this purpose are available on the Web. One such program is called QuickView. It's a full version of the quick viewers supplied with Windows 9x. QuickView is available at www.avantstar.com.

Notepad files used to be limited in size to about 50KB. That's no longer the case. Even very large files can be loaded into Notepad 5.

RUNNING NOTEPAD

To run Notepad, click Start, More Programs (or just Programs, depending on how you have your taskbar settings), Accessories, Notepad. Notepad then appears on your screen (see Figure 5.1). When it does, you can just type away.

Figure 5.1
You can use Notepad to edit simple text. I've entered some text already.

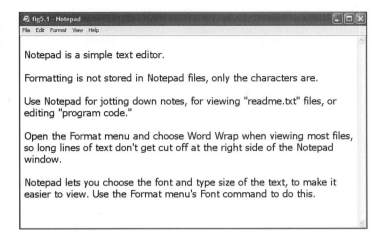

Of course, you can choose File, New to start a new file at any time. If you've made changes in the current file and haven't saved them, Notepad asks if you want to save it before creating the new file. You use the standard File, Open and File, Save As commands. You can have only one document open at a time in Notepad.

You should turn on word wrap when you enter text unless you're entering program code that is line oriented. When you do, by choosing Format, Word Wrap, the text wraps within the constraints of the window. If you resize the window, the text rewraps to fit the available space. Note that the word wrap setting doesn't affect the text file itself. That is, Notepad doesn't insert line feeds or carriage returns at the points where the lines wrap.

As with most Windows text programs, the keys shown in Table 5.1 have the effects shown here.

TABLE 5.1   KEYS IN NOTEPAD

Key	Moves Insertion Point to
Home	Start of the line
End	End of the line
PgUp	Up one window
PgDn	Down one window
Ctrl+Left Arrow	Start of previous word
Ctrl+Right Arrow	Start of next word
Ctrl+Home	Start of the file
Ctrl+End	End of the file

continues

TABLE 5.1   CONTINUED

Key	Moves Insertion Point to
F5 (particular to Notepad)	Inserts the time and date
Ctrl+Backspace	Deletes a word to the left
Del	Deletes letter right
Backspace	Deletes letter left

 If you can't see all the text in a Notepad window, see "My Text Is Chopped Off" in the "Troubleshooting" section at the end of this chapter.

SETTING MARGINS AND ADDING HEADERS AND FOOTERS

Despite the paucity of formatting options for onscreen display, you can format printed output to some degree. Use the File, Page Setup command to establish headers and footers. Enter your desired footing and heading text. Margin changes and header and footer settings aren't visible onscreen but do print. You can also include the special codes shown in Table 5.2 in the header and footer fields. You can enter these codes alone or within a text string.

TABLE 5.2   FORMATTING CODES FOR NOTEPAD

Code	Effect
&d	Includes the current date
&p	Includes the page number
&f	Includes the filename
&l	Forces subsequent text to left-align at the margin
&r	Forces subsequent text to right-align at the margin
&c	Centers the subsequent text
&t	Includes the time of the printing

Here's an example of a string you could enter:

```
Page &p Printed at &t  Filename is & f
```

The result would look like

```
Page 13 Printed at 10:33 Filename is My Document.txt
```

When you print a document, Notepad lets you choose the page range, the number of copies, and the printer to which the job is sent. See Chapter 6, "Printing and Faxing," for more details.

WORDPAD

For more capable word processing than Notepad can accomplish, you can use WordPad. Though it's not Word or WordPerfect, it works fine for most everyday writing chores. It includes most of the formatting tools people need for typical writing projects, and the price is right. You can edit documents of virtually any length, it supports drag-and-drop editing, and it can accept graphics pasted to it from the Clipboard. WordPad supports the following:

- Standard character formatting with font, style, and size
- Standard paragraph formatting with changing line spacing, indents and margins, bullets, justification, and right and left alignment
- Adjustable tab stops
- Search and replace
- Headers and footers
- Pagination control
- Insert and edit graphics
- Undo
- Print preview

It doesn't do tables, columns, indexes, master documents, outline view, legal line numbering, or anything really groovy, though. Go get Word or WordPerfect if you have that level of need.

SAVE AND OPEN OPTIONS

WordPad can save and open files in several formats:

- **Rich Text Format**—This choice is the default. The Rich Text Format is used more and more as a common format for exchanging documents between word processors, though few, if any, use it as their primary format (it's sort of like an Esperanto for word processors). The Rich Text Format preserves the appearance as well as the content of your document. Graphics and other objects are saved in the file along with the text but might be lost when you open the file with another application.
- **Text Files**—See the discussion of text files earlier in the chapter in the discussion of Notepad.
- **Unicode**—See the discussion of Unicode earlier in the chapter in the discussion of Notepad.

WordPad also can open the following document types (although it must save changes to these files as RTF, Text, or Unicode documents):

- **Word for Windows**—This choice opens documents stored in the format used by Microsoft Word for Windows, version 6.0 and Microsoft Word 95 (.doc). If you have any version of Microsoft Word installed, incidentally, double-clicking a .doc file opens it in Word, not WordPad.

- **Windows Write**—This choice opens documents stored in the .wri format used by Windows Write, the simple word processor supplied with Windows 3.x. This feature enables you to read README.wri files supplied with some older Windows applications.

- **Text documents (MS-DOS Format)**—This choice opens text documents stored with the MS-DOS version of the ASCII character set.

WordPad correctly opens even incorrectly named (wrong extension) RTF and Word 6 files if you select the All Documents option in the Files of Type area in the Open dialog box or type the document's full name. If WordPad doesn't detect a file's format, it opens it as a text-only file. Note that if a document contains formatting information created by another application it will likely appear as garbage characters mixed with the document's normal text.

RUNNING WORDPAD AND EDITING WITH WORDPAD

To run WordPad, choose Start, Programs, Accessories, WordPad. The WordPad window then comes up. Figure 5.2 shows an example of a Notepad file.

Figure 5.2
WordPad includes moderately sophisticated word processing features.

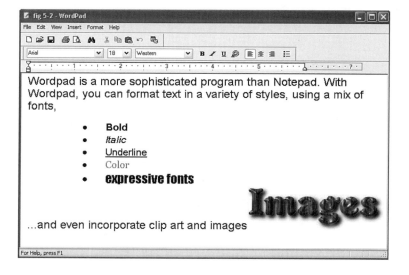

As with most Windows programs these days, you don't have to memorize what each button on the toolbar does. Just position the mouse pointer over the button and a pop-up screen tip will appear. In WordPad, look at the status bar at the bottom of the screen for a description.

When you're doing lots of editing and formatting in WordPad, check the View menu. You can turn on as many of the toolbars as you need to quickly change formatting, tab locations, and so on. A check mark next to a bar's name means it's on. They are toggle settings.

You can drag and drop or "tear off" the various toolbars. Just position the mouse pointer over the far left edge of any bar (don't click a button); then drag the bar where you want it.

Editing is simple in this program and complies with Windows standards and then adds a few rules of its own. I'll outline them very quickly. Just enter your text as usual. Lines of text occur automatically and are readjusted if you resize the window, change the margins, or change the font size. You can move the cursor around with a click of the mouse or by using the control codes listed for Notepad in Table 5.2.

You can double-click a word to select the whole word. To select the entire document quickly (select all), move the cursor to the left edge of the document until the arrow changes direction, and then Ctrl+click. To select an arbitrary area, click and drag the pointer over the text. Release when the text is highlighted. You can also select areas of text by pressing Shift and using the arrow keys. The spot where you first click (beginning of the selection) is called the *anchor point*. You can triple-click to select a paragraph. After text is selected, you can format it with the toolbars and format menu commands.

To move blocks of text, either select the text and use Cut, Copy, and Paste from the Edit menu, or drag it with the mouse to the new location and drop it.

TIP

> To insert characters that aren't available on your keyboard, such as ™, ®, or ©, use the Character Map accessory, covered later in this chapter in the section "Character Map."

WordPad handles each paragraph as a separate entity, each with its own formatting information, such as tab stops. To apply changes to multiple paragraphs, select them first.

To undo the last command, choose Edit, Undo; click the Undo button (the curving arrow) on the toolbar; or press Ctrl+Z.

Undo can undo the following errors: block deletions, anything removed by pressing Del or Backspace (as a unit), blocks replaced by typing, new text typed (back to the last time you issued a command), and character and paragraph formatting changes (if you select the Undo command immediately after making the change).

ADDING GRAPHICS TO A WORDPAD DOCUMENT

You can insert a graphic—and other *OLE* objects—into a WordPad document in one of two ways: by creating the object from scratch as you insert it or by inserting an existing object stored in a disk file. The basic steps required are similar for either method, but they vary slightly in detail.

- Select Edit, Paste to insert a graphic you've put on the system Clipboard.
- Select Insert, New Object to create a new graphic using another program or an existing file. In the Insert Object dialog box, choose the type of graphic object you want from the list, and click OK. At the insertion point, an area opens for the graphic. You create

the graphic in the second program and then exit the graphics program using the appropriate command (typically Exit and Return) and return to WordPad.

■ Click the graphic, and then drag the picture's handles (the small black squares along the edges) to resize the image.

After you've pasted the graphic, you have only crude control over positioning it where you want it in the document. You can't move a graphic around with the mouse, and no menu command is available for this purpose. Instead, you must push the picture around in your document with ordinary typing, the Backspace key, or the Tab key, or you can cut and paste it into a new location.

TIP

> When you insert an existing object from a file, the Insert Object dialog box offers a Link check box. If you check this box, any changes to the source file are reflected in the WordPad file. This is called Object Linking and Embedding (OLE), and is different than the usual Cut, Copy, and Paste commands. It's not used very often, so it's not covered in this book. For more information about OLE, check the Windows Help system, and search for linking and embedding.

Display Options

A few WordPad preferences affect viewing of files. You can check the View, Options dialog box to see them. All the tab pages except General Options in the Options dialog box pertain to the various types of documents that WordPad can open: Text Only, Rich Text Format, Word for Windows, Windows Write, and Embedded. Each of these pages offers identical choices. These settings affect display only; none of these choices affect the way your document prints.

 If you have trouble inserting tab stops where you want them, see "Adding and Modifying Tab Stops" in the "Troubleshooting" section at the end of this chapter.

Paint

Paint is a simple drawing program that creates and edits bitmapped images (BMP files). Using free-form drawing tools, text, and special effects, you can create projects such as invitations, maps, signs, and wallpaper for your desktop.

Let me explain why Paint is called a bitmapped image editor. Your computer's screen is divided into very small dots (*pixels* or *pels*) that are controlled by the smallest division of computer information—bits. A *bitmap* is a collection of bits of information that creates an image when assigned (*mapped*) to dots on the screen. This bitmap is similar to one of those giant electronic billboards in Times Square, New York, that can display the score, a message, or even a picture by turning on and off specific light bulbs in the grid.

Being a bitmapped drawing program, rather than an object-oriented drawing program, Paint has some significant limitations to keep in mind—also some advantages. After you paint a shape, you can't move it independently. You can use the computer to remove an area of the painting and place it somewhere else—as if you were cutting out a piece of the canvas and pasting it elsewhere. But all the dots in the area get moved, not just the ones in the shape you're interested in.

Windows XP Home doesn't come with an object-oriented graphics program. Simple object-oriented graphics modules are included in some word processors and spreadsheets.

An addition to Paint that appeared in the Windows 2000 version and carries over to Windows XP is the capability to save files in JPG and GIF formats in addition to the usual bitmapped (BMP) formats. You can also edit and save files in the TIF and PNG files formats. Table 5.3 lists the file types and typical uses.

TABLE 5.3   GRAPHICS FILE TYPES

File Format	Full Name	Typical Use
BMP	Bit-Mapped Picture	BMP files store graphics in a format called DIB. They tend to be large in file size, and are used by Windows for things such as screen wallpaper.
JPG	Joint Photographic Experts Group	Highly compressed means of storing graphics files, and often compress to about 5% of uncompressed size. This is a "lossy" format, meaning that some of the detail is lost as a sacrifice for small sized files. Often used on the Web or for storing photos from digital cameras.
GIF	Graphics Interchange Format	Often used on Web pages for graphics. Like JPG, GIF files can be stored with compression, making them very efficient in terms of storage space and email or Web transmission.
PNG	Portable Network Graphics	A relatively new bitmapped graphics format similar to GIF and created by the World Wide Web Consortium (W3C) as a freely usable, unlicensed form for storing graphics and photos.
TIF	Tagged Image File Format	This is one of the most widely supported and cross-platform file formats for images on PCs (including Macs). These files are not used on the Web. Web browsers can't display them, and they often are large. Digital cameras sometimes store highest quality, uncompressed images in TIF format.

If what you want to do is edit photo images (typically JPG, TIF, or GIF) created with a digital camera or scanner, you should use another program such as Adobe Photoshop, Adobe Elements, or PhotoDeluxe, Paint Shop Pro, Kai Photo Soap, or another of the many popular programs designed specifically for photos. Some versions of Microsoft Office comes with a photo editor, called Microsoft Photo Editor, that can do the job, too.

TIP

Using the Image Preview feature (discussed in Chapter 7, "Multimedia and Imaging") you can view, rotate, and perform basic tasks with image documents. You can transfer pictures to your computer from a digital camera or scanner, view your pictures in a slideshow, and annotate your fax documents. The Photo Printing Wizard, in Windows XP, can walk you through the process of printing your digital photos or scanned images. We cover that in Chapter 7 also.

STARTING A NEW IMAGE

To bring up Paint, choose Start, More Programs, Accessories, Paint. When the Paint window appears, maximize it. Figure 5.3 shows the Paint window and its component parts. I've loaded a BMP-file photograph into the program by double-clicking on a BMP file I found using the Search tool. (See Chapter 4, "Using the Windows XP Interface," and Chapter 9, "Browsing the World Wide Web with Internet Explorer," for discussion of the Search tool.)

Figure 5.3
The Paint window.

WORK AREA, TOOLBOX, TOOL OPTIONS, COLOR PALETTE

You create the drawing in the central area (or *work area*). Down the left side, the *Toolbox* holds a set of tool buttons for painting, drawing, coloring, and selecting. You choose colors from the *Color Box* at the bottom of the window. The status bar offers help messages on menu choices and displays the coordinates of the mouse pointer.

The object is to choose a tool and start fiddling around. You'll soon learn which tool does what. Hovering your mouse pointer over a tool displays some pop-up text with the tool's name. Some of the tools are a little difficult to figure out, but if you open Help and look up the tool, you can find descriptions there for each of them.

When you start a new picture, you must attend to a few details; then you can get on with painting.

1. If a picture is open, choose File, New to erase the previous image.

2. Choose Image, Attributes to set the picture size and whether it's color or black and white.

You can alter the size of the overall canvas when you're painting, so don't lose any sleep over perfecting it before you start. An image prints smaller on paper than it appears onscreen because the printer's resolution is much higher (each dot is smaller). So if you're aiming to print out your creation, you might want to do a little experimentation.

Setting the printed size of your image is easy. You used to have to calculate it based on the resolution of your printer and the pixel size of the image. Now, you can just choose Image, Attributes and set the size in inches (or cm, or pixels). You can check that the size looks about right at any time, by choosing File, Print Preview. Remember, though, that if your picture is wider than it is tall, and if its printed width is more than about 8 inches, you need to change the page orientation for printing from Portrait to Landscape. To do so, just choose File, Page Setup, and select the appropriate button.

The maximum picture size is limited by available memory and color setting. Black-and-white pictures use far less memory than color pictures do, so they can be much larger. Paint lets you know if you set a picture size that's too large to fit in memory. A black-and-white image is not the same as a grayscale image, in which you can paint with 16 or more separate shades of gray. Black and white has only two colors—black and white. Duh. To create a grayscale image, you must place the desired shades of gray on the palette.

TIP

You can resize a picture with the mouse by dragging the handles on the edges of the white workspace; however, the direct entry method in the dialog box is more accurate.

WORKING WITH THE PAINTING TOOLS

Before beginning to use a tool, you set the color to paint with. You need to set two colors: background and foreground. One of the most fundamental techniques to learn is selecting a color to paint with. In Paint, you control both foreground and background colors independently.

The foreground or drawing color is the main color you paint with. For example, when you add strokes with Paint's paintbrush, draw lines or shapes, or even when you type text, these items appear in the currently selected foreground color. The term *background color* is somewhat different. Many of the tools (such as the Brush, Pencil, and the Shape tools) let you paint with the so-called background color just as you would with the foreground color. All you have to do is hold down the right mouse button instead of the left one as you paint. The background color also determines the fill color for circles, squares, and other enclosed shapes; the fill color inside text frames; and the color with which you erase existing parts of the picture. If you select a section of the picture and drag it to another location, the resulting "hole" is filled with the background color. You can change the background color as many times as you like.

An alternative technique for selecting colors is using the Eyedropper tool, which lets you "suck up" a color that already appears in the picture. That color becomes the new foreground or background color for use with any of the painting tools.

TIP

> You can start a new picture with a certain color as the "canvas." Before you paint anything on the picture, choose the desired background color, and click anywhere over the work area with the Paint Can tool.

After you have the colors selected, you can use the tools to draw:

1. Click the tool you want to use to select it.
2. Position the pointer in the work area where you want to start painting, selecting, or erasing, and then click and hold the mouse button.
3. Drag to paint, select, or erase. Release the mouse button when you are through.

Some tools (for example, the polygon tool) require multiple clicks. When some of the tools are selected, the area below the grid of buttons provides options for the selected tool. The options are different for each tool.

UNDOING MISTAKES

Every addition you make to an image eventually melds into the picture and can't be undone. However, the program does keep track of the three most recent additions, allowing you some small degree of rethinking. Each time you make a new change, Paint "forgets" the fourth most recent change, and it becomes permanent.

To undo a change, press the fairly-universal Undo command key, Ctrl+Z, or choose Edit, Undo. You can undo an undo by choosing Edit, Repeat.

OPENING AN EXISTING PICTURE

You might often use Paint simply as a viewer of BMP files. Web browsers do not open BMP files for display, so when you double-click a BMP, it runs Paint (unless the system association for BMP files has been set to another program) and opens the file.

To see the maximum image amount at once, choose View, View Bitmap. All the other screen elements, including the title bar, menu bar, and scrollbars, disappear. Clicking anywhere on the screen or pressing any key returns you to the working screen.

 If you have opened a photographic picture for work in Paint, and it looks splotchy and uneven, see "Photos Look Terrible in Paint" in the "Troubleshooting" section at the end of this chapter.

ZOOMING IN FOR DETAIL WORK

One of the best features of Paint is pixel editing. You can zoom in closely to edit a picture, dot by dot, and can choose from five magnification levels: normal, 2×, 4×, 6×, and 8×(800). Figure 5.4 shows a detail of a full-face portrait, showing only the person's eye. This is at highest magnification, 8×(800). In Paint, you can use any of the standard painting tools at any magnification level. Use the Pencil tool to best change the color of one dot at a time. This feature is most useful when you have a little touchup to do (such as photo retouching), but you can't seem to control the mouse well enough to do it in normal view.

Figure 5.4
An image magnified for pixel editing.

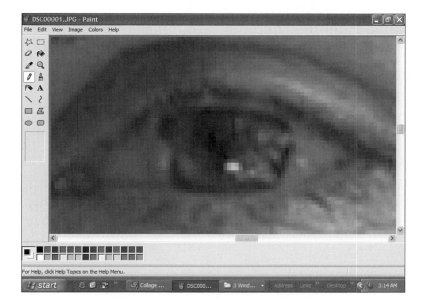

SAVING YOUR WORK

You can choose from several BMP formats for saving Paint files; the variations pertain to the number of colors stored in the file. Normally, you can just let Paint choose the correct format for you, but sometimes knowing which format to use comes in handy.

The following are the available formats and their descriptions:

- **Monochrome bitmap**—Use when you have only two colors (black and white) in your picture.
- **16-color bitmap**—Use when you have 16 colors or fewer in your picture.

- **256-color bitmap**—Use when you have more than 16 and fewer than 257 colors in your picture.
- **24-bit bitmap**—Use when you have more than 256 colors in the picture.

Use the lowest possible setting, based on the number of colors with which you have been painting. The more colors you save, the larger the file. However, saving a picture with a format that has fewer colors might ruin it, causing it to lose detail. You can also save in a variety of other formats, as mentioned earlier. As a rule, save your image in a format that in which your target audience (or program) uses to view it. For example, if you intend to send an image to someone in email or put it on a Web page, stick with GIF, JPG, or PNG. These are the most universal image formats.

> **TIP**
>
> When a picture is displayed in the Paint window, you can set it to be the wallpaper on the computer's desktop. Just choose File, Set as Background (tiled) or Set as Background (centered) , depending on how you want it displayed. For large pictures, I would choose Centered.

CALCULATOR

The Calculator is a quick and dirty onscreen version of two traditional pocket calculators: a standard no-brainer calculator and a more complex scientific calculator used by statisticians, engineers, computer programmers, and business professionals. They are good for adding up your lunch bill, a list of inventory items, or the mortgage payment on your office building. But neither calculator sports a running tape that you can use to backtrack through your calculations.

To run the Calculator, choose Start, Programs, Accessories, Calculator. A reasonable facsimile of a hand-held calculator then appears on your screen, as shown in Figure 5.5. You can switch between modes by choosing View, Standard or View, Scientific. The program always remembers which type was used last and comes up in that mode.

> **TIP**
>
> To quickly see a little help about any Calculator button, right-click the button, and choose What's This?
>
> To add a series of numbers or to find their mean, use the statistical functions on the Scientific Calculator. This way, you can see all the numbers in a list before you perform the calculation instead of having to enter them one at a time. And don't let the idea of statistics make you nervous; the technique is very simple.

Most of the operations on the Standard Calculator are self-explanatory, but a couple of them—square roots and percentages—are just a bit tricky. Check the Help file for more information. Table 5.4 provides a quick reference chart of keyboard shortcuts.

Figure 5.5
The Scientific Calculator is the often-unseen mode in which the Windows Calculator can appear. Many additional functions appear in this mode.

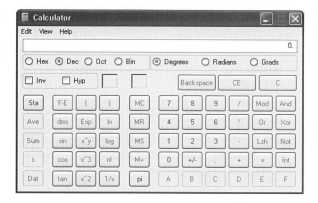

TABLE 5.4   KEYBOARD SHORTCUTS FOR THE CALCULATOR

Button	Key	Button	Key	Button	Key
%	%	cos	o	MR	Ctrl+R
(	(	Dat	Ins	MS	Ctrl+M
)	)	Dec	F6	n!	!
*	*	Deg	F2	Not	~
+	+	dms	m	Oct	F7
+/-	F9	Dword	F2	Or	|
-	-	Qword	F12	PI	p
.	. or ,	Exp	x	Rad	F3
/	/	F-E	v	s	Ctrl+D
0 to 9	0 to	Grad	F4	sin	s
1/x	r	Hex	F5	SQRT	@
=	= or Enter	Hypo	h	Sta	Ctrl+S
A to F	A to F	Int	;	Sum	Ctrl+T
And	&	Inv	I	tan	t
Ave	Ctrl+A	In	n	Word	F3
Bin	F8	log	l	Xor	^
Byte	F4	LSH	<	x^2	@
Back	Backspace	M+	Ctrl+P	x^3	#
C	Esc	MC	Ctrl+L	x^y	y
CE	Del	Mod	%		

5

COPYING YOUR RESULTS TO AND FROM OTHER DOCUMENTS

You can prepare a complex equation in a text editor such as Notepad and then copy it to the Calculator for execution. For example, you can enter the following in Notepad:

`((2+8)+16)/14=`

or

`(2+(8+16))/14=`

Mind your parentheses, and make sure to include the equal sign, or click = on the calculator after you paste in the equation; otherwise, the result will not appear. You can omit the parentheses if you use extra equal signs, like this:

`2+8=+16=/14=`

Some special characters can be included in your equations to activate various Calculator functions as shown in Table 5.5.

TABLE 5.5 CALCULATOR FUNCTION KEYS

Character	Function
:e	If the Calculator is set to the decimal system, this sequence indicates that the following digits are the exponent of a number expressed in scientific notation; for example, 1.01:e100 appears in the Calculator as 1.01e+100.
:p	Adds the number currently displayed to the number in memory.
:c	Clears the Calculator's memory.
\	Places the number currently displayed into the Statistics box, which must already be open.
:m	Stores the number currently displayed in the Calculator's memory.
:q	Clears the Calculator.
:r	Displays the number stored in the Calculator's memory.

TIP

You can copy information to and from the Calculator using the Windows Clipboard. Just use the standard Windows Copy and Paste commands.

CHARACTER MAP

Character Map is a utility program that lets you examine every character in a given font and choose and easily insert into your documents special characters, such as trademark (™ and ®) and copyright symbols (©), foreign currency symbols and accented letters (such as é) and nonalphabetic symbols (such as fractions, 3/4), DOS line-drawing characters (+), items from specialized fonts such as Symbol and Wingdings, or the common arrow symbols (↑, ↓, ←, and →). Some fonts include characters not mapped to the keyboard. Character Map lets you choose them, too, from its graphical display. The Program Map displays Unicode, DOS, and Windows fonts' characters.

Character Map for Windows XP Home is larger and updated from the one in Windows 98. Now you can choose the character set, rearrange the items in a font (such as grouping all currency types together) to eliminate hunting, and search for a given character.

Character Map works through the Windows Clipboard. You simply choose a character you want to use, click Copy, and it moves onto the Clipboard. Switch to your destination application (typically a word processing file), position the cursor, and choose Paste.

USING CHARACTER MAP

To run Character Map, follow these steps:

1. Choose Start, Programs, Accessories, System Tools, Character Map. When the window appears, check the Advanced View box to see more. The window then appears with all the characters included in the currently selected font displayed.

2. Choose the font you want to work with from the Font list.

3. By default, the Character Set is Unicode. This means all the characters necessary for most of the world's languages are displayed. To narrow down the selection, choose a language from the drop-down list.

4. To examine an individual character, click a character box, and hold down the mouse button to magnify it. You can accomplish the same thing with the keyboard by moving to the character using the arrow keys (see Figure 5.6).

5. Double-click a character to select it, transferring it to the Characters to Copy box. Alternatively, after you've highlighted a character, you can click the Select button or press Alt+S to place it in the Characters to Copy box. You can keep adding characters to the copy box if you want to paste several into your document at once.

6. Click the Copy button to place everything from the Characters to Copy box onto the Windows Clipboard.

7. Switch to your destination application, and use the Paste command (typically on the application's Edit menu) to insert the characters into your document. In some cases, you might then have to select the inserted characters and format them in the correct font, or the characters won't appear as you expected. You can, of course, change the size and style as you like.

TIP

If you know the Unicode number of the item to which you want to jump, type it into the Go to Unicode field. The display scrolls as necessary, and the desired character is then highlighted, ready for copying.

5

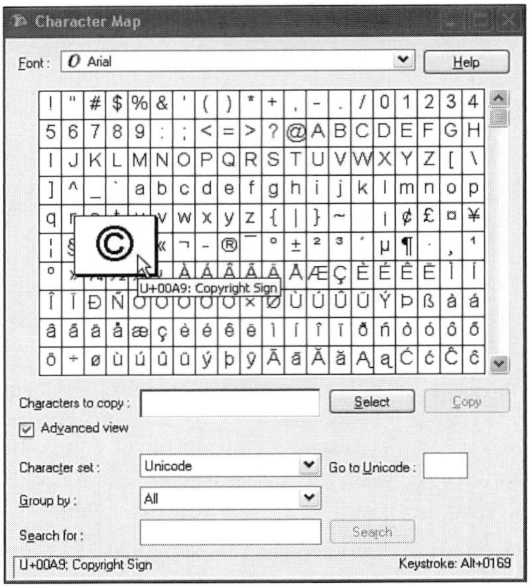

Figure 5.6
Character Map with Advanced options showing. You can double-click a character to put it in the copy list.

CHOOSING FROM A UNICODE SUBRANGE

A useful feature of Character Map lets you choose a subrange from the Unicode. Unicode was designed intelligently with characters grouped in sets. You can choose a subset of a font's characters to help you locate a specific symbol. To check out this feature, open the Group By list, and choose Unicode Subrange. When you choose this option, a box like the one in Figure 5.7 pops up.

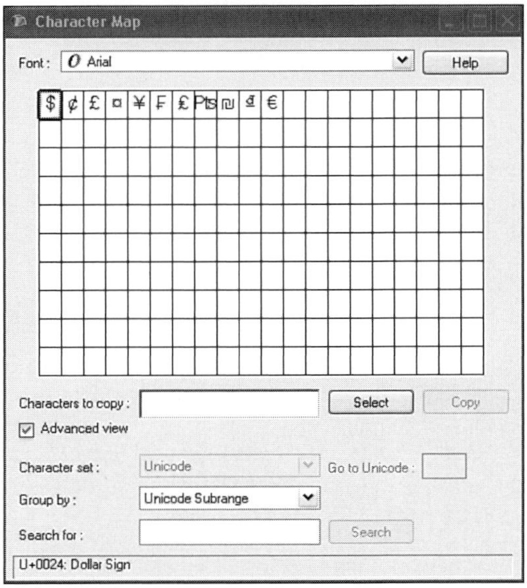

Figure 5.7
Choosing a subset of a font from which to select a character.

Click the subgroup that you think will contain the character you're looking for. Good examples are currency or arrows. Make sure to open the Group By list again, and choose All when you want to see all the characters again.

ENTERING ALTERNATIVE CHARACTERS FROM THE KEYBOARD

At the bottom right side of the Character Map dialog box is a line that reads

`Keystroke:`

For nonkeyboard keys (typically in English, anything past the ~ character), clicking a character reveals a code on this line—for example, `Alt+1060`. This line tells you the code you can enter from the keyboard to quickly pop this character into a document. Of course, you must be using the font in question. For example, say you want to enter the registered trademark symbol (™) into a Windows application document. Note that with a standard text font such as Arial or Times New Roman selected in Character Map, the program lists the keystrokes for this symbol as Alt+0174. Here's how to enter the character from the keyboard:

1. Press Num Lock to turn on the numeric keypad on your keyboard (the Num Lock light should be on).

2. Press and hold Alt, and then press 0+1+7+4 (that is, type the 0, 1, 7, and 4 keys individually, in succession) on the number pad. (You must use the number pad keys, not the standard number keys. On a laptop, you must activate the number pad using whatever special function key arrangement your laptop uses.) When you release the Alt key, the registered trademark symbol should appear in the document.

> **TIP**
>
> Not all programs accept input this way. If this approach doesn't work with a program, you'll have to resort to the standard means of putting characters into the Clipboard explained previously.

VOLUME CONTROL

The Volume Control accessory is basically a no-brainer. It provides a pop-up volume control sporting balance, mute, and other controls for your audio subsystem. Whether you're playing radio stations from the Web, CDs from your CD drive, listening to TV if you have a TV tuner card, doing online conferencing with NetMeeting, or recording sound files, you need access to these controls from time to time. Of course, if you don't have a working sound card installed, this accessory isn't available, or at least it won't do anything. A little known fact for many people is that this accessory has two sets of controls—one for recording and one for playback.

1. To open the volume controls, choose Start, Programs, Accessories, Entertainment, Volume Control. A shortcut is to double-click the little speaker icon in the system tray on the Windows XP taskbar.

Your sound system's capabilities and possible changes that past users have made to the application's settings determine the format of the volume controls you see. On one of my computers the controls look like what you see in Figure 5.8.

Figure 5.8
The basic volume controls for setting playback volume. Another set is available for record levels.

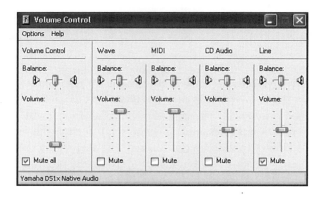

2. You can alter any volume control's setting by dragging the volume up or down. Change the balance between right and left channels by dragging the Balance sliders left or right. Mute any source input by checking the Mute box in its column.

3. Controls for some input sources are probably not showing. Check out the Options, Properties command. It offers options for turning on various volume controls and possibly special features. Figure 5.9 shows an example. Because audio controls operate differently for different sound cards, check out any Help files that might be available from your audio controls.

Figure 5.9
The Properties dialog box for typical volume controls.

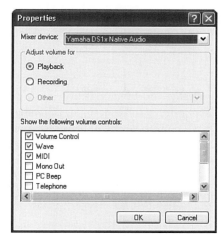

If you are doing any sound recording, be sure to see the recording controls, too. Open the Properties dialog box, and choose Recording.

TIP

Sometimes you want to see the playback and the recording controls at one time. To do so, run the Volume Control application twice. Set one for playback and the other one to record. Then adjust them onscreen so that you can see each side-by-side.

NOTE

Some sliders in one module are linked to sliders in other modules. Adjusting the Volume setting on one affects Volume settings on the other mixers. For example, adjusting the playback volume in Media Player or your audio CD player or MP3 player typically will alter the "Wave" or the master Volume control slider position on the system Volume Controls.

To quickly adjust or mute the sound output from your system, or to adjust the master volume level (useful when the phone rings), click the little speaker icon in the system tray, near the clock, as shown in Figure 5.10. If the speaker icon isn't showing, then you have to turn it on. To turn it on, click Start, Control Panel, Sounds Speech and Audio Devices; click Sounds and Audio Devices, then turn on 'Place volume icon in the taskbar notification area' and OK the dialog box.

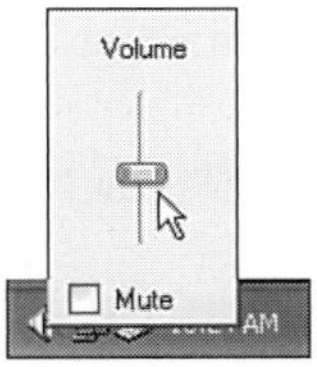

Figure 5.10
Quickly setting the master output volume.

 If your system suddenly doesn't have any sound at all, **see** *"No Sound" in the "Troubleshooting" section at the end of this chapter.*

5

WORKING WITH THE WINDOWS CLIPBOARD

Although not an application per se, the Clipboard is an integral part of Windows, and typically is used when working with applications. Chapter 4, "Using the Windows XP Interface," introduced the Clipboard indirectly, explaining how to cut, copy, and paste items, particularly files and folders within the Windows GUI.

Because transferring data between applications and documents is such a common task, this chapter offers some additional detail on the techniques you can use to facilitate the process.

The most basic sort of information sharing relies on the Windows Clipboard. As you're probably well aware, you can cut, copy, and paste information from one application to another with relative abandon—assuming both applications allow you to work with the kind of information you're transferring (text, graphics, or musical notes, for example).

Almost all Windows applications use the Clipboard for everyday, on-the-fly data-transfer operations. The Clipboard lets you move text, graphics, spreadsheet cells, portions of multimedia files, and OLE objects from one location to another. It supports both 16-bit and 32-bit Windows programs and can even move text to and from non-Windows programs, within the constraints I explain later in this chapter.

Information cut or copied to the Clipboard goes into system memory (RAM and virtual memory), waiting there until you paste it to a new location elsewhere in the same document or in another document. Even then, the data remains on the Clipboard until it's replaced by new cut or copied information, or until you exit Windows. The upshot of this arrangement is that you can paste the same information as many times as needed, into as many different locations in your documents as necessary.

Want to know what information currently resides on the Clipboard? Run the Clipbook Viewer utility that comes with Windows XP to view the Clipboard contents as well as to store Clipboard information on disk (in CLP files or Clipbooks) for later retrieval. You won't find that program on your All Programs menus, but if you Click Start, Run, and enter `clipbrd`, it should come up. Double-click on the Clipboard's title bar (which is probably minimized at the bottom of the Clipbook Viewer window), and you can see what's in the Clipboard at any given time. Although you might seldom use it, the Clipbook Viewer can be used to share Clipboard contents over the local area network. Doing so is a little tricky, however, and rarely used. Figure 5.11 shows an example of some text on the Clipboard.

Figure 5.11
Checking the contents of the Clipboard using the Clipbook Viewer application.

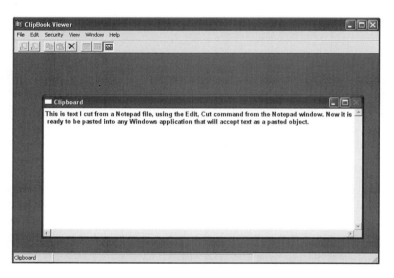

NOTE

Some Windows applications maintain their own independent Clipboard-like storage areas for cut or copied data. These proprietary clipboards overcome some of the weaknesses of the main Windows Clipboard. For example, whereas the Windows Clipboard can hold only one chunk of cut or copied data at a time, Microsoft Office 2003/XP has its own clipboard that stores up to 12 chunks. In Office 2003/XP apps, a special toolbar pops up as the Office clipboard fills up. The toolbar displays each chunk of data with an icon identifying the data's source application, and you can paste the chunks in any order you need them into your Office 2003/XP documents.

COPYING, CUTTING, AND PASTING IN WINDOWS APPLICATIONS

Windows XP maintains time-honored Windows standards (most of them date all the way back to Windows 2.0) for selecting, cutting, copying, and pasting information. This section offers a brief review of the techniques you need. In summary, four steps are required to transfer data from one place to another using the Clipboard:

1. Select the data. The techniques required to select data depend on the type of information in question and the application you're using. If you're working with text, you can drag across the characters to be selected. If you prefer a keyboard approach, hold down the Shift key while you use arrow keys and other cursor movement keys to expand or reduce the selection. Many programs let you select entire lines or paragraphs using techniques such as clicking or double-clicking in the left margin. Selected text appears in reverse colors.

   With graphics and other nontext information, selection techniques vary, but you typically just click on the item you want to select, Shift+click to select a series of adjacent items, or drag over adjacent items to select them together. In many applications, you also can Ctrl+click to select nonadjacent items. You usually can tell that an item has been selected by the appearance of an outline or small rectangles on its perimeter.

2. Cut or copy that data to place it on the Clipboard. Choose Edit, Copy to place the selected data on the Clipboard without disturbing the original. You also can choose Edit, Cut to put the information on the Clipboard and remove it from the source document. As mentioned in Chapter 4, many applications let you right-click over the selection and choose Copy or Cut from the shortcut menu that pops up. With the keyboard, the standard shortcuts are Ctrl+X for Cut and Ctrl+C for Copy; however, some applications don't abide by these conventions.

3. Identify the destination for the information by selecting the destination document and, if appropriate, navigating to a specific location in that document.

4. Paste the data into the destination document. With the mouse, choose Edit, Paste or choose Paste from the shortcut menu. Using the keyboard, pressing Ctrl+V does the trick, except in the odd, nonstandard application. With any of these techniques, the contents of the Clipboard will appear in the new location.

5

If the Paste command fails to paste the data into the destination document, see "Paste Command Doesn't Work" in the "Troubleshooting" section at the end of this chapter.

 If the pasted data doesn't look like you expected, see "Pasted Data Doesn't Look Right" in the "Troubleshooting" section at the end of the chapter.

N O T E

> Almost all Windows applications have Cut, Copy, and Paste commands on their Edit menus, but that doesn't mean these commands are always available. If you haven't selected anything to be cut or copied, for example, the Cut and Copy commands will be inactive—they appear grayed out on the Edit menu and you can't choose them. For its part, the Paste command can be grayed out even if data is currently on the Clipboard. This happens when the application doesn't recognize the data format in which the Clipboard data is stored.

N O T E

> Many Windows applications place cut or copied information onto the Clipboard in multiple formats. For example, suppose you copy some text from Microsoft Word. When the copy operation is complete, the Clipboard will contain at least four representations of that same text: a "plain text" (nonformatted) version, a version in the Rich Text format, a version in HTML, and a picture (an image of the text stored as a line, or *vector*, graphic). When you paste, the destination application communicates with the Clipboard to decide which format to use. In some cases, the application also has a command that lets you take manual control and decide the right format for yourself. At any rate, the availability of all these formats means that you have a better chance of successfully pasting the data into the destination document.

USING THE SEARCH APPLET

One of the first rules of organization is to know where things are and how to keep them in their rightful places. The Search command (or Companion, as it's now called), accessible from the Start menu or toolbar in any folder, is a tool often used in this mission. We think of the Search Companion as a supplied application, because it has grown into something formidable, despite the impression the cute little animated Search Assistant gives. Although we mentioned it briefly in Chapter 4 as a way to find and run programs, we wanted to cover this powerful feature more thoroughly in general terms here.

As mentioned in Chapter 1, "Introducing Windows XP Home Edition," Windows XP's Search feature is new and wholly superior to anything in any version of Windows to date. In Windows 9x and NT 4, Search was called *Find*. The name has changed, as has the functionality of the look of the window. The Search Companion can find a needle in a haystack, and it doesn't much matter where the haystack is or what else is in it. The Search window will find people, computers, Web pages, files, folders, and programs. It will look on the Web, on the local machine, or across the intranet (LAN). In the context of this chapter, let's focus on searching for your multimedia files, document files, and folders, however. In the chapters covering network issues (Part IV) and the Web section (Part III), we'll cover searching out other kinds of information.

Just click Start and choose Search (or as a shortcut I use all the time, press Windows+F). This will bring up the Search Companion window, as shown in Figure 5.12. Notice that this is essentially an Explorer window, but with a Search panel on the left side. By default, you have a little Search Companion there to help entertain you while a search is going on, in the form of a dog. He does tricks, and occasionally makes noise as he scratches himself, so don't be alarmed. You can choose another Search Companion, make him perform a trick, or turn him off by double-clicking on him and choosing from a menu, or clicking on "Turn off animated character".

Figure 5.12
The new Search Companion is multi-talented. Use it to seek out multimedia files, documents, folders, people, computers, and other stuff.

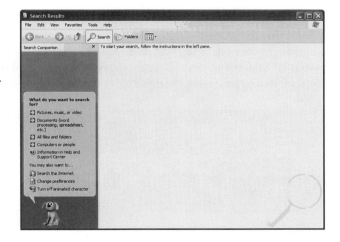

Like a Web page, the Search Companion has links and Back buttons to move from page to page. In the previous versions of Search or Find, you filled in boxes more like a traditional dialog box, but no longer. It's all HTML-based now and very Webby-looking. There are numerous pages and links within the Search window to explore.

Let's try a simple search for files on the computer. This is the most frequent kind of search (outside of Web surfing). Suppose I wanted to search for any music on my computer that was by Beethoven (see Figure 5.13).

Notice that I found three files, as indicated in Figure 5.13. After a search is complete (this could take some time as Windows searches through all your hard disk files, but the doggie sure looks cute turning those book pages), the found files are listed to the right. You are asked by the Search Companion whether you are finished searching. If you are satisfied, click Yes; the Search Companion disappears and is replaced by the normal view of an Explorer window, yet the found files remain in the right-hand pane for you to work with as you will (copy, cut, open, run, edit, and so on) by clicking or right-clicking on them. If you

5

are not satisfied with the results of the search (either no hits, or too many hits), notice the several options:

- **Change the file name or keywords**—This is the most likely thing to do. You might have spelled the file or other item incorrectly. Use a smaller amount of the filename, don't specify the extension, or try a different spelling if you don't know how it's spelled. Maybe specify just the extension, such as *.tif.

- **Look in more locations**—Well, this is not likely going to help much, because normally a search is conducted on all your local hard disks. But it might be worth a try. Click this to see what options you have. Click the check mark in the resulting box to open a list of places you can look in. Then click Browse to open a box that lets you look all around, including on the local area network.

- **Change whether hidden and system files are included**—There are numerous files on your computer that are normally hidden so that you (or someone else) don't mess with them and mangle your operating system. If you're searching for DLL files or some other system-related things, you can choose this option. You won't need it for sleuthing out typical documents and programs, though.

Figure 5.13
Here I'm searching for all music with Beethoven in the file name. I'm also showing you the result of the search.

You get the idea with the multimedia files. If you're a worker bee who doesn't have time for photos, videos, and MP3 music files, you're probably looking for those business reports you've been slaving over and are freaking out about whether your computer ate them. This happens to me all the time, especially because today's programs want to put your files in weird places that never see the light of day (like somewhere inside My Documents under some strange user name). So, you'll want to experiment with conducting another search, this time for Documents (this is the second option listed when you first bring up the Search Companion). Notice that it offers two criteria categories for searching—file name and when it was modified. Actually, this makes a lot of sense, because people generally remember at least a little bit about their work-related documents this way—at least I do. "Gee, I worked on that thing two days ago, and I probably would have called it something like Bob's Pleading with the IRS for Mercy." So, I click on Within the Last Week and in the document name area I type in **IRS**. The results are good (see Figure 5.14). (I've hit the Back button, so you can see both the results and the search criteria.)

Figure 5.14
Here I've done a search for that file I hope will keep me out of debtor's prison. I used the "time modified" and "file name" criteria, together.

SEARCHING FOR TEXT WITHIN A DOCUMENT

Now for something a little more complicated. Suppose I wanted to find any files that I've modified in the last week, are related to this book, and also contain the word "Passport" in them. This is a real need for me, because I'm working on the Passport topic and don't want to repeat myself in the chapter I'm writing now. Can the Search Companion help me? Yup. Here's how:

1. I run the Search Companion.
2. I choose to search for Documents.
3. I click on Within the Last Week for the last time it was modified.
4. I enter the file name **ch*.doc**, because I know that all my chapter files start with the letters "ch" and are Word or WordPad files (so they end with .doc).
5. I click on Use Advanced Search Options. The box changes a bit to show some advanced settings. I enter **Passport** in the lower area of the box (see Figure 5.15).

TIP

> When specifying file and folder names during searches of the hard disk, note that * (asterisk), is a DOS wildcard that replaces any number of characters. The ? replaces one character.

Figure 5.15
Here I'm searching for all files in the past month that start with "ch" and end with ".doc" (Word or WordPad files) and have the word "Passport" within the file.

LOOKING FOR ANY KIND OF FILE

If you're looking more generally for files or folders (that are not documents or multimedia files), choose the All Files and Folders option from the first page of the Search Companion. He'll now look through more of your folders. This will result in a more exhaustive search, because every file and folder will be examined, not just those that are popular document types.

NARROWING THE SEARCH

Just as with the Find box in Windows 9x and NT, you have to be a bit crafty when filtering the search. If you enter a long filename with spaces between the words, the search will likely end up becoming too broad. For example, if you entered

Annual Report 2

in the Search For area, the result would be any file with the word *Annual*, *Report*, or *2* in any part of its name. This is annoying. Also, using quotes around the string, as when conducting a Web search, doesn't help either, unfortunately. I was trying to find a folder called Ch 3 and the only way to exactly find it was to enter **Ch*3** as the criterion. So, keep in mind that you should use DOS-style wildcards when searching for items that contain spaces in their names.

Experiment with other aspects of the Search box, such as searching the Internet or turning on the Indexing Service. The Indexing Service was introduced in Windows 2000 Professional. This tool scans files and folders on your hard disk and builds a database of the words it finds in those documents. This database helps speed up file and directory searches when you're looking for words within files or keywords in file descriptions. The database also helps the Internet Information Services Web server perform Web site searches. To turn it on, do this:

1. From the first page of the Search Companion, click on Change Preferences.
2. Choose With Indexing Service (for faster local searches).
3. Click Back.
4. Begin your search.

The Indexing Service can index the following types of documents in several languages:

- Text
- HTML
- Microsoft Office 95 and later
- Internet mail and news
- Any other document for which a document filter is available

The Indexing Service is designed to run continuously and requires little maintenance. After it's set up, all operations are automatic, including index creation, index updating, and crash recovery if there's a power failure.

→ To learn more about the Windows Indexing Service, **see** "Indexing," **p. 917**.

TIP

> You can save any search you have conducted by choosing File, Save Search. It will prompt you to save the search in My Documents and will suggest a filename for it, such as "Files named CH05.doc." When you want to rerun the search, open the folder where you stored the file and double-click it. It will open in the Search Companion. Then, click the Search button.

TROUBLESHOOTING

MY TEXT IS CHOPPED OFF

I can't see all the text in a Notepad window. Where did it go?

You must manually turn on word wrap to get the text in a file to wrap around within the window. By default, word wrap is turned off, which can be annoying. The good news is that word wrap is now a persistent setting. After you turn it on and then close Notepad, it should be on the next time you run it. If you need to edit program code, make sure to turn it off, or your program lines will wrap, making editing and analysis of code more confusing.

If you still can't see enough text, remember that Notepad 5 now supports font changing for display. Change the display font from the Format menu. Choosing a monospaced font (for example, Courier) might help you line up columns. Choosing a smaller font and/or a proportional font (for example, Times) crams more text into the window.

ADDING AND MODIFYING TAB STOPS

Inserting and adjusting tab stops in WordPad is a pain. Is there an easy way?

You can easily insert and adjust tabs in WordPad by clicking in the ruler area. Choose View, Ruler to turn on the ruler. Then click in the ruler area where you want to insert a tab stop. You can drag the cursor left and right to see a vertical rule to align the stop. To kill a tab stop, drag it out of the ruler area into the document.

PHOTOS LOOK TERRIBLE IN PAINT

I've opened a photo in Paint, and it looks terrible. Why?

You probably have your display set to too few colors. When too few colors are available to the video display, it "bands" the colors, making photos look like a topographic map. Each sharp delineation between similar colors in the picture is called a *band*, for obvious reasons. Normally, the colors would blend together evenly. But if the video display's driver is set to 16, or even 256 colors, this is too few to render most photographic images properly.

Typically, photos have well over 256 colors. You need thousands of colors to display an attractive photograph. As I said earlier, to edit photos in any professional manner, you should use a program designed for photographic retouching. Still, you can cut and paste, do some pixel editing, add text and so forth, with Paint. First, however, check your display settings by right-clicking the desktop, choosing Properties, and then Settings. Make sure you have your system set to run in 16-bit color or higher.

NO SOUND

I'm adjusting the volume control from the system tray icon, but I just don't get any sound.

Total loss of sound can be caused by myriad goofs, settings, hardware conflicts, or program malfunctions. Troubleshooting your sound system isn't always easy as a result. You should consult other chapters in this book that deal with the Control Panel and the Device Manager for serious problems. One tip is in order here: If you're using a laptop computer, ask yourself whether the sound stopped working after you hibernated or suspended the system. I've noticed this problem on several laptops, and this bug might not have been worked out of Windows XP Home for your sound chip set. Try rebooting the computer, and see whether the sound comes back to life. Another thing to look for is a manual volume control on the computer. Many laptops have a control you can turn or push, that's often found along the right or left side of the computer itself. Such settings override any settings within Windows.

PASTE COMMAND DOESN'T WORK

I'm sure I placed information on the Clipboard but the Paste command won't work.

The problem is that the destination document doesn't recognize the format of your Clipboard data. You might be able to work around this obstacle by first pasting the data into another application that does accept the information and then copying and pasting from this way station app into the intended destination document. Alternatively, try saving the selected information to disk in a file format that the destination app can import.

PASTED DATA DOESN'T LOOK RIGHT

My pasted data sometimes looks quite different in the destination document than it did in the original.

You might be able to get better results by pasting the data in another format, if the destination application allows this. Look for a command in the destination app such as Edit, Paste Special that lets you select from all the Clipboard formats the application recognizes. Try each format in turn to see which gives the best results.

CHAPTER 6

PRINTING AND FAXING

In this chapter

WINDOWS XP PRINTING PRIMER

During Windows setup, a printer might have been detected and installed automatically, eliminating the need for you to install a printer manually. In this case, a default printer is already installed, and printing should be fairly effortless from your Windows applications. You can just print without worrying about anything more than turning on the printer, checking that it has paper, and choosing the File, Print command from whatever programs you use.

If you didn't have your printer on or connected during setup, or it isn't a Plug and Play printer, this process might not have happened successfully. Sometimes simply plugging in a new printer or having Windows do a scan for new hardware is enough to get things rolling. I'll talk about installation procedures later, but regardless of your current state of printer connectedness, as a user of Windows XP, you should know how to control your print jobs, print to network-based printers, and share your printer for others to use. This chapter covers these topics.

When you print from an application, the application passes the data stream off to Windows, which in turn *spools* the data to a specified printer. Spooling is the process of temporarily stuffing onto the hard disk the data to be transmitted to the printer, and then delivering it at the relatively slow pace with which that printer can receive it. Spooling lets you get back to work with your program sooner. Windows passes the stored information from the queue through a *driver* program, which sends the printer the specific codes and commands it needs to render, or draw, your document. Meanwhile, additional documents can be added to a printer's queue, either from the same computer or from users across the LAN.

THE PRINTERS AND FAXES FOLDER

Windows gives you control over the printing system through the Printers and Faxes folder, shown in Figure 6.1. You can add printers, check the status of the queue, and manage print jobs by clicking Start, Control Panel, Printers and Other Hardware, Printers and Faxes.

> **TIP**
>
> If you use Printers and Faxes frequently, you can add it to your Start Menu. Right-click the Start button and select Properties. View the Start Menu tab and click Customize. Select the Advanced tab, and check Printers and Faxes under Start Menu Items. Customizing the Start Menu is discussed in more detail in Chapter 21, "Tweaking the GUI," under "Start Menu Pizzazz!"

After you open the folder, you can view the Task menu for a particular printer by clicking a printer's icon.

The print spooler system takes control of all printing jobs, whether from Win32, Win16, OS/2, POSIX, or DOS applications. In cases of trouble (for example, ink or paper outage or paper jams), it also issues error or other appropriate messages to print job originators.

Figure 6.1
The Printers and Faxes folder is the starting point for printer setup and management. Open it from the Control Panel item "Printers and Other Hardware."

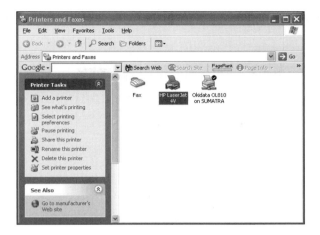

NOTE

I'll refer to the spooling and other printer management capabilities of Windows XP's GUI, taken as a whole, as *Print Manager*.

The Print Manager in Windows XP has the following features:

- It lets you easily add, modify, and remove printers right from the Printers and Faxes folder by using the Add Printer Wizard.

- The intuitive user interface uses simple icons to represent printers that are available to use, whether they're connected directly to your computer or are available via a network. You don't need to worry about the relationship of printer drivers, connections, and physical printers. You can simply add a printer and set its properties. After it is added, it appears as a named printer in the Printers and Faxes folder.

- Multiple applications can send print jobs to the same printer, whether local or across a LAN, at the same time. Additional documents are simply added to the queue and are printed in turn.

- Default settings for such options as number of copies, paper tray, page orientation, and so on can be automatically used during print jobs, so you don't have to manually set them each time.

- You can easily view the document name, status, owner, page count, size, time of submission, paper source and orientation, number of copies, and destination port of jobs. You also can pause, resume, restart, and cancel jobs; plus, you can rearrange the order of the print queue. In addition, you can temporarily pause or resume printing without causing printer time-out problems.

- You can set color profiles for color printers, ensuring accuracy of output color. Associating the correct color profile with all your publishing tools helps to ensure consistent color application throughout the publishing process.

6

If you have a local area network (LAN) set up in your home or office, you can take advantage of the more advanced features:

- Browsing for LAN-based printers to which to connect has been made very simple. In most cases, icons for printers that other computers on your network share automatically appear in your Printer and Faxes folder.

- You can easily share a printer over the LAN by modifying a few settings on the printer's Properties sheet. Your printer then acts as a printer server for other computers. Shared printers can be given a meaningful name and a comment, such as *LaserJet in Ted's Office*, which identifies them to other users of your network.

- The priority level of a print job can be increased or decreased.

→ To learn more about using a printer on the network, **see** "Using Printers on the Network," **p. 552**.

- With the Web printer feature Internet Printing Protocol (IPP), remote printers can be reached over the Internet.

→ To learn more about IPP, **see** "Using Printers over the Internet with IPP," **p. 556**.

INSTALLING AND CONFIGURING A PRINTER

If your printer is already installed and operational at this point, you can skip this section and skim ahead for others that may be of interest. However, if you need to install a new printer, modify or customize your current installation, or add additional printers to your setup, read on.

You might want to add a printer in a few different instances, not all of which are obvious:

- You're connecting a new physical printer directly to your computer (obvious).

- You're connecting a new physical printer to the network (obvious).

- You want to print to formatted disk files that can later be sent to a particular type of printer (not so obvious).

- You want to set up multiple printer configurations (preferences) for a single physical printer, so that you can switch among them without having to change your printer setup before each print job (timesaving idea).

6

TIP

> As discussed in Chapter 2, "Getting Your Hardware and Software Ready for Windows XP," and Chapter 3, "Installing Windows XP Home," before you buy a new piece of hardware, it's always a good idea to check the Microsoft Windows Catalog or the Windows 2000 Hardware Compatibility List (HCL) on the Web, or use the compatibility tool on the Windows XP CD. You should at least check with the manufacturer or check the printer's manual to ensure that it's compatible with Windows XP or Windows 2000.
>
> You should know, though, that Windows XP comes with preinstalled drivers for more printers than are listed in the HCL. Before assuming that your old printer isn't supported, go through the manual installation procedure to see whether your printer make and model is listed as an installation choice.

The basic game plan for installing and configuring a printer is as follows:

■ Read the printer's installation manual and follow the instructions for Windows XP or Windows 2000. Some printer manufacturers ask you to install their driver software *before* you plug in and turn on the printer for the first time. *Heed their advice!*

■ Plug it in. Many newer printers are detected when you simply plug them into the parallel or USB port. Your printer might be found and then configure itself fairly automatically. If it does, you can skip on down to "Printing from Windows Applications," later in this chapter.

■ If the printer doesn't configure itself, you can run the Add New Printer Wizard (or use a setup program, if one is supplied with your printer). We'll go over this procedure in detail in the next section.

At this point, you should have a functioning printer. You might want to make alterations and customizations to the printer setup, though. For example, you can do the following:

■ If you have more than one printer installed, select the one you'll use most often as the Default Printer.

■ Set job defaults pertaining to paper tray, two-sided printing, scaling, type of paper feed, halftone imaging, printer setup information (such as a PostScript "preamble"), and paper orientation.

■ Check and possibly alter device-specific settings such as DPI (dots per inch), memory settings, and font substitution.

■ Share the printer, and specify its share name so that other network users can use your printer.

How you go about adding the printer depends on how you'll be connecting to it:

■ If your printer is connected directly to your computer with a USB, parallel, or serial printer cable, you are installing a *local printer*. Installing a local printer is covered in the next section.

■ To use a printer that's physically attached to another computer on your network, you still need to set up a printer icon on your own computer. This is called installing a *network printer*.

6

NOTE

Windows should automatically locate and install icons for the shared printers on your LAN without you needing to do anything. (You can disable this behavior—open My Computer, select Tools, Folder Options, and select the View tab. You can check or uncheck Automatically Search for Network Folders and Printers.) You also can add icons for networked printers manually, as described in Chapter 16, "Using a Windows XP Network."

→ For detailed instructions on installing a network printer, **see** "Using Printers on the Network," **p. 552**.

- A printer that's physically connected to the network wiring itself and not cabled to another computer is called a "local printer on a network port," just to make things confusing. We'll cover the installation of these in Chapter 16 as well.

INSTALLING A LOCAL PRINTER

Installing a local printer is a bit more complex than connecting to an existing network printer. For starters, unless Windows finds the printer automatically (via Plug and Play), you have to specify the location where the printer is physically connected, what you want to name it, and a few other pieces of information.

The procedures vary, depending on how the printer is connected to your computer:

- Parallel printer port
- USB/FireWire (IEEE 1394)
- Serial port
- Infrared

> **TIP**
>
> A restricted user can't add a local printer to a computer, so you must start by logging on as a Computer Administrator user.

Here's the basic game plan, which works with most printers. A restricted user can't add a local printer to a computer, so you must start by logging on as a Computer Administrator user. Then, do the following:

1. Read the printer's installation instructions for specific Windows XP or Windows 2000 instructions. You might be instructed to install software *before* connecting the printer to your computer for the first time. This is especially important if your printer connects via USB.

2. Connect the printer to the appropriate port on your computer according to the printer manufacturer's instructions.

3. Read the description that applies to the kind of connection your printer uses and proceed as directed:

    Parallel Port   Connect the printer to your computer (typically you don't have to shut down the computer to attach parallel devices, though doing so might be a good idea). Windows might detect and install the printer. If it doesn't, open the Printers and Faxes folder, and select Add New Printer to start the wizard. Now click Next. Click Local Printer, and turn on Automatically Detect My Printer. Then click Next again to start the Found New Hardware Wizard. Follow the instructions on the screen to finish installing the printer. The printer icon is then added to your Printers and Faxes folder.

USB or FireWire	Just connect the printer's cable to your computer. Windows will detect it and automatically start the Found New Hardware Wizard. Because USB and FireWire are hot-pluggable, you don't need to shut down or restart your computer. Simply follow the instructions on the screen to finish installing the printer. The printer icon is then added to your Printers and Faxes folder.
Infrared	Be sure your printer is turned on and within range of your computer's infrared eye. Also, make sure your infrared service is installed properly.
	Windows may detect the printer automatically and create an icon for it. If not, see Chapter 17, "Windows Unplugged: Remote and Mobile Networking," for more information on infrared printers.
Serial Port	Some antique laser and daisywheel printers use a serial data connection. (If you're still using one of these, I like you already.) Follow the instructions in the next section.

If Windows can't detect the make and model of your printer, it will ask you to assist in selecting the appropriate type. If you can't find your printer's make and model in the list of choices, see step 5 in the next section.

IF THE PRINTER ISN'T FOUND OR IS ON A SERIAL (COM) PORT

If your printer isn't found using the options in the preceding section, or if the printer is connected via a COM port, you have to fake out Plug and Play and go the manual route. To do so, just follow these steps:

1. Open the Printers and Faxes folder, and run the Add New Printer Wizard.
2. Click Next.
3. Click Local Printer, make sure that Automatically Detect My Printer is *not* checked, and then click Next.
4. Select the port the printer is connected to in the resulting dialog. Figure 6.2 shows the port dialog box; the options and what they mean are as follows:

6

Options	Notes
LPT1:, LPT2:, LPT3:	The most common setting is LPT1 because most PC-type printers hook up to the LPT1 parallel port.
COM1:, COM2:, COM3:, COM4:	If you know your printer is of the serial variety, it's probably connected to the COM1 port. If COM1 is tied up for use with some other device, such as a modem, use COM2. If you choose a COM port, click Settings to check the communications settings in the resulting dialog box. Set the baud rate, data bits, parity, start and stop bits, and flow control to match those of the printer being attached. Refer to the printer's manual to determine what the settings should be.
File	This is for printing to a disk file instead of to the printer. Later, the file can be sent directly to the printer or sent to someone on floppy disk or over a modem. When you print to this printer name, you are prompted to enter a filename. (See the section "Printing to Disk Option.")
Create a New Port	Create a New Port is used to make connections to printers that are directly connected to your LAN and are to be controlled by your computer. Its use is covered in Chapter 16.

Figure 6.2
Choosing the port for a printer. Ninety-nine percent of the time it is LPT1.

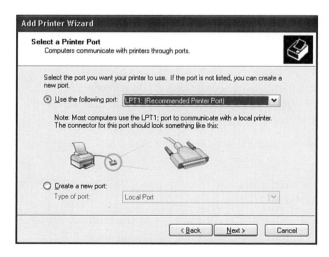

5. Select the manufacturer and model of your printer in the next dialog, as shown in Figure 6.3. You can quickly jump to a manufacturer's name by pressing the first letter

of the name, such as E for Epson. Then use the up- and down-arrow keys to home in on the correct one.

If you can't find the appropriate model, you have two choices: You can choose a similar compatible model and risk getting less-than-perfect output, or you can try to get the correct driver. If you have an Internet connection, click Windows Update to see if Microsoft has a driver available. Otherwise, get the manufacturer's driver on a floppy disk or CD-ROM or download it from the Internet, and then click Have Disk. Locate the driver (look for an INF file, the standard type for driver setup programs) and click OK.

→ For more information on dealing with unlisted printers, **see** the next section, "What to Do If Your Printer Isn't Listed."

Figure 6.3
Choose the make and model of your printer here.

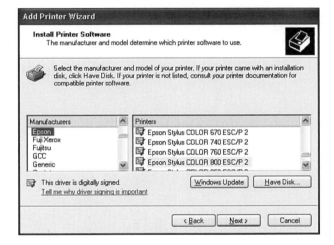

If the wizard finds that the appropriate driver is already installed on your machine, you can elect to keep it or replace it. It's up to you. If you think the replacement will be better, go for it. By contrast, if no driver is listed on the machine, you may be prompted to install it or insert a disk, such as the Windows XP setup disk. On the whole, manufacturer-provided drivers tend to be better than the default ones provided with XP.

6. Name the printer. The name will appear in LAN-based users' browse boxes if you decide to share this printer. Some computers have trouble with names longer than 31 characters, so if you intend to share the printer, keep the name short and sweet.

7. Set whether you want this printer to be your default printer.

8. Click Next. Choose whether you want to share the printer on the LAN. If not, skip to step 10. If so, click Share As and enter a name for sharing—this name will also be visible to network users. If you're connected to any old DOS or 16-bit Windows

computers, limit this name to 12 characters because that's the maximum length those users can see.

→ To learn more about sharing your printer on a network, **see** "Sharing Printers," **p. 564**.

9. Click Next. Now you can fill in additional information about the printer that people can see when browsing for a printer over the LAN. Something like `Joe's Laser Printer in Room 23` might be useful (as long as your name is Joe). These fields are optional. Be creative.

10. Click Next. You then are asked whether you want to print a test page. Doing so is a good way to confirm the printer is now operational. Choose Yes or No, and then click Next.

11. Assuming that everything looks good, be sure your printer is turned on and ready to print, and click Finish. Some files will be copied between directories. You might be asked to insert disks again.

12. If you chose to print a test page, your printer should start up and print a single page. You will be asked whether it printed okay. If it did, click Yes and you're finished. If it didn't print correctly, click Troubleshoot, and follow the wizard's instructions to identify the problem.

When you're finished, the icon for the printer appears in your Printers and Faxes folder.

TIP

> If you're going to share the printer with LAN users running Windows 95, 98, Me, or NT 4 on Intel or Alpha platforms, they'll need different printer drivers than Windows XP and 2000 machines do. You can preinstall the drivers needed by other operating systems so that other users don't have to hunt around for driver files, and so that they're not prompted to insert disks into their machines when they try to connect to your printer. Do do this, open the Properties sheet for the printer, click the Sharing tab, and then click Additional Drivers.

→ For more details about sharing printers for use by workstations running other operating systems, **see** "Installing Extra Printer Drivers," **p. 565**.

WHAT TO DO IF YOUR PRINTER ISN'T LISTED

If your printer isn't detected with Plug and Play, and isn't listed in the selection list, you'll have to find a driver elsewhere.

First of all, your printer probably came with a floppy disk or CD-ROM with driver software. On the printer manufacturer selection dialog box (Figure 6.5, shown later), click Have Disk, and then click Browse to find the Windows XP or Windows 2000 driver files for your printer. Select the appropriate INF file and click OK.

If you can't find the disk or it doesn't contain a Windows XP or 2000 compatible driver, don't worry; there's still hope. Windows XP has been out long enough that *all* currently manufactured printers have XP-compatible drivers. Even many older printers have Windows XP or 2000 driver support.

Your next step should be to visit the printer manufacturer's Web site. Check out the Product Support section, and look for a way to locate and download drivers. If you can find the appropriate driver, follow the manufacturer's instructions for downloading it. It will probably come as a compressed or executable file that has to be expanded or run, and this will put the installation files into a folder on your hard drive. You can then use the Have Disk feature discussed earlier to point Windows to this folder.

If this fails, check Microsoft's download site page at www.microsoft.com/downloads. Click Drivers in the left column and search from there.

If neither Microsoft nor the manufacturer provides a driver, hope is fading. Still, some off-brand printers or models are designed to be compatible with one of the popular printer types, such as the Apple LaserWriters, Hewlett-Packard LaserJets, or one of the Epson series. Also, many printer models are very similar and can use the same driver. Check the product manual or manufacturer's Web site to see whether your printer supports an *emulation mode*. This might help you identify an alternative printer model, and you can try its driver.

TIP

Use the Internet to see whether other people have run into the same problem and have found a solution. For instance, you might use Google to search for Windows XP printer driver *manufacturer model*, substituting in the manufacturer's name and model number. However, don't download a driver from some random site: It could be infected with a virus. Download drivers *only* from a credible corporate Web site.

Assuming that you have obtained a printer driver, follow these instructions to install it:

1. Open the Printers and Faxes folder, and run the Add Printer Wizard.
2. Click Next, choose Local Printer, and then turn off the check box for autodetect.
3. Choose the correct port, and click Next.
4. Click the Have Disk button.
5. You're now prompted to insert a disk in drive A:. Insert the disk, or click Browse to get to a disk or network volume that contains the driver files. The wizard is looking for a file with an .INF extension, which is the standard file extension for the installer setup file provided with all drivers.
6. Click OK. You might have to choose a printer model from a list if multiple options exist.
7. Continue through the wizard dialog boxes as explained previously.

CHANGING A PRINTER'S PROPERTIES

Each printer driver has a Properties sheet of associated settings (typically enough to choke a horse). The basic settings are covered in this chapter, whereas you'll find those relating to network printer sharing in Chapter 16. Printer drivers dictate, among other things, the particular options available on their Properties sheet. Because of the variations possible, the following sections describe the gist of these options without necessarily going into detail about each printer type. (In other words, your fancy new printer might have options we've never even heard of).

The settings pertaining to a printer are called properties. When you add a printer, the wizard puts the icon for it into the Printers and Faxes folder, and it's ready to go. At that point, you can accept the default properties or alter the properties as follows:

1. Open the Printers and Faxes folder by clicking Start, Control Panel, Printers and Other Hardware, View Installed Printers or Faxes. (For quicker access, you can put Printers and Faxes on your Start menu. See "Start Menu Pizzazz" in Chapter 21).

2. Select the printer's icon and choose Set Printer Properties from the task list. Or, right-click the printer icon and select Properties. The printer's Properties dialog box then appears, as shown in Figure 6.4.

Figure 6.4
A typical printer's Properties dialog box. The settings available vary between printers. Some have more or fewer tabs.

3. Change any of the text fields as you see fit. (Their significance was explained earlier in this chapter.)

Any printer's Properties sheet can have as many as eight tabs: General, Sharing, Ports, Advanced, Color Management Device Settings, and Utilities. Table 6.1 shows the general breakdown. Again, the tabs can vary depending on the capabilities of your printer.

TABLE 6.1	PROPERTIES SHEET TABS
Tab	**What It Controls**
General	This tab lists the name, location, model number, and features of the printer. From this tab, you can print a test page. You also can set default printing preferences, including the paper size, page orientation, paper source, pages per sheet (for brochure printing), affecting all print jobs. (You should rely on your application's Print Setup commands to control an individual print job's choice of paper orientation, paper source, and so on, which will override these settings.) Some color printers may have settings for paper quality, color control, and buttons for maintenance functions on this tab.
Sharing	On this tab, you can alter whether the printer is shared and what the share name is. You also can provide drivers for users of other operating systems by clicking the Additional Drivers button. (See Chapter 16 for more.)
Ports	On this tab, you can add and delete ports; set time-out for LPT ports; and set baud rate, data bits, parity, stop bits, and flow control for serial ports.
Advanced	This tab controls time availability, printer priority, driver file changes, spooling options, and advanced printing features such as booklet printing and page ordering. The first two settings are pertinent to larger networks and can safely be ignored. Additional Advanced settings vary from printer to printer, depending on its capabilities. Booklet printing is worth looking into if you do lots of desktop publishing. Using this option, you can print pages laid out for stapling together small pamphlets. Also, the New Driver button on the Advanced tab lets you replace the current driver with a better one, if necessary.
Color Management	On this tab, you can set optional color profiles on color printers, if this capability is supported. (See "Color Management" later in this chapter.)
Device Settings	The settings on this tab vary greatly between printers. For example, you can set paper size in each tray, tell Windows how much RAM is installed in the printer, and substitute fonts.
Utilities	This tab, if present, probably contains options for inkjet nozzle cleaning, head cleaning, head alignment, and so on.

6

We'll discuss the most important of the settings in more detail in the next section.

TIP

> Each time you add a printer, Windows creates an icon for it in the Printers and Faxes folder. Although each is called a printer, it is actually a "virtual" printer, much the way a shortcut represents a document or application in the GUI. A given *physical* printer can have multiple icons, each with different default settings. For example, one could be set to print in landscape orientation on legal-size paper, whereas another printer would default to portrait orientation with letter-size paper. Of course, you can always adjust these settings when you go to print a document, but that can get tedious. With multiple printer icons, you can choose a setup by just selecting the appropriate printer icon.

→ For more details about printer sharing, printer pooling, port creation and deletion, and other server-related printing issues, **see** Chapter 16.

COMMENTS ABOUT VARIOUS SETTINGS

Table 6.2 describes the most common settings from the Properties dialog box for both PostScript and HP-compatible printers.

TABLE 6.2 THE OPTIONS IN THE BASIC SETUP DIALOG BOX

Option	Description
2 Sides	This option enables or disables double-sided printing for printers that support this feature.
Configure Port, LPT Port Timeout	This option specifies the amount of time that will elapse before you are notified that the printer or plotter is not responding. If printing from your application regularly results in an error message about transmission problems, and retrying seems to work, you should increase the setting. The maximum is 999,999 seconds.
Configure Port, Serial Port Settings	Settings here pertain to network ports' and serial ports' communications settings, such as baud rate and parity. The serial port's baud rate, data bits, parity, stop bits, and flow control must match that of the printer's, or you're in for some garbage printouts.
Default Datatype	This setting usually doesn't need changing. The default is RAW. A very specialized application might ask you to create a printer with another data type setting for use when printing its documents. The EMF data types can result in faster transmission over slow networks (for example, VPN by modem).
Enable Advanced Printing Features	When this option is checked, metafile spooling is turned on, and options such as Page Order, Booklet Printing, and Pages Per Sheet may be available, depending on your printer. For normal printing, you should leave the advanced printing feature set to the default (Enabled). If compatibility problems occur, you can disable the feature.
Enable Bidirectional Support	This option lets the computer query the printer for settings and status information.

Option	Description
Font Cartridges	For this option, you choose the names of the cartridges that are physically installed in the printer.
Font Substitution	TrueType Font Substitution Table: Used for PostScript printers to declare when internal fonts should be used in place of downloaded TrueType fonts to speed up printing.
Form-to-Tray Assignment	For this option, you click a source, such as a lower tray, and then choose a form name to match with the source. When you choose a form name (such as A4 Small) at print time, the printer driver tells the printer which tray to switch to and you don't have to think about it. You can repeat the process for each form name you want to set up.
Hold Mismatched Documents	This option is used mostly with dot-matrix forms printers, and directs the spooler to check the printer's form setup and match it to the document setup before sending documents to the print device. If the information does not match, the document is held in the queue. A mismatched document in the queue does not prevent correctly matched documents from printing.
Keep Printed Documents	This option specifies that the spooler should not delete documents after they are printed. This way, a document can be resubmitted to the printer from the printer queue instead of from the program, which is faster.
New Driver	Use this button to install an updated driver for the printer. It runs the Add Printer Driver Wizard.
Orientation	This option sets the page orientation. Normal orientation is Portrait, which, like a portrait of the Mona Lisa, is taller than it is wide. Landscape, like a landscape painting, is the opposite. Rotated Landscape means a 90° counterclockwise rotation of the printout.
Page Order	This option determines the order in which documents are printed. Front to Back prints the document so that page 1 is on top of the stack. Back to Front prints the document so that page 1 is on the bottom of the stack.
Page Protect	If turned on, this option tells the printer to forcibly reserve enough memory to store a full page image; some intense graphics pages otherwise might not be able to print if the printer gives too much memory over to downloaded fonts and macros.
Print Directly to the Printer	This option prevents documents sent to the printer from being spooled. Thus, printing doesn't happen in the background; instead, the computer is tied up until the print job is completed. There's virtually no practical reason for tying up your computer this way, unless your printer and Windows are having difficulty communicating or you find that printing performance (page per minute throughput) increases significantly when this option is enabled. When a printer is shared over the network, this option isn't available.

continues

TABLE 6.2 CONTINUED

Option	Description
Print Spooled Documents First	This option specifies that the spooler should favor documents that have completed spooling when deciding which document to print next, even if the completed documents are a lower priority than documents that are still spooling.
Printer Memory	This option tells Windows how much memory is installed in the printer.
Printing Defaults	You click this option to view or change the default document properties for all users of the selected printer. If you share your local printer, these settings are the default document properties for other users.
Priority	Printers can have a priority setting from 1 to 99. The default setting is 1. Print jobs sent to a printer that has a priority level of 2 always print before a job sent to a printer with a level 1 setting if both setups use the same physical printer.
Resolution	Some printers can render graphics and images in more than one resolution. The higher the resolution, the longer printing takes, so you can save time by choosing a lower resolution. For finished, high-quality work, you should choose the highest resolution. On some printers, this choice is limited by the amount of memory in the printer.
Separator File	A preassigned file can be printed between jobs, usually to place an identification page listing the user, job ID, date, time, number of pages, and so forth. Files also can be used to switch a printer between PostScript and PCL (HP) mode for printers that can run in both modes.
Use Printer Halftoning	Halftoning is a process that converts shades of gray or colors to patterns of black and white dots. A newspaper photo is an example of halftoning. When the arrangement of dots (pixels) on the page is varied, a photographic image can be simulated with only black and white dots. Because virtually no black-and-white printers and typesetters can print shades of gray, halftoning is the closest you get to realistic photographic effects. Normally, Windows processes the halftoning of graphics printouts. Only printers that can do halftoning offer halftone options.

If you can't figure out what an option does, you can always click the Help button in the upper-right corner of the Properties dialog box and then click an option. A description of the option should appear.

TIP

> You can access the Printing Defaults tab through two paths: one by choosing Printing Defaults from the Advanced tab and the other by choosing Printing Preferences from the General tab. What's the difference? Printing Defaults are the baseline settings offered to each user. Printing Preferences hold your own personal preferences, overriding the Printing Defaults (but are not forced on other users of that printer).

TIP

> Another set of properties is available for shared printers. To locate it, right-click an empty spot within the Printers folder, and choose Server Properties. The Server Properties list ports and show the collective list of all installed drivers in use. Here, you can define forms and set events and notifications. Because it is a network topic, this last tab is covered in Chapter 16.

REMOVING A PRINTER FROM THE PRINTERS AND FAXES FOLDER

You might want to remove a printer setup for several reasons:

- The physical printer has been removed from service.
- You don't want to use a particular network printer anymore.
- You had several definitions of a physical printer using different default settings, and you want to remove one of them.
- You have a nonfunctioning or improperly functioning printer setup and want to remove it and start over by running the Add Printer Wizard.

In any of these cases, the approach is the same:

1. Open the Printers and Faxes folder.
2. Be sure nothing is in the print queue. You have to clear the queue for the printer before deleting it. If you don't, Windows will try to delete all jobs in the queue for you, but it unfortunately isn't always successful.
3. Select the printer icon you want to remove, and choose File, Delete (or press the Del key).
4. Depending on whether the printer is local or remote, you see one of two different dialog boxes. One asks whether you want to delete the printer; the other asks whether you want to delete the connection to the printer. In either case, click Yes. The printer icon or window disappears from the Printers and Faxes folder.

TIP

> The removal process removes only the virtual printer setup from the Registry for the currently logged-in user. The related driver file and font files are not deleted from the disk. Therefore, if you ever want to re-create the printer, you don't have to insert disks or respond to prompts for the location of driver files. On the other hand, if you are having problems with the driver, deleting the icon won't delete the bad driver. Use the New Driver on the Advanced properties tab to solve the problem in this case.

6

PRINTING FROM WINDOWS APPLICATIONS

When you print from 16-bit or 32-bit Windows applications, the internal Print Manager kicks in and spools the print job for you, adding it to the queue for the selected printer. The spooler then feeds the file to the assigned printer(s), coordinating the flow of data and keeping you informed of the progress. Jobs are queued up and listed in the given printer's window, from which their status can be observed; they can be rearranged, deleted, and so forth. All the rights and privileges assigned to you, as the user, are applicable, potentially allowing you to alter the queue (as discussed later in this chapter), rearranging, deleting, pausing, or restarting print jobs.

If the application doesn't provide a way to select a specific printer (typically through a Print Setup dialog box), then the default printer is used. You can select the default printer from the Printers and Faxes folder by right-clicking a printer and choosing Set as Default Printer.

PRE-PRINTING CHECKLIST

To print from Windows applications, follow these steps:

1. Check to see that the printer and page settings are correct and the right printer is chosen for your output. Some applications provide a Printer Setup or other option on their File menu for this task. Recall that settings you make from such a box override the default settings made from the printer's Properties sheet. If the application has a Print, Preview command, use it to check that the formatting of the document is acceptable.

2. Select File, Print from the application's window, and fill in whatever information is asked of you. Figure 6.5 shows the Print dialog for WordPad. (Print dialogs for other applications may differ.) Notice that you can just click a printer's icon to choose it. When you do, its printer driver kicks in, changing the options on the tabs. You can also find a printer on the LAN or print to a file, using their respective buttons. Two other tabs, Layout and Paper/Quality, could be useful. For advanced options such as half-toning and color matching, select the Layout tab and click Advanced.

3. Click OK (or otherwise confirm printing). The data is sent to the spooler, which writes it in a file and then begins printing it. If an error occurs—a port conflict, the printer is out of paper, and so on—Windows displays a message indicating what the problem is, as shown in Figure 6.6.

You can attempt to fix the problem by checking the cable connection, the paper supply, and so forth. Then click Retry. If you run into more serious trouble, you can run the Troubleshooting Wizard from the Help menu.

For most users, following these steps is all you'll ever need to do to print. The remainder of this chapter deals mostly with how to work with the printer queues of your own workstation printer or of network printers, and how to alter, pause, delete, or restart print jobs.

Figure 6.5
Preparing to print a typical file.

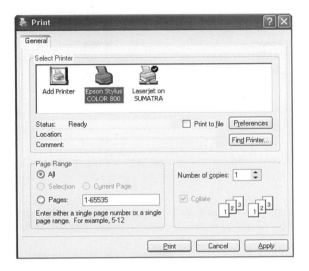

Figure 6.6
Typical error message resulting from a printer problem.

 If you receive printer errors when attempting to print a document, see "Printer Errors" in the "Troubleshooting" section at the end of this chapter.

 If nothing happens when you send a print job to the printer, see "Nothing Happens" in the "Troubleshooting" section at the end of this chapter.

PRINTING BY DRAGGING FILES INTO THE PRINT MANAGER

As a shortcut to printing a document, you can simply drag the icon of the document you want to print either onto an icon of a printer or into the printer's open window (from the Printers and Faxes folder). You can drag the file from Explorer right onto the chosen printer's icon or open window to see it added to the print queue for that printer.

When you drop the document, Windows realizes you want to print it, and the file is loaded into the source application, the Print command is automatically executed, and the file is spooled to the Print Manager. Figure 6.7 shows an example of dropping a Word document on a PostScript printer.

6

TIP

> Documents must have associations linking the filename extension (for example, `.doc` or `.bmp`) to the application that handles that file type; otherwise, printing by dragging them to Print Manager doesn't work. Also, you obviously don't have the option of setting printing options when you print this way. All the defaults are used.

→ For more information about file associations, **see** "Setting Folder Options," **p. 730**.

 If you're having trouble printing, you're getting "garbage" printouts, or you're getting only partial pages, see "Printer Produces Garbled Text" in the "Troubleshooting" section at the end of this chapter.

 If only half of the page prints correctly before the printer starts printing garbage text, see "Only Half of the Page Prints Correctly" in the "Troubleshooting" section at the end of this chapter.

Figure 6.7
You can print a document or a number of documents by dragging them onto a destination printer in the Printers and Faxes folder. The files must have application associations.

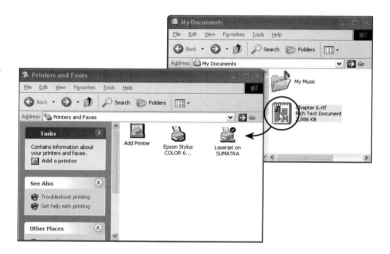

PRINTING OFFLINE

If your printer is disconnected, you can still queue up documents for printing. You might want to do this while traveling, for instance, if you have a laptop and don't want to drag a 50-pound laser printer along in your carry-on luggage.

If you try this, however, you'll quickly find that the Print Manager will beep, pop up messages to tell you about the missing printer, and otherwise make your life miserable. You can silence it by right-clicking the printer's icon in the Printers and Faxes folder and selecting Use Printer Offline.

Windows will now quietly and compliantly queue up anything you "print." (Just don't forget that you've done this or nothing will print even when you've reconnected your printer. You'll end up yelling at your unresponsive printer, when it's only doing what it was told.)

When you've reconnected the printer, uncheck Use Printer Offline (with the same steps used above) and the output will flow forth. It's a nifty feature, but only available for local printers, not networked printers.

PRINTING FROM DOS APPLICATIONS

If you are still using MS-DOS applications, printing is one of the more problematic areas. Many modern inexpensive inkjet and laser printers don't even support output from DOS programs because they don't have enough built-in smarts to form the character images by themselves. If you need laser or inkjet output from a DOS application, be sure that any new printer you buy uses a page-description language supported by your application, such as PostScript, Hewlett-Packard's PCL, or one of the Epson text formats.

Furthermore, most DOS application can print only to LPT ports. If you want to use a printer that is on a USB port or is out there somewhere on a LAN, nothing will come out! To direct a DOS program's output to a USB or network printer, share the printer (even if it's attached to your own computer) and issue the following command from the Command Prompt window:

```
net use lpt2: \\computername\sharename
```

Then direct your DOS program to use LPT2. (You should select an LPT port number that does not have an associated physical LPT port in your computer.)

→ For more information about the `net use` command, **see** "Mapping Drives with `net use`," **p. 568**.

WORKING WITH THE PRINTER QUEUE

After you or other users on the network have sent print jobs to a given printer, anyone with rights to manage the queue can work with it. If nothing else, it's often useful to observe the queue to check its progress. This way, you can better choose which printer to print to, or whether some intervention is necessary, such as adding more paper. By simply opening the Printers and Faxes folder, you can see the basic state of each printer's queue, assuming you display the window contents in Details view.

For each printer, the window displays the status of the printer (in the title bar) and the documents that are queued up, including their sizes, status, owner, pages, date submitted, and so on.

TIP

You can drag a printer's icon from the Printers and Faxes window to your desktop, for easy access. Click Yes when Windows asks if you want to create a shortcut.

Figure 6.8 shows a sample printer's folder with a print queue and related information.

6

Figure 6.8
A printer's folder showing several print jobs pending.

TIP

When print jobs for a workstation are pending, an icon appears in the system tray, near the clock. You can hover the mouse pointer over it to see the number of documents waiting to print. Right-click it to choose a printer's queue to examine in a window.

To keep network traffic down to a dull roar, Windows doesn't poll the network constantly to check the state of the queue. If you are printing to a network printer and want to check the current state of affairs on the network printer, choose View, Refresh or press F5 to immediately update the queue information.

TIP

By default, all users can pause, resume, restart, and cancel printing their own documents. However, to manage documents printed by other users, your system administrator must give you the Manage Documents permission.

DELETING A FILE FROM THE QUEUE

After sending a document to the queue, you might reconsider printing it, or you might want to re-edit the file and print it again later. If so, you can simply remove the file from the queue. To do so, right-click the document and choose Cancel, or choose Document, Cancel from the menu. The document is then removed from the printer's window.

If you're trying to delete the job that's printing, you might have some trouble. At the very least, the system might take some time to respond. Sometimes canceling a laser printer's job while it's printing in graphics mode necessitates resetting the printer to clear its buffer. To reset, either turn the printer off and then on, or use the Reset option (if it's available).

NOTE

Because print jobs are spooled to the hard disk, they can survive powering down Windows XP. Any documents already in the queue when the system goes down, whether due to an intentional shutdown or a power outage, reappear in the queue when you power up.

CANCELING ALL PENDING PRINT JOBS ON A GIVEN PRINTER

Assuming you have been given the privilege, you can cancel *all* the print jobs on a printer. In the Printers and Faxes folder, right-click the printer, and choose Cancel All Documents. A confirmation dialog box appears to confirm this action.

PAUSING, RESUMING, AND RESTARTING THE PRINTING PROCESS

If you need to, you can pause the printing process for a particular printer or even just a single document print job. This capability can be useful in case you have second thoughts about a print job, want to give other jobs a chance to print first, or you just want to adjust or quiet the printer for some reason.

To pause a print job, right-click it and choose Pause. Pretty simple. The word Paused then appears on the document's line. The printing might not stop immediately because your printer might have a buffer that holds data in preparation for printing. The printing stops when the buffer is empty. When you're ready to resume printing, just right-click the job in question, and choose Resume.

TIP

Pausing a document lets other documents later in the queue proceed to print, essentially moving them ahead in line. You can achieve the same effect by rearranging the queue, as explained in the section titled "Rearranging the Queue Order."

In some situations, you might need to pause all the jobs on your printer, such as to add paper to it, to alter the printer settings, or just to shut up the printer for a bit while you take a phone call. To pause all jobs, open the Printer's window and choose Printer, Pause Printing. You have to choose the command again to resume printing, and the check mark on the menu goes away.

Should you need to pause (due to a paper jam or other botch), you can restart a printing document from the beginning. Just right-click the document, and choose Restart.

REARRANGING THE QUEUE ORDER

When you have several items on the queue, you might want to rearrange the order in which they're slated for printing. Perhaps a print job's priority has increased because you need it for an urgent meeting, or you have to get a letter to the post office. Whatever the reason, as long as the document hasn't yet started to print, you can easily rearrange its position in the print queue like this:

1. Click the file you want to move, and keep the mouse button pressed.
2. Drag the file up or down to its new location. A solid line moves to indicate where the document will be inserted when you release the mouse button.
3. When you release the mouse button, your file is inserted in the queue, pushing the other files down a notch.

6

VIEWING AND ALTERING DOCUMENT PROPERTIES

Like everything in Windows, each document in the printer queue has its own properties. For a more detailed view of information pertaining to each document, you can open the Properties sheet for it by right-clicking it and choosing Properties. You can change only two settings from the resulting dialog box (see Figure 6.9):

- The print priority. Documents with higher priority numbers get printed ahead of documents with lower numbers.
- The time of day when the document can be printed.

Figure 6.9
Altering the properties for a print job on the queue.

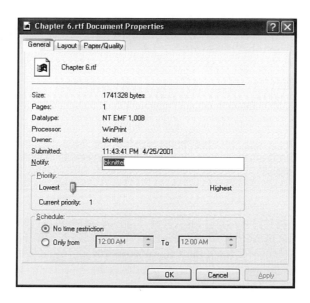

> **NOTE**
>
> As a shortcut, you can open a document's properties by just double-clicking it.

PRINTING TO DISK OPTION

Sometimes printing to a disk file rather than to a printer can be useful. What does printing to a disk file mean? It means that the same data that normally would be sent to the printer is shunted to a disk file, either locally or on the network. The file isn't a copy of the document you were printing; it contains all the special formatting codes that control the printer. Codes that change fonts, print graphics, set margins, break pages, and add attributes such as underline, bold, and so on are all included in this type of file. Print files destined for PostScript printers typically include a PostScript preamble, too.

The primary use of print-to-disk is to send formatted PostScript files to a service bureau for professional printing. You don't even need to own a PostScript printer to do this.

In some applications, this choice is available in the Print dialog box. If it isn't, you should modify the printer's configuration to print to a file rather than to a port. Then, whenever you use that printer, it will use all the usual settings for the driver but send the data to a file of your choice instead of to the printer port. Just follow these steps:

1. In the Printers and Faxes folder, right-click the printer's icon, and choose Properties.
2. Click Ports.
3. Set the port to File, and close the dialog box.

   The next time you or another local or network user prints to that printer, you'll be prompted to enter a filename, as you can see in Figure 6.10. You should specify the full path with the filename. The file will be stored on the machine where the print job originated.

Figure 6.10
Enter the full path and filename for the printer output file.

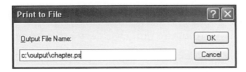

TIP

> If you want to create an encapsulated PostScript file (.eps), go through the Add New Printer procedure, selecting an appropriate PostScript printer model, such as the Apple LaserWriter or the QMS PS-810—your service bureau should suggest which model to use. You don't need to have such a printer attached to your computer. Then, modify the properties of the printer via the Properties, Details, Job Defaults, Options dialog box to set an encapsulated PostScript filename.

COLOR MANAGEMENT

Color management is the process of producing accurate, consistent color among a variety of input and output devices. In Windows, the color management system (CMS) maps colors between devices such as scanners, monitors, and printers; transforms colors from one color space to another (for example, RGB to CMYK); and adjusts tints displayed or printed for correctness. For most of us, this kind of precision isn't very important, but for graphic artists and designers, it's an essential part of preparing proofs and professional output.

Just like a printer needs a printer driver or a scanner needs a TWAIN driver, each piece of hardware needs its own color *profile*. A profile is a file made by the hardware manufacturer (or Microsoft), specifically for the device, and it contains information about the color characteristics of the hardware. You simply associate the profile with the device via the device's Properties sheet, and the color system does the rest. Only if a device supports color management does its Properties sheet have a Color tab on it, however.

Even though some profiles are included with Windows XP, you might need to obtain a profile for your particular hardware. Check with the manufacturer. You can use the following procedure to add a color profile to a printer:

1. If you obtain a custom color-profile file from your manufacturer, copy it to *%systemroot%*\system32\spool\drivers\color, where *%systemroot%* is your Windows folder.

2. Open the Printers and Faxes folder by selecting Start, Control Panel, Printers and Other Hardware, Printers and Faxes.

3. Right-click the printer that you want to associate with a color profile, click Properties, and then click the Color Management tab. Notice that the tab has two settings: Automatic and Manual. Normally, Windows uses the Automatic setting, in which case it assigns a color profile to the printer from those it has on hand. If you want to override the default, click Manual.

4. Click Add to open the Add Profile Association dialog box.

5. Locate the new color profile you want to associate with the printer. You can right-click a profile and choose Properties to read more about the profile. Because the filenames are cryptic, this is the only way to figure out what device a color profile is for.

6. Click the new profile, and then click Add. Keep in mind that you can associate any number of profiles with a given piece of gear. Only one can be active at a time, however. After you open the profile list, select Manual and click the one you want to activate. For sophisticated setups, you may have reason for multiple profiles, but it's not likely that many users who are not designers or artists will bother.

You can use the same approach to add profiles for other hardware pieces, such as displays and scanners. Just bring up the Color Management tab of each item through its Properties sheet.

NOTE

> For a video display, open the Settings tab, click Advanced, and then click the Color Management tab.

FAXING

If your computer has a modem installed, you can use it to send and receive faxes. Windows XP comes with fax software built in. (You might have to go through an extra step to install it, though—we'll cover that shortly).

To send a fax from Windows XP, you just write a document using your favorite application, choose the Fax icon from the printer folder, and print. Windows asks for the appropriate fax phone number and makes the call—no paper is involved. The fax service can even add a cover sheet to your document on the way out. To receive faxes, your modem can be set to answer calls. When a fax arrives, you can view its image onscreen or print it, or even have it printed automatically.

Third-party fax software, such as Symantec's WinFax Pro, has more bells and whistles and can provide fax services for the whole network, but the basic version that comes with Windows will take care of most home and small office users' needs. Windows XP faxing can't be shared among several users on the LAN the same way you can share regular printers, though. If you want to provide a shared FAX modem for your LAN, you should look for a third-party product. See the following note for some links.

NOTE

> I should tell you that, although computer-based faxing is great for documents you're typing up in your word processor, it's not so great for handwritten documents, which you need to scan and then "print". There's still a lot to be said for inexpensive dedicated fax machines, at least for sending. If you frequently need to fax hardcopy, you might also consider getting an all-in-one printer/fax/scanner.

INSTALLING THE FAX SERVICE

All you need to get started faxing is a fax device, such as a fax modem. (All modems sold in the last several years have fax capability, so the odds are slim that you'll have to buy a replacement.) There are also some combination scanner/printer/faxing machines that can serve as a Windows Fax device.

In this day of Plug and Play, just installing a modem or attaching a fax device will probably induce Windows to install the modem software, fax service, and a fax printer icon automatically. If, for some reason, Windows doesn't sense that you've attached a fax modem even when you reboot, you can use the Add/Remove Hardware Wizard. (See Chapter 27, "Installing and Replacing Hardware," for coverage of the Add/Remove Hardware applet and the Modem applet, both in the Control Panel.)

NOTE

> For more information on modem compatibility with faxes, see the Microsoft Windows Hardware Compatibility List at the Microsoft Web site (`http://www.microsoft.com/whdc/hcl`).

6

When a functioning fax modem or multifunction printer has been installed, check to see if a Fax icon has appeared in your Printers and Faxes folder (you get there from Start, Control Panel, Printers and Other Hardware). If it's not there, you'll need to install the fax service by following these steps:

1. Log on as a Computer Administrator user.
2. Open the Printers and Faxes folder by clicking Start, Printers and Faxes. If this isn't on your Start menu, click Control Panel, Printers and Other Hardware, and then View Installed Printers or Fax Printers.

3. Click Install a Local Fax Printer in the Printer Tasks List.

4. You may need to insert your Windows XP installation disc if Windows needs to copy the Fax service files.

NOTE

> If you have a functioning Fax modem installed but the Fax icon doesn't appear in Printers and Faxes, or if you inadvertently delete the Fax icon from that folder later on, select Set Up Faxing or Add a Local Fax Printer from the Printer Tasks menu.

When the fax service has been installed, a Fax icon appears in your Printers and Faxes folder, and a set of Fax management programs are installed under Start, More Programs, Accessories, Communications, Fax. Table 6.3 lists these commands and their purposes.

TABLE 6.3 FAX-RELATED COMMANDS

Command	Action
Fax Console	Displays a queue of outgoing faxes and lists received faxes.
Fax Cover Page Editor	Lets you design custom cover pages for your faxes.
Send a Fax…	Used by itself, sends only a cover page; you can use this to send a short memo. It's mainly invoked by other applications to send whole documents.

In addition, there is a Fax Configuration Wizard that asks you for setup information to be used in cover sheets and selects devices to be used for sending and receiving faxes. We'll discuss all of these programs in the following sections.

GETTING SET UP

After you install your fax hardware, you can get started by entering your fax-related settings using the Fax Configuration Wizard (see Figure 6.11). Open it by clicking Start, More Programs, Accessories, Communications, Fax, Fax Configuration Wizard.

1. Enter the relevant information into the User Information tab. You can skip the stuff that is not relevant. This data will be printed on your cover pages. Click Next.

2. Select the modems or other fax devices you want to use. If there are more than one, you can prioritize them with the arrow buttons. Click Next when you're finished.

3. Enter an identifying string (TSID) for your fax transmissions. This is displayed by receiving fax machines. Enter up to 20 characters and click Next.

4. If you'd like to receive faxes automatically, check the box corresponding to your fax modem. If you do, your modem will answer any incoming calls on its line (you can select the number of rings before it answers). If you leave the box unchecked, your computer won't be able to receive faxes. If you decide to receive faxes, enter a Called Station Identifier—this will be displayed on a sender's fax machine. Click Next.

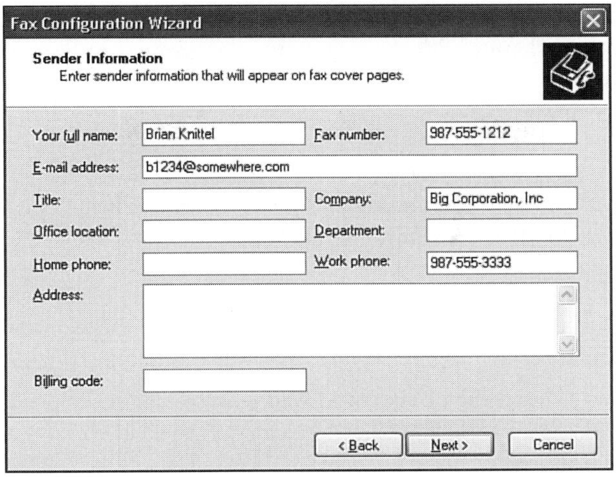

Figure 6.11
The Fax Configuration Wizard sets up your cover page particulars.

5. If you chose to receive faxes, indicate what you'd like done with them as they arrive. You can choose to print them by checking Print It On and selecting a printer, or you can save a copy of the fax in a designated folder.

6. Finally, click Finish.

NOTE

> There is one other configuration option you might want to set. By default, Windows will save its own copy of each fax it sends and receives. To alter this, open the Printers and Faxes folder, right-click the Fax icon, select Properties, and view the Archives tab. Here, you can select where and whether to store copies of incoming and outgoing faxes.

If you can't get your fax printer installed, see "Fax Printer Can't Be Added" in the "Troubleshooting" section at the end of this chapter.

IMPORTING FAXES FROM WINDOWS 9X/ME

If you used Personal Fax for Windows in Windows 95, 98, or Me and you want access to the archived faxes you sent and received with it, you can import these faxes into the new Fax service. Follow these steps:

1. Open the Printers and Faxes folder and double-click the Fax icon. This opens the Fax Console.

2. Select File, Import, and then select either Sent Faxes or Received Faxes.

3. In the Browse dialog box, locate the folder containing your sent or received faxes. When you have selected the folder, click OK.

6

4. The imported faxes are not deleted from their original location. If the import is successful and you're happy with the new setup, you can delete the old archives later to recover disk space.

SENDING A FAX

The Fax service should now be running and your fax printer installed. You should now be ready to send a fax. To do so, just follow these steps:

1. Open the document you want to send.

2. Choose File, Print. In the standard Print dialog box, in the Name field, select Fax. Set up the particulars as necessary (page range, and so on), and click OK.

3. The Send Fax Wizard then begins and walks you through the process of preparing the fax. (If you haven't run the Fax Configuration Wizard yet, you'll get the pleasure of going through it now.)

4. Fill in the recipient and dialing information as prompted, as shown in Figure 6.12. You can add multiple names to the list. If you have fax numbers in your address book, you can use it as a source for your list. If you set up your area code and Dialing Rules when you installed your modem, just enter the fax recipient's area code and number. If you didn't, uncheck Dialing Rules and enter the recipient's number, including a 1 and area code if needed. Click the Add button to add the first recipient, and repeat the process for each additional recipient. (This way, you can do a bulk faxing if you need to. This feature is one of the true advantages of faxing with a computer rather than a hardware fax machine.) When you've entered all the recipients, click Next.

Figure 6.12
Adding recipients to the fax transmission list.

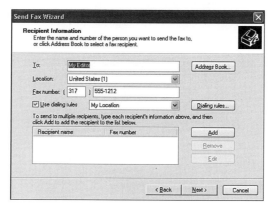

→ Windows can automatically manage area codes and special features such as outside-line access by setting up Dialing Rules. This is really handy when you're on the road. For more information, **see** "Dialing Rules," **p. 765**.

5. If you'd like to add a cover page to your fax, check Select a Cover Page and choose one of the predefined formats from the drop-down list. Enter the subject and any notes you

want to appear on the cover page. If you'd like to alter your personal information, click Sender Info.

6. Click Next. Choose when you'd like to send the fax. Typically, it is Now, but the When Discount Rates Apply option is interesting. (See the description of Fax Service Management in the following section to see how to set the timing.) Alternatively, you can specify a time in the next 24 hours.

7. Click Next. If you'd like to be notified if the fax is successfully sent or fails to go out, choose the desired notification method, and then click Next.

Windows then will prepare the print job for faxing. You can follow its progress by watching the Fax Console, which I discuss in the next section.

TIP

> You can send a quick note via fax without using a word processor at all. Just click Start, All Programs, Accessories, Fax, Send a Fax. This sends just a cover sheet. You can type your message into the Send Fax Wizard's Note field, which appears on the cover sheet.

FAX MANAGEMENT UTILITIES

For detailed control of how the Fax service sends and receives faxes, and to set up shared cover sheets that can be used by all the computer's users, there's a management tool called Fax Console.

To run it, double-click the Fax icon in Printers and Faxes, or choose Start, More Programs, Accessories, Communications, Fax, Fax Console.

You then see the window shown in Figure 6.13.

Figure 6.13
Fax Console lets you manage outgoing and received faxes.

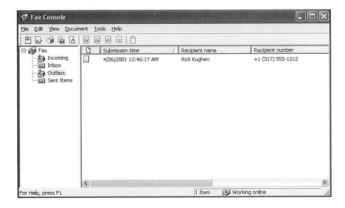

Poke around in this application to familiarize yourself with it. As you can see, you can browse through outgoing and received faxes by opening their Explorer folder views. The most important use of Fax Console is to delete outgoing faxes if you change your mind. To do this, just highlight the entry in the Outbox listing and press the Del key.

The Tools menu also offers several management options, as listed in Table 6.4

TABLE 6.4   FAX CONSOLE TOOLS

Tools Menu Item	Lets You...
Sender Information	Change your contact information used on cover sheets
Personal Cover Pages	Edit personal cover sheets not shared with other users of your computer
Fax Printers Status	(Not terribly useful)
Configure Fax	Run the Fax Configuration Wizard again
Fax Printer Configuration	Edit Fax Printer Properties
Fax Monitor	Monitor the progress of outgoing faxes

COVER SHEETS

Windows XP comes with several fax cover sheet forms predefined for typical business use: Generic, Confidential, Urgent, and so on. You can modify these cover sheets using the Fax Cover Page editor from the Fax menu or from Fax Console, as noted in Table 6.4. I can't go into much detail on this program, except to give you few hints:

- From the Fax Console, select Tools, Personal Cover Pages to start the Cover Page Editor. You can select an existing cover sheet, or you can click New to create a new one.

- For new cover pages, it's easiest to start with one of the predefined cover sheets and modify it. First, open Windows Explorer and click Tools, Folder Options, and select the View tab. Select Show Hidden Files and Folders. Now, back in the Cover Page Editor, click File, Open and browse to one of the files in this spectacularly-named folder: \Documents and Settings\All Users\Application Data\Microsoft\Windows NT\MSFax\Common Coverpages.

- Use the text button (labeled "ab1") and graphics button to draw items that never change, such as a confidentiality clause. Use the Insert menu to drop in information that is specified when each fax is sent, such as the recipient name.

- When you've finished editing, use Save or Save As to store the personalized cover sheet in My Documents\Fax\Personal Coverpages.

INCOMING FAXES

Each fax is converted to a file using the TIF file format when it arrives. Because TIF is a nonproprietary format, you can view or edit it with almost any graphics program. However, using the Windows Picture and Fax viewer and editor is easy enough.

There are two ways to set up the fax service for receiving faxes: It can answer your modem's phone line whenever it rings, or you can do a one-time receive.

To set up auto-answering, follow these steps:

1. Log on as a Computer Administrator user.
2. Open the Printers and Faxes folder, right-click the Fax icon, and select Properties.
3. Select your fax modem on the Devices tab and click Properties.
4. View the Receive tab. Check Enable Device To Receive. You can enable auto-printing here as well, as discussed later in this section.

If you don't want the fax modem to answer every call, you can enable a one-time receipt this way:

1. Open the Printers and Faxes folder.
2. Wait for the phone line to ring, or use a telephone handset to call the sender and him to press the Start button on his fax machine.
3. Double-click the Fax icon to open the Fax Console, and choose File, Receive a Fax Now.

This is the software equivalent of using a regular fax machine's handset and pressing its Start button.

 If your system refuses to receive incoming faxes, see "Cannot Receive a Fax" in the "Troubleshooting" section at the end of this chapter.

TIP

> As long as the fax service is running, and you have enabled your fax modem to receive faxes, the fax icon appears in the system tray. Double-clicking it brings up the Fax Monitor.

By default, incoming faxes are converted to TIF files and are dumped into the Fax Console's Inbox. But you can configure a fax setup to actually print your documents on paper as they come in. To shunt all incoming faxes to a physical printer for automatic printing, follow these steps:

1. Log on as a Computer Administrator user.
2. Open the Printers and Faxes folder, right-click the Fax icon, and select Properties.
3. Select your fax modem on the Devices tab and click Properties.
4. View the Receive tab. Check the Print and/or Save a copy options, as shown in Figure 6.14, and click OK. Use Save a Copy only to store an *extra* copy of received faxes, because they'll also be stored in the Fax Console's inbox.

6

Figure 6.14
Use this dialog box to configure automatic printing of received faxes. You can have incoming faxes printed automatically, and/or store a copy in a folder.

VIEWING RECEIVED FAXES

As I mentioned in the previous section, you can configure the fax service to automatically print incoming faxes. You can also view them on your monitor at any time.

There are two ways to view faxes. First, you can use the Fax Console, shown previously in Figure 6.13. There are three ways to open the Fax console:

- If the Fax Monitor icon appears in the Notification area of your task bar, right-click it and select Fax Console
- Select Start, All Programs, Accessories, Communications, Fax, Fax Console
- Use a shortcut created by right-clicking and dragging the Fax Console menu item to your Start Menu or desktop

In the Fax Console window's left pane, select Incoming to view received faxes, or Sent Items to view faxes you've sent. Double-click any item in the right pane to display the fax with the Windows Picture and Fax viewer.

The Picture and Fax Viewer tool sports a toolbar across the bottom. Figure 6.15 shows the functions of the most important toolbar buttons. You can print the fax with the small Printer icon.

TIP

> To forward a received or sent fax to another recipient, view the fax, click the Print button, and use the use the Photo Printing Wizard's instructions to print the fax images through your Fax printer.

Figure 6.15
The Picture and Fax Viewer toolbar lets you flip through the pages of a received fax, as well as rotate, scale, and print it.

Zoom

Page forward and back

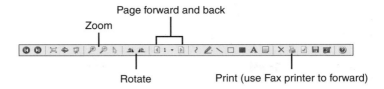

Rotate

Print (use Fax printer to forward)

Another way to view received faxes is to open the received fax folder directly. By default, the folder—get ready for this—is \Documents and Settings\All Users\Application Data\ Microsoft\Windows NT\MSFax\Inbox. Double-click on any listed file to display the fax. If you receive a lot of faxes, you can create a shortcut to this folder.

(To see into the Application Data folder you have to tell Windows Explorer to show hidden files. To do this, open Windows Explorer and click Tools, Folder Options; then select the View tab and select Show Hidden Files and Folders.)

Fax Resolutions

With all the talk about digital cameras, scanners, and cameras these days (and their respective resolutions), you might be wondering about fax resolution. Here's the skinny on that: The standard resolution for faxes is 3.85 scan lines/mm (approximately 98dpi vertically) with 1728 pixels across a standard scan line of 215mm (about 8 lines/mm or 204dpi horizontally).

An additional, popular setting on many fax machines is called "fine" resolution. This setting scans 7.7 lines per millimeter (approximately 196 dpi vertically) with the same resolution horizontally as with the normal setting.

Can some fax machines go higher? Yes. Many so-called Group III fax machines use nonstandard frames to negotiate higher resolutions. Some go as high as 300 × 300dpi (similar to older laser printers) and even 400 × 400dpi, but have to be talking with other fax machines made by the same manufacturer for this scheme to work. Manufacturers are working to set standards to support this level of resolution between machines of dissimilar manufacture.

The resolution you get on your printouts or as viewed on your computer screen depends on many factors. First, the screen resolution depends on the resolution of the source fax machine or computer. Second, it depends on the group of fax your system is employing and, finally, on the resolution of your display or printer. If what you intend to send someone is a high-resolution picture, you should always try to acquire a good color or grayscale scan of the image. Then you can attach it to an email as a GIF, TIF, or JPEG file. Generally speaking, it will look better than sending it as a fax.

Sending Faxes Over the Internet

The problem with sending faxes is that you don't always have a phone line available (as when you are in an office connected to the Internet via a LAN), or you don't want to pay for long-distance phone calls or high per-page charges to use a hotel fax machine. The problem with receiving faxes is that you aren't always there to receive the fax when it comes in. Isn't there a way to send faxes over the Internet?

Internet faxing is in development as of this writing, and there are various ways of both sending and receiving faxes using the Internet. If you're using an email program capable of faxing (such as newer versions of

6

Microsoft Outlook), you can configure it to send and receive faxes. Several services (commercial as well as free) offer to accept email messages and fax them to the specified phone number. Some even let you fax from portable, wireless devices such as Palm Pilots.

The following are some links to information about email-based faxing services:

```
www.j2.com
www.onebox.com
www.efax.com
```

You can read a FAQ about this topic, courtesy of Kevin M. Savetz at `www.savetz.com/fax`

TROUBLESHOOTING

PRINTER ERRORS

I receive error messages when I try to print. What's wrong?

When an error occurs during a print job, Windows tries to determine the cause. If the printer is out of paper, you might see a `Paper Out` message in the status area. At other times, the message is ambiguous, and the word `Error` might appear in the status area. Add paper; make sure that the printer is turned on, online, and correctly connected; and make sure that the settings (particularly the driver) are correct for that printer.

NOTHING HAPPENS

I try to print, but nothing happens. How do I proceed?

If your print jobs never make it out the other end of the printer, work through this checklist:

- First, ask yourself whether you printed to the correct printer. Check to see whether your default printer is the one from which you are expecting output. If you're on a LAN, you can easily switch default printers and then forget that you made the switch.
- Check the settings in the Print dialog box carefully before you print. Is there something to print? Do you have to select some portion of your document first?
- Next, check to see whether the printer you've chosen is actually powered up, online, and ready to roll.
- If you're using a network printer, is the station serving the printer powered up and ready to serve print jobs?
- Then check the cabling. Is it tight?
- Does the printer need ink, toner, or paper? Are any error lights or other indicators on the printer itself flashing or otherwise indicating an error, such as a paper jam?

PRINTER PRODUCES GARBLED TEXT

When I print, the printout contains a lot of garbled text.

If you're getting garbage characters in your printouts, check the following:

- You might have the wrong driver installed. Run the print test page and see whether it works. Open the Printers and Faxes folder (by choosing Start, Control Panel, Printers and Other Hardware, Printers and Faxes), open the printer's Properties sheet, and print a test page. If that works, then you're halfway home. If it doesn't, try removing the printer and reinstalling it. Right-click the printer icon in the Printers and Faxes folder, and choose Delete. Then add the printer again, and try printing.

- If the printer uses plug-in font cartridges, you may also have the wrong font cartridge installed in the printer, or your text might be formatted with the wrong font.

- Some printers have emulation modes that might conflict with one another. Check the manual. You may think you're printing to a PostScript printer, but the printer could be in an HP emulation mode; in this case, your driver is sending PostScript, and the printer is expecting PCL.

ONLY HALF OF THE PAGE PRINTS CORRECTLY

My printer prints about half of a page, and then it starts printing garbage.

This problem is a rare occurrence nowadays, but it's still possible if you're running a printer off a serial port. If your printer regularly prints about the same amount of text or graphics and then flips out, suspect a buffer-related problem. On serial printers, buffer problems can often be traced to cables that do not have all the serial-port conductors (wires), or they're not in the correct order. Make sure the cable is the correct kind for the printer.

FAX PRINTER CAN'T BE ADDED

I can't add a fax printer.

If you are unable to add a fax printer, you might not have sufficient user rights. See your system or fax server administrator. Also, be sure that your modem is fax-capable.

CANNOT RECEIVE A FAX

My system can't receive a fax. What's wrong with it?

Here's a quick checklist of common stumbling blocks:

- Have you plugged in the phone line properly?

- Is your modem installed and working properly?

- Is it a true fax modem, not just a data modem?

- Did you enable fax reception via the Fax Configuration Wizard (the default setting is off)?

- Is another device (for example, an answering machine) picking up the phone before your fax modem is? Check the ring settings for the fax modem and/or answering machines. Consider using the option that lets you screen for a fax first and then activate it manually (see the faxing section earlier in the chapter).

- If your computer goes into standby mode and doesn't wake up to receive incoming faxes, you might need to turn on an option in the computer's BIOS to "wake on ring." This option wakes up the computer any time it senses the ringer voltage on the phone line. If a fax is coming in, it takes the call. If it's not a fax, the computer goes back to sleep.

Tips from the Windows Pros: Does the Green Ink Have You Seeing Red?

If you're shopping for or currently use one of those inexpensive color inkjet printers that are so popular these days, you might find that your pleasure over their low purchase price fades quickly when you find out how much the ink cartridges cost. It's the overall cost per page that matters, and this can range from $.05 to $.15 per page for black-and-white printing, and *lots* more for color. If you print, say, an average of 10 pages per day, a printer that costs $.05 per page less than a competing model will save you $180 a year. That can *way* more than make up for a higher initial purchase price. This same argument goes for laser printers, too, by the way. Some monochrome laser printers on the market sell for not much more than $100 now, but the cost of the consumables—ouch!

My advice is, when you're shopping for any printer, check out online reviews and estimate your actual cost of operation before you buy. You can find reviews at www.pcmag.com, www.zdnet.com, www.consumersearch.com, www.consumerreports.com (which requires a subscription), and many other sites. An hour or two invested in research now can save you a bundle later.

But suppose you already have a printer and find that it's been rated as the biggest ink-sucking pig on the market. If you use it heavily, consider trading it for a less-thirsty model. Remember, you might recoup the cost in short order. You also can look into using recycled, refilled ink or toner cartridges, or even get one of those fill-your-own kits. (I would probably accidentally stick myself with the needle and end up with unintentional multicolored tattoos, but you might be braver than me.)

Finally, right-click the printer's icon in the Printers and Faxes folder, click Properties, and look at the various properties tabs. Most color inkjet printers have a special settings page that lets you choose to print everything in black and white only, or to print in a "thrifty" mode that saves ink. Use the color and letter- or photo-quality output modes only when you really care about what you're printing.

MULTIMEDIA AND IMAGING

MULTIMEDIA, IMAGING, AND WINDOWS

When Windows was first developed in the mid-1980s, none of the hardware we use today to capture and transform still and video images was available. However, as time passed, still photographers, and more recently, videographers have discovered the computer and its ability to edit, transform, organize, and store their work.

Whether you're a serious photographer with a portfolio that rivals Ansel Adams, a videographer inspired by Stanley Kubrick, or just a casual camera user who's looking for a way to organize the family photo album, Windows XP contains built-in tools and features that are designed to make the marriage of images and pixels a happy one. Even if you plan to replace the multimedia and imaging tools in Windows XP with higher-powered third-party solutions, Windows XP's architecture makes it easier to use the tools you want to use with the photos and video you love to create.

If you're upgrading from Windows Me, some of Windows XP's features will be familiar, although many are new and advanced. If you're upgrading from other versions of Windows, prepare for a brand-new world of Windows, where the operating system is designed to work with photo and video data as well as the other types of data you've traditionally used with your computer.

HOW WINDOWS IMAGE ACQUISITION WORKS

Windows XP works with virtually any type of imaging device you can connect to your computer, including

- Scanners
- Digital cameras
- Web cameras
- DV camcorders

How does Windows XP interface with these devices to capture photos or video? Windows XP uses a technology called Windows Image Acquisition (WIA), originally introduced with Windows Me, which provides a standard method for all types of imaging devices to communicate with Windows.

WIA is designed to go beyond what's been possible with older types of imaging hardware/software interfaces, such as TWAIN and ISIS. If you've used scanners or digital cameras before, you might be familiar with TWAIN (developed by the TWAIN Working Group; www.twain.org), which has been used by most flatbed scanners and some digital cameras to communicate between a host application (such as Adobe Photoshop or other image editors) and the imaging device. TWAIN drivers are available for both Windows and Macs. A similar interface preferred by some scanner and imaging-device vendors is Pixel Translation's Image and Scanner Interface Specification (ISIS; see www.pixtran.com for more information). ISIS supports Windows applications.

7

Although WIA-compatible scanners and digital cameras show up in program image acquisition menus just as TWAIN and ISIS-compatible devices do, there are major differences between WIA and TWAIN:

- WIA is activated immediately when a supported device is connected to the computer or turned on. For example, when you attach your digital camera to your computer and turn it on in Connect mode, WIA immediately brings up a menu of choices for working with your camera's images or starts your preferred application. This makes image transfer easier, even for inexperienced computer users.

- TWAIN and ISIS rely on your application's File/Acquire menu option to scan or retrieve pictures. This makes image transfers more difficult for inexperienced users.

- WIA can offer users a choice of options: copying, viewing, or editing pictures, whereas TWAIN is designed for users who want to edit pictures before saving them.

- WIA supports all types of imaging devices, including video, whereas TWAIN is designed for still image cameras and scanners only.

- WIA provides a universal interface for all types of imaging devices, whereas the details of TWAIN support vary a great deal from device to device.

Although this chapter focuses on Windows XP's built-in WIA support for imaging devices, you might still prefer to use TWAIN or other device-specific support for your imaging device if WIA doesn't support all of its functions.

WHAT'S BUILT IN TO WINDOWS XP FOR PHOTOGRAPHS?

Like digital photography? Own a scanner? Windows XP supports the immense popularity of digital photography and scanning with the following features:

- Scanner and camera wizard—Provides a unified interface for working with all types of digital imaging devices, including digital cameras, card readers, scanners, Web cameras, and DV camcorders with still image options.

- Imaging preview—See your pictures within Windows Explorer.

- My Pictures folder—Provides sorting, organizing, email, Web site publishing, slideshow, and screen saver options for your digital and scanned photos.

- New Photo Printing wizard—High-quality printing using templates for layout.

- Integrated CD burning—Create your own CD-R or CD-RW image archive.

No matter where your digital images come from, these features can help you have more fun and get more use from your photographs. In the following sections, you'll learn how each of these features works.

7

USING THE SCANNER AND CAMERA WIZARD

Windows XP's Scanner and Camera Wizard, originally introduced with Windows Me, provides you with a unified interface for copying pictures from your imaging devices to your computer, your network, or to the World Wide Web.

If you have more than one imaging device supported by Windows XP, the Camera and Scanner wizard displays all supported devices when you start it from the Start menu and allows you to choose the one you want to use (see Figure 7.1). Web cameras, scanners, digital cameras, and card readers are some of the devices the Scanner and Camera Wizard can recognize. It also starts automatically when you press the Scan button on a supported scanner or connect a supported digital camera.

If the Scanner and Camera Wizard is not available on your system, no supported imaging devices have been installed.

Figure 7.1
Click the device you want to use, and click Properties to configure it or OK to capture pictures.

> **TIP**
>
> If you have a choice between a USB-based scanner and other interface types such as SCSI and parallel, choose USB. The Scanner and Camera Wizard automatically detects and uses many USB devices, but may not work with other interface types unless specific Windows XP–compatible drivers are available. If you set up other scanner types with Windows XP/2000 drivers, you might need to use the scanner's own TWAIN interface to scan photos and other media.

USING THE SCANNER AND CAMERA WIZARD WITH A SCANNER

To start the wizard with your scanner, you can push the Scan button on your scanner, open the Scanner and Camera Wizard and choose the scanner from the Scanner and Camera Wizard menu (refer to Figure 7.1), or use the image acquisition feature from within your favorite photo editor or paint program. Image acquisition is located in the File menu of most applications.

When the wizard starts, click Next to continue. Follow this procedure to scan your pictures:

1. On the Choose Scanning Preferences screen, select the picture type and select Preview to prescan your picture with default settings. With some scanners, you may need to press the Scan button to perform the preview (see Figure 7.2).

Figure 7.2
The preview scan has been completed. Use the Custom Settings button to adjust resolution, brightness, and contrast.

2. Click Custom settings to adjust the contrast, brightness, and resolution for the scan (I recommend 75 dpi for scans you plan to use in slideshows, and 150–300 dpi for scans you want to print). Click OK to return to the Choose Scanning Preferences screen and click Next to scan the picture with the settings you've chosen.

3. On the Picture Name and Destination screen, enter a name for the group of pictures you're scanning, select a file format (BMP, JPG, TIF, and PNG are the options), and select a location. The default location is a subfolder beneath the My Pictures folder (see Figure 7.3). Click Next to scan your picture and save it. Each picture is numbered as it is scanned and saved.

TIP

Which file format should you choose? The default, JPEG, creates very small file sizes but does so by discarding fine image detail. Unless you're short on disk space, I recommend TIF, which creates large file sizes but retains all picture detail. Use BMP if you're saving files for use on the desktop. Use PNG for use on Web pages. If you save the file in one format and need to convert it into another later, retrieve the file into Windows Paint and save it in the format you need.

4. After the picture is scanned, the Other Options screen appears (see Figure 7.4). You can choose to publish your pictures online, order prints from a photo printing Web site, or finish working with the pictures. You can also use the Back button to return to previous menus so you can scan more pictures.

7

Figure 7.3
Select a group name, file type, and location for your pictures.

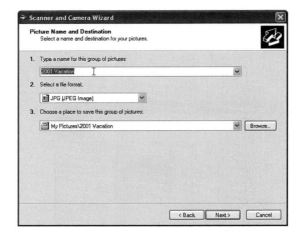

Figure 7.4
To learn more about Windows XP's picture tools, click the Working with Pictures link.

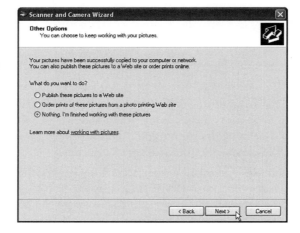

5. Click Next, and the Scanner and Camera Wizard provides an on-screen report of the number of pictures copied (scanned) and their location. Click the link provided to open the folder.

→ For details about the My Pictures folder, **see** "Viewing Images," **p. 219**.

USING THE SCANNER AND CAMERA WIZARD WITH A DIGITAL CAMERA

Start the Scanner and Camera Wizard to retrieve pictures from your digital camera:

1. Connect your device and turn it on.

2. Click Start, All Programs, Accessories, Scanner and Camera Wizard.

3. If you have more than one imaging device, select your digital camera from the opening menu shown in Figure 7.1 and click OK.

4. If you have only a digital camera, after the wizard locates your device, the opening screen of the wizard appears, as shown in Figure 7.5. To continue, click Next.

Figure 7.5
The Scanner and Camera Wizard identifies your device and offers you the option to work directly from the device or use the default wizard interface.

5. By default, all pictures are selected for copying to your computer. To skip a picture, clear the checkmark. To rotate it or see its properties, click the buttons below the picture area (see Figure 7.6).

Figure 7.6
The second and third pictures will not be copied because the user has cleared the check marks. The currently selected picture has a heavy border around it.

6. On the next screen, you can supply a name for the group of pictures (replace the default "Picture" with your own name) and specify where to store the pictures. If you use the default location (a folder beneath the My Pictures folder), you can use My Picture's multimedia and printing enhancements. You can also have the wizard delete the pictures from your device to free up space after copying them to your system.

7

7. The wizard displays each picture while it copies the selected pictures and provides a status display onscreen, shown in Figure 7.7.

Figure 7.7
The wizard displays the process of the copying task.

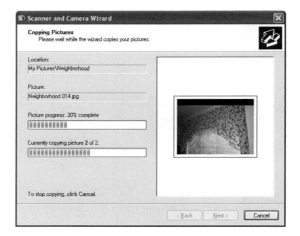

8. If you chose to delete the pictures from your imaging device, the wizard will also delete them and inform you of its progress.

9. When the pictures have been copied, you can choose to publish your pictures online, order prints from a photo printing Web site, or finish working with the pictures. You can also use the Back button to return to previous menus so you can copy pictures you skipped (refer to Figure 7.4).

10. Click Next, and the Scanner and Camera Wizard provides an on-screen report of the number of pictures copied and their location. Click the link provided to open the folder.

→ For details about the My Pictures folder, **see** "Viewing Images," **p. 219**.

USING A CARD READER

When you plug a flash memory card containing pictures into your card reader, you can choose from several actions (see Figure 7.8):

- **Start the Scanner and Camera Wizard**—The wizard works with flash memory cards the same way it does with digital cameras. For more information, see "Using the Scanner and Camera Wizard with a Digital Camera," earlier in this chapter.

- **View a slideshow**—This displays each picture on-screen for a few seconds and continues until you press the Esc key. For more information about slideshows, see "Using Slideshow," later in this chapter.

- **Print pictures directly from the media with the Photo Printing wizard**—For more information about printing, see "Using the Photo Printing Wizard," later in this chapter.

Figure 7.8
When you insert a flash memory card containing photos into your card reader, Windows XP displays options to help you copy, view, and print your photos.

- **Open folder to view files**—This option starts the Windows Explorer. For more information about using this option, see "Using the Windows Explorer to View Your Photos," later in this chapter.

- **Take no action**—Select this option to leave the contents of the flash memory card alone until you decide what you want to do.

Check Always Do the Selected Action after you choose an action if you want to make that action the default.

TIP

> Use the Always Do the Selected Action option only if you're sure you always want to perform the same task with your pictures. If you leave this box unchecked, you can choose the task you want every time you insert your flash memory card. It takes only a couple of mouse clicks, so my advice is to keep your freedom and don't choose a default action to perform.

VIEWING IMAGES

Windows XP provides you with two ways to view your pictures:

- Through Windows Explorer
- As a slideshow

Which one is better for you? That depends on whether you're looking for immediate gratification or for long-term storage and enjoyment of your pictures. The following sections show you how to use both options.

7

USING WINDOWS EXPLORER TO VIEW YOUR PHOTOS

If you select the Windows Explorer option when you read the photos from your flash memory card, view pictures stored in My Pictures folder or a subfolder, or view the contents of a folder containing photos, Windows Explorer activates several special features designed to make working with your image files easier.

Instead of the normal large icons display of files, Windows Explorer switches to a special Filmstrip display option, which uses a large window on the right side of the screen to display the selected picture and shows other pictures in smaller size below navigation and image-rotation buttons (see Figure 7.9). You can use the navigation buttons to select which photo to display, or click on the photo you want to see in the large view.

Figure 7.9
The filmstrip view is used automatically by Windows XP when you view a folder containing photos.

TIP

If the filmstrip view isn't selected automatically, click the View tool or the View menu and select Filmstrip. If Filmstrip isn't available because the images are not the correct type or the folder has a mixture of image files and other files, Filmstrip won't be listed as an option.

The File menu in Explorer also changes when you select a photo, providing the following options:

- **Preview**—Opens the photo in the Windows Picture and Fax Viewer
- **Edit**—Opens the photo in an image editor
- **Print**—Opens the photo printing wizard

- **Refresh thumbnail**—Generates a new thumbnail preview of the picture (useful if you've edited the picture)
- **Rotate clockwise/counterclockwise**—Rotates picture in 90-degree increments
- **Set as Desktop Background**—Puts your digital masterpiece on the Windows desktop
- **Open with**—Selects another program to open this picture
- **Send to**—Sends photo to a compressed folder, removable-media drive, or My Documents folder; creates a desktop shortcut; or provides other destinations
- **Properties**—Displays file properties

TIP

> By default, the Edit menu in Explorer uses Windows Paint to edit photos. If you prefer another image editor (and who wouldn't?), right-click a photo and select Open With. Windows XP will display Paint and Windows Picture and Fax Viewer, as well as Choose Program. Click Choose Program and select the program you want to use if it's listed, or click Browse to locate the program you prefer. To keep this choice for all files of the same type, check the Always Use the Selected Program box. You also can search the Web for a suitable program. Click OK when you're finished.

USING SLIDESHOW

Making a slideshow of your pictures once required you to fire up a program like PowerPoint and click and paste your way through your digital stack of photos. If all you want to do is view your photos on-screen, you no longer need any third-party software: just select the slideshow option when it's available within a folder or from the card reader's menu.

Windows XP's slideshow option is very simple: It sequences the images in a folder with five seconds per photo and continues to show the pictures in a loop until you press the Esc key on your keyboard.

An on-screen toolbar lets you play, pause, move to the previous photo or next photo, or exit the show. You can also use the following keyboard commands to control the show as shown in Table 7.1.

TABLE 7.1   SLIDESHOW CONTROL KEYS

Action Desired	Keys to Press
Go to the previous picture in the folder.	Left arrow or Page Up or up arrow
Go to the next picture in the folder.	Right arrow or Page Down or down arrow
Rotate picture 90 degrees clockwise.	Ctrl+K
Rotate picture 90 degrees counterclockwise.	Ctrl+L

7

continues

TABLE 7.1 CONTINUED

Action Desired	Keys to Press
Play or pause the slide show (press once to pause, again to play).	Spacebar
Go to the next picture.	Enter
Exit the show.	Esc
Hide or display toolbar on or off (toggle).	Tab

TIP

> If you don't want to display all the images in a folder during your slide show, just select the ones you want to view with Ctrl-Click or Shift-Click, and then click the Slideshow button on the left side of the Explorer screen or choose Slideshow from the menu. Only the slides you've selected will be displayed.

USING THE PHOTO PRINTING WIZARD

Windows XP's Slideshow feature can show you your digital photos immediately. How about instant prints from your digital photos? Thanks to the brand-new Photo Printing wizard, you can have pictures as fast as your printer can produce them, and get them in a variety of sizes.

You can start the Photo Printing wizard from

- The flash memory card opening menu
- The Picture Tasks menu in a photo folder
- The pull-down menu in a photo folder
- The File and Folder tasks menu in a regular folder

When the wizard starts, here's how to use it:

1. The Photo Printing wizard displays its opening screen. Click Next to continue.
2. The Picture Selection screen lets you select the pictures you want to print. Clear or add checkmarks to select the pictures you want to print and click Next to continue.
3. On the Printing Options screen, select the printer you want to use (if you have more than one printer). Click the Properties button to select the paper type, print quality, and other document properties (see Figure 7.10). Click the Advanced button to adjust the number of copies to print and other advanced printer features. Click OK to return to the Printing Options menu, then click Next.

7

Figure 7.10
For best results in photo printing, choose the paper type you're using from the list of paper types.

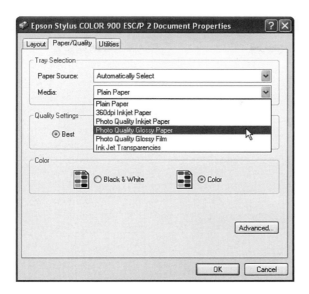

TIP

> If you haven't used your inkjet printer for several days, or your printouts are of poor quality, you should click the Utilities tab (if available) and run your printer's head cleaning or nozzle test options with plain paper inserted in your printer (take out the photo paper until you're ready to print a good print). Head and nozzle clogs will ruin your printout and waste expensive photo paper, and most recent printers also offer a cleaning routine on this tab. If your printer doesn't have a menu option for head cleaning, check the instruction manual for the correct method to use. You might need to press buttons on the printer to activate a built-in head-cleaning routine.

4. Use the Layout selection screen to select how your photos should be laid out on the photo paper. Select from full-page; contact sheets; or sizes such as 3.5×5, 4×6, 5×7, and 8×10, and wallets. The preview shows you how your pictures will be laid out on each page. If you select a size which allows for multiple photos on a page, each image will be laid out once unless you specify a larger number (see Figure 7.11). Click Next to print your photos.

COPYING YOUR PICTURES TO A CD-RW DRIVE

CD-RW drives, which can use either rewritable CD-RW media or recordable CD-R media, have become some of the hottest peripheral options on the market. While previous versions of Windows couldn't use these drives until you installed CD-mastering software, Windows XP has built-in features which allow you to use a supported CD-RW drive as soon as you install or connect it and turn on your computer.

7

Figure 7.11
Select the layout you want, and the print preview displays your photos accordingly.

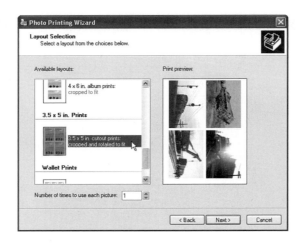

When Windows XP detects a supported CD-RW, the Picture Tasks menu lists Copy to CD as an option. Here's how to use it:

1. If you want to copy only some of the pictures in your folder, select the pictures you want to copy and click Copy to CD.

2. To copy all photos in the folder to CD, don't select any pictures first. Then click Copy all items to CD.

3. The pictures are copied to the CD-RW folder

4. Repeat steps 1–3 for other folders that contain pictures you want to add to the CD.

5. Click My Computer in the Other Places menu.

6. Double-click the CD drive where you will store your pictures.

7. The folders you are going to copy are displayed under Files Ready to Be Written to the CD. If you've used the CD for other pictures previously, they will also be listed (see Figure 7.12).

> **TIP**
>
> To see a small preview of your picture files as shown in Figure 7.12, select Thumbnails from the View menu or View tool instead of the default Icons view. This provides you with an easy way to make sure you're copying only the pictures you want.

8. Click Write these files to the CD from the CD Writing Tasks menu at the left side of the screen and the CD Writing Wizard opens.

9. Enter the name of the CD on the opening screen. If you want to create just one CD, select Close the Wizard. Otherwise, click Next to continue.

7

Figure 7.12
Displaying the files to be written to the CD and those already on the CD with Thumbnail view.

10. If your pictures were stored in a folder, the wizard creates a folder on the CD for the pictures. While the wizard writes the files to the CD, it displays a progress indicator onscreen (see Figure 7.13).

Figure 7.13
The CD Writing Wizard provides you constant updates on its progress in creating your CD.

11. The system ejects your CD after copying your picture(s). Click Yes to create another CD if you want or close the wizard. If you elected to close the wizard in Step 9, the wizard closes automatically.

Your photo folders act as regular folders once they've been copied to the CD. If you want to use the special imaging features such as slideshow or photo printing discussed earlier in this chapter, select a file in the folder, open the File menu and select Preview. The picture is

7

loaded into the Windows Picture and Fax Viewer, which has buttons for photo printing, slide shows, image rotation, editing, and other imaging options, as shown in Figure 7.14. You can use the forward and back buttons to select other files in the folder.

Figure 7.14
The Windows Picture and Fax Viewer provides access to imaging features for picture folders on your CD or pictures located in regular folders anywhere on your system.

WORKING WITH YOUR PICTURES ONLINE

If you're like most photographers, you don't want your pictures to spend their life inside a shoebox (or inside a folder on your hard disk). Windows XP offers two online options that help other people enjoy your pictures:

- Publish photos to the Web
- Ordering prints online

PUBLISHING YOUR PHOTOS TO THE WEB

When you open a folder containing photos, one of the File and Folder Tasks available in the left-hand side of your screen is "Publish this folder/file to the Web."

Here's how to use this feature to make your pictures available on the Web:

1. If you want to publish only some of your photos, select them first, and then click Publish. Otherwise, click Publish.

2. The Web Publishing Wizard starts and makes your Internet connection (if you're not already connected). Click Next to continue.

3. Files which will be published are check-marked. Add or remove checkmarks if desired, then click Next.

4. Select a service provider from those listed, such as MSN and Xdrive. If you select MSN and you don't have a .NET Passport yet, you must complete the .NET Passport wizard that appears and continue. See Chapter 10, "Sending Email with Outlook Express," for details.

5. On the File Destination screen, select the destination folder you want to use, or create a new folder. Click Next to continue.

6. On the Adjust picture size dialog box, you can choose to resize your pictures to fit either a Small (640×480 browser window; default), Medium (800×600 browser window), or Large (1024×768 browser window). Clear the checkbox to leave your photos at their original size.

TIP

> The most common screen size today is 800×600. If you want to create a fast-loading Web page that maximizes screen area for most users, select Medium.

7. Click Next to publish your photos to your chosen provider. If you are publishing only a few pictures or have a broadband (cable modem, DSL, or two-way wireless or satellite) connection, the copying process may take only a few seconds. If you are using an analog (56Kbps or slower) modem or are copying many pictures, the process could take several minutes. Photos stored in the JPEG (.JPG) format use less disk space and can be published faster than other types of photos. JPEG photos also can be viewed over the Web by standard browsers without using special software. If you plan to publish your photos to the Web, save a copy of each photo as a JPEG file.

8. At the end of the process, a URL for your pictures is displayed and a matching shortcut is added to your My Network Places folder (see Figure 7.15). Close the wizard and your site is displayed.

Figure 7.15
Web Publishing Wizard displays your pictures' URL.

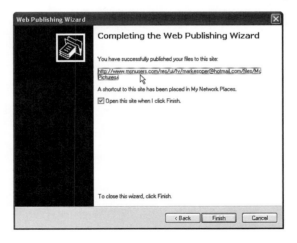

9. If you want to show off your pictures to others, just click on the shortcut in My Network Places, or enter the URL when you're with friends and family (you must provide your username and password assigned by the service you selected for your photos). Any computer with Internet access becomes a virtual photo album.

7

TIP

> The Web Publishing Wizard's not the way to go if you're trying to share pictures with other users when you're not present. If you want to share your photos with everyone, look into a free Web site from www.tripod.lycos.com or www.freehomepage.com. These services also offer Web-page building programs which can help you organize your pictures with more options than Microsoft's Web Publishing Wizard provides.

ORDERING PRINTS ONLINE

If your inkjet printer is saying "enough already!" as you insert yet another stack of 4×6 snapshot photo stock or if your printer is simply not up to the task, you might want to try the Online Print Ordering Wizard.

To use the wizard, follow these steps:

1. Click Order Prints Online from the Picture Tasks menu.
2. When the opening screen of the Online Print Ordering Wizard appears, click Next to continue.
3. Select the pictures you want to use for reprints.
4. Select the service from those listed (see Figure 7.16).

Figure 7.16
Choosing a printing company for reprints of your digital images.

5. Complete the order form that the vendor provides and enter your payment and shipping information when prompted. Depending on the vendor you choose, you can order prints, enlargements, gifts, and novelty items (such as mugs, T-shirts, jigsaw puzzles, and mousepads) from your pictures.

TIP

> Digital pictures printed by an online vendor are higher quality than those you can produce with your inkjet printer, but the quality of the images you send to the vendor affect the prints you'll get back. For best results:
>
> - Scan your prints at 150 dpi for snapshots; use 300 dpi if you're scanning only part of a picture.
> - Scan 35mm slides and negatives (which are much smaller than prints) at 1350 dpi or higher for 4×6-inch prints.
> - Use a two-megapixel digital camera (1536×1024) or greater resolution for 4×6-inch or larger prints, and set the camera to use highest quality and high resolution. The minimum camera resolution recommended for 4×6-inch prints is 640×480 (the "VGA" setting on some cameras); remember, more pixels in the original image means better quality in the final print.
> - The digital still mode on most DV camcorders is usually not nearly high enough quality for printing, although the results will look acceptable on-screen.
> - Order just a few digital prints from a new vendor and evaluate the quality before you place a big order.

GOING BEYOND WINDOWS XP'S BUILT-IN IMAGING TOOLS

Windows XP's imaging tools make it easy to get digital images into your computer and keep them organized, but unless you're a perfect photographer, some of those images will need cropping, color-correcting, and other enhancements that Windows XP's tools don't offer.

Because WIA-compatible devices can be used from the Acquire menu of your favorite image editor, just as TWAIN-compatible digital cameras and scanners can be, you can use virtually any third-party photo-editing program you prefer to acquire your pictures, or retrieve them from a photo folder for editing after you copy them to your system with the Camera and Scanner Wizard or other Windows XP tool.

My favorite is Adobe Photoshop (www.adobe.com), which is immensely powerful, offering layers, automation, and many different ways to control brightness, contrast, and image appearance, but is also quite expensive. If you're on a budget, some capable alternatives include Jasc Software's Paint Shop Pro (www.jasc.com) and Corel PhotoPaint (www.corel.com), which is part of CorelDraw.

In addition to the product sites listed above, check out these online resources:

- **Imaging Resource (www.imaging-resource.com)**—Covers the gamut of imaging hardware and software products, and has the unique "Comparometer" feature which compares the actual output of any two digital cameras from their huge database.
- **DPReview (www.dpreview.com)**—The interactive buying guide helps you get the digital camera that matches the features you want, and its unique "Timeline" shows you when the camera you own was introduced.

7

- **FocalFix (`www.focalfix.com`)**—The new name for Focus Online, where readers review their favorite products.
- **John Cowley's Lonestardigital.com**—A long name for a great site with product reviews and tutorials on both digital imaging hardware and software.

VIDEO CAPTURE AND EDITING WITH MICROSOFT MOVIE MAKER 2

If you prefer moving images to stills, or combining the two, Windows XP provides a video-friendly environment. By using the Windows Movie Maker program, Windows XP can capture video from

- Web cameras
- DV camcorders
- Analog camcorders
- VHS and other video players
- Little movie-ettes that many still cameras make

Windows Movie Maker can then be used to edit your video into movies you save on your hard disk, removable-media drive, prepared for a Web page or for emailing, or to burn to a CD for playback on systems using Windows Media Player.

The editing process that Windows Movie Maker and other digital video editing programs use is often referred to as *non-linear editing (NLE)*, because you can arrange different digital movie sources in any order, and don't need to physically cut or damage video tape or film to edit your movies.

Windows Movie Maker has evolved greatly since version 1. We suspect that Microsoft is trying to keep up with Apple's iMovie, which runs on the Mac only. I've compared the two programs and, risking being written hate mail by Mac defenders, I will report they are roughly comparable in features. Each has its strengths, but with either program, you can become proficient at producing eye-catching videos within a day's time. Movie Maker actually has some very cool output options that exceed those of iMovie. For example, you can output a movie for a PocketPC, email, Web streaming, or playback on CD-ROM drives.

Of course, professionals spend a lifetime learning their trade and there is no replacement for experience, good judgment, an artistic eye, and a studio-grade NLE system. But just the fact that today's computers are powerful enough to do non-linear editing *and* a decent program comes *free* with Windows XP is a mind blower, as far as I'm concerned. But I guess I'm dating myself. I remember when a word processor was a big deal. Now we're talking about a video processor, essentially.

Just a little caveat here. This book isn't big enough to include full-blown coverage of Movie Maker. I've worked with it for quite some time and have discovered how rich a program it is. If you're interested in playing with video editing, I suggest you do the same. I'll just get you going in this section; you'll have to take it from there.

The Hardware You Need

You will need a video capture card or USB device to capture video from an analog camcorder or video tape player. Some video cards, such as the All-in-Wonder series from ATI, and an increasing number of desktop computers have TV-in jacks that can also be used for analog video capture.

If your Web camera is supported by Windows XP, you can use it for video capture without any additional hardware.

You will need a supported IEEE-1394 (FireWire) port or add-on card to capture video from a DV camcorder, and Windows XP also must have support for the DV camcorder if you want to interface directly with Windows Movie Maker.

I have made numerous movies based on only the little 30-second videos my tiny pocket digital still camera takes. Although the source files the camera shoots aren't as high a resolution as, say, a DV camcorder, they are not terrible. And because the camera fits in my shirt pocket, I always have it. Many people overlook the 'movie' feature in their digital still cameras, but if they knew it was so easy to create a clever movie of virtually any length (by combining the short clips), with special effects, background music, and titles, they might think again. On the day after an event like a wedding or party, when I show up with a CD that has a 15-minute movie of the event, complete with background music, transitions, effects, and titles, people are stunned. They didn't even see that I was shooting video.

> **TIP**
>
> If Windows Movie Maker doesn't support your video hardware but it can be used with third-party software, capture your data with third-party software and save it in a Windows-Movie-Maker–compatible format, such as `.mpeg`, `.mpg`, `.m1v`, `.mp2`, `.mpa`, `.mpe`, `.asf`, `.avi`, or `.wmv`. You can import these types of files into Windows Movie Maker. Note that you can only create (or output) .WMV files, however.

Using a Laptop to Capture and Edit DV

Some new laptops have FireWire ports, but not many, at this point. Most of the Sony VAIO models do, but that's about it. Don't have a VAIO? Not a problem. Adding a FireWire port to your laptop is easy. Not only that, if you have a relatively fast laptop you can do DV capture on it, and even nonlinear editing in the DV format (even broadcast-quality stuff).

First, get yourself a mini-FireWire card that plugs into the PCMCIA slot on the side of your laptop. A laptop FireWire card will run you less than $100 and open up a whole new world in both video and storage options. I have two FireWire cards—one from SIIG and one from KeySpan. I have two because I do lots of laptop video capturing and have a couple of computers I work with.

When I've shot my video and am ready to pull it into the computer for editing, I plug in my DV camcorder, launch my capture program, (Ulead Media Studio Pro) and suck in the DV video directly to my computer's hard disk. My 1GHz HP laptop has nary a hiccough while keeping up with large amount of incoming data from

7

the camera. This amazed me, because previously I was using a desktop computer with 512MB RAM and 100GB of hard disk space to do this. People will try to sell you all kinds of fancy, expensive, SCSI hard-disk arrays to capture and edit full-frame (720×480) DV, but it's not necessary. My HP laptop's 4200-RPM 30GB internal drive does quite fine.

For additional storage space (which you'll need if you intend to produce feature movies or even hour-long home movies, and so on), you easily can add disk space to your laptop or desktop computer. I am very keen on the new Maxtor line of external FireWire drives. They are small, quiet (no fan), and attractive. And, because a single FireWire port can have 63 devices *daisychained* (connected in series), believe me, you needn't run out of space to store your videos. In my video business, I have successfully recorded and edited many hours of video on the external FireWire drives I have stacked up. Setting up a home video-editing system doesn't take a million bucks anymore. You can even edit high-class movies while sipping a cappuccino at your favorite cafè.

The first time you attach a supported DV camcorder to your Windows XP system and turn it on, WIA displays the menu shown in Figure 7.17. You can start Windows Movie Maker or take no action. To make Windows Movie Maker the default action, select it, and then checkmark the Always perform the selected action box below the displayed options.

Figure 7.17
Digital video device actions in Windows XP.

When you select Windows Movie Maker, the Windows Movie Maker opening screen is displayed briefly, then, the Video Capture Wizard box is displayed.

1. You might be offered the choice between different video and audio inputs for your capture. (If not, go to step 2.) If you have more than one video or audio source, you can choose between them. Depending on the sources you have (such as analog or digital video), you see different options. In general, DV gives you very few options because they are unnecessary. After choosing the source and related options, click Next.

2. Enter the name of the file to record to and select the destination folder. By default, captured files go into My Documents/My Videos. Make sure there is plenty of room (think gigs, not megs) on the destination drive because video files are large. Browse to a different drive or folder if necessary. Click Next.

3. In the next dialog box, choose the movie quality (see Figure 7.18). This setting determines how the file is captured, how large the file size on disk is, and ultimately the output quality level of the resulting movie. The Other Settings option gives you a raft of options for target device, such as Pocket PCs, Web streaming, and so on. The information panel at the bottom of the dialog box helps you decide between the options. (You can also click the link Learn More About Video Settings.) Click Next.

Figure 7.18
Setting quality for
your movies.

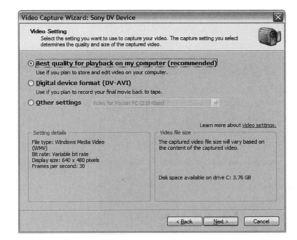

4. In the next dialog box, you decide whether to let the capture driver rewind the entire tape and record it automatically (breaking it into clips you can rearrange, easily cut and paste, and so on) or whether you want to manually select sections of tape to import. Click Next.

5. If you chose the manual approach, you now see a dialog box with device controls and some other information and options in it. You can advance, rewind, and preview the picture using this dialog box. You can also use the controls on your video camera or playback device instead. Either works. Advance the tape to the start point and then use the Start Capture and Stop Capture buttons in the dialog box to create your clips. Movie Maker can also be instructed to make clips from the section you captured. It does this by making a separate clip each time you press the Start Capture and Stop Capture buttons. Notice also that the dialog box reports the available disk space on the target drive. This is only somewhat useful because it doesn't tell you how many minutes of tape you can capture on that drive using the selected quality. That depends on the capture settings you chose. You have to experiment to figure this out, unfortunately.

Each file you save is referred to as a collection of one or more clips in Windows Movie Maker.

7

IMPORTING DIGITAL STILL CAMERA MOVIES, SNAPS, AND SOUND FILES

As I mentioned earlier in the chapter, if you want to import videos you shot on your digital still camera, you can do it. Once imported, use those as the basis of your movie or to spice up your other imported video. Simply do this:

1. In the left panel of Movie Maker, expand the Capture Video section and click Import Video.

2. Browse to the video file(s) you want, and select them.

3. Click Import.

They are added to your working collection to later be put on the movie timeline.

When I make movies, I often want to pull in still images, too. Many folks have digital cameras these days, so images are easy to come by. These add richness to your productions. Use the same technique as before, but click Import Pictures instead of Import Video.

You can import audio tracks, too, for enhancing your movies by adding theme songs, background music, speech, and so forth. Do the following:

1. Click Import Audio or Music and browse to the file. Many popular sound file formats are supported (not QuickTime or Real Media, but the oh-so-common MP3 is, at least).

2. Select the file(s) and click Import (or just double-click the file).

ORGANIZING YOUR CLIPS

The next task is to get organized. You need to get your video clips, stills, and audio into the same collection so you can easily see them in the collection bin. This makes pulling them onto the timeline in the order you want easier. Follow these steps:

1. Click the Collections button in the toolbar. The collections panel appears on the left.

2. Right-click Collections (in the left panel), and select Create New Collection. Give it a name, such as `Dan's Birthday Party`.

3. Now drag all your captured video clips, audio clips, and stills for this video production into this collection. (There are other ways to organize collections, such as keeping all the video clips in one collection, audio in another, and so forth, but glomming them all together for a given project is the one I use most often.) Move objects around just as you do in Windows Explorer. That is, drag the thumbnails in the middle pane over to the destination collection in the left pane. Or, import them into a collection by highlighting the new collection name and then clicking File, Import into Collections. You can also drag files from a Windows Explorer window. Figure 7.19 shows my collection setup for making my Birthday Party movie.

NOTE

> You can resize the sections of the Movie Maker window, such as the Preview pane and Collections pane, by dragging the dividing lines.

Figure 7.19
Getting your clips organized into a collection makes putting them on the timeline an easier job.

TURNING YOUR VIDEO CLIPS INTO A SIMPLE MOVIE

Next, you start piecing together your movie by dragging your movie clips and still images into the Windows Movie Maker storyboard, which is the filmstrip-like area at the bottom of the screen. The clips you drag to the storyboard are positioned left-to-right (you can change the order later). The movie eventually plays starting with the leftmost clip and moves to the right, through all the clips in order.

Figure 7.20 shows the storyboard area after adding various clips from DV video I captured while making a movie called Dan's Birthday Party.

To play only the currently-selected video clip in the Collections pane, click the triangular Play button beneath the preview window. To play the entire storyboard, click Play, Play Storyboard/Timeline from the top-level menu. Use the keys in Table 7.2 to control playback:

TABLE 7.2   WINDOWS MOVIE MAKER PLAYBACK CONTROL KEYS

Key	Action
Spacebar	Toggles pause/playback
Period	Stop playback
Alt+Left arrow	Display previous frame
Alt+Right arrow	Display next frame

continues

7

TABLE 7.2   CONTINUED

Key	Action
Alt+Ctrl+Left arrow	Moves to previous clip
Alt+Ctrl+Right arrow	Moves to next clip
Alt+Enter	Toggles full screen display

Figure 7.20
A simple movie built from various video clips displayed in storyboard view.

EDITING YOUR MOVIE

After you drag your clips and images to the storyboard, you can use various tools to adjust the length of each clip, the order of your clips, and the transitions between each clip. I like to trim my clips at least roughly before I add transitions between them, add background music, credits, and so on.

To change the length of each clip (called *trimming*) , you must use timeline view; click View, Timeline or click the Show Timeline button just above the storyboard. The timeline replaces the storyboard at the bottom of your screen. To change the order of clips, you should be in storyboard view. To edit and trim clips and adjust details of the timing of clips, use Timeline view.

When you have your clips in the basic order you want, you typically have to make adjustments such as these:

- Trim off the beginning and end of a clip.
- Split a clip into two or more clips so you can move them around on the timeline independently, do transitions between the sections, or apply different effects to each portion.
- Combine two clips together if you accidentally split them or because working with a smaller number of clips is easier.

To adjust the length of each clip, do the following:

1. Switch to timeline view if necessary.
2. Click the + or – symbols just above the timeline or select the View/Zoom commands to zoom in or out (making the clips appear larger or smaller). Zooming lets you accurately adjust the clip. You might have to scroll the timeline left and right a bit to find your clip. Use the scrollbar at the bottom of the Movie Maker window.
3. Click the clip in the timeline. Notice that, if you hover the mouse pointer over the right or left edge of the clip, a red sizing arrow appears. Now you can drag the clip.
4. To delete the end of the clip, move the trim handle at the start of the clip to the right to the point where you want the clip to start; to delete the end of the clip, drag the trim handle at the end of the clip to the left until you reach the point where you want the clip to end.

TIP

If you're trying to shorten the end of a video clip, play the video clip from start to finish, then play it again and stop it at the point where you want to cut it. A vertical line in the timeline shows the playback location. Move the trim handle at the end of the clip until it is lined up with the vertical line.

You can't make a video clip be longer than its original length—you can only trim it. (Well, you can make it play in slow motion; see the "Adding Video Effects (Filters) to Your Clips" section.) However, still images can play for any length of time. Just drag the still image's edge down the timeline. By default, stills have a length of 5 seconds.

You can scrub across the timeline and see your movie play. Just position the pointer on the time area (it looks like a ruler) of the timeline view. Then click and drag. The video plays sort of jerkily. If you click a spot in the timeline ruler and then click the Play button in the Preview window, the preview starts from that point. This is useful for working on a specific area of the movie.

To move a clip from one position to another, you can use either drag and drop or cut and paste. I prefer drag and drop if I can see the source clip and destination location at the same time. Otherwise, I use cut and paste. To use drag and drop, do this:

1. Switch to storyboard view (it is not required but is easier to use than timeline view).
2. Drag the clip left or right on the timeline. A vertical line indicates where it will be inserted (always just *before* any clip you are hovering over).

7

To use cut and paste, do this:

1. Switch to storyboard view (not required, but easier to use than timeline view).
2. Right-Click the clip in the storyboard.
3. Choose Cut.
4. Click the clip in the timeline that will be *behind* the clip when you paste it in.
5. Click Edit, Paste.

ADDING TRANSITIONS BETWEEN CLIPS

Movie Maker comes with 60 transition effects to use between clips. *Transitions* control how one clip blends into the next. The default transition is called a *flat cut*. Actually, most film and TV transitions are flat cuts—they happen so quickly we barely notice them. Transitions add life to your creations. Like fonts, though, you can easily overuse transitions. However, an occasional transition is useful, especially between still images or for a special effect such as in a music video.

> **TIP**
>
> You can download more from various online sources such as this one:
>
> ```
> http://www.microsoft.com/windowsxp/downloads/powertoys/
> mmcreate.mspx
> ```

There are several ways to add transitions to your production. To create a transition effect from one scene to another:

1. Switch to Storyboard view. Zoom in as necessary. Notice the little box between each clip; this is the placeholder for a transition.
2. In the Collections pane, click Transitions. A bunch of transitions appear in the middle pane. Double-click any one of them to see the effect played in the Preview window. When you find the one you want, drag it to the little box between the two clips you're transitioning between. In Figure 7.21, I have just added a checkerboard transition between two clips marked by the pointer.

> **TIP**
>
> You can drag transitions between transition placeholders on the timeline, and you can remove a transition by right-clicking it and selecting Delete.
>
> You can control the length of a *dissolve* (one clip fades into the next) by overlapping the clips on the timeline.

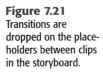

Figure 7.21
Transitions are dropped on the placeholders between clips in the storyboard.

Adding Video Effects (Filters) to Your Clips

Video effects are fun to play with. If you've used Photoshop filters, you know what these are. They change the look of a clip, for example from color to black and white. The nearly 30 supplied effects run the gamut from painterly, to old fashioned, to slow motion, to even psychedelic. For still shots, there are a few transitions that add a sense of motion. This approach is often used in professional documentaries. Filters are also available for fading in and out, rotating clips, and increasing and decreasing brightness.

When you apply an effect, it alters the way the entire clip plays back. It does not alter the actual clip file on your hard disk; it is just applied as the movie runs and to the final output file you create when you save the movie after editing. You can remove effects at any time, so don't hesitate to experiment. If you split the clip, both halves keep the effect.

Here's how to apply a video effect:

1. Switch to storyboard view. (Timeline view works, but I think it's graphically easier to use storyboard view.)

2. In the Collections pane, click Video Effects. The middle pane should show thumbnails of the available effects (see Figure 7.22). (You can select View/Details to see descriptions of each effect instead of thumbnails.)

3. Double-click an effect to see how it works. If you like it, drag and drop it on a clip and then click the Play button on the Preview pane to see the effect on the actual clip. If you don't like the effect, right-click the clip and select Video Effects to bring up a dialog box. Click the effect you dislike and click Remove.

7

4. You can add multiple video effects to a single clip. Effects for that clip are processed in the order listed in the Video Effects dialog box.

Figure 7.22
Applying effects to clips is easy. Just drag and drop the effect on the clip.

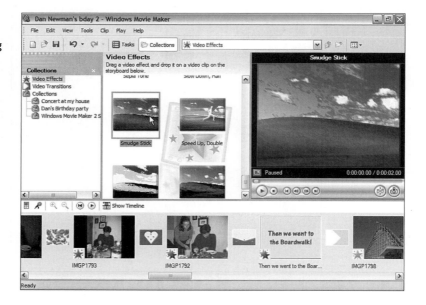

ADDING NARRATION TO YOUR MOVIE

You can record narration for your movie when the movie is in timeline mode if you have a microphone attached to your computer. To record narration:

1. Select Timeline mode.

2. Position the cursor somewhere on the timeline where there is no other audio track. (The Audio/Music track is visible below the video track.) Click File, Record Narration.

3. The Record Narration Track pane appears (see Figure 7.23). Click Show More Options to see the default audio device and input source, as shown in Figure 7.23. To change the defaults, use the drop-down lists.

4. You should click Mute Speakers if you have your sound turned up because it prevents feedback between the speakers and the microphone.

5. Adjust the recording level as desired (the level should be somewhere near the middle of the colorful Input level meter).

6. Click Start Narration to begin. Click Stop Narration when you're finished. You are asked to name the file. It's saved as a .wma (Windows Media audio) file and then automatically dropped into the timeline in exactly the place where you started narration.

7

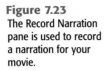

Figure 7.23
The Record Narration pane is used to record a narration for your movie.

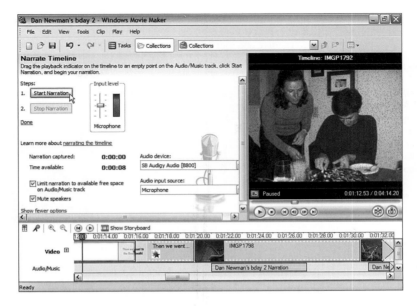

ADDING TITLES TO YOUR MOVIE

Although Windows Movie Maker version 1 doesn't have built-in titling features, version 2 does. And they are pretty spiffy. There are many styles to choose from. You can have titles appear over the top of clips and stills or as separate slides (like in an old silent movie). You can also create opening and closing animated titles and credits just like in real movies or TV shows. You can spend a few hours just playing with the titling options, so I'll just point you in the right direction.

To add an opening title sequence, select Tools, Titles and Credits. In a few seconds the titler loads into the left pane.

Notice the options you have now. You can add a title

- At the beginning of the movie
- Before a selected clip
- On the selected clip
- After the selected clip
- At the end of the movie

Click the desired option. As you enter your titles, they immediately show up in the Preview pane as they will appear in your movie. The real key lies in the options near the bottom of the titler pane: Change the Title Animation and Change the Text Font and Color. Play with these to get some fun effects. See Figure 7.24 for an example.

7

TIP

A Title Overlay track is on the timeline, below the audio track. You can slide titles around down there and trim their lengths, just as you can stills and video clips.

Figure 7.24
The titler pane, for creating overlays, intro credits, and ending credits, hosts a myriad of built-in animated title looks.

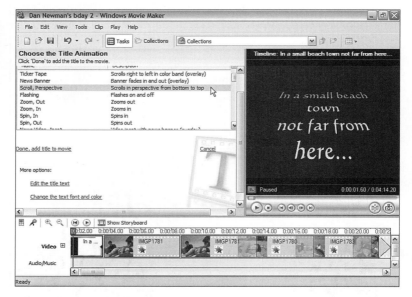

SAVING YOUR PROJECT AND SAVING YOUR MOVIE

There are two ways to save your work in Windows Movie Maker. To save the various parts of your movie (the clips on the timeline and the storyboard), click File, Save Project. By default, your Windows Movie Maker Project (.MSWMM) file will be saved to the My Videos folder. Give your project a name, and save it.

You should save your projects frequently during the creation and editing process. If you don't, and a system lockup or power outage takes place, your clips will remain, but the structure and timing of your film will be lost, and it will be back to the digital "cutting room" to start over.

Here's how to save your movie:

1. Click File, Save Project.
2. Give it a name and location and click Save.

Now your project is saved and safe. You can open it again and fine-tune the project, add to it as you capture more video, or whatever. You can close Movie Maker if you want and then open it and open the project. All the items in the collection should appear, as will the timeline and storyboard, just as it was when you saved it.

Next, you should make sure you are happy with the movie. When you are, you can *render* it, which means to output it in the desired format. This can take a little time, so be ready to take a coffee break while your computer chugs away. Because rendering does take time, you should do a dry run of your final movie beforehand. You can see it in the preview window or at full screen. Simply select Play, Play Timeline. If you're happy with it, great. If not, edit it as necessary. When you're satisfied with the movie, try outputting it to the target medium and see how it looks:

1. The easiest way to render is to bring up the Movie Tasks sidebar (click Tasks in the toolbar). Then expand the Finish Movie section. You'll see these choices: Save to My Computer, Save to CD, Send in Email, Send to the Web, and Send to DV Camera. Select the option you desire, and move ahead.

2. A wizard runs, asking you for additional details that pertain to your choice. For example, if you chose to make the movie available to viewers over the Web, you have to decide what connection speed your viewers will likely be using (see Figure 7.25). Also reported are the size of the final file and how much space is left on your hard drive (the hard disk is always used as the intermediary for rendering). The file is written from the hard disk to the target destination.

NOTE

Movies saved to a recordable CD are saved by using Microsoft HighMAT technology. A HighMAT (High-performance Media Access Technology) CD can contain audio, video, and pictures. HighMAT-compatible consumer electronic devices recognize how the content is organized on the CD and enable users to play content using the displayed menus. The recordable CD can be played back on a computer as well. Be aware that some older standalone DVD players don't recognize this format and fail to play the movie. You have to experiment and do a little research. Newer consumer DVD players recognize more formats (for example, rewriteable CDs and DVDs), but older ones don't. As for burning actual DVDs, at this time, Movie Maker doesn't write to DVDs. You have to use one of the many DVD-writing programs for that, assuming you have a DVD burner connected to your computer. The procedure for making a DVD from Movie Maker is a two-stage one. First, you write the movie to the hard disk from Movie Maker. Then you use a DVD authoring program to convert the WMV file (the program has to know how to deal with WMV files, obviously) to DVD.

TIP

Typically for Web posting, you output several versions and allow the viewer to choose between them, based on his connection speed. You also need a Web server that can handle the bandwidth of uploading video. Some services on the Web will do this. Check with your ISP or Web server administrator. If you really get interested in producing experimental videos and sharing them with the world at large, check www. atomfilms.com.

7

3. Just work through each wizard as necessary. Except when outputting to DV tape (make sure to put a tape in the DV camcorder that is not write protected and doesn't have your source material on it because it will be overwritten), your movie is output in the proprietary Windows Media Video (WMV) format.

4. A progress bar meter informs you of the process. After the movie is saved, click Yes to view it immediately. Windows Media Player loads the movie and plays it for you.

Figure 7.25
The options for saving a movie for Web distribution.

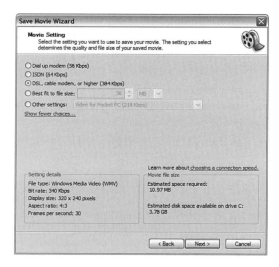

Regardless of the destination of your movie (such as in an email), you'll probably want to make a copy for safekeeping. Consider saving it on your computer or on a CD. You might also want to back up the project file and possibly the source files.

BEYOND WINDOWS MOVIE MAKER

Windows Movie Maker provides an enjoyable and even pretty powerful way to experiment with digital moviemaking. Movie Maker 2 is actually powerful enough that I have started using it for small projects rather than using my favorite full-blown video editor. If you get hooked on video creation (which is likely to happen if you have the patience, eye, and disposition), you might want to try more powerful editing programs. Some video editors are now available in versions that work directly with DVD-R recorders and have fancy multitrack timelines for editing multicamera shoots, zillions of effects, color correction, and industry-standard SMPTE timecode; produce edit decision lists (EDLs); and do all kinds of other stuff.

Some of the more popular low-priced video-editing programs on the market include Ulead's Video Studio, MGI's VideoWave, and Dazzle's DV-Editor SE. Some IEEE-1394 DV capture cards, TV capture cards, and VGA/TV capture cards may also include various video editing programs, including the ones mentioned above.

More powerful DV-editing programs you might consider Ulead media Studio Pro, Sony Vegas Video (highly rated), or Adobe's Premiere 6.0 (which can be paired with Adobe AfterEffects for exciting special effects). To get more information about

- Media Studio Pro and Video Studio see www.ulead.com.
- VideoWave, see www.roxio.com.
- Dazzle's lineup of digital video editing programs and hardware, see www.dazzle.com.
- Keyspan 1394 FireWire laptop card, see www.keyspan.com.
- SIIG 1394 FireWire laptop card, see www.siig.com.
- Maxtor external 1394 FireWire hard drives, see www.maxtor.com.

HELP SITES AND RESOURCES FOR DIGITAL VIDEO

In addition to the product Web sites listed previously, check out these resources:

- **Digital Video Magazine**—Look for the big "DV" on the cover for news, reviews, and tips for great digital video. The Web companion to the magazine is located at www.dv.com.
- **VideoMaker Magazine**—Get advice on good videographic techniques as well as buyer's guides and reviews. The Web companion to the magazine is located at www.videomaker.com.
- **Codec Corner**—The first stop if you're looking for the last word on streaming media compression algorithms (codecs) and technologies for video and Web animations. Find it online at www.codeccorner.com.

WINDOWS MEDIA PLAYER

Windows Media Player has grown into a pretty amazing app with multiple personalities. Its talents include playing music and video files from online sources or local drives (including DVDs), playing online radio and TV stations, displaying specialized Web pages, organizing music files (MP3s and WMAs), burning music CDs, copying and synching to portable MP3 players, and providing a conduit to online media shopping sites. Windows Media Player was extensively retooled for the initial release of Windows XP and appears as version 8. Since then, WMP has been upgraded to Media Player 9. Even at the time of this book revision, version 10 was on board for imminent release. It will probably be available a few months after this book goes to press, in which case you should upgrade to it.

Keeping up with the ever-burgeoning media player wars (WMP competes with iTunes, Real Jukebox, WinAMP, Music Match, and others) is almost impossible for us writers. Books just don't come out as fast as easily downloadable new software releases do. Still, here are the basics of Windows Media Player.

Compared to version 8, Media Player 9 has a somewhat spiffed-up (although a little less confusing) user interface, as shown in Figure 7.26, to support its many features.

7

Figure 7.26
Windows Media Player 9 defaults to the Media Guide view when you have a working Internet connection, providing links to popular audio and video content.

MEDIA TYPES COMPATIBLE WITH MEDIA PLAYER

Windows Media Player can play the file types shown in Table 7.3.

TABLE 7.3 WINDOWS MEDIA PLAYER–SUPPORTED FILE TYPES	
File Type	**File Name Extension(s)**
Music CD (CD audio)	`.cda`
Intel Indeo video	`.ivf`
Audio Interchange File Format (digitized sound)	`.aif, .aifc, .aiff`
Windows Media (audio and video)	`.asf, .asx, .wax, .wm, .wma, .wmd, .wmv, .wvx, .wmp, .wmx, .wpl`
Windows Media Center video	`.dvr-ms`
Windows video and audio	`.avi, .wav`
Quicktime content*	`.mov, .qt`
Windows Media Player skins	`.wmz, .wms`
MPEG (Motion Picture Experts Group) video	`.mpeg, .mpg, .m1v, .mp2, .mpa, .mpe, .mp2v, .mp2`
AU (Unix audio)	`.au, .snd`

7

File Type	File Name Extension(s)
MP3 (digital audio)	.mp3, .m3u
MIDI (Musical Instrument Digital Interface)	.mid, .midi, .rmi
DVD video	.vob

Formats not supported: RealNetworks supports .ra, .rm, *and* .ram.

* Only QuickTime files version 2.0 or earlier can be played in Windows Media Player. Later versions of QuickTime require the proprietary Apple QuickTime Player.

N O T E

> XP doesn't come from Microsoft with DVD playback capability, except in the Media Center Edition of XP. For a stock version of XP to play back DVD video and .mp2v files, first you must install a hardware or software DVD decoder on your system. If you insert a DVD and it doesn't run, that's probably the problem. Installing a decoder is typically a simple software update you can download from the Web. The easiest way to do it is to click Start, Help (on the XP taskbar). In the Help window, search for DVD. Under Fix a Problem in the list of topics, you'll see If you do not have a DVD decoder. Click that. The resulting article has a list of decoder sources near the bottom. If this doesn't work, search the Web for WinDVD or Power DVD. The decoder will cost you a few bucks (probably around $10). (Although current boxed editions of both players are around $50-$60.)

Major Features of Media Player

The major features of Media Player are accessible from the mode selection buttons on the left side of the default (full-view) display. Here's what they do:

- **Now Playing**—When you select online or locally stored content for playback, the Now Playing window displays a list of the content you're playing. An optional Visualizations feature can be used to display album art (when available) or various animated abstractions that change in response to the music. Open the top-level View menu to enable other features, such as titles, lyrics, graphic equalizer, video settings, and others. Figure 7.27 shows Media Player with a typical selection of Now Playing options.

- **Media Guide**—As shown in Figure 7.26, this option enables you to select from a wide variety of online content.

- **Copy from CD**—Click this button to copy all or selected tracks from your favorite music CDs to the My Music folder on your system.

7

Figure 7.27
Now Playing mode of Windows Media Player with visualization, playlist, and graphic equalizer options enabled.

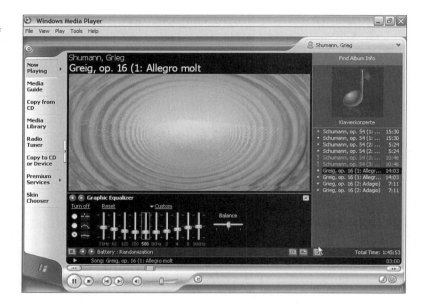

TIP

When you copy music, Windows Media Player, by default, prevents copied tracks from being played on any other computer. If you want to disable this feature so you can move copied music from one PC to another, check the box labeled Do Not Add Copy Protection in the dialog box that appears when you click Copy Music. You have to agree to the copyright warning before you can copy the music. As of Media Player 9, you have two new encoding options: Lossless and Variable Bit Rate (VBR). Audiophiles will likely want to use lossless (no loss of data results from this compression scheme, but the files are large). VBR creates smaller file sizes than non-VBR .wma encoding with the same audio quality. Note that to rip your CDs into MP3 format, you have to buy a plug-in for the Media Player. Microsoft wants you to use its own .wma format for your music. This can be a pain if you want compatibility with other music players such as iPods or many others that do not decode .wma files. The plug-ins are not that expensive (at little as $10), but still, come on, Microsoft!

- **Media Library**—Use this feature to organize and locate your favorite media types you've downloaded or created with Copy from CD. As you download and create music, Media Player automatically creates album and artist information for audio and video content. You also can view content by type and by genre.

- **Radio Tuner**—Use this feature to connect with the wide world of Internet radio. Featured stations offer a wide variety of music formats, and you also can locate stations by format or by searching for keywords. The Today's Hits section highlights the top pop, *Billboard Magazine*, R&B, and country hits. This is a very neat feature, a little like having a satellite radio. Type a country name into the Search Keyword box (for example, Africa or Denmark) and you'll be amazed at how many radio stations are streaming online! Click a station to see a description; then click Play to sample it. Click +Add to My Stations to set up your own set of favorite radio stations to easily come back to.

- **Copy to CD or Device**—After you download or convert music tracks to WMA format, use this feature to transfer your music mix to either writable CDs (CD-R or CD-RW media) or to WMA-compatible portable audio players.

TIP

> Be sure you fill your CD with all the music you want to play; unlike conventional CD-mastering programs or Windows XP's Copy to CD feature in other parts of the operating system, Windows Media Player's Copy to CD feature closes the CD (so it no longer can accept data) after you copy your selected music to it, even if you use only a small portion of the CD. Why? Standalone CD players are designed to handle single-session CDs and won't work if you add music later. If you want to create a CD for playback on your computer, use Windows Explorer's Copy to CD feature instead, which will allow you to copy music over several sessions.

- **Premium Services**—From this button, you can quickly sign up for and receive subscription-based services such as sports highlights, hit tunes, and thousands of movies on demand.

- **Skin Chooser**—If you're tired of the default Windows Media Player full view, as seen in Figure 7.28, use this option to select a completely new look (called a *skin*) for the Media Player. From artistic to sci-fi, from minimalist to charming, Media Player provides lots of choices by default. Click More Skins to see downloadable options available on Microsoft's Web site. Click Apply Skin to use the selected skin; a Return to Full Mode button lets you switch back whenever you want. Figure 7.27 shows the Media Player in its Windows XP skin.

Figure 7.28
The Windows XP skin for Media Player features a visualization window and the most commonly used control buttons.

7

CUSTOMIZING MEDIA PLAYER

In addition to changing its default playback mode and appearance, you can adjust many other features of Windows Media Player.

Use the View menu to adjust menu bar and taskbar options when Media Player is in full mode and to see statistics for your average connection speed. You can adjust the default for the connection speed in the Tools menu.

Use the Tools menu's Options selection to adjust most of the defaults for Media Player, including

- **Player tab**—Selects how often to check for Media Player updates, Internet options such as media licensing, and general player settings.

> **TIP**
>
> If you play a favorite tune and want to add it to your Media Library, check the Add Items to Media Library when Played box in the Player Settings section of the Player tab.

- **Copy Music**—Adjusts the default location and bit-rate used to copy music. Also enables you to compare WMA to other formats and to download the optional MP3 plug-ins, which will allow you to create MP3 files with Windows Media Player 9.
- **Devices**—Configures playback and copying settings for CD-RW, CD, and portable audio players. With CD-ROM and similar optical drives, you can select analog or digital copying and playback, and whether or not to enable error correction. With portable audio players, you can specify the quality level to use for copying music. With CD-RW drives, you can specify where to store CD images, the recording speed, and whether to eject the CD after recording.
- **Performance**—Configures the connection speed, network buffering settings, and video acceleration used for Internet content.
- **Media Library**—Configures access rights for the library and specifies whether to automatically add purchased music to the Media Library.
- **Visualizations**—Adds and configures visualizations. You can set the screen size and offscreen buffer size for each collection to match your screen resolution or the preferred window size you use for Media Player.
- **File Types**—Configures which file types compatible with Media Player will use Media Player as the default player program.

> **TIP**
>
> If you prefer a program such as WinAmp, iTunes, Real Jukebox, or Music Match (all of which can rip MP3s from your music CDs as well as play them without needing plug-ins), clear the checkbox for MP3 Format Sound. Then, your preferred MP3 program can be used instead of Media Player to work with MP3 files.

- **Network**—Configures network protocols, TCP port numbers, and proxy settings to be used for streaming media. Use this menu to manually configure Media Player if your corporate network prevents Media Player from working when using its normal settings.

TIP

> Contact your network administrator for help in configuring this tab, because the allowable settings can vary from network to network.

A rich point of optimization is in the Now Playing enhancements. Figure 7.26 shows the graphic equalizer, for example. But there are many more options. See the left and right arrows at the upper-left corner of the equalizer? Click those to cycle through the other control panels. (If the panel isn't showing, select View, Enhancements, Show Enhancements.) One of the newer ones is Play Speed Settings. With this, you can slow down or speed up videos without shifting the pitch of the voice or music. Another is Quiet Mode, which reduces the difference in volume of movies, radio, CDs, and recorded CDs as you play them back. This allows you turn down the volume of your computer speakers and still hear things without the quiet passages dropping too low to hear.

Media Player has many options. Check the Help file for the program, and check for updates regularly. The Help file will evolve as the program is updated.

TIP

> Select Help, Getting Started to read more about Media Player and configuration settings and to see some tutorials.

7

PART III

WINDOWS XP AND THE INTERNET

CHAPTER 8

INTERNET AND TCP/IP CONNECTION OPTIONS

In this chapter

8

GOING WORLD WIDE

Hooking up to the Internet used to be a privilege afforded only to universities and corporations. Now, it's an essential part of owning and using any PC, and it's available to virtually everyone.

In this chapter, you find information about choosing an Internet service provider (ISP), making the connection through a modem or other link, installing and configuring your system, and making it safe and secure. This chapter tells how to select and Internet connection technology and connect a single computer to the Internet. However, this isn't your only option. You can take any one of several routes:

- If your computer is part of an existing local area network (LAN) with Internet access, you can skip this chapter entirely because Internet access comes along as part of your Windows XP network installation.

- If you are setting up a LAN for your home or office, you can provide Internet access to the entire LAN through one connection. Read Chapter 18, "Connecting Your LAN to the Internet," to help you decide whether you want to connect your LAN. Use the instructions in this chapter to set up the initial connection; Chapter 18 tells you how to share it with the rest of your workgroup.

- If want to use your existing ISP account and connection technology, you can skip the introductory sections of this chapter and go right down to "Installing a Modem in Windows XP" or, for broadband connections, "Installing a Network Adapter."

- If you need to make a clean start with the Internet, read on!

NOTE

> The built-in Windows Firewall—actually, all aspects of Windows Internet security—was significantly improved in Windows XP Service Pack 2. It's essential that you use this updated version of Windows. The Internet used to be a congenial, trusted community designed to permit easy collaboration and open communication. But now, spammers, con-artists, hackers, and other bottom-feeders have infested its every nook and cranny, and you have to protect yourself against them.
>
> The procedures in this chapter assume that you have Service Pack 2 installed. To see whether Service Pack 2 (or higher) is installed on your copy of Windows XP, open Windows Explorer and click Help, About Windows. If the version number doesn't say "Service Pack 2" or higher, see Appendix A, "Installing Service Pack 2," for instructions on obtaining and installing this critical security update.

CONNECTION TECHNOLOGIES

Not long ago, you had one choice to make for your Internet connection: which brand of modem to buy. Now, options abound, and you can choose among several technologies, speeds, and types of Internet service providers. A huge technology shift is taking place, as high-speed digital (*broadband*) connection services are being deployed worldwide.

Let's take a look at the basic Internet connection technologies appropriate for an individual user or workgroup. After describing each one, I show you roughly what they cost to set up and use.

ANALOG MODEM

Standard, tried-and-true dial-up modem service requires only a telephone line and a modem in your computer. The connection is made when your computer dials a local access number provided by your Internet service provider (ISP). The downside is that this ties up a telephone line while you're online. Furthermore, if you have call waiting, the "beep" that occurs when someone calls while you're online can make the modem drop its connection. To avoid these hassles, many people order an additional line just for the modem, and this adds to the monthly expense.

NOTE

> Some modems and ISPs provide a service called Internet call waiting. The modem detects the call-waiting beep and notifies you through a pop-up window that a call is coming in; you can ignore it or suspend your Internet connection for a time while you take the call. This requires a modem supporting the V.92 standard and a participating ISP. The service costs upward of $8 per month, if it's even available, so it's not a big win as far as I can see.

Modems transmit data at a top speed of 33Kbps and can receive data at up to 56Kbps (56 thousand bits per second). In real life, you will usually obtain download speeds of 40 to 50Kbps. This speed is adequate for general Web surfing—that is, reading text and viewing pictures. It's woefully inadequate for viewing video and for voice communication.

To use standard dial-up service, you'll need a modem and a telephone cable. Modems come in internal, external, USB, and PC-Card varieties by dozens of manufacturers. Most computers made for home use come with one pre-installed.

ISDN

Integrated Services Digital Network (ISDN) is a special digital-only telephone service that can carry two independent voice or data conversations over one telephone wire. ISDN service is actually a different type of telephony; you can't plug ordinary telephones into an ISDN line. ISDN modems can carry data at 64 or 128Kbps, depending on whether you use one or two of its channels to connect to your ISP. Until broadband solutions like DSL and cable modems came along, that was pretty impressive. Thanks to the worldwide spread of cable and DSL service, ISDN's star is fading rapidly. Still, IDSN is a good interim solution if you need higher speed than an analog modem can provide, and DSL and cable aren't yet available.

To use ISDN service, you'll need an internal or external ISDN modem, or an ISDN router device and a network adapter. Your ISP can help you choose compatible equipment. In addition, you'll need the special ISDN telephone line wired into your home or office.

DSL

Digital Subscriber Loop (DSL) service sends a high-speed digital data signal over the same wires used by your telephone line, while that line is simultaneously used for standard telephone service. This means that you can get DSL service installed without needing an extra telephone line. The most common DSL service is called *asymmetric* or ADSL because it receives data at 128Kbps to 1200Kbps and sends at a lower rate. (This is fine, because most Web surfing involves sending out a very small request and receiving a large amount of data back.)

> **NOTE**
> DSL varieties include Asymmetric, Symmetric, High-Speed, and DSL-over-an-ISDN-line, so you'll see the acronyms *ADSL, SDSL, HDSL,* and *IDSL,* or the collective *xDSL*. For this chapter, these distinctions are unimportant, so I just call it DSL.

DSL service is not available everywhere yet, but it's spreading rapidly. However, DSL has at least one Achilles heel in that its availability is restricted by your distance from the telephone company's central office, and isn't available when the distance is more than a couple of miles (as the wires run, not as the crow flies). DSL's reach can be extended by optical fiber lines and special equipment, but this is expensive for the telephone companies to install. DSL might never make it into rural areas.

> **NOTE**
> U.S. readers can see reviews of various DSL providers and check for DSL service availability at `http://www.dslreports.com`.

DSL modems come in two varieties, internal and external. Internal modems fit inside your computer's PCI slots, just like internal dial-up modems and other adapter cards. External units connect to your computer through a network adapter or a USB cable. Before you buy an additional network adapter, check with your DSL provider, because they often include one in their installation kit. Also, before you decide to pay extra to get service for multiple computers, read Chapter 18 to see how you can share a single connection with all of your computers.

CABLE MODEM

Cable modem Internet service is provided by your local television cable company, which sends high-speed data signals out through the same distribution system it uses to carry high-quality TV signals.

Cable modem service has none of the distance limitations of ISDN or DSL. One criticism of cable service is that data speeds can drop during high-use times like the early evening, because everyone in a given neighborhood shares a single network "pipe." Recent surveys show, however, that cable subscribers on the average get 2.5 times the download speed of DSL subscribers.

→ For more information on ISDN, xDSL, and cable modem service, **see** Chapter 18. That chapter describes these technologies with a focus on using them to connect a LAN to the Internet, and you might find the information helpful.

Cable modems generally are external devices that connect to your computer through a network adapter or a USB cable. Before you buy a network adapter, though, check with your ISP as they may include one in their installation kit. Some ISPs charge extra to lease you the modem. The price of a cable modem has dropped to the $60 range, so leasing one from your cable company isn't as good a deal as it once was. Also, before you decide to pay extra to get service for multiple computers, read Chapter 19, "Network Security," to see how you can share a single connection with all of your computers. This is especially important for cable users. Multiple-computer cable service has some serious problems that I'll discuss in Chapter 18.

SATELLITE SERVICE

Satellite Internet service uses microwave signals and small (roughly two-foot diameter) dish antennas to connect to an orbiting communication satellite. There are two types of satellite service: *unidirectional*, which receives high-speed data through the dish but transmits outgoing data by modem over a phone line, and *bidirectional*, which uses the satellite dish for both sending and receiving. Bidirectional service is the way to go! It's currently available in most parts of the world.

Satellite's big advantage is that it's available wherever there's a good view of the southern sky (in the northern hemisphere), or northern sky (in the southern hemisphere). The disadvantages are that installation requires both a rocket scientist and a carpenter, the equipment and service plans can be expensive, and the system suffers from the same slowdowns that affect cable service.

NOTE

> In the U.S., check out www.starband.com and www.direcway.com. In Australia, check www.telstra.com. In Europe, Southern Africa, the Middle East, the Indian subcontinent, and Southeast Asia see www.europestar.com. Satellite services are often resold through regional companies.

Satellite service requires you to purchase a receiving dish antenna, a receiver, and a USB or network adapter to connect the setup to your computer. These devices will be furnished by your ISP. For one-way satellite service, you'll also need to have a phone line near your computer.

TIP

> To get the full scoop on satellite and wireless Internet service, check out *The Complete Idiot's Guide to High-Speed Internet Connections* by Mark Soper, published by Que.

8

WIRELESS

In some major metropolitan areas, wireless Internet service is available through a regional network of small radio transmitters/receivers. Cell phone companies are getting into this in a big way, so it's going to spread rapidly. The wireless modem connects to a small whip or dish antenna, and data transfer rates are typically over 1Mbps with setups with fixed antennae.

NOTE

Check www.sprintbroadband.com for more information.

Wireless is similar to satellite service. You'll have to purchase a receiving dish antenna, a receiver, and a USB or network adapter to connect the setup to your computer. These devices will all be furnished by your ISP. You'll also have to pay for professional installation.

CHOOSING A TECHNOLOGY

With all the options that are potentially available to Windows users for Internet access, making a choice that fits your needs and limitations can become a bit confusing. You should research the options provided by local and national ISPs, and then start narrowing them down. Table 8.1 summarizes the costs and speeds of the different ways for a single computer user to access the Internet. The prices shown are typical costs for the service in question after applying the usual discounts and special offers.

TABLE 8.1   INTERNET CONNECTION OPTIONS FOR THE INDIVIDUAL USER

Method	Approximate Cost, $ per month	Approximate Setup and Equipment Cost	Time Limits in hours	Availability	Download Speed
Analog Modem	$0*–$25	$50	10 to unlimited	Worldwide	33 to 56Kbps
ISDN	$40 plus ISDN toll charges	$300	10 to unlimited	Limited, unlikely to expand	64 to 128Kbps
DSL	$30 and up	$100	Unlimited	Limited but growing	312Kbps to 6Mbps
Cable Modem	$30–$40	$100	Unlimited	Limited but growing	1 to 10Mbps
Satellite	$50–$150	$200–$800	25 and up	Almost worldwide	400Kbps

There are some "free" ISPs; I discuss them later in this chapter.

Remember that you have three or four costs to factor in:

- The cost of hardware required to make the connection
- The cost of installation and setup
- The monthly ISP cost for Internet service
- The cost of telephone or ISDN lines, if you order a separate line just for Internet access

Try to estimate how long you'll keep the service, and amortize the startup and equipment costs over that time frame when comparing technologies. If you are going to share the connection among several computers, plan to download lots of large files, or want to play games online, a faster service might make more sense, even if it's a bit more expensive.

CHOOSING AN INTERNET SERVICE PROVIDER

Several different kinds of businesses offer Internet connections, including large companies with access points in many cities, smaller local or regional Internet service providers, and online information services that provide TCP/IP connections to the Internet along with their own proprietary information sources (I'm talking about AOL here, of course).

You might notice that Windows XP comes with pre-installed software to use Microsoft's MSN service. The New Connection Wizard (which we'll discuss later) might try to steer you to an ISP that paid Microsoft to be listed. Also, your computer reseller might have installed icons for other preferred services. Remember, you don't *have* to use any of these providers. Windows has all the software it needs to connect to any ISP except AOL, and AOL is easy to add on, if that's the way you want to go. (Getting its software is certainly no problem. If you're like me, you probably have at least 50 AOL CDs lying around. They come in magazines, newspapers, take-out pizzas....) Do your own research to find out the best fit for you.

The following are a few points to consider in choosing an ISP:

- Does the ISP offer the connection technology you want?
- Can you have multiple email accounts for family members or employees? If so, how many?
- Does the ISP provide you with a news server so you can interact with Internet newsgroups?

→ To learn more about Newsgroups, **see** Chapter 11, "Reading Newsgroups with Outlook Express."

- What is the charge for connect time? Some ISPs offer unlimited usage per day. Others charge by the hour or have a limit on continuous connect time.
- Does the ISP have local (that is, free) phone numbers in the areas you live, work, and visit? If not, factor in the toll charges when you're comparing prices.
- Can you get a discount by signing up for a year or longer term contract?

If you have access to the Web, try checking the Web page www.thelist.com. It shows comparative pricing and features offered by ISPs, along with links to their pages for opening an account. Another good site is www.boardwatch.com.

Finally, you should know that there some ISPs that give you free dial-up Internet access. These providers install software on your computer that displays a small window of advertising the entire time you're connected. If you're pinching pennies, this isn't a terrible way to go. You might check out http://www.freedomlist.com/ for a list of free (and cheap) ISPs in your area.

TIP

> In my opinion, getting good customer service is more important than saving a few dollars a month. As you narrow down your list of potential ISPs, call their customer support telephone number and see how long it takes to get to talk to a human being. This experience can be very illuminating.

TRAVEL CONSIDERATIONS

If you're a frequent traveler and have a laptop or other device with which you want to connect to the Internet while on the road, remember that broadband service is wired into place. In other words, it doesn't provide for access when you travel or roam about town, unlike many national dial-up ISPs that offer roaming. However, some broadband ISPs include a standard modem dial-up account at no extra charge just to compensate for this factor.

If you want Internet connectivity when you travel, consider these options:

- For occasional or personal travel, you can forgo national access. Just find an Internet cafe or get Internet access at your hotel. Wireless hotspots are appearing everywhere, so you might do well just to buy a wireless network adapter.

- If you want to use your own computer for occasional travel, you can always place a long-distance call to your own ISP. Subtract the cost from the money you might save using a less expensive local ISP, versus the higher prices of a national ISP, to see which solution is best.

- If you travel frequently, choose a national ISP with local access numbers in the places you visit frequently or toll-free access with an acceptable surcharge.

At the end of this chapter, I'll give you some advice about getting Internet access while traveling overseas.

AOL

If you're a current dial-up AOL user, you know how painfully slow it is at accessing non-AOL Internet Web sites (or maybe you don't—maybe you think everyone suffers this way!). You should know that you can get a fast broadband connection or even standard dial-up service, which gives you fast Internet access, and still allows for use of AOL for email and their exclusive content.

Relying on the New Connection Wizard

Windows XP includes a Wizard that can connect via modem to a toll-free line operated by Microsoft, offer you a choice of ISPs, and sign you up for service, without your having to lift much more than a finger.

Before you let the wizard narrow the range of choices for you, remember that its range of choices is narrow to begin with. You'll probably want to do some research on your own. Then you can use the wizard to see if it recommends your ultimate choice. If it does, you can let it help you set up the account.

Choosing Equipment

You need to purchase equipment that's compatible with the particular type of Internet service you'll be using. If you're going to use dial-up service, your computer probably came with a modem pre-installed, so you don't have any choices to make. If you are going to buy new connection hardware, here are some points to consider:

- Most broadband services require specific hardware that your ISP provides. (You can sometimes buy a DSL or cable modem independently, but be sure it's compatible with the equipment your ISP uses). In addition, broadband modems connect via USB or through an Ethernet network adapter. If your service needs a network adapter, be sure it's Windows XP compatible. This isn't such a great concern now that Windows XP has been around for a while because every vendor has had time to become XP compatible. However, not all of them have invested the effort to get Microsoft certified, so it's still worth checking the list.

- If you're going to share your Internet connection with other computers via a LAN, please read Chapter 18 before making any hardware purchases, as there are some nifty special hardware setups you might want to consider.

- Above all, be sure any hardware that you plug directly into the computer (modem or LAN adapter) appears in the Windows Catalog (www.windowsmarketplace.com) or in the Windows XP Hardware Compatibility List (http://www.microsoft.com/hcl). This isn't such a great concern now that Windows XP has been around for a while, as every vendor has had time to become XP compatible. However, not all of them have invested the effort to get Microsoft certified, so it's still worth checking the list before you make any purchases.

- For dial-up service, choose a modem that is compatible with the fastest service level provided by your ISP. They should be using V.90 modems for 56Kbps service. If your ISP still uses X2 or K6Flex modems, they're way behind the times. Some ISPs support the new V.92 call-waiting protocol. If you have a modem that supports this feature, ask prospective ISPs if they support it and if there's an additional charge.

8

ORDERING THE SERVICE

Ordering standard dial-up modem Internet service is really quite simple. Just call the ISP, talk to the sales department, and ask the sales representative to mail or fax you instructions for configuring Windows XP. In fact, it's easy enough that they might just talk you through it over the phone.

Ordering ISDN service is quite a different matter. The most difficult part is getting the ISDN telephone line ordered and installed correctly, because ISDN service has a bewildering number of options, all specified in telephone-companyese. What you want is standard "2B+D, two data and voice" service with no extra-cost features.

TIP

> Your best bet is to have your ISP order an ISDN line for you. If they won't, some ISDN modem manufacturers—for example, 3COM—will order your ISDN service for you.

Ordering cable, DSL, or satellite service is also quite easy because the ISP takes care of all the details for you. The provider first checks to see whether your neighborhood qualifies for the service. They call you back with the news and then either send you a self-installation kit or schedule an installation appointment. (Getting DSL installers to actually show up, though, can be a nightmare. But don't let me discourage you from trying. The service is really nice.)

After the service is installed, you're ready to configure your Windows XP computer. I discuss modems first, and then I cover setting up broadband equipment.

INSTALLING THE HARDWARE

No matter what kind of Internet connection you'll be using, you'll need a modem, a network adapter, or some other sort of connection hardware. If you're lucky, your computer came with this preinstalled and you can just skip ahead to "Configuring Your Internet Connection." Otherwise, you'll be adding some hardware. For most types of high-speed service, your ISP will either come install everything for you, or they'll give you detailed instructions. For the basic service types, I'll give you some generic installation instructions in the next few sections. Your connection hardware might come with detailed instructions. If it does, by all means follow those.

INSTALLING A MODEM IN WINDOWS XP

Installing a modem is a pretty painless process these days. If you had to undergo the experience in the mid-'90s, you might remember worrying about interrupt conflicts, having to set jumpers, and needing to navigate the computer's setup screen. Plug and Play has pretty much eliminated this mess. Your modem should come with straightforward installation instructions. Follow those and you'll be online in no time.

8

For an internal modem, they'll have you pop open your PC's case and insert the modem card into a free expansion slot inside the computer. For an external modem, it's a more simple matter of cabling it to a USB or serial port on your PC. (Don't forget to connect the power supply and turn it on.) A PC card modem simply plugs into your portable.

→ For more information about installing new hardware, **see** Chapter 27, "Installing and Replacing Hardware."

From that point, here's what you'll need to do. These procedures apply to analog modems as well as external ISDN modems.

If your modem is Plug and Play (PnP) compatible, Windows XP should automatically detect it when you turn on your computer and log in using a Computer Administrator account.

→ For more details on Administrator privileges, **see** "User Account Types," **p. 882**.

If Windows XP cannot find a set of drivers that match your brand and model of modem, you might be asked to insert a CD or floppy disk provided by the modem manufacturer into the appropriate drive.

If you're using an older modem, you might need to add it to the configuration manually by following these steps:

1. Choose Start, Control Panel, Network and Internet Connections, Phone and Modem Options.

2. Select the Modems tab, as shown in Figure 8.1.

Figure 8.1
The Modems tab on the Phone and Modem Options control panel identifies the modems currently installed in your system.

8

3. If Windows has already detected your modem, its name appears in the Modems tab. If the correct modem type is listed, skip to step 8. If the wrong modem type is listed, skip down to the next section, "Changing the Modem Type."

   If no modem is listed, click the Add button to run the Install New Hardware Wizard.

4. Click Next, and Windows will locate the COM port and determine the type of modem you have. If this is successful, Windows will tell you. In this case, continue with step 7.

5. If Windows detects your modem incorrectly and doesn't offer you the chance to correct the mistake, skip down to step 7, and then correct the problem using the instructions in the next section. If you are given the opportunity, though, click Change and locate the manufacturer and model of your modem in the dialog box. If you find the correct make and model, select them and click OK. If your modem came with a driver diskette for Windows XP or 2000, click Have Disk, and locate the installation file for the modem.

   If your modem isn't listed, try to download the proper driver from Windows Update or from the modem manufacturer (using another computer, of course!). Or, you might try selecting a similar model by the same manufacturer.

6. After you select the modem type, click OK and then Next.

7. Click Finish to complete the installation. The modem then appears in the list of installed modems in the Phone and Modem Options dialog box.

8. Select the Dialing Rules tab.

9. Select New Location, and click Edit.

10. Enter the General tab information for your current location, as shown in Figure 8.2.

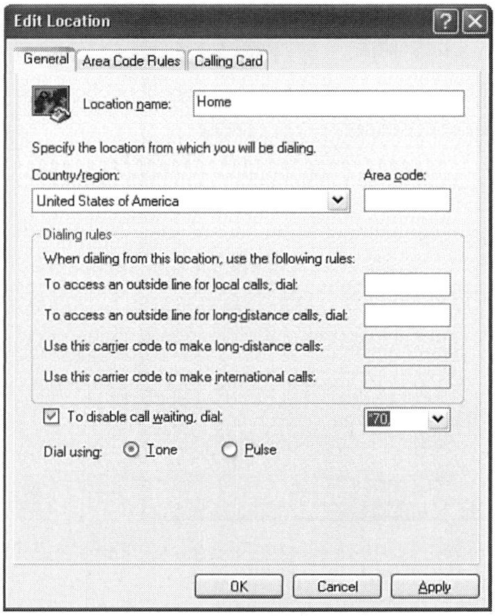

Figure 8.2
In the Edit Location dialog box, you can record the dialing instructions for your current location. The important settings are Country/region, Area code (and the rules for accessing for an outside line), and the check box to disable call waiting.

8

11. Enter the name of your location—for example, Home, the name of your city, or another name that distinguishes the current telephone dialing properties. Set the Country, Area code, and Dialing rules information.

    If your telephone system, for example, requires you to dial a 9 to make an outside local call, enter 9 in box labeled To Access an Outside Line For Local Calls, Dial. Make a corresponding entry for long-distance access.

    If your telephone line has call waiting, check To Disable Call Waiting, Dial and choose the appropriate disable code.

    I'm going to assume that your ISP access number is a local call in the same area code. If this is not the case, you might want to fill in the Area Code Rules table for the ISP access number. (If you don't know the number yet, don't worry; you can come back and fix it later.)

12. Click OK.

Now your modem is installed, and you can continue with "Configuring Your Internet Connection," later in this chapter.

CHANGING THE MODEM TYPE

If Windows incorrectly determines your modem type, you can change it by selecting the appropriate line in the Modem list (see Figure 8.1) and clicking Properties. Then

1. Select the Driver tab and click Update Driver.
2. Check Install from a List and click Next.
3. Check Don't Search, and click Next.
4. Uncheck Show Compatible Hardware, and either select your modem make and model, or click Have Disk and locate the proper .INF setup file. Click Next, then Finish.

INSTALLING INTERNAL ISDN ADAPTERS

Internal ISDN modems or adapters are treated by Windows as network adapters, not modems. Plug and Play adapters should be set up automatically the first time you log on after installing the adapter. Log on as a Computer Administrator to be sure that you have sufficient privileges to install hardware drivers.

For older non-Plug and Play adapters, you must get up-to-date Windows XP drivers from the manufacturer's Web site, along with installation instructions. (But, if your ISDN adapter is that old, don't count on finding any.)

Modern ISDN driver software might be able to get the ISDN line's telephone number and other necessary information right over the line from the phone company, but you might be prompted for setup information. In this case you need the SPID (Service Profile Identification, a number assigned by the telephone company), directory number, and switch-type information provided by your telephone company.

8

INSTALLING A NETWORK ADAPTER

Some DSL and cable modems use a USB connection and can just be plugged into your computer this way.

However, most DSL and cable service providers require an Ethernet network adapter for use by their modems. If you're lucky, they supply and install this for you. You don't have to lift a finger, in fact, as long as the installer is familiar with Windows XP. You just need to log on using a Computer Administrator account, and supervise while the installer does his or her stuff.

TIP

> If a professional installer configures your computer or adds software to it, be sure to take thorough notes of what he or she does. Don't hesitate to ask questions—you have a right to know exactly what they're doing. And be sure to test the setup before the installer leaves.

If you want to purchase or install the network adapter yourself, install it according to the manufacturer's instructions. This process should involve no more than inserting the card into your computer, powering up, and logging on as a Computer Administrator. The Plug and Play system should take care of the rest for you.

After installation, confirm that the network adapter is installed and functioning by following these steps:

1. Click Start, right-click My Computer, and then select Manage.
2. Select the Device Manager in the left pane. The list in the right pane should show only "first-level" items. Under Network Adapters, you should see no items listed with an exclamation mark icon superimposed.

If the network adapter appears and is marked with a yellow exclamation point, follow the network card troubleshooting instructions in Chapter 20, "Troubleshooting Your Network."

For DSL service with self-installation, you are provided with *filters*, which are devices that plug into your telephone jacks and block the DSL signal from reaching your telephones and answering machines. You need to identify every phone jack that is connected to the line your DSL service uses and install a filter on every one but the one that plugs into your DSL modem. If you need to plug a phone into the same jack the DSL modem uses, use a dual jack adapter with a filter on the side that connects to the phone.

Alternately, the service installer might connect your telephone line to a device called a *splitter* outside the house, and install a separate cable to bring the DSL signal to your computer. These devices separate the high-frequency DSL carrier signal from the normal telephone signal. The phone line is connected to a DSL modem, which then plugs into a USB port or a LAN adapter on your computer.

CAUTION

> After a LAN adapter or USB connection is made, you must be sure that the Windows Firewall is enabled to protect your computer against hackers. I'll mention this again later in the chapter. You can read more about firewalls in Chapter 19.

INSTALLING A SATELLITE OR WIRELESS CONNECTION

Installing satellite or wireless modems is not terribly tricky, but the procedure is very specific to the type of hardware you're using. Unfortunately, I have to leave you at the mercy of the manufacturer's instruction manual.

I can give you one bit of advice: Installing a satellite dish is difficult, and it's best to hire a professional dish installer for this task. (My executive editor, Rick Kughen, didn't have the benefit of this sage advice when he installed his, and his conclusion was: "About halfway through the ordeal, I decided that I really wished I had paid the $199 installation fee.")

CAUTION

> After your satellite connection is set up, you must be sure that the Windows Firewall is enabled to protect your computer against hackers. I'll mention this again later in the chapter. You can read more about firewalls and network security in Chapter 19.

CONFIGURING YOUR INTERNET CONNECTION

Now that your modem is installed and ready to go, it's time to head off to see the wizard. The New Connection Wizard, that is.

TIP

> Have your Windows XP Installation CD handy, even though it's unlikely that the wizard will need to install some Windows files to set up your Internet connection.

The New Connection Wizard runs the first time you try to open Internet Explorer. You can also fire it up at any time by clicking Start, All Programs, Accessories, Communications, New Connection Wizard. Click Next, Connect to the Internet, and Next again. You should see the wizard screen shown in Figure 8.3.

Your path from here depends on whether you want Microsoft to give you a list of suggested ISPs or you want to set up an account for your chosen ISP manually.

The first alternative is for analog modem or ISDN access only. If you want to take this route, go on to "Using a Referral ISP."

Otherwise, skip to "Making and Ending a Dial-Up Connection," or "Configuring a High-Speed Connection" later in this chapter.

8

Figure 8.3
The New Connection Wizard has ways to set up a new Internet connection.

USING A REFERRAL ISP

If you want the New Connection Wizard to help you choose an ISP, select Choose from a List of Internet Service Providers (ISPs), and click Next. Then, you can choose to buy Microsoft's MSN Internet service, or you can check Select from a List of Other ISPs. Click Next to display a window that has shortcuts, where you have another chance to make the same choice—double-click either the MSN or Refer Me icon. You might see other choices as well, placed there by your computer vendor.

If you choose MSN, you are walked through the subscription process for Microsoft's own Internet service. If you choose Select from a List, Windows makes a toll-free call to Microsoft's ISP referral server and downloads a list of ISPs in your area.

Internet Explorer then displays a list of available ISPs in your area, as illustrated in Figure 8.4. You can follow the onscreen instructions to establish an account with one of them, if you choose. If you choose not to, or if none are available, you are given the chance to manually configure an ISP account.

Figure 8.4
The Microsoft ISP Referral service lists ISPs operating in your area—but just the ones who paid to be listed.

MANUALLY CONFIGURING AN ISP ACCOUNT

If you already have an ISP account or need to set up a new one, select Set Up My Connection Manually on the New Connection Wizard screen, and click Next. Select Connect Using a Dial-Up Modem, and click Next. You now need to complete three dialog boxes, using the information provided by your ISP.

The first asks for the name of your ISP. I like to use the name of the ISP and the city name from which I'm calling—for instance, SBC Internet - Berkeley—because I travel occasionally and have to add extra connection setups for other cities with different dial-up numbers. Enter a name and then click Next.

The second dialog box asks for the local access telephone number for your ISP. Enter the local number, optionally preceded by any other codes needed to dial the call. For instance, in the United States I enter 1 followed by the area code, as shown in Figure 8.5. You can enter dashes (-) between the parts of the number if you want; the modem ignores them.

CAUTION

> Be sure to use a local number. Your ISP will not help pay your phone bill if you choose a toll number by mistake!

TIP

> If your phone line has call waiting, you might want to precede the telephone number with the code you use to disable call-waiting so your online session won't be disrupted. For many areas, the code is *70. Add a comma after this to make the modem pause. The combined entry might be something like this: *70, 1-510-555-4999.
>
> However, a better way to handle the area code and call-waiting settings is to edit the connection's properties after the wizard has finished. I'll mention this again later in "Adjusting Dial-Up Connection Properties."

Figure 8.5
In the manual Internet account connection information dialog box, enter the local access number for your ISP.

8

The third dialog box asks for your ISP account logon name and password, as shown in Figure 8.6. Two options are enabled by default:

- **Use This Account Name and Password when Anyone Connects to the Internet from This Computer**—By default, this Internet account information is usable by anyone who uses the computer. Uncheck this if you don't want other users to access your dial-up account.
- **Make This the Default Internet Connection**—This becomes your account's default Internet connection. If you are setting up a secondary connection you won't use every time, you can uncheck this option.

Figure 8.6
Enter the logon name and password assigned by your ISP.

Click Next and then Finish to complete the New Connection Wizard. The wizard immediately dials your ISP. If you don't want to do this, click Cancel when the dialing dialog box appears.

That's it. Your connection is ready to use. If you have no other LAN or dial-up connections, you can simply fire up Internet Explorer to automatically dial. You can choose Start, Control Panel, Network and Internet Connections to use or modify your dial-up configuration at any time.

If you have several ISP accounts, ISP access numbers for different cities, or both personal and business dial-up connections, you can add additional connections by repeating the New Connection Wizard process for each additional access telephone number or account.

TIP

If you find yourself frequently having to dig into Network Connections to get to a connection icon, you can make a desktop or quick-launch shortcut for it. Right-click and drag the connection icon from Network Connections to the desktop or Quick-Launch bar and choose Create Shortcut Here from the shortcut menu that appears after releasing the right mouse button.

NOTE

You can also make it appear in the Start menu. To do this, right-click the Start button and select Properties. Click Customize, select the Advanced tab, and find Network Connections in the list of Start Menu Items. Check either Display As Connect-To Menu (which lets you dial a connection right from the Start menu) or Link to Network Connections Folder.

TIP

For maximum protection against hackers, I suggest that you read Chapter 19. But at the very least, follow the steps in the next section to ensure that the Windows Firewall is enabled. It ought to be enabled by default, but you should check just to be safe.

ADJUSTING DIAL-UP CONNECTION PROPERTIES

As configured by the wizard, your dial-up connection is properly set up for most Internet service providers. The wizard doesn't do a good job of setting up the area code and call-waiting settings, so you might need to manually adjust these. It's unlikely that you would need to change any of the other settings, but just in case, and because I know you're curious, I will walk you through the various settings and properties that are part of a dial-up connection. I explain dial-up connection properties in more detail in Chapter 17, "Windows Unplugged: Remote and Mobile Networking."

You can view a connection's properties by selecting Start, Control Panel, Network and Internet Connections, Network Connections. This displays all dial-up connections you've configured (see Figure 8.7). Right-click the icon for your dial-up connection and select Properties. You see five tabs, as shown in Figure 8.8, which I run through in order in which they appear. Only a few settings ever need to be changed for an ISP connection. Here is a list of the ones that do matter:

Figure 8.7
Network Connections shows icons for each of your dial-up accounts and high-speed links.

Figure 8.8
A dial-up connection's Properties page lets you change dialing rules, set network parameters, and manage the Windows Firewall.

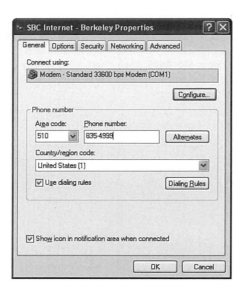

- The General tab contains modem properties and the ISP telephone number. If you travel with your computer, check Use Dialing Rules, be sure the area code is set correctly and is not entered in the Phone Number field, and click Dialing Rules if you want to enable Call Waiting control.

- If you have multiple modems, at the top of this page you can choose which of one or more of these modems is to be used for this particular connection.

- Using the Configure button for the modem, you can set the maximum speed used to communicate from the computer to the modem. For *external* modems connected to a COM port, if you don't have a special-purpose high-speed serial port, you might want to reduce this speed from the default 115200 to 57600.

- Using the Alternates button for the telephone number, you can add multiple telephone numbers for your ISP, which can be automatically tried, in turn, if the first doesn't answer.

- On the Options tab, you can change the time between redial attempts if the connection fails:
  - You can select a time to wait before hanging up the line when no activity occurs. By doing so, you can help cut costs if you pay an hourly rate to your ISP by having your computer disconnect itself from the Internet if it detects that you've not been using your connection for a set amount of time.
  - To maintain a permanent or *nailed-up* dial-up connection, check Redial If Line Is Dropped and set the disconnect time to Never. (Do this only with the consent of your ISP.)

- The Security tab controls whether your password can be sent in unencrypted form. It's okay to send your ISP password unsecured. *Don't* check Automatically Use My

Windows Login Name and Password if you use a commercial ISP. That's only for connections to corporate networks.

- The Networking tab determines which network components are accessible to the Internet connection. If you're dialing a standard ISP, you should leave File and Printer Sharing… unchecked. You learn more about that in Chapter 19.

- On the Advanced tab, you can share this dial-up connection automatically with other users on a LAN. (You learn more details on that in Chapter 18). You can also manage the Windows Firewall, which protects your computer from hackers while you're connected. For details on configuring the Windows Firewall, see Chapter 19.

Click OK to save your changes.

CAUTION

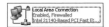

> While I strongly recommend that you read the Windows Firewall section in Chapter 19, if you don't, at least be sure to check the Network Connections window to ensure that the Windows Firewall is enabled on every connection icon that is used to connect directly to the Internet.
>
> Each Internet connection icon should be labeled `Firewalled`, as in the example shown here. If it doesn't, click Change Windows Firewall Settings in the Network Tasks list. Be sure that the On (Recommended) choice is selected. Select the Advanced tab, and be sure that each of the direct Internet connections is checked.
>
> For home and small office networks, all of your network connection icons can and should be firewalled.

CONFIGURING A HIGH-SPEED CONNECTION

If you're using an Ethernet network adapter to connect your computer to a DSL or cable Internet service, the installer may set up your computer for you. "Self-install" providers will give you a set of instructions specific to your service. In the next several sections, I give you a general idea of what's required.

You start by installing and configuring a network adapter to connect to the modem or by plugging in a USB-based modem and then setting up the connection with the New Connection Wizard. Configuring the network adapter goes something like this:

1. If your computer has a built-in Ethernet network adapter that you're not already using for a home or office LAN, you can use the built-in adapter to connect to your broadband modem, so you can skip ahead to step 3. Otherwise, you have to install an additional plug-in Ethernet adapter. This might be provided by your ISP, or you might have to purchase one.

8

2. For an internal adapter, shut down the computer, insert the card, turn the computer back on, and log on as a Computer Administrator. In most cases, Windows automatically installs and configures drivers for the adapter. For an external or PCMCIA (PC Card) adapter, just log on as a Computer Administrator and plug it in.

3. Configure the network adapter according to the instructions given by your ISP. In most cases you can leave it with all the default settings, although in some cases you might need to configure a specific IP address as described in the later section "Setting Up Dynamic IP Addressing."

CAUTION

If your broadband service uses a network adapter (that is, an Ethernet adapter) to connect to a cable or DSL modem, you must take these additional steps to secure your computer from hackers:

1. Open the Network Connections window. You can get to this from the Control Panel by clicking Network and Internet Connections, then Network Connections.

2. Locate the icon that corresponds to the network adapter that connects to your DSL or cable modem—it's probably labeled Local Area Connection. Right-click it and select Properties.

3. Under This Connection Uses the Following Items, only QoS Packet Scheduler and Internet Protocol (TCP/IP) should be checked. If any other entries have check marks, click the check marks to remove them.

4. Double-check to be sure that neither "Client for Microsoft Networks" nor "File and Printer Sharing for Microsoft Networks" is checked.

5. Click OK, then OK again, then close Network Connections.

Although I strongly recommend that you read the Windows Firewall section in Chapter 19, if you don't, at least be sure to take these steps.

When the adapter has been configured and attached to the DSL or cable modem with a network cable, you must configure the connection. The procedure depends on whether your ISP uses PPPoE or an always-on connection. The procedures are described in the next two sections.

CONFIGURING A PPPoE BROADBAND CONNECTION

Most DSL and some cable Internet providers use a connection scheme called *PPPoE (Point-to-Point Protocol over Ethernet)*. This is a technology that works a lot like a standard dial-up connection, but the "call" takes place through the DSL circuit or TV cable rather than over a voice connection. Windows XP has PPPoE software built in, but the setup process will vary from provider to provider. They should give you clear instructions.

NOTE

> Some ISPs give you a CD-ROM with installation software that does the next setup procedure for you. I intensely dislike this practice because you never know what other software—including adware and "customer support" spyware—they're installing. I lie to them, telling them I'm installing the connection on a Macintosh or Linux computer and can't use their software; then I ask for the information necessary to perform the setup manually. Sometimes this works, and sometimes it makes life very difficult. Southwest Bell DSL, for instance, requires you to set up the service account through a special Web site, so if you want to shun their software, you need Internet access to set up your Internet access.

If you perform the procedure manually, these are the steps you should perform:

1. Open the Network Connections window by clicking Start, My Computer, My Network Places, View Network Connections. Be sure that the Local Area Connection icon for the network adapter that connects to your DSL modem says `Firewalled`. Be sure to read the cautions on page xxx and xxx. [The immediately preceding two cautions]

2. Click Create a New Connection. Select Connect to the Internet and click Next.

3. Select Set Up My Connection Manually and click Next.

4. Select Connect Using a Broadband Connection That Requires a User Name and Password, and click Next.

5. Enter your ISP's name and click Next.

6. Enter the username and password assigned by your ISP, and click Next; then click Finish.

At this point, you are prompted to sign on. The procedure for signing on and off is the same as for dial-up Internet service and is described later in this chapter in the section "Making and Ending a Dial-Up Connection."

INSTALLING AN ALWAYS-ON BROADBAND CONNECTION

If you have "always-on" DSL or cable service, your ISP will provide different installation instructions. You'll most likely perform these steps:

1. In the New Connection Wizard, select Set Up a Connection Manually, and click Next.

2. Check I Connect through a Local Area Network and click Next.

3. Uncheck Automatic Discovery of a Proxy Server, and click Next, then Finish. These steps tell Windows that it doesn't need to dial a modem connection.

Now, you might need to configure the Ethernet card using information specified by your ISP. Your ISP will tell you whether your network card must be manually configured or if the DHCP protocol is available through its service.

8

> **NOTE**
>
> Installing a network adapter to connect to a broadband modem doesn't give you a Local Area Network—it's just a way of connecting to the modem. If you want to set up a LAN in addition to an Internet connection, please see Chapter 18.

SETTING UP DYNAMIC IP ADDRESSING (DHCP)

In most cases, your ISP will use the DHCP protocol to configure client network adapters. This is the default setting for all new network adapters. To confirm the setting, do the following:

1. Log on as a Computer Administrator. Open the Network Connections window—for example, from Start, My Computer, My Network Places, View Network Connections.

2. Right-click the icon for the local area connection that corresponds to the adapter connected to your DSL or cable modem, and select Properties.

3. Highlight Internet Protocol (TCP/IP) and click Properties.

4. Ensure that Obtain an IP Address Automatically and Obtain DNS Server Address Automatically are selected.

Some ISPs require you to give them the MAC address of your network adapter. This is an identification number built in to the hardware that uniquely identifies your particular network adapter. To find this number, follow these steps:

1. Open a Command Prompt window by clicking Start, All Programs, Accessories, Command Prompt.

2. Type `ipconfig /all` and press Enter.

3. You might need to scroll back, but find the title that is something like `Ethernet Adapter Local Area Connection`. Look for the name of the adapter that goes to your broadband modem. This might be `Local Area Connection 2`, if you've installed an extra adapter. Ignore any entries that mention the word `Miniport`. If you have multiple adapters and can't tell which is which, unplug the network cable from all but the one that goes to the modem and type the command again.

4. Find the line titled `Physical Address`. It will be followed by six pairs of numbers and letters, such as `00-03-FF-B9-0E-14`. This is the information to give to your ISP.

Alternatively, you might be instructed to set your computer's name to a name provided by the ISP. To do this, follow these steps:

1. Log on as a Computer Administrator. Click Start and right-click My Computer. Select Properties.

2. Select the Computer Name tab and click Change.

3. Enter the computer name as supplied by your ISP, as shown in Figure 8.9

4. Click More, and enter the domain name specified by your ISP, as shown in Figure 8.10.

8

After you close all of these dialog boxes by clicking OK, you need to let Windows restart. When it restarts, your Internet connection should be up and running.

Figure 8.9
Specify a required computer name in the Computer Name Changes dialog box.

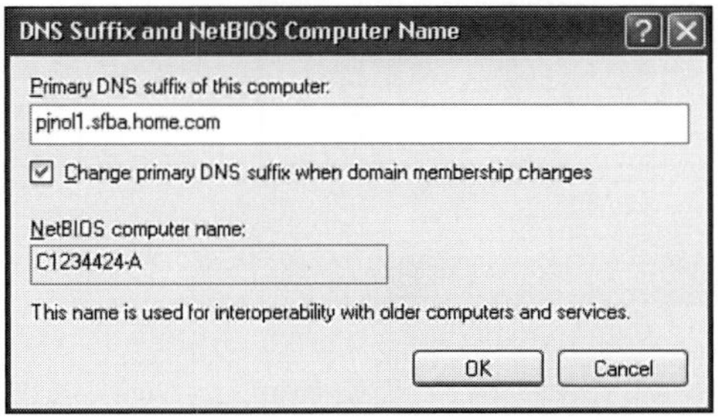

Figure 8.10
Enter your ISP's full domain name in the DNS suffix dialog box.

SETTING UP A FIXED IP ADDRESS

In some cases, your ISP will require you to set your LAN adapter to a fixed IP address. This might be required with either PPPoe or always-on service. To set the address, follow these steps:

1. Log on as a Computer Administrator. Choose Start, Control Panel, Network and Internet Connections, Network Connections.

2. Right-click the Local Area Connection icon, and select Properties. View the General tab, as shown in Figure 8.11.

3. Select Internet Protocol and click the Properties button.

4. Select Use the Following IP Address, and enter the IP address, Subnet mask, and Default gateway information provided by your ISP, as shown in Figure 8.12.

TIP

If you use your computer at work and at home and have a fixed IP address at home, leave the IP address and DNS settings set to Obtain Automatically for work and make the fixed IP address entries for home on the Alternate Configuration tab that appears when Obtain Automatically is selected.

Figure 8.11
Select Internet Protocol and click Properties to set the LAN adapter's IP address and network information.

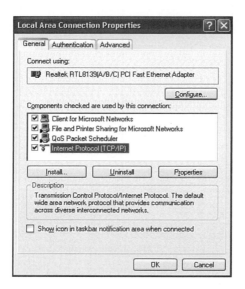

Figure 8.12
Here, you can add the network address, subnet mask, and DNS information supplied by your ISP.

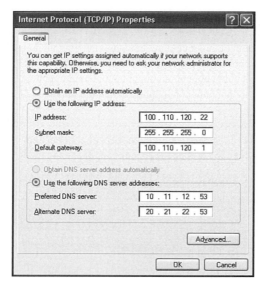

T I P

> When you enter TCP/IP dotted-decimal numbers like 1.2.3.4, the spacebar advances the cursor across the periods. This technique is much easier than using the mouse to change fields.

5. Select Use the Following DNS Server Addresses, and enter the two DNS addresses provided by your ISP.
6. Click OK to return to the Local Area Connection Properties dialog box.

When you have completed this procedure, return to the PPPoE setup steps, or, if you have always-on service, open Internet Explorer to test-drive your new connection.

MAKING AND ENDING A DIAL-UP CONNECTION

If you use a dial-up connection with an analog modem or ISDN line, after you've set up an icon for your ISP, making the connection is a snap. You'll use this same procedure if you use a broadband connection with PPPoE that requires you to log on:

1. Select (double-click) the connection icon in Network Connections.
2. When Windows displays a connection dialog box (see Figure 8.13), enter the login name and password assigned by your ISP. If you're the only one using your PC (or you don't care who uses your account) check the Save Password check box so that you don't need to retype it every time you dial.

T I P

> Put your dial-up connections on your Start menu for quick access. To do this, right-click the Start button. Click Customize, select the Advanced tab, and find Network Connections in the list of Start Menu Items. Check either Display As Connect-To Menu (which lets you dial a connection right from the Start menu) or Link to Network Connections Folder.

3. For dial-up connections only, check that the phone number is correct, including area code and any required prefix numbers. You might need to correct your current location (Dialing From) and/or the Dialing Rules if the prefix or area code isn't correct; to do this, click Properties, and then, optionally, Dialing Rules.
4. If you want other users of your computer to be able to use this same ISP account and password, or if you are going to use Internet Connection Sharing to share this connection, check Save This User Name and Anyone Who Uses This Computer.
5. Click Dial or Connect to make the connection.

Figure 8.13
When you want to initiate a dial-up connection, enter your username and password, and check Save Password to simplify connecting in the future.

Windows then dials your ISP and establishes the connection; if it works, a connection icon appears in the System Tray with a temporary note indicating the connection speed, as shown in Figure 8.14. (Unfortunately, on some computers—mine for instance—this shows the wrong number. It shows the speed the computer is using to talk to the modem, not the actual speed of the Internet connection.)

 If your modem doesn't attempt to connect to your ISP, see "Modem Didn't Dial ISP" in the "Troubleshooting" section at the end of this chapter.

Figure 8.14
The icon beneath this information bubble indicates an active dial-up Internet connection. The bubble itself indicates the connection name and speed.

If the connection fails, Windows displays a (usually) sensible message explaining why: there was no dial tone because your modem in unplugged, there was no answer at the ISP or the line is busy, or your username and password failed. In the latter case, you get three tries to enter the correct information before Windows hangs up the phone.

 If the modem dials, but fails to establish a connection, see "Modem Dialed ISP but the Connection Failed" in the "Troubleshooting" section at the end of this chapter.

(Of course, if you use a dedicated, always-on Internet connection, you don't have to fool with dialing and hanging up connections at all. To be honest, I don't know which I like more about my DSL connection—its lickety-split speed or the fact that I don't have to wait for a modem connection to be made.)

After your connection is made, you should be able to browse Web sites, check your email, and so on.

 If your Internet connection seems to be working but you can't view any Web pages, see "Can't Reach Any Web Sites" in the "Troubleshooting" section at the end of this chapter.

CHECKING THE CONNECTION STATUS

The System Tray connection icon shows two tiny computer screens, which are normally black. They flicker when data activity occurs on the dial-up connection, momentarily turning green to show that the modem is active. The two indicators represent data you're sending and data returned from your ISP, respectively. This icon is actually a decent troubleshooting tool because you can immediately see whether modem activity is taking place.

If you let your mouse cursor hover over the connection icon, a small pop-up window shows the number of bytes transmitted and received over the current connection.

If you right-click the connection icon, a pop-up menu appears. This menu contains the following options:

- **Disconnect**—Hang up the connection
- **Status**—View the Connection Status dialog
- **Open Network and Dial-Up Connections**—Bring up the whole dial-up networking control panel

Choosing Status from this menu opens the Status dialog box, which shows the number of bytes transmitted and received during the connection and the number of transmission errors detected; it also has buttons to let you disconnect or adjust the connection properties. Its Details tab lists technical information such as the connection's IP address.

HANGING UP A DIAL-UP CONNECTION

After you finish with your Internet connection, simply right-click the connection icon in your System Tray, and select Disconnect. Windows hangs up the dial-up connection and removes the icon from the System Tray in a few seconds.

CHANGING THE DEFAULT CONNECTION

If you don't establish a connection manually before using an Internet program like Internet Explorer, Windows goes ahead and dials your ISP automatically when you start these programs. If you don't want Windows to dial automatically, or if you have defined multiple dial-up connections, you can tell Windows which, if any, of the connections you want it to dial automatically.

To change the default settings, follow these steps:

1. Open the Control Panel, select Network and Internet Connections, and click Internet Options. Alternatively, within Internet Explorer, you can choose Tools, Internet Options.

2. Select the Connections tab, and highlight the dial-up connection you want to use for Internet browsing (see Figure 8.15).

Figure 8.15
In the Internet Properties dialog box, you can specify which dial-up connection to use automatically when an Internet application is started.

3. If you use a standalone computer or a portable computer that sometimes has Internet access via a LAN, select Dial Whenever a Network Connection Is Not Present.

   If you want to use the modem connection even while you're connected to a LAN, you can select Always Dial My Default Connection.

   Finally, if you don't want Windows to dial automatically at all but prefer to make your connection manually, you can choose Never Dial a Connection.

4. If you have changed the default dial-up connection, click Set Default.

5. Click OK.

MANAGING MULTIPLE INTERNET CONNECTIONS

Life would be so simple if computers and people just stayed put, but that's not the way the world works anymore. Portable computers now account for more than half of the computers sold in the United States. Managing Internet connections from multiple locations can be a little tricky.

I talk a bit more about the ins and outs of traveling with your computer in Chapter 17 where the topic is remote networking.

The issue comes up with plain Internet connectivity as well, so let me share some tips:

- If you use a LAN Internet connection in the office and a modem connection elsewhere, bring up the Connections tab of the Internet Properties dialog box, and choose Dial Whenever a Network Connection Is Not Present, as I discussed in "Changing the Default Connection."

- If you use different LAN connections in different locations, see "Multiple LAN Connections" in Chapter 17.

- If you use a dial-up Internet service provider with different local access numbers in different locations, life is a bit more difficult. It would be great if Windows let you associate a distinct dial-up number for each dialing location, but it doesn't—dialing locations just adjust the area code and dialing prefixes.

  The solution is to make separate connection icons for each location's access number. After you set up and test one connection, right-click its icon and select Create Copy. Rename the icon using the alternate city in the name; for example, I might name my icons My ISP Berkeley, My ISP Freestone, and so on. Finally, open the Properties page for the new icon, and set the appropriate local access number and dialing location.

  In this case, it's best to tell Windows never to automatically dial a connection (as shown in "Changing the Default Connection") because it doesn't know which of several connections is the right one to use; and you don't want it to dial a long-distance number without your noticing.

Moving around from one network to another or from one ISP to another can also cause major headaches when you try to send email. The reason is that outgoing email has to be sent from your email program to a mail server called an SMTP server. These servers are set up to reject incoming email from an unidentified user who is not directly connected to or dialed-up to their own network. For example, if you have Outlook Express set up to send email through your company's mail server and you try to send mail from home, your company's server will see that you're connected from a foreign network—that is, your IPS's network—and reject the message, calling it an "attempt to relay mail."

Likewise, you might experience the same problem if you are set up to send through your ISP's mail server and then try to send mail from a wireless connection at an Internet café.

→ For some tips on handling this problem, **see** "All Your Mail Is in a Laptop," **p. 364**.

TROUBLESHOOTING

MODEM DIDN'T DIAL ISP

When I attempted to make a connection to my ISP, the modem didn't make an audible attempt to connect.

There are four possible problems here:

- Your phone line may not be correctly plugged into the modem. Be sure the phone cable is plugged into the correct jack on the modem.

- The phone line may not be working. Try an extension phone in the same wall jack to see if there's a dial tone.

- The modem may be working but its speaker volume may be turned down. (This has fooled me more than once!) Some external modems have volume knobs. You can set the volume on an internal modem by opening Control Panel, Phone and Modem Options. View the Modems tab and select Properties. Select the Modem tab and adjust the volume control.

- There may be a hardware problem with the modem. Open the Modem Properties as described in the previous paragraph. View the Diagnostics tab and click Query Modem. After 5 to 15 seconds, you should see some entries in the "Command / Response" list. If an error message appears instead, your modem is not working properly. If it's an external modem, be sure it's powered up. If it's an internal modem, see Chapter 27. Try to update the modem's driver software.

MODEM DIALED ISP BUT THE CONNECTION FAILED

When I attempted to make a connection to my ISP, the modem made the call, but the Internet connection still failed.

Windows should indicate what sort of problem was encountered. You may have typed your account name and password incorrectly. Try one or two more times. If it still doesn't work, a call to your ISP is the best next step. Your ISP may require you to enter the account name information in an unintuitive way (Earthlink, for example, requires you put "ELN\" before your account name). Their customer support people will help you straighten this out.

CAN'T REACH ANY WEB SITES

My Internet connection seems to be established correctly but I can't reach any Web sites.

Troubleshooting connection problems is such a large topic that an entire chapter is devoted to it. If you're having trouble, turn to Chapter 13, "Troubleshooting Your Internet Connection," for the nitty-gritty details.

TIPS FROM THE WINDOWS PROS: STAYING CONNECTED WHILE TRAVELING ABROAD

As I said earlier, you can choose an ISP with regional local access numbers to let you connect without toll charges wherever you roam in your home country. But what about when you travel overseas?

Actually, you usually don't have to go far to find an Internet terminal. You can rent PCs with Internet connections for roughly $1 to $10 per hour almost anywhere. Listings of Internet cafés and computer parlors are now a required element in guide books (for example, the fantastic *Rough Guide* series), and tourism information centers in most towns can direct you to the nearest rental centers.

If you want to connect your own computer, however, connecting is a bit more difficult. The following are some tips I've picked up in travels through Mexico, Australia, and Europe:

- Do your research before you leave. Search the Internet to find at least one Internet location and/or ISP in each area you'll be visiting. Print these pages and bring them along, being sure to get the local addresses and telephone numbers. You might find a more convenient location or better service after you arrive, but this way you have a place to start.

- Most Internet cafés won't let you hook up your own computer. Some will. You can find Kinko's Copy centers, for example, in many large cities in North America, Europe, and Asia; they're outfitted with fast computers, fast connections, and at least one bay with an Ethernet cable that you can use to connect your own laptop. Bring a PCMCIA (PC Card) Ethernet card, and you're set. (You will have to configure it using the Local Area Connection icon in Network and Dial-Up Connections, as you learn in Chapter 15, "Creating a Windows XP Home Network" using the settings provided by the rental center.)

- Bring some formatted floppy disks with you. If you need to transfer files and can't hook up your own computer, you can at least use the floppy disks.

- If you normally receive email through a POP mail server at your ISP, use one of the free email services such as Hotmail or Yahoo! Mail to view your home email via the Web while you're traveling. Use a different password, not your regular password, for the free account. Set up the free service to fetch mail from your ISP, using what is called *external* or POP mail. Set the mail service to "leave mail on the server" so you can filter through your mail the normal way when you get home. Delete the free account, or change its password when you return home.

  These steps will (a) let you read your mail from virtually any Internet terminal in the world and (b) protect your real mail password from unscrupulous types who might be monitoring the network traffic in the places you visit.

- If you're staying a reasonable length of time in one country, you can sign up for a month of Internet service. For example, in Australia, I used ozemail.com, which gave me local access numbers all over the Australian continent. A month's service cost only $17, with no setup fee. After I found an adapter for Australia's curious telephone jacks, I was all set.

■ If you do use a foreign ISP, configure your email software to use the foreign ISP's outgoing mail (SMTP) server, but keep your incoming POP server pointed to your home ISP. (This step is important because most ISPs' mail servers won't accept mail from dial-up users outside their own networks. You need to use *their* SMTP server to *send* mail, and *your* home POP server to *pick up* mail.)

■ Get power plug adapters and telephone plug adapters from a travel store, telephone accessory store, or international appliance store before you leave, if you can.

CHAPTER **9**

BROWSING THE WORLD WIDE WEB WITH INTERNET EXPLORER

In this chapter

ORIGINS AND DEVELOPMENT OF THE WORLD WIDE WEB

The World Wide Web (also called WWW or the Web) has worked its way into virtually every aspect of modern life, an astounding fact considering that just a short decade ago it was nothing more than an idea living inside a computer scientist's head. That scientist was Tim Berners-Lee, who, while working at the European Laboratory for Particle Physics (or CERN, from its original name, *Conseil Européen pour la Recherche Nucléaire*), needed to devise a way in which scientific data could easily be shared simultaneously with physicists around the world. Along with Robert Cailliau, he designed the first Web browser in 1990 to allow scientists to access information remotely without the need to reformat the data.

This new communications technology developed by Berners-Lee and Cailliau transmitted data to viewers via the Internet, which by the early 1990s already existed as a global network linking numerous educational and government institutions worldwide. The Internet served for decades as a means for exchanging electronic mail (email), transferring files, and holding virtual conversations in newsgroups, although data shared online was typically static and text only. The new idea provided data in hypertext format, which made it easier for far-removed scientists to view the electronic library at CERN's information server. The hypertext data could even incorporate graphics and other file formats, a practice virtually unknown to Internet users of the time.

Despite a relatively small initial audience, the hypertext concept quickly caught on and by 1993 more than 50 hypertext information servers were available on the Internet. That year also saw the development of Mosaic, the first modern and truly user-friendly hypertext browser. Mosaic was produced by the National Center for Supercomputing Applications (NCSA) at the University of Illinois with versions for the X Window System, PC, and Macintosh. Mosaic served as the basis for a number of browsers produced by commercial software developers, with Netscape Navigator and Microsoft Internet Explorer eventually becoming Mosaic's best-known offspring.

The world was eager when the first commercial Web sites began appearing in 1994. President Bill Clinton and Vice President Al Gore had already popularized the idea of an "information superhighway" during their 1992 political campaign, and by the next year it seemed that everyone wanted to get online and see what this new World Wide Web of information had to offer. A high level of media coverage meant that by 1995 most of the general public knew what the World Wide Web was, and they wanted to be part of it.

The rest, as they say, is history. In its current form, the Web exists on hundreds of thousands of servers around the world. The system of naming and addressing Web sites is implemented by a number of private registrars contracted by the United States Government. Today you can go shopping, play games, conduct research, download tax forms, check the status of a shipment, find directions to a new restaurant, get advice, or just plain goof off on the World Wide Web.

The hypertext concept has grown as well, even outside the confines of the Internet. These days, Microsoft structures much of the Windows interface in a Hypertext Markup Language (HTML) format. This makes interfacing with the Web more seamless and allows you to use the same program—in this case, Internet Explorer 6—to browse the World Wide Web, your company's intranet, the contents of your own computer, the online Help system, Control Panel, and other network resources.

WHAT'S NEW IN INTERNET EXPLORER 6?

If you have used Internet Explorer 5, IE6 will be very familiar to you. Some of its new features are behind-the-scenes, not readily apparent but designed to make IE run more smoothly. Others are enhancements that you will see:

- The Integrated Web searching tool formerly called the Search Assistant has been spiffed up and is now called the Search Companion. You'll notice some changes in the interface, but it works essentially the same way. (See "Effectively Searching the Web," later in this chapter.)
- The Media button on the Explorer Bar is new. Click on it to bring up the Radio Guide and your music and video folders in a side-pane. The media player control buttons are also included in the pane for ease of use.
- A new pop-up menu for images makes it simpler to save or email them. (For more about this tool, see "Dealing with Multimedia Browsing and Downloading," later in this chapter.
- Playback support for Flash and Shockwave files is built into IE6.

NOTE

> The Department of Justice Consent Decree has brought about some changes in the way that middleware applications are handled. As of SP-1 you can configure your computer to show only Microsoft middleware applications (Outlook Express, Internet Explorer, and so on), to show only non-Microsoft middleware applications (Netscape Navigator, Eudora, and so forth), or to show some combination of both. See Chapter 22, "Configuration via Control Panel Applets," for more information on how to make these changes to your Windows XP computer.

INTERNET EXPLORER 6 QUICK TOUR

Because Web browsers have become ubiquitous, we'll assume here that you are already comfortable with the basics of Web browsing. And because many Windows XP elements such as Windows Explorer, the Control Panel, and My Network Places use the background code of IE6, you are probably already familiar with the location of common toolbar buttons, menus, and other screen elements.

Still, IE6 does have some new features, so an overview of how to use some of them is provided here. This overview will be especially useful if you are switching from an even earlier version of Internet Explorer or another Web browser such as Netscape Navigator.

→ You must have a connection to the Internet configured on your computer before you can connect to the Web. **See** "Configuring Your Internet Connection," **p. 269**.

You can begin browsing the Internet by launching Internet Explorer from the Start Menu.

If you connect to the Internet via a dial-up connection, you may be prompted to connect. When the connection is established, Internet Explorer probably opens, by default, to the MSN (The Microsoft Network) home page, as shown in Figure 9.1. Some PC manufacturers—such as Compaq—customize IE before delivery so that you see their home page instead.

→ To change the home page so that you see a personal favorite when IE opens, **see** "Customizing the Browser and Setting Internet Options," **p. 313**.

Figure 9.1
Internet Explorer opens with MSN, the default home page, displayed.

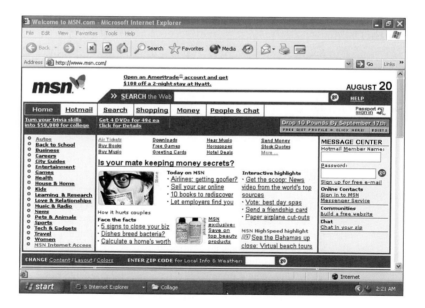

 Did a Web page freeze your browser? See "Internet Explorer Crashes on Certain Web Pages" in the "Troubleshooting" section at the end of the chapter.

As you probably know, Web pages change frequently, so the page you see will almost certainly look different from Figure 9.1. The general layout of the IE6 window might also be somewhat different from what is shown here, although if you have performed a standard installation of Windows XP and have not done any customizations, it should look like this.

Want even more space to view Web pages? Press F11 to change the view to get rid of some screen elements and make more room for Web documents. If you don't like what you see, press F11 again to toggle back.

Consider creating buttons for the Web pages you visit most frequently on the Links bar. In order to see the Links bar more fully, you must first unlock the toolbars, by going to View, Toolbars, and unchecking "Lock the Toolbars." Then, click and drag the Links bar to a more visible position on the screen. It should look something like Figure 9.2. Before you customize the Links bar, keep these tips in mind:

- The Customize Links button merely takes you to a Microsoft-hosted Web page that provides instructions on how to do what is already described here. Consider removing that button to make room your own favorites.

Drag a Web site icon from the Address bar.

Figure 9.2
The Links bar is a handy place to store your most frequently visited Web sites.

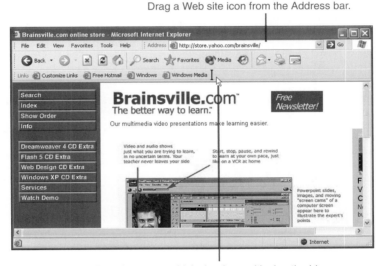

Drop it onto your Links bar by positioning the I-beam cursor where you'd like the new link to appear.

- You can remove unwanted Links buttons by right-clicking them and choosing Delete from the menu that appears.
- Make space for more Links by right-clicking an existing Links button and choosing Rename from the menu that appears. Type in a shorter name or abbreviation and click OK.
- To save more room, reduce the length of your Address bar and move it to share a "line" with another toolbar. (The main toolbar, on the top line, is a good place for the address bar.) Experiment with the placement of all of the toolbars so that you have as much space as possible to view Web pages.

- The easiest way to add a Web page to the Links bar is to drag the icon for the page from the Address bar and drop it onto the Links bar. Figure 9.2 demonstrates this technique.

As you probably know, you can navigate around the Internet by typing Web addresses into the Address bar or by clicking hyperlinks on a page. The mouse pointer changes from an arrow into a hand whenever it is over a link. Among the most useful features of the IE6 interface are the Back and Forward buttons. When you click the Back button, you return to the previously visited page. Clicking Forward moves you ahead once again. (To move around even faster, Alt + back arrow and Alt + forward arrow have the same function, and if you have a new mouse, it may have special Back and Forward buttons on it.)

Are you frustrated because Internet Explorer tells you that a site you visit often is unavailable? See "What Happened to the Web Site?" in the "Troubleshooting" section at the end of this chapter.

Notice that next to both the Back and Forward buttons are downward-pointing arrows. If you have been browsing through several Web pages, click the down arrow next to the Back button. A menu similar to that shown in Figure 9.3 should appear showing a backward progression of the Web pages you have visited. Click a listing to move back several pages simultaneously rather than one at a time.

Figure 9.3
The Back and Forward buttons allow you to navigate more easily through recently viewed Web pages.

ENTERING URLs

Every Web document you view in IE6 is identified by a unique address called a *Uniform Resource Locator (URL)*. When you visit a Web page, for example, the URL for that page appears in the Address bar of Internet Explorer. URLs for links also appear in the status bar when you hover the mouse pointer over a hyperlink.

URLs are broken down into three main components. To illustrate, consider these URLs:

```
http://www.quepublishing.com/
http://www.irs.treas.gov/formspubs/index.html
http://www.zen-satsang.org/
http://store.yahoo.com/brainsville/index.html
```

Each of the listed addresses conforms to this scheme:

```
protocol://domain/path
```

The protocol for all World Wide Web documents is `http`, short for *Hypertext Transfer Protocol*. The protocol is followed by a colon, two forward slashes and the domain name.

The domain often—but not always—starts with www. Following the domain is the path to a specific document file. You may notice that the first URL listed here does not actually show a path; this is usually okay because Internet Explorer automatically looks for a file called `default.htm`, `index.htm`, `home.html`, or something along those lines in the root directory of the domain.

TIP

> If you get an error message when trying to visit a URL, remove the path from the address and try again. Although the exact link might have changed, it's quite possible that the main page for the site still exists and that you will be able to find the information you seek there.

9

When you type a URL into the IE Address bar, a built-in feature automatically reviews your browsing history and presents a number of possible matches. A list appears directly under the Address bar and shrinks as you type more characters, narrowing the search. If you see a desired URL appear in the list, click it to go directly to that page. This feature, called AutoComplete, can save keystrokes, but it can also be incriminating if others use your computer and user profile. I mean, do you really want the rest of your household to know you visited `industrialstrengthwhoopicushions.com`? AutoComplete works with Web form data as well, which means that others could see your user IDs, passwords, and other sensitive data for various sites.

If you are concerned about others viewing your data, disable AutoComplete by doing the following:

1. Choose Tools, Internet Options.
2. Click the Content tab to bring it to the front, and then click AutoComplete.
3. Remove check marks next to the items you do not want affected by AutoComplete.
4. You can further safeguard existing information by clicking either of the two Clear buttons in the AutoComplete Settings dialog box. Click OK when you are finished.
5. To prevent existing Web URLs from being compromised, select the General tab in the Internet Options dialog box, and click Clear History. Click OK to finish.

NOTE

> If no one else has access to your Windows XP user profile or you really don't care who sees where you've been browsing, AutoComplete doesn't present a security problem. In this case, you should be able to safely leave the feature enabled.

BROWSING OFFLINE

If you have a permanent Internet connection that is never interrupted or shut off, consider yourself fortunate. A permanent connection—such as what you might have through your company's network—allows you a great deal of flexibility in terms of what and when you download from the World Wide Web.

Alas, not all users have this sort of flexibility in their daily computing, so IE offers you the ability to download Web pages into cache for offline viewing. This feature can be useful in a variety of situations. For example, you can set up IE to download specific Web sites in the background every time you go online. You can also download Web sites onto your portable computer so that you can view them later—while you're on the plane, for example.

NOTE

> Internet Explorer works just fine whether or not an Internet connection is available. However, if no connection is available, it can view only files stored on the local computer or other available network resources. The IE6 status bar displays this icon when you are working offline.

The process of downloading a Web site for offline browsing is fairly simple. Your first step, obviously, is to browse to the Web site you want to make available offline. For best results, open the main or index page of the Web site first. Now try the following:

1. Choose Favorites, Add to Favorites.

2. In the Add Favorite dialog box, place a check mark next to Make Available Offline, as shown in Figure 9.4. You can also change the name so that you will be able to easily identify the page. The name entered here is what will be shown in your Favorites list.

Click here to make the page available for offline viewing   Click here to set offline viewing options

Figure 9.4
In this dialog box, you can select this Web page for offline viewing and choose how this Web page will appear offline.

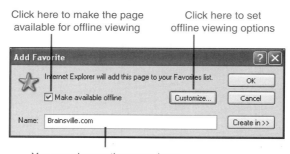

You can change the name here to something you will recognize easily

3. To set up offline browsing options, click Customize to start the Offline Favorite Wizard. Click Next in the introductory dialog box to open the window shown in Figure 9.5. Depending on the layout of the site, this screen could contain the most important options that you will set.

Figure 9.5
Here, you can choose how many link levels you want to make available offline.

4. Usually, you will want to choose Yes when asked whether you want to download pages that are linked to the one you are making available offline. For example, if the main page is a list of news stories, the next level of links probably contains the actual stories. Viewing a list of stories won't do you much good without also being able to read the stories!

5. If you chose Yes in the preceding step, select the number of levels you want to download. The exact number will depend on the layout of the site.

TIP

> If you aren't sure how many levels to download, cancel this process, and browse the Web site to get a feel for it. Too many levels could result in a lot of unwanted content, and too few will leave you frustrated, trying to click links that are unavailable.

6. Click Next after you have chosen how many link levels you want to download. In the next window, you must choose between downloading the pages manually or automatically. If you will browse offline only occasionally—say, on a laptop—choose the first option, Only When I Choose Synchronize from the Tools Menu, and skip to step 8. Otherwise, select the second option, I Would Like to Create a New Schedule, and click Next to create a schedule for downloads.

7. Select a schedule to synchronize the download process. You may want to set a schedule that will download the pages when the computer is least likely to be in use. You can also choose to have the computer automatically connect to the Internet for you if the computer is not connected at synchronization time.

8. Click Next when you are finished setting your schedule. If the Web site requires a username and password, you must enter it in the last window of the wizard. Click Finish. If the Add Favorite dialog box is still open, click OK to close it.

9

VIEWING PAGES OFFLINE

Now that you've set up a schedule and have downloaded some pages for offline viewing, you are ready to actually read them offline. To do so:

1. Open Internet Explorer.

2. If you are prompted to establish an Internet connection, click the Cancel button. Internet Explorer may load a copy of your home page from cache, so it could appear as if you are online even though you are not. On the other hand, IE may open with a message that says "The page cannot be displayed." If so, go to File and click Work Offline.

3. To view a synchronized offline page you have set up and downloaded, click Favorites and choose the page's listing from the Favorites menu. You can view the page and click links that have been downloaded.

4. Notice that if you move the mouse pointer over a link that has not been downloaded, this "not available" symbol will appear.

If you click a link that has not been downloaded, you will be asked whether you want to connect or remain in offline mode. If you do not or cannot connect, you cannot open the link.

SAVING A SINGLE WEB PAGE FOR LATER VIEWING

Sometimes you want to save only a single Web page, not a whole site, for offline viewing. Say you want to just reference a page, defer the reading of a page, save a page that shows proof of an online purchase, or print it later when you're offline. Here's how:

1. In IE, select File, Save As.

2. In the Save As type section of the dialog box, select Web Page, Complete.

3. Then select the folder, name the file, and click Save.

What happens now depends on your page. The Web page itself (the HTML file) is stored in the folder you specified. If images, scripts, and other supporting files exist on the page, IE creates a folder just *under* the target folder and puts those items in it. Then IE modifies the HTML code in the HTML page to point to that subfolder instead of across the Web. This lets you open the Web page without being online, and it should still look correct.

It's important to understand that, by default, the HTML file and its subfolder are linked and act as a single entity. Moving one or the other moves both of them. This prevents the entity from becoming nonfunctional if you move them around separately.

If you have Microsoft Office installed, you have three options for altering this linkage behavior:

1. Open a Windows Explorer window and select Tools, Folder Options.

2. Click the View tab.

3. Scroll down to Managing Pairs of Web Pages and Folders. Double-click it if it's not showing the following three options:

- Show and Manage the Pair As a Single File (default setting)
- Show Both Parts and Manage Them Independently
- Show Both Parts but Manage Them As a Single File

NOTE

If you try to change the name of either the HTML page or the underlying subfolder containing the associated files, you are warned that this will break the page.

9

DEALING WITH MULTIMEDIA BROWSING AND DOWNLOADING

When the World Wide Web first debuted as a method for sharing scientific data among physicists, the hypertext format of the data was specifically chosen to lend itself to sharing information in many different formats. For early Internet users, the ability to download pictures and other graphics in conjunction with Web pages was both exciting and profound.

Today, Web pages with pictures in them are commonplace. Web developers continue to push the multimedia horizon, with many sites now featuring audio and video. You can even listen to radio stations and watch other broadcasts live over the Web.

In addition to multimedia-rich Web sites, you'll find that the Web is a good place to download software. You can find many places to download freeware, shareware, software updates, and sites to purchase and download full versions of programs.

IMAGES

Believe it or not, graphics-rich Web sites used to be controversial. Some people believed that graphics would put too much of a strain on the bandwidth capacity of the Internet, but those gloom-and-doom predictions have not come to pass. Backbone improvements have helped the Net keep pace with the ever-growing appetite for multimedia on the Web, and images are now both commonplace and expected.

Internet Explorer supports three basic graphics formats used in Web pages:

- **JPEG**—Short for Joint Photographic Experts Group, this format allows pictures to be compressed significantly (reducing download time and bandwidth, but also image quality) so it is used often for photos on Web pages.
- **GIF**—Short for Graphical Interchange Format, this format is often used for buttons and other simple icons used on Web pages.
- **PNG**—Short for Portable Network Graphics, was developed to help images load faster and to enable them to look the same on different platforms.

The exact format used for each image is not apparent when you view the page. Usually, the specific format used is not important unless you plan to copy the graphics and use them for some other purpose. For Web use, the formats are essentially interchangeable.

By default, IE6 displays graphics used in Web pages. Although the idea of disabling this feature to allow speedier downloads might seem appealing, many Web pages now rely so heavily on graphics that they do not include text links. This means you cannot navigate the site without the images. Don't disable this feature unless you deem it absolutely necessary.

 What if some graphics on a page open, but others don't? See "Some Graphics Don't Appear" in the "Troubleshooting" section at the end of the chapter.

You can do a variety of things with online graphics. You will notice a new feature in IE6: When you mouse-over a graphic, a pop-up window will appear. Click the appropriate icon if you'd like to save the image to your hard drive, print it, email it, or just open the My Pictures folder. If you find this toolbar annoying, disable it by going to Tools, Internet Options. Under the Advanced tab, scroll down to Multimedia and deselect Enable Image Toolbar. Click OK to save and close the window.

Also notice a little square with four arrows on it, in the lower-right corner of some pictures. This happens only on pictures that, if shown full size, wouldn't fit on the screen. IE6 thoughtfully auto-sizes such pictures so that you can see the whole image at once. Click on the little box and the image will scale up to its full size, in higher resolution. When it's full size, click on the little box again, and the image you're viewing returns to the compressed size.

CAUTION

> Before you use any graphics you find on the Web, check the Web site for a copyright statement or other information about terms of use. You should obtain permission before you use any copyrighted material.

AUDIO AND VIDEO

A growing number of Web sites offer audio or video content in addition to standard text and graphics. The terms *audio* and *video* when used in conjunction with Web content can mean a few different things:

- Basic audio files—such as MIDI music files—that play in the background while you view a Web page.
- Video files on Web sites that download and play automatically or play when you click a Play button.
- Video media that plays using the Windows Media Player.
- Animated GIFs that give the appearance of a video signal but with a significantly reduced bandwidth requirement. They display a series of static GIF frames that simulate video and are often used in logos.

- Flash movies that also appear to be video but are actually vector-based instructions requiring very little bandwidth. Vector-based simply means that they have small mathematical descriptions (much the same way fonts do in Windows) that can be manipulated to animate the objects.

- Streaming audio or video that you choose to open and listen to or watch.

You might have noticed that, when you visit some Web sites, a song starts to play while you read the page. Audio isn't nearly as common as graphics in Web pages because some people find it annoying. If you come across a Web page that contains a song you would rather not hear, the most obvious solution is to simply turn your speaker volume down or mute the Windows volume control. If you're listening to music on your computer (such as from a CD or MP3 file) and don't want to can your entire audio experience by turning off the speakers, see the note below.

→ To disable audio, video, or other multimedia from automatically downloading when you visit a Web site, **see** "Customizing the Browser and Setting Internet Options," **p. 313**. By disabling these "features" you also might notice that Web pages will load faster. Note that some Web pages use media playback programs that IE settings won't touch. For example, if a page has a RealMedia or QuickTime sound or video file in it, auto-playback of those files will commence regardless of IE settings.

Likewise, some Web sites contain video files and animations set to download and play automatically. MPEG and AVI video files are usually very large, and if you have restricted bandwidth capacity, you might want to consider disabling them.

Web-based video seems to be improving almost daily, but most broadcasts are still lower in quality than that produced by a plain old television set. Whereas a broadcast TV signal may deliver 30 or more frames per second (fps), typical Web-based streaming videos provide just 5–15fps. In contrast to streaming, many sites will give you the option of downloading a video clip before playing it. Usually the clip in this format is much larger and of a higher quality than the streaming video. Once the entire clip has been downloaded, it can be played and may appear as a high-quality image, depending on how it was produced. Playback will typically be in the Windows Media Player, QuickTime Player, or RealPlayer. The ranges of file sizes, frame sizes, and compression techniques all of which affect the quality of the picture, abounds. Unlike the TV standard we are all accustomed to, the Web is the wild, wild West of video non-standards.

→ To learn more about using the Windows XP audio controls, **see** "Volume Control," **p. 159**.

MPEG, AVI, AND WMV VIDEOS

By default, MPEG, AVI, and WMV (Windows Media Video) files are played using Windows Media Player. Windows Media formats are sort of the new kid on the block and are Microsoft's attempt to be a big player in the Internet multimedia market. Just as movies encoded in Apple's QuickTime format or RealNetworks' RealPlayer format require those companies' proprietary player, Microsoft's proprietary format only plays in Microsoft's player.

NOTE

> Windows Media Player is covered in depth in Chapter 7, "Multimedia and Imaging," but because how you deal with online video is relevant to mastering Web browsing, I'll briefly mention its use in this context. Be sure to check Chapter 7 for more about the Media Player.

Snarfed Media Associations

When you install players such as RealPlayer, they want to alter your file associations. Each of the popular media players (QuickTime player, RealPlayer, or Windows Media Player) is engaged in a war of kidnapping your filename associations and wants to become your player of choice. They do this in hopes of garnering your business, (a.k.a. $) one way or another. They either do this by selling you upgrades to the fancier model of the player, or by selling advertisements that show up in their content—or both. These incentives behoove them to offer a quick means to reclaim any file associations that have been hijacked by another player. You don't have to play their game though. You can always change those associations back to the player of your choice. The easiest way to reset media file association is via the preferences dialog box for the media player in question. In Windows Media Player, for example, choose Tools, Options, File Types, and check off the file types (such as MPEG and "video file") you want played by Media Player. Some players try to reclaim associations each time you run them, which can really be annoying. Be aware, though, that not all players can play all the popular file formats. You'll need RealPlayer for Real format, QuickTime for QuickTime. Windows Media Player plays the greatest number of audio and video formats, by far, however.

Most Web pages featuring videos online will give you links for Real, QuickTime, or Media Player, letting you choose, such as the one in Figure 9.6. Some sites will give you links for downloading MPEG or AVI files. These don't stream, and must first download. Depending on your connection speed, downloading could take awhile. These files tend to be very large. Just be prepared for a long download, especially if using a dial-up connection.

Figure 9.6
Choose the target player of your choice, and connection speed, from the drop-down list.

You might notice that Media Player opens as soon as you click the link. Earlier versions of Media Player (prior to ver. 8) would remain blank, however, until the entire file was downloaded. Now with some types of files such as .WMV (Windows Media Video), movies can start playing more quickly even though they are not technically streaming. (See the next section to read about streaming.) Instead, they are doing a *progressive download*. This is less reliable than streaming, but at least you don't have to wait until the movie is completely downloaded before you start seeing it. It might hang up a few times, though, if your connection speed is slow. QuickTime movies have had this feature for some time. Now Media Player does too.

If you click on the Media button in the toolbar, a miniature version of the Media Player will open in the left pane of your IE window, along with a bunch of links for supposedly interesting media. When you click on a Web page link for an audio or video file, you'll be asked if you want it to play in this tiny Media Player or you'd rather it open in a regular Media Player window. The choice is up to you. The advantage of its opening in the small window is that it lets you neatly play some tunes or movie trailers or whatever, over in the left pane while you continue your Web surfing.

Streaming Broadcasts

As mentioned earlier, another type of sound or video you might play over the Internet is *streaming audio* or *streaming video*. Streaming audio/video is a format in which a signal "plays" over your Internet connection starting after a few seconds after you click, instead of playing from a file that was first downloaded to your hard drive.

When you first click a streaming signal, a portion of the signal is buffered in *RAM* on your computer. This buffer helps provide a steady feed if connection quality wavers. If the signal is received faster than it can be played, the additional data is buffered. However, if your connection deteriorates significantly, the video may not play smoothly. Streaming broadcasts are not written to the disk, so retrieving the signal later from your own PC will be impossible.

Although the minimum requirement of many streaming audio signals is typically 56K these days, a quicker connection is desirable. A lower speed delivers a lower-quality broadcast, skipping and jumping of video, or stopping altogether.

Streaming audio signals are often used to play various types of audio signals over the Web. For example, most online music retailers offer you the ability to listen to sample audio tracks from many of the CDs it sells. Also, you can listen to many radio stations and programs—such as those on National Public Radio (www.npr.org)—over your Internet connection instead of a radio.

Streaming video is used by a number of information providers to send newscasts and other broadcasts across the Web. Many news sites, such as www.cnn.com, allow you to watch news stories online. You'll notice that you can continue to surf the Web while a current audio or video is playing.

MSN (windowsmedia.msn.com) provides links to a number of online video resources, streaming and otherwise.

To access streaming audio or video signals, you need to have an appropriate plug-in program for IE6, such as the RealPlayer from Real Broadcast Network (www.real.com), QuickTime from Apple (www.apple.com/quicktime/), or Windows Media Player, included with Windows XP. After you have downloaded and installed the appropriate streaming player following the installation instructions provided by the player's publisher), you can access the streaming signals over the Web.

Although the Windows Media Player can handle many formats, most broadcasts require a specific player. Check the Web site that hosts the streaming media you want to play for specific requirements. Some Web sites offer a choice of player formats, and often, the Web site will have a convenient link for downloading the necessary freeware. RealPlayer is a common application used for streaming audio, and QuickTime is used by many streaming video providers.

Although the look may be different due to custom "skins" used on flashier sites, the basic functions are similar. You'll be able to tell whether it's Windows Media Player, Real Player, QuickTime, or another player if you look closely. Sometimes you'll have to wait for the file to download, and sometimes it will stream right away. QuickTime gives you the choice to download the entire file first so you can avoid glitches when you watch it. Notice that the play slider can go at a different rate than the progress bar, which indicates how much of the file has been downloaded. When it's downloaded, you can play the clip easily again and again without interruption. Note that the Windows Media Player can be encoded right into a Web page these days, so the video might just play with little ado when you hit a particular URL.

→ To learn about downloading programs from the Web, **see** "Downloading Programs," **p. 306**.

To use a streaming media player, follow these steps:

1. Locate a link to an audio clip or video signal you want to access, and click it.

2. Your streaming media player should open automatically. The RealPlayer, the Windows Media Player, and Apple QuickTime include standard Play, Pause, and Stop buttons.

3. When you are finished listening to the streaming signal, click the Close (x) button for the player.

When you access a streaming signal from the Web, notice the bandwidth requirements. Many signal providers provide scaling of signals from as low as 14.4Kbps up to 300Kbps and higher. Choosing a signal that is scaled higher will only provide a higher quality broadcast if your connection can handle it. If you choose a larger signal than you have bandwidth for, the signal will arrive too fragmented to use. For example, suppose you use a dial-up connection that typically runs at 24Kbps to 26Kbps, and the broadcaster offers signals in either 14.4 or 28.8 flavors. Although you might be tempted to opt for the 28.8Kbps signal because your connection is *almost* up to it, you will probably find that the 14.4Kbps broadcast provides a more usable signal.

9

MP3 Audio

MP3 is an audio file format whose name refers to files using MPEG Audio Layer 3, a coding scheme for audio tracks. MP3 files are small (about one-twelfth the size of CD audio tracks) but they maintain a high sound quality. One minute of CD-quality MP3 music requires only 1MB of storage space.

Controversy has surrounded MP3 since its introduction. The small size of MP3 files makes it easier for people to slide behind copyright laws, pirate music, and illegally distribute it over the Internet. These days, authorities are working on ways of controlling this. However, this had only lead to Napster spinoffs that are harder to control and much more difficult to track down or prosecute. It will be interesting to see how the Justice Department handles the impending and unavoidable new age of intellectual property protection.

The bottom line is this: Distributing or downloading MP3 files from any artist without permission is, well, technically, a violation of the law. Although there are artists (particularly new artists) who willingly provide audio tracks for free download as a means for building a fan base, many MP3 sites contain audio files that have been pirated. If you have questions about the legality of MP3 files you find on the Internet, you'll have to be the judge. Probably the most ethical thing for you to do is not to download them, but I don't want to sound like a prude. As I say, it's a brave new world out there in copyright protection. I believe that free music on the Web probably drives the purchase of new CDs and of concert ticket sales. I'm a musician myself, and while I would want my music (and my books) protected, I wouldn't mind more people becoming acquainted with my works, either. It could pay off in the long run. In any case, you might want to be careful about sharing your MP3s of other people's music on the Web, since it could be a little bit dicey, legally.

The MP3 format has become extremely popular, with tiny portable players (such as the iPod from Apple) available that can contain endless hours of music. It is possible to load all of your music into your computer, and create your very own jukebox. Software for recording and organizing your music is available at `www.real.com/player/`, `www.itunes.com`, `www.winamp.com`, and `www.musicmatch.com`, to name a few. MP3 files can be played by many different applications, including Windows Media Player, RealPlayer, and QuickTime. A number of consumer electronics companies are also now producing devices that allow you to play MP3 files away from your computer. Samsung makes a single device (called a Digimax) that functions as three: a digital camera, a PC camera to use for video conferencing, and an MP3 player. A wide variety of MP3 players are available, with varying storage capacities—some units as small as a pen. You can transfer MP3 files to the player's storage via a Universal Serial Bus (USB), parallel, or serial port connection.

For a good resource, free downloads, and to learn more about the MP3 format, go to `www.mp3.com`. After you have downloaded an MP3 file, you can play it using the Windows Media Player, RealPlayer, QuickTime, or any other MP3-compatible player.

TIP

> Sound quality is affected not only by your hardware, but also by the player application. Experiment with several different programs to find the one that works best for you.

When you click a Web page link for an MP3 file, your default MP3 application will probably open. It may or may not be the application you want to use. Also, the MP3 file will be inconveniently saved in IE's cache. You can exercise more control over the process by following these steps:

1. When you see a link for an MP3 file, right-click the link and choose Save Target As.
2. Select the location in which you'd like to save the file download.
3. When the download is complete, open the desired player application manually, and choose File, Open to listen to the file. If you click Open in the File Download dialog box, your default MP3 player will open.

NOTE

> Another new kid on the block, incidentally, is called MP3 Pro. This is an audio format that uses half the storage space per minute without reducing quality.

DOWNLOADING PROGRAMS

Although the World Wide Web is most often thought of as a source of information and entertainment, it is also an excellent place to obtain new software or updates for existing programs.

You can find numerous excellent resources for downloading free or trial versions of software. Good sources are www.tucows.com and www.download.com. It is necessary to follow the specific instructions for installation provided by the software publisher (and offered on most download sites), but when you're downloading, these general rules apply:

- Some Web sites require you to choose from a number of *mirror sites* for your download. Mirror sites are servers in different parts of the world that have the same files on them. The redundancy prevents traffic jams on a single server when many people hit it for the same program downloads. You are asked to select a location that is geographically close to you, but you're usually free to choose any site you want. The closer ones are sometimes faster, but not always. Sometimes I'll download from a mirror site in another country whose citizens are sleeping, and I get quicker downloads.

- To begin the download, typically you just click on a link that says something like Download Now. This should open a dialog box asking whether you want to open or save the file. Choose to Save. Select a location for saving the download files that you will remember—it is a good idea to create a "downloads" folder. Within the Downloads file, I create a new folder with the name of the program, and then switch to that and save the program there. This way, all my downloads are organized and I know where each one is.

- Check with your network administrator before installing any new software to find out what your company policies are.

- Scan all downloads with virus-scanning software before you install them.

- Many downloads come in a compressed .ZIP format. If you download such a file, you can run it easily in XP, because ZIP files are supported without having to install a Zip program such as WinZIP or TurboZIP. Just double-click the Zip file and it will open in a folder window. Then, examine the contents. You'll probably double-click the installer or Setup program to begin installing the program into XP.

TIP

Downloads are fastest when Internet traffic is low, such as late at night. If you are given a choice of mirror sites for a download, keep in mind the local time for each site and choose a server located where current traffic is likely to be lower.

During the download process, a window appears showing the download progress and an estimation of the time remaining in the download. If you can't wait that long, click Cancel and try again later.

In addition to downloading new software, you can also download updates to software you already own. Check the manufacturer's Web site from time to time to see whether new updates, patches, or bug fixes are available (this is especially important for entertainment software).

TIP

Create a Software folder in your Favorites list, and add to it the manufacturers' Web sites for software you own. Doing so will make it easier to periodically check for updates.

PROTECTING AGAINST BAD DOWNLOADED PROGRAMS

As of SP-2, a new feature in IE helps protect your computer from potentially malicious software. When you use Internet Explorer to download a file, a message might appear in the information bar just below the Address Bar saying To help protect your security, Internet Explorer blocked this site from downloading files to your computer. Click here for options.

Clicking the information bar opens a drop-down list of options (see Figure 9.7).

If you choose to allow the page to download a program, you see another dialog box warning you about downloaded programs and asking whether you want to run the program from its remote location across the Web or save it to your hard disk, as you see in Figure 9.8.

Figure 9.7
IE now offers to block downloads from the particular page.

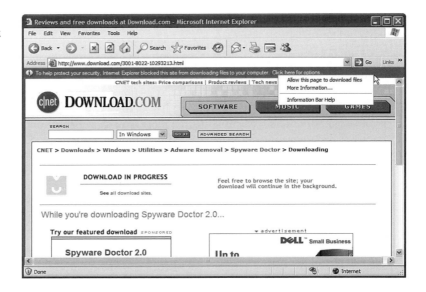

Figure 9.8
After you decide to accept downloads from that page, you see another warning and some options at the bottom of the dialog box.

If you choose to run the program from the site, rather than save it, you're likely to see the dialog box shown in Figure 9.9. All executable files that are downloaded are checked for publisher information, using a scheme called Authenticode. Authenticode checks a database of known good software publishers, checks this against the digital signature of the file you are downloading, and gives you some advice about the file. After being presented with the information, you can then make a more informed decision about running the file.

Some publishers of programs have been black listed and are prevented from running in your PC under Windows XP. Executable files with blocked publishers are not allowed to run.

Figure 9.9
If a publisher is not verified, you are prompted if you try to run the program from the Web page.

TIP

> You can unblock a publisher by using Manage Add-ons in Internet Explorer. This is explained later in this chapter, in the section "Viewing and Managing Your IE Add-ons."

PROTECTING AGAINST DRIVE-BY DOWNLOADS OF IE ADD-ONS

A recurring cause of instability in Windows machines is attributable to what's sometimes called *drive-by downloads* from the Web. How many times have you visited a Web site, only to see a pop-up dialog box saying you need to install some software for the Web site to work on your browser? Sometimes it's clearly stated why this is necessary (for playing a video, proprietary sound file, or Flash animation for example), but other times the reason is not so clear. All you know is that you are faced with the decision of either letting some (typically) unknown source install some software on your computer so you can enjoy the Web page or opting out and moving on. Maybe you assume it can do no harm because it's only an addition to IE and not to your operating system per se. But because IE is often the back door through which viruses, adware, spyware, and Trojan horses infect your computer, being cautious at this juncture is extremely important.

These spur-of-the-moment additions Web sites can push at you are called IE *add-ons* and are typically ActiveX controls, although not all are. ActiveX controls and active script (sometimes called script or JavaScript) are small programs used extensively on the Internet. Without scripts, Web sites would be much more static and boring. Script and ActiveX controls enable all sorts of animation and other entertaining features on the Internet. Web sites become more interactive by offering customized content based on information about your computer, your browser, and so on. Common add-ons include extra toolbars, animated mouse pointers, stock tickers, and pop-up ad blockers.

TIP

> IE now has its own pop-up blocker, by the way. See the section "Blocking Pop-ups and Pop-unders," later in this chapter.

Add-ons can be installed from a variety of locations and in several ways, including these:

- Download and installation while viewing Web pages
- Installation by the user by way of an executable program
- As preinstalled components of the operating system
- As preinstalled add-ons that come with the operating system

The downside is that these programs can also be used to collect information from your computer for harmful purposes. After six months or a year of cruising the Web with IE, many users don't recall what add-ons they authorized, and what those might be doing to compromise the stability of their systems.

Unbeknownst to you, you could have many add-ons installed. This can happen if you previously gave permission for all downloads from a particular Web site or because the add-on was part of another program you installed. Some add-ons are installed with Microsoft Windows.

Post SP-2, you are sometimes given more information about potentially damaging add-ons so you can make an informed decision about installing one. Some add-ons have digital signatures that verify who wrote them. This is called a *certificate*. IE verifies a signature and call tell you whether it's valid. If a signature is reported as invalid, you definitely shouldn't trust the publisher as asserting a truthful identity. Allowing installation of ActiveX controls that have invalid signatures obviously is not recommended and introduces additional risk to your computer.

Internet Explorer blocks file downloads in these circumstances when you are using the default security settings:

- When a file has an invalid signature on its certificate
- When a file has no signature on its certificate
- When you or someone else who uses your computer has blocked the source of the file

Even if an add-on has a legitimate certificate, it doesn't mean the program won't mess up your computer. In the end, whether you choose to install an add-on or not is your choice. Make the decision based on whether you know the source to be trustworthy. If, after installing an add-on, your system or IE becomes unstable, use the information in the following section to track and remove the add-on.

NOTE

Certificates are explained in more detail, in the section "Using Encryption" later in this chapter.

ALLOWING ADD-ONS WITH INVALID SIGNATURES

Some add-ons are known to be bad and have been blocked by Microsoft intentionally. You can't install or run add-ons from blocked publishers on the computer. If you really want to, you can force the use of an add-on that has an invalid signature, like so:

1. In Internet Explorer, select Tools, Internet Options; then click the Security tab.
2. In the Security level for this zone box, click Custom Level.
3. Scroll down to Download Unsigned ActiveX Controls and choose Enable or Prompt.

Another approach is to unblock a *specific* publisher. This is a safer approach, obviously, because it doesn't open you up to all invalidated signatures. To do this, follow these steps:

1. Select Tools menu, Manage Add-ons.
2. Select the publisher you want to unblock, and then click Enable.

VIEWING AND MANAGING YOUR IE ADD-ONS

You can review all your add-ons, update selected ones, choose ones to ditch, and (if you've been having IE crashes) potentially see which one was responsible for your last IE crash. (Crashing can happen if the add-on was poorly built or created for an earlier version of IE.) You work with your add-ons using the IE Add-on Manager. The Add-on Manager even shows the presence of some add-ons that were previously not shown and could be very difficult to detect.

To see all add-ons for Internet Explorer, do the following:

1. Select View, Manager Add-ons. You'll see the Add-on Manager window, as shown in Figure 9.10.
2. In the Show box, click the set of add-ons you want to see.

Add-ons are sorted into two groups in the Show box. Installed add-ons are a complete list and include all the add-ons that reside on your computer. Loaded add-ons are only those that were needed for the current Web page or a recently-viewed Web page.

Some add-ons can crash your IE session. If you notice this after you've installed an add-on, you have three options:

- **Update it**—If the add-on is an ActiveX control, you should check whether the item has been updated. You can use the Manage Add-ons dialog box to update an add-on if an update is available. Click the Show arrow, and then click Add-ons That Have Been Used by Internet Explorer. In the list of add-ons, click the add-on you want to update, and then click Update ActiveX. Windows searches for an update at the location where the original control was found. If a newer version is found at that location, Internet Explorer attempts to install the update.

- **Disable it**—If an add-on causes repeated problems, you can disable the add-on. Click the add-on you want to disable and then click Disable. Some Web pages, or Internet

Explorer, might not display properly if an add-on is disabled. It is recommended that you disable an add-on only if it repeatedly causes Internet Explorer to close. Add-ons can be disabled but not easily removed.

NOTE

If you disable an add-on and then realize it was needed, click the add-on you want to enable and then click Enable.

■ **Report it**—When prompted, you might want to report the glitch to Microsoft. This is completely anonymous and requires nothing from you but permission. Microsoft claims the info is used to improve their products and to encourage other companies to update and improve theirs.

Figure 9.10
The new Add-on Manager in SP-2 lets you see and control the IE add-ons you've either wittingly or unwittingly down-loaded and installed.

Internet Explorer Add-on Crash Detection attempts to detect crashes in Internet Explorer that are related to an add-on. When the add-on is successfully identified, you are informed of it. You then have the option of disabling add-ons to diagnose crashes and improve the overall stability of IE.

TIP

You can turn off notifications about browser add-ons if you don't want to be bugged about them. Choose Tools, Internet Options and then click the Advanced tab. Under Browsing, clear the Notify when Add-on's Disabled check box.

CUSTOMIZING THE BROWSER AND SETTING INTERNET OPTIONS

One of the most important features of Internet Explorer is the capability to tailor it to your own specific needs. Every user sets up IE differently based on programs used, favorite Web sites, bandwidth capability, security needs, and so on.

You can make most customizations in the Internet Options dialog box, which you can access either through the Windows Control Panel or by choosing Tools, Internet Options in IE6. The dialog box contains seven tabs, each holding a number of unique preference settings. Figure 9.11 shows the General tab.

Type a new URL here to change the home page

Figure 9.11
On the General tab, you can set general preferences for your home page, temporary cache files, history, and browser view options.

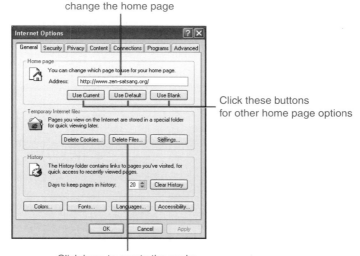

Click these buttons for other home page options

Click here to empty the cache

Check each tab in the dialog box to customize your own IE6 settings. Table 9.1 describes some of the key preference settings you can change.

TABLE 9.1   IMPORTANT INTERNET OPTIONS

Tab	Option	Description
General	Home Page	The home page is the first page that appears when you open Internet Explorer. It is probably set to MSN or has been customized by your PC's manufacturer. Consider changing this page to your company's home page or something else you find more useful.

continues

9

Tab	Option	Description
TABLE 9.1	**CONTINUED**	
	Temporary Internet Files	When you view a Web page, the files for the page are saved on your hard drive as *Temporary Internet Files* (also called *cache*). You can clear all files from the cache or change the amount of disk space they are allowed to consume.
	History	A record of the Web sites you have visited is maintained by IE6. You can change the length of time these records are kept or clear the history altogether.
	Colors, Fonts, and so on	You can customize default colors, fonts,languages, and set accessibility options here.
Security	Zones and Levels	You can set security options for IE6. See "Setting Security and Privacy Preferences" later in this chapter.
Privacy	Settings and Web Sites	This area allows you to determine how and under what conditions cookies are sent. See "Setting Security and Privacy Preferences" later in this chapter.
Content	Content Advisor	You can control the capability to view objectionable content on your computer. See "Controlling Objectionable Content" later in this chapter.
	Certificates	When a Web page tries to run a script or install a piece of software on your computer, you can accept certificates from the publisher to authenticate their identity and trustworthiness. See "Setting Security Preferences" later in this chapter.
	AutoComplete	You can enable or disable AutoComplete when typing Web URLs, email addresses, or form data.
	My Profile	You can create a profile for yourself in the Microsoft Address Book.
Connections		You can set up preferences for your Internet connection, whether it be through a dial-up or network connection.
Programs		You can select default programs for various actions. See "Setting Default Mail, News, and HTML Editor Programs" next.
Advanced		You can set various (but obscure) options for browsing, multimedia, printing Web pages, searching from the address bar, and security.
	Multimedia	This is where you can disable automatic downloading of graphics, videos, audio, and more.

SETTING DEFAULT MAIL, NEWS, AND HTML EDITOR PROGRAMS

Using the Programs tab of the Internet Options dialog box, you can decide some default programs for a variety of Internet-related tasks. If you have not installed any other Internet software packages, you probably won't have too many choices here, but if you use different programs, these options can be useful. Figure 9.12 shows the default program settings you can make on the Programs tab, and Table 9.2 describes the various options you can set.

Remove this check mark if you want another installed Web browser (such as Netscape Navigator) to remain the default

Figure 9.12
On the Programs tab, you can choose the default programs for the various Internet tasks you perform.

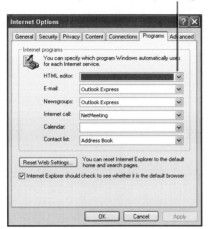

TABLE 9.2 DEFAULT INTERNET PROGRAMS

Program	Description
HTML Editor	If you are a Web developer, make sure the correct editor is listed here. This will simplify editing during your testing process. The list might include Word, Notepad, FrontPage, or another installed editor.
Email	This program will open when you click the Mail button on the IE6 toolbar or when you click an email link on a Web page.
Newsgroups	If you link to or open a newsgroup URL, the reader listed here will open.
Internet Call	Microsoft NetMeeting is the default Internet Call client, but if you have another call program, you can select it here.
Calendar	If you have a calendar program such as Outlook, you can set it here.
Contact List	The default list is the Microsoft Address Book. You should set this to the Address Book used by your favorite email and calendar program.

 Email links in Web pages can cause many frustrations. See "Email Link Troubles" in the "Troubleshooting" section at the end of the chapter.

SETTING SECURITY AND PRIVACY PREFERENCES

In many ways, the World Wide Web is a safer place than the "real" world, but it does present its own unique dangers as well. The greatest hazards involve sensitive and private information about you or your company being compromised, or in having your computer infected with a software virus. IE6 incorporates a number of security features to protect you from these hazards, and those features can be customized to suit your own needs, browsing habits, and company policies.

Begin by opening the Internet Options dialog box from the IE6 Tools menu, and click the Security tab to bring it to the front. Click Default Level in the lower-right corner of the dialog box to show the slider, as seen in Figure 9.13, that allows you to set a security level for each zone.

You first need to select a zone for which you want to customize settings. The four zones are shown in Figure 9.13.

Internet	This zone applies to all resources outside your LAN or intranet.
Local Intranet	This zone applies to pages available on your company's intranet. They are usually more trustworthy and can justify less restrictive settings.
Trusted Sites	You manually designate these sites as trusted. To designate a trusted site, browse to the site, open this dialog box, select the Trusted Sites zone, and click Sites. Here, you can add the site to your Trusted Sites zone list. Trusted sites usually allow lighter security.
Restricted Sites	Designated in the same manner as Trusted Sites, Web sites listed here are ones you specifically find untrustworthy. They should have the strictest security settings.

CAUTION

> Before you designate a Web page as trusted, try to remember that even the most diligently maintained sites can be compromised. Recent "hacker" attacks at Web sites of the FBI, U.S. Army, and others make the practice of designating any Web site as "trustworthy" questionable.

Each zone has its own security preferences, which you set. The easiest way to set preferences is to choose one of the four basic levels offered in the dialog box. The default level is Medium, and for most Web users, this setting works best because it provides a good balance of security and usability. The High setting offers the greatest possible security, but you might find that the level is so restrictive that it's difficult to browse your favorite Web sites.

Select a zone here to change its settings

Figure 9.13
On the Security tab, you can customize security settings for various Web zones.

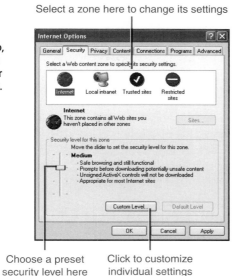

Choose a preset
security level here

Click to customize
individual settings

Likewise, the Low and Medium-Low levels make browsing much easier because you aren't presented with dialog boxes and warnings every time a potentially hazardous activity begins. Because these two levels leave too many doors open to virus infection and other dangers, they are not advisable in most situations.

Besides setting a basic security level, you can customize individual settings. First, choose a basic level (such as Medium), and then try these steps:

1. Click Custom Level to open the Security Settings dialog box, as shown in Figure 9.14.
2. Browse through the list of options, and apply custom settings as you see fit.
3. Click OK when you're finished. A warning dialog box appears, asking whether you really want to apply the changes. Choose Yes.

Figure 9.14
You can scroll through this list to make custom security setting changes.

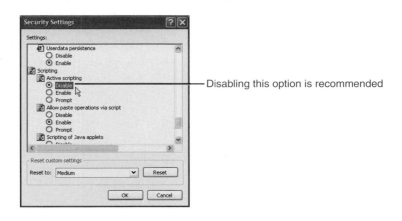

Disabling this option is recommended

The items in the Security Settings dialog box that most deserve your attention are those pertaining to ActiveX controls and Java applets. Review these settings carefully, especially those for ActiveX controls, because of the unique hazards they can present. The ActiveX standard contains loopholes, so unsigned controls can run virtually any OLE-compliant operation on your system. Java, on the other hand, is relatively—but not entirely—secure.

You also should consider what level of cookie security you are willing to live with. A *cookie* is a small text file that some Web sites can leave on your computer in cache. Because cookies are text only, they cannot contain a virus or other harmful content. However, they can contain personal information such as a record of Web pages you have visited, how long you spent at a page, how many times you have visited, personal preferences for a Web page, and even user IDs and passwords. It is for these reasons that cookies are regarded by many people as an invasion of privacy.

You can disable cookies, or you can choose to have IE prompt you every time a site attempts to leave a cookie in your cache. However, keep in mind that some Web sites make such heavy use of cookies that you could find it difficult—if not impossible—to browse the Web normally.

To set your cookie preferences, go to Tools, Internet Options, and click on the Privacy tab. The Settings area enables you to determine how and under what conditions cookies are sent. Choose a level you are comfortable with, or click the Advanced button to always accept, block, or prompt you before enabling first-party or third-party cookies. (For more on first-party and third-party cookies, see "Getting a Passport to Microsoft Country" later in this chapter.)

There might be certain Web sites for which you'd like to override your other cookies settings. If so, go to the Web Sites area of the Privacy tab and click the Edit button. In the text box, carefully enter a complete Web site address. Then, click the Block or Allow button to specify Web sites for which you want to never or always allow cookies.

TIP

> A major security hole in IE involves the option Allow Paste Operations via Script, which is enabled in all security levels but High. It allows any Web site to see the contents of your Windows Clipboard via a scripted Paste operation. If you have been working with sensitive information in another program and used a Copy or Cut command, that information could be compromised by unscrupulous Webmasters. To be on the safe side, change this setting to Disable or Prompt no matter which security level you use.

USING ENCRYPTION

The Advanced tab of the Internet Options dialog box has a number of other security settings that deserve your attention. In particular, most of the security settings here deal with *certificates*. Certificates can be saved on your computer and serve to authenticate your identity or the identity of the server you are connected to. They also provide for secure encrypted communication over secure Web connections.

IE supports *Secure Socket Layer (SSL) encryption* technology developed by Netscape. It supports 128-bit encrypted SSL sessions, the highest level of data encryption available in the online world. SSL encryption works using a pair of encryption keys, one public and one private. One key is needed to decrypt the other. Certificates facilitate this use by including the following information:

- The issuing authority, such as VeriSign
- The identity of the person or organization for whom the certificate is issued
- The public key
- Time stamps

Thus, the certificate provides and authenticates the basis for an encrypted session. The identity is reverified, the private key is shared, and encryption is enabled.

Another encryption protocol supported by IE is *Private Communication Technology (PCT)*, developed by Microsoft. PCT is similar to SSL encryption, except that it uses a separate key for identity authentication and data encryption. Thus, in theory, PCT should provide slightly enhanced security versus SSL.

Again, encryption protocols can be enabled or disabled on the Advanced tab of the Internet Options dialog box. If you disable a protocol, any page you try to access on a secure server that uses that protocol will not open in IE.

→ Learn how to obtain a digital certificate for yourself in "Sending and Receiving Secure Messages," **p. 352**.

BLOCKING POP-UPS AND POP-UNDERS

Pop-up windows are an intrusive means by which advertisers on the Web can ensure that you see their plug. We've all seen pop-up windows that come up unexpectedly, sometimes blaring music or flashing to catch our attention. Usually they pop up when you've clicked a link to go to another page. Another form of less intrusive though a little more insidious window is called the *pop-under* window. You don't discover it until you close the window you're looking at. This way, it's harder to tell which site actually spawned the pop-under, so you don't know who to blame.

Many power users have figured out ways to prevent pop-ups, such as by installing the Google toolbar or one of the many add-ins or installing some other browser, such as Opera, that blocks pop-ups. AOL's browser does this, as do Netscape and Mozilla's Firefox. Oddly enough, 70% or more of Web surfing is done with IE, even though it hasn't until now had the modern nicety of pop-up blocking and still doesn't have tabbed browsers like Opera and some others do. The good news is that the latest IE now has a pop-up blocker built in.

9

TIP

Tabbed browsers let you have any number of Web pages open at one time, all contained within a single browser window. You just click tabs to switch between them. To add tabbing to IE, you might want to try Netcaptor, AvantBrowser, or Maxthon.

Without even having the latest version of IE (that includes a pop-up blocker), there's a quick solution to stop the pop-ups dead in their tracks: Turn off Active Scripting (JavaScript). This works because pop-up windows require Active Scripting to launch. Even though other browser functions need Active Scripting as well, you can surf effectively on most sites without it. You can turn off Active Scripting by clicking Tools, Internet Options. Then select the Security tab, change your Internet security level to High, and click OK. Five quick steps, no pop-ups, and you haven't spent a dime on a blocker or to have the latest version of IE. Of course, using the latest IE is a better idea, due to the improved security features and add-in management.

IE's pop-up blocker is turned on by default. When a pop-up window tries to launch, you see an indication of this in the IE yellow information bar (just below the Address bar). It informs you that that a pop-up has been blocked and gives the steps you can take to allow it through if you wish. Click the information bar to see the options (see Figure 9.15).

Figure 9.15
IE now blocks pop-ups. When a pop-up is blocked, you can click the information bar for options.

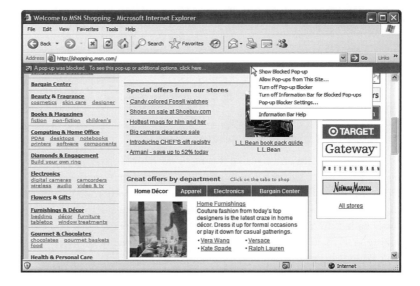

Sometimes it's useful to see blocked pop-ups. Just follow these steps to do so:

1. Click the information bar.
2. From the menu, select Show Blocked Pop-ups.

Suppose you want to see any and all pop-ups from the site you're on; you'd do the following:

1. Choose Tools, Pop-up Blocker, Allow Pop-ups from This Site.
2. Answer the dialog box appropriately.

If you want to always allow pop-ups from one or more specific sites, you can authorize this. You just add those site(s) to an exception list, like this:

1. Select Tools, Pop-up Blocker, Pop-up Blocker Settings.
2. In the resulting box, enter the URLs from which you want to allow pop-ups, and click Add.
3. Repeat for each URL you want to see pop-ups from.

A FEW NOTES ABOUT POP-UP EXCEPTIONS

Sometimes the pop-up blocker isn't able to preclude a pop-up from appearing. There are several possible reasons for this. First, you might have software on your computer that is launching pop-ups. To stop these pop-ups, you must identify the software and remove it or change its settings to stop launching pop-ups. Try installing an adware and spyware sleuthing program such as Spybot Search and Destroy or Ad-aware.

Second, some pop-ups are written cleverly enough that they can circumnavigate the IE pop-up blocker.

Third, Internet Explorer does not block pop-ups from Web sites that are in your Intranet or Trusted Sites zone. If you want to specifically remove such a site from your trusted zone, you can do that from the IE settings dialog boxes:

1. In IE, choose Tools, Internet Options, and then click Security.
2. Click the zone from which you want to remove a Web site. Then click Sites.
3. Skip this step unless you chose Intranet Zone in the last step. Click Advanced and then go to step 4.
4. In the Web Sites box, click the Web site you want to remove; then click Remove.

CONTROLLING OBJECTIONABLE CONTENT

The World Wide Web holds the most diverse range of information and content of any library in the world. That diverse range includes a great deal of material that you might deem objectionable, and there is no perfect way of protecting yourself from it short of never going online. However, Internet Explorer incorporates a feature called the Content Advisor, a tool to help you screen out much of the things you or the other people using your computer would rather not see.

9

The Content Advisor evaluates Web content based on a rating system. The included rating system is developed by RSACi (Recreational Software Advisory Council on the Internet), but you can add others if you want.

You must enable the Content Advisor manually, but after it is set up, the Advisor can be password-protected so that only you can adjust the settings. To enable the Content Advisor, open the Internet Options dialog box, and perform the following:

1. Click the Content tab to bring it to the front, and click Enable to open the Content Advisor dialog box.

2. The Content Advisor dialog box contains four tabs, as shown in Figure 9.16. On the Ratings tab, you can move the slider back and forth to set a rating level in each of the four categories presented.

Select a rating category here

Figure 9.11
On the Ratings tab, you can move the slider back and forth to change the rating level.

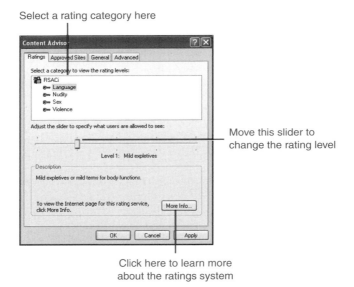

Move this slider to change the rating level

Click here to learn more about the ratings system

3. Click the Approved Sites tab to bring it to the front. List specific Web sites here to control access to them. Click Always to make it easily acceptable, or click Never to restrict access.

4. On the General tab, choose whether unrated sites can be viewed. Keep in mind that many objectionable sites will not be rated. You can also set a password to let people in unrated or restricted sites on a case-by-case basis, or you can add another rating system here.

5. Click the Advanced tab. If you plan to use a ratings bureau or PICSRules file you obtain from the Internet, your ISP, or another source, add it here. Click OK when you're finished.

RSACi and other organizations provide content rating systems based on the PICS (Platform for Internet Content Selection) system developed by the World Wide Web Consortium, or W3C (www.w3.org/PICS/). They work using meta tags in the code of a Web page. The tags are usually generated by the rating organization after a site developer follows a brief rating procedure. Developers can then place the PICS meta tag in the header of their HTML code, where it is identified by IE's Content Advisor when you try to open the page. The tag identifies the types and levels of content contained in the site, and the Content Advisor allows or disallows the site based on the content settings you have chosen. If you want to screen Web sites using a system other than RSACi's, you must install an appropriate PICSRules file provided by the rating organization.

Of course, rating is voluntary. Developers set the rating levels in the meta tags based on their own evaluation of the site content, so you never really get a surefire guarantee that the tag accurately represents the site. RSACi periodically audits rated sites, and Web developers generally *try* to rate their sites as accurately as possible. It is a voluntary system, after all, and providing inaccurate ratings defeats the purpose of voluntary rating in the first place.

OTHER INTERNET SETTINGS

Several other settings deserve your attention. On the Content tab of the Internet Options dialog box, check the AutoComplete option to make sure it does not contain information that you are concerned about being compromised. AutoComplete makes it easier to fill in data fields on forms and URLs in the Address bar, but if other people use your user identity, they could end up seeing your personal information because of these settings.

One setting you probably should *not* enable is the Print Background Colors and Images option. If a Web page uses anything but a plain white background, a printed copy of it will waste a considerable amount of printer ink and probably be harder to read.

Review the Search settings on the Advanced tab. In earlier versions of Internet Explorer, if you wanted to visit a Web site with a fairly simple URL like www.quehelp.com, all you had to type was **quehelp** and press Enter. Internet Explorer would assume the missing www. and .com and fill it in for you. But now, if you type only **quehelp** in the Address bar, IE6 opens a Search window in the Explorer bar. In theory, this is supposed to make searching easier, but if you've been using IE for a while, you might find it annoying.

TIP

> If you press Ctrl+Enter after typing a word in the Address bar, IE6 will assume that it is preceded by www. and followed by .com to create a URL.

You cannot completely restore the previous function of "assuming" the missing bits of the URL, but you can modify the way in which this feature works by altering settings under the Advanced tab. The different search options will have the following results:

- **Display results and go to the most likely site**—The default setting, it opens the Explorer bar search window. In some cases, the "most likely" site will also appear in the main window, but it may or may not be what you were hoping for.
- **Do not search from the Address bar**—No search is made of any kind. Typing a single word in the Address bar will generally result in a `Page not available` error.
- **Just display the results in the main window**—No attempt is made to find a close match, nor is the Explorer bar opened. A search engine will open in the main window.
- **Just go to the most likely site**—In theory, this setting should work as in previous IE versions, but in practice it does not. It first looks for a match within the Microsoft Web domain and then tries to find a match at large. Select this option, and then type `quehelp` in the Address bar to see what we mean.

Under Security, check Empty Temporary Internet Files Folder When Browser Is Closed to discard cache files you don't want others to see. This setting can also be useful if disk space is limited, but you shouldn't use it if you want to be able to view pages in offline mode later.

EFFECTIVELY SEARCHING THE WEB

You've probably heard that you can find virtually anything on the Web, and if you've spent much time online, you're probably left wondering where it all is. Finding information on the World Wide Web is a fine art, but Internet Explorer 6 makes the process much simpler than it used to be.

The Search Companion (formerly Search Assistant) in IE6 can be a great help. Click the Search button on the IE toolbar to open the Search Companion in the Explorer bar on the left side of Internet Explorer, as shown in Figure 9.17.

To begin searching, enter a word, phrase, or even a question in the search text box, and click the Search button. If you type a single word—such as `antiques`—the search probably will yield a list of results too big to be useful. Using more words, and more descriptive words, will narrow your search. You probably will get better results by searching for `antique furniture` or `antique French furniture` instead. Search results are displayed in the main IE window, 15 at a time. You can click directly on a search result to link to that site, or you can click Next to see the next 15 results.

An advantage to using the Search Companion instead of the browser to go to individual search engines is its ability to easily search through several search engines for a single topic.

Notice that the Search Companion gives you more options and suggestions for helping you find what you're looking for. You can click on the options to "Automatically send your search to other search engines" or to "Highlight words on the results page," which is handy to locate the exact word you're looking for or to do a search within a page you navigated to. When you click the option to go to other search engines, you will see a short list to choose from. Click on one of them to conduct your search at that site. If you would like to reset your preferences so that the Search Companion always visits your favorite site first, click

Change Preferences on the main Search Companion screen, and then click Change Internet Search Behavior. Select a default search engine from the list, and click OK.

Figure 9.17
The Search Companion opens and allows you to search for several different kinds of information.

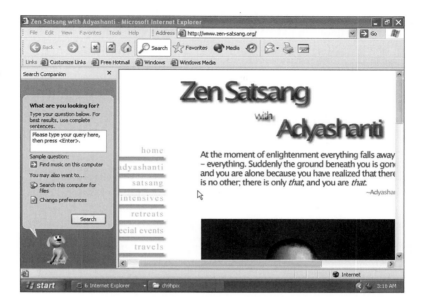

To start a new search, click on Start a New Search, near the bottom of the Search Companion pane. If you'd like to go back to a previous option in the Search Companion, click the Back button near the bottom of the Search Companion pane. Clicking the Back button in the main IE window, however, will take you to the previous Web page.

The Search Companion will search for files and other resources on the local computer or network as well. Click Search This Computer for Files in the Search Companion pane to select categories for the local search. To return to Web searching, click Search the Internet.

When you're finished searching, close the Search Companion to get it out of the way. To revisit a previous search, click on the History button on the IE toolbar, and go to the search folders. Depending on the search engine(s) you used, you could find information in folders labeled search.msn, search.yahoo, and northernlight. Another way to find previous search results is by clicking the Search button at the top of the History pane and entering a word to search among the pages you've visited recently.

As helpful as the Search Companion can be, when you've become familiar with the Internet, you are likely to discover your own favorite search engine. You could set the Search Companion to use it, as explained above, or you could add it to your Links bar for easy access. Many search engines have advanced options that allow you to perform a more directed search.

Try these helpful search engines, directly from a Web page:

- `www.hotbot.com` (includes a drop-down list for more effective searching)
- `www.google.com` (has a Web Directory which works much like Yellow Pages do in a phone book, and Google Groups, which searches newsgroups)
- `www.northernlight.com` (categorizes search results into folders for ease in refining your search)

SAFER ALTERNATIVES TO IE

In that more than 70% of Web surfing is done with IE (some say as much as 95%), Microsoft's browser has become the obvious target for hackers the world over. Because a large proportion of viruses and other malware can enter your computer through Web sites (typically through exploitation of Microsoft ActiveX controls), switching to a different browser might no longer be just a goofball suggestion your propeller-head Linux evangelist friends push on you. It might be a necessity.

Even though ActiveX was meant to extend the capability of IE in exciting ways, such as into the area of multimedia, it has instead become an enticing target for hackers. Due to this fact, the U.S. Computer Emergency Readiness Team (US-CERT), a partnership between the tech industry and the Department of Homeland Security, recently began advising computer users to consider switching browsers. Whether you do, US-CERT advises upping your Internet Explorer security settings.

It might take a little work to get a non-IE browser to properly display all the sites you want to view, but it might well be worth it. For example, you'll probably have to reinstall plug-ins for some sites and install Sun's Java engine for viewing Java-powered sites.

In general, make sure you're switching to a browser that isn't simply a shell on top of IE. That will still leave you vulnerable. You need an entirely new browser, such as Firefox, Opera, or Maxthon.

For more information about browser security, visit `http://www.us-cert.gov/`.

MSN EXPLORER BROWSER—THE TOUCHY-FEELY ALTERNATIVE TO IE

In addition to Internet Explorer, Microsoft has included its new breed of Web browser in the XP package. Dubbed MSN Explorer, it is more personalized than IE6: To use it, you need to have a Microsoft "Passport" or Hotmail address, which is covered in the next section.

Begin by opening MSN Explorer from the Start menu; click the butterfly icon. If you are online, a wizard will guide you through the procedure to set up MSN Explorer. You will only need to do this once: Signing on in the future will be simpler and can be automated.

After you are signed in to MSN Explorer, you will see a window similar to Figure 9.13. Notice that it is already customized somewhat, giving you a personal greeting tailored to your time zone. Information about the city in which you live (according to the ZIP Code you gave when you signed up for Hotmail) is also prominent. The toolbar shows how many new Hotmail messages are waiting for you. Simply click the mail button to display your Web-based Hotmail inbox. If you have MSN Messenger buddies, a number next to the icon will show you how many of them are online. By clicking the icon, a drop-down list appears with Messenger options to connect you with your buddies.

The downside to all of this customization is that you cannot choose your own home page in MSN Explorer. The home page is permanently set to http://www.msn.com, although you can personalize it by choosing the MSN features and news you want to see. In addition, if you are frustrated that a significant portion of the main MSN Explorer screen is used for tool and navigation bars, you can make a bit more room for viewing Web pages by minimizing the one on the left (see Figure 9.18).

Figure 9.18
MSN Explorer is Microsoft's "personalized" browser.

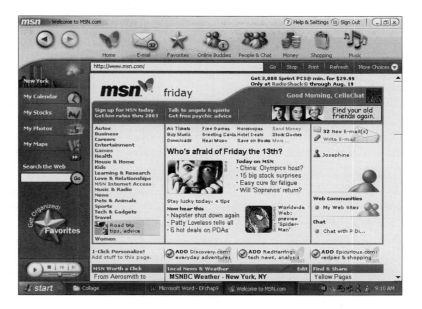

Fans of Internet Explorer who open multiple IE windows while surfing the Web might be frustrated with the multiple-window format that MSN Explorer uses. The easiest way to open up additional windows is to press Ctrl+N while within MSN Explorer. Or, you can click More Choices to the right of the address bar and select New Window from the drop-down list. Each new window that opens will be in a different format from the main MSN Explorer window—the My Stuff and main toolbars will not appear, leaving more room to view Web pages. It's all connected, more so than in other programs: Closing the main MSN Explorer window will close all its subwindows.

9

MSN Explorer does have its advantages: with personalized content and the possibilities of multiple users on a single computer, you can sign on and be sure to see all of the information that you want to see. This includes email, an integrated calendar, your MSN buddy list, favorite Web sites, stock quotes, and more. Since the information is Web-based, it is particularly handy when traveling. You can sign on to MSN Explorer from any computer and have all your personalized settings at your disposal. The information about your home town will make it easier to keep in touch, get local weather forecasts and news, and possibly alleviate homesickness.

To add a user, click Add New User from the opening screen of MSN Explorer. (You will need to sign out if you are already signed in.) Each User chooses a unique picture, which is used as an identifying icon, making it easier to see who's who.

Getting a Passport to Microsoft Country

Using MSN Explorer is only one reason to get a Microsoft Passport. These days, Microsoft requires the use of the Passport in order to use several of their sites and services including MSN Calendar, MSN Messenger, MSN Communities, MSN Wallet, and more. If you already have a Hotmail or MSN email address, you already have a Passport. If not, you can just go to www.passport.net and create one. If you only use an email address (such as a yahoo.com address), though, when setting up your account, you can't get into MSN Hotmail, which is another Passport site. If you open a Hotmail account at www.hotmail.com, you automatically get a Passport and Hotmail at the same time. Parents might be comforted to learn that a Kids Passport also is available, which can help parents protect the online identity of their children. Go to http://www.passport.net to sign up for one.

However, some might be understandably concerned that Passport is yet another way Microsoft is trying to invade our space and privacy to increase their profits. You can minimize the effect by entering the bare minimum of personal information when you sign up for a Passport. We were able to sign up using a single letter for a first name and last name. You also must enter a birth year and a ZIP code, but the Microsoft stormtroopers are not going to knock down your door in the middle of the night if you don't enter it truthfully. Personally, I'd avoid using Microsoft Wallet—I just don't want my credit card information floating around, regardless of how secure Microsoft says it is.

Hey, Who's Afraid of Microsoft Passport?

The Microsoft Passport is a simple way of making it easy to sign on and purchase items and services from a growing number of sites affiliated with (read "owned by") Microsoft. Because people are so darned tired of having to remember tens of passwords (maybe even hundreds if you're a Web addict like me) the idea of using a simple MS Passport that stores your username, password, credit card info, and so forth, and promises to effortlessly log you on at all kinds of Web sites and services, might sound pretty alluring. I mean, I forget my passwords all the time, don't you? In fact, I keep a Notepad file on my computer of nothing but my passwords and other such stuff. If I don't have access to this file when I'm traveling and I want to, say, purchase a plane ticket, I'm out of luck, because I can't remember how to log into Travelocity. (Of course, I keep this file in an encrypted file folder running under Windows XP, so it's not going to be easy for someone to liquidate my IRA. After the "substantial penalty for early withdrawal," it's not going to amount to that much anyway!)

But I'll suggest to you that Passport isn't all it's cracked up to be. In fact, it's a whole lot less. In fact, if you were concerned about cookies, you'll really be scared of Passport. As mentioned earlier, there are these things called cookies, which are small text files stored locally on your computer used to store a bit of info about you. When you go to a Web site that uses cookies, the Web server and your computer agree to exchange a little information, based on what you do on the Web site. Suppose you set up an account at Jack's Pizza with your name and address, or just that you like pepperoni pizza. Only the information you give to that site, along with possibly when you viewed the site, what you purchased, and what server you were coming in from will be stored in the cookie. The idea is to make it easier for the site to recognize you the next time you visit. This is why you can go to some sites and the Web page says "Hi Karen!" It simply looks in your cookie directory on your hard disk (the cookie jar) and looks for the one it stored there. It opens the cookie, and sees that your name is Karen (because you typed that into its site the last time you visited), and then displays it. It also knows that last time, you bought an extra-large pepperoni pizza and a bag of fries. This time it automatically suggests an extra-large pepperoni pizza and fries. Neat. Convenient. It's like going into your favorite restaurant, and the waiter knows what you like.

The important point to remember is this: The agreement is that this information is only transacted between you and the Web site you're visiting. You have some privacy of information. Jack's Pizza's Web server is not talking to Jill's Soda Pop Company's Web server and then generating email to you trying to sell you a soda to wash your pizza down with. (Okay, so maybe you want a soda with your pizza, so not a bad idea. But it can get out of hand. Keep reading.)

The idea of Passport is totally different. Although it contends otherwise, I don't think Microsoft is just trying to offer a better "user experience" on the Web by offering you a Passport to keep your passwords and stuff all tidy. With Passport, you sign on in one place, essentially Microsoft, even if you're clicking the "Sign in through Passport" link on your favorite Web site. Really, you're signing in at Microsoft's Passport, which in turns links you back to the site you wanted. Then, you start hopping around between sites. Although most of the Passport sites are now MS sites like Hotmail, they hope to entice other vendors to become Passport enabled. (With any luck on Microsoft's site, Jack and Jill will both fall down this slippery slope.) When that happens, the Web servers are linked to one another. Garnering lots of valuable customer information (such as your buying patterns, net worth, geographical location, age, sex, hobbies, medical history, and other such private info) can be more and more easily aggregated into one large database. Do you think that kind of information is valuable? You bet it is, and Microsoft knows it!

Let's consider some examples. Log into Microsoft's Investor site (http://www.investor.com) and look in the upper-right corner. There's a logon button for Passport. Now, I'm not saying this is happening now, but it's possible. Suppose you're buying a house, refinancing your current one, or buying a new car, through a Passport-affiliated site. It is possible using today's technology that the selling agent can determine your net worth by checking your portfolio on Investor.com and bargain harder with you. This kind of thing actually happened with Amazon, who raised it prices on DVDs for people who regularly bought DVDs from them. The practice was based only on cookies (and was stopped, by the way, after customers discovered what was going on).

If you want to read that story, here's a brief quote and URL: "Amazon customers on DVD Talk reported that certain DVDs had three different prices, depending on which so-called cookie a customer received from Amazon."

`http://news.cnet.com/news/0-1007-200-2703210.html?tag=st.ne.1002.tgif.ni`

In essence, the idea of cookies being private is being circumnavigated by the Passport. What's particularly scary about all this is that there is one entry point (or gatekeeper) to all Passport sites—Microsoft. Over time, look to see more and more sites (and even IE itself) incorporating Passport. I think we should be wary of the aggregation of information about us, and allowing that information to be passed around freely between corporations. Even umpteen-page-long privacy statements can't protect you when a Web company goes bankrupt and the court orders sale of its valuable database with your buying patterns or other private information in it.

TROUBLESHOOTING

WEB PAGE ERRORS

An error occurs when I try to visit a specific Web page.

Try clicking the Refresh button to reload the page. If you still don't have any luck, remove the path information (that would be everything after the domain name) from the URL in the Address bar, and press Enter.

EMAIL LINK TROUBLES

When I click an email link, Outlook Express opens, but I prefer a different email program.

Choose Tools, Internet Options to open the Internet Options dialog box, and change the default mail program on the Programs tab. You should be able to select any installed email client (such as Outlook, Outlook Express, Eudora, Netscape Mail, and so on) here.

SOME GRAPHICS DON'T APPEAR

Some pictures on a page don't open.

If the Web page contains many pictures—say, a dozen or more—the graphics at the bottom of the page often do not open. Right-click the placeholder boxes for the images that didn't download, and choose Show Picture from the menu that appears.

INTERNET EXPLORER CRASHES ON CERTAIN WEB PAGES

A Web page freezes Internet Explorer.

Some Web pages contain poorly developed scripts or ones that needlessly strain your Internet connection. Scripts that try to detect the brand and version of browser you are using frequently cause this problem. Click the Stop button on the IE toolbar, and close and reopen the program if necessary. You can try disabling most scripting operations in the Security settings dialog box, but doing so might cause the offending Web page not to display properly. Read the section "Viewing and Managing Your IE Add-ons," earlier in this chapter, for information on how to deactivate specific scripts.

WHAT HAPPENED TO THE WEB SITE?

I get a lot of `Page not available` *errors, even on major commercial sites.*

The most obvious suggestion is to check your Internet connection. Your server may also be having a temporary problem, or high Internet traffic is preventing your access. But another thing you should consider is whether the page you are trying to visit is on a secure Web server. Choose Tools, Internet Options, and click the Advanced tab to bring it to the front. Scroll down to the group of security settings, and see whether any of the encryption protocols supported by IE are disabled. If, for example, you are trying to visit a page that uses PCT encryption but Use PCT 1.0 is disabled, that page will not open.

TIPS FROM THE WINDOWS PROS: FINDING AND USING PDF DOCUMENTS ON THE WORLD WIDE WEB

Perhaps you saw the photograph on the cover of *Time* magazine a few years ago of Bill Gates in a forest, sitting atop a tree-sized stack of papers while holding a single compact disk in his hand, suggesting that digital information storage could save trees. It can, but it isn't easy.

The problem with digital documents is that, even with the best available technology, they are still not as easy to read as a paper book. Computer monitors put considerably more strain on your eyes, and even laptop PCs can be too bulky or clumsy to carry with you to a comfortable reading location. Furthermore, current digital storage technologies have a shorter shelf life than paper. Most CDs begin to deteriorate and lose their data after 10 to 20 years, but properly stored paper can last for centuries.

Still, digital documents have many advantages. First and foremost is cost: A single compact disc can contain hundreds of books yet cost less than $1 to manufacture. Printing the same amount of data on paper would cost hundreds, if not thousands, of dollars. Electronic books can be searched quickly, efficiently, and more thoroughly than printed ones. And, of course, digital documents are much easier to distribute.

One of the most popular methods for producing and distributing electronic books online is via PDF (Portable Document Format) files. PDF documents can be read using the Adobe Acrobat Reader, a free program offered by Adobe Systems, Inc. (www.adobe.com). PDF books can have the appearance and properties of a paper book but without the paper. They also have the advantage of being compatible across many platforms, with versions of the Reader software available for Windows, Macintosh, OS/2, and various incarnations of UNIX. A PDF document link on a Web page is usually identified by the PDF icon.

PDF is used for a wide range of documents:

- It is used for government documents such as tax forms and educational materials.
- Technology companies such as Intel distribute technical documents and white papers in PDF.
- Private and commercial publishers produce and distribute electronic libraries of PDF books both on CD and the Web.
- News agencies produce PDF weather maps and other news material.

You can obtain the Acrobat Reader from many sources. If you own any other Adobe software—such as Photoshop or PhotoDeluxe—the reader is probably already installed on your computer. Look for a program group called Adobe or Adobe Acrobat in your Start menu. You can also download it for free from the Adobe Web site.

Even if you find Adobe Acrobat on your computer, it's best to download the latest version of the Acrobat Reader. Later versions integrate nicely with Internet Explorer to read PDF documents directly over the Web, and include the "Find" feature. When you're choosing the version to download, click the box next to "Include option for searching PDF files and accessibility support." The file size is just a little larger, and the additional features are well worth it. Some features are dependent on the writer of the PDF file. For example, "bookmarks" only work with PDF documents that have been indexed.

Acrobat Reader works as a plug-in for Internet Explorer. When you click a link for a PDF document, it opens Acrobat Reader within IE, but the tool bars and menu will change, as you can see in Figure 9.19. Just click the back button to bring you back to the Web page you were viewing.

It is not uncommon to have problems with this whole procedure, although it does run more smoothly with the latest version. If you have trouble reading PDF documents over the Web, first save the PDF document to your hard drive. Instead of clicking the PDF link to open the file in a browser, right-click it and choose Save Target As from the shortcut menu that appears. After saving the document to the location you choose, open it manually using the Acrobat Reader outside the IE session. Saving the PDF document in this manner has the added advantage of making the document easily available to you for future reference, and available offline.

Figure 9.19
PDF files can be
viewed within a Web
page.

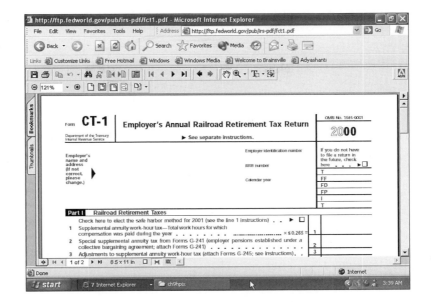

CHAPTER 10

SENDING EMAIL WITH OUTLOOK EXPRESS

In this chapter

CHOOSING AN EMAIL CLIENT

From the start, the Internet has been touted as a means for enhancing human communications, and among the many communication tools available in the online world, few have had the impact of electronic mail (email).

To fully understand the nature of email, you should keep in mind that, at its most basic level, it is simply a way for users to send messages to each other over a network. This network could be a local area network (LAN) run by your company using MS Exchange Server software. In this situation, the network server manages all message traffic. The server can also act as a gateway to other servers, allowing you to send mail beyond the local network. If you have an email account with an Internet service provider (ISP) or other Internet-based service, the provider's server acts as your gateway to other mail servers across the Internet.

Email has been criticized by some as diminishing the art of written communication by making letter writing into a less formal exchange. On the positive side, the ease of use of email communication seems to be connecting people who'd lost touch with each other and were not using other forms of communication—and you can't beat the price and speed of delivery for reaching someone on the other side of the world. In addition, the feasibility of home offices is due in large part to the fact that email can facilitate business communication. Given that email is here to stay, you must decide which email client you plan to use for reading, composing, and sending messages. You have a number of options available to you, and which one you ultimately choose will depend not only on your personal preferences but also professional needs.

Windows XP includes an excellent email client called Outlook Express 6 (OE6), which is actually a companion program to Internet Explorer 6 (IE6). It is a multifeatured program designed to appeal to a variety of email users, but it isn't for everyone. OE6 can also function as a newsgroup client, making it a "one-stop" program if you routinely communicate via email and use newsgroups.

→ To learn more about using Outlook Express to read newsgroups, **see** Chapter 11, "Reading Newsgroups with Outlook Express."

Outlook Express is relatively compact as Windows applications go. If you want an efficient program that can handle your email needs without a lot of extra fluff, OE6 is a pretty good choice. However, it does lack a few features that you might want or need, so read the next couple of sections to find out if you should be using a different client.

NOTE

This discussion assumes you have a choice in email clients. If you're using Windows XP Home in an office environment, check with your company's Information Systems (IS) manager to find out whether you must use one specific client.

WHAT IF YOU LIKE OUTLOOK 97, 98, 2000, OR 2003?

If you use Microsoft's Office suite, you're probably familiar with Outlook. Outlook is the primary communications tool included in the Office package, and many professional PC users like it. However, don't be misled by the name similarity between Outlook and Outlook Express. OE6 is not a "lite" version of Outlook; these two applications are actually quite different. Aside from the name and a few basic interface similarities, the only thing they have in common is the capability to handle email.

Outlook includes many features that Outlook Express does not, such as the following:

- A personal calendar
- An electronic journal
- Fax capability
- Compatibility with Microsoft Exchange Server

In addition, Outlook's system of managing personal contacts is far more advanced than that of Outlook Express. If the ability to integrate a heavy email load with your personal scheduler on a daily basis is important to you, Outlook is the clear choice.

If you are already using Outlook and like the Calendar and Journal, stick with it. For those of you using XP Home in an office setting, it is worth noting that if your company's network or workgroup uses Exchange Server for mail services, Outlook is the only fully compatible upgrade to that system. Outlook is also Messaging Application Programming Interface (MAPI) capable, which means it can share mail with other MAPI-capable programs on your system. Outlook Express is not MAPI-capable. Because Outlook is bigger than OE, it requires more disk space, more RAM, and slightly more patience on the part of the user. If you find that you don't use Outlook for anything but email, you might be better served by Outlook Express.

OTHER EMAIL CLIENTS

Microsoft isn't the only company producing high-quality email clients. One of the most popular alternatives is Eudora Pro from Qualcomm (www.eudora.com). Eudora offers an excellent package of mail management and filtering features, as well as compatibility with the latest Internet mail standards. Like Outlook Express, it is considerably more compact than Outlook, but it does not incorporate a newsgroup reader. Some unique Eudora features include the following:

- Voice messaging capability
- Integrated McAfee VirusScan protection for viruses propagated in mail attachments
- Built-in compression agent to shorten download times on slow dial-up connections

A free version of Eudora called Eudora Light is available, but it lacks so many of the features available in the identically priced Outlook Express that, at this point, it isn't worth your consideration.

10

Another popular email client is Netscape Messenger, which comes as part of the Netscape Communicator package and is available as freeware. Messenger is comparable to Outlook Express in terms of mail management and newsgroup capability, and its interface is clean and uncluttered.

Numerous other email clients exist. A simple search on the Web or of www.download.com will flush them out.

OUTLOOK EXPRESS QUICK TOUR

Because covering the many different email clients that are available would be beyond the scope of this book, we will assume that you have chosen Outlook Express 6. It comes free with Windows XP and will meet many of your electronic mail needs.

Outlook Express is installed during a clean installation of Windows XP, so it should be ready to open. You can launch it by clicking the Outlook Express icon near the top of the Start menu, labeled Email.

NOTE

In Windows, there is something called your "default email program." This is the program used to generate email from other programs. For example, it will be used if you click a link in IE to send an email to someone. As installed, Windows XP assumes that OE is your default email program. If you upgraded your previous version of Windows to XP, and had been using another email program such as Outlook or Eudora for email, that program will be your default email program instead.

Still, this does not mean it will necessarily appear at the top of the Start menu next to Email. If it doesn't, you can simply change that by right-clicking the Start button, choosing Properties, clicking Start menu, and then the Customize button, and finally changing the Email drop-down list to the program of your choice. If you don't see the program you expected, then it's not installed into XP.

→ If you have not yet set up an Internet connection, you will need to do so. The New Connection Wizard will pop up to guide you through the process. **See** Chapter 8, "Internet and TCP/IP Connection Options," for more information.

If you are online and you already have an email account set up, OE automatically checks for new mail when you open the program. If you don't yet have an account set up, when you open OE for the first time the (poorly named) Internet Connection Wizard opens to help you set up a mail account. For now, click Cancel to close this screen and take a look at Outlook Express. I'll talk about setting up your account in the next section, "Setting Up an Email Account." The OE window will appear as in Figure 10.1.

→ If you haven't yet set up an account, **see** "Setting Up an Email Account," **p. 340**.

If this is the first time you've opened OE6, notice that you have one unread mail message. Click the link to go to your Inbox and read the message, which is actually just a welcome letter from Microsoft.

Figure 10.1
The opening view of Outlook Express is not very useful. You can configure the program to open directly to the Inbox instead.

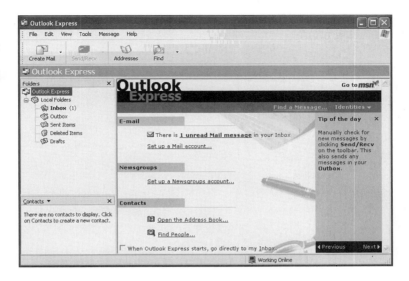

TIP

> You'll probably find that you spend more time in the Inbox than in any other place in Outlook Express. For that reason, on the default OE startup screen, place a check mark next to When Outlook Express Starts, Go Directly to My Inbox.

When the Inbox opens, as shown in Figure 10.2, you'll see that the right side of the window is divided. The upper half is a list of messages in your Inbox, with unread messages shown in boldface. The lower half is the Preview Pane, which shows a preview of whichever message is selected above. You can use the scrollbar to read more of the message.

The Preview Pane is useful, but some people don't like it because it crowds the message headers a bit. Before SP-2, the Preview pane came with some security risks, potentially alerting spammers that you were reading their mail, or even running malicious code. If you haven't upgraded to SP-2 and you use OE, this is an excellent reason to upgrade. To open a message in a separate window, double-click it. If you always prefer to read mail in this manner, you can hide the Preview Pane to make more room to view the list of Inbox messages. To hide that pane or make a variety of other adjustments to the Outlook Express interface, try these steps:

1. Choose View, Layout.

2. In the Window Layout Properties dialog, select or deselect the screen elements you want to show or hide. We suggest you deselect the Folder Bar (duplicated with more clarity in the Folder List), as well as the Preview Pane if you don't plan to use it. You may also want to deselect the Contacts pane, since OE can be set to auto-complete an address that is in your Address Book.

3. Experiment with the settings, and click OK when you have OE6 looking the way you want it.

Figure 10.2
The Inbox includes a list of new messages and a Preview Pane that you can use to read them. The Folders list can serve as a directory to virtually all Outlook Express resources.

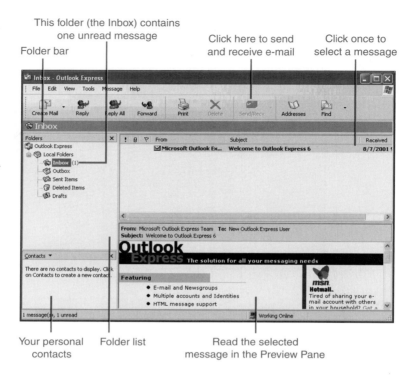

This folder (the Inbox) contains one unread message

Folder bar

Click here to send and receive e-mail

Click once to select a message

Your personal contacts

Folder list

Read the selected message in the Preview Pane

Take a look at the other screen elements. The Folders list shown in Figure 10.2 is handy because you can use it to quickly jump to any part of Outlook Express, including newsgroups if you have an account set up.

 Does Outlook Express always seem to check for new mail at the wrong time? See "Making OE6 Less Automated" in the "Troubleshooting" section at the end of the chapter.

SETTING UP AN EMAIL ACCOUNT

Before you can send or receive electronic mail, you need to have an email account. There is a good possibility that your account has already been configured by your company's IS department or that some software from your ISP took care of it for you. Otherwise, you'll have to set it up yourself.

You can set up an account directly from Outlook Express by following the instructions listed here. These steps also work for setting up a second or third account or mail identity on the same machine.

1. In Outlook Express, choose Tools, Accounts.
2. In the Internet Accounts dialog (see Figure 10.3), click the Mail tab to bring it to the front.
3. Click Add, Mail.

Click the Mail tab   Click here to add an account

Figure 10.3
You can review your
email accounts here or
add a new one.

Only one e-mail account has been configured

4. The Internet Connection Wizard opens to a dialog asking for your display name. This is the name that other people will see when you send them mail, so choose carefully. Click Next after you've entered a name.

5. The next wizard box asks for your email account address, which should have been provided by your company or ISP. Click Next after you've entered the address.

6. You must enter the types and names of your email servers in the next dialog, which is shown in Figure 10.4. Again, this information is provided by your company or ISP. See the next section for an explanation of the different server types.

Figure 10.4
You can enter the
types and names of
your email servers
here.

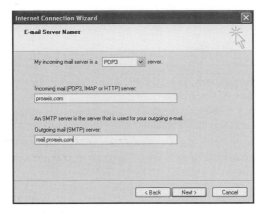

7. The next dialog asks for your login name and password. Do not check the option Remember Password if other people have access to your computer. Check the SPA (Secure Password Authentication) option if required by your email provider; then click Next. Click Finish in the final dialog. Your new account should now be listed in the Internet Accounts dialog.

10

NOTE

> Secure Password Authentication (SPA) is used by some email services to prevent unauthorized users from getting or sending your email. When you attempt to receive your mail in OE, a screen pops up asking for you to enter a username and password. Both Outlook Express and MS Outlook have this feature. Most email (POP) servers do not use this feature, so you should probably leave it turned off.

The only other piece of information that Outlook Express needs is which network or dial-up connection it should use when sending and receiving mail. You probably don't need to select this connection because OE6 automatically assigns your default connection to all mail accounts.

→ If you don't have a connection set up, **see** "Configuring Your Internet Connection," **p. 269**.

 If you routinely encounter server errors when sending or receiving mail, see "Missing Mail Servers" in the "Troubleshooting" section at the end of the chapter.

WHAT ARE POP, IMAP, SMTP, AND HTTP?

You've probably noticed the veritable alphabet soup of acronyms that exist for the many different kinds of email servers. Unlike so many other cryptic terms thrown around in the PC world, these acronyms are actually worth remembering.

First, a basic understanding of how email flows across networks (including the Internet) is important. Usually, when you send a message, Outlook Express transfers it to a *Simple Mail Transfer Protocol (SMTP)* server. An SMTP server is controlled by the sender, meaning that it waits for you to push mail through it. After you send the message to your SMTP server using OE6's Send/Recv or Send All command, no other interaction is required to deliver the message to its final destination.

NOTE

> The Send command must be used in the main program, not just in an individual email. Otherwise, the mail you've written will simply pile up in your Outbox. You can click on the Outbox in the Folder list to see if there are messages waiting to be sent. If so, click the Send/Recv button on the toolbar.
>
> If you click Tools, Options, and select the Send tab, you can click the Send Messages Immediately check box to configure OE so that it sends out messages immediately after you send them to the Outbox.

Mail sent to your computer doesn't just go from the sender to your PC. Since your PC is likely not always online, and certainly not always ready to receive email, messages must go to an interim server (usually maintained through your Internet service provider). To receive mail, you probably use either a *Post Office Protocol (POP)* or *Internet Message Access Protocol (IMAP)* server. POP and IMAP differ in that POP servers forward all messages directly to your local machine, whereas IMAP servers maintain the messages on the server until you delete them. When you check for mail on an IMAP server, a list of message headers is downloaded, but the actual message bodies stay on the server (like newsgroup messages, as explained in the next chapter). An IMAP server comes in handy if you travel a lot and want to be able to check messages on the road with your laptop or PDA, but don't want to remove them from the server until you can download the mail to a more permanent location on your home desktop.

Another type of email server is a *Hypertext Transfer Protocol (HTTP)* server, such as those offered by Yahoo!, Hotmail, and others. An HTTP mail account is useful for those who wish to travel light because it is not necessary to take a computer or software with you. You can access your HTTP account using a Web browser on any computer with access to the Internet, and generally the only information you will need to provide is your login name and password. Outlook Express can also be used to read and send mail using an HTTP account.

 Having trouble with a stubborn account password dialog? See "Password Trouble" in the "Troubleshooting" section at the end of the chapter.

SETTING UP AN HTTP MAIL ACCOUNT

HTTP mail accounts have their advantages. They usually are free, and it is possible to access these accounts on the road from any computer with Internet access. These accounts historically have had limits to the server space they allow you to use for free. There's a space war going on at this point (100MB on Yahoo!, 250MB on Hotmail). In any case, it's worth remembering that your HTTP email address might eventually top out when receiving large quantities of mail or big file attachments. Monitoring your remaining capacity and deleting old mail regularly is a good idea. When your mailbox fills up, messages will be bounced back to the sender.

There are many free email providers. Two of the most popular are at www.yahoo.com and www.hotmail.com. To find others, do an online search for "free email," and you'll see a seemingly limitless list. Alternatively, go to this site that lists the top five free email providers:

http://www.iopus.com/guides/bestpopsmtp.htm

Be prepared to provide information such as your name and geographic location. You will also be asked for your age, but testing has shown that you can pretty much enter anything you want into that field.

When your new account is configured, you can use it directly from the Web or add it to OE as described previously, in the section, "Setting Up an Account." You enter the HTTP server address in the same location where you would otherwise enter the POP or IMAP server address. In terms of downloading and deleting messages, HTTP mail accounts work in a similar manner to IMAP accounts.

TIP

> You can always check your HTTP account from another computer by visiting its Web site and entering your username and password. If you are checking mail away from home, you can leave the messages you receive on the server so that they will still be available for download later using OE6.

One point to keep in mind about most free HTTP mail accounts is that although they can be helpful when you're traveling, you must use your account periodically to keep it active. For example, you need to log on to your Hotmail account at least once during the first 30 days of membership and once every 90 days beyond that.

READING AND PROCESSING INCOMING MESSAGES

After you have an account set up, you are ready to begin downloading and reading mail. To get started, open Outlook Express, and go to the Inbox. By default, Outlook Express automatically checks for new mail when it first opens. If your installation is configured otherwise, click the Send/Recv button on the toolbar. As your mail is coming in, a dialog box appears indicating which account is being checked, and shows the progress of the sending and receiving. It will also tell you how many messages are being transferred. New messages will then appear in your inbox, as shown in Figure 10.5.

Figure 10.5
The Inbox shows seven new messages.

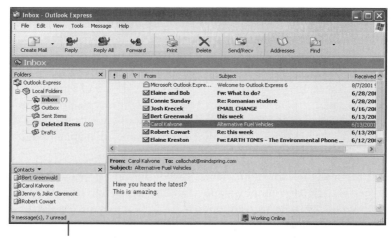

The open folder contains nine messages total; seven of them have not been read.

TIP

> If you receive a message from someone you plan to communicate with regularly, right-click his or her name in the message header, and choose Add Sender to Address Book. By doing so, you add the person to your contacts list so that sending him or her mail in the future will be easier.

When you reply to a message, you need to be wary of a few things. First, note that if the incoming message was sent to a group of people, clicking the Reply button will send your message to the single person who sent it to you; clicking Reply All will send your message to the entire list of people who received the original message. Although this can be a helpful tool when communicating with a group of people, it could get you in trouble if you think you are writing to a specific person and accidentally click the Reply All button. Before you send any message, make sure the correct person or persons are listed in the To: and Cc: fields. Anyone listed in those two fields will receive a copy of the message as well as a list of the other recipients and their email addresses, so make sure you aren't airing your dirty laundry any more publicly than you intended. The section "Creating and Sending New Mail" discusses addressing messages more thoroughly.

The rest of the reply process is fairly straightforward. You just type in your own text and click Send on the toolbar when you are ready to deliver the message. By default, Outlook Express automatically places the text of the original message in the reply.

When you're composing your reply, you should keep in mind these important points:

- Consider editing the quoted text in the reply by cutting it down to the text you actually intend to respond to. Most people don't appreciate reading four pages of quoted text followed at long last by "Me too."

- Include enough of the original text to help the recipient understand exactly what you are replying to. If the recipient doesn't read your reply for several days, he or she might not remember what his or her original statements were.

- Breaking up quoted text with your own inserted comments is usually acceptable, but make sure it is obvious which words are yours. Figure 10.6 illustrates this reply technique.

Figure 10.6
Quoted text and reply text are interspersed throughout the message, but there is little doubt as to who wrote what.

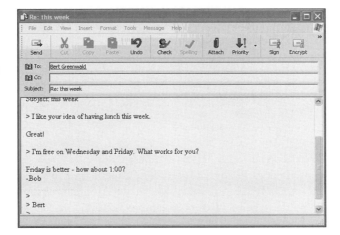

DELETING MESSAGES

How and when messages are deleted depends on what kind of mail server you use. If you receive mail from a POP server, deleted messages remain in the OE6 Deleted Items folder indefinitely, similar to "deleted" files in the Windows Recycle Bin.

You can permanently delete them by right-clicking the Deleted Items folder and choosing Empty 'Deleted Items' Folder from the shortcut menu that appears. If you have an IMAP mail server, the Deleted Items folder is emptied automatically when you log off the mail server.

You can change the way Outlook Express handles items in the Deleted Items folder. To do so, choose Tools, Options, and select the Maintenance tab to customize when and how mail messages are deleted.

CREATING AND SENDING NEW MAIL

The process of creating and sending new mail is almost as easy as receiving it. To open a New Message composition window, click the Create Mail button on the OE6 toolbar.

NOTE

You might find it helpful to have OE spell-check your email before sending it. OE does have a spelling checker, but it is available only if you also have Microsoft Word, Excel, or PowerPoint installed on your computer. Once enabled, you can click the Spelling icon in the message window when composing a message. Adjust your spelling options by going to Tools, Accounts, and clicking on the Spelling tab.

Addressing messages properly is extremely important. A single misplaced character, or an extra one, in an email address can send the message to the wrong person or to no one at all. A typical email address looks like this:

bob@mcp.com

TIP

Some mail servers are case sensitive. If you're not sure, just type the whole address in lowercase letters.

Notice that OE6 has two address fields that appear by default, To: and Cc: . Cc: is short for Carbon Copy or, these days when that messy blue paper is nearly extinct, Courtesy Copy. The address field is the only required field when sending email; all the others, including the subject and even the message body, can be blank. The To: field usually contains the email address of the primary recipient, although it can contain more than one address, as shown in Figure 10.7. You separate multiple addresses with a semicolon (;).

To send email to several people without allowing its recipients to see the names or email addresses of others who also received it, enter addresses in the Bcc: field (Blind Carbon/ Courtesy Copy) . In an email window, choose View and select Show All Headers. The Bcc: field will now appear in the email window.

Figure 10.7
A new message with an attachment has been addressed to several people.

Two people are listed in the To: field

One person will receive a carbon copy

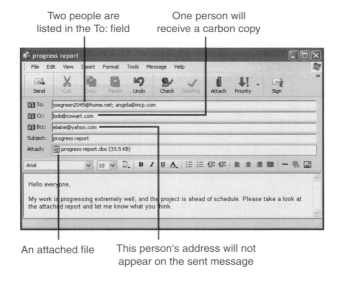

An attached file

This person's address will not appear on the sent message

When you are finished composing the message, just click Send on the toolbar. If you do not want your message sent right away, choose File, Send Later. The message is then sent to the Outbox folder and will be sent to your mail server the next time the Send command is given.

 If you don't like the name that is being assigned to your outgoing mail, see "Identity Crisis" in the "Troubleshooting" section at the end of the chapter.

SENDING AND RECEIVING ATTACHMENTS

Of the many features that make email a versatile method for communication, perhaps the most useful is the capability to send files along with an email message. You can attach any electronic file stored on disk to an email message in Outlook Express and then send it to someone else.

NOTE

> Some email accounts do not allow you to send or receive file attachments with messages. Others, particularly HTTP accounts, limit the number and size of attachments allowed. Check with your account provider to find out whether you have this capability. Also, make sure that the recipient has the capability to receive attachments.

Attaching a file to an outgoing message is easy. In the message composition window, click the Attach button on the toolbar, and locate the file you want to send in the Insert Attachment dialog. After you have selected the file, click Attach. The file attachment should appear in the header information, as shown earlier in Figure 10.7.

Before you send any attached files, consider the bandwidth it will require. Even if you have a very fast network or Internet connection, if the recipient connects to the Internet via a dial-up modem, downloading the attachment could take a long time. In general, you should avoid sending any attachments that are larger than one or two megabytes unless you are sure the recipient can handle them or knows in advance that they're about to receive some rather large files. It's best to ask your recipient first. Many mail servers (especially Web-based accounts) limit the total amount of space a person can use, and many also set a limit to the size of attachments allowed.

One more thing: If you or the recipient uses a 56Kbps or slower Internet connection, it is usually a good idea to compress large attachments before you send them. Simply right-click on the document(s) you wish to send, choose Send To, and then Compressed (zipped) Folder. Attach the compressed version to your email.

To open an attachment in a message you receive, right-click the attachment (listed in the header) and choose Save As to save it to disk, or simply open it. If the attachment is a picture file, it often appears in the body of the message as well.

10

CAUTION

Computer viruses often propagate themselves through email attachments. Hackers seem to get their jollies out of slowing down the Internet or bringing corporate business to a crawl. One way to do this seems to be targeting the most popular email programs, such as Outlook and Outlook Express. As a result, the bulk of email–borne contagion exists in the form of attachments whose payloads sneak through weaknesses in those two programs. Personally, I think that both these programs are excellent email clients, so I don't suggest changing your email program just to avoid the onslaughts of malicious Internet hackers.

As you might suspect, Microsoft doesn't want to lose customers either, so it makes a point of looking for viruses and posting critical updates to its site for easy download. A good approach is to run a Windows system update regularly. As of SP-2, Automatic Updates are turned on for just this reason.

In addition, security has been improved in OE6 to specifically combat this problem. By going to Tools, Options and clicking the Security tab, you'll notice the addition of Virus Protection since the previous version of OE. By default, OE6 will warn you if another program attempts to send a message to contacts in your Address Book. As you might have heard, this is a common way for viruses to spread. I recommend that you keep this option selected.

There is also an option that deals with potential threats from inborne email attachments. If you click the box next to Do Not Allow Attachments To Be Saved or Opened That Could Potentially Be a Virus, you'll be more protected, but your ability to access any attachment to email in OE will be quite limited. If you're diligent about it, a better way of dealing with the possibility of attachment-borne viruses is to carefully look over your incoming email before opening any attachment by following the tips below. I've found that when enabling the automatic feature in OE6, even the most innocuous attachments are prevented from opening. (You can regain access to these attachments simply by returning to the Security dialog box and deselecting this option.)

Yet another option is to download and use one of many available anti-virus programs. http://www.mcafee.com is a reliable source, and its Web site is another good place to check for the latest discovered viruses and how to protect your computer from them.

Contrary to popular belief, simply downloading an infected attachment virtually never harms your computer. With few exceptions, there could be dire consequences only if you open an attached executable file. If possible, save the file attachment on a separate disk, and then scan it with antivirus software.

Be especially wary of

- Attachments you weren't expecting (even from people you know). If in doubt, write back to the sender and ask if they intended to send you the attachment. Their computer might have a virus they are unaware of. Ask if the attachment is safe, and if they've run it on their computer.

- Executable attachments (filenames ending in .exe, .vbs, or .js). Be aware that sometimes file names are misleading on purpose. For example, you might see an attachment such as party.jpg.vbs. This is not a picture. The final extension is the one that counts.

- Emails with cryptic or odd subjects and messages such as "I Luv U," "Here's that document you requested," or "CHECK THIS OUT!!!"

- Anything that comes from a source you are unfamiliar with.

→ **See** "Additional Security Features in Post-SP2 Outlook Express," **p. 357**, for further discussion of this important topic.

SETTING UP A SIGNATURE

If you use email for much of your personal and business communication, you may like to "sign" outgoing messages with an electronic signature file. These signatures frequently include additional information about you, such as an address, title, phone number, company name, Web URL, or a witty quote. Outlook Express makes it easy to set up a standard signature that will be included in every message you compose. You can configure your own signature by following these steps:

1. Choose Tools, Options. Click the Signatures tab to bring it to the front.

2. Click New to begin typing a new signature. Type your signature information as shown in Figure 10.8.

3. If you have multiple email accounts, click Advanced and select the account or accounts you want this signature to be used with.

4. Place a check mark next to Add Signatures to All Outgoing Messages to enable this feature. Notice that, by default, your signatures will not be added to replies and forwards. Click OK when you're finished.

TIP

Consider creating several signatures, with varying levels of personal information. You can then choose a signature in the message window by selecting Insert, Signature.

Figure 10.8
You can create a standard signature for your outgoing messages here.

REQUESTING RECEIPTS

It is possible for OE to send a request along with email you send, asking the recipient to simply click a box to notify you that your email message has been read. This is called a "read receipt." When typing a message, go to Tools, Request Read Receipt. If there is not already a check mark next to it, click on Request Read Receipt.

Note that this is a request only: The recipient has the option of refusing to send the receipt. Still, it is a helpful tool: If you don't get a receipt, you can follow-up with another email or a phone call.

If you intend to request a read receipt every time you send email, you can change your settings to make it simple. In OE, go to Tools, Options, and click on the Receipts tab. Click the box at the top of the window that says "Request a read receipt for all sent messages." Consider this carefully; your Inbox could get filled quickly with read receipts, and the significance of receipts could be diluted (and recipients irritated) if a request is attached even to the messages of minor importance that you send. In addition, this window allows you to select your preference for returning read receipts. If you find the pop-up windows to be annoying, choose an option to "never" or "always" send a receipt when requested.

FORMATTING OPTIONS FOR MAIL

A simple way to enrich email is to apply message formatting using HTML code, the same type of code used to construct Web pages. HTML is the default format for new messages you create in OE6, although replies are typically formatted in whatever manner they were originally sent to you.

Applying special formatting to HTML messages is easy. Outlook Express provides a formatting toolbar similar to what you would see in a word processing program, where you can choose such formatting options as bold, italic, and so on. You also can give HTML messages graphic backgrounds by choosing one of several varieties of "stationery" provided by OE6. To do this, choose Format, Apply Stationery. You can even generate email that looks much like a Web page, complete with pictures (and, heaven forbid, banner ads), as well as links.

→ **See** the "Tips from the Windows Pros" section at the end of this chapter for details on how to create Web-page–like HTML email.

CAUTION

Although you don't have to worry about accidentally generating malicious HTML-formatted email, you might want to know that HTML email can carry scripts that might damage your system or invade your privacy. Some viruses (such as the infamous bubble-boy virus) have used HTML mail to propagate. Also, HTML emails can be used to track how people view their email. For example, some emails have links to pictures in them that automatically download from the Internet when you click on the message. These links can be used by advertisers (if they care to notice) to track when you've opened an email. They can also track how often you read that email. Some people consider this a breach of privacy.

One problem with HTML messages is that not all modern email clients can view them properly. Messages formatted in this manner may appear with a huge quantity of gibberish at the end of the message if the recipient doesn't have an HTML-compatible client. Likewise, mailing lists usually cannot handle HTML formatting in messages that are sent to them.

There are two types of plain text message formatting available. Until a few years ago, all email was formatted as simple text, with no special characters or fancy formatting. These early emails utilized a message format called *uuencode*, short for Unix-to-Unix encode. You don't need to be running UNIX to read uuencoded messages, though; virtually any email client you are likely to encounter—including OE6—can read and send messages in this format.

To address the shortcomings of ASCII-based uuencode email, the *Multipurpose Internet Mail Extensions (MIME)* specification was developed. MIME, which is supported by most modern email clients, allows the use of graphics, file attachments, and some special non-ASCII characters in email messages.

Most mailing lists and users in general can handle MIME messages. To change the default sending formats for outgoing messages, open the Options dialog in OE6. On the Send tab, choose HTML or Plain Text. If you choose Plain Text, your default message format will actually be MIME. If you want to change to uuencode, click the Plain Text Settings button, and choose the appropriate options in the dialog that appears.

TIP

> If you happen to know that your recipient is using some truly ancient technology to download and read email, such as Telnet and a text reader, send messages to that person uuencoded.

 Is the formatting of your outgoing messages creating discontent among your recipients? See "Recipients Don't Like My Mail Formatting" in the "Troubleshooting" section at the end of the chapter.

SENDING AND RECEIVING SECURE MESSAGES

Email has fast become an essential method of communication, but for some uses, it might not be secure enough. Hiding or falsifying one's identity on the Internet is easy enough that some unscrupulous person could be masquerading as you or one of your associates. To combat this problem, several companies offer *digital IDs* that help verify the identity of the sender.

Another threat to the privacy of email is the possibility that messages will be intercepted and read by others (think digital wiretapping). Sending *encrypted* email will prevent your mail from being read by anyone on the way to your intended recipient.

A digital ID is made up of a private key, a public key, and a digital signature. When you digitally sign a message, two of these three things are added to your email: a public key and your digital signature. Together, these are called a *certificate*. The private key stays with you.

When you send secure mail, recipients use your digital signature to verify your identity. They use your public key to send encrypted email to you. When you receive the encrypted email, you use your private key to decrypt the message.

The mechanics of how this works are elaborate and a topic that can entertain the most advanced cryptologists and software engineers. What's important is that you will need to have a digital ID to send or receive secure mail. To encrypt messages you send, your Address Book must contain a digital ID for each recipient.

You can obtain a digital ID for yourself by following these steps:

1. In OE, choose Tools, Options.
2. On the Security tab, click Get Digital ID, as shown in Figure 10.9. Choosing this option will launch your browser and automatically go to a Microsoft Web page that contains links to various certification authorities. Among those listed are VeriSign, GlobalSign, and Thawte Certification.
3. Select one of these companies and go to its Web site. Follow the instructions provided there to obtain and install a digital ID.

Click here to obtain a digital ID

Figure 10.9
Get a digital ID, and adjust your security preferences, on the Security tab of the Options dialog box.

Click here to set advanced security settings
(such as checking the validity of digital IDs)

10

When you have a digital ID, adding it to a message is simple. To do so

1. Open OE and click Create Mail.
2. In the New Mail window, go to Tools and click Digitally Sign.
3. Compose and send your message.

Outlook Express will automatically add your digital ID to your email account when you send your first digitally signed message, by searching your computer for a valid digital ID which matches the email address from which you are sending. If more than one valid digital ID is found, you must choose which ID to add to that email account. Also note that if you have more than one email account, you will need to have a different digital ID for each account from which you want to send secure email.

NOTE

> When sending secure email, your reply address must match the account from which you send digitally signed email. If you have set up a different reply address (on the General tab of your account properties dialog box), message recipients won't be able to use your ID to reply with encrypted email.

When others send digitally signed email to you, messages are marked with a red seal in the message header. Outlook Express shows you an explanatory message about digital signatures before displaying the message. If you are online, you can check the validity of the digital ID of the sending party. To do this, choose Tools, Options, Security tab, Advanced, Check for revoked Digital IDs, Only when online.

USING THE ADDRESS BOOK

You don't have to communicate via email for very long before you mistype someone's address. Suddenly, spelling has become more important than ever before. Your local mail carrier can direct your parcel to you when the label is misspelled, tattered, and torn, but email with a misspelled address just gets bounced back to you. Email addresses can also be cryptic and long, and some are even case sensitive. The Address Book feature in Outlook Express is a big help with all of this.

Before going through the inner workings of the Address Book, keep in mind that this single feature goes by two different names within OE6. Sometimes it is called the Address Book, and other times it is called the Contacts list.

You can open the Address Book in its own window by choosing Tools, Address Book, or by clicking the Address Book icon in the toolbar.

 If you have too many unwanted entries in your Address Book, see "Thinning Your Contacts List" in the "Troubleshooting" section at the end of the chapter.

ADDING, EDITING, AND REMOVING ENTRIES

By default, OE adds an entry to your address book whenever you reply to an email you've received. This is an easy way to fatten up your address book quickly. Before your Address Book grows to an unmanageable size, you might want to turn off that feature (see the "Troubleshooting" notes at the end of this chapter). If you do this, you'll need to know how to add contacts in other ways. A fool-proof way to add someone to your Address Book is by doing the following:

1. Open a message sent to you by someone you want to add to the Address Book.

2. Right-click the individual's name or email address in the message header, and choose Add to Address Book.

3. A Properties sheet opens for the entry, but don't close it yet. Click the Name tab to bring it to the front, as shown in Figure 10.10. If the person uses a nickname, you might need to edit the name entries on this tab so that they are displayed correctly in your Contacts list. Pay special attention to the Display field.

4. Review all the other tabs in the Properties sheet, and enter any other information about this person you feel appropriate. Click OK when you're finished.

You also can add someone to your address book the old-fashioned way—that is, manually from a business card or other source. In Outlook Express, click on the Addresses icon. This will open up the Address Book. Click on the New icon, and select New Contact. The Properties window, described above, will open for you to enter information.

To edit a contact later, click on the Addresses icon to open the Address Book. Select the contact that you wish to edit by double-clicking that person's name. The Properties window will now open with a summary of that person's contact information. To change or add information, you need to click on one of the other tabs along the top of the window—the information cannot be changed on the Summary tab.

Figure 10.10
Go through all the tabs on the Properties sheet, and enter any information about this contact you feel appropriate.

Click here to indicate this contact prefers to receive plain text messages

You might find duplicate listings or unwanted contacts in your Address Book. Deleting a contact is simple: Just highlight the entry and click Delete. Be certain you've selected the correct contact, because this action cannot be undone.

CREATING DISTRIBUTION LISTS — Groups

Sending a single email message to several people is not unusual. However, entering multiple addresses can get tiresome, especially if you frequently send messages to the same group of people.

To simplify this task, you can create *distribution lists* in the OE6 Address Book. You can group many people into a single list, and when you want to send a message to the group, you simply choose the distribution listing from your Address Book. Distribution lists can be created for co-workers, customers, friends and family, or any other group you communicate with. To create a list, just follow these steps:

1. Open the Address Book.
2. Click New, and select New Group from the menu that appears.
3. On the Group tab of the Properties dialog that opens, type a descriptive name. For example, consider using the name of your daughter's soccer team or that of your department at work.
4. Click Select Members. In the Select Group Members dialog, pick a name from your Address Book, and click Select. Repeat until you have selected all the names you want in the distribution list.

5. Click OK when you are finished selecting names from the Address Book. As you can see in Figure 10.11, each member is listed under Group Members. Check the Group Details tab to see whether you should enter any information there, and click OK when you're finished.

Figure 10.11
A distribution list has been created for sending group emails.

A listing for the group then appears in your Address Book. When you are composing email for the group, simply select the group name from your Address Book to automatically send the message to all group members. To delete a group, highlight the group name and click Delete. Note that this deletes the group, but not the group's members, from your Address Book.

FINDING PEOPLE WHO AREN'T IN YOUR ADDRESS BOOK

A number of people-search directories exist on the Internet to help you locate individuals. Outlook Express does a good job of integrating these search engines into the program, making it easy for you to search for people and add them to your Contacts list.

TIP

> No matter how obscure a name may seem, you would be amazed at how many other people in the world share it. When you locate someone in an online directory, first send that person an email inquiry to confirm that he or she is indeed the person you are seeking *before* you share any sensitive information with him or her. Unfortunately, you'll also find that the information given by some online directories is frustratingly out of date. (So much for the speed of the Internet.) If you suspect the information is not current, try a different search engine.

To find people who aren't in your Address Book, follow these steps:

1. Open the Address Book. Click Find People on the Address Book toolbar.

2. In the Find People dialog, click the drop-down arrow next to Look in, and select a directory service. No single directory is ideal, so you might need to try searching through several directories before you find the person you are looking for.

3. Click Find Now. A search of the directory service you selected in step 2 is conducted, and results are displayed. If the person is not found, a dialog tells you so. Try another directory or a different spelling for the name.

4. After you have located the person you are looking for, select his or her listing, and click Add to Address Book. Click Close when you are finished searching.

ADDITIONAL SECURITY FEATURES IN POST SP-2 OUTLOOK EXPRESS

As of Service Pack 2, Outlook Express included a couple of security features worth knowing about. Click Help, About Outlook Express, and check the revision number. If your Outlook Express revision is later than 6.00.2900, you have the updated version. The post SP-2 version deals with two essential problems: spam and unsafe email attachments.

Of course, one way around most viruses and other intrusive *malware* (uninvited programs that do harm to your computer) is to switch to the Mac and Linux operating system and hardware. The degree to which hackers are interested in writing malicious code for a platform is directly proportional to the size of the installed based of a platform, and Windows wins that competition by a long shot. However, if, like us, you really enjoy the broad base of applications and utilities available for the Windows platform, switching to a Mac or Linux system simply to avoid viruses seems self-defeating. It's better to understand how to protect yourself from malware's ravages by taking reasonable security measures. Spam is another issue, one that affects most anyone who uses email.

LIMITING SPAM

Some estimate that *spam* (unsolicited email) constitutes as much as 60% of all Internet traffic. This is an unbelievable waste of bandwidth that could be better used. Then again, look at how much paper spam we get in our physical mailboxes every week, and that consumes trees. Don't get me started!

Spammers are very clever about distinguishing between live addresses and dead ones. Spammers often use programs that generate thousands of potentially accurate email addresses, based on known domain names (such as AOL.com, Mindspring.com, or other domains in the publicly viewable domain registries). As explained earlier, one way of mining a real address is to send an email that has image links in it. You might not know that email images can be sent in two ways: stored in the email itself or pointed to by placeholders in the email that direct the email reading program (in this case, Outlook Express) to download the images from a server on the Internet. The former is a good way of ensuring that recipients can see the images even if they are not online at the time they read the email. However, this approach slows down the transmission of the emails because the images increase the file size of the emails. Pumping out spam in this way takes too much time, so spammers use the second method, with an additional benefit. When the recipient views an email (assuming she is online), the links download the images from the spammer's Web server. At that point, the

10

spammer's server notes who is downloading the images and then updates its spam database, marking that address as live.

One way around this problem is to use a less popular email *client* (program), such as Eudora, Pegasus, or a Web-based client such as Yahoo! mail or Hotmail. But I have found that there are incompatibilities of various kinds that I prefer not to deal with. Again, I'd prefer to buttress my defenses and continue to use the industry-standard Outlook or Outlook Express. Outlook 2003 already had a defense against this image downloading issue, and it has migrated into Outlook Express. Here's how to use it:

1. In Outlook Express, Open Tools/Options. Click the Security tab.

2. Notice the check box labeled Block Images and Other External Content in HTML email (see Figure 10.12). Make sure that this option is on.

3. When you receive an email with images in it, the images will be blank and will indicate that you can right-click the image and select Download Images after you have determined that you can trust the sender of the email. The images are downloaded and stored with the email on your computer and can later be viewed.

Figure 10.12
Turning off auto-downloading of external images and other HTML items helps decrease spam.

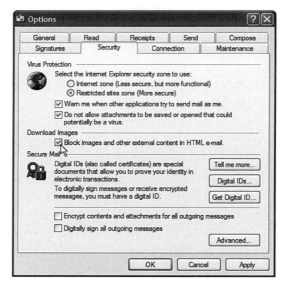

Another advantage of this arrangement pertains to folks using dial-up connections to the Net. In previous Outlook Express versions, viewing an HTML email with external images (that download from a server) caused the computer to begin a dial-up session. This was annoying.

See more spam-battling techniques at the end of this chapter.

PROTECTING AGAINST HTML SCRIPTS

Email programs that can read and execute HTML-formatted email are potential targets for virus authors because HTML email can include scripts. These scripts are little programs that can run when the email is viewed. Microsoft attempts to thwart such vulnerabilities in Internet Explorer and Outlook Express via security patches and system updates disseminated via the Windows Update site, but people don't check it as often as they could, and a delay often occurs between the outbreak of a virus across the Net and the availability of a fix. However, a more failsafe approach is to turn off Outlook Express's ability to execute HTML email altogether.

As of SP-2, Outlook Express can do this via a setting that causes emails to be read using a rich text editor instead of the HTML editor. This turns off the part of Outlook Express that executes malicious HTML code (typically code stored in the HTML header). You won't see images or things like font styles, sizes, and color, but you can still read the text just fine.

Here's how to turn off the HTML editor/viewer:

1. Choose Tools, Options. Then click the Read tab.
2. Select the Read All Messages in Plain Text check box.

Now whenever you read emails, they will not have HTML formatting displayed, but potential malicious HTML headers won't be executed, either.

Sometimes you want to display HTML effects, however, because it can make reading the message easier when it's formatted. Just do this:

1. Ask yourself: Is this email from a trusted source? If yes, proceed.
2. Choose View, Message in HTML. The message is displayed in all its glory. (This can't be reversed, incidentally.)

HANDLING UNIQUE MAIL SITUATIONS

Outlook Express 6 has features that go well beyond the most common email-related tasks of reading and composing mail, addressing and sending messages, or using the Address Book. For example, you might have more than one email account. You can set preferences for these accounts, choose to keep them separate, or to bring them all into the same OE Inbox. You'll also learn ways to organize and filter your mail, check your mail while traveling, and how to make an alternate back-up location for the mail you want to save and protect. In this section, we'll describe these more advanced situations and capabilities. Even if you don't intend to use these features, skim through the sections just so you know what features are available. Once you know what features are built in, you might want to come back and try them out later.

MODIFYING AN EXISTING EMAIL ACCOUNT

After setting up an email account or two, you might find that you'd like to change a few things, such as the server name, password, connection preference, and more. To do this, go to Tools, Accounts, click the Mail tab, and click Properties. Poke around in here to see all the characteristics that you can change.

Under the General tab, you can change how your name will appear on outgoing mail. Whatever you enter in the Name box will be what the recipient sees. Think about whether you'd like your email to be listed in recipients' Inboxes in a casual or formal way, or even with your business name instead. (In other words, enter "Bob Cowart" or "Mr. Robert Cowart" or "Bob's Car Care.")

You might want to send mail from one email address, but have replies go to a different email address (when recipients click Reply). To do this, enter the outgoing email address in the Email address box, and the alternate email address in the Reply address box.

Some email accounts (university accounts, for example) require you to connect to the Internet using a specific connection in order to access your email. If you need to change the connection used for an account, open the Internet Accounts dialog and follow these steps:

1. Click the Mail tab to bring it to the front, and select the account you want to change. Click the Properties button on the right side of the dialog.

2. Click the Connection tab. If you need to use a specific connection, place a check mark next to Always Connect to This Account Using, and select a connection from the drop-down menu.

3. Click OK and Close to exit all the open dialog boxes.

HANDLING MULTIPLE EMAIL ACCOUNTS FOR THE SAME USER

Increasingly, individuals have more than one email account. Outlook Express can be configured to handle multiple email accounts, even if they are on separate servers. For example, I have four email accounts, one from each of my Internet service providers. I can pull all my email into one Inbox, by setting up the various accounts under a single user identity. When I click on Send/Receive Mail on the OE toolbar, OE goes out and pulls in all the new mail from all four accounts automatically. It's just that simple. How do you set up your system so it can do this? Read on.

Each email account needs to be set up and configured in Outlook Express as explained earlier in this chapter. Simply set up an account for each email address and server you have, using the information provided by each ISP (or email account, if a single ISP has given you multiple email accounts).

Normally, OE6 checks all accounts when looking for new mail, even if they use different servers. Sending and receiving email from different accounts normally will happen automatically and without impediments. You connect to the Internet (whether by dial-up service or over your LAN or cable/DSL modem), click Send/Receive, and OE will try to access each server one after another, using the currently active Internet connection. However, there are a couple instances where this gets more complicated:

- If you have specified that an account must use a specific connection, you will see a dialog box when you try to use that account on another connection. Here, you must decide whether you want to switch connections or try to locate the server on the current connection.

- Some services require that you be actually dialed into their Internet connection service before you can send email through their SMTP (mail sending) service. This is to prevent "spoofing" or "spamming" by nonpaying users who jam up SMTP servers sending their unwelcome advertisements. It's sort of like hijacking the U.S. Postal Service to send free bulk mail. Such services check to see that you are connected to the Internet through them, and logged in. When you are, you can send mail through that account. Sometimes, such services will let you *receive* mail regardless of how you are connected to the Net, because that doesn't infringe on their services. Typically, only the *sending* is restricted. If a unique connection is needed for a given email account, you must specify this in the account's properties dialog boxes. Click the Connection tab and choose the Always Connect to This Account Using option. Then, choose which connection the account in question should use.

You can set up an unlimited number of email accounts in OE6. You can even set up multiple accounts using the same email address and server information. Each account can serve a separate identity for you.

When you compose a new mail message, it is automatically addressed for your default mail account. The default account can be set in the Internet Accounts dialog. You can change the account used for an individual message manually, as follows:

1. Click Create Mail in Outlook Express to begin composing a new message.
2. In the New Message window, select an identity from the drop-down menu next to From: in the header, as shown in Figure 10.13. The identity used here appears on your outgoing mail and also determines the Reply to: address used if the recipient replies.

Figure 10.13
You can choose an identity for your new message here.

Does Outlook Express check for new mail in some of your accounts but not in others? See "Checking Mail in Multiple Accounts" in the "Troubleshooting" section at the end of the chapter.

ORGANIZING YOUR MAIL

You don't have to receive very much mail to realize that your Inbox can get cluttered in a hurry. The best way to save important mail and stay organized is to organize your mail into folders, just like files are organized on your hard drive.

The process of creating folders and storing messages in them is quite simple:

1. Right-click the Inbox in the OE6 Folder list, and choose New Folder. The Create Folder dialog opens.

2. Type a descriptive name for your folder under Folder Name. Look at the folder list in the lower half of the dialog to make sure that the correct parent folder is selected.

3. Click OK to create the folder.

The new folder appears in the OE6 Folder list under the parent folder. You can simply drag and drop messages from the message list to the designated storage or project folder.

CAUTION

> Compacting messages in the background automatically can be dangerous, so we choose to turn off this option. To do so, go to Tools, Options, and click the Maintenance tab. Uncheck Compact Messages in the Background. The reason this can be dangerous is because if the computer crashes or the phone connection is interrupted when message compaction is in progress, it can kill the crucial folders.dbx file or corrupt the entire message store. In addition, you may notice a significant drop in the computer's performance each time background compacting begins.
>
> It is important to compact folders regularly, however. By choosing a time to clean them up manually, you can minimize the risk of corruption while compacting. Go back to the Maintenance tab and click the Clean Up Now button. Compacting folders can take several minutes. It is best not to use your computer during this time. If an error occurs, such as "cannot compact, folder in use", close OE, wait a moment, reopen OE, and restart the process.

FILTERING YOUR MAIL

Many email users—especially those who subscribe to mailing lists—receive dozens or even hundreds of messages per day. Wading through all this mail for the really important stuff can be challenging (to say the least), so OE6 includes a mail filtering feature similar to Outlook's Inbox Rules that helps you direct certain kinds of mail to specific locations. For example, you might want to direct all mail from a list you are subscribed to into a special folder where it can be read later.

You can even use mail filters to delete mail you don't want to see at all. Mail can be filtered by content, subject, or sender information. If you are frequently being bothered by someone, you can simply set up OE6 to send all messages from that person to the Deleted Items folder.

To set up a filter: *Filter*

1. In Outlook Express, choose Tools and select Message Rules, Mail. You will see the window shown in Figure 10.14. If there are already one or more Mail Rules set up, the Message Rules dialog opens first. In that case, click New to get to the New Mail Rule window, or Modify to change an existing rule.

2. Select a condition from box 1 of the New Mail Rule dialog. Place a check mark next to the condition or conditions you want to apply.

3. Select an action in box 2. This action will happen if the condition specified in box 1 is met.

4. Follow the instructions in box 3. They will be specific to the conditions and actions you set in boxes 1 and 2. As you can see in Figure 10.14, we have set up a rule that automatically files certain incoming messages in a specific folder. The reply states that we are away from the office until a certain date.

Figure 10.14
You can create mail rules to filter your mail and automate certain tasks.

5. Check the description in box 3 to make sure the correct action will take place. Name the rule in box 4, and click OK when you are finished.

The rule then appears in the Message Rules dialog with a check mark next to it. You can open this dialog at any time to edit, disable (by clearing the check box), or remove any rules.

TIP

> An "out of office" auto reply rule can be created in mail rules to automatically respond to all incoming messages, stating that we are away from the office until a certain date. Although this can be useful, do not enable such a rule if you are subscribed to any mailing lists. (For more on mailing lists, see "What About Mailing Lists?" in Chapter 11.)

Block Mail

To block mail from a specific sender, you can use the Blocked Senders tab of the Message Rules dialog. You can open this tab directly by choosing Tools, Message Rules, Blocked Senders List in Outlook Express. Click Add in the dialog, and type the person's email address in the Add Sender dialog. After you add the address, that person's name appears in your Blocked Senders list. Notice that you can opt to block newsgroup messages from that person as well.

CHECKING YOUR MESSAGES WHILE TRAVELING

If you are traveling away from home, consider setting up a message rule in Outlook Express to forward all incoming messages to your HTTP mail account (such as Hotmail or Yahoo!). That way, you can read all of your mail on the road, regardless of which of your addresses to which the messages are sent. Of course, in order for this method to work, your computer must remain on while you are away, and OE must be set to check for new messages regularly. This is not the best idea, environmentally speaking, but there are conditions where it will work with no wasted energy, such as if the computer you will leave behind will be in use by others in your absence.

A better way to check email while away from your computer is to set up POP mail in your HTTP mail account. At your HTTP account online, go to options (or something similar) to enter your POP server settings. Some servers let you differentiate between different mail accounts with color coding of messages. Once this is set up, simply click on the online Inbox or, in some cases, Check Other Mail.

ALL YOUR MAIL IS IN A LAPTOP

If you're like me, though, you'll want to keep all your mail in the same computer, not scattered around in places like Hotmail, Yahoo! Mail, and Google Mail as well as in your laptop or desktop in Outlook or Outlook Express. I have two ultimate solutions to this depending on how you work.

If all your work is on a laptop and that is your primary computer, all you have to do when traveling is ensure that you have an email account that lets you send mail from the road, using the various connections you'll find along the way (typically Wi-Fi connections in airports, hotels, and cafes). Although Wi-Fi hotspots are becoming ubiquitous, the problem is when you try to send mail on your usual email account and you find out (usually much to your chagrin) that it won't go. Why is this? It's because many ISPs, in an attempt to thwart spammers, don't let just anyone use their SMTP (outgoing mail) servers. You have to be connected directly to the ISP's server to do so.

For example, I have cable at home, using Comcast. Until recently, I couldn't send email through Comcast unless I was actually communicating through the cable connection. This was a bummer because I like to work in cafes. But cafes usually don't have SMTP servers available. Why? Because spammers would sit in cafes and deluge the cafe's SMTP server with outgoing spam—sad but true. When on the road, I have two options. I checked with Comcast and found that they now have an authenticated SMTP server. I went into the account settings for my email (Tools, Accounts, Mail tab, Servers). In the lower section I selected My Server Requires Authentication, which enables me to send outgoing mail through Comcast's server even when I'm connected to the Net through another ISP such as a Wi-Fi hotspot.

My backup solution is to have a dial-up connection I can use from hotels and friends' houses. The trick here is that I must have a separate email account for that server. In my case, it's Earthlink. So, using the techniques explained in the previous section ("Handling Multiple Email Accounts for the Same User"), I created an Earthlink account. When I write an email, it's automatically set to be sent by the default mail account, which is usually Comcast for me. I have to make a point of either changing the default email account or manually choosing the account I'm going to send each new email with. (If you have multiple email accounts, you'll see a drop-down list on the From field in your new emails. Click open the list and choose the email account that has the SMTP server that corresponds to your current Internet connection at the time of sending the message(s).

ALL YOUR WORK IS IN YOUR DESKTOP

My other and newer solution is this: I have so much work on my desktop computer that I decided to leave it all there and not worry about taking some email folders with me on the road. I'm doing video editing and have all my MP3s and photos on my desktop. It's too much to carry with me. Transferring stuff onto my laptop prior to a trip is always a last-minute hassle. What's more, I'm running beta operating systems on the desktop using Virtual PC and don't want that to potentially confuse things on my laptop. So here's what I do (and, no, I'm not getting paid for this shameless advertising):

1. I subscribed to GoToMyPC.com. It costs about $20 a month, which is worth it for the convenience it affords me.

2. I leave my desktop at home, on and running. I make sure it's not going to power down (check the Control Panel's Power Options). (The desktop computer has to be connected to the Net with a cable or DSL connection for this to work reasonably fast enough, by the way.)

3. When I'm on the road, I get online (preferably on a high-speed connection such as in a cafe), go to www.gotomypc.com, and log in. In a few seconds, my desktop computer screen comes up on my laptop, and I'm working as though I'm at home, only a tad slower. The speed degradation is not too bad if both computers have DSL, cable, T1, and so on. It's livable.

Of course, you can achieve similar results using Remote Desktop (see the section "Remote Desktop" in Chapter 17, "Windows Unplugged, Remote and Mobile Computing"), but with a little more elbow grease to get it working. Notably, routers get in the way and have to be set up carefully to allow the signal to pass through, and the desktop has to be running Windows XP Professional. But once it's set up, it's free. Remote Desktop also connects the com ports, printer ports, disk drives, and sound cards of the host computer to the remote computer. However, for a simple, easy-to-connect solution to the email issue we're addressing here, my vote is for GoToMyPC. Virtually any Web browser-enabled computer can function as the remote machine. I have logged on to my desktop PC from afar using both Macs and PCs in libraries, for example. All my email is still safe and sound at home, and I can run any programs I like.

NOTE

Other remote control programs such pcAnywhere (Symantec) offer similar functionality. VNC is another similar though somewhat crippled tool. But it's free. Timbuktu is another remote control program. You can find all of these on the Web.

BACKING UP MESSAGES

One of the unique aspects of electronic mail is that it can serve as a permanent record of your communications. Mail that seems insignificant now may be invaluable in the future, and many people back up all their correspondence on a regular basis to ensure that a record is kept for all time.

You can save copies of individual messages by choosing Save As from the File menu in the message window. Choosing this option opens a standard Windows Save dialog, where you can choose a location and name for the file. It is saved with the `.eml` extension.

BACKING UP ALL YOUR OUTLOOK EXPRESS MESSAGES

The easiest and perhaps safest way to back up your mail is to make a backup copy of all your Outlook Express email message files. (It's complicated to backup and restore just individual folders.) To begin making a backup copy of all of your OE messages

1. In OE, go to Tools, Options, and click the Maintenance tab.
2. Click the Store Folder button.
3. Copy the folder location that appears in the box (highlight the entire line and then press Ctrl+C).
4. Click Cancel twice to close the dialog boxes.
5. From the Start menu, click Run, press Ctrl+V (to paste the folder location into the Run dialog box), and click OK. This opens the mail folder in a new window.
6. On that window, open the Edit menu, and click Select All.
7. Open the Edit menu and click Copy.
8. Close the window.

9. Create a new folder on your hard drive or alternate back-up drive, and name it ("Bob's email backup," for example).

10. Open the new folder, and choose Edit, Paste. All the mail files will be copied into the new folder, leaving the originals in place.

11. Close the window.

> **TIP**
>
> You might want to make one backup folder on your hard drive and another on a CD-R or Zip disk.

RESTORING YOUR BACKED-UP MESSAGES

Restoring the folder is a multi-step process. Even Microsoft doesn't tell you how to do that in its Help file for OE. Here's how.

> **NOTE**
>
> If you're restoring the data into a new computer, or newly installed operating system, you'll want to first decide which Identity is going to reclaim the messages. Create the Identity if you need to. Then follow these instructions to pull in the messages.

To import your OE email messages from your backup folder, open OE, go to the File menu, click Import, and then click Messages. In the box that appears, select an email program to import from, and click Next. Click Import mail from an OE6 store directory, and click OK. Browse to your mail backup folder and click OK, and Next. Choose All Folders, click Next, and click Finish.

> **TIP**
>
> For more thorough (and more advanced) ways of backing up and restoring data, go to these Web sites. If no longer available, perform a search by entering "OE backup restore" in the window of a search engine such as `www.hotbot.com`.
>
> Answers to dozens of questions about OE:
>
> > `http://www.chasms.com/mskb/mskbol.htm`
>
> How to back up and restore mail folders:
>
> > `http://support.microsoft.com/default.aspx?scid=kb;EN-US;`
> > `q270670`
>
> Advanced backup instructions here:
>
> > `http://insideoe.tomsterdam.com/`

To make the process easier, there is software available that will back up files for you with a single click (once you've set up your preferences). An added perk is its ability to synchronize OE message folders on multiple computers. The program even includes a system that will remind you to back up files regularly.

One of these programs, Express Assist, is available for downloading here:

`http://www.ajsystems.com/oexhome.html`

DEALING WITH SPAM

A hot topic in email circles today is the subject of commercial advertisements mass-delivered via electronic mail. This type of unsolicited mail is generally referred to as *spam*, a name attributed in Internet lore to a Monty Python musical skit pertaining to the pink meat product of the same name. This type of mail is so offensive to some people that a few states have even enacted laws against it.

Some groups are also working with the U.S. Federal Government to ban unsolicited electronic mail and place identification requirements on people and organizations who send advertisements via email. Countless anti-spam organizations exist, with one of the foremost being CAUCE, the Coalition Against Unsolicited Commercial Email (`www.cauce.org`).

The real problem with spam is that scam operations are rampant and difficult to detect. Spam also has an impact on Internet traffic, requiring a considerable amount of bandwidth that many people feel would be better used for other purposes.

If you have been online for very long, you've almost certainly received some spam yourself. You can protect yourself from receiving a lot of spam by taking some basic precautionary measures:

- Avoid giving out your email address whenever possible. Some Web sites funnel you through pointless registration procedures that do little else than collect email addresses.

- If you post to newsgroups periodically, alter your Reply to: email address for your news account in such a way that "spam bots" searching newsgroups for email addresses will not be able to send you mail correctly. Many people put "Nospam" or other phrase in front of their address (nospambob@mcp.com), a modification that will be easy for humans to correct when sending you a valid reply.

- Don't register with too many online directories. Some directories can be used as email address archives for spammers. The trade-off is that someone looking for you will have a harder time.

Alas, no matter how careful you are, some spam will get through. Many spams contain instructions for getting yourself removed from their lists. Beware that following their instructions can result in even more spam, because some unscrupulous spammers use this trick to find active addresses. To avoid this, simply delete the messages.

You can also check with your local, state, or federal laws from time to time to find out whether there are regulations against spam that apply to your account. If so, you may have legal recourse against spammers. The CAUCE organization mentioned earlier is a good starting point to search online for information about laws in your area.

TROUBLESHOOTING

PASSWORD TROUBLE

The server will not accept my password.

Many email servers are case sensitive. If the Caps Lock key on your keyboard is on, it could cause the password to be entered in the wrong case. Sometimes an inadvertent space can be the culprit as well. This is true even if you have configured Outlook Express to remember your email address so that you don't have to type it in every time you check mail.

IDENTITY CRISIS

I don't like the name Outlook Express is using to identify me in outgoing messages.

The name Outlook Express uses could be indicative of several things. First, if you have multiple accounts or identities configured in Outlook Express, make sure that you are selecting the desired one in the From: field when you send the messages. You can also open the Internet Accounts dialog and check the Properties sheet for your email address(es). The Name field under User Information on the General tab is the name used to identify you on outgoing mail.

CHECKING MAIL IN MULTIPLE ACCOUNTS

I have several mail accounts, but OE6 doesn't check all of them when I click Send/Recv.

Open the Properties sheet for each of your mail accounts in the Internet Accounts dialog. On the General tab is an option labeled Include This Account When Receiving Mail or Synchronizing. Make sure a check mark appears next to this option for each of your mail accounts.

THINNING YOUR CONTACTS LIST

Several people in my Contacts List shouldn't be there, including spammers.

By default, OE6 adds an entry to the Address Book for every source to which you reply. You can disable this feature by opening the Options dialog in the Tools menu. On the Send tab, disable the option labeled Automatically Put People I Reply to in My Address Book. Then, to remove unwanted entries from your Address Book, highlight the contact and click Delete.

RECIPIENTS DON'T LIKE MY MAIL FORMATTING

People on my mailing list are sending me hate mail because of machine characters or strange attachments that accompany each of my posts.

HTML messages are not compatible with most electronic mailing lists. Change your default mail-sending format to Plain Text on the Send tab of the OE6 Options dialog.

Alternatively, you can have OE remind you of specific people in your address book that request Plain Text messages. Open the Address Book and click on the name of a person who requests Plain Text mail. Click on the Name tab, and put a check mark in the box next to "Send Email using plain text only." When you try to send HTML email to this person, a reminder window will pop up asking if you'd like OE to reformat the email to Plain Text.

MISSING MAIL SERVERS

When I try to go online and check mail, an error occurs stating that the server could not be found.

Assuming that the server information for your account is correct, you probably have a problem with your connection. OE6 should automatically dial a connection if one is not present, but if it doesn't, open the Internet Properties icon in the Windows Control Panel. On the Connection tab, select the option Dial Whenever a Network Connection Is Not Present, and click OK to close the dialog.

MAKING OE6 LESS AUTOMATED

I want/don't want Outlook Express to automatically check for mail periodically.

Go to the General tab of the Options dialog. If the option Check for New Messages Every XX Minutes is checked, OE6 automatically checks for new mail at the specified interval. Just below that option, you can also specify whether you want OE6 to automatically dial a connection at this time.

TIPS FROM THE WINDOWS PROS: HOW TO CREATE FORMATTED EMAIL

So, you know a lot about email. What about the fancy-looking messages you get in your Inbox—the ones that look like Web pages? This type of email is created with HTML formatting.

And how do you create fancy HTML email messages, anyway? In its simplest form, HTML mail lets you format the font and other goodies like color and background. Well, we already talked about stationery. So you know that this is HTML mail. You can also use the Insert Picture button on the OE toolbar to insert an image. But your ability to design a document with much control is still quite limited.

If you want to create a more elaborate email, with tables, text that wraps around pictures, and lots of links in it, you'll probably want to use a Web-design program such as FrontPage or DreamWeaver. After you've designed a page there

1. Start a new email in OE.
2. Select and copy the new page you designed in your Web design program and paste into the new email you're constructing. As you paste in the text and images, they should appear in your email.
3. Adjust as necessary.

Test the look of the email you created by sending the sample mail to yourself; see how it looks when you open it. Be sure to test it by sending it to another computer, too. That way, you can determine whether there are any missing images. Your test can be deceptive if you send and receive from the same computer, because the images you use are already on the source computer. If the images are missing from the email, they are still likely to show up if you use the source computer to test it, simply because they are being called up from your local hard drive.

To keep your email easy to read, keep the page fairly narrow. Also, don't expect your message to display with as much predictably as it does in a Web browser because HTML-capable email programs just aren't as polished in their capability to render HTML. It's a good idea to check your mail in various email clients first to get an idea of how it will look to a variety of readers.

TIP

> Some folks don't have programs that can read HTML mail. In the subject line of HTML mail, I like to include the words "HTML version" so people will know not to bother reading it if their email program isn't HTML savvy. Then, I send another message that is plain text, with a subject line that includes the words "Plain text version."

Much spam HTML email only downloads the HTML code and the text portion into OE. The rest of the images are not loaded until you look at the mail (assuming you are online at the time). When you click on the mail to read it, the images stream in because the HTML code in the message "points" to the image sources, which are out on Web servers somewhere across the Internet. This is an acceptable way to construct your HTML mail, but it assumes your readers are online. If you want to be sure people can read your mail offline, you should include the images in the email itself. However, this does make the file larger, and can slow down the transfer time. Be sure to keep your images relatively small and compressed (as a rule, your images shouldn't exceed about 25KB). Use a program such as Fireworks, FrontPage, or Photoshop to optimize photos and other images for transmission over the Web.

CHAPTER 11

READING NEWSGROUPS WITH OUTLOOK EXPRESS

In this chapter

NEWSGROUPS AND THE INTERNET

With the overwhelming and still growing popularity of the World Wide Web since its inception in the early 1990s, you might easily forget that the Internet was around for more than two decades before the first Web page saw the light of a cathode ray tube. Before the inception of the Web, people used the Internet to access newsgroups. Newsgroups began in 1979 as a forum in which Unix users could communicate with each other, and the concept grew steadily from there into what is now a global assemblage of people sharing information on virtually every topic imaginable.

Originally, news servers exchanged articles using Unix-to-Unix Copy Protocol (UUCP), which involves direct modem dial-up over long-distance phone lines. In 1986, the Network News Transport Protocol (NNTP) was released, allowing news to be transported via TCP/IP connection over the Internet. Most modern newsgroups use the NNTP protocol, and it is the only news protocol supported by Outlook Express.

Newsgroups are scattered on servers around the world, and the rough network used to carry newsgroup bandwidth is generally referred to as *Usenet*. We're not implying, however, that some authority provides oversight of Usenet. "Usenet is not a democracy" is one of the first statements you will read in virtually any primer or Frequently Asked Questions list (FAQ) on the subject, alluding to the virtual anarchy in which this medium exists. Usenet has become so large and diverse that a simple definition cannot possibly do justice.

What we can do, however, is roughly describe the types of newsgroups and news servers that you can access using Outlook Express 6 (OE6). Basically, the administrator of your news server determines which news feeds you will have access to. Feeds are passed along to the server from adjacent servers, providing a decidedly decentralized structure to Usenet. Each server maintains a list of message IDs to ensure that new articles are received at a given server only once. An individual server can control which feeds it propagates, although the interconnectivity of Usenet servers ensures that a lone server has little or no control of the overall distribution. Thus, the authority of a news server is generally limited to what clients (that would be you) can access and what kind of material those clients can post. Likewise, the decentralization of servers means that an article you post may take hours—or even days—to circulate among all other news servers.

> **NOTE**
>
> The terms *newsgroup* and *Usenet* are used almost interchangeably in today's online world, but it is useful to know that *newsgroup* refers to individual groups, whereas *Usenet* refers to the entire network of groups as a whole.

WHAT ABOUT MAILING LISTS?

Are newsgroups the same as mailing lists, or *listservs*, as some people call them? No. So here's a little digression about those, just to make the distinction. The very openness that makes newsgroups desirable has its drawbacks: privacy and security are almost nonexistent.

Mailing list posts are less public because usually the only people who can read them are other list members, and lists are generally less susceptible to spam and objectionable material. Furthermore, mailing list traffic comes into your email reader (your inbox in OE), making lists easier to deal with for some people.

Mailing lists are simple; you send a message to the list address, which is then forwarded to every other list member. Every time another member posts a message to the list, you receive a copy. The list is managed by a list administrator who often, but not always, works directly with the mail server hosting the list. Often the administrator can be reached via the email address `listproc` or `majordomo` followed by @ and the name of the domain server.

Virtually any topic imaginable has a mailing list. If you want to find one to join, a good place to start would be CataList available online at `http://www.lsoft.com/lists/listref.html`.

Lists vary widely in terms of message volume, ranging anywhere from only a few messages per month up to hundreds of posts each day. Many lists let you opt to receive one or two daily list compilations rather than a string of individual posts. These compilations are called *digests* and are especially useful with high-volume lists.

USING MAILING LISTS

Before you join and start to participate in mailing lists, you need to keep two main issues in mind: security and netiquette. Security is largely determined by the list administrator, so you should check list policies for concerns before you join. You should also exercise caution when posting sensitive information to a list because, generally speaking, you won't know who is actually subscribed.

Netiquette is a little trickier. You've probably already read volumes on such topics as flame wars and the public airing of private laundry, but you should be aware of some issues unique to mailing lists:

- **Don't post attachments**—Most mailing lists, especially those offering a digest mode, forbid file attachments, and for good reason. If you want to send a file to someone, do it off list.

- **Send posts in plain text format**—HTML formatting can wreak havoc on recipients' systems. Check with the list administrator to find out whether MIME or uuencode plain text formatting is best.

- **Read and save the FAQ**—Every list has a different procedure for subscribing, unsubscribing, switching to digest mode, or changing various other options. This information is usually contained in a list FAQ, which should also include guidance regarding list content and rules.

- **Be conscious of the reply procedures for your list**—Some mailing lists are configured so that a Reply action goes only to the original sender, and you must click Reply All to post a reply to the list. But with other lists, clicking Reply sends your response directly to the list. Again, double-check your list's FAQ to find out the correct procedure.

11

■ **Do not use an "Out of Office" auto-reply rule for your Inbox**—Automatic replies to incoming messages can cause destructive feedback loops in lists that you are subscribed to. (Since every incoming message from the list triggers a response from Outlook Express, those responses go back to the mailing list, generating more list traffic that will be sent to your account, resulting in more auto replies, and so on.) If you feel that you must use such a rule, unsubscribe or suspend your mailing lists before enabling it.

TIP

> Because mailing lists can dump dozens—or even hundreds—of posts into your email account daily, set up a separate folder in OE for each mailing list, and use Message Rules to direct incoming messages to that folder. (For more on Rules, see Chapter 10, "Sending Email with Outlook Express.")

→ Spam is a fact of life in both mailing lists and newsgroups. To learn more about spam, **see** "Avoiding Spam," **p. 386**.

SETTING UP A NEWSGROUP ACCOUNT IN OUTLOOK EXPRESS

Outlook Express 6 (OE6) is included free with XP and serves quite well as a news reader. If you already use OE6 for email services, you're probably already familiar with the basics of using this program. If not, you may benefit from a quick review of Chapter 10, which will help you master the fundamentals of using OE6.

You first must set up a news account in OE6. You might do so at the same time you set up an email account, but if not, you can configure it any time. Before you can configure your news account, you need to obtain a news server address, which should look something like this:

```
news.domainname.com
```

Your company might also have a news server account with a commercial provider. You can configure multiple server accounts in OE6, just as you can set up multiple email accounts.

As mentioned earlier, a news server provides you with news feeds from other news servers. Which feeds are available to you depends on decisions made by your server's administrator. For example, some news servers restrict feeds for all `alt.` (alternative) newsgroups because some of them contain highly objectionable material.

→ If you do not have a news server you can access, **see** "Locating News Servers," **p. 389**.

To set up your account in Outlook Express, follow these steps:

1. Open Outlook Express, and choose Tools, Accounts to open the Internet Accounts dialog. Click the News tab to bring it to the front, and then select Add, News.

2. Follow the instructions in the Internet Connection Wizard for inputting your display name and email address (the wizard may provide this information for you).

3. Type the name of your news (NNTP) server, as shown in Figure 11.1.

Type your NNTP server name here

Figure 11.1
Enter the name of your news server here. If you use multiple news servers, you must set up an individual account for each one.

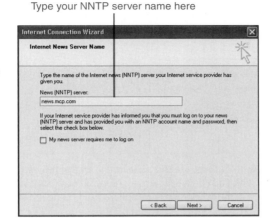

4. Click Next, and then click Finish.

Downloading the Newsgroup List

After you have configured Outlook Express for your news server, your next step is to download a list of newsgroups from the server. Depending on how many groups the server allows access to, this list could contain more than 75,000 newsgroups. In reality, most servers list less than half that number.

Why aren't they all listed? As you've already seen, some content might be censored by the server's administrator. In many cases, though, it is a much more practical matter: New groups are created so frequently that your server simply might not be aware of them. If you become aware of a newsgroup you would like to join, but it is not currently available on your server, try dropping an email message to the administrator and ask for the group to be added. Assuming the group falls within the administrator's guidelines for acceptable content, adding the group will take only a few seconds.

To begin downloading your server's list, follow these steps:

1. Click the listing for your news account in the OE6 Folders list.

2. A message appears stating that you are not currently subscribed to any newsgroups and asking whether you would like to view the list. Click Yes.

3. If this is the first time you have viewed the list, a dialog appears, as shown in Figure 11.2. Depending on the size of the list and the speed of your connection, downloading could take several minutes. You probably have time to go get another cup of coffee.

When the process is finished, the list is downloaded, and you are ready to locate and subscribe to newsgroups.

Figure 11.2
The list of news-groups downloads from your news server.

TIP

Although new newsgroups are created daily, the list that has been downloaded to your computer is static and doesn't show new groups. To make sure you have a current list, click Reset List in the Newsgroup Subscriptions dialog periodically.

FINDING AND READING NEWSGROUPS

Usually, when you read a newsgroup, you must first subscribe to it. A subscription simply means you've placed a bookmark of sorts in Outlook Express for that group, making it easy to return to and follow conversations whenever you are using OE6.

Before you can subscribe to a newsgroup, you need to find one that piques your interest. Searching for a group in your downloaded list is fairly simple in OE6 (see Figure 11.3). If the list isn't already open, you can open it by clicking your news account in the Folders list. If the list doesn't open automatically, you can click the Newsgroups button on the toolbar.

As you type a word in the Display Newsgroups Which Contain field (Figure 11.3), the list of newsgroups shrinks. You can experiment by typing a keyword you are interested in, paus-ing after each keystroke.

Newsgroups are usually—but not always—named descriptively. In Figure 11.3, you can see the option to search newsgroup descriptions as well as their names, but very few groups actually have descriptions listed in this window.

TIP

If you don't find a newsgroup that interests you, try a search at `http://groups.google.com/` or another Web source to see whether other groups not cur-rently available on your news server exist. There is no such thing as a "complete" list of newsgroups, so a search of several different resources will yield the best results.

Type a word here

Figure 11.3
You can begin typing a word to search the newsgroup list. The list automatically gets smaller as you type, showing only those groups with names that match what you typed.

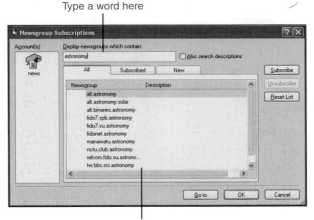

The list shows only groups with names that match what you typed

SUBSCRIBING TO NEWSGROUPS

OE6 does not require you to subscribe to a group to view its contents. You can simply select a group from the list and click Go To to see messages posted to the group, but you might find it easier to manage the process by simply subscribing anyway. Subscribing to a newsgroup does not require any great level of commitment on your part because you can always unsubscribe with just two mouse clicks.

When you find a newsgroup you want to subscribe to, do the following:

1. Click once on the newsgroup name to select it, and then click the Subscribe button. An icon should appear next to the group name, as shown in Figure 11.4.

2. Click Go To at the bottom of the Newsgroup Subscriptions window. The window closes, and the 300 most recent posts are downloaded to your computer.

Actually, only the message headers are downloaded, and they appear listed in the OE6 window. The message contents are not downloaded until you choose to view a specific message.

MANAGING YOUR SUBSCRIPTIONS

Newsgroups you are subscribed to are listed in the OE6 Folders list, under the news account listing, as shown in Figure 11.5. If you have multiple news server accounts, individual subscriptions are listed as subfolders under the server you used to subscribe to them.

When you click a newsgroup's listing in the Folders list, the 300 most recent headers are downloaded.

→ If you want to change the number of headers shown, **see** "Customizing Outlook Express for Newsgroups," **p. 388**.

Figure 11.4
You can select a news-group and subscribe to it here. When you click Go To, this window automatically closes.

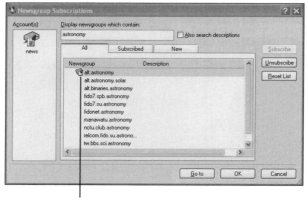

This icon indicates that you have subscribed

Figure 11.5
Subscribed news-groups appear in the Folders list.

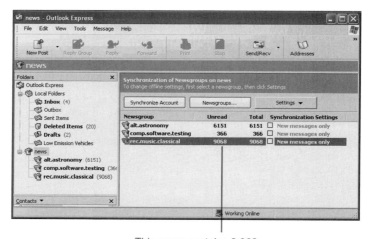

This group contains 9,068 messages

If you decide that you don't want to remain subscribed to a group, unsubscribing is easy. Just right-click the group's listing in the Folders list, and choose Unsubscribe from the shortcut menu that appears.

READING AND POSTING MESSAGES TO A NEWSGROUP

As you learned previously, when you first access a newsgroup using OE6, only the first 300 message headers are downloaded. You can download additional headers by clicking Tools, Get Next 300 Headers.

If you want to read a message, you need to manually open it. If you are using the Preview Pane, all you have to do is click once on the message header to cause it to download. If you are not using the Preview Pane, you can double-click a message to open it in a separate message window.

→ To learn how to show or hide the Preview Pane, **see** "Outlook Express Quick Tour," **p. 338**.

As you peruse the list of messages in the group, you need to understand the concept of *discussion threads*. A thread occurs when someone responds to a message. Others respond to the response, and this conversation becomes its own discussion thread. Messages that are part of a thread have a plus (+) sign next to them, and you can click this icon to expand a list of other messages in the thread. Figure 11.6 shows several expanded threads.

Figure 11.6
Threaded messages.

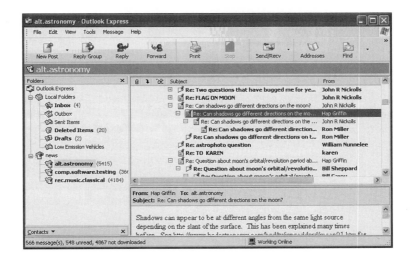

Posting messages to a newsgroup is quite simple. Perhaps the easiest way to post is to reply to an existing message. This process works much the same as replying to regular email, except that you must take extra care to ensure that your reply is going to the right place. Notice that the toolbar has a new button—the Reply Group button—as shown in Figure 11.7.

Each reply button serves a unique purpose:

Reply Group	Sends a reply back to the group
Reply	Sends a reply only to the original sender
Forward	Forwards the message to a third party

One aspect to watch carefully is that messages you post to a newsgroup are relevant. If the newsgroup is moderated, someone reviews all posts and removes those posts that are deemed inappropriate. Look for a newsgroup FAQ (Frequently Asked Questions) for more information on netiquette and any rules that might apply to the groups you are subscribed to.

Forward message to another party
Reply to Group

Figure 11.7
You must choose your
reply mode carefully.

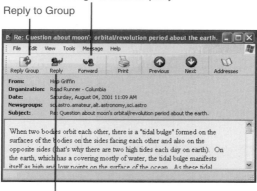

Reply to Single Sender

CAUTION

Information posted in newsgroups can be viewed by anyone, and we do mean *anyone!* Never post personal or sensitive information in a newsgroup.

NOTE

The default news message format is Plain Text. You should maintain this setting to ensure that your message can be read by other news readers.

MANAGING MESSAGES

By default, OE6 deletes messages from your computer five days after you download them, but you can change this option easily. Likewise, you can also set up Outlook Express to delete read messages every time you leave the group. You can review these settings by choosing Tools, Options. In the Options dialog, click the Maintenance tab to bring it to the front, as shown in Figure 11.8.

 If a message you read earlier becomes unavailable, see "Message No Longer Available" in the "Troubleshooting" section at the end of this chapter.

 If you're not sure which messages have been read and which haven't, see "Which Ones Are New?" in the "Troubleshooting" section at the end of the chapter.

If you want to maintain a record of the messages in your newsgroup, remove the check marks next to each Delete option shown in Figure 11.8. Messages remain in OE6 indefinitely if you deselect both of these options, but keep in mind that if the group has high traffic, these messages could eventually eat up a lot of disk space.

The better option is to save individual messages that you want to maintain. To do so, create a new folder for storing news messages under Local Folders in the OE6 Folders list, and then drag any messages you want to save into the folder. You can also drag and drop newsgroup messages to any of your email folders, but you might find it easier to keep newsgroup and email correspondence separate.

Figure 11.8
You can review your message management settings here.

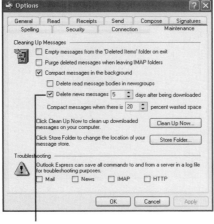

Adjust the length of time read messages are saved

READING NEWS OFFLINE

In Chapter 9, "Browsing the World Wide Web with Internet Explorer," you learned that you can download Web pages for offline viewing. You can do the same with newsgroup messages, a capability that makes especially good sense if you must limit your Internet connection time or will be traveling with your laptop. OE6 calls this feature *synchronizing*.

CAUTION

Before you synchronize a newsgroup for offline viewing, check the size of the messages you will download. Some people post pictures and other large files into newsgroups, and they can add significantly to download time.

To begin downloading a newsgroup for offline viewing, click your news server account in the Folders list. A list of the groups you are subscribed to then appears, as shown in Figure 11.9. Now follow these steps:

1. Select the newsgroup(s) you want to synchronize, and review the synchronization settings. By default, only new messages will be synchronized, but you can change this setting by clicking the Settings button and choosing another option.

2. Place a check mark in the box(es) under Synchronization settings, as shown in Figure 11.9.

3. Click Synchronize Account. Messages are downloaded based on the synchronization settings you choose. Keep in mind that if you choose to synchronize all messages, the download could take awhile.

Figure 11.9
You synchronize messages for offline viewing by choosing options as shown here.

Click here to change synchronization settings

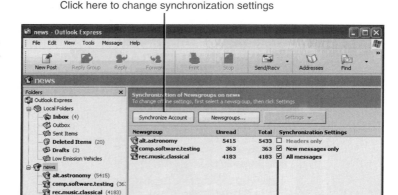

Place a check mark here for groups you want to synchronize

When the download is complete, you can get offline to read the downloaded messages. If you try to open a message that isn't available offline, a warning advises you of this fact.

 If, after you synchronize a newsgroup, some messages are not available, see "Some Messages Are Unavailable After Synchronizing" in the "Troubleshooting" section at the end of this chapter.

You also can select individual messages for offline reading. Choosing particular messages may be a better course of action, especially if the newsgroup has thousands of messages and you want to download only the first few. Select several message headers in the newsgroup by Ctrl+clicking or Shift+clicking. Then right-click the selection and choose Download Message Later from the menu that appears. When you later choose Synchronize Account from the server account window shown in Figure 11.9, only the selected messages are downloaded. Note that if you select to download all messages in your synchronization settings, all messages will be downloaded, not only the ones you selected.

NEWSGROUP SAFETY

It is no secret that many potential hazards exist in the online world, and nowhere is this more evident than in Usenet. Objectionable Web pages get all the media attention, but nowhere is objectionable—and often illegal—content more readily available than in newsgroups. You can avoid most objectionable content simply by staying away from certain newsgroups, but you might still find the need to filter some of the content you receive.

Besides objectionable content, you must also consider that you become more vulnerable to victimization (or, for that matter, prosecution) when you participate in newsgroups unless you take some basic precautions. Remember, anyone in the world who has access to an Internet connection can see what you post in a newsgroup.

FILTERING UNWANTED MESSAGES

OE6 allows you to set up some message rules to filter certain messages. You can set up this feature, which is similar to mail message rules, as follows:

1. In Outlook Express, choose Tools, Message Rules, News.

2. In the New News Rule dialog, choose conditions for your rule in box 1. As you can see in Figure 11.10, you can select more than one condition. In this case, we're looking for messages in the alt.astronomy newsgroup that contain the word *Hubble* in the subject line.

3. In box 2, choose what you want to happen to messages that meet your conditions. In this case, matching messages will be highlighted in yellow. If the condition were looking for objectionable material, we would probably choose to delete it instead.

4. In box 3, review the rule description and enter any required information. For example, you will probably have to specify words or other pieces of information pertaining to the conditions you set.

5. Click OK when you're finished, and click OK in the Message Rules dialog to close it.

Figure 11.10
You can create rules for filtering your news messages here. Be sure to look through each box for relevant information.

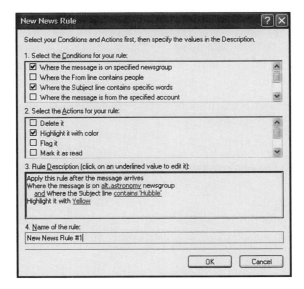

You can modify or disable a rule at any time by using the Tools, Message Rules, News command.

→ You can also filter news by restricting senders. To learn how, **see** "Filtering Your Mail," **p. 362**.

PROTECTING YOUR IDENTITY

Besides objectionable content, the other great hazard involved with using newsgroups is the threat to your identity and personal information. You can avoid having personal information compromised on Usenet by simply not posting it. Don't post your home address or phone number, age (especially if you are young), or financial information (such as a credit card number).

You can also hide your identity if you do not want to reveal it. Outlook Express identifies you in all outgoing posts by whatever username you entered when you configured the account. If you are concerned about protecting your identity in newsgroups, consider changing the username for your news account to a nickname that your friends or associates will recognize but strangers won't. Figure 11.11, in the next section, shows such a nickname in use.

Of course, there are limits to how much anonymity can be provided by simply changing the username and email address for your news account in OE6. Any message you post to a newsgroup can be easily traced back to your server, and your server maintains transaction logs that allow your real identity to be ascertained.

A better way to protect your identity is by signing up for a Web-based email account, such as those available at Yahoo! or Hotmail, and register for a rather bland address. When you do this, limit the amount of information that you give.

Using a *pseudonymous remailer* can be an even more secure solution. A pseudonymous remailer is a server that assigns you an ID based on a proprietary scheme, and you send and receive through the server. However, finding a remailer can be challenging because of their tendency to have a short lifespan, perhaps because of their low profitability. Also, some remailers require you to use a specific news application, and it never seems to be OE.

At the time of this printing, it was possible to find a list of pseudonymous remailers, and FAQs, online at the following site:

```
http://www.andrebacard.com/remail.html
```

Some remailer choices include: `www.ziplip.com`, `www.securenym.net`, and `www.hushmail.com`.

AVOIDING SPAM

One of the most pervasive threats to your identity that exists in Usenet is spam (see "Dealing with Spam" in Chapter 13, "Troubleshooting Your Internet Connection," for more information).

Programs called *spambots* do nothing but scan Usenet message headers for email addresses. These addresses are compiled and sold to companies that send out unsolicited advertisements via email. If you post frequently to newsgroups, your email address could get "vacuumed" in this manner, resulting in a greater volume of spam in your Inbox.

Fortunately, spambots aren't intelligent, so defeating them is relatively simple. The most common tactic is to add a word to your email address that actual human beings will recognize as an anti-spam measure. It would look something like this:

```
bob@nospam_mcp.com
```

A person who wants to respond to you can easily remove the "nospam_" from your email address, but most spambots won't be able to recognize it, and the spam that was meant for you will end up bouncing back to the sender. There are rumors that some spambots may have become savvy to this technique, and can remove text such as "nospam" from an email address. You might want to try another approach, if you find that nospam isn't working. Use something odd such as

```
bob@myhatmcp.com
```

In your postings, you can say "to respond to me, just remove myhat and use the remaining address."

You can change your reply address by clicking Tools, Accounts to open the Internet Accounts dialog. Then click the News tab, select your news account, and click Properties. Type the modified email address in the Reply Address text box, as shown in Figure 11.11, and click OK to close the dialog.

Figure 11.11
You can type a modified identity and reply address in this dialog to avoid spam and protect your identity somewhat in Usenet.

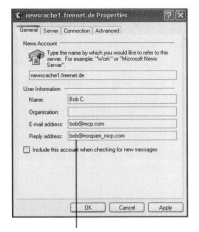

Modified e-mail address

NOTE

> Outlook Express will probably show you a warning that the Reply To address is not valid. Click Yes to use the modified address despite the apparent problem.

RESPONDING TO ANONYMOUS POSTERS

You're not the only person trying to remain anonymous in Usenet. Trying to respond to a message you read can cause you a few problems, especially if you are trying to respond directly to the poster.

Obviously, there are different levels of anonymity. If the person is simply using a nickname, you should be able to respond to him or her normally. But if that person is also trying to conceal his or her email address, responding can get trickier. If an error message is returned to you when you try to send someone email (often called a *bounce*), check that person's email address to see whether he or she is using an anti-spam scheme as shown here:

```
bob@nospam_mcp.com
```

People who use this naming scheme usually have something in their signature files that says "To reply, remove 'nospam_' from the domain" or something to that effect.

If the email address is obviously not valid, and no clues to the individual's real address exist, your last resort might be to post to the newsgroup. But don't use this situation as an excuse to share a private response in a public forum. A typical response would look something like this:

```
Attn: bob@nospam_mcp.com
I wish to send you a response. Please contact me directly at rick@mcp.com.
```

This message should get the individual's attention. If not, there's not much else you can do.

CUSTOMIZING OUTLOOK EXPRESS FOR NEWSGROUPS

Outlook Express 6 comes with a fairly good package of preset options for reading and participating in newsgroups. Still, what works for the "average" user might not suit you. You can customize virtually every aspect of news reading in this program by reviewing the various settings available to you. To do so, follow these steps:

1. In OE6, choose Tools, Options.

2. Click the General tab to bring it to the front, and then remove the check mark next to Notify Me If There Are Any New Newsgroups if you already plan to reset your group list periodically without input from OE6.

3. Click the Read tab, as shown in Figure 11.12. OE6 automatically downloads the first 300 headers at a time, but you can change that number here. You also might want to check the option Mark All Messages as Read When Exiting a Newsgroup. If you routinely ignore some posts in the group, selecting this option will help you determine which messages are actually new the next time you open the group.

4. Switch to the Send tab to make your default news-sending format HTML if you like, but doing so is not recommended because most news readers can't read HTML formatting.

5. Click the Signatures tab to bring it to the front, and create a new signature to be used exclusively with newsgroups. Your news signature could include instructions for removing anti-spam measures from your email address. After you have created the new signature, click the Advanced button to open the dialog shown in Figure 11.13. Here, you can select your news account to "assign" the signature to it. After you have assigned a signature, it will be used only with that account.

Adjust this number to
get more or fewer headers

Figure 11.12
You can set the num-
ber of message head-
ers that will be
downloaded when you
open a group here.

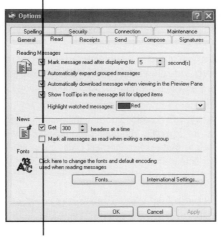

Click here to clarify which messages
are new when downloading headers

Figure 11.13
You can assign a spe-
cific signature to your
news account here.

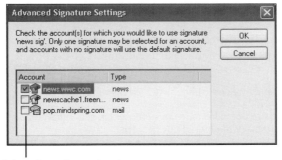

11

Place a check mark here to assign a signature

6. On the Maintenance tab, check the two news-related Delete options if you want to save disk space.

→ To learn more about setting the Delete options, **see** "Managing Messages," **p. 382**.

7. Click OK to close the dialog and save your settings changes.

LOCATING NEWS SERVERS

Many ISPs and companies provide news server accounts to their Internet users, but you still might find yourself looking for a server on your own. This may be the case even if you have a news account available to you; some service providers censor the news content that is available, and if you want uncensored news, you must rely on a different source.

Censorship, Big Brother, and NNTP Servers

News feeds are censored for a variety of reasons. For example, your company's server might restrict feeds from `alt.`, `rec.`, and `talk.` groups to reduce the number of work hours lost to employee abuse or simply to reduce bandwidth. Many other servers restrict feeds that contain pornographic content for both legal and moral reasons.

Even if your news server provides a relatively unrestricted news feed, you should exercise care when deciding which articles you download from the server. Virtually all servers maintain logs of the activities of each login account. This means that your service provider can track which articles you download, and in most cases these logs can be subpoenaed and used against you in court.

In other words, Big Brother might be watching you download porn, bomb making instructions, and bootleg copies of the latest Hollywood blockbuster. Be especially paranoid if you access a company news server; hours spent receiving otherwise legal content such as fruit cake recipes, Bill Gates jokes, and the like could still land you in hot water if the boss is logging your online activities.

Many news servers are available through virtually any Internet connection, but you'll pay for that connection. Typically, monthly charges for a personal news server account range from $10 to $20 per month and get higher for corporate or higher bandwidth accounts. If you plan to use newsgroups frequently, you might want to factor in this cost when you're shopping for an ISP. You can find a good list of commercial news servers at the following URL:

`http://freenews.maxbaud.net/forfee.html`

However, if you have an Internet connection and would simply like a different news server, you can find a list of free news servers available online. The list of free servers can change daily:

`http://freenews.maxbaud.net/newspage.html?date=today`

 If Outlook Express has trouble locating your news server, see "No News Server Connection" in the "Troubleshooting" section at the end of this chapter.

A free alternative to commercial news servers is a Web-based news service, such as the one created by deja.com. An advantage of using a Web-based news service is that a search brings back results from many newsgroups, not only one. It's a terrific way to find expert postings on just about anything from open-heart surgery, to child adoption, to what people think of the new car you're considering buying. However, messages are not brought into your news client program (such as OE) for reference offline. Deja was bought out and redesigned by Google awhile back, so until recently, you couldn't post new messages to Usenet, but now you can again. Just go to `http://www.google.com` and click the Groups link. Another Web-based news server is findable at `http://newsguy.com/news.asp`

 If you cannot locate a particular newsgroup on your news server, see "Newsgroup Isn't Available on News Server" in the following "Troubleshooting" section.

TROUBLESHOOTING

NEWSGROUP ISN'T AVAILABLE ON NEWS SERVER

A newsgroup I want to access isn't available on my server.

Click Reset List in the Newsgroup Subscriptions window. The newsgroup may be new and simply not shown in your current list. If the group still isn't there, try contacting the ISP or other service that hosts the list and ask that service to add it. Often new groups simply go unnoticed because so many of them are out there. Many news servers are willing to respond to such a request, unless they have a rule restricting or censoring the particular group.

Try paying for an alternative dedicated news server that does carry the newsgroup you're interested in.

SOME MESSAGES ARE UNAVAILABLE AFTER SYNCHRONIZING

I tried to synchronize the group, but some messages I click aren't available.

Obviously, you should first check that the settings for the group are correct. If the group isn't set to All Messages, and the Synchronize check box isn't checked, this could easily explain the missing message bodies. Another possibility is that the message was removed from the host server sometime after the header list was distributed. It can take up to 72 hours after a message is physically removed before it disappears from the header list.

News servers only have so much disk space. To allow them to continually add incoming files to their lists, they must continually discard old files. If your server is missing a few articles you may "ask" for a repost of the incomplete files, but while the poster is expected to service reasonable repost requests there is no requirement to do so. Sometimes a regular poster might not service repost requests at all, but will instead indicate an FTP, ICQ, or IRQ service where you can pick up missing files. And in many cases a repost request will be answered by a person who just happens to have downloaded the same file set and is willing to help support the group.

Finally, if you are doing everything right and your server is not gathering all the articles that were posted, consider informing your ISP's support desk of the problem. It does not do any good to complain to everyone else in the newsgroup if you are not telling the few people who are actually paid to help you. Servers and the connecting routers are sensitive electronic equipment and their only guarantee is that they will fail at some point. Help your ISP monitor the network.

If your server is very poorly connected and misses a lot of articles, as I stated above, you should consider hiring a dedicated news service as a secondary server.

MESSAGE NO LONGER AVAILABLE

A message I read earlier is no longer available.

The default settings in Outlook Express delete read messages five days after you have downloaded them. You can change this option on the Maintenance tab of the OE Options dialog.

WHICH ONES ARE NEW?

I can't tell which messages are new.

Open the Options dialog by choosing Tools, Options. On the Read tab, place a check mark next to Mark All Messages as Read When Exiting a Newsgroup.

NO NEWS SERVER CONNECTION

Outlook Express cannot locate my news server.

Do you need to use a separate Internet connection to access the news server? If so, choose Tools, Accounts, and then click the News tab in the Internet Accounts dialog. Look at what is listed under Connection next to your news account listing. If it says Any Available, click Properties and select the Connection tab. Place a check mark next to Always Connect to This Account Using, and select the appropriate connection from the drop-down list.

TIPS FROM THE WINDOWS PROS: NEWSGROUPS...FOR MORE THAN JUST NEWS

Newsgroups began innocently enough as forums for university, government, and science research folks to find and offer various kinds of support and share info over the precursor to the 'Net. However, it didn't take long for Usenet to explode as a means of online recreation. Today, no matter how obscure you think your hobby or personal interest may be, a newsgroup is probably already dedicated to it. And one of the great advantages of newsgroups is the fact that files can be easily attached to posts. Attachments can be in the form of pictures, sound files, movies, text documents, programs, or anything else imaginable. In this respect, newsgroups really shine when compared to mailing lists; most mailing lists strictly forbid attachments, but in Usenet they are welcome.

Newsgroups with the word *binaries* in their address are good places to find attachments. The word Binary refers to a non-text attachment, some kind of a data or program file. Naturally, you need to exercise some care before you download any messages with large attachments. First, ask yourself whether you have enough bandwidth to download the message. The OE6 message list doesn't show a paper clip icon until you've downloaded a message with an attachment, but it does tell you the size of each individual message, as shown in Figure 11.14. It is a fair assumption that a large file size would indicate the presence of an attachment.

After you have determined that you can handle the message download, you should also keep virus safety in mind. If the attachment is a standard multimedia format, such as JPEG, WAV, GIF, MP3, or AVI, it should be safe. But if the attachment is an unknown format or is an executable program (.EXE and .VBS are common extensions for these), you should follow your standard anti-virus procedures.

Large news attachments are posted as multi-part files, to get around the message-size limitations of news servers. These postings break up the large attachment over several consecutive posts. You can usually identify these types of posts by the Subject field, which identifies the message as part of a series. For example, you might see something like, "xfiles.avi (1/3), xfiles.avi (2/3)...", and so on.

Figure 11.14
This newsgroup contains a message with a large attachment.

Note the message size here

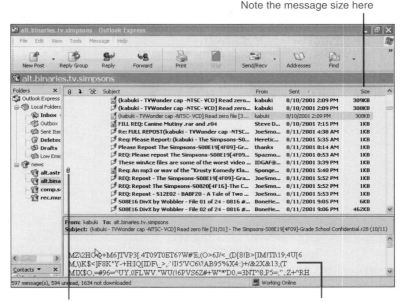

The paper clip icon appears here when a message with an attachment has been downloaded

Binary data

Multi-part attachments only open properly if downloaded and then combined together. Your first step is to identify each part of the series; if you miss even one portion of the series, it will not open properly. Use Ctrl+click and/or Shift+click to select each member of the series. After you've selected all of them, right-click the series, and choose Combine and Decode from the shortcut menu, as shown in Figure 11.15.

You are next presented with a dialog asking you to put the series members in order. They should be in numeric order, starting with part one at the top of the list. Use the Move Up and Move Down buttons to place them in the correct order. Depending on the size of the multipart attachment, the download may take some time. When it is complete, a message window opens with a single attachment listed. This doesn't make much sense, since it looks as though you're going to send the file to someone. But typically you want to save it to your hard disk. So just right-click on that file icon in the attachment line, and choose Save As. Then save the file with the name and location you wish.

Multimedia attachments in Usenet can be a lot of fun. For example, the group alt. binaries.tv.simpsons usually contains WAV and AVI files of popular sound bites and catchphrases—or even an entire episode—from the television series *The Simpsons*. If you save downloaded WAV files in the \WINNT\Media folder of your hard drive, you can later assign those sounds to various Windows events. Wouldn't Windows be more enjoyable if each critical stop were accompanied by Bart Simpson's "Aye Carumba" rather than the monotonous Chord.wav?

Figure 11.15
You must be sure you select every member of a multi-part attachment series before attempting the download.

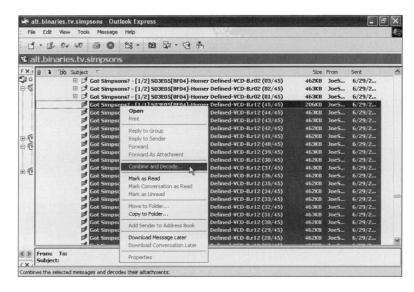

Another gem to be on the lookout for in Usenet is MP3 music. MP3 files offer CD-quality music, but because they use about one-twelfth the storage space, they can be transported efficiently over the Internet. You probably know about MP3s from all the hoopla about MP3 players such as the iPod and the old Napster court case, but you may not have known that MP3s were also available over newsgroups. Look for any newsgroup with *mp3* in the address, but watch out for those bootlegs!

If you become a serious newsgroup junkie, especially if you're into downloading (or uploading) large files, you'll have some boning up to do:

■ Check out the news stuff at `groups.google`, or go to Google and click the Groups tab. Start by corresponding with heavy news posters on your group of choice. When you post large files, split them up into smaller chunks. In OE, choose Tools, Accounts. Click the News tab and Choose the news server you use. Click Properties, and the Advanced tab. Notice the setting there for Posting: Break Apart Messages Larger Than ____KB. This specifies to break up large messages, so that each part is smaller than the file size indicated. Some older servers cannot handle messages larger than 64KB. By breaking large messages into smaller messages, you ensure that the messages are transmitted and received correctly. Make sure this option is selected.

■ Secondly, if you are seriously into newsgroups, you'll want to bag OE and use it only for your email. Download and get familiar with one of the serious programs designed for news, such as Xnews (download.com), News Rover (download.com), or Agent (forteinc.com/agent/index.php). Among other benefits, these specialized products automate the process of finding, grouping, downloading, and decoding file attachments split across multiple messages. They are serious time savers. Here's a list of URLs for a couple other alternative newsreaders:

- NewsRover ($)

  http://www.newsrover.com/

- Newsbin Pro ($) and "classic" Newsbin (free)

  http://www.newsbin.com/

Figure 11.16 shows an example of Xnews.

TIP

> Some news readers, such as Agent-MP3, are specifically made to search Usenet and quickly find all the MP3 files.

Notice how the icons on the left indicate whether all the portions of a message are on the server. If the block icon is full, all the pieces of an attachment are present, and you can begin downloading. If not, skip it, and try to find it on another news server, or ask the poster to re-post that portion. This saves you from having to visually examine and count to be sure all the attachments are there. Also, assuming the postings are named correctly, Xnews doesn't require you to rearrange them before downloading and decoding. It does so automagically.

Indicates missing attachments

Figure 11.16
Xnews makes downloading, combining, and decoding multi-part news messages far less laborious than OE does.

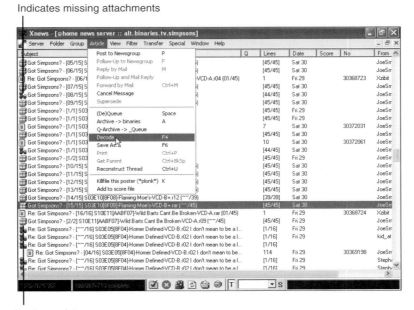

Attachment set complete

CHAPTER **12**

CHATTING AND CONFERENCING WITH WINDOWS MESSENGER

In this chapter

An Overview of Windows Messenger

Windows Messenger is an online, real-time communication program that lets you talk with friends and coworkers across the house or across the world, over the Internet. For starters, Windows Messenger lets you keep track of which of your friends are online at any given time. When they're online, you can type messages which appear instantly on your friends' screens.

Depending on your interest and the speed of your Internet connection, you and a friend can also communicate by voice, and even use two-way video so you can see as well as talk to each other. You can share a virtual electronic "whiteboard" or chalkboard to make collaborative drawings, or work interactively with a program, using a feature called Application Sharing. All of these capabilities are part of Windows Messenger.

Messaging is a great way to stay in touch with friends and family. It's a way to make new friends and pen-pals. Messaging has also become very popular in the business world as a way of communicating with coworkers, for reducing travel costs through videoconferencing, and for demonstrations and customer support.

Before we get into these details, though, we should talk a bit about the whole phenomenon of messaging itself.

What Is Messaging, Anyway?

Messaging fills a niche somewhere between email and the telephone. Like email, it can travel anywhere around the globe, essentially for free. Unlike email, though, it requires you and the person you're communicating with to be online at the same time. Like the telephone, it's immediate, interactive, and conversational. But unlike the telephone, it doesn't have to occupy your full attention—with it, you can carry on several conversations at once, or you can divide your attention between a conversation and other work.

Messaging has been around since the early 1980s when the first computer networks and "bulletin board" computer systems appeared. When the Internet became a public phenomenon, programs like IRC (Internet Relay Chat) and ICQ ("I seek you") became popular. But messaging really took off as America Online soared in popularity, and today millions of people, both AOL subscribers and non-subscribers alike use AOL's "Instant Messenger" service. Microsoft, which may join revolutions late but always brings bigger guns, came up with several attempts to move into the field: Microsoft Chat, then NetMeeting, and now Windows Messenger.

NOTE

Windows Messenger is one of the programs that got Microsoft in some anticompetitive hot water a few years ago, so it's now one of the programs that can be enabled, disabled, or hidden by vendors and by you. If you've just purchased a new computer, you might find that the manufacturer hid Windows Messenger and replaced it with another product. If you want to use Windows Messenger and find that it's not on your Start menu, just click Start, All Programs, Set Program Access and Defaults. Click Custom, and enable access to Windows Messenger.

You can, and should, try different chat programs; do a survey of your friends, coworkers, or family and select the one or two that most of them are using. If you find the need to communicate with people on different systems, be sure to read the last section in this chapter.

Also, you'll see references to the .NET Messenger Service. That's the technology and user directory behind both Windows Messenger and MSN Messenger.

WHAT WINDOWS MESSENGER CAN AND CAN'T DO

Messenger has several options for communicating. You can choose any or all of them, so you can start out with the simple stuff and work your way up, if you want. With Messenger and an Internet connection, you can

- Type text messages.
- Communicate with voice and video even over a dial-up Internet connection. (It's not quite TV quality but you can, say, stick your tongue out at someone, and within a few seconds, they'll more likely than not be able to tell.) Over a cable or DSL connection or a corporate LAN, you can get up to 15 video frames per second, which is nearly TV quality, with excellent voice quality.
- Receive video and sound even if you don't have a camera or microphone of your own.
- Transfer pictures and files of any type.
- Collaboratively draw on a shared "whiteboard," which can be saved or printed out for permanent storage.
- Collaborate on a single application, or even share your entire screen with another. The desktop-sharing feature lets multiple people collaborate on, say, a word processing document, each being able to see the contents of a shared window, grab the cursor, and make edits. It's great for training and demonstrations too.

TIP

A free download is available that adds some additional features to Windows Messenger, such as the automatic notification of new mail arrivals on Hotmail, public chat profiles, and text messaging with pagers and cell phones. You can add those features to Windows Messenger by visiting www.microsoft.com/windows/messenger/addin.asp.

NOTE

Microsoft has another free chat program called MSN Messenger, which has an additional feature: the capability to place telephone calls through the service. The programs share a common pool of chat users. You can download and install MSN Messenger if you want.

Just to be clear, though, this chapter is exclusively about Windows Messenger, and from this point forward, when I say "Messenger," I mean Windows Messenger.

12

Although Messenger lets you communicate with several people at a time with text chat (as many as you want, actually), it does *not* have a group videoconference conference feature that lets several people participate in one collective voice or video conversation. For that, you'll need to turn to third-party software like CU-See-Me.

Also, in my experience, audio and video communication with Messenger isn't perfect. I've found it to be picky and unpredictable: Sometimes the audio comes through, and sometimes it doesn't. Connections can drop out at random intervals. Audio "echoing" occurs sometimes, as well as other irritating sound glitches. But when it works, it works very well, and after all, it's free. If you look at it as a super CB radio rather than as a telephone, you should have a great time with it.

NOTE

> Messenger uses the newly developed SIP Protocol (Session Initiation Protocol) for voice and video. SIP provides a standard way for messaging, telephony (voice), and video programs to communicate. Check your router's manual to see whether it supports Universal Plug-and-Play (UPnP). You might have to upgrade its internal software (firmware) to get this support. Windows Internet Connection Sharing software doesn't have this limitation: It's already SIP aware. For more information about this topic, see "Windows Messenger, Shared Connections, and Firewalls," later in this chapter.

SYSTEMS REQUIREMENTS AND PLATFORM COMPATIBILITY

To use the audio and video features of Messenger, your computer must meet the following minimum hardware requirements:

- The most current Windows Messenger version runs only on Windows XP Home Edition or Professional. It's not available on the 64-bit (Itanium and AMD) versions of Windows XP. Older Messenger versions are available for other Windows operating systems, as is a Macintosh version of MSN messenger, so you can communicate with people who use those programs. (At least, you can communicate via text messages—video and audio chat might not work with earlier versions.)

- Any computer capable of running Windows XP has enough memory and processing power for Messenger.

- For text communication only, any connection speed is fine. If you want to use voice or video, you'll need a 33,600bps or faster modem, ISDN, DSL, cable, or LAN Internet connection—the faster the better.

- To establish voice or video connections, you need a sound card, a microphone, and speakers. A sound card is required for both audio and video support. Without a sound card, you can only use text chat and desktop sharing.

- To transmit video with your calls, you need a video capture card or camera that provides a Video for Windows capture driver. Any recent USB- or FireWire-connected camera should meet this requirement. Older parallel-port cameras are very unlikely to have compatible drivers (see the manufacturer's Web site).

12

TIP

> Owing to the growing use of Messenger, NetMeeting, and other videoconferencing software, numerous companies now sell inexpensive add-on products such as cameras, microphones, headsets, video cards, and software additions. For example, I got a free color video camera as a bonus for buying a $99 hard drive!

TIP

> You should install any new audio or video hardware, and, if necessary, update your audio and video device drivers, *before* you run Messenger for the first time, if possible. Getting it to recognize newly installed hardware isn't always effortless.

Before we go any further, I should warn you that Messenger's voice and video communication might not work properly if you use a shared Internet connection made through a cable/DSL Sharing Router device. Voice and video should work with the Internet Connection Sharing and Windows Firewall systems built in to Windows XP—or, as mentioned previously, if your Internet connection router is SIP aware, supports UPnP, and UPnP is enabled on the device. For more information, see "Windows Messenger, Shared Connections, and Firewalls," later in this chapter.

If your hardware router doesn't support UPnP, you will be able to communicate with text chat, but you will not be able to use voice, video, or desktop sharing.

With Whom Can I Communicate?

Messenger works with the .NET Passport system which was described in Chapter 9, "Browsing the World Wide Web with Internet Explorer." You can only chat or voice/videoconference with people who have registered for a Passport. As mentioned in Chapter 9, you don't need to use Microsoft's Hotmail or MSN service, but you both need to register with Microsoft. Remember, if you're concerned about privacy, you can submit an absolute minimum of information when you register—only your email address is really required. (Of course, without your name on file, your friends can't search for you by name if they want to chat you up. They'll need to know your email address.)

The type of messaging you can use is limited by what equipment you and your friend(s) have in common. At the very least, you can always type text messages back and forth. Obviously, if you don't have a camera attached to your computer you can't send video, but if your friends do, you can still receive video when you chat with them, and vice versa. You'll need a microphone and speakers or a headset if you want to communicate by voice.

Text messaging may be the slowest way to communicate but at least it's a guaranteed thing. Personally, I find that I use it more than voice or video, by far. It's the least obtrusive form of Messenger communication—I can have a chat window or two open and pop off questions and answers while I continue to work on my projects.

12

Getting Started with Windows Messenger

To fire up Messenger, look at the bottom-right corner of your screen for the tiny Messenger icon—it looks like two tiny people—in the Notification area, as shown in Figure 12.1.

Figure 12.1
Double-click the tiny people to start Messenger.

If this icon doesn't appear in your Notification area, click Start, All Programs, and see if Windows Messenger appears in the menu. If it does, click it. (If it isn't listed, it might have been hidden using the Set Program Access and Defaults tool. See the note at the beginning of this chapter to see how to fix this.)

The first time you start Messenger, you'll see a blank window that says "Click Here to Sign In." Click there, and Messenger will walk you through a setup wizard to gather your personal information. You'll want to be sure you're connected to the Internet before proceeding.

Signing In with Your .NET Passport

If you haven't already signed up for a Passport, you'll have to do that now. Messenger will walk you through the .NET Passport Wizard to get this set up.

→ To learn about Passport and the .NET Passport Wizard, **see** "Getting a Passport to Microsoft Country," **p. 328**.

To link up with Passport, you'll have to provide an email address. You can use your current email address, or you can set up a Microsoft Hotmail or MSN email address. If you have already set up a Passport, you'll only need to enter your email address and password, following the .NET Passport Wizard's instructions. Then whenever you log on, Windows will use this Passport automatically.

N O T E

You can change the Passport associated with your Windows user account (and the email address it's linked to) from the User Accounts control panel. To do this, click Start, Control Panel, User Accounts. Click on your account's icon, and then click Change My .NET Passport.

If you're concerned about privacy, you can always create a Hotmail or other free email account just to use for your .NET Passport and Messenger.

SIGNING IN TO MESSENGER

When the Passport setup process is finished, or if you had already set up your Passport earlier, Messenger will ask you to sign in, as shown in Figure 12.2. It may seem odd that you have to sign in to Windows, and then sign in to Messenger separately. The reasons the process is separate are (a) so you can choose whether or not you want to be available to others who might want to use Messenger to contact you, and (b) you might have several Passport accounts that you want to use at various times.

Figure 12.2
The Messenger Sign In screen asks for your Passport password. You can also choose to have Messenger sign in automatically when you log on to Windows XP.

By default, Windows will display your Passport email address. If you happen to have multiple passports, you can select an alternate one from the drop-down list, or you can just type in a different email address.

You can also choose to have Messenger sign on automatically when you log on to Windows. If you always want Messenger active and available when you're using your computer, check Sign Me In Automatically. You can always change this selection later on.

Finally, enter your Passport password and click OK.

 If Messenger can't sign in, see "Messenger Gives Connection Error When I Sign In" in the "Troubleshooting" section at the end of this chapter.

When you've signed on to Windows Messenger, you'll see a screen similar to the one shown in Figure 12.3. The Messenger screen shows you your current passport account or the name you want to display to others (I'll show you how to change this later in the chapter).

Finally, the window shows you which of your contacts are presently online and which are not. What are contacts? Read on.

ADDING CONTACTS

A *contact* is a person whom you've identified as someone you want to be able to chat with. Before you can communicate with Messenger, you'll need to add your friends, family, or coworkers to your Messenger contact list.

Figure 12.3
The Messenger screen shows you who's online and who's not.

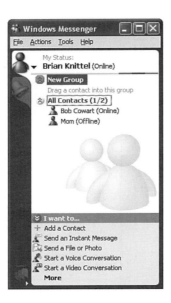

To add a contact, click the Add a Contact button at the bottom of the Messenger window or click Tools, Add a Contact. Windows will ask you whether you want to select a contact by their email address (if you know their Passport sign-in name), or whether you want to search for them by name. Right now you can only search through the .NET Messenger (Passport user) directory or your own personal Address Book, but Microsoft may add other search directories later on. Select a method, and click Next.

In the next step, enter the person's email address or Passport sign in name and click Next, or fill out the search form, which is shown in Figure 12.4. Fill in as much information as you can to help narrow things down, select the desired directory under Search For This Person At, and then click Next.

After a moment, Windows will show you a list of matching names and locations. If you don't see your friend listed, select Back and change some of your selection criteria. If you do see the entry for your friend, select it and click Next.

As a matter of privacy, your new contact will be notified that you have added them to your contact list. Likewise, you'll be notified if others add you to their contact list. (For your own privacy, if you want to you can block them from knowing if you're online and from sending you messages. I'll show you how in the next section.)

Of course, to add them to your list, your contacts must already have signed up for a Passport account. (This, I'm sure, is part of Microsoft's Grand Plan.) In fact, if you select a contact by searching your own Windows Address Book and the associated email account isn't registered with Microsoft Passport, Messenger asks whether you want it to send the contact an email asking him to sign up. (Don't worry—you'll be able to cancel this if you don't want it to happen.)

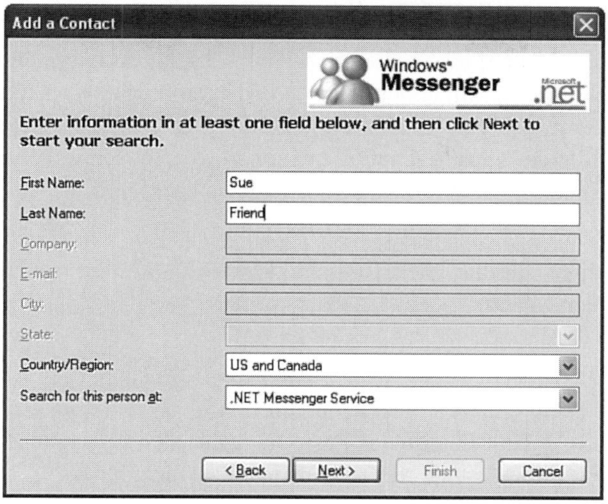

Figure 12.4
To search for a contact in the .NET Messenger directory or your Address book, fill in as much information as you can.

Add a Contact

Windows®
Messenger .net

Enter information in at least one field below, and then click Next to start your search.

First Name: Sue

Last Name: Friend

Company:

E-mail:

City:

State:

Country/Region: US and Canada

Search for this person at: .NET Messenger Service

< Back | Next > | Finish | Cancel

Add as many contacts as you wish. Once contacts are added to your list, when any of them sign in, you'll receive notification, as shown in Figure 12.5. If you find this annoying, you can disable notifications using the Preferences settings, which I'll discuss in the next section.

Figure 12.5
When your contacts sign in, you'll receive notification.

change

Bob Cowart
has just signed in.

NOTE

Throughout this chapter, I'll usually refer to your contacts as "friends." Of course, you can use Messenger to contact acquaintances, pen-pals, relatives, coworkers, or enemies too, for that matter.

12

SETTING MESSENGER OPTIONS AND PREFERENCES

Messenger has the potential to intrude upon your workday and upon your privacy. You can control how much information about you is revealed, and what ways Messenger is allowed to notify and interact with you. In this section, I'll cover the Messenger options including its privacy settings. Remember that if you use Hotmail, you'll need to configure your Hotmail privacy settings (such as whether or not your name is listed in the Member directory) on the Hotmail site.

To change Messenger options, click Tools and Options, and then view the six options tabs. I'll go through them in turn.

PERSONAL INFORMATION

The Personal tab (see Figure 12.6) lets you choose the name others see when you're signed in to Messenger. By default this is your Passport name; that is, your email address. For privacy reasons, you want to change this to your name or nickname.

Figure 12.6
The Personal tab lets you change your displayed name and some other preferences.

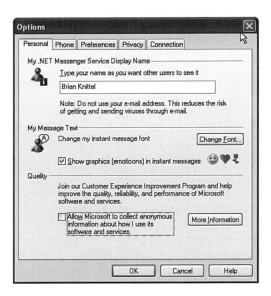

You can also select the font used to display chat messages, can enable or disable the automatic display of "smilies" or emoticons (with graphics enabled, if your friend types :) you'll see), and optionally, let Messenger send (anonymously) information to Microsoft about how well it's working, information that presumably will be used to improve the software.

PHONE CONTACT INFORMATION

The Phone tab lets you enter home and work telephone numbers that your contacts will be able to view. If you're using Messenger for business purposes, you'll probably want to enter your work telephone number here. Otherwise, I suggest leaving this page blank. You can always give out your phone number later on if you think it's appropriate.

MESSENGER PREFERENCES

The Preferences tab, shown in Figure 12.7, lets you control how Messenger starts, and how and when it's allowed to alert (or you might say "annoy") you as contacts and messages come and go. The options you are most likely to want to think about changing are

- **Run Windows Messenger When Windows Starts**—This is enabled by default. Uncheck to prevent Messenger from starting up automatically. (Automatic sign-in must be changed separately, from the Sign In window. To change that setting, click File, Sign Out, and then File, Sign In.)

- **Show Me As Away**—If your computer sits idle for 5 minutes, by default your contacts will see a notification that you're "away." This is another privacy issue. You can change the time, or block the message entirely by unchecking this option.

- **Alerts**—You can enable or disable pop-up messages and sounds for when contacts sign on and off or send messages with the options in the Alerts section. If you have installed the Messenger add-in pack, you can also control the alerts for new mail.

- **File Transfer**—This lets you change the folder where any files your contacts send you land. The default folder is My Received Files inside My Documents.

Figure 12.7
The Preferences tab lets you change Messenger startup, alert, and file transfer options.

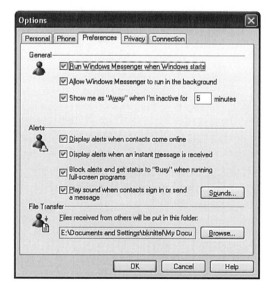

PRIVACY OPTIONS

The Privacy tab lets you choose to prevent specific contacts, or all unknown contacts, from seeing your status and from sending you messages. Additionally, you can also see who has added you to their contact list, configure an alert to occur when someone adds you to her contact list, configure security for your passport by instructing Messenger to always prompt you for your password, and prevent Messenger from downloading *tabs* (announcement areas that display information such as new email announcements) if you are using a public computer. All these options have been provided to allow you to control the amount of security you feel you need.

Figure 12.8 shows the Privacy tab's Allow and Block lists. By default all of your contacts and "All Other Users" are in the Allow List, which lets them see when you sign in and out, and lets them send you messages. You can move individual contacts over to the Block List to shut them out. Move an entry by selecting it in one list or the other, and clicking Allow or Block.

Figure 12.8
The Privacy tab lets you control who knows you're online.

You also can move the Other .NET Messenger Users entry. Other .NET Messenger Users applies to people who have added you to their contact lists but whom you haven't yet added to yours. In other words, these are unverified strangers. By default, Other .NET Messenger Users is put on the Block side. Unless you're concerned that other people will look you up by name and contact you, you can probably move this entry to the Allow side.

CONNECTION OPTIONS

The Connection tab can normally be ignored. If, however, your computer is on a network that uses a SOCKS or Web proxy server, you might need to make entries here in order to use Messenger. Your ISP or network administrator will tell you if you need to do this.

Finally, when you've enlisted your friends, signed in to Messenger, and gone over your privacy options, you're ready to chat.

ORGANIZING YOUR CONTACTS

By default, Messenger displays all the contacts you enter under the title All Contacts. If you have many contacts, you might want to separate them into categories such as Business, Family, Friends, Political Commentators, or whatever. It's pretty easy to do:

1. Right-click a group name, such as All Contacts, and select Create a New Group.
2. Enter a name for the group.
3. Drag contacts from All Contacts to the new group. Contacts can be entered in more than one group.

It's easier to view and manage large contact lists when they're organized this way. To remove a contact from a group, right-click the name and select Remove Contact from Group. This doesn't delete the contact; it remains in All Contacts. To completely delete a contact, right-click and select Delete Contact.

CHATTING WITH TEXT

To chat with one of your contacts, she has to be signed on. That is, she has to appear in your contact list with (online) next to her name. To start up a conversation with one of your contacts, double-click her name in the Online list, or click Actions, Send an Instant Message and select her name from the drop-down list.

When you do this, a text chat conversation window appears, as shown in Figure 12.9. Enter your message in the bottom part of the window, and press Enter, or click Send to send the message to your friend. The first message you send will start the conversation.

Figure 12.9
The Conversation window lets you carry on a text conversation.

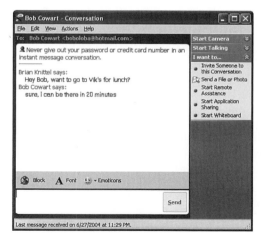

12

If someone starts a conversation with you, a notification will appear as shown in Figure 12.10. Click it open the Conversation window and begin chatting. You can also open the window by clicking on the new button that appears in your taskbar.

Figure 12.10
When someone starts up a conversation with you, a notification will appear. Click it to open up the Conversation window.

The messages you type to each other will appear in the upper part of the window, as shown in Figure 12.9. This is pretty much all there is to know about text chat. Before we move on to other topics, though, there are a few tips:

- Unless you're certain of the identity of the person you're chatting with, don't give out any personal information, especially your telephone number, Social Security number, credit card info, and so on.
- You can save the text of your conversation by clicking File, Save As.
- You can change the size of the displayed text with View, Text Size.
- You can instantly add the person you're talking with to your Block list by clicking the Block icon or selecting File, Block. This is handy if someone contacts you out of the blue and you don't care to hear from them again.

CHAT ETIQUETTE

Online chatting has an etiquette all its own. In face to face conversations, whether we realize it or not, facial expressions and body language communicate almost as much as the words we use. When we're using text chat, many of those emotional cues are missing. Sometimes it's hard to tell from a written message whether a person is joking, angry, sad, or sarcastic, and misunderstandings can follow.

One way to help with this is to spice up your text chat with the popular little punctuation-mark faces called emoticons or smilies. A wry comment might sound too sharp in plain written form, but if it's followed by a winking smiley face signified by ;-), the reader knows the remark was made in jest. Some of the most popular emoticons are listed in Table 12.1. (If they don't make sense, try rotating the page 90° to the right.)

TABLE 12.1	BASIC EMOTICONS
:-)	I meant that in the nicest possible way
;-)	Wink! Wink!
:-O	Horrors!

Click the Emoticons button on the conversation window to select from the most commonly used possibilities. There are actually many more that can be sent only by entering a text shortcut, such as (y) for a thumbs-up icon or my current favorite (D), which sends a little martini glass picture. To view the full list of emoticons, click Help, Help Topics; then search for the word "emoticons," and select Use Emoticons in Messages to Show Feelings from the resulting list.

Because we tend to type these messages off the top of our head and fire them off instantly, rather than considering them the way we do when writing a letter, it's especially important to think about how your remarks will be perceived. And before you write anything that could come back to haunt you, remember that these chat messages can be saved as files, and they could conceivably reappear as Exhibit A in court someday.

MY STATUS, OR OUT TO LUNCH AND BACK AGAIN

If you're signed in to Messenger but are planning on stepping away from your computer for a while, you can tell Messenger so that it can tell your friends. This is the polite thing to do—otherwise, if someone tries to contact you while you're away, they'll think you're ignoring them when you don't respond.

To change your status, click File, My Status in the Messenger window, or click the Messenger icon in the Notification area and select My Status. Choose one of the messages, as shown in Figure 12.11. When you select one of the away messages, it will appear in your friends' contacts lists, as shown in Figure 12.11. This lets them know not to expect an immediate reply from you.

Figure 12.11
When you select a status message (left), it appears on your friends' contact lists (right).

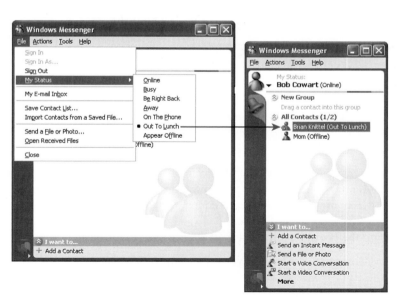

Change your status back to Online when you're ready to be contacted again.

SIGNING OUT

If you're finished with Messenger, if you don't want to be disturbed at all, or if you don't want anyone to know you're at your computer, you can sign off from Messenger completely. However, just closing the Messenger window *does not sign you out.* Messenger will stay active—you can still see the little person icon in the Notification area.

To sign out completely, choose File, Sign out in the Messenger window, or right-click the Messenger icon in the Notification area and select Sign Out. Now, you're signed out and no one can contact you. You can sign on again by double-clicking the Messenger notification icon again.

You can also completely close Messenger by right-clicking the Messenger notification icon and selecting Exit.

GROUP CHAT

Messenger will let you open several Conversation windows at once and carry on several separate conversations. Sometimes, though, you'll want to have a conversation with several people together. Messenger lets you do this. Like conference-calling on the telephone, group chat lets everyone in the conversation see what anyone types. It's great for discussing anything from dinner plans to business proposals.

To set up a group conversation, set up a chat connection to one person. Then, click Invite Someone to This Conversation in the right part of the Conversation window or in the Action menu. You can select another name from your contact list or select the Other tab and enter an email address as you would in the Add New Contact procedure. You can add as many people as you want by extending additional invitations.

You can't remove someone from the group, but individuals can leave the group at any time by closing their Conversation window.

SENDING AND RECEIVING FILES

While you're chatting with someone, you can easily transfer files back and forth using Messenger. You can use this exchange documents, pictures, movie files, or anything else you please.

To send a file to a person you're chatting with, you can drag the file from the desktop or Explorer to the Conversation window. Or, you can click Send A File on the right side of the Conversation window, or select Actions, Send a File or Photo. In this case, a file selection dialog box will appear. Locate the file and click Open to send it. Your friend will have to permit the file to be sent, and then the file will be transferred.

If someone attempts to send you a file, a message will appear in your Conversation window as shown in Figure 12.12. You can click on Accept or Decline. A pop-up message will warn you that you should check files from unknown sources with a virus scanner. I'll emphasize that warning here:

12

Don't accept files from people you don't know! Don't accept executable program files with extensions ending in .exe, .wsh, .com, .vbs, or .bat unless you are *certain* that they're safe. You should scan any files you receive with a virus checker before opening them, in any case.

Figure 12.12
If someone attempts to send you a file, you can accept or decline the transfer.

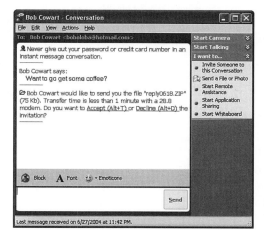

NOTE

If you're using a shared Internet connection, you can't receive files unless your connection sharing system supports UPnP. See "Windows Messenger, Shared Connections, and Firewalls," later in this chapter, for more information.

You can explore the folder into which received files arrive by clicking File, Open Received Files. By default, files received by Messenger are placed in My Received Files inside My Documents, but you can change this location using Tools, Options, Preferences.

 If file transfer fails, see "File Transfer Doesn't Work" in the "Troubleshooting" section at the end of this chapter.

COMMUNICATING WITH VOICE

Although text chat is fun and useful all by itself, you can have even more fun using voice chat. If you and one of your friends have computers outfitted with a sound card, speakers, and a microphone, you can converse over your Internet connection.

Now, before you get too excited about this, take note that AT&T and the other telephone carriers haven't sued Microsoft over this intrusion into their territory. Why? Internet voice chat isn't quite up to telephone quality standards. Over a dial-up Internet connection, you may find that the sound is choppy, that you miss phrases, or that the sound connection doesn't work at all. Over a high-speed Internet connection or a local area network, it's better, but still far from perfect. Still, it's free (well, you're paying for you Internet connection, but using Messenger doesn't cost any more), and when it works, it's fun.

To use voice chat, as I mentioned, your computer will have to be outfitted with sound hardware (most are, these days), and you'll need speakers and a microphone that's compatible with your sound card. Your local computer store can show you what you need. You'll have even better luck if you use a headset designed for computer use, with an earphone and microphone that hangs in front of your mouth.

NOTE

> The voice transmission system used by the version of Messenger in Windows XP is not compatible with older versions of Messenger. Your friends may have to upgrade their copy of Messenger if they're not using Windows XP. They should check for updates at www.windowsupdate.com or www.microsoft.com.

Before you try to use Messenger to talk to a friend for the first time, you should check out your sound equipment using the Audio and Video Tuning Wizard.

TUNING UP AUDIO HARDWARE

Getting your microphone and speaker volume controls set up correctly is an important factor in being able to use Messenger for voice communication. If your microphone isn't set up correctly or its volume control is incorrect, your friends may near horrendous noise or nothing at all. If your speakers are set too high, they may feed back into the microphone causing weird echoes. Messenger can help you check this out before you try to make your first call.

Click Tools, Audio and Video Tuning Wizard in the Messenger menu, then follow these steps:

1. Be sure to close any programs that use sound or video, such as Windows Media Player. Be sure your speakers and microphone (and camera, if you have one) are plugged in. Then click Next.

2. If you have a video camera or video capture hardware installed, the wizard will ask you to adjust your picture. I'll talk about this later in the chapter. You can skip this part now by clicking Next until you get to the screen that discusses speaker placement.

3. Read the instructions about proper speaker and microphone placement and click Next.

4. Select the microphone and speakers you're currently using, if you have multiple sets. If you are *not* using headphones, uncheck I Am Using Headphones. Then click Next.

5. Click the button marked Click to Test Speakers and adjust the volume slider (indicated in Figure 12.13) until you can head the sound clearly. Then click Stop, and Next.

6. Read into the microphone in a normal speaking voice, and move the microphone until the indicator touches the yellow region at times while you're talking (see Figure 12.14). Windows will adjust the volume control automatically. When the level is correct, click Next, and then Finish to end the wizard.

Figure 12.13
Test and adjust your
speaker volume here.

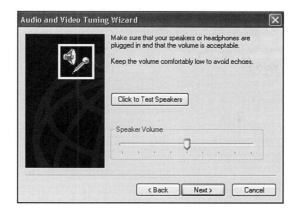

Figure 12.14
Adjust the micro-
phone until the indi-
cator bar touches the
yellow region while
you're speaking.

 If the green, yellow, and red microphone indicator bar doesn't appear, see "No Sound Picked Up from Microphone" in the "Troubleshooting" section at the end of this chapter.

When your speaker and microphone volume have been adjusted, you're ready to call someone.

CHATTING BY VOICE

If your and a friend's computers are both equipped with a microphone and speakers, or preferably combination headsets that contain a built-in microphone, you can use Messenger to converse for free. The quality of this type of voice connection can vary, and never equals real telephone quality, but it usually works. It's a great low-budget way to talk to friends or family.

TIP

Be sure you use the Audio/Video Tuning Wizard to get your speaker and microphone volume set correctly *before* you make a call, as I discussed in the previous section. This step may save you some frustration later on. If the sound doesn't work at least you'll know it's Messenger and not your hardware.

To use voice chat, you'll need to have your friend, relative, or coworker already listed as a contact in Messenger. Use the instructions I gave earlier in the chapter to add contacts. And, your contact has to be online.

There are two ways you can initiate a voice call:

- You can click Actions, Start a Voice Conversation. All of your online contacts are listed there. Select your friend's name and choose Computer. This opens up a Conversation window and starts up a voice chat connection.

- If you already have a Conversation (text chat) window open, you can select Start Talking on the right side of the window.

This sends an "invitation" to your contact to start voice chat. They'll need to accept the invitation by clicking on the word Accept in their chat window, as shown in Figure 12.15. Likewise, if one of your friends invites you to start voice chat, you'll see the same message.

When the invitee clicks Accept, the voice conversation is started. The screen changes to show a speaker volume control, and a microphone mute button, as shown in Figure 12.16. You can use these to adjust the incoming sound, and to temporarily mute your microphone as you see fit.

Figure 12.15
An invitation to start voice chat requires you to click Accept or Decline.

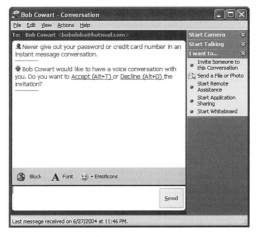

12

Figure 12.16
When you have begun voice chat, sound controls appear in the Conversation window.

You can continue to use text chat in the Conversation window, if you wish. In fact, you may need to as sometimes the voice connection just doesn't work correctly.

If the voice connection doesn't work for you, see "Voice Chat Doesn't Work" in the "Troubleshooting" section at the end of this chapter.

When you're finished chatting (or give up trying), you can click Stop Talking on the right side of the Conversation window, or you can just close the window entirely.

COMMUNICATING WITH VIDEO

If your computer has a "Web" camera installed, or if you have video capture hardware connected to a video camera, you can send pictures of your smiling self while you chat with a friend. Likewise, if your friend has a camera, you'll be able to see them while you chat. It's pretty nifty. It's just like the futuristic Videophone service that the telephone company promised (but never delivered) way back in the 1960s!

NOTE

> The video and voice transmission system used by the version of Messenger in Windows XP is not compatible with older versions of Messenger. Your friends may have to upgrade their copy of Messenger if they're not using Windows XP. They should check for updates at www.windowsupdate.microsoft.com or www.microsoft.com.

Video chat is an extension of voice chat, so all of the caveats and setup instructions I gave in the previous section apply to video chat. Remember, you don't need a camera yourself to accept video chat calls from friends. You only need to worry about this section if you want to send video to your friends.

12

TIP

> I suggest that you use voice chat by itself a few times to get the hang of it before trying video. Video is slower and more troublesome, so you'll have better luck with audio the first time around.

TUNING VIDEO HARDWARE

Before you try to use video chat to connect to a friend, you'll need to set up your Web camera or video camera according to the manufacturer's instructions. I prefer the little eyeball-sized cameras that connect through your computer's USB port. You can pick these up for $25–$40 at office supply stores; sometimes they're even free-after-rebate. Chapter 27, "Installing and Replacing Hardware," has some tips on adding and replacing hardware, if you haven't already installed the camera.

When the camera's installed, follow these steps:

1. Open Messenger and click Tools, Audio and Video Tuning Wizard. Click Next.
2. If you have more than one video input device installed, select the one you'd like to use. Click Next.
3. The Wizard will activate your camera and display your picture. Adjust the picture as needed. Center your face in the image, adjust the lighting, focus, brightness or anything else needed to get a good picture.
4. Click Next to proceed through the Audio tune-up portion of the Wizard, as I discussed earlier in the chapter.

When you know your picture and audio equipment are adjusted correctly, you can try to contact a friend.

CHATTING WITH PICTURES AND VOICE

Chatting with friends using video uses a procedure just like the one to use voice chat. Your friend will have to be online first, of course. Click Actions, Start a Video Conversation to initiate a video conversation with your friend. Alternatively, you can click the Start Camera button if you already have an open Conversation window.

Windows will inform your friend that you wish to begin a video and voice conversation. They'll have to click Accept or Decline, just as with a voice conversation.

 If the video connection can't be established, see "Video Chat Doesn't Work" in the "Troubleshooting" section at the end of this chapter.

When the connection has been made, a video window appears on the right side of the Conversation window, with sound controls underneath, as shown in Figure 12.17. By default, your own picture will appear in the lower right-hand corner of the video window. You can turn this screen-in-screen display off, and also temporarily stop sending a picture to your friend, by clicking on the Options menu just below the video screen.

Figure 12.17
With a video connection, you can see your own picture as well as your friend's. Click the Options button to change this display setup.

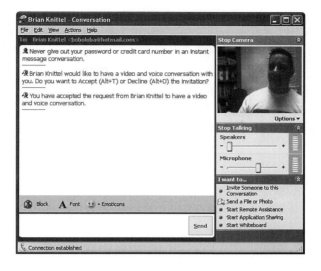

To end a video connection, click Stop Camera, or close the Conversation window.

CONFERENCING OPTIONS

Messenger provides a few features of the old NetMeeting program that are very useful for collaborating with another user, or for business presentations. From the Messenger Actions menu, you can select one of the following:

- **Start Application Sharing**—Application Sharing lets you and your friend both view the window of a program running on your computer. You can both use your mouse and keyboard to control the application. This is helpful for training, software demonstrations, or just plain collaboration on a project.

- **Ask for Remote Assistance**—Remote Assistance, which I will discuss in more detail in Chapter 17, "Windows Unplugged: Remote and Mobile Networking," lets a friend view and manipulate your entire screen. Remote Assistance is great when you need help configuring or using Windows; a friend or coworker can show you what to do, or can just go ahead an fix problems for you.

- **Start Whiteboard**—The Whiteboard is a drawing application that lets both you and a friend "scribble" on a window. You can then save or print the results of your efforts.

Remote Assistance is covered in Chapter 17. I'll briefly discuss Application Sharing and the Whiteboard in the next two sections.

APPLICATION SHARING

If you want a friend, coworker, or consultant to help you work with a Windows program (such as Excel, WordPerfect, or Netscape Navigator) or even to help set up Windows itself, you can issue them an invitation to *share* the application or desktop. Application Sharing displays your program's window or your entire screen on your friend's computer. Either of you can take control of the program to make changes with the mouse and keyboard.

NOTE

Application Sharing is similar to the Remote Assistance feature, although it's based on older technology. It's slower to use than Remote Assistance, but it does offer you a bit of privacy when you only want to share one application window—your friend won't be able to see the rest of your desktop unless you explicitly share it.

To use Application Sharing, your friend must be online. Start Application Sharing and select your friend's name from the list of online contacts (or, click Other and enter their Passport address).

Windows will display a "Do you want to Accept" message in the other user's Conversation window. When they click Accept, Application Sharing will start up.

When the connection is established, you will see two new pages open, as shown in Figure 12.18 and Figure 12.19. In Figure 12.18, clicking App Sharing will open the Sharing page (see Figure 12.19) if it is not already open. From the Sharing page, you can select a window name and click Share to share it, or select the Desktop to share all applications at once. Shared windows appear on your friend's screen as shown in Figure 12.20. If you click the Whiteboard button in Figure 12.18, you will start and share the Whiteboard application.

Figure 12.18
Click App Sharing to open the Sharing page.

When you first share an application or the desktop, your friend will be able to see the shared windows, but not change anything. If you want to let them actually manipulate the program you're sharing, click the Allow Control button in the Sharing dialog. If you want to work with an application someone has shared with you, click Control, Request Control. When you have control, you can use your mouse and keyboard to make changes in the your friend's program.

Normally, when the remote user requests to take control of the application, Windows asks the program's owner if this is okay. You can let your friend have control at will by checking the Automatically Accept Requests for Control button, which you can see in Figure 12.19. You can take control back at any time by pressing the Esc key.

Figure 12.19
Select individual applications or the entire Windows desktop to share with your friend.

Figure 12.20
When someone shares an application with you, their application appears on your screen.

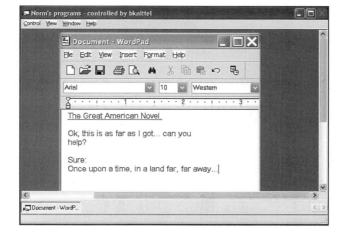

TIP

Application Sharing works best if the person who is sharing an application has their desktop resolution set to the same or a lower value than the person who's being invited to share.

12

WHITEBOARD

When people started using computer conferencing to replace face-to-face meetings, everyone was happy about the travel money they saved, but noticed that it was tough to really interact. Some of the most productive parts of meetings occur at the chalkboard, where you can write down brainstorming ideas or sketch out ideas and get immediate feedback. To give the same sort of shared writing tool to online meetings, Messenger includes a "virtual chalkboard" called the Whiteboard that lets you and your chat partner draw on a common screen, as shown in Figure 12.21.

Figure 12.21
Whiteboard lets the members of a conversation draw on a common window.

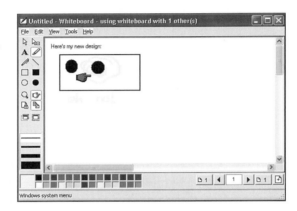

To start up the Whiteboard, you can select Tools, Send an Invitation, To Start Whiteboard in the Messenger window, or if you're already chatting with someone, you can click the Invite button and select To Start Whiteboard in the conversation window.

Whiteboard is very similar to Windows Paint, but I don't have enough space in this book to go into any further detail. I'll leave it to you investigate its menus and drawing tools.

WINDOWS MESSENGER, SHARED CONNECTIONS, AND FIREWALLS

There are two issues with Windows Messenger that you should be aware of: First, it can be subject to restrictions placed by Windows Firewall or other network firewalls. Second, as I've mentioned elsewhere in this chapter, Windows Messenger can have problems with Internet connections that go through a firewall or use NAT to share an Internet connection. Specifically, this means that anyone using a connection sharing router or anyone on corporate network might have to take special steps to get the advanced Messenger features to work. This section discusses some of the technical details.

First, I'll give you the executive summary:

- If you want to use text chat, you should have no problems even if you and your friends are using a shared Internet connection. All shared connections can handle this.

- If you are using Windows Internet Connection Sharing (ICS), you're golden because ICS copes with all the problems this section discusses.

- If you want to send files to someone else, your router must support UPnP or you must manually set up port forwarding in your router. Also, you probably have to enable UPnP because it's most often disabled by default. UPnP is considered by many to be a security risk, because rogue software on your computer could potentially subvert your firewall's protection. It's a tradeoff you have to make between security and utility.

- If you want to use voice, video, application sharing, or the whiteboard, your router must support UPnP or be SIP aware.

- If your router can't support UPnP and can't be made SIP aware, you might be able to replace it with one that can for very little cost these days. If that's not possible, you could use Windows's Internet Connection Sharing instead. Or, just appreciate the extra security these devices offer and consider giving up voice and video chat as a small price to pay.

- Receiving files, audio, and video from others requires your computer to receive data from the Internet. By default, Messenger instructs the Windows Firewall to permit this data to pass. Only if you've deliberately unchecked Windows Messenger in the Windows Firewall Exceptions list do these services fail to work. If your network has some other sort of firewall set up, you need to ensure that certain network port numbers are open to use Messenger services. Table 12.2 lists these ports.

NOTE

> All this also applies to the people you want to chat with if they also use a shared Internet connection.

12

Now, for the terminally curious, here's the technical background.

The Internet routes data back and forth between computers identified by a number called an *IP address*. When several computers share a single Internet connection, all the communications share a single IP address and the router takes care of directing incoming data to the appropriate computer. It's a lot like the telephone switchboard of a large company: There's one public telephone number, and the operator takes care of routing incoming phone calls to the internal extensions. This is what NAT is all about, whether it's performed by a hardware connection sharing router device or Windows's Internet Connection Sharing service.

When an Internet connection is initiated by your computer and directed to a computer elsewhere on the Internet, NAT sees your outgoing data and expects data to come back; it knows to send the returned data to your computer. Basic text chat works fine with NAT because each computer in the conversation makes a connection to an outside chat server run by Microsoft (or by your company if you're using a corporate network). NAT sees this connection as it's made, and the chat server sends text back and forth through the established data connection. Likewise, if you use File Transfer to send a file to a friend, NAT sees your attempt to contact your friend's computer and tracks the conversation.

Unfortunately, if another computer spontaneously attempts to establish a connection directly to yours, the NAT "operator" won't be expecting the call and won't know to whom to direct the incoming data. Sending a file via Messenger's File Transfer option involves an incoming connection initiated by the remote computer directly to yours (to pick up the file), so without special preparations or help, it won't work over a shared Internet connection. Likewise, audio and video chat, the whiteboard, and application sharing services all have problems with NAT.

There are two ways they can work, though. You can manually configure your sharing router to forward incoming connections that use certain port numbers to your computer by entering the port number and your IP address on the router's Applications or Forwarding setup screen.

However, if your router or connection sharing service supports the UPnP protocol, it's much easier. Windows Messenger automatically tells the router to expect an incoming connection, and the router knows to forward it to your computer. UPnP is built in to the Windows Internet Connection Sharing service, which is why Messenger works with ICS right out of the box. If you use a hardware sharing router, check whether it supports UPnP. Nowadays, most routers do. However, you might have to upgrade the router's firmware to get UPnP support; check the manufacturer's Web site for update information.

Messenger's audio and video chat, whiteboard, and application sharing have an additional problem. These services use the Session Initiation Protocol (SIP), in which each computer in the conversation tells the other its IP address in a way that NAT normally can't see and translate. The result is that the two computers attempt to send data to IP addresses that don't exist on the Internet and the chat session never gets off the ground. If your connection sharing service or router supports UPnP, Messenger gets around this problem by asking the router for its external, public IP address and uses this inside the SIP message. If your router doesn't support UPnP, in addition to forwarding the required connection ports, the router must also be SIP–aware—that is, it has to know to look specifically for SIP data and to modify it as it's passed through. SIP support is much less common than UPnP in inexpensive connection sharing routers, so it's unlikely that voice and video will work over a manually forwarded connection.

NOTE

If two NAT routers exist between your computer and the Internet, UPnP will not save the day for you because Messenger can negotiate with the first router but not the second. This might be the case when, for example, someone shares her Internet connection with a neighbor and the neighbor uses his own router. (I've actually seen this in friends' apartments; one person buys DSL service and they snake network cables out the windows and all over the rest of building.) In this case, you can probably just forget about voice, video, and the rest.

Finally, here's some technical data. I highly recommend using UPnP, but if you have the masochistic urge to set up manual port forwarding, Table 12.2 lists the ports used by Messenger services. If your network uses a firewall, you also have to ensure that these ports are open to use the associated Messenger services.

TABLE 12.2   NETWORK PORTS USED BY MESSENGER SERVICES

Service	Uses SIP	Data Protocol	Port(s)
Text chat	No	TCP	1863
File Transfer	No	TCP	6891–6900*
SIP	—	TCP or UDP	5060
Audio chat	Yes	UDP	500–65534†
Video chat	Yes	UDP	500–65534†
Whiteboard	Yes	TCP	1503
Application sharing	Yes	TCP	1503
Remote Assistance	Yes	TCP	3389

*The sending Messenger listens on a port in the range 689–6900 for a connection initiated by the receiving Messenger.
†Audio and video chat use a UDP port determined by SIP; it's impossible to determine it in advance. A SIP-aware router handles it automatically; otherwise, it's not possible to manually forward the audio/video data.

You can read more about this topic by searching Microsoft's Web site for the article "Windows Messenger 5.0 in Windows XP: Working with Firewalls and Network Address Translation Devices."

WHAT ABOUT NETMEETING?

As I mentioned at the beginning of this chapter, Messenger is meant as a replacement for Microsoft's previous chat/voice/video conferencing program called NetMeeting. If you use and like NetMeeting, you'll be happy to know that even though it doesn't appear on the

Start menu, it's still present on your Windows XP computer. (The Whiteboard and Application Sharing features in Messenger use parts of NetMeeting, in fact.) If you want to continue to use NetMeeting, just follow these steps to create a shortcut for it:

1. Right-click on the desktop and select New, Shortcut.

2. Click the Browse button, and browse in turn into My Computer, the drive containing Windows, the Program Files folder, and the NetMeeting folder. Select conf, click OK, and then click Next.

3. Enter "NetMeeting" as the name of the shortcut and click Finish. A NetMeeting shortcut will appear on your desktop.

4. You can drag the shortcut from your desktop to your Quick Launch bar, or into your Start Menu. I suggest that you drag it to the Start button and hold it there. When the Start Menu opens, drag it to All Programs, Accessories, and Communication before letting it go.

When you start NetMeeting for the first time, it will walk you through its setup wizard. You'll need to enter personal information (only as much as you want to), and run the Audio/Video Tuneup Wizard. When this is done, you're ready to go on the air.

One significant difference between this version of NetMeeting and versions you may have used in the past is that the Directory system is gone. You no longer can log on to the ILS (Internet Locator Service) or search for chat buddies. NetMeeting now uses the same contact list that Windows Messenger uses. So, you have only two ways to choose a partner for chatting and conferencing: You can select from your list of MS Messenger contacts, or you can directly enter the IP address of someone else running NetMeeting. Of course, this makes NetMeeting more difficult to use, and that's probably intentional ("You will use Passport. Resistance is futile").

Also, if you use a shared Internet connection, you need to know that Netmeeting is not firewall aware—that is, it doesn't know how to use UPnP to open ports in your firewall or NAT router to permit incoming connections. Visit `msdn.microsoft.com` and search the Knowledge Base for article 878451 for more information.

TROUBLESHOOTING

MESSENGER GIVES CONNECTION ERROR WHEN I SIGN IN

When I click Sign In, I get an error message saying Messenger can't connect.

Be sure you're connected to the Internet when you try to sign on with Messenger. If your computer connects to the Internet through a network with a firewall (in a business environment), you may need to contact your network administrator for help.

FILE TRANSFER DOESN'T WORK

When I attempt to receive a file from another user, Messenger says `You have failed to receive file so and so`, or when I attempt to send a file, Messenger says `This file could not be sent because the connection was blocked`. The person who is sending the file might a problem with his firewall or connection sharing router. This could be caused by a router that doesn't support Universal Plug and Play. See "Windows Messenger, Shared Connections, and Firewalls" earlier in this chapter for the details.

If the dialog box shown in Figure 12.22 appears, you were sending a file and Messenger was not previously authorized to pass through the Windows Firewall. Click Unblock and try the file transfer again.

Figure 12.22
If the Windows Firewall blocks a file transfer, this dialog box appears.

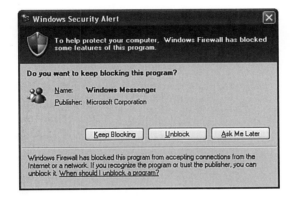

If the Windows Messenger entry in the Firewall exception list is present but unchecked, there will be no pop-up message explaining why the file transfer fails.

NO SOUND PICKED UP FROM MICROPHONE

When I speak into the microphone, the green yellow and read indicator bar doesn't appear. Or, when I use voice chat, my friend doesn't hear any sound.

First, be sure that your microphone is plugged into the correct jack on your computer or sound card. There are usually three jacks: Line Out, Line In, and Mic. You want to plug into the Mic jack. Be sure that you're using a microphone designed for computer use.

If you have multiple sound cards or sound input devices, be sure you've selected the device that your microphone is actually plugged into.

If that doesn't help, click Start, Control Panel, Sounds Speech and Audio Devices, and Adjust the System Volume. Select the Audio tab, and click Volume in the Sound Recording section. Be sure that the Microphone volume slider is moved up and the Select button under it is checked.

VOICE CHAT DOESN'T WORK

When I initiate or accept a voice conversation, the connection fails with an error message, or I hear no sound.

First of all, if you or your friend is using a shared Internet connection, you can't use voice chat if the sharing system doesn't support Universal Plug and Play or if UPnP is disabled. For more information, see "Windows Messenger, Shared Connections, and Firewalls" earlier in this chapter.

Otherwise, if there is no clear indication of what the problem is, see if your friend is hearing anything. Use the text chat window to ask them what they hear, while you speak. Check your screen's microphone indicator be sure that it's lighting up while you speak. If it doesn't, your microphone is probably not connected. If it does, have them check their speakers and volume settings. If you or your friend still don't hear anything, try disconnecting and starting the connection again. That sometimes fixes the problem.

VIDEO CHAT DOESN'T WORK

When I initiate or accept a video and voice connection, the connection fails with an error message, or I see no picture.

Video connections are even more troublesome than audio connections. There's so much more data to send that any little bit getting lost along the way can foul up the whole process.

First, check the comments in the previous "Troubleshooting" note, "Voice Chat Doesn't Work." Get the audio portion working before you try video.

If you get a good audio connection but still don't get a video connection, be sure that each person with a camera can see themselves in the lower right-hand corner of the Conversation Window's video area. If they don't, the camera is at fault. If the see-myself area is working but the other user isn't receiving video, disconnect and try making the connection again.

TIPS FROM THE WINDOWS PROS: EXTENDING YOUR CHAT COMMUNITY

If you spend a lot of time working at your computer, you may find that messaging is a powerful and effective tool for communicating with colleagues, clients, family, and friends. Messaging is much more immediate than email, yet much less intrusive and demanding than the telephone. I use messaging on a daily basis to keep in touch with friends and colleagues all over the country.

Although messaging is free, it costs the providers big money to develop and run. Why do they pay to make this a free service? Well, if you haven't noticed yet, these services are tied into their manufacturers' other ventures. For example, AOL Instant Messenger (IM) displays a constant parade of advertisements for AOL and other products, and occasionally, a video ad with loud audio accompaniment. (I immediately shut it down when it pulls this on me—this is totally inappropriate behavior for a program used in the workplace.) Microsoft's Messenger forces you to sign up for Passport and not so subtly steers you toward using Hotmail, MSN, and other Microsoft services, where you'll again be barraged with advertising that Microsoft collects on.

There's absolutely nothing wrong with this, in itself. The problem is that the messaging companies want you all to themselves, and have steadfastly refused to let their systems interoperate. Microsoft did make headlines by trying to make Messenger work with AOL's IM for a while (perhaps to lure away its users?). AOL modified their software to block Messenger users, and Microsoft fixed that until AOL changed their software yet again; lawsuits followed and it all got very ugly. The bottom line is that AOL Instant Messenger, Windows Messenger, and ICQ don't work together, so their users are in separate, noncommunicating camps.

If you find that you have friends and co-workers scattered across all the major systems, you can either get a third-party program that can connect to all the systems at once or load all the separate programs at the same time.

Multiple-system programs make life simpler because they merge all your contacts into one list and let you use a single user interface for all chatting and file transfers. You also save time when you log on because you don't have to wait for several programs to start up (AOL Instant Messenger, in particular, has a really ugly startup time; it freezes my desktop for about 15 seconds every time I log on). The downside is that the message service providers might eventually decide that these third-party programs are cutting into their cross-selling profits and might take steps to prevent them from connecting.

Some multiple-service programs you might want to check out are listed here:

- **Odigo Messenger for Windows (`www.odigo.org`)**—It can connect with AIM, ICQ, MSN, and Yahoo!, as well as the Odigo community. Free download.

- **Sealquest Messenger (`www1.sealquest.com`)**—It can connect to MSN and Yahoo! Messenger. It can also encrypt messages so that others (for example, the service providers) can't monitor or record them. Free download; a secure chat option costs $14.95 per month.

- **Trillian (`www.trillian.cc`)**—It can connect to AIM, ICQ, MSN (Windows Messenger), Yahoo! Messenger, and IRC. Encryption available. The basic version is free; the Pro version costs $25.00.

NOTE

Always be suspicious of free software; it might come with unsavory adware that pops ads up onto your screen. Even worse, it might come with spyware that monitors your online activity and sends the information to marketing companies.

Personally, because most of the people I contact are on one IM system and I only occasionally need to use others, I've found it best to use the various providers' own chat programs. If you want to use separate chat clients, here are some tips to help you get set up:

- **AOL Instant Messenger**—You can download it from www.aol.com, getting it separately or as part of the full Netscape browser program. AIM's advantage is its huge community, and the ability to search for chat pals by areas of interest, should you want to.

- **ICQ**—This program is now owned by America Online, but its community is totally separate from AOL. ICQ's advantage is its extreme configurability, as well as its search-for-a-pal features. You can download it at www.icq.com.

- **Yahoo! Messenger**—It can be downloaded from messenger.yahoo.com.

Regardless of which IM clients you use, remember to take steps to protect your privacy. Think twice about listing your email address, telephone number, or full name in any of these service's directories. I prefer to contact my friends directly and give them my chat identification info, rather than making it public.

You can also configure these programs to prevent unknown people from contacting you without your permission. It's your computer, your time, and your connection, so you should be in control of who uses it.

Finally, when you register for one of these services, be sure to opt out of any marketing email lists the provider wants to sign you up for.

TROUBLESHOOTING YOUR INTERNET CONNECTION

In this chapter

IT'S GREAT WHEN IT WORKS, BUT...

Browsing the Internet is great fun—and very useful, too. In fact, watch as I instantly transfer millions of dollars from my secret Swiss bank account to…. Wait a minute, what's a 404 Server Not Found Error? What's going on? Did the modem disconnect? Is the IRS closing in on me? Help! *Where's my money?!*

If you've used the Internet for any length of time, this scene may seem all too familiar—except for the bit about the Swiss bank account (a guy can dream, can't he?). Connecting to the Internet and using the Web is an amazingly user-friendly experience, yet we can't escape the basic fact that it's a staggeringly complex system. If something goes wrong at any step along the way between your fingertips and a server somewhere off in cyberspace, the whole system comes to a crashing halt. Where do you begin to find and fix the problem?

In this chapter, I'll show you the basic strategies to use when tracking down Internet problems, and then I'll briefly discuss some of the diagnostic tools available to help you pinpoint the trouble.

TIP

> Experiment with the diagnostic tools when your network and Internet connection are operating correctly to learn how the programs work and what sort of output you should expect. This way, as we'll discuss in the next section, if you run into trouble later, you can compare the results to what you saw when things were working.

BEFORE YOU RUN INTO TROUBLE

The best tool to have on hand when you're diagnosing Internet problems is information about what you should expect when your connection is *working*.

First, I suggest that you invest a bit of time learning about networking in general—for the Internet is nothing but an overgrown computer network—by reading Chapter 14, "Overview of Windows XP Networking." In that chapter I'll define the networking terms that I'll be using in this chapter.

Then, it's very helpful to collect correct output of the TCP/IP diagnostic programs, which I'll discuss later in this chapter, and store the copies in a notebook for reference purposes. You can use the PrntScrn key to take snapshots of the output and setup windows, and then paste the pictures into a WordPad document as a super-fast way of documenting this stuff.

Here are some things to record:

- The output of `tracert` to a sample Web site. The tracert tool records all the intermediate steps that Internet data takes getting from your computer to a site out on the Net. Knowing what the route looks like when things are working can help you tell whether a problem is in your computer or out somewhere on the Internet, beyond your control.

- The output of `ipconfig /all` on each of your computers, while you're connected to the Internet. Ipconfig lists all your networking settings so you can check for mistakes.

- The network hardware and protocol configuration dialog boxes in Network Connections, as pictures snapped with PrntScrn. If you have a network or a network adapter that you use for a broadband cable or DSL Internet connection, it's handy to record the setup information in case you need to re-enter it at a later date. You might need to do that if you replace your network adapter, for example.

- The configuration of any routers or network connection equipment. If you have an Internet connection sharing device, it's a good idea to record its correct settings in case they are accidentally changed, or if you update or replace the device. You can do this by printing each of its setup screens from your Web browser.

- The settings for any dial-up connections used. Many ISPs talk you through their setup, and it's important to record the setup information in case you need to reconstruct it someday.

- Diagrams showing network cabling, hubs, routers, and computers. If your three-year-old niece is a budding network installer and rewires your computer, it's handy to have a diagram of the correct setup to help you get the all the wiring spaghetti back in order.

I'll tell you how to gather this information in the sections that follow.

By the way, If you're using Windows XP in a business setting, documentation of your LAN configuration is a "due diligence" issue—it's not optional. Keep it up-to-date, and if you hired someone to set up your computer, be sure that they give you good documentation.

This way, you'll be armed with supportive information if a problem does occur.

TROUBLESHOOTING

A functioning Internet connection depends on a whole chain of correctly functioning hardware and software components that reach all the way from your keyboard to a computer that might be halfway around the world. Troubleshooting is a real detective's art, and it's based more on methodical tracking down of potential suspect problems than intuition. If something goes wrong, you have to go through each component in turn, asking, "Is this the one that's causing the problem?"

Let's assume that you are having trouble using a certain Web site. It could be that one of the following is happening:

13

- You can view some of its pages but not others, or you see text displayed but, say, not the streaming video or sound.

    In this case, you know that your Internet connection itself is fine, as evidenced by the fact that text and some pages do appear. The problem is that the video or sound application isn't working. To fix this problem, check the appropriate chapter in this book or see if the Web site itself has any online help.

- Nothing on this particular site is responding.

    In this case, see if you can view *any* other Web site—for example, www.google.com or www.quepublishing.com; use your imagination.

    If you get a response from even *one* Web site, your Internet connection is fine. The problem is most likely with the site you're trying to use or with your ISP. Check that Internet Explorer isn't set up to block access to the site you're interested in (see Chapter 9, "Browsing the World Wide Web with Internet Explorer," for more help on this topic).

- You can't view any Web pages on any site at all. If you poke around and find that you can't view any Web site at all, you know that your Internet connection itself is at fault. This chapter will help you find out what's wrong.

To that end, Figures 13.1 and 13.2 show flowcharts to help direct you to source of the problem. The first chart is for dial-up connections to an ISP, and the second is for LAN connections. If you're having Internet connection trouble, follow the appropriate flowchart. The endpoints in each flowchart suggest places to look for trouble. I'll discuss these in the sections that follow.

IDENTIFYING SOFTWARE CONFIGURATION PROBLEMS

Software configuration problems can easily be the cause of Internet connection problems, and it's fairly easy to determine that this is the problem—you can't make any Internet connection whatsoever, although the Device Manager says your network card or modem seems to be working correctly. The potential problems depend on the type of Internet connection you use.

TROUBLESHOOTING A DIAL-UP CONNECTION

If your modem appears to connect to your ISP but, even though connected, you still can't access any Web pages or Internet services, here are some steps you can take:

1. In Internet Explorer, select Tools, Internet Options. Select the Connections tab. Be sure you have selected the correct dial-up connection. Click LAN Options and be sure that Use a Proxy Server is not checked, as shown in Figure 13.3.

2. In Network Connections (click Start, All Programs, Accessories, Communications, Network Connections), select your Dial-Up connection, right-click Properties, and select the Networking tab. The type of dial-up server should be PPP, and under Components Used By This Connection, only Internet Protocol and QoS Packet Scheduler should be checked, as shown in Figure 13.4.

3. On the Security tab of your connection's Properties sheet (refer to step 2), be sure that Validate My Identity As Follows is set to Allow Unsecured Password.

Figure 13.1
A flowchart for diagnosing dial-up Internet connection problems.

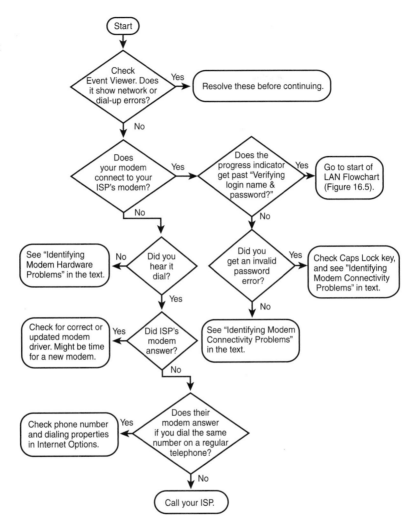

If none of these steps identifies a problem, it's time to call your ISP for assistance. You might have to spend half an hour listening to really bad music on hold, but at this point, it's their job to help you get online and they should help you cheerfully and expertly.

Figure 13.2
A flowchart for diagnosing broadband or LAN-based Internet connection problems.

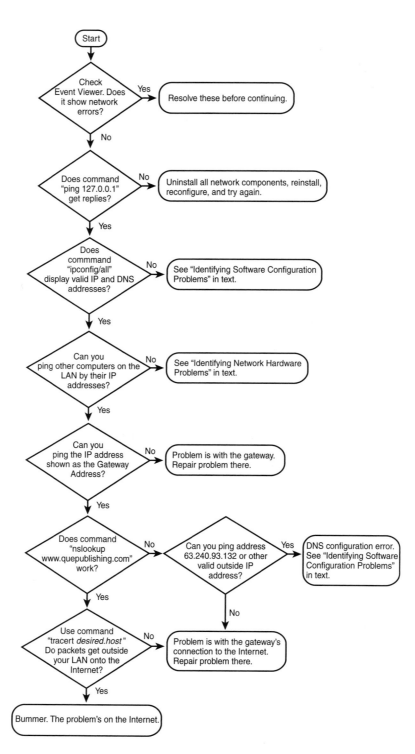

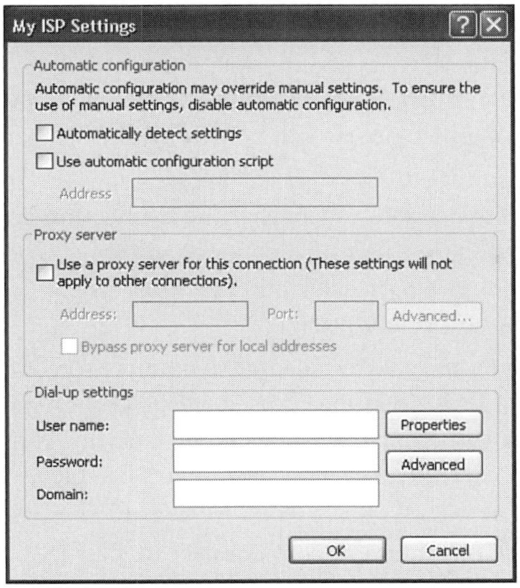

Figure 13.3
For a dial-up Internet connection, Proxy Server should not be checked.

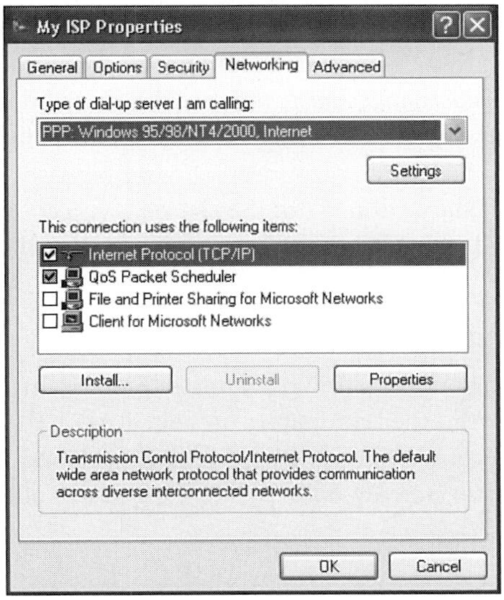

Figure 13.4
For a dial-up Internet connection, only Internet Protocol and QoS Packet Scheduler should be checked.

13

TROUBLESHOOTING A CABLE OR DSL MODEM CONNECTION

If your computer connects to a cable or DSL modem, you may have one or two network cards installed in your computer, depending on whether you're sharing the high-speed connection on a network as described in Chapter 18, "Connecting Your LAN to the Internet."

Here's how to check for the proper settings:

1. In a command prompt window, type ipconfig /all. Be sure that your IP address and DNS information for the network card that connects to your high-speed modem is accurate. Your ISP's tech support people can help you confirm this.

2. If your DSL provider requires you to "sign on" before using the Internet, you'll be using a sort of "dial-up" connection, except that the connection is made digitally over the DSL network. You will have to set up a connection using "Connect using a broad-band connection that requires a user name and password" as described in Chapter 8, "Internet and TCP/IP Connection Options."

   If this is the case, and if you use a LAN adapter to connect to your DSL modem, this LAN adapter will have an IP address that is used *only* to communicate with your DSL modem. Be sure to check with your ISP to be certain that this computer-to-modem connection is configured correctly; if it's not, you won't be able to make the connection to your ISP.

   Then, be sure to use the Connection icon to connect to your ISP. You can get to it quickly using Start, Connect To.

   When the logon process has completed, ipconfig should show a dial-up connection with a different IP address. This is your real, public Internet address for the duration of the call.

3. If you're sharing a high-speed connection to a network using two network cards in your computer, be sure that you've enabled sharing on the correct connection! The connec-tion to check as "shared" is the one that connects to your high-speed DSL or cable modem. The network-side connection is not the shared connection and should have an IP address of 192.168.0.1. Internet Connection Sharing is described in Chapter 18.

TROUBLESHOOTING A LAN CONNECTION

If you connect to the Internet through a wired or wireless local area network, the first ques-tion is, can you communicate with other computers on your LAN? To test this, use the ping command. Open a Command Prompt window and type the command ipconfig. The output of ipconfig lists a number called a *gateway address*. Test the gateway address with the ping command. Here's an example:

```
ping 192.168.0.1
```

This tests the connection to the computer or router that is sharing its Internet connection. If ping says Request timed out rather than listing for successful replies, you have a LAN problem that you need to fix first. If you are using a wireless network connection, be sure that your wireless connection is working correctly, that you are connected to the correct wireless network, and that you have the correct network key entered. Chapter 20, "Troubleshooting Your Network," is devoted to LAN troubleshooting.

TIP

> Windows has a repair function that resets all the software components of a LAN connection, including the DHCP address assignment. This often solves LAN problems. To use it, open the Network Connections page, find your LAN or wireless connection, right-click it, and select Repair.

If you can communicate with other computers on the LAN but not the Internet, can anyone else on your network access the Internet? If no one can, the problem is in the shared connection to the Net. If your LAN uses Internet connection sharing, go to the sharing computer and start diagnosing the problem there. Otherwise, follow these steps:

1. Open a command prompt window and type **ipconfig /all** to view your TCP/IP settings. The output will appear similar to that shown in Listing 13.1.

LISTING 13.1   OUTPUT FROM THE ipconfig /all COMMAND

```
Windows IP Configuration

        Host Name . . . . . . . . . . . : ambon
        Primary Dns Suffix . . . . . . . :
        Node Type . . . . . . . . . . . : Unknown
        IP Routing Enabled. . . . . . . : No
        WINS Proxy Enabled. . . . . . . : No

Ethernet adapter Local Area Connection:
        Connection-specific DNS Suffix  . : myisp.net
        Description . . . . . . . . . . : Realtek RTL8139 Family PCI Fast
                                          Ethernet NIC
        Physical Address. . . . . . . . : 00-C0-CA-14-09-7F
        Dhcp Enabled. . . . . . . . . . : Yes
        Autoconfiguration Enabled . . . . : Yes
        IP Address. . . . . . . . . . . : 192.168.0.102
        Subnet Mask . . . . . . . . . . : 255.255.255.0
        Default Gateway . . . . . . . . : 192.168.0.1
        DHCP Server . . . . . . . . . . : 192.168.0.1
        DNS Servers . . . . . . . . . . : 192.168.0.4
                                          207.155.183.72
                                          206.173.119.72
        Lease Obtained. . . . . . . . . : Sunday, August 19, 2001 5:57:56 PM
        Lease Expires . . . . . . . . . : Monday, August 20, 2001 5:57:56 PM
```

13

Check the following:

- The DNS suffix search list and/or the connection-specific DNS suffix should be set correctly for your ISP's domain name or your company's domain name. (This is helpful but not crucial.)
- The IP address should be appropriate for your LAN. If you're using Internet Connection Sharing, the number will be 192.168.0.xxx. If you're using a hardware connection sharing device, the number may be different.

- If your IP address appears to be 169.254.0.*xxx*, the sharing computer or router was not running the connection-sharing service when you booted up your computer or is no longer set up to share its connection. Get the sharing computer or router restarted and then skip to step 2.

- The default gateway address should be the IP address of your router or sharing computer, usually something such as 192.168.0.1 or 192.168.1.1.

- The default gateway address and your IP address should be identical for the first few sets of numbers, corresponding to those parts of the subnet mask that are set to 255. That is, both might start with 192.168.0 or 192.168.1.

- If your computer gets its IP address information automatically, a DHCP Server should be listed. If your computer has its IP address information entered manually, no DHCP Server should be listed.

- If you're using Connection Sharing, the DNS server address will be 192.168.0.1. Otherwise, the DNS server numbers should be those provided by your ISP or network administrator.

  If your computer gets its settings automatically or uses a shared connection, continue with the next two steps.

2. Be sure that your DSL or Cable modem is on and connected, and that the computer that shares its Internet connection is running, or that your connection sharing router is turned on. It might help to power your DSL modem off, then back on. Wait a couple of minutes until its lights indicate that the connection to the central office has been re-established. Then, in the Network Connections window, click your Local Area Connection icon and select Repair This Connection from the task list. This may solve the problem.

3. Repeat the ipconfig command and see whether the correct information appears now. If it does, you're all set. If not, the master computer or the router is not supplying the information that I described above, and needs to be set correctly before you can proceed.

These steps should take care of any software configuration problems, and there isn't much more that could be causing a problem, as long as your network hardware is functioning correctly. If none of these steps indicates or solves the problem, check that your network or modem hardware is functioning correctly.

IDENTIFYING NETWORK HARDWARE PROBLEMS

If you suspect hardware as the source of your Internet connection problems, check the following:

- Log on as a Computer Administrator. On the Start menu, right-click My Computer and select Manage to open Computer Management. Select Device Manager. Look for any yellow exclamation point (!) icons in the device list; if your network adapter is marked with this trouble indicator, you'll have to solve the hardware problem before continuing. See Chapter 23, "Maintaining and Optimizing System Performance," for hardware troubleshooting tips.

■ Still in Computer Management, check Event Viewer for any informative error message that might indicate a hardware problem.

■ Use `ipconfig` on each of your computers to check that all the computers on your LAN have the same gateway and network mask values and similar but distinct IP addresses (refer to Listing 13.1).

■ If your LAN has indicator lights on the network cards and/or hubs, open a command prompt window and type `ping -t x.x.x.x`, where *x.x.x.x* is your network's Default Gateway address. This forces your computer to transmit data once per second. Confirm that the indicator lights blink on your LAN adapter and the hub, if you have one. This test may point out a cabling problem.

■ If your hub or LAN card's indicator doesn't flash, you may have a bad LAN adapter, the wrong driver may be installed, or you may have configured the card incorrectly. You can stop the Ping test by typing Ctrl+C when you're finished checking.

IDENTIFYING MODEM HARDWARE PROBLEMS

Modems can have a greater variety of problems than network adapters. Here are a few steps you can take to determine what the problem might be:

1. Before getting too frustrated, check the obvious one more time: Is a functioning telephone line connected to the right socket on the modem? Unless you're using an ISDN modem, it also doesn't hurt to plug in an extension phone and listen in as the modem dials and your ISP answers. You must somehow put the extension on the "line" side of the modem, though, because most modems disable the "telephone" jack when dialing.

   If dialing was actually taking place but you couldn't hear it, run the Phone and Modem Options (open the Control Panel and select Network Connections). Select the Modems tab, select Properties, and then turn up the speaker volume.

   If you have a voicemail system that uses a stutter dial tone to indicate that you have messages waiting, your modem may not dial when the stutter is active. If this is the case, in this same Control Panel dialog, disable the Wait for Dial Tone Before Dialing option.

2. If you have an external analog or ISDN modem, be sure that it's plugged in and turned on. When you attempt to make a connection, watch for flickering in the Send Data LEDs. If you don't see flickering, your modem cable might not be installed correctly.

3. Check the Event Viewer for informative error messages that may indicate a hardware problem.

4. In the Start menu, right-click My Computer, select Manage, and select Device Manager. Look for any yellow exclamation point (!) icons in the device list; if a modem or port is marked with this trouble indicator, you'll have to solve the hardware problem before continuing. See Chapter 23 for hardware troubleshooting tips.

13

N O T E

> If you'd like to learn more about troubleshooting hardware conflicts, I recommend that you pick up a copy of Scott Mueller's *Upgrading and Repairing PCs* published by Que. As I write this, it's about to be published in its 16th edition!

5. In the Dial-Up Connection's Properties Option tab, check Prompt for Phone Number and try to make the connection. This will show you the actual number being dialed. Verify that the call waiting code, outside line access codes, and area code are correct. These are set on the connection's General tab and in the Phone and Modem Options control panel (on the Dialing Rules dialog box, select the proper location and click Edit).

6. If you have an analog or ISDN modem, and dialing is taking place but no connection is made, in the Device Manager or Control Panel Phone and Modem Properties, view the modem's Properties dialog. Select the Diagnostics tab, and check Append to Log. Close the dialog, and try to make the connection again. Go back to the Properties dialog, and select View Log. This log may indicate what is happening with the modem. Be sure to uncheck Append to Log when you're finished or the file that stores this information could grow to enormous proportions.

7. Try reducing the Maximum Port Speed (computer-to-modem connection speed) setting in Modem Properties to 19200. If this solves your problem, you need a new modem, or, if you have an external serial modem, a higher-quality serial port card.

IDENTIFYING MODEM CONNECTIVITY PROBLEMS

Modems are much more reliable these days than they were in the 1980s and 1990s. Still, compatibility problems and trouble due to poor telephone line quality still occur from time to time. If your modem fails to make a connection, or disconnects by itself, here are a few things to look for:

■ If the ISP's modem answers but you don't establish a connection, your modem may be incompatible; call your ISP for assistance.

■ If your modem disconnects and you are told that there was a problem with your username or password, try to connect again and check these entries carefully. If you try two or three times and still can't connect, contact your ISP for help. I've known them to disable accounts for various reasons, from non-payment to, well, no reason at all.

■ Create and view a log file of modem activity and look for error messages indicating a protocol negotiation error. Your ISP can assist with this as well.

■ If your modem makes screeching sounds for about 15 seconds and hangs up, your modem is probably incompatible with the equipment used at your ISP, and one of you needs to get an updated modem. Before you buy a new one, note that some modems can be updated via software. Check the manufacturer's Web site for information.

13

- If your connection works but the modem disconnects after a certain amount of time, there are two possible causes. If your connection was sitting idle, you may have run into the Windows inactivity timer. View the dial-up connection's properties in Network Connections and select the Options tab. Check the entry Idle Time Before Hanging Up. Increase the time (or stay busier!). You might enable the modem log and see whether it provides an explanation if this recurs. Your ISP also might have set up its equipment to disconnect you after a certain period of inactivity.

- If you don't think that idle time was the cause, your connection may have been interrupted by call waiting. On the connection's General tab, check Use Dialing Rules and select Rules and Edit. Verify that you've chosen to disable call waiting and have selected the proper call waiting turn off setting (for example, *70). Some newer modems are able to cope with call waiting, and even alert you to a call coming in. If you really rely on call waiting, it might be time for an upgrade.

- If none of these are the cause, you may simply have a scratchy telephone line or a flagging older modem. This is an annoying problem and difficult to diagnose. Try changing modems.

If your modem is making contact with your ISP, but despite a solid modem connection you still can't use the Internet, see the next section for tips on diagnosing Internet connectivity problems.

Troubleshooting Internet Problems with Windows TCP/IP Utilities

If you think you are connected to your ISP but still can't use Internet applications, you can use some of the command-line tools provided with Windows XP to trace TCP/IP problems. (TCP/IP is the network language or *protocol* used by the Internet; see Chapter 14 for an introduction to networking and protocols). To run the command-line utilities, open a Command Prompt box with Start, More Programs, Accessories, Command Prompt. Then type in the commands described next. If you're not familiar with command-line utilities you might take a look Launch Windows Help (Start, Help and Support), and search for the command names, e.g. "ping" and "tracert." You can also open a Command Prompt window and type the command name followed by /?, as in

```
Ping /?
```

Now, let's go through some of the Windows XP TCP/IP diagnostic and command-line utilities.

NOTE

> If you're a Unix devotee, you'll find these utilities very familiar, if not identical, to their Unix counterparts. If you're new to TCP/IP networking or debugging, you might find these utilities a little unfriendly. (Welcome to the world of networking!)

13

IPCONFIG

Ipconfig is one of the most useful command-line utilities available with Windows XP, because it displays the current IP address information for each of your computer's network adapters and active dial-up connections. On networks that assign addresses automatically (which includes most dial-up ISPs), ipconfig provides the only way to find out what your computer's IP address is, should you ever need to know it.

After opening a command prompt window, typing the command

```
ipconfig
```

returns the following information (of course the specific information ipconfig provides will be different for your computer, and you might see a dial-up connection listed rather than a LAN adapter):

```
Windows IP Configuration
Ethernet adapter Local Area Connection:

        Connection-specific DNS Suffix  . : mycompany.com
        IP Address. . . . . . . . . . . . : 202.201.200.166
        Subnet Mask . . . . . . . . . . . : 255.255.255.224
        Default Gateway . . . . . . . . . : 202.201.200.190
```

You can get an even more detailed listing by using the /all switch with ipconfig. Type Ipconfig /all and Windows displays a listing like that shown in Listing 13.1. The entries include the following information:

Host name	The name you gave your computer.
Primary DNS suffix	The Internet domain to which your computer primarily belongs. (You might temporarily belong to others as well while using a dial-up connection.) This might be blank; it's not a problem.
Node type	The method that Windows uses to locate other computers on your LAN when you use Windows Networking. This should be Hybrid if you have a Windows Server or a WINS server on your LAN; otherwise, the node type should say Broadcast.
DNS suffix search list	Alternative domain names used if you type just part of a host name and the default domain does not provide a match.
Connection-specific DNS suffix	The domain name for this particular connection. This is most applicable to dial-up connections.
DHCP enabled	If set to Yes, this adapter is set to receive its IP address automatically. If set to No, the address was set manually.
DNS servers	IP addresses of domain name servers.

Ipconfig displays most of the information in the Network and Dial-Up Connection Properties dialog box, but it shows their real-world values. This makes it an invaluable "first stop" when troubleshooting any network problem. If you determine that an Internet connection problem lies in your equipment somewhere (because you cannot access *any* Internet destinations), typing `ipconfig /all` will tell you whether your network setup is correct. You'll want this information at hand before calling your ISP for assistance.

PING

If you try to browse the Internet or share files with other computers on your LAN and get no response, it could be because the other computer isn't getting your data or isn't responding. After ipconfig, ping is the most useful tool to determine where your Internet connection or your home network has stopped working.

TIP

> You can type `ping` *x.x.x.x*, replacing *x.x.x.x* with the default gateway address or the address of any other operational computer on the Internet or on your home network, if you have one, and in an instant know whether your dial-up or high-speed modem, computer, network hardware, and cabling are operating properly. If echoes come back, the physical part of your network is functioning properly. If they don't, you can use tracert and other tools, explained later in this chapter, to see why.

Here's how it works:

1. The `ping` command sends a few packets of data to any computer you specify. (Packets are the basic little blocks of data that Internet and network computers communicate with. If you ever passed notes back and forth with a friend in grade school, you were communicating with packets.)
2. The other computer should immediately send these packets right back to you.
3. Then, ping lets you know whether the packets come back.

Therefore, ping tests the low-level communication between two computers. If ping works, you know that your network wiring, TCP/IP software, and any routers in between you and the other computer are working. Ping takes several options that can customize the type and amount of output it reports back to you. There are three especially useful variations of these options, the first two of which are

```
C:\> ping hostname
```

and

```
C:\> ping nnn.nnn.nnn.nnn
```

These variations transmit four packets to the host or IP address you specify and tell you whether they return. This command returns the following information:

13

```
C:\> ping www.mycompany.com
Pinging sumatra.mycompany.com [202.222.132.163] with 32 bytes of data:
Reply from 202.222.132.163: bytes=32 time<10ms TTL=32
Reply from 202.222.132.163: bytes=32 time<10ms TTL=32
Reply from 202.222.132.163: bytes=32 time<10ms TTL=32
Reply from 202.222.132.163: bytes=32 time<10ms TTL=32
```

In this example, the fact that the packets returned tells us that the computer can communicate with www.mycompany.com. It also tells us that everything in between is working as well.

NOTE

It's not uncommon for one packet of the four to be lost; when the Internet gets congested, sometimes ping packets are discarded as unimportant. If *any* come back, the intervening networks are working.

Another useful variation is to add the -t option. This makes ping run endlessly, once per second, until you press Ctrl+C. This is especially helpful if you're looking at indicator lights on your network hub, changing cables, and so on. The endless testing lets you just watch the screen to see whether any changes you make cause a difference.

Ping is a great quick test of connectivity to any location. If the ping test fails, use tracert or pathping to tell you where the problem is.

NOTE

Ping is a good quick tool to use to learn whether an Internet site is alive. (However, some large companies have made their servers not respond to ping tests at all. ping www.microsoft.com doesn't work, ever, even with a good Internet connection. (I guess Microsoft got tired of being the first site everyone thought of to test their Internet connections.)

TRACERT

Tracert is similar to ping: It sends packets to a remote host and sees whether packets return. However, tracert adds a wrinkle: It checks the connectivity to each individual router in the path between you and the remote host. (Routers are the devices that connect one network to another. The Internet itself is the conglomeration of a few million networks all connected by routers). If your computer and Internet connection are working but you still can't reach some or all Internet sites, tracert can help you find out where the blockage is.

In tracert's output, the address it tests first is your local network gateway (if you connect to the Internet via a high-speed connection or a LAN) or the modem-answering equipment at your ISP's office (if you're using a dial-up connection). If this first address responds, you know your modem, LAN, or broadband connection is working. If the connection stops after two or three routers, the problem is in your ISP's network. If the problem occurs farther out, there may be an Internet outage somewhere else in the country.

Here's an example that shows the route between my network and the Web server www.fictitious.net. Typing

```
C:\> tracert www. fictitious.net
```

returns the following:

```
Tracing route to www.fictitious.com [204.179.107.3]
over a maximum of 30 hops:

1    <10 ms   <10 ms   <10 ms   190.mycompany.com [202.201.200.190]
2    <10 ms   <10 ms    10 ms   129.mycompany.com [202.201.200.129]
3     20 ms    20 ms    20 ms   w001.z216112073.sjc-ca.dsl.cnc.net [216.112.73.1]
4     10 ms    10 ms    10 ms   206.83.66.153
5     10 ms    10 ms    10 ms   rt001f0801.sjc-ca.concentric.net [206.83.90.161]
6     10 ms    20 ms    20 ms   us-ca-sjc-core2-f5-0.rtr.concentric.net
                                [205.158.11.133]
7     10 ms    20 ms    10 ms   us-ca-sjc-core1-g4-0-0.rtr.concentric.net
                                [205.158.10.2]
8     10 ms    20 ms    20 ms   us-ca-pa-core1-a9-0d1.rtr.concentric.net
                                [205.158.11.14]
9     10 ms    20 ms    20 ms   ATM2-0-0.br2.pao1.ALTER.NET [137.39.23.189]
10    10 ms    20 ms    20 ms   125.ATM3-0.XR1.PAO1.ALTER.NET [152.63.49.170]
11    10 ms    10 ms    20 ms   289.at-1-0-0.XR3.SCL1.ALTER.NET [152.63.49.98]
12    20 ms    20 ms    20 ms   295.ATM8-0-0.GW2.SCL1.ALTER.NET [152.63.48.113]
13    20 ms    20 ms    20 ms   2250-gw.customer.ALTER.NET [157.130.193.14]
14    41 ms    30 ms    20 ms   www.fictitious.com [204.179.107.3]
Trace complete.
```

You can see that between my computer and this Web server, data passes through 13 intermediate routers, owned by two ISPs.

TIP

> When your Internet connection is working, run tracert to trace the path between your computer and a few Internet hosts. Print and save the listings. Someday when you're having Internet problems, you can use these listings as a baseline reference. It's very helpful to know whether packets are stopping in your LAN, in your ISP's network, or beyond when you pick up the phone to yell about it.

I should point out a couple of tracert's oddities. First, notice in the example that I typed www.fictitious.net, but tracert printed www. fictitious.com. That's not unusual. Web servers sometimes have alternative names. Tracert starts with a reverse name lookup to find the *canonical* (primary) name for a given IP address. There's another glitch you might run into. For security reasons, many organizations use firewall software or devices, which block tracert packets at the firewall between their LAN and the Internet. In these instances, tracert will never reach its intended destination even when regular communications are working correctly. Instead, you'll see an endless list that looks like this:

```
14       *        *        *     Request timed out.
15       *        *        *     Request timed out.
16       *        *        *     Request timed out.
```

13

This continues up to tracert's limit of 30 probes. Just press Ctrl+C to cancel the test if this happens. If tracert was able to reach routers outside your own LAN or PC, your equipment's fine and that's all you can hope for.

PATHPING

Pathping is relatively new to Windows's toolkit, having first appeared in Windows 2000. It provides the function of tracert and adds a more intensive network traffic test.

Pathping performs the route-tracing function faster than tracert because it sends only one packet per hop, compared to tracert's three.

Then, after determining the route, pathping does a punishing test of network traffic at each router by sending 100 ping packets to each router in the path between you and the host you're testing. It measures the number of lost packets and the average round trip time for each hop, and it displays the results in a table.

The results tell you which routers along the way are experiencing congestion, because they will not be able to return every echo packet they're sent, and they may take some time to do it. Performing the pathping test can take quite a while. Fortunately, you can cancel the test by pressing Ctrl+C, or you can specify command-line options to shorten the test. A reasonably quick test of the path to a site, say www.quepublishing.com, can be performed using just 10 queries instead of the default 100, using this command:

```
pathping -q 10 www.quepublishing.com
```

You can type

```
pathping /?
```

to get a full description of the command line options.

ROUTE

Most of us have at most one modem or one LAN adapter through which we make our Internet and other network connections, but Windows Networking components are sophisticated enough to handle multiple LAN and dial-up adapters in one computer. When multiple connections are made, Windows has to know which connections to use to speak with another remote computer. For the TCP/IP or Internet Protocol (IP) data, this information comes from the *routing table*. This table stores lists of IP addresses and subnets (blocks of IP addresses) as well as indicates which adapter (or *interface*) Windows used to reach each of them.

Now, this is getting into some hardcore networking that only a few readers will be interested in; please don't think that you'll need to know about this tool (there will be *no* quiz next Friday). I'm discussing this only to get the details down for those few people who have a complex network setup and only need to know how to go to this information. You don't have to worry about routing unless one of the following scenarios is true:

- You use a dial-up connection *and* a LAN adapter simultaneously.

- You use multiple LAN adapters.

- You use Virtual Private Networking connections, as discussed in Chapter 17, "Windows Unplugged: Remote and Mobile Networking."

If you have trouble reaching an Internet destination and fall into any of these three categories, type route at the command line. You'll be shown a table that looks something like this:

```
===========================================================================
Interface List
0x1 ........................ MS TCP Loopback interface
0x2 ...0e c3 24 1f 09 3f ...... NDIS 5.0 driver
===========================================================================
===========================================================================
Active Routes:
Network Destination        Netmask          Gateway       Interface  Metric
          0.0.0.0          0.0.0.0  202.201.200.190  202.201.200.166       1
        127.0.0.0        255.0.0.0        127.0.0.1        127.0.0.1       1
  202.201.200.160  255.255.255.224  202.201.200.166  202.201.200.166       1
  202.201.200.166  255.255.255.255        127.0.0.1        127.0.0.1       1
  202.201.200.255  255.255.255.255  202.201.200.166  202.201.200.166       1
        224.0.0.0        224.0.0.0  202.201.200.166  202.201.200.166       1
  255.255.255.255  255.255.255.255  202.201.200.166  202.201.200.166       1
Default Gateway:      202.201.200.190
===========================================================================
Persistent Routes:
  None
```

There's a lot of information here, but for our purposes, we can boil it down to this: The entry for network destination 0.0.0.0 is the effective gateway address for general Internet destinations. This *can* be different from your LAN's specified default gateway, especially while a dial-up or VPN connection is active. That, in turn, may mean that you can't get to the Internet. If you have multiple LAN adapters, the issues are more complicated. Contact your network administrator for assistance.

→ If the gateway address is incorrect after you've made a dial-up connection, **see** "Routing Issues," **p. 600**.

THIRD-PARTY UTILITIES

Besides the utilities provided with Windows XP, there are some third-party tools that you can use to help diagnose your connection and gather Internet information. I'll describe three Web-based utilities and one commercial software package.

SPEED CHECK

Ever wondered how to find the real-world transfer rate of your Internet connection? Intel Corporation has a nifty Web-based program to measure transfer speeds using a Java applet. Check out www.intel.com/personal/do_more/broadband/speedtest.htm. (Every time I put this URL into print, Intel seems to feel the need to change it. If you get a `page not found` error, search the Intel site for "broadband speed test.")

WHOIS DATABASE

Anyone registering an Internet domain name is required to file contact information with a domain registry. This is public information, and you can use it to find out how to contact the owners of a domain whose customers have sent spam mail or with whom you have other concerns.

Finding the registrar for a given domain name can be a bit difficult. You can find the registrar information for any `.aero`, `.arpa`, `.biz`, `.com`, `.coop`, `.edu`, `.info`, `.int`, `.museum`, `.net`, or `.org` domain via the following Web page:

`www.internic.net/whois.html`

The search results from this page indicate the URL of the whois lookup page for the associated domain registrar. Enter the domain name again on *that* page and you should see the contact information.

It's a bit harder to find the registrar associated with two-letter country code domains ending in, for example, `.au`, `.de`, `.it`, and so on. The InterNIC site recommends searching through `www.uwhois.com`.

You can find the owner of an IP address through a similar lookup at `www.arin.net/whois`. Enter an IP address to find the owner of the block of IP addresses from which the specific address was allocated. This is usually an ISP or, in some cases, an organization that has had IP addresses assigned to it directly.

REVERSE TRACERT

As I discussed earlier, the tracert program investigates the path that data you send through the Internet takes to read another location. Interestingly, data coming back to you can take a different path. Users of older satellite Internet service know this already as their outbound data goes through a modem, while incoming data arrives by satellite. It turns out that this can happen even with standard Internet service, depending on the way your ISP has set up their own internal network.

It's handy to know how the path data takes coming to you. If you record this information while your Internet connection is working, if you run into trouble you can have a friend perform a tracert to you (you'll need to give him or her your IP address, which you can find using the ipconfig command). If the results differ you may be able to tell if the problem is with your computer, your ISP or the Internet.

You can visit `http://www.traceroute.org` for a list of hundreds of web servers that can perform a traceroute test from their site to you. Don't be surprised if the test results take a while to appear as these tests typically take a minute or more.

WS_PING PRO PACK

If you want to be really well equipped to handle Internet and general networking problems, you can buy third-party utilities that are really much easier to use than the standard ones built into Windows. I really like WS_Ping ProPack from Ipswitch Software (www.ipswitch.com). This one utility packs almost all the TCP/IP tools into one graphical interface and adds other features such as whois for domain registration lookups, SNMP probing, and network scanning. The registration fee is $37.50 U.S. for a single-user license. I rarely use or like add-ons like this, but I use this program every few days for one reason or another, and it quickly made my "must have" list.

TIPS FROM THE WINDOWS PROS: PINGING WITH LARGER PACKETS

I have a DSL connection in my office, and one night it appeared that my Internet connection had stopped working. After a closer look, I saw that only downstream communication was affected, meaning my browser could contact Web sites, but information from the Web wasn't reaching my computer.

I first tried pinging my ISP at the gateway address of my DSL modem. It worked just fine. In fact, I could ping any site in the entire Internet but still could not view a single Web page. I called my Internet service provider and they found out that pings from their network into my LAN worked, too. The guy I spoke to suggested that I must have a software problem.

That didn't make sense to me, especially because everything was working fine just minutes before. Then I had a hunch. Ping, by default, sends very small packets: 32 bytes each, plus a few bytes of IP packet packaging. Requests for Web pages are very small, too (maybe 100 bytes). However, responses from Web servers are big and come in the largest packets possible—about 1500 bytes each. This meant the problem might not be the direction the data was taking. Instead, it could be the size of the data that was causing the problem: If a lot of interference was on my DSL line, it could be that small packets would likely make it through between bursts of electrical interference but larger packets would be much more likely to be garbled.

I vaguely remembered that ping has a bunch of command-line options, so I looked up "ping" in Windows Help and saw that I could increase the size of its packets with the -1 option. Typing

```
ping -l 300 www.someplace.com
```

tells ping to send 300-byte packets. Aha! I found that only about 50 percent of these packets made the roundtrip. When I sent 500-byte packets, the success rate dropped to 10 percent. When I called tech support with this news, the guy at my ISP tried the same test, and got the same result when he tried to ping my computer from his network. Now, we knew that there was a physical problem that the ISP was responsible for fixing.

13

It turned out that there was a bad connection in the telephone wiring down the street from my office. The connection had suddenly failed, making it difficult for the modem to send more than a few bytes at a time without interference. They fixed the problem a few days later.

The moral of this story is to be familiar with your friendly neighborhood command-line utilities.

Networking

CHAPTER 14

OVERVIEW OF WINDOWS XP NETWORKING

In this chapter

NETWORK CONCEPTS

A revolution is going on now, and it compares to the one Johannes Gutenberg started in 1456 when he pioneered the use of movable type. The ability to print in quantity made it possible for the first time for the common man to gain knowledge by himself. This new revolution is based on global connectivity, and its impact is on our ability to *disseminate* information by ourselves. We now take it for granted that we can share information, preach, publish, talk, and touch the rest of the world through our computers. Networks have radically changed the way the world communicates.

Networks aren't limited to just the work environment anymore. Many homes with a computer quickly end up with two or more, and it's not long before it seems sensible to tie them together with a network. So, whether or not you have one now, a network is probably in your future. In this chapter, you'll learn how networking works and how Windows XP provides the tools to help you become part of the connected world.

NOTE

> This chapter is designed to provide some basic networking concepts. If you have been networking computers for some time, feel free to skip ahead. If you are new to networking, read on. This chapter will help get you pointed in the right direction.

WHY YOU REALLY NEED A NETWORK

I probably don't have to convince you of the value of tying your computers together with a network, even if you have only two. With a network, you can do the following:

- Use any printer attached to any computer.
- Share files, that is, get at files stored on one computer from another. At home, having this capability might mean you can finish that letter you were writing yesterday using your kids' computer because they're now using yours to manage their stock portfolios.
- Play multi-user games within your home or across the Internet.
- Share CD-ROMs.
- Back up networked computers with one common backup system—for example, a tape drive.
- Use network-enabled application software, such as databases, workgroup scheduling and calendar programs, and email. Network-enabled software is designed to give multiple users simultaneous access to information that is updated in real-time.
- Share a single Internet connection among several computers, saving on telephone lines and connection costs.

A network can justify its cost with printer or Internet connection sharing alone. But how hard is it to put together?

14

No Longer a Dark Art

It doesn't seem possible that it's now nearly 15 years since I installed my first network in a client's office. It was a nerve-wracking experience because it had cost my client thousands of dollars in hardware and software above the cost of the computers alone, and although he didn't know, I had never installed networking software or a file server before. Networking was reputed to be a costly, mystical, and dark art, and I soon found that this reputation was well-deserved. The network eventually worked. For several thousand dollars, my client got 10 computers that could read and write to the same database file.

Now a network card can cost less than half the price of a movie ticket, you can buy network cables at the corner hardware store, and first-class networking software is, well, nearly free…it's free if you were going to buy Windows anyway. And you can probably take it for granted that you should be able to just plug and play.

In the next few chapters, you'll learn how to use Windows networking to connect to the computer in your basement, to the rest of your office workgroup, or to a worldwide corporate enterprise. You may still need to learn an incantation or two, but fear not, they're no longer in Latin.

One other point: I'll be using the word *resource* frequently in this chapter. By *resource*, I mean a shared folder or printer on someone else's computer, which you can access through the LAN.

Network Neighborhoods

Windows XP has, right out of the box, all the software you need to communicate and share information with other computers. Windows XP Home Edition can fill several roles, depending on the way it's connected to other computers. It can be any of the following:

- A standalone computer working in complete isolation. An example might be a simple home computer.

- A standalone computer connected to others via a modem. An example is a laptop computer with a modem used to connect to an office or to the Internet. This computer works in isolation some of the time but can socialize when needed. You can think of this type as a *remote workstation*.

- A member of a small workgroup of computers with no central "server." An example might be a computer in a small office or home office, one of say 2 to 10. The computers share resources with each other but are essentially independent. This computer is a *peer* in what is called a *peer-to-peer* network; no one computer has an intrinsically special role in making the network work. All the participants are on equal footing; they are peers. Not all the computers need to use Windows XP either; Windows XP can peer with older versions of Windows and other operating systems such as Mac OS and Linux.

14

Windows XP Home Edition has all the stuff to participate in any of these network environments. What it can't do is take part in Windows "domain" networks, which large organizations use. For that, you need Windows XP Professional.

Also, Windows XP Home Edition's file sharing service can make a network connection with at most 10 other computers. If you need to share a network resource (such a printer or file folder) with more than 10 computers, you'll need Windows Server 2003 or one of the other Windows Server versions.

In the next few chapters, you'll learn how to configure and tune up Windows XP in each of these environments. Check out the following sections for an introduction to the concepts and terms you should know.

NETWORK FORM AND FUNCTION

What makes a network tick? Let's start by looking at Figure 14.1, the first sort of network you probably built.

Figure 14.1
Did your first network look like this?

Don't laugh! A tin-can telephone has many of the attributes of a computer network. The basis of a network is a *physical transport medium*: a means of carrying raw information (for example, words) over a medium (string) between hardware interfaces (cans). When you first used a tin can phone, you found out right away that you couldn't speak at the same time as the person on the other end, so you had to work out a *protocol* to coordinate your conversation: You probably said "over" after you spoke, like the astronauts and pilots you saw in the movies. Finally, you found that there's a limit to how long the string could be for the phone to work. If the string was too long, you couldn't hear.

Computer networks have these components and limitations, too. The raw information in a network is digital data (bits), carried over a physical medium (usually wires or optical fibers, but sometimes radio waves) between hardware interfaces (network adapters plugged into your computer), according to a mutually agreed-upon protocol that coordinates the computers' conversations.

SIZE MATTERS

A computer network is often called a *local area network*, or *LAN*. A LAN is a group of computers connected by a physical medium that supports a relatively high rate of data transmission, say 1 million bits per second (Mbps) or more, in relatively close proximity, say within one building, all able to communicate directly with each other. (Imagine 10 cans on strings, all tied together in the center!) Most home and small office LANs transmit data at 10Mbps or 100Mbps (million bits per second). This is fast enough that loading and saving large word processing documents to a remote computer isn't noticeably slower than using your own hard drive. Hot-rod networks can run as fast as 1000Mbps. This kind of blazing speed is used mostly in corporate settings and by digital-media mavens.

The electrical nature of LAN communication limits the physical distance allowed between computers to at most a few hundred yards. LANs can be extended much farther using optical fiber cables, which carry data as pulses of light, to connect groups of computers sharing a more traditional (and inexpensive) electrical connection. You might hear this arrangement called a *campus network* or *metropolitan area network*.

A *wide area network*, or *WAN*, is a group of two or more LANs tied together over even longer distances. Historically, these connections were much slower, between 56 thousand bits per second (Kbps) and 1Mbps because long-distance connections were extremely expensive. (A 56Kbps connection between San Francisco and Chicago with a guaranteed throughput of only 16Kbps cost about $2,500 per month in 1996.) Now that the telecommunications companies have installed optical fiber cables all over the world, even WAN connections can be as fast as LAN connections these days. Using the Internet, a 400Kbps connection between any two points in the U.S. can be made for as little as $300 per month.

In addition to your data, LANs carry quite a bit of "chatter" as the member computers broadcast questions, asking for the location of needed resources, and as servers broadcast announcements of the services they provide. This communications overhead could use up most of the carrying capacity of a slow WAN connection, so special devices called *routers* examine and make decisions about what data to send back and forth between the disparate geographical areas.

NETWORK CONNECTION TECHNOLOGIES

As you know, a LAN consists of a group of computers connected together using some sort of electrical medium. Most home and office networks use a technology called *Ethernet* that was developed by Xerox, Intel, and Digital Equipment Corporation.

If you're using Windows XP Home to construct your own network at home or in a small office environment, you'll use Ethernet in one form or another. The choice you'll have to make is which kind of physical medium to use. I discuss the pro's and con's of the most common alternatives in more detail in Chapter 15, "Creating a Windows XP Home Network." Here, I'll just give you an overview of the technologies that are available for home use.

14

PHYSICAL MEDIA

The signals transmitted across a LAN are generated and interpreted by electronics in each computer. Some computers have built-in network interfaces; otherwise, each computer in a LAN needs a *network interface card*, or *NIC*. I may also refer to them as *network cards*.

These electrical signals have to be carried from computer to computer somehow.

The original design for Ethernet used a *very* expensive, 1/2-inch thick cable that could carry a 10Mbps (million bits per second) Ethernet signal up to 500 meters. (It was named 10BASE5 for reasons that make sense only to an engineer). Thinner coaxial cable, similar to that used by cable TV, also was used for Ethernet. Some coaxial cable is still around, but it's almost never used for new network installations.

Today's network interface cards are designed to use one of several inexpensive varieties of network cabling, or use radio waves to avoid the need for wiring altogether. The following sections list the various types of media you're likely to encounter.

UNSHIELDED TWISTED-PAIR

Unshielded Twisted-Pair, or UTP, has become the most common network carrier, and is so called because like-colored pairs of wires inside the cable are gently twisted together for better immunity to electrical interference from fluorescent lights, radio signals, and so on. This inexpensive type of cable is also used for telephone connections, although the network variety is of a higher quality and is certified for its capability to carry high data rates. UTP cables are terminated with eight-wire RJ45 connectors, which are wider versions of the ubiquitous modular telephone connectors you can find on any phone at home or in the office.

UTP cable quality is categorized by the highest data rate it's been designed and certified to carry reliably. The most common cable types are shown in Table 14.1.

TABLE 14.1 UTP CABLE CATEGORIES

Designation	Highest Data Rate	Application
CAT-1	Less than 1Mbps	Telephone (voice)
CAT-2	4Mbps	IBM Token Ring
CAT-3	16Mbps	10Mbps Ethernet (10BASE-T)
CAT-4	20Mbps	16Mbps Token Ring
CAT-5	100Mbps	100Mbps Ethernet (100BASE-T), ATM, others
CAT-5E or -5x	250Mbps	Gigabit Ethernet (1000BASE-T)*
CAT-6	250Mbps	Gigabit Ethernet*

Gigabit Ethernet uses four pairs of wire each carrying 250Mbps, providing an aggregate speed of 1000Mbps.

The thing to remember here is that you can't use just any old wiring you find in your walls to carry a network signal: You have to look for the appropriate "CAT-something" designation, which will be printed on the cable jacket every foot or so. UTP Ethernet devices are connected to a central device called a *hub*, as shown in Figure 14.2.

Figure 14.2
Unshielded twisted-pair network with a hub.

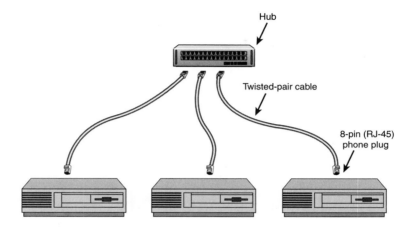

For home networking, you can buy two varieties of UTP-based Ethernet hardware, denoted 10BASE-T and 100BASE-T. I'll discuss the 10BASE-T variety first.

10BASE-T

The odd name 10BASE-T is geek-speak for network technology that sends data at 10Mbps over twisted-pair cable. The maximum permitted cable length is 100 meters, or 330 feet.

In a home network, 100 meters is usually long enough to reach from a single hub to every computer you own. In a large building or campus LAN, groups of computers have to be connected by hubs, which in turn are connected to each other with fiber-optic cable or more UTP cable (see Figure 14.3).

100BASE-T or Fast Ethernet

Fast Ethernet is a 100Mbps version of Ethernet over UTP cable. It is also called 100BASE-T or 100BASE-Tx. Most current hardware can actually work at either speed and is labeled 10/100BASE-T or -Tx. (The x stands for full-duplex, which is standard with 100BASE-T networking hardware, with or without the x.)

The hardware is 10 times faster than 10BASE-T hardware. The CAT-5 cable and connectors required to carry this high-speed signal are a bit more expensive than CAT-3 and require more care in their installation, but the cost has fallen so much in recent years that it's really no longer a consideration. 100BASE-T hubs and network cards used to be more expensive as well, but again, they're manufactured in such enormous volumes now that the

14

price differential has disappeared. In fact, most new computers have a 10/100BASE-T adapter built right into the motherboard.

TIP

> It doesn't make sense to buy new 10BASE-T parts now. For new networks, or if you're adding on to an existing 10BASE-T network, these dual-speed network cards are the way to go.

Figure 14.3
In larger LANs, hubs are connected together to span larger distances. Hubs can be connected using UTP or fiber-optic cabling.

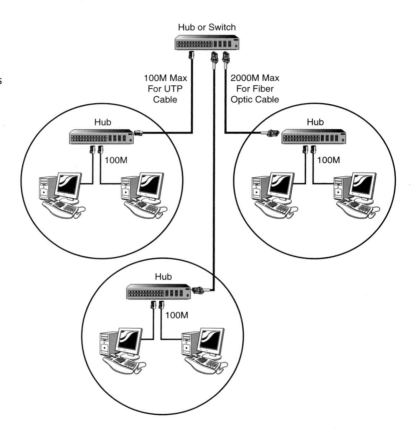

1000BASE-T OR GIGABIT ETHERNET

Gigabit Ethernet, as you might guess, sends data at 1000Mbps. It's relatively expensive (now), but another tenfold increase in speed is nothing to sneeze at if you're involved in high-speed videoconferencing or other such intensive communication work. It's also used for the backbones of large networks and for fast server-to-server connections.

Some higher-end workstations, such as Mac G5s, and most server-class machines now come with a 10/100/1000BASE-T adapter built in. This adapter works at any of these three speeds, depending on the abilities of the hub to which it's connected. Gigabit Ethernet requires CAT-5E- or CAT-6-quality cable and connectors and is overkill for home and small office networks.

WIRELESS ETHERNET

It always seemed silly to me to have a portable computer tied down by network and power wires. Now, it doesn't have to be. Ethernet-over-the-proverbial-ether—that is, wireless networking—has become amazingly inexpensive and ubiquitous. Using wireless network adapters, you can connect computers in a small area (such as your home or office) via radio, as illustrated in Figure 14.4. With modern equipment, the data rate can reach a respectable 54Mbps.

Wireless access is especially handy for users of laptop computers, Palm Pilots, and other mobile users who visit several offices in the course of a day. A device called an *access point* can be installed at each location to make the connection between wireless devices and a standard wired network or the Internet. Then, to quote Buckaroo Banzai, "wherever you go, there you are."

Hot spots—sites with wireless access to the Internet—are springing up everywhere. In fact, a certain big coffee chain from Seattle is rolling this out nationwide…they'll connect you to the Internet for a small hourly fee while you sip a latte! (Your humble authors would never set foot in one of these places, of course, preferring to patronize locally owned establishments and the original Peet's Coffee & Tea. But I digress.)

Figure 14.4
Wireless Access Point connecting computers to a standard twisted-pair network.

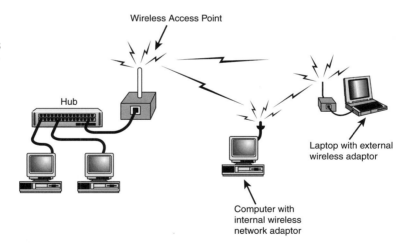

NOTE

The wireless network manufacturer's organization is called the Wi-Fi Alliance. *Wi-Fi* stands for wireless fidelity, and in a loose way *Wi-Fi* is used to refer to wireless networking.

14

One thing you have to watch out for is that currently there are three wireless standards, named 802.11a, 802.11b, and 802.11g. The "standard" part refers to the fact that the technology is governed by an international standards committee, and equipment made by one manufacturer *should* work correctly with equipment made by another. (This didn't actually hold true a few years ago, but today it largely does.)

However, equipment designed for one standard won't necessarily work with equipment designed for a different standard, as shown in Table 14.2. 802.11a equipment can communicate only with other 802.11a devices. 802.11b and 802.11g equipment can interoperate, but only at the lowest-common-denominator speed.

TABLE 14.2   WIRELESS NETWORKING STANDARDS

Wireless Standard	Data Rate*	Compatible with
802.11a	Up to 54Mbps	802.11a only
802.11b	Up to 11Mbps	802.11b at 11Mbps; 802.11g at 11Mbps
802.11g	Up to 54Mbps	802.11g at 54Mbps; 801.11b at 11Mbps

Some manufacturers have tweaked their wireless devices to let them communicate at double the standard's maximum speed, but only when connected to equipment by the same manufacturer.

If you're considering wireless, you should get 801.11g (also called *wireless-g*) for home and small office networks. Wireless-a equipment tends to be expensive. The price differential between -b and -g is miniscule, but -g can go five times faster *and* it's compatible with -b adapters.

Given the complexity of it, and knowing that just a few years ago it cost about $400 *per computer* to go wireless, I think today's prices for wireless gear are insanely low: about $20–$40 per computer for adapters and $20–$100 for an access point, the wireless network's hub. In fact, even though it isn't as fast as 100Mbps Ethernet and has trouble reaching more than 100 feet or so indoors, wireless is so much easier to install that it's competitive with wired networks even in the home and office.

However, there are two things that you must keep in mind. First, a wireless network is not as reliable as a wired network. In my experience and that of many friends, it simply stops working at random intervals; sometimes once a day, sometimes once a week. It may start working again by itself after a few seconds or minutes or hours, or you may have to restart your computers and wireless router to get it back on the air. In contrast, unless someone trips over a cable and yanks the connector off, a wired Ethernet network should run for years without a single glitch.

Secondly, unless you take explicit steps to secure it, a wireless network is "open to the public," and it's a trivial matter for random passers-by to browse through your shared files and borrow your Internet connection. Making a wireless network secure takes some effort, and to be frank, it can be difficult and confusing for even for networking pros, let alone the technologically-challenged. As a result, many people skip the security step just to get their network working, and end up getting their computers hacked-into. A wired network has neither the setup headaches nor the security risks.

PHONELINE AND POWERLINE NETWORKING

Wireless networking equipment can have problems reaching the far corners of the house, and standard twisted Ethernet wires can be a pain to put through walls and doorways. For the home market, networking equipment manufacturers have responded with network adapters that send network data using radio signals carried over your home's telephone wiring or your electrical power wiring. The technologies are called HomePNA and HomePlug, respectively. The radio signals don't interfere with normal phone conversations, modem connections, or even DSL Internet service. The adapters are relatively inexpensive (about $50 each). I dissed this equipment in the first two editions of this book, but the technology has improved and the prices have fallen to the point where it makes perfect sense to use it in the average home.

These products are easy to install, but they do have some drawbacks. Phoneline networking requires you to have the same phone extension installed at each computer's location. And powerline networking can't pass a signal through a power company's transformer, so you might be in trouble if some of your outlets are on different branch circuits from the others.

IEEE-1394 (FIREWIRE) NETWORKING

The blazingly fast IEEE-1394 data transfer system used to connect computers to digital movie cameras and hard drives can also carry network data. IEEE-1394 (also called FireWire by Apple and iLink by Sony) is similar to USB, but transfers data at 100, 200, or even 400Mbps. Many new laptop computers come with IEEE-1394 adapters, and Windows XP has the necessary networking software built-in. Computers equipped with 1394 adapters can be networked just by plugging them together with the appropriate 1394 cables.

In summary, there are several different network technologies involved in any network: data transmission format standards like Ethernet, and electrical wiring standards like 10BASE-T and ThinNet. Networks depend on an agreement to use several specific technologies, each of which relies on another to help it do its job. For example, a file-sharing standard relies on a network protocol, which depends on a data transmission format, which requires a wiring standard.

In fact, there's even a standardized way of talking about the way these standards interrelate. In case you haven't guessed already, engineers like nothing more than forming committees to create standards.

THE OSI MODEL

If you've read about networks in any other computer book, you've probably seen a diagram similar to the one in Figure 14.5, the OSI Standard Network Model. The International

14

Organization for Standardization (ISO) and Institute of Electrical and Electronic Engineers (IEEE) developed this model—I think to help computer book authors fill lots of pages trying to explain it. It's in every computer book I've ever seen.

Figure 14.5
The OSI Standard Model for Computer Networks–a required figure in every computer book. Networks are built from components, each of which performs a job for a higher-level component in the "stack."

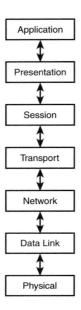

I will spare you the usual long explanation of this diagram because I don't think it's very helpful as an introduction to networking. But I do think it helps illustrate that networks are composed of modular components, *conceptually* stacked one on top of the other, each performing a job for the component above it, using the components below. The parts are interchangeable in that you may often choose one of several available technologies to do the given job of a given layer. As long as the job is done correctly, the higher layers don't really care how it's done.

The components in this "stack" communicate with their corresponding components in the other computers on the network. As you go down in these stacks, the layers are less concerned with *interpreting* the data they handle and more with simply *moving* it somewhere. The higher level components interpret and communicate with each other to reassure each other that the data they have sent was correctly received, and they rely on the lower levels to actually transport that data from one computer to another.

That's the OSI network model in two paragraphs.

In the real world—at least in the Windows world—the "stack" of components that make up Windows networking isn't just a concept, it really does exist. Figure 14.6 shows the Windows network model. When you want to access a remote network resource somewhere inside the operating system, the following actions occur:

- A *network client* composes data messages to communicate these desires to the remote computer, using an agreed-upon file sharing protocol.

- These messages are packaged according to a *transport protocol*, which specifies how messages are to be broken into manageable pieces, how the pieces are to be addressed to member computers, and how to re-request missing or garbled pieces as they are received.

- The packaged message pieces are called *packets* and are physically carried by a *data link or framing protocol* that determines how to arrange the bits of information in each packet for transmission.

- The bits are converted into electrical pulses, radio waves, or flashes of light and carried from one computer to another through a *physical medium* that carries the pulses or flashes to another computer.

- The pulses or flashes are received at the other end and the data work their way up the network component stack on the other side and are finally delivered to a *server* component. The server sends a response back through the same path to the client.

The Data Link level is handled entirely by the hardware in a *network interface card (NIC)*, When you buy a network card, you're buying a data link protocol and the attachment to the physical medium. Because the card is what you'll actually see and have to describe to Windows, from this point on, I'll talk about adapters rather than data link protocols.

Figure 14.6
A practical Windows network model, with actual Windows network components.

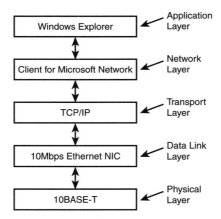

NETWORK CLIENTS

A network client is one of the most important top-level parts of Windows networking. The *client* is responsible for making remote files, folders, and printers available to your computer. To do this, it communicates with a corresponding *server* component on another computer, whose job it is to deliver file and printer information to client computers. Your Windows XP computer actually has both components built in, as it can both share files and printers, and use shared files and printers.

14

Microsoft provides one network client with Windows XP Home Edition: the Client for Microsoft Networks. (The Client for Novell NetWare networks, which is used on some corporate networks, is only provided with Windows XP Professional).

The client component, at the top of the network stack, communicates with its corresponding top-level server component in other computers to read and write files, queue printer data, read the contents of folders for display in Explorer, and so on. The Client for Microsoft Networks uses the *Server Message Block (SMB)* and *NetBT (NetBIOS over TCP/IP)* protocols to speak to other Windows computers, Windows 200x Servers, and IBM OS/2 LAN Manager Servers. You won't ever encounter SMB or NetBIOS directly in your dealings with Windows Networking; they're part of the client and server software.

The client package uses a transport protocol to carry messages between your workstation and a remote computer's sharing service.

PROTOCOLS

As you learned previously, transport protocols define how data is arranged and sent in a coordinated fashion between computers. There are three transport protocols commonly used on Windows-based computers:

- **Transport Control Protocol/Internet Protocol (TCP/IP)**—It's the transport protocol that forms the basis of the Internet. TCP/IP is actually a set of many protocols that are used to provide the services that higher-level network components need: resolving computer names into network card and IP addresses, guaranteed transmission, and internetwork routing. The *TCP* part, or *Transmission Control Protocol*, is the method an IP-based network uses to guarantee that data is sent end-to-end without errors. I'll go into more detail about TCP/IP in a little bit.

- **Internetwork Packet Exchange/Sequenced Packet Exchange (IPX/SPX)**—Was developed by Novell for its NetWare network software. Windows can use IPX/SPX for its file sharing services as well. Like TCP/IP, IPX/SPX is really a set of protocols that provide many services, including name resolution, guaranteed transport, and Internetwork routing.

- **NetBIOS Enhanced User Interface (NetBEUI)**—Was developed by IBM for its original IBM PC Network; it provides similar services to TCP/IP and IPX/SPX, except that it doesn't have a mechanism to route data to remote networks. NetBEUI can transport data between computers only on the same physical LAN. NetBEUI was supported by previous versions of Windows, but has been dropped in Windows XP (well, almost dropped—it's on the Windows XP installation CD in case you have to use it, but it's not easy to find).

14

The Client for Microsoft Network can use either TCP/IP or IPX/SPX to send its messages to a file server; all that's required is that both the client computer and server computer have at least one installed protocol in common.

The following are some other protocols and acronyms you might run across:

- **Point-to-Point Protocol (PPP)**—Used to carry Internet Protocol data packets across a dial-up modem connection. This protocol is used to establish most all modem connections to Internet service providers. PPP is part of the TCP/IP suite and a standard part of Windows's Dial-Up Networking support.

- **Point-to-Point Protocol over Ethernet (PPPoE)**—Used by some DSL and cable modem Internet service providers to link your computer to the ISP's routing equipment. Its purpose is to limit the number of computers connected to the Internet to just those being actually used. For previous versions of Windows, ISPs provided their own PPPoE software. PPPoE is now built into Windows XP as part of its Broadband Connection support.

- **Wired Equivalent Privacy (WEP)**—An encryption protocol used by wireless networks to protect data from being intercepted by eavesdroppers and to prevent random passers-by from being able to connect to and use your network without permission. In urban areas, computers can commonly pick up half a dozen or more wireless network signals. That means that half a dozen or more random other people can pick up *your* wireless signal, and you don't want them poking into your files. WEP helps prevent that. It's unfortunately not completely unbreakable—a hacker with a laptop can park herself in front of your house or office for a few hours and eventually be able to get on your network, so another encryption standard was developed, and is becoming more common (see next bullet).

- **Wi-Fi Protected Access (WPA)**—An improved encryption scheme for wireless networking. Windows XP Service Pack 2 includes WPA support. Most wireless equipment vendors now support it as well; however, if you have existing equipment, you might have to download upgraded software to get it.

- **Universal Plug and Play (UPnP)**—Lets networked computers and networked devices such as network routers, printers, and household appliances automatically configure themselves to join whatever network they find themselves plugged into. It can, for example, automatically configure your computer to use an Internet connection shared by another computer on the LAN. UPnP also lets these "smart" appliances tell your computer what they do and can let you configure them from your Windows PC.

- **Point-to-Point Tunneling Protocol (PPTP)**—Used to create *Virtual Private Networks*, or *VPN*s. PPTP takes data destined for a private, remote network, repackages the data for transmission across the Internet, and at the other end unpackages the data to be released into the private, protected network. I'll go into greater detail explaining VPNs in Chapter 17, "Windows Unplugged: Remote and Mobile Networking."

- **AppleTalk**—With its Ethernet-based counterpart *LocalTalk*, it's used in Apple Macintosh networking and by Apple printers. XP Home Edition doesn't come with support for AppleTalk.

By the way, XP Professional has some more advanced networking features that aren't provided with Windows XP Home Edition. These features are useful mainly only on a

14

corporate network run by one of the more advanced Server versions of Windows, Windows NT, Windows 2000 Server, or Windows Server 2003 (for some unfathomable reason, Microsoft changed the ordering of the name between 2000 and 2003).

NOTE

> To avoid having to type all those names again and again, when I'm referring to the Server versions of Windows, I'll call them collectively Windows 200x Server.

NETWORK ADAPTERS

Earlier in the chapter, when I described UTP and coaxial cable media, I described the popular physical media and data link protocols used in LANs, and mentioned the Ethernet data link protocol. When you buy a network adapter, they come lumped together: You're buying a piece of hardware that performs both data-link and physical transport functions.

At the physical level, network cards send packets of data through their physical medium from one card to another. Network cards have two ways of sending data: *unicast*, which sends data directly from one card to another specific card, and *multicast* or *broadcast*, which sends the same data packet to *every* card on the network. Each network card has an address (like a phone number) that is actually built right into the hardware of the network card. It is called the *physical network address* or *media access control (MAC)* address.

When a unicast data packet is addressed directly to a MAC address, only the one intended computer receives and examines the data. When a broadcast is made, every computer receives the packet. When a packet arrives by either means, the network adapter uses a hardware interrupt to inform Windows that data has arrived. Windows reads the data out of the network card and passes it up to the next higher layer in the protocol stack to be examined and acted upon.

IP ADDRESSES AND ROUTING

When we tell our computer to connect to another, how does it know how to send data there? For example, if I direct Internet Explorer to view www.quepublishing.com, how does it get the Web page request to Que's server in Indianapolis? Because the MAC addresses built into network adapters are essentially random numbers, knowing a remote computer's MAC address doesn't help you find it—you'd have to send the request to every computer in the world to locate the destination!

The solution to this problem is that each computer in an IP network is given an *IP address*, which I'm sure you've seen before; it's a number like 198.70.146.70. These are like street addresses, and can be interpreted by routers all over the world to get data packets where they need to go. As the postal service first sends mail to a given state, then a city, then a street, then your house, so a router only has to know where to deliver data for all IP addresses starting with 198. Once it gets there, the 198 router sends the packet to the router responsible for all addresses starting with 198.70, which sends it to the router for

14

198.70.146, which finally sends it to computer 198.170.146.70. (I'm oversimplifying this, but it should give you the picture.)

On an IP network, each of the computers on an individual local network has an IP address that starts with the same digits. The *network mask*, a series of numbers you may have seen like 255.255.255.0, indicates how many of the digits must match. When an individual computer wants to send data to another, if the IP address of the destination computer starts with the same digits, it knows the destination computer is local and it can send the data directly through the local LAN. This is how computers in your home or office send data when you're sharing files.

Otherwise, if the first digits don't match, the computer sends the data to a *gateway*, which routes the data out to the Internet and on toward its destination. The nice thing about this is that individual computers like yours need only to know their own IP address and the IP address of a gateway in order to reach any computer on the entire Internet. The gateway and the worldwide network of routers take care of the details of delivery. This is how data intended for `www.quepublishing.com` gets from your home to Indianapolis.

DHCP AND IP ADDRESSING

As I mentioned earlier, a network card's MAC address is physically "burned in" to the adapter's hardware. But IP addressing must somehow be set up in software. We can't just pull a number out of a hat, because each computer on a LAN must use a number with the same leading digits (the same subnet number), but different final digits than others on its local network. Also, it needs to know the address of its local gateway router, and the addresses of any name-resolving servers.

There's no simple automatic way for a computer to reliably determine this information. It can be assigned and entered manually, but on large networks, this is a cumbersome and difficult task.

To solve this problem the Internet community developed a protocol called BootP. Microsoft "embraced and extended" the BootP protocol and called the result *DHCP* (*Dynamic Host Configuration Protocol*). DHCP services can be provided by Windows 200x Server and the Internet Connection Sharing service, as well as virtually all routers and hardware Internet connection sharing devices. When a computer using DHCP is started (booted) up, it broadcasts a request for an IP address on its local network. A computer running a DHCP server responds to this request with a reply packet that specifies an appropriate IP address, network mask, and other setup information. Since broadcasts aren't passed by routers to other connected networks, only the local DHCP server hears the request and responds with an appropriate local network address. Each DHCP server keeps track of which IP addresses it has assigned to local computers, to avoid handing out the same number twice. It's also responsible for recycling addresses when a computer leaves the network and stops using an address it's been given. So, it places a time limit during which a computer can use a given IP address—it's called a *lease*. Before the time limit runs out, the computer must either contact the DHCP server to either renew its lease or obtain a new number.

14

NOTE

> Just when you thought things couldn't get more complex... they do. Small IP-based LANs with only Windows computers don't even really need a DHCP server. If Windows is set up for automatic (DHCP) IP configuration, and no DHCP server responds to the request for configuration information within 30 seconds or so, it *does* pull an IP address out of a hat. It picks a random IP address in the range 169.254.0.0 through 169.254.255.255.
>
> Windows continues to ask for DHCP service every three minutes, and if a DHCP response does eventually arrive, Windows reconfigures itself accordingly.
>
> Although this works, it's ugly: The boot process is delayed a while, and every three minutes the network will seem to "lock up", over and over. The fix is to manually assign IP addresses in each computer.

NAME RESOLUTION AND DNS

To continue with the example I used earlier, we're trying to connect to www.quepublishing.com. We've seen how packets are routed from a computer through the Internet based on IP addresses, but how do we know what IP address to use for www.quepublishing.com? That answer is provided by a name resolution service.

If we needed someone's telephone number we'd dial Directory Assistance. In computer parlance, the good people at 411 *resolve* names like Mary Smith into telephone numbers. On the Internet, we have *DNS*, the *Domain Name Service*. DNS servers are computers set up to accept electronically formatted requests like "what is the IP address of www.quepublishing.com" and return the desired information. And just as we have to know that Directory Assistance's phone number is 411, we have to tell our computer the IP address of a functioning DNS server. These have to be entered into the computer's IP information setup before the computer can find Web sites and other computers by name. Sometimes an ISP will have you enter the information manually. With dial-up connections and on networks with DHCP servers, though, it is delivered automatically.

NOTE

> Microsoft provided another name resolution service for corporate networks called *WINS (Windows Internet Naming Service)*, but it's very unlikely that you'll run across it for two reasons: First, Windows XP Home Edition isn't designed to connect to corporate networks, and second, Microsoft is encouraging corporate networks to use DNS for internal as well as public use.

For small LANs it's too much trouble to set up a DNS server to resolve the names of local computers. For example, in a home LAN, you might name your computers Kids, Kitchen, and Den, and you should be able to view the files in these computers just by typing their names.

Windows has a trick up its sleeve to resolve names that aren't available by DNS. It broadcasts a message to each computer on the network asking the desired computer to identify itself. This makes it possible to find a name without any setup, and while it's not terribly efficient, it works very well on small networks.

WAYS OF CONNECTING TO WINDOWS XP NETWORKS

Now you know the basics of what makes a network work. I've described how a network is composed of layers of software and hardware whose purpose is to let the network provide useful services to you.

The following sections describe different ways that Windows XP Home Edition can be used to connect to a network.

THE WINDOWS PEER-TO-PEER NETWORK

With a direct connection on a peer-to-peer network, Windows XP Home Edition is a terrific member workstation, and you can set up shared folders with just the click of a mouse. Windows XP is also quite friendly with Windows 2000, NT, and 9x, and treats them as peers, too. It can attach to Unix/Linux computers as well, if they're part of your network and run the appropriate file-sharing software.

The downside of the peer-to-peer network is that each Windows computer manages its own separate username/password database. Because there's no centralized control over user privileges, obtaining access to shared folders and printers on your LAN can be hit or miss. If you haven't been added as a user of the computer whose shared resources you want to use, you're out of luck.

Because networks are becoming so common even in the home, Microsoft has introduced a feature with Windows XP called Simple File Sharing. With Simple File Sharing, passwords are dispensed with across the network. That is, files made available across the network are available to one and all. This is a fair compromise between simplicity and security for homes and small offices. The feature is optional on Windows XP Professional in a workgroup network and is always enabled on Windows XP Home Edition.

THE WINDOWS REMOTE NETWORK

Windows XP can behave like a standalone computer when you're working at home or toting your laptop around in the field, and then it can act like a network member when connected to the network by modem or docking port.

In fact, you can use Windows XP's built-in software to connect from your home computer to your office computer, by modem or the Internet, to pick up files and work. (Due to the risk from hackers, however, this type of access may be prohibited by your company if running Windows XP Home in an office environment. You'd best check before trying to set this up).

You can also instruct Windows XP to answer an incoming modem call, or receive connections through the Internet from other computers.

14

CAUTION

> Enabling access to any computer from the "outside" is a significant security risk. Please don't do this without first reading Chapter 19, "Network Security."

WHAT ABOUT CORPORATE DOMAIN NETWORKS?

Corporate networks run by Windows Server 2003, Windows 2000 Server, or Windows NT, have another network security mechanism called *domain security*. These networks have a centralized list of users and passwords, so any authorized person can log on to any computer on the network and security is handled in the exact same way in all cases.

Windows XP Home Edition can't completely participate in a domain network as a full member. If you connect your XP Home Edition computer to a domain network (via direct network connection or through a dial-up or VPN connection), you can still use it and access network resources, but you'll be prompted for a domain username and password every time you open a network resource.

TIP

> If you use a domain network at work, you might consider upgrading even your home computer to run Windows XP Professional. Pro gives you features that can help if you bring your computer to work, such as domain access and Offline Files.

WINDOWS XP'S NETWORK SERVICES

Besides file and printer sharing, Windows XP provides many other network services. You might never interact with some of these services directly, but their presence makes Windows the amazing application platform it is.

Let's take a tour of Windows network services. I'll describe what each service is, why it's useful, perhaps a bit about how it works, and I'll tell you where to find out how to install, configure or use it, if appropriate.

FILE AND PRINTER SHARING

Networking software was originally developed to share and transfer files between computers (America Online Buddy Chat came later, if you can believe that!). Windows XP comes with the following features:

- Client for Microsoft Networks, which gives access to files and printers shared by other Windows computers as well as OS/2, Unix, Linux, and so on.
- File and Printer Sharing for Microsoft Networks, which lets Windows XP share files and printers with users of the aforementioned operating systems. Windows XP Home

14

Edition is limited to 10 simultaneous connections from other computers; the Server version is required for larger LANs.

■ Print Services for Unix, which lets you use and share printers with computers using the Unix operating system's LPR protocol.

→ For information about installing, configuring, and using Microsoft network software, **see** Chapters 15–18.

.NET

The .NET (pronounced "dot net") initiative is Microsoft's most recent replacement for COM, DCOM, and RPC. .NET is an entire software framework for Internet-enabled software application development. Again, it's something you will probably never interact with directly, but it is making possible a whole new generation of software applications.

VIRTUAL PRIVATE NETWORKING

Windows XP Home Edition can connect to remote LANs (for example at your home or office) through the Internet using *Virtual Private Networking (VPN)*. This very secure technology makes it safe to use Microsoft networking over the Internet.

→ If you're interested in learning more about Virtual Private Networking, **see** "Virtual Private Networking," **p. 596**.

REMOTE ACCESS

If you travel with a laptop or often work from a location outside your physical LAN, you can use RAS (Remote Access Service) to connect to remote networks by modem.

→ For more about RAS, **see** "Dial-Up Networking," **p. 574**.

INCOMING CONNECTION BY MODEM

Windows XP Home Edition allows you to configure a modem for incoming connections as well as outgoing. You can provide access to your LAN via modem, for example, to retrieve files from your office while you are at home or in the field. At most, two incoming connections are permitted with Home Edition.

→ To configure Remote Access, **see** "Enabling Dial-In and VPN Access to Your Computer," **p. 586**.

INCOMING VPN

Windows XP Home Edition also allows you to connect to your LAN via the Point-to-Point Tunneling Protocol (PPTP); that is, it lets you create a Virtual Private Network. If your LAN has a full-time Internet connection, it will (or it should) have a firewall installed, thus preventing you from using file sharing directly from the outside world. A VPN connection lets you safely penetrate the firewall to gain access to your LAN over the Internet. The VPN service is often used to connect to corporate networks from home.

I'll discuss how to make VPN connections in Chapter 17 and will explain more about firewalls and virtual private networking in Chapter 19.

14

REMOTE ASSISTANCE AND WINDOWS TERMINAL SERVICES

All Windows XP versions provide a sort of remote-control system called, variously, Windows Terminal Services, Remote Desktop, and Remote Assistance. Terminal Services let you use a computer remotely. Your applications run on the remote computer, while you use your local computer's display, keyboard, and mouse. There are three names for what is basically the same piece of software, because it's used three different ways:

- **Terminal Services**—A Windows Server 2003 system can be set up to host applications used by remote clients. For example, one beefy computer can run complex software, while the remote computers, which only need to provide a display and keyboard, can be relative lightweights. Terminal services is also great for remote administration of a server—a manager can sit in front of one computer, but can control and configure servers anywhere in the world.

   Although the service is provided only by Windows Server 2003, the client software can be run on XP Home Edition and older Windows versions.

- **Remote Desktop**—Windows XP Professional has a Remote Desktop feature, which is a copy of the Terminal Services server limited to *one* incoming connection. You can use XP Home Edition to connect to an XP Professional computer at work, for example.

- **Remote Assistance**—Windows Home Edition's Remote Assistance feature is based on—you guessed it—Terminal Services again, also limited to one connection. An incoming connection can only occur when the Home Edition computer owner emails a remote user an electronic invitation, which is good for one connection only. This makes the service useless for general remote-employee-type work, but handy for one-time assistance.

INTERNET CONNECTION SHARING

Windows XP has a handy feature that first appeared in the Windows 98 Second Edition: Internet Connection Sharing. This feature lets one Windows XP computer with a modem or high-speed Internet connection provide Internet access to all users of a LAN. This access is somewhat limited, however. It requires that the LAN use the Windows built-in automatic IP address configuration system, so it's incompatible with WAN configurations. It also requires that the computer with the modem or high-speed connection be left turned on all the time.

Connection sharing is described in more detail in Chapter 18, "Connecting Your LAN to the Internet."

WINDOWS FIREWALL

With Service Pack 2, Microsoft has significantly beefed up the Internet security features of Windows XP. Windows Firewall replaced the earlier Internet Connection Firewall. Among other things, Windows Firewall addresses one of the more stunning deficiencies in the older firewall, which left computers unprotected for 10–30 seconds during the bootup process.

You might not think that 10–30 seconds is much, but with millions of Windows-based computers connected to the Internet, thousands of computers became infected by computer viruses and worse through that window of opportunity.

Windows Firewall is discussed in Chapters 18 and 19.

UNIVERSAL PLUG AND PLAY

Windows XP includes support for Universal Plug and Play, a network protocol that lets "smart" networked devices advertise their presence on the network. For instance, many of the inexpensive Internet connection sharing routers on the market are UPnP-enabled. Windows XP automatically detects their presence and can, to a limited extent, let you configure them through the Windows interface. More importantly, UPnP lets network-dependent application software such as Microsoft Messenger function correctly across an Internet router; UPnP provides a means for the application and router to talk to each other.

There is some discussion of UPnP in Chapter 12, "Chatting and Conferencing with Windows Messenger," and more in Chapters 19 and 21.

INTRANET/INTERNET SERVICES AND TOOLS

Finally, Windows XP comes with a full complement of applications and tools that Internet and Unix users expect on a TCP/IP-based computer. They're not part of Windows Networking, technically speaking, because they don't use the Networking Clients. They communicate with other computers using TCP/IP directly. These tools include the following:

- Internet Explorer (Web browser)
- SNMP Agents
- Telnet
- Ping
- FTP
- NetMeeting
- nslookup
- pathping
- tracert
- Outlook Express (SMTP/POP mail client)

These programs are discussed in Part II of this book, "Getting Your Work Done."

WINDOWS PEER-TO-PEER NETWORKING

With an unfortunate and confusing name (because this relatively new networking addition has nothing to do with the peer-to-peer networking we've been discussing so far in this chapter), Windows Peer-to-Peer Networking is a new service that lets software developers

14

write applications that run on multiple computers. The potential applications include number-crunching tools that can take advantage of unused processing power on other people's computers, file and media sharing tools (think Napster), and discussion/collaboration/communication tools.

XP PROFESSIONAL FEATURES NOT FOUND IN HOME EDITION

Windows XP Home Edition does not include some of the advanced features of Windows XP Professional. These features include

- Ability to log on to domain networks directly, by modem, or VPN. (You can still use domain network resources by typing in usernames and passwords when you're prompted to. You won't have access to other domain features like user profiles, automatic program installation and active directory searching, however.)
- Client for Novell Networks
- Offline Folders
- Ability to connect to your computer via Remote Desktop. (The Remote Desktop client is included—you can still connect to other computers).
- Roaming User Profiles
- L2TP Virtual Private Networking and IPSec Network encryption
- IIS Web Server and Web Folder Sharing

Also, Home Edition has *no* tools to directly share files with Apple Macintosh computers or to use Macintosh shared folders. For that, you need to install Windows-compatible file sharing software on your Macs.

TIPS FROM THE WINDOWS PROS: BECOMING A NETWORKING PROFESSIONAL

I've found that modern network software works perfectly the first time about 99% of the time. When things go wrong, however, you quickly find that the diagnostic tools are nowhere near as sophisticated, automated, or helpful as the installation tools. You need a more complete understanding of network technology and structure to diagnose a broken network than you do to install one, and more to the point, a more complete understanding than I can give you in a general-purpose book like this.

So, the big tip for this chapter is this: If you're planning to set up a network for more than a few computers, or you're setting up a network in a business situation, you should have some pretty solid expertise at hand for the times when problems arise. You might have a consultant install and maintain your network, or you might at least establish a relationship with a consultant or technician whom you can call if you run into trouble.

If you want to become a networking professional yourself, I recommend the following books as places to continue your training:

Upgrading and Repairing Networks, Fourth Edition, ISBN: 0-7897-2817-6, Que

Practical Network Cabling, ISBN: 0-7897-2233-X, Que

Practical Network Peer Networking, ISBN: 0-7897-2247-X, Que

Practical Firewalls, ISBN: 0-7897-2416-2, Que

14

CREATING A WINDOWS XP HOME NETWORK

In this chapter

15

CREATING OR JOINING A NETWORK

In the previous chapter, I discussed the benefits of having a network. In this chapter, I'll show you what you'll need to buy to install your own home or small-office network using Windows XP Home Edition. Later in the chapter, I'll cover the actual network installation.

This chapter is written for a small group of users, at home or at work, who want to set up a LAN for themselves. This type of LAN is called a *peer-to-peer network* because no one computer has a central role in managing the network. Windows XP Home Edition doesn't have all the sophisticated corporate network capabilities of Windows XP Professional and 200x Server, but unless you have more than 10 computers to network, you probably don't *need* all those capabilities. For you, a peer-to-peer network is just the thing to let you share files and printers with your housemates or co-workers. Creating a speedy, useful network isn't nearly as hard or expensive as you might think. In fact, after you've done the planning and shopping, you should be able to get a network up and running in an hour or two.

If you're adding a computer to an existing network, you can skip ahead to the section titled "Installing Network Adapters." If you're setting up a new network, though, just read on. This chapter should give you all the information you need.

> **NOTE**
>
> Windows has a feature called a *direct network connection* that lets you use a serial, parallel, or infrared port to connect two computers without requiring a network adapter. It's not very fast, but it's adequate for one-time file transfers. I'll cover direct connections in Chapter 17, "Windows Unplugged: Remote and Mobile Networking."

> **NOTE**
>
> If you need to network more than 10 computers, you probably should use Windows XP Professional instead of Home Edition, with at least one computer running Windows 200x Server. (By the way, when I say "Windows 200x Server" I mean Windows 2000 Server, Windows Server 2003, or its successors.)

Instant Networking

If your goal is to share printers, files, and maybe an Internet connection between a few computers that are fairly close together, and you don't want to make any decisions, here's a recipe for instant networking. Get the following items at your local computer store, or at an online shop such as www.buy.com. Chain computer or office supply stores are also a good bet if a sale or rebate offer is available.

- One 10/100BASE-T network adapter for each computer that doesn't already have a network interface. These cost $5–$15 for internal PCI cards, and $40 for PCMCIA or USB adapters. (The buy.com category is Computers-Networking-NIC Cards, PC Cards (for laptops), or USB Networks. Choose one of the featured or sale items.)

- A 10/100BASE-T hub with four or more ports for about $10–$40, or a DSL/Cable-sharing or a dial-up gateway router with a built-in four switch/hub, for $20–$90.. (The buy.com category is Computers-Networking-Hubs or Cable/DSL.) I recommend using a router even if you aren't setting up a shared Internet connection.

- One CAT-5 patch cable for each computer. You'll place the hub next to one of the computers, so you'll need one short four-foot cable. The other cables must be long enough to reach from the other computers to the hub. (The buy.com category is Computers-Accessories-Cables.)
- If you have only two computers to hook up and no DSL or cable modem, you can skip the hub and patch cables, and instead get a single *crossover* cable to connect your network adapters directly. (I'll discuss this in more detail under "Connecting Just Two Computers," later in the chapter.)

When you have these parts, skip ahead to the "Installing Network Adapters" section later in this chapter. By the way: I'm not getting a kickback from buy.com! I've just found that buying from them is a no-brainer. Their prices are low enough that it's hardly worth the time to shop around, and more importantly, their service is ultra-reliable and fast.

CHOOSING A NETWORK AND CABLING SYSTEM

For a simple home or small office network, there are three main choices for the type of network connection you'll use:

- 10/100BASE-T (Fast Ethernet), over high-quality CAT-5 UTP wiring
- Phoneline or powerline networking
- 802.11g Wireless networking

I described how these systems work in Chapter 14, "Overview of Windows XP Networking." The 100Mbps wired option is the fastest option, but for the average home or small office network, all three options provide perfectly adequate performance. In the next sections, I'll go over the pros and cons of each type.

TIP

> If your network is small and/or temporary, you can run network cables along walls and desks. Otherwise, you probably should keep them out of the way and protect them from accidental damage by installing them in the walls of your home or office. As you survey your site and plan your network, consider how the network cabling is to be routed.

 If you can't or aren't allowed to drill through your home's or building's walls, see "Can't Drill Through Walls or Ceilings" in the "Troubleshooting" section at the end of this chapter.

10/100BASE-T ETHERNET

10/100BASE-T Ethernet networks use *unshielded twisted-pair cabling*, commonly called *UTP*, *twisted-pair*, or *phone wire*. This last name is a little dangerous because I'm not talking about the thin, flat, ribbon-like cable used to connect a phone to a wall jack, nor is it likely that phone wires installed in the 1930s will work either. The "10/100" part of the name means the equipment can run at 100Mbps but can automatically slow down to 10Mbps if it's connected to older 10BASE-T equipment.

15

These networks require a cable and connectors designated "CAT-5" or better. You can buy premade network cables in lengths from 3 to 50 feet, or you can buy bulk cable and attach the connectors yourself. I'll discuss this more in the "Installing Network Wiring" section later in this chapter.

→ To learn more about UTP wiring, **see** "Unshielded Twisted-Pair (UTP)," **p. 460**.

A cable is run from each computer to a *hub*, which is a small connecting box that routes the signals between each computer. You'll need to get a hub that has at least as many *ports* (sockets) as you have computers, plus a spare or two. 10/100BASE-T hubs cost roughly $5 to 10 per port. A typical setup is shown in Figure 15.1.

Figure 15.1
A 10/100BASE-T network connects each computer to a hub with UTP cabling. It sounds sophisticated, but remember, you can buy this stuff at just about any office supply store.

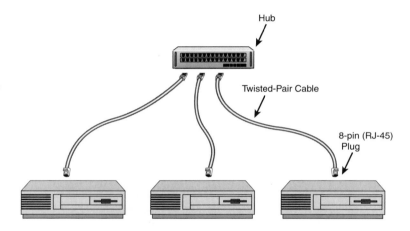

Hub

Twisted-Pair Cable

8-pin (RJ-45) Plug

TIP

> Multiple hubs can be connected if your network grows beyond the capacity of your first hub. You can just add on rather than replace your original equipment.

TIP

> If you have DSL or cable broadband Internet connection, see Chapter 18, "Connecting Your LAN to the Internet," for some advice about hardware connection sharing devices before making any decisions about your network. Some connection sharing routers have a built-in hub, sparing you the expense of buying a separate one.

10/100BASE-T network interface cards (NICs) are available for as little as $5 each (if you catch a sale) and are made by companies such as Intel, 3COM, NETGEAR, Farallon, SMC, Kingston, D-Link, Linksys, Boca, and Cnet. Most "nameless" cheap-o cards are based on one of a handful of standard chipsets, so they'll usually work even if they're not listed in the Windows Catalog at www.windowsmarketplace.com or the Windows 2000 Hardware Compatibility List at www.microsoft.com/hcl.

NOTE

Adapters come in four styles: external adapters that you connect with a USB cable, thin credit-card sized PCMCIA (PC Card) adapters for laptops, and internal PCI cards for desktop computers. If your computer is so old that it has only ISA slots, you need to get a 10BASE-T ISA adapter.

And again, if you want to use existing in-wall wiring for your network, you should be sure it's at least CAT-5 certified.

When you're shopping for a hub, you might see devices called *switches*. Switches are hubs on steroids. Whereas a hub is a simple repeater that forwards received data to every device on the LAN, a switch can route data between several pairs of computers simultaneously, if all are transmitting at once. Switches used to be more expensive than hubs, but the circuitry inside is now mass-produced and cheap enough that there is no longer a price difference. Get the switch type if you can.

TIP

Even if you're not going to set up a shared broadband Internet connection, I recommend that instead of a hub you buy an Internet connection sharing router to use as your network's hub, just to get the DHCP service it provides (more on that later in the chapter). On sale, these routers cost no more than a plain hub. And, in fact, as I write this, today's newspaper has an ad for a router for $20 with a $20 mail-in rebate.

Overall, 10/100BASE-T networking is as inexpensive as it gets—hooking up three computers should set you back under $75. It's easy to set up, and it's very reliable. On the down side, though, you do have to run those wires around and any connectors and wall data jacks used have to be CAT-5 certified as well. If you use in-wall wiring, the work should be done by someone with professional-level skills.

PHONELINE AND POWERLINE NETWORKING

HomePNA (Home Phoneline Networking Association) devices send network data by transmitting radio signals over your existing telephone wiring, using a network adapter that plugs into a telephone jack (see Figure 15.2). These devices don't interfere at all with the normal operation of your telephones; the extra signal just hitchhikes along the wires.

TIP

If you use Phoneline networking, be certain to get only HomePNA 2.0 compatible adapters, or better. This will ensure that your equipment will operate at at least 10Mbps, and will work with other manufacturers' products. Don't get any device that connects through your computer's parallel port: It's too slow!

15

Phoneline networking is intended primarily for home use. The products are relatively inexpensive—about $40–$70 per computer—and don't require you to string cables around the house. However, they have some disadvantages:

- All your adapters must be plugged into the same telephone line. So, the same extension must be present at a phone outlet near each of your computers. If you have to call in a wiring contractor to add a phone extension, you haven't saved much over a wired network.

- "Access Point" devices, used to link standard wired-networked computers to your phoneline network, are relatively rare.

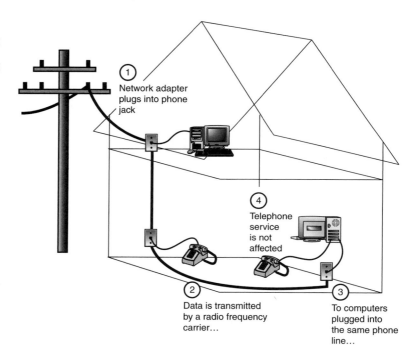

Figure 15.2
Phoneline networking uses existing household telephone wiring to carry a radio frequency signal between networked computers.

① Network adapter plugs into phone jack

④ Telephone service is not affected

② Data is transmitted by a radio frequency carrier…

③ To computers plugged into the same phone line…

Without a hardware access point it's difficult to use a hardware Internet connection sharing device, or to add standard wired computers to your network. However, Windows XP can manage this in software, if necessary. I'll discuss this later in this chapter under "Bridging Two Network Types with Windows XP."

HomePlug (HomePlug Powerline Alliance) adapters work in a similar fashion, sending signals through your electrical wiring, and are plugged into a wall socket. These also provide 10MBps performance and are somewhat more flexible than the phone line system because you don't have to worry about having a phone jack near your computers, just a nearby electrical outlet.

In addition, for about $60 you can get HomePlug devices called *bridges*, which are specifically designed to link a wired network to the powerline network—the Linksys Powerline EtherFast 10/100 Bridge is an example. This means you can easily add a shared Internet connection router or mix in wired computers. Figure 15.3 shows how this would look in a typical home network.

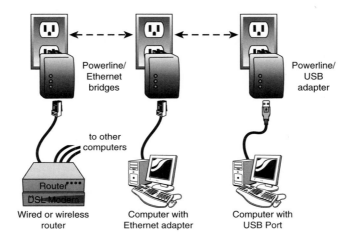

Figure 15.3
Typical powerline networking setup, showing HomePlug adapters and bridges.

802.11G WIRELESS NETWORKING

One way to build a network without hubs, cables, connectors, drills, swearing, tools, or outside contractors is to go wireless. Blocks of radio frequencies in the 2.4GHz (802.11b) and 5GHz (802.11a) band is reserved for close-range data communications, and standardized products from cordless telephones to computer networks are now available to take advantage of this. Prices have fallen to the point that wireless connectivity is now competitive with wired networks, even before the installation cost savings are factored in.

But let me warn you: A wireless network is not anywhere near as reliable as a wired network. Unless you or your dog chews through the cable, after a wired Ethernet network is set up, it should work indefinitely with nary a hitch. Despite the lack of wires, a wireless network is harder to set up, and for your pains, you can expect it to simply stop working for no apparent reason every day or two or three, often requiring you to restart your computers and power cycle the access point. The cost of networking hardware is now so low—no matter what type you choose—that I encourage you to consider the long-term maintenance costs and hassle as major factors in deciding which type of network to set up.

Today's high-speed 802.11g equipment operates at up to 54Mbps and is compatible with older 802.11b (11MBps) equipment. Some manufacturers offer Wireless-G equipment that operates at up to 108Mbps. This is great, but you should know that you get the speed boost only when you buy all your equipment from the same manufacturer (and even then, you have to read the packaging carefully to see whether the double-speed function works with

15

the particular parts you're buying). You also might read about 802.11a equipment. Wireless A is used mainly in corporate environments and is much more expensive than the more modern Wireless G equipment I am recommending.

Wireless networking products typically

- Give actual throughput of about half the advertised speed
- Can transmit data about 100 feet indoors and up to 300 feet outdoors
- Are available for both desktop and laptop computers, in PCI, PCMCIA (PC Card), or USB formats
- Cost between $25 and $70 per adapter
- Can be bridged to a wired LAN through an optional device called an *Access Point*, router, bridge, or base unit, costing $40 and up. (That's not a typo: $40, if you catch a good sale)
- Don't work well between floors of a multistory building.

TIP

> If you do decide to set up a wireless network, regardless of whether you're going to set up a shared Internet connection, you'll save time and money by using a Wireless Internet connection sharing router as your network's access point. A router includes a DHCP server (more on that later) that simplifies setting up your network.

Figure 15.4 shows a typical family of wireless products: a wireless access point (Ethernet bridge), a wireless router that can also share a DSL or cable Internet connection, an internal wireless network adapter for desktop computers, and a PCMCIA adapter for laptops.

Figure 15.4
Typical wireless networking equipment. Clockwise from upper left: access point, router with Internet Connection Sharing capability, PCI adapter, PCMCIA adapter. (Photo used by permission of D-Link.)

15

IEEE-1394 (FIREWIRE) NETWORKING

In addition to the three primary networking options described in the preceding sections, if all you have to do is copy a few files on a one-time basis, there is one other option for "quick and dirty" networking: IEEE-1394. IEEE-1394 is a very high-speed connection technology used primarily to connect portable hard disks and video cameras to computers. This technology is also called FireWire by Apple, and i.LINK by Sony. By any name, it's fast—up to 400Mbps. If two or more of your computers are outfitted with IEEE-1394 (FireWire) ports, you can simply attach your computers together with 1394 cables and forgo the use of network adapters entirely, as Windows XP supports IEEE-1394 for networking use. Because the cables can't be made very long, you'd probably only use this as a temporary arrangement to copy files between two computers.

With 1394, you don't have to worry about hubs and you can connect your computers together in any fashion as long as each computer is connected to at least one other, and as long as there's only one cable connecting any two given computers. Figure 15.5 shows a typical 1394 wiring setup. Connecting computers to computers rather than accessories requires the use of special cables with six pins on each end, called "6-6" cables.

Figure 15.5
Computers net-worked with IEEE-1394 (FireWire) can be connected in any convenient way. The maximum cable length of 15 feet limits the usefulness of 1394 for networking, however, and the price of the cables could bring tears to your eyes.

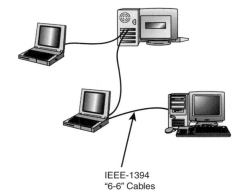

IEEE-1394
"6-6" Cables

If you want to add computers without IEEE-1394 adapters to this sort of network, you'll have to have one computer with both a 1394 port and a standard network adapter. Use the Bridging feature, described later in this chapter, to connect the two network types.

IEEE-1394 is fast and convenient. However, the computers have to be within 15 feet (4.5 meters) of each other, as this is the maximum permitted length of IEEE-1394 cables. And the price of those cables—ouch! I found 15 foot 6-6 cables online at buy.com for $15, but at the local CompUSA, I had to pay $25 for a *three foot* cable! Adding an IEEE-1394 adapter to a computer can cost you an additional $60 or more. With these limitations and prices, I wouldn't buy this stuff just to build a network, or to connect more than two or three computers.

If your computer does have an IEEE-1394 adapter, you'll find an icon for it in the Network Connections page, which we'll discuss later in the chapter. Wherever I mention using an icon for a network adapter, you can use your computer's 1394 Connection icon.

MIXED NETWORKING

If you are updating an existing network or are connecting two separate types of networks, you should consider several factors.

If you have some existing 10Mbps-only devices and want to add new 100Mbps devices without upgrading the old, you can buy a dual-speed (10/100) hub, which connects to each computer at the maximum speed it permits.

But be wary of some so-called *Autosensing 10/100Mbps Hubs*, which purport to let you connect both 10 and 100Mbps devices. Some of these hubs force the entire network to run at 10Mbps if any one device runs this lower speed. Read the specifications carefully. You want a hub that's labeled either "N-way autosensing" or "switching".

TIP

> To speed up a 10Mbps network, instead of replacing all the wiring and network cards in all your computers, upgrade just the network card in your primary computer (file server) to a 100Mbps device. Get a 10/100 switching hub to connect the server to the workstations, and use a CAT-5 cable to connect the server to the new hub. This effectively gives every computer its own full 10Mbps channel to the file server at a minimal cost.

Finally, if you want to mix standard Ethernet, wireless and/or IEEE-1394 devices on your network, you can use the Bridge feature built into Windows XP, or you'll need one of the bridges or access points I mentioned in the previous section. I'll discuss bridging in the section "Bridging Two Network Types with Windows XP," later in this chapter.

PRINTING AND FAXING

Shared printers simply need to be connected their host Windows XP computers with a standard USB or parallel printer cable. If the printer needs to be farther than 10 feet away from a computer, you have three choices:

- Get a really long cable, and take your chances. The electrical signal for printers is not supposed to be stretched more than 10 feet, but I've gotten away with 25 feet in the past. Buy a high-quality shielded cable. You may get data errors (bad printed characters) with this approach.

- Use a network-capable printer. You can buy special network printer modules for some printers, or you can buy special third-party "print server" modules, which connect to the printer port and to a network cable. Network supply catalogs list a myriad of these devices. Some of the newer DSL/cable sharing routers and wireless access points have a print server built in. These are great for small offices.

- Use a printer-extender device. These devices turn the high-speed parallel data signal into a serial data connection somewhat as a modem does. I don't like these as they result in very slow printing.

If your network includes Windows 95, 98, NT 3 or 4, or Windows 3.1 computers, take the time to collect the CDs or floppy disks containing the printer drivers for all the operating systems you use, for each of your printers. Windows XP lets you load in the printer drivers for the older operating systems and lets these computers automatically download the proper printer driver when they use the shared printer. We'll cover this slick feature in Chapter 16, "Using a Windows XP Network."

PROVIDING INTERNET CONNECTIVITY

You probably will want to have Internet access on your LAN. It's far less expensive and far safer security-wise to have one connection to the Net for the entire LAN than to let each user fend for himself or herself.

Windows XP has a built-in Internet Connection Sharing feature that lets a single computer use a dial-up, cable, or DSL modem and make the connection on behalf of any user or users on your LAN. You can also use an inexpensive hardware device called a *router* to make the connection. I strongly prefer the hardware devices over Windows Internet Connection Sharing. This topic is important enough that it gets its own chapter. I recommend that you read Chapter 18 before you buy any equipment.

You also must be sure to study Chapter 19, "Network Security," to build in proper safeguards against hacking and abuse. This is especially important with full-time cable/DSL connections.

PROVIDING REMOTE ACCESS

You also can provide connectivity *in* to your network from the outside world, either through the Internet or via modem. This connectivity lets you get at your LAN resources from home or out in the field, with full assurance that your network is safe from outside attacks. Chapter 17 covers remote access.

If you need to get to your network from outside and you aren't planning to have a permanent direct Internet connection, you might want to plan for the installation of a telephone line near one of your Windows XP computers so that you can set up a dedicated modem line for incoming access.

INSTALLING NETWORK ADAPTERS

If you're installing a new network adapter, follow the manufacturer's instructions for installing with Windows XP or Windows 2000. Even if it does not come with specific Windows XP instructions, the installation should be a snap. Just follow these steps:

1. If you have purchased an internal card, shut down Windows, shut off the computer, unplug it, open the case, install the card in an empty slot, close the case, and restart Windows.

   TIP

   > If you've never worked inside your computer, jump ahead to Chapter 27, "Installing and Replacing Hardware," for advice and handy tips.

   If you are adding a PCMCIA or USB adapter, be sure you're logged on with a "Computer Administrator" account, and then just plug it in while Windows is running.

   If you're using your computer's IEEE-1394 port, there's nothing to install or configure.

2. When you're back at the Windows login screen, log in as a Computer Administrator. Windows displays the New Hardware Detected dialog box when you log in.

3. When Windows boots or detects the device, the New Hardware Detected dialog might instruct you to insert your Windows XP CD-ROM. If Windows cannot find a suitable driver for your adapter from this CD, it might ask you to insert a driver disk that your network card's manufacturer should have provided (either a CD-ROM or floppy disk).

   If you are asked, insert the manufacturer's disk and click OK. If Windows says that it cannot locate an appropriate device driver, try again, and this time click the Browse button. Look for an "INF" file in the floppy disk's top folder, as shown in Figure 15.6. If that fails, look inside any folders named WindowsXP, Windows2000 (or some reasonable approximation), W2K, or NT5. When you've located the setup file, click OK.

   NOTE

   > The exact name of the folder containing your device driver varies from vendor to vendor. You might have to poke around a little on the disk to find it.

4. After Windows has installed the card's driver software, it automatically configures and uses the card. Check the Device Manager (explained earlier) to see whether the card is installed and functioning. Then you can proceed to "Installing Network Wiring" later in this chapter.

→ For more detailed instructions about installing drivers, **see** Chapter 27.

Figure 15.6
If Windows needs help finding the appropriate driver setup file, find the INF file on the floppy disk.

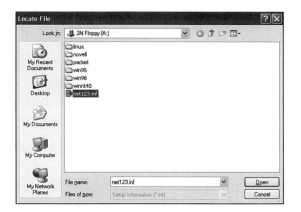

CHECKING EXISTING ADAPTERS

If your adapter was already installed when you set up Windows XP, it might be ready to go, in which case you can skip this section and jump down to "Installing Network Wiring." Follow these steps to see whether the adapter is already set up:

1. Right-click My Computer and select Manage.
2. Select Device Manager in the left pane, and open the Network Adapters list in the right pane.
3. Look for an entry for your network card. If it appears and does not have a yellow exclamation point (!) icon to the left of its name, the card is installed and correctly configured. In this case, you can skip ahead to "Installing Network Wiring."

   If an entry appears but has a yellow exclamation point icon by its name, the card is not correctly configured.

NOTE

> If you see a yellow exclamation point icon in the Network Adapters list, skip ahead to Chapter 20, "Troubleshooting Your Network," for tips on getting the card to work before proceeding. Here's an additional tip: Network adapters are *really* inexpensive. If you're having trouble with an old adapter, just get a new one.

4. If no entry exists for the card, the adapter is not fully plugged into the motherboard, is broken, or is not plug-and-play capable. Be sure the card is installed correctly. If the card is broken or non–plug-and-play, you should replace it. Check out Chapter 27 for troubleshooting tips.

15

INSTALLING MULTIPLE NETWORK ADAPTERS

You might want to install multiple network adapters in your computer if

- You want to simultaneously connect to two or more different networks with different IP addresses or protocols. You'd use a separate adapter to connect to each network.

- You want to share a broadband cable or DSL Internet connection with your LAN without using a hardware sharing router. I strongly recommend using a hardware router, as I'll discuss in Chapter 18, but you can also do it using one adapter to connect to your LAN and another to connect to your cable or DSL modem.

- You have two different network types, such as Phoneline and Ethernet, and want the computers on both LAN types to be able to communicate. You could use a hardware Access Point, but you could also install both types of adapters in one of your computers, and use the Bridging feature to connect the networks. I'll discuss bridging later in this chapter.

I suggest that you use the following procedure to install multiple adapters:

1. Install and configure the first adapter. If you're doing this to share an Internet connection, install and configure the one you'll use for the Internet connection first. Configure and test the Internet connection as well.

2. Click Start, Control Panel, Network and Internet Connections, Network Connections. Select the icon named Local Area Connection and choose Rename This Connection in Network Tasks. (Or, right-click the icon and select Rename.) Change the connection's name to something that indicates what it's used for, such as "Connection to Cable Modem" or "Office Ethernet Network."

3. Write the name on a piece of tape or a sticky label and apply it to the back of your computer above the network adapter, or to the edge plate of the network card.

4. Install the second adapter. Configure it and repeat steps 2 and 3 with the new Local Area Connection icon. Name this connection appropriately, for example "LAN" or "Wireless Net" and put a tape or paper label on the computer too.

If you follow these steps, you'll be able to distinguish the two connections easily in the future, instead of having to remember which "Local Area Connection" icon is which.

INSTALLING NETWORK WIRING

When your network adapters are installed, the next step is to get your computers connected together. Installing the wiring can be the most difficult task of setting up a network. How you proceed depends on the type of networking adapters you have:

- If you're using wireless adapters, of course you don't have to worry about wiring at all. You can just skip ahead to "Installing a Wireless Network," later in this chapter.

15

- If you're using Phoneline networking, plug a standard modular telephone cable into each Phoneline network adapter and connect them to the appropriate wall jacks. The adapter must be plugged directly into the wall jack, and then additional devices such as modems, telephones, and answering machines can be connected to the adapter. Remember that each of the phone jacks must be wired to the same telephone line. Then, skip ahead to the section "Configuring a Peer-to-Peer Network" later in the chapter.

- If you're using a powerline networking adapter, follow the manufacturer's installation instructions. If you're using a powerline bridge, plug the bridge into a wall socket and connect it to your computer or other networked device with a CAT-5 patch cable. Follow the manufacturer's instructions for configuring the adapter's security features. You should enable encryption if it's available. Then, skip ahead to the section "Configuring a Peer-to-Peer Network" later in the chapter.

- If you're using IEEE-1394 networking, buy certified IEEE-1394 cables and plug your computers together as shown in Figure 15.5. Then, skip ahead to the section "Configuring a Peer-to-Peer Network" later in the chapter.

Otherwise, you're using UTP Ethernet adapters and you have to decide how to route your wiring and what type of cables to use. The remainder of this section discusses UTP wiring.

CABLING FOR ETHERNET NETWORKS

If your computers are close together, you can use pre-built *patch cables* to connect your computers to a hub. (The term patch cable originated in the telephone industry—in the old days, switchboard operators used patch cables to temporarily connect, or patch, one phone circuit to another. In networking, the term refers to cables that are simply plugged in and not permanently wired.)You can run these cables through the habitable area of your home or office by routing them behind furniture, around partitions, and so on. Just don't put them where they'll be crushed, walked on, tripped over, or run over by desk chair wheels. Hardware stores sell special cable covers you can use if you need to run a cable where it's exposed to foot traffic, as well as covers for wires that need to run up walls or over doorways.

If the cables need to run through walls or stretch long distances, you should consider having them installed inside the walls with plug-in jacks, just like your telephone wiring. I'll discuss this later in this section.

TIP

As you install each network card and plug it into the cables running to your hub, you should see a green light come on at the hub and on the network adapter. These lights indicate that the network wiring is correct.

 If you don't get green lights, stop immediately and get the wiring fixed. See "Hub Lights Do Not Come On" in the "Troubleshooting" section at the end of this chapter.

15

GENERAL CABLING TIPS

You can determine how much cable you need by measuring the distance between computers and your hub location(s). Remember to account for vertical distances, too, where cables run from the floor up to a desktop, or go up and over a partition or wall.

CAUTION

If you have to run cables through the ceiling space of an office building, you should check with your building management to see whether the ceiling is listed as a *plenum* or air-conditioning air return. You may be required by law to use certified *plenum cable* and follow all applicable electrical codes. Plenum cable is specially formulated not to emit toxic smoke in a fire.

Keep in mind the following points:

- Existing household telephone wire probably won't work. If the wires are red, green, black, and yellow; no way. The cable jacket must have CAT-5 (or higher) printed on it. It must have color-matched twisted pairs of wires; usually, each pair has one wire in a solid color and the other white with colored stripes.

- You must use CAT-5 quality wiring and components throughout: Not just the cables, but also any jacks, plugs, connectors, terminal blocks, patch cables, and so on must be CAT-5 certified.

- If you're installing in-wall wiring, follow professional CAT-5 wiring practices throughout. Be sure not to untwist more than half an inch of any pair of wires when attaching cables to connectors. Don't solder or splice the wires.

- When you're installing cables, be gentle. Don't pull, kink, or stretch them. Don't bend them sharply around corners; you should allow at least a one-inch radius for bends. And don't staple or crimp them. To attach cables to a wall or baseboard, use rigid cable clips that don't squeeze the cable, as shown in Figure 15.7. Your local electronics store can sell you the right kind of clips.

Figure 15.7
Use rigid cable clips or staples that don't squeeze the cable if you nail it to a wall or baseboard.

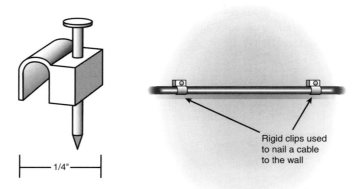

1/4"

Rigid clips used to nail a cable to the wall

■ Keep network cables away from AC power wiring and away from electrically noisy devices such as arc welders, diathermy machines, and the like.

NOTE

If you really want to get into the nuts and bolts, so to speak, of pulling your own cable, a good starting point is Que's *Practical Network Cabling*, which will help you roll up your shirtsleeves and get dirty (literally, if you have to crawl around through your attic or wrestle with dust bunnies under too many desks at the office).

WIRING WITH PATCH CABLES

If your computers are close together and you can simply run prefabricated cables between your computers and hub, you've got it made! Buy CAT-5 cables of the appropriate length online or at your local computer store. Just plug (click!), and you're finished. Figure 15.1, earlier in this chapter, shows how to connect your computers to the hub.

If you have the desire and patience, you can build custom-length cables from crimp-on connectors and bulk cable stock. Making your own cables requires about $75 worth of tools, though, and more detailed instructions than I can give here. Making just a few cables certainly doesn't make buying the tools worthwhile. Factory-assembled cables are also more reliable than homemade ones because the connectors are attached by machine. They're worth the extra few dollars.

For the ambitious or parsimonious reader, Figure 15.8 shows the correct way to order the wires in the connector.

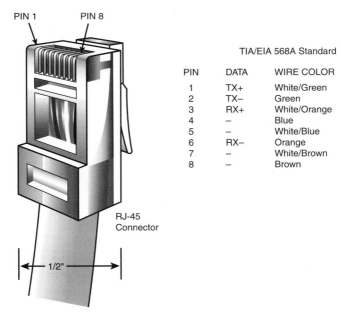

Figure 15.8
Standard wiring order for UTP network cables.

PIN 1   PIN 8

RJ-45 Connector

1/2"

TIA/EIA 568A Standard

PIN	DATA	WIRE COLOR
1	TX+	White/Green
2	TX–	Green
3	RX+	White/Orange
4	–	Blue
5	–	White/Blue
6	RX–	Orange
7	–	White/Brown
8	–	Brown

INSTALLING IN-WALL WIRING

In-wall wiring is the most professional and permanent way to go. However, this often involves climbing around in the attic or under a building, drilling through walls, or working in an office telephone closet. If this is the case, calling in a professional is probably best. Personally, I find it a frustrating task and one I would rather watch someone else. Hiring someone to get the job done might cost $30 to $75 per computer, but you'll get a professional job, and if you consider that the price of network cards has gone down at least this much in the last few years, you can pretend that you're getting the wiring thrown in free.

TIP

> Look in the yellow pages under Telephone Wiring, and ask the contractors you call whether they have experience with network wiring. The following are some points to check out when you shop for a wiring contractor:
>
> - Ask for references, and check them out.
> - Ask for billing details up front: Do they charge by the hour or at a fixed rate? Do they sell equipment themselves, or do you have to supply cables, connectors, and so on?
> - Ask for prices for parts and labor separately so that you know whether you're getting a good deal and can comparison-shop.
> - Find out what their guaranteed response time is, should problems or failures occur in the future.
> - Ask what the warranty terms are. How long are parts and labor covered?

At each computer, in-wall wiring is brought out to special network-style modular jacks mounted to the baseboard of your wall. These "RJ-45" jacks look like telephone modular jacks but are wider. Near the hub, the cables will either be fitted with RJ-45 connectors, or they'll end in a special "patch panel," as shown in Figure 15.9. You'll need patch cables to connect the jacks to your computers and hub.

Figure 15.9
Connect your computers and hub to the network jacks using short patch cables.

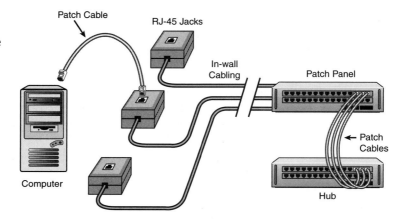

Patch Cable

RJ-45 Jacks

In-wall Cabling

Patch Panel

Patch Cables

Computer

Hub

OUT OF THE (PHONE) CLOSET

If you're wiring an office, running all your network wiring alongside the office's phone system wiring to a central location—the phone closet—may be most sensible. You might be able to put your hub near the phone equipment in this case. Your building might even already have CAT-5 wiring in place.

In most office buildings, telephone and data wiring are run to a central location on each floor or in each office suite. Connector blocks called *punchdown blocks* are bolted to the wall, where your individual telephone extension wires are joined to thick distribution cables maintained by the phone company or the building management.

These commercial wiring systems are a little bit daunting, and if you aren't familiar with them, it's best to hire a wiring contractor to install your network wiring.

CONNECTING JUST TWO COMPUTERS

If you're making a network of just two computers, you might be able to take a shortcut and eliminate the need for a network hub or additional special hardware. If you want to add on to your network later, you can always add the extra gear then.

If you're connecting two computers with IEEE-1394, you have the simplest possible cabling setup: Just plug one end of a "6-6" cable into a free IEEE-1394 socket on each computer.

If you are connecting two computers with Ethernet, yours is the second easiest possible network installation: Simply run a special cable called a *crossover cable* from one computer's network adapter to the other, and you're finished. This special type of cable reverses the send and receive signals between the two ends, and eliminates the need for a hub. You can purchase a crossover cable from a computer store or network supply shop, or make one as shown in Figure 15.10. The cable in Figure 15.10 can be used with 10, 100, or 1000BASE-T network adapters.

TIP

> Be sure your crossover cable is labeled as such, as it won't work to connect a computer to a hub and you'll go nuts wondering what's wrong if you try. Factory-made models usually have yellow ends. When I make them myself, I draw three rings around each end of the cable with a permanent-ink marker.

NOTE

> Windows has a feature called a *Direct Network Connection* that lets you use a serial, parallel, or infrared port to connect two computers without a network adapter. This type of connection lets you copy files but isn't as convenient as a full-fledged network setup. I'll cover Direct Network Connection in Chapter 17.

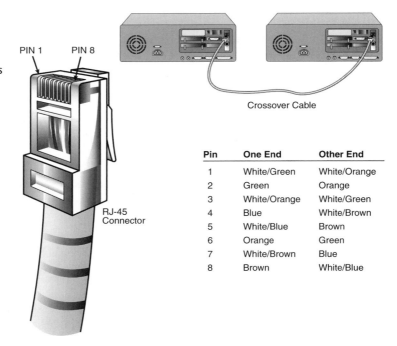

Figure 15.10
Wiring for a UTP crossover cable. The cable reverses the send and receive wires so that two network cards can be directly connected without a hub. Note that the green/orange and blue/brown pairs are reversed across the cable.

PIN 1   PIN 8

RJ-45 Connector

Crossover Cable

Pin	One End	Other End
1	White/Green	White/Orange
2	Green	Orange
3	White/Orange	White/Green
4	Blue	White/Brown
5	White/Blue	Brown
6	Orange	Green
7	White/Brown	Blue
8	Brown	White/Blue

CONNECTING MULTIPLE HUBS

You might want to use more than one hub to reduce the number of long network cables you need if you have groups of computers in two or more locations. For example, you can connect the computers on each "end" of the network to the nearest hub, and then connect the hubs to a main hub. Figure 15.11 shows a typical arrangement using this technique.

> **NOTE**
>
> A cascade port is a hub connector designed to be connected to another hub. Some hubs have a separate connector for this purpose, whereas others make one of the hub's regular ports do double-duty by providing a switch that turns the last hub port into a cascade port. Refer to your hub's manual to see what to do with your particular hardware.

If you have to add a computer to your LAN and your hub has no unused connectors, you don't need to replace the hub. You can just add an additional hub. To add a computer to a fully-loaded hub, you must unplug one cable from the original hub to free up a port. Connect this cable and your new computer to the new hub. Finally, connect the new hub's *cascade* or *uplink port* to the original hub's free port, as shown in Figure 15.12. The instructions included with your hub will describe how to connect two hubs. Some hubs have a dedicated uplink port, whereas others have a switch that turns a regular port into an uplink port.

Figure 15.11
You can connect groups of computers with multiple hubs to reduce the number of long cables needed. Use the cascade port on the remote hubs to connect to the central hub.

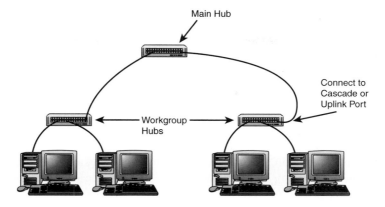

Main Hub

Connect to Cascade or Uplink Port

Workgroup Hubs

Figure 15.12
You can expand your network by cascading hubs. The instructions included with your hub describe how to connect two hubs using a patch cable. Some hubs have a dedicated uplink port, whereas others have a switch that turns a regular port into an uplink port.

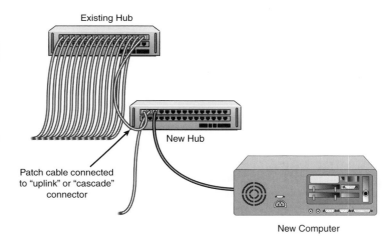

Existing Hub

New Hub

Patch cable connected to "uplink" or "cascade" connector

New Computer

Now, skip ahead to "Configuring a Peer-to-Peer Network."

INSTALLING A WIRELESS NETWORK

If you are installing a wireless network, after installing your network adapters you have to configure wireless security and networking options.

NOTE

This section describes how to set up a wireless network in a home or small office. On a corporate wireless network, your network administrator will most likely be the one to configure the wireless adapter and security settings.

15

CAUTION

> If you want to use file and printer sharing on your wireless network, you must make the network secure by assigning a cryptographic key to the network. Otherwise, random people will be able to get at your computer.
>
> If you want to set up an open wireless hotspot to share your Internet connection with friends, neighbors, or the world, that's great, but you must not use file and printer sharing on the same network. Please see Chapter 18 for safer options.

Here's the scoop: It can easily happen that separate groups of people with wireless network gear set up within radio range of each other. In my office, I can pick up signals from four separate wireless networks: mine, the office next door's, a friend's from nearly a block away, and one other (I can't tell whose it is). Even in the suburbs, it's not uncommon to be able to receive signals from several neighbors. And people do actually drive around with laptops in their cars, looking for free Internet access.

So, to distinguish your network's signal from others, and to secure your network, you must make four choices when you set up a wireless network:

- **A service set identifier (SSID)**—A short name that you give your network, up to 32 characters in length. This could be your last name, company name, pet's name, or whatever makes sense to you.

- **An encryption type**—A choice of the protocol and "strength" of the code used to secure the network against eavesdropping. The choices are, in order of increasing security: none, WEP 40-bit (also called 64-bit), WEP 128-bit, and WPA 128-bit. WEP stands for Wired Equivalent Privacy, but that turned out to be overoptimistic because WEP security can be broken in as little as a few hours by a determined interloper. Wi-Fi Protected Access (WPA) is the new, improved encrypting scheme, but not every network adapter and driver supports it. Select the highest security method supported by all your network gear, including any access points or routers. (If your router doesn't support WPA, you might be able to install updated firmware to get it. Windows XP Service Pack 2 provides WPA support for Windows XP. You need to download updated driver software to get WPA support for older versions of Windows.)

- **An encryption key**—A string of hexadecimal digits, that is, the numbers 0–9 and the letters A–F. Some wireless networking software lets you generate a key from an ordinary text password, but this method doesn't work when you use equipment from different manufacturers. I recommend that you just deal with the cumbersome numeric key. 40-bit security requires a 10-character key, which would look like this: `47A014C65F`. 128-bit security requires a 26-character key. (If you're doing the math, you're right, that adds up to only 104 bits, but that's the way it works.)

  This should be kept secret because it's the key to your network and shared files.

- **A channel**—It selects the frequency used to transmit your network's data. In the United States, this is a number between 1 and 11; the numbers might be different in other countries. The most common channels used are 1, 6, and 11. Start with channel 6.

15

If you have a router or an access point, you are setting up what is called an *infrastructure network*. Windows XP has a wizard to help you choose the correct settings. If you have an access point or a router, skip ahead to the next section, "Using the Wireless Network Setup Wizard."

JOINING AN AD HOC NETWORK

If you aren't using an access point or a wireless router, you're setting up what's called an *ad hoc* network. In this case, you have to configure each computer manually, using this procedure:

1. The Notification area at the bottom of your screen should show a small Wireless Network icon with a red X that indicates that there is no active connection. Right-click this icon and select Open Network Connections.

2. Right-click the Wireless Network Connection icon and select Properties.

3. Select the Wireless Networks tab and click Add.

4. In the Wireless Network Properties dialog box (see Figure 15.13), enter your chosen network name (SSID). Set Network Authentication to Open and Data encryption to WEP or WPA (only if all your devices support WPA).

Figure 15.13
Enter your choice of a network name and security settings.

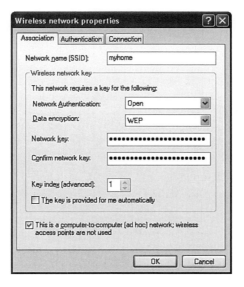

5. Uncheck The Key Is Provided for Me Automatically. Enter your chosen network key of 10 or 26 hexadecimal digits (numbers 0–9 and/or letters A–F). Enter it again to confirm.

6. Check This Is a Computer to Computer (Ad Hoc) Network, and then click OK.

15

7. If other people's networks are listed in the top of the dialog box, click Advanced, select Computer-to-Computer (Ad Hoc) Network Only), and click OK. This prevents your computer from recognizing access points.

Now with your ad-hoc network established, go to your other computers and repeat this process.

NOTE

> If you use the Advanced setting Computer-to-Computer (Ad Hoc) Networks Only and later want to use wireless networking in an office, home, or Internet café, you have to change this setting back to Any Available Network before you can use those networks.

USING THE WIRELESS NETWORK SETUP WIZARD

As mentioned in the previous section, you have to select four things to set up a wireless network: an SSID (name), an encryption type, an encryption key, and a channel number. If you're using a wireless access point or router, starting with Windows XP Service Pack 2 you can use the Wireless Network Setup Wizard to help you select and copy these settings to each computer on your network, and even to your router if it supports automatic configuration via a USB memory device.

If you want to add a computer to an existing wireless network, see the next section, "Joining an Existing Wireless Network."

To set up a new wireless network, follow this procedure:

1. Open My Network Places from the Start menu. In the Network Tasks list, select Set Up a Wireless Network for a Home or Small Office. When the wizard appears, select Set Up a New Wireless Network.

2. In the first screen (see Figure 15.14), enter a name for your wireless network and indicate whether you want Windows to create a random key for you or you want to enter your own. Also, if all your wireless equipment supports WPA encryption, check the Use WPA box at the bottom of the screen. Then, click Next.

3. If you elect to enter the key manually, Windows displays a page asking for the network key. Unless you're concerned that someone is peeking over your shoulder, uncheck Hide Characters As I Type. Enter 10 or 26 hexadecimal digits (digits 0–9 and/or letters A–F; upper/lower case doesn't matter), as shown in Figure 15.15, and enter them again to confirm. Click Next to proceed.

4. Now for the clever part (see Figure 15.16). If you have a USB-based keychain Flash memory device or have a USB-connected digital camera memory card reader that presents the memory cards as disk drives on your computer, you can use this device to copy the settings from one computer to another, and even to your wireless router if it has a USB port. Windows copies a file containing the settings and an "autoplay" program that loads the settings when you plug the card into each computer. (You can also

make this selection and use a floppy disk, if you want.) You can also choose to copy the settings manually. Make your selection and click Next.

Figure 15.14
The first page of the Wireless Network Setup Wizard lets you select a network name and choose which type of encryption to use.

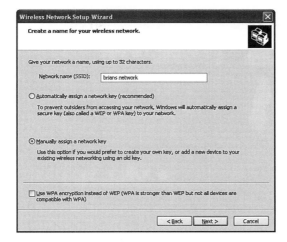

Figure 15.15
If you're entering a key manually, uncheck Hide Characters As I Type so you can see what you're typing.

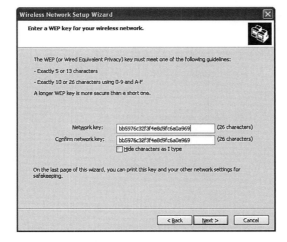

5. If you chose to use the USB device, Windows asks you to insert the device and then select the corresponding drive letter. You can also select your floppy drive here. Click Next and Windows copies the necessary files.

   After Windows copies the files, click Print Network Settings to get a copy of the settings. You'll need this as a backup and might need it to configure your router. Click Next; Windows prompts you to configure your access point and other computers before proceeding. (When you've done that, come back to this computer, reinsert the USB drive, and click Next so Windows can erase the secret key information from the USB drive.)

15

Figure 15.16
Select the means you want to use to copy the wireless settings.

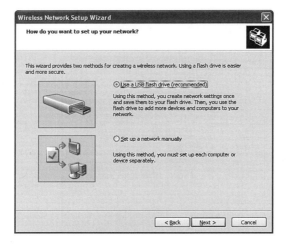

If you chose to copy the settings manually, click the Print button. Windows opens a Notepad window containing the wireless settings. Click File, Print to print a copy. The printout will look like this:

```
Wireless Network Settings

Print this document and store it in a safe place for future reference.
You may need these settings to add additional computers and devices to
your network.

Wireless Settings

Network Name (SSID): brians network
Network Key (WEP/WPA Key): bb5976c32f3f4e8d9fc6a0a969
Key Provided Automatically (802.1x): 0
Network Authentication Type: open
Data Encryption Type: WEP
Connection Type: ESS
Key Index: 1
```

6. At this point, the wizard has already set up the Windows XP computer you're using to automatically connect to your new network after it's up and running.

7. Configure your router or access point next. If it has a USB port and you're using a USB device, plug the USB memory unit into the router. It should blink its lights and load the settings within 30 seconds. If you're using a manual setup, use the printed list of settings and enter this information into your router's setup screens.

8. Finally, configure the other computers on your network, using one of these methods:

   • If you're using a USB device, plug the device into the computer. The Wireless Network Setup Wizard should run automatically and add the computer to the wireless network.

15

- If you're using a floppy disk, insert the disk in each computer and use My Computer or Windows Explorer to locate and double-click the file SetupSNK.EXE. This adds the computer to the wireless network.
- If you're adding computers manually, go to each computer. Use the printed sheet of setup information to add the computer to the network. I'll cover this procedure in the next section.

9. If you're using a USB device, when you're finished with the other computers, go back to the first computer, reinsert the disk, and click Next on the screen remaining from when you first ran the wizard. This erases the sensitive key information from the USB drive.

If you later need to add more computers to the network, you can rerun the wizard on the computer you started with, and it will walk you through the process of reinstalling the setup software on your USB drive or reprinting the instruction sheet. Or, you can follow the procedure in the next section to join them to the network manually.

When all of your computers have joined the wireless network, skip to next section and continue with "Configuring a Peer-to-Peer Network."

JOINING AN EXISTING WIRELESS NETWORK

If you are using a wireless connection on a corporate network, your wireless configuration can and should be managed by your network administrators. Most likely, your administrator will install a security certificate file that identifies your computer as one authorized to use the wireless network. It's also likely that you won't have to make any manual settings to use the network.

However, if your home or small office wireless network has already been configured and you're just adding a new computer—or, if you are taking your computer into someone's work or home and want to use her wireless network—you have to take some steps to be able to use the network. You can use the Wireless Network Setup Wizard discussed in the previous section, or you can connect to and use the network by following this manual procedure:

1. In the notification area at the bottom corner of your screen, locate the Wireless Connection icon (shown here to the right). Double-click it.

2. Windows displays a list the names (SSIDs) of the wireless networks it "hears," as shown in Figure 15.17. Click the network you want to use and click Connect.

NOTE

If the network you want to use doesn't appear, it could be because the signal is too weak. Also, some people prevent their routers from broadcasting the SSID names over the airwaves. (This doesn't really provide much extra security because hackers can find the network anyway.) If the network you want to use isn't broadcasting its SSID, you have to enter the information manually. Follow the procedure under "Joining an Ad Hoc Network" earlier in the chapter, except don't check This Is a Computer-To-Computer (Ad Hoc) Network in step 6.

Figure 15.17
Windows displays the names of the networks whose signals it can receive.

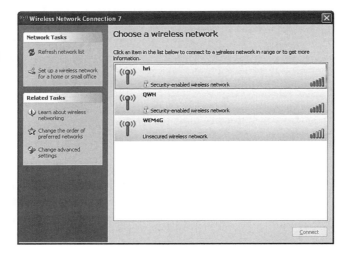

3. Windows determines which type of security the network is using and, if the network is encrypted, it prompts you to enter the network key. Enter the 10- or 26-digit key that was used to set up the network to begin with.

NOTE

We'll talk more about managing connections to multiple wireless networks in Chapter 17.

After the wireless connections are made, you can continue setting up the rest of your network, as described in the following sections.

CONFIGURING A PEER-TO-PEER NETWORK

When you're sure that the physical connection between your computers is set up correctly, you're ready to configure Windows XP. With today's Plug and Play network cards and with all the needed software built into Windows, this configuration is a snap.

You have two choices for configuring your network software. You can make the settings manually, or you can let the Network Setup Wizard do the work for you.

NOTE

You *must* run the Network Setup Wizard at least once. Windows XP's networking features are initially disabled in order to protect you from Internet hacking. The Wizard enables networking after ensuring that your Internet connection is secure.

If you want to set up your network manually, you still must run the wizard first and then go through the network settings.

15

CONFIGURING THE TCP/IP PROTOCOL

After your network adapters are installed—and, if you're using a wired network, cabled together—you need to ensure that each computer is assigned an IP address. This is a number that uniquely identifies the computer on the network. The three ways that these numbers can be assigned are as follows:

- If the network has a computer that uses Windows Internet Connection Sharing to share an Internet connection, or if there is a hardware Internet sharing router, each computer should be assigned an IP address automatically—they're doled out by the DHCP service that runs on the sharing computer or in the router. This is why I recommend using a router even if you aren't setting up a shared Internet connection.

- Each computer can be given an address manually, which is called a *static* address as opposed to dynamic (automatic).

- If no static settings are made, but there is no DHCP server on the network, Windows automatically assigns IP addresses anyway. However, even though the network will work, this is not an ideal situation and can slow down Windows.

If you're setting up a new computer on an existing network, just use whatever scheme the existing computers use; check their settings and follow suit with your new one. The following procedures show you how. If you're setting up a new computer, follow these steps to ensure that the network is set up correctly:

1. Open the Network Connections window. Right-click the Local Area Connection or Wireless Connection icon corresponding to your LAN connection and select Properties.

2. Highlight Internet Protocol (TCP/IP), as shown in Figure 15.18, and click Properties.

Figure 15.18
Highlight your LAN connection's Internet Protocol entry and click Properties to configure TCP/IP.

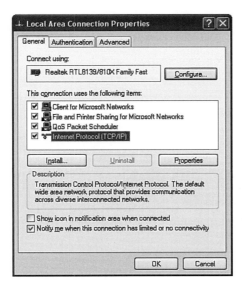

Figure 15.19
Internet Protocol
(TCP/IP) Properties is
the place to make IP
Address settings.

3. Make the appropriate settings in the Properties page, shown in Figure 15.19:

- If you are going to use Windows Internet Connection Sharing, first set up the one computer that will be sharing its connection, as described in Chapter 18.

  All the computers, including the one sharing its Internet connection, should be set for automatic configuration, as shown in Figure 15.19.

- If you are going to use a hardware router, configure the router first, following the manufacturer's instructions. Enable its DHCP feature. Set the starting DHCP IP address to 100, so that numbers from 2 to 99 can be used for computers with static settings. Also, if your ISP has provided you with static IP address settings, be sure to enter your ISP's DNS server addresses in the router's setup screens so it can pass them to the computers that rely on the router for their IP setups. (For more information about configuring a shared Internet connection, see Chapter 18.)

  Then, all your computers should be set as shown in Figure 15.19.

- If you will not have a shared Internet connection, you should configure your network with static IP address information. Assign a unique number to each of your computers, starting with 2 and counting up. Make the following settings in the Internet Protocol Properties page:

  - **Use the Following IP Address**—Select this item.

  - **IP Address**—Enter **192.168.0.x**, replacing *x* with the number you chose for this particular computer.

- **Subnet Mask**—Enter `255.255.255.0`.
- **Default Gateway**—Leave this blank.
- **Obtain DNS Server Address Automatically**—Select this.

TIP

> If your computer will move back and forth between networks that use automatic configuration and a network that uses static settings—for example, between work and home—make the static settings in the Alternate Configuration tab. This way, Windows will use the static settings only when a DHCP server is not present.

USING THE NETWORK SETUP WIZARD

Windows XP comes with a Network Setup Wizard program you must run after installing your network. Its purpose is to configure your computer based on its relationship to other computers on your network and to the Internet.

Even if you want to manage all the setup details yourself, on a Workgroup-type network you still have to run the Network Setup Wizard at least once; until you do, file and printer sharing is disabled. Then, after running the wizard, you can skip to "Manually Configuring Your Network," later in this chapter.

NOTE

> If you're going to use Microsoft's Internet Connection Sharing, configure the computer that will be sharing its Internet connection first. Establish and test its Internet connection, and only then configure the other computers. I'll describe this procedure in detail in Chapter 18. Otherwise, you can configure your computers in any order.

To start the wizard, click Start, Control Panel, Network and Internet Connections. From the task list, select Read the Checklist for Creating a Network if you wish, and then click Next again. Follow the wizard through the following steps.

SELECTING A CONNECTION METHOD

The wizard asks you to select a statement that best describes your computer's relationship to other computers on your network and to the Internet. The choices offered by the wizard are confusing, so I'll give a more detailed list of the various ways your computer might be set up. Identify the scenario in Table 15.1 that describes the particular computer you're setting up, and make the indicated selection in the wizard.

TABLE 15.1   CONNECTION SCENARIOS FOR THE NETWORK SETUP WIZARD

Your Computer...	Make This Selection in the Wizard
...will connect to the Internet via its own modem. You want to share this Internet connection with the rest of the network.	This Computer Connects Directly to the Internet. The Other Computers on My Network Connect to the Internet Through This Computer.
...has two network adapters: one for the LAN and a second one that connects to a cable or DSL modem. You want to share this Internet connection with the rest of the network.	
...will connect to the Internet via its own modem. It is not to share its Internet connection with the rest of the network.	Other, Next, This Computer Belongs to a Network That Does Not Have an Internet Connection.
...will be participating on the network for file and printer sharing only, and no computer on the network uses the Internet.	
...has no *direct* Internet connection of its own. It is to use a shared Internet connection that is made by a hardware Internet connection sharing router (wired or wireless), or by some other computer on the network that is set up to share its connection.	This Computer Connects to the Internet Through a Residential Gateway or Through Another Computer on the Network.
...is on a corporate network. The Internet is available via the network, it has a firewall, and there are people who ensure your connection is safe.	
...will be using the network for file and printer sharing only and won't use the Internet. However, other computers on the network do use the Internet.	
...has one network adapter. A cable modem is connected directly to the network (to the same network hub), and you're paying for multiple computers to use the cable Internet service.	Other, Next, This Computer Connects to the Internet Directly or Through a Network Hub. Other Computers on My Network also Connect to the Internet Directly or Through a Hub.

Your Computer...	Make This Selection in the Wizard
...has two network adapters: one for a LAN and a second one that connects to a cable or DSL modem (directly or through a separate hub). This computer is not to share the Internet connection with the rest of the network.	→ You must take additional steps to secure your computer from hackers. **See** the following note for details.
...uses a wireless Internet connection provided by a router or an access point, and no WEP or WPA security key is required for this connection.	

15

CAUTION

If you have a network adapter that connects directly to the Internet via a cable or DSL modem or through an unsecured Wireless connection, you should select This Computer Connects to the Internet Directly or Through a Network Hub. Windows offers to turn off file and printer sharing; you should accept this offer. Windows also turns on the Windows Firewall to offer some protection against hackers.

However, this is not enough because some other people on the same Internet service—people you don't know—will still be able to read and possibly change your shared files! You must ensure that file and printer sharing are disabled on the connection that goes to the Internet.

To disable File and Printer sharing, use the following procedure:

1. Open the Network Connections window.

2. Right-click the icon for the connection that goes directly to the Internet; this will be a Wireless Connection icon, or the Local Area Connection icon for the adapter that goes to the Cable/DSL modem. Select Properties.

3. Uncheck Client for Microsoft Networks and File and Printer Sharing for Microsoft Networks. Then, click OK.

4. If you have another wireless or local area connection that goes to a separate LAN that you'll use for file and printer sharing, repeat this process for that connection, but this time ensure that Client for Microsoft Networks and File and Printer Sharing for Microsoft Networks are checked.

After making the appropriate connection selection, click Next and continue.

SELECTING YOUR INTERNET CONNECTION

If you indicated that you will be sharing your computer's Internet connection or two network adapters exist in your computer, Windows asks you to select the one that is used to connect directly to the Internet (see Figure 15.20). If you use a dial-up or PPPoE connection (a type of DSL service), select the appropriate dial-up connection. Otherwise, select the network adapter that connects to your Internet service. Then, click Next.

Figure 15.20
Choose the appropriate connection to be used for your Internet service.

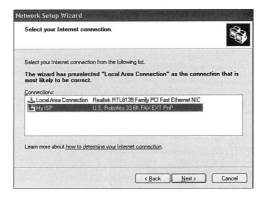

GIVING THIS COMPUTER A DESCRIPTION AND NAME

Enter a brief description of the computer (such as its location or primary user) and a name for the computer. For the name, use just letters and/or numbers with no spaces or punctuation. Each computer on your LAN must have a different name.

Some Internet service providers, especially cable providers, require you use a name that they'll provide. (If you have a hardware connection sharing device hooked up to your cable modem, the hardware device will use that name and you can use any names you want on your LAN).

NAMING YOUR NETWORK

Choose a name for your network workgroup. The wizard always tries to get you to use the name MSHOME, but you can change it. This name is used to identify which computers should appear in your list of network choices later on. All computers on your LAN should have the same workgroup name, so if you don't use MSHOME, be careful to enter the selected name on every computer. If you have an existing network, be careful to enter the same workgroup name that the other computers use.

NOTE

The workgroup name must be different than all the computer names.

READY TO APPLY NETWORK SETTINGS

Review the list of selections you've made and either click Back to correct them or click Next to proceed.

YOU'RE ALMOST DONE

You'll need to run the wizard on the other computers on your LAN. If all the computers use Windows XP, select Just Finish the Wizard, and repeat the wizard process on the other computers. If you have computers running versions of Windows 95, 98, Me, NT, or 2000, you can create a diskette that will let you run the wizard on these older machines, or you can use your Windows XP CD-ROM in these computers.

NOTE

> To create a diskette for an older version of Windows, choose Create a Network Setup Disk, and insert a blank, formatted floppy disk. If you ran the wizard earlier and just changed some of the settings, choose Use the Network Setup Disk I Already Have, and re-insert the Setup Disk you created earlier.

When the Network Setup Wizard is complete, you should verify that the Windows Firewall is correctly set up to protect your network from Internet hackers.

CONFIGURING THE WINDOWS FIREWALL

After running the Network Setup Wizard, you must check that the Windows Firewall is set up correctly; otherwise, you could end up exposed to Internet hacking or find that your network is so locked down that you can't use file and printer sharing. The Windows Firewall is discussed in detail in Chapter 19.

In this section I'll assume that your network is not protected by a professionally installed firewall. Home and small office users should go through this quick checklist of steps to confirm that your network will function safely. The critical points are highlighted in boldface:

1. Open the Windows Firewall window. You can get there from Start, Control Panel, Security Center, Windows Firewall.

2. **On the General tab, be sure that On is checked.** Don't Allow Exceptions should normally be unchecked to use your LAN for file and printer sharing.

3. On the Exceptions tab, be sure that the File and Printer Sharing entry is checked. Highlight this entry and click Edit. **The dialog box that appears should list the word Subnet four times, as shown in Figure 15.21. If any entry says Any rather than Subnet, you must change it.** Highlight the entry, click Change Scope, and select My Subnet Only.

   Other entries present might also be checked, and they should also be set for subnet access only.

Figure 15.21
The File and Printer Sharing service must be open to the local subnet only.

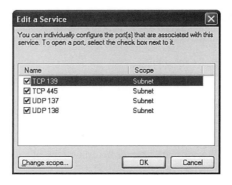

4. **On the Advanced tab, every connection name should have a check mark next to it.** Check any that are missing.

5. Click OK to close the Windows Firewall dialog box and the Security Center window.

6. If your computer connects to the Internet only via the LAN—that is, through a connection shared by a router or some other computer on your network—you can stop here. Otherwise, continue.

   If you computer connects directly to the Internet via a modem or network adapter that connects to a broadband modem, **Windows Firewall is not sufficient to protect you from hacking by other people who use your same ISP!** You must take the following steps to protect yourself.

7. Open the Network Connections window; if it's not on your Start menu, click Start, Control Panel, Network and Internet Connections, Network Connections.

8. For each icon that represents a direct connection to the Internet (dial-up icons or local area connections that connect directly to a broadband modem), right-click the icon and select Properties.

9. On the General tab, be sure that the only two items checked are Internet Protocol (TCP/IP) and QoS Packet Scheduler, as shown in Figure 15.22. **Be sure that File and Printer Sharing and any Client for items are not checked.** Check all the connections that lead directly to the Internet itself.

This completes the procedure for setting up Windows networking on one Windows XP computer. Repeat the wizard procedure on your other computers, and you'll be able to start using your network.

If the other computers are running a version of Windows earlier than XP, you need to use either the network setup disk you created earlier or the Windows XP CD-ROM. To fire up the wizard from a disk, insert the disk into the older computer, click Start and Run, type **a:setup**, and press Enter.

Figure 15.22
Connections that lead directly to the Internet must have only the Internet Protocol and QoS items checked.

To use the CD-ROM, insert the CD-ROM in the older computer and wait for it to autorun the Windows setup program. Select Perform Additional Tasks, and then select Set Up Home or Small Office Networking.

MANUALLY CONFIGURING YOUR NETWORK

When it first detects your network card, Windows installs most of the necessary network software components automatically. This can occur during the initial installation of Windows XP or when you later add a network card. I suggest that you go through the installed components, as I'll describe below, to be sure that everything is set up correctly.

ADDING NETWORK CLIENTS, SERVICES, AND PROTOCOLS

When your network card and its drivers are installed, Windows knows the card is there but doesn't have any networking software attached to it. Use the following procedure to attach the networking protocols and services you'll need.

Choose Start, Control Panel, Network and Internet Connections and Network Connections. Double-click Local Area Connection and select Properties. You should see a Properties dialog with your network card named at the top under Connect Using. The list below This Connection Uses the Following Items probably will contain at least four items, as shown in Figure 15.23:

- Client for Microsoft Networks
- File and Printer Sharing for Microsoft Networks

15

- QoS Packet Scheduler
- Internet Protocol (TCP/IP)

Figure 15.23
Default Network components installed with Windows XP.

These components will suffice for most home or office LANs:

- **Client for Microsoft Networks**—Lets your computer use files and printers shared by other computers.

- **File and Printer Sharing for Microsoft Networks**—Lets your computer share files or printers with others. (If you definitely don't need to share files or printers from this computer, you can uncheck this item—this will help protect your computer from unwanted visitors.)

- **QoS Packet Scheduler**—Used on some networks to assign varying priorities for different type of network traffic. (It's not necessary for small networks but it doesn't hurt to leave it in.)

- **Internet Protocol (TCP/IP)**—The basic network protocol used for all Internet services, and usually for Microsoft file and printer sharing as well.

There are some additional components required in certain situations:

- If you have an existing network that uses the IPX/SPX protocol for file sharing, you must add the NWLink IPX/SPX protocol.

- The Network Monitor Driver protocol allows your computer's network communications to be monitored by a network supervisor, for diagnostic purposes. It's of no use on a home or small office network.

If you need to add any of these components, or if any were inadvertently removed, use this procedure to add them:

1. Click Install. From the list shown in the Select Network Component Type dialog box, choose Client, Service, or Protocol, then click Add. (You might need to search through the list of components under each of these three categories to find the component you're after.)

2. From the list of Network Clients, Services or Protocols, select the desired entry and click OK.

TIP

> If Windows asks whether it can restart, select Yes. For previous versions of Windows, I would have suggested selecting No because you would face further restarts as you added other network components. With Windows XP, you're rarely asked to restart more than once, so you might as well get it over with right away.

In addition to these standard components, there are some advanced components available through Windows Setup.

- Management and Monitoring Tools:
  - **Simple Network Management Protocol**—Used on larger networks to monitor computer and router configuration. Install this only if required by your network administrator, as it can reveal sensitive information to hackers if there is no firewall in place.
  - **WMI SNMP Provider**—Permits Windows Management Interface application software access to SNMP data.
- Networking Services:
  - **Internet Gateway Device Discovery and Control Client**—Lets your Windows XP computer control devices such as Internet connection sharing routers and Windows Internet Connection Sharing through the My Network Places window. We'll talk more about this component in Chapter 18.
  - **Peer-to-Peer**—Provides services for future applications that could let several computers on a network work collaboratively on a shared problem. (It's unrelated to the peer-to-peer file sharing we're talking about in this chapter.)
  - **RIP Listener**—Lets Windows configure its TCP/IP routing tables to adjust to varying network router availability as broadcast by the Router Information Protocol (RIP).
  - **Simple TCP/IP Services**—A set of primitive TCP/IP services such as character stream generation and data echo. They're rarely needed and can make you an easy target for Denial of Service (DOS) attacks by hackers if installed.

15

- **UPnP User Interface**—Lets your computer automatically discover and connect to networked appliances and other new network devices. UPnP is a new technology that lets network hardware and future network-ready appliances communicate without manual setup. More about this in Chapter 18.
- Other Network File and Print Services:
  - **Print Services for Unix**—Lets Unix/Linux users use your computer's printers (and other shared printers on your network).

In general, the only two of these components you might ever need are the Internet Gateway discovery service and the UPnP User Interface. We discuss them in Chapter 18. Otherwise, it's best not to install any components unless you're sure you need them. If any are required on your network, do the following:

1. View the Network Connections window and select Advanced, Optional Networking Components.
2. Select the appropriate category (for example, Networking Services) and click Details.
3. Check the boxes next to the desired components, and click OK.
4. Click Next to complete the installation. Windows may require you to insert your Windows CD-ROM.

ADDING ON TO AN OLDER NETWORK

Microsoft has removed support for the old NetBEUI networking protocol from Windows XP. If you're adding a Windows XP computer to an older network that contains computers running Windows 95, 98 and/or Me, look at the network configuration of your other computers and see if they use NetBEUI for networking. It's best if all of your computers use the exact same list of network protocols, so you may wish to remove NetBEUI from your older computers and either rely entirely on TCP/IP, or add the NWLink IPX/SPX protocol to *all* of your computers. Personally, I've found that the latter approach makes for a more reliable network.

To add NWLink IPX/SPX, view the network properties on each computer. Click Add or Install, select Protocols, and select NWLink IPX/SPX from the list of available protocols.

TIP

Microsoft says that it's enough for all of the computers to share at least one common protocol. But my experience is that unless every computer has the *exact same* protocol or set of protocols installed, it's very common for your computers to not be able to "see" each other on the network. Standardizing on one protocol list makes your network much more reliable.

Microsoft does supply a NetBEUI protocol driver on the Windows XP installation disc but does not support its use. It might be become nonfunctional at some point in the future due to changes in Windows XP. Still, if you absolutely have to use NetBEUI on your older network, you can install NetBEUI on Windows XP with the following disagreeable procedure. The first seven steps copy the two omitted files into subfolders of your Windows directory:

1. Insert your Windows XP Installation CD-ROM into your CD drive.
2. Open Windows Explorer and select Tools, Folder Options. Select the View tab. Scroll down through the Advanced Settings and, if it isn't already checked, check Show Hidden Files and Folders. Click OK. If you don't see the folder view in the left pane, click the Folders button.
3. Browse into your CD-ROM drive into folder \VALUEADD\MSFT\NET\ NETBEUI.
4. Right-click NBF.SYS and select Copy.
5. Browse into your hard drive's \WINDOWS\SYSTEM32\DRIVERS folder. Select Edit, Paste from the menu.
6. Browse back to the NETBEUI folder on the CD-ROM, right-click NETNBF.INF, and select Copy.
7. Browse into your hard drive's \WINDOWS\INF folder (this folder is normally hidden). Select Edit, Paste from the menu. Close Windows Explorer.
8. Open Network Connections by clicking Start, My Computer, My Network Places, View Network Connections. Right-click Local Area Connection, and then select Properties.
9. Select Install, highlight Protocol, and select Add. Select NetBEUI Protocol from the list and click OK. Then you can close Local Area Connection Properties.

CONFIGURING NETWORK COMPONENTS

After adding or checking your network components, you might need to configure them with appropriate network settings.

You should only need to make configuration settings for the Internet Protocol (TCP/IP) entry. Select it from the list of installed network components and click Properties.

If your network provides a *DHCP (Dynamic Host Configuration Protocol)* server, you can leave the TCP/IP parameters on their default Obtain Automatically setting. DHCP service is provided by most Internet routers, connection sharing devices, and Windows computers providing Internet Connection Sharing.

15

TIP

> As discussed in the sidebar, if computers are set up for automatic (dynamic) addressing but no DHCP server is found on the network, Windows uses automatic private IP addressing to make the network operational. You can force Windows to use static addressing as its fallback option on the Internet Protocol (TCP/IP) Properties Alternate Configuration tab. This is helpful if you carry your computer between a network that has DHCP and one that doesn't. On the Alternate Configuration tab, you can set up static addressing for, for example, your home network, and still leave Windows set up to try dynamic addressing first, so it will also work on your office network.

If you have a small network with no DHCP server and you're not using Internet Connection Sharing or a hardware connection sharing device, you can still leave the TCP/IP settings alone and Windows will choose appropriate automatic-configuration values.

If your computer is part of a network with predetermined IP addresses (such as if you have already built a LAN with set IP addresses, or if you're using routed broadband Internet service like some cable-based Internet providers), you might have to manually enter IP information. You'll need the following information from your network manager or your Internet service provider:

- IP address
- Subnet mask
- Default gateway
- DNS domain name
- Preferred DNS servers

Automatic Configuration Without DHCP

Dynamic Host Configuration Protocol, or DHCP, is a network service that lets computers receive their TCP/IP configuration automatically over the network. It's great because a network administrator can make all the settings once in a DHCP server configuration program and not have to deal with managing individual setups for tens, hundreds, or even thousands of computers. DHCP service can be provided by Windows XP, 200x and NT Server, Unix servers, and even many Internet gateways and network routers. Computers running Windows Internet Connection Sharing also provide DHCP service for their LAN.

If a computer is set for automatic configuration, it broadcasts a message on the LAN when it boots, basically saying "Help! Who am I?" The LAN's DHCP server responds, assigns an IP address to the computer, and sends other information such as DNS server addresses, the domain name, and so on.

What's interesting is that a Windows TCP/IP network will still work even without a DHCP server.

Here's what happens: When each computer on the LAN is booted up, during its startup, it cries "Help!" as usual. But this time, there's no answer. The computer repeats the request a couple of times, to no avail. So, it picks an IP address at random from the range 169.254.0.1 through 169.254.0.254. (These addresses were reserved by Microsoft for this purpose and will never conflict with other computers on the Internet.) The computer sends a broadcast to the LAN asking whether any other computer is using this address. If none answers, then the computer continues on its merry way. If the address is already in use, the computer tries others until it finds one that is unclaimed. This scheme is called Automatic Private IP addressing (APIPA).

Each computer on the LAN is able to obtain an IP address this way, but doesn't get network gateways, domain names, or DNS server information. But because this system is only for the simplest of LANs with no server and no permanent outside connections, that's fine. The other information comes if and when these computers dial out to the Internet independently.

Just to be on the safe side, each computer bleats its "Help!" request every five minutes in the hope that there really was a DHCP server that had just been temporarily indisposed. If a DHCP server actually does come online later (perhaps the server computer had been turned off while the others booted up), then the Windows computers discard their made-up IP configuration for the real thing. This makes the network self-healing, but at a cost: The continual checks for a DHCP server can slow down Windows significantly.

When Internet Connection Sharing is in use, the picture is a little different. The sharing computer actually acts as a DHCP server because it has to give the others its own IP address as the gateway and DNS server address for the LAN. This topic is covered in Chapter 18.

If you are setting up a shared LAN connection to the Internet, see Chapter 18 for a discussion of TCP/IP configuration.

If you have to join your computer to an existing TCP/IP network, you might have to do a little more work. If your network has a DHCP server, or if your other computers are already set up for automatic configuration, you can leave the TCP/IP settings on Automatic, and your computer will obtain all its network settings from the DHCP server. (This is *so* slick!)

Otherwise, you'll have to add an additional IP address following the scheme you used when you initially set up your network. You'll need to determine the required settings for the five parameters listed above.

To configure settings for the TCP/IP protocol, follow these steps:

1. In Local Area Connection Properties, select the Internet Protocol (TCP/IP), and click Properties to open the dialog shown in Figure 15.24.

2. Select Use the Following IP Address, and enter the required IP address, subnet mask, and default gateway address, as shown in Figure 15.24. Of course, you need to enter *your* IP address information.

TIP

> When you're entering IP addresses, if you enter three digits, the cursor moves to the next part of the address field automatically. If you enter one or two digits, press the period (.) or spacebar to move to the next address field.

3. Select Use the following DNS server addresses and enter one or two DNS server addresses.

Figure 15.24
To configure TCP/IP parameters, select Internet Protocol and click Properties.

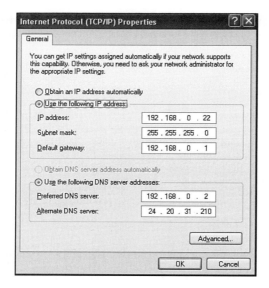

4. If your LAN is not connected to the Internet, you're finished, so just click OK. Otherwise, if your LAN has access to the Internet via a direct connection or Connection Sharing, click the Advanced button, and select the DNS tab, as shown in Figure 15.25.

5. Be sure that Append Primary and Connection Specific DNS Suffixes is selected and that Append Parent Suffixes of the Primary DNS Suffix is *not* checked.

6. Under DNS Suffix for This Connection, enter your Internet provider's domain name, such as myisp.com.

7. Click OK when you've made all the required entries.

Figure 15.25
You can enter your LAN's registered Internet domain name here, if you have a permanent connection on your LAN.

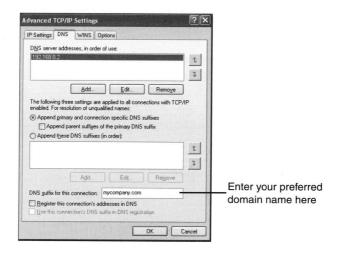

Enter your preferred domain name here

The other TCP/IP parameters are used only on larger corporate networks, and it's very unlikely you'd need to change them.

SETTING YOUR COMPUTER IDENTIFICATION

After you've configured your network, the next step is to make sure that each of the computers on your network are correctly named and are members of the same workgroup.

Click Start, right-click My Computer, and select Properties. On the Properties dialog, click the Computer Name tab. Check each of the Windows computers on your network. Do they each have a different full computer name and the same workgroup name? If so, you're all set. If not, click the Change button, and select a computer name and a workgroup name.

You can use a cute name such as HOCKEYTOWN, or leave the default setting MSHOME in place.

TIP

> If you have a mixture of Windows XP Professional and Windows XP Home Edition computers on your network, be especially careful to check the workgroup name. The default names are different between Professional and Home Edition (WORKGROUP versus MSHOME). It's easy to overlook this.

Click Next and then click Finish to complete the setup. You need to let Windows restart your computer if you changed the Workgroup name setting.

CAUTION

> You must be sure that every computer on your network uses the same workgroup name if you want them to share files and printers.

NETWORK SECURITY

Now that you have a LAN—even if it's just a simple peer-to-peer LAN—you should be worried about network security and hackers. Why? Because you'll certainly be connecting to the Internet, even if only intermittently, and when you do, you risk exposing your network to the entire world. These risks are not as far-fetched as you might think.

Refer to Chapter 19 to find out what risks you'll be exposed to and what you can do to protect your LAN. If you use Internet Connection Sharing or a connection sharing router, you're in pretty good shape, but in any case please go through Chapter 19 very carefully. It is *very* important.

CHECKING OUT THE NEIGHBORHOOD

Your network is finally ready to go. After you have configured, connected, and perhaps restarted your computers, you'll want to add My Network Places to your Start menu. This is a quick way to view networked folders and printers. To do this

1. Right-click the Start button and select Properties.
2. Click Customize, and view the Advanced tab.
3. Scroll down the list of Start Menu items and find My Network Places.
4. Check the box next to My Network Places and click OK, and OK again.

Now, click Start and select My Network Places.

Select View Workgroup Computers from the Network Tasks list. If your network is up and running, you should see one icon for every computer you've connected, as shown in Figure 15.26.

Figure 15.26
When your Workgroup network is up and running, you should see at least one icon for every other computer you've set up.

 If you don't see other computers in the View Workgroup Computers window, see "View Workgroup Computers Shows No Other Computers" in the "Troubleshooting" section at the end of this chapter, and read Chapter 20.

If your computers appear, congratulations: Your network is up and running! But before you continue on to Chapter 16, there's one unpleasant task left: backups. I suggest making a backup right now.

INSTALLING AND CONFIGURING BACKUP SOFTWARE

Now that your network is up and running, it's a good time to set up a backup system and create a full system backup. Get in the habit of backing up at regular intervals. I suggest backing up your entire system *at least* once a month. You should consider backing up the folders containing your documents even more often.

NOTE

> Windows XP comes with a backup program, which you'll find on the Windows XP installation CD-ROM. Instructions for installing and using it are in Chapter 26, "Managing the Hard Disk." If you're interested, you can buy better backup software, or it might be supplied with an add-on tape backup system.

Your backup will be smaller, and just as useful, if you can configure your backup software to exclude certain files:

~*.*	Any file starting with a tilde
*.tmp	Any file with extension .tmp
hiberfil.sys	The Hibernation system data file
pagefile.sys	The Windows swap file
*.bak	Any backup file
.ff	Fast-find index files
.ci	IIS Index Server index files

Test your backup system periodically by viewing a tape directory or by restoring a single file from the tape. This will not only ensure that your backup system is functioning properly, but will maintain your skill in operating the backup-and-restore software.

BRIDGING TWO NETWORK TYPES WITH WINDOWS XP

Windows XP has a feature new to Windows: the ability to connect or *bridge* two different network types through software. This can eliminate the need for buying a hardware device to connect two disparate networks. Figure 15.27 shows an example of what bridging can do. In the figure, one Windows XP computer serves as a bridge between an Ethernet LAN and a Phoneline LAN.

Figure 15.27
Bridging a Phoneline and Ethernet network with Windows XP. Computers on either network can communicate as if they were directly connected.

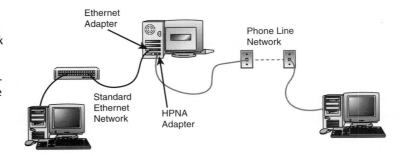

Ethernet Adapter

Phone Line Network

Standard Ethernet Network

HPNA Adapter

Bridging is similar to *routing*, but it's more appropriate for small LAN's because it's easier to configure and doesn't require different sets of IP addresses on each network segment. Technically, bridging occurs at the physical level of the network protocol stack, so it forwards broadcasts and packets of all protocol types, including TCP/IP, IPX/SPX, AppleTalk, and so on.

→ To learn more about protocol stacks, **see** "The OSI Model," **p. 465**.

To enable bridging in your Windows XP computer, install and configure two or more network adapters, as described under "Installing Multiple Network Adapters" earlier in this chapter. Don't, however, worry about setting up the Internet Protocol (TCP/IP) parameters for either of the adapters. An IEEE-1394 (FireWire) adapter may be bridged as well. Then

1. View the connection icons by clicking Start, Control Panel, Network and Internet Connections, Network Connections.

2. Select the icons you wish to bridge by clicking on the first, holding down the Shift key, and clicking on the second.

3. Right-click on one of the icons and select Bridge Networks.

4. A new icon will appear as in Figure 15.28. Select the new bridge icon, and if you want, rename it appropriately, for example "Ethernet to Phoneline."

Figure 15.28
The Network Bridge icon appears when you have bridged two network connections together.

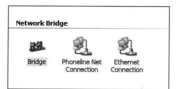

5. Double-click the bridge icon. Select Internet Protocol (TCP/IP) and configure your computer's TCP/IP settings if necessary. You must do this, as any TCP/IP settings for the original two adapters are lost.

When you've created a bridge, your two network adapters function as one and share one IP address, so Microsoft disables the "network properties" of the individual network adapters. You must configure your computer's network properties with the bridge's icon.

Remember that the connection between the two networks depends on the computer with the bridge being powered on.

You can remove the bridge later on by right-clicking the network connections and clicking Remove from Bridge. When you've removed both connections, you can right-click the bridge icon and delete it.

TROUBLESHOOTING

CAN'T DRILL THROUGH WALLS OR CEILINGS

My lease or the physical limitations of my building prevent me from drilling through walls or the ceiling to install network cabling.

In this case, you can install wires along baseboards, around doors, and so on. It's not as pretty, but because network wiring is low voltage, it's not risky to do so as it is with power wiring. (My office has a cable shamefully strung through a skylight, across the ceiling, and into a closet.) You also can use products called *wiring channels* to conceal the wires run along baseboards and rubber guards to protect them where they might be trod upon. You can find these products in the hardware store or in business product catalogs. Of course, you can also consider using a wireless network.

HUB LIGHTS DO NOT COME ON

One or more UTP hub link lights do not come on when the associated computers are connected.

The problem lies in one of the cables between the computer and the hub. Which one is it? To find out, do the following:

1. Move the computer right next to the hub. You can leave the keyboard, mouse, and monitor behind. Just plug in the computer, turn it on, and use a commercially manufactured or known-to-be-working patch cable to connect the computer to the hub. If the light doesn't come on regardless of which hub connection socket you use, you probably have a bad network card.

2. If you were using any patch cables when you first tried to get the computer connected, test them using the same computer and hub socket. This trick can identify a bad cable.

3. If the LAN card, hub, and patch cables are all working, then the problem is in whatever is left, which would be your in-wall wiring. Check the connectors for proper crimping, and check that the wire pairs are correctly wired end-to-end. You might have to use a cable analyzer if you can't spot the problem by eye. These devices cost about $75. You connect a "transmitter" box to one end of your cabling, and a "receiver" at the other. The receiver has four LEDs that blink in a 1-2-3-4 sequence if your wiring is correct.

VIEW WORKGROUP COMPUTERS SHOWS NO OTHER COMPUTERS

The View Workgroup Computers display doesn't show any other computers when I boot up.

If you've eliminated the network card and any UTP wiring as the source of the problem, you can use Windows own built-in diagnostic tools to help. Here's how:

1. The first thing to check is whether the LAN hardware itself is working. Check the Device Manager to be sure that your network card is operating properly. Be sure you're using an approved network card and have up-to-date drivers for it. If the Device Manager gives you a message that reads The Card Is Not Functioning, you almost certainly have the wrong drivers. Check with the vendor to see whether up-to-date Windows XP or Windows 2000 drivers are available for you to download over the Internet.

2. If you have a UTP LAN, make sure all the expected indicators on your hub are lit.

3. On each computer, start a command prompt. Then type the command `ipconfig`.

4. When you see IP addresses listed, be sure each computer has a different IP address. They should all be similar but different. For example, they might look like 209.203.104.x, where the x is different for each computer. If not, check the Internet Protocol properties on each computer to be sure each was correctly configured.

5. Type ping *x.x.x.x*, where *x.x.x.x* is the computer's own IP address. It should have four "replies," which look like this:

```
Reply from x.x.x.x: bytes=32 time<10msec TTL=128
```

   If not, remove, reinstall, and reconfigure the TCP/IP protocol.

6. Type ping *x.x.x.y*, where *x.x.x.y* is one of the IP addresses of the other computers on your LAN. If the replies don't come back, your network hardware is at fault. Check the wiring as follows:

   On a 10BASE-T or 100BASE-T LAN, see whether an "activity" LED flashes on your network card when you type a ping command. If it doesn't, the problem is your network card. If it does, you might have to get a cable testing device to find out what's wrong with the wiring. (A professional installer will have one…it's time to call for help!)

   Another possibility with combination 10/100BASE-T network cards is that the cards might not have decided to use the correct speed. You can force them to use one speed or the other in the Device Manager by viewing the network card's Properties page and selecting the Advanced tab. This tab usually has a Link Speed/Duplex Mode property. Set all the cards to the appropriate value for the type of hub you are using.

7. If the ping commands work between computers, be sure that each computer's Network Identification has the same workgroup name. This information is on My Computer's Properties page.

8. If none of these steps help, see whether the Event Log has any helpful error messages. To do so, right-click My Computer, select Manage, and view the logs under the System Tool Event Viewer.

9. Finally, you can use a diagnostic provided with Windows. Click Start, Control Panel, Network and Internet Connections. In the Troubleshooters panel, select Network Diagnostics.

For more troubleshooting tips, see Chapter 20.

TIPS FROM THE WINDOWS PROS: GRASSROOTS NETWORKING

Despite their becoming so inexpensive and simple to install, networks are extremely complex systems "under the hood." It's hard enough to solve the problems that creep up from time to time in an existing, functional LAN, but new LANs are worse because *everything* is untested, and a little problem in any one part can mess up the whole thing. Where do you start looking for the problem?

The answer is an exercise in delayed gratification! It's exciting to see all the new equipment, parts, and cables all over the place, but as much as I'd like to hook it all up and see what happens when I turn on the switch for the first time, I've found that it's best to start small.

Whenever I build a new network, I put two computers side-by-side on one desk. They can be two regular computers for a peer-to-peer network, or a Windows 200x Server and a regular workstation for a Server-based network. I wire them together in the simplest possible way, usually with two short patch cables and a hub.

This technique gives me the smallest possible, least complex system to start with. It's much easier to solve a networking problem when you can see both computers' screens at the same time.

When I have these two computers completely configured and tested, I start adding components one at a time: a network printer, an Internet connection, a tape backup system, an uninterruptible power supply, and so on.

When something goes wrong during this technique, I know it must have something to do with the last component I added, and I'm not searching for a needle in a haystack.

Finally, when I have all the parts working, I take the two computers to their final locations and see whether they still work with the real-world wiring. Then I add workstations to the network one at a time. Attaching them this way is not as much fun as assembling the whole thing at once, but I've found that staying up all night diagnosing problems on a new network is even less fun.

CHAPTER 16

USING A WINDOWS XP NETWORK

In this chapter

16

WINDOWS XP WAS MADE TO NETWORK

Aside from finally finding a use for the right button on the mouse, almost all the advancements in the Windows platform over the last 10 years have been made in the area of networking. Back in Windows version 3.1, network software was an expensive add-on product—an afterthought—cumbersome to install and manage. Not so anymore! Networking is built right into the heart of Windows XP, such that Windows is hardly even *happy* without a network attached.

Okay, I'm exaggerating. But the truth is, Windows XP's personality does change for the better when it's connected to a network. In this chapter, I'll show you how to use Windows XP networking, and share tips for making the most of whatever type of network you have.

In Windows XP, using files and printers on the network is exactly the same as using files and printers on your own hard drive. The "look and feel" are identical. The only new tasks you have to learn are how to find resources shared by others and how to make your own computer's resources available to others on the network. I'll use the word *resource* frequently in this chapter. When I say *resource*, I mean a shared folder or printer on someone else's computer, which you can access through the LAN or the Internet. *The American Heritage Dictionary* defines a resource as "an available supply that can be drawn upon when needed." That's actually a perfect description of a network resource: It's there for you to use—provided you can find it, and provided you have permission.

N O T E

> In the next couple of sections, I'll be giving some background information on Windows networking. If you're new to networking, I'd rather that you see how easy it really is before plowing through technical details you may never need to deal with. You might want to skip these technical sections for now and come back to them later. The good stuff starts in the "My Network Places" section of this chapter.

The ways of finding resources and managing permissions change depending on the type of network you have. I talked about these network models in detail in Chapter 14, "Overview of Windows XP Networking," but here's a quick review of the ways you can base a network on Windows:

- **Workgroup network (peer-to-peer)**—A workgroup network, also called a peer-to-peer network, does not have a central server computer to perform user/password verification. On this network, each computer manages its own user list and security system. Home users and small offices usually use workgroup networks. Networks mixing Windows computers with Macintosh, Linux and Unix computers also fall into this category.

- **Domain network**—A domain-based network uses Windows 2003/2000/NT Server to provide a centralized user security database. All computers on the network look to a *domain controller*, or primary server, for usernames, group memberships, and passwords.

A Windows XP Home Edition computer can't be a real member of a domain network but it can access resources on one as it does on a peer-to-peer network.

- **Remote network**—Windows XP Home Edition functions very well on a standalone computer, but it also lets you connect to and disconnect from networks, or get remote access by modem to the Internet. Windows provides special services to help you deal with this "on again/off again" network relationship.

WORKGROUP VERSUS DOMAIN NETWORKING

On a Windows domain-based network (that is, a network managed by a Windows NT, 2000 or 2003 Server), user accounts are set up on the domain servers. Domain users are known by every computer on the network. When the network managers are establishing who can and can't have access to files, they can choose users and groups from the entire list of all users in your organization. They can grant access to specific individuals, departments, sites, or other groupings even though those users might be scattered around the globe.

The Windows XP Professional version can also enforce user-specific security, even though it's a bit more work to manage it on a peer-to-peer network.

With Windows XP Home Edition, however, it's a different story. Windows XP Home edition forgoes user-level security and lets anyone on a networked computer access the shared files and folders of any other computer. This is less secure than networks based on the more advanced versions of Windows, but it's *much* less work to set up and use on a day to day basis.

NOTE

> The Simple File Sharing feature eliminates the ability to restrict access to shared files and folders based on passwords. If you need to be able to enforce user permissions over your network, you have to upgrade to Windows XP Professional, at least on the computer(s) that are sharing sensitive files. Then, you can disable Simple File Sharing on the XP Pro computer(s).

TRADITIONAL VERSUS WEB SHARING

In Windows XP, you can actually get at shared folders and printers in two ways: through traditional LAN methods or via the World Wide Web. This last method shouldn't come as much of a surprise these days; I think even washing machines come with a Web interface now.

The traditional methods are based on the Microsoft Networking protocol (called NetBT, or NetBIOS over TCP/IP, also called SMB, or Server Message Block), which has been around for a very long time.

The new Internet-based file sharing technology is called WebDAV (Web Distributed Authoring and Versioning) or Web Sharing; and the new printer sharing technology is called Internet Printing Protocol (IPP). They're both based on the Hypertext Transfer Protocol (HTTP) that most Web sites use, which means that file and print operations can be carried out safely across the Internet, even through corporate firewalls. They require Web server software on the computer that is sharing the files or printers—for example, a computer in your corporate office.

With Web sharing, you can work with files and folders shared by a remote computer just as you would with files found in My Computer, Explorer, or traditional network shared folders. Using IPP Printing, you can connect to a shared printer over the Internet and use it exactly as you would a local or LAN-based printer.

Although the look and feel are virtually identical to traditional LAN sharing, the Internet-based methods are not as speedy as ordinary LAN sharing, so they're meant only for remote users who need to get at shared files and printers at their home base.

There is another significant difference. Traditional networking provides *file and record locking* to mediate access to a file when multiple users try to read and write data at the same time. Database programs like Microsoft Access depend on this. Web Sharing doesn't permit con-current access, so only one person can modify a given file at a time.

WHAT'S IN A NAME?

Virtually the only difference you'll notice between local and networked files is their names. If you've found the use of the backslash character to be an annoying and peculiar conven-tion, you'd better hang on to your hat because slashes of all persuasions are in your future in a big way.

Let's look at the names of shared network folders and files. Each computer on your network (or on an intranet or the Internet) has a name, and every folder or printer that is offered up for shared use on the network must be given a *share name* as well. For example, if I want to give officemates the use of my business documents, I might share my hard disk's folder c:\documents and give that folder the share name "docs."

> **NOTE**
>
> It might seem confusing to use a different name for the share name than for the folder. The reason for this is that while folder names can be very long and can contain spaces in them, share names should be 12 characters or less and have no spaces. This isn't very user friendly, but it's the way it is.

Figure 16.1 shows the relationship between my computer named Ambon, its hard disk, and the shared folder, from the point of view of another computer named Bali.

Figure 16.1
Sharing makes a folder, or even a whole hard drive, accessible to the LAN. Ambon shares folder \documents as "docs," and Bali can use this folder by its network name \\ambon\docs.

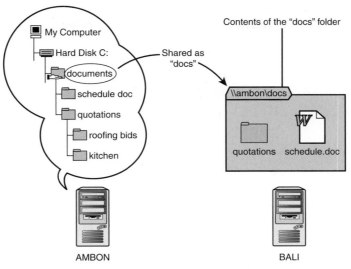

A folder shared from one computer…   …can be viewed on another

THE UNC NAMING CONVENTION

I can specify the location of a file on my hard drive with a drive and path name, like this:

```
c:\documents\roofing bids.xls
```

A user on another computer can refer to this same file using a syntax called the *Universal Naming Convention*, or UNC:

```
\\ambon\docs\roofing bids.xls
```

The double backslash indicates that the name "ambon" is the name of a computer on the LAN rather than the name of a folder in the top directory of the local hard disk. "Docs" is the share name of the folder, and everything past the \\ambon\docs part specifies the path and file relative to that shared folder.

Or, if you know only the remote computer's IP network address, you can even use a notation like this:

```
\\192.168.0.10\docs\roofing bids.xls
```

No matter which way you specify the remote computer, Windows finds it and locates its shared folder "docs."

NOTE

Elsewhere in this chapter, I'll use UNC names like \\server\folder as a generic sort of name. By "server" I mean the name of any computer that's sharing a folder. You'll need to use your network's actual computer names and shared folder names.

Shared printers are also given share names and specified by their UNC path. For example, if I share my HP LaserJet 4V printer, I might give it the share name *HPLaser*, and it will be known on the network as \\ambon\HPLaser. Here, it's not a folder, but rather a printer, and Windows keeps track of the type of resource.

NAMING FOR WEB-BASED SHARING

The new Internet-compatible technologies are based on the World Wide Web's Hypertext Transfer Protocol (HTTP) and use the Web's traditional forward slash rather than the backslash.

A Web folder name looks just like a standard Web URL:

```
http://ambon/docs
```

or

```
http://ambon.mycompany.com/docs
```

When you open a Web folder, instead of just displaying a listing of files, as it might if you visited a regular Web page, Windows displays the files in a standard Explorer folder view. You can do anything to the files that you would do in a normal folder: delete, rename, drag files in and out, and open and save files with applications, providing you have the appropriate permissions.

IPP printers shared by Windows 200x Server and Professional use the built-in Web server on those operating systems, and use a similar naming scheme, but I'll wait until the section "Using Other IPP Printers" later in this chapter to get into the messy details about that. If you're connecting to a Windows 2000 or XP computer from across the Internet, it's enough to view the "printers" page by typing

```
http://ambon.mycompany.com/printers
```

This allows the Web server software to take care of all the work for you.

MY NETWORK PLACES

How do you find the folders and printers floating around out there somewhere in the Network Twilight Zone? If you've been using Windows for any length of time, you may have guessed by now that you can do the job in several ways.

The most straightforward way is through the My Network Places display. It appears as a choice on the Other Places list of My Computer after you install any network components in Windows XP and it's the starting place for finding network resources.

My Network Places gives you a way to browse, search, and bookmark network resources, including shared folders, Web pages, FTP sites, and so on. To open My Network Places, view My Computer, and then select My Network Places from the Other Places menu.

TIP

> If you find yourself using My Network Places frequently, you can add it to your Start Menu. Just right-click Start, select Properties, and then Customize. Select the Advanced tab and scroll the Start menu items list down to My Network Places. Check it and click OK. You can also drag a shortcut to My Network Places from your Start menu onto the desktop or the quick launch bar.

When you select My Network Places from the My Computer window, you get the "folder" view of My Network Places, as shown in Figure 16.2.

My Network Places is meant to be a place to collect shortcuts to commonly used remote network resources like shared folders, Web Folders, FTP sites, and the like. When you first install Windows, My Network Places doesn't have any of your personalized shortcuts, of course. By default, Windows sets up an icon for each shared folder on your network.

My Network Places organizes your network resource shortcuts and also lists several commonly used tasks:

- **Add a Network Place**—Opens a wizard to create network or Internet shortcuts. I discuss the Add Network Place wizard later in this chapter.

- **View Network Connections**—Displays and configures your dial-up connections or LAN adapter.

Figure 16.2
My Network Places is the starting point for searching and opening network resources. By default, Windows locates and displays icons for all shared folders.

- **Set Up a Home or Small Office Network**—Runs the Network Setup Wizard. (For more information, see "Using the Network Setup Wizard," in Chapter 15, "Creating a Windows XP Home Network.")

■ **Set Up a Wireless Network for a Home or Small Office**—Runs the Wireless Network Setup Wizard to create or add to an existing wireless network. (For more information, see "Using the Wireless Network Setup Wizard" in Chapter 15.)

■ **View Workgroup Computers**—Provides a quick way to view the list of computers in your workgroup.

■ **Show (or Hide) Icons for Networked UPnP Devices**—Installs or removes the optional Universal Plug and Play User Interface (UPnPUI), which lets you manage and configure UPnP-enabled devices like routers. The UPnPUI is discussed in Chapter 18, "Connecting Your LAN to the Internet."

I suggest that you browse through My Network Places to check out the computers and resources on your network.

> **TIP**
>
> You can drag shortcuts to any of the icons in My Network Places to your desktop for convenience.

USING SHARED FOLDERS

File sharing lets users on a network browse through and use files and folders, no matter which computer's hard drive the files actually reside on. The look and feel are exactly the same.

Let's say I want to share a folder named C:\bookstuff. I have to give it a *share name* by which it'll be known on the network. For its share name, I might give the folder the name "book," as shown in Figure 16.3.

Figure 16.3
Sharing a folder on my computer.

When other network users browse through their My Network Places display, they will see that Book is a shared folder on my computer. It looks like any folder on their own computers.

If they open it, they'll see the same folders and file listings I see in c:\bookstuff, as illustrated in Figure 16.4. The information about filenames, dates, and contents is sent over the network. If anyone drags a file into this folder, all other users will see it appear there. If anyone edits a file in this shared folder, the next time another user opens the file, they'll get the changed version. That's network file sharing in a nutshell; the rest is just a matter of details.

Figure 16.4
A network user examining the shared folder (left) sees the same files the owner of the shared folder sees (right).

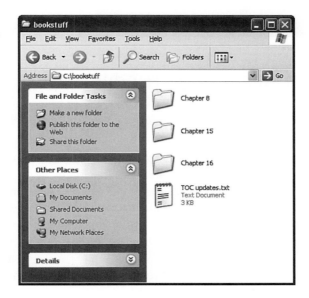

Home users might not even need to go to the trouble to set up shared folders, because Windows automatically makes each computer's Shared Documents folder available over the network, as shown in Figure 16.5.

→ To learn more about shared documents, **see** "Sharing Files Among Users," **p. 891**.

TIP

> If you put files into your Shared Documents folder, not only will other users of your computer be able to view and use these files, so will other users on your network.
>
> Likewise, you can get to other computers' shared documents by looking for folders named SharedDocs in My Network Places.
>
> This is a pretty intuitive way to organize things, and you might not need to set up or use any other shared folders.

Figure 16.5
Your computer's Shared Documents folder is shared with the network by default. You can view other computers' Shared Documents folders in My Network Places.

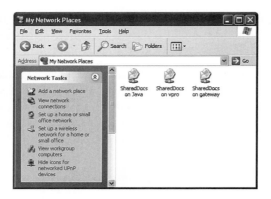

EXPLORING AND SEARCHING THE NETWORK

Of course, before you can use a network resource, you have to know where to find it. You can look through your network for shared folders and printers by exploring in the following areas in turn:

- If you have a workgroup LAN, view My Computer and select My Network Places in the Other Places list. By default, Windows can automatically display an icon for each shared folder on each of your networked computers. (This can be enabled or disabled by selecting View, Folder Options. On the View tab, check or uncheck Automatically Search for Network Folders and Printers). You can open these icons to view and use these folders just like the folders on your own hard drive.

- From there, select View Workgroup Computers in the Network Tasks list to peruse all the computers with the same workgroup name as yours. Opening the computer icons displays any folders and printers they're sharing.

- If you're part of a larger network, including domain-type networks, you can select Microsoft Windows Network in the Other Places list to view all of the workgroups on your LAN. You can double-click any of these to see the computers in that workgroup.

- Select Entire Network from the Other Places list to view all of the computers on your LAN. You can dig into the Microsoft Windows Network folder, and if your organization uses other network operating systems like Novell NetWare, you can delve into the Novell folder as well.

If you'll be using shared folders, Web sites, FTP sites, or Web folders repeatedly, you add them to My Network Places for a quick return later. You can use the Add A Network Place Wizard to do so; the Wizard is listed in the Network Tasks list. Even easier, you can just drag a shortcut from Explorer's Address bar into My Network Places, into any folder or even to the desktop, as shown in Figure 16.6.

Figure 16.6
You can drag the folder icon from Explorer's Address bar to My Network Places, to the desktop, or to another folder to make an instant shortcut to a network folder.

You can also explore your network from the Folders view of Explorer, as shown in Figure 16.7. (You can bring up the Folders view in any Explorer window by clicking the Folders button. Folder views are discussed in Chapter 4, "Using the Windows XP Interface"). This view lets you see that your network is structured like the folders of your hard drive.

UNDERSTANDING SHARED RESOURCES

If you do a bit of poking around, you might find that some computers share folders that may not make much sense. Table 16.1 shows some of the unusual shared resources you might see and what they do. You don't really need to worry about these. Windows sets them up and manages them automatically.

Figure 16.7
The Folders view in Explorer lets you browse through your network. This view shows the shared folder "cdrive" on the computer named Sumatra.

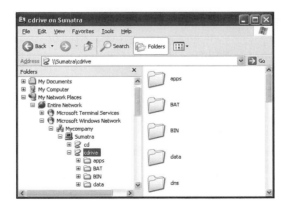

16

TABLE 16.1   TYPICAL ADMINISTRATIVE FOLDERS SHARED ON A WINDOWS XP NETWORK

Folder	Description
Printers	Mirrors the computer's Printers folder; can be used by an administrator to install or control printers across the LAN.
Scheduled Tasks	Mirrors the computer's Scheduled Task list; can be used by an administrator for remote maintenance.
ADMIN$	Used by remote administration software
IPC$	Used for remote procedure calls, a network software system built into Windows.
print$	Shared folder containing print drivers for the computer's shared printers. This lets Windows automatically load the appropriate driver software for each shared printer.
C$, D$, etc	Entire hard drives, shared for administrators' use. However, these are not usable on Windows XP Home Edition computers because Simple File Sharing treats all network users as "guest" users, granting no Administrator privileges.

NOTE

> Share names ending with $ are usually hidden from being displayed in Explorer's browsing lists.

Of these folders, only Printers and Scheduled Tasks are of interest, and then only to administrators. The operating system uses the others, which should not be modified.

Windows XP computers also will have a SharedDocs folder. This is the computer's Shared Documents folder as presented to the network. Windows does this automatically. If you see any other shared resources, the computer's users must have put them there.

SEARCHING THE NETWORK

You can locate shared folders or printers by exploring My Network Places, or you can use the search links under Start, Search. The Windows Search function can explore folders on the network just as efficiently as it searches your hard disk.

SEARCHING FOR FILES OR FOLDERS

When you use Search to look for files and folders, you can tell Windows to look on the network as well as on your own computer.

When entering your search request, under Look In, choose Browse. In the Browse for Folder dialog, open My Network Places. You can select Entire network, if you want Windows to scan every shared folder on every computer of your network. You can also dig down to a specific computer or shared folder to narrow things down—on a large network, it could take some time to search through every shared folder on every computer. (On the other hand, if you don't know where look, it's nice to know that Windows can do the schlepping for you.)

As Windows finds matching files, it displays them along with the computer name on which the files were found, as shown in Figure 16.8.

Figure 16.8
When searching the network for files or folders, Windows displays the names of the computers on which the matches were found.

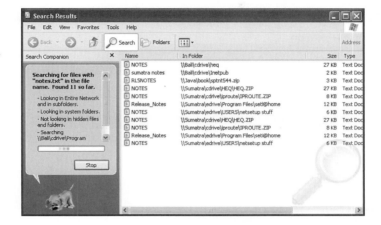

You can view or open the files you've found on the network just as you can files you've found on your own computer.

ADDING NETWORK PLACES

By using the Add a Network Place Wizard, you can add shortcuts in My Network Places to network shared folders, for a quick return when you need them in the future. I find Windows a bit hyper-helpful with its Favorites, Histories, Shortcuts, and now Network Places. However, this aid is actually useful because entries in My Network Places appear in the list of choices in every application's Save As dialog, as shown in Figure 16.9.

NOTE

> The shortcuts in Network Places differ from those in Internet Explorer's "favorites" list. When you open an IE "favorite" location, you are shown a Web-based *view* of the contents of the location. When you open a "network place," you can actually *manipulate* the files in the remote folder.

Windows should automatically add locations to Network Places whenever you open a remote folder by name using Windows Explorer or Internet Explorer's Web Folder view. If you want to add a network place shortcut yourself, do the following:

1. Open My Network Places and select Add a Network Place from the task list.
2. When asked where you want to create the network place, select Choose Another Network Location and click Next.

3. The Add Network Place Wizard asks for the name of the network resource. Enter one of these three types of network resource names:

- A UNC name for a shared folder, such as `\\server\share`
- A URL for a Web Sharing folder, such as `http://host/share`
- The name of an FTP site, such as `ftp://host` or `ftp://host/subfolder`

You can also choose Browse to search through an Explorer-like view of the Entire Network.

4. Click Next, and enter a name for your Network Place Shortcut. Then select Finish. A shortcut icon appears in My Network Places, and Windows pops up an Explorer window showing the contents of the remote shared folder or site.

Figure 16.9
My Network Places is handy because you can select network folders when you're saving files in any application. You can delve deeper into the shared folders, if necessary.

TIP

> When you're browsing through your network or browsing the Internet using Internet Explorer, you can drag network folders or Web page addresses to My Network Places to instantly make a Network Place shortcut without the Add Network Place Wizard.
>
> Likewise, you can drag the address from the Explorer window's Address bar to your desktop or to a folder to make an instant network shortcut.

USING A SHARED DISK DRIVE

Shared folders don't have to be subfolders. Computer owners can share the *root folder* of their disk drives, making the entire drive available over the network. This is especially useful with CD-ROM, floppy, and Zip disk drives. If an entire CD-ROM drive is shared, for example, you can access the entire CD from any computer on the network. Sharing the root folder of the hard disk containing your \Windows folder is not a good idea—it could let hackers or even other network users mess around with Windows itself.

TIP

> If you need to install CD-ROM-based software on a computer with a broken CD-ROM drive but a good network connection, you can put the CD-ROM in another computer's drive, and share the entire drive. See the section "Mapping Drive Letters," later in this chapter to see how to access the CD from the disabled computer.

Using Internet-Based File Storage Services

Starting with Windows XP, Microsoft has added the ability to make Network Places shortcuts to commercial services that provide file storage space over the Internet. To use these services, you must first visit the provider's Web site to obtain a username and password (and to take care of small details like payment!). When your account is set up, you can use the Add Network Place Wizard to create a shortcut to the services.

Then, when you're online, you can easily move files to and from your personal folder on the provider's network, simply by opening the service's Network Place icon. I'll talk more about this type of service in Chapter 17, "Windows Unplugged: Remote and Mobile Networking."

Mapping Drive Letters

If you frequently use the same shared network folder, you can make it a "permanent house-guest" of your computer by *mapping* the network shared folder to an unused drive letter on your computer—one of the letters after your hard drive's "C:" and the CD-ROM drive's "D:" (assuming you have one hard drive and one CD-ROM drive and have not already changed your drive mappings). You can give the shared folder \\server\shared the drive letter J:, for example, so that it appears that your computer has a new disk drive J:, whose contents are those of the shared folder.

Mapping gives you several benefits:

- The mapped drive appears along with your computer's other real, physical drives in My Computer for quick browsing, opening, and saving of files.

- Access to the shared folder is faster because Windows maintains an open connection to the sharing computer.

- MS-DOS applications can use the shared folder through its assigned letter. Most legacy DOS applications can't accept UNC-formatted names like \\server\shared\subfolder\file, but they can use j:\subfolder\file.

- If you need to, you can map a shared folder using an alternate username and password to gain access rights you might not have with your current Windows login name.

If you used Novell or older Windows networks in the past, this may be the only way you've ever used a network! Good news: you still can.

To map a drive, select Tools, Map Network Drive in any Explorer window (such as My Computer). Or you can right-click My Network Places and select Map Network Drive.

Next, select an unused drive letter from the drop-down list, as shown in Figure 16.10. If possible, pick a drive letter that has some association for you with the resource you'll be using: P for Pictures, S for Shared Documents—whatever makes sense to you.

Figure 16.10
You can select an unused drive letter to use for the drive mapping.

Then select the name of the shared folder you want to assign to the drive letter. You can type the UNC-formatted name if you know it already—for example, \\servername\ sharename—or you can click Browse to poke through your network's resources and select the shared folder. Find the desired shared folder in the expandable list of workgroups, computers, and share names, as shown in Figure 16.11, and click OK.

Figure 16.11
Browsing for a shared folder. You can open the list view to see network types, workgroups, computers, and shared folders.

After you select the shared folder and click OK, the folder name appears in the dialog, and you have two options:

■ If you want this mapping to reappear every time you log in, check Reconnect at login. If you don't check this box, the mapping disappears when you log off.

■ If your current Windows username and password don't give you sufficient permission to use the shared resource, or if your username won't be recognized at the other computer because your account name is different there, select Connect Using a Different User Name. Choosing this option displays a Connect As dialog, as shown in Figure 16.12. Here, you can enter the alternative username and password, and click OK.

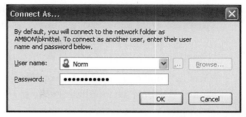

Figure 16.12

After you map a drive letter, the drive appears in your My Computer list along with your local disk drives. You might notice a couple of funny things with these drives:

- If you haven't used the network drive for a while, 20 minutes or so, it might turn gray, indicating that the network connection to the remote computer has been disconnected. When you use the drive again, it will reconnect and turn black.

- If the remote computer (or you) really go offline, a red X appears over the drive.

If you enjoy the more esoteric aspects of networking, there are a couple of nifty features for you—mapping a drive to a subfolder and mapping shared folders with no drive letter.

MAPPING A DRIVE TO A SUBFOLDER

When you're setting up a mapped drive and you browse to find a shared folder, notice that Windows lets you delve into the shared folders themselves. If you drill down into a subfolder and select it as the location to use in mapping a drive letter, you'll find that the mapped drive starts at the subfolder. The subfolder becomes the mapped drive's "root directory," and you can't explore upward into the shared folder that contains it.

NetWare users call this the *map root* function. See Figure 16.13, in which I've selected the subfolder h02\images from the shared folder \\java\book. If I map drive M: to that folder, drive M: will contain the contents of folder \\java\book\h02\images, and it can't be made to see up into \\java\book\h02 or higher. The root, or top-level, directory of M: will be the images folder.

Figure 16.13
By delving into a shared folder, you can map the root directory of a drive letter to a deeper point in the share.

Mapping a subfolder can be a good thing because it makes any program that uses the mapped drive letter see just that subfolder as the drive's root directory.

Mapping a Shared Folder Without a Drive Letter

You can make an established connection to a shared folder, keeping it readily available for quick response without assigning it a drive letter. Follow the procedure shown earlier for mapping a drive letter. When you select the letter to map, go all the way to the bottom of the Drive letter drop-down list, and select (None), the last choice. Continue through the rest of the process as described.

Mapping a shared folder to (None) doesn't add a drive to your My Computer list, but it does make for speedier response from the server when you're accessing that folder.

Using Web Folders

Windows XP Professional and Windows NT4/2000/2003 Server computers running Internet Information Services (IIS) can share folders using another file sharing system called WebDAV (Web Distributed Authoring and Versioning), or Web Sharing. Because it's based on the standard HTTP protocol, you can access Web folders on those computers from your XP Home Edition computer or office PC, from home, over the Internet, or from another LAN halfway around the world.

Web Folders let you view, use, and manage files and folders over the Internet just as if you were using them on your PC or on your LAN. You get exactly the same look and feel. You can use Microsoft Office 2000 or later, FrontPage, and Internet Explorer version 5 or higher to access Web folders. You don't even have to be using Windows XP; you can use these three applications on earlier versions of Windows as well.

To use a folder that has been shared using Web Sharing, you need to know the folder's URL, which the manager of the Web server you'll be using sets. In Internet Explorer, you can't use a link in a Web page to pop open a Web Folder. You have to use the following procedure instead:

1. Select File, Open.
2. Enter the Web folder's URL, being sure to start with `http:`, and check the Open as Web Folder box, as shown in Figure 16.14.

Figure 16.14
When opening a Web folder, always type `http:` at the beginning of the URL.

3. Click OK.

4. You might be prompted to enter your login name and password. It's safe to do so, even over the Internet.

An ordinary folder view will appear, as in Figure 16.15. You can treat it in the usual way: drag files in and out, create new folders, and rename and delete files, providing you have the appropriate permissions to do these things. These operations take much longer than with LAN file sharing, however.

One peculiar thing to note is that after you open a Web folder from Internet Explorer, the window changes to Windows Explorer view. The File menu will no longer have an Open choice. If you want to open another Web folder, you'll have to start Internet Explorer again.

Windows will automatically add the Web folder address you used to My Network Places, and the Web Folders list in Other Places. This is a convenient way to return to the folder later.

Figure 16.15
The Web Folder view looks just like an ordinary Explorer folder view.

You can also view a Web folder using the Add Network Place Wizard in My Network Places. When you're asked for the location of the network place, enter the Web folder URL starting with `http:`.

N O T E

> After you open a Web folder, you might be tempted to create a shortcut to it by dragging the address from the Address bar in the Explorer window. This approach doesn't work if you opened the Web folder by choosing File, Open; you get a Web page shortcut instead.
>
> If you opened the Web folder by using the Add Network Places Wizard, however, or by opening an existing Web Folder icon, you get a working folder shortcut. Strange!

If you see an empty folder, or if you see a plain listing of filenames and dates without icons, see "Web Folder Appears to Be Empty" or "Directory Listing Appears Instead of Web Folder" in the "Troubleshooting" section at the end of the chapter.

16

USING PRINTERS ON THE NETWORK

Whether you're part of a large corporation or have a home network with just two computers, network printing is a great time and money saver. Why connect a printer to each computer, when it will spend most of its time idle? By not having to buy a printer for each user, you can spend the money you save more constructively on faster, higher quality, and more interesting printers. You might add a color photo-quality printer or a transparency maker to give your network users more output choices.

Windows XP really excels at network printing. Here are some of the neat features of Windows XP network printing:

- Windows can print to any of hundreds of printer models, whether they're attached to a computer or connected directly to the LAN.

- It can send printer output to other operating systems. OS/2 and Linux/Unix printer support is built in to Windows XP. Linux/Unix and Macintosh users can access your shared printers if they get software that enables them to access Windows networks.

- If you select a printer shared by a computer running Windows XP, the necessary printer driver software will be installed on your computer automatically.

- Users of older versions of Windows can attach to a Windows XP network printer, and the correct printer driver for their operating system can be installed for them automatically as well.

- You can print to and monitor a Windows XP printer over the Internet with new Internet Printer Protocol (IPP) support.

→ To learn more details about monitoring a printer via an Internet connection, **see** "Using Printers over the Internet with IPP," **p. 556**.

- Printer data is sent to a spooler on the computer that shares the printer. The printer data is stored on the hard disk while the printer catches it, making printing seem faster to user applications. More than one person at a time can send output to the same shared printer; their print requests simply queue up and come out in first-come, first-served order. (You can raise or lower a user's or an individual print job's priority, though, to give preference to some print jobs over others.)

Because the software to do all this comes with Windows XP Home Edition, and you can hook computers together for about the cost of a movie ticket, printer sharing alone is a good enough reason to install a network.

The best part is that from the user's standpoint, using a network printer is no different than using a local printer. Everything you learned about printing in Chapter 6, "Printing and Faxing," applies to network printers; the only difference is in the one-time step of adding the printer to Windows. Later in the chapter, I'll describe how to share a printer attached to your computer; right now, let's look at using a printer that has already been shared elsewhere on the network.

USING SHARED PRINTERS

Windows can directly attach to printers shared via Microsoft Networking services, whether from Windows XP, 2000, NT, 95, 98, Windows for Workgroups, OS/2, or even the Samba service from Linux and Unix.

To use a shared printer, you have to install the printer in your Printers folder, just as you would with any printer, as I described in Chapter 6. To start, display the Printers and Faxes window from the Start Menu or from Control Panel. (If Printers and Faxes doesn't appear on your start menu, you can add it by customizing the Start Menu, as explained in Chapter 23, "Maintaining and Optimizing System Performance." I put Printers and Faxes and My Network Places on my Start menu, as I use them all the time).

NOTE

> Windows may already have automatically installed icons for printers shared by other Windows XP computers on your network. If that's the case, you can stop right here. Just use the printer(s) as you would one attached directly to your computer.
>
> You might want to rename the icons, though, removing the word "Auto" from their names.

To add a network printer, select the Add a Printer task, and click Next. Select Network Printer rather than Local Printer, and choose Next.

Next, you have to identify the shared printer. If you know its network name already, you can type it into the Name box in UNC format—for example, \\sumatra\laserjet—as shown in Figure 16.16.

Figure 16.16
You can enter a UNC shared printer name if know it, or you can leave the Name field blank and choose Next to browse the network for a shared printer.

After you've identified the shared printer, click Next to finish installing it.

LOCATING A SUITABLE PRINTER

If you don't know the name of the printer you want to use, you can browse through the network. You went through something like this already when you were mapping shared folders to drives, but this time there's no Browse button. Just leave the Name field blank, and choose Next.

On a workgroup network, the network display appears, as shown in Figure 16.17, to let you probe into domains or workgroups, computers, and their shared printers.

Figure 16.17
You can browse your workgroup network for shared printers by opening the list view of networks, domains, workgroups, and computers. Shared printers are found listed under each computer. It helps that the list includes only computers with shared printers.

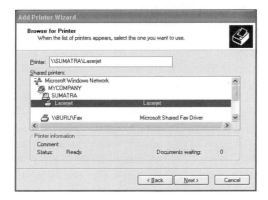

From here, just select the printer you want, and click Next to finish the installation.

SELECTING A PRINTER DRIVER

When you've chosen a printer, Windows automatically looks to the computer sharing that printer for the correct software driver for Windows XP. If it finds the driver, that driver is instantly downloaded to your PC, and the installation completes without you having to look up the printer's model number, hunt for the right driver diskettes, or otherwise lift a finger.

You might hit a snag, though, if the sharing computer doesn't have the correct Windows XP printer driver for you. You might have this problem if the remote computer isn't running Windows XP. In this case, Windows pops up a message saying: "The server on which the printer resides does not have the correct printer driver installed. If you want to install the driver on your local computer, click OK."

If you want to use the printer, well, now you will have to lift a finger. Click OK, and Windows displays the Add Printer Wizard with its list of known printer manufacturers and models, as discussed in Chapter 6. Choose the correct make and model from the list, and then click OK.

→ If you can't locate the correct printer model in this list and need more detailed instructions on installing printer drivers, **see** "If the Printer Isn't Found or Is on a Serial (COM) Port," **p. 179**.

FINISHING THE INSTALLATION

If you are adding a second or subsequent printer, Windows asks whether you want this newly installed printer to be set as your default printer. You can choose Yes or No, as you like; then select Next. You can always change your choice of default printer later, as I'll show you in the next section.

When you click Finish, the wizard adds the printer to your list of printer choices, and you're finished. The network printer is ready to use in any application. The whole process usually takes about 15 seconds from start to finish.

> **NOTE**
>
> When the new printer appears in your printer window, you might want to verify that you can actually use the printer and that its output is correct. To do so, right-click the printer icon and select Properties. Select Print a Test Page to ensure that the network printer is working correctly.

SETTING A DEFAULT PRINTER

If you've installed more than one printer, you can choose one to be the default printer in your Windows applications like this:

1. Right-click your preferred printer.
2. Choose Set Default Printer.

You might select the printer closest to you as your default printer and select alternate printers only when you need one for its special features, or when your usual printer is backlogged.

USING THE NETWORK PRINTER

When the network printer is set up, you can use it in exactly the same way as you use a locally attached printer, so all the printer management discussion in Chapter 6 applies to network printers, too. The only difference is that you probably won't have management privileges on someone else's shared printer, so you can't change the printer's properties or manage the printer owner's print jobs. The reason is that Windows XP Home Edition's Simple File Sharing feature treats all remote network users as the "Guest" user, and Guest has very restricted access to the computer.

It's probably best that you don't have that capability anyway, as it's considered bad form to change the hardware setup of someone else's printer without permission. If you connect to a computer that doesn't use Simple File Sharing (such as Windows 2000 Server), view the printer's Properties page and have access to all the usual printer configuration tabs—Sharing, Ports, Advanced, Security and Device Settings—don't make any changes without the permission of the printer's owner. Changing the port, for example, will certainly make the printer stop working, and the printer's owner probably won't figure out why for quite some time (when they do, leave town).

You can view and manage the printer's list of pending documents by double-clicking the printer icon. However, you can't cancel or alter the properties of anyone's print jobs but your own.

USING PRINTERS OVER THE INTERNET WITH IPP

A fairly new feature in Windows is the capability to install and print to a shared printer through the Internet as easily as you can through a LAN. The Internet Printing Protocol (IPP) was developed by a group of network and printer technology companies at the initiative of Novell Corporation and Xerox Corporation. They saw the need for a standardized way to provide reliable, secure, and full-featured print spooling functions over the Internet.

The idea is that business travelers should be able to send reports back to their home offices via the Internet and use the same technology to print reports or presentations in a hotel's business center or a commercial copy service center. I use it myself to print to my office's laser printer from home. Some printers are even manufactured with IPP built in, so you can simply connect them directly to your network and use them from any of your computers.

IPP is based on the Hypertext Transfer Protocol (HTTP), which runs the World Wide Web, so it's simple and it passes safely through network firewalls. In Windows, IPP uses Windows's own safely encrypted username and password security, so your printers are protected from abuse by anonymous outsiders.

As with all the shared resources I'm discussing, using and providing these services are really separate things. You can use IPP to reach a printer without providing the service yourself, and vice versa. In this section, I'll talk about *using* the service.

The blessing of IPP is that once you've installed the printer icon, you can use the remote printer in exactly the same way as you use any Windows printer. The printer queue, management tools, and other operations are all exactly the same, as long as you're connected to the Internet or the appropriate intranet LAN.

SELECTING AN IPP PRINTER BY ITS URL

You can connect to a remote printer via IPP in either of two ways. If you know the URL of the IPP-connected printer, you can use the Add Printer Wizard, as I discussed earlier in this chapter. You'll need to get the URL from the printer's owner, that is, your network manager at work, or from the hotel or service bureau.

1. Follow the instructions I gave earlier for adding a network printer.
2. When you are asked to enter the printer name, choose Connect to a Printer on the Internet or on a Home or Office Network.
3. Enter the URL provided by the network administrator or the service you are using, as shown in Figure 16.18, and select Next.
4. You might be prompted for a username and password. If so, enter the name and password supplied by the vendor or, if the printer is on your own network, your network username and password.
5. Continue with the installation procedure described above; you might need to select a print driver if the remote print server doesn't provide it automatically.

Figure 16.18
Adding an Internet-connected printer using IPP. This URL is fictitious, but the hope is that soon you will be able to send output to a printer at a copy center or service bureau as easily as to a printer in your own home or office.

When the new printer icon is installed, you have a fully functional Windows printer. You can view the pending jobs and set your print and page preferences as usual as long as you're connected to the Internet (or the LAN, in a service establishment).

TIP

> If you use a printing service, remember to delete the printer from your Printers folder when you leave town; you don't want to accidentally print reports in Katmandu after you've returned home.

SELECTING AN IPP PRINTER OVER THE WEB

If you can reach a service bureau or a Windows XP/2000 Professional or Server computer that sports both Internet Information Services (IIS) and a shared printer, Internet printing is a snap.

TIP

> If you use Windows XP Professional or Windows 200x Server at work, and Windows XP Home Edition at home, you can use this feature to print to your office printer from home, as long as the office computer's Web server is reachable over the Internet.

If you view the URL `http://computername/Printers`, replacing *computername* with the actual hostname of the remote computer, you get a display like the one shown in Figure 16.19.

Selecting one of the printers brings up a detailed printer status page, as shown in Figure 16.20. The printer status page lists queued print jobs and current printer status. If you're using Internet Explorer as your Web browser and have IPP printing software installed in Windows, clicking Connect sets this printer up as a network printer on your computer, drivers and all. You can select the printer and use it immediately, right over the Internet.

Figure 16.19
Windows 2000/XP Professional and Server versions provide a Web Interface for printer management. The home page gives a quick overview of all shared printers. You can select a printer to view or manage for more detail.

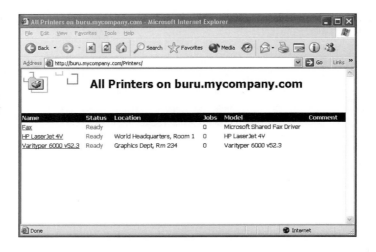

Figure 16.20
The printer status page shows current print jobs; using it, you can manage the printer and queued documents. The Connect hyperlink installs the printer on your computer.

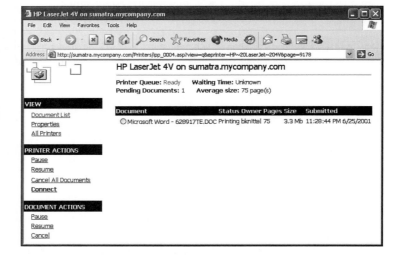

 If you view a Windows XP computer's Printers Web page, and can select printers but don't have the Connect option, see "No Connect Option for Web Printing" in the "Troubleshooting" section at the end of this chapter.

USING OTHER IPP PRINTERS

You can buy an IPP-capable printer and plug it directly into your LAN. An IPP-capable printer will probably provide Web-based management and status, which is a great way to monitor its health from across the country (or across the room).

In a workgroup network, the printer might not have a registered hostname, so you might need to refer to it by its assigned IP address, as in `http://192.168.0.24/hplaser4`. The installation instructions for the printer tell you what URL to use.

When you know the URL for the intranet- or Internet-accessible printer, follow the instructions from earlier in this chapter. You don't have to search for the printer, though. When you get to the screen shown in Figure 16.16, choose Connect to a Printer on the Internet or on a Home or Office Network. Enter the URL, and then go on installing the printer as instructed earlier.

When it is set up, you can use the printer as if it were directly connected to your PC.

> **TIP**
>
> Connect to the printer this way with just *one* of your Windows XP computers. Share the printer from that computer with the rest of your LAN. This way, you can make installation easier for everyone else.

USING UNIX AND LPR PRINTERS

In the Unix and Linux world, most shared printers use a protocol called LPR/LPD, which was developed at the University of California at Berkeley during the early years of Unix and the TCP/IP protocol.

> **NOTE**
>
> If you have a Unix background, you might be happy to know that the familiar `lpr` and `lpq` utilities are available as command-line programs in Windows XP.

Manufacturers such as Hewlett-Packard make direct network-connected printers that accept the LPR protocol, and many companies sell small LPR-based print server devices that can attach to your printer as well. You can connect one of these printers to your LAN, configure its TCP/IP settings to match your LAN, and immediately print without running a cable from a computer to the printer. This way, you can place a printer in a more convenient place than could be reached by a 10-foot printer cable. Better yet, you can use these networked printers without requiring a Windows computer to be left turned on to manage it.

You can install a Windows printer that directs its output to an LPR print queue or device as easily as you can install a directly connected printer. Follow these steps:

1. For the first LPR-based printer you use, you have to install LPR support. Open My Network Places and select View Network Connections. Select Advanced, Optional Networking Components. Check Other Network File and Print Services and click Next. You may need to insert your Windows XP Installation CD-ROM.

2. View Printers and Faxes and select Add a Printer.

3. Select Local Printer. (You choose Local because Network connects only to Windows and IPP shared printers.) Uncheck Automatically Detect and Install My Plug and Play Printer, and click Next.

4. Select the Create a New Port option, and choose LPR Port in the Type of Port box, and click Next.

5. In the Add LPR Compatible Printer dialog, enter the IP address or hostname of the Unix or print server, and the name of the print queue on that server, as shown in Figure 16.21.

Figure 16.21
In this dialog box, enter the IP address or hostname of the LPR print server and the queue or printer name.

6. Select the manufacturer and printer model as usual, and proceed with the rest of the printer installation.

NOTE

If you enter the wrong IP address, hostname, or print queue name, Windows will not let you change this information. To correct the problem, bring up the printer's Properties page, select the Ports tab, highlight the LPR port, and select Configure Port. If Windows doesn't display a dialog to let you change the IP information, uncheck the LPR port. Delete the port, and add a new LPR port with the correct information. Then check the port to connect your Windows printer to the LPR server.

USING APPLETALK PRINTERS

If your network has AppleTalk printers attached, you probably have Macintosh users on your LAN.

Windows XP Home Edition doesn't offer services to let your computer share files or printers with Mac users, so the burden is on the Mac. Mac users may be able to obtain SMB protocol software to let use printers and files shared by Windows.

NOTE

Before giving up, however, check the documentation on your networked printer. Some printers support access via all three standard protocols: AppleTalk, NetBIOS (SMB), and TCP/IP.

USING OTHER NETWORK-CONNECTED PRINTERS

Windows XP can use other types of network-connected printers as well. Some printer models come with a built-in network connection, and others have a network adapter option. You can also buy network printer servers, which are small boxes with a network connector and one to three printer connection ports. These devices let you locate printers in a convenient area, which doesn't need to be near a computer.

The installation procedures for different printer and server models vary. Your networked printer or print server will come with specific installation instructions. When you install it, you have a choice about how the printer will be shared on your network:

- You can install the network-to-printer connection software on *one* of your Windows computers, and then use standard Windows printer sharing to make the printer available to the other computers on your network.
- You can install the printer's connection software on *each* of your computers.

With the first method, you will guarantee that print jobs will be run first-come-first-served, because one computer will provide a queue for the printer. Another plus is that you'll only have to do the software setup once, it's much easier to set up the other workstations to use the standard Windows shared printer. The one computer will have to be left on for others to use the printer, however.

With the second method, each computer will contact the printer independently, so there may be contention for the printer. However, no computers need to be left on, since each workstation will contact the printer directly.

You can use either method. The first one is simplest, and is best suited for a busy office. The second method is probably more convenient for home networks and small offices.

USING NETWORK RESOURCES EFFECTIVELY

Tips are scattered throughout this chapter, but I want to collect a few of the best ones here for easy reference. The following tips and strategies will help you make the most of your LAN.

USE MY NETWORK PLACES

My Network Places not only serves as a convenient place to collect shortcuts to network resources, but it also appears under My Computer when you open or save files in any application. This feature can save you lots of time when you use the same network folders over and over.

You can make shortcuts in My Network Places for the handful of the network shared folders that you use most frequently.

16

You can add the names of subfolders when you make these shortcuts, if you find that you always have to drill your way into the main shared folder to get to the folder you actually want.

MAKE FOLDER SHORTCUTS

You can drag the icon appearing in the Address bar from any shared folder view to your desktop, to My Network Places, or any other convenient place for reuse later. (The Address bar may not appear on your Explorer windows. You may need to right-click the toolbar and check Address Bar. You also might need to uncheck Lock the Toolbars to drag it into a visible position.)

I like to organize projects into folders on my desktop and put related network resources in each. For example, I might have three project folders on my desktop, and in each one, three shortcuts to related shared folders.

Because shortcuts aren't the "real thing," you can have shortcuts to the same network places wherever you need them.

PUT TOOLS AND DOCUMENTATION ONLINE

Power users and Administrators might want to management batch files, Registry installation and setup files, special program utilities, and documentation in a shared network folder, for convenient access from any computer on the network. Your network's users don't need to know it's there unless you want them to.

SHARING FOLDERS AND DRIVES

Windows automatically makes your computer's Shared Documents folder available on the network. However, you may wish to share other folders with your network cohorts. This capability is built right into Explorer.

CAUTION

> When you share folders on a computer running Windows XP Home Edition, anybody can see the files, and if you allow modification, anybody can modify them. They don't even need a user ID or password—just a connection to your network. (If you have an unsecured wireless network, this includes random people driving by your home or office.) Be very careful to share folders that contain only files you want others to be able to see.

To share a folder, just follow these steps:

1. Select a folder in Explorer, or select the name of the CD-ROM, floppy, Zip, or hard drive itself at the top of the Explorer view, if you want to share the entire disk.

   Microsoft recommends that you only share folders found inside your My Documents folder, but I think that's too restrictive. You can safely share any folder on your hard drive except Documents and Settings, Program Files and your Windows folder. You should not share the entire hard drive that contains your Windows folder.

2. Right-click the folder, and choose Sharing and Security.

3. Select Share This Folder on the Network. Windows fills in the Share Name field with the name of the folder. If the name contains spaces, it may not be accessible to Windows for Workgroups users, so if you still have computers running this old operating system, you might want to shorten or abbreviate the name. You also can enter a comment to describe the contents of the shared folder, as shown in Figure 16.22.

4. If you want remote users to be able to add, delete, and edit files in your shared folder, check Allow Network Users to Change My Files. Otherwise, uncheck it.

Figure 16.22
When sharing a location, be sure to enter a share name. Comments are optional.

TIP

> You can prevent other users from seeing your shared folder when they browse the network by adding a dollar sign to the end of the share name—for example, `mystuff$`. They have to know to type in this name to use the shared folder. However, this convention alone does *not* prevent them from seeing your files if they know the share name.

Before clicking OK to make the folder accessible, you should consider file security and the ability of other users to access your files. I'll continue this discussion in the next section.

 If you receive a File Is in Use By Another error when attempting to use one of the files in a folder you have shared, see "File Is in Use by Another" in the "Troubleshooting" section at the end of this chapter.

16

NOTE

You do have to run the Network Setup Wizard at least once to share any of your computer's files, even if you've set up your network manually. The Network Setup Wizard was discussed in Chapter 15.

SHARED FOLDER SECURITY

Sharing security is frequently misunderstood. You can specify the rights of remote users and groups to read or change (that is, write, delete, rename, and so on) the files in your shared folder when you enable sharing, as shown in Figure 16.22. It works like this:

- If you check Allow Network Users to Change my Files, remote users will be able to delete, edit, or rename files in your shared folders just as they would if they were logged on to your computer directly.

- If you don't check Allow Network Users they'll only be able to view and read files.

Network security is a serious matter, and if you use the Internet, you should be very sure to understand the risks you're exposing your files to and the ways you can protect them. I suggest that you be sure to read Chapter 19, "Network Security."

After you've chosen whether to permit write-access by network users, click OK to make the share available on the network.

Finally, when you have shared a folder, its icon changes to a hand holding the folder like an offering. This is your cue that the folder is shared. You can right-click the folder later on to select Sharing and Security if you want to stop sharing or change the sharing permissions.

SHARING PRINTERS

You can share any local printer on your computer. It can be a printer directly cabled to your computer or one connected via the network using LPR or other network protocols.

To enable printer sharing, do the following:

1. Choose Start and view the Printers and Faxes folder.
2. Right-click the printer icon and choose Sharing, or select Properties and then select the Sharing tab.
3. Select Share This Printer, and enter a network name for the printer, as shown in Figure 16.23. Enter up to 14 characters, using letters, numbers, and hyphens. Avoid spaces if you have Windows 3.x computers on your network. 8.3 naming is recommended if Windows 3.x computers need to access the share.
4. If your network has only Windows XP/2000 computers, click OK, and you're finished. Other network users can now use the shared printer.

Otherwise, continue to the next section to add extra printer drivers for other operating systems.

Figure 16.23
Enabling sharing for a printer.

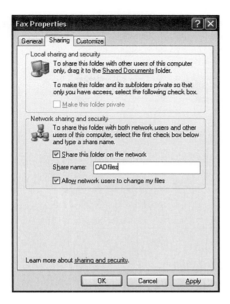

INSTALLING EXTRA PRINTER DRIVERS

If you have computers running other versions of Windows or other CPU types, you can load the appropriate printer drivers for those operating systems now, and network users will receive them automatically when they connect to your printer. This step is optional, but it's the friendly thing to do.

View the Sharing tab in your printer's Properties dialog box, and select the Additional Drivers button. Windows displays a list of supported operating systems and CPU types, as shown in Figure 16.24. (By the way, "Intel" refers to any Intel or compatible chips like those made by AMD.)

Figure 16.24
You can install drivers for additional operating systems or CPUs to make it easy for network users to attach to your printer.

Check the boxes for the CPUs and operating systems you want to support, and click OK. Windows then goes through any additional operating systems you chose one-by-one and asks either for your Windows XP CD-ROM, or other operating system installation disks to locate the appropriate drivers, as shown in Figure 16.25.

Figure 16.25
In this dialog box, you are asked to locate the appropriate drivers for each operating system as requested.

You can find these drivers on the original installation disks for the alternate operating system, or often on disks provided with the printer, which may contain support for many operating systems on the same disk.

When installed, the alternate drivers are sequestered in your Windows folder and delivered to users of the other operating systems when necessary.

NOTIFYING USERS WHEN PRINTING IS COMPLETE

You can have Windows send a pop-up message to remote users when print jobs they send to your printer have completed. By default, this feature is turned off when you install Windows XP.

To enable remote user notification, do the following:

1. Open the Printers and Faxes window.
2. Choose File, Server Properties.
3. Select the Advanced tab.
4. Check Notify When Remote Documents Are Printed.
5. If users on your network tend to use more than one computer at a time, check Notify Computer, Not User, When Remote Documents Are Printed. This option sends the notification to the computer where the print job originated rather than to the user who submitted the print job.
6. Click OK.

With remote notification enabled, when a print job has completed, a notification pops up on the sender's desktop, as in Figure 16.26. No message is sent if the print job is canceled, however.

Figure 16.26
Remote Notification tells a user that his or her print job submitted over the network has completed.

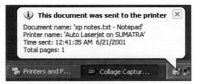

CHANGING THE LOCATION OF THE SPOOL DIRECTORY

When jobs are queued up to print, Windows stores the data it's prepared for the printer in a folder on the computer that's sharing the printer. Data for your own print jobs and that for any network users will all end up on your hard drive temporarily. If the drive holding your Windows directory is getting full and you'd rather house this print data on another drive, you can change the location of the spool directory.

To change the location of the Windows print spooler folder

1. View the Printers and Faxes folder.
2. Select File, Server Properties and select the Advanced tab.
3. Enter a new location for the Spool Folder and click OK.

MANAGING NETWORK USE OF YOUR COMPUTER

If you've shared folders on your LAN, you might want to know who's using them. You could need to know this information if, for example, someone were editing a file in your shared folder. If you tried to edit the same file, you'd be told by your word processor that the file was "in use by another." But by whom?

Computer Management can help you out. Open the Start menu, right-click My Computer, select Manage, and open the Shared Folders system tool. It displays the shared folders that your computer offers and the number of users attached to them.

You can add new shared folders using the Shares tool with a right-click.

You also can view the current users (sessions) and the files they have in use with the Sessions and Open Files views. This will let you know whom to ask to close a file, or, in an emergency, you can disconnect a user or close an open file with the Delete key. (This is a drastic measure and is sure to mess up the remote user, so use it only when absolutely necessary.)

MANAGING NETWORK RESOURCES USING THE COMMAND LINE

If you find yourself repeating certain network and file operations over and over, day after day, it makes sense to try to automate the process. You might be so used to the graphical interface that you've forgotten the command line, but it's still there, and you can perform drive mappings and printer selections with the command line almost as easily as from the GUI. Batch files, which were so familiar in the old DOS days, are still around and are a great way to perform repetitive administrative tasks.

I use batch files to perform simple computer-to-computer backups of important files. Let's say I want to back up the folder c:\book on my computer to a shared folder of the same name on another computer named abalone. Here's what a batch file to do this might look like:

```
@echo off
net use q: /delete 1>nul 2>nul
net use q: \\abalone\book
xcopy c:/book q: /e /r /c /y
net use q: /delete
exit
```

Of course, I could bring up Explorer, locate my c:\book folder and the abalone book folder, drag the folder from one computer to the other, and repeat this process every time I want to make a copy of my files. But a shortcut to the above batch file on my desktop will do the same job with a double-click, and I can add the batch file as a Scheduled Task to run automatically every night. *Now* which seems more convenient—that nifty GUI or the humble command-line batch file? Knowing the net utilities gives you an extra set of tools to work with, and their ancient origins shouldn't make them seem less worthy!

The net command comes to us virtually unchanged since the original PC network software developed by Microsoft and IBM back in the early 1980s. There are so many variations of the net command that I think of them as separate commands: net view, net use, net *whatever*. Each net command contains a word that selects a subcommand or operation type.

You can get online help by typing net /? or net *command* /?, where *command* is one of the net subcommands.

MAPPING DRIVES WITH net use

The net use command is the most useful of the command-line network functions. net use makes and disconnects drive mappings, and establishes printer redirection for command-line programs. The basic command is as follows:

```
net use drive sharename
```

The following example

```
net use q: \\abalone\book
```

maps drive letter q to the shared folder \\abalone\book. You can't replace the shared folder attached to an already mapped drive, so it's best to place commands in the batch file to delete any previous mapping before trying to make a new one:

```
net use q: /delete
net use q: \\abalone\book
```

The /delete command prints an error message if there was no previous message. An elegant solution to this is to redirect the output of the first net command to NUL, which discards any output. I usually redirect both standard output and standard error output with

```
net use q: /delete 1>nul 2>nul
```

to ensure that this command will do its work silently.

You can add the /persistent:yes option to a net use command to make the drive mapping return when you log off and back on, matching the function of the Reconnect at Login check box in the graphical drive mapping tool.

16

You can also map a drive to a subfolder of a shared folder—mimicking the "map root" function familiar to Novell NetWare veterans. Subfolder mapping lets you run legacy DOS applications that require that certain files or directories be placed in the root directory of a hard disk. You can fool them into running with data on a shared network folder. I like to do this because it lets me store data in a centralized place where it will get backed up regularly.

For example, suppose the hypothetical program runit needs to see its data files in the current root directory, and runs from directory \startdir. I want all the files to reside in a shared network folder, in a subdirectory oldprog of a shared folder named \\server\officedata. This batch file does the trick:

```
@echo off
net use e: /delete 1>nul 2>nul
net use e: \\server\officedata\oldprog
e:
cd \startdir
runit
c:
net use e: /delete
exit
```

Creating a shortcut to this batch file in Windows XP lets me run the old program with a double-click.

net use also maps network printers to the legacy DOS printer devices LPT1, LPT2, and LPT3. The capture printer setting found in Windows 9x is not available, and the only way to redirect DOS program output to a network printer is through net use.

The following command directs DOS application LPT1 printer output to the network printer:

```
net use lpt1: \\server\printername
```

The following command cancels it:

```
net use lpt1: /delete
```

TROUBLESHOOTING

NO CONNECT OPTION FOR WEB PRINTING

I can view a Windows XP computers/printers Web page and select a printer, but Connect is not shown as an option.

This problem should only occur when you're trying to establish the connection using an older version of Windows. This won't be a problem with Windows XP or Windows 2000. If you are using an older version of Windows, first of all, you must be using Internet Explorer version 5 or higher. Then, you need to have IPP software installed on the computer that is viewing the Web page, and you must be using Internet Explorer as your Web browser. Windows 95, 98, and NT 4 can get IPP software from http://www.windowsupdate.com. Download the Internet Printing update. Then, when you view the Web page with IE, you can connect and use the printer.

WEB FOLDER APPEARS TO BE EMPTY

When I view a Web folder known to contain files, it appears to be empty. What's wrong?

The Web server that is sharing the folder does not have Directory Listing enabled on the shared folder. The manager of this Web server (who could be you) needs to set this property in the Web Sharing Properties dialog box for the folder.

DIRECTORY LISTING APPEARS INSTEAD OF WEB FOLDER

When I view a Web folder, I see a columnar text listing of filenames, sizes, and dates instead of the expected folder view with icons.

You did not view the folder using the Open dialog box with Open as Web Folder checked, or the Web site you visited does not have WebDAV, FrontPage, or Office server extensions installed. This can also happen if you opened the folder using a shortcut you created by dragging the Address icon from Explorer when you first viewed this Web folder. Get your shortcut from My Network Places instead.

FILE IS IN USE BY ANOTHER

When I attempt to edit a file in a folder I've shared on the network, I receive an error message indicating that the file is in use by another user.

You can find out which remote user has the file open by using the Shared Folder tool in Computer Management, as I described earlier in this chapter under "Managing Network Use of Your Computer."

You can wait for the remote user to finish using your file, or you can ask that person to quit. Only in a dire emergency should you use the Shared Folder tool to disconnect the remote user or close the file. The only reasons I can think of to do this would be that the remote user's computer has crashed, but your computer thinks the connection is still established, or that the remote user is an intruder.

TIPS FROM THE WINDOWS PROS: USING COMMAND-LINE UTILITIES

Setting up a new network can be a grueling task. If you've ever set up a dozen computers in a day, you know what I mean. Think how long it took you to set up Windows, install applications, set up printers and network information, and get the desktop just so…then multiply that work by 10 or more. Then repeat the process any time a new computer is installed, or repaired and reformatted.

Network managers do anything they can to minimize the amount of work they need to do to set up and maintain computers. Windows 200x Server offers a remote installation service that can set up a completely outfitted Windows XP Professional workstation in a new computer, over the LAN, without laying a finger on it. This is a blessing for them, but what about those of us with peer-to-peer workgroup LANs?

The rest of us rely on whatever handy labor-saving tricks we can find to minimize the amount of work needed. Batch files can go a long way to help ease the pain of installing, and they also have two other benefits: They let you make more consistent installations, and they serve as a sort of documentation of whatever configuration they're performing.

If you're responsible for setting up lots of computers for friends or for a business, my first tip is to learn the Windows XP command-line utilities; you can set up batch files to make some consistent settings on new computers. It doesn't hurt to learn how to use Windows Scripting Host. And, the Windows XP Resource Kit offers a big pile of extra command line utilities. Every power user should have a copy of the resource kit.

Put any batch files and scripts you develop in a shared network folder, and you'll have an installation and configuration toolkit. If a user accidentally disconnects a mapped network drive, that person can visit your folder of handy icons, click MAPDRIVES, and easily reset everything. This can be done with net use commands in a batch file.

You also can install printers with the command line. The entire functionality of the Install Printer Wizard is available at the command line; you can pop up graphical utilities like the queue manager, and you even can perform installations and configure printers with a batch file.

Type the following at the command prompt for a full listing of the printer configuration utility's commands:

```
rundll32 printui.dll,PrintUIEntry /?
```

Scroll to the bottom of the list for an eye-popping list of examples. (I warn you, it's ugly. Some experimentation is required to get some of the commands to work, even with the examples given here.)

One really handy use of this command is to install a connection to a network shared printer. This example sets up the local computer to use the shared printer \\bali\laserjet:

```
rundll32 printui.dll,PrintUIEntry /n "\\bali\laserjet" /in
rundll32 printui.dll,PrintUIEntry /n "\\bali\laserjet" /y
```

The first command installs the printer, and the second makes it the default printer.

If you put commands like these in a batch file (using your own network's printer names, of course) and put the batch file in a shared network folder, you can add the printer(s) to any computer just by double-clicking the batch file icon. This capability can be a real time-saver when you're configuring many workstations. You could also put these commands in a common login script batch file on your network so that they are executed when your users log in. (For a discussion of logon scripts, see Chapter 25, "Managing Users.")

WINDOWS UNPLUGGED: REMOTE AND MOBILE NETWORKING

In this chapter

GOING UNPLUGGED

LANs once were so expensive and difficult to manage that they were found only in big corporations. Now, networks are found in most businesses and many homes. Internet access is available nearly everywhere, even in coffee shops and airports. We're becoming more and more used to being connected. In fact, with the advent of wireless networking, some people believe that the Internet is going to evolve into the *Evernet*: a global network that's available everywhere, all the time.

We don't have an Evernet yet, but it's become easy—and even expected—that we should be able to connect to our office and home LANs and work wherever we are. Windows XP has several features to help make this possible:

- Dial-Up Networking lets you connect by modem to a remote network and use it as if you were directly connected. File sharing and network printing are available just as if you were wired right to the LAN.

- Virtual Private Networking lets you exploit the Internet or a wide area network to get from a computer to your own LAN, with a high degree of security.

- Offline Web pages let you mark Web pages and sites for perusal when you're disconnected from the Net.

- Remote Desktop lets you connect to a Windows XP Professional computer from afar as if you were there; you might use this to connect to your office from home, for instance.

- Remote Assistance lets you remotely see and control another user's desktop to render assistance or to work cooperatively.

- Built-in support for secure wireless and infrared connectivity lets you walk into remote offices (or coffee shops) and just start surfing and working…no wires.

Going "unplugged" is not perfectly effortless, but it's very close, and you'll find you take to it very quickly. You learned about Offline Web pages in Chapter 9, "Browsing the World Wide Web with Internet Explorer." Now it's time to tackle the network features.

DIAL-UP NETWORKING

Windows XP can connect to a remote Windows network via modem. All file sharing, printing, and directory services are available just as if you were directly connected. Just dial up, open shared folders, transfer files, and email as if you were there, and disconnect when you're finished.

The receiving end of Dial-Up Networking can be handled by the Remote Access Services (RAS) feature in Windows 200x or NT4 Server, or by third-party remote connection hardware devices manufactured by networking companies such as Cisco and Lucent.

Windows XP Home Edition comes with a stripped-down version of RAS, so you can also set up your own Windows XP computer to receive a single incoming modem connection.

You can do so, for example, to get access to your home computer and LAN from out of town or from the office, provided your company permits this access.

I'll discuss incoming calls later in the chapter. First, though, let me tell you how to connect to a remote Windows network.

SETTING UP DIAL-UP NETWORKING

To create a dial-up connection to a remote network or computer, you need an installed modem. You learned how to install modems in Chapter 8, "Internet and TCP/IP Connection Options," so start there to install and configure your modem.

You also must get or confirm the information shown in Table 17.1 with the remote network's or computer's manager.

TABLE 17.1   INFORMATION NEEDED FOR A RAS CONNECTION

Information	Reason
Telephone number	You must know the receiving modem's telephone number, including area code.
Modem compatibility	You must confirm that your modem is compatible with the modems used by the remote network; check which modem protocols are supported (V.90, V.32, and so on).
Protocols in use	The remote network should use TCP/IP and/or IPX/SPX. Windows XP can currently be made to use the NetBEUI protocol, but it's not guaranteed to work in the future.
TCP/IP configuration	You should confirm that the Remote Access Server assigns TCP/IP information automatically (dynamically) via DHCP. Usually, the answer is yes.
Mail servers	You might need to obtain the IP addresses or names of SMTP, POP, Exchange, Lotus Notes, or Microsoft Mail servers if you want to use these applications while connected to the remote network.
User ID and password	You must be ready to supply a username and password to the remote dial-up server. If you're calling a Windows XP, 200x, or NT RAS server, then use the same Windows username and password you use on that remote network.

Armed with this information, you're ready to create a dial-up connection to the remote network. To do so, just follow these steps:

1. Choose Start, My Computer, My Network Places and select View Network Connections. (Note: You might need to close the left Folders pane to see the Task list.)

NOTE

If this is the first time you've made any sort of dial-up connection, you will be asked to enter your area code before proceeding.

2. Select Create a New Connection, and click Next.

3. Select Connect to the Network at my Workplace (see Figure 17.1), and then click Next. Choose Dial-Up Connection, and then click Next.

Figure 17.1
Choose Connect to the Network at My Workplace from the New Connection Type selections.

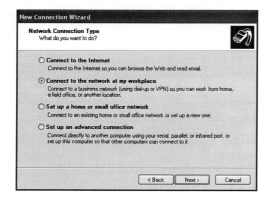

4. Enter a name for the connection, for example Office LAN, and click Next.

5. On the Phone Number To Dial dialog box, enter the telephone number of the remote dial-in server. You can enter the number directly, including any necessary prefixes or area codes. Select Next.

6. The final page asks if you want Windows to put a shortcut to this connection on your desktop. Check this if you want, and select Finish.

NOTE

You can delete a connection shortcut later if you don't want it and can drag the connection icon from Network Connections to your desktop later if you do.

7. After you've clicked Finish, Windows immediately wants to open the connection. You must first check the connection properties, so click the Properties button.

When the properties dialog box appears, review it to ensure that all the settings are correct. The next section discusses the most important connection properties.

SETTING A DIAL-UP CONNECTION'S PROPERTIES

There are two ways you can edit the properties for a dial-up connection from the Network Connections window: You can open the connection icon and click the Properties button, or you can right-click the icon and select Properties.

The Dial-Up Connection's properties page has five tabs and a heap o' parameters. Most of the time, the default settings will work correctly, but you might need to change some of them. I'll walk you through the most important parameters.

→ For detailed instructions on establishing locations and dialing rules, **see** "Phone and Modem Options," **p. 764**.

GENERAL

On the General tab of the Properties dialog (see Figure 17.2), you can set your choice of modems if you have more than one installed. You also can set telephone numbers and dialing rules.

Figure 17.2
General Properties include dialing and modem settings.

The significant parameters are as follows:

- **Connect Using**—If you have more than one modem installed, choose which modem to use for this connection. The Configure button lets you set the maximum speed (data rate) to use between the computer and the modem, and other modem properties.

- **Area Code, Phone Number, and Country/Region Code**—If the remote server has more than one phone number (or more than one hunt group), you can click Alternate to specify alternate telephone numbers. It's a neat feature if your company has several access points or provides emergency-use-only toll-free numbers.

- **Use Dialing Rules**—Check to have Windows determine when to send prefixes and area codes. If you want to use this, enter the Area code and Phone number in their separate fields. This feature is useful if you will be calling the same number from several locations with different dialing properties.

- **Show Icon in Notification Area**—This option lets you keep a small connection monitor icon in your task tray when you're connected to the remote network. Opening it lets you quickly disconnect the remote connection, so it's best to leave Show Icon checked.

OPTIONS

The Options tab of the Properties dialog (see Figure 17.3) includes dialing options, choices for being prompted for phone number and passwords, and redialing settings.

Figure 17.3
The Options tab includes dialing and prompting options.

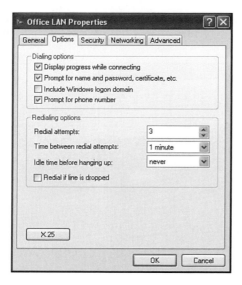

The important options are as follows:

- **Prompt for Name and Password**—If this box is checked, Windows always prompts for your remote connection user ID and password. If it is unchecked, after the first successful connection, Windows stores your password and uses it automatically later on. If you are worried that someone might dial the connection by gaining unauthorized access to your computer, leave this box checked; otherwise, you can uncheck it to skip the password step when connecting.

- **Include Windows Logon Domain**—Be sure to check this box if you are calling a Windows 200x/NT4 domain-type network and want to use your domain login name. When this box is checked, the dialing dialog box will have a space for you to enter the remote domain's name. (XP Home Edition doesn't support full Windows domain security. You can connect but you'll have to enter your domain username and password repeatedly to use network resources.)

- **Prompt for Phone Number**—If this box is checked, Windows displays the phone number it's about to dial. Leave it checked if you don't trust Windows to use the correct area code, prefixes, and so on. It's best to leave it checked until you're convinced.

- **Redialing Options**—If the remote server frequently gives you a busy signal, increase the number of attempts from 3 to, say, 20, and lower the delay from 1 minute to 15 seconds to get quicker redialing action.

- **Idle Time Before Hanging Up**—If you tend to wander off for hours with your modem still online, you can set this option to a reasonable time, and Windows will automatically disconnect you if no network traffic occurs for the specified time.

- **Redial If Line Is Dropped**—This option makes Windows redial immediately if your modem connection fails. It's good if you have lousy phone connections but bad if the remote computer disconnects you because its "idle time" runs out before yours does.

SECURITY

On the Security tab, you can select which encryption methods are required or permitted when you're logging on to the remote connection server. You will probably never need to change the default settings unless instructed to by a network administrator.

NETWORKING

The Networking tab of the Properties dialog (see Figure 17.4) defines which network protocols and network services are connected through the dial-up connection.

Figure 17.4
On the Networking tab, you can choose which network protocols and services are enabled for the dial-up connection. Check everything, and set the TCP/IP protocol's properties if necessary.

Usually, all protocols and services should be checked except File and Printer Sharing. This option should be disabled so remote network users cannot use your computer's shared folders and printers. If you really do want to let the remote network's users see them, check File and Printer Sharing.

Normally, a Remote Access Server automatically assigns your connection the proper IP address, DNS addresses, and other TCP/IP settings through DHCP, so you don't need to alter the Internet Protocol properties. In the very unlikely event that the network administrator tells you that you must set TCP/IP parameters yourself, select Internet Protocol from the Components list, and click Properties. Enter the supplied IP address and DNS addresses there.

ADVANCED

The Advanced tab configures Internet Connection Sharing and the Windows Firewall. These utilities might not be needed when you're connecting to a remote network.

If the network to which you're connecting is a safe, protected corporate network with its own firewall, you should disable Windows Firewall just for this particular dial-up connection. To do this, view the Advanced tab, click the Settings button, view the Windows Firewall's Advanced tab, and uncheck the dial-up connection that corresponds to your corporate network, as shown in Figure 17.5.

Figure 17.5
If you are connecting to a secure corporate network, you can disable Windows Firewall for just this connection.

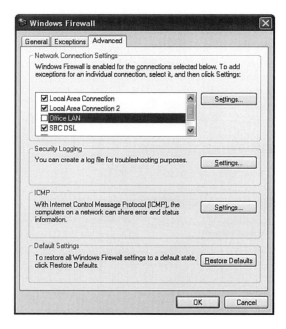

Finally, after you've finished making any changes to the connection's options, select OK. The connection icon is then installed in Network Connections for use anytime.

MANAGING DIAL-UP CONNECTIONS FROM MULTIPLE LOCATIONS

As you've seen already, Windows lets you enter your current telephone area code and dialing prefix requirements so that it can make modem calls using the customs appropriate for your local phone system. This capability is great if you use a portable computer. For example, at home, you might be in area code 415. At the office, you might be in area code 707 and have to dial 9 to get an outside telephone line. When you're visiting Indianapolis, you're in area code 317 and might need to use a telephone company calling card when making long-distance calls.

Windows offers great support for these variations by letting you define "locations," each with a separate local area code and dialing rules. When you use one of your Network Connections icons, as long as you've told Windows your current location, it can automatically apply the correct set of rules when making a dial-up connection.

➔ For detailed instructions on establishing locations and dialing rules, **see** "Phone and Modem Options," **p. 764**.

However, if you use an ISP with access points in various cities, or your company has different access numbers in various regions, you'll find that this Locations system does not let you associate a different dial-up number with each location. It would be great if it did, but no such luck.

If you want to use different "local" dial-up numbers for the various locations you visit with your computer, you must set up a separate Network Connections icon for each access number and use the appropriate icon when making a connection at each location.

TIP

> Set up and test the first access number you need. Then, when you need to add a new access number, right-click the first one, select Create Copy, rename it, and change its telephone number. I name my icons based on the location of the local number: Office-Berkeley, My Office-Seattle, and so on.
>
> When you travel and want to make a dial-up connection, select the appropriate dial-up icon, and set your location before you click Dial.

TIP

> If you travel, you'll find that having your Internet Options set to dial a particular connection automatically is not a great idea. It would dial the chosen connection no matter where you were (and remember, if there's a 50-50 chance of things going wrong, 9 times out of 10 they will). So, if you travel with your computer, you might want to open Internet Explorer and select Tools, Internet Options. Select the Connections tab, and choose Never Dial a Connection. This way, you won't be blind-sided by an inadvertent call to Indiana while you're in India.

17

MAKING A DIAL-UP CONNECTION

Making a remote network dial-up connection is no more difficult than connecting to the Internet. If you're a mobile user who moves between area codes, check your current location first, and then dial.

CHECK YOUR CURRENT LOCATION

If you've changed area codes or phone systems since the last time you made a modem connection, check your location setting by following these steps before dialing into the network:

1. Open the Control Panel, and select Printers and Other Hardware, then Phone and Modem Options.
2. Check your current location in the list of configured dialing locations using the Dialing Rules tab.
3. Click OK to close the dialog.

Windows should now use the correct area code and dialing prefixes.

CONNECTING TO A REMOTE NETWORK

To connect to a remote network, just follow these steps:

1. Open the connection from the Start Menu "Connect to" list, from Network Connections, or from a shortcut to the connection.

TIP

> Windows puts a "Connect to" menu on the Start menu when you've defined a dial-up connection. You can select a connection to dial, or right-click it to edit its properties. This is a real time saver.

2. Windows will open the connection dialog, as shown in Figure 17.6. Enter your login name and password. You can also select Properties to adjust the connection's telephone number or dialing properties. (The Dialing From choice appears only if you checked Use Dialing Rules and have defined more than one dialing location.)

TIP

> If you're connecting to a Windows 200x domain server, you can enter DOMAIN\ username or username@domain in the User name field. XP Home Edition doesn't support full Windows domain security. You can connect but you'll have to enter your domain username and password repeatedly to use network resources.

Figure 17.6
In the Connect dialog, you can enter your username and password for the remote network. You also can tell Windows to remember your password and change the dialing properties.

3. You can choose to let Windows remember your password, if you're not worried that other people might use your computer to gain inappropriate access to the remote network. (Giving access to "anyone who uses this computer" is usually used only for a shared ISP connection, not remote networks.)

4. Select Dial. Windows shows you the progress of your connection as it dials, verifies your username and password, and registers your computer on the remote network.

   If the connection fails, unless you dialed the wrong number, you'll most likely get a reasonable explanation: The password or account name was invalid, the remote system is not accepting calls, and so on. If you entered an incorrect username or password, you are usually given two more chances to re-enter the information before the other end hangs up on you.

   If the connection completes successfully, a new connection icon appears in your System Tray, indicating the established connection speed, as in Figure 17.7.

You can now use the remote network's resources, as I'll discuss next.

Figure 17.7
A connection icon appears in the task tray while the dial-up connection is connected.

CALLBACKS

For security purposes, some networks don't permit you to just call in; they want to call you, so you not only need the right login name and password, but you also must be at the right location to gain access to the network. This type of access also generates an audit trail through phone company records.

When this type of security is in force, your network manager will contact you to arrange the predetermined telephone number to use to call you. You cannot access the network from any other location unless you arrange for call forwarding from the original number.

Callbacks can also be used to make the remote host pay for a long phone call. Some businesses use callbacks so that employees can dial in from the field at the company's expense.

When callbacks are in effect, you'll dial up the remote network as I described earlier, but as soon as the network accepts your password it will hang up. Within 30 seconds it will call back, and your modem will pick up the line and establish a connection.

If your network manager says that callbacks are optional, you can tell Windows how you want to exercise the option. In Network Connections, select the Advanced menu, choose Dial-Up Preferences, and select the Callback tab. You can indicate that you want callbacks on or off, or that you want to be asked each time you make a connection.

USING REMOTE NETWORK RESOURCES

When you're connected, you can use network resources exactly as if you were on the network. My Network Places, shared folders, and network printers all function as if you were directly connected.

The following are some tips for effective remote networking by modem:

- Don't try to run application software that is installed on the remote network itself. Starting it could take hours!

- If you get disconnected while using a remote network, it's a bummer to have to stop what you're doing and reconnect. You can tell Windows to automatically redial if you're disconnected while you're working. In Network Connections, from the Advanced menu, choose Dial-up Preferences, and select the Autodial tab. Check any locations you work from where you would like Windows to automatically reconnect you.

> **TIP**
>
> If you get disconnected while you are editing a document that was originally stored on the remote network, save it on your local hard disk the moment you notice that the connection has been disrupted. Then, when the connection is reestablished, save it back to its original location. This will help you avoid losing your work.

- You can use My Network Places to record frequently visited remote network folders. You can also place shortcuts to network folders on your desktop or in other folders.

- If the remote LAN has Internet access, you can browse the Internet while you're connected to the LAN. You don't need to disconnect and switch to your ISP. You might need to make a change in your personal email program, though, as I'll note later under "Email and Network Connections."

- If you use several different remote networks, you can create a folder for each. In them, put shortcuts to the appropriate connection and to frequently used folders on those networks. Put all of these folders in a folder named e.g. "Remote Networks" on your desktop. This way you can open one folder and be working within seconds.

EMAIL AND NETWORK CONNECTIONS

If you use your computer with remote LANs as well as an ISP, you might need to be careful with the email programs you use. Most email programs don't make it easy for you to associate different mail servers with different connections.

Although most email servers allow you to retrieve your mail from anywhere on the Internet, most are very picky about whom they let send email. Generally, to use an SMTP server to send mail out, you must be using a computer whose IP address is known by the server to belong to its network. You can usually only send mail out through the server that serves your current connection.

See if your favorite email program can configure separate "identities," each with associated incoming and outgoing servers. If you send mail, be sure you're using the identity that's set up to use the outgoing (SMTP) server that belongs to your current dial-up connection.

→ For some tips on sending mail through different ISPs, **see** "All Your Mail Is in a Laptop," **p. 364**.

MONITORING AND ENDING A DIAL-UP CONNECTION

While you're connected, note that the System Tray connection icon flashes to indicate incoming and outgoing data activity. It's a true Windows tool, which means you can have it do pretty much the same thing in about five different ways.

NOTE

If the connection icon is missing, open Network Connections. Right-click the connection you're using, select Properties, and check Show Icon in Notification Area When Connected.

- If you hover your mouse cursor over the connection icon, a box appears, listing the connection name, speed, and number of bytes sent and received.
- If you double-click it, the connection status dialog box appears, as shown in Figure 17.8. From the status dialog, you can get to the connection properties or disconnect.
- If you right-click it, you can select Disconnect, Status, or Open Network Connections. This is the way to go.

Actually, all I ever do with the taskbar icon is make sure it blinks while I'm working and right-click Disconnect when I'm finished. When you disconnect a remote network connection, the taskbar icon disappears.

17

ENABLING DIAL-IN AND VPN ACCESS TO YOUR COMPUTER

Windows XP Home Edition has a stripped-down Remote Access Server (RAS) built in, and you can take advantage of it to get access to your work computer from home or from the field, or vice versa. You can also enable remote access temporarily so that a system administrator can maintain your computer.

Figure 17.8
The connection status dialog displays current connection statistics and lets you disconnect or change connection properties. Right-clicking the connection icon in the taskbar is a quicker way to disconnect.

17

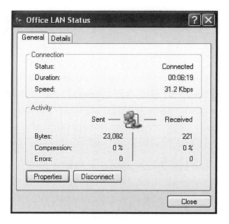

> **CAUTION**
>
> RAS is not too difficult to set up, but beware: Permitting remote access opens up security risks. Before you enable dial-in access on a computer at work, be sure that your company permits it. In some companies, you could be fired for violating the security policies.

To enable dial-in access, you must be logged on as a computer administrator. Then follow these steps:

1. In Network Connections, select the Create A New Connection task to start the New Connection Wizard. Click Next.

2. Choose Set Up An Advanced Connection, and click Next. Choose Accept Incoming Connections, and click Next.

3. Check the modem to be used for incoming connections.

> **TIP**
>
> Despite what the wizard dialog box seems to say, you can choose at most one modem. You *can* choose one of each different type of connection: modem and direct parallel port.

4. If you want to disconnect incoming connections that sit idle (unused) for too long, click the Properties button and check Disconnect a call if idle more than *XXX* minutes, and then click OK.

5. You then are asked whether you want to additionally permit Virtual Private Network connections to your computer. I'll discuss Virtual Private Networking later in this chapter. You can read ahead to decide whether you want it, or check Do Not Allow Virtual Private Connections now. You can always repeat this process to enable it later. It's best to not allow virtual private connections now if you're not sure.

6. Windows then displays a list of your computer's users. Select the ones who will be permitted to access your computer remotely, as shown in Figure 17.9. This step is very important: Check only the names of those users whom you really want and need to give access. The fewer accounts you enable, the less likely that someone might accidentally break into your computer.

Figure 17.9
Here, you can choose users who will be granted the right to remote access of your computer. Check only the names of those users really needing access, and don't check Guest.

CAUTION

Under no circumstances should you enable Guest for remote access. Guest is used for general network access. There's no way you would ever want to give unprotected access to your network via modem or VPN!

Check only the names of users who need access and who have good (long, complex) passwords.

7. You can enable or enforce callbacks for individual users if you like. Select the username, click Properties, then select the Callback tab. If you do enable callbacks, you must enter any required dialing prefixes and area codes. Windows doesn't use dialing rules when making callbacks.

8. Windows displays a list of network protocols and services that will be made available to the dial-up connection. Generally, you can leave all protocols and services checked.

View the properties page for each checked protocol to specify whether callers have access only to your computer or have access to the LAN via your computer. Unless you have a reason to ban a remote caller (usually you) from reaching the rest of your LAN, you have no reason to disable these services.

NOTE

> If you use or want to use incoming VPN connections and your Internet Connection Sharing or a connection sharing router between the Internet and your computer, you'll have to forward incoming VPN connections to your computer. For details, see "Making Services Available" in Chapter 18, "Connecting Your LAN to the Internet."

When someone connects to your computer using a VPN connection, there is a networking issue that has to be addressed if they are to be able to contact other computers on your home network.

Access to your other computers using the IPX/SPX protocol is handled without difficulty. However, the TCP/IP protocol presents a significant problem. Incoming callers must be assigned IP addresses that are valid on your LAN if they are to be able to communicate with computers other than your own.

If your network has a DHCP server, or if you are using Internet connection sharing or a gateway device, then a caller will automatically receive a valid IP address. You don't have to worry about setting the TCP/IP address.

If you do not have a true DHCP server on the network, you must manually assign a valid subnet of at least four IP addresses taken from the IP address range of your network. If you don't, incoming callers can access only your computer. (And if that's sufficient, then you don't need to worry about this.)

Unfortunately the process of assigning subnet addresses is more complex than I can go into here in any detail, and the articles on this topic in Windows XP's online help are worse than useless. You'll have to get a network manager to assign the subnet for you.

NOTE

> You also can read more about TCP/IP networking in *Upgrading and Repairing Networks, Fourth Edition*, published by Que.

TIP

> Look up your LAN adapter's IP address. If it starts with 192.168, you might try this trick for assigning IP addresses for incoming connections. For the starting and ending addresses, use the first three numbers of your IP address followed by 220 and 223, respectively. For example, my IP address is 192.168.0.34. I'd enter 192.168.0.220 and 192.168.0.223 as the From and To addresses.

When the incoming connection information has been entered, a new icon appears in your Network Connections window. You can edit its properties later or delete it to cancel incoming access. When someone connects to your computer, yet another icon appears in Network Connections showing their username. If necessary you can right-click this to disconnect them.

WIRELESS NETWORKING

One great way to work "unplugged" is to maintain your network or Internet connection with wireless networking. Radio-based networking technology has advanced rapidly in recent years, and it's being deployed in schools, universities, corporations, airports, and even coffee houses. Whether you're at a client's desk or in an overstuffed chair sipping a *café latte*, as long as you're within hundred feet or so of a network access point, you're online.

For a portable computer, what you'll need is a PC-card based radio transmitter/receiver. Windows XP has built-in support for the 802.11a, 802.11b, and 802.11g security and signaling protocols used in Wireless networking. These protocols ensure that the data rate is adjusted up and down as the quality of the radio signal reception varies. If you're in the market for a new adapter, you should buy the 802.11g variety because this type of adapter can work at 54Mbps when it talks to other "g" equipment but can also work with 802.11b equipment at 11Mbps.

→ To learn more about wireless networking, **see** "802.11g Wireless Networking," **p. 487**.

Data sent on a wireless network isn't confined to a network cable. It can be received by any other wireless-equipped computer up to several hundred feet away. To protect networks from eavesdropping, the previous generation of wireless network cards employed an encryption technique called WEP (*Wired-Equivalent Privacy*), but the word "equivalent" proved to be over-optimistic: Researchers found that the encryption could quickly be broken by a determined eavesdropper. Newer adapters (and old adapters with a software update) can use Wireless Protected Access (WPA), which is a significant improvement. Windows XP supports both types of encryption.

In the following sections, I tell you how to manage Windows when you carry your computer between different wireless networks. If you plan on using a wireless connection in a hotel, airport, café, or other public place, be sure to read "Using a Public Wireless Network" on page 592.

MANAGING WIRELESS NETWORK CONNECTIONS

If you use wireless networking with a portable computer you carry between home and work or use while traveling, you will probably find that you want to be able to connect to any of several wireless networks. Windows XP remembers the names and encryption keys of each network you use and can be told to automatically connect to whichever network it finds itself in range of. This makes moving from one network to another almost effortless.

When you double-click the Wireless Connection icon in the Notification Area, Windows displays the names of any wireless networks it detects, as shown in Figure 17.10. (Networks that don't broadcast their names do not appear. If you want to use a network that hides its name, see the instructions under "Advanced Wireless Network Settings" later in this chapter.)

Figure 17.10
Windows displays the names of all the wireless networks in the receiving range.

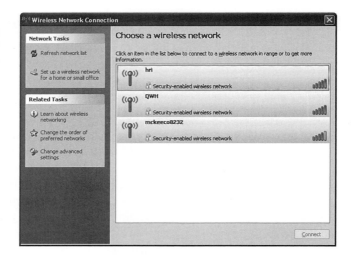

To use the network, click its name and click the Connect button. If necessary, Windows prompts you for the encryption key, as shown in Figure 17.11. (You don't have to enter a key if the network is unsecured or the network access certificate was already installed onto your computer or wireless adapter by your network manager.)

Figure 17.11
Enter the networks WEP or WPA key. This is usually a string of hexadecimal digits (0–9 and A–F).

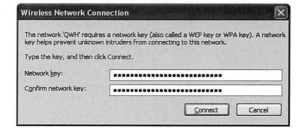

The key is provided by the manager of the wireless network and takes one of the forms listed in Table 17.2.

TABLE 17.2   WEP/WPA KEY FORMATS

Encryption Strength	Key Format
40-bit (also called 64-bit)	5 ASCII characters (any character) or 10 hexadecimal digits (0–9, A–F)
104-bit (also called 128-bit)	13 ASCII characters or 26 hexadecimal digits
232-bit (also called 256-bit)	29 ASCII characters or 58 hexadecimal digits

Enter the key twice, and click OK. Windows should connect to the network.

This is now a preferred network, and Windows should automatically connect to it whenever it is in range.

SELECTING PREFERRED NETWORKS

If you travel and connect to different networks, you will soon collect a list of several preferred (preconfigured) networks. To view the list of preferred networks, double-click the Wireless Connection icon in the task tray and select Change the Order of Preferred Networks under Related Tasks. (Alternatively, you can open Network Connections, double-click the Wireless Connection icon, and view the Wireless Networks tab.) The Wireless Connection Properties dialog box appears, as shown in Figure 17.12.

Figure 17.12
The Wireless Connection Properties dialog box lets you manage preferred networks.

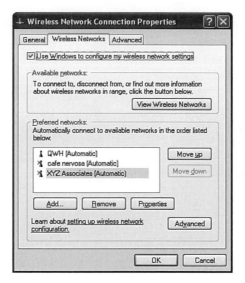

When Windows is not currently connected to any wireless network, Windows scans through this list of preferred networks in order and automatically connects to the first one that is in range. In most cases, you will be within range of only one of the networks you want to use, and this system will work without any adjustments. Windows automatically connects to a network you have previously selected and ignores any other networks that are in range.

SWITCHING BETWEEN WIRELESS NETWORKS

If you find that your computer is in range of more than one of your preferred networks, you might have to manually instruct Windows as to which one you want to use because, given a 50/50 chance of picking the wrong one, 9 times out of 10 it will. One way to do this is to view the list of available networks by double-clicking the Wireless Connection icon in the Notification Area (or by clicking View Wireless Networks on the Wireless Networks Properties page).

If you really don't want Windows to connect to the original network, select the current network (as shown in Figure 17.13) and click Disconnect. Then, select the desired network and click Connect.

This has a permanent side effect: From this point on, Windows will not automatically connect to the original network when it becomes available. To use the original network in the future, you have to manually select it in this list and click Connect.

Figure 17.13
Disconnecting from a network marks it for manual connection only.

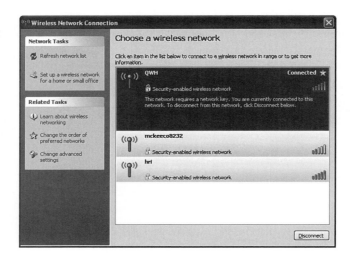

To switch networks without disabling the original one, don't use the Disconnect button; just select the desired network and click Connect.

USING A PUBLIC WIRELESS NETWORK

If you're going to use a public wireless Internet provider, say in an airport, a hotel, or a coffee shop, you are responsible for securing your computer.

CAUTION

> Windows Firewall does protect your computer from distant hackers, but it has a fatal flaw: It doesn't protect you from other wireless users on the same network—that is, in the same airport lounge, or hotel! Your shared files could be completely exposed to these strangers.
>
> If you use your wireless connection in an office or a home setting and in public settings, you must always take care to reconfigure the wireless connection's Networking properties and Windows Firewall every time you move back and forth between the public and private environments.

If you are going to use a public wireless network to obtain Internet access, you must take these steps to disable File and Printer Sharing from your wireless network connection:

1. Open the Network Connections window—for example, by clicking Start, My Network Places, View Network Connections.

2. Right-click the icon that corresponds to your wireless network adapter and select Properties.

3. Uncheck File and Printer Sharing and Client for Microsoft Network; then click OK.

4. Be sure that the Windows Firewall is enabled; the icon should say `Firewalled`. If it doesn't, see Chapter 19, "Network Security," for instructions on how to enable the firewall.

Now, File and Printer sharing services will not function over the wireless connection.

When you return to your private network and want to share and use shared files and printers, repeat the previous process but in step 3, check File and Printer Sharing and Client for Microsoft Networks.

(And, while you're at it, write a letter to Microsoft complaining about the need to do this. Tell them that firewall and network configuration selections should be able to be set independently for each wireless network you attach to!)

ADVANCED WIRELESS NETWORK SETTINGS

In this section, I list some of the more advanced wireless network configuration options. These can come in handy if you work with crowded or unconventional wireless network situations.

SETTING PREFERRED NETWORK ORDER

If you work in a place where multiple preferred networks are available and find that Windows is consistently connecting to the wrong network, you can change the ordering of the preferred network list. Viewing the preferred network list (see Figure 17.12), select the network you want to use most often and click Move Up to raise it above the less-commonly used network(s).

You can also delete a network from the list if you don't plan on using it again in the future.

SELECTING AUTOMATIC OR MANUAL CONNECTIONS

If you work in an area that has more than one wireless network you actually do use, you can leave the less-commonly used networks in the preferred network list and indicate that Windows is just not to connect to them automatically. To do this, double-click the Wireless Connection icon in the task tray and select Change the Order of Preferred Networks under Related Tasks. This brings up the Wireless Networks dialog box shown in Figure 17.12. Select a network in the Preferred Networks list, click Properties, view the Connection tab, and uncheck Connect When This Network Is in Range.

17

Now, Windows will not connect to this network unless you deliberately select it from the list of available networks and click Connect.

ADDING A NETWORK MANUALLY

A network that does not broadcast its network name (SSID) does not appear in the list of available networks. To connect to such a network, you must enter its connection information manually, by following these steps:

1. Bring up the Wireless Connection Properties dialog box by double-clicking the Wireless Connection icon in the Notification area and clicking Change the Order of Preferred Networks under Related Tasks. (Alternatively, view Network Connections, double-click the Wireless Connection icon, and select the Wireless Networks tab.)

2. Click the Add button.

3. Enter the network name (SSID).

4. If the network is an ad hoc network (uses no base station, router, or access point), check This Is a Computer-to-Computer Network at the bottom of the dialog box.

5. If the network is unencrypted, change the Data Encryption setting to Disabled and click OK, and you're finished.

6. If the network is encrypted, in most cases you have to manually enter the encryption key. Uncheck The Key Is Provided for Me Automatically, leave Network Authentication set to Open, change Data Encryption to WEP or WPA, and enter the encryption key twice. Then click OK.

The network now appears in the list of available networks when it is in range.

AD HOC VERSUS INFRASTRUCTURE NETWORKS

Most wireless networks use a wireless router, base station, or access point. These are called *infrastructure* networks; all communications on the network are between the computers and the access point. You can also tie a group of computers together without an access point; this is called an *ad hoc* network. In this type of network, the computers talk directly to each other.

By default, Windows connects to either type of network but assumes that networks you define manually are infrastructure networks.

To connect to an ad hoc network, follow the procedure described previously under "Adding a Network Manually." You must select This Is a Computer-to-Computer Network while you are adding the preferred connection; you can't change this setting afterward.

To limit the available networks display to ad hoc or infrastructure network connections only, double-click the Wireless Connection icon in the task tray and select Change the Order of Preferred Networks under Related Tasks. This displays the Wireless Network Connection properties dialog box shown in Figure 17.12. Click the Advanced button and make the desired selection under Networks to Access.

AUTHENTICATED WIRELESS NETWORKS

In corporate environments, in addition to using encryption to protect data, security is also obtained by *authentication*—permitting only authorized computers to connect to the corporate wireless LAN. The authorization is based on identifying the computer itself via a certificate and/or identifying you, based on your Windows logon and password or a certificate. This topic is beyond the scope of this book, but I can at least provide some driving directions.

Authentication settings are part of the properties of each preferred connection. To change them, view the Wireless Connection Properties page and select the Wireless Networks tab. Select a preferred connection and click Properties. As long as encryption is enabled, authentication properties can be set on the Authentication tab. Your network manager will provide you with the required settings for your corporate network. They might also be installed automatically via Group Policy while your computer is connected to a wired network.

PROMISCUOUS CONNECTIONS

In some circumstances, you might want Windows to attempt to connect to any available wireless network, regardless of whether it appears in the preferred connection list. To enable this, double-click the Wireless Connection icon in the task tray and select Change the Order of Preferred Networks under Related Tasks. This displays the Wireless Network Connection properties dialog box shown previously in Figure 17.12. Click the Advanced button and check Automatically Connect to Non-Preferred Networks. Now, Windows will attempt to automatically connect to any available unrecognized network if a preferred network is not in range.

WARDRIVING

With the proliferation of wireless networks in urban and suburban areas, many people are wondering why they should pay for Internet service when so many people—intentionally or not—make their Internet connections available without encryption? Good point. In my office, I can often attach to an unsecured network located in a friend's house down the street, and at home, there are two to choose from. I don't know whom they belong to, but when my DSL line is down, I have used these to stay connected.

An entire community has sprung up to share information about the location of unsecured wireless networks. The terminology is peculiar: *Wardriving* is the act of driving around with a laptop in your car, seeking a free Internet connection, and w*archalking* is the practice of making cryptic chalk marks on the sidewalk in front of an obliging residence or business. The marks tell those in-the-know that a connection is available nearby. Interesting, but also disturbing.

If you choose to take advantage of someone else's unsecured wireless network, follow the instructions under "Using a Public Wireless Network" earlier in this chapter to protect your computer from whomever else might be using the network. Remember that if found out, you might be considered to be a trespasser and might be subject to legal prosecution or even vigilante harassment.

WEB FOLDERS AND WEB PRINTING

If a remote computer has Internet Information Services (IIS) installed, has enabled Web Sharing on any folders, and is accessible over the Internet or a corporate Internet, you can access its shared files through Internet Explorer version 5 or higher. This technology lets you copy files to and from a remote computer with a high degree of security, through firewalls that normally block access to file sharing protocols.

When IIS is installed, the computer's shared printers may also be used through the Internet using the Internet Printing Protocol, or IPP. IPP lets remote computers print to shared printers across the Internet, again through firewalls.

You can use these technologies to great advantage if your office computer or server has dedicated Internet access because you access its shared folders over the Internet without using a modem or VPN connection.

These applications are all described elsewhere in this book; I just wanted to be sure they were mentioned here as they're great resources for the "unplugged" user.

Using Web Folders and Web Printing is covered in Chapter 16, "Using a Windows XP Network."

VIRTUAL PRIVATE NETWORKING

You know that you can use dial-up networking to connect to your office LAN or home computer from afar. But, with the Internet providing network connections and local modem access nearly all over the world, why can't you reach your network through the Internet instead of placing a possibly expensive long-distance call?

Well, in fact, you can. Microsoft networking can use the Internet's TCP protocol to conduct its business, so you can use an Internet connection to access shared files and printers, if the computer you want to reach has an Internet connection up and running.

But the Internet is not a friendly place. With tens of millions of people using it every day, you must expect that some percentage of them are up to no good. Network break-ins are everyday news now. If your computer's file sharing services are exposed to the Internet, any number of people thousands of miles away could just try password after password in the hope of guessing one that will give them access to your files. How do you take advantage of the convenience of accessing network services over the Internet without, figuratively speaking, putting out a big welcome mat that says "Please Rob Me?"

The answer is by the use of firewalls and Virtual Private Networking. I'll describe these concepts in detail in Chapter 19, but in a nutshell, a Virtual Private Network (VPN) lets you connect to a remote network in a secure way. Access by random hackers is blocked by a network firewall, but an authorized user can penetrate the firewall. Authorized data is *encapsulated* in special packets that are passed through the firewall and inspected by a VPN server before being released to the protected network. VPNs create what is effectively a *tunnel* between your computer and a remote network, a tunnel that can pass data freely and securely through potentially hostile intermediate territory.

Figure 17.14 illustrates the concept, showing a Virtual Private Network connection between a computer out on the Internet and a server on a protected network. The figure shows how the computer sends data (1) through a VPN connection which encapsulates it (2) and transmits it over the Internet (3). A firewall (4) passes VPN packets but blocks all others. The VPN Server (5) verifies the authenticity of your data and transmits the original packet (6) on to the desired remote server. The encapsulation process allows for encryption of your data, and allows "private" IP addresses to be used as the endpoints of the network connection.

Figure 17.14
A Virtual Private
Network encapsulates
and encrypts data
that is passed over
the Internet.

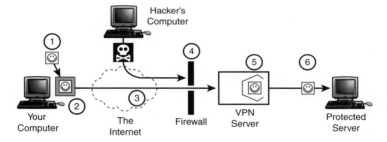

On Windows XP, VPN connections work like dial-up connections. Once you have an Internet connection established (via modem or a dedicated service), a dial-up connection icon establishes the link between your computer and a VPN server on the remote network. Once connected, the VPN service transmits data between your computer. In effect, you are part of the distant LAN.

You can use Windows XP's VPN service to allow incoming connections to your computer as well. You can use the Internet Connection Firewall or a firewall on your LAN to protect against hackers, yet still connect to your computer through the Internet to retrieve files from afar.

NOTE

> Along the way, you may hear the term *Point-to-Point Tunneling Protocol*, or *PPTP*. PPTP is the data formatting protocol that Microsoft uses to establish VPNs.

SETTING UP FOR VIRTUAL PRIVATE NETWORKING

To establish a VPN connection from your computer to another network, you must know the hostname or IP address of the remote VPN server. This information corresponds to the telephone number in a dial-up connection; it lets you specify the endpoint of the tunnel. VPN connections are set up by the New Connection Wizard. Just follow these steps:

1. Open Network Connections. You can view My Network Places and select the View Network Connections task, or, if Connect To appears on your Start menu, choose Connect To, Show All Connections.

2. Select Create A New Connection from Network Tasks.

3. Select Connect To The Network At My Workplace and click Next. (This is a poorly named choice—you might be connecting to your home computer!)

4. Select Virtual Private Network Connection, and click Next.

5. Enter a name for the connection, such as "VPN to Office."

6. If you use a dial-up connection to connect this computer to the Internet, you can select Automatically Dial This Initial Connection to ensure that your Internet connection is up before attempting the VPN connection, as shown in Figure 17.15. If you have a dedicated Internet connection, use a shared connection from another computer, or want to make a dial-up connection manually, choose Do Not Dial and click Next.

Figure 17.15
You can have Windows automatically dial a selected Internet connection before making a VPN connection.

7. Enter the hostname or IP address of the remote dial-in server—for example, vpn.mycompany.com—and select Next.

8. Click Finish to close the wizard.

NOTE

You can delete a connection shortcut later if you don't want it and can drag the connection icon from Network Connections to your desktop later if you do.

Windows immediately opens the Dialer dialog. Before establishing the connection for the first time, verify the connections properties pages.

VPN Connection Properties

To modify a VPN connection's properties, click the Properties button on the dialer dialog, or right-click the connection icon in Network Connections and select Properties.

The properties page has five tabs. Most of the time, the default settings will work correctly, but you should check some of them. In this section, I'll walk you through the most important parameters.

General Properties

The General tab of the Properties dialog holds the hostname or IP address of your VPN connection server, and if needed, the name of a dial-up connection to use to carry the VPN connection. If you are establishing the VPN connection over a LAN or dedicated Internet connection, you can uncheck Dial Another Connection First.

Options

The Options tab includes dialing and redialing options. The two important options are

- **Prompt for name and password**—If you tell Windows to remember your username and password when dialing, and after you've made a successful connection once, you can uncheck this option to bypass the Dialing dialog. When you select the connection icon, Windows will just make the connection.

- **Include Windows logon domain**—If the VPN server is a Windows NT or 200x server, you may need to provide your login domain name with your username. You can also enter *domain\username* or, with Windows 2000/2003 servers only, *username@domain*.

Security

It's unlikely that you will need to change any security settings. The data in a VPN connection is usually carried across the Internet, and a high level of security is required. Your password and data should be encrypted in the strongest fashion possible. Be sure that Require Secured Password and Require Data Encryption are set on the Security tab.

If you use the same logon name and password on your local computer as you use on the remote network, you can check Automatically Use My Windows Logon Name and Password so that you don't have to enter it whenever you use the connection.

Networking

It's likely that you want to participate as a full member of the remote network, so leave all Components checked on the Networking tab of the Properties dialog.

17

As I mentioned, Windows XP and 2000 use two types of VPN protocols. Generally, you can leave the Type of VPN server set to Automatic, and Windows will determine to which type it's connected when it makes each call.

If the remote network is a complex, multi-subnet network, or if you want to browse the Internet while you're using the VPN, you also must deal with the gateway issue, which I'll discuss later in this chapter under "Routing Issues." To change the gateway setting

1. Select Internet Protocol, and choose Properties. Leave the IP address and DNS information set to Obtain Automatically, and click Advanced.

2. If the remote network has only one subnet, *or* if you will set routes to multiple subnets manually, uncheck Use Default Gateway On Remote Network.

DIALING A VPN CONNECTION

Making a VPN connection follows the same procedure as making a dial-up connection:

1. Select the desired VPN connection icon from Network Connections.

2. If this VPN connection requires a dial-up connection, you are prompted with the username and password for your dial-up connection to your ISP. Check for the proper location and dialing rules, and then select Dial. After the connection has been made, Windows proceeds to make the VPN connection.

3. Enter the username and password for access to the remote network. Select Connect.

   Windows then contacts the remote VPN server, verifies your username and password, registers your computer on the network, and creates a connection status icon in the notification area, just as for a standard dial-up connection.

You can use the remote network now, access shared files and folders, access printers, and so on.

When you're finished, right-click the connection icon, and select Disconnect.

ROUTING ISSUES

If the remote network you want to use is a simple, small network with only one subnet or range of IP addresses, you can skip this section. Otherwise, I must address an issue with TCP/IP routing here, as much as I fear it's a real can of worms.

When you establish a VPN connection to another network, your computer is assigned an IP address from that other network for the duration of your connection. This address might be a private, non-Internet-routable address like 192.168.1.100. All data destined for the remote network is packaged up in PPTP or L2TP packets and sent to the remote host. But what happens if you want to communicate with two servers—a private server through the tunnel and a public Web site on the Internet—at the same time?

When you send data to an IP address that doesn't clearly belong to the private network's range, Windows has two choices: It can pass the data through the tunnel and let the network on the other end route it on, or it can pass the data without encapsulation and let it travel directly to the Internet host.

It would seem sensible that Windows should always use the second approach because any IP address other than, say, 192.168.1.*xxx* obviously doesn't belong to the private network and doesn't need protection. That's right as long as the remote network has only one such subnet. Some complex corporate networks have many, with different addresses, so Windows can't always know just from the address of the VPN connection which addresses belong to the private network and which go direct.

If you plan to use a VPN connection and the Internet at the same time, you must find out whether your remote network has more than one subnet. Then follow this advice:

- If the remote network has only one subnet, tell Windows not to use the remote network as the gateway address for unknown locations. This is the easy case.

- If the remote network has more than one subnet, tell Windows to use the remote network as its gateway, so you can connect to all servers on the remote network. But Internet access goes through the tunnel, too, and from there to the Internet. It slows things down.

- Alternatively, you can tell Windows not to use the remote network gateway and you can manually set routes to other subnets while you're connected. It's tricky and inconvenient. I'll show you how I do it at the end of the chapter, under "Tips from the Windows Pros."

When you know how you'll resolve the gateway issue, refer to the VPN Connection Properties earlier in this chapter to make the appropriate settings on the connection's Networking properties tab.

ENABLING VPN ACCESS TO YOUR COMPUTER

You can enable incoming VPN connections to your computer if it has a dedicated Internet connection. Your Windows XP computer can act as a VPN server for one incoming connection at a time. You can connect to your computer through the Internet from home or in the field from a computer running Windows 9x, NT, 2000, or, of course, XP.

To function correctly, however, your computer must have a known IP address, and if its Internet connection is made through a router, Internet Connection Sharing, or a connecting sharing device, then PPTP packets must be forwarded to your computer. I'll discuss this in more detail shortly, under "Enabling Incoming VPN Connections with NAT."

The process for enabling VPN access is exactly the same as for enabling dial-in access, so see the section "Enabling Dial-In and VPN Access to Your Computer" earlier in this chapter. Follow those instructions, being sure to enable an incoming VPN connection. You don't need to choose any modems to receive incoming modem calls.

When Incoming Calls is configured, your computer can be contacted as the host of a VPN connection. To connect to it, establish a VPN connection as you learned in the preceding section, using your computer's public IP address or hostname as the number to dial.

NOTE

> You must configure the Internet protocol to assign valid IP addresses for incoming connections. This topic, which was discussed in "Enabling Dial-In and VPN Access to Your Computer," applies to VPN access, too.

NOTE

> Windows Firewall doesn't have to be told to permit incoming VPN connections, as it knows to let them in.

ENABLING INCOMING VPN CONNECTIONS WITH NAT

Microsoft's Internet Connection Sharing and the commercial DSL/cable sharing routers known as Residential Gateways use an IP addressing trick called Network Address Translation (NAT) to serve an entire LAN with only one public IP address. Incoming requests, as from a VPN client to a VPN server, have to be directed to a single host computer on the internal network.

This means if you use a shared Internet connection, only one computer can be designated as the recipient of incoming VPN connections. If you use Microsoft's Internet Connection Sharing, that computer should be the one sharing its connection. It will receive and properly handle VPN requests.

If you use a hardware sharing router, the VPN server can be any computer you wish to designate. (Remember that once the VPN connection is established, you can communicate with any of the computers on the LAN.) Your router must be set up to forward the following packet types to the designated computer:

TCP port 1723

GRE (protocol 47. This is not the same as port 47!)

Unfortunately, many of the inexpensive commercial DSL/cable connection sharing routers (residential gateways) don't have a way to explicitly forward GRE packets. If you use one of these devices you will need to designate the VPN target computer as a DMZ host, which will receive *all* unrecognized incoming packets.

CAUTION

> If you designate a computer as a DMZ host, that computer can be vulnerable to hacker attacks. You *must* also configure your router to block Microsoft File Sharing packets, at the very least. Set up filtering to block TCP and UDP ports 137 through 139.

→ To learn more about forwarding network requests on a shared Internet connection, **see** "Making Services Available," **p. 648**.

REMOTE DESKTOP

Windows XP has a spiffy feature called Remote Desktop that lets you connect to and use a Windows XP Professional or 200x Server computer from another location. If you use Windows XP Professional at work, for instance, you can use Remote Desktop at home to attach to your work computer. You'll be able to see your work computer's screen, move the mouse and type on the keyboard just as if you were there. This is just what you need when you're out of town and need to read a file you left on the computer back home, or if you have to catch up on work at the office while you're at home changing Alexa Marie's diapers. I've been using this feature a lot while writing this book, and I love it.

You can also use the Remote Desktop client program to attach to computers running Windows NT Terminal Server Version and Windows 200x Server's Terminal Services. The client program lets you log on to these computers to access special applications or for administration and maintenance.

Third-party programs such as Carbon Copy, PC Anywhere, Timbuktu and VNC have been doing this for years, and some of them have more sophisticated features, but Remote Desktop is supplied with Windows XP Professional and it's essentially free. It's a scaled-down version of Windows Terminal Services, a component of the Windows NT/200x Server version that lets multiple users run programs on one central server. By stripped down, I mean that only one person can connect to Windows XP Professional at a time, and it forces a local user off.

While the host computer (the computer you'll take control of) has to be running Windows XP Professional or Windows 200x Server, the Remote Desktop Client software (that you use to view the XP computer) can run on 16- and 32-bit versions of Windows from 3.1 up to XP Home Edition. Figure 17.16 shows how this works.

Figure 17.16
You can use Remote Desktop to connect to and control a Windows XP Professional or Windows Server computer at work.

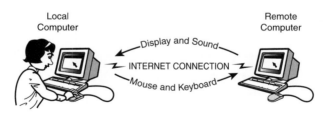

To use Remote Desktop, the host computer must be reachable over the Internet, and this means that it will need a dedicated Internet connection with a known IP address (or, you'll need someone to make an Internet connection at the computer and tell you what the IP address is).

CONNECTING TO OTHER COMPUTERS WITH REMOTE DESKTOP

To establish a connection to another computer (or another Remote Desktop server), you'll need a copy of the Remote Desktop Client, also called the Terminal Services Client. There are several ways you can get this program:

- It's preinstalled on Windows XP computers. Select Start, All Programs, Accessories, Communications, Remote Desktop Connection.

- It's on your Windows XP CD-ROM. Insert it in another computer, and from the setup program select Perform Additional Tasks, then Set Up Remote Desktop Connection. This will run the installation program.

- You can download a slightly less-capable version from www.microsoft.com. Search for "Terminal Services Advanced Client." This is handy if you're traveling and don't have an XP disc with you.

When you run the Remote Desktop Client, you'll see the Remote Desktop Connection dialog box, as shown in Figure 17.17.

Enter the IP address or register DNS name of the computer you'd like to use. Entering a username and password is optional. If you don't enter them now, you'll be asked for them when the connection is established. Click Connect to establish the connection immediately, or click Options to adjust the connection properties first. The properties tabs are described in Table 17.3.

Figure 17.17
The Remote Desktop Connection dialog box lets you configure the connection and select the remote computer to use.

TABLE 17.3 REMOTE DESKTOP CONNECTION PROPERTIES

Tab	Properties
General	*Connection Settings* saves the configuration for a particular remote computer as a shortcut for quick access later.
Display	Sets the size and color depth of the window used for your remote connection's desktop. Display size can be set to a fixed window size or Full Screen.
Local Resources	Connects devices on the local computer so that you may use them as if they were part of the remote computer. (This feature does not work when connecting to Windows NT and Windows 2000 Terminal Services.) The Keyboard setting determines whether special Windows key commands like Alt+Tab apply to your local computer or the remote computer.
Programs	Lets you automatically run a program on the remote computer upon logging on.
Experience	Lets you indicate your connection speed, so that Windows can appropriately limit display-intense features like menu animation.

When you establish the connection, you'll see a standard Windows logon dialog. Enter your username and password to sign on. It may take a while for the logon process to complete, if Windows has to shut down a logged-on user.

When you're logged on, you'll see the remote computer's desktop, as shown in Figure 17.18, and can use it as if you were actually sitting in front of it. Keyboard, mouse, display and sound should be fully functional. If you maximize the window, the remote desktop will fill your screen. It all works quite well—it can even be difficult to remember which computer you're actually using!

In addition, any printers attached to your local computer will appear as choices if you print from applications on the remote computer, and the local computer's drives will appear in the list in My Computer. You can take advantage of this to copy files between the local and remote computers.

Finally, your local computer's serial (COM) ports will also be available to the remote computer. (My friend Norm syncs his Palm Pilot to his Windows XP Professional computer from remote locations using this feature.)

While you're connected, you may want to use keyboard shortcuts like Alt+Tab to switch between applications. This can confuse Windows, which won't know whether to switch applications on the local computer or the remote computer. You can specify where special key combinations should be interpreted on the Local Resources page, as I described earlier, or you can use alternate key combinations to ensure that the desired actions take place on the remote computer. The alternate keyboard shortcuts are shown in Table 17.4.

Figure 17.18
When connected to Windows XP via Remote Desktop, your local computer's drives and printers are available for use.

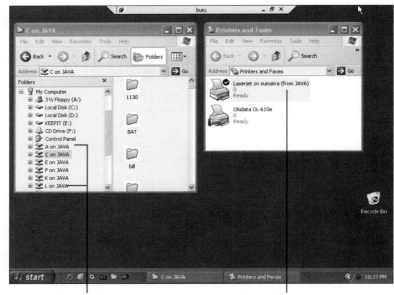

Drives on local computer   Printer on local computer

TABLE 17.4 SOME OF THE REMOTE DESKTOP KEYBOARD SHORTCUTS

Use These Keys:	To Transmit This to the Remote Computer:
Alt+PgUp, Alt+PgDn	Alt+Tab (switch programs)
Alt+End	Ctrl+Alt+Del (task monitor)
Alt+Home	(Displays the Start menu)
Ctrl+Alt+Break	Alt+Enter (toggle full screen)
Ctrl+Alt+Plus	Alt+PrntScrn (screen to clipboard)

When you've finished using the remote computer, choose Start, Log Off to end the connection. If you want the remote computer to continue running an application, though, you can simply close the Remote Desktop window or select Disconnect. Your account will stay active on the remote computer until you reconnect and log off, or until a user at that computer logs on.

NOTE

If you attempt to connect to a Windows XP computer with Remote Desktop while another user is logged on, you'll have the choice of disconnecting or forcing them off. Windows XP Professional only permits one person to use each computer. If Quick User Switch is enabled, they'll be switched out; otherwise they're summarily logged off. This is somewhat brutal; the other user might lose work in progress. If you log on using the same username as the local user, though, you simply take over the desktop without forcing a logoff.

If someone logs on to the remote computer while you're connected from afar, you'll be disconnected. If Quick User Switch is enabled, you can reconnect later and pick up where you left off. Otherwise, the same deal applies: If it is a different user, your applications will be shut down.

REMOTE ASSISTANCE

Remote Assistance lets two people work collaboratively on one Windows XP computer—one at the computer and one remotely, over the Internet. The feature is intended to let people get technical assistance from someone at a remote location, and it's based the same technology as the Remote Desktop feature I described in the previous section. There are several significant differences, however:

- With Remote Assistance, both the local and remote users see the same screen at the same time, and both can move the mouse, type on the keyboard, and so forth.

- Remote Assistance doesn't make the local computer's drives appear in the drive list, nor does it transmit sound back, as Remote Desktop does.

- Remote Assistance connections can't be made *ad lib*. One Windows XP user must invite another through email or Windows Messenger. Or, one user can offer assistance to another using Messenger. In any case, the procedure requires the simultaneous cooperation of users at both ends of the connection.

- Remote Assistance can be used to connect to Windows XP Home Edition. Users of any version of Windows XP can assist each other.

- Remote Assistance allows you to use text chat or to establish voice communication while the desktop session is active.

If you're familiar with NetMeeting's Desktop Sharing function, this may all sound familiar. The difference is that Remote Assistance is based on the more modern Terminal Services technology that powers Remote Desktop, so it's only available to Windows XP users. Also, it just plain works better than Desktop Sharing.

NOTE

If your computer gets its Internet connection through a residential gateway (a hardware device also called a *router*), your friend won't be able to connect to you unless the Universal Plug and Play (UPnP) protocol is installed on your computer and enabled on the router. For more information on UPnP, see Chapter 18.

→ To learn more about forwarding network requests on a shared Internet connection, **see** "Making Services Available," **p. 648**.

REQUESTING REMOTE ASSISTANCE

To invite a friend or colleague to work with you on your computer, first contact your friend and confirm that they have Windows XP and are ready to work with you. If you want help making system or network settings, or installing software, you should log in with a Computer Administrator user account before going any further. Then, follow these steps:

1. Select Start, Help and Support.

2. Click Invite a Friend To Connect To Your Computer with Remote Assistance.

3. Select Invite Someone To Help You.

4. You can issue an invitation via Windows Messenger, if you and your friend both have accounts, or via email. Select your friend's name from the Messenger Online list, or enter her email address, as shown in Figure 17.19. Then, click Invite This Person.

5. Enter a message to send to the person (such as "I can't get Space Quest III to install properly"), and click Invite This Person.

6. If you have chosen to send the invitation by email, Windows will pop up a rather alarming message warning you that a program is attempting to send email. Choose Send (and thank the guy who wrote the Melissa virus for making this necessary).

Figure 17.19
Select a Windows Messenger user ID or enter an email address to invite someone to connect to your computer.

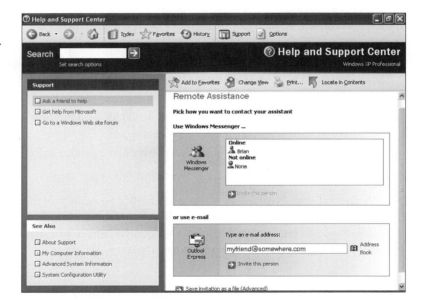

NOTE

> If you use a dial-up Internet connection or a DSL service that requires you to sign on, your Internet IP address changes every time you connect. Remote Assistance invitations use this address to tell the other person's computer how to contact you, so they will only work if you stay connected from the time you send the invitation to the time your friend responds. If you have a fixed (static) IP address, this won't be a problem.

If you sent your request via Windows Messenger, you should get a response within a few seconds. If you sent the request by email, it could be some time before the other party reads and receives it.

You also can select Save Invitation as a File to transfer the invitation by other means such as a network or floppy disk. The invitation, whether sent by Messenger, email, or file is actually an XML file containing the IP address of your computer and some encrypted information that specifies how long the invitation remains valid.

If you want to view the list of invitations you've sent by email, select View Invitation Status on the Remote Assistance page. You can then select invitations to delete, expire (disallow), or resend. You can also view the details of who sent the invitation, how long it's valid, and so on.

When someone responds to your request for assistance, a dialog will appear on your screen asking if it's okay for them to connect. Click Yes, and after a minute or so a window will appear with which you can control the Remote Assistance session, as shown in Figure 17.20.

Figure 17.20
When your Remote Assistant has connected, you can use this window to chat and control the connection.

You can use this dialog to type text messages back and forth, initiate a voice connection or a file transfer, or terminate the connection. When the remote user wants to take control of your mouse and keyboard, you'll be asked and can permit or deny this. Even then you can still type and move the mouse yourself, and can end the remote user's control by pressing the Esc key or by clicking End Control on the Remote Assistance window.

RESPONDING TO AN ASSISTANCE REQUEST

When someone invites you to connect by Remote Assistance, you'll either see a pop-up box in Windows Messenger, or you'll receive an email, as shown in Figure 17.21.

Figure 17.21
You might receive an instant message or email invitation requesting Remote Assistance. To accept an email invitation, open the attachment.

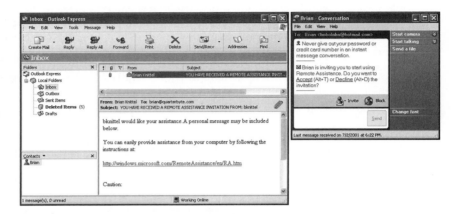

You can directly respond to an instant message invitation as indicated in the message window. To accept an email invitation, open the attachment. (How you do that depends on your email program—in Outlook Express 6, click on the paperclip icon, and select the attachment labeled `rcBuddy.MsRcIncident`. When the Attachment Warning dialog appears, select Open It.) Opening the attachment should activate the Remote Assistance connection.

> **NOTE**
>
> You can absolutely prevent others from manipulating your computer when they connect using Remote Assistance—they'll be able to see your screen but not control it. To do this, right-click My Computer and select Properties. View the Remote tab and click Advanced. Uncheck Allow This Computer To Be Controlled Remotely and click OK. In any case, you have to grant the other user permission to manipulate your computer each time a connection is made.

You will be asked if you wish to proceed with the connection, and when it's been established, the remote user will be asked if they want to permit you to connect. Assuming you both say yes, at this point patience is called for as it can take more than a minute for the required software to load up and for the other user's desktop to appear on your screen, as shown in Figure 17.22.

The Remote Assistance window has several sections. On the left is a text chat window through which you and the other party can type to each other. Enter messages in the Message Entry window.

Figure 17.22
The Remote Assistance screen has a control panel on the left, and a view of the remote user's screen on the right. Click Take Control if you want to manipulate the remote computer.

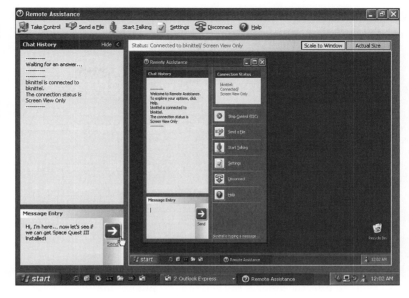

Across the top is a menu of controls. The choices are

- **Take Control**—Click this to begin using the other computer's mouse and keyboard. The remote user will be asked to grant permission. Once you have control of the other computer, both of you can use your mouse and keyboard. The remote user can cancel your control at any time by pressing the Esc key.
- **Send a File**—Brings up a dialog to let you transfer a file to the remote computer. You can select a file to send, and the remote user must select a place to store it, as shown in Figure 17.23.

Figure 17.23
File Transfers during Remote Assistance require the sender to select the file and the recipient to select a destination folder.

- **Start Talking**—Establishes a voice connection. If both of you have a microphone, speakers, and a sound card, you will be able to speak to each other over your Internet or LAN connection.
- **Settings**—Lets you change the audio settings for voice communication and the default screen scaling setting.
- **Disconnect**—Ends the Remote Assistance connection.

Most of the window is devoted to a view of your friend's screen. You can click Scale To Window to fit his entire screen in this window, or click Actual Size to see a normal size view, which you'll probably have to scroll up and down from time to time.

COPYING FILES BETWEEN TWO COMPUTERS

If you need to transfer files between two computers but you don't already have a LAN in place, you may think you'll have shuttle a floppy disk back and forth 50 times. You do have some other options:

- Use an external high-capacity drive such as a USB-connected hard drive or a Zip disk.
- Install network adapters in the two computers and connect them with a *crossover cable*, as described in Chapter 15, "Creating a Windows XP Home Network." The cable will cost about $7.50, and if you need to buy network adapters, this might set you back another $10 to $30. You'll eventually want the network hardware anyway, though, and with this mini-LAN you can copy mega-files in minutes.
- If both computers have FireWire (IEEE-1394) ports, you can get a so-called "6-6" cable to directly connect the computers, and use the IEEE-1394 ports to set up a LAN. (The price of the cable might bring tears to your eyes, though.)
- You can use the "Direct Connection" networking feature to connect two computers through their parallel, serial, or Infrared ports. Parallel or serial connections require special "Direct Connection" parallel or serial data crossover cables—these cables are needed to hook input wires to output wires on each computer and vice versa.

To establish a Direct Connection, connect the cable or point the infrared ports at each other. Then, on the computer that has the files you want to copy, called the Host computer, follow these steps:

1. Open the Network Connections window and select the Create a New Connection task to start the New Connection Wizard. Click Next to get going.
2. Select Set Up an Advanced Connection and click Next.
3. Choose Connect Directly to Another Computer and click Next.
4. Choose Host and click Next.
5. Choose the device for the connection: a parallel, serial, or infrared port. If you're using a serial connection, click the Properties button, select a reasonable serial port speed (19200, 38400, or 57600 bps), and click OK. Click Next to proceed.
6. Check the boxes next to the user or users who should be permitted access and click Next.
7. Click Finish. An Incoming Connections icon will appear in your Network Connections window. Now, configure the Guest computer.

Then, on the computer to which you want to transfer files, called the Guest computer, follow these steps:

1. Open the Network Connections window and select the Create a New Connection task to start the New Connection Wizard. Click Next to get going.

2. Select Set Up an Advanced Connection and click Next.

3. Choose Connect Directly to Another Computer and click Next.

4. Choose Guest and click Next.

5. Choose the device for the connection: a parallel, serial or infrared port, and then click Next, Finish. A Direct Connection icon will appear, and the connection dialog box will open.

6. If you're using a serial cable connection, click the Properties button, click Configure, and select the same serial port speed you chose on the Host (19200, 38400, or 57600 bps). Click OK twice.

7. Enter a username and password that is valid on the Host computer. You have to use one of the usernames you selected when setting up the Host. Then, click Connect.

When the connection is established, you can use Windows Explorer to browse the Host computer's shared network folders and copy files, as described in Chapter 16.

When you're finished, close the connection by right-clicking on the connection icon in the notification area on the Guest computer. On the Host computer, you can disable incoming connections by opening the properties page for the Incoming Connection icon and unchecking the device you chose earlier.

If you can add an infrared adapter to your desktop, you can also use Windows's built-in support for quick wireless infrared file transfers. This technique isn't as involved as the networking approach I've just described. I'll explain it in the next section.

Finally, if you want to move both your files and your preferences and settings, see "Moving Profiles with the Files and Settings Transfer Wizard" in Chapter 25, "Managing Users."

INFRARED FILE TRANSFERS

Most portable computers include an infrared data transmission device similar to that used on TV remote controls. Using a data transmission standard called IrDA (after the Infrared Data Association), computers, printers, and handheld organizers can communicate with each other without LAN wiring. Just point them at each other. LAN connections are much faster, so I recommend using them over IrDA any day, but if you don't have a LAN connection, IrDA can give "point and shoot" a whole new meaning.

IrDA comes in two flavors: SIR (Serial Infrared), which tops out at 112Kbps, and FIR (Fast Infrared), which runs up to 4Mbps. Most new portables support both protocols. The advantage of using SIR is that you can attach an expensive adapter to a standard serial port on a desktop computer and get infrared capability.

NOTE

> An FIR adapter connects to an SIR adapter by automatically lowering its transfer rate. The two standards interoperate quite nicely.

Windows XP includes support for IrDA file transfers between two capable devices such as laptops, digital cameras, and so on. Because most laptop computers have IrDA hardware, you can transfer files between two Windows XP/2000 laptops just by bringing them near each other.

SETTING UP AN INFRARED DEVICE

If your computer has IrDA-compatible hardware installed, Windows detected it and installed support for it during installation. You can tell by checking for a Wireless Link applet in the Control Panel under Printers and Other Hardware.

NOTE

> The use of the word *wireless* in Wireless Link is unfortunate because it could be confused with 802.11x wireless networking. The Wireless Link feature we're discussing here refers to infrared file transfers only.

If you've added an external serial port IrDA adapter, choose Add/Remove Hardware in the Control Panel, select Add Hardware, choose the device manually, and select Infrared Devices. Finally, choose the proper IrDA device type and serial port information.

 If the Wireless Link icon is not present in the Control Panel, see "Wireless Link Is Not Present in Control Panel" in the "Troubleshooting" section at the end of this chapter.

Open the applet, and confirm that Windows thinks the device is operating properly (see Figure 17.24). If it's not, select Troubleshoot to diagnose and fix the problem.

The applet has three tabs. On the first two, you can select the destination folder for files and images received from other computers and digital cameras. The default folder for received files is your desktop. The default folder for received images is the My Pictures folder inside your My Documents folder. You can change these defaults by clicking Properties and selecting a different folder.

On the Hardware tab, you can set the maximum speed for wireless transfers. If you experience a high error rate, try changing the speed from the default 115200bps to 57600 or lower.

INFRARED FILE TRANSFER

When another infrared-capable computer is in range of your computer's beam, your computer makes an interesting sound, a Send Files to Another Computer icon appears on the desktop, and a small control icon appears in the notification area (see Figure 17.25). You can instantly send files to the other computer by dragging files to the Wireless icon. Pretty neat!

Figure 17.24
Using the Wireless Link Control Panel applet, you can configure file transfer directories and the transfer speed.

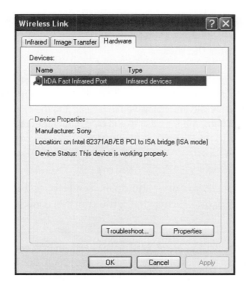

 If the Send Files icon doesn't appear when you think it should, see "Send Files Icon Doesn't Appear" in the "Troubleshooting" section at the end of this chapter.

Send Files icon appears when another infrared file transfer device is in range.

Figure 17.25
When another infrared file transfer device is in range, the Send Files icon (left) appears on the desktop, and the Wireless control icon (right) appears in the notification area.

The Wireless control icon appears in the notification area

To send files to another computer, you can use any of these three methods:

- Drag and drop the files onto the Send Files icon on the desktop.
- Select and right-click a file, choose Send To, and select Infrared Recipient.

- Open the Send Files icon, or select Transfer Files from the control icon in the taskbar to bring up the Wireless Link dialog. This lets you browse for and select the files to transfer. Click Send to transfer the files.

N O T E

The Wireless Link dialog is a standard Open File dialog; it's really a little Explorer window. If you drag a file into this dialog, you're moving it to the displayed folder on your own computer. To transfer a file via drag and drop, you must drag it to the Send Files icon.

After you've selected files to transfer via drag and drop, Send To, or the dialog, progress dialogs appear on both computers, indicating that a file transfer is taking place.

N O T E

When infrared file transfers are enabled, anyone with an IrDA-equipped Windows XP or 2000 computer can zap files onto your computer's desktop. Don't worry, though, because files are never overwritten. If someone sends you a file with the same name as an existing file on your desktop, it's named something like Copy 1 of *XXXXXX*.

DIGITAL CAMERA IMAGE TRANSFER

When you bring a digital camera with a compatible IrDA interface near your computer, the image transfer utility appears. Follow your camera manufacturer's instructions to copy images from the camera to your computer.

You can specify the directory for image transfers in the Wireless Link properties, from the Control Panel, or from the Wireless Link task tray icon. The default is the My Pictures folder inside your My Documents folder.

INFRARED PRINTING

When your computer has an IrDA interface, you can print to infrared-connected printers. To make a connection to an infrared printer, follow these steps:

1. Power up the printer and point your computer's IR beam at it. Windows may detect and install the printer automatically. If it doesn't, proceed with step 2.
2. In Printers, select Add Printer. Choose Local Printer, and uncheck Automatically Detect.
3. Under Use the Following Port, choose IR (Local Port).
4. Select the printer's manufacturer and model. If it's not listed, and you have a disk from the manufacturer, select Have Disk and locate the Windows XP printer drivers.
5. Supply a name for the printer, choose whether it will be the default printer, and choose whether to share the printer to your LAN.

Now you can use the printer whenever it's in visible range of your computer.

MULTIPLE LAN CONNECTIONS

Most desktop computers sit where they are installed, gathering dust until they're obsolete, and participate in only one LAN. But portable computer users often carry their computers from office to office, docking or plugging into several different local LANs. Although Microsoft has made it easy for you to manage several different dial-up and VPN connections, it's difficult to manage connections to several different LANs if the network configuration settings are manually set.

Internet Protocol settings are the difficult ones. If your computer is set to use automatic TCP/IP configuration, you won't encounter any problems; your computer will absorb the local information each time you connect.

If your TCP/IP settings are set manually, things aren't so simple. Microsoft has come up with a partial solution called Alternate Configuration. You can configure your computer for automatic IP address assignment on most networks, and manual assignment on one. The way this works is that Windows looks for a DHCP server when it boots up, and if it doesn't find one it uses the Alternate Configuration. This can be a static IP address, or the default setting of Automatic Private IP address assignment, whereby Windows chooses a random address in the 169.254 subnet. (The automatic technique was the only option in Windows 98, Me, 2000 and XP.)

What this means is that your computer can automatically adjust itself to multiple networks, at most one of which requires manual IP address settings.

To set up Alternate Configuration, open Network Connections, view Local Area Connection's properties, and double-click Internet Protocol. Be sure the General tab uses the Obtain an IP Address Automatically setting. View the Alternate Configuration tab and choose User Configured to enter the static LAN's information.

If you need to commute between multiple networks that require manual configuration, you'll have to change the General settings each time you connect to a different network. I suggest that you stick a 3-by-5-inch card with the settings for each network in your laptop carrying case for handy reference.

NOTE

> While it appears that Microsoft isn't going to solve this problem for us, we can hope that third-party software developers will come up with a tool to manage multiple LAN connections properly. Back on Windows 95 I used a program called Network Hopper that let you choose from a list of multiple network setups. It changed not only the IP address info but even email setups, so that the appropriate mail servers were used on each network. A tool like that for Windows XP would be a real blessing. Attention developers: Care to take this on?

TROUBLESHOOTING

VPN CONNECTION FAILS WITHOUT CERTIFICATE

When I attempt to make a VPN connection, I receive the message `Unable to negotiate the encryption you requested without a certificate.`

You are trying to connect to a VPN server with a higher level of encryption than your computer or the other computer is configured to carry out.

If you are attempting to contact a Windows 200x VPN server, contact your network administrator to get the appropriate certificate installed. If you are calling a Windows NT 4 VPN server, this error probably occurred because you enabled IPSec on the Options tab of the Advanced Internet Protocol properties. In this case, disable IPSec.

WIRELESS LINK IS NOT PRESENT IN CONTROL PANEL

I have a wireless adapter in my desktop (or portable computer), but Wireless Link does not appear in the Control Panel.

The IrDA adapter is probably disabled in your computer's BIOS. Shut down and restart your computer. When your BIOS is setting up, press the indicated key to enter its setup utility.

Look at its Built-In Peripherals screen for IrDA options. You must enable IRDA 1.1 support. It might require a DMA and Interrupt port as well, so you might not be able to use infrared and ECP printing at the same time. Save and exit the setup program.

When you restart Windows, it will detect and install support for the infrared connector.

SEND FILES ICON DOESN'T APPEAR

When another computer with an infrared IRDA port is brought near my computer, the Send Files To Another Computer icon doesn't appear.

In this case, the problem could be with either computer. If one of the two computers *can* make a wireless link with at least one other computer, then you know the fault lies with the other.

The following are a few points to check:

- Be sure that the wireless optical ports are within a few feet of each other, are pointed relatively directly at each other, with a clear line of sight between them.
- Check the Device Manager on both computers to be sure that both IrDA ports are working correctly.
- Be sure that both computers have wireless file transfers enabled.
- If all else fails, borrow a handheld video camcorder. These cameras can often "see" the infrared light emitted by IrDA ports. Check to see that the ports on both computers are blinking. If you see one blinking but not the other, you know one computer isn't set up correctly.

Tips from the Windows Pros: Access to Your Computer When You Travel

It never fails: I can't leave town without getting a phone call from a client: "We *need* you to send us such and such right away!" Even if I take my laptop along, that "such and such" is probably the one file I didn't bring or didn't keep up-to-date. If you depend on your computer for your livelihood, you've probably had this happen to you too. With the Internet being available all over the world, though, there's no reason you can't take care of these emergencies in short order. You have to prepare ahead of time, of course.

First of all, in order to reach your computer by the Internet, it has to be turned on and connected. This means you'll need an able assistant at home, or you'll have to leave your computer turned on and use an always-on DSL or cable connection. We Californians are sensitive about wasting energy, so if you take the second approach, be sure your computer's hard drive is set to power down after an hour or so (see the section "Power Options" in Chapter 22).

Then you'll need a way to connect. There are three ways you can do it:

- If you're traveling with a laptop, you can use Windows's VPN software. Enable incoming VPN connections on your home computer, and set up a Dial-Up connection to it on your laptop. When the connection is established, open Explorer, select Tools, Map Network Drive, and view *name*\SharedDocs with Windows Explorer, where *name* is the computer name of your home computer. You'll able to browse through the "shared documents" folder to get the file you want.

- If your home-base computer uses Windows XP Professional, you can use enable incoming Remote Desktop connections on it, and use Remote Desktop Connection to call it. With Remote Desktop, you can use all features of the computer.

- If your home computer uses XP Home Edition and you want that full remote-control experience, buy a third-party package like PC Anywhere. For the peace of mind they give, they're worth the money. You'll need to install the software on your laptop too. If you're not bringing your own computer, bring the software's installation CD-ROM with you.

  There is also a free, public-domain program called VNC that takes a little more know-how to set up.

- If you're not bringing a laptop along, there's another spiffy way to connect to your computer at home. Check out www.gotomypc. This Internet-based service lets you access your home computer from afar over the Web, with *no* additional software needed at the remote site. Talk about cool! You could also store files you might need on an Internet-accessible file sharing service like www.magicaldesk.com.

Now, these are the most important bits of advice I can give you:

First, *test* your setup before you leave. And secondly, you *must* protect your computer with good passwords on *every* account, and you *must* be sure that your Internet connection has a firewall in place to prevent hackers from getting in (see Chapter 19).

CHAPTER 18

CONNECTING YOUR LAN TO THE INTERNET

In this chapter

IT'S A GREAT TIME TO CONNECT YOUR LAN TO THE INTERNET

In the 1980s, only big corporations and universities had Internet connections, and then, a single 64Kbps connection was probably shared by hundreds of users. Now, accessing the Internet is as much a daily requirement as coffee and the morning paper. We expect to have instant access from any keyboard we can get our fingers on, and personally, I get grumpy using anything less than a 400Kbps connection. That's progress, I suppose.

In today's homes it's common to have two or more computers, and you're sure to want Internet access on all of them. It seems wasteful to make each computer connect to the Internet separately—this ties up two or more telephone lines, or costs lots extra for multiple high-speed cable or DSL hookups. Is there a better way? You bet: You can share a single Internet connection with several computers using your home/office local area network. The money you'll save not needing several telephone lines can pay for the network in a few months. I think it's worth setting up a network just for this.

You have a host of options for shared Internet connections. You can use a high-speed connection to serve the entire LAN, or you can share a modem connection made from one designated Windows XP computer. Either way, shared access makes online life simpler and safer for everyone.

A shared Internet connection can actually provide better protection against hackers than an individual connection. In this chapter, I show you why. I also cover your Internet connection options and discuss the pros and cons of each.

TIP

> You should also read Chapter 19, "Network Security," for more details on protecting your network from hacking.

THE NUTS AND BOLTS OF THE CONNECTION

You're probably familiar with using a modem to connect your own PC to an Internet service provider and thence to the Internet. When you're connecting an entire network of computers, the process is a little more involved. We'll address five main issues, starting with the physical connection itself. We'll discuss the pros and cons of each of the most common and reasonable alternatives.

THE NEED FOR SPEED

Of the several connection technologies, each has advantages and disadvantages in reliability, speed, and cost.

Speed is everything on the Internet now, and the need for raw speed will become even more important in the future. Remember that everyone on your LAN will be sharing a single connection. Now, most of the time you're using the Internet you're just staring at the screen and downloading only intermittently, so a single modem connection shared by two or three people probably would feel fast enough. Most of the time, when you clicked on a new page, the modem wouldn't be busy downloading stuff for other people, so you'd get its full speed. Sometimes the modem would have to work for two or more people simultaneously, and your download speeds would drop for a while, but overall, you wouldn't notice the difference.

However, if you have more than a handful or computers, if you spend lots of time downloading large files, if you want to use voice or videoconferencing, or if you want to view online streaming audio or video, you'll probably find a modem connection isn't fast enough. In this case, if you can get it, high-speed DSL, cable, or satellite service will provide a much better experience than a dial-up setup. It costs a bit more per month, but when you take into the account that one shared broadband connection can replace several dial-up accounts and free up several phone lines, it might turn out to be the least expensive alternative as well as the most fun.

WAYS TO MAKE THE CONNECTION

When you're using a single computer, you use its analog modem or a broadband cable, DSL, or satellite modem to connect to your ISP as needed. When you share your Internet connection on a network, you either designate one computer running Windows XP to make the connection or use an inexpensive hardware device called a *connection sharing router* or *residential gateway* to serve as a bridge between your network and a dial-up, cable, or DSL modem. Whichever method you choose, the designated computer or router automatically sets up the connection anytime it's needed by anybody on your network.

As an overview, Figure 18.1 shows six ways you can hook up your LAN to an Internet service provider. They are

A. Microsoft Internet Connection Sharing (ICS) with an analog or ISDN dial-up connection. In this scenario, the built-in software in Windows automatically dials your ISP from one computer whenever anyone on the LAN wants to connect to the Internet. This is called *demand-dialing*. (By the way, the modem doesn't have to be an external one, it could be an internal modem; I just wanted it to show up in the figure).

B. ICS with a broadband DSL or cable modem. The computer that hosts the shared connection uses a second LAN adapter to connect to a broadband modem. This type of connection might be always-on, or, if your ISP uses a connection-based setup called PPPoE, Windows will establish the link whenever anyone wants to use the Internet.

→ To learn more about PPPoE, **see** "Configuring a High-Speed Connection," **p. 275**.

C. Connection Sharing Router with a broadband, analog, or IDSN modem. You can use a small hardware device that costs somewhere in the range of $20–$100 to do the same job as Internet Connection Sharing. The advantage of this is that you don't have to leave a particular Windows XP computer turned on for other users to reach the Internet. It is also more secure because a separate device is shielding Windows from the Internet.

18

Figure 18.1
Six ways to connect
your LAN to the
Internet.

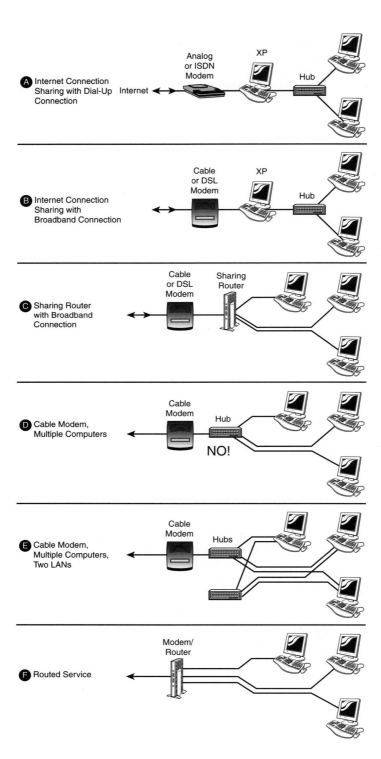

D. Cable Service with multiple, directly connected computers. This is the setup most cable Internet providers recommend for a home with more than one computer, but it is a *bad idea*! You can't use this method and also use file and printer sharing. Use scheme B, C, or E instead. See "Special Notes for Cable Service" later in this chapter for more information.

E. Cable Service with multiple, directly connected computers and a separate LAN for file and printer sharing. If you don't use connection sharing (scheme B or C), this is the only safe way to share files and printers *and* also have an "unfiltered" broadband Internet connection.

F. Routed Service with a router. Some ISPs provide routed Internet service through DSL, cable, Frame Relay, or other technologies. There's usually an extra charge for this type of service because it provides a separate public IP address to each computer on the LAN. This has some advantages, which I discuss next, but it also incurs a risk of exposing your network to hackers, unless you're vigilant in setting it up.

I discussed the pros and cons of dial-up, ISDN, and broadband connections themselves in Chapter 8, "Internet and TCP/IP Connection Options," so I won't repeat that discussion. Here, I'll discuss the costs and benefits of these six connection-sharing strategies.

NOTE

> While I really prefer using the shared connection strategies—the first three schemes in Figure 18.1—they have a drawback: It's more difficult to enable incoming access to your computer. In particular, it makes it difficult for someone to work with you using Remote Assistance. I'll show you how to make it work at the end of the chapter, under "Making Services Available."

18

Now, let's look at the issues involved in having a single ISP connection serve multiple computers.

MANAGING IP ADDRESSES

Connecting a LAN to the Internet requires you to delve into some issues about how computers are identified on your LAN and on the Internet. You'll find some background on this topic in Chapter 14, "Overview of Windows XP Networking," under "IP Addresses and Routing." In this chapter, we'll focus on how your LAN relates to the Internet as a whole.

As discussed in Chapter 14, each computer on your LAN uses a unique network identification number called an *IP address* that is used to route data to the correct computer. As long as the data stays on your LAN, it doesn't matter what numbers are used; your LAN is essentially a private affair. On LANs with no shared Internet connection, in fact, Windows just makes up random IP address numbers for each computer and that's good enough.

When you connect to the Internet, though, those random numbers can't be used to direct data to you; *public* IP addresses have to be assigned to you by your ISP so that other computers on the Internet can properly route data to your ISP and then to you.

Now, when you establish a solo dial-up connection from your computer to the Internet, this isn't a big problem. When you dial up, your ISP assigns your connection a temporary public IP address. Any computer on the entire Internet can send data to you using this number. When you want to connect a LAN, though, it's not quite as easy. There are two approaches:

- You can get a valid public IP address for each of your computers, so they can each participate in the Internet at large

- You can use *one* public IP address and share it among all the users of your LAN

The first approach is called *routed* Internet service, because your ISP assigns a fixed block of IP addresses for your LAN—one for each of your computers—and routes all data for these addresses to your site. The second approach uses a technique called *Network Address Translation* or NAT, in which all of the computers on your LAN share one IP address and connection.

NAT AND INTERNET CONNECTION SHARING

Microsoft's Internet Connection Sharing system and the popular devices called *residential gateways* or *connection sharing routers* all use Network Address Translation to carry out all Internet connections using one public IP address. The computer or device running the NAT service mediates all connections between computers on your LAN and the Internet (see Figure 18.2).

To explain NAT, it's helpful to make an analogy to postal mail service. Normally, mail is delivered to each house according to its address, and the mail delivery person stops at each separate house on a given block. This is analogous to routed Internet service where each of your computers has its own public IP address. Data is routed to your LAN, and then delivered to each computer independently.

NAT works more like a large commercial office building, where there's one address for many people. Mail is delivered to the mail room, which sorts it out and delivers it internally to the correct recipient. With NAT, you are assigned one public IP address, and all communication between your LAN and the Internet uses this address. The NAT service takes care of changing or translating the IP addresses in data packets from the private, internal IP addresses used on your LAN to the one public address used on the Internet.

Using NAT has several significant consequences:

- You can hook up as many computers on your LAN as you wish. Your ISP won't care, or even know, that more than one computer is using the connection. You will save money because you only need to pay for a single-user connection.

- You can assign IP addresses inside your LAN however you wish. In fact, all of the NAT setups I've seen provide DHCP, an automatic IP address service, so that there's virtually no manual configuration needed on the computers you add to your LAN.

- If you want to host a Web site, VPN, or other service on your LAN and make it available from the Internet, you'll have some additional setup work to do. When you contact a remote Web site, NAT knows to send the returned data back to you, but when an unsolicited request comes from outside, NAT has to be told where to send the incoming connection. I'll discuss this later in the chapter.

- NAT serves as an additional firewall to protect your LAN from probing by Internet hackers. Incoming requests, to read your shared folders for example, are simply ignored if you haven't specifically set up your connection sharing service to forward requests to a particular computer.

- Some network services can't be made to work with NAT. For example, you might not be able to use audio and video chat with Windows Messenger and NetMeeting. These programs expect that the IP address of the computer they're running on is a public address. Windows Internet Connection Sharing and some hardware sharing routers can work around this problem using the Universal Plug and Play protocol, which I discuss later in the chapter.

- A hardware connection sharing router can provide better security than Windows Internet connection sharing because, as a special-purpose device, its software is simpler and less likely to be buggy than Windows. Also, when used with Windows Firewall, you have two separate lines of defense against hackers rather than just one.

Figure 18.2
A NAT device or program carries on all Internet communications using one IP address. NAT keeps track of outgoing data from your LAN to determine where to send responses from the outside.

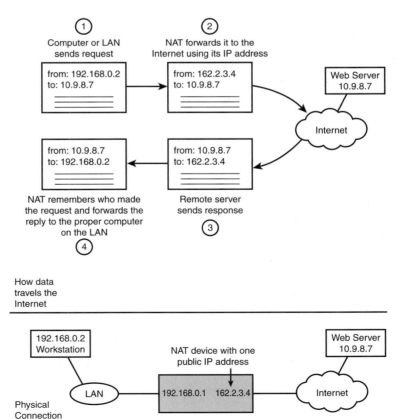

Starting with Windows 98, Microsoft has provided a NAT service through its Internet Connection Sharing feature. In addition, Windows XP Service Pack 2 introduced Windows Firewall, an additional security feature that prevents outside people from accessing your LAN. I'll talk more about Windows Firewall in Chapter 19.

Given the choice between Microsoft's Internet Connection Sharing (ICS) service and an external hardware router, I recommend that you use a router, for two reasons:

■ First, to use ICS, you have to leave one of your Windows computers turned on so that other computers can reach the Internet. Connection sharing routers have to be left on too, but they consume very little power compared to what a PC sucks up.

■ More importantly, connection sharing routers provide better security than Windows. These little boxes have very little going on inside them, so it's more likely that any security flaws have been noticed and fixed. Windows, on the other hand, is hugely complex, and Microsoft finds security flaws at the rate of one or two a week. If you use ICS and host a Web site on the connection-sharing computer, you're inviting outside people to run complex software on the same computer that's protecting your network. If they find a way to circumvent NAT or Windows Firewall, they're already inside your computer. With the hardware router, they have to break into the router and then break into Windows.

I won't go so far as to say that you shouldn't trust ICS, and I will show you how to hook up your LAN using all of the methods I described earlier. I'll just put in as my final word on this issue that I use DSL/Cable Sharing Routers at my own home and office.

If you decide to use a router, look at the products made by Linksys, D-Link, SMC and Netgear. You can find them at computer stores, office supply stores, and online (check www.buy.com), and on sale you can pick one up for $20 or less. Wireless versions that include an 802.11g Wireless networking base station as well as a hub for wired Ethernet connections don't cost that much more—I'm looking at the ads in my Sunday paper right now and see prices ranging from $40 to $60.

In addition, more advanced (and expensive) versions include additional features like a built-in print server or virtual private networking (VPN) service. For example, the D-Link DI-713P Wireless Broadband Router provides NAT (connection sharing), a three-port switching Ethernet hub, a print server, and a wireless access point all in one box. But, while combination devices might be less expensive when you look at the total cost of getting separate devices, separate units give you more flexibility in where you locate the devices. Also, if one device fails, you don't lose all the functions at once.

NOTE

> By the way, while most connection sharing routers on the market are designed for use with cable or DSL Internet service, some can connect with an analog or IDSN modem. If you use dial-up service, you're not left out. Netgear and SMC make devices that can be hooked up to a modem.

RUNNING YOUR OWN WEB SERVERS

If you want to host your own public Web or email servers on your LAN, or if you want to reach your LAN through a VPN connection, you need to have an always-on connection so the network can always be reached from the outside. A demand-dialing modem connection is not a good choice for this use because the connection is established only when you try to reach out. Many years ago it was cost-effective to use a permanently connected dial-up service, but it's no longer cost-effective. Broadband is really the only way to go. Routed Internet service is a big advantage here because each computer gets a fixed, public, always-on IP address, but you can get by with a shared connection, too.

You'll probably also want to be able to reach your Web site or computers by typing in a standard domain name, such as www.mysitename.com. For this, you need to register a domain name and need Domain Name Service (DNS) to give the Internet the means of finding your computer's public IP address. You can have your ISP provide domain name service, but it will probably cost you an extra $5–$20 per month. You also might check out the free public DNS services hosted by www.dyndns.org and others (do a Google search for free DNS service and check out the sponsored links).

Whether you use NAT or a routed Internet service, it's best if you can get your ISP to assign you a permanent, or *static*, IP address so that your computers' IP addresses don't change from day to day as a dial-up connection's does. This way, your DNS information can be set up once and will work as long as you keep your ISP. Static IP addressing is not available with every connection technology or ISP, though, so you have to ask when shopping for your service provider.

If you have dial-up, cable, or nonstatic DSL service, you have to get dynamic DNS service because your network's public IP address changes every time your connection is reestablished.

Inverse DNS

If you go for dedicated Internet access, and your ISP assigns you a block of fixed IP addresses, you might want to ask your ISP to enter *Inverse DNS* information for you as well as register your domain name.

The domain name service (DNS) is called into play whenever you use an Internet address like www.microsoft.com. DNS looks up this name in a directory and returns some computer's IP address—for example, 207.46.131.137. The DNS system can also work in reverse and return the name of a computer given its IP address. For example, the name 4.3.2.1 turns out to be durham2-001.dsl.gtei.net.

When you get routed Internet access, the "inverse" lookup names for the IP addresses assigned to you either are left undefined or are set to some generic names like cust137.dsl131.someISP.com. If you ask, your ISP can set up names that identify your computers and domain so that anyone on the Internet to whom you connect can find out the name of your computer.

Using inverse DNS has some pros and cons. One pro is that some email servers on the Internet don't accept email from systems without a valid inverse DNS entry. If you run an email server on your network, at least that computer should have an inverse DNS entry. One con is that Web site managers can tell the name of your computer and domain when you visit Web sites, so you give up some privacy.

The choice is up to you. If you want to register your computers, talk to your ISP.

18

SPECIAL NOTES FOR WIRELESS NETWORKING

If you're setting up a wireless network, you *must* enable WEP or WPA encryption to protect your network from unexpected use by random strangers. People connecting to your wireless network appear to Windows to be part of your own LAN and are trusted accordingly.

If you really want to provide free access to your broadband connection as a public service, provide it using a second, unsecured wireless router plugged into your network, as shown in Figure 18.3. Use a different channel number and SSID from the ones set up for your own wireless LAN. Set up filtering in this router to prevent Windows file sharing queries from penetrating into your own network. See "Scheme F—Routed Service Using a Router," later in this chapter, for the list of ports you must block.

(And remember that someone might use your connection to send spam or attack other networks. If the FBI knocks on your door some day, don't say I didn't warn you.)

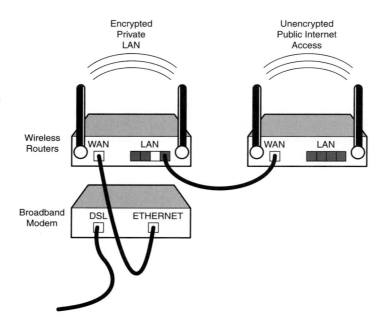

Figure 18.3
If you want to provide unsecured, free wireless Internet access to strangers, use a second wireless router to protect your own LAN.

SPECIAL NOTES FOR CABLE SERVICE

Although some cable Internet providers can provide you with multiple IP addresses so you can connect multiple computers directly to your cable modem, I strongly urge you *not* to use this type of service. There are two reasons for this.

First, when you order more than one IP address on cable service, some providers assign IP addresses that have different IP subnet addresses. This is like giving you telephone extensions with different area codes, and it makes it very difficult to use Microsoft Networking (file sharing) on your LAN.

More importantly, this type of setup requires you to connect your cable modem directly to your LAN, without any firewall protection between the Internet and your computers. You would have to disable file and printer sharing on each computer. If you didn't, you would expose all of your computers to a *severe security risk.*

CAUTION

> Do not connect a cable modem directly to your LAN. Anyone on the Internet would be able to read and change your shared files and folders, and could possibly infect your computer with viruses and other nasty software.

Now, if you don't care about file and printer sharing, this isn't a big loss. But, if you do want the full advantage of having a LAN in your home or office, you can solve this dilemma in three ways:

- You could set up two separate networks: one to connect each computer to the cable modem and the other to connect the computers for file sharing (see Figure 18.1-E). With Ethernet network adapters costing as little as $5 each, this isn't a bad solution. You would have to take great care to configure the two networks correctly. I'll discuss this shortly.

- You could install two network adapters in one computer—one going to the cable modem and the other to your LAN—and use Windows Internet Connection Sharing, as shown in Figure 18.1-B.

- You could install an inexpensive cable/DSL sharing router to provide the connection, as in Figure 18.1-C.

Some cable ISPs don't want you to use a router, but I think it provides superior protection against hacking, and that needs to be your first priority. You can always pay your ISP for the extra computers and use just the one, safe connection to provide service to your other computers.

SPECIAL NOTES FOR ORDERING ISDN SERVICE

If you are ordering ISDN service, you should know what kind of ISDN modem or router you will be using before you order an ISDN line from the phone company. ISDN provisioning is complex, and most telephone companies can determine the options you need if you tell them the brand of equipment you're using. Also, your ISDN equipment manual may list a special "quick order" code to give your telephone company. You will probably order "2B+D, Data and voice, 64K data" service with no special call functions.

18

When your ISDN line is installed, be sure to ask the installer for the following information:

- Switch type
- SPID (Service Profile Identifiers) numbers
- Directory numbers

You'll need these when you install your ISDN modem.

CONFIGURING YOUR LAN

You waited weeks for installation day, and the installer finally came. Now all you can think of is all those bits, just waiting to blast their way onto your network. Hang on; we're almost done.

You now need to set up your network's TCP/IP software to let your computers talk through the Internet connection in a coordinated way. This step depends not so much on the connection type you chose but on the sharing system and the IP address system you'll use.

In the following sections, I'll describe how to set up each of the connection schemes diagrammed in Figure 18.1. If you're still in the planning stages for your network, you might want to read all six sections to see what's involved. If your LAN is already set up and your Internet service is ready to go now, just skip ahead to the appropriate section.

SCHEME A—MICROSOFT INTERNET CONNECTION SHARING WITH A DIAL-UP CONNECTION

This section shows how to set up the Internet connection method illustrated in Figure 18.1 (letter A).

The Internet Connection Sharing feature provided with Windows XP can share modem, ISDN, or broadband connections that require a sign-on procedure. The connection is made automatically whenever any user on the network tries to access the Internet; this is called demand-dialing. The following section describes how to set it up.

SETTING UP THE SHARED CONNECTION

To set up a shared connection, first install and test your modem and ISP information on the computer that will be used to share the connection. To do this, set up a standard dial-up connection using the procedure described in Chapter 8. Be sure that you can access the Internet properly by viewing at least one Web page. When you know this is working, you're ready to set up Internet Connection Sharing. You can do this with the Network Setup Wizard, or set it up manually. To use the wizard, follow these steps:

1. Click Start, My Network Places and then select Set Up a Home or Small Office Network.
2. In the Network Setup Wizard, click Next twice. Select the first choice—This Computer Connects Directly to the Internet—and then click Next.

3. In the list of network connections, select the listing for the connection to your ISP as shown in Figure 18.4 and click Next. (Your display will not look exactly like the one in the figure because it will list the dial-up connections *you've* defined.)

Figure 18.4
In this dialog box, select the ISP Internet Connection that you want to share.

4. Complete the rest of the Network Setup Wizard as described in Chapter 8. If you have an existing LAN, be sure to enter the same Workgroup name you used originally, as the Wizard wants to change the setting to MSHOME every time you run it.

   If you have older Windows 95 or 98 computers on your network, you might want to create a diskette with the Network Setup Wizard for these computers by following the instructions you'll encounter in the wizard.

5. When the wizard completes, restart your computer.

6. Log on again, and try to view any Web page (such as www.google.com). Your computer should automatically dial your ISP. If the Web page appears, proceed to step 7. If it doesn't, you'll have to resolve the problem before continuing.

 If your modem doesn't dial up when you try to view a Web page, see "Shared Connection Doesn't Happen" in the "Troubleshooting" section at the end of this chapter.

7. When the sharing computer can connect properly, repeat these steps on your other computers, except for one detail: when you run the wizard, select This Computer Connects to the Internet Through Another Computer on My Network or Through a Residential Gateway.

Connection sharing is now set up. You might want to walk through the manual process described next, just to confirm that all of the settings were made correctly. Otherwise you may skip ahead to the section titled "Configuring the Rest of the Network."

If you don't want to or can't use the Network Setup Wizard on the connection-sharing computer, you can use the manual configuration process described next. Here is the procedure:

1. Click Start, My Network Places and select View Network Connections. Right-click the icon for the connection to your ISP, and select Properties.

2. Choose the Advanced tab. Check all of the boxes, as shown in Figure 18.5.

Figure 18.5
On the computer that is going to share its connection, enable Windows Firewall and Internet Connection Sharing.

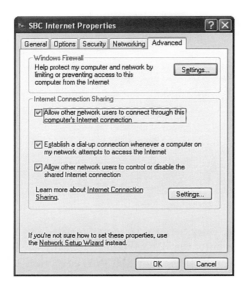

3. Select the Options tab. Uncheck Prompt For Name And Password and Prompt for Phone Number. This will let the connection start up without user intervention.

4. If you want an always-on 24/7 connection, make these settings: Check Redial If Line Is Dropped. Set the number of Redial Attempts to 99, Time Between Redial Attempts to 10 seconds, and Idle Time Before Hanging Up to Never. Be aware that if you pay per-minute charges, this can result in an astounding phone bill!

   Usually, though, you'll want an intermittent demand-dialing connection. Make these settings: Uncheck Redial if Line Is Dropped, Set the number of Redial Attempts to 10, Time Between Redial Attempts to 10 seconds, and Idle Time Before Hanging Up to 10 minutes. (I recommend using 10 minutes; you can increase it later if you find that the line disconnects too frequently while you're working.)

CAUTION

The following step is a crucial part of protecting your computer and LAN from hacking over the Internet. Omitting this step could make your computer vulnerable to hacking.

5. Select the Networking tab. In the list of Components used by the connection, be sure that *only* Internet Protocol (TCP/IP) and QoS Packet Scheduler are checked, as shown in Figure 18.6. This will prevent file sharing from being exposed to the Internet. The Firewall will do that too, but it doesn't hurt to be extra safe.

Figure 18.6
Be sure that on your Internet connection the Client and Sharing components are not checked.

6. Click OK. Windows then warns you that it is changing the network address of your LAN adapter to 192.168.0.1. This is now the IP address for this computer on your LAN.

I suggest restarting your computer and confirming that your computer connects to your ISP when you try to view a Web page. Then, proceed by configuring the other computers on your LAN.

CONFIGURING THE REST OF THE NETWORK

Once the shared connection is setup, configuring the rest of your LAN should be easy. The computer sharing its Internet connection is now running the Internet Connection Sharing service, which makes it

- A DHCP server, which parcels out IP addresses and setup information
- The network gateway, which forwards to the Internet any network traffic that isn't directed at local computers
- A DNS server, which assists the other computers in converting domain names into IP addresses

Its IP address is 192.168.0.1 and all your other computers simply refer to it for network services.

To configure the other computers on the network, you can use the Network Setup Wizard, or configure manually. First, I'll give the steps for using the wizard. On each of your other computers, (all except the connections-sharing computer), follow these steps:

18

1. Open My Network Places from the Start Menu, and select Set Up a Home or Small Office Network. If you are setting up older Windows 95/98/2000 computers that don't have a Network Setup Wizard, you can use the diskette you prepared when you setup connection sharing.

2. Select This Computer Connects to the Internet Through Another Computer as the connection method, and then select Next.

3. Complete the rest of the Network Setup Wizard as described in Chapter 15, "Creating a Windows XP Home Network." If you have an existing LAN, be sure to enter the same Workgroup name you used originally, as the wizard wants to change the setting to MSHOME every time you run it.

4. When the wizard finishes, you might want to restart your computer. Then, you should be able to open Internet Explorer and view a Web site. When you try, the connection-sharing computer should dial out.

NOTE

> When you're using a shared dial-up connection, it takes a while for the dialer to go through its paces if the connection wasn't already up, and before it can finish you might get an error from Internet Explorer saying it can't open the page. If this happens, just wait a few seconds and click Refresh to try again.

If you are using Microsoft Internet Connection Sharing or a connection sharing router that supports Universal Plug and Play (UPnP), the Network Connections window of all the other computers on your network should have an icon that represents the shared Internet connection, as shown in Figure 18.7. Normally, Windows automatically establishes and drops the shared connection as needed. If necessary, you can right-click this icon to control the connection manually (unless the owner of the shared connection disabled the remote-control feature on the shared connection's Advanced properties page).

Figure 18.7
The other computers on your network can control the shared connection from their Network Connections windows.

If you're a networking hotshot want to configure other computers manually, you can use this procedure:

1. Open My Network Places and select View Network Connections. Open Local Area Connection's Properties. (On versions of Windows other than XP, you may have to use different selections to get to your network adapter's settings; check online help or your copy of the corresponding *Special Edition Using* book.)

2. Select Internet Protocol (TCP/IP), and then select Properties.

3. Check Obtain an IP Address Automatically and Obtain DNS Server Address Automatically.

4. Click OK. The computer should reconfigure itself with a new IP address obtained from the computer with the shared dial-up connection.

Now test the shared connection from a computer on your LAN by trying to browse a Web page.

 If the computer can't browse Web pages, see "Can't Access a Shared Modem Connection from the LAN" in the "Troubleshooting" section at the end of this chapter.

→ If you want to make services available to the Internet, **see** "Making Services Available," **p. 648**.

SCHEME B—MICROSOFT INTERNET CONNECTION SHARING WITH A BROADBAND CONNECTION

This section shows how to set up the Internet connection method illustrated in Figure 18.1 (letter B).

The procedure for configuring a shared high-speed cable or DSL Internet connection with Microsoft ICS is very similar to that for setting up a shared dial-up connection. To prepare, be sure to install and test your DSL or cable connection on the computer you'll use to host the shared connection, as described in Chapter 8. It's essential that you have this working before you proceed to set up your LAN and the shared connection.

TIP

> If your broadband service uses a LAN adapter rather than USB to connect your computer to the DSL or cable modem, you'll be installing two LAN adapters in this computer: one for the LAN, and one for the modem. I suggest that you install them one at a time. Install the one you'll use for your broadband connection first. View the adapter's icon in Network Connections, right-click it, and rename it `DSL Connection`, `Internet Connection`, or some other name that indicates what it's used for, as shown in Figure 18.8. Then, install the network adapter you'll use to connect to your LAN. Rename this connection `LAN Connection` or leave it as `Local Area Connection`. This will help you later on in the setup process when you need to know which connection goes to your ISP.

18

Figure 18.8
Install and rename your network adapters one at a time, indicating what purpose they'll serve. DSL Connection or Internet Connection is much more informative than Local Area Connection #2.

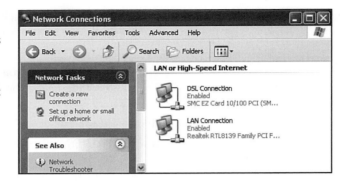

Verify that the broadband Internet connection is not connected to Windows file and printer sharing. To do this, follow these steps:

1. Open the Network Connections window by clicking Start, My Network Places, and selecting View Network Connections.

2. Right-click the icon that corresponds to your broadband connection and select Properties. Be sure that *only* QoS Packet Scheduler and Internet Protocol (TCP/IP) are checked, as shown in Figure 18.6.

When your broadband connection is configured correctly and is working, follow these steps:

1. Click Start, My Computer. Select My Network Places and then select View Network Connections. Select Set Up a Home or Small Office Network.

2. In the Network Setup Wizard, click Next twice. Select This Computer Connects Directly to the Internet as the connection method, and then click Next.

3. In the list of network connections, select the listing for the connection to your ISP as shown in Figure 18.9 and click Next. (Now you see why it's helpful to have renamed the connection icons.)

Figure 18.9
In this dialog box, select the network connection that corresponds to your broadband connection.

4. Complete the rest of the Network Setup Wizard as described in Chapter 8. If you have an existing LAN, be sure to enter the same Workgroup name you used originally, as the wizard wants to change the setting to MSHOME every time you run it.

   If you have older Windows 9x or Me computers on your network, you might want to create a diskette with the Network Setup Wizard for these computers by following the instructions you'll encounter in the wizard.

5. When the wizard completes, you may want to restart your computer.

6. Log on again, and try to view any Web page (such as www.google.com). If it appears, proceed to step 7. If it doesn't, you'll have to resolve the problem before proceeding. You should check the appropriate connection icon to be sure it's still configured correctly for your ISP.

7. When the sharing computer can connect properly, repeat these steps on your other computers, except for one detail: when you run the wizard, select "This computer connects to the Internet through another computer on my network or through a residential gateway."

When Connection Sharing has been set up, follow the instructions under "Configuring the Rest of the Network" in the section immediately preceding this one.

Because it's so important with these always-on broadband connections that Windows Firewall is actually working, I suggest that you view the icons in Network Connections to be sure that at least the broadband connection has the word "Firewalled" next to it, as shown in Figure 18.10. If it doesn't, use the following manual configuration steps to set it up.

Figure 18.10
Be sure that your shared broadband connection says Firewalled.

If you want to confirm that the wizard did its job properly, or if you want to configure Connection Sharing manually, rather than using the wizard, you can follow these steps on the computer with the broadband connection:

1. Locate the icon for the adapter that goes to your broadband modem in Network Connections. Right-click it and select Properties.

2. Choose the Advanced tab. Check all of the boxes, as shown in Figure 18.5.

3. Select the Networking tab. In the list of Components used by the connection, be sure that *only* Internet Protocol (TCP/IP) and QoS Packet Scheduler are checked. (This will prevent file sharing from being exposed to the Internet. Windows Firewall will do that too, but it doesn't hurt to be extra safe.)

4. Click OK. Windows then warns you that it is changing the network address of your LAN adapter to 192.168.0.1. This is now the IP address for this computer on your LAN.

5. Select Change Windows Firewall Settings in the Network Tasks list. Be sure that Windows Firewall is On and that Don't Allow Exceptions is unchecked.

I suggest restarting your computer and confirming that your computer connects to your ISP when you try to view a Web page. Now, skip back to the section titled "Configuring the Rest of the Network" earlier in this chapter.

SCHEME C—SHARING ROUTER WITH A BROADBAND OR DIAL-UP CONNECTION

This section shows how to set up the Internet connection method illustrated in Figure 18.1 (letter C).

Your router's manufacturer will provide instructions for installing and configuring it. If you're using cable or DSL Internet service, you'll connect your broadband modem to the router using a short Ethernet patch cable. If you're using a dial-up or ISDN account, you'll need to set up the router and a modem. Then, you'll connect the router to your LAN using one of the two methods shown in Figure 18.11.

If you connect your router to a separate hub, be sure that the "Link" indicators come on at both the hub and the router. If they don't you might need to switch the hub end of the cable from a regular port to an uplink port or vice versa.

You'll then configure the router, telling it how to contact your ISP, and what range of IP addresses to serve up to your LAN. Every device will use a different procedure, but I can show you the basic steps used by the Linksys Cable/DSL Sharing Routers that I have been so happy with.

The procedure will go something like this: When the router is attached to your network, you'll set up one of your computers' LAN adapters to obtain its IP address information automatically. Then you will use Internet Explorer to connect to the router by viewing http://192.168.1.1. (The address may be different for your router). A password is required; on my router the factory default value was admin. (On some routers you have to enter both a username and a password.)

You'll fill in your ISP's IP and sign-on information, if any, on a Web page similar to the one shown in Figure 18.12.

Figure 18.11
Connecting a
Connection Sharing
Router to your LAN.

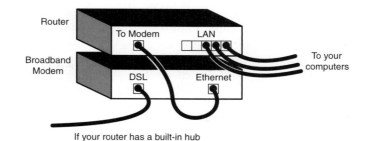

Figure 18.12
Sample setup page for
a Cable/DSL
Connection Sharing
router.

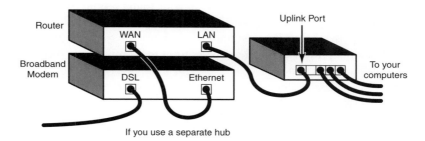

You might need to enter a static IP address, if one was assigned to you by your ISP. If your ISP uses DHCP to assign IP addresses dynamically, the router may need to be assigned the host and domain name expected by your provider. This is common with cable Internet setups.

If your ISP uses PPPoE to establish a connection, you'll need to enable PPPoE and enter your logon and password. Most DSL service works this way. If your DSL provider does use PPPoE, you should enable the router's auto-signon feature, and you can optionally set up a "keep-alive" value that will tell the modem to periodically send network traffic even if you don't, in order to keep your connection active all the time. (This might violate your service agreement with the DSL provider—better check before you do this.)

If you use cable Internet service and your ISP didn't provide you with a special hostname that you had to give to your computer, your ISP probably identifies you by your network adapter's MAC (hardware) address. You'll probably find that your Internet connection won't work when you set up the router. One of your router's setup pages should show its MAC address. You can either call your ISP's customer service line and tell them that this is your new adapter's MAC address, or you can configure the router to "clone" your computer's MAC address—that is, copy the address from the computer you originally used to set up your cable connection.

CAUTION

> Be sure to change the factory-supplied password of your router after you install it. (And write the password down somewhere in the router's manual.) Also, be sure to disable outside (Internet) access to the router's management screens.

18

As you are configuring your router, you might want to enable Universal Plug and Play (UPnP). I'll discuss this later in this chapter.

You might also opt for even better hacker protection by having your router filter (block) Microsoft file and printer sharing data. This is usually done on an advanced set up screen labeled Filtering. See "Scheme F—Routed Service Using a Router" later in this chapter for the list of ports that you must block.

When the router has been set up, go to each of your computers and follow the instructions under "Configuring the Rest of the Network" earlier in this chapter. You can configure all of the computers manually, or you can use the Network Setup Wizard. If you use the wizard, select My Computer Connects Through Another Computer or a Residential Gateway. If you use the manual method, select Obtain an IP Address Automatically, and Obtain DNS Information Automatically.

USING UNIVERSAL PLUG AND PLAY

If you use a hardware connection sharing router, consider enabling a feature called Universal Plug and Play (UPnP). UPnP provides a way for software running on your computer to communicate with the router. Here's what UPnP can do:

- It provides a means for the router to tell software on your computer that it is separated from the Internet by network address translation. Some software—Remote Assistance and the video and audio parts of Windows Messenger in particular—ask the computer on the other end of the connection to establish a connection back to your IP address. On a network with a shared connection, however, the IP address the computer sees is not the public IP address the shared Internet connection uses. UPnP lets software such as Remote Assistance find out what its public IP address is. It also provides a way for the router to suggest alternative port numbers if several computers on the network want to provide the same service (for example, if several users send Remote Assistance requests).

- It provides a means for software running on the network to tell the router to forward expected incoming connections to the correct computer. Remote Assistance and Windows Messenger again are two good examples. When the computer on the other end of the connection starts sending data, the router does not know to send it to your computer. UPnP lets UPnP-aware application programs automatically set up forwarding in the router.

- UPnP provide a means for other types of as-yet-undeveloped hardware devices to announce their presence on the network, so Windows can automatically take advantage of the services they provide.

UPnP has a downside, however: It has no built-in security mechanism, so any program on any computer on your network could potentially take control of the router and open holes for incoming connections. (I am confident that we will soon see computer viruses and Trojan horses that take advantage of this.) However, Windows Firewall still provides some protection and warns you if an undesired program attempts to receive incoming network connections, so this is not a serious problem. If you use Remote Assistance or Windows Messenger, the benefits UPnP provides outweigh the risks.

To use UPnP, you must enable the feature in your router. It's usually disabled by default. If your router doesn't currently support UPnP, you might have to download and install a firmware upgrade from the manufacturer. Most routers now do support UPnP.

By default, Windows XP provides support for detecting UpnP-enabled routers. If you have a UPnP router or Windows Internet Connection Sharing running on your network, the Network Connections screen should display an icon for the router, as shown in Figure 18.13.

NOTE

If the icon doesn't appear, click Advanced, Optional Networking Components; then select Networking Services and click Details. Be sure that Internet Gateway Device Discovery and Control Client is checked. While you're here, check UPnP User Interface as well—this enables support for future UPnP devices.

Then, on the task list, click Change Windows Firewall Settings. View the Exceptions tab and be sure that UPnP Framework is checked.

Figure 18.13
If your router supports UPnP, an Internet Gateway icon should appear in Network Connections.

If you right-click the Internet Connection icon and select Status, you see a dialog box similar to the one shown in Figure 18.14, displaying the status of the router's connection. If your Internet service uses a connection-based system such as PPPoE or standard dial-up service via a modem, this dialog box might display a buttons that lets you connect to and disconnect from your ISP.

Click Properties and then Settings to display a list of network services for which the router is forwarding incoming connections to computers on your network. This list shows only forwarding settings made via UPnP. Services forwarded by the setup screens on your router—a process discussed later in this chapter under "Making Services Available"—do not appear here. Also, new settings need not be made here; they might disappear when the router is reset.

Figure 18.14
Router Status displayed via UPnP.

SCHEME D—CABLE INTERNET WITH MULTIPLE COMPUTERS

This section shows how to set up the Internet connection method illustrated in Figure 18.1 (letter D). As I mentioned earlier in the chapter, you cannot safely use file and printer sharing with this setup. You should use this setup only if you don't want file and printer sharing at all and just want to have several computers with Internet access.

Here is the procedure to follow:

1. If your computers do not already have LAN adapters, install a network adapter in each of your computers. Configure the adapters as instructed by your ISP. In most cases, you won't need to make any adjustments to the default settings.

2. Connect your computers and your cable modem to an Ethernet hub. Chapter 16, "Using a Windows XP Network," provides details on installing network wiring.

3. On each computer, run the Network Setup Wizard. Click Next twice.

4. On the Select a Connection Method screen, select Other and click Next. Select the first choice—This Computer Connects to the Internet Directly or Through a Network Hub. Click Next.

5. If your ISP has given you a specific name to use with each computer, enter it in the Computer Name field. Otherwise, provide your own name and click Next.

6. Leave the workgroup name set to MSHOME and click Next.

7. Select Turn Off File and Printer Sharing and click Next.

8. Confirm the settings and click Next. Select Just Finish the Wizard and click Next.

9. When the wizard finishes, don't have it restart your computer right away. Instead, open the Network Connections window, right-click the Local Area Connection icon, and uncheck the Client and Sharing items, as shown in Figure 18.6. Click OK and then restart Windows.

If you later decide you want to use file and printer sharing, *do not* simply enable the Client and Sharing items. Instead, set up a shared connection using scheme B or C or install a second LAN as described in the next section.

SCHEME E—CABLE INTERNET WITH MULTIPLE COMPUTERS AND A SEPARATE LAN

This section shows how to set up the Internet connection method illustrated in Figure 18.1 (letter E). If you want to have file and printer sharing *and* have multiple computers on a cable Internet connection but for some reason do not want to use a connection sharing setup, you must set up a second, private network for file sharing that is physically separate from the network used for the Internet connection.

To do this, set up and test the LAN for the cable service as described in the previous section. Then, on each of the computers that is to participate in file and printer sharing, perform the following steps:

18

1. View the Network Connections screen, right-click the icon that corresponds to the network adapter, and select Rename. Change the name to **Internet Connection**.

2. Shut down the computer and install a second network adapter. Connect this adapter to a *separate* network hub.

3. Run the Network Setup Wizard again. Make the same choices, except this time turn *on* file and printer sharing.

4. On the Network Connections window, right-click the Internet Connection icon, select Properties, and be sure that it is still configured as shown in Figure 18.5.

5. Right-click the Local Area Connection icon (which corresponds to your new, second network), select Properties, and be sure that all the component items are checked.

   You also might want to assign each computer a static IP address. To do this, select Internet Protocol and click Properties. Click Use the Following IP Address. For the first computer, enter **192.168.0.1**. Set the Network Mask to **255.255.255.0** and leave the Default Gateway Address blank. Leave the DNS setting on automatic. For the second computer, enter address **192.168.0.2**, and so on.

6. In the Network Tasks list, select Change Windows Firewall Settings. Be sure the firewall is set to On.

7. On the Exceptions tab, check File and Printer Sharing. Click OK to close the dialog box.

Now, file and printer sharing will use your second, private LAN while the first LAN is used only for Internet service.

SCHEME F—ROUTED SERVICE USING A ROUTER

This section shows how to set up the Internet connection method illustrated in Figure 18.1 (letter F).

Some Internet service providers will sell you service that provides multiple, fixed IP addresses. This is usually the case for higher-priced business-class DSL service. You should really have a good reason for going this way, beyond just wanting to connect multiple computers—it's not as secure as a single shared connection. A good reason might be that you want the reliability of this class of service, or you want fixed IP addresses in order to host Web, email, or other Internet based services on several computers.

For this type of service, if you are using a cable, DSL, or satellite modem with a built-in router, your ISP will help you configure your network. In this setup, you will be provided with a fixed set of IP addresses, which you'll have to parcel out to your computers. Your ISP should help you install all of this, but I can give you some pointers.

First of all, it is *absolutely essential* that your router be set up to protect your network. You must ensure that at least these three items are taken care of:

1. The router must be set up with filters to prevent Microsoft file sharing service (NetBIOS or NetBT) packets from entering or leaving your LAN. In technical terms, the router must be set up to block TCP and UDP on port 137, UDP on port 138, and TCP on ports 139 and 445. It should "drop" rather than "reject" packets, if possible. This helps prevent hackers from discovering that these services are present but blocked. Better to let them think they're not there at all.

2. Be absolutely sure to change your router's administrative password from the factory default value to something hard to guess, with uppercase letters, lowercase letters, numbers, and punctuation. Don't let your ISP talk you out of this; you should, however, let them know what the new password is so they can get into the router from their end if need be.

3. Disable SNMP access, or change the SNMP read and read-write community names to something other than the default. Again, use something with letters, numbers, and punctuation.

CAUTION

> If your router is not properly configured to filter out NetBIOS traffic, your network will be exposed to hackers. This is absolutely unacceptable. If you're in doubt, have your ISP help you configure the router. Also, after setting things up, visit http://www.grc.com and use the "Shields Up!" pages there to be sure your computers are properly protected.
>
> For more information about network security please see Chapter 19.

Second, you'll need to manually set up a fixed IP address for each computer that is to host a service reachable from the "outside." You can make address settings manually in all of your computers, or just the ones that are hosting services, with your router providing DHCP service to configure the other computers. Make a list showing the name of each computer that is to get a static IP address, and the IP address you want to assign. You'll also have to manually enter the network mask, gateway IP address, and DNS server addresses supplied by your ISP, on each of these computers.

Follow these steps on each computer that is to get manual settings:

1. View My Network Places and select View Network Connections.
2. Right-click the Local Area Connection icon and select Properties.
3. Select the General tab, select Internet Protocol (TCP/IP), and then click Properties.
4. Enter an IP address and other assigned information. Figure 18.15 shows an example; you'll have to use the information provided by your ISP.

Finally, be sure to run the Network Setup Wizard on every one of your computers, however configured. When asked to choose a connection method, select Other, and on the next page, select This Computer Connects to the Internet Directly or Through a Network Hub.

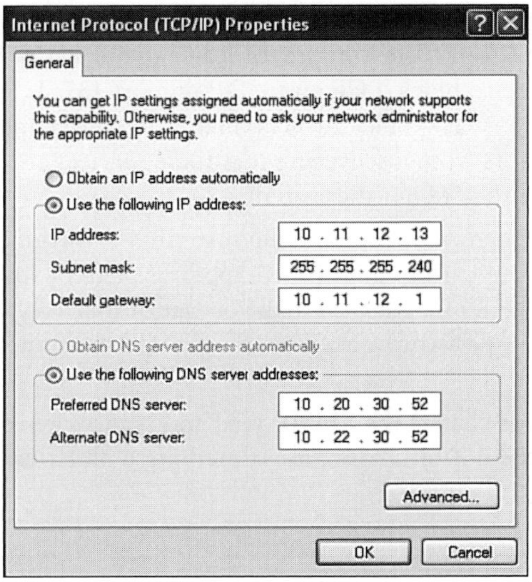

Figure 18.15
Setting up static
assigned IP address
information.

The wizard will give you some grief about the security risk involved in your Internet setup and will enable Windows Firewall on your LAN adapter. Don't let it disable File and Printer sharing—leave it turned on.

MAKING SERVICES AVAILABLE

You might want to make some internal network services available to the outside world through your Internet connection. You would want to do this if

- You want to run a Web or email server at home
- You want to enable incoming VPN access to your LAN so you can securely connect from home or afield
- You want to enable have someone help you through Remote Assistance
- You want to play multi-user games that depend on incoming connections to a game server that you run

If you have set up routed Internet service with a router, (as in the fourth setup in Figure 18.1), you don't have to worry about this because your network connection is wide open and doesn't use Network Address Translation. As long as the outside users know the IP address of the computer hosting your service—or its DNS name if you have set up DNS service—you're on the air already.

Otherwise you have either Windows Firewall, Network Address Translation or both in the way of incoming access. In order to make specific services accessible, you'll need to follow one of the sets of specific instructions in the next few sections, depending on the type of Internet connection setup you've used. Skip ahead to the appropriate section.

Enabling Access with Internet Connection Sharing

When you are using Microsoft's Internet Connection Sharing feature your network is protected from outside access. This is a good thing when it blocks attempts by hackers to get to your shared files and folders. It also blocks access to some of the neat services you might *want* the outside world to have access to: Virtual Private Networking, Remote Assistance, and if you've got them set up, Web and FTP servers, and so on.

Two steps are needed to provide outside access to a given service provided by a computer on your network. First, the connection sharing system (ICS) must be told which computer on your network is to receive incoming connection requests for a particular service. Then, on the computer that provides the service, Windows Firewall must be told to let these requests through.

Some services, such as Remote Assistance and Windows Messenger, use UPnP to automatically perform this setup work by communicating with the computer that is sharing its connection. So, when you are using ICS to share you network connection, these services simply work.

However, most server-type functions, such as Remote Desktop and Internet Information Services, require manual setup. On the computer providing the service itself, you must tell Windows Firewall to allow incoming connections to the service by following these steps:

1. Open the Windows Firewall screen by viewing Network Connections and clicking Change Windows Firewall Settings.
2. View the Exceptions page. See whether the service this computer is providing is already listed and checked. If so, you can proceed to configure the computer that is sharing its Internet connection.
3. If the service isn't already listed, click Add Port, enter the service name and port number, and select TCP or UDP, as shown in Figure 18.16. Common service numbers and protocols are listed in Table 18.2. (For the FTP and DNS services, you have to make two entries.)
4. Click Change Scope and select Any Computer (Including Those on the Internet). Click OK, and then click OK again.

Figure 18.16
Add a service's port number and protocol type to the Windows Firewall on the computer running the service.

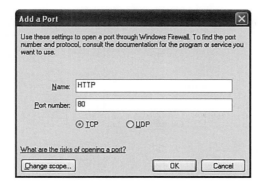

TABLE 18.2   COMMON SERVICES AND PORT NUMBERS

Protocol	Port	Associated Service
TCP	20 and 21	File Transfer Protocol (FTP)
TCP	23	Telnet
TCP	25	Simple Mail Transfer Protocol (SMTP)
TCP and UDP	53	Domain Name Service (DNS)
TCP	80	World Wide Web (HTTP)
TCP	110	Post Office Protocol (POP3)
TCP	3389	Remote Desktop
TCP and UDP	5631 5632	Symantec PCAnywhere

Then, you must instruct the computer sharing its Internet connection to forward incoming requests to the designated computer. On the computer that physically connects to the Internet, follow these steps:

1. Click Start, select My Network Places, and then select View Network Connections.

2. Right-click the icon for the shared Internet connection and select Properties. View the Advanced tab, and under Internet Connection Sharing, click Settings.

3. On the Advanced Settings dialog, view the Services tab (shown in Figure 18.17).

Figure 18.17
The Services tab lets you specify which services are to be forwarded through Internet Connection Sharing.

4. Check the Service entry for each service for which you want to permit access and for which you have servers on your LAN. If you have a computer running XP Professional on your network, the most common service to select is Remote Desktop; if you have set up IIS, the most common services are FTP Server and Web Server.

5. When you select a check box, a dialog appears, as shown in Figure 18.18.

Figure 18.18
The Service Settings dialog box lets you specify the name or IP address of the computer that is to handle incoming connections for a particular service.

6. Enter the IP address of the computer that is hosting this service, if your LAN uses fixed IP addresses. If your LAN uses automatically-assigned addresses from Internet Connection Sharing, you can enter the computer's name and the software will locate the correct computer.

7. If you want to use an incoming VPN connection, you must set it up on the computer that hosts the Internet Connection Sharing or Firewall service. You can't forward VPN connections to other computers.

8. If the service you want to use isn't listed, you'll need to find out what TCP and/or UDP ports the service communicates with. You'll have to search through the service software's documentation or the Internet to find these port values. For example, Symantec PC Anywhere uses TCP Port 5631 and UDP Port 5632.

   To add an unlisted service, click Add. Enter the name of the service, the IP address or host name of the computer which is running this service, and the port number, as shown in Figure 18.19. Generally, you'll want to use the same number for the port number the public sees (external port) and the port number used on the LAN (internal port). Check TCP or UDP, and then click OK.

   In the PC Anywhere example I'm using, after creating an entry for TCP Port 5631, I'll have to add a second entry to forward UDP Port 5632.

When you've enabled the desired services, incoming requests using the selected service ports will be forwarded to the appropriate computer on your LAN. Windows Firewall will know to let these services through.

18

Figure 18.19
Enter port information for a new service in this dialog box.

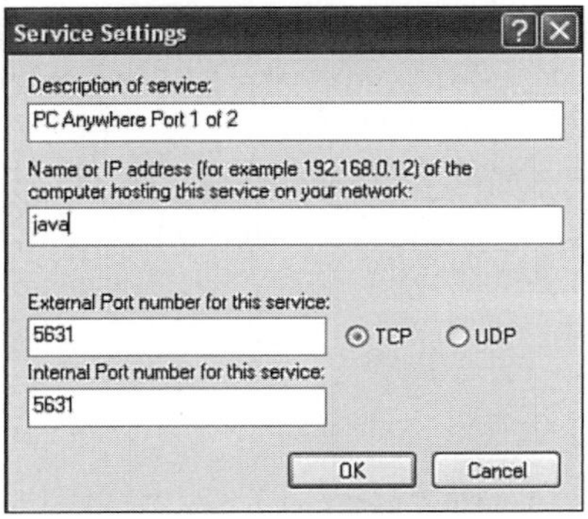

CAUTION

> With the exception of incoming VPN connection service, I suggest that you don't run any other services on the computer that manages your Firewall and/or Internet Connection Sharing. There's too great a risk that a security flaw in the service might let hackers compromise the Firewall.

TIP

> If you're not sure which port a given service uses, you can use the Firewall's logging feature to find out what ports are used. To do this, open the Advanced Settings page again and view the Security Logging tab. Check Log Dropped Packets and click OK. Then attempt to connect to the sharing computer from outside on the Internet using the service of interest. View the log file (by default, c:\windows\pfirewall.log). The eighth column in this file lists the "destination port" that you tried to use. This is the port your service needs to have forwarded.

ENABLING ACCESS WITH A SHARING ROUTER

If you use a connection-sharing router on your LAN, you need to follow a somewhat different procedure to enable outside access to services on your network.

You must still open the Windows firewall on the computer(s) providing services, as described in the first four-step procedure in the previous section.

Then you must use a manufacturer-specific procedure to set up forwarding for services you want to expose to the Internet.

One difficulty with these devices is that you must forward services by IP address, not by computer name. Normally, you set up computers to obtain their IP addresses automatically. This makes the computers moving targets because their IP address could change from day to day.

So, you have to make special arrangements for the computers on your LAN that you want to use to host services. On your router's setup screens, make a note of the range of IP addresses it will hand out to computers requesting automatic configuration. Most routers have a place to enter a starting IP address and a maximum number of addresses. For instance, the starting number might be 2, with a limit of 100 addresses. For each computer that will provide an outside service, pick a number between 2 and 254 that is *not* in the range of addresses handed out by the router, and use that as the last number in the computer's IP address.

To configure the computer's network address, follow these steps:

1. View its Network Connections window, right-click the icon that corresponds to its network adapter, and select Properties.
2. Select Internet Protocol and click Properties.
3. Check Use the Following IP Address.
4. Enter the selected IP address. For the first three numbers, use the same numbers set up in the router (usually 192.168.0 or 192.168.1), and follow it with the fixed number you selected for this computer. The final result might be something like 192.168.0.250.
5. For the network mask, enter `255.255.255.0`.
6. For the Default Gateway, enter `192.168.0.1` or `192.168.1.1`, again using the same first three numbers set up on the router.
7. Leave the DNS setting on Automatic.
8. Click OK and then click OK to close the dialog boxes.

Then you need to use the router's setup screens to set up forwarding to this computer. There are two ways you can set up forwarding. One is appropriate for services that use standard, well-known TCP or UDP protocol ports (like a Web server or Remote Assistance), and the other is appropriate for access to services that use non-standard protocols (like Microsoft VPN connections).

FORWARDING STANDARD TCP AND UDP SERVICES

For standard services with a known TCP or UDP port number, view the Forwarding setup page on your router's internal configuration screen. Enter the appropriate port number, protocol type and target IP address. For example, Figure 18.20 shows a router set up to forward a whole slew of services into computers on my LAN. Table 18.3 shows what is being forwarded here.

Of course, your gateway router may use different configuration screens—you'll have to check its documentation for examples appropriate for your setup.

18

Figure 18.20
Service Forwarding
configuration for a
typical connection
sharing router.

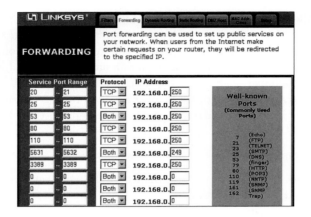

TABLE 18.3 SERVICES BEING FORWARDED IN FIGURE 18.20

Port	Service
20–21	FTP (file transfer protocol)
25	SMTP (simple mail transfer protocol)
53	DNS (domain name service)
80	HTTP (web server)
110	POP3 (mailbox server)
3389	Remote Desktop
5631–5632	Symantec PC Anywhere

FORWARDING NONSTANDARD SERVICES

For services that use TCP/UDP in unpredictable ways, you'll have to use another approach to forwarding on your LAN. Some services, such as Remote Assistance and Windows Messenger, communicate their private, internal IP address to the computer on the other end of the connection. When the other computer tries to send data to this private address, it fails. To use these services with a hardware router, you must enable UPnP as described earlier in the chapter.

Other services use network protocols other than TCP and UDP, and most routers can't be set up to forward them. Incoming Microsoft VPN connections fall into this category. Some routers have built-in support for Microsoft's PPTP protocol, which is the basis of VPN. If yours has this support, your router's manual will tell you how to forward VPN connections to a host computer.

Otherwise, to support nonstandard services of this sort, you have to tell the router to forward all unrecognized incoming data to one designated computer. This in effect exposes that computer to the Internet, so it's a fairly significant security risk. In fact, most routers call this targeted computer a *DMZ host*, referring to the notorious Korean no-man's-land called the demilitarized zone and the peculiar danger one would face standing in it.

To enable a DMZ host, you'll want to use a fixed IP address on the designated computer, as described in the previous section. Use your router's configuration screen to specify this selected IP address as the DMZ host. The configuration screen for my particular router is shown in Figure 18.21; yours may differ.

Figure 18.21
Enabling a DMZ host to receive all unrecognized incoming connection requests.

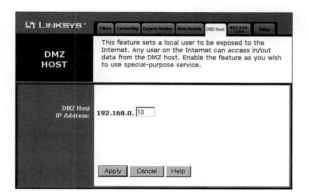

Now, designating a DMZ host means that this computer is now fully exposed to the Internet, so you must protect it with a firewall of some sort. You can enable Windows Firewall on this computer's LAN Connection, but you must also block access to Windows File and Printer sharing. You could disable these services on this computer by disconnecting them from the network adapter, as shown in Figure 18.5. You should also set up filtering in the connection sharing router to block ports 137 through 139 and 445. Figure 18.22 shows how this is done on my Linksys router; your router may use a different method.

TIP

> It's not a bad idea to enable filtering for these ports even if you're not using a DMZ host. It's *essential* to do so if you set up a DMZ host.

Figure 18.22
Configuring filters to block Microsoft file sharing services.

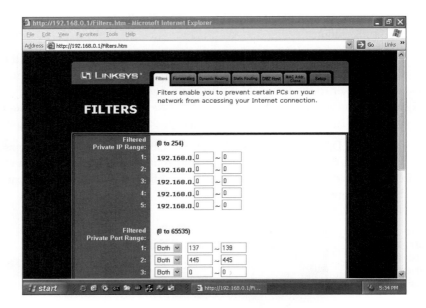

TROUBLESHOOTING

CAN'T ACCESS A SHARED MODEM CONNECTION FROM THE LAN

When I attempt to view an Internet page from a LAN computer, my Web browser doesn't get past "Looking up host www.somewhere.com."

A delay of 30 seconds or so is normal while the dial-up connection is established when you first start using the Internet.

If the connection doesn't progress after 30 seconds, be sure of the following: The sharing computer was turned on when you booted up your computer, the sharing computer is logged in, and your computer is set to obtain its IP address automatically.

Try to make the connection from the sharing computer to be sure the modem is connecting properly. If it's not, see the "Troubleshooting" section at the end of Chapter 8 to diagnose the dial-up connection problem.

CAN'T ACCESS A SHARED DSL OR CABLE CONNECTION FROM THE LAN

When I attempt to view an Internet page from a LAN computer, my Web browser doesn't get past "Looking up host www.somewhere.com."

Be sure that the sharing computer was turned on when you booted up your computer, that the connection to the DSL or cable modem is the one marked as "shared," and that your computer is set to obtain its IP address automatically.

Try to view Web pages from the sharing computer to be sure the high-speed connection is functioning. If it's not, see the "Troubleshooting" section at the end of Chapter 13, "Troubleshooting Your Internet Connection," to diagnose the Internet connectivity problem.

If you are using a connection-sharing router, view the router's built-in Status Web page (usually by viewing http://192.168.0.1 or http://192.168.1.1 with Internet Explorer). See whether the router has been able to connect to your ISP. You might have entered an incorrect password, or for cable systems, you might need to clone the MAC address of the computer that was originally used to set up the Internet connection.

SHARED CONNECTION DOESN'T HAPPEN

When I attempt to view a Web page on a network with a shared connection, no Internet connection is established.

If you are using a modem to establish the shared connection, listen to the modem to see if it's trying to establish the connection. If it is, you may just need to wait a bit and try to view the page again. Sometimes Internet Explorer gives an error message before the modem has had enough time to make the connection.

If the modem makes the connection but Web browsing still fails, it may be that the dial-up connection on the shared computer is not set up with a saved password. On that computer, open My Network Places, select View Network Connections, and attempt to make the connection manually. Be sure that you've checked Save This User Name and Password and selected Anyone Who Uses This Computer.

If the modem isn't attempting to make the connection at all, run the Network Setup Wizard again on the sharing computer.

TIPS FROM THE WINDOWS PROS: SQUEEZING TOP SPEED FROM YOUR HIGH-SPEED CONNECTION

If you're using a high-speed connection such as DSL or cable, you can make an adjustment to your computer's networking software to get the best speed from your new connection.

Internet TCP/IP software sends data in chunks called *packets*, which are sent in a stream from, say, a Web server to your computer. The receiving computer sends acknowledgments every so often to indicate that the data has been received correctly or to indicate that something was lost or garbled during transmission.

A server sends only a limited amount of data before it expects to receive an acknowledgment. If the limit is reached before an acknowledgment is received, the sender has to stop and wait for one. Ideally, for the fastest possible transfers, the sender should never have to stop sending because acknowledgments for data sent earlier should arrive before this limit has been reached. Then the sender can go on sending, again hoping that the data will be acknowledged before the limit is reached.

For cable and DSL modems, the data rate is so high and the cross-country travel times so long that a considerable amount of data can be "in flight" before an acknowledgment could possibly be returned. So, to get the maximum use of your DSL or cable connection, you must tell Windows to make the limit larger than normal for a LAN connection.

This limit, called the *receive window*, should be larger than the data rate times the roundtrip time for data traveling back and forth between the two computers. This number is the maximum amount of data "in flight." A typical round trip time is .100 seconds for interstate Internet traffic, so for various data rates, the receive window should be at least

At 100Kbps * 0.100 sec /bits per byte	= 1.2KB
500Kbps	6KB
1.5Mbps	19KB
4Mbps	75KB

The default value used by Windows 9x, NT, and 2000 is only about 4KB! This means that Windows sends or lets a remote server send only 4KB and then sits and waits while your high-speed connection sits idle.

Windows 2000 and XP slowly boost the window size all by themselves during long file transfers, but when you're browsing Web pages with lots of small graphic images, they never get a chance to boost the window size enough for you to realize the full potential of your fast connection.

The maximum window size that you can specify in Windows 2000 and XP is greater than 64KB, but 64KB is a practical maximum for DSL or cable service. To set the receive window, you must use the Registry Editor, which is described in Chapter 29, "The Registry." You must add a Registry value to a key that contains TCP/IP software parameters.

CAUTION

> Before adding a Registry value, be sure to read Chapter 29, with its dire warnings about the risks of editing the Registry and its urgings for you to back up the Registry before making a change of this sort.

SETTING THE RECEIVE WINDOW IN WINDOWS XP AND 2000

To set the receive window in Windows XP and 2000, do the following:

1. Open Registry key HKEY_LOCAL_MACHINE\System \CurrentControlSet\ Services\Tcpip\Parameters.

2. Select Edit, New, DWORD value, and name it `GlobalMaxTCPWindowSize`. Set its value to 20000 (hexadecimal). See Figure 18.23 to see this entry in the Registry Editor.

Figure 18.23
You set the
`GlobalMaxTCP-`
`WindowSize` value in
this dialog. Note that
Hexadecimal must be
checked.

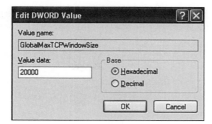

You must restart your computer for the setting to take effect.

CHAPTER **19**

NETWORK SECURITY

In this chapter

WHO WOULD BE INTERESTED IN MY COMPUTER?

Most of us don't give security risks a second thought. After all, who is a data thief going to target: me or the Pentagon? Who'd be interested in my computer? Well, the sad truth is that there are thousands of people out there who'd be delighted to find that they could connect to your computer. They might be looking for your credit card information, passwords for computers and Web sites, or a way to get to other computers on your LAN. Even more, they would love to find that they could install software on your computer, which they could then use to send spam or probe other peoples' computers. They might even use your computer to launch attacks against corporate or governmental networks. Don't doubt that this could happen to you.

Much of the spam you receive is sent from home computers that have been taken over by criminals through the conduit of an unsecured Internet connection. The problem has gotten so bad in the past few years that starting with Windows XP Service Pack 2, when you install Windows software, Microsoft is now enabling the strictest network security settings by default, rather than requiring you to take explicit steps to enable them. There were just too many Windows computers—perhaps millions—with no protection whatsoever. And with the advent of high-speed, always-on Internet connections, the risks are increasing because computers stay connected and exposed for longer periods of time.

In this chapter, I'll explain a bit about how network attacks and defenses work. I'll tell you ways to prevent and prepare for recovery from a hacker attack. And most importantly, I'll show you what to do to make your Windows XP system secure.

Even if you're not too interested in this, and you don't read any other part of this chapter, you should read and carry out the steps in the section titled "Specific Configuration Steps for Windows XP."

19

Think You're Safe? Think Again.

I want to give you a practical example of what can happen over the Internet. Just to see how easy it might be, one night at 1 a.m., I scanned the Internet for computers with unprotected Windows File Sharing. I picked a block of IP addresses near mine and used common, completely legal programs to find computers that were turned on and connected. Within a few minutes, I had found 20. I went through these 20 to see whether they had shared files or folders. My efforts didn't take long; on the fourth try, I was presented with the contents of someone's entire hard drive. Of course, I immediately closed the display, but not before noticing that one of the folders on the hard drive was named Quicken and probably contained all this person's checking and savings account information.

Within 10 minutes I had hacked into someone's computer, and I wasn't trying very hard or using one of the many sophisticated tools available. I didn't even have to attempt to break a password. But even if I'd had to, would that person have noticed his or her computer's hard disk light flickering at 1 a.m.? Would you?

To make matters worse, in a business environment, security risks can come from *inside* a network environment as well as from outside. Inside, you might be subject to highly sophisticated eavesdropping techniques or even simple theft. I know of a company whose entire customer list and confidential pricing database walked out the door one night with the receptionist, whose significant other worked for the competition. The theft was easy; any employee could read and print any file on the company's network. Computer security is a real and serious issue. And it only helps to think about it *before* things go wrong.

TYPES OF ATTACK

Before I talk about how to defend your computer against attack, let's briefly go through the types of attacks you're facing. Hackers can work their way into your computer and network using several methods. Here are some of them:

- **Password cracking**—Given a user account name, so-called "cracking" software can tirelessly try dictionary words, proper names, and random combinations in the hope of guessing a correct password. This doesn't take a modern fast processor very long to accomplish.

- **Address spoofing**—If you've seen the Caller ID service used on telephones, you know that it can be used to screen calls: You only answer the phone if you recognize the caller. But what if telemarketers could make the device say "Mom's calling"? There's an analogy to this in networking. Hackers can send "spoofed" network commands into a network with a trusted IP address.

- **Impersonation**—By tricking Internet routers and the domain name registry system, hackers can have Internet or network data traffic routed to their own computers rather than the legitimate Web site server. With a fake Web site in operation, they can collect credit card numbers and other valuable data.

- **Eavesdropping**—Wiretaps on your telephone or network cable, or monitoring of the radio emissions from your computer and monitor can let the more sophisticated hackers and spies see what you're seeing and record what you're typing.

- **Exploits**—It's a given that complex software has bugs. Some bugs make programs fail in such a way that part of the program itself gets replaced by data from the user. Exploiting this sort of bug, hackers can run their own programs on your computer. It sounds farfetched and unlikely, but exploits in Microsoft's products alone are reported about once a week. The hacker community usually hears about them a few weeks before anyone else does, so even on the most up-to-date copy of Windows, there are a few available for use.

- **Back doors**—Some software developers put special features into programs intended for their use only, usually to help in debugging. These back doors sometimes circumvent security features. Hackers discover and trade information on these, and are only too happy to use the Internet to see whether they work on your computer.

- **Open doors**—All the attack methods I described up to here involve direct and malicious actions to try to break into your system. But this isn't always necessary: Sometimes a computer can be left open in such a way that it just offers itself to the public. Like leaving your front door wide open might invite burglary, leaving a computer unsecured by passwords and without proper controls on network access allows hackers

19

to read and write your files by the simplest means. Simple File Sharing, which I'll discuss later in the chapter, mitigates this risk somewhat.

- **Viruses and Trojan horses**—The ancient Greeks came up with it 3200 years ago, and the Trojan Horse trick is still alive and well today. Shareware programs used to be the favored way to distribute disguised attack software, but today email attachments are the favored method. Most email providers automatically strip out obviously executable email attachments, so the current trend is for viruses to send their payloads in `.zip` file attachments.

- **Social engineering**—A more subtle approach than brute force hacking is to simply call or email someone who has useful information and ask for it. One variation on this approach is the email that purports to come from a service provider like AOL, saying there was some sort of account glitch and could the user please reply with their password and social security number so the glitch can be fixed. P.T. Barnum said there's a sucker born every minute. Sadly, this works out to 1,440 suckers per day, or over half a million per year, and it's not too hard to reach a lot of them with one bulk email.

  Recently there has been an upsurge in a new form of social engineering called *phishing*, where spammers send an email that purports to be from your bank, eBay, or some other such vendor with a link to a Web site that looks official and a request that you sign on with your username, password, and other personal information.

- **Denial of service**—Finally, not every hacker is interested in your credit cards or business secrets. Some are just plain vandals, and it's enough for them to know that you can't get your work done. They may erase your hard drive, or more subtly, crash your server or tie up your Internet connection with a torrent of meaningless data. In any case, you're inconvenienced. For an interesting write-up on one such attack, see www.grc.com/dos.

If all this makes you nervous about hooking your computer up to the Internet, I've done my job well. Before you pull the plug, though, read on.

YOUR LINES OF DEFENSE

Making your computer and network completely impervious to all these forms of attack is quite impossible, if for no other reason than there is always a human element that you cannot control, and there are always bugs and exploits not yet anticipated.

You *can* do a great deal, however, if you plan ahead. Furthermore, as new software introduces new features and risks, and as existing flaws are identified and repaired, you'll have to keep on top of things to maintain your defenses. The most important part of the process is that you spend some time thinking about security.

The following sections delve into the four main lines of computer defense. They are

- Preparation
- Active defense

- Testing, logging, and monitoring
- Disaster planning

You can omit any of these measures, of course, if you weigh what you have at risk against what these efforts will cost you, and decide that the benefit isn't worth the effort.

What I'm describing sounds like a lot of work, and it can be if you take full-fledged measures in a business environment. Nevertheless, even if you're a home user, I encourage you to consider each of the following steps and to put them into effect with as much diligence as you can muster. Just think of that poor sleeping soul whose hard disk I could have erased that morning at 1 a.m. (if you missed this poignant example, see the sidebar titled "Think You're Safe? Think Again" earlier in the chapter).

PREPARATION

Preparation involves eliminating unnecessary sources of risk before they can be attacked. Steps you should take include these:

- **Invest time in planning**—If you want to be really diligent about security, for each of strategies I describe in this chapter, outline how you plan to implement each one.

- **Structure your network to restrict unauthorized access**—If you can minimize the number of ways to get into and out of your home or office network, you can focus your security attention on the remaining ways. Do you really need to have each computer use its own modem to connect to the Internet, when you could share one Internet connection? Do you want to permit access from the Internet directly in to your network, indirectly via a Virtual Private Network (VPN), or not at all? Eliminating points of access reduces risk, but also convenience. You'll have to decide where to strike the balance.

  If you're concerned about unauthorized in-house access to your computers, be sure that every user account is set up with a good password—one with letters and numbers or punctuation. Unauthorized network access is less of a problem with Simple File Sharing, as *all* network users are treated the same, but you must ensure that an effective firewall is in place between your LAN and the Internet. I'll show you how to use the Windows firewall later in this chapter.

→ To learn more about simple file sharing, **see** "Simple File Sharing," **p. 893**.

- **Install only needed services**—The less network software you have installed, the less you'll have to maintain through updates, and the fewer potential openings you'll offer to attackers.

  For example, don't install software like ICQ unless you really need it. The optional "Simple TCP Services" network service provides no useful function, but only archaic services that make great denial of service attack targets. Don't install it.

- **Use software known to be secure and (relatively) bug free**—Use Windows's Automatic Updates feature. Update your software promptly when fixes become available. Be very wary of shareware and free software, unless you can be sure of its pedigree and safety.

■ **Properly configure your computers, file systems, software, and user accounts to maintain appropriate access control**—We'll discuss this in detail later in the chapter.

■ **Hide from the outside world as much information about your systems as possible**—Don't give hackers any assistance by revealing user account or computer names, if you can help it. For example, if you set up your own Internet domain, put as little information into DNS as you can get away with.

TIP

> The most important program to keep up-to-date is Windows XP itself. I suggest that you keep up-to-date on Windows XP bugs and fixes through the Automatic Update feature *and* through independent watchdogs. Configure Windows to notify you of critical updates. Subscribe to the security bulletin mailing lists at `www.microsoft.com/security`, `www.ntbugtraq.com`, and `www.sans.org`.
>
> If you use Internet Information Services to host a Web site, pay particular attention to announcements regarding Internet Explorer. Of all Microsoft products, Internet Explorer has had the lion's share of security problems.

If you're running a business you should think of security as partly a technical issue and partly a matter of organizational policy. No matter how you've configured your computers and network, one user with a modem and a lack of responsibility can open a door into the best-protected network. Even in a home environment, this is something to think about. A parent might want to discuss with children the importance of not downloading and running software without permission.

You should decide which security-related issues you want to leave to your users' discretion, and which you want to mandate as a matter of policy. The following are some issues to ponder:

■ Do you trust users to create and protect their own shared folders, or should this be done by an administrator/parent only?

■ Do you want to let users run a Web server, FTP server, or other network services, each of which provides benefits but also increases risk?

■ Are your users allowed to create simple alphabetic passwords without numbers or punctuation?

■ Are users allowed to install software they obtain themselves?

■ Are users allowed to share access to their desktops with Remote Desktop, Remote Assistance, NetMeeting, Carbon Copy, PCAnywhere, or other remote-control software?

If you are using Windows XP Home Edition in a business setting, you should make public your management and personnel policies regarding network security and appropriate use of computer resources.

If your own users don't respect the integrity of your network, you don't stand a chance against the outside world. A crucial part of any effective security strategy is making up the rules in advance and ensuring that everyone knows them.

ACTIVE DEFENSES: BLOCKING KNOWN METHODS OF ATTACK

Active defense means actively resisting known methods of attack. Active defenses include

- Firewalls and gateways to block dangerous or inappropriate Internet traffic as it passes between your network and the Internet at large
- Encryption and authentication to limit access based on some sort of credentials (such as a password)
- Keeping up-to-date on security and risks, especially with respect to Windows XP

When your computer or LAN is in place, your next job is to configure it to restrict access as much as possible. This task involves blocking network traffic known to be dangerous and configuring network protocols to use the most secure communications protocols possible.

SET UP FIREWALLS AND NAT (CONNECTION SHARING)

Using a firewall is an effective way to secure your computer or network. From the viewpoint of design and maintenance, it is also the most efficient tool because you can focus your efforts on one critical place, the interface between your internal network and the Internet.

A firewall is a program or piece of hardware that intercepts all data passing between two networks—for example, between your computer or LAN and the Internet. The firewall inspects each incoming and outgoing data packet and only permits certain packets to pass through. Generally, a firewall is set up to permit traffic for safe protocols like those used for email and Web browsing. It blocks packets that carry file sharing or computer administration commands.

NAT (Network Address Translation), the technology behind Internet Connection Sharing and connection sharing routers, also insulates your network from the Internet by funneling all your LAN's network traffic through one IP address—the Internet analogue of a telephone number. Like an office's switchboard operator, NAT lets all of your computers place outgoing connections at will, but intercepts all incoming connection attempts. If an incoming data request was anticipated, it's forwarded to one of your computers, but all other incoming network requests are rejected or ignored. Microsoft's Internet Connection Sharing and hardware Internet connection sharing routers all use a NAT scheme.

→ To learn more about this topic, **see** "NAT and Internet Connection Sharing," **p. 626**.

19

The use of either NAT or a firewall, or both, can protect your network by letting you specify exactly how much of your network's resources you'll expose to the Internet.

Windows Firewall

One of Windows XP's new features is the built-in Windows Firewall software. Windows Firewall was introduced in Windows XP Service Pack 2 to replace the more primitive Internet Connection Firewall that originally shipped with XP. (Among other things, Internet Connection Firewall left computers unprotected for 5–20 seconds during bootup, and untold thousands of computers were infected by viruses as a result.)

Windows Firewall is enabled, or attached, to any network adapter or dial-up connection that directly connects to the Internet. Its purpose is to block any traffic that carries networking-related data, so it prevents computers on the Internet from accessing shared files, Remote Desktop, remote administration and other "sensitive" functions.

In fact, Windows Firewall is designed so it can be connected to all network interfaces without interfering with day-to-day networking use. This can help prevent the spread of viruses from one computer to another across your LAN, should one become infected.

Windows Firewall is enabled by default when you install XP Service Pack 2 or a copy of Windows XP that has Service Pack 2 built in. You can also enable or disable it manually by selecting the Change Windows Firewall Settings task on the Network Connections window. (I'll tell you how to do this later in the chapter under "Specific Configuration Steps for Windows XP.") You also can tell the firewall whether you want it to permit incoming requests for specific services. If you have a Web server, for example, you'd need to tell Windows Firewall to permit incoming HTTP data.

NOTE

> Windows Firewall has the advantage that it automatically opens up to permit incoming connections for programs like Remote Assistance and Windows Messenger. On the other hand, it's part of the very operating system it's trying to protect, and if either Windows XP or the firewall gets compromised, your computer's a goner.
>
> If I had the choice between using Windows Firewall and an external firewall device such as a commercial firewall server or a connection sharing router with filter rules, I'd use the external firewall. But Windows Firewall is definitely better than no firewall at all.

Simple File Sharing

Windows XP introduced a new network security model called Simple File Sharing. Before I explain this, I'll give you some background. In the original Windows NT/2000 workgroup network security model, when you attempted to use a shared network resource, Windows would see if your username and password matched an account on the remote computer. One of four things would happen:

- If the username and password exactly matched an account defined on the remote computer, you'd get that user's privileges on the remote machine for reading and writing files.

- If the username matched but the password didn't, you'd be prompted to enter the correct password.

- If the username didn't match any predefined account, or if you failed to supply the correct password, then you'd get the privileges accorded to the Guest account, if the Guest account was enabled.

- If the Guest account was disabled, and it usually was, you would be denied access.

The problem with this system is that it required you to create user accounts on each computer you wanted to reach over the network. Multiply say five users times five computers, and you had 25 user accounts to configure. What a pain! (People pay big bucks for a Windows Server–based domain network to eliminate this very hassle.) Because it was so much trouble, usually people would enable the Guest account.

The problem is that Guest is a member of the group Everyone, and usually Everyone has read/write or at least read privileges on the entire hard drive; and full privileges on FAT-formatted disks which have no user-level security at all. This means the user account headache invited people to make their entire computers vulnerable to abuse over their LAN and the Internet. (And, as I mentioned earlier, this is where most of your spam comes from.)

Enter Simple File Sharing. On all Windows XP Home Edition computers, and as the default option on XP Professional, Simple File Sharing does three things:

- It treats anyone who attempts to use shared resources over the network as Guest.

- The Guest account is enabled by default for network use only. (You can separately choose whether Guest can log on at your keyboard. This is disabled by default on both XP Home and Pro.)

- Windows removes Everyone from the permission lists for access to the hard drive's root folder and Windows directory. This means that only authorized locally-logged-on users can access most of the disk, and the Windows directory in particular.

- When you share folders, Windows in most cases automatically applies the correct permissions to the shared folder so that Everyone (for example, Guest) can read and optionally write to the folder. For folders it knows aren't safe to share, it doesn't do this.

Only a few folders are shared, and while anybody with access to the network can access them, the damage an intruder can do is limited to stealing or modifying just the files in a few folders that are known to be public.

It's also much easier to use shared files and folders for your LAN. You won't be called on or able to select which individual users get access and which don't. If you share a folder, you share it with read-only or read/write access. It's very simple indeed, and it's perfectly appropriate for home and small office LANs. Microsoft's reasoning here is that it's better to configure a somewhat looser LAN correctly than a stricter LAN poorly. For tight user control, corporations use Server-based networks.

There are two downsides to Simple File Sharing: First, and most important, it's *crucial* that you have a firewall in place. Otherwise, everyone on the Internet will have the same rights in your shared folders as you. (That's one of the reasons for Windows Firewall, and why the Network Setup Wizard is so adamant about either installing the Firewall or disabling file sharing.)

The second downside is less troublesome and probably less noticeable to most people: If you attempt to use a shared folder from another computer on which you have the same username and password, you won't get the full rights that you'd have locally. You'll be a guest like anyone else. In particular, the handy whole-drive administrative shares such as "C$" do not work thanks to Simple File Sharing.

PACKET FILTERING

If you use a hardware Internet connection sharing router (also called a residential gateway) or a full-fledged network router for your Internet service, you can instruct it to block data that carries services you don't want exposed to the Internet. This is called *packet filtering*. You can set this up in addition to NAT to provide extra protection.

Filtering works like this: Each Internet data packet contains identifying numbers that indicate the protocol type (for example, TCP or UPD) and the IP address for the source and destination computers. Some protocols also have an additional number called a port, which identifies the program that is to receive the packet. The WWW service, for example, expects TCP protocol packets addressed to port 80. A domain name server listens for UDP packets on port 53.

A packet arriving at the firewall from either side is examined; then it is either passed on or discarded, according to a set of rules that list the protocols and ports permitted or prohibited for each direction. A prohibited packet can be dropped silently, or the router can reject the packet with an error message indicating the requested network service is unavailable. (If possible, I prefer to specify the silent treatment. Why tell hackers that a desired service is present even if it's unavailable to them?) Some routers can also make a log entry or send an alert indicating that an unwanted connection was attempted.

Configuring routers for filtering is beyond the scope of this book, but I'll list some relevant protocols and ports in Table 19.1. (If this seems a bit complex, don't worry—if you use a router for your Internet service, you can ask your ISP to help set up filtering protection.)

If your router lets you block incoming requests separately from outgoing requests, you should block incoming requests for all the services listed in Table 19.1, unless you are sure you want to enable access to them. If you have a basic gateway router that doesn't provide separate incoming and outgoing filters, you probably only want to filter those services that I've marked with an asterisk (*).

TABLE 19.1 SERVICES THAT YOU MIGHT WANT TO BLOCK

Protocol	Port	Associated Service
TCP	20–19	FTP—File Transfer Protocol.
TCP *	23	Telnet—Clear-text passwords are sent by this remote terminal service, which also is used to configure routers.
TCP	53	DNS—Domain Name Service. Block TCP mode "zone" transfers, which reveal machine names.
TCP+UDP	67	BOOTP—Bootstrap Protocol (similar to DHCP). Unnecessary.
TCP+UDP	69	TFTP—Trivial File Transfer Protocol. No security.
TCP	110	POP3—Post Office Protocol.
UDP * TCP *	137–8 139	NetBIOS—Three ports are used by Microsoft File Sharing.
UDP *	161–2	SNMP—Simple Network Monitoring Protocol. Reveals too much information and can be used to reconfigure the router.
TCP*	445	SMB—Windows XP and 2000 File Sharing can use Port 445 as well as 137-139.
TCP	515	LPD—UNIX printer sharing protocol supported by Windows XP.
UDP TCP	1900 5000	Universal Plug and Play—can be used to reconfigure routers.

As I said, if you use a hardware router to connect to the Internet, I can't show you the specifics for your device. I can give you a couple of examples, though. My Linksys Cable/DSL Sharing Router uses a Web browser for configuration, and there's a page for setting up filters, as shown in Figure 19.1. In this figure, I've blocked the ports for Microsoft file sharing services.

If you use routed DSL Internet service your ISP may have provided a router manufactured by Flowpoint, Netopia, or another manufacturer. As an example, filtering is set up in a Flowpoint router through a command line interface, as shown below:

```
remote ipfilter append input drop -p udp -dp 137:138 internet
remote ipfilter append input drop -p tcp -dp 139 internet
remote ipfilter append input drop -p tcp -dp 445 internet
```

These are complex devices and your ISP will help you set yours up. Insist that they install filters for ports 137, 138, 139, and 445 at the very least.

USING NAT OR INTERNET CONNECTION SHARING

By either name, Network Address Translation (NAT) has two big security benefits. First, it can hide an entire network behind one IP address. Then, while it transparently passes connections from you out to the Internet, it rejects all incoming connection attempts except those that you explicitly direct to waiting servers inside your LAN. Packet filtering isn't absolutely necessary with NAT, although it can't hurt to add it.

→ To learn more about NAT, **see** "NAT and Internet Connection Sharing," **p. 626**.

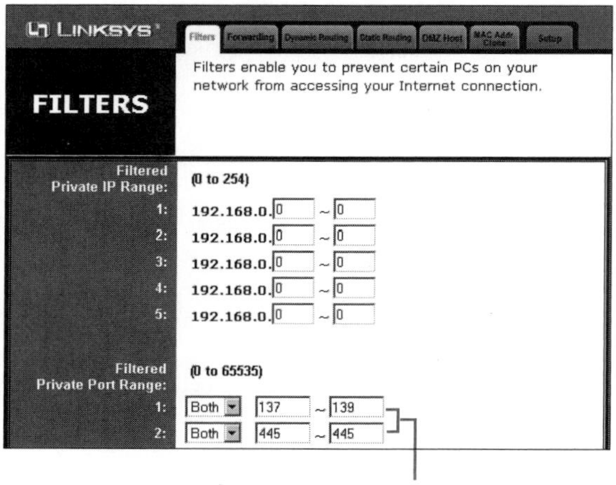

Figure 19.1
Configuring packet filters in a typical Internet connection sharing router.

Settings to filter ports 137-139 and 445

You learned how to configure Windows Internet Connection Sharing in Chapter 18, "Connecting Your LAN to the Internet," so I won't repeat that information here.

CAUTION

Microsoft's Internet Connection Sharing (ICS) blocks incoming access to other computers on the LAN but unless Windows Firewall is also enabled, it does *not* protect the computer that is sharing the Internet connection. If you use ICS you must enable Windows Firewall on the same connection. Together, they provide adequate protection for all of your computers.

If you have built a network with another type of router or connection sharing device, you must follow the manufacturer's instructions or get help from your ISP to set it up.

TIP

Not all ISPs will help you set up a connection-sharing router. These devices just cut into their revenues. Your ISP may even forbid their use. Better check first, before asking for help in installing one. Personally, I think the additional security they provide justifies their use even if the ISP doesn't like them.

ADD-ON PRODUCTS FOR WINDOWS

There are many commercial products called *personal firewalls*, designed for use on PCs. Products such as Zone Alarm and Zone Alarm Pro (www.zonelabs.com), McAfee Personal

Firewall (www.mcafee.com), Sygate Personal Firewall (www.sygate.com), Norton Personal Firewall (www.symantec.com), and BlackIce Defender (www.networkice.com) range in price from free to about $50. Now that Windows includes an integral firewall, these add-on products may no longer be necessary, but you might still want to investigate them for the additional reporting and outbound traffic monitoring they provide.

SECURE YOUR ROUTER

If you use a router for your Internet connection and rely on it to provide network protection, you *must* make it require a secure password. If your router doesn't require a password, *anyone* could connect to it across the Internet and delete the filters you've set up. Most routers, as configured by the manufacturers and ISPs, *do not* require a password.

To lock down your router, you'll have to follow procedures for your specific router. You want to do the following:

- Change the router's administrative password to a combination of letters, numbers, and punctuation. Be sure to write it down somewhere!
- Change the SNMP read-only and read-write community names (which are in effect passwords) to a secret word.
- Prohibit Write access via SNMP or disable SNMP entirely.
- Change all Telnet login passwords, whether administrative or informational.

If you don't want to attempt to lock down your router, your ISP should do it for you. If your ISP supplied your router, and you change the password yourself, be sure to give the new password to your ISP.

SET UP RESTRICTIVE ACCESS CONTROLS

Possibly the most important and difficult step you can take is to limit access to shared files, folders, and printers. You can use the guidelines shown in Table 19.2 to help organize a security review of every machine on your network. I've put some crucial items in boldface.

TABLE 19.2   RESTRICTING ACCESS CONTROLS

Access Point	Controls
File Sharing	Don't share your computers' entire hard drives. Share only folders that need to be shared, and if possible choose only folders in your My Documents folder (for simplicity).
Passwords	Set up all accounts to require passwords. You can configure your computers to require long passwords if you want to enforce good internal security. I'll show you how to do this later in the chapter.

continues

TABLE 19.2   CONTINUED

Access Point	Controls
Access Control	Don't use Computer Administrator accounts for your day-to-day work. If you accidentally run a Trojan horse or virus program using an Administrator account, the nasty program has full access to your computer. Instead, create and use Limited User accounts to the extent possible.
SNMP	This network monitoring option is a useful tool for large networks but it also poses a security risk. If installed, it could be used to modify your computer's network settings and, at the very least, will happily reveal the names of all the user accounts on your computer. Don't install SNMP unless you need it, and if you do, change the "community name" from public to something confidential and difficult to guess.

KEEP UP-TO-DATE

New bugs in major operating systems and applications software are found every week, and patches and updates are issued almost as frequently.

Software manufacturers including Microsoft have recently become quite forthcoming with information about security risks, bugs, and the like. It wasn't always the case, as they mostly figured if they kept the problems a secret, fewer bad guys would find out about them, and so their customers would be better off. (That, and it saved them the embarrassment of admitting the seriousness of their bugs.) Information is shared so quickly among the bad guys now, however, that it has become essential for companies to inform users of security problems as soon as a defensive strategy can be devised.

You can subscribe to the Microsoft Email Updates security bulletin service at `www.microsoft.com/security`. The following are some other places to check out:

```
www.ntbugtraq.com
www.sans.org
www.cert.org
www.first.org
www.cs.purdue.edu/coast
www.greatcircle.com
Usenet newsgroups: comp.security.*, comp.risks
```

Some of these sites point you toward security-related mailing lists. You should subscribe to Microsoft Security Advisor Bulletins and the SANS and CERT advisories at least, and perhaps other lists in digest form. Forewarned is forearmed!

TESTING, LOGGING, AND MONITORING

Testing, logging, and monitoring involve testing your defense strategies and detecting breaches. It's tedious, but who would you rather have be first to find out that your system is hackable: you or "them"? Your testing steps should include

- Testing your defenses before you connect to the Internet
- Monitoring Internet traffic on your network and on the connection to your Internet service provider or other networks
- Detecting and recording suspicious activity on the network and in application software

You can't second-guess what 100 million potential "visitors" might do to your computer or network, but you should at least be sure that all your roadblocks stop the traffic you were expecting them to stop.

TEST YOUR DEFENSES

Some companies hire expert hackers to attempt to break into their networks. You can do this too, or you can try to be your own hacker. Before you connect to the Internet, and periodically thereafter, try to break into your own system. Find its weaknesses.

Go through each of your defenses and each of the security policy changes you made, and try each of the things you thought they should prevent.

First, connect to the Internet, visit www.grc.com and view the Shields Up page. This Web site attempts to connect to Microsoft Networking and TCP/IP services on your computer to see whether any are accessible from the outside world. Click the Test My Shields! and Probe My Ports! buttons to see whether this testing system exposes any vulnerabilities. This is a great tool. (Its author, Steve Gibson, is a very bright guy and has lots of interesting things to say, but be forewarned, some of it is a bit hyperbolic.)

As a second test, find out what your public IP address is. If you use a dial-up connection or Internet Connection Sharing, go to the computer that actually connects to the Internet, open a Command Prompt window, and type **ipconfig**. Write down the IP address of your actual Internet connection (this number will change every time you dial in, by the way). If you use a sharing router, you'll need to get the actual IP address from your router.

Then, enlist the help of a friend, or go to a computer *not* on your site but out on the Internet. On Windows Explorer (*not* Internet Explorer) and in the Address box, type \\1.2.3.4, except in place of 1.2.3.4 type the IP address that you recorded earlier. This will attempt to connect to your computer for file sharing. You should not be able to see any shared folders, and you shouldn't even be prompted for a username and/or password. If you have more than one public IP address, test *all* of them.

 If you are able to view your computer's shared folders, see "Shared Folders Are Visible to the Internet" in the "Troubleshooting" section at the end of this chapter.

If you have installed a third party Web or FTP server, attempt to view any protected pages *without* using the correct username or password. With FTP, try using the login name anonymous and the password guest. If you are able to access files this way, check your server software documentation for instructions on securing your site. Try to copy files to the FTP site while connected as anonymous—you shouldn't be able to.

Use network testing utilities to attempt to connect to any of the network services you think you have blocked—for example, SNMP.

 If sensitive network services are found to be accessible, see "Network Services Are Not Being Blocked" in the "Troubleshooting" section at the end of this chapter.

Attempt to use Telnet to connect to your router, if you have one. If you are prompted for a login, try the factory default login name and password listed in the router's manual. If you've blocked telnet with a packet filter setting, you should not be prompted for a password. If you are prompted, you want to be sure that the factory default password does not work, because you should have changed it.

 If you can access your router, see "Router Is Accessible via Telnet" in the "Troubleshooting" section at the end of this chapter.

Port scanning tools are available to perform many of these tests automatically. For an example, see the Shields Up Web page at www.grc.com. I caution you to use this sort of tool in addition to, not instead of, the other tests I listed here.

MONITOR SUSPICIOUS ACTIVITY

If you use Windows Firewall, you can configure it to keep a record of rejected connection attempts. Open the properties page of the firewalled connection, select the Advanced tab, click Settings, select the Advanced tab, and under Security Logging click Settings (phew!) to get to the Log Settings dialog box shown in Figure 19.2.

Figure 19.2
Enable logging to see what Windows Firewall is turning away.

Inspect the log file periodically by viewing it with Notepad.

NOTE

If you use a dial-up connection, the firewall log is less useful. It will accrue lots of entries caused by packets left over from connections made by the dial-up customer who had your temporary IP address before you got it. They'll continue to arrive for a while, just as junk mail does after a tenant moves out.

Disaster Planning: Preparation for Recovery After an Attack

Disaster planning should be a key part of your security strategy. The old saying "Hope for the best, and prepare for the worst" certainly applies to PC or network security. Murphy's law predicts that if you don't have a way to recover from a network or security disaster, you'll soon need one. If you're prepared, you can recover quickly and may even be able to learn something useful from the experience. Here are some suggestions to help you prepare for the worst:

- Make permanent, archived "baseline" backups of exposed computers *before* they're connected to the Internet and anytime system software is changed.
- Make frequent backups once online.
- Prepare written, thorough, and tested computer restore procedures.
- Write and maintain documentation of your software and network configuration.
- Prepare an incident plan.

A little planning now will go a long way toward helping you through this situation. The key is having a good backup of all critical software. Each of the points discussed in the above list are covered in more detail in the following sections.

Make a Baseline Backup Before You Go Online

You should make a permanent "baseline" backup of your computer before you connect with the Internet for the first time, so you know it doesn't have any virus infections. This backup should be kept permanently. It can be used for recovery if your system is compromised.

→ To learn more about making backups, **see** "Backup Tools and Strategies," **p. 923**.

Make Frequent Backups

I hate to sound like a broken record on this point, but you should have a backup plan and stick to it. Make backups at some sensible interval and always after a session of extensive or significant changes (for example, after installing new software or adding users). In a home environment you might want to make backups once every few weeks, at least.

Write and Test Restore Procedures

I can tell you from personal experience that the only feeling more sickening than losing your system is finding out that the backups you've been diligently making are unreadable. Whatever your backup scheme is, be sure it works!

This step is really difficult to take, but I really urge you to try to completely rebuild a system after an imaginary break-in or disk failure. Use a sacrificial computer, of course, not your main computer, and allow yourself a whole day for this exercise. Go through all the steps: Reformat hard disks, reinstall Windows, and restore the most recent backups. You will

19

find this a very enlightening experience, well worth the cost in time and effort. Finding the problem with your system *before* you need the backups is much better than finding it afterwards.

Also, be sure to document the whole restoration process so that you can repeat it later. After a disaster, you'll be under considerable stress, so you might forget a step or make a mistake. Having a clear, written, tested procedure goes a long way toward making the recovery process easier and more likely to succeed.

WRITE AND MAINTAIN DOCUMENTATION

It's in your own best interest to maintain a log of all software installed on your computers, along with software settings, hardware types and settings, configuration choices, network number information, and so on. (Do you vaguely remember some sort of ordeal with a DMA conflict when you installed the tape software last year? How *did* you resolve that problem, anyway?)

> **TIP**
>
> Windows has no utilities to print out the configuration settings for software and network systems. I use Alt+PrntScrn to record the configurations for each program and network component and then paste the images into WordPad or Microsoft Word.

Then, print out a copy of this documentation, so you'll be able to refer to it if your computer crashes.

Make a library of documentation, CD-ROMs, repair disks, startup disks, utility disks, backup CDs, Zip disks, tapes, manuals, and notebooks that record your configurations and observations. Keep them together in one place and, in a business setting, locked up.

PREPARE AN INCIDENT PLAN

A system crash or intrusion is a highly stressful event. A written plan of action made now will help you keep a clear head when things go wrong. The actual event probably won't go as you imagined, but at least you'll have some good first steps to follow while you get your wits about you.

If you know a break-in has been successful, you must take immediate action. First, disconnect your network from the Internet. Then find out what happened.

Unless you have an exact understanding of what happened and can fix the problem, you should clean out your system entirely. This means that you should reformat your hard drive, install Windows and all applications from CDs or pristine disks, and make a clean start. Then you can look at recent backups to see whether you have any you know aren't compromised, restore them, and then go on.

SPECIFIC CONFIGURATION STEPS FOR WINDOWS XP

Many of the points I've mentioned so far in this chapter are general, conceptual ideas that should be helpful in planning a security strategy, but perhaps not specific enough to directly implement. The following sections provide some specific instructions to tighten security on your Windows XP computer or LAN. These instructions are for a single Windows XP computer or a home/small office LAN without a Windows 200x Server.

IF YOU HAVE A STANDALONE WINDOWS XP HOME EDITION COMPUTER

If you have a standalone system without a LAN, you need to take only a few steps to be sure you're safe when browsing the Internet:

- Enable Macro Virus Protection in your Microsoft Office applications.

- Be wary of viruses and Trojan horses in email attachments and downloaded software. Install a virus scan program, and discard unsolicited email with attachments without opening it. If you use Outlook or Outlook Express, you can disable the "preview" pane that automatically displays email. Several viruses have exploited this open-without-asking feature. (The version of Outlook provided with XP Service Pack 2 is better in this regard.)

- Keep your system up-to-date with Automatic Updates (see the Automatic Updates tab on the System control panel applet), Windows Update, service packs, application software updates, and virus scanner updates. Check for updates every couple of weeks at the very least.

NOTE

> Unfortunately, the Automatic Updates pop-up appears only when you are logged in using a Computer Administrator account. Unless you've configured Automatic Updates to automatically install the updates, you need to log on as an administrator at least once every week or two to see whether anything new has been downloaded.

19

- Use strong passwords on each of your accounts. For all passwords, use letters and numbers or punctuation; don't use your name or other simple words.

- Be absolutely certain that Windows Firewall is enabled on any icon in your Network Connections folder that connects directly to the Internet. To enable Windows Firewall, use the steps shown later in this chapter under "Enabling Windows Firewall."

IF YOU HAVE A LAN

If your computer is connected to others through a LAN, follow the first four suggestions from the list in the preceding section.

Because Windows XP Home Edition uses the Simple File Sharing system that I discussed earlier in this chapter, the security situation is quite different than it was in any previous version of Windows. Since *all* access to shared files over any network or Internet connection is granted or denied access without a password, your one and only line of defense is having a firewall in place between the Internet and your computer. It's *absolutely essential* that you have a firewall in place, either Windows Firewall or a third-party product.

CAUTION

> If you use cable Internet service with multiple IP addresses provided by your ISP, but have no hardware firewall device in place, you cannot share files on your LAN. For this reason, I urge you not to use this type of arrangement. See Chapter 18 for details.

Finally, if you use a wireless network, you must use WEP or WPA encryption to protect your network. Otherwise, thanks to Simple File Sharing, random people passing by could have the same access to your shared files as you do.

ENABLING WINDOWS FIREWALL

If you use the Internet, whether directly from your computer or through a network connection, you must be sure that some sort of firewall is in place to prevent Internet denizens from reaching into your computer. If you use a hardware Internet connection sharing device, that will protect you to some extent, and I gave specific tips for adding additional protection in the previous section. But unless you use a third-party firewall product, you should also use Microsoft's Windows Firewall.

Starting with Windows XP Service Pack 2, Windows Firewall is turned on by default, so you might already be using it. You can use the following procedure to verify or manually enable the firewall. Follow these steps:

1. Click Start, My Network Places, View Network Connections.
2. Find the icon that represents your actual connection to the Internet. This could be a dial-up connection or a local area connection that is used to connect to a LAN, router, DSL, cable or satellite modem.
3. The icon for this connection should have the word Firewalled next to it. If it does, you're all set.
4. If it doesn't say `Firewalled`, click Change Windows Firewall Settings. Check On (Recommended), as shown in Figure 19.3.
5. Click OK. The icon now should say `Firewalled` next to it.

Then, if you want to run a Web server, email system, or other network services that you want to be made available to the outside world, you have to "open" the firewall for these services. See the next section for details.

Figure 19.3
Click On to enable
Windows Firewall.

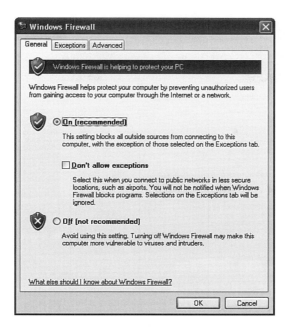

CONFIGURING WINDOWS FIREWALL

The purpose of Windows Firewall is to examine all incoming network data looking for attempts to connect to your computer. The firewall maintains a list of networking services for which incoming connections should be permitted, within a given range of network addresses. For example, by default, Windows Firewall permits file sharing connections only from computers on the same subnet or local area network as your computer. Attempts by users outside your immediate network to contact your computer are rebuffed. This prevents Internet users from examining your shared files. (Outgoing requests, attempts by your computer to connect others, are not restricted.)

The firewall also monitors application programs and system services that announce their willingness to receive connections through the network. These are compared against a list of authorized programs. If an unexpected program sets itself up to receive incoming network connections, Windows displays a pop-up message similar to the one shown in Figure 19.4, giving you the opportunity to either prevent the program from receiving any network traffic (Keep Blocking) or add the program to the authorized list (Unblock). This gives you a chance to prevent spyware and Trojan horses from doing their dirty work. Firewall-aware programs such as Windows Messenger automatically instruct the firewall to unblock their data connections.

To view Windows Firewall's setup dialog boxes, open the Network Connections window and select Change Windows Firewall Settings, or open the Windows Security Center and select Manage Security Settings for Windows Firewall.

Figure 19.4
Windows Firewall displays a pop-up message if an unauthorized program asks to receive network connections.

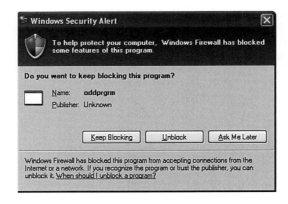

The remainder of this section discusses the various setup options for Windows Firewall.

ENABLING AND DISABLING THE FIREWALL

The Firewall's General tab (refer to Figure 19.3) lets you enable or disable the firewall function. When on, you can additionally check Don't Allow Exceptions to prevent all incoming connections from other computers. This can provide an extra level of safety when you are using an unsecured public network such as a wireless hotspot in a hotel, an airport, or a café.

 If Windows Messenger file transfer fails after enabling Windows Firewall, see "Windows Messenger Can't Send Files" in the "Troubleshooting" section at the end of this chapter.

ENABLING EXCEPTIONS

In most cases you *do* want other computers to be able to make connections to yours; for instance, this is how other people get to folders and printers you are sharing. Windows Firewall lets you determine which network services it will let in and, for each, which other users (as specified by their computers' network addresses) will be allowed to make contact. These are called *exceptions*.

Exceptions can be defined in terms of network protocols and port numbers, which correspond to particular network services or in terms of specific application program filenames. When a protocol and port are listed, any program that wants to receive connections for that network service is permitted to. When a program filename is listed, that program is permitted to receive connections for any protocol or port it wants to.

The range of network addresses allowed to contact your computer is called a *scope* and can be specified as any of the following:

- Any computer (including those on the Internet)
- My Network (subnet only)
- Custom list (a list of network addresses or subnet specifications separated by commas)

CAUTION

The My Network selection permits access by any computer in the same subnet (local network group) of any of your computer's network connection, which can include more than just your own LAN. When your computer has a direct broadband or dial-up Internet connection, in most cases up to 252 other random computers can be assigned to the same subnet as your computer, and they'll have access to your computer.

The workaround is to not run sensitive services on a computer that is sharing its own Internet connection. This is not a problem when you are using a shared connection or a sharing router.

On the Firewall's Exceptions tab, shown in Figure 19.5, is a predefined list of programs and network services for which the firewall will allow incoming connections. These are listed in Table 19.3.

Figure 19.5
Exceptions permit incoming connections to particular network services or specified application programs.

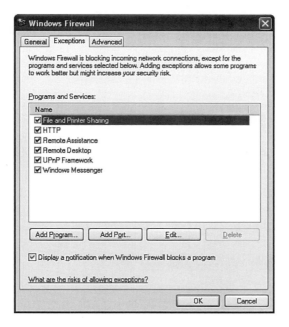

19

TABLE 19.3 PREDEFINED WINDOWS FIREWALL EXCEPTIONS

Entry	Selected by Program or Port?	Scope	Protocols/Ports
File and Printer Sharing	Port	Subnet	TCP 139
		Subnet	TCP 445
		Subnet	UDP 137
		Subnet	UDP 138
Remote Assistance	Program	Any	

continues

TABLE 19.3	CONTINUED		
Entry	**Selected by Program or Port?**	**Scope**	**Protocols/Ports**
Remote Desktop	Port	Any	TCP 3389
UPnP Framework	Port	Any	TCP 2689
		Any	UDP 1900
Windows Messenger *	Program	Any	

Windows Messenger appears automatically the first time Windows Messenger is used.

If you run a service such as a Web server or an application program that needs to receive network connections, you can get an exception placed in this list by letting Windows display a pop-up warning similar to the one previously shown in Figure 19.4, or you can manually add an exception for this program.

To manually add an application exception, which lets the program receive any network connections it wants, view the Exceptions tab and click Add Program. Click Browse to locate the program's executable (.exe) file, and click Change Scope to set the range of network addresses that should be able to access the program's services.

To manually add a port (service) exception, which lets any program receive network connections on the specified network ports, view the Exceptions tab and click Add Port. Enter a name to describe the network service, enter the port number, and select TCP or UDP. Click Change Scope to set the range of network addresses that should be able to access this service.

For example, to permit access to a Web server running on your computer, add the information shown in Figure 19.6. The Scope could be set to Any to permit access by the entire Internet or Subnet to restrict access to your LAN only.

Figure 19.6
Adding an exception
for a Web server.

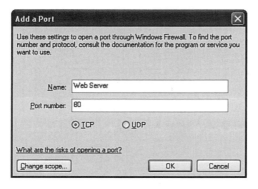

You can later highlight any entry and select Delete or Edit to remove or modify these settings. You can also uncheck an entry to temporarily block the program or service.

TIP

> Curious to know which programs and services on your computer are listening for incoming network connections? Log on as a Computer Administrator, open a Command Prompt window, and type the command `netstat -ab ¦ more`. (This can take quite a long time.) If you don't recognize a program's name, use Google to see whether it's discussed on any Web pages; this can help you determine whether it's a legitimate Windows program or some sort of malware.

Advanced Firewall Settings

The Firewall's Advanced tab lets you remove the firewall from particular network connections, enable logging of rejected data, control how Internet control packets are treated, and restore the firewall to the default factory-fresh settings.

Network Connection Settings

You can remove some network connections from the firewall's scrutiny by unchecking these connections in the Network Connection Settings list. This leaves the other connections still protected by the firewall. You might want to do this when, for instance, your LAN is professionally protected by a hardware firewall and you use network services on your LAN the firewall has trouble with.

In general, though, it's best to leave all your network connections protected by the firewall to help prevent the spread of viruses and Trojans around your network should one computer be compromised.

The Settings button lets you change forwarding and ICMP packet filtering for the highlighted connection. This is not useful unless you are using Internet Connection Sharing and the selected connection is the one being shared. (To be honest, it's hard to understand what Microsoft was thinking here. It would have been very useful if this button let you configure exceptions on an interface-by-interface basis, but that's not what it does.)

Security Logging

You can have Windows Firewall keep a record of connection requests it receives and rejects, or even of connections accepted and rejected. This can be useful in determining why network connections to your computer are failing and also in identifying when your computer is under attack. This feature was discussed earlier in the chapter in the section "Monitor Suspicious Activity."

ICMP

In addition to TCP, UDP, and other data transmission protocols, the Internet makes extensive use the Internet Control Message Protocol (ICMP), which takes care of housekeeping details like informing computers of routing problems and data transmission errors. It's also used by the `ping` program, an important networking diagnostic tool.

19

By default, Windows Firewall does not permit any ICMP data to pass through the firewall. This prevents outside computers from sending you bogus ICMP data that could disrupt your use of the network. You can click ICMP Settings to instruct the firewall to pass any particular ICMP messages that your computer definitely needs to process.

In most cases, ICMP Echo Request (ping) is the only ICMP message you want to process. And, happily, you don't have to manually check this because Windows Firewall automatically passes these packets if the exception for File and Printer Sharing is enabled.

DEFAULT SETTINGS

You can restore the firewall to the default settings provided by Microsoft by clicking Default Settings.

However, you should be aware that this removes entries for programs that might have added their own firewall settings. Furthermore, it unchecks most of the default entries listed in Table 19.3, including File and Printer Sharing. You need to recheck the entries for any services you want to make available.

LEARN MORE ABOUT SECURITY

This chapter just barely scratched the surface of what there is to know and do about network security. There are many great books on the topic. For a good introduction to firewalls and Internet security in general, I recommend *Practical Firewalls*, published by Que, *Maximum Security, Third Edition*, published by Sams, and *Firewalls and Internet Security: Repelling the Wily Hacker*, published by Addison & Wesley.

You also can get lots of information on the Web. First, www.sans.org and www.cert.org are great places to start looking into the security community. Steve Gibson has plenty to say about security at www.grc.com—it's an educational and entertaining site.

Finally, you might look into additional measures you can take to protect your computer and your network. There are many ways to configure networks. It's common, for example, to keep any public Web or email servers you have separate from the rest of your LAN. For additional security, you even can buy or build special-purpose firewall routers to place between your LAN and the Internet. The site www.linux-firewall-tools.com/linux/ shows one nifty way to do this.

In any case, I'm glad you're interested enough in security to have read this far down in the chapter!

TROUBLESHOOTING

SHARED FOLDERS ARE VISIBLE TO THE INTERNET

When I use Explorer to view my computer across the Internet, I am prompted for a username and password, and/or shared folders are visible.

If you have this problem, Microsoft file sharing services are being exposed to the Internet. If you have a shared connection to the Internet, you need to enable Windows Firewall, or enable filtering on your Internet connection. At the very least you must block TCP/UDP ports 137 through 139 and 445. Don't leave this unfixed!

If you have several computers connected to a cable modem with just a hub, and no connection sharing router, you should read Chapter 18 for alternative ways to share your cable Internet connection.

NETWORK SERVICES ARE NOT BEING BLOCKED

I can connect to my computer across the Internet with remote administration tools such as the Registry Editor, with SNMP viewers, or with other tools that use network services. How do I prevent this access?

Look up the protocol type (for example, UDP or TCP) and port numbers of the unblocked services, and configure filters in your router to block these services. Your ISP might be able to help you with this problem. You might have disabled Windows Firewall by mistake.

ROUTER IS ACCESSIBLE VIA TELNET

I can connect to my Internet service router through Telnet across the Internet without providing a secret administrative password. How do I prevent this access?

Configure your router to require a sensible password for access. Choose a password with letters and numbers. Be sure you write it down, and also give it to the technical support department of your ISP. The ISP might even be able to help you change the password.

CHAPTER **20**

TROUBLESHOOTING YOUR NETWORK

In this chapter

WHEN GOOD NETWORKS GO BAD

Today's networks are so easy to install and configure that you can just Plug and Pray, er, I mean Play. But when good networks go bad, it's another story, one with all the makings of a Fox Network special.

Every time I get a call from a client with a network problem, I cringe. I never know whether it's going to take 10 minutes or a week to fix. Sometimes the problem isn't so bad; I've fixed more than one "broken" computer by turning it on. If such an easy fix doesn't present itself immediately, though, a bit of a cold sweat breaks out on my forehead. The problem could be anything. How do you even start to find a nasty problem in the maze of cards, wires, drivers, and hidden, inexplicable system services?

Well, if you were on a corporate network with a network support staff, of course, the answer to that question is "Call the Help Desk!" or "Call Bob!" or call whatever or whomever is responsible for network problems in your organization. For a home or small office network, you still could hire a network consultant or a neighborhood teenager to help you out. This isn't a bad idea. Still, if you want to go it alone, there are some tools provided with Windows that can help you find the problem. After talking about troubleshooting in general, I'll show you how to use them. Then, in the "Tips from the Windows Pros" section at the end of the chapter, I'll give you a checklist to follow to help narrow down what the problem might be.

Three Engineers in a Car

There's an old joke about three engineers in a car that I have to tell you before I get on with the chapter. It seems they were driving down the street together when the engine suddenly stopped and wouldn't start again. Each engineer figured he had the right stuff to fix the problem. The first said, "I'm an electrical engineer. This probably is a wiring problem, so I'll check the fuses and test all of the wires for shorts." The second engineer said, "I'm a mechanical engineer, and I think this is a problem with the transmission. I'll take it out, look at the mechanism, and repair the gears." The third engineer says, "Look, I'm in software. Let's just get out of the car, get back in, and see if that fixes it."

Sometimes, software problems do go away just by getting out and back in. Although it's irritating and doesn't engender much trust in these complex systems, it's actually not a bad first stab at solving a computer problem. With software as complex as that in Windows, there are bound to be bugs, and sometimes we run into them. It seems to happen at random, but somewhere, some subtle sequence of events takes place and triggers a problem. Logging off or restarting might be enough to reset the software and get it back on its feet… until the next time it falls into the same trap.

This definitely can happen with networking, so the next time you run into a problem, remember the three engineers in the car and try a logoff or reset. If it works, well, you can only hope that someone up there in Redmond runs into the same bug–hope springs eternal that maybe the next Service Pack or download from Windows Update will solve the problem for real.

GETTING STARTED

As a consultant, I've spent many years helping clients with hardware, software, and network problems. The most common—and frustrating—way people report a problem is to say "I can't..." or "The computer won't..." Usually, knowing what *doesn't* happen isn't very helpful at all. To solve a mystery, you have to start with what you *do* know. I always have to ask "What happens when you try...?" The answer to that question usually gets me well on the way to solving the problem. The original report usually leaves out important error messages and symptoms that might immediately identify the problem.

Also, as you work on a problem, pay as much attention to what *does* work as to what doesn't. Knowing what *isn't* broken lets you eliminate whole categories of problems. It also helps you to see whether a problem affects just one computer or all the computers on your local area network (LAN).

The following are some other questions I ask:

- Does the problem occur all the time or just sometimes?
- Can you reproduce the problem consistently? If you can define a procedure to reproduce the problem, try to reduce it to the shortest, most direct procedure possible.
- Has the system ever worked, even once? If so, when did it stop working, and what happened just before that? What changed?

These questions can help you determine whether the problem is fundamental (for example, due to a nonfunctioning network card) or interactive (that is, due to a conflict with other users, with new software, or confined to a particular subsystem of the network). You might be able to spot the problem right off the bat if you look at the scene this way. If you can't, you can use some tools to help narrow down the problem.

Generally, network problems fall into one or more of these categories:

- Application software
- Network clients
- Name-resolving services
- Network protocols
- Addressing and network configuration
- Driver software
- Network cards and hardware configuration
- Wiring/hubs

→ To learn more information about networks and network components, **see** Chapter 14, "Overview of Windows XP Networking."

If you can determine the category in which a problem falls, you're halfway there. At this point, diagnostic tools and good, old-fashioned deductive reasoning come into play.

You might be able to eliminate one or more categories right away. For example, if your computer can communicate with some other computers but not all, and your network uses a central hub, you can deduce that at least your computer's network card and the wiring from your computer to the hub are working properly.

Windows comes with some diagnostic tools to further help you narrow down the cause of a network problem. In the rest of this chapter, I'll outline the tools and suggest how to use them. (You might also peruse Chapter 13, "Troubleshooting Your Internet Connection," for tips on diagnosing network problems specific to the Internet [TCP/IP] protocol.) Finally, at the end of the chapter, in "Tips from the Windows Pros," I'll give you a checklist to go through to help narrow down the problem.

DIAGNOSTIC TOOLS

Each diagnostic tool I'll describe tests the operation of one or more of the categories I mentioned in the preceding section. I'll go through these tools in roughly the order you should try them.

Some tools can be used to find problems in any of the many networking components. These tools quickly identify many problems.

MY NETWORK PLACES

You might not think of it as a diagnostic tool, but My Network Places can be one. It can quickly tell you whether your computer can communicate with any other computers on your LAN using the file and printer sharing client services. If at least one other computer is visible and online, then you can be pretty sure that your computer's network card and cabling are okay.

To use it, open My Network Places (if you haven't customized your Start menu to show My Network Places, you get to it by opening My Computer, then click on My Network Places in the task list). Open View Workgroup Computers from the Network Tasks list. See whether any computers are listed.

If you see at least one other computer displayed here, your network cabling and network card are probably okay, and you need to check to be sure that each computer on your network has the same set of network protocols installed; skip "Network Protocols and Bindings" later in this chapter. If no other computer appears, My Network Places won't tell why, so you have to begin the process of diagnosing connectivity or higher-level problems. The next place to go is the Event Viewer, which might have recorded informative error messages from network components.

EVENT VIEWER

The Event Viewer is another very important diagnostic tool, one of the first to check, as Windows often silently records very useful information about problems with hardware and software in its Event Log. To display the Event Log, click Start, right-click My Computer, select Manage, and select the Event Viewer system tool. (Alternatively, if you've added Administrative Tools to your Start menu, you can choose Start, All Programs, Administrative Tools, Event Viewer.)

20

On the left pane, select the System, Application, and Security logs in turn. The Event Viewer displays Event Log entries, most recent first, on the right (see Figure 20.1).

Figure 20.1
The Event Viewer might display important diagnostic information when you have network problems. View the System, Application, and Security logs in turn.

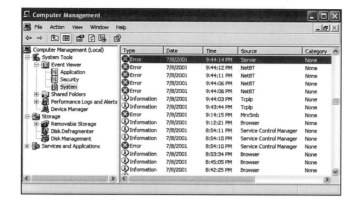

Log entries for serious errors are displayed with a red X circle; warnings appear with a yellow ! triangle. Informational entries (marked with a blue *i*) usually don't relate to problems. Double-click any error or warning entries in the log to view the detailed description and any associated data recorded with the entry. (The Error entries in Figure 20.1 told me that my computer had the same name as another computer on the network: problem solved!)

These messages are usually quite significant and informative to help diagnose network problems; they may indicate that a network card is malfunctioning or a DHCP server for configuration can't be found, and so on. The Source column in the error log indicates which Windows component or service recorded the event. These names are usually fairly cryptic. A few of the more common nonobvious ones are listed in Table 20.1.

TABLE 20.1   NETWORK SOURCES OF EVENT LOG ENTRIES

Source	Description
NetBT	Client for Microsoft Networks
MrxSmb	Client for Microsoft Networks
Browser	Name resolution system for Client for Microsoft Networks
Application Popup	(Can come from any system utility; these warning messages are usually significant)
RemoteAccess	Dial-Up Networking
SNMP	Simple Networking Monitoring Protocol, an optional networking component
IPNATHLP	Internet Connection Sharing

continues

20

TABLE 20.1 CONTINUED	
Source	**Description**
NWCWorkstation	Client for Novell Networks
NwlnkIpx	SPX/IPX Network transport layer
W32Time	Computer clock synchronization service
Dnsapi	DNS client component
Dnscache	DNS client component
atapi	IDE hard disk/CDROM controller

If you're at a loss to solve the problem even with the information given, check the configuration of the indicated component, or remove and reinstall it to see whether you can clear up the problem.

→ To learn more details about the Event Log, **see** "Event Viewer," **p. 854**.

> **TIP**
>
> A problem with one network system usually causes other problems. Therefore, the oldest error message in a sequence of errors is usually the most significant; subsequent errors are just a result of the first failure. Because the Event Log is ordered most-recent-first, you might get the most useful information down a bit from the top of the list.
>
> The real cause of your problem might reveal itself at system startup time rather than when you observe the problem. Reboot your system, and note the time. Then reproduce the problem. Check the Event Log for messages starting at the reboot time.

DEVICE MANAGER

Hardware problems with your network card will most likely be recorded in the Event Log. If you suspect that your network card is the culprit, and nothing is recorded in the Event Log, check the Device Manager.

To use it, click Start, right-click My Computer, select Manage, and choose the Device Manager system tool. Any devices with detectable hardware problems or configuration conflicts appear with a yellow ! icon when you display the Device Manager. If no yellow icons appear, you don't have a *detected* hardware problem. This doesn't mean that you don't have any, but the odds are slim that your network card is the problem.

If devices are shown with ! icons, double-click the device name to see the Windows explanation of the device status and any problems.

→ For more detailed instructions and tips on device troubleshooting, **see** Chapter 27, "Installing and Replacing Hardware."

TESTING NETWORK CABLES

If your computer can't communicate with any other on your LAN, and the Device Manager doesn't indicate a faulty network card, you might have a wiring problem. Wiring problems can be the most difficult to solve, as it's quite difficult to prove that data is leaving one computer but not arriving at another. The `ping` program, which I'll discuss later in this chapter, can help with this problem.

→ To learn how you can use the `ping` command to diagnose Internet-related network problems, **see** "ping," **p. 445**.

If your computer is not properly wired into the LAN, in many cases, Windows displays an offline icon right on the system tray and indicates that your network card is disconnected. It might not, though, so you shouldn't take a lack of this kind of message to mean that no wiring problems exist.

If your network uses UTP (10BASE-T or 100BASE-T) cabling plugged into a hub, there's usually a green LED indicator on each network card and at each port on the hub. Be sure that the lights are on at each end of your network cable and those for the other computers on your LAN.

You also can use inexpensive (about $75) cable test devices that check for continuity and correct pin-to-pin wiring order for UTP wiring. They come as a set of two boxes. One gets plugged into each end of a given cable run, and a set of blinking lights tells you whether all four wires are connected and in the correct order. (If you install your own network cabling or make your own patch cables, these tools are quite handy to have to check your work.)

NOTE

> If you really want to get into the guts of your network cabling or are planning a major installation and want to learn more details so that you can oversee a professional installation, I recommend that you read *Upgrading and Repairing Networks, Fourth Edition*, published by Que.

CHECKING NETWORK CONFIGURATION

If hardware isn't at fault, you may have a fundamental network configuration problem. Often the Event Log or Device Manager gives these problems away, but if they don't, you can use another batch of tools to check the computer's network configuration.

IPCONFIG

If your computer can't communicate with other computers on your LAN, after you check the Event Log and Device Manager, use the `ipconfig` command-line utility to see whether your computer has a valid IP address. Check others on the LAN, too, to ensure that they do as well.

20

At the command prompt (which you open by choosing Start, All Programs, Accessories, Command Prompt), type the following command:

ipconfig /all

The results should look something like this:

```
Windows IP Configuration
        Host Name . . . . . . . . . . . . : AMBON
        Primary DNS Suffix  . . . . . . . : mycompany.com
        Node Type . . . . . . . . . . . . : Broadcast
        IP Routing Enabled. . . . . . . . : Yes
        WINS Proxy Enabled. . . . . . . . : No
        DNS Suffix Search List. . . . . . : mycompany.com

Ethernet adapter Local Area Connection:
        Connection-specific DNS Suffix  . : mycompany.com
        Description . . . . . . . . . . . : Realtek RTL8139(A) PCI Fast Ethernet
                                            Adapter
        Physical Address. . . . . . . . . : 00-C0-CA-14-09-7F
        DHCP Enabled. . . . . . . . . . . : No
        IP Address. . . . . . . . . . . . : 202.201.200.166
        Subnet Mask . . . . . . . . . . . : 255.255.255.204
        Default Gateway . . . . . . . . . : 202.201.200.190
        DNS Servers . . . . . . . . . . . : 201.202.203.72
                                            201.202.213.72
```

The most important items to look for are the following:

- **Hostname**—This should be set to the desired name for each computer. If you can correspond with computers but not others, be sure that the ones that don't work are turned on and correctly named.

- **IP address**—This should be set appropriately for your network. If your LAN uses Internet Connection Sharing, the address will be a number in the range 192.168.0.1 through 192.168.0.254. If your LAN uses DHCP for automatic configuration, your network manager can tell you whether the IP address is correct. Networks with cable/DSL sharing routers usually use numbers starting with 192.168.0 or 192.168.1.

  If you see a number in the range 169.254.0.1 through 192.254.0.254, your computer is set for automatic configuration but no DHCP server was found, so Windows has chosen an IP address by itself. This is fine if your LAN uses this automatic configuration system. However, if there should have been a DHCP server, or if you use Internet Connection Sharing or a hardware Internet connection router, this is a problem. Restart the ICS computer or the router, and then restart your computer and try again.

- **Network mask**—This usually looks like 255.255.255.0, but other settings are possible. At the very least, all computers on the same LAN should have the same network mask.

Each computer on the same LAN should have a similar valid IP address and the same network mask. If they don't, check your network configuration.

20

The "Repair" network task also can be used to help fix problems with DHCP-based (automatic) IP address assignment.

→ To learn more details about IP addressing, network masks, and configuration, **see** "IP Addresses and Routing," **p. 470**, and "Configuring Network Components," **p. 521**.

NETWORK TROUBLESHOOTER

Windows XP features a Network Troubleshooting Wizard that can check for some common network setup problems. Sadly, it holds more promise than good advice. I suggest that you do give it a try, because one of these days it might surprise us all and propose a solution that actually fixes the problem.

To run it, click Start, My Network Places. From the Network Tasks list select View Network Connections. Then, under See Also, select Network Troubleshooter. The troubleshooter is shown in Figure 20.2. At the very least, it will walk you through some helpful, if generic steps to diagnose your network.

Figure 20.2
The Network Troubleshooter can be reached from the Network Connections window.

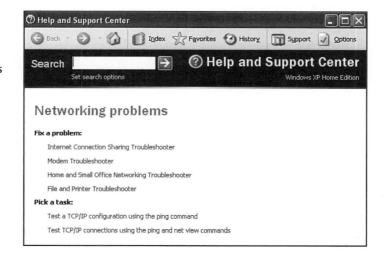

NETDIAG

`netdiag` is a comprehensive network connectivity and configuration diagnosis tool included with the Windows XP Resource Kit, a set of extra utility programs and diagnostic tools sold by Microsoft. It's also provided as one of the optional Support tools on your XP installation CD.

To install it, browse your Windows XP installation CD and double-click `\SUPPORT\TOOLS\`
`SUPTOOLS.MSI`. Be sure to select the Complete setup mode, as opposed to Typical. This installs a set of diagnostic and maintenance tools, including the `netdiag` program I'm about to describe.

20

N O T E

> If the \SUPPORT\TOOLS folder isn't on the Windows XP Installation CD provided by your computer vendor, check whether this folder has been copied to one of your hard disk partitions. Click Start, Search, and look for the file SUPTOOLS.MSI.
>
> In any case, you also might want to get a copy of the Windows XP Professional Resource Kit. It costs a few bucks, but every organization or serious computer geek with a LAN should have a copy, period. Besides netdiag, it has enough nifty tools and utilities to keep the most tweak-happy computer user satisfied for weeks.

To use netdiag, issue the command

```
netdiag >x & notepad x
```

This runs the diagnostics and displays the results with Notepad. The output of netdiag is long—over 180 lines on my computer—because it tests quite a number of network subcomponents. Scroll through the output looking for tests marked Failed. They help point you toward fixing a network problem.

You can get even more detailed information with this command:

```
netdiag /v >x & notepad x
```

MY COMPUTER

You can check your computer's identification and workgroup membership setup by using My Computer. To do so, right-click My Computer, select Properties, and view the Computer Name tab. You should see your computer's name and the name of your workgroup. The workgroup name should be the same on all computers on your network. If any computer has a different workgroup name, change it to match the others. Unless you really want to use a different workgroup name, you should use MSHOME because that's the name that the Network Setup Wizard wants to use.

N O T E

> None of your computers can use the Workgroup name as its computer name. For example, if your workgroup is MSHOME, you also can't name a computer MSHOME. If you find this on one of your computers, change the computer name.

NETWORK AND DIAL-UP CONNECTIONS

You can manually check all installed network protocols and services and their configuration by viewing Network Connections and viewing the properties for Local Area Connection. Confirm that each required protocol is installed and correctly configured. In general, the settings on each computer on your LAN should match, except that the IP address differs usually only in the last of its four dot-separated numbers. If your LAN uses Automatic IP address configuration, you need to use the ipconfig command, which I described earlier, to check the settings.

NETWORK PROTOCOLS AND BINDINGS

One common source of problems on Windows networks is a mismatch between the network protocols installed on the network's computers. This often leads to a situation in which the network is fundamentally okay, but the computers still can't "see" each other. It's especially common when the computers are running different versions of Windows.

On each computer that should be participating in file and printer sharing, view the Network Connections window, select the Local Area Connection icon (or Wireless Connection icon, if you have a wireless network), right-click it, and select Properties.

Each computer should have the same network protocol(s) installed—preferably just one, but possibly two or more of the following:

- Internet Protocol (TCP/IP)
- NWLink IPX/SPX/NetBIOS Compatible Transport Protocol
- NetBEUI

There should be a check mark to the left of the protocol so it is bound (connected) to the network adapter.

(The procedure to check these protocols is somewhat different for older versions of Windows.)

In any case, if some of the computers have different protocols or mix of protocols installed, Windows has a hard time getting the computers to communicate with each other.

If your network is okay at the electrical level (that is, if the ping test described in the next section works and Internet connection sharing works) and you have computers running Windows 95, 98, or Me but you still can't find all your computers in the View Entire Network display, try installing NetBEUI on all the computers. NetBEUI can be installed on Windows XP by following the procedure described in `\VALUEADD\MSFT\NET\NETBEUI\ NETBEUI.TXT` on your Windows XP installation CD-ROM.

WINDOWS FIREWALL

Another configuration setting that could prevent File and Printer sharing from working correctly is the Windows Firewall. To ensure that File and Printer sharing aren't blocked, open the Windows Firewall window by opening the Network Connections window and clicking Change Windows Firewall Settings. On the General tab, be sure that Windows Firewall is enabled (On is checked) and Don't Allow Exceptions is not checked. View the Exceptions tab, and be sure that a check appears next to File and Printer Sharing. Highlight File and Printer Sharing and click Edit. Be sure that the Scope for each of the four listed items is set to Subnet.

→ For more information about configuring the firewall, **see** "Configuring Windows Firewall," **p. 681**.

20

TESTING NETWORK CONNECTIVITY

A few tools can help you determine whether the network can send data between computers; these tools test the network protocols as well as low-level network hardware layers.

PING

`ping` is a fundamental tool for testing TCP/IP network connectivity. Because most Windows XP home networks use the Internet (TCP/IP) protocol for file and printer sharing services, as well as for Internet access, most Windows XP users can use the `ping` test to confirm that their network cabling, hardware, and the TCP/IP protocol are all functioning correctly. `ping` sends several data packets to a specified computer and waits for the other computer to send the packets back. By default, it sends four packets and prints the results of the four tests.

To see whether the network can carry data between a pair of computers, use the `ipconfig` command (described previously) to find the IP address of the two computers. Then, on one computer, open a Command Prompt window by choosing Start, All Programs, Accessories, Command Prompt.

Next, type the following command:

```
ping 127.0.0.1
```

This command tests the networking software of the computer itself, by sending packets to the special internal IP address 127.0.0.1; this test has the computer send data to itself. It should print the following:

```
Reply from 127.0.0.1: bytes=32 time<10ms TTL=128
Reply from 127.0.0.1: bytes=32 time<10ms TTL=128
Reply from 127.0.0.1: bytes=32 time<10ms TTL=128
Reply from 127.0.0.1: bytes=32 time<10ms TTL=128
```

If it doesn't, the TCP/IP protocol itself is incorrectly installed or configured; check the computer's IP address configuration, or, if that seems correct, remove and reinstall the Internet Protocol from Local Area Connection in Network Connections. (I have to say, in more than 10 years of working with PC networks, I've never seen this test fail.)

If your computer can send data to itself, try another computer on your LAN. Find its IP address by running `ipconfig` on that computer; then issue the `ping` command again on the first computer, as in this example:

```
ping 192.168.0.23
```

Of course, you should use the other computer's real IP address in place of 192.168.0.23. You should get four replies as before:

```
Reply from 192.168.0.23: bytes=32 time<10ms TTL=32
Reply from 192.168.0.23: bytes=32 time<10ms TTL=32
Reply from 192.168.0.23: bytes=32 time<10ms TTL=32
Reply from 192.168.0.23: bytes=32 time<10ms TTL=32
```

These replies indicate that you have successfully sent data to the other machine and received it back.

20

If, on the other hand, the ping command returns Request timed out, the packets either didn't make it to the other computer or were not returned. In either case, you have problem with your cabling, network adapter, or the TCP/IP protocol setup.

You can use ping to determine which computers can send to which other computers on your LAN or across wide area networks (WANs) or the Internet. ping works when given a computer's IP address or its network name.

DIAGNOSING FILE AND PRINTER SHARING PROBLEMS

If the tests in the previous section don't point to a problem—that is, if basic network connectivity is fine but you're still having problems with file or printer sharing—there are a few things you might try. Here are some tips:

- Did you run the Network Setup Wizard on each of your computers? To ensure that you don't inadvertently expose your network to the Internet before it's correctly configured, file and printer sharing is disabled until you've run the Network Setup Wizard at least once. You can change your configuration however you like after it's run, but Microsoft wants the first shot at giving you a secure network.

- If you use Internet Connection Sharing, restart the computer that's sharing your Internet connection and wait a minute or two after it's booted up. Then, restart your other computers. This may help. The ICS computer needs to be up and running *before* any other computers on your LAN start up.

- If you don't see other computers in the View Workgroup Computers window, wait 10 to 20 minutes (really) and then select View, Refresh. Sometimes it takes up to 20 minutes for the list of online computers to be updated.

- If you're used to seeing shared folders and printers appear in My Network Places and Printers and Faxes automatically but they're missing now, again, wait a few minutes, then select View, Refresh. You might also want to make sure that the "network crawler" is enabled. Select Tools, Folder Options, then select the View tab. Be sure that "Automatically Search for Network Folders and Printers" is still checked. If it wasn't, check it, log off, and back on. Wait a few minutes, then view My Network Places again.

TESTING NETWORK THROUGHPUT

If your network works but works slowly, you might have a problem with your network cabling or hubs. First of all, if you are using 10/100Mbps Ethernet adapters, you'll get full speed only if your network hub is also 100Mbps capable. If you are using a 10Mbps hub, your network will run at the slower speed. In this case, if you can't live with it, you'll have to update your hub to a 100Mbps or 10/100 dual-speed unit.

If that's not the problem, you can diagnose slow network throughput by using the Windows Performance monitor tool. The Performance Monitor can display utilization statistics collected from your network card and its drivers. You must first install the Network Monitor Driver to enable the collection of network driver performance statistics. Do this on the most-used computer on your network:

1. In Network Connections, right-click Local Area Connection, and select Properties.
2. Select Install, choose Protocol, click Add, and select the Network Monitor Driver.
3. Click OK to close the Properties dialog.

Now run the Performance Monitor by choosing Start, All Programs, Administrative Tools, Performance. You can use the Performance Monitor to measure network utilization and other network statistics.

(If Administrative Tools doesn't appear, right-click the Start button and select Properties. Click Customize and view the Advanced tab. Find System Administrative Tools in the Start Menu Items list and check Display on the All Programs Menu. Then run the Performance Monitor as described earlier.

MEASURING NETWORK UTILIZATION

In the right pane of the Performance console, you can add an item to the graph of performance statistics like this:

1. Right-click in the graph pane, and select Add Counters.
2. Check Use Local Computer Counters.
3. Select the performance object named Network Interface.
4. Select a counter such as Bytes Received/Sec, Packets Received Errors, and so on.
5. Check Select Instances, highlight your LAN adapter interface name, and click Add.
6. Select Close.

The Performance Monitor then graphs the amount of data traffic on your network connection or connections and the plot is updated as you watch. Now you can visually monitor the traffic on your network.

→ To learn more details about this nifty system-monitoring application, **see** "Measuring System Performance with Performance Monitor," **p. 784**.

20

NOTE

To learn more about network design and maintenance, take a look at *Upgrading and Repairing Networks, Fourth Edition*, (from Que).

To remove counters from the Performance graph, you can select the items in the legend below the graph and click the X icon at the top of the graph. Alternatively, you can right-click the graph and select Properties; next, select the Data tab, select Counters, and then click Remove.

TIPS FROM THE WINDOWS PROS: A NETWORK TROUBLESHOOTING CHECKLIST

The most common problem with Windows networking is the inability to locate or contact other computers on the network. Sometimes it's hard to tell where to start when you're troubleshooting a broken network, so I'll give you a checklist to follow to help find the problem. I can't guarantee that this will work to find *every* problem, but it should help you get started:

1. Be sure you've run the Network Setup Wizard (Set Up a Home or Small Office Network on the Network Tasks list) on each of your computers, even if you've configured it manually. File and printer sharing are disabled until you've run the wizard at least once.

2. If the problem is that some computers appear in My Network Places or View Workgroup Computers, while others don't, wait 20 minutes and check again. If all computers still don't appear, and you have older Windows 9x or Me computers on your network, restart the Windows XP computers, wait a minute or two, and then restart the older computers. Wait a few minutes and check again. (By the way, this happens fairly often in Windows networking, and I've never found a reliable way of fixing it. Sometimes you just have to boot up your computers in the correct magic order.)

3. On each of your computers, click Start, My Computer, select My Network Places, and then select View Network Connections. Find the Local Area Connection icon, and see if the icon says "Disconnected." If it does, you have a cabling problem or a bad network adapter. Fix this before proceeding.

4. See if any of your Local Area Connection icons say "Firewalled" next to them. If so, the Windows Connection Firewall might be blocking file and printer sharing on that computer. See the section titled "Windows Firewall" earlier in this chapter.

5. Click Start, right-click My Computer, and choose Properties. View the Computer Name tab. Each computer should have a different computer name, and the same workgroup name. If this isn't so, fix the names as I described earlier in this chapter under "My Computer," and restart the computers you adjusted. This might fix the problem.

6. On each computer, click Start, All Programs, Accessories, Command Prompt. In the Command Prompt window, type **ipconfig** and press Enter. Under the Local Area Connection entry, Windows should report a different IP address on each computer. If any computers have the same address, or if the addresses aren't similar (they all should start with similar numbers), you'll have to fix this before proceeding. See "Configuring Network Components" in Chapter 15 for details.

7. From one of your computers, use the `ping` command to see if that computer can communicate with each of the others. To do this, type

   `ping x.x.x.x`

   into the command prompt window, substituting the actual IP addresses of your other computers for `x.x.x.x` in turn. This might look like something like **ping 192.168.0.10**.

20

You should see several "Reply from" lines listed each time you do this. If any computer doesn't respond, it has a cabling or network hardware problem and you'll need to fix this before proceeding.

8. Be sure that each of your computers has the same network protocols installed, as described in the section "Network Protocols and Bindings" earlier in this chapter.

These steps should help you find the problem in most cases. If you still can't make it work, I suggest calling in either a network professional or an experienced friend to lend a hand.

20

SYSTEM CONFIGURATION AND CUSTOMIZATION

CHAPTER 21

TWEAKING THE GUI

In this chapter

GUI: TO TWEAK OR NOT TO TWEAK

I wanted to start this chapter with something cute or meaningful, but all I could think was that, if you know what this title means, you qualify for the Geek-of-the-Year award. For the rest of you, let's get our minds out of the gutter; tweaking the graphical user interface (GUI) doesn't mean anything lascivious. This chapter describes the graphical user interface and some interesting, useful, and fun stuff you can do with it—changes to help increase your computing efficiency and perhaps even make your computer more fun to use.

As you know, the GUI is the translator that interprets human input into commands the computer can interpret. It's also responsible for displaying output from computer programs and the operating system so that you can understand the results. The Windows XP GUI is set up with factory defaults that 90% of users will never touch, despite its being highly programmable and easily modifiable through the Control Panel, Folder Options, Properties sheets, and so on. If you're a GUI hacker, you know who you are, and if all you want to do is get your work done, well, more power to you because you're the one who's going to get the raise. But playing with the GUI can be fun.

Most folks won't modify their GUIs, but it's a shame they don't. Often, not even knowing there is a recourse, users develop headaches from screen flicker, come down with eyestrain from tiny screen fonts, or they live with color schemes they detest. With a little effort, they can rectify these problems. Likewise, means for managing zip archives, altering the right-click Send To options, and handling numerous other functions users have to deal with every day are just a few clicks, Net downloads, Registry hacks, or Properties sheet settings away. Just for fun, you can choose from hundreds of desktop themes, screen savers, wallpaper images, and so on.

Some of this chapter deals with standard display options. Other portions deal with deeper GUI tweaks and tricks. Just skim for the part that interests you. Or, if you are not inclined to alter the way things work right-out-of-the-box, then skip this chapter altogether.

→ This chapter doesn't cover multimonitor support because it's related more to hardware upgrades than the GUI. **See** "Installing and Using Multiple Monitors," **p. 966**, for coverage of multiple monitors.

START MENU PIZZAZZ!

The default Start menu of Windows XP is much improved over the classic style (in my opinion). I dread returning to Windows 2000 or earlier OSes for whatever reason simply because of the now-old-fashioned Start menu. For those of you who like the classic view, you can get back to it in a flash. But, for those willing to give the new look and feel a solid go, there are many nifty improvements you can take advantage of and even customize.

Accessing Properties for the Start menu involves a right-click over the Start button to select the Properties command from the pop-up menu. This reveals the Taskbar and Start Menu Properties dialog box. The Start Menu tab is selected by default (which is strange since it's not the first tab of the dialog box). This tab offers the selections of Start menu and Classic Start menu. The Start menu option is the new Luna visual stylings of Windows XP. The

Classic Start menu is that of Windows 2000. A quick click and you can be back in the land of Windows 2000 out-of-date fashion before you can say baggy jeans.

For those of you sticking with Windows XP's new classy stylings, slam the Customize button to see all the options available to you. From the Customize Start Menu dialog box, you can choose between large (default) and small icons, the number of recently accessed applications to be displayed (5 by default), and which Internet (IE by default) and email (Outlook Express by default) application shortcuts to display.

The Advanced tab (see Figure 21.1) of the Customize Start Menu dialog box controls the following:

■ Whether to open submenus on mouse over (default) or only when clicked.

Figure 21.1
The Advanced tab of the Customize Start Menu dialog box.

■ Whether to highlight newly installed programs (enabled by default).
■ Which items to include on the Start menu: Control Panel (enabled by default), Favorites menu, Help and Support (enabled by default), My Computer (enabled by default), My Documents (enabled by default), My Music (enabled by default), My Network Places, My Pictures (enabled by default), Network Connections, Printers and Faxes, and Run command (enabled by default). Some of these can be normal links or displayed as submenus themselves (see "Cascading Elements Off the Start Menu," later in this chapter).
■ Whether to list the most recently opened documents (and to clear out this list).

With a bit of experimentation, you'll find the combination of features that best suits your preferred Start menu population and function.

21

WORKING WITH THE TASKBAR

The taskbar itself has configurable options; these are contained on the Taskbar tab of the Taskbar and Start Menu Properties dialog box. The taskbar can be locked so stray mouse actions won't alter its placement or configuration; it can be auto-hidden to maximize desktop area; and it can be set to always appear on top of other maximized windows. You'll probably recall these controls from previous Windows OSes. The latest taskbar feature is the automatic grouping of similar taskbar items. Instead of listing task buttons in their order of launch, they are grouped by similar interface. For example, if you have Control Panel, My Computer, and Windows Explorer open, they can appear as a single button. This single button displays a number indicating how many applications are accessed through it (I just love the grouping feature). You can elect to show or hide the clock and even hide inactive system tray icons.

If you're experienced with previous Windows OSes, you might be familiar with how quickly the system tray (next to the clock) can fill up with icons. I've had systems with more than a dozen. Windows XP manages its system tray much more intelligently by allowing inactive icons to be hidden. Plus, instead of displaying a long stream of active icons, only two or so are displayed with a double-arrow button, which can be used to access the hidden icons. By enabling Hide inactive icons (which is the default) you can also customize which icons are hidden or displayed.

As with previous versions of Windows, you can still drag the taskbar to any edge of your desktop: top, bottom, or sides. You can also still expand the thickness of the taskbar to allow multiple rows of task buttons. Just hover the mouse pointer near the edge of the taskbar so that it turns into a double arrow, and drag it up or down.

CUSTOMIZING THE START MENU

As new applications are installed, the All Programs section of the Windows XP Start menu can become horribly cluttered. Almost every application will create its own Start menu submenu and propagate itself with numerous shortcuts—often to worthless documentation or sales promotions. I rarely let an installed application dictate the state of my Start menu, and I'll tell you how you can take control, too.

The Start menu is little more than a folder hierarchy full of shortcuts. Changing the layout of the Start menu (or at least the All Programs section) is just a matter of folder and shortcut manipulation—easy. Just right-click over the Start button and select Open or Explore. You'll be dropped into a My Computer or Windows Explorer interface pointing to the …\Documents and Settings\<username>\Start Menu folder. Any item you add to this folder (that is, at the same level as the Programs folder) will be displayed above the dividing line within the All Programs submenu. Any item you add within the Programs folder or any of its subfolders will appear as you expect in the Start menu hierarchy. Be sure only to create shortcuts within this folder hierarchy.

You should also be aware that there are actually two Start menus for every user. There is the Start menu which is associated with your user profile (the one stored in the …\Documents and Settings\<username>\ folder, where <username> is your user account name), and there is the Start menu stored in the ...\Documents and Settings\All Users\Start menu folder. The latter Start menu includes items that appear in every user's Start menu. When you need to make a change for everyone on this system, make it within the All Users area. If it is for only one user, make that change within their personal Start menu.

DISPLAY PROPERTIES

The most obvious means for altering your GUI display settings is the Display Properties dialog box. From there, you can reach a multitude of GUI settings, mostly affecting visual stylings rather than GUI functionality per se:

- Screen saver settings
- Desktop background
- Colors and fonts for GUI elements
- Active Desktop setting
- Color depth and resolution
- Special GUI effects such as menu sliding
- Energy-saving settings
- Device drivers
- Advanced properties such as hardware acceleration

You can most easily reach the display properties by right-clicking the desktop and choosing Properties. The resulting dialog box appear in Figure 21.2.

Figure 21.2
You can alter a multitude of display attributes from the Display Properties dialog box (Themes tab shown). Programs such as virus protectors or video drivers may introduce additional tabs to this dialog box.

21

NOTE

You also can get to the display properties from the Control Panel. Click Start, Control Panel, Appearance and Themes, and Display.

I'll briefly describe this dialog box tab by tab. You've probably used it before, so I won't belabor it; however, I will point out the basics and mention any specifics you should be aware of.

THEMES TAB

To quote the dialog box itself, "A theme is a background plus a set of sounds, icons, and other elements to help you personalize your computer with one click." That just about sums it up, I think. All the settings you make on the other tabs of the Display Properties dialog box can be saved to a theme file on the Themes tab (refer to Figure 21.2). Windows XP includes a few themes, such as the default Windows XP scheme (a.k.a. Luna) and the classic theme (similar to the default theme of Windows 2000). Microsoft offers several other themes for download, and many third parties have created themes for Windows XP as well. To download additional themes from Microsoft, select the More Themes Online option from the Theme pull-down list and Windows XP will take you to the online theme stash.

DESKTOP TAB

The desktop is used to express your inner personality. "Hanging wallpaper" (a picture of your kids, your car, a sunset, a nebula, and so forth) on your desktop gives the environment a more personalized feeling. Microsoft includes dozens of options for you. These include small tiles (a.k.a. patterns) that are repeated across and down your screen to make a pattern as well as larger single images centered on the screen (some of which are quite stunningly beautiful). If the image is too small to fill up your desktop, you can always set the Position control to Stretch.

NOTE

Stretching takes a picture smaller than your screen resolution and enlarges it so that it fills the screen. Stretching can distort the picture or cause it to pixelate, so if you want it to look good, make sure to shoot the picture at, or convert it to, a size roughly matching the resolution setting of your display. Then choose the Center option.

TIP

If the image is larger than the screen's resolution, stretching actually shrinks the image to fully fit on the desktop. If stretching is turned off, and the image is larger than the screen, you'll only be able to see the center portion of the image that fits within your display.

21

If you don't want a pretty picture (or you need to hide the image of the sultry pin-up before your spouse returns), you can select None in the list of backgrounds to view a solid background color. That solid color can be altered on this tab, using the Color button on the

Desktop tab or via the Appearance tab's Advanced button. The color setting will be hidden if you use a tiled image or a full-screen size image. But it will show up as the background color for the names of shortcuts populating your desktop.

If you don't like the images offered by default, you can always add your own spicy image. Just click the Browse button to find images elsewhere. You can select BMP, JPG, GIF, DIB, and PNG images, or even entire HTM Web pages. In addition to files already on your local system (or accessible over your local network), you can grab any image from a Web site by right-clicking over it and selecting Set as Background from the pop-up menu.

 If you've used a photo as a background for your desktop, but it appears blocky, see "Stretched a Bit Thin" in the "Troubleshooting" section at the end of this chapter.

Clicking on the Customize Desktop button at the bottom of the Desktop tab opens the Desktop Item dialog box (see Figure 21.3). On the General tab of this dialog box, you can select from four common shortcut icons to appear on the desktop: My Documents, My Computer, My Network Places, and Recycle Bin. You can also manage the icons used for these desktop shortcuts using the Change Icon and Restore Default buttons.

Figure 21.3
The Desktop Item dialog box, General tab.

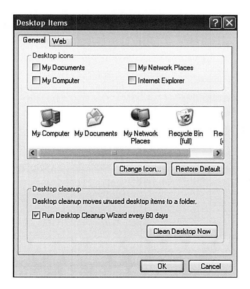

Another interesting feature of Windows XP's new user experience is the Desktop Cleanup Wizard. By default it is launched every 60 days to prompt you to remove items you've not been using. If you elect to remove items from the desktop, they are moved into an Unused Desktop Shortcuts folder the wizard adds to the desktop. You can disable the 60 day launch by clearing the checkbox (that's one of the first settings I change!). You can also force a desktop cleanup by clicking the Clean Desktop Now button.

The Web tab of the Desktop Items dialog box is used to configure the Web components on the desktop (this used to be called Active Desktop). From here you can add new Web

21

components or remove old ones. Desktop Web components are miniature Web browsers which can be resized and moved around, plus they actively update their content as long as an Internet connection is available. To add a new Web page item, click the New button. From the New Desktop Item dialog box, click Visit Gallery to see a collection of Microsoft pre-selections, enter your own URL, or click Browse to add a locally stored image or HTML document. After you've added all the items you wish, you can close this dialog box and drag the components around on the desktop to arrange them as you desire. Once you have the components arranged as you please, reopen the Desktop Items dialog box to lock the desktop items so a stray mouse click won't rearrange them.

After you've added a Web component (via a URL) to the available items to display on your desktop, you can customize the schedule and download restrictions through their Properties dialog box. Desktop Web components can be synchronized automatically on a custom defined schedule or manually. You can also specify what to download, such as everything, only the front page, or only up to a specific number of kilobytes. All of these configuration settings are very self-explanatory, so take a few minutes and explore them.

SCREEN SAVER TAB

We all know what screen savers are. On the Screen Saver tab of the Display Properties dialog box, you can choose from several supplied screen savers and perhaps others that you have installed from other sources. In the old days when phosphors would "burn," screen savers actually did something useful. They prevented a ghost of the image on the screen from being burned into the screen for all time, no matter what is being displayed. Most modern CRTs don't actually need a screen saver to save anything because the phosphors are more durable. Also, LCD monitors don't need them either because they don't have any phosphors on the screen at all.

So, what good is a screen saver nowadays, you ask? Well, some older monitor/card combinations go into low-power states when the screen is blanked, so if you choose Blank Screen, there could be some advantage.

The SETI@home Screen Saver

Interested in space exploration? Think life might exist on other planets? If you want to become part of the largest global experiment in massive parallel processing, you can download the SETI@home screen saver to harness your computer's otherwise wasted CPU cycles to sift through signals from outer space, searching for signs of intelligent life out there. (Go to http://setiathome.ssl.berkeley.edu/ if you're interested in participating.)

SETI@home is a scientific experiment that harnesses the power of hundreds of thousands of Internet-connected computers in the Search for Extraterrestrial Intelligence (SETI). The screen saver downloads and analyzes radio telescope data captured at the world's largest radio telescope in Arecibo, Puerto Rico. There's a small but captivating possibility that your computer will detect the faint murmur of a civilization beyond Earth.

Your computer gets a "work unit" of interstellar noise that it analyses when the screen saver comes up. A work unit requires approximately 20 hours of computing time on most computers. If an unnatural noise is detected, you and the people back at the University of California will be alerted. The scientists will attempt to confirm the finding by doing their own analysis and ruling out man-made radio sources such as radar and such. If it is finally confirmed, you and the team can pack up and head for Sweden to pick up your Nobel Prize. If nothing is found (which is somewhat more likely), your system moves on to the next work unit.

As of this writing, five million computers were participating. This huge, collective-computing model has set the standard by which massively parallel-processing experiments using small computers are based. There are dozens of sites which use this scenario to perform calculations on encryption codes, calculating PI, and even performing Internet searching and indexing.

Now that beats the old days of screen savers featuring flying toasters, doesn't it?

Because far too many people leave their computers on all the time (it's not really true that they will last longer that way), efforts have been made by power regulators and electronics manufacturers to devise computer energy-conservation schemes. And, of course, some screen savers are fun to watch. The 3D-Pipes screen saver that comes with Windows XP is pretty mesmerizing actually.

Some screen savers are mindless; others are more interesting. Some, such as the Marquee, have additional options, such as font, size, and color. You can check out each one as the spirit moves you. Just highlight it on this tab, and click Preview. Don't move the mouse until you're ready to stop the preview. If a particular screen saver has configuration elements, click on the Settings button.

If you're looking to find the actual screen saver files on your hard drive, most of them have an .scr extension and are stored in the windows\system32 folder. Most files are 100KB or smaller in size. Double-clicking a screen saver runs it. Just press a key or click the mouse to stop it from running.

The Web is littered with screen savers. Just do a search. The following are some sources:

- Screen Saver Heaven:
  http://www.galttech.com/ssheaven.shtml
- Screensaver.com:
  http://www.screensaver.com/

Between those two sources alone, you have access to more than 2,500 screen savers. Plus, most of the screen savers designed for Windows 3.x, Windows 9x/Me, Windows NT, and Windows 2000 will work on Windows XP.

In addition to selecting the screen saver du jour, you should also define the length of time the system must be idle before the screen saver is launched, as well as whether to display Welcome screen or return to the desktop when the system is resumed (that is, when the keyboard or mouse is activated by a user).

→ The Energy Star settings for monitors are covered under the Power applet discussion. **See** "Working with Power," **p. 721**.

If you are working from a portable system or are an energy conservationist (why do you have a computer in the first place?), the Screen Saver tab also offers quick access to the power saving properties of Windows XP via the Power button. This opens the Power

21

Options Properties dialog box, which is a Control Panel applet in its own right. The Power Options applet is discussed a bit later in this chapter.

APPEARANCE TAB

From the Appearance tab (see Figure 21.4), you can radically alter the look of your entire Windows machine. You can do some serious mischief here, creating some egregious color schemes that will attract the fashion police. Or you can design or choose schemes that improve readability on screens (or eyes) with certain limitations. If, perchance, you're using a monochrome monitor (no color), altering the colors may still have some effect (the amount depends on how you installed Windows), so these settings are not just for systems with color screens.

Figure 21.4
The Display
Properties dialog box,
Appearance tab.

In most cases your desktop is set to the Windows XP style by default, which is fine for most screens and users. If you prefer the stylings of Windows 2000, you can go retro by selecting Windows Classic style from the Windows and buttons pull-down list.

The Windows Classic style offers all of the color scheme pre-defined options you remember, such as Desert, Eggplant, and Wheat. But even if you stick with the new XP styling, there are the default, Olive Green, and Silver color schemes, and even these can be customized through the Advanced button.

The final pull-down selection box on this tab is Font size. I bet you can guess what it's for. So, if you have trouble reading the names of icons or dialog boxes, increase the size of the font!

21

The Effects button opens the Effects dialog box. From here, you can set the following:

- Whether menus and ToolTips are animated or not, and whether the animation is fade or scroll. Set to Fade effect by default.
- Whether screen fonts are smoothed using the standard Windows method, or using ClearType. ClearType often improves the visibility range on older LCD displays. The Standard method is selected by default.
- Whether to use large icons. Not selected by default.
- Whether to show shadows under menus. Enabled by default.
- Whether to show the contents of a window while dragging. Enabled by default.
- Whether to hide the underlined letters for keyboard shortcuts until the Alt key is pressed. Enabled by default.

The Advanced button opens the Advanced Appearance dialog box, which is used to alter the color settings, component size, and fonts of each individual component of a windowed display. By using the various pull-down lists or clicking in the preview area, you can fine-tune the color and font scheme.

TIP

If you spend considerable time creating a color, component, and font styling, be sure to save it as a theme on the Themes tab. Otherwise, if you switch to another view, even for a second, you'll lose all of your previous settings.

Choosing a color called Other brings up the Color Refiner dialog box (this is true on the Desktop tab as well). You work with two color mix controls here. One is the *luminosity bar* (which looks like a triangle arrow pointing left), and the other is the *color refiner cursor* (which looks like a set of crosshairs).

You simply drag around these cursors one at a time until the color in the box at the lower left is the shade you want. As you do so, the numbers in the boxes below the color refiner change.

- **Luminosity**—The amount of brightness in the color.
- **Hue**—The actual shade or color. All colors are composed of red, green, and blue.
- **Saturation**—The degree of purity of the color; it is decreased by adding gray to the color and increased by subtracting gray.

You also can type in the numbers or click the arrows next to the numbers if you want, but using the cursors is easier. When you like the color, you can save a color for future use by clicking Add to Custom Colors.

21

SETTINGS TAB

On the Settings tab (see Figure 21.5) of the Display Properties dialog box, you can tweak the video driver's most basic settings—screen resolution (desktop size) and color quality (color depth).

Figure 21.5
The Display
Properties dialog box,
Settings tab.

> **TIP**
>
> Unless you have a very fast computer or an intelligent co-processed AGP video card, you will find that running in true color at a high resolution, such as 1280x1024, can be annoying if you have Show window contents while dragging turned on. When you move a window, it moves jerkily across the screen. If you play videos such as QuickTime, MPEG, or RealPlayer movies, you'll also notice that these higher color depths can slow down the movies or make them play jerkily. Try using a setting of 16-bit color depth (also known as "high color") for movies and photos. If you don't view movies and photos but only do non-photographic tasks such as word processing, spreadsheet work, and so on, you might even want to try 256 colors.

Assuming that Windows XP has properly identified your video display card and that the correct driver is installed, the Color quality drop-down list box should include all the legitimate options your card is capable of. Your color depth options are limited by the amount of video RAM on the card and the resolution you choose. The higher the resolution, the more memory is used for pixel addressing, limiting the pixel depth (number of colors that can be displayed per pixel). With many modern cards, this limitation is no biggie, and it's likely that many Windows XP users will not have to worry about it except in cases when they have large monitors displaying 1600x1200 and want 32-bit color *and* a high refresh rate. If you find that setting the color scheme up to high color or true color causes the resolution slider to move left, this is the reason. All modern analog color monitors for PCs are capable of displaying 16 million colors, which is dubbed true color.

 If you've changed the screen area only to find that you can no longer see some icons or open windows on the desktop, see "Where Did Those Icons Go?" in the "Troubleshooting" section at the end of this chapter.

You must click the Apply button before the changes are made. When you do, you are warned about the possible effects. The good thing about the no-reboot video subsystem, first introduced with Windows 98, is that the driver settings should revert within 15 seconds unless you accept them. So, if the screen goes blank or otherwise goes bananas, just wait. It should return to the previous setting.

 If, after toying with the screen resolution, you notice that your once-speedy computer seems to have lost its zip, see "Moving in Slow Motion" in the "Troubleshooting" section at the end of this chapter.

The Screen resolution setting makes resizing your desktop a breeze. Obviously, we all want to cram as much on the screen as possible without going blind. This setting lets you experiment and even change resolution on-the-fly to best display whatever you're working on. Some jobs, such as working with large spreadsheets, databases, CAD, or typesetting, are much more efficient with more data displayed on the screen. Because higher resolutions require a trade-off in clarity and make onscreen objects smaller, you can minimize eyestrain by going to a lower resolution, such as 800x600 pixels (a pixel is essentially one dot on the screen). If you find the dialog box doesn't let you choose the resolution you want, drop the color palette setting down a notch and try again.

TIP

> All laptop and notebooks and an ever-increasing percentage of desktop computers have LCD monitors these days. Unlike their more versatile yet clunky CRT-based progenitors, these energy- and space-saving displays are optimized for one resolution, called their *native* resolution.
>
> On LCDs I don't suggest changing the setting from the native, (sometimes called *suggested*), resolution. Although choosing a lower resolution results in screen elements being larger (and thus easier for some people to see), it also produces a blockier, fuzzier display. This effect is mitigated somewhat on more intelligent displays by intelligent engineering that provides antialiasing.
>
> Trying a higher resolution than the native one typically does not work. There is a discrete number of pixels on the display, and these are of a predetermined size. Trying to jam more pixels on the screen works, if it works at all, by creating a virtual screen that is larger than the actual one. This requires you to pan and scroll the screen image about. Check the computer's or monitor's manual if you're in doubt about which external monitor resolutions are supported.

21

 If you've connected an external TV monitor to your computer but cannot read the fonts on the screen, see "What Does That Say?" in the "Troubleshooting" section at the end of this chapter.

If you are experiencing any problems with your video system, from pop-up errors blaming the video system, to a flickering display, to even trouble resetting the resolution and color, click on the Troubleshoot button. This button launches the Video Display Troubleshooter. It's a Q&A type of wizard that helps you discover solutions to problems. Overall, I've found the Windows XP troubleshooters worth their weight in gold.

 If the screen flicker really annoys you, see "Reducing Screen Flicker" in the "Troubleshooting" section at the end of the chapter.

Windows XP boasts the Dual View feature. Dual View allows Windows XP to display the same desktop view on two or more monitors. On a notebook, where it was common to display the desktop both on the LCD panel and an external, this is nothing new. But, on desktop PCs equipped with multiple video cards, you can now use multiple monitors. The screen resolution of each monitor is controlled from the Settings tab. Just select the monitor to set the context for the screen resolution and color quality controls.

The Advanced button on the Settings tab opens the Monitor and Adapter Properties dialog box. This dialog box has five tabs—General, Adapter, Monitor, Troubleshoot, and Color Management.

TIP

> Contrary to some advertising accompanying flat-panel monitors, LCDs don't give a hoot about high refresh speed. In fact, they don't like high speeds. LCDs use a completely different technology, typically with a transistor for each pixel. The dots don't have to be refreshed as they do in a CRT. I noticed a blurry display on a desktop LCD screen once and tracked down the problem to a 72Hz refresh rate on the video card. I lowered it to 60Hz, and the image cleared up. This advice applies only to LCDs that are attached to analog display cards. Some outboard LCD monitors are driven by their own digital adapter cards, and refresh settings don't affect those cards.

The General tab is used to alter the display's DPI setting and how display changes are handled. The DPI or Dots Per Inch changes the size of items displayed on your screen. The Handling of display changes option simply sets the system to restart before applying, apply without restarting, or ask about restarting whenever changes are made to the display settings.

CAUTION

> If you specify a refresh rate that is too high for your monitor, it could damage the monitor. Also, trying to expand the desktop area to a larger size might not work. You just get a mess on the screen. If you have this problem, try using a setting with a lower refresh rate, such as 60Hz or "interlaced." The image may flicker a bit more, but at least it will be visible.

The Adapter tab displays information about the video card and offers access to configure, uninstall, update, or rollback the video driver through the Properties button. The List All

Modes button is used to view the color, resolution, and refresh rate combinations supported by this video adapter.

 If, while you're tinkering with the refresh rates for your monitor, the monitor goes blank, don't panic; instead, see "Uh-Oh, My Monitor Died" in the "Troubleshooting" section at the end of this chapter.

The Monitor tab offers access to configure, install, upgrade, or rollback the monitor driver and to set the screen refresh rate. Use the screen refresh rate with caution as it can damage older monitors or render your desktop unviewable. Higher refresh rates reduce the flickering of the display.

 If, after you install a new LCD monitor, you discover that the image is blurry, see "Blurry Images in LCD" in the "Troubleshooting" section at the end of this chapter.

The Troubleshoot tab is used to set the hardware acceleration rate, anywhere between None and Full. Basically this indicates how much video processing is offloaded to the video adapter instead of being performed by Windows XP on the CPU. The more you can offload processing to the video card, the more smoothly your system will function. If you have problems with jitters or lockups, you may need to reduce the amount of hardware acceleration.

The Color Management tab is used to set the color profile used to manage colors for your adapter and monitor. If you are performing high-end image processing you may want to investigate this feature in the Windows XP Resource Kit.

→ If you have a new driver for your display card or monitor and want to install it, **see** "System Device Manager" or "Add Hardware," **p. 750**.

WORKING WITH POWER

The Power Options applet is the tree-hugger's dream. Well, it's at least a necessary feature for users of portable systems, and increasingly handy for desktop users over the last few years as those larger machines have evolved to become more miserly with electricity. This applet is designed to help the computer consume electricity at a more modest pace. This conservation is accomplished by powering down the monitor and hard drives after periods of inactivity. Several pre-defined power schemes are included, but with just two controls (one for the monitor and one for the hard disks) it's not hard to define your own.

In addition to turning off the energy guzzling components, the Power Options applet also manages standby, hibernation, APM, and UPS.

Standby is a feature of most notebook systems that allows the system's state to be saved to RAM and the monitor and hard drives to be powered off. A system can return to fully active state from standby at any point before the batteries are drained. Once power is lost, the system state is lost as well, because it is only stored in RAM. The Power Options applet's Advanced tab offers a single control relative to standby—whether to require a password to resume from standby.

Hibernation is a feature that is a cross between standby mode and shutting down a system. With hibernation, the system state is saved to the hard drive, and then the system is

21

powered down. Once the system is powered back on, the system state is restored. Since the system state data is stored on the hard drive, it is not dependant on constant power to be maintained, and you can return days later and jump back into working right where you left off. The Power Options applet's Hibernate tab offers a single control to enable or disable hibernation. Keep in mind that no passwords are required to resume from hibernation, so it is not a secure feature. Also, take note that this tab displays the amount of drive space required to save the system state. If the required space approaches your available free space, you might lose data or be completely unable to reboot from hibernation.

If your system supports APM (Advanced Power Management) and virtually all modern PCs do, the APM tab allows you to enable or disable APM. APM allows for finer tuning of power consumption by your system and its components. It also supplies battery power status information so you can keep track of your portable juice. APM is typically available on portable systems and some "green" desktops or server systems.

You may have a UPS tab. This offers control and interface configuration for uninterruptible power supplies. These wonderful tools are an essential part of any production environment where computers are used. The nation's power grid is not always up to par. Blackouts, brownouts, spikes, dips, and even noisy electricity can damage or destroy computer equipment. Just ask residents of California! A UPS conditions the incoming electricity so a consistent regulated flow reaches its delicate circuits. You may already know that a shock from static electricity can destroy your system; just think what a surge from a nearby lightning strike will do. UPSes can be integrated into Windows XP by a serial or USB cable. These connections feed data about the power levels of the UPS's battery to the computer and allow the UPS to inform the system when the power is out. When the city electricity goes out, the UPS will supply the computer with power from its battery. If properly configured, the UPS can instruct the system to automatically shut down or hibernate after so many minutes of battery supplied life force. That way, the system will have a graceful shutdown instead of an abrupt loss of power.

NOTE

> When no one is logged in to the system, what power saving settings does Windows XP use? When no one is logged in, Windows XP automatically uses the power saving options set for the last user who logged in with computer administrator privileges. So, when the next computer administrator level user logs in, their power options settings are stored as the global defaults on the log in screen, overwriting any previous settings.

If you can't reduce your power consumption through the Power Options applet to suit your needs then you need to turn off the computer and go chop some wood instead.

21

TWEAK UI

Many Windows experts have become fond of an unsupported Microsoft product called Tweak UI, which is available and freely downloadable from the Microsoft site. Tweak UI is one of the Microsoft "Power Toys" developed by programmers at Camp Bill in Redmond,

Washington. Tweak UI works fine on Windows XP as it did on Windows 2000 and Windows 98. Version 2.10.0.0 of Tweak UI is the newest available for download as of the time of this writing, and it has been fully optimized for usage on Windows XP.

Tweak UI enables you to make more than 100 changes to the Windows XP user environment. For example, you can do the following:

- Scroll smoothly in Windows Explorer
- Enable the mouse wheel for scrolling
- Speed up the display rate of menus
- Add special folders to your operating system that have mouse setting refinements
- Add more types of "New" documents when you right-click a folder and choose New
- Add or remove installed programs from the list of available programs through the Add or Remove Programs applet
- Repair Start menu and desktop hotkeys, font folders, and icons
- Cover your tracks by erasing temp files, document lists, and history files
- Control whether CDs play automatically when you insert a disk
- Add or remove drives from being displayed in My Computer
- Configure auto-logon

You can download the Tweak UI Power Toy from the Power Toys home page at http://www.microsoft.com/windowsxp/downloads/powertoys/xppowertoys.mspx.

1. Double-click on the TweakUiPowertoySetup.exe file.
2. Click Next to dismiss the opening page, acknowledging that you are about to install the Tweak UI power toy.
3. Accept the licensing agreement and click Next to continue.
4. Provide your username and organization information and then click Next to continue.
5. The default installation type is Complete (which is really the only type because there are no installation options); click Next to continue.
6. Click Install to start the installation.
7. Click Finish to end the installation process.
8. You can now access the Tweak UI power toy from the Power Toys for Windows XP folder located on your Start menu.

When you run it, you see the dialog box displayed in Figure 21.6.

NOTE

If you want to uninstall Tweak UI, be sure to read its Help file under "How to Uninstall."

21

Figure 21.6
Tweak UI offers lots of fun stuff to play with here!

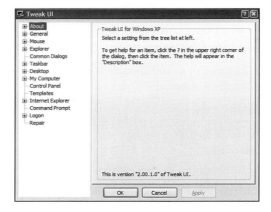

The following are issues with Tweak UI as it pertains to Windows XP:

- If you do not have permission to alter the list of drives that appear in My Computer, the My Computer tab is not shown.
- Depending on the security permissions granted to the current user, some Tweak UI features may not have any effect. For example, if the current user doesn't have permission to edit the part of the Registry that contains the desktop, then changes to the desktop don't have any result.

TIP

> You might want to check out the other Power Toys, too—not just Tweak UI. The following additional tools are available:
>
> Super-Fast User Switcher, "Open Command Window Here" Shortcut, Power Calculator, Task Switcher, Image Resizer, CD Slide Show Generator, Virtual Desktop, Manager, Taskbar Magnifier, HTML slide show wizard, Webcam Timershot. We think the most useful Power Toy is the Task Switcher. It enhances the existing Alt+Tab application switching mechanism of Windows XP. It provides a thumbnail preview of windows in the task list and is compliant with the new Windows XP visual style.

MISCELLANEOUS GUI TIPS

Windows XP offers lots of new features and capabilities. But you don't have to settle for the out of the box defaults, you can customize to your heart's content. In the following sections, we provide you with several tips to help you soup up your Windows XP installation.

If you've become really frustrated because single clicks are interpreted by Windows as double-clicks (and you can't seem to find any mention of the problem in this chapter), never fear; there's an easy solution. See "Single- or Double-Click?" in the "Troubleshooting" section at the end of this chapter.

FONTS PREVIEW TRICK

If you've ever tried to see what a font looked like before you printed it, you know how frustrating it can be. But, getting a preview of a font is now easier than ever before. There are actually two ways to view the output of a font through the OS itself. The first method is enabled by default on the system. Just open the Fonts applet through the Control Panel, and then double-click on any listed font. A dialog box displays details about the font, a sample of most characters, and several sizes of characters (see Figure 21.7).

Figure 21.7
A font sampling dialog box.

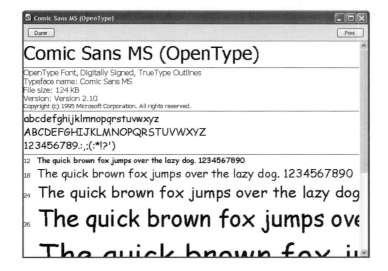

The second method for viewing a font sample requires that your system be configured for single-click mode. This is done through the Folder Options applet from the Control Panel. Once single-click mode is enabled, open the Fonts applet. The View menu will now have a Preview command. When Preview is selected, you will see a small sample of each font as you position your mouse cursor over its icon. It only displays the line "The quick brown fox" in the selected font. I don't like the single-click mode, so I don't use this feature.

WHICH WINDOWS ARE YOU USING?

If you're dual- or multi-booting between Windows XP (using the classic interface style) and other Windows products, you may sometimes wonder which operating system you're running at any given time because the GUIs of the post-Windows 95 OSes are often virtually indistinguishable. Yes, you'll see a few giveaways, such as My Network Places versus Network Neighborhood (assuming your desktop is visible), but in essential look and feel the similarities easily outweigh the differences.

21

To determine what's running, you could open the Control Panel, open the System applet, and read the dialog box. But that's a pain. Instead, you can use these techniques to remind yourself.

- Although many people like to turn off large icons on the first level of the Start menu, leaving them on displays the operating system name when you click Start. You can locate this option by right-clicking the taskbar and clicking Properties. Then select the Start Menu tab and click Customize.

- Executing `winver` from the Run command or a Command Prompt opens a dialog box that displays the OS name, version, applied Service Packs, and the amount of physical RAM installed in the system.

- Click Start and right-click the My Computer icon. From the menu that appears, click Properties. The first set of information on the General tab is labeled System, and names the version of Windows you're currently using.

Tweaking the Clock to Add Your Company Name

You can put your company's name or abbreviation on the taskbar next to the clock, or even an identifier if you have different machines, different operating systems, or different departments. Here's how you do it:

1. Select the Date, Time, Language, and Regional Options applet in the Control Panel and select the Regional and Language Options icon.
2. On the Region Options tab, click Customize.
3. Click the Time tab.
4. Set the time format as h:mm:ss tttttttt (each t is a placeholder for one character in your message, with eight characters max).
5. Set both AM and PM symbols to your message (leave the AM/PM text in place if you want them to remain in the clock display).

For example, I have mine set to AM- LANW and PM- LANW respectively, because LANW is the name of my company (see Figure 21.8). Because you have only eight characters to work with, you may end up obliterating the display of AM or PM, so you might want to change your time code to 24-hour format. Don't worry about time stamps being messed up in other programs, however. Windows internally uses 24-hour time codes, and even though Outlook Express mail might appear to go out stamped 8:07 LANW, for example, it really goes out with 24-hour time. The options you are setting on the Time tab of the Regional Options really affect only the display.

Because this tag also affects programs that have an "insert time stamp" function, you could use it to your benefit, for example, to track not only when a file was opened or edited, but from what department.

ADMINISTRATOR TOOLS NOT SHOWING UP

Windows XP is designed as an end-user operating system. Thus, most of the system-level management tools are not made readily accessible by being placed in plain sight on the Start menu. Instead, they are all contained within a sub-folder of the Control Panel known as Administrative Tools. Open the Control Panel, click Performance and Maintenance, and choose Administrative Tools to open a folder containing these management tools.

Figure 21.8
You can embed a message in the system clock to identify a machine or operating system.

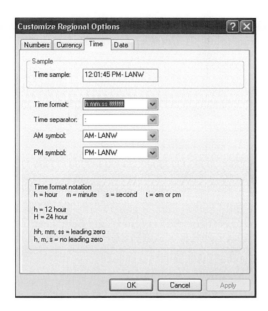

Other than manually creating a shortcut to the Administrative Tools folder, there is no easy way to add this item to the Start menu's top level. Well, that's true as long as you are using the new Luna display styling. If you revert to the Classic Start menu, you'll be able to enable the display of the Administrative Tools item within the Start menu through the Start menu's Properties, Start menu tab, Customize button.

However, there is a bit of a back-road method, which can allow you to gain access to Administrative Tools without having to open the Control Panel first. By setting the Control Panel to Display as a menu (Start menu's Properties, Start menu tab, Customize button, Advanced tab), whenever you select the Control Panel item in the Start menu, it will display a fly-open menu of all the applets it contains, thus offering you quick access to all of the tools there, including Administrative Tools.

CHANGING THE LOCATION OF THE MY DOCUMENTS FOLDER

This is a very cool tip. As you know, many applications default to saving or opening files in the My Documents folder. If you are like me, you employ your own organizational scheme for saving documents and files, which does not include the My Documents element. Having

21

every Save dialog box default to My Documents is a huge annoyance! It's almost enough to make you throw up your hands and surrender to saving your documents where Microsoft wants you to. In fact, that location may be pretty well hidden. In a multi-user system, XP creates the My Documents folder under the user's name, like this:

```
C:\documents and settings\bob\my documents
```

If you're the only person using the computer, this is particularly annoying, since having to "drill down" through those folders every time you want to open a document is a pain. Well, fret no more. In earlier versions of Windows, you had to hack the Registry to change the location of the My Documents folder, but now changing the location is much simpler.

All you have to do is the following:

1. Right-click the My Documents icon on the desktop or through My Computer or Windows Explorer.
2. Choose Properties.
3. Click Move, then select the new destination.

This action doesn't move the original My Documents folder, it just redefines where the My Documents variable actually points to. In other words, it lets you declare another preexisting folder as the default Save As and Open folder. If you already have documents stored in the original location, you'll need to copy or move them to the new location of the My Documents folder.

CASCADING ELEMENTS OFF THE START MENU

Cascading is the ability to expand certain folders right off of the Start menu. These expanded menus are also called fly-open menus. The native Windows XP interface can be configured to add cascading menus for the Control Panel, My Computer, My Documents, My Music, My Pictures, and Network Connections. This is the same feature we discussed earlier to gain direct Start menu access to Administrative Tools.

The process is simple: Just open the Properties for the Start menu (right-click over the Start menu button and then select the Properties command from the pop-up menu). Select the Start Menu tab, click Customize, and then select the Advanced tab. Scroll down the list of Start menu items and change the settings for the desired items to Display as a menu.

VIRTUAL DESKTOP

If you find yourself running out of space on your sole monitor and you've already maxed out the resolution, there is still more room to be had. Cool Desk from ShellToys Inc. brings the acreage of nine virtual desktops to your fingertips. Switching between virtual desktops occurs with a mouse click. You can even move applications from one virtual desktop to another. This simple tool can greatly expand your workspace. Its like having nine monitors stacked on your computer desk.

You can grab this nifty tool from http://www.shelltoys.com/.

AUTOPLAY

AutoPlay is the feature of Windows which automatically launches or plays a CD once it is inserted into the CD-ROM drive. Under Windows XP, you have more control than ever over AutoPlay. By opening the Properties dialog box of a CD-ROM drive from Windows Explorer or My Computer, you'll be able to access the AutoPlay tab. From here, you can define for each type of CD (music files, pictures, video files, mixed content, or music CD), whether to take no action, play, open folder to view files, print, launch slide show, and more.

AUTO SCROLLING WITH A THREE-BUTTON MOUSE

Do you have a three-button mouse and wish you had a wheel mouse to make it easier to scroll your Web pages? Don't bother coveting your neighbor's wheel mouse because Internet Explorer and your three-button mouse can do the next best thing. When you're working in an Internet Explorer window, just click the center mouse button. The cursor changes to a two-headed arrow shape. Now move the mouse away or toward you, and the page scrolls. Click again or click another mouse button, and the scrolling function is terminated.

CUSTOMIZING FOLDER VIEWS

Windows XP offers a wide range of options for customizing how files are displayed through the My Computer and Windows Explorer utilities. The View menu (see Figure 21.9) offers the following controls:

- **Toolbars**—This control is used to display or hide the standard buttons, address bar, and links bar. You can also lock the bars (so stray clicks don't alter your layout) or fully customize the button toolbar.

- **Status bar**—This control enables the display of an information bar at the bottom of the utility which shows object details, file size, free space, and so on.

- **Explorer bar**—This control sets the folder item to be displayed in the right-hand pane. No selection displays the context-sensitive quick access menus of File and Folder Tasks, Other Places, and Details. Selections in this control include: search, favorites, history, contacts, and folders.

- **Views**—This section allows quick change of the view used to display file objects: thumbnails, tiles (default), icons, list, and details.

- **Arrange Icons by**—This command is used to sort file objects by name, size, type, or modification date. There are also settings for show in groups, auto arrange (maximize layout starting from upper left corner), or align to grid.

- **Choose Details**—This command sets the details that appear in ToolTips, details, and Tile view. The defaults are name, size, type, and modification date. Among the 33 options included are attributes, owner, subject, company, and file version.

- **Customize this Folder**—This command is used to define custom attributes for the selected folder (see next section).

21

Figure 21.9
The View menu of
Windows Explorer.

Figure 21.9
The View menu of
Windows Explorer.

- **Go to**—This menu is used to navigate back, forward, up one level, to the home page, or to recently visited locations.

CUSTOMIZE THIS FOLDER

If you have a complex organizational structure to your personal files, you might find this feature quite intriguing. Customizing folders allows you to select from six templates designed for a specific type of file (document, image, or music) or collection of files (all, one artist, one album). These templates set how the contents of these folders are displayed as well as the context for the menu commands. Additionally, you can define a custom image for thumbnails and a unique icon for the folder. All these customizations can help you keep track of what you've got stored where.

SETTING FOLDER OPTIONS

Folder Options should be seen as more of a superset of controls over all folders on a system, while folder customization is on an individual or parent and sub-folder basis. Folder Options is a Control Panel applet that can also be accessed from the Tools menu of My Computer and Windows Explorer. This applet is used to set a wide range of file system features.

The General tab of the Folder Options dialog box defines whether common tasks are shown in folders or whether only classic Windows folders are displayed; whether folders are opened in the same or a new window; and whether single-clicks or double-clicks are used to open items. If you make changes to this tab, you can always return to the default by clicking the Restore Defaults button.

NOTE

> The common tasks view or the view which displays the File and Folder Tasks, Other Places, and Details context panels is an interesting and useful feature of Windows XP. However, in the releases since Beta 2 of Windows XP, the common tasks pane disappears whenever you select any other item from View menu's Explorer Bar submenu. I find this highly frustrating because I want both the common tasks pane and the Folders pane. Perhaps someday Microsoft will release an update to Windows XP that re-enables this functionality. So far, even in SP-2 this is not the case.

The View tab (see Figure 21.10) performs two major functions—folder view management and advanced settings management. For folder view management, all folders can be reset to their default views, or the currently selected folder's view can be applied to all folders. Advanced settings management contains a long checklist of settings.

Figure 21.10
The View tab of
Folder Options.

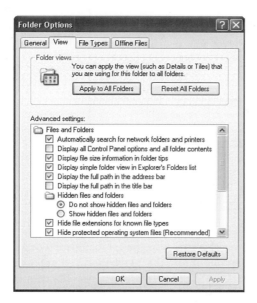

Because I like seeing every file on my system, I always enable Show hidden files and folders, and disable the Hide file extensions and Hide protected OS files. You need to make your own choice on what you want the OS to show you and hide from you. If you want to return to the defaults, just click the Restore Defaults button.

NOTE

> If you've tried to delete a folder that looked like it was empty but an error message states the folder still contains files, you are probably dealing with hidden files. To see what's not being shown, go change the Hidden files and folders Advanced setting. I've run into this issue a few times with downloaded applications that must be extracted to a temporary folder before being installed. They sometimes include files pre-marked as hidden.

The File Types tab (see Figure 21.11) is where the registration of file extensions or file types is managed. All registered file types are listed. Because changing a file type is just defining which application is used to open or view the file type, you can alter these settings as you see fit. The Advanced button is used to manipulate more advanced features of file type registration, such as displayed file type name, icon, and actions (such as open, play, display, install, and so on). New file types can be created manually. Existing file types can be deleted. In most cases, the registration of file types is managed by the OS and by applications as they are installed.

Figure 21.11
The File Types tab of Folder Options.

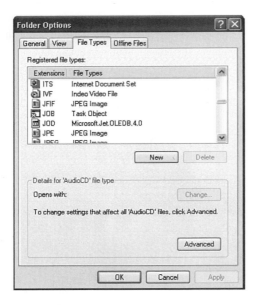

In some instances you'll discover that one file type can be opened or accessed by more than one application. And nine times out of ten, the application you don't want will be the one launched when you double-click on the file. To associate the file with the tool of your choice, modify the file type's application association through the Change button.

If you want to learn more about file type management, consult the Windows XP Resource Kit.

The Offline Files tab configures the caching of network content on the local system in order to maintain access to cached files while disconnected. This feature is discussed in Part IV of this book.

21

CONFIGURING THE RECYCLE BIN

The Recycle Bin holds recently deleted files to provide you with a reasonable opportunity to recover them. As we talked about in Chapter 4, the Recycle Bin will hold the last deleted files that fit within its size restriction. That restriction by default is 10% of the drive space for each partition or volume on the system. However, you can and should customize the Recycle Bin for your specific needs.

The Recycle Bin's Properties dialog box (accessed by right-clicking over the icon, and then selecting Properties) has a Global tab and a tab for each partition/volume on the system. The Global tab offers a control that allows you to configure your drives independently or to use one setting for all drives (the default). If you've never deleted a file by mistake and don't think you ever will, you can elect to delete files immediately without storing them in the Recycle Bin. If you'd rather just limit how much space Windows uses to store deleted files, you can set a maximum size for the Recycle Bin as a percentage of drive space. A final control enables a deletion confirmation dialog box—I think this should be left enabled.

Remember, if you select to configure the properties for each drive independently, you must use the provided tabs labeled for each drive on your system. Each drive will display the size of the drive and the space reserved for the Recycle Bin along with the other controls we just discussed.

When limiting the amount of space to use for deleted files, the default percentage is 10%. This is usually a good size, but as hard disk sizes increase, you may want to reduce this to 5%. Keep in mind that files moved to the Recycle Bin are not actually deleted. Instead, their path information is removed from the normal interfaces and moved into the Recycle Bin. Deleted files still remain on the drive exactly where they were before the deletion operation. This means they take up space on the drive. So, if you leave the default percentage setting at 10% on a 20GB hard drive, you can have up to 2GB of deleted files still sitting on the drive slowing down the drive's seek time.

TUNING VISUAL EFFECTS

In addition to the controls we've already mentioned in the Display applet, there are additional visual effect controls in the System applet from the Control Panel. On the System applet's Advanced tab, click on the Settings button in the Performance area. This opens the Performance Options dialog box. The Visual Effects tab (see Figure 21.12) can be set to allow Windows to manage effects, set for best appearance, set for best performance, or set your own custom settings.

When Custom settings is selected, you can then enable or disable a long list of effects. These effects include animate resizing of windows, fade ToolTips, show shadows under menus, and use visual styles on windows and buttons.

Unless your system is low on physical RAM, uses an old non-AGP video card, or uses a video card with less than 8MB of native RAM, there is little need to modify the default settings for these controls in respect to performance. However, if you think no shadows or no animation looks better, you can customize the look and feel of the user environment all you want.

21

Figure 21.12
The Visual Effects tab of Performance Options.

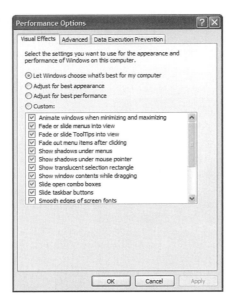

TROUBLESHOOTING

REDUCING SCREEN FLICKER

My CRT is flickering and annoying me. How can I change it?

Increase the refresh rate of the display subsystem to at least 70Hz. Right-click the desktop, choose Properties, and then choose Settings, Advanced, Monitor. Finally, change the refresh rate.

WHERE DID THOSE ICONS GO?

I changed the screen resolution, and now I can't find items off the edge of the screen and I have windows I can't close.

You might have this problem when you switch to a lower resolution from a higher one. Theoretically, Windows is good about relocating desktop icons, but some applications might not do the same. For example, the small AOL Instant Messenger dialog can be off the edge of the screen somewhere, and when it is, you can't get to it. Closing and rerunning the program doesn't help. One trick is to switch to the application by pressing Alt+Tab. Then press Alt+spacebar, and press M. This key combination invokes the Move command for the window. Then you can use the arrow keys on the keyboard to move the window (typically to the left and/or up). When you have the title bar of the window in view, press Enter. If this trick doesn't work, switch back to the previous higher resolution, reposition the application window in question closer to the upper-left corner of the screen, and then switch back to the lower resolution. It may help to remember that your screen is always decreased or increased in size starting from the lower-right corner and moving up or down diagonally.

What Does That Say?

I want to use an external TV monitor, but the output text is illegible.

Some video cards and laptops can be plugged into a TV monitor or regular TV that has video input. But displaying computer output on a TV monitor is problematic for a couple of reasons. For starters, some video display cards don't let you run the TV at anything higher than 640x480 resolution. Also, TV sets (as opposed to professional TV monitors) often *overscan*, pushing the edges of the image off the edge of the screen. The following are a few points to remember when you're using a TV or video projector; whether you're doing presentations, playing games, or giving your eyes a break by moving your focal plane back a bit:

- If your computer and TV have "S" (Super VHS) inputs, use them. They increase the clarity a bit. Don't expect miracles, though. If you're using a video projector and the computer and projector have Digital Video Interface (DVI) connectors, use those. The image should be much clearer.
- Use Display Properties to switch to 640x480 resolution.
- Check to see whether your Display Properties dialog has buttons to center the image on the TV. It's most likely off center or needs resizing when you first try it. Some drivers, such as those from ATI, have advanced properties for fine-tuning TV display.
- Your application may have a "zoom" control for easily increasing the size of text onscreen, without the hassle of reformatting the entire document. MS Office tools such as Excel and Word, for example, have such a feature. Try bumping up the zoom size to increase legibility.

Single- or Double-Click?

I seem to accidentally run programs and open documents with a slip of the finger.

You probably have Single-Click selection turned on. As a result, one click (or tap, if you're using a touch pad) runs the program or opens the document that is highlighted. Change to Double-Click selection mode by opening a folder window, choosing Tools, Folder Options, and selecting Double Click to Open an Item.

Uh-Oh, My Monitor Died

I changed my resolution or refresh rate, and now the screen is blank.

Normally, you shouldn't have this problem because Windows XP asks you to confirm that a screen resolution works properly and switches back to the previous resolution if you don't confirm. If somehow you changed color depth and resolution, and the system is stuck with a blank screen, you can reboot, press F8 during boot, and choose Safe Mode. Access the Device Manager on the Hardware tab of the System applet. The System applet is accessed either through the Control Panel or by opening the Properties dialog for My Computer. Select the video display, and reset the properties to what the computer was running at before the change. Be sure to reset both the screen resolution *and* the color depth. In the worst case scenario, start with 640x480 and 16 colors. After you've booted successfully, then right-click the desktop, choose Properties, click Settings, and increase the settings one step at a time. Don't change resolution *and* color depth at the same time, though. Increase one first and then the other.

MOVING IN SLOW MOTION

I increased the resolution, but now the screen updates slowly when I drag windows around.

Unless you're doing high-resolution photographic-quality work, you don't need the high-resolution 24-bit or 32-bit color depth settings. These settings just serve to slow down screen redraws when you move windows about. On the Settings tab of the Display Properties dialog, try dropping to 16-bit color or even 256 colors, and enjoy the speed increase.

BLURRY IMAGES IN LCD

I switched to an LCD screen, and the image is blurrier than I expected.

Unlike CRTs, LCDs do not benefit from higher refresh rates. Don't try to use anything above a 60Hz refresh rate for an LCD monitor. Also, check the LCD monitor's internal settings (check its manual) for a "phase adjustment" or focus adjustment to help clear up fuzziness on small text.

STRETCHED A BIT THIN

I set up a picture for my desktop wallpaper, but it looks blocky.

You're stretching a small bitmap. Either use a larger image, or turn off the Stretch setting for the image. See the Display Properties, Background, Picture Display option.

CONFIGURATION VIA CONTROL PANEL APPLETS

In this chapter

22

SIZING UP THE CONTROL PANEL

As most experienced Windows users know, the Control Panel is the central location for making systemwide modifications to everything from accessibility options to user profiles. Microsoft has moved some features around in Windows XP from where you might expect them from your experience with Windows 2000, NT, 98, and so on. Most of these movements have resulted in new or expanded applets in the Control Panel. So, before throwing up your hands in frustration, check there (and Table 22.1 in the next section). The Help system also has a "Where is it now?" feature, which will help you locate seemingly vanished items.

Not all the settings the Control Panel handles are pivotal to effective or reliable operation of the system. In fact, many of the adjustments you can make from the Control Panel applets are interface improvements rather than related to system reliability and functionality. For example, the Display applet, among other things, can be used to make Windows a little easier to use or tolerate. Other applets are more imperative, such as applets for setting user rights, installing new hardware, or running system diagnostics.

The preference settings you make via the Control Panel applets are stored in the Registry. Some are systemwide, whereas others are made on a per-user basis and go into effect when you log in. Many Control Panel applets can be accessed through other utilities. For example, Printers and Faxes can be added to your Start menu, the Display applet can be accessed by right-clicking the desktop and clicking Properties, Folder Options can be accessed through the Tools menu of My Computer and Windows Explorer, and Internet Options can be accessed through Internet Explorer's Tools menu. Although the paths may be multifarious, the results are the same; you usually end up running a Control Panel extension (files with .CPL extensions) to do your bidding.

Keep in mind that you must have high-level permissions to modify many of the settings in the Control Panel. User-level settings such as display appearances are not a big deal. However, system-wide settings such as addition and removal of hardware are governed by the security monitor, and you must have the requisite administrator permissions to successfully make modifications. For information on user permissions, see Chapter 25, "Managing Users."

TIP

> As you learned in Chapter 4, "Using the Windows XP Interface," you can opt to "expand" the Control Panel, making the applets appear in a fly-out window (by choosing Start, Control Panel), thus allowing you to avoid opening the whole Control Panel as a window. Using this fly-out window is worthwhile if you use the Control Panel a lot. To make this your default setting, right-click the Start menu and select Properties. In the dialog box that appears, click Customize, select the Advanced Tab, and then select the Display As a Menu radio button under Control Panel in the list of Start menu items.
>
> If you use a particular applet a lot, you can drag it into the Start menu or the Quick Launch bar for even faster access.

22

Not all the Control Panel settings are discussed in detail in this chapter. Because a few of the Control Panel options pertain to other topics, such as networking or printing, or fall under the umbrella of system management, performance tweaking, or system applications, you'll find them in later chapters. Table 22.2, in the next section, lists each applet and where to look in this book for coverage of those not discussed here. Also, I won't bore you by covering each and every option in the dialog boxes. Many of the settings are intuitively obvious.

OPENING THE CONTROL PANEL

One of the most common ways to access the Control Panel is to click Start, Control Panel. But there are several other ways, such as using the Control Panel link in the Other Places quick access menu or, in Windows Explorer folder view, clicking on the Control Panel sub-element of My Computer. If you have opted to expand the Control Panel in your Start menu, you can still right-click over the Control Panel name and select Open from the pop-up menu to open the regular Control Panel window.

THE NEW CONTROL PANEL

No matter how you get there, the Control Panel in Windows XP is displayed by default in category view. Category view organizes the most commonly accessed functions of Control Panel applets into groups. In Windows XP, the Category view is the default method of navigating the Control Panel applets. If you are new to configuring a Windows OS, the Category view offers a natural language guide to finding the right location to make an intended change. Within each category is a list of tasks and related Control Panel icons. As you can see from Figure 22.1, this view is much different from the Control Panel that appeared in previous versions of Windows (which is now referred to as the Classic view).

Selecting a task or its icon in Category view takes you to another Control Panel screen containing either a more specific breakdown of tasks you can select or a screen where the configuration setting described by the selected task must be performed (see Figure 22.2).

If you need to make a change within the category but the task is not listed in the task list, you can open one of the offered Control Panel icons to open the applet and find the correct tab for your desired setting change.

BREAKING DOWN THE CATEGORY VIEW

There are ten categories in the category view. Tables 22.1 through 22.8 list the tasks for each category, as well as the applet tab or application the task opens. Table 22.9 lists the Control Panel icons displayed within or related to a category.

NOTE

> The Add or Remove Programs category does not display a task list; instead it opens the Add or Remove Programs applet directly. The User Accounts category opens the multi-function task User Accounts utility. Please see Chapter 26, "Managing the Hard Disk," for a discussion of this tool.

Figure 22.1
The Control Panel in the default Category view (top), and in the Classic view (bottom).

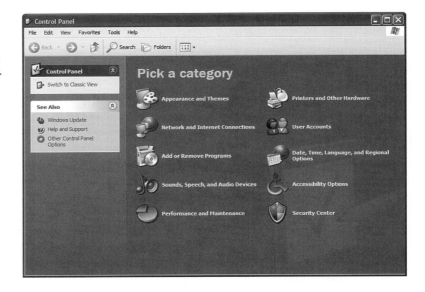

More tasks from which to choose

Figure 22.2
Clicking the Appearance and Themes category takes you to this screen.

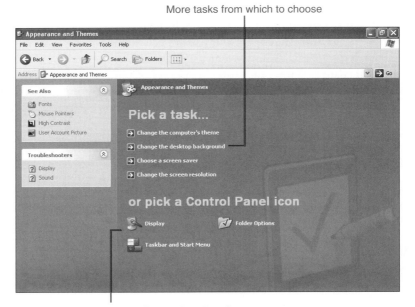

These icons open specific Control Panel applets

TABLE 22.1   APPEARANCE AND THEMES CATEGORY VIEW

Task	Applet	Tab
Change the computer's theme	Display	Themes
Change the desktop background	Display	Desktop
Choose a screen saver	Display	Screen Saver
Change the screen resolution	Display	Settings

TABLE 22.2   NETWORK AND INTERNET CONNECTIONS CATEGORY VIEW

Task	Applet	Tab/Wizard
Set up or change your Internet connection	Internet Options	Connection
Create a connection to the network at your workplace	Network Connections	New Connection
Set up or change your home or small office network	Network Connections	Network Setup
Change Windows Firewall	Windows Firewall	General Settings

TABLE 22.3   SOUNDS, SPEECH, AND AUDIO DEVICES CATEGORY VIEW

Task	Applet	Tab
Adjust the system volume	Sounds and Audio Devices	Volume
Change the sound scheme	Sounds and Audio Devices	Sounds
Change the speaker settings	Sounds and Audio Devices	Volume

TABLE 22.4   PERFORMANCE AND MAINTENANCE CATEGORY VIEW

Task	Applet	Tab
See basic information about your computer	System	General
Adjust visual effects	Performance Options	Visual Effects
Free up space on your hard disk	Disk Cleanup	(application)
Back up your data	Backup or Restore Wizard	(application)
Rearrange items on your hard disk to make programs run faster	Disk Defragmenter	(application)

TABLE 22.5   PRINTERS AND OTHER HARDWARE CATEGORY VIEW

Task	Applet	Wizard
View installed printers or fax printers	Printers and Faxes	(none)
Add a printer Printer	Printers and Faxes	Add

TABLE 22.6   DATE, TIME, LANGUAGE, AND REGIONAL OPTIONS CATEGORY VIEW

Task	Applet	Tab
Change the date and time	Date and Time	Date & Time
Change the format of numbers, dates, and times	Regional and Language Options	Regional Options
Add other languages	Regional and Language Options	Languages

TABLE 22.7   ACCESSIBILITY OPTIONS CATEGORY VIEW

Task	Applet	Tab
Adjust the contrast for text and colors on your screen	Accessibility Options	Display
Configure Windows to work for your vision, hearing, and mobility needs	Accessibility Options	(wizard)

TABLE 22.8   SECURITY CENTER CATEGORY VIEW

Task	Applet	Tab
Turn Firewall on/off	Windows	General Firewall
Automatic Updates on/off	System	Automatic Updates
Turn virus protection on/off	Security Center	

TABLE 22.9   CONTROL PANEL ICONS WITHIN CATEGORIES

Category Wizard	Related Applets
Appearance and Themes Folder	Taskbar and Start menu, Options, Display
Network and Internet Connections	Network Connections, Internet Options
Add or Remove Programs	Add or Remove Programs
Sounds, Speech, and Audio Devices	Sounds and Audio Devices, Speech

Category Wizard	Related Applets
Performance and Maintenance Scheduled	Administrative Tools, Tasks, Power Options, System
Printers and Other Hardware	Printers and Faxes, Scanners and Cameras, Game Controllers, Mouse, Keyboard, Phone and Modem Options
User Accounts	User Accounts
Date, Time, Language, and Regional Options	Regional and Language Options, Date and Time
Accessibility Options	Accessibility Options
Security Center	Security Center

As you can see, the category view offers an alternate route to the Control Panel applets and several other useful utilities. Windows XP defaults to category view, so it is important to be familiar with how to navigate through this new mechanism.

For those who prefer the old Control Panel display, Windows XP does offer a classic view where all the applets are displayed as they were in previous versions of Windows (refer to Figure 22.1). To access the Classic view, click on the Switch to Classic View command in the Quick List to the left the categories within Control Panel. Then, to return to the category view, click on the Switch to Category View command in the Quick List.

As you can see, Windows XP often offers multiple means to access a control, setting, application, or display of information. Understanding the default paths (such as with Category View of the Control Panel) and the alternates (such as the Classic View of the Control Panel or direct access through an object's Properties), will aid you in extracting the most productivity out of the OS possible.

WHAT SHOULD YOU USE?

Working with the Control Panel in Category view may simplify access to common configuration controls. However, not all of the controls for Windows XP can be accessed through category view (at least not directly). So, in order to provide an exhaustive discussion of the applets, this chapter focuses on reviewing each applet as listed in the Classic View. If you want to use the Category view, refer to the tables we just presented.

Table 22.10 shows a list of all the standard Control Panel applets and what they accomplish. Your Control Panel may include other applets which are installed by other products from Microsoft and third parties. Following the table, I'll cover each of the included applets (the ones not covered in other chapters) in alphabetical order.

TABLE 22.10   CONTROL PANEL APPLETS

Applet	Description
Accessibility Options	Sets keyboard, mouse, sound, display, and other options for increasing ease of use by those who are visually, aurally, or motor impaired.
Add Hardware	Installs or troubleshoots a wide variety of hardware devices such as sound, video, CD-ROM, hard and floppy disk controllers, SCSI controllers, display adapters, keyboard, mouse, and ports.
	Installation of printers is covered in Chapter 6, "Printing and Faxing."
Add or Remove Programs	Adds, removes, or modifies applications or Windows XP components from Microsoft or a third-party. It supports remote application installation over the LAN.
Administrative Tools	Provides shortcuts to the administrative tools—Component Services, Computer Management, ODBC settings, Event Viewer, Local Security Policy, Performance, and Services. Administrative Tools is covered in Chapter 24, "System Utilities." Component Services are not covered in this book.
Date and Time	Sets the current date, time, and time zone for the computer. It can also synchronize system time with an Internet time server.
Display	Sets colors of various parts of Windows display elements, as well as other display-related adjustments, such as desktop background, screen saver, display driver, screen color depth and resolution, refresh rate, energy-saving modes, and color schemes or themes.
	The Display applet is covered in detail in Chapter 21, "Tweaking the GUI."
Folder Options	Sets systemwide folder view options, file associations, and offline files.
	The Folder Options applet is covered in detail in Chapter 21.
Fonts	Adds and deletes typefaces, and displays examples of system-installed typefaces for screen display and printer output.
Game Controllers	Adds, removes, and configures game controller hardware, such as joysticks and gamepads.
Internet Options	Sets Internet Explorer options.
	Internet Options are covered in Chapter 9, "Browsing the World Wide Web with Internet Explorer."
Keyboard	Sets key repeat rate, cursor blink rate, language of your keyboard, keyboard type, and drivers, and includes keyboard troubleshooting wizards.

22

Applet	Description
Mouse	Alters mouse properties such as motion speed, double-click, button orientation, cursor shapes, and other proprietary settings dependent on your mouse driver.
Network Connections	Manages all network connections, including LAN, dial-up, WAN, and VPN. Networking components (clients, services, and protocols) are configured. These connections are covered throughout Part IV, "Networking."
Phone and Modem Options	Adds, removes, and sets the properties of the modem(s) connected to your system. Using this applet, you can declare dialing rules (long-distance numbers, call waiting, credit card calling, and so on). You also can add and remove telephony drivers. Installing and configuring a modem are covered in Chapter 8, "Internet and TCP/IP Connection Options." The other features of this applet are discussed here.
Power Options	Provides options for setting the Advanced Power Management (APM) and Advanced Configuration and Power Management (ACPM) functions. Using this applet, you can set timeouts for monitor, hard disk, system standby, and hibernation. The Power Options applet is covered in detail in Chapter 21.
Printers and Faxes	Adds, modifies, removes, and manages printer and fax devices. Using this applet, you can manage the print queue for each printer and enable direct faxing from applications. The Printers and Faxes applet is covered in Chapter 6.
Regional and Language Options	Sets how Windows displays times, dates, numbers, and currency through region/country settings and language preferences.
Scanners and Cameras	Adds, removes, sets properties for, and troubleshoots scanners and digital cameras.
Scheduled Tasks	Sets up automatic execution of applications, utilities, disk cleanup, and so on. Task scheduling is covered in Chapter 24.
Security Center	(New applet as of XP Service Pack 2) A central location for control of Windows Firewall, Automatic Updates, and antivirus programs (if you have one installed). Firewall is covered in Chapter 19, "Network Security." Automatic Updates are covered in Chapter 24.
Sound and Audio Devices	Assigns sounds to system events and manages sound devices.
Speech	Sets voice options for text-to-speech translation.

continues

TABLE 22.10   CONTINUED

Applet	Description
System	Examines and changes your identification (workgroup name, domain name, computer name), installed devices, amount of RAM, type of processor, and so on. Using this applet, you can add, disable, and remove specific devices using the Device Manager; set up hardware profiles; set up user profiles; optimize some parameters of system performance; set environment variables; and set emergency startup options.
	The use of the System applet is rather complex and thus is partially covered in this chapter and partially in Chapter 24.
Taskbar and Start Menu	Sets the properties for the taskbar and Start menu.
	This was covered in Chapters 4 and 21.
Users Accounts	Adds, deletes, or alters users. Using this applet, you can assign groups, manage passwords, and set logon mode.
	Passwords and security are covered in Chapter 25.
Windows Firewall	Use this applet to turn on and off and fine-tune the firewall that protects your computer from uninvited invasion from the Internet. See the section "Security Center," later in this chapter, as well as the firewall discussion in Chapter 19.
Wireless Network Setup	This applet makes setting up a wireless network much easier than before SP-2. See Chapter 17, "Windows Unplugged: Remote and Mobile Networking."

TIP

Windows NT 4 and 9x included a PCMCIA applet in the Control Panel. That applet was dropped in Windows 2000 and was not included in Windows XP. It didn't do much anyway, other than let you control whether PC cards beeped when installed and removed. If your system has PC card slot services installed, the system tray contains an icon for PC card control and for starting and stopping PC card devices. See Chapter 23, "Maintaining and Optimizing System Performance," for details.

NOTE

Many Control Panel dialog boxes have a question mark button in their upper-right corners. You can click this button and then click an item in the dialog box that you have a question about. Windows then shows some relevant explanation about the item.

In those dialog boxes where no question mark appears in the title bar, click F1 to open the Help system. The Help window will include information relevant to the applet in use.

ACCESSIBILITY OPTIONS

Microsoft has made a point of increasing computer accessibility for people who are physically challenged in one way or another. Over the last half decade, Microsoft has increasingly included accessibility options in its operating systems, with features that allow many handicapped people to use Windows without major machine or software modifications.

Many people have difficulty seeing characters on the screen, and others have trouble typing on the keyboard or controlling the mouse. People who are partially paralyzed or who have muscle-coordination problems have been at a disadvantage with computers for a long time. Now, with these accessibility options, the playing field is being leveled at least somewhat. Even if you are not disabled, some of the Accessibility options may prove useful for you.

Accessibility options are broken down into several categories, with their respective tabs: Keyboard, Sounds, Display, Mouse, and a few others on the General tab.

ACCESSIBILITY KEYBOARD SETTINGS

The keyboard settings deal with such problems as accidentally repeating keys or pressing combinations of keys. These options fall into three categories: *Sticky keys*, *Filter keys*, and *Toggle keys*.

Sticky keys are settings that, in effect, stay "down" when you press them once. They are good for controlling the function of the Alt, Ctrl, and Shift keys if you have trouble pressing two keys at the same time. To use them, set the Sticky keys option on; then choose the sub-options as you see fit. For some users, the shortcut of pressing the Shift key five times is a good way to activate Sticky keys. If you turn on this activation method, note that pressing the Shift key five times again turns off Sticky keys. This trick isn't explained clearly in the dialogs. Also, if you choose the Press Modifier Key Twice to Lock option, that means you press, for example, Shift twice to lock it. You can then press Shift twice again to unlock it.

Filter keys let you "filter" (remove) accidental repeated keystrokes in case you have trouble pressing a key cleanly once and letting it up. This feature prevents you from typing multiple keystrokes. The shortcut key for turning on this feature works like the one for Sticky keys; it's a toggle.

TIP

> Filter keys, when activated, can make it seem that your keyboard has ceased working unless you are very deliberate with keypresses. You have to press a key and keep it down for several seconds for the key to register. If you activate this setting and want to turn it off, the easiest solution is to use the mouse to run or switch to the Control Panel (via the taskbar), run the Accessibility Options applet, turn off Filter Keys, and click Apply or OK.

The Toggle keys option, when turned on, sounds a high-pitched tone when Caps Lock, Scroll Lock, and Num Lock keys are activated and a low-pitched tone when they're turned off again.

Each of these three keyboard features can be used independently or together. Note that a slowdown in performance occurs at the keyboard if sounds are used, since the sound is generated by playing a WAV file that briefly eats up your system resources. Processing of key-presses doesn't commence until after the keyboard sound finishes, which can result in jerky performance.

When Sticky keys or Filter keys are turned on, a symbol appears in the system tray. The Sticky keys feature is indicated by the three small boxes, representative of the Ctrl, Alt, and Shift keys. The Filter keys feature is represented by the stopwatch, which is representative of the different key timing that goes into effect when the option is enabled.

ACCESSIBILITY SOUND SETTINGS

The two Accessibility sound settings—Sound Sentry and ShowSounds—are for those with hearing impairments. Instead of playing a sound when an error message or other event that causes a sound occurs, some type of visual display appears onscreen.

With Sound Sentry, a portion of the normal Windows screen blinks, typically the window or application that is generating the error. With ShowSounds turned on a text caption or special icon will pop up over a window or dialog box when a sound is played. The information in the pop-up window will inform you of the sound played and whether the audio clue as a warning, error, and so on.

If you choose Sound Sentry, you have a choice of the visual warning to use. The options are offered in a pull-down list, which includes Flash active caption bar, Flash active windows, and Flash desktop. Typically, you'll want the window of the application or at least its title bar to flash. Don't make the desktop flash because it won't indicate which program is producing the warning.

TIP

> Some programs are finicky about the sound options, especially ShowSounds. If they're not programmed correctly, they don't display a sound. Think of it like closed captioning for TV. Not all shows have it.

ACCESSIBILITY DISPLAY SETTINGS

Special display settings in the Accessibility Options applet increase the screen contrast by altering the display scheme. Using this applet really is just an easy way to set the display color scheme and font selection for easier reading, just as you could do from the Display applet, as discussed in Chapter 21. The big plus of setting the contrast here is that you can quickly call it up with a shortcut key combination when you need it. Just press Left-Alt, Left-Shift, Prnt Scrn, and the settings go into effect. I have found this feature useful for when my eyes are tired or in imperfect lighting situations. Figure 22.3 shows the effect it had while I was writing this chapter.

Figure 22.3
The effect of turning on the default high-contrast setting.

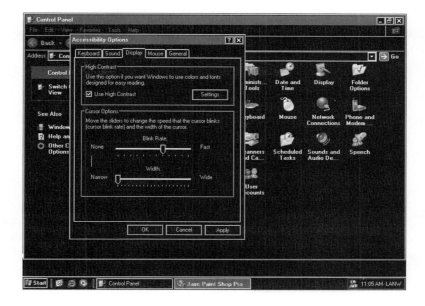

TIP

You get to select which predefined color scheme (both Windows provided and ones you've created through the Display applet) will be used as the high contrast scheme. It's easier to observe the look of the schemes using the Display applet than in the Accessibility Options applet. Do it there, and then decide which one you like best. Then come back to the Accessibility dialog box and make your choice.

ACCESSIBILITY MOUSE SETTINGS

Using the Mouse Settings tab, you can control the mouse with the keypad, in case you have problems controlling your mouse's movements. This feature can bail you out in case your mouse dies for some reason, too, or if you simply don't like using the mouse. As is covered in Chapter 4, you can execute many Windows and Windows application commands using the keyboard shortcut keys. But sometimes an application still responds only to mouse movements and clicks. Graphics programs are a case in point. When you use this Accessibility option, your arrow keys do double duty, acting like pointer control keys.

To use this option, simply turn on Mouse Keys from the dialog box, and apply the change. Then, to activate the keys, press Left-Alt, Left-Shift, and Num Lock at the same time. The system tray should show a new icon. If the icon has a red line through it, Mouse keys are disabled, so press the Num Lock key to enable them.

Now you can move the pointer around the screen using the arrow keys on the numeric number pad. If you're using a laptop, you'll have to consult its manual to determine how to activate the numeric keypad. The normal arrow keys won't cut it.

22

Click the Settings button if you need to adjust the speed settings for the arrow keys. Turn on the Ctrl and Shift options for speeding up or slowing down the mouse, assuming you can press two keys simultaneously. This setting really speeds things up.

If you adjust the configuration on the Settings dialog box, you have to click OK and then click Apply before the changes register. Then you can go back and adjust as necessary.

OTHER ACCESSIBILITY SETTINGS (GENERAL TAB)

The final Accessibility tab is General, which is divided into four sections, each of which is described in Table 22.11.

TABLE 22.11   OTHER ACCESSIBILITY SETTINGS

Setting	Description
Automatic Reset	If multiple people are using the same computer, it's a good idea to have the Accessibility features time out if they're not used for a while. If you turn off this option, the settings stay in operation until you manually turn them off, even surviving reboots.
Notification	This setting determines how you're alerted to a feature being turned on or off. By default, a little dialog box appears, but you can change it to a sound.
Serial Key Devices	You can opt to use special input devices designed for the disabled. Just connect such a device to a free serial port, and choose the port (COM1 through COM4) and baud rate.
Administrative Options	The first option applies your Accessibility settings (such as high contrast, and so on) to the *logon deskto*p. The logon desktop is what you see when a user is logging on or when you press Ctrl+Alt+Del. It is a different desktop than the user desktop. If you choose this option, all users of the machine have the benefit (or annoyance) of seeing the settings when they are logging on. The second option, when activated, copies the current Accessibility settings for each new user an administrator adds to the computer.

ADD HARDWARE

The Add Hardware applet is used to install new devices as well as troubleshoot hardware-related problems. The ability to disable or remove hardware devices has been relegated to the Device Manager (see the System applet later this chapter).

In general, Windows XP detects new hardware during bootup. If drivers are not located automatically (typically only for non-Plug-and-Play devices), you'll be prompted for a location to search (such as floppy, CD, or the Windows Update site). Once drivers are located, they are installed and the device is activated. In some cases, you'll be prompted to reboot the system for the new hardware to be fully functional. Sorry, even under Windows XP hardware level device drivers often require a reboot. Think of it as changing a rung on the ladder you are climbing; it's always a good idea to step off of it while the repair is being made.

The Add Hardware applet is for use when the manufacturer does not supply an installation tool and when the installed device is not automatically detected during bootup. If you meet these criteria, you can use the Add Hardware applet to install the device drivers for your new equipment.

When you first launch the applet, it attempts to locate new hardware by performing a system scan for yet unidentified devices. If none are found, you'll be asked if the hardware has already been installed or is it still outside the computer (in other words, not installed). If you select that the hardware is not yet installed, the wizard informs you that you must install the hardware to continue with the installation. I always knew Microsoft could develop a sense of humor.

TIP

> The System applet is used to fine-tune device settings (such as IRQ and port) and updating devices and drivers. The Add Hardware applet is only for adding hardware. Also, note that there are other locations throughout Windows for installing some devices, such as printers—which can be installed from the Printers folder—or modems—which can be installed from Phone and Modem Options—even though the effect is the same as using this applet.

It is always a very good idea to read the manufacturer supplied manual for installation and operational procedures. If none were provided, check the vendor's Web site. If you still can't find any guides for installation, go ahead and try the Add Hardware applet.

It's always a good idea to save your work and stop any applications when performing driver installations or upgrades, or when making configuration changes to hardware. It is possible for a new driver to crash the system, but under Windows XP this is a rare occurrence.

For non-Plug and Play hardware or for Plug and Play stuff that, for some reason, isn't detected or doesn't install automatically, you need to run the applet. The typical scenario is as follows:

1. Launch the Add Hardware applet.
2. Click Next. A search is performed for new hardware.
3. If none are found, you are asked whether the hardware is already installed. If not, you'll be asked to install the hardware in order to proceed.
4. A list of installed hardware is presented. To install new equipment, scroll down and select Add a new hardware device. Otherwise, select an existing item to troubleshoot. Click Next.

22

5. If you elected to troubleshoot an existing item, you'll see a status report and a message stating that clicking Finish will launch the troubleshooter for this device.

6. If you selected the Add a new hardware device item, you'll be asked where the system should search again for the device, or you may manually select the device from a list.

7. There is only a slight chance that the second automated search will detect the new device. In most cases, you'll have to proceed with the manual method.

8. The manual installation method requests that you select a general type of hardware or the Show All Devices item. Click Next.

9. A list of manufacturers and device models is displayed. If your product is listed, select it, and then click Next. Otherwise, click the Have Disk button.

10. The Have Disk button opens a dialog box where you provide the path to the new device drivers.

11. From this point you'll need to follow the prompts as they appear, because each type of device has different requirements. Some need no additional settings while others require the defining of ports, IRQs, and so on. You may also be prompted to provide the Windows XP distribution CD, so keep it handy.

TIP

> In some cases, you are given the option of adjusting settings after the hardware is installed and possibly adjusting your hardware to match. (Some legacy cards have hardware settings [via dip switches or jumpers] or software adjustments that can be made to them to control the I/O port, DMA address, and so forth.) You may be told which settings to use in order to avoid conflicts with other hardware in the system.
>
> If, for some reason, you don't want to use the settings the wizard suggests, you can manually set your own settings. You can do so via the Device Manager (from the System applet). See "System: Device Manager" later in this chapter for coverage of the Device Manager.

CAUTION

> In general, be cautious about configuring resource settings manually. When you change settings manually, the settings become fixed, and Windows XP's built-in device contention resolution is less likely to work. Also, if you install too many devices with manually configured settings, you might not be able to install new Plug and Play devices because no more settings are available. In the worst-case scenario, the system might not even boot if conflicts occur with primary hardware devices such as hard disk controllers or video cards. If you decide to use manual configuration, make sure you know what you're doing, and have in hand the specs for the hardware in question.

In cases in which the wizard detects a conflict, you are alerted upon finishing the wizard. You then have the option of bailing or continuing despite the conflict. You could also back up and choose a different model of hardware, one you think is compatible with what you're attempting to install.

ADD OR REMOVE PROGRAMS

As you know, many programs come with their own installation (Setup) programs that handle all the details of installation, such as file copying, making Registry additions, making file associations, and adding items to the Start menus. There are an ever growing number of applications which even provide their own uninstall routine which appears as a unique icon within their Start menu folder. You'll rarely add programs through the Add or Remove Programs applet. Most of what you'll use this applet for is to remove applications or portions thereof when a dedicated tool is not provided by the vendor.

CHANGE OR REMOVE PROGRAMS

You've probably noticed that not all programs show up in the Add or Remove Programs applet. They don't appear because only programs complying with the 32-bit Windows API standard for installation get their filenames and locations recorded in the system database, allowing them to be reliably erased without adversely affecting the operation of Windows. Many older or less-sophisticated applications simply install in their own way and don't bother registering with the operating system.

Most modern applications are written in compliance with the Microsoft Windows standards for installation and removal. Thus, you see them in your installed applications list in the Add or Remove Programs applet. This list is mainly the result of the PC software industry's response to kvetching from users and critics about tenacious programs that are hard to root out after they're installed. Some ambitious programs spread themselves out all over your hard disk like oil on your garage floor with no easy way of reversing the process. Users complained about the loss of precious disk space, unexplained system slowdowns, and so forth.

 If you need help removing a program because it doesn't show up in the Add or Remove Programs list, see "Program Doesn't Show Up" in the "Troubleshooting" section at the end of this chapter.

This problem was the inspiration for such programs as Uninstaller, CleanSweep, and other utilities that monitor and keep a database of the files a program installs; they wipe out these files effectively when you decide to remove the program, also returning any modified Windows settings to their previous state with any luck. This process is better relegated to those writing the operating system, I feel, and Microsoft rightly set up standards for installation and removal of applications, overseen by this applet. Even if an application isn't installed via the Add or Remove Programs applet per se, if well behaved, it should still make itself known to the operating system and register changes it makes, enabling you to make changes and/or uninstall it from there.

22

TIP

> Never attempt to remove an application from your system by deleting its files from the \Program Files folders (or wherever you installed it). Actually, never may be too strong. Removal through manual deletion should only be as a last resort. Always attempt to use the Add or Remove Programs applet or the uninstall utility from the application first. For tips on manually removing programs, see "Program Doesn't Show Up" under the "Troubleshooting" section at the end of this chapter. If you must manually uninstall, contact the vendor for specific instructions.

What's more, the built-in uninstaller lets you make changes to applications, such as adding or removing suboptions (assuming the application supports that feature).

Use of the uninstall feature of the applet is simple:

1. Run the Add or Remove Programs applet from the Control Panel.
2. Check the list of installed applications. A typical list is shown in Figure 22.4. Note that you can sort the applications by some interesting criteria in the sort box, such as frequency of use. (That one helps weed out stuff you almost never use.)

Figure 22.4
Choosing the program to uninstall or change.

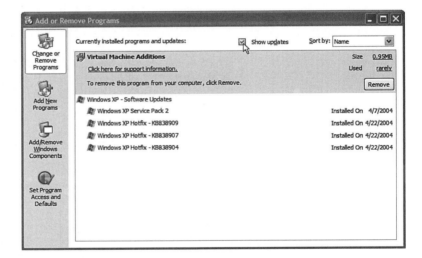

3. Select the program you want to change or uninstall.
4. Click the Change/Remove button.
5. Answer any warnings about removing an application as appropriate.

TIP

> Obviously, removing an application can't easily be reversed by, say, restoring files from the Recycle Bin because settings from the Start menu and possibly the Registry are deleted.

Some applications (for example, Microsoft Office) prompt youto insert the program CD when you attempt to change or remove the app. These prompts can be annoying, but what can you do? The setup, change, and uninstall programs for some large suites are stored on their CDs, not on your hard disk. So, just insert the disc when prompted.

NOTE

> Incidentally, Add or Remove Programs can be run only by users with Administrator credentials on their local computers. Although some applications can be installed or removed by nonadministrators, most do require administrative privilege.

SHOW/HIDE UPDATES

As of Service Pack 2 (SP-2), this applet evolved to provides a means for you to select whether updates, such as security updates downloaded from the Microsoft Web site, are displayed in the Currently installed programs list. This applies to the operating system as well as to applications whose vendors provide removable updates.

A new Show Updates check box appears above the list, which enables you to toggle between showing or hiding installed updates. This is helpful because, before SP-2, the list of installed programs was overwhelmed by the list of installed updates. The new option to filter out the updates from the list and only show installed programs makes this list easier for users to read.

By default, Change and Remove Programs does not show installed updates to Windows. To see the updates that have been installed, you can select the Show Updates check box at the top of the list.

ADD NEW PROGRAMS

As you know, installation of new programs is usually as simple as inserting a CD into the drive. The autorun program on most application CDs does the rest. Or, when it doesn't, you can run the Setup file on the disk, and the rest is automatic. Ditto for programs you download off the Net. Still, you can install from the Add or Remove Programs applet if you want or if the program's instructions suggest it. This part of the applet provides a front end for running an application's Setup program. Big Whoop. But, what launching a setup through the applet does is gather uninstall data for applications that otherwise don't properly register with the OS for uninstallation. Here's what you do:

1. Click Add New Programs in the left panel of the opened Add or Remove Programs applet.

2. Choose the source:

    • **CD or Floppy**—Choose this option for CD, floppy, or hard disk folder. You have to browse through your hard disk to get to the right folder.

    • **Windows Update**—This option runs Internet Explorer, connects to the Microsoft site, and runs Windows Update just as though you had started that

22

process from the Start menu. Don't choose this option unless you're trying to update your Windows installation.

3. The wizard is looking for any file named setup or install. If it finds this file on the CD or floppy, just choose the desired file, and follow the instructions you see. If the setup program you're looking for isn't called setup or install, then you have a little more work to do. Change the Files of Type drop-down list to Program Files or All Files, and poke around a bit more. But make sure you choose a file that's actually a setup file. If you point to a regular old application, it will just run normally. Nothing weird will happen; you just won't be installing anything.

4. Click Finish to complete the task and make the new software's installation or setup procedure run. Instructions vary depending on the program. If your program's setup routine isn't compatible with the applet, you are advised of this fact. After installation, the new program appears in the list of removable programs only if it's compatible with Windows XP's install/remove scheme.

ADD/REMOVE WINDOWS COMPONENTS

In addition to managing add-on products and applications through the Add or Remove Programs applet, the components of Windows XP itself are installed and removed here. Clicking the Add/Remove Windows Components button opens the Windows Components Wizard dialog box (see Figure 22.5). From here, you can install additional Windows XP components by marking their check boxes. Plus, you can remove existing components by clearing their check boxes. However, be careful since there are often many sub-levels of selections. Click on the name of an item, not its checkbox, and then click the Details button to view its sub-components. Marking or clearing a top-level item will install or remove all of its subcomponents.

Figure 22.5
The Windows
Components Wizard
dialog box.

After you've made your selections and clicked Next, the system will install or remove components based on your instructions. You may be prompted for the Windows XP distribution CD, so be prepared.

SET PROGRAM ACCESS AND DEFAULTS

This new feature in Windows XP, added with Service Pack 1, enables you to choose your own default middleware applications. For more on how to do this, see the section "Department of Justice Consent Decree Compliance" in Appendix B.

DATE AND TIME

Date and Time is a simple applet you're sure to have used in the past to adjust the system date and time. That is, it adjusts the hardware clock in the computer, which is maintained by a battery on the motherboard. The system date and time are used for myriad purposes, including date- and time-stamping the files you create and modify, stamping email, controlling the scheduler program for automatic application running, and so on.

NOTE

The Date and Time applet doesn't change the format of the date and time, only the actual date and time stored on your computer's clock. To change formats, see the description of the Regional applet later in this chapter.

When you're a member of a Microsoft network domain, you should never need to set the clock. It is kept synchronized to the domain controller (Windows 2000, Windows NT, or Windows Server 2003). Many network services, including authentication protocols and replication, require exact or close synchronization of all systems within the network.

If your system is part of a workgroup or just a standalone, you can sync your clocks with an Internet time server. The Date and Time applet includes a new third tab for doing just that. However, this capability is not available on domain clients. The ability to sync with an Internet time server through the Date and Time applet is reserved for workgroup members, stand-alone systems, and domain controllers.

The Date and Time applet can also be accessed by double-clicking on the clock on the taskbar or right-clicking over the clock and selecting Adjust Date/Time. To set the date and time, follow these steps:

1. Run the Date/Time applet.
2. Alter the time and date by typing in the corrections or by clicking the arrows. The trick is to click directly on the hours, minutes, seconds, or AM/PM area first, then use the little arrows to the right of them to set the correct value. So, to adjust the a.m. or p.m., click AM or PM, and then click the little up or down arrow. After setting the month and year, you can click the day in the displayed calendar.
3. Click the Time Zone tab to adjust the zone. Why? It's good practice to have your time zone set correctly for programs such as client managers, faxing programs, time synchronizing programs, or phone dialing programs. They may need to figure out where you are in relation to others and what the time differential is. Also, if you want your

computer's clock to be adjusted automatically when daylight saving time changes, make sure the Automatically Adjust Clock for Daylight Saving Changes check box is selected.

4. Click the Internet Time tab. On this tab you can enable clock synchronization with an Internet time server. Two known time servers are provided in the pull-down list, but you can type in others. If you want to force a sync, click the Update Now button.

5. Click OK to save changes and close the applet.

When Internet synchronization is enabled, your clock is reset to match the time servers once each week. Internet synchronization should only be configured on systems with an active Internet connection. Clock synchronization will not initiate a dial-up connection. Plus, if there is a firewall or proxy server between your client and the Internet, the clock synchronization packets may be blocked.

TIP

> You can also adjust the time and date using the TIME and DATE commands from a DOS command prompt. For example, open a DOS box (click Start, All Programs, Accessories, Command Prompt), type **time**, and press Enter. This command displays the current time and a prompt to enter the new time, as shown here:
>
> ```
> The current time is: 21:39:31.78
> Enter the new time:
> ```
>
> Enter the new time or press Enter to leave the time as it is. The same process applies to the date. Type **date** and press Enter. The current date is displayed with a prompt to enter the new date, as shown here:
>
> ```
> The current date is: Thu 11/04/2001
> Enter the new date: (mm-dd-yy)
> ```

FONTS

Managing fonts through the Fonts applet involves viewing, adding, and deleting fonts. To view a font, simply double-click on its font name in the Fonts applet. The Font Viewer will display the font's details, its character set, and several sizes of characters.

Adding a font to your system can be performed through several means. Many font collections have their own installation utility. You can use the File, Install New Font command. Or, you can copy or move the font into the \windows\fonts folder.

Removing a font is even easier. Just select one or more fonts from the Fonts applet and press Delete.

CAUTION

> Don't just delete fonts willy-nilly. There are several key system fonts required by native dialog boxes and other functions which should never be deleted. These include Courier, MS Sans, MS Sans Serif, Small Fonts, and Symbol. These all have the H (hidden) attribute set. They will not even appear in the Fonts applet unless you've configured Folder Options to show all hidden files (see Chapter 21).

Thousands of fonts are available on the Internet for free or for a small fee. Using the keyword "font" on any search tool will locate more sites than you could ever explore.

GAME CONTROLLERS

If you're serious about playing games on your computer, you need a game controller (and often more than one); that means something more than a mouse. Typical controllers include joysticks, flightsticks, gamepads, driving wheels, and other hardware devices designed specifically for the games of your choice. If you're an extreme gamer, the type of controller you need can vary greatly with the types of games you play. High-tech gaming these days requires high-tech controls. Game controllers have reached the point at which serious flight simulator enthusiasts hook up a flightstick, throttle, and separate rudder foot pedals to more accurately simulate the flying experience. Sports gamers usually go for handheld digital gamepads with quick response times. And fans of racing games just aren't getting the full experience without a force feedback steering wheel with its own set of foot pedals for the gas and break (and possibly even a clutch).

This book doesn't cover gaming to any extent, but if you are a gamer, and you buy a game controller, it likely comes with an installation program. If not, Windows XP may detect it automatically or you may need to run the Add Hardware applet. If that doesn't seem to work, you can try adding it through the Game Controllers applet. In most cases, USB devices have no-brainer installations. Just plug it in and you are good to go.

For the last several years, heavy gamers have opted for Windows 95 and 98 as their platforms because of their more extensive support for games. The kinds of direct hardware access and the display driver optimizations that games expect have traditionally been unsupported on the NT platform. The DirectX support on Windows 9x has been superior in this regard.

With Windows 2000, the NT platform began to change this legacy. As a result, options such as game controller settings in the Control Panel have appeared. There has been some migration to the Windows 2000 platform for gaming, but Windows XP is even more gamer friendly and promises a solid following.

As of SP-2, Windows XP supports DirectX 9.0c, including accelerated video card and sound card drivers that provide better playback for different types of games, full-color graphics and video, and 3D animation. DirectX automatically determines the hardware capabilities of your computer and then sets your programs' parameters to match. This allows multimedia applications to run on any Windows-based computer and at the same time ensures that the multimedia applications take full advantage of high-performance hardware.

Low-level functions of DirectX 8.0 are supported by the components that make up the DirectX Foundation layer—namely the following:

- DirectDraw
- Direct3D

22

- DirectSound
- DirectMusic
- DirectInput
- DirectPlay
- DirectShow

Of particular interest to gamers are DirectDraw (which provides extremely fast, direct access to the accelerated hardware capabilities of a computer's video adapter), DirectInput (for quick processing of game controller input), Direct3D (which supports advanced, real-time, three-dimensional graphics), and DirectPlay (which supports game connections over a modem, the Internet, or a LAN).

TIP

When you upgrade to Windows XP, the system doesn't always automatically set up previously installed game devices. You need to manually add your devices through the Control Panel.

NOTE

If you want to optimize your computer for gaming or want to build one from the ground up, I suggest you pick up a copy of *Maximum PC's Guide to Building a Dream PC*, published by Que. This book will walk you through the building, configuring, and optimizing of a high-powered gaming PC that can squeeze every drop of performance from Windows, DirectX, and DirectSound.

After you install a game controller, you can click the Advanced button if you need to alter the controller ID and/or the port to which it's connected. Each game controller should be assigned a different ID. You can share the same game port for a number of controllers by disconnecting one and connecting another. You might be prompted to remove a game controller from the list before a new one can be connected, however, depending on the kind of controller and the port to which it's connected.

- For a custom controller (one not listed in the Add list), click Add, and then click Custom. Fill in the settings for controller type, axes, and number of buttons; then give the controller a name.
- To choose from a list of brand-name controllers, click Add Other, and choose a manufacturer and model. (Some of the devices that show up in this list aren't game controllers, but many are.) If you have a disk for your game port or game controllers, click Have Disk, insert the diskette if necessary, or browse to the appropriate folder location.

KEYBOARD

The Keyboard applet (see Figure 22.6) lets you fine-tune the way the keyboard behaves, check the keyboard driver, and perform some keyboard troubleshooting. The Input Locales tab has been removed from this applet; to change your language settings, you must use the Regional and Language Options applet (later in this chapter).

Figure 22.6
Adjusting key-repeat speed and delay can be useful for avoiding unwanted characters.

The main attractions here are the repeat rate, the repeat delay, and the cursor blink rate. By altering the key-repeat delay (the time after pressing a key before it starts to repeat) and the repeat speed, you can calm down an ill-behaved keyboard or improve usability for someone with a mobility impairment. Altering the delay before the repeat sets in might be helpful if you use applications that require extensive use of, say, the PgUp and PgDn, Enter, or the arrow keys (perhaps in a point-of-sale situation).

You might also want to change the cursor blink rate if the standard blinking cursor annoys you for some reason. You can even stop it altogether (the setting is "none"). I prefer a non-blinking one myself.

The defaults for these keyboard settings are adequate for most users and keyboards.

MOUSE

With each passing year, it seems that the mouse, trackpad, roller, graphics tablet, or pointing stick has become more and more the means through which users interact with the computer. I remember when the mouse was an option. Nowadays, you can barely shut down a computer without a mouse, much less use it effectively.

Obviously, then, the mouse being a major means of interface with your computer, it behooves you to optimize its functioning. The Control Panel's Mouse applet (located under the Printers and Other Hardware option in the Control Panel) lets you do just that, with many aspects of your mouse's operation being adjustable (see Figure 22.7):

- Left/right button reversal
- Double-click speed
- ClickLock
- Look of the pointers
- Pointer scheme
- Pointer speed
- Enhance pointer precision
- Snap to the default button of dialog boxes
- Display pointer trails and length
- Hide pointer while typing
- Show location of pointer when Ctrl is pressed
- Set wheel scroll to number of lines or screen at a time
- Troubleshooting
- Access device properties (same controls as through Device Manager)

The options vary based on pointing device type, and sometimes you are supplied with even fancier options if your pointing device comes with a custom driver. For example, the Synaptics touchpads let you scroll a window by sliding your finger down the right side of the trackpad.

Poor lefties never get a fair shake in life, what with all the right-handed scissors and tools around. Well, they get one here (except for some types of weird, ergonomically shaped mouse devices that don't work well in the left hand). If you're left handed, you can move the mouse to the left side of the keyboard and then reverse the function of the buttons on the Buttons tab of the Mouse applet. Right-clicks then become left-clicks. Of course, DOS programs don't know squat about this mouse setting, but for Windows and Windows programs, the button reverse will work.

On the same tab, you can set the double-click speed. A middle-range setting is appropriate for most folks. Double-click the folder icon to try out the new double-click speed. The folder opens or closes if the double-click registered. If you're not faring well, try adjusting the slider, and then try again. You don't have to click Apply to test the slider settings. Just moving the slider instantly affects the mouse's double-click speed.

If all else fails and you just can't find a double-click speed to suit your needs or abilities, then forget double-clicks altogether. Instead, click on an icon or any selectable object in the Windows XP environment. A single click will usually highlight the option. Think of this as getting the object's attention. Then pressing Enter on the keyboard will launch, open, or execute the selected object.

Figure 22.7
Setting mouse properties can help you get your work done more efficiently, though the defaults usually work fine without modification.

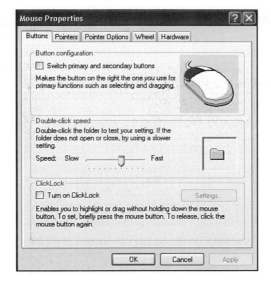

As you know, the pointer cursor changes based on the task at hand. For example, when you're editing text, it becomes an I-beam. You can customize your cursors for the fun of it or to increase visibility. You can even install animated cursors to amuse yourself while you wait for some process to complete. Just as with icons and screen savers, the Web is littered with Windows cursors, in case you would like to collect a few thousand. Windows XP comes with enough to keep me happy, organized into schemes. You can change individual cursors or change a set of them in one fell swoop by using the *cursor schemes*.

Like color schemes and sound schemes, cursor schemes are collections of cursor shapes. When you select a scheme, all the cursors in the scheme go into effect at once. You can choose from about 20 canned schemes.

NOTE

Use one of the Extra Large cursor schemes if you have trouble seeing the pointer. Also, some of the schemes change the pointer into things that don't resemble pointers and can make selecting or clicking small objects difficult because the pointer's hotspot is difficult to locate. Sometimes the cursor is very distracting and can obscure the very item you want to select or click.

You can change individual cursors in a scheme, if you like. To change a cursor assignment, click a cursor in the list. Then click Browse. The default location is ...\windows\cursors. Animated cursors move for you in the Browse box (a thoughtful feature). After you custom tailor a set of cursors to your liking, you can save the scheme for later recall. Click Save As, and name it.

TIP

> In the olden days of Windows, if you used DOS programs that required the mouse, they required DOS mouse drivers. If the DOS mouse driver and the Windows mouse driver's speed settings were different, using the mouse could be annoying because your body would learn hand-eye coordination with one environment that didn't match the other. Some DOS mouse drivers let you adjust the speed in that environment, so you could match the two. In Windows XP, DOS-environment mouse support is provided by Windows. As my co-author Brian says, DOS support under Windows XP is one of the marvels of the modern world because it is so well thought out and extensive.

If you're frustrated because the mouse pointer still appears on the screen while you're in DOS, see "Using DOS Programs with a Mouse" in the "Troubleshooting" section at the end of the chapter.

TIP

> If you use an external serial mouse on your laptop, it might not wake up after your laptop goes into a suspended state. For example, if you close the lid to a laptop running Windows XP, it will probably go into Standby or Hibernate, depending on your laptop and Windows settings. When you wake it up, your external mouse might not wake up along with it because the mouse driver may not know to reinitialize the mouse. Here's a way around that problem, short of rebooting: Choose Control Panel, System, Hardware, Device Manager. Next, click Computer. Then choose Action, Scan for Hardware Changes to do a search for new hardware. Because the mouse was not initialized, it fell off the list of current hardware. Doing the scan finds it and reinitializes it. The mouse should now work.

PHONE AND MODEM OPTIONS

The Phone and Modem Options applet lets you add, remove, and set the properties of the modems connected to your system. You can also declare dialing rules (long-distance numbers, call waiting, credit card calls, and so on), and add and remove telephony drivers.

If you can't get your modem to connect, see "Cannot Connect" in the "Troubleshooting" section at the end of this chapter.

THE WINDOWS TELEPHONY INTERFACE

The Phone and Modems applet in the Control Panel offers a central location for altering some TAPI settings, as well as for installing and configuring modems and telephone devices. Installing and configuring a modem were covered in Chapter 8, so I'll dispense with the basics of modem installation here. Refer to that chapter if you're hooking up a new modem.

TIP

You can use cell phones for data communications, for example, from a laptop in the field. Remember two points, though. The phone must be set to run in analog mode. Also, in the best of circumstances, you will get only 9600bps throughput because of limitations in the cellular transmission channel.

To set up cellular communications, you need a modem that is compatible with the cell phone you have and a cable designed specifically for connecting your model of phone to that modem. I use a standard Motorola "flip phone" with a Megahertz cellular-ready modem. With this combo, not much fiddling is required, but I made sure *before* I purchased the modem that it would work with my make and model phone.

As for settings, I did drop down the transfer rate to 9600 baud, and because my phone is analog/digital, I have to force it into analog mode for each call. This extra step is a bit of an annoyance, but I'll survive. Then I connect the cell phone to the modem, power up the phone, and initiate the dialing sequence. With any luck, I get on the Internet. Don't forget the per-minute cost of cellular connections! The charges can add up. If you do a lot of on-the-road connecting, check out one of the wireless connection options such as Ricochet's or Hughes's service, which are typically offered at a reasonable flat rate for a full 24x7 connection.

Windows XP supports *modem aggregation*, which is also called *PPP multilink dialing*. It essentially allows you to group modems together to increase the connection bandwidth. This process is a little tricky and requires multiple phone lines and multiple ISP accounts to work, as well as an ISP that supports synchronization of multiple modems.

In general, your default TAPI and modem properties will probably work fine and won't need to be changed. If you do need to change them, remember that changes affect all applications that use the modem whose properties you modify. To change the modem properties after installation is complete, open the Control Panel, and double-click the Phone and Modem Options icon.

DIALING RULES

On the Dialing Rules tab of the Phone and Modem Options dialog, you can set up your dialing locations and rules pertaining to those locations, such as phone number prefixes for outside lines, calling card access codes, and so on. If you move around (road-warrior style), you can add some new locations to the default one that's already set up for you as the current user.

You can either edit or add a dialing location from this tab. Table 22.12 describes the settings.

22

TABLE 22.12 SETTING DIALING RULES FOR EACH LOCATION

Option	Description
Location Name	This field specifies the name of each configuration set. To create a new configuration, use the New button and type a name in the Create New Location dialog box.
Country/Region	This field contains a drop-down menu that lists the international dialing codes for most countries of the world. Choose the name of the country from which you will be originating calls. The United States, Canada, and many Caribbean countries all use the same Country Code.
Area Code	Type your own area code in this field.
To Access an Outside Line for Local Calls	If your modem line is in an office where you must dial 9 for an outside line or some other code for long distance, type that number here. If you have a direct outside line, leave this field blank.
To Access an Outside Line for Long-Distance	If you have to dial 9 or 8 for long-distance calls, enter that number. Remember that you need to use this field only when your modem is connected to a PBX or other telephone system that uses a special code for toll calls. Do *not* use this field for the 1 prefix that you dial before making long- distance calls. The dialer adds that code automatically.
Use this carrier code to make long-distance calls	If you use one of the long distance services which require a carrier code to be dialed, such as 10-10-811 or 10-10-220, use this field to provide it. The dialer adds that code automatically.
Use this carrier code to make international calls	If you use one of the international calling services which require a carrier code, use this field to provide it. The dialer adds that code automatically.
To Disable Call Waiting, Dial	If your phone service has call waiting, it can be a nuisance and cause your data connection to fail when a phone call comes in while you're online. Most call waiting services let you turn off the service for the duration of the current call by entering *70, 70#, or 1170 before making the call. If you have call waiting, you should turn on this option and enter the code your phone company tells you, or choose the correct code. Often your local telephone directory has the necessary code listed. The comma after the code causes a 1- or 2-second pause after dialing the special code, often necessary before dialing the actual phone number.
Tone or Pulse Dialing	Most pushbutton telephones use tone dialing (known in the United States as TouchTone dialing). However, older dial telephones and some cheap pushbutton phones use pulse signaling instead. Chances are good that your telephone circuit will accept tone dialing even if a dial telephone is connected to it. Try it if in doubt. Change to pulse if it doesn't make a connection.

AREA CODE RULES TAB

On the Area Code Rules tab, you can set details about the use of an area code, specifically the use of the 1 prefix for certain exchanges. If you have to dial 1 (but no area code) for certain areas, you can add those prefixes here.

Click New to create a new rule, and fill in the resulting dialog box.

CALLING CARD TAB

You might not need to worry about calling cards at all if you travel using an ISP that has many points of presence. The larger ISPs such as Mindspring, CompuServe, and AOL have local dial-up numbers from most major cities. Some also have 800 numbers that you can use when connecting phones from remote locations. If you need to bill your connection to a telephone company (or long-distance service) calling card, though, you set those options on the Calling Card tab.

> **TIP**
>
> If you use more than one calling card, you can create a different location for each one. Telephony programs, such as Phone Dialer or the Send Fax Wizard, normally let you change the location before dialing.

As you probably know from using a calling card for voice calls, to place and charge a call with a calling card, you dial a special string of numbers that includes a carrier access code, your account number, and the number you're calling. In some cases, you have to call a service provider, enter your account number, and wait for a second dial tone before you can actually enter the number you want to call.

To assign a calling card, follow these steps:

1. Click the location you are assigning it to on the Dialing Rules tab of the Phone and Modem Options dialog.
2. Click Edit.
3. Fill in the general information and any area code rules.
4. Click the Calling Card tab.
5. Choose the card type you have. If it's not listed, click New and fill in the resulting dialog box, using the ? (question mark) button for assistance. If your service is one of the presets, all the necessary settings, such as pauses and dialing codes, are made for you.
6. Enter your Account Number and Personal ID Number (PIN) if necessary. Not all calling card options require them, so these options may be grayed out.

SETTING OR EDITING CALLING CARD SCRIPTS

If you get into editing the calling card rules for a location, you're in pretty deep. There's not enough room here to walk you through a description of every setting and how the

22

dialog box works, but I can give you a few tips. For more details, consult the Windows XP Resource Kit.

Basically, you can set up and edit a sequence of events, like a script, in the Edit Calling Card dialog. You can not only change the sequence of events, but you can also enter any specific numbers or other codes. When you make the call, the events progress from the top of the box to the bottom. You can set up a script for each kind of call: local, long distance, and international.

You can use the Edit Calling Card dialog box when you have to fine-tune a calling card's dialing script. Do so only if the presets for your calling card service don't already work. The six buttons below the steps list insert new steps into the script.

Some services require you to wait for a "bing" tone before continuing with the dialing. If the tone your carrier plays isn't detected by your modem, try experimenting with different pause lengths instead. You typically are allowed a few seconds to enter the remainder of the sequence, so the pause amount may not be critical as long as you have waited for the bing.

If a connection isn't working, and you're fine-tuning these events, it sometimes helps to lift the receiver of a phone on the same line and listen (or turn on the modem's speaker), monitoring the sounds. You'll be better able to figure out where a sequence is bombing out.

SETTING MODEM PROPERTIES

So much for dialing rules. The second tab in the Phone and Modem Options dialog—Modems—is for setting modem properties. Accessing a modem's properties opens the same dialog box as when accessing a device's properties through the Device Manager. Typically, you don't need to change your modem properties, so unless you're having difficulty, remember this old adage: If it ain't broke, don't fix it.

To alter a modem's properties, follow these steps:

1. Click the Modems tab.
2. Choose the modem.
3. Click Properties.

> **TIP**
>
> Notice that you can add and remove modems from this Properties dialog box, too, although you can do so just as easily from the Add Hardware applet.

You can dig pretty deeply into the tabs on a modem's Properties dialog box, especially the Advanced one. As per usual Microsoft strategy on its communications stuff, if you're used to pre-Windows XP dialogs, you'll find things have shifted around, and you'll have to do a little hunting. Table 22.13 lists a few notes about some of the more salient settings.

TABLE 22.13   MODEM PROPERTIES SETTINGS

Setting	Description
Port	You can use the drop-down Port menu to specify the COM port to which your modem is connected. If you don't have a drop-down list box, you don't have a choice of ports.
Speaker Volume	The Speaker Volume control is a slide setting that sets the loudness of the speaker inside your modem. In some cases, you will have only Off and On as options rather than a variable speaker volume.
Maximum Port Speed	When your modem makes a connection, it tries to use the maximum speed to exchange data with the modem at the other end of the link. As a rule, if you have a 38400bps or faster modem, the maximum speed should be three or four times the rated modem speed (for example, set your modem speed to 115200) to take advantage of the modem's built-in data compression. Note that the Advanced settings' Port Speed setting interacts with this one.
Dial Control	You can choose whether the dialer should wait to detect a dial tone before proceeding.
Extra Initialization Commands	The Extra Settings section is a place to send additional AT commands to your modem. In most cases, you don't need to add any special commands. Because different modem manufacturers use slightly different command sets, you'll have to consult your modem manual for specific commands.
Data Protocol	If you're using a cellular phone with the modem, choose Cellular Protocol in the default settings page's Data Protocol drop-down list. Cell phones use special data error compression and correction protocols to increase connection speed. The modem still works with this setting turned off, but the connection may improve if it's turned on. Don't use Cellular Protocol if your cell phone service doesn't support it.
Change Default Preferences	The Data bits, Parity, and Stop bits settings must be the same at both ends of a data link. The most common settings are 8 data bits, no parity, and one stop bit. These are set on the Advanced tab" of the Default Preferences dialog box. On the General tab of this dialog box, call preferences options control when idle calls are disconnected and how long to attempt a connection before canceling. Also on this tab are settings for port speed, data/protocol, compression, and flow control—consult the modem's manual for specifics on these settings.

continues

22

TABLE 22.13 CONTINUED	
Setting	**Description**
Advanced Port Settings	Clicking this button brings up the Advanced Port Settings dialog box. These settings determine how incoming and outgoing data is buffered by the COM port UARTS. Leave them alone unless you have information from your ISP or modem manufacturer, or you suspect that dropping them will help with connection success. Before you change these settings, drop the maximum port speed, which controls the data transmission speed between the modem and the port. If you do experiment with them, and your throughput drops significantly, return to this screen, and click Defaults to set the sliders and check box back to the original suggested settings.
Distinctive Ring	A tab for this option appears only if your modem supports the feature. "Distinctive ring" is a service from your phone company that provides different ring patterns for different kinds of incoming calls. Depending on the kind of modem you have, you can have between three and six numbers, or addresses, for one telephone line. Each number can have a distinctive ring pattern. You can also assign each ring pattern to a specific type of program. For example, if you have two rings assigned for fax calls, any call received with that ring pattern could be automatically sent to your fax program. Some phone companies have distinctive ring patterns based on the duration of the ring rather than the number of rings. Some modems support this scenario. In general, you should choose the desired number of rings for each kind of incoming call based on settings you get from your phone company. Then check your modem's manual for details on using this feature. You'll have to enable the distinctive ring feature first by clicking the check box before you can alter the ring settings.

DIAGNOSTIC PROPERTIES

You can click the Diagnostics tab in the original Modem Properties dialog box to make it active. The Diagnostics tab asks the modem to identify itself. It can further test the modem's capability to respond to the standard AT command set, display the contents of its internal registers, and display its settings. Click Query Modem to make it so. The results of the diagnostics query will make sense only if you compare them to the expected results in the modem's manual. If things don't look square, you should look for troubleshooting information in the manual or contact the vendor for modem specific repair options.

REGIONAL AND LANGUAGE OPTIONS

The Regional and Language Options settings affect the way Windows displays times, dates, numbers, and currency. When you install Windows, chances are good that the Regional settings are already set for your locale. This will certainly be true if you purchase a computer with Windows XP preinstalled on it, from a vendor in your country or area.

Running this applet from the Control Panel displays the dialog box you see in Figure 22.8.

To change the settings, simply click the appropriate tab, and then click the drop-down list box for the setting in question. Examples of the current settings are shown in each section, so you don't need to change them unless they look wrong. The predefined standards are organized by language, then by country. If you can't find a standard to your liking, you can always create a customized format.

Figure 22.8
Making changes to the Regional settings affects the display of date, time, and currency in Windows applications that use the internal Windows settings for such functions.

SCANNERS AND CAMERAS

Using the Scanners and Cameras applet, you can add, remove, set properties for, and troubleshoot your connection to scanners and digital cameras. As scanners and digital cameras become as omnipresent as the trusty printer, provisions are being made to assist in the transfer of documents and images from them into the computer. Especially with the advent of the digital still camera, many new convenient methods for facilitating the transfer of captured images are being made available. This is a must if the digital camera is to become as prevalent as the standard film camera.

The Scanners and Cameras applet is used to install scanners, digital still cameras, digital video cameras, and image-capturing devices.

After a device is installed, Scanners and Cameras can link it to a program on your computer. For example, when you press Scan on your scanner, you can have the scanned picture automatically open in the program you want.

22

With some cameras and scanners, you can create linked events that execute when you do something on the camera or the scanner. Typically, this means pressing a button on the scanner or camera.

In the best of all worlds, detection of your scanner or camera will occur automatically as Windows Plug and Play detection notices the device. But as you know, sometimes running the Add Hardware wizard is required to force a search. To do that, use this applet to install a scanner device like this:

1. Run the Scanners and Cameras applet, and click Add an imaging device. (Ideally, you should hook up the device before doing so.) Follow the wizard, and choose the make and model if necessary.

2. Choose the port the device is connected to. You can use the option Automatic Port Select if you don't intend to be consistent with which port you use for this connection, or you don't want to bother guessing which port it's on.

3. When an item is installed, the drivers are added to the boot list at startup, and appropriate features in the operating system are modified for gaining access to the device.

You can check and test a scanner or camera by selecting it and clicking the Properties button. The Properties dialog for the device appears. Here, you can alter the port number if you need to and check other settings as applicable. If color profiles are available for the device, you can add or remove them using the Color Management tab.

 If your camera or scanner doesn't show up in the installed devices list, see "It's Not Here" in the "Troubleshooting" section at the end of this chapter.

GETTING IMAGES INTO THE COMPUTER

How you acquire images from the device into the computer varies depending on the product. Some cameras use a USB connection, some use a serial cable, and some use FireWire, while others use PC Card memory sticks or even high-density floppies.

When the physical connection is made, it's a matter of triggering the correct "event" to initiate communication between the system and the digital imaging device for image transfer. To link a program to a scanner or digital camera event, follow these steps:

1. Open the Scanners and Cameras applet.

2. Click the scanner or camera you want to use, click Properties, and then click the Events tab.

3. In Scanner Events or Camera Events, click the event you want to link to a program.

4. In Send to This Application, click the program you want to receive the image from the scanner or camera. If the Events tab isn't displayed, you're out of luck; the feature isn't available for the selected scanner or digital camera. Also, at this point, most applications don't support linking to scanners and digital cameras using this new technique. It may take some time for software makers to incorporate it, just as it took awhile for *TWAIN*

to be supported by the PC industry at large. Also, note that linking is available only with the programs that appear in Send to This Application.

SECURITY CENTER

With the onslaught of spam and malicious viruses and other code, Microsoft realized that XP users needed a single place to turn to for monitoring and controlling their systems' security. True, XP already incorporated an Internet firewall and the Windows Update technology. And also true, various antivirus programs such as Norton and McAfee were available from third parties. The problem is that too many users got lost poking around Windows to make adjustments to each of these services. Many purchased third-party firewalls, not knowing one was built in to XP. (Admittedly, however, Norton's and Zone Alarm's firewalls have more features.) The Security Center applet was added as an antidote for this shortfall. When opened from Control Panel, it appears as shown in Figure 22.9.

Figure 22.9
The Security Center provides central access to firewall, Windows updates, and virus protection settings.

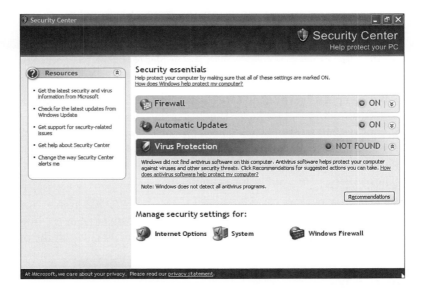

Notice that handy links are also provided for other security concerns such as Internet security (usually only reachable from the Internet Options applet or the Tools menu in Internet Explorer), and there's a link to the System applet. As mentioned earlier in this chapter, you'll find coverage of Firewall and Auto Updates in other chapters. Virus protection is not provided by Microsoft with XP. Maybe in the future it will be, in Microsoft's inimitable style of co-opting other non-MS technologies. In the meantime, click the Recommendations button if you want antivirus protection. You'll be led to sites from which purchasing of third-party applications is made easy. After you install an antivirus program, you most likely can alter its settings through this control panel interface. As the dialog box states, however, not all programs are recognized by Windows. If yours isn't, you must resort to the antivirus program interface to make adjustments.

SOUNDS AND AUDIO DEVICES

The Sounds and Audio Devices applet is your stopping place when it comes to adjustments to your sound system and the sounds the computer makes to alert you of errors, new mail, and so on.

NOTE

As you might know, you adjust the volume of your computer speakers (and other inputs and outputs) by choosing Start, All Programs, Accessories, Entertainment, Volume Control. Alternatively, you can simply double-click the little speaker next to the clock in the system tray. By single-clicking the same little speaker, you can quickly adjust the master volume control. The Volume Controls are covered in Chapter 5, "Using the Simple Supplied Applications."

There's a bunch of fun to be had from this applet, should you like to twiddle with your sounds. Most of what people do with this applet is change the goofy sounds their computers make in response to specific events.

If your computer had a sound card (or motherboard-based sound chipset) when you installed Windows XP, it's likely Windows established a default set of rather boring sounds for your system, most of which you've probably grown tired of already. Aside from making life more interesting, having different sounds for different types of events is also more informative. You know when you've made an error as opposed to when an application is acknowledging your actions, for example.

The sounds the system uses are stored on disk in the .WAV format. You can create, purchase, or download just about any sound you can think of from the Internet. I downloaded the sound of Homer Simpson saying "Doh!" and the theme from the original TV show *Star Trek* the other day, for example.

THE VOLUME TAB

The Volume tab is used to set the master volume. This is the same master volume control which appears in the Volume Control tool and when you single-click the speaker in the system tray. Clicking the Advanced button opens the Volume Control tool so you can access all of the input and output audio controls.

Also on this tab are speaker controls. If you have a special speaker system, such as surround sound or 3-D audio, these controls help you fine tune your settings.

THE SOUNDS TAB

The Sounds tab is used to associate Windows events with sounds. Windows XP comes with tons of sound files, a big improvement over the measly assemblage of WAV files supplied with some earlier versions of Windows. In fact, just as with the color schemes, you can create and save sound schemes by using the Control Panel's Display applet (covered in Chapter 21); you can set up and save personalized schemes to suit your mood. Microsoft supplies a fairly rich variety of sounds for your auditory pleasure.

Despite the diverse selection, I still use a few of the sounds I've put together using the Sound Recorder. I have one, for example, that says "New Mail" when I receive email. Sometimes I didn't notice the generic "boop" sound when new mail arrived, so I changed it.

If you want to get fancy, you can record from a CD or tape recorder rather than from a microphone. This way, you can sample bits and pieces from your favorite artists by popping the audio CD into the computer and tapping directly into it rather than by sticking a microphone up in front of your boom box and accidentally recording the telephone when it rings. Just check out the Volume Control applet, and figure out which slider on the mixer panel controls the input volume of the CD. Then use the Sound Recorder applet to make the recording. I have a few good ones, such as James Brown's incomparable "Ow!" for an error message sound.

> **TIP**
>
> You should be sure that WAV files you intend for system sounds aren't too large. Sound files *can* be super large, especially if they are recorded in 16-bit stereo. As a rule, you should keep the size to a minimum for system sounds because it takes a few seconds for a larger sound to load and play.

You assign sounds to specific Windows "events" like this:

1. Open the Control Panel, and run the Sounds and Audio Devices applet. Select the Sounds tab as shown in Figure 22.10.

2. The Program Events section lists the events that can have sounds associated with them. Several classes of events are listed on a typical computer, such as Windows, NetMeeting, Windows Explorer, and so on. As you purchase and install new programs in the future, those programs may add their own events to your list. An event with a speaker icon next to it already has a sound associated with it. You can click it and then click the play button (the one with the triangle pointing right, just like the play button on a VCR or stereo) to hear the sound. The sound file that's associated with the event is listed in the Sounds box.

3. Click any event for which you want to assign a sound or change the assigned sound.

4. Open the drop-down Sounds list, and choose the WAV file you want to use for that event. Some of the event names may not make sense to you, such as Asterisk, Critical Stop, or Exclamation. These names are for the various classes of dialog boxes that

22

Windows XP displays from time to time. The sounds you're most likely to hear often will be Default Beep, Menu Command, New Mail Notification, Question, Open Program, Close Program, Minimize, Maximize, and Close program. You might want to start by assigning sounds to them and then add others as you feel like it.

Figure 22.10
The Sounds and
Audio Devices
Properties dialog box,
Sounds tab.

5. Repeat these steps for each item you want to assign or reassign a sound to. Then click OK to close the dialog box.

TIP

> The default folder for sounds is \windows\media. If you have a WAV file stored in another folder and want to assign it to an event, use the Browse button to locate it. You don't have to move your sound files to the \windows\media folder for it to work. However, if you're planning on reassigning sounds regularly, you'll find that the process is easier if you move your WAV files into the media folder first.

At the top of the list of available sounds is an option called <none>, which has the obvious effect: No sound will occur for that event. Assigning all events to <none> effectively silences your laptop for use in a library or other silent setting. You can also silence all sounds easily by choosing the No Sounds sound scheme as explained next.

In the same way that the Display Properties page lets you save color schemes, the Sounds and Audio Devices applet lets you save sound schemes. You can set up goofy sounds for your humorous moods and somber ones for those gloomy days. I often tire of a sound scheme, so I have a few setups that I can easily switch to. The ones supplied with Windows XP are pretty decent, actually, and considering the amount of work required to set up your own schemes, you'll probably make out best just trying a scheme to see if you like it. To choose an existing sound scheme, just use the Sound scheme pull-down list and select one.

You can set up your own sound schemes by assigning or reassigning individual sounds, as I've already explained. But unless you *save* the scheme with the Save As button, it'll be lost the next time you change to a new one. So, the moral is that after you get your favorite sounds assigned to system events, save the scheme. Then you can call it up any time you like.

THE AUDIO AND VOICE TABS

On both the Audio and Voice tabs, you can declare the default hardware you want to use for audio playback, recording, MIDI playback, voice playback, and voice recording. Most systems offer minimal choices in these departments because typical computers have only a single sound system. You might find something strange in the sound playback and recording settings, such as the option to use your modem for these purposes (if your modem has voice messaging capability). Don't bother trying to use your modem for voice messaging unless you have multiple sound cards in the computer.

The Advanced buttons for these categories could be useful, however, depending on your sound system's chipset. Some offer options to adjust bass and treble; expanded stereo (sort of a wider sound based on adjustment of the "phase" of the signal going to the amplifier); sample-rate conversion options; equalization optimization based on the kind of speakers you have; and hardware acceleration (use full acceleration if you're a gamer because it affects DirectSound used in some games).

The Use only default devices option determines which sound card or cards your programs will use. If you use programs that require a specific type of sound card, and that sound card is selected as a default device on this tab, select this check box. That way, if for some reason your preferred devices aren't available, the program doesn't bomb or freak out by trying to use a sound card that Windows thinks is a reasonable replacement. For any situation I've been in, leaving the check box cleared has never been a problem.

THE HARDWARE TAB

The Hardware tab of the Sounds and Audio Devices Properties dialog simply lists all the sound, video, DVD, and other multimedia hardware items currently installed. You can check their properties and current status, as well as troubleshoot them. You can get to the same properties dialog boxes offered here via the Device Manager, but this tab limits the device list only to multimedia-related hardware.

SPEECH

The Speech applet is used to configure the voice that you'll hear whenever the text-to-speech translation feature is used. Now, the voice offered is still too jerky and coarse for my taste. I remember my first voice enabled computer game "Parsec" for the TI; that was more than 20 years ago. And the voice it used is just about the same as what is offered here in Windows XP. I can't wait until the sultry voice of the *Star Trek: The Next Generation* computer becomes the standard.

The Microsoft SAM voice is limited in its configurability. But, Windows XP will accept third-party voices which may offer greater end-user control.

Currently, text-to-speech or TTS is only available through Microsoft Office. To use it, you must enable the Speak Text command in the Language bar under Options. Once enabled, highlight the section of the document you want read to you, then issue the Speak Text command from the Language bar.

SYSTEM: DEVICE MANAGER

The System applet is covered in Chapter 24, but we wanted to mention an important element accessed through the System applet here—the Device Manager. The Device Manager is accessed from the System applet's Hardware tab by clicking on its name-sake button. When launched, you are presented with a category list of the devices installed in the system (see Figure 22.11). When there are no problems, the display is a bit bland. To see the individual devices, expand any of the listed categories. Then, to access a device's Properties dialog box, just double click on it.

Figure 22.11
The Device Manager.

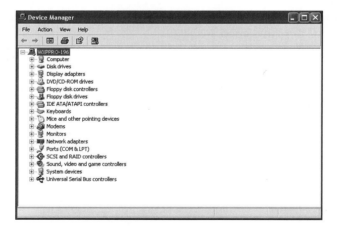

The Device Manager serves several functions, the foremost of which is to aid in the resolution of hardware problems. When any device fails to function as expected it will be highlighted with a yellow triangle or a red stop sign. The yellow triangle indicates a warning or a possible problem. A red stop sign indicates a device conflict or other serious error. When the Device Manager is launched and a device has an outstanding issue, its category will be expanded so you can easily see the warning or error icon.

When a device's Properties dialog box is opened, the General tab displays basic information about the device, plus details on the device's current status. In most cases, the status report will point out exactly what is preventing the device from functioning normally. You may be able to correct the issue on your own, or if you need help or guidance, click the Troubleshoot button for a wizard. You'll be amazed how useful these wizards are! Merlin would be proud.

Depending on the device, there can be many other tabs in addition to the General tab. In most cases, you'll see a Driver tab, and almost as frequently you'll see a Resources tab. The Driver tab offers details about the currently installed driver for this device and enables you to update, roll back, or uninstall the driver.

Device driver roll back is a new feature to the Windows product line. Roll back will remove the current driver and restore the previous driver (assuming there was one). The ability to remove the current or newly installed driver to return to the previously used driver is often a lifesaver. I can't remember how many times I've had to remove a new driver, then had to go through the process of re-installing the hardware just to get the old driver back. The Roll Back Driver button now performs this operation with a simple click. No muss, no fuss.

→ For more information on Device Driver rollback, **see** "Device Driver Rollback," **p. 959**.

The Resources tab specifies the system resources to which the device is assigned. These include IRQ, I/O ranges, DMA, and more. On PnP devices, you can switch the settings from automatic to either a predefined configuration set or a fully customized setting. On legacy cards, you may need to alter the physical device settings (such as dip switches or jumpers) first, then set the Resources tab to match. For some PnP cards, the settings on the Resources page are read-only. Meaning you must use a vendor-supplied configuration utility to change the settings away from automatic control.

As for any other tabs that may appear in a device's Properties dialog box, be sure to consult the respective user manual.

From the main Device Manager view, you can perform a few helpful actions:

- Change views between devices by type, devices by connection, resources by type, and resources by connection
- Force a scan for hardware changes
- Update the driver for the selected device
- Disable the device in the current hardware profile
- Uninstall the device from the system
- Eject or unplug a device

NOTE

> A hardware profile is similar to a user profile except it focuses on the presence or absence of devices. Hardware profiles are typically used on portable systems that have interchangeable PC card devices or which use a docking station or other transient external devices. Each hardware profile contains active device drivers for a specific set of devices. Upon bootup, the system attempts to match the located device set with a known hardware profile. Hardware profiles are discussed in Chapter 23.

TROUBLESHOOTING

PROGRAM DOESN'T SHOW UP

A program I'm trying to kill doesn't show up in the Add or Remove Programs applet. How can I remove it?

This is often the case with programs that don't announce themselves thoroughly to Windows as they are being installed. You have to find the program on the hard disk and eliminate it using the Windows Explorer. Finding a program is often as simple as browsing to the Program Files folder, opening it, and looking around for a folder holding the program in question. Often, deleting the folder is all you have to do. Look for an "uninstall" application there first because it will do a more complete job of removal than just killing the folder, most likely, because some stray DLLs and other support files may be scattered about, not to mention shortcuts in your Start menus that you'll want axed.

As a second (and possibly quicker) means of discovering the location of an unlisted program, you can use its Start menu shortcut to lead you to the application's source. Open the Start menu, and click your way to the application. When you see it, *right-click* it. Now choose Properties from the context menu. Then click Find Target to go directly to the folder where the program resides. Then you can start your dirty work.

If you're trying to kill a program that seems to start up all on its own when you boot up, choose Start, Programs, Startup. Anything in this group autoexecutes upon bootup. Right-click the offending item, and choose Delete. This trick doesn't remove the program from your hard disk, but it prevents the program from starting at boot time.

NO BATTERY ICON IN SYSTEM TRAY

I don't see a battery icon in the system tray. My laptop seems to be brain dead about batteries and power conservation.

Be sure APM is enabled for the computer via the Power Options applet in the Control Panel. Also, make sure the computer complies with APM (check your BIOS settings).

CANNOT CONNECT

My modem isn't connecting for some reason.

More often than not, modem problems are caused by incorrect phone numbers and/or a bad phone line connection. Assuming Windows detected and installed your modem, don't get esoteric in your troubleshooting. Just as you're most likely to find a lost item where you think it should be, it's the silly things that keep modems from working—a bad or incompletely inserted phone wire, bad wall jack, or splitter; or a phone number that's missing an area code (or has an unnecessary area code) being dialed. Another typical goof is to specify an external access number (typically 9), which might be necessary at the office but not on the road. Check the properties for the dial-up networking connection you're trying to use. Also, of course, double-check the user ID and password. You might be dialing in and physically connecting just fine, but the remote server is kicking you off because of incorrect user ID or password.

Finally, recall that a number of troubleshooters are built into Windows XP. One of them is for modems. Choose Start, Help, and in the right pane, click Troubleshooting.

IT'S NOT HERE

My camera or scanner doesn't show up.

Sometimes starting with the obvious is easiest. Does the device have power? Is your scanner or camera plugged in and turned on? Check the power cables and the data connection. Does the camera have a good power source? Digital cameras eat up batteries at a ravenous rate. Either use fresh batteries or an external power source. (I recommend getting nickel-metal hydride batteries for digital cameras. They work much longer than normal alkalines or Ni-Cad batteries.) If the connection is an infrared one, make sure the camera and computer IR sensor are lined up properly.

Some devices don't connect correctly unless they're turned on. See your device documentation if you need more information.

As per my usual admonition, check your cables! Make sure you have the correct type of cable plugged into the correct ports on both the device and your computer. See your scanner or camera documentation for more information. Your device may be connected to a port that is disabled. A serial port, for example, is often disabled to allow an internal modem to work.

Next, check to see whether the driver for your device is installed. Virtually all cameras and scanners are Plug and Play these days, so Windows XP should install the drivers for them automatically. However, you might need to install drivers for some devices manually. See the section in this chapter covering the Scanners and Cameras applet for details on installing a driver. If that doesn't help, and the device is listed as installed (in Control Panel, Scanners and Cameras), try removing it and reinstalling it via that applet and then reinstalling it (by clicking Remove and then Add).

USING DOS PROGRAMS WITH A MOUSE

Why is the mouse pointer still on the screen while I'm in DOS?

Lots of folks still run DOS programs, even under Windows 9x, NT, 2000, and now XP. Most DOS programs are keyboard driven and don't require a mouse. Normally, however, when you run DOS programs in a window, the mouse pointer sits annoyingly on the screen, even though it's useless.

You can hide the mouse pointer when running an MS-DOS program, assuming you don't need it. To hide it, right-click the title bar of the MS-DOS window to display the menu, and then click Hide Mouse Pointer. (If the program switches between character-based and graphics modes, you might need to hide the mouse pointer again.) When the mouse pointer is hidden, you can't see it inside or outside the program's window. To display the mouse pointer, press Alt+Spacebar, and choose Display Mouse Pointer from the resulting menu.

CHAPTER 23

MAINTAINING AND OPTIMIZING SYSTEM PERFORMANCE

In this chapter

RUNNING A TIGHT SHIP

If you're reading this chapter, you are probably the kind of user who is interested in keeping your Windows PC spinning like a top. Or maybe you are responsible for maintaining a myriad of computers on a LAN, and your charges insist that you do the same for them. You probably like to install and test new video cards, experiment with USB devices, or set up multiple hardware profiles. In short, you like to—no, *need* to—tinker with your hardware. You're also likely to be looking for ways to boost the performance of your system through tweaking system software.

In this chapter, I'll start by discussing some of the techniques that will best serve you in the process of improving system stability and performance.

The remainder of the chapter deals with configuration of the various program application subsystems—Win32, Win16 and DOS.

MEASURING SYSTEM PERFORMANCE WITH PERFORMANCE MONITOR

Before you can improve your system's performance, you need to find out how well it's currently performing. Use Windows XP's integrated Performance Monitor to learn what's happening inside your system in much more detail that is available from the Task Manager's Performance tab (that is, from the display you get to by typing Ctrl+Alt+Del).

Performance Monitor creates a graphical or numeric display of essential system information, such as memory usage, hard disk transfer rates, CPU activity, network traffic, and many other quantifiable aspects of your computer's real-time operations. You can display the gathered information in line graph, bar chart, or numeric format. Displaying this information is useful for trying to get a handle on what's happening with your computer, particularly when you're troubleshooting or tracking down bottlenecks.

Not only does Performance Monitor put up a real-time display, it also interacts with Performance Logs and Alerts (another administrative tool). Using the combination of the two, you can record performance data for later analysis, set up system alerts to send a message, run a program, or start a log specifying whether a counter's value is above, below, or equal to a defined threshold.

To start the Performance Monitor, click Start, Control Panel, Performance and Maintenance, Administrative Tools, and finally, double-click Performance.

When you start the Performance Monitor, the default display shows three counters, as down in Figure 23.1. These counters are

- **Memory Pages/second**—This counter indicates how may times per second Windows has to move programs or data between memory and the hard disk. Much of the activity measured by this counter is the swapping of data between memory and the hard disk's page file, which holds active programs and data that can't currently fit into memory. If this value frequently rises above 20, your system might have a memory bottleneck.

Figure 23.1
The Performance monitor displays operating system and hardware performance measurements in a chart format.

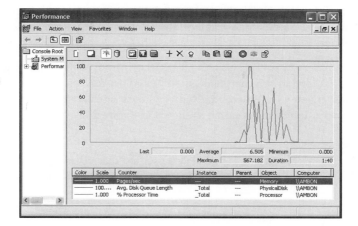

- **Average Disk Queue Length**—The number of blocks of data waiting to be written to your hard disk. Generally, it should be no higher than 2 plus the physical number of hard drives on your system. If it frequently rises higher, your disk's transfer speed is too low.

- **% Processor Time**—The percentage of time that your processor is actually busy doing your work. If this value frequently exceeds 85%, consider adding a faster processor.

Each measurement is color-coded, and the default graph of current activity uses a moving vertical red stripe to indicate where the latest information is displayed.

To add additional counters, click the + (plus) button on the toolbar. From the resulting dialog box, choose a computer to measure, the performance object (the choices include various system components such as Memory, Network Interface, and Processor), and then the specific performance counter.

What can you measure with the Performance Monitor?

- Processor activity, including the percentages of time the processor handles many different types of activities.

- Network activity, including data transfer rates to and from the specified computer.

- Pagefile activity, including what percentage of your pagefile is in use at a given time.

All together, there are more than 40 different performance objects whose activity can be tracked with the Performance Manager, and many offer ten or more counters that measure different aspects of the object's performance. It's almost overwhelming what you can measure. Performance Monitor is a hugely flexible tool. And you can mix and match counters and objects from different computers on the same graph. Therefore, you could, for example, compare some interesting statistics such as disk hits, print jobs, or network requests from different computers on the same graphical display to help you get a sense of bottlenecks in data throughput.

As you add counters to your display, the list at the bottom of the window grows, and each new counter is added to the chart and assigned a color. You can sort the list by clicking the column heads. If you wonder what a given counter is actually measuring, click Explain. You then see a description of the counter, as shown in Figure 23.2.

TIP

You can keep the Explain window open and click around on counter names to quickly learn about them, without clicking the Explain button each time.

Figure 23.2
This dialog box lets you select from the myriad of possible counters to display. Click Explain to read a description of a selected counter.

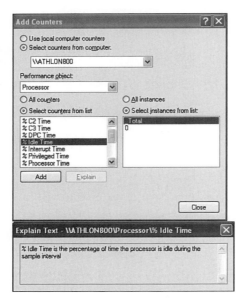

To change the format of the display, click the toolbar icons labeled View Graph (which displays a performance vs. time graph), View Histogram (which is a misnomer; it's actually just a bar chart of current values), or View Report (which displays current values in a table of numbers).

T I P

To single out one counter in a chart, click the Highlight button in the toolbar; then click the object's name in the list at the bottom of the window.

TUNING WINDOWS PERFORMANCE WITH THE SYSTEM APPLET

Once you discover how your system is performing, it's time to consider ways to speed up your system if you're not satisfied.

The System Applet provides several ways you can improve your system's performance without wielding a screwdriver or opening up your system.

To open the System applet, click Start, Control Panel, Performance and Maintenance and System, or just right-click My Computer and select Properties. The System properties sheet's General tab appears in Figure 23.3. The General tab lists the processor type, processor speed, and the amount of physical RAM (memory) installed.

Figure 23.3
This system has only the minimum amount of RAM necessary to run Windows XP Home Edition acceptably.

If your system has 128MB of RAM or less, your first move to increase performance should be to upgrade your system's RAM to at least 256MB. Windows XP really, *really* likes to have lots of memory, and with today's prices, you can add an additional 128MB for as little as $20. Memory modules come in larger increments as well, if your computer is designed for them. You'll notice a big improvement in performance when you step up to 256MB. It can't hurt to add even more, although you probably won't notice as great an improvement as the jump from 128MB to 256MB, unless you use memory-hungry applications such as Adobe Photoshop and Microsoft Access.

TIP

> If you're using a computer with its video built in to the motherboard (rather than located on a separate card), your effective memory is reduced by as much as 10MB or more because your system's memory is shared with the video card. For example, a system with 64MB of RAM that uses shared video memory (sometimes referred to as Unified Memory Architecture [UMA]) can have as little as 54MB of available RAM, or even less! This is another good reason to consider a memory upgrade, or at least stay away from chipsets with integrated video (except those that use NVIDIA's nForce chipset).

If you already have at least 256MB of memory or are looking for ways to fine-tune Windows to find more performance, click the Advanced tab. This tab has five sections:

- Performance
- User Profiles
- Startup and Recovery
- Environment Variables
- Error Reporting

Click the Settings button in the Performance section to get started.

Adjusting Visual Effects for Performance

If you have a modern, reasonably fast processor (that is, at least 500MHz), you can take full advantage of all the visual niceties provided by Windows XP's Visual Effects menu. However, if you're running with less than 128KB of RAM, have a processor under 500MHz, or have a slow video card (such as a PCI-based video card or typical motherboard-integrated video circuits), you might want to adjust Windows XP's defaults so that less graphics processing is required (see Figure 23.4).

If you select Adjust for best performance, all of the animations and effects shown in Figure 23.4 are turned off. If you select Adjust for best appearance, all of the animations and effects are turned on. If you use Let Windows choose what's best for my computer, none, some, or all of the animations and effects will be enabled, depending on the speed of your hardware. Select Custom to choose the options you want turned off or on.

You can speed up screen displays by turning off options in the Visual Effects menu.

Figure 23.4
Windows XP Home Edition's Visual Effects menu offers several animation and effects settings.

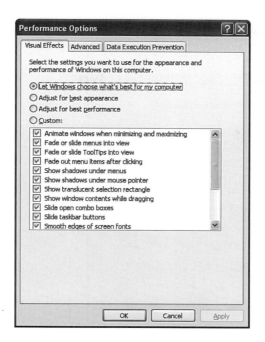

TIP

> If you enable Smooth Edges of Screen Fonts, you can further fine-tune its behavior through the Appearance tab of the Display properties sheet. Click Effects and select either Standard or ClearType for the smoothing method, or disable it if you prefer. Standard or disabled are best for CRT displays and many presentation projectors. ClearType can be a better choice for LCD displays. (I say "can be" because it's a matter of individual perception whether you think ClearType improves the display or makes it look fuzzier.)

ADJUSTING PROCESSOR, MEMORY, AND VIRTUAL MEMORY USAGE

To improve the performance of your computer by adjusting processor, memory, and virtual memory usage, click the Advanced tab (see Figure 23.5). The Advanced tab provides three ways to affect the performance of your system:

- **Processor scheduling**—Adjusts the balance of processor time between programs and background processes

- **Memory usage**—Adjusts the balance of memory usage between programs and system cache

- **Virtual memory**—Adjusts the size and location of the paging file, which uses the hard disk to hold active applications and data that can't currently fit into memory.

These options are covered in the following sections.

23

Figure 23.5
The Advanced dialog box allows you to adjust three factors to improve system performance.

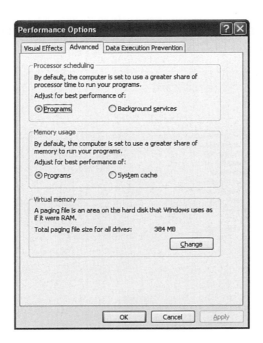

Optimizing Virtual Memory (Paging) File Size

Windows XP Home Edition—like Windows 2000, Windows NT, Windows Me, Windows 9x, and Windows 3.x—incorporates a virtual memory scheme. As you might know already, virtual memory is a method for tricking the operating system into thinking it has more apparent RAM for use by applications than is physically present in the computer. Windows XP uses a hard disk file called pagefile.sys to simulate RAM. Windows XP's Virtual Memory Manager (VMM) constantly tracks the amount of free RAM, and when the available RAM is exhausted, the VMM begins swapping out 4KB chunks of data and instruction code to pagefile.sys. As portions of the data or code are needed, they are swapped back into RAM chips, where they can be used by the CPU. This activity is called *paging*. The upshot is that more applications and services can run simultaneously than would normally be the case. Paging is a big benefit when the memory required by programs that are actually doing real work at any given time is less than the amount of physical memory. On the other hand, CPU access to the page file on your hard drive is monumentally slower than to your physical system memory, so when paging activity is high, performance plummets.

The default VMM settings applied when you install Windows XP Home Edition are based on your hard disk space and partition designations. Windows 9x and Me allowed only a single page file, although its size could vary. On Windows XP, however, a page file is created in the root of the partition containing the operating system, each additional partition can also have a `pagefile.sys` file, and the size of the each file is dynamic. So, if you have several disks or partitions, Windows XP Home Edition can decrease the size of a pagefile on one partition and shift paging onto another one as available hard disk space decreases.

Because Windows XP Home Edition is such a huge operating system and today's office suites, games, movie, and graphics editors are bigger than ever before, it's imperative that paging be intelligent and plentiful. This is especially important if your system barely exceeds the minimum RAM recommendation, as you learned in Chapter 2, "Getting Your Hardware and Software Ready for Windows XP."

If you want to ensure that your hard disk doesn't thrash itself to death and that the system runs efficiently, not making you wait every time you switch between windows or move something around on the screen, you should install at *least* 256MB of RAM, let Windows manage the pagefile size, and keep lots of free space on your drive.

The default pagefile size is equal to the amount of RAM in your computer plus 12MB. As disk space dwindles, the file can shrink. The minimum can be no less than about 2MB. Usually, you should leave the pagefile at its recommended size, although you might increase its minimum size if you routinely use programs that require a lot of memory—this lets Windows allocate the page file space immediately when there is less chance of having a fragmented pagefile. You can check with the software maker for information about how demanding applications might benefit from increasing the allocation.

You can optimize virtual memory use by dividing the space between multiple drives and especially by removing it from slower or heavily accessed drives. To best optimize your virtual memory space, you should divide it across as many physical hard drives as possible. When you're selecting drives, keep the following guidelines in mind:

- Try to avoid having a large pagefile on the same drive as the system files. You should have at least a 2MB pagefile on the boot volume. The system requires this to write events to the system log, send an administrative alert, or automatically restart after a system Stop error occurs in the event of a system failure.

- Avoid putting a pagefile on a fault-tolerant drive, such as a mirrored volume; some of today's high-performance systems come with mirrored IDE drives (where the second drive immediately reflects changes to the first drive). Pagefiles don't need fault tolerance, and some fault-tolerant systems suffer from slow data writes because they must write data to multiple locations.

- Don't place multiple pagefiles on different partitions on the same physical disk drive. This only makes your hard drive work even harder. Most systems have only one physical drive, so this is not usually a problem. If you have split the drive into more than one drive letter, be careful where you place pagefiles.

TIP

If you have multiple drive letters, it can be difficult to tell whether drive letters above C: are located on a second physical drive or are partitions of your first hard drive. Use the Microsoft Computer Management program (which you can access from the Administrative Tools folder in the Control Panel) and run the Disk Management tool to view local drives and their drive letters.

The following are some other points to consider when you're adjusting the pagefile:

- Setting the pagefile's initial size and maximum size to the same value increases efficiency because the operating system does not need to expand the file during later processing. Setting different values for initial and maximum size can contribute to disk fragmentation. Expanding the default size of the pagefile can increase performance if applications are consuming virtual memory and the full capacity of the existing file is being used. To determine how large your pagefile should be based on your system workload, you should monitor the Process (_Total)\Page File Bytes counter in the Performance Monitor. This counter indicates, in bytes, how much of the pagefile is being used.

- Don't put a large pagefile on a disk that is used a lot, such as one used for serving applications and databases. It slows down overall performance.

- The operating system always needs 5MB free on its partition. Make sure you don't use up the whole system boot drive.

- Change the file size a little at a time, and test the performance.

TIP

For additional speed improvements, consider defragmenting your hard disk and upgrading your hard disk, hard disk controller, or motherboard for faster disk performance. Before installing a new IDE hard drive, find out which transfer protocol it uses. If the new drive uses Ultra DMA/66 or Ultra DMA/100, and your present IDE controller doesn't, you could have booting problems. See whether the drive manufacturer has provided a method of reverting to an Ultra DMA level supported by your system. If not, you might have to turn off DMA support completely in your system BIOS and suffer a large performance hit. Sometimes when you're upgrading a hard drive, upgrading the motherboard at the same time will serve you well, for just this reason.

Serial ATA drives currently offer even faster performance.

To change the initial and maximum size of the workstation's pagefile, the file locations, and the number of pagefiles, follow these steps:

1. Open the Control Panel, and run the System applet, or right-click My Computer and select Properties.

2. View the Advanced tab; then click Settings under Performance Options. View the Advanced tab and in the Virtual Memory area, click Change, then Custom Size. You then see the dialog box shown in Figure 23.6.

3. Edit the initial size and maximum size if you want to change them, and click Set.

TIP

Short on disk space? If you're seriously short on space, you can turn off the VMM and then delete the pagefile. You can't delete it while it's in use, though. So, first, you have to turn it off using the Control Panel's System applet. Then, reboot, and delete the inactive file using Windows Explorer.

You can use the Performance Monitor discussed earlier in this chapter to get a sense of how much virtual memory is being used. To get started, open the Performance Monitor and click the + (plus) button on the toolbar. Choose Paging File from the Performance Object drop-down list. Then add Usage and Usage peak. View the statistics in whatever way you like. Figure 23.7 shows an example. In this figure, you can see that even with 15 programs running, I'm still only at 3.354 percent usage, with a peak of 6.212 percent.

Figure 23.6
You can set Pagefile sizes and locations in this dialog box.

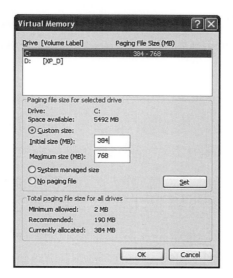

Figure 23.7
You can check virtual memory usage via the Performance Monitor by adding paging file monitoring for display in the chart.

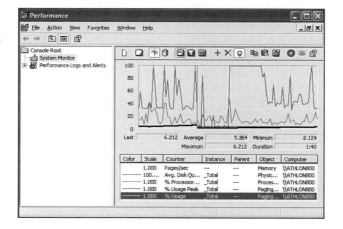

SETTING MULTITASKING PRIORITIES

As you know, Windows XP Home Edition is a multithreaded, preemptive multitasking operating system. Left to its own devices, it does an extremely good job of balancing user requests with the need for internal system operations and control. The result from the user's point of view is performance that appears to be highly responsive, even though some internal sleight of hand and task juggling may be going on under the hood.

One setting can slightly improve overall smoothness of Windows XP Home Edition's multitasking, depending on what you use your computer for. To set it, do the following:

1. Click Start, right-click My Computer, and select Properties.
2. Select the Advanced tab and click the Settings button in the Performance section.
3. View the Advanced tab, as shown in Figure 23.5. In this dialog box, you can set the tasking priority for your applications.

    Click either Background Services or Programs, and save the change by clicking OK.

Normally, Programs is selected, ensuring that the foreground application (the window you're currently working with) gets more CPU time slices than programs running in the background. Time slices are also shorter and variably sized, which results in more responsive action from an application as you work in it. Unless you have CPU-intensive applications running in the background, though, you won't notice a difference in foreground performance.

If you're running something important in the background that bogs down too much when you're doing other foreground work on the computer, choose the Background Services option. Examples might be data acquisition programs, communications programs, Internet Connection sharing, a Web server, or a backup utility. The time slices are doled out in longer portions with this setting.

SETTING MEMORY USAGE

By default, Windows XP devotes more memory to running programs than to the system cache (the memory used for disk caching and handing background operations). If your computer is used entirely as a workstation and doesn't share folders, drives or its Internet connection with other computers on a network, this setting should be left alone. However, if your computer is used as a server, and particularly if you have 256MB of RAM or more, change the default for Memory Usage (see Figure 23.5) from Programs to System Cache to improve performance for shared resources.

When you're finished customizing Performance settings, click OK to close the Performance Options dialog box and return to the Advanced tab of the System Properties window.

ENABLING DATA EXECUTION PREVENTION

Since the early days of computing, most computer designs have allowed program instruction codes and data to be mixed together in memory. This has many advantages, but it's also made possible a whole category of security disasters, wherein hackers exploit program bugs to write new instructions into the program's data areas and then fool the program into executing these new instructions. These program bugs take a lot of time to identify and eliminate, and untold numbers of them are still lurking about, so programs and operating systems remain vulnerable.

To answer the security threat, some recent microprocessors now have as part of their memory-management hardware a feature that lets the operating system mark the data storage sections of memory as nonexecutable, so the operating system can be notified if a program attempts to execute instructions in them. Starting with Service Pack 2, Windows XP can take advantage of this hardware feature and calls it the Data Execution Prevention (DEP) option. At the time this was written, only Intel's and AMD's 64-bit processors provided Execution Protection support, so DEP was available on the 64-bit version of Windows XP and the 32-bit versions of XP only while running on the Opteron and Athlon-64 processors in 32-bit mode. However, it also might be provided by newer 32-bit processors, so you should check to see whether Data Execution Prevention is available on your computer.

To manage DEP, log on as a Computer Administrator, open the Control Panel, open the Security Center, and at the bottom of the screen double-click the System icon to view the dialog box shown in Figure 23.8. (You can also get to the Data Execution Prevention tab from the System Options/Performance dialog box we've been discussing in the previous sections.)

Figure 23.8
If Data Execution Prevention is available on your computer, you can control it from the System Performance Options dialog box.

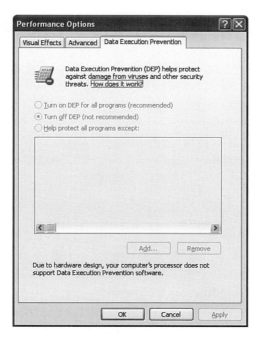

If Windows indicates that your processor does not have the necessary hardware support, the dialog box's options will all be grayed out, and you can simply close it and forget about it.

23

If the options are not grayed out, you should check Turn On DEP for All Programs to enable the feature. Thereafter, if an application program attempts to execute instructions from protected memory regions, Windows will display a dialog box informing you of the program failure and terminate the application.

In almost all cases, executing instructions in writable data memory occurs only as a consequence of a serious bug or during a hacking attempt. In some rare instances application programs legitimately write and execute instructions-on the-fly—"just-in-time" compilers like Java are an example. Also, some graphics processing applications use self-modifying code to squeeze out every last bit of performance. These programs should be updated by their manufacturers to work correctly under DEP. Until they're updated, however, DEP will not let them run. If you know you can trust a given application, you can disable DEP just for the one application by making an entry in the DEP configuration dialog box. Click Add, and then locate the application's executable filename.

If a device driver fails with DEP enabled, you get the dreaded blue screen of death with the message ATTEMPTED_EXECUTE_OF_NOEXECUTE_MEMORY, and you have to restart Windows. If this happens, I suggest that you restart Windows in Safe Mode and attempt to identify and then disable or update the device driver that failed.

→ To learn more about starting in Safe Mode, **see** "Boot Options," **p. 1040**.

SETTING ENVIRONMENT VARIABLES

Settings that you're not likely to use but could still prove handy are the environment variables. What do environment variables do? They're a way to communicate setup information to application programs, from the days before the Registry. They indicate where temporary files are stored, what folder contains Windows program files, and other settings that affect program operation and system performance. In particular, batch files and application programs can use them to find where certain system files and folders are located.

Windows sets up a set of environment variables for you, including the ones listed in Table 23.1.

TABLE 23.1 SOME WINDOWS XP ENVIRONMENT VARIABLES

Variable Name	Contains
ALLUSERSPROFILE	The path to the folder that contains files visible to all users, including desktop items, start menu items, and the Shared Documents folder.*
COMPUTERNAME	The network name of this computer.*
OS	Windows_NT, provided to let you write batch files that know when they're running on Windows NT, 2000, or XP as opposed to MS-DOS, Window 3.1, or Windows 9x.*
PATH	The list of folders that Windows searches when you try to run a program by entering only its name.

Variable Name	Contains
PATHEXT	The list of file extensions Windows considers to indicate runnable programs: .com, .exe, .bat, and so on.
PROMPT	A specification of how Windows is to display the prompt in a command prompt window. By default, it is PG, which displays the current drive and folder behind the >.
TEMP	The folder in which applications are to create temporary (scratch) files.
TMP	Like TEMP. (Some applications look at the TMP variable, and other applications look at TEMP to get the name of the temporary file folder.)
USERNAME	The logon name of the current user.*
USERPROFILE	The path to your profile folder, the folder that contains My Documents, your Start menu, and so on.*
SystemRoot	The path to the system32 folder in the Windows installation folder.*
windir	The path to the Windows installation folder.*

These variables are informational only; changing their value doesn't change the corresponding location or name.

In DOS and Windows 9x, environment variables usually were set up in the AUTOEXEC.BAT file, using lines like this:

```
SET PROMPT=$P$G
SET TEMP=C:\TEMP
SET PATH=C:\WINDOWS;C:\DOS;C:\MOUSE;C:\BIN
```

In Windows XP, environment variables for Windows applications are set up using a nifty graphical user interface. In addition, old DOS and Windows 3.x applications will see any environment variables set up by the AUTOEXEC.NT file, which we'll discuss later in this chapter, under "Configuring the MS-DOS Environment."

By clicking the Environment Variables button on the System applet's Advanced tab, you can change the environment variables in the resulting dialog box (see Figure 23.9).

In Figure 23.9, you can create new variables, delete a variable, or edit a variable using the corresponding buttons. Notice that this dialog box has two sections, System Variables and User Variables. Environment variables set in the System Variables area are the default settings provided for every user account. This section can be edited only while logged on to a Computer Administrator account. The User Variables section applies just to the currently logged-on user (that is, *you*), and each user can edit her own settings.

Figure 23.9
Examining the
Environment Variables
for the current user
(top) and for all users
of the system
(bottom).

If you need to alter a variable, you need to understand what happens if there's a conflict between environment variables defined in more than one place. As a rule, Windows examines several locations for definitions and the last definition seen wins. Windows XP sets variables in the following order:

1. System-level variables.

2. User-level variables. (However, at this step, the PATH variable is treated specially. See the next section for details.)

3. AUTOEXEC.NT-declared variables (seen only by MS-DOS or Windows 3.x applications). AUTOEXEC.NT contains commands similar to those used in the AUTOEXEC.BAT file used by older versions of Windows. We'll discuss AUTOEXEC.NT later in this chapter.

4. Subsequent definitions, issued by set commands typed at the command prompt or encountered in a batch file. Environment changes made in a batch file persist at the command prompt, unless the batch file uses the SETLOCAL command.

CAUTION

I need to make an important distinction here. AUTOEXEC.NT settings (such as the SET BLASTER command, which sets up sound support) do not affect the default variables seen in the standard Command Prompt window, which is actually a 32-bit environment running the 32-bit CMD.EXE shell program. The AUTOEXEC.NT variable settings go into effect only when the execution of an MS-DOS or Windows 3.x program causes a Virtual DOS Machine (VDM) to be created and are seen only by the program(s) running inside the VDM. The Virtual DOS Machine subsystem is described in more detail later in this chapter.

You can view the effective MS-DOS environment by opening a Command Prompt window, running the old MS-DOS shell program command.com, and typing **set** to list the defined variables.

Why modify system variables? Good question. Not many people need to. Probably the most likely reasons to modify these variables are to change the folder applications use to create temporary work files and to add directories to the system's search path. Or, you might have particular applications that require special environment variables set. Finally, some command-line utilities look for environment variables to set the default value of certain options. For example, copy checks to see whether an environment variable named COPYCMD has been defined, and if it has, it interprets COPYCMD as containing command-line switches that can be used, for instance, to determine whether copy should prompt before overwriting files. I discuss these options in the next several sections.

Chances are, you'll never need to adjust environment variables, but if you want to send temporary files to a drive besides C:, this is where you do it.

NOTE

> The environment variables defined here are used by every Windows application, and are the initial environment variables set for each Command Prompt window. If you change environment variables in the Command Prompt window (say, in a batch file), the changes apply only to that window and will disappear when the window is closed.

Specifying the Location of Temporary Files

Many applications create temporary files to hold information while you're working. These files are usually deleted when the application exits. Sometimes, however, they're not deleted, and they can accumulate, taking up a lot of disk space. To make management simpler, you may wish to control where they are stored. By custom, most applications that do create temporary files create them in the folder named by either the TMP or TEMP environment variable.

By default, both TMP and TEMP are defined in the System Settings list as %userprofile%\ Local Settings\Temp. %userprofile% is an environment variable that contains the full path to your user profile folder. The net result is that, for my account, temporary files are created in C:\Documents and Settings\bknittel\Local Settings\Temp.

Now, for maximum security, placing each user's temporary files in a different folder is a good idea. Also, with Fast User Switching active, several users could have applications running at the same time, so placing temporary files in a different folder for each user avoids the possibility of conflicts in the filenames. On my own computer, however, I am not worried about inter-user security, and to make cleanup easier, I personally prefer to place temporary files for all users in a folder named \temp on the hard drive with the most space. On my computer this is D:\temp.

To specify the location of temporary files for your account alone, set the values of variables TEMP and TMP in the User Settings section. To specify the same location for *all* accounts, set the values in the System Settings section and delete any settings in the User Settings section.

23

NOTE

If you designate a folder in a partition that is formatted with the NTFS file system, be sure that the user or users who are set up to use it have read and write permissions on the folder! Ensure this by editing the folder's security properties, adding the group Users, and giving Users all permissions except Full Control. You may need to temporarily disable Simple File Sharing to view the Security properties.

NOTE

You might be inspired to create a separate folder for each user with a setting like D:\temp\%username%. This will work, but you must create the folder for each user in advance. Windows will *not* create the folders automatically, and if the folder specified by TEMP or TMP does not exist, most applications either fail or create temporary files in seemingly random locations.

SETTING THE PATH ENVIRONMENT VARIABLE

Another important environment variable is called PATH. This variable lists the folders Windows is to search whenever you attempt to run a program by typing its name without a path specification. For example, if I type regedit into a command prompt window or into the Start, Run dialog box, the Registry Editor window appears. But how does Windows know that regedit means C:\windows\system32\regedit.exe? The answer is the *PATH* variable. On my computer, *PATH* contains this:

```
D:\Perl\bin;C:\WINDOWS\system32;C:\WINDOWS;C:\WINDOWS\system32\WBEM;
 "C:\program files\scripts";
"C:\Program Files\Symantec\pcAnywhere";c:\progra~1\winzip;"c:\Documents and
  Settings\bknittel\scripts";c:\bin;c:\bat
```

The value of the PATH variable is a list of folder names separated by semicolons. If a folder name has a space in it, it is enclosed in double quotes, as "C:\program files\scripts" and "C:\Program Files\Symantec\pcAnywhere" are on my computer.

Now, when I type regedit as a command name, Windows searches the folders named in the PATH variable in order, looking for the first one that contains an executable program whose name is regedit. It finds the standard Windows utility in the second folder, c:\WINDOWS\system32.

NOTE

The PATH variable is used for Windows programs as well as DOS programs; it's used any time a program is not specifically specified with a full path.

Many applications add their own installation folders to the path during installation. Thus, you seldom if ever need to modify the PATH to provide access to programs designed to run from the command line. If you write batch files or scripts, however, it's useful to put all these into one folder and to enter this folder name into the PATH, so you can run your batch files and scripts simply by typing their names.

Because it's so common for users to want to put a personal folder into the PATH, and because misediting the PATH variable can prevent Windows from being able to find applications it needs to run, Windows gives the User Variables PATH definition special treatment:

- For the PATH variable, the User Variables definition is appended to the System Variables definition.

- For all other environment variables, a User Variables definition overrides a System Variables definition.

In other words, you can enter your own personal folder(s) into the User Variables definition of PATH without worrying about messing up the standard definitions.

For example, a few paragraphs back I showed my computer's PATH setting. It's set up this way: the System Variables PATH definition is

```
D:\Perl\bin;C:\WINDOWS\system32;C:\WINDOWS;C:\WINDOWS\system32\WBEM;
"C:\program files\scripts";"C:\Program Files\Symantec\pcAnywhere";
c:\progra~1\winzip;"%USERPROFILE%\scripts"
```

These folders are used for every user on my computer. The User Variables PATH definition contains only my personal folders:

```
c:\bin;c:\bat
```

When I log on, Windows automatically adds my personal folders after the system-wide folders.

> **TIP**
>
> To make it even easier to have personal PATH folders, you can automatically give each user a place to store her own personal programs by placing %USERPROFILE%\scripts in the System Variables PATH definition. This gives each user the option of creating a folder named scripts in her profile folder, into which she can put commonly used batch files, programs, and scripts.

You can also modify the PATH variable by directly setting the environment variable at the command prompt. It's best to do this by adding a new folder at the beginning or end of the existing path list, rather than by replacing the list entirely. Type the string %path% where you want the original PATH contents to appear. For example, you can add the folder c:\myfolder to the head of the path list by typing

```
set path=c:\myfolder;%path%
```

or to the end of the path by typing

```
set path=%path%;c:\myfolder
```

You also can use this technique to modify the path from within a batch file.

PROGRAM COMPATIBILITY WIZARD

One of the biggest concerns any user of a new Windows version has is, "Will it run my software?" This fear goes all the way back to the birth of Windows, when Windows 386 was unable to run some programs designed for Windows 286, and Windows 3.x couldn't run all Windows 3.0 programs.

Fortunately, Windows XP Home Edition includes a Program Compatibility Wizard that can help you run your "golden oldie" Windows 95, Windows 98/Me, Windows NT 4.0, or Windows 2000 programs under Windows XP.

By default, Program Compatibility is turned off for all the programs you install, since most 32-bit Windows programs will run with Windows XP without any problems. If you have problems with a particular program (game and education programs are the most common culprits), start the wizard by clicking Start, All Programs, Accessories, Program Compatibility Wizard.

When the wizard (which is part of Windows XP's Help and Support Center) starts, click Next after you read the introduction.

You can select the program that needs compatibility help from a list of programs already installed, or choose the program currently in the CD-ROM drive, or by locating the program manually. Once you select a program and click Next, choose the version of Windows you want Windows XP to emulate (note that Windows NT 4.0 compatibility is for NT 4.0 with Service Pack 5 installed) as shown in Figure 23.10.

Figure 23.10
The Program Compatibility Wizard lets you run your program in any of four modes compatible with recent Windows versions.

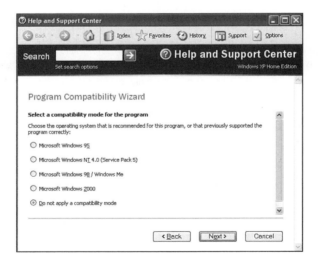

After you select the compatibility mode, select any special display options needed by the program. For example, you can run the program in 256-color mode, 640x480 screen resolution, or without Windows XP visual themes without resetting your normal screen settings (see Figure 23.11). This is a great benefit if you have programs that normally require you to change these options before they'll work correctly.

Figure 23.11
Select color depth and resolution needed for your game, or disable the Windows XP visual themes if your program requires these special settings.

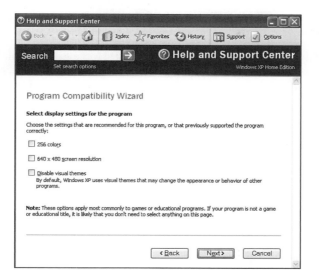

After you choose the display options, click Next to test the program. If you chose display options, the screen may blank briefly as the monitor resets to the color depth and resolution you selected. When you close the program, you have the option to save the compatibility settings, discard them, or stop the process.

NOTE

There are still some application incompatibilities that the wizard can't fix. I've found a few older Windows programs that simply won't run under Windows XP under any setting of the Program Compatibility Wizard. There's nothing to be done in this case but contact the manufacturer. Some manufacturers are eager to hear bug reports and gracious about providing updates. Some—Epson Corporation is notable for this—basically tell you to go jump in a lake. That's life, I guess.

For incompatible but critical older applications, you can actually run them under the older operating system right on your Windows XP computer, using a PC emulation program such as VMWare or Microsoft Virtual PC.

→ For more information about emulation, **see** "The Virtual Machine Approach," on **p. 1005**.

CONFIGURING THE PROGRAM ENVIRONMENTS

Chapter 21, "Tweaking the GUI," and Chapter 22, "Configuration via Control Panel Applets," covered quite a few of the adjustments that you can make to the Windows XP user environment. Those chapters also addressed a variety of settings that affect the operation of Windows on a more rudimentary level, such as Properties sheets for printers and other devices you may have installed on a typical system or network. In addition to all these settings and properties, Windows XP allows for fine-tuning of program and system handling under the various operating system environments that Windows XP can control.

As discussed in Chapter 1, "Introducing Windows XP Home Edition," and Chapter 2, in addition to standard 32-bit Windows applications, Windows XP can also run programs designed for MS-DOS and Windows 3.x. If you download and install the Services for Unix (Interix) package, it can additionally run POSIX-compliant character-based applications. Chances are that you'll seldom, if ever, encounter POSIX-based software at home, but you might sometimes run Windows 3.x or MS-DOS based programs, especially older games, on your computer. (I have a cherished copy of Space Quest III, myself).

How does Windows XP handle programs written for different operating systems? Windows XP has a feature called *environment subsystems*, which enables Windows XP to emulate a particular operating system's operation and translate a program's request for services into Windows XP commands. For MS-DOS applications, this includes monitoring the program's attempts to access hardware registers and memory locations that had special meaning to MS-DOS and taking the appropriate action.

Some optimization and configuration of the various environments are possible, typically to allow for higher compatibility with non–Windows XP programs. Or, in some cases, the adjustments possible are purely aesthetic or convenience factors. The following sections describe options for configuring applications and subsystems. They also describe some specific programs or classes of programs (such as DOS-based TSRs) and how best to run them under Windows XP.

In the following sections, you'll learn about settings for the following subsystems:

- Windows 16-bit
- DOS

32-bit Windows tuning was covered earlier in this chapter in the section, "Tuning Windows Performance with the System Applet."

VDM—The Virtual DOS Machine

Windows XP provides support for old MS-DOS and Windows 3.x applications through a program subsystem called the Virtual DOS Machine, or VDM. VDM is a program that mimics the hardware and software of a computer running MS-DOS. This program then loads and executes MS-DOS and Windows 3.x programs in a controlled environment. The "virtual" part signifies that an old program running in the VDM thinks it can directly control hardware such as the video card and keyboard, when in fact, the VDM intercepts all hardware control attempts and uses Windows XP to carry out the desired operations safely.

An illegal or dangerous hardware operation can simply be rejected. No user application program can directly manipulate hardware on Windows XP—that's why it's so sturdy. When you run a Windows 3.x application or an MS-DOS program, Windows XP runs it through the VDM, where it can do whatever it wants without the risk of actually crashing the computer.

The Virtual DOS Machine can be configured by several settings and setup files, which are discussed in the following sections.

CONFIGURING THE WINDOWS 3.X ENVIRONMENT

Windows XP runs Windows 3.x programs without a hitch, thanks to its Windows-on-Windows (WOW) system, which lets these older Windows programs see the 16-bit Windows operating system environment that they expect. WOW, in turn, depends on the Virtual DOS Machine to provide emulated hardware support. This sounds complex, and it is, but from the user's point of view, you can just run an older Windows application and it just plain works.

One significant thing that WOW does is monitor the old configuration files WIN.INI and SYTEM.INI. Old Windows programs expect to see Windows's system settings in these files in the Windows directory. Windows XP therefore keeps copies of these files up to date with your system's current settings. It also tries to detect changes made to these old configuration files made by legacy programs that are attempting to signal Windows to make changes.

One thing that WOW can't completely fix is the filename length limitation that hearkens back to DOS. If you run Windows 3.x applications on Windows XP, you'll see truncated file and folder names in any program that looks at the hard disk directory. You see these shortened names because Windows 3.x applications were hostage to the limitation of DOS's 8.3 file-naming conventions. This limitation can be annoying, especially in a Browse box, but there's absolutely nothing you can do about it, short of upgrading to a 32-bit Windows version of the program.

TIP

> The term "32-bit Windows" describes programs that are designed to run on Windows 9x, Windows NT, Windows Me, Windows 2000 or Windows XP.

If you can't upgrade, at least understanding how the truncated names are generated helps a bit. Following are some of the rules governing truncated NTFS and DOS file-naming rules and some hints for using them.

First, consider the rules of Windows 9x, NT 4, Windows 2000, and Windows XP long filenames:

23

- Files and directory names can be up to 256 characters in length.
- You can include a file type or extension, separated from the rest of the name by a period, such as *2002 Sales Reports.WKS*. (If associated file extensions are hidden via the Folder Options, the extension is invisible in listings, however.) Windows XP doesn't care how many periods are in a name, and only considers the last one when looking for the file type: Sales.Reports.xls and Salesreports.xls are both taken to be Excel files.
- Special characters not allowed are as follows:

  ?, ", \, /, <, >, *, |, and :
- Spaces can be included. No problem.
- Uppercase and lowercase are both allowed, and they appear in listings. However, they aren't interpreted by Windows XP or its applications as being different from one another. In other words, you can't store a file called mybudget.xls and another one called MYBUDGET.XLS in the same folder, because Windows XP interprets both files as having the same name. If you tried to copy or move one file into the folder containing the other file, you would be asked if you wanted to replace the original file.

Windows XP automatically generates shorter DOS-compatible filenames when needed by a Windows 3.x program by doing the following:

- Removing illegal characters and replacing them with _ (an underscore).
- Removing any spaces in the name.
- Using only the last period that has three consecutive letters after it as the extension.
- Truncating the first name to six letters and adding a tilde (~) and a single-digit number as the last two characters of the first name; the digit is chosen to make the name distinct from other similar filenames. Consider these examples:

Windows XP Name	DOS/Windows 3.x Name
Quarterly Sales Reports.WK3	QUARTE~1.WK3
Quarterly Sales Reports. Atlanta.Georgia.WK3	QUARTE~2.WK3
Qrtr[Sales]Reports from Atlanta,Georgia.WK3	QRTR_S~1.WK3

When you use any programs that generate documents you're going to use with DOS and Windows 3.x applications, you might want to adopt a naming convention that makes sense to you when the longer names are converted to shorter DOS names. Try to use only one period, and use the extension that the application expects. Because the first six letters are retained, pack as much description into them as possible. And if you stick to filenames of eight letters or less, plus a three character extension, they'll most likely look identical under the Windows 3.x and DOS applications.

ALLOTTING INDEPENDENT MEMORY SPACE FOR WINDOWS 3.X APPLICATIONS

Windows XP creates a separate instance of the VDM program for each MS-DOS program that you run, but normally all 16-bit Windows 3.x applications are run by one VDM. This is necessary because the old Windows depended on being able to directly transfer data back and forth between programs in ways that modern Windows programs aren't allowed (again, for reliability's sake). The result is that, just like in a real Windows 3.x machine, one crashing Windows 3.x application can take down the whole VDM, crashing any other Windows 3.x programs (but not, thankfully, Windows XP itself).

Well, unlike death and taxes, this isn't necessarily a fact of life. If you don't need your Windows 3.x applications to communicate with each other, you can cause an application to request its own VDM. The memory space that it runs in is then totally isolated, protected from other applications that might run amok. The upside is that one errant Windows 3.x application can't take down another. The downside is that any Windows 3.x applications running in their own memory space can't communicate with other Windows 3.x applications as they would in a true Windows 3.x computer. Dynamic Data Exchange (DDE) and services provided by shared Dynamic Link Libraries (DLLs) do not work, thus data passing between applications is quashed. However, this isn't a big problem for most Windows XP users, because you'll probably seldom use more than one or two Windows 3.x applications at once anyway.

You make the setting to the properties for the Windows 3.x program. As an example, I'll use a Windows 3.x version of the popular Pretty Good Solitaire shareware program. To change the setting, follow these steps:

1. Create a shortcut for the program in question; to make a shortcut, right-click the program icon in Windows Explorer and select Create Shortcut.

2. Right-click the shortcut, and choose Properties. In the Shortcut Properties dialog box, choose the Shortcut tab and then click Advanced. You then see the dialog box shown in Figure 23.12.

Figure 23.12
You can set this option to give a Windows 3.x application its own memory space. You can do so only from a shortcut for the application.

TIP

> Many Windows 3.x programs were developed for 256-color displays, and may not function properly with the 65,536 or 16.8 million color displays now used by Windows. If necessary, you can also use the Compatibility tab to select 256-color or other display settings, or to choose compatibility mode settings described earlier in this chapter in "Program Compatibility Wizard."

From this dialog box, you have only to put a check in the Run In Separate Memory Space check box.

CONFIGURING THE MS-DOS ENVIRONMENT

If you still use DOS programs, you'll be glad to know that the DOS environment that Windows XP uses is highly configurable. I discussed the Virtual DOS Machine, or VDM, in the previous section. It provides a simulated MS-DOS computer environment in which your old DOS applications run. It's also run "underneath" the simulated Windows 3.x environment, so it's used by old 16-bit Windows applications as well. You can configure it in several ways:

- By configuring the user variables in the System dialog box, as discussed in the section "Setting Environment Variables"
- By making selections from the DOS window's Control menu
- By making settings in the Properties sheet for a shortcut to the DOS application
- By making settings stored in custom AUTOEXEC.NT and CONFIG.NT files you can create for programs that require special memory or environment variable settings
- By entering environment-altering commands at the command prompt

You can choose from a great number of settings, including the following, all of which can be set for an individual program or as defaults to be used any time a Command Prompt window or DOS program is run. You can make the following settings:

- Set the window font (including TrueType and bitmapped font styles).
- Set the background and foreground colors for normal text.
- Set the background and foreground colors for pop-up boxes.
- Choose window or full-screen viewing.
- Set the default window position on the screen.
- Use or turn off the QuickEdit mode, which lets you copy text to the clipboard by highlighting it on the DOS window and pressing Enter.
- Use or hide the Windows XP mouse pointer in the application.

In addition to these settings, you can set the search path and other environment variables, specify memory requirements (for EMS and XMS), and set other nitty-gritty options using

Program Information Files (PIF files) and the System option in the Control Panel. Unless specified otherwise, Windows XP uses the file _DEFAULT.PIF, stored in the default Windows folder (usually either \WINDOWS or \WINNT), as the basis for MS-DOS sessions and running applications that don't have a PIF. When you alter the "properties" for DOS applications by right-clicking the application and making settings, you create a customized PIF file for that application. The result of running any DOS application, however, is that Windows XP Home Edition creates a PIF on-the-fly and assigns the default settings to it unless other settings are specified.

If your MS-DOS program gives error messages when it tries to open files, see "MS-DOS Program Can't Open Enough Files" in the "Troubleshooting" section at the end of this chapter.

If your older MS-DOS application displays lots of strange characters on the screen, especially the combination ←[, see "MS-DOS Application Displays Garbage Characters" in the "Troubleshooting" section at the end of this chapter.

CUSTOMIZING AUTOEXEC.NT AND CONFIG.NT

You can choose to further configure the MS-DOS and Windows 3.x environment by modifying XP's equivalent of the old CONFIG.SYS and AUTOEXEC.BAT files. In Windows XP, as in Windows NT and Windows 2000, these files are called CONFIG.NT and AUTOEXEC.NT. They are the files used to configure each DOS VDM when it starts up.

When you run a DOS or 16-bit Windows application, Windows XP creates a DOS VDM by loading the DOS environment subsystem and sort of booting up DOS. In the process, it reads in settings from CONFIG.NT and AUTOEXEC.NT in just the same way the original DOS read CONFIG.SYS and AUTOEXEC.BAT when it booted. The differences are the filenames and the file locations. In this case, the files are in the SYSTEM32 directory (usually \WINDOWS\ SYSTEM32 or \WINNT\SYSTEM32) instead of the root directory. Each time you run a DOS application in a new window (that is, each time a new VDM is created), Windows XP reads the CONFIG.NT and AUTOEXEC.NT files. The great thing about this capability is that you can change the settings and rerun a program, and the new settings get read and go into effect immediately. It's like rebooting DOS after fine-tuning CONFIG.SYS and AUTOEXEC.BAT— except faster.

Just remember these points:

- The files CONFIG.SYS and AUTOEXEC.BAT in your hard drive's root folder are ignored by Windows XP. They're there only to fool really old applications that won't run unless they see that these files exist.

- The files CONFIG.NT and AUTOEXEC.NT in \WINDOWS\SYSTEM32 are used but only when Windows needs to start up an MS-DOS or Windows 3.x application. The settings in these files affect only the one DOS or Win3.x application you're running at the time because they're read by the VDM program before it starts up the old application.

The standard settings in CONFIG.NT that are set up when Windows XP is installed are shown in the following listing. The REM comments have been removed for brevity. (If you upgraded your computer from an earlier version of Windows, your CONFIG.NT might be different because the installer might have retained some of your previous operating system's settings):

```
dos=high, umb
device=%SystemRoot%\system32\himem.sys
files=20
```

TIP

> On my computers, I always change the file setting to files=100 and add the line device=%SystemRoot%\system32\ansi.sys.
>
> For more information about ansi.sys, see the next section.

TIP

> If you need to specify different CONFIG.NT and AUTOEXEC.NT settings for various MS-DOS programs, see "Custom Startup Files" later in this chapter.

You can edit the CONFIG.NT and AUTOEXEC.NT files with a simple text editor like Notepad. Microsoft, for some reason, chose not to provide a comprehensive list of the settings permitted in CONFIG.NT in the online Help and Support, so I've listed them in Table 23.2.

TABLE 23.2   COMMANDS AVAILABLE FOR CONFIG.NT

Command	Description
country=	Sets the language conventions for the session.
device=	Installs loadable device drivers. Be careful with drivers that attempt to address hardware directly; they very likely won't work. However, you can load display drivers such as ANSI.SYS and memory managers such as EMM.SYS and HIMEM.SYS.
dos=	Tells Windows 2000 what to do with the upper memory area (where to load DOS, as in dos=high).
dosonly	Allows only DOS programs to be loaded from a COMMAND.COM prompt. POSIX, OS/2, and Windows programs don't run. Note that a COMMAND.COM prompt and a Windows XP command prompt are not the same. If you run COMMAND.COM, you get a DOS VDM window running the DOS command interpreter. Command prompt windows run Windows XP's command interpreter (CMD.EXE), whose command set differs and expands on MS-DOS's.
echoconfig	Tells the VDM to print CONFIG and AUTOEXEC commands as they are executed from the files.
EMM	Configures the Expanded Memory Manager (EMM). Applies only when the program's properties specify that the value for EMS memory is greater than 0.

Command	Description
fcbs=	Sets the maximum number of file control blocks (FCBs). This setting is required only for truly ancient DOS programs.
files=	Sets the maximum number of open files. I recommend setting this to 100.
install=	Loads a memory-resident (TSR) program into memory before the window comes up or an application loads.
loadhigh=	Loads a device driver into the High Memory Area (HMA).
lh=	Same as loadhigh=.
ntcmdprompt	Replaces the COMMAND.COM interpreter with the Windows XP interpreter, CMD.EXE. After you load a TSR or when you shell out of an application to DOS, you get CMD.EXE instead, from which you have the added benefits of the Windows XP interpreter.
rem	Marks a line as a comment, causing the system to ignore it when booting the file.
stacks=	Indicates the amount of RAM set aside for stacking up hardware interrupts as they come in.

If you enter CONFIG.NT into the Search box in Windows XP Home Edition's Help and Support Center, some of the previous terms are listed under the Full-Text Search Matches section of Search Results. Click the individual term for more information.

The standard settings in AUTOEXEC.NT that are set up when Windows XP is installed are shown in the following listing. The REM comments have been removed for brevity. (And again, if you upgraded your computer from an earlier version of Windows, your AUTOEXEC.NT might be different):

```
REM Install CD ROM extensions
lh %SystemRoot%\system32\mscdexnt.exe

REM Install network redirector (load before dosx.exe)
lh %SystemRoot%\system32\redir

REM Install DPMI support
lh %SystemRoot%\system32\dosx
REM The following line enables Sound Blaster 2.0 support on NTVDM.
SET BLASTER=A220 I5 D1 P330 T3
```

Here's what these do:

- mscdexnt gives DOS programs access to CD-ROM and DVD-ROM data discs.
- redir gives DOS programs access to shared network resources.
- dosx provides expanded and extended memory services.
- SET BLASTER tells DOS programs, through an environment variable, how to use the emulated Sound Blaster–compatible sound services provided by the VDM.

TIP

> Editing these files properly is no piece of cake. You need to read about the configuration commands in Windows's Online Help and Support, and I suggest you have at hand a good DOS reference like Que's *Special Edition Using DOS 6.22, Third Edition*.

ISSUES WITH DOSKEY AND ANSI.SYS

Two of the most common enhancements used on MS-DOS computers were DOSKEY and ANSI.SYS. DOSKEY provided enhanced command-line editing—for example, the use of the up and down arrow keys to recall previous commands. ANSI.SYS gave DOS applications a way to easily control the position and color of text output onto the screen. Both enhancements are provided with Windows XP, although, they don't work exactly as you might expect.

ANSI.SYS can be made available for MS-DOS programs simply by adding the line device=ansi.sys to CONFIG.NT (or an alternative CONFIG file). Unfortunately, no ANSI cursor support is provided for 32-bit Windows character mode (console) applications.

Conversely, DOSKEY—which has been enhanced significantly from the old DOS days— functions only in the 32-bit Windows console environment. Even if you attempt to load it in AUTOEXEC.NT, it does not function within the MS-DOS COMMAND.COM shell; that is, after you've run any MS-DOS program in the command prompt window.

You can work around this limitation by instructing Windows to use CMD.EXE as the MS-DOS shell. Just add the line NTCMDPROMPT to your CONFIT.NT file. However, this might not work if you need to load terminate-and-stay-resident (TSR) programs before your DOS application.

SETTING THE COMMAND PROMPT WINDOW PROPERTIES FROM A WINDOW

The Command Prompt window displays a text-mode window that looks a lot like a DOS computer's screen. This window actually is a true 32-bit Windows application, although it also can execute old MS-DOS applications. Settings you make in the Command Prompt window affect both the window itself and any DOS programs that run it. In fact, by far the simplest means for altering the DOS environment is via the Properties dialog box of a DOS window. If you need to fine-tune the DOS environment, this is most likely the way you will do it.

When you open a Command Prompt window or run a DOS-based program, the window defaults to a standard size, background color, and font. Configuration options on the window's Control menu allow you to alter settings for the specific session. Options in the dialog boxes also let you save the settings to establish new defaults. You can set the properties like this:

1. Choose Start, Run.
2. Enter cmd, and press Enter. This runs the Windows XP command prompt, a true 32-bit Windows program. The settings you'll make here are applied to the VDM as well.

3. On the resulting Command Prompt window, click the upper-left corner to open the Control menu, and choose either Properties or Default.

- Properties sets the properties for this box and optionally all other boxes with the same title (as seen in the box's title bar) in the future.

- Default applies the settings to all DOS-based programs and Command Prompt windows from here on out (even with other programs running in them).

The resulting dialog box is the same in either case; only the window title is different. You can see it in Figure 23.13.

Figure 23.13
Here, you can set the default properties for all command prompt windows.

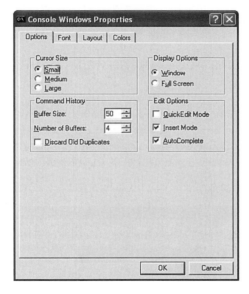

4. Click through the four tabs, and notice the settings. You can click the ? (question mark) button in the dialog box and then click any of the settings to learn more about them. Some of the more useful settings are listed in Table 23.3.

5. Make changes as necessary, and click OK.

TABLE 23.3   SOME USEFUL CONSOLE WINDOW PROPERTIES

Tab	Item	Description
Options	QuickEdit	Check it to enable copying to the Windows clipboard by selecting text and pressing Enter. Uncheck it if you need to use the mouse with an MS-DOS application.
	Insert Mode	Check it to set insert mode as the default for command-line editing; uncheck it to overwrite by default. (Press the Ins key while editing to toggle.)

continues

TABLE 23.3	CONTINUED	
Tab	**Item**	**Description**
	AutoComplete	Check it to have the Tab key automatically complete a partial filename you've typed on the command line.
Font	Size, Font	Sets the character size in the window.
Layout	Screen Buffer Size	Sets the width and number of lines of text that are stored for the screen; if larger than the window size, you can scroll back to view previously displayed text.

If you're changing the properties for a specific window, the default is to change the properties for this window only. If you want to use these settings every time you launch this program, select Modify Shortcut That Started This Window, and then click OK.

When you make this choice, Windows edits the PIF for the DOS application in question (or the _DEFAULT.PIF in the case of a CMD window), storing the settings.

NOTE

> The Control menu's Edit command and its associated cascading menu options are covered in Chapter 5, "Using the Simple Supplied Applications," which describes the use of the Clipboard and OLE.

TIP

> Setting a large buffer size can be a real boon if you run batch files or other programs that normally cause text to scroll off the top of the screen. A large buffer enables you to scroll back the screen and check program flow and error messages.

EDITING ADVANCED SETTINGS FOR A DOS APPLICATION

If you're experiencing difficulties while running specific DOS programs, you should read this section to learn about making deeper changes to the properties settings for them. When you manipulate the properties (via the PIF) for a program, Windows XP Home Edition fine-tunes the VDM environment for the particular application, allowing it to run more smoothly, or in some cases simply allowing it to run at all.

MS-DOS applications were designed to run in solitude. They assume that they are the only applications running and usually are memory hogs. Often they want at least 640KB of RAM and perhaps even extended or expanded memory. Running several non-Windows programs simultaneously—especially DOS programs—is just asking for territorial conflict.

To successfully accommodate the DOS-based applications still in use, Windows XP Home Edition must be ingenious in managing computer resources such as RAM, printers, modems, mouse devices, and display I/O. Significant sleight of hand is required to pull off this task smoothly, but Microsoft has done this fairly well, partly due to the use of PIFs.

PIFs (program information files) are small files stored on disk, usually in the default Windows folder (\WINDOWS or \WINNT) or in the same folder as the application. They contain settings Windows XP Home Edition uses when it runs a related application. When you modify the properties of a DOS executable or shortcut, Windows XP, in turn, edits the associated PIF. With the correct settings, the program runs properly, sparing you the aggravation caused by program crashes, sluggish performance, memory shortages, and other annoying anomalies. PIFs have the same initial name as the application but use .PIF as the extension (123.PIF, for example). When you run an MS-DOS application (using any technique), Windows XP searches the application's directory and the system search path for a PIF with the same name as the application. If one is found, this file's settings are applied to the DOS environment by the DOS environment subsystem before running the application. If no PIF is found, Windows XP uses the default settings stored in a file named _DEFAULT.PIF, stored in the \WINDOWS or \WINNT directory. These settings work for most DOS applications, but not all; games and educational programs are likely to need the most modifications.

TIP

In earlier versions of Windows, you had to edit a PIF using the PIF Editor. You no longer need to do so. For all intents and purposes, you can forget about the existence of PIFs and focus on a DOS application's properties instead by right-clicking the application and choosing Properties. However, if you have specific instructions provided with an older application for making PIF file settings, follow the advice provided for the program in configuring the application's properties.

DOS property settings can affect many aspects of an application's operation, such as (but not limited to) the following:

- The drive and folder (directory) that is selected as the default when an application starts
- Full-screen or windowed operation upon launch
- Conventional memory usage
- Expanded or extended memory usage
- The application's multitasking priority level
- The application's shortcut keys
- Foreground and background processing

Some DOS programs come with PIFs, knowing you might run them under Windows. PIF settings from a Windows 3.x computer work under the Windows XP environment, so you can copy them to the appropriate directory, or take note of the settings on the Windows 3.x machine and reenter them on the Windows XP machine.

Earlier versions of Windows (namely Windows 3.x) sported more settings for DOS programs, but because Windows XP Home Edition is more intelligent than its now-obsolete sibling, many of them are history.

To edit these properties for a DOS program, do the following:

1. Find the program file or a shortcut to it.

2. Right-click and choose Properties. You then see a dialog box like the one shown in Figure 23.14. (In this example, I adjusted the properties for a DOS shareware game.)

Poke through each tab, and use the ? (question mark) button for help on the settings. Educational and game programs will most often require you to adjust the Memory and Compatibility settings.

Figure 23.14
Setting the property settings for a DOS application.

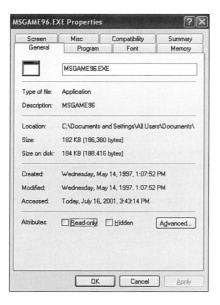

KEEPING A COMMAND PROMPT WINDOW OPEN AFTER EXECUTION

When you run a command-line program or batch file from the command prompt window, the window stays open after the program completes and you can read any messages the program has printed.

However, if you run the program or batch file from a shortcut or by entering its name in the Start, Run dialog box, by default the command window closes automatically as soon as the program exits. To keep the window open, follow these steps:

1. Create a shortcut to the DOS program or batch file.
2. Right-click the shortcut, and select Properties.
3. Select the Program tab.
4. Uncheck Close on Exit. The window will now stay open after the program exits. You'll have to close it manually when you're finished reading its output.

TIP

> If the command prints more text than fits on the screen and some scrolls off, you can usually scroll the window up to see the first part of the output. If more text is generated than the scrolling function can keep track of, you can increase the amount of stored text by editing the shortcut's properties. Select the Layout tab, and increase the Screen Buffer Size Height value. Alternatively, run the program from a batch file and send its output through the `more` command by adding ¦ `more` to the end of the command line. This displays one screen at a time. Press Enter to see each successive page.

CUSTOM STARTUP FILES

If you don't want every application's VDM to use the same `AUTOEXEC.NT` and `CONFIG.NT` settings, you can specify alternate `AUTOEXEC` and `CONFIG` files to be used instead, on an application-by-application basis. Here's how:

From the application's Properties page, select the Program tab and click the Advanced button. You then see the dialog box shown in Figure 23.15; here, you can name alternative files to be used. Just enter the names of the files. You should create your own modified files for this use. Start by copying CONFIG.NT and AUTOEXEC.NT from the \WINDOWS\ SYSTEM32 folder to a new folder (the folder of the DOS application in question is a good spot). Then edit them with a plain text editor such as Notepad.

Figure 23.15
You can specify a custom `CONFIG.NT` and `AUTOEXEC.NT` file for a given application.

THE WINDOWS XP COMMAND LINE

Despite the ease of use of the Windows graphical user interface, the command-line interface provides a useful way to perform many maintenance, configuration, and diagnostic tasks. Many of the most important diagnostic tools such as ping, tracert, and nslookup are only available from the command line, unless you purchase third-party graphical add-ons to perform these functions. Using batch files remains a useful way to encapsulate common management functions; batch files (or shortcuts to batch files) can be placed in shared folders as a way of distributing management functions on a network. Together, command-line utilities and scripts run with either Windows Scripting Host (wscript.exe) or the command-line-based scripting host (cscript.exe) provide a complete set of building blocks from which you can build very high-level utilities if norm al Windows commands aren't sufficient for your needs.

The Windows XP command-line utilities include many of the same programs found in DOS and earlier versions of Windows. In many cases, the programs have been enhanced considerably. Utilities not found in DOS or Windows 9x are also available.

Command-line programs fall into five categories, as shown in Table 23.4.

TABLE 23.4 CATEGORIES OF COMMAND-LINE PROGRAMS

Types of Commands	Description
Built-in	These commands are built into the command interpreter; for example, dir, copy, and rename.
Native	These commands call .EXE files; for example, sort.exe, net.exe, and more.exe.
Subsystem	These commands are .EXE files from older operating systems that were designed to adjust the environment or interface. They run inside the virtual DOS machine. Examples are DOSKEY, SETVER, himem.sys, and dosx.exe.
Batch file	These commands direct the flow of execution in batch files; for example, for, goto, if, and else.
Configuration	These commands go in AUTOEXEC.NT, CONFIG.NT, and CONFIG.SYS in the root drive. They tune the subsystem during startup.

The command interpreter (the shell) in Windows XP is, by default, CMD.EXE. The CMD.EXE command interpreter is similar to DOS's old COMMAND.COM shell but has enhanced batch file functions and also has built-in command-line editing and a command history function similar to that provided by DOSKEY in DOS and Windows 9x. You don't need DOSKEY in Windows XP, unless you want to use its command aliasing feature.

Many of the built-in commands are significantly enhanced since Windows 9x and NT 4. However, Microsoft made the amazingly poor decision to exclude most of the documentation for command-line utilities from the online help in Windows XP Home Edition.

You can get to the command-line program index in the Windows XP Help system using these steps.

1. Click Start, Help and Support. Search for fsutil.

2. Select the suggested topic "Managing Disk Quotas from the command line."

3. In the text that's displayed, select the link "Command-line reference." That will display an alphabetical listing of all of Windows XP's command-line utilities.

Some of the programs listed in the help index might not be included in Windows XP Home Edition, but the index will give you a good place to find out what's available.

> **TIP**
>
> To learn how to get the most from the scripting and the command-line environment, get Brian's book *Windows XP Under the Hood: Hardcore Windows Scripting and Command Line Power*, published by Que.

WHAT'S NEW OR DIFFERENT FROM MS-DOS

Windows XP retains and enhances almost all the functionality of MS-DOS. The following sections explain new Windows XP commands not found in MS-DOS, changes to MS-DOS commands, and unavailable MS-DOS commands.

> **TIP**
>
> You can see the command-line syntax and options for most commands by typing the command name followed by /? in a command prompt window. For example, `rasdial` /? lists the options for the `rasdial` command.
>
> The online command-line reference provides more detail. See the previous tip to find out how to view the command-line reference.
>
> Also, try typing `help` *xxxx*, where *xxxx* is the name of the program you're interested in. Some commands are documented this way.

WINDOWS XP COMMANDS

Table 23.5 lists some of Windows XP's command-line commands. Some of these can be used only by a Computer Administrator. Many of these are used mostly in corporate environments, but you might want to take a look through the whole thing in any case, just to get an idea of the wide variety of things command-line programs can do. Then, you can look into the ones that seem most interesting.

23

TABLE 23.5   WINDOWS XP COMMAND-LINE COMMANDS

Command	Function
arp	Displays and edits the ARP cache.
attrib	Displays and sets file/folder attributes.
cacls	Clears the command prompt window.
cipher	Encrypts and decrypts files and folders.
cmd	Command shell.
compact	Enables and disables file and folder compression.
convert	Schedules the conversion of a volume from FAT to NTFS.
cscript	Windows Scripts Host (command-line version).
defrag	Defragments a disk volume.
driverquery	Lists the installed device drivers.
endlocal	Restores environment variables.
eventcreate	Adds an event to the event log.
eventquery	Lists events from the event log.
expand	Expands a file from a .cab file.
find	Finds text in files.
findstr	Finds text in files using regular expressions.
for	Repeat command (many options).
forcedos	Runs a program in the MS-DOS environment.
format	Formats a fixed or removable disk.
ftp	File Transfer Protocol.
getmac	Displays network adapter MAC addresses.
goto	Goes to the label in a batch file.
help	Displays command-line program usage information.
hostname	Displays the local computer's TCP/IP hostname.
iexpress	Creates simple Installer applications.
if	Executes a command conditionally.
ipconfig	Displays the TCP/IP configuration and manages DHCP leases.
label	Sets the volume label on a disk or mount point.
logoff	Logs off from Windows.
makecab	Compresses files into a .cab file.
md	Creates a directory, (same as mkdir).

Command	Function
mkdir	Creates a directory, (same as md).
more	Displays text a page at a time.
mountvol	Creates, deletes, and lists volume mount points.
move	Moves files or folders.
msg	Sends a message to another user.
net	Networking management utility.
netsh	Network-configuration utility.
netstat	Displays the current TCP/IP connections and open sockets.
nslookup	Queries DNS servers.
openfiles	Displays files in use by local processes or network users.
path	Sets the command search path.
pathping	Tests TCP/IP connectivity.
pause	Stops a batch file until the user presses Enter.
ping	Tests TCP/IP connectivity.
popd	Restores the current directory.
prompt	Sets the command-line prompt.
pushd	Saves the current directory.
rasdial	Starts and ends dial-up networking connections.
rd	Removes a directory, (same as rmdir).
rem	Remarks or comments text.
ren	Renames files or folders (same as rename).
rename	Renames files or folders (same as ren).
replace	Replaces files.
rmdir	Removes a directory, (same as rd).
runas	Runs a program with another user's credentials.
sc	Displays and manages installed services.
set	Sets environment variables.
setlocal	Saves the current environment.
shift	Deletes and moves command-line arguments.
shutdown	Shuts down, logs off, or restarts a computer.
sort	Sorts text files alphabetically (filter).
start	Runs a command or opens a document in a new window.

continues

23

TABLE 23.5 CONTINUED

Command	Function
taskkill	Terminates a process.
tasklist	Lists active processes.
telnet	Establishes a command-line session on another computer.
time	Displays and sets the time of day.
title	Sets the window title.
tracert	Checks TCP/IP connectivity.
tree	Displays the directory structure.
type	Copies a text file to the console window.
wscript	Windows Script Host (windowed version).
xcopy	Copies multiple files.
&	Separates multiple commands on the command line.
&&	Separates multiple commands. The command following && runs only if the command preceding && succeeds.
¦	Separates commands. The output of the command preceding ¦ is sent as input to the command after ¦.
¦ ¦	Separates commands. The command following ¦ ¦ runs only if the command preceding ¦ ¦ fails.
( )	Groups commands.
; or ,	Separates parameters.
^	Escape character. It removes special meaning from characters like & and ¦. For example, ^¦ is treated as ordinary text ¦.

CHANGES TO MS-DOS COMMANDS

Table 23.6 lists some changes and improvements to command-line programs that date back to MS-DOS.

TABLE 23.6 CHANGES TO MS-DOS COMMANDS IN WINDOWS XP

Command	Changed Features
chcp	This command changes code pages for full-screen mode only.
cmd	CMD.EXE replaces COMMAND.COM.
del	New switches provide many more functions.
dir	New switches provide many more functions.
diskcomp	Switches /1 and /8 are not supported.

Command	Changed Features
diskcopy	Switch /1 is not supported.
doskey	DOSKEY has several enhancements. However, it functions with 32-bit Windows command-line (console) applications only and is not active in the 16-bit MS-DOS environment.
format	Switches /b, /s, and /u are not supported. Adds new filesystem and cluster-size switches.
label	The symbols ^ and & can be used in a volume label.
mode	This command has had extensive changes.
more	New switches provide many more functions.
print	Switches /b, /c, /m, /p, /q, /s, /t, and /u are not supported.
prompt	New character combinations allow you to add ampersands ($a), parentheses ($c and $f), and spaces ($s) to your prompt.
recover	This command recovers files only.
rmdir	The new /s switch deletes directories containing files and subdirectories.
sort	This command does not require the TEMP environment variable. File size is unlimited.
xcopy	New switches provide many more functions.

I talk a bit more about some enhanced commands at the end of this chapter, under "Tips from the Windows Pros."

UNAVAILABLE MS-DOS COMMANDS

The MS-DOS commands in Table 23.7 are not available at the Windows XP command prompt.

TABLE 23.7 MS-DOS COMMANDS NOT AVAILABLE IN WINDOWS XP HOME EDITION

Command	New Procedure or Reason for Obsolescence
assign	Not supported in Windows XP.
backup	Not currently supported.
choice	Not currently supported.
ctty	Not currently supported.
dblspace	Not supported.
deltree	The rmdir /s command deletes directories containing files and subdirectories.
dosshell	Unnecessary with Windows XP.

continues

23

TABLE 23.7	**CONTINUED**
Command	**New Procedure or Reason for Obsolescence**
drvspace	Not currently supported.
emm386	Extended memory support is provided for MS-DOS applications through EMM.SYS, which should appear in CONFIG.NT.
fasthelp	This MS-DOS 6.0 command is the same as the Windows XP command help. Windows XP also provides an online command reference.
fdisk	Disk Management prepares hard disks for use with Windows XP.
include	Multiple configurations of the MS-DOS subsystem are not supported.
interlnk	Not supported. Use the Network Connections wizard to configure a direct connection via parallel, serial, or infrared (IR) ports.
intersrv	Not supported. Use the Network Connections wizard to configure a direct connection via parallel, serial, or infrared (IR) ports.
join	Filesystems can be joined from the Disk Management console.
memmaker	Windows XP automatically optimizes the MS-DOS subsystem's memory use.
menucolor	Multiple configurations of the MS-DOS subsystem are not supported.
menudefault	Multiple configurations of the MS-DOS subsystem are not supported.
menuitem	Multiple configurations of the MS-DOS subsystem are not supported.
mirror	Not supported in Windows XP.
msav	Not supported.
msbackup	Windows XP Home Edition provides the optional NTBackup utility (under the Administrative Tools in the Control Panel) for computers with tape drives or the xcopy command for computers without tape drives. Install NTBackup from the \3RDPARTY\MSFT\NTBACKUP folder of the Windows XP CD-ROM.
mscdex	CD-ROM support for MS-DOS applications is provided by mscdexnt, run within AUTOEXEC.NT.
msd	You can use the System Information snap-in instead. To start System Information, choose Start, Run, and then type msinfo32. System Information is much more accurate and much more complete than msd.
numlock	Not currently supported.
power	Not supported.
restore	Not currently supported.
scandisk	Not supported.
smartdrv	Windows XP automatically provides disk caching for the MS-DOS subsystem.
submenu	Multiple configurations of the MS-DOS subsystem are not supported.

Command	New Procedure or Reason for Obsolescence
sys	Windows XP does not fit on a standard 1.2MB or 1.44MB floppy disk.
undelete	Not supported in Windows XP.
unformat	Not supported in Windows XP.
vsafe	Not supported.

Speeding Up Legacy Programs

Read on if you want to learn how to monitor a 16-bit Windows-based program or an MS-DOS–based program. In Windows XP Home Edition, 16-bit Windows-based programs run as separate threads in a multithreaded process called Windows Virtual DOS Machine (NTVDM). The NTVDM process simulates a 16-bit Windows environment.

An MS-DOS–based program runs in its own NTVDM process. You can monitor a 16-bit program or an MS-DOS–based program running on your computer with System Monitor by monitoring the NTVDM instance of the Process performance object. Note that 16-bit programs running in an NTVDM appear only if they are started in a separate memory space. If you find that your 16-bit programs are not performing well under Windows XP Home Edition, you can access some of the program's properties by right-clicking the name of the program in Windows Explorer and configuring the properties as follows:

- If the program is in a window, and the display performance is slow, on the Screen tab, click Full-Screen.
- If the program is in a window and seems to pause periodically, click the Misc tab, and set the Idle Sensitivity slider to Low.

You can turn off Compatible Timer Hardware Emulation for the program if performance does not improve by changing the previously described settings. To do so, right-click _DEFAULT.PIF or the program name, select Properties, point to Program, and click Advanced. In the dialog box that appears, clear the Compatible Timer Hardware Emulation check box. This change typically causes a decrease in performance and should be made only if other efforts fail.

TROUBLESHOOTING

ADJUSTING PROGRAM SETTINGS

I can't get my Windows 95 program to work, even if I use the Program Compatibility Wizard.

The Program Compatibility Wizard isn't a cure-all for program compatibility problems, although it can help many otherwise-incompatible programs to run.

Before you decide you simply can't use the program at all with Windows XP, try the following:

1. Try using additional compatibility settings—When Windows 95 was first introduced, many system still used standard VGA (640 × 480) resolution with only 256 colors. If you didn't select these options before, or didn't disable the visual themes, try running the wizard again and make these additional settings.

2. Try using a different Windows version when you run the compatibility wizard—If your program specifies "Windows 95 or Windows NT 4.0", for example, try both compatibility mode settings before you give up.

3. Reinstall the program—It's possible that when Windows XP was installed that your program's installation was damaged.

4. Be sure you have installed the latest patches and updates from the program vendor.

These same steps will help you with any program compatibility problem you encounter.

MS-DOS Program Can't Open Enough Files

When I run my MS-DOS application, I get the error "Too Many Files Open" or a similar message.

By default, MS-DOS applications run by the VDM are allowed to open only 20 files. Some older programs, especially database programs, want to open more. In DOS or Windows 9x, you'd have added the line

```
FILES=100
```

to your CONFIG.SYS file. In Windows XP, you must add this line to your CONFIG.NT file. Use Search to find this file on your computer, or look in \WINDOWS\SYSTEM32. Of course, if you specified an alternative setup file for this application, you'll want to change that file rather than CONFIG.NT.

MS-DOS Application Displays Garbage Characters

When I run an old MS-DOS application, I see lots of junk characters on the screen, and many occurrences of ←[.

Some older programs that displayed text on the computer screen depended on the assistance of a display driver program called ansi.sys. Ansi.sys isn't installed by default in CONFIG.NT, so you're seeing the control message that your program was intending for ansi.sys to interpret; these should have resulted in color changes or cursor movements.

You need to add the line

```
device=ansi.sys
```

to your CONFIG.NT file. Use Search to find this file on your computer, or look in \WINDOWS\SYSTEM32. Of course, if you specified an alternative setup file for this application, you'll want to change that file rather than CONFIG.NT.

NOTE

If you're a software developer, you should know that ANSI.SYS works for MS-DOS applications only. There is no support for ANSI escape sequences for Win32 console applications.

TIPS FROM THE WINDOWS PROS: GETTING MORE OUT OF THE COMMAND PROMPT WITH COMMAND EXTENSIONS

If you grew up with MS-DOS, like I did, you may find that even Windows XP's many enhancements to Windows aren't enough to keep you out of command-prompt-land permanently.

Believe it or not, you still can't make a printout of the files and folders stored in a given folder from Windows Explorer. And, when it comes to switching drives and folders, the command is quicker than the mouse.

If you want to move around your system faster than Explorer can do it, take advantage of the enhancements to Prompt provided by the Command Extensions activated by default with Windows XP Home Edition.

Command Extensions make lots of your favorite command-line utilities a lot more powerful in Windows XP Home Edition than they were in Windows 9x/Me.

Command extensions can be turned off by typing the command cmd /y and pressing Enter at a command prompt. To turn them back on again, type cmd /x and press Enter.

COMMANDS AFFECTED BY COMMAND EXTENSIONS

When command extensions are enabled, the following commands have new features or are available for use. Commands with an asterisk (*) are available only when command extensions are enabled.

ASSOC *	IF
CALL	MD or MKDIR
CD or CHDIR	POPD
COLOR *	PROMPT
DEL or ERASE	PUSHD
ENDLOCAL	SET
FOR	SETLOCAL
FTYPE *	SHIFT
GOTO	START

If you like to write batch files, you'll find that changes to the FOR command alone will make your head spin with possibilities. Type help for >x & notepad x to read all about it.

In the following sections, you'll see how to use some of the other enhanced commands to get more done at the command-prompt level.

TIP

> For a list of valid commands at the command prompt, type `help | more` and press Enter.

COMMAND EXTENSIONS MAKE cd (CHANGE DIRECTORY) EASIER

The `cd` (Change Directory) and `md` (Make Directory) commands allow you to change to a different folder and make a new folder from the command prompt as an alternative to using the Windows Explorer.

When command extensions are enabled, you can change to a long directory (folder) without putting quote marks around the name:

```
cd \My Documents\My Music\My MP3s
```

Without command extensions, you'd need to enter the following command:

```
cd "\My Documents\My Music\My MP3s"
```

Forget the quotes, and you'd see an error message.

Normally, `md` (Make Directory) can create just one folder (directory) at a time. When command extensions are enabled, you can create a nested series of folders with a single command. For example, this single command creates a series of folders below your current folder. You could use a command like this within the \My Documents folder to create folders for your home budget:

```
md "My Budget\4th Quarter\Travel"
```

(Yes, you need the quote marks!)

COMMAND EXTENSIONS MAKE PROMPT MORE POWERFUL

When you open a command-prompt session in Windows XP, the default prompt pg uses $p (current drive and path) and $g (greater-than sign) to display your current location:

```
C:\Documents and Settings\All Users>
```

But, if you've mapped a network drive to a drive letter, either with Windows Explorer or the command-prompt NET USE command, all you normally see is a drive letter when you change to the network drive:

```
S:\>
```

When command extensions are enabled, you can use the following `prompt` command to display the server name (if any):

```
prompt $m$p$g
```

Now, the prompt displays the true network path and the drive letter you're using to access it.

Figure 23.16 shows you how this special prompt command makes life easier for you when you work with network drives.

Figure 23.16
Using the mp$g prompt to display the actual path to a mapped network drive.

COMMAND EXTENSIONS CAN CHANGE THE COLOR OF THE COMMAND PROMPT WINDOW

Very experienced DOS users might remember when the ANSI.SYS device driver and complex batch file commands were needed to change the screen color in a command-prompt session. When command extensions are enabled, you can use the COLOR command to do the same thing. And, if you want to use more than one command-line session at the same time, you can color-code each one.

To see a complete list of the color codes you can use, type color /? and press Enter.

Here are two examples:

To change the color of the screen to light blue and the text to light aqua (very easy on the eyes), enter color 9B.

To reset the screen color to its original colors, enter color by itself.

The color command affects only the current command prompt window. If you later open a new window, the colors are reset to the defaults set on the Color tab of the command prompt window's properties page.

SYSTEM ADMINISTRATION AND MAINTENANCE

SYSTEM UTILITIES

GETTING UNDER THE HOOD

Windows XP is rife with system management and administrative utility programs—so many, in fact, that you can easily become overwhelmed by the number of tools and the multitudinous paths for reaching those tools. As writers who have pounded on Windows systems since the days of version 1.1, my co-author and I can easily report that the mandate of effectively discussing the administrator tools for Windows XP was a bit daunting, even to us.

If you're the kind of user who likes to pop the hood, see what's inside, and do a little tinkering, or if you're an administrator who has the job of managing computers in a corporation, this is the chapter for you. You'll want to read through the descriptions of the various tools covered here and learn a bit about how to use them.

Thus far, you've learned about the basic Control Panel utilities and many of the configuration and maintenance tools and applets. Dividing the tools into clearly delineated chapters was somewhat difficult, as many do not fall neatly into a category. The following is how it all shook out in the end:

- Chapter 21, "Tweaking the GUI," discusses most of the user environment alteration tools, most of which are display or formatting oriented Control Panel applets.

- Chapter 22, "Configuration via Control Panel Applets," discusses a majority of the Control Panel applets not already covered in Chapter 23.

- Chapter 23, "Maintaining and Optimizing System Performance," discusses a number of primarily hardware-related tools.

- This chapter discusses the balance of the computer management tools, some of which are very powerful, especially the Microsoft Management Console (MMC), which is a highly customizable toolbox you can customize for your own sleuthing purposes. If you did not find a tool you were looking for by skimming the other chapters, it is likely here.

NOTE

> The Microsoft Management Console or MMC is not directly covered in this book. This is a technology incorporated into Windows 2000 which has been retained in Windows XP. Unless you are planning to create custom interfaces or tools, there is little you really need to know about MMC. However, if you want to customize your own tools, Microsoft has done a great job of discussing this in the Windows XP Resource Kit.

If you're a Windows 9x or NT maven, some tools that you are likely familiar with in those interfaces have changed names and locations in Windows XP. But, if you are stepping over from Windows 2000, you'll find things reassuringly familiar. Most of the system-level control tools, with the exception of the System applet, are Microsoft Management Console (MMC) tools.

Table 24.1 describes each of the system management tools. With the exception of the Recovery tool (which is described in Chapter 26, "Managing the Hard Disk"), each of these tools is discussed later in this chapter.

TABLE 24.1   SYSTEM MANAGEMENT TOOLS

Tool	Description
Task Manager	A tool for killing crashed applications, listing currently running processes, and checking system performance.
Computer Management	A subset of Microsoft Management Console, for extensive control of the local machine.
Windows Update	Online tool for ensuring your system is running the latest software additions and bug fixes.
Scheduled Tasks	A utility program for automating execution of programs.
File Signature Verification tool	A tool that prevents critical system files from being altered.
System File Checker	A command-line executable that verifies system file versions are aligned properly.
System Monitor	(a.k.a. Performance) A tool that creates a graphical and/or numeric display of essential system information, such as memory usage, status of the hard disk usage, CPU activity, and network traffic. This tool is discussed in Chapter 23.
Event Viewer	A tool for viewing system-generated log files.
Recovery Console	A tool that attempts to recover a broken or otherwise nonbooting system. This tool is discussed in Chapter 26.
System applet	This applet offers access to controls for system name, network membership, hardware management, system restoration, automatic updates, working remotely, and more.
Services	Manages how services are launched within the XP environment.
System Tools	A section of the Start menu used to access several tools: Files and Settings Transfer Wizard, Backup, Disk Cleanup, Disk Defragmenter, System Restore, Activate Windows, and System Information.
System Information	This tool provides a detailed view into the configuration and status of the systems hardware and software.
Accessibility	This section of the Start menu contains tools for the visual and mobility impaired.

These tools are scattered throughout the Windows XP environment. To stick to some semblance of order, we will try to discuss these tools in the following order based on their location or execute/access point: Control Panel applets, Administrative Tools, Start menu items, and then Run command/Command Prompt utilities. However, most of these tools can be accessed through more than one of these means.

Scheduled Tasks

Scheduled Tasks is found in the Control Panel and in the Start menu (All Programs, Accessories, System Tools, and Scheduled Tasks). Using the Scheduled Tasks, you can set up any program or script (or even open a document) to be run automatically at predetermined times. This utility is very useful for running system maintenance programs or your own scripts and programs when you can't be around to execute them manually.

NOTE

When the Scheduled Tasks runs a task as a different user, the logged-on user cannot see or interact with the program. Be sure that scheduled tasks can operate without user input and exit cleanly when they've done their work. And keep in mind, when an application or service is running, even if it was launched through a scheduled task, it still will affect system performance as if you ran it manually.

After you declare tasks to run, the Scheduled Tasks sits in the background, checking the computer's system clock, and when a predetermined time for a task rolls around, the Scheduled Tasks runs it as though executed from the specified user.

After you've defined a task to be executed, the Scheduled Tasks service will be automatically launched at startup each time the computer boots. The Scheduled Tasks service does not significantly affect system performance. The service is required to monitor the time and other system events that are defined as triggers to launch applications, scripts, and so on. The Scheduled Task service cannot be configured to load based on a logged-on user because it is a systemwide service. Even if a user without scheduled tasks is logged on, a scheduled task from another user may execute in the background.

NOTE

Obviously, the computer has to be alive to run a task, so if you expect to do a disk cleanup at 4 a.m., make sure you've left the computer on. If you turn on the system at 4:01 a.m., you missed the execution. The scheduler will not inform you of missed launchings; you'll have to view the information in the Last Run Time column within the Scheduled Tasks window to figure it out for yourself.

TIP

If you upgraded from Windows 98/SE/Me/NT/2000 and had automated tasks assigned there, they should have been converted or imported to the Windows XP Scheduled Tasks automatically.

To learn how to assign tasks to the Scheduled Tasks applet, follow these steps:

1. Run the Scheduled Tasks by choosing Start, All Programs, Accessories, System Tools, Scheduled Tasks. If you have any scheduled tasks, they appear in the list already.

2. Click Add Scheduled Task to invoke a wizard that walks you though adding a new task. Click Next to see a list of programs (see Figure 24.1). If the program isn't listed in the resulting list, click the Browse button to find it. (For system-related applications, the most likely browse locations are in the \windows or \windows\system32 folders. For programs you've installed, try the Program Files subfolders.)

Figure 24.1
The Scheduled Task Wizard's program selection page.

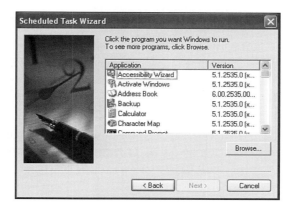

3. Click Next, and choose how often you want the program to run (see Figure 24.2). Click Next again, and then specify applicable time options, such as time of day, as required.

Figure 24.2
The Scheduled Task Wizard's execution schedule page.

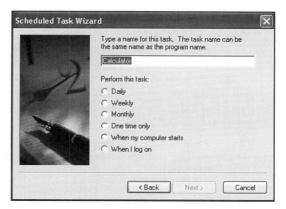

4. Click Next, and you are prompted to enter the user's name and password so that the task can be executed as though the user (typically, you) were there to run it. (It may

already be entered for you, using the current user's name, preceded by the computer name.) After a username and password are set, another user cannot cancel or delete the task unless that user has the correct permissions. If you are working with a user account without a password, don't type in anything in the password field.

5. Click Next. If you want to set advanced options such as idle time, what to do if the computer is running on batteries, and what to do after the task completes, mark Open Advanced Properties For This Task When I Click Finish.

6. Click Finish to close the wizard. The task is then added to the list and will execute at the preassigned time.

If you chose to open the task's advanced properties upon clicking Finish, its dialog box now opens. To open this same dialog box manually, open the Scheduled Tasks applet, right-click the task in question, and choose Properties. The three tabs on this dialog box enable you to modify it as follows:

- From the Task tab on the Properties dialog, you can disable the task temporarily, without having to delete it, by clearing the Enabled check box.

- Use the Schedule tab to change the task's timing. You can change the scheduled time using the options present, or use the Advanced button to access more advanced scheduling options. There is also a check box that allows you to enable multiple schedules for the task.

- Use the Settings tab to set whether to delete the task after completion, to stop the task after it runs for a specified length of time, to start the task only if the system is idle, and to not start the task if running on batteries.

Click OK when you're finished to save any changes made to the properties sheet. Now that you've established a task, though, there are still more issues to consider.

If you want to remove a task from the Scheduled Tasks list, right-click it, and choose Delete. Choosing Delete here doesn't remove the executed application from your hard disk, it just removes the task from the list of tasks to be executed.

To use controls that affect all tasks in the Scheduled Tasks applet, use the commands on the Advanced menu from the main Scheduled Tasks window's menu bar. You'll see a number of useful items there, as shown in Table 24.2.

TABLE 24.2   ADVANCED SETTINGS FOR THE SCHEDULED TASKS

Option	Description
Stop Using Scheduled Tasks	This option turns off the scheduler, preventing it from running any added tasks. The scheduler won't start automatically the next time you start Windows XP. To reactivate it, you have to open the Scheduled Tasks and choose Start Using Scheduled Tasks.

Option	Description
Pause Scheduled Tasks	This option temporarily suspends added tasks in the task list. This capability is useful if you are running a program whose operation could be slowed down or otherwise influenced by a scheduled task. To resume the schedules for all tasks, choose Advanced, Continue Scheduled Tasks. If a task's execution time is now past, it will run at the next scheduled time.
Notify Me of Missed Tasks	If a task can't complete for some reason, a dialog box pops up, letting you know what was missed. For example, if the computer was turned off when a task should have been run, you'll be told of this situation when you boot up next.
AT Service Account	The Scheduled Tasks runs any commands scheduled using the `at` command-line utility, which is a carryover from Windows NT. By design, commands scheduled by `at` all run under the same login account. This option lets you specify which account is to be used. You can leave it set to the default `LocalSystem` setting, or you can turn on This Account to specify a user account.
View Log	This option brings up a text file in Notepad, listing tasks completed, date, and other information about the tasks. Note that some tasks listed in the log might not appear in the Scheduled Tasks list. This omission can result from system tasks initiated by other services such as synchronization (such as Web page subscriptions and offline folders). For coverage of these issues, see Chapter 9, "Browsing the World Wide Web with Internet Explorer," and Chapter 17, "Windows Unplugged: Remote and Mobile Networking. "

TIP

You can run one of your tasks immediately by right-clicking the task in question and choosing Run.

You also can reach Scheduled Tasks via the Explorer by going to the \windows\tasks folder.

 If the Scheduled Tasks fails to activate properly, see "The Scheduled Tasks Doesn't Activate Correctly" in the "Troubleshooting" section at the end of this chapter.

You can view scheduled tasks on a remote computer by opening My Network Places, opening the computer in question, and then opening the Scheduled Tasks folder. You need administrative privileges if you want to view the settings on a remote machine. If you want to edit remote settings, the requirements are greater; you can edit tasks on a remote computer running Windows 95 or later, Windows NT 4.0, Windows 2000, or Windows XP only if that remote computer has remote Registry software installed and shares the *x$* share, where *x* is the hard disk on which the Scheduled Tasks folder resides. That is, it must be shared with an "Administrative Share."

Unlike under Windows 2000, Windows XP tasks do not have task-level ACLs. However, if the user account defined as the "run as" account does not have access to the executable, the task will not be able to run.

SYSTEM APPLET

The System applet offers a wide range of functions through its multi-tabbed interface. The System applet is accessed through the Control Panel. When the Control Panel is in Classic view, double-click on the System icon to open the System applet. When the Control Panel is in Category view, either switch to Classic view or open the Performance and Maintenance category, and then click on the System icon. Let's take a look at each tab and the options on each.

The General tab (see Figure 24.3) displays the system OS version, registration details, and basic computer info (CPU type, speed, and RAM).

Figure 24.3
The System applet (or System Properties) dialog box, General tab.

SETTING THE COMPUTER NAME

The Computer Name tab is the same interface as is accessed through the Network Identification command of the Network Connections applet's Advanced menu. This interface is used to change the computer name and manage workgroup membership. The Change button opens the Computer Name Changes dialog box where the computer name and workgroup membership is defined with simple text fields.

MANAGING AND CONTROLLING HARDWARE

The Hardware Tab has four buttons. The Device Manager button launches the Device Manager; this is also discussed in Chapter 22. The Hardware Profiles button opens the Hardware Profiles dialog box where hardware profiles are managed. This is discussed in Chapter 23. The Windows Update button brings up a dialog box asking whether and when XP should go onto the Internet to look for drivers in the event that you connect new hardware to your system. The Driver Signing button opens the Driver Signing Options dialog box.

Driver Signing is a security feature that aids in preventing malicious rogue or Trojan horse drivers from being installed onto a mission-critical system. By enabling driver signing, you can configure a system to refuse all device drivers except those that are "signed" by Microsoft or other MS-approved vendors. This dialog box offers three settings: Ignore, Warn, and Block. Ignore allows the installation of any driver. Warn prompts you each time you attempt to install a non-signed driver. Block only allows signed drivers to be installed.

CAUTION

The default setting of Driver Signing is Warn. Keep in mind that this safety feature is designed from the Microsoft perspective. In their eyes, the only legitimate and safe drivers are those that have been approved by their labs. In many cases, drivers that are not preapproved by Microsoft are perfectly safe and legitimate. However, ignore this security at your own risk. If you don't trust the vendor or fully trust the distribution method, don't install unsigned drivers.

ADVANCED SYSTEM PROPERTIES

The Advanced Tab of the System applet has five buttons. Three of these buttons are labeled Settings and are contained within sections titled: Performance, User Profiles, and Startup and Recovery. The other two buttons are below these sections, they are labeled Environmental Variables and Error Reporting.

The Settings button under the Performance heading opens the Performance Options dialog box. The Visual Effects tab of this dialog box is discussed in Chapter 21. The Advanced tab of this dialog box is used to set memory usage parameters and is discussed in Chapter 23.

The Data Execution Prevention (DEP) tab is new as of SP-2 and is used for settings that prevent malicious applications from executing programs in protected areas of RAM. Protected areas of RAM, supposedly reserved for the operating system and other programs that are running, can potentially be invaded by malware that then tries to load and execute itself in the legitimate memory space. This new SP-2 feature prevents this from happening, if it's turned on.

There are two levels of DEP: hardware and software. To use hardware DEP, your CPU has to have execution protection capability. You can check whether yours does by reading the

DEP tab page. Hardware DEP works by virtue of the CPU tracking where the operating system and legitimate programs are operating in RAM, and it blocks other programs from trying to load and execute in those address blocks. If a detection occurs, the offending program is simply shut down.

If your CPU doesn't support DEP, XP does its best to do DEP in the software, if it's turned on from the DEP tab. Software DEP isn't turned on by default because some programs don't run properly with it turned on. This isn't as complete a form of protection, but it's better than nothing.

Normally, only Windows programs and services are monitored by DEP. If you want to be extra safe, choose the second option—Turn On DEP for All Programs and Services Except Those I Select.

As stated, however, the problem with software DEP is that some legit programs might not run with it turned on. When DEP shuts down a program, the first thing you should do is run a virus check on your computer. Do a complete sweep. If some threat is detected, remove the offensive program. If nothing is detected, try running the offending program again. If DEP closes it again, you have three choices:

- If available, purchase an updated, DEP-compatible version of the program.
- Set up an exception list to run the program by clicking Add (on the DEP tab) and adding the program.
- Don't use the program.

If you take the second course of action, you should check frequently for an updated version of the program and, after you update it, turn on DEP for that program again by highlighting it in the DEP tab and clicking Remove.

The Settings button under the User Profiles heading opens the User Profiles dialog box. This interface is used to manage local and roaming profiles stored on the local computer. This is discussed in Chapter 25, "Managing Users."

The Settings button under the Startup and Recovery heading opens the Startup and Recovery dialog box. This interface is used to configure multibooting actions and how system failures are handled. This is discussed in Chapter 28, "Multibooting Windows XP with Other Operating Systems," and Chapter 30, "Troubleshooting and Repairing Windows XP."

The Environmental Variables button opens the Environmental Variables dialog box. This interface is used to define user and system variables. These include TEMP and TMP, which point to storage locations where Windows can create temporary files. In most cases you should not edit the system variables. There are some application installations that may require this activity, but specific details should be included in that application's installation instructions.

TIP

> If the storage volume where your main Windows directory resides is becoming full, you can perform three operations to improve performance and keep the risk of insufficient drive space to a minimum. First, move the paging file to a different volume on a different hard drive (see Chapter 23 for details on this). Second, define the TEMP and TMP variables to point to a \Temp folder you create on a different volume on a different hard drive. Third, through Internet Options, define a location for the temporary Internet files within the alternate \Temp folder. After rebooting, the new locations will be in use. However, you may need to delete the old files from the previous temporary file locations (typically \Documents and Settings\<username>\Local Settings\Temp and \Documents and Settings\<username>\Local Settings\Temporary Internet Files\).

The Error Reporting button opens the Error Reporting dialog box. On this interface you can define whether Windows XP automatically reports system problems to Microsoft. This information is submitted anonymously and is used to help Microsoft fine tune the system and to create fixes and patches. As you might expect, it's enabled by default. You can choose just to submit OS related issues or to include (all or some) Program issues as well.

CONTROLLING SYSTEM RESTORE SETTINGS

The System Restore tab is used to track and reverse damaging changes made to your system, and it enables you to set the defined space usage for the System Restore feature. This feature is discussed in Chapter 30. The System Restore command is also found in the Start menu under All Programs, Accessories, and System Tools.

SETTING AUTOMATIC UPDATES

The Automatic Updates tab defines how Windows XP handles critical Windows Update downloadable modules. Windows Update is an online OS fixing and patching tool. This feature has grown more and more comprehensive over the years and, as of XP SP-2, incorporates more push technology than it did when XP was first released. This move is mostly in response to the continued onslaught of viruses and other hacking strategies that destabilize Windows machines. Windows Update can now push not only new system updates and security patches for the operating system, but also less-critical software such as device drivers and updates to Microsoft Office (if Office is installed on the target computer).

If you're wondering whether Automatic Updates is the same as Windows Update, the answer is well, sort of. Automatic Updates is actually a subset of Windows Update. Windows Update is a Web site you visit and interact with. From the site, you can see what's available for your machine and then choose what you want to download. As the name implies, Automatic Updates handles some of that for you, eliminating the need to visit the Windows Update site manually or make decisions about what to download. Automatic Updates delivers only the highest-priority updates, in hopes of keeping more Windows systems up-to-date and operating smoothly. If you want to download optional updates (fun stuff or lower-priority items), you still need to visit the Windows Update Web site, even if Automatic Update is turned on.

NOTE

> The Windows Update technology is very rich. Among other things, systems administrators can use it to control updating many machines across a network using a Windows Update Services server. Outside of a corporate setting, though, most users simply use Microsoft's online update server via its Web site.

Upon installing a post-SP-2 version of XP or upon upgrading to SP-2, you're prompted to confirm settings for Automatic Updates. Microsoft does its level best to push you into allowing it to keep your system up-to-date automatically. You'll see a dialog box strongly recommending that you leave automatic updates turned on (the default). If you do so, information about your computer is uploaded to Microsoft's Windows Update database. Then, security patches, critical updates, Office updates, drivers, and operating system service packs all are automatically downloaded and installed to your computer. If you choose to deactivate this feature, you're going to be bugged incessantly about it, anyway, so why fight a good thing? We believe this is good thinking on Microsoft's part.

NOTE

> Windows does not use your name, address, email address, or any information that can be used to identify you or contact you.
>
> In Windows XP Home Edition, you have to be logged on as an administrator to install components or modify Automatic Updates settings. If your computer is connected to a network, network policy settings might also prevent you from completing this procedure.

Allowing Windows to download and install updates automatically keeps you up-to-date without having to remember to initiate an update check. It doesn't matter whether you use a dial-up or broadband connection. Microsoft has developed efficient means to ensure that your other downloads aren't slowed, through the use of small patch download sizes and a new compression scheme called delta patching. Under the previous scheme, Windows Update examined your system, determined which patches you needed, and downloaded all of them. The problem was, such downloads were often quite large. The new Windows Update downloads just the files you need, or just the parts of the files you need, thereby keeping the downloads as small and fast-moving as possible. The system is made additionally efficient by ensuring that the system downloads and installs the most crucial updates before less-important patches. So, when the next virus outbreak hits, Windows users are immediately protected. To make the most of your connect time, if you disconnect from the Internet before your updates are finished, nothing is lost. The download process continues the next time you connect to the Internet.

Microsoft states that security updates are published every month, unless there is more radical threat, in which case it releases an update as soon as possible.

Of course, it's possible that an update could damage your system. Microsoft can't control all the variables that might appear on John Q. Public's system, and updates, although they often fix bugs, can introduce new ones.

If this should happen, you can always roll back a system to its state before the update (see "Using Rollback to Uninstall a Windows Update," later in this chapter), or use the System Restore feature (see Chapter 30), so using automatic updates is not necessarily a poor choice.

As you see from the dialog box in Figure 24.4, there are three levels of manual updating. The default settings are as you see in the figure. That is, every day at 3 a.m., updates are automatically downloaded and installed. This is the recommended setting. If the computer isn't on at that time, downloads occur when you first turn on your computer and connect to the Net. You can choose a specific day of the week and a different time, if you want.

Figure 24.4
The Windows Automatic Updates applet.

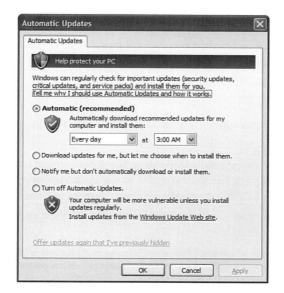

NOTE

> If you need to accept an end user license agreement (EULA) before an update can be installed, you are prompted to do so. Some updates might require a reboot, too. If the download happens at the predetermined time (for example, 3 a.m.) and a reboot is needed, the computer reboots at that hour. This could be a problem if you need to have the computer available as a full-time server or you're using a remote-control program from afar because, after booting, the computer might require user login for a given remote application to be functional.

If you want to choose when to install updates (because you can't reboot or be distracted for whatever reason), choose the second option. Downloads happen in the background, but you don't know about it. You see a balloon pop up from the system tray indicating that there is an update ready to install. Just click the balloon and you are told what to do.

Some users prefer to at least know whether an update is being performed, so they select Notify Me But Don't Automatically Download or Install Updates. This way, they can more likely correlate some strange new system behavior with an update that just took place.

When would you use the third option, to turn off updates altogether? In general, I'd rule that out as an intelligent option, with two exceptions.

- If you have a computer that is almost always off the Internet or a LAN and is "mission critical" (has to be up and running), and rarely if ever has new software (including email) added to it, this is a potential candidate. Once I get such a dedicated system running, I haven't much interest in tempting fate with software or system upgrades.

- You're running and maintaining PCs in a corporate setting. These PCs *are* connected to the Internet and probably on a corporate network. You want to rigorously test updates before you install them across the corporation's PCs, because Microsoft patches and updates can sometimes break your applications' features in subtle ways.

To use the Windows Update site manually, do the following:

1. Click Start, Help and Support Center.
2. Then select Keep Your Computer Up to date with Windows Update.
3. A Web page appears. Click Scan for Updates.
4. A list of possible updates for your computer appears. Sift through the list and click Add to select the update of your choice and add it to the collection of updates you want to install. You can also read a full description of each item by clicking the Read More link.
5. When you have selected all the updates you want, click Review and Install Updates; then click Install Now.

You can hide an update if you want to get it off the screen. Click Hide Update. If you want to see hidden updates again, click Restore Hidden Updates. Sometimes hiding a critical update doesn't really stick. You'll be reminded about such an update later and prompted to install it.

NOTE

> Note that some updates are exclusive—that is, you must install them separately, and sometimes even reboot afterward. Then you can go back to the Windows Update site and install other updates.

USING THE REMOTE TAB: REMOTE ASSISTANCE

Remote Assistance allows you to grant dual-control over your desktop with another computer over a network or the Internet. The Remote tab controls whether Remote Assistance is enabled. When enabled, the other client can see your desktop, conduct a real-time chat with you, and even use their mouse and keyboard to make changes and operate your system. Remote Assistance was designed to allow a system administrator, tech support specialist, instructor, or even a knowledgeable computer buddy to aid end-users with tasks without having to leave their workspace.

Remote Assistance works through the exchange of time-sensitive invitation scripts via email. To initiate an invitation

1. Click the Start menu, All Programs, Remote Assistance. The Remote Assistance help page opens (see Figure 24.5).

TIP

This page also can be accessed through Help and Support by clicking on the Invite a Friend to Connect to Your Computer with Remote Assistance link under Ask for Assistance.

Figure 24.5
The Remote Assistance page of the Help and Support Center.

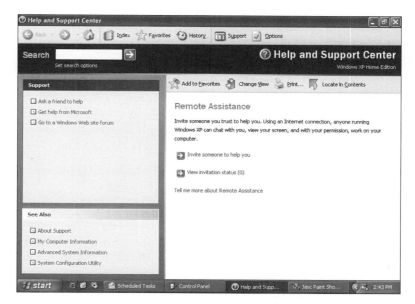

2. Click Invite someone to help you. The invite page opens (see Figure 24.6).

NOTE

Remote Assistance requires a compatible OS on the remote system (currently only Windows XP and the Server 2003 family are compatible), with either Windows Messenger Service or a MAPI-compliant email utility (such as Microsoft Outlook or Outlook Express). Remote Assistance also requires that both systems have Internet access.

Figure 24.6
The invite page for
Remote Assistance.

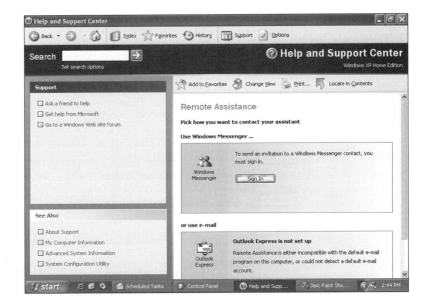

3. If you have MSN Messenger installed and a contacts list defined, you can select an invitee from Messenger. Or, you can provide an email address to send an invitation. Since Outlook Express (OE) is installed by default and MSN Messenger is not, we'll use OE.

   Type in an email address to send a Remote Assistance initiation, and then click Invite this person. The email invitation page opens.

   NOTE

   > The invitation can also be saved as a file. When saved as a file or included as an email attachment, the invitation is a 900KB file named rcBuddy.MsRcIncident.

4. Provide a From name and a message to include in the email invitation, such as "Please help me configure my new printer through Remote Assistance." Then click Continue.

5. Define the invitation's expiration period in minutes, hours, or days.

6. Select whether to require a password to connect, then provide the password. Defining a password will prevent anyone who doesn't have the password from using your invitation to gain access to your system. Click Send invitation.

7. A warning prompt appears, stating that another application is attempting to send an email message on your behalf, click Send.

When the invitation appears in the invitee's inbox, they only need to execute the attachment.

CAUTION

Microsoft warns to only execute attachments from people you trust or from whom you are expecting an attachment. It is very easy to create a malicious utility masquerading as a valid Remote Assistance invitation.

When it's executed, you'll be prompted for a password (if required) and whether you want to initiate a Remote Assistance connection. Once you click Yes, the connection attempt commences. If a connection is started, the invitor is prompted whether to allow the connection to continue. After clicking Yes, the Remote Assistance floating tool window appears on the original system (see Figure 24.7) and the Remote Assistance remote desktop utility (see Figure 24.8) appears on the invited system. If someone attempts to use an invitation after the expiration time has passed, they will see a message stating the Remote Assistance invitation has expired.

Figure 24.7
The Remote Assistance floating tool window as it appears on the original or host system.

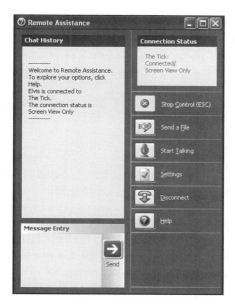

From either system, you can send chat text, stop the session, transmit a file, initiate voice chat, or disconnect the session. From the remote system, you can request full control of the original desktop and control it with the remote system's mouse and keyboard. This is a great tool for walking someone through a complex task or training them on software usage.

Remote Assistance should only be used when both system are connected by a fairly high-bandwidth link, such as over a 10+MB LAN or via ISDN, DSL, or Cable modem Internet link. It will work over slow modem connections, but you are more likely to experience significant performance delays and disconnects. The faster the connection, the more responsive the remote assistance will be and the higher resolution the remote visuals. Unless blocked by a firewall, proxy, or other security screen between the two systems, Remote Assistance can link two systems on a LAN or over the Internet.

Figure 24.8
The Remote Assistance remote desktop utility as it appears on the invited or remote system. Notice that the host's desktop can be seen in the background of the invitee's screen.

ADMINISTRATIVE TOOLS

The Administrative Tools are a collection of system control and configuration utilities that Microsoft deemed powerful and technical enough to separate into its own category from the Control Panel applets. The Administrative Tools include Component Services, Computer Management, Data Sources (ODBC), Event Viewer, Performance, and Services. Each of these is discussed in the following sections, with the exception of Component Services and Data Sources (ODBC), which are not discussed in this book. You might want to consult the Windows XP Resource Kit for details on these two items. These two tools are fairly complex and are used by program developers and network database integrators. In most cases, these controls are beyond what most end users or administrators will need or use.

COMPUTER MANAGEMENT

In addition to the Task Manager and Control Panel, another tool named Computer Management (see Figure 24.9) is probably the most likely candidate for configuring and administering your PC. To get to it, open the Control Panel (in Category view), select Performance and Maintenance, then Administrative Tools, and finally, double-click Computer Management. A simpler method is to right-click your My Computer icon (on your desktop or in your Start menu) and select Manage from the pop-up menu.

Figure 24.9
The Computer
Management utility
from Administrative
Tools. Shared Folders
node selected.

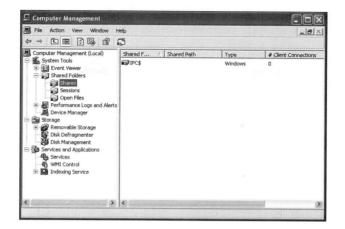

NOTE

> The Computer Management utility is just one of many MMC (Microsoft Management Center) tools. The MMC is a powerful programming infrastructure for creating system control utilities. You can even create your own custom tool sets using MMC consoles and taskpads. Creating tools for MMC is a complex subject. We've covered it *Special Edition Using Microsoft Windows XP Professional* (should you have access to that book), and you can also find in-depth coverage of the topic in the Windows XP Resource Kit.

Computer Management provides easy access to the following tasks:

- Managing shared devices and drives
- Checking system event logs containing information such as logon times and application errors
- Seeing which remote users are logged in to the system
- Viewing currently running system services, starting and stopping them, and setting automatic startup times for them
- Managing server applications and services such as the Indexing service

The Computer Management tool looks similar to the familiar Windows Explorer. It uses a two-pane view, with the *console tree* (for navigation and tool selection) in the left pane and details of the active item shown the right pane.

Items in the tree are called *nodes* (akin to folders in Explorer). The three nodes in Computer Management are as follows:

- System Tools
- Storage
- Services and Applications

As you would expect, you can conduct administrative chores by selecting a tool in the console tree and then clicking items in the right pane. When you select an item in the right pane, toolbar and menu options change as appropriate for that item, typically displaying attributes of the item or tool you selected. For example, the System Information branch can show you which IRQs are assigned already, and the Local Users and Groups branch can display the names and properties of all the users on the machine.

In previous versions of Windows NT, you had to hunt around through Control Panel applets to discover properties and settings that are now conveniently grouped together in Computer Management. I'll be honest; things are still a little confusing just because some of the properties available from Computer Management can also be reached via the Control Panel. An example is the Device Manager, which you can get to from the System applet in the Control Panel as well as the System Tools node in Computer Management. It's the same tool, and having multiple paths to the same destination is nothing new in Windows.

TIP

> You must be assigned Administrator privileges to fully utilize the Computer Management tools. If you have lesser privileges, you'll have limited access to system properties and are locked out of making certain administrative changes to the system.

Explore with the interface to uncover all that is available from these three "little" nodes in the left pane. However, avoid making any changes or modifications (where possible) unless you know what affects your alterations will have. You'll be surprised. Open each node by clicking the boxed + (plus) sign. If you choose View, Details, some helpful information about various items in the right pane is displayed along with the items.

By default, you manage the local computer. To manage a remote computer (assuming you have permission), right-click the topmost item in the tree (Computer Management), and choose Connect to Another Computer.

Also by default, the view is set to Basic. To gain access to more advanced settings in the console, choose View, Advanced.

A few points about each node are listed in the following sections.

SYSTEM TOOLS NODE

This node includes five subnodes:

- **Event Viewer**—Used to view the event details contained in the Application, Security, and System logs. This tool is discussed later as an Administrative Tools utility in its own right.

- **Shared Folders**—Used to manage shared folders and remote users accessing shared folders.

- **Performance Logs and Alerts**—Used to define logs and alerts related to system performance. This tool is identical to that accessed through the Performance tool (a.k.a. System Monitor interface). This tool is discussed in Chapter 23.

- **Device Manager**—Used to troubleshoot device problems and configure device and drivers settings. This is identical to the Device Manager accessed through the System applet. This tool is discussed in Chapter 22.

The Shared Folders node (refer to Figure 24.8) amounts to what used to be NetWatcher in previous Windows versions. The three folders under the Shared Folders node are as follows:

- **Shares**—Allows you to manage the properties of each shared resource. For example, you can alter the access rights for a shared resource so that certain users have read-only access. You can also change share permissions for a resource in the Properties dialog box of any shared resource by right-clicking the resource and clicking Properties.

- **Sessions**—Allows you to see which users are connected to a share and optionally disconnect them.

- **Open Files**—Allows you to see which files and resources are open on a share. You also can close files that are open.

STORAGE NODE

This node includes three subnodes:

- Removable Storage
- Disk Defragmenter
- Disk Management

The Removable Storage is used to check the physical location of removable storage devices (such as CD-ROM, DVD-ROM, JAZ, Zip, tapes, and optical disks), check the existence of media pools (typically robot-controlled multidisk gadgets), and check properties of offline media. This node also provides a means for labeling, cataloging, and tracking all your removable media; controls library drives, slots, and doors; and provides drive-cleaning operations.

This node can work together with data management or backup programs like the one supplied with Windows XP (the Backup program is covered in Chapter 26, "Managing the Hard Disk"), conveying information about storage properties.

The Disk Defragmenter node runs the disk defragmenter program. This is the same tool with a slightly different interface as the Disk Defragmenter on the Tools tab of a drive's Properties dialog box.

The Disk Management node runs Disk Management (known as Disk Administrator under Windows NT). This tool is used to define new drives as Basic or Dynamic, create/delete/manage partitions and volumes, format, assign drive letters, and so on.

All three of these nodal tools are discussed in Chapter 26.

24

SERVICES AND APPLICATIONS

Through the Services and Application node, you can view and manage the properties of any server service or application that is installed on the computer, such as the file indexing service.

EVENT VIEWER

The Event Viewer is an administrative application used to view the log files that record hardware, software, and system problems and security events. You can think of an event as any occurrence of significance to the operating system. Logs are very useful because, like a seismograph in earthquake country or a black box in an airplane, they provide a historical record of when events occurred. For example, you can see when services were started, stopped, paused, and resumed; or when hardware failed to start properly; when a user attempts to access protected files; or an attempt to remove a printer over which he or she doesn't have control. The logs report the level of danger to the system, as you can see in Figure 24.10. For a shortcut to the Event Viewer, you can choose Start, Control Panel (in Category view), Performance and Maintenance, Administrative Tools, Event Viewer.

Figure 24.10
The System log viewed through the Event Viewer.

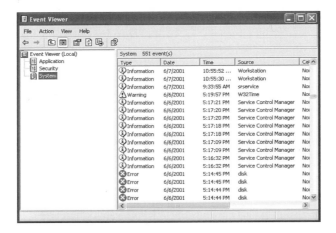

As you know, Windows XP has an intelligent internal security design. So, as you might expect, numerous more subtle events than those described here can generate messages internal to the operating system that are not directly reported to the user. Events such as applications being run, drivers being loaded, or files being copied between directories are common examples. Though kept out of sight, these events are monitored and recorded in log files available for later examination by the system administrator. Many events are stored in the log by default. Others are optional and can be set within dialog boxes pertaining to specific operations.

TYPES OF LOG FILES

Windows XP generates three primary logs (files), though others are possible. These logs are explained in Table 24.3.

TABLE 24.3   WINDOWS LOG FILES

Type of Log	Description
Application log	The application log contains events logged by applications or programs. For example, a database program might record a file error in the application log. The program developer decides which events to record.
Security log	The security log can record security events such as valid and invalid logon attempts, as well as events related to resource use such as creating, opening, or deleting files. An administrator can specify which events are recorded in the security log. For example, if you have enabled logon auditing, attempts to log on to the system are recorded in the security log.
System log	The system log contains numerous entries pertaining to system events such as booting up, shutting down, loading drivers, and errors with hardware conflicts such as conflicts between ports, CD-ROMs, SCSI cards, or sound cards. For example, the failure of a driver or other system component to load during startup is recorded in the system log. The event types logged by system components are predetermined by Windows XP and cannot be altered by the user or administrator.

Now that you have a basic understanding, let's consider the Event Viewer. The Event Viewer is an application that displays each of the log files. Aside from simply displaying a log file, the Event Viewer also lets you do the following:

- Apply sorting, searching, and filtering that make it easier to look for specific events
- Control settings that affect future log entries, such as maximum log size and the time old entries should be deleted
- Clear all log entries to start a log from scratch
- Archive logs on disk for later examination and load those files when needed

NOTE

Only a user with Administrative privileges can work with the security log. Other users can view the application and system logs, however. By default, security logging is turned off. You can use Group Policy to enable security logging. The administrator can also set auditing policies in the Registry that cause the system to halt when the security log is full.

WORKING WITH EVENT VIEWER LOGS

The following steps explain how you can use the Event Viewer to open the three available logs and more easily view specific events:

1. Open the Event Viewer program in Administrative Tools via the Control Panel. When you run it, the basic Event Viewer window comes up. (The meaning of each column is explained in the following section.)

2. Choose the log you want to view by clicking it in the left pane.

3. Just as with the File Manager, changes to the log that occur while you're examining it are not always immediately reflected. Press F5 to update the log if you suspect that some system activity has occurred while you've been running the program.

4. Normally, the list is sorted with the most recent events at the top of the list. You can reverse this order if you want by choosing View, Oldest First.

5. You can optionally filter out events that you don't want to wade through. For example, you can show events that occurred only during certain times of the day, events pertaining to a specific user or event ID, or only a certain event type (such as only errors or warnings). Just choose View, Filter and fill in the dialog box. (The options are explained in the section titled "Filtering Events.")

6. You might want to search for a specific event. To do so, choose View, Find, and enter the relevant information in the resulting dialog box.

7. If you want to see more information about an event, double-click it. Another dialog box then appears, listing details. An example is shown in Figure 24.11.

Figure 24.11
An Event Properties or event details properties dialog box.

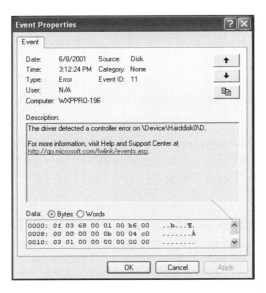

Details of your security log won't make much sense if you're not a programmer. Even then, the messages are cryptic. The system and application logs offer more in the way of understandable English. Most useful is information about drivers failing to load (often leading you to IRQ and port conflict resolutions).

VIEWING A REMOTE COMPUTER'S LOGS

By default, the local computer's log is displayed. If you want to examine a networked computer's log, just right-click over the Event Viewer (local) node and select Connect to another computer from the pop-up menu.

LOG INTERPRETATION

Careful monitoring of event logs can help you predict and identify the sources of system problems. For example, if log warnings show that a disk driver can read or write to a sector only after several retries, this information could be a foreshadowing that the hard disk sector may die eventually. Logs can also confirm problems with software. If a program crashes, a program event log can provide a record of activity leading up to the event. When a program does crash, you often see a system message informing you that a log entry is being made.

Essentially, each log file consists of a database table with eight columns, which are described in Table 24.4.

TABLE 24.4   DECIPHERING EVENT LOGS

Column Name	Meaning
Type	Indicates the type of event. The five types of events are described in Table 24.5.
Date	Reports the date the event was logged (according to the system clock).
Time	Reports the time that the event occurred.
Source	Lists the name of the application software or device driver that reported the problem.
Category	Shows the general classification this event falls under. Each of the three logs has different categories of events.
Event	Lists an event number. Event numbers are assigned to events based on a coding system Microsoft has designed. The event ID matches a message file. The message is displayed in the details box for the event.
User	Indicates the specific user for whom the event applies. Many events are related to a specific user.
Computer	Specifies the computer where the event happened.

As mentioned in Table 24.4, five different icons characterize an event type, as shown in Table 24.5.

24

TABLE 24.5   EVENT TYPES

Type of Event	Meaning
Error	Indicates serious trouble of some sort, such as the device driver not loading, IRQ or other hardware conflicts, missing network cards, and so forth.
Warning	Indicates non-serious trouble, but worthy of attention soon, such as being low on hard disk space (which could bring down the system).
Information	Indicates a non-serious situation. Typically, these notices concern successful operations achieved by applications, drivers, or services. For example, when a network driver loads successfully, an Information event is logged.
Success Audit	Indicates success of a procedure.
Failure Audit	Similar to a success audit but reversed; indicates that failed attempts are logged. Failures typically occur because the user making the attempt doesn't have the correct privileges.

TIP

> Many typical hardware problems—such as conflicting protocols, network card conflicts, and IRQ conflicts—are reported in the system log. The Event Viewer can help you sleuth out possible entries explaining the problem.

FILTERING EVENTS

One way of seeing several similar events you're interested in (for example, to see how many times the same event occurred) is to click the relevant column head in the Event Viewer. Clicking the head sorts the listing according to the column's data. As in Windows Explorer and other Windows programs, the column sorter toggles between ascending and descending order.

A more powerful approach for culling out the items you're interested in is to use filtering. When logs get quite large or if you have a server that supports a high density of workstation activity, this approach might be the most effective technique for ferreting out what you need to examine. The System Log Properties dialog box you use for filtering is shown in Figure 24.12.

After you set up a filter, don't be alarmed if all your entries suddenly seem to have disappeared; they're probably just being filtered. Check the View menu, and you'll see the Filter option selected. Choose it again to eliminate the filter.

SETTING LOGGING OPTIONS

You can stipulate a few settings that affect how log entries are recorded. These settings are most useful in managing the size of your logs so that they don't eat up too much disk space. There are potentially so many loggable events that even a typical day on a busy network server could produce far larger log files than you would want to wade through, or that you would want to devote disk space to.

Figure 24.12
On the Filter tab of the System Log Properties dialog box, you can limit the listing to specific conditions.

To view or change options for a log file, right-click the log file in question, and choose Properties. Then click the General tab to see the dialog box shown in Figure 24.13.

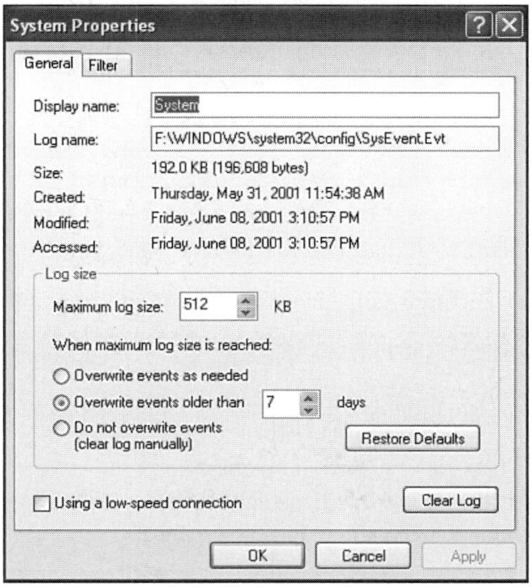

Figure 24.13
Setting a log's options.

If you don't archive the log (see the next section), then you should probably have the log "wrap" around after it reaches the maximum log size. The Overwrite Events as Needed option ensures that, when the log fills up, a new event takes the place of the oldest preexisting log entry.

If you really want to ensure that you get to see the log entries, choose the Do Not Overwrite Events option. After the maximum size is reached, subsequent events are not written, and thus lost. If so, you have to use the Action, Clear All Events command to make room for new entries.

Using Archived Log Files

A final option in the Event Viewer lets you create archives of log files and to reload those files for later examination. As a rule, archiving log files isn't of much use unless you're running a very secure operation in which extensive background records of system or network usage are mandated by the government or the corporation where you work. Most likely, in such a secure operation, you'll be doing regular tape or other forms of backup, which might include backups of the log files anyway. In this case, this regimen might meet your security requirements, depending on your tape rotation scheme. If it doesn't, you can archive your event logs. Archiving is a relatively simple process.

TIP

> One case to be made for archiving is that logs can be useful in isolating network or machine failures. By keeping copies of past logs, you have something to compare with current versions that list new failures. By comparing logs, you can perhaps notice how and when the errors began to accumulate. Generally speaking, a network failure starts simple and then increases in frequency until a catastrophic failure occurs. Old logs can help here.

You can store archives as text files, comma-delimited files (text files with a comma between each field for use in database or spreadsheet programs that can import this format), or binary files with the .EVT extension. Only the .EVT files retain all the property information for each event. If you want to reload the file for later use, save it as an .EVT file.

Note that the file created by the archiving process isn't affected by any filtering active at the time. That is, all events in the log are written into the archive file. The Action, Save Log File As command can save the log as a .EVT, .TXT, or .CSV file. The Action, Export List command can save into .TXT or .CSV as plain text or Unicode text.

NOTE

> After you save, the log is archived, but the current log isn't cleared. Its contents are unaffected. If your log is full, you have to clear it manually.

To recall an archived log for later examination, open it using the Open Log File command from the Action menu.

 If your security log file is empty, see "No Events in Security Log" in the "Troubleshooting" section.

SERVICES

As you learned in Chapters 1 and 2, Windows XP is highly modular. Many of the inner housekeeping chores of the operating system are broken down into services that can be added, removed, started, and stopped at any time, without requiring a reboot. A typical Windows XP system has 80 or more services running at any one time. You can view which services are running by using the Services tool. Use this tool to start and stop services. Figure 24.14 shows a typical Services listing. To start, stop, pause, or restart a service, you can use the context menu or the VCR-like buttons on the toolbar. For deeper control of a service, such as to declare what automatic recovery steps should be taken in the case of the service crashing, which hardware profiles it should run in, and more, open its Properties dialog box. Within the Properties dialog box are several controls. You can set a service's startup type (automatic, manual, or disabled), and you'll find start/stop/pause/resume buttons and a startup parameters field. You also can set the account under which the service is executed (Log On tab), define how a service recovers from failures (for example, restart, run a program, reboot system)(Recovery tab), and view a list of service, program, and driver dependencies (Dependencies tab).

Figure 24.14
While you're checking the status of services, you can start, stop, and pause system services from this screen.

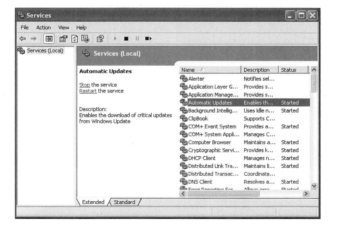

SYSTEM TOOLS

The System Tools section of the Start menu (All Programs, Accessories, System Tools) includes several interesting tools. Most of these are discussed in other chapters (such as Chapter 25 [Files and Settings Transfer Wizard], and Chapter 26, [Disk Cleanup, Disk Defragmenter, and System Restore]). But, two tools from this menu are discussed in the following sections: Activate Windows and System Information.

ACTIVATE WINDOWS

Recall from Chapter 3, "Installing Windows XP Home," that I discussed the issue of Windows activation. If you failed to activate your system during installation, for whatever reason, you can use this tool to activate Windows XP. Keep in mind that you have 30 days to activate your system after the installation before it will no longer function. Also remember that if you try to activate the same copy of Windows XP on multiple computers, Microsoft's storm troopers may come a knockin' at your e-door.

Just be sure to have Internet access when you start this tool if you want to activate online. You also can activate over the phone. This wizard will walk you through the simple but necessary process of activating Windows XP. It will even provide you with the phone number to call if you don't have Internet access for online activation.

SYSTEM INFORMATION

System Information, which made its debut in Windows 98, is a simple but elegant tool. Opening this tool reveals a complex hierarchy of four folders, which in turn lead to a zillion lower folders containing an exact blueprint of your system, hardware, system components, and software environment. (You might have additional nodes in your system because some software you install may add nodes of their own.)

This tool is the first place I go whenever I have to install hardware, especially when it's a legacy device that requires manual configuration of its system resources. Even for PnP devices, you may discover that they are not infinitely configurable. Instead, many devices have only three or four system resource combination sets (these include IRQ, memory address space, I/O, DMA, etc). If your system does not have available resources to match one of these sets, the device will not function. If a device is limited to certain configuration sets, this will be detailed in the user manual and will appear as options on the Resource tab of the device's Properties dialog box.

The top level, labeled "System Summary," shows you basic information about your computer, operating system revision number, CPU, RAM, virtual memory, pagefile size, BIOS revision, and so on (see Figure 24.15).

Figure 24.15
See a summary of your system properties easily from the System Summary node.

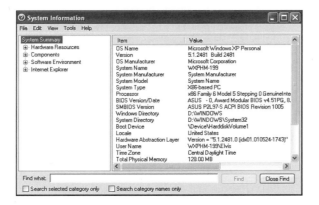

Four nodes appear in the right pane of this figure:

- **Hardware Resources**—Displays hardware-specific settings, such as DMA, IRQs, I/O addresses, and memory addresses. The Conflicts/Sharing node identifies devices that are sharing resources or are in conflict. This information can help you identify problems with a device. Some IRQs can be shared between devices successfully.

- **Components**—Provides a truly powerful view of all the major devices in your system. Open any subfolder and click an item. In a few seconds, information pertaining to the item is displayed, such as drive IDs, modem settings, and video display settings. In some cases, you can also see driver details. Check the folder called Problem Devices to see a list of all devices not loading or initializing properly.

- **Software Environment**—Similar to a super Task Manager. It displays details of twelve categories of software settings. You can see the system drivers, certified drivers, environmental variables, print jobs, network connections, running tasks, loaded modules, services, program groups, startup programs, OLE registration, and Windows error reporting.

24

TIP

> Ever wonder why some darned program starts up when you boot, even though it's not in your Startup group (click Start, All Programs, Startup)? It's probably hiding the Software Environment, Startup Programs folder.
>
> Travel down the path from System Information, Software Environment, Startup Programs, and take a look. I just checked mine and found RealTray and RealJukeboxSystray there. Hey, I don't want these things slowing down my bootup process! Office Startup is there, too. Unfortunately, you can't remove these startup utilities by right-clicking and choosing Delete. You have to use their related Setup programs. For example, to disable RealJukeboxSystray, I had to right-click its icon in the system tray and choose Disable Start Center.
>
> There also is a helpful tool within Help and Support that can be used to enable or disable startup items. It's called the System Configuration Utility. To get to it, open Help and Support and click Use Tools to View Your Computer Information and Diagnose Problems under the Pick a Task section. Scroll down in the Tools menu and click System Configuration Utility, and then click Open System Configuration Utility in the right pane. Finally, select the Startup tab.

ACCESSIBILITY

The Accessibility section of the Start menu (All Programs, Accessories, Accessibility) includes several tools to ease, simplify, improve, or enable computer interaction for those users who are visually, audibly, or mobility impaired. These tools are in addition to the system settings available through the Accessibility Options applet in the Control Panel.

The Accessibility wizard is a great tool to help you quickly configure the system so it is at its most beneficial to you, no matter what your disability affects you. This wizard walks you step-by-step through a decision making tree to determine fonts, screen size, colors, sounds, mouse actions, keyboard responsiveness, and so on. The results from this wizard make changes to the environment. These are the same changes you could manually adjust through the Accessibility Options applet in the Control Panel.

The Magnifier is a desktop looking glass that magnifies portions of the display by two times or more. When launched, a view window is created at the top of the desktop. The Magnifier can follow the mouse cursor, or focus on keyboard activities for text editing. This tool is a must for those with a slight visual impairment who need just a bit of magnification to read displayed text.

The Narrator is a text-to-speech program design to aid computer usage for the visually impaired. The Narrator will read aloud English text from most programs. Just highlight the text then press Ctrl+Shift+Spacebar. It can also be set to read screen events (that is, read everything on the active window) and typed characters. The voice is the same controlled through the Speech applet. It's a bit coarse, but you can understand it.

The On-Screen Keyboard is just that, a point-and-click keyboard. It is designed to aid those with mobility impairment who's computer control is restricted to a joystick type mouse. With just a mouse, the On-Screen Keyboard can be used to "type" out text or perform key-sequences.

The Utility Manager is used to manage the three accessibility tools (Magnifier, Narrator, and On-Screen Keyboard). These tools can be set to launch at login, at desktop lock, or when Utility Manager is launched.

These tools provide basic functionality for those with visual or mobility impairments. However, Microsoft warns that these tools should only be used as stop-gap measures. Those needing consistent aid in interacting with their computers should employ a dedicated specialty solution. Microsoft maintains a Web site with information on accessibility solutions at `http://www.microsoft.com/enable/`.

WINDOWS UPDATE

Windows Update serves to synchronize your operating system files with the newest developments for it at Microsoft. These can include free programs, security updates, bug fixes, drivers, or other extensions to the operating system. Using the Internet and Web technologies for updating your operating system means you don't have to wait for the next release of the operating system or install service packs to get interim updates.

OBTAINING NEW UPDATES

The Windows Update command is found in several places, including the top of the All Programs section of the Start menu and on the Tools menu of Internet Explorer. Manually launching Windows Update gives you the ability to selectively download offered updates. However, you can easily configure Windows XP to download all relevant updates automatically. This setting is made on the Automatic Updates tab of the System applet (see earlier this chapter).

NOTE

> Another Start menu item in the same category as Windows Update is Windows Catalog. This tool opens an Internet Explorer window to the Windows Catalog Web site. This site maintains a database of products made for Windows, including applications, devices, and complete PCs.

Microsoft is very keen on having you visiting the update Web site regularly. To do so, you can simply connect to the Net, and choose Start, All Programs, Windows Update. A typical page at the Web site looks like the one shown in Figure 24.16. The look of the pages and the list of updates obviously change from week to week, so what you see there might differ slightly from what you see here.

Figure 24.16
Visit the Windows Update site regularly to keep Windows XP up-to-date.

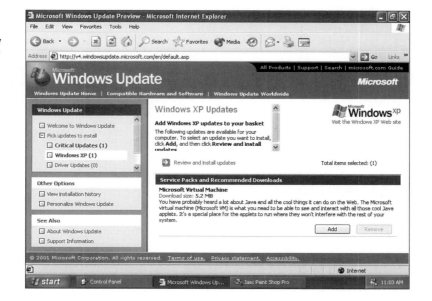

The ActiveX components that run when you visit the site scan your computer to determine what updates have been made in the past and which ones are outstanding. According to Microsoft, no corporate espionage or personal eavesdropping ensues during the process of system analysis. This is accomplished by downloading a master list of available updates and allowing a client-side component to determine which items are applicable to your system. Other than making requests for the master list of updates and for downloading the selected updates, no information is sent to Microsoft.

If you're seeing Windows Update in the wrong language, see "Wrong Language" in the "Troubleshooting" section at the end of this chapter.

The first time you run it, the update tool creates a database of consummated updates on your computer. This information allows the installer to do the following:

- More quickly determine which updates you haven't installed the next time you visit the site
- Remove items you no longer want
- Roll back the system to its previous state in case an update causes troubles

Look for a History button on the Web page (not the History button on the Internet Explorer toolbar, obviously) to see what you installed and when.

USING ROLLBACK TO UNINSTALL A WINDOWS UPDATE

If you notice unruly system behavior after updating drivers, patches, or system files from Windows Update, you'll probably want to roll back your system to its previous state. You can remove such items by using the Update site. Look for instructions about uninstalling items there. You might have to display past updates by clicking the View Installation History button on the Web page. Then you can scroll down to the update and click Uninstall.

If you don't have Web access, are you sunk? No. Good thing, because you could conceivably make an update only to find it kills your networking or Web access. Some items, such as standalone programs, can be removed via the Control Panel's Add/Remove Programs applet, so check there to remove something such as FrontPage Express or non-Microsoft applications. Of course, you can't use this approach to roll back system files, patches, or drivers. To do that, you can use System Restore capability of Windows XP. Please see Chapter 30, "Troubleshooting and Repairing Windows XP," for details.

TASK MANAGER

The Task Manager is one tool you're bound to frequent, perhaps more than any other. Whenever an application crashes, you believe you're running some suspect process that you want to kill, or you want to check on the state of system resources (for example, RAM usage), you can use the Task Manager. Even as nothing more than an educational tool, the Task Manager is informative.

The Task Manager is always available, with a simple press of the "three-finger salute" (Ctrl+Alt+Del) and up pops the Task Manager (see Figure 24.17). Note that this is different from Windows NT and Windows 2000 where the Windows Security dialog box appeared following this keystroke pattern. You can also launch the Task Manager by pressing Ctrl+Shift+Esc or right-clicking over an empty area on the Taskbar and selecting Task Manager from the pop-up menu.

The Task Manager of Windows XP has five tabs, two more than that of Windows NT and Windows 2000. Plus, there is a new menu—Shut Down. The Shut Down menu performs many of the same operations that the Windows Security dialog box performed under

Windows NT/2000 when you pressed Ctrl+Alt+Del. This menu offers quick access to Stand By, Hibernate, Turn Off, Restart, Log Off current user, and Switch User. You'll note that all of these functions can also be accessed through the Start menu's Log Off and Turn Off Computer commands.

Figure 24.17
The Task Manager shows you which applications and processes are running and lets you terminate hung programs. It also indicates some important aspects of system performance.

The other menus of File, Options, View, Windows, and Help all contain the items you've become accustomed to. These menus are somewhat context sensitive, meaning they have different elements depending on which tab is selected. You are smart enough to figure out what most of these commands do, so take the time to explore each menu from each tab. However, I will point out a few interesting commands when appropriate.

APPLICATIONS TAB

You can click the Applications tab of the Task Manager to see a list of the programs currently running on the computer. Not a lot of information is displayed, only the application name and the status (running or not responding). However, this tab does provide a more complete report than you'll get by glancing at the taskbar buttons or via the dialog box you see if you press Alt+Tab.

You can sort the list by clicking the column heads. If an application has multiple documents open, the application appears only once in the list, probably with the name of the document that is foremost at the time (has the focus). Some applications don't comply with this single-document interface (SDI) approach, listing each new document as a separate application. Some examples of non-SDI applications are MS Office programs such as Word, Excel, and PowerPoint.

From this list, you can kill a hung application. If an application has hung, it is probably reported in the list as Not responding (although this is not always true). Click the End Task button to terminate the task. If a document is open and unsaved, and if, for some unexpected reason, the program responds gracefully to Windows's attempt to shut it down (which is unlikely), you might see a dialog asking whether you want to save. More likely, Windows XP will just ask for confirmation to kill the application.

 If you have killed applications and they still appear in the Applications tab listing, see "The Task Manager Is Stalled" in the "Troubleshooting" section at the end of this chapter.

Dr. Watson, Come Quick!

You might want to know about a debugging program called Dr. Watson, which is supplied with Windows XP. It's primarily designed for programmers or for technical support people who might be helping you resolve a software conflict on the workstation. The program sits in memory, keeping an eagle eye on applications as they run. If one bombs or breaches security, Windows XP shuts down the errant program, and Dr. Watson creates an entry in a special log file named Drwtsn32.log found in the \Documents and Settings\All Users\Application Data\Microsoft\Dr Watson folder by default. The entry contains key information about what the application did wrong, and some other details of your computer's operation at the time of the error. If you are getting application crashes on a specific program, you can contact the vendor and ask whether the tech support people want to see the log. To start the Dr. Watson program to set up preferences, you can choose Start, Run, and enter drwtsn32. The default settings are fine under most circumstances.

Incidentally, two Dr. Watson programs are actually included with Windows XP. You'll find both 32-bit and 16-bit versions for the corresponding Windows applications. The programs are named drwtsn32.exe (for 32-bit programs) and drwatson.exe (for 16-bit programs).

By default, drwtsn32.exe creates a Crash Dump file for each error that is generated. It is a binary file that can be opened and examined in a debugger program. These files can be quite large, however. They take up space on your disk and cause a bit of a system slowdown while writing the files to disk. The last time I checked one of these files on one of my machines, it was 45MB. If you don't expect to be debugging a program, you can turn off this feature by running drwtsn32.exe and turning off the Create Crash Dump File option.

TIP

Before you give an application its last rites, pause for a bit. In general, it's not a good idea to kill an application if you can avoid doing so. Terminating an application can cause instability in the operating system (even though it shouldn't). Or at the least, you can lose data. Try "jiggling" the application in various ways, in hopes of being able to close it gracefully first. Switch to it and back a few times. Give it a little time. Maybe even do some work in another application for a few minutes, or take a trip to the water cooler. Try pressing Esc while the application is open.

When executing some macros in Word, for example, I noticed that one of my macros hangs for no apparent reason. It seems to crash Word. So, I killed it from the Task Manager, losing some work. I later realized the solution was to press Esc, which terminated the macro. Having slow network connections and attempting to link to nonexistent Web pages, printers, or removable media can also cause apparent hangs. Try opening a drive door, removing a network cable, or performing some other trick to break a loop a program might be in before resorting to killing the program from the Task Manager. This is especially true if you've been working on a document and you might potentially lose data.

> Some applications will so intensely perform calculations that the Task Manager will list them as Not Responding. If you suspect this, give the program five minutes or so to complete its thinking, I've learned the hard way to be patient with some applications.

Notice that you can also switch to an application in the list or run a new one. Just double-click the application you want to switch to (or click Switch To). Similarly, to run a new application, click New Task, and enter the executable name or use the Browse dialog box to find it. This dialog is no different from the Start, Run dialog box, even though its name is different.

 If you're frustrated because you cannot send the Task Manager to the background, see "Sending the Task Manager to the Background" in the "Troubleshooting" section at the end of this chapter.

PROCESSES TAB

Whereas the Application tab displays only the full-fledged applications you're running, the Processes tab shows *all* running processes, including programs (for example, Photoshop), services (for example, Event Log), or subsystem (for example, wowexec.exe for running Windows 3.x applications). In addition to just listing active processes, Windows XP displays the user or security context (that is, the user, service, or system object under which the process is executing) for each process—a great new feature not present in previous OSes. Also by default, the percentage of CPU utilization and memory utilization in bytes is listed. You can change the displayed information through the View, Columns command.

Almost any listed process can be terminated by selecting it and then clicking the End Process button. There are some system-level processes which even you as administrator don't have sufficient privileges to kill. You might also discover at times that an application will fail to be killed, typically due to a programming error or a memory glitch. In those cases, you should reboot the system. You might find that sometimes a hung application will also prevent a normal shutdown. If your attempt to reboot fails, you'll have to resort to manually turning the power off, and then back on. Hopefully, you saved often and didn't lose too much work.

TIP

> At the bottom of the Processes tab is a check box labeled Show processes from all users. If you've switched users, you can see not just the processes under your user account and those of the system, but also those of other active users. Plus, once displayed, you can also terminate them using the End Process button.

By studying the entries in the process list, you can learn some interesting facts about the operating system. For starters, you might be shocked to see just how many separate processes the operating system has to multitask just to keep going (see Figure 24.18). Notice that the highlighted process is ntvdm (NT Virtual DOS Machine); also, notice that wowexec.exe is running in it and is indented a bit (it appears just above ntvdm). The processes running along with the wowexec (three instances of Alarm, listed below wowexec) are also indented. All Windows 3.x processes run in the same VDM (by default), with wowexec.exe (WOW means "Windows on Windows") being the process that emulates Windows 3.x. Terminating the ntvdm or wowexec process will terminate all three Windows 3.x applications.

For more details on managing DOS and Windows 3.x environments, please jump to Chapter 23.

If the true identity of some of the processes is something you're dedicated to uncovering, check the Services snap-in described later in this chapter. Many of the entries in the processes list are system services, the bulk of which load during bootup.

Figure 24.18
Examining running processes. Notice the wowexec.exe process, which is the Windows 3.x subsystem, and the three Windows 3.x programs.

ALTERING THE PRIORITY OF A TASK

In the beginning, all tasks are created equal. Well, most of them, at least. All of the processes under your user account's security context will have Normal priority by default. Most kernel or system processes will have High priority. You might want to increase or decrease the priority of a process, though changing the priority typically isn't necessary. To do so, right-click the task and choose the new priority through the Set Priority sub-menu. Avoid altering the priority of any task listed with a user name of SYSTEM. This indicates the process is in use by the kernel. Altering the execution priority of such processes can render your system nonfunctional. Fortunately, process priority settings are not preserved across a reboot, so if you do change something and the system stops responding, you can reboot and return to normal. In some cases, raising the priority of an application or game can improve its performance. However, increase the priority in single steps instead of automatically setting it to the maximum. Throwing another top-priority application into the mix of kernel-level activities can render the system dead too.

There are six priority levels you can assign to processes: Realtime, High, AboveNormal, Normal, BelowNormal, and Low. Realtime is restricted for use by administrators. You should keep away from High since it can interfere with essential OS operations (especially if you have several user processes set to High). More details about process priorities is discussed in Chapter 23.

TIP

> If you have a multiprocessor computer, and you want to assign a task to a given processor, right-click the process and choose the Set Affinity command. Choosing this command guarantees that the process receives CPU time only from the CPU you choose.

PERFORMANCE TAB

24

The Performance tab of the Task Manager indicates important conditions of your operating system. It shows a dynamic overview of your computer's performance, including CPU usage; memory usage; and totals of handles, threads, and processes (see Figure 24.19).

Figure 24.19
The Performance tab displays some interesting statistics and a chart of CPU and page file usage over time.

From the Performance tab, the View menu includes CPU History and Show Kernel Times. The former command is used to show different graphs for each CPU (only useful on multiple CPU systems). The latter command sets the display to show kernel (operating system) activity in red and user activity in green on the CPU and Page file usage graphs. You should also notice that paging file usage is shown instead of memory usage.

Although CPU usage is interesting, the most important of these numbers is memory usage. You can easily check in the Physical Memory area to see how much memory is installed in your system, how much is available for use by applications before disk caching begins, and how much the system is using for caching.

NOTE

> System cache is the total current swap and RAM area allocated for system operations. When your computer has to go to a disk cache to access information, it significantly slows down overall system performance, which is why having more system RAM is almost always better.

The Kernel Memory area reports the memory in use strictly by the operating system for running the operating system internals. Nonpaged kernel memory is available only to the operating system. This memory is in physical RAM and can't be paged out to the hard disk because the operating system always needs fast access to it, and it needs to be highly protected. Paged memory can be used by other programs when necessary. Commit memory is memory allocated to programs and the system. Because virtual memory increases the amount of actual memory available, the Commit Peak memory can exceed the maximum physical memory.

In the Totals section, you can see the number of handles, threads, and processes. Threads are discussed in more detail in Chapter 2. Handles are tokens or pointers that let the operating system uniquely identify a resource, such as a file or Registry key, so that a program can access it.

Most of these size reports are of use only to programmers. However, the charts can offer strong, telltale signs of system overstressing. If you see, for example, that your page file usage is consistently nearing the top of its range, you are running too many programs. If the CPU is topped out most of the time, you also could be in trouble. Perhaps you have a background task running that is consuming way too much CPU time. An example could be a background program doing statistical analysis or data gathering.

TIP

> When the Task Manager is running, even if minimized, a green box appears in the system tray, indicating CPU usage. It's a miniature bar graph.

NETWORKING TAB

The Networking tab (see Figure 24.20) displays a bandwidth consumption history graph. As network operations occur, this graph will plot the levels of usage. The View menu includes a Network Adapter History sub-menu. This sub-menu offers the ability to include bytes sent (red), bytes received (yellow), and bytes total (green) on the graph (shown by default). At the bottom of this tab, a list of all network connections along with details is displayed.

The Columns command from the View menu is used to add or remove data columns from this display. This tab can give you a quick heads up if you suspect a network slowdown.

Figure 24.20
The Networking tab shows network traffic activity.

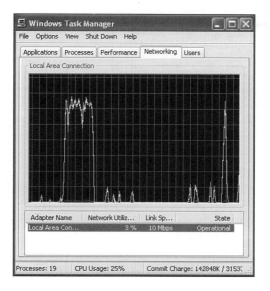

USERS TAB

The Users tab shows a list of all active users on this system or connected via the network. From here you can disconnect a network user, log a local user off, or send a user a text message.

The Users tab will be visible only if you have not disabled Fast User Switching.

PROTECTING THE SYSTEM FILES

We are all familiar with the problem of an operating system becoming suspiciously unstable after the installation of a new application or a driver or after a system crash. Microsoft has been painfully aware of this problem for some time, and many a technician (whether a Microsoft employee or not) has been forced to instruct a PC user to "reinstall Windows" as the only solution. We all know how much fun that is. If you think Windows operating systems sometimes seem like a house of cards stacked level upon level, waiting for a single *.DLL or other system file to fail, well, you're right. This kind of vulnerability is wholly unacceptable in mission-critical settings, so Microsoft had to come up with preventive measures.

NOTE

> Windows XP also supports a new side-by-side DLL feature. This automatic feature keeps track of the DLL versions used by installed applications. If a system update or an application install attempts to change the version of a DLL that is needed by a service or application, XP automatically places a copy of these necessary DLLs in the \Windows\WinSxS folder. Each time an application is launched, XP checks its list to see what version of each required DLL is needed and loads those DLLs into that application's virtual machine. No more "DLL hell." This feature is completely automatic and invisible to the user.

Windows has means for setting up options that prevent the often-unintentional destabilization of the operating system from applications or driver installations or, in the worst case, the introduction of viruses that intentionally alter or overwrite system files. Windows XP's Security Manager and file system work in symphony to help protect critical system files and drivers. Several areas of system functionality help prevent damage from the installation of untested drivers or from modification of system executables such as dynamic link libraries (DLLs). They are as follows:

- **Windows File Protection service**—This service is a function of the operating system that continually monitors protected system files, standing guard against attack.

- **System File Signature Verification tool**—You can use this command-line executable to check the signatures on your essential system components.

- **System File Checker tool**—You can use this command-line executable to verify that system file versions align properly.

The essential (and automatic) portion of this trio is the first one. Windows XP's file protection system is enabled by default, and it prevents the replacement of the protected system. Windows File Protection runs in the background and protects all files installed by the Windows XP setup program—.SYS, .DLL, .OCX, .TTF, .FON, and .EXE files. If one is replaced or altered, by default, a dialog box alerts you that a program is attempting to alter a system file.

In Chapter 23, you learned about setting up the three levels of overwrite protection for Windows File Protection: ignoring, warning, or preventing modification of all system files. Here, I'll talk a bit about a standalone utility supplied with Windows XP that you can use to scan for modified files that may have slipped through the detection process.

Running the File Signature Verification Tool

To verify that system files have a digital signature, follow these steps:

1. Choose Start, Run, and then enter **sigverif** to launch the File Signature Verification tool.

2. Normally, the program searches for any system files not signed, and when you close the program, the results are saved in SIGVERIF.TXT. If you want to search for nonsystem

files as well or append to an existing log of found items, click the Advanced button and set up the log file's name, append option, and other related options.

3. Back in the File Signature Verification dialog, choose Start. The tool then checks to see which system files are digitally signed and displays its findings. Typically, you see the message displayed stating that files have been scanned and verified as digitally signed. Otherwise, you'll see a list of files that have not been digitally signed. If you have logging enabled, these search results are also written to SIGVERIF.TXT in the <system root>\Windows directory (by default).

USING THE SYSTEM FILE CHECKER

Another program, closely related to the File Signature Verification tool, is the System File Checker. This tool looks for protected system files and verifies that their version numbers link up with the operating system and that they haven't been replaced or trashed accidentally. The System File Checker is a command-line program that you set up using a keyboard-entered command. It then runs the next time you boot.

> **NOTE**
> You must be logged in as a system administrator to run this program.

If the System File Checker discovers that a protected file has been overwritten, it retrieves the correct version of the file from the <systemroot>\system32\dllcache folder and then replaces the incorrect file. It uses the following syntax for program execution:

```
sfc [/scanonce] [/scanboot] [/cancel] [/quiet]
```

The details for these parameters are as follows:

```
/scanonce
```

The preceding syntax scans all protected system files once.

```
/scanboot
```

The preceding command scans all protected system files every time the computer is restarted.

```
/cancel
```

The preceding command cancels all pending scans of protected system files.

```
/quiet
```

This command replaces all incorrect file versions without prompting the user.

> **NOTE**
> What if something or someone has trashed the \system32\dllcache folder? No problem. The `sfc /scanonce` or `sfc /scanboot` commands repair the contents of dllcache if it's unreadable.

Windows File Protection, if turned on, normally prevents any kind of intrusion that might result in a corrupted file, at least from an outside source such as a third-party program installation. If all is working as planned, you don't have to worry about running this program or the File Signature Verification program with any regularity. If you want to play it super safe, though, protecting also against microscopic bit loss on the hard disk or crafty hacking, you can use the /scanboot option to check each time you boot. The verification process doesn't take very long to complete.

TROUBLESHOOTING

THE TASK MANAGER IS STALLED

My Task Manager seems stuck. It doesn't reflect newly opened or closed applications.

You might have this problem if you've paused the Task Manager. Choose View, Update Speed, and then choose any setting other than Paused. Another approach, if you want to keep it paused, is to choose View, Refresh Now.

SENDING THE TASK MANAGER TO THE BACKGROUND

My Task Manager doesn't drop into the background when I click another program.

Like some Help files, the Task Manager has an Always on Top option. Choose Options, and turn off this setting.

WRONG LANGUAGE

I'm seeing Windows Update in the wrong language. Why?

You're probably having this problem because of settings in Windows and Internet Explorer. But let's start at the beginning. The first thing to know is that every copy of Windows has a language tag associated with it. If you're running an English version of Windows XP, then Windows Update is only going to offer to download English-based add-ins for the operating system.

Now with that said, yes, you can change the language in which you view the Windows Update pages. If you have the wrong Regional settings in Windows and/or in Internet Explorer, you might be dishing up Greek or Italian when you want English. Here's the order in which Windows Update checks for your language preference:

1. Language tag of your copy of Windows and Internet Explorer

2. Your system's Regional Settings

3. Internet Explorer's auxiliary language preferences setting

The catch is that Internet Explorer has a feature called Accept Language, which supersedes the Windows Regional Settings. If you are viewing Windows Update (which is available in multiple languages), Internet Explorer looks to the list of languages in your language preference settings to determine which language to display. This list is prioritized, so if you have

Greek as the first language and English as the second, Windows Update is displayed in Greek.

To see the Windows Update site in a different language, you can adjust your Internet Explorer's language preference settings as shown here. Note that changes here affect other multilanguage sites that you view.

1. In Internet Explorer, choose Tools, Internet Options.
2. On the General tab, click the Languages button.
3. Select the language you want, and then use the Move Up button to place your selection at the top of the list of languages. Click OK.
4. Click OK in the Internet Options dialog, and restart your browser.
5. Reload the Windows Update page.

In Windows Update, I Can't View Update Details, Installation History Details, or Troubleshooting Articles

This is probably because you have a pop-up blocker set either in IE or another program. That prevents Windows Update's site from opening new browser windows from links you click. To change the Pop-up Blocker settings (available only for Internet Explorer 6), in Internet Explorer, on the Tools menu, point to Pop-up Blocker. Then click Pop-up Blocker Settings. Then do one of the following:

- To allow pop-up windows only when using Windows Update, under Address of Web Site to Allow, type (or copy and paste) this URL: `https://windowsupdate.microsoft.com`. Then click Add.
- To allow new browser windows to open when using any secured (`https://`) Web sites, in the Filter Level list, click Low: Allow Pop-ups from Secure Sites.

If you use other pop-up blocking software, find out whether you can change your settings just for links you click within a Web site. If not, you might need to allow pop-ups while using Windows Update.

The Scheduled Tasks Doesn't Activate Correctly

My Scheduled Tasks doesn't seem to activate correctly. What's the problem?

You can check several things when a Scheduled Tasks job doesn't activate correctly. Here's the rundown; check these steps in order:

1. Open the Scheduled Tasks window, and then open the properties for the task. Make sure the task is actually enabled via the Enabled check box on the Task tab.
2. On the Schedule tab, verify that the schedule is set correctly.
3. Check the permissions for all the items involved in running the task, such as scripts, executables, and so on. Be sure the permissions for those items match those of the user account assigned to the task.

4. If a user whose account a task is set to run in is not logged on at the time the task is scheduled to run, the task runs but is not visible. Check the task log file to see whether the task was running but you didn't know it.

5. Some commands hang, waiting for user input, unless launched with command-line arguments. Research the command or executable you are trying to run. Check the Help file for the program or issue the command from a Command Prompt window, followed by /?, -?, or ? to see a display of options.

6. Check or ask your administrator to check that Scheduled Tasks service is turned on (by choosing My Computer, Manage).

7. Check the Status column in the Scheduled Tasks window, and look for the task in question. (Use the Details view.) Table 24.6 describes the status types.

TABLE 24.6   SCHEDULED TASK STATUS TYPES

Status	Description
Blank	The task isn't current running, or it already ran and encountered no obstacles.
Running	The task is currently being run.
Missed	One or more attempts to run this task was missed, possibly because the computer was not turned on, or the scheduler was paused at the time.
Could not start	The most recent attempt to start the task failed for some reason. Check the log file if you care to investigate further. The log file, named schedlgu.txt, is stored in the \Windows folder. This file is used to record the activity of scheduled tasks.

NO EVENTS IN SECURITY LOG

No events are showing in my security log.

By default, security logging is turned off in Windows XP. Therefore, no security events are monitored or recorded, and your security log is devoid of entries even if you *do* have the administrative rights required to view them. See Chapter 19, "Network Security," for details on auditing and the recording or logging of security events into the Security log.

TIPS FROM THE WINDOWS PROS: POWER USER TRICKS

The following tricks are two of my personal favorites. The first is helpful if you frequently work with a laptop computer and want to add a serial mouse without closing all your applications and rebooting.

The second tip is especially helpful if you want to deter workgroup users from using the Windows Update feature without first checking with the system administrator.

ADDING A SERIAL MOUSE WITHOUT REBOOTING

Due to the cramped or otherwise uncomfortable position I have to assume to use my laptop keyboard, I very often plug in an external, ergonomic keyboard with a trackpad on it. Then I can sit back in my chair, keyboard on my lap, or even stand the computer up sideways. In any case, I don't always want to power down and then reboot just to plug in the keyboard and mouse.

Now, if the mouse and keyboard were USB devices, this wouldn't be a problem because USB supports hot docking. Keyboards, mouse devices, graphics tablets, and many other external devices such as cameras, printers, scanners, and PDAs are available in a USB-enabled version, but that doesn't mean you own them.

My keyboard plugs into the PS/2 port, which is no problem. Although making PS/2 connections with a computer turned on is not advisable (it can blow the driver chip for the port), I do it anyway, and on my Dell 7000, it hasn't posed a problem. The keyboard is immediately recognized and works fine. But the rub is that the trackpad, which connects to the serial port (a second PS/2 port for a mouse is not available on my machine), isn't recognized. Connecting the mouse doesn't result in anything at all, functionally. For a while, I resorted to rebooting Windows XP. Hibernating or suspending didn't force a hardware redetection. Another approach was to run Add/Remove Hardware, but that's a pain because it takes too long.

I discovered that the Device Manager can scan hardware and see whether anything new is lying around, without its driver. After I had installed the trackpad software, it was part of the Device Manager's list for the computer. But when the mouse is sensed as unplugged, the operating system marks it as not functioning (with an exclamation mark in the Device Manager). To get it going again, no reboot is necessary. I just had to do the following:

1. Reconnect the mouse.
2. Get to the Device Manager (you can do so from Control Panel, System, Hardware tab).
3. Click somewhere on the computer's tree, such as the top level, the icon showing the computer name. (This step is imperative, or the next step isn't possible.)
4. Choose Action, Scan for Hardware Changes.
5. Wait about 10 seconds while Windows does its thing. Now the external mouse should work.

By the way, this trick works on the desktop system too!

REMOVING WINDOWS UPDATE FROM THE START MENU

As good an idea as Windows Update is, unauthorized use of it could be annoying to a system administrator. Corporate system administrators who are responsible for hundreds of PCs need to control what goes on their machines, especially in the way of core operating system updates. It is possible to remove the Windows Update icons that appear in the Start menu, and even prevent the users from accessing the Windows Update site (`http://windowsupdate.microsoft.com`) from anywhere within Windows.

By using the Windows XP Microsoft Management Console's snap-in called Local Computer Policy, you can disable Windows Update on the Start menu. Although you can modify and configure MMC to view policies in many ways, the most generic way to configure a new console root is as follows:

1. Choose Start, Run. Then enter MMC and click OK.
2. From the console, choose Add/Remove Snap-in.
3. Choose Add, Choose Group Policy. Then click Add, Close, and finally OK.
4. Navigate down by expanding the Local Computer Policy by expanding User Configuration, then expand Administrative Templates, and then select Start Menu and Taskbar.
5. Double-click Remove Links to Windows Update.
6. Select the Disabled radio button.
7. Click OK.
8. Click File, Exit. If prompted to save settings to the Console, click No.

CHAPTER **25**

MANAGING USERS

In this chapter

MULTIPLE USERS ON ONE MACHINE

In many instances, a single computer is used by more than one user, which creates some challenges. While we sometimes use computers to share information, we often want to keep information confidential. We want to customize our desktop settings, and want the computer to look and behave the same way every time we use it, no matter who has used it in the meantime. Furthermore, we might want to prevent other users and network visitors from seeing or changing our files. These issues can make sharing a computer troublesome, and the Windows 9x product line addressed them poorly. Windows XP is a great improvement thanks to the following features:

- **User accounts**—Let you set up access for each individual who wants to use the computer. Each account has its own name and optional password.
- **User profiles**—Let users configure their own personalized desktop scheme, icons, preferences, and settings, and give users their own personal My Documents folder.
- **Private folders and Shared folders**—Let users control just who is permitted to have access to which of their files.

In this chapter, we'll go over these features so you can decide how much control you want to exercise over your computer. Using these features is optional—you can make your system as secure or as open as you wish.

First, though, there is a bit of background on accounts that we need to cover. If you already know about user accounts (or don't care to know about them), you can skip ahead to the section "Working with Passwords."

USER ACCOUNT TYPES

Each user identifies him- or herself to Windows with a username and an optional password. Windows keeps track of each user in its list of *accounts*, or known users. For each user, Windows associates information such as whether the user has Administrator privileges, the user's desktop and sound preferences, and the location of the user's My Documents file folder.

When you installed Windows XP Home Edition, you had the opportunity to enter the names of several users. At that time, Windows created accounts for each person. These users were all designated Computer Administrators, which means that when logged on they can install hardware and software, create and delete any other user's account, view any file on the computer, and in general, do just about anything they want. Computer Administrator users can do anything. This is just like Windows 95, 98, and Me in that regard.

You also can designate that some accounts are Limited Users. People using these accounts can run but not install software, can view their own private My Documents folder but not others', can use printer and networks but not install them, and cannot change the settings for other user accounts. The Limited User concept might be new to you, but you'll find that it's a great help because it lets you restrict the amount of damage, intentional or otherwise, that others might cause.

→ Folder privacy works only if your hard drive was formatted with or updated to use the NTFS file system. For more information about NTFS, **see** Chapter 26, "Managing the Hard Disk."

In addition to any individual users you specified, a special user accounts is created on your machine, named Guest.

The Guest user account provides access to your computer by people who don't have a pre-defined username and password. This account is turned off by default, but when enabled, it allows visitors restricted (Limited User) access to your computer without your needing to set up a new account for them. This is fine for home use but in a business environment I strongly urge you to leave the Guest account turned off. Even though the Guest account has lower privileges than a normal user account and can't modify system settings or install soft-ware, it's still risky to let random people have access to a computer in a business setting.

NOTE

During installation, an account with the name Administrator is also set up by Windows, but it cannot be viewed, used or changed on Windows XP Home Edition, except if you boot Windows in Safe Mode. As you'll hopefully never encounter it, you can just ignore its existence. For this chapter, we'll just concern ourselves with normal users as Computer Administrators.

WHY USE SEPARATE USER ACCOUNTS?

Windows XP requires you to add a separate user account for each person that uses your computer. You created at least one when you installed Windows. Using separate accounts makes good sense:

- Each user can set their desktop, color, sound, and application preferences separately.
- Each user has their own "desktop" so downloads and icons won't accumulate from other users (I know some people whose desktop is completely covered with icons. This would drive me crazy!)
- Email, My Documents, and other files are stored separately, so each user has some measure of privacy.

When you create accounts, you should consider what kind of privileges to grant the users. As I mentioned earlier, Windows XP Home Edition provides two types of account privilege levels:

- **Computer Administrators**—Can install hardware and software, read system files, and add and change user accounts.
- **Limited Users**—Can't install programs or make changes to important system settings.

Children and nontechnical users, for example, probably should have Limited privileges, so they don't accidentally erase files or programs. In a business setting, *no* regular day-to-day user account should have Administrator privileges—the risk of someone running virus-infected software from a highly-privileged account is too great.

For reasons that I can't quite fathom, Microsoft decided to make all users "Administrators" by default in Windows XP. This may have been to reduce the number of support calls from people who said "My computer won't let me install this new hardware," but I think it's a *very bad* idea to have users operate with Administrator privileges on a day-to-day-basis. To name just one reason, any Trojan Horse virus software that you might accidentally run will have full access to your system.

I suggest that you set up only one account as a Computer Administrator, use it only for installing software and hardware, and make all of your regular user accounts Limited users. It's easy to change them after the fact, if you set up accounts when you first installed Windows.

NOTE

> Because any Computer Administrator-level user can change the password of any user account, Administrator users can ultimately get into the files and folders of any user on the computer, even if the users have chosen to make their documents private. If confidentiality is an issue for you, this is another reason to have only one Computer Administrator.

I recommend that you use a Administrator level account only when you:

- Don't have permission to access a file you need
- Need to create or change the password of another user account
- Need to install new hardware or software

Microsoft gave all users Administrator privileges to make these actions easier for you, but I think they're needed seldom enough that it's not worth the added risk.

 If you are told that your user account doesn't have permission to accomplish some necessary maintenance task, see "Can't Install Hardware or Software" in the "Troubleshooting" section at the end of this chapter.

THE RUN AS COMMAND

If you find that you are logging in and out frequently to do administrative tasks, try using the Run As command. You can do so by opening the Start Menu or Windows Explorer and locating the program that you want to run as an Administrative user. (It could be a Control Panel item, the Microsoft Management Console, or any other application.) Right-click the program name, and select Run As, as shown in Figure 25.1. (If Run As doesn't appear, try pressing the Shift key while you right-click). You then can type the username and password of the privileged account you want to use.

Figure 25.1
You can choose to run selected applications in the security context of a different user.

NOTE

Run As doesn't work with Windows Explorer, the Printers folder, or desktop icons.

You can also run programs in the context of another user account through the command line. For instance, you can open a command prompt window and type something like this:

```
runas /user:Administrator "control userpasswords"
```

This runs the User Accounts control panel as the Administrator.

WORKING WITH PASSWORDS

By default, Windows does not create passwords for user accounts when they're created. You should set a password for every account on your computer. You can set up or change your account's password at any time. Just follow these steps:

1. Click Start, Control Panel, User Accounts.

2. Select your account icon if necessary, and choose Create a Password or Change My Password.

3. If you're adding a password for the first time, you'll be asked to enter the password twice, to be sure of the spelling. You also should enter a password hint, something that will remind you (and *only* you) what your password is. The hint will be displayed on the Welcome screen if you mistype your password when you try to log on. Remember that anyone can see the hint, so "My husband's name" is not a good choice. Then, click Create Password.

If you're changing your password, you'll have to enter your current password, and then type in your desired new password twice as indicated. Then click Change Password.

4. If you're entering a password for your own account for the first time, you'll be asked if you want to make your My Documents folder private. (This privacy feature works only if your hard disk was formatted with or updated to use the NTFS file system, as discussed in Chapter 26.) If you choose to make it private, other users will not be able to see it or view its files.

If you change your mind about this later, open My Computer, right-click your My Documents folder, select the Sharing tab, and check or uncheck Make This Folder Private. Click OK to confirm the change.

Because passwords aren't created when you first install Windows, you'll probably want to create one the first time you log on. That's also a good time to create a password reset disk if you think it will be necessary down the road.

PREVENTING PASSWORD DISASTERS

Your password is the key to all of the information your have stored in the computer. This includes not only private files and email, but also additional security information like your Microsoft .NET Passport, Wallet, network passwords, and passwords to Web sites you've visited. The use of passwords to protect this information is essential. Then again, people tend to forget passwords or to leave jobs, so there has to be a way to gain access to a user's files without the password.

To this end, a Computer Administrator can reset any other user's password. But a security system wouldn't be worth much if the administrator could then log on as that user and go on a shopping spree using his or her Passport and Wallet. The compromise reached in Windows XP is that an Administrator can change a user's password to regain access to an account, but there is a cost: As a security measure, Windows will erase any other passwords it has associated with that user. Why? Since Windows offers to remember the passwords you type for Web sites, network computers, email, and other protected resources, these would become available to anyone who was able to change your Windows password. Erasing them after a forced password change eliminates this risk.

You and other users can protect yourselves from all this by creating *password reset disks* before a password emergency occurs. With a reset disk, you can change even a forgotten password without the risk of losing your passwords and access to your .NET passport.

To create a Password Reset Disk, you will need a blank, formatted floppy disk. Then, follow these steps:

1. Click Start, Control Panel, User Accounts.

2. Select your own account, and from Related Tasks, choose Prevent a Forgotten Password.

3. Follow the wizard's instructions to insert a floppy disk and create the password reset disk.

When the wizard has finished, be sure to label the disk clearly; for example, "Mary's password disk for Computer XYZ." The disk is as good as your password for gaining access to your computer, so be sure to store it in a safe place.

You don't have to re-create the disk if you change your password in the future. The disk will still work regardless of your password at the time. However, a password disk works only to get into the account that created it, so each user should create one for him or herself.

IF YOU FORGOT YOUR PASSWORD...

Forgetting the password to your computer account is an extremely unpleasant experience. It's definitely no fun to have your own computer thumb its proverbial nose at you and tell you it's not going to let you in to get your own files. If this happens to you, take a deep breath. You might be able to recover from this. Here are the steps to try, in order of preference:

1. If you have created a password reset disk, as I described in the previous section, you're in good shape. Follow the instructions under "Using a Password Reset Disk."

2. Log on with any Computer Administrator user account and follow the procedure outlined under "Creating and Managing User Accounts" later in this chapter to reset your account's password.

3. If you don't remember the password to *any* Computer Administrator account, or you can't find someone else who does, you're in big trouble. There are programs available that can break into Windows XP and reset the Guest or Administrator account password. It's a gamble—there's a chance these programs might blow out your Windows installation. Still, if you're in this situation, you probably will want to risk it. Here are some programs you might look into:

   - ERD Commander from Winternals.com can replace the Administrator or Guest password through an easy-to-use GUI interface.

   - Windows XP/2000/NT Key from LostPassword.com works just as well on Windows XP as it does on Windows NT and Windows 2000. In fact, this little guy saved my own you-know-what a couple of years ago. It creates a Linux boot disk, which pokes through an NTFS or FAT volume, finds the windows security registry file, and replaces the administrator's password so you can reboot and log on.

   - There are some other password-reset programs that I haven't personally tested, but you might be able to use: NTAccess from www.sunbelt-software.com and NTAccess from www.mirider.com.

4. If you only need to retrieve files, you can remove the hard drive and install it in another Windows XP or 2000 computer as a *secondary* drive. Boot it up, log on as a Computer Administrator, and browse into the added drive.

5. If you get this far and are still stuck, things are pretty grim. You'll need to reinstall Windows using the Clean Install option, which will erase all of your user settings.

25

Then, as a Computer Administrator, you can browse into the Documents and Settings folder to retrieve files from the old user account folders.

You remember the old saying about 28 grams of prevention being worth 454 grams of cure. To prevent the disaster from occurring in the first place, create that password reset disk, or at least record the password of an Administrator-level account in a safe and secure place.

USING A PASSWORD RESET DISK

If you have lost your password and have a password reset disk, you can use it to log on and reset your password. Here's the procedure:

1. Attempt to log on using an incorrect password.
2. If you're using the Welcome screen, click the message "Click here to use your password reset disk." If you're using the old-style "classic" logon, click the Reset button when you get the Logon Failed dialog box.
3. The Password Reset Wizard launches. Click Next.
4. Insert your password reset disk for this account, and click Next.
5. Provide a new password, and click Next.
6. Click Finish.
7. You will be returned to the logon prompt. Provide your newly set password, and log on.
8. Pat yourself on the back for having the forethought to have made the password disk in the first place.

When you're finished, store the password reset disk away for another day. You don't need to make another recovery disk after using it.

CREATING AND MANAGING USER ACCOUNTS

Windows XP excels in the home environment, where more than one person might want to use a single computer. Windows can set up individual user accounts, so each person's files, preference settings, and desktop look will be kept separate.

To create new user accounts or to modify an existing account, log on as a Computer Administrator user. Keep in mind that you don't need to log on as a Computer Administrator to manage your *own* account.

User accounts are administered with a Control Panel tool. To run it, select Start, Control Panel, User Accounts.

Using the User Accounts control panel applet shown in Figure 25.2, you can perform three tasks:

1. To modify the password, name, picture or security level of an account, or to delete an account, select Change an Account or click on one of the account icons.

2. To create a new account (no surprise here), click Create a New Account.

3. To choose between the Welcome Screen (the graphical Windows XP Welcome login screen) and the older Windows logon dialog box, choose Change the Way Users Log On or Off.

Microsoft has done a good job of designing the Windows XP account management tool, and most of the dialogs are self-explanatory. I'll go through them here to show you what's possible.

Figure 25.2
The User Accounts control panel applet lets you create, delete, and modify user accounts on a workgroup computer.

CHANGING AND DELETING ACCOUNTS

You can alter an account's settings at any time using the User Accounts control panel. You can always change your own account settings. In addition, Computer Administrator users can adjust any user's account.

Selecting Change an Account or clicking on an account icon displays the Change Account task list, as shown in Figure 25.3. Here you can

- Change the name of a login account.

- Add, change or remove an account's password. Changing another account's password has consequences—please see the note later in this section.

- Change the picture associated with an account. These pictures appear on the Welcome screen. You can select one of several provided by Microsoft, or select Browse to select one of your own digital photographs. You can use any image file in BMP, GIF, JPG, or PNG format. The picture will be displayed at about postage-stamp size, so it's best to choose fairly small images of an object or person that fills the picture.

- Change the account type from Computer Administrator to Limited or vice versa.

Figure 25.3
Manage account settings with the Change User Account screen.

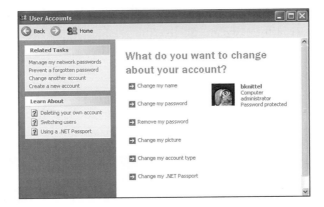

- Delete the account. (This option is only available when you're logged on with a different, Administrator-level account. You can't delete the account you're currently using, and you can't delete a Computer Administrator account if it's the only one.) When you delete an account you have the option of retaining or deleting the user's personal files stored in their My Documents and Desktop folders. If you want to keep them, they'll be put into a folder on your desktop.

- Change your Microsoft .NET Passport. This is where your user account is matched up with a Passport email address. You can use this task to assign a Passport or change your Passport settings. (This task is only available when you're changing your own account.)

- Modify passwords stored for access to other network resources, by clicking the Related Tasks option.

NOTE

> Although Microsoft doesn't seem to encourage you to, I recommend that you create passwords for *all* the accounts on your computer.
>
> If you change another account's password, Windows will erase any stored network passwords, Web site passwords, and security certificates associated with the account—this ensures that you can't then use their account to impersonate them. It's best if a user changes his or her own password. Only change another user's password if they have forgotten it.

Automatically Logging On at Startup

Your computer can automatically log itself on and go directly to the desktop when it boots up, bypassing the sign-on process entirely. You might want do this if you have only one account on the computer and you are completely unconcerned about security or you are setting up a computer that will not directly interact with users, such as a kiosk or an industrial control system.

You can't actually eliminate the need for a user account and logon name. What you can do is tell Windows to automatically log on for you, by following this procedure:

1. Click Start, Run and enter **cmd** into the run field. With the Command Prompt window open, type the following command:

   `control userpasswords2`

   If you are not currently logged on as a Computer Administrator, you are prompted for the Administrator password.

2. On the Users tab, uncheck Users Must Enter a User Name and Password to Use This Computer.

3. Click OK. You are prompted for the username and password to use when the system starts up. If the account has no password, leave the password field blank.

Now, every time Windows boots up, it automatically logs on with the specified username and password. If you want to use a different account, simply log off; you then see the Welcome Screen or logon dialog box as usual.

You can go back to the normal logon-at-boot system by repeating this procedure and checking the box in step 2.

SHARING FILES AMONG USERS

When you set up multiple users on your computer, you'll notice that every user gets his or her own clean Desktop and My Documents folder. In fact, if your hard drive is formatted using the NTFS file system, users have the option of making their My Documents folders private when they create a password, so other users can't see into them.

That's great for keeping everyone's stuff separate, but what do you do when you want to have files that anyone can get to? This might come up when different people are working on a collaborative project, or when you want to keep common nonconfidential information in a shared place.

Windows provides a simple solution to this with the Shared Documents folder. In Figure 25.4, you can see that My Computer shows each user's My Documents folder, and the common Shared Documents folder. Shared Documents is a place to put files and folders that you want to make available to each user on the computer. (This folder also automatically is made available to your other computers, if you have installed a home or office network.)

Inside Shared Documents are folders named Shared Music and Shared Pictures, to help you start organizing your common files. You can create other folders in there as well, as you see fit.

Figure 25.4
My Computer shows each user's My Documents folder, plus the common Shared Documents folder.

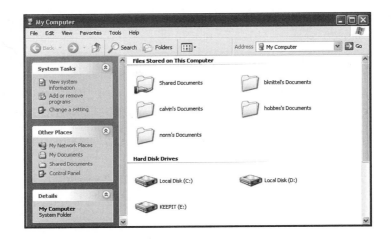

Computer Administrator users can browse into other users' personal My Documents folders as long as they didn't choose to make them private when they created their passwords. In Figure 25.5, you can see the personal My Documents folders for several other users, along with my own. Limited Users can't view any other user's My Documents folder, so they are limited to using their own folder or Shared Documents.

→ For more information about making your My Documents folder private, **see** "Working with Passwords," **p. 885**.

Of course, you also can create other folders anywhere on your computer's hard drive, and any user can view and use these folders. The advantage of Shared Folders is that it appears on everybody's My Computer display, so it's quite convenient.

WORKING WITH PRIVATE FILES

If your hard drive is formatted using the NTFS (New Technology File System) directory structure, Windows can let you prevent or allow others to access to your My Documents folder. The first time you create or change the password for your own account using the User Accounts control panel applet, Windows asks whether you want to make your files and folders private.

If you say yes, other users will not be able to browse into your My Documents folder (more precisely, they will not be able to get into your User Profile folder, which will be discussed later in this chapter). You still can share documents with other users and with network users using the Shared Documents folder, by creating new folders on the hard drive or by using the other network shared folders.

You can change the Private/Public setting of your My Documents folder at any time. Just open My Computer, right-click your My Documents folder, select the Sharing tab, and check or uncheck Make This Folder Private. Click OK to confirm the change.

If your hard drive is formatted with the FAT file system, private folders will not be available. Any user can read any file on a FAT-formatted hard drive.

→ To learn more about NTFS, **see** "Choosing a File System: FAT, FAT32, or NTFS?," **p. 68**.

→ To learn how to convert a FAT-formatted disk to NTFS, **see** "Convert," **p. 915**.

There are a couple of things you should consider, though, if you are counting on this feature for privacy. First, remember that any Computer Administrator user can change your account's password and log on as you. They will be able to see your files without any problems. Folder privacy doesn't make your files completely inaccessible to everyone else, only a bit more difficult to get to.

Second, Windows manages private folder security with the industrial-strength file protection system used by Windows NT, 2000, and XP Professional and their various server versions. In XP Home Edition, you don't have access to the settings and controls that let the users of these operating systems adjust and manage file security. That's fine, because these features are complex and easy to mess up.

However, there is one confounding situation that could arise as a result of this. When you create files in a private My Documents folder and then move them to the Shared Documents folder or another public folder, the "privacy" attribute is moved along with the files. If you move the files with Windows Explorer (or My Computer or any of Explorer's other guises), you're OK because Explorer will take care of adjusting the files' security settings, and other users then will be able to read the files. However, if you move the files using the command line—that is, with the "move" command—the files' security settings will not be reset and other users will be see these files listed, but will not be able to open, edit, or delete them.

 If you have files that can't be opened because they were moved out of a private My Documents folder, see "Access Is Denied Opening a File" in the "Troubleshooting" section at the end of this chapter.

SIMPLE FILE SHARING

Although home users are typically happy letting anyone at any computer read or modify any file, business users usually need to restrict access to files with payroll, personnel, and proprietary information. Windows XP's predecessors Windows NT and Windows 2000 were designed for business use, so they have a security system that lets computer owners restrict access to sensitive files on a user-by-user basis.

Unfortunately, this is difficult to set up and manage. Microsoft gave Windows XP Home Edition a new security system called "Simple File Sharing." (It's available in Windows XP Professional, too, where it can be turned on or off.) The strong security foundation of Windows 2000 is still present in Windows XP Home Edition, but it's been pre-configured.

With Simple File Sharing

- Network users are not prompted for a username or password. Instead they are automatically granted access to shared folders using the permissions granted to the Guest account, even if Guest is disabled for direct logins.

- The Security properties tab used to assign per-user permissions to files and printers in Windows 2000 and Windows XP Professional is not available.

- Windows automatically assigns appropriate security permissions to folders and printers when you share them. There are two options: "Others can read and write the shared files," or "Others can only read the shared files."

Simple File Sharing vastly simplifies managing a workgroup or home network, but makes it extremely important that you take steps to be sure your computer and network is secured from Internet hackers. Be sure to read Chapter 19, "Network Security," for more information.

USER PROFILES

User profiles contain all the information that the computer needs to personalize your system's look and feel. Your user profile contains your desktop icons, shortcuts, personalized Start menu, and your personal file folders such as My Documents and My Pictures. The profile also contains your network settings, network printer definitions, and desktop settings, which are stored in a Registry file named NTUSER.DAT. This file is accessed as part of the Windows Registry when you are logged in.

Normally, user profiles are stored under C:\Documents and Settings, in folders with the same name as the user account. For example, the user profile for my account is stored in C:\Documents and Settings\bknittel. When accounts are deleted and recreated, when Windows is reinstalled, or when users log on to domain accounts with the same name as local accounts, Windows may append something to the user name—usually the name of the local computer, the domain, and/or a number.

A profile is really just an ordinary folder. It just contains some important stuff and it's used in a special way—the contents of its Desktop subfolder, for instance, appear on your desktop when you log on, and the contents of its Start Menu subfolder appear when you click the Start button. The contents of a user profile are shown in Table 25.1. (Some of the listed folders are hidden. To see them in Windows Explorer, click Tools, Folder Options. Then select the View tab, and select Show Hidden Files and Folders.)

TABLE 25.1   CONTENTS OF A USER PROFILE FOLDER

Item	Contains
Application Data	User-specific files needed by application programs such as Explorer and Outlook Express.
Cookies	Internet Explorer (IE) data.

Item	Contains
Desktop *	Icons and files displayed on the desktop. This is where desktop stuff is actually stored.
Favorites	Lists of shortcuts used by the Favorites menu in IE.
Local Settings	Like Application Data; includes temporary files.
Documents **	User's My Documents folder.
NTUSER.DAT	User's Registry data (HKEY_CURRENT_USER).
NetHood	Shortcut icons used by My Network Places.
PrintHood	Shortcut icons used by Printers and Faxes.
Recent	Shortcuts to recently accessed documents.
SendTo	Shortcuts used to fill the "Send To" context menu.
Start Menu	Shortcuts displayed on the user's Start menu.
Templates	Templates used by various applications to create blank documents.

Actually Windows displays the contents of your profile's Desktop folder, plus the contents of the All Users Desktop folder. I'll discuss this later in the chapter.
** *Windows Explorer displays this folder's name as "My Documents" or "Bob's Documents", but the folder's real name is just Documents. Explorer displays what it deems a more understandable name.*

The "documents" folder in your profile is displayed on My Computer and Windows Explorer as My Documents. In fact, Windows displays all user' documents folders in Explorer, as shown in Figure 25.5. Each is displayed with an appropriate user name. Your account folder will appear with your user name; this is the same folder as My Documents. Shared Documents belongs to a special user profile which I'll discuss below under "Making Icons Available to All Users."

Figure 25.5
My Computer displays each profile's Documents Folder with an appropriate name.

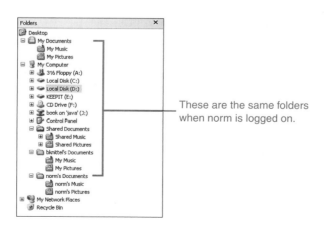

These are the same folders when norm is logged on.

The Profile Manager will let you copy profile data from one account to another. To run the Profile Manager, you must log on as a Computer Administrator. Select Start and right-click My Computer. Select Properties and view the Advanced tab. Click Settings in the User Profile section. The Profile Manager will appear as shown in Figure 25.6.

Figure 25.6
User profile folders contain the user's Registry settings, My Documents, desktop, and so on. They can only be copied using the User Profiles tool.

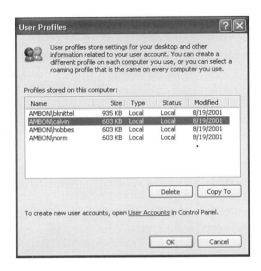

You can copy or delete user profile folders by selecting a listed profile and clicking Delete or Copy To.

Delete a profile only if the account is no longer being used, or if you are certain you want to delete the account's My Documents folder and other personal information.

You can copy profiles to set up preconfigured accounts. I'll give an example of this in the "Tips from the Windows Pros" section at the end of this chapter.

NOTE

> You can't just manually copy the files and subfolders from one user profile to another. The files have exclusive security permissions, and the Registry file has security data inside it that makes the profile unusable by other users. The Profile Manager works because it changes the security data as it copies the profile.
>
> If you have a LAN, you might be tempted to store each user's profile on a shared network folder. This doesn't work because the users will have a different *SID (security identifier)* on each computer, even if she has the same login name on each computer. The Registry file NTUSER.DAT is tied to the SID, so the profile will not function on machines other than the one that created it. This is one of the reasons to buy Windows Server 2003 or XP Professional: Domain network users have a global SID that follows them from computer to computer, and this makes "roaming" profiles possible.

MOVING PROFILES WITH THE FILES AND SETTINGS TRANSFER WIZARD

You can copy your user profiles between computers using the Files and Settings Transfer Wizard. You might want to do this if you

- Upgrade computers or operating systems
- Switch between your home computer and a portable computer rented for a trip
- Decide to erase your hard drive and start over with a fresh copy of Windows.

The wizard can copy your user profile (My Documents folder, Registry settings, and so on) to a floppy disk, but it's best to store the wizard's data on a zip drive, CD-RW, or a shared network folder because the amount of information can be quite large. You can also use a direct serial cable connection between two computers, but this requires you to purchase a "Serial PC to PC File Transfer Cable" from a computer store or other vendor.

Run the wizard first on the "old" computer, the one whose settings you want to move or save. The older computer can be running Windows 95, 98, 98SE, ME, NT, 2000, or XP. If it's running older versions of Windows, insert your Windows XP CD-ROM, and run the wizard from the Setup menu. On Windows XP, click Start, All Programs, Accessories, System Tools, Files and Settings Transfer Wizard. The wizard will give clear instructions as you go.

You can choose to copy settings only, files only, or both files and settings. Windows will display the list of file types and settings it will copy. You can choose Let Me Select a Custom List if you want to modify the list of files or directories to transfer.

Then, run the wizard on the "new" computer to transfer the documents and settings into your Windows XP user account.

MAKING ICONS AVAILABLE TO ALL USERS

If you find that you want to make the same desktop icons and Start menu applications available to all users on your computer, rather than for just your own account, you don't have to make copies for each user. Instead, you can take advantage of the All Users profile.

When Windows displays your desktop, it's actually displaying the merged contents of two folders: Your profile's Desktop folder, and the All Users desktop folder, stored in C:\Documents and Settings\All Users\Desktop. If you have an icon or shortcut that you'd like to share with all of your computer's users, you can store it in the All Users folder rather than make a copy for each user. Of course, if any user deletes the icon... it's gone for everybody.

The All Users profile contains four folders, listed in Table 25.2.

25

TABLE 25.2   CONTENTS OF THE ALL USERS PROFILE

Item	Contains
Desktop	Files, Icons and shortcuts that will appear on every user's desktop.
Documents *	The Shared Documents folder.
Favorites	Shortcuts that will appear on every user's Favorites list.
Start Menu	Shortcuts that will appear on every user's Start menu. Shortcuts in the Programs\Startup subfolder will be run when any user logs on.
Application Data **	User-specific files needed by application programs such as Explorer and Outlook Express. Quick Launch bar shortcuts, for example, are in Application Data\Microsoft\Internet Explorer\Quick Launch.
Templates	Templates used by various applications to create blank documents.

Windows Explorer displays this folder's name as "Shared Documents", but that's done with smoke and mirrors. The folder's real name is Documents.
**Some folders are hidden. To see them in Explorer, you have to select View Hidden Files in Tools, Folder Options, View.*

TROUBLESHOOTING

CAN'T INSTALL HARDWARE OR SOFTWARE

When I try to install new software, use a Control Panel or Computer Management tool, or set up hardware such as a printer or network adapter, I get an error message telling me I don't have sufficient privileges to perform the operation.

Limited user accounts are not allowed to perform many management functions or to make changes to the Windows software folder. In general, this is a good thing because it prevents unauthorized people (such as young children, visitors, or meddlesome in-laws) from making changes to your computer setup. More subtly, it can help prevent rogue software from taking over your computer without your knowledge.

If you are using a Limited User account and run into a roadblock because of this, you can either get a Computer Administrator user to perform the task for you, or you can have them change your account to make you a Computer Administrator as well. If you know the password to an Administrator account, just log off and log on again using that account.

ACCESS IS DENIED OPENING A FILE

When I attempt to open a document, I get the message Access is Denied.

This can sometimes occur if you are using Fast User Switching and the document is in use by another logged-on user, or if the document was in use by a crashed application. If this is the case, have the other user close the application, or use the Task Manager to kill the errant application.

This also can occur if your disk is formatted with the NTFS file system and you move files from a private My Documents folder to a public folder using the command-line move command. In this case, the file's security attributes have been moved with the file, so it's still "private." One way to fix this is for the original owner of the file to locate the file in Windows Explorer. She or he needs to drag the file to her or his My Documents folder, and then drag it back to the shared location. Explorer then will fix the security settings.

A Computer Administrator user also can use the cacls command to change the file's security settings. In a command prompt window, change to the directory containing the file, and type the following command:

```
cacls filename /G Everyone:F
```

where filename is the name of the file you're trying to fix.

You could also boot your computer in Safe Mode and log on as Administrator (no password). Now, an additional Security tab appears on each file and folder's Property page. With this tab you can adjust file permission settings. For instance, you can add Everyone to the list of users authorized to access a file.

TIPS FROM THE WINDOWS PROS: SETTING UP FOR MULTIPLE USERS

I have a lot of (quirky, I'm told) preferences that I like to make when I set up a new computer: Start menu settings, application settings, icon placement, and so forth. If you are setting up multiple users for your computer, you can save everyone a lot of configuration-tweaking time by setting up the default user profiles before the users log on for the first time. To do this:

1. As a Computer Administrator, create the new user accounts. Then, log off and log back on using one of the new users.

2. Make the changes to the computer that you want all users to have, such as power management settings, desktop icons, Start menu, wallpaper, and so on. Install application software, load up shortcuts, whatever you want each user to have.

3. Log off, and log back on with the Computer Administrator account you used to create the accounts in step 1.

4. Open My Computer, select Tools, Folder Options, select the View tab and check Show hidden files and folders. Click OK.

5. Open the Start menu, right-click My Computer, and select Properties (or select View System Information from the System Tasks list). View the Advanced tab and click Settings in the User Profile section. The Profile Manager appears (refer to Figure 25.6).

6. Select the profile for the user you just configured and click Copy To.

7. Click Browse, and browse to \Documents and Settings\Default User. Click OK.

8. Click OK.

Now, when users log on for the first time, Windows creates the user profile by making a copying of the Default Users folder, which now contains all the settings you made. The user starts out with a nicely configured computer.

Unfortunately, on standard installations of Windows XP, Microsoft puts some icons like the Windows Media player icon back on the desktop and the quick-launch bar even if you deleted them in the Default User profile.

CHAPTER 26

MANAGING THE HARD DISK

HARD DISK MANAGEMENT

For many users and system administrators, intelligent hard disk management really forms the core of efficient system management. Until a new technology evolves to replace the hard disk, we're stuck with the problems and limitations created by what is in a sense a crude system of motors, spinning platters, and very delicate parts such as read/write heads floating just microns above a flying surface that can be easily ruined by particles as small as those found in a puff of cigarette smoke. Perhaps some day hard disks will be relics of the past, bookends, like the 5MB drives I have on my bookshelf. (They make good doorstops, too.) Until that time, though, we're stuck with the peculiar vagaries of hard disks. The good news is that high-capacity drives are cheap and plentiful these days.

No doubt, the majority of Windows XP users will never set up RAID arrays or multiple-booting arrangements or need to do any remote disk administration. Perhaps they will perform occasional disk cleanups and defragmenting as well as learn to share folders over a small network. These tasks are enough to get by with. Yet, with a bit more knowledge gleaned by reading through this chapter, you will learn how extensive Windows XP's hard disk configuration capabilities are.

For users with access to both operating systems, note that Windows XP Home omits some hard disk–related features found in Windows XP Professional. These include support for dynamic storage, encryption, and file level security. Although it is possible to live without these, I recommend using Windows XP Home only as a stand-alone system. If you have any need for security, you should use Windows XP Professional.

> **NOTE**
>
> RAID is short for *redundant array of independent* (or *inexpensive*) *disks*. In this hard disk scheme, two or more drives are connected together in combination for higher fault tolerance and performance. RAID arrangements are used frequently on servers but aren't generally necessary for personal or client computers.

This chapter describes the following:

- Using Windows XP Home's disk management tools
- Learning organizational strategies for arranging files and partitions on your hard disk
- Working with the supplied Disk Management utility
- Managing removable storage
- Cleaning up your drives
- Defragmenting and repairing your drives
- Converting NTFS
- Compressing files

- Freeing up space
- Backing up your data
- Zipping files
- Using third-party filesystem tools
- Troubleshooting hard disk problems

WINDOWS XP FILE AND STORAGE SYSTEMS

Windows XP Home uses the traditional storage model (known as basic storage) of disk structure employing partition tables. Each hard drive can hold up to four *primary partitions* or up to three primary partitions and one *extended (secondary) partition*. Within this extended partition, logical drives are created. The total number of primary partitions and logical drives cannot exceed 32 per hard drive. This disk structure is understood and can be accessed by any Microsoft OS. The annoyances and limitations of this partition table methodology are artifacts of Microsoft operating systems, incidentally, not something imposed by hard disks themselves or their manufacturers. One of the most annoying issues related to basic storage is the fact that you must reboot every time you alter partition configuration. A serious limitation of basic storage is the inability to expand the size of a partition with unallocated space from anywhere. Basic storage only allows expansion using contiguous space.

NOTE

> As mentioned earlier, Windows XP Home does not support the dynamic storage mechanism that Windows XP Professional and Windows 2000 both support. In fact, Windows XP Home cannot even see dynamic storage drives created by other OSes. In case you don't know, dynamic disk storage is a clever scheme that overcomes some of the annoyances and limitations of basic storage. For example, dynamic disk volume management does not require reboots. Plus, volumes can be expanded with space from anywhere within the system, include space from other drives.

26

Within the confines of basic storage, only *simple* volumes and *extended* volumes can be created. A simple volume uses free space available on a single disk. This space must be a single contiguous region. Each partition or logical drive is assigned a separate and distinct drive letter and functions as a distinct region of disk space. An extended volume is a simple volume that has been expanded by adding additional space. The added space must be contiguous, unallocated space located on the same physical drive as the simple volume and that space must be located after the simple volume. To make this clearer, think of a hard drive as a yard stick. A basic partition which is located at inches 19 through 31 can only be expanded by the available space in between 32 and 36, not with the space of 1 through 18.

NOTE

If you use only the tools supplied with XP, expanding a volume must be performed from a command line window. The Disk Management interface does not even offer a GUI-based volume-expanding function. I don't recommend expanding volumes; instead, delete and then re-create them. But, if you must, the procedure is outlined in the Help system from Computer Management under Disk Management, How To, Manage basic volumes, Extend a basic volume. If you use a third-party program such as Partition Magic, you can resize partitions and volumes non-destructively, though, using a GUI.

ORGANIZATIONAL STRATEGIES

Most Windows XP users will end up setting up their systems with standard partitions (that is, basic storage) and the NTFS file format. But what about other filesystems? How should you organize multiple disks? What about preparing your disks, and what kinds of strategies should you consider?

If you're not going to stick with the straight and narrow of running only NTFS on your hard disk, consider these alternative strategies and rules to follow:

- Whenever possible, create a separate partition for your data files. This tip has particular relevance to users who test new software or operating systems. If you store your data on a separate partition, reinstalling an operating system is a simple matter of formatting your system partition and starting from scratch. Although you still have to reinstall your programs, using a separate data partition eliminates the need to fuss and ensures you didn't miss a data file somewhere along the line. It also makes backups simple and straightforward. You can do one backup of your system partition; you then need to update this backup only when you add a new device or software program. Data backups can be run on a daily or weekly basis (as determined by how often your data changes) and set to run on your data partition.

TIP

When you have a data partition in place, right-click the My Documents icon in your Start menu, select Properties, and reset the target folder location to your data partition. Resetting it ensures that all your favorites, application settings, and history files are also kept separate from the system partition.

- Buy a disk image program (such programs are discussed toward the end of this chapter). You can purchase one for less than $75, and it is worth its weight in gold if you like to "tinker" with your system and program configurations. After you have your operating system set up, your principle applications installed, and everything tweaked and configured to perfection, you can create an image of your system on a separate drive or partition. If you need to reinstall your operating system for whatever reason, the complete process—from beginning to end—should take no more than 20 minutes. Couple this program with the separate data partition discussed in the preceding bullet, and you have a system that you can rebuild from scratch with minimal effort or time loss. However, note that it is important for the hardware comprising the system to remain the same so the restored disk image can fully function properly.

When you add, delete, or reconfigure a program, be sure to update your disk image.

Some clients I know have gone so far as to buy and install a separate hard drive just for image storage. At about $100 or less for a 150GB drive (if you shop around at a site such as www.pricescan.com), a hard drive is probably one of the best investments in crash protection you can buy. As a matter of fact, I'm considering making dedicated image drives a standard system configuration for all computers I maintain.

- If you have more than two IDE hard drives, put both drives on your primary IDE controller and your CD-ROM on the secondary controller. Configuring a system this way puts all the strain on one IDE bus when copying data from drive to drive, but mixing a CD-ROM drive and a hard disk on the same channel is worse. CD-ROM drives transfer data at a much slower rate than hard disks. Mixing fast and slow devices on the same controller forces the controller to run at the slower of the two rates. If you really want good performance with complex drive scenarios (multiple hard disks and CD-R or CD-RW), I suggest that you look into SCSI controllers or get an add-on IDE controller, such as the fast ATA controllers card from Promise Technology. These controllers enable you to add several more ATA (IDE) drives to what would otherwise be a maxed-out system, and are competitive in speed to SCSI drive/card systems at significant cost savings. Don't overlook the newer serial-ATA arrangements. Another way to go is with external FireWire-based drives (sometimes called IEEE 1394 spec). A handful of manufacturers such as Maxtor make such drives. They can perform as well as internal drives because the FireWire cable can transfer data at up to 400Mbps, and you can daisy-chain up to 63 drives on one cable. External FireWire enclosures are available from companies such as Pyro allowing you put standard IDE-based CD-RW or hard drives of varying capacities on the FireWire channel. If you have both a CD or DVD-ROM and a CD-R/CD-RW drive, you should consult the documentation packaged with your drive to determine the optimum configuration for copying from CD to CD. USB 2.x drives are even faster than FireWire 1.x drives by a bit (440Mbps versus 400Mbps). My external FireWire drive has both USB2 and FireWire 1.x connectors.

26

TIP

> Beware that sometimes external drives cause data storage problems with XP, though, dropping out of view of the operating system. I have had this happen with a handful of Maxtor 1394 drives. The only trick I know is to keep the drive from spinning down into energy-saving mode and turning off write-caching for the drive (drive properties). Maxtor has some information about this problem in its knowledgebase, but I have yet to find a consistent solution. So for backup, an external drive seems to be fine. For doing online work such as video capture, it's a little dicier, in our experience.

- If you want to install Windows XP in a dual-boot configuration with other OSes, please jump over to Chapter 28, "Multibooting Windows XP with Other Operating Systems." In Chapter 28, all the ins and outs of multibooting, including which filesystems to use in various scenarios, are discussed.

WINDOWS XP'S DISK MANAGEMENT TOOLS

Windows XP comes equipped with a handful of disk management tools, ranging from very powerful ones that can create hard disk stripe sets, create mirror disks, or beat your disk into submission, to a couple of tools that are simply convenience items.

The most oft-used ones are available right off the Tools tab of a drive's Properties sheet. To reach the Properties sheet, right-click a drive in Windows Explorer or My Computer. Figure 26.1 shows the Properties tabs for drives that are formatted with both a FAT and an NTFS partition. Notice the difference in the number of tabs. NTFS has more options because of its support for quota management.

Figure 26.1
Properties sheets for FAT and NTFS volumes.

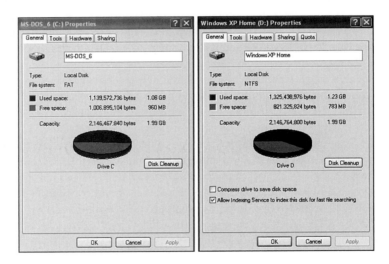

The following sections explain the use of the bulk of hard disk management tools included in Windows XP.

DISK MANAGEMENT

The Disk Management utility, shown in Figure 26.2, is responsible for the creation, deletion, alteration, and maintenance of storage volumes in a system. This tool is located within the Computer Management interface of Administrative Tools. To get there, click Start, Control Panel, Performance and Maintenance, and Administrative Tools. Double-click Computer Management, and then select Disk Management from the Console Tree. Another means is by right-clicking My Computer in your Start menu and choosing

Manage. Using the Disk Management utility, you also can assign the drive letters used by your CD and hard disk drives.

Figure 26.2
The Disk Management tool as part of Computer Management.

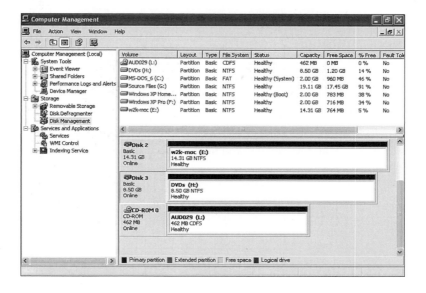

TIP

If the Administrative Tools menu selection is not displayed on the Start menu, right-click the Start menu and select Properties, click Customize, click Advanced tab, scroll down to the System Administrative Tools items, then select the appropriate radio button.

If you enable the Control Panel to act as a menu, Administrative Tools can be accessed through it off the Start menu as well.

26

THE DISK MANAGEMENT INTERFACE

As discussed in Chapter 24, "System Utilities," this single interface lets you manage both local and remote computers using the various administration utilities shown in the left pane. Using this interface, I will show you how to perform different procedures on your existing and new hard disks. The process is quite simple for most of the operations because you are presented with a wizard to complete them.

Most operations on disks can be performed by right-clicking the disk or volume you want to affect. As usual, you are presented with a context-sensitive menu from which you can perform any actions relating to the volume or disk you clicked. You can also see, from the graphical layout in the Disk Management, just what is going on with your disks at any given time. As always, you can select the Help option from within any menu to get an explanation of the operations available to you.

TIP

> You can tweak the way volumes are displayed in the Disk Management tool. You can do this by clicking the Settings button at the end of the button bar. From there, you can select the color you would like to use to represent any of the various disk states that are shown in Disk Management. By selecting the Scaling tab from the Settings dialog box, you can also change the way in which the Disk Management shows the scaling of each disk. This capability is particularly useful if you would like the scale display to be more representative of the actual physical sizes of your disks.

ASSIGNING DRIVE LETTERS AND JOINING VOLUMES

Windows automatically assigns letters to the drives. However, this assignment might not suit your system; for example, you might have mapped a network drive to the same letter Windows assigns to a new drive.

Using Disk Management, you can easily assign logical drive letters to your hard disks and removable drives such as CD-ROMs. You can't change the drive letter of your boot drive (usually the C: drive), but you can change any of the others (except the floppy letter[s]).

CAUTION

> Note that many MS-DOS-based and Windows-based programs make references to a specific drive letter (for example, environment variables). If you modify the drive letter of a drive with these programs installed, they might not function correctly.

To change the letter, right-click the disk volume or drive in the bottom-right pane of the Disk Management, and select Change Drive Letter and Paths. A dialog box appears, listing the current drive letter assignment. Click Change. Under Assign a Drive Letter, choose the desired new letter. Click OK and confirm that you really do want to make the change.

The "Path" part of "Change Drive Letter and Path" is in addition to or instead of assigning a drive letter to a disk drive or partition, you can "graft" the disk volume onto another. Windows lets you specify a folder that will become the mount point for the new drive. For example, I might create a folder named C:\TEMP. Because I want lots of space for it, I can install a new hard drive and, instead of assigning it a drive letter, tell Windows to access it through C:\TEMP. My C:\TEMP files and subfolders are then stored on the alternative drive.

TIP

> By using a mount point, you can add space to the folders under the mount point folder using an available hard drive. This is a good way to add space in a controlled fashion for a specific purpose, such storing scratch files or Web page images.

Mount points graft subsequently added drives at a folder, sort of like grafting two trees by tying together a branch from each tree. Figure 26.3 illustrates this approach. Here I've grafted my music files from drive G:\MUSIC into the mount point on drive H:\MP3.

NOTE

You can graft new volumes or disks onto a folder only on an NTFS-formatted drive. The new volume can have any format, however.

Figure 26.3
Assigning a partition or volume to a folder rather than a drive letter joins the volume to an existing volume. The contents of the added volume appear as subdirectories of the mount point folder.

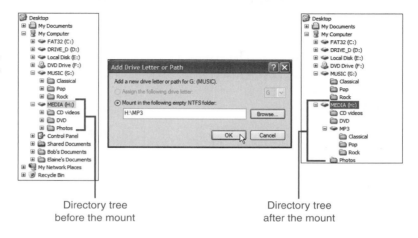

Directory tree before the mount

Directory tree after the mount

NOTE

If the folder you specify as the mount point already contains files, they are inaccessible as long as the drive-to-path mapping exists because that folder is now remapped into the new location. The original files reappear if you delete the drive path. Thus, it's usually a good idea to create a new folder as a mount point or delete all of the contents of an existing folder before establishing the mount point.

Even if you have several hard drives and CD-ROM drives, you can graft them all together onto your C: drive, making it look like one big filesystem. It's a great management concept: You can add space to your filesystem by attaching new disk volumes right into the original folder structure. (Unix users are probably smirking at this point because the Unix operating system has worked this way since it was written in the 1970s.) The original or main drive must be formatted with NTFS, but the mapped drive (the one to which the mount point links) can be formatted with FAT, FAT32, or NTFS.

To graft a disk volume to an existing filesystem, follow these steps:

1. Create the folder that is to serve as the mount point for the new drive or volume on the existing drive that needs additional space.
2. Highlight the drive or volume that will be linked to in Disk Management.
3. Right-click, select Change Drive Letter and Paths, and click Add.
4. Select Mount in the following empty NTFS Folder.
5. Enter the folder's pathname, or click Browse to locate it.
6. Click OK to save the path.

26

TIP

> When Explorer shows you free disk space on the original drive, it measures only the space on the physical drive, not space on any grafted drives. You'll actually have more space than you think because files on the grafted folders are stored on another volume. If you want, you can also assign a drive letter to the added volume so that you can view and monitor its free space directly.
>
> Alternatively, you can use the command prompt, change to the folder in the grafted volume, and use the DIR command. The DIR command lists free space on the actual current volume.

NOTE

> In the Explorer, notice that the icon for the folder mount point shows up as a hard disk. This icon appears simply so that you can differentiate between a mounted folder and a plain folder.

You can assign a given drive or volume to at most one drive letter, but an arbitrary number of paths. (It's a little strange to see the same files appear in several different places, so I recommend that you not go nuts with this feature.)

TIP

> If you're running out of room on your C: drive, see whether it makes sense in your situation to add lots of space to just one folder (for example, My Documents). If it does, install and format a new hard drive, and assign it a letter. Copy the original folder to the new drive. Then add a path (that is, mount point) to the new hard drive using the name of the original folder. This way, you can preserve your original data and have lots of room for growth.
>
> Another really good time to use this feature is when you've backed up application data onto a CD-R or CD-RW. If you want to use the backed-up data in an emergency, you can add a path for your CD-ROM drive to make its files appear in the original data location expected by your application. That way, you can use the data off the CD-R without restoring it to disk or reconfiguring your application. Later, you can delete the path to regain access to the "real" folder.

REMOVABLE STORAGE

Removable storage is another tool within Computer Management. Its job is to track and catalog the data stored on removable storage devices. These devices can take the form of tape backup drives, MO drives, Jaz drives, or the changers that control many removable storage devices. The Removable Storage Manager works by allowing you to create *media pools*—collections of media to which the same management properties (such as security permissions or backup routines) apply. These are devices and schemes that serious data management professionals need to worry about, not the typical Windows XP Home user.

The Removable Storage is another of those "buried" Windows XP features that you're not likely to know about unless you know where to look (using the Control Panel or My Computer methods described earlier). In the right pane of Computer Management, expand Storage and click Removable Storage. From here, you can create and manage media pools and also get information about the physical locations for media.

NOTE

> If you're not certain whether a given removable device is compatible with Windows XP, check the Hardware Compatibility List (HCL) and/or catalog at the Microsoft Web site http://www.microsoft.com/windows/catalog/.

As implemented, the Removable Storage tool is limited to the small scope of hardware supported under it. But like many other Windows XP features (the Indexing Service, for example), it has tremendous potential when third-party vendors develop hooks to its functions and interface. At the moment, it stands as a useful tool to catalog backup media, such as tapes and optical cartridges, but little else.

For more typical backup needs, consult the Backup Tools and Strategies section later in this chapter.

DISK DEFRAGMENTER *See next page for process*

When an operating system stores data on a hard disk, it places that information in the first available "hole" it can find that isn't already occupied by another file's data. If the disk already contains several other files, however, that location might not be large enough for the complete file. When this happens, the operating system places as much of the file as it can in the space available and then searches for another open hole for the balance of the file. This process continues until the entire file has been written to disk. Any files not written to a contiguous disk location are considered "fragmented."

The problem with fragmentation is that it slows down the rate at which your hard disk can retrieve information and supply it to the requesting program. Hard disks remain largely mechanical devices and are governed by the laws of physics. To access files stored on a disk, the drive must physically move a small arm to the correct location on a spinning platter. These movements are measured in milliseconds, but milliseconds add up, especially when a file is spread over 100 unique locations.

Fragmentation is not always a bad thing. If an operating system had to find a contiguous section of disk space for each and every file it stored, as your drive filled, your system would get even slower. Eventually, your system would reach a point where the disk still had ample free space, but none of this space would be in contiguous blocks big enough to hold a file.

Disk Defragmenter addresses this fragmentation problem by reorganizing all the files on your hard disk so that they are stored as complete units on a single area of the disk. To do so, it identifies any remaining free areas, moves small files there to open up more space, and

26

uses this newly opened space to consolidate larger files. This shuffling process repeats until all the files are shuffled around in this manner and the entire disk is defragmented.

TIP

> Defragmenting a large drive with many files on it can take a lot of time. This is the kind of process to use the Task Scheduler to handle, running at night when you're not around and don't need access to your hard disk drive. However, the defragmenter included with Windows XP cannot be automated because it does not have command-line parameters. It must be operated or controlled manually. You'll need to purchase a full-blown commercial defragmenter to take advantage of automated scheduling. I've had great success with Symantec's Norton Speed Disk which is a part of SystemWorks (www.symantec.com) and Executive Software's Disk Keeper (www.execsoft.com). By the way, the native Windows XP defragmenter is a limited version of Disk Keeper.

When should you defragment your drive? In reality, because today's drives are so fast, you're not likely to notice slowdowns unless you're using very large data files, you're capturing video onto your hard drive, or you use the same files or applications regularly, which can fragment them. But for typical users who are hopping around between programs, creating new files, and deleting files on a regular basis, the average access times they experience with a drive will be acceptable, even when fragmented.

If you start to notice a general hard disk access slowdown, the first thing to suspect is a RAM shortage, or that you have too many files open and your drive's pagefile is being hit too much (that is, swapping between system memory and virtual hard disk memory is going on). After ruling that out, however, take a trip down defrag lane. Run the program, and it will tell you whether it is worth your time to defragment.

To run Disk Defragmenter, follow these steps:

1. Select Disk Defragmenter from the Storage section of Computer Management.

2. Click to select a drive in the list of volumes.

3. Click the Analyze button. In a few minutes, the result of the analysis appears. You'll see a screen like the one shown in Figure 26.4.

4. Click the View Report button if you're the curious type. You can really get into the numbers here, viewing statistics about the drive, and checking to see where the maximum fragmentation is occurring, the number of fragments, the file sizes, and so on. Figure 26.5 shows an example from my hard disk. You can save the report or print it if you like.

5. If you decide to go ahead and defragment, click the Defragment button and get ready to wait. As the defragmenting progresses, you'll see the progress reported across the bottom graph in the window. The graphic display slowly becomes primarily blue, indicating that most files are now contiguous. You will see some areas of green, indicating system files (possibly a large area if a pagefile is on the drive). You might have some small areas of fragmentation left over as well.

Figure 26.4
Running Defrag's analysis on a drive indicates whether you would net any advantage from defragmenting.

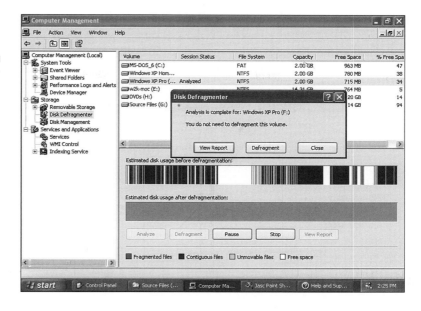

Figure 26.5
Details of a defrag analysis can be helpful in determining where most of your fragmentation is occurring. Scroll the top pane, and check to see whether your pagefile is fragmented. Typically, it won't be, but if it is, this is a good reason to defragment.

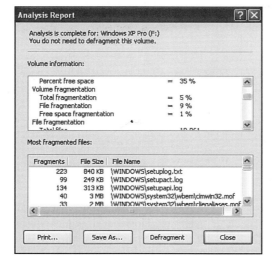

DETECTING AND REPAIRING DISK ERRORS

NTFS was introduced and billed as a "robust and self-healing" filesystem (as opposed the FAT system, which isn't). All in all, I would have to agree with Microsoft on this one. I have yet to have an NTFS partition go "sour" on me in any way, shape, or form. I've had NTFS partitions that would not boot and key system files that would not run, but for the most part these errors were self-inflicted and usually brought on by playing with fire.

Some other versions of Windows have the ScanDisk program whose job it is to detect and repair the file allocation table (FAT) when you shut down improperly. In these versions, you also could set the Task Scheduler to run it periodically, or run it manually as needs dictated. This program, which hearkens back to DOS days, now appears within the Windows XP GUI as an error checking utility in a hard drive's Properties sheet.

Error Checking in Windows XP checks the filesystem for errors and checks the drive for bad sectors (bad spots). To run the program, do the following:

1. In My Computer or the Explorer, right-click the drive you want to check.
2. On the context menu, choose Properties.
3. Click the Tools tab.
4. In the Error-Checking section, click Check Now. A dialog box appears, as shown in Figure 26.6.

Figure 26.6
Checking a disk for errors in the filesystem and bad spots on the disk.

You can run the error check with neither of the option boxes turned on. You are not required to close all open files and programs. However, if you check either of the boxes, you are told that all files must be closed for this process to run. You are given the option of deferring the check until the time you restart your system, however.

The meaning of the options is as follows:

Automatically Fix File System Errors	If file directory errors (for example, lost clusters, files without end-of-file markers, and so on) are found, this option specifies whether the program should fix them.

Scan for and Attempt Recovery — This option specifies whether the program of Bad Sectors should attempt to locate bad sectors, mark them as bad, and recover data from them, writing it in a known good area of the disk. If you select this option, you do not need to select Automatically Fix File System Errors; Windows fixes any errors on the disk.

TIP

> If your volume is formatted as NTFS, Windows automatically logs all file transactions, replaces bad clusters automatically, and stores copies of key information for all files on the NTFS volume.

CONVERT

After formatting a volume with FAT or FAT32 and storing files on that volume, you later can decide you really want NTFS on that volume. To make this change, you have two options. One is to back up all the files, reformat the volume, and then restore all the files. Another and more preferable option is to use the Convert tool to transform the volume from FAT/FAT32 to NTFS without disturbing the files stored on the volume. Convert is a command-line program that converts an existing FAT16 or FAT32 partition to NTFS.

CAUTION

> This conversion process is a one-way street. The only way to revert an NTFS partition back to a FAT partition with the native tools is to reformat the drive. To revert and *not* lose your data, you have to use a program such as Partition Magic (from Symantec).

The command-line syntax for the Convert program is as follows:

```
CONVERT volume /FS:NTFS [/V]
```

The arguments are as follows:

volume	Specifies the drive letter (followed by a colon), mount point, or volume name
/FS:NTFS	Specifies that the volume to be converted to NTFS
/V	Specifies that Convert should be run in Verbose mode (unless you are a programmer, running the Convert program in Verbose mode will not be of interest to you)

These are not all the parameters for Convert. For more details, see the Help and Support center or issue **CONVERT /?** from the command prompt. Considering the work the Convert program has to do, it's surprisingly fast, even on a well-populated disk.

26

COMPRESSION: HOW IT WORKS, HOW TO USE IT

Windows XP ships with a built-in provision for file compression that is implemented via NTFS. It's not strictly true that only NTFS files and folders can be compressed because a command-line program called compress can compress FAT-based files and folders. However, you must, in turn, use the expand command to decompress the resulting files and folders before you can use them. This procedure is awkward. So, for practical purposes, compression is implemented seamlessly into the operating system only on NTFS-formatted volumes.

File compression works by encoding data to take up less storage space. Digital data is compressed by finding repeatable patterns of binary 0s and 1s. The more patterns found, the more the data can be compressed. Text can generally be compressed to about 40 percent of its original size and graphics files from 20 to 90 percent. Some files (namely .EXE files) compress very little because of the lack of repeating data patterns within the program. The amount of compression depends entirely on the type of file and compression algorithm used.

NOTE

> Compression in this context is different from the zip-compressed files you may be familiar with. This is all rather confusing, thanks to Microsoft. See the section later in this chapter on zipping and unzipping files if that is what you are interested in doing.

Compressing a file or folder in Windows XP is a simple and straightforward process:

1. Open Windows Explorer (or a My Computer window), and select the file or folder you want.
2. Right-click, and select Properties from the context menu.
3. Select the Advanced button at the bottom of the Properties dialog.
4. In the Advanced Attributes dialog that appears, put a check mark in front of the Compress Contents to Save Disk Space option (see Figure 26.7).
5. When you click OK, if this item is a folder, you are prompted to choose whether you want to compress this folder only, or to compress this folder, subfolders, and files within those subfolders.

By default, compressed files are shown in blue. If you open the Control Panel, select the Tools menu, Folder Options and then select the View tab on the Folder Options dialog box, you can find an option to Show Encrypted Or Compressed NTFS Files In Color.

NOTE

> By the way, even though this option mentions encryption, Windows XP Home does not support encryption. If you need encryption, you should use Windows XP Professional.

Figure 26.7
The Advanced Attributes dialog box where the Compress check box can be accessed.

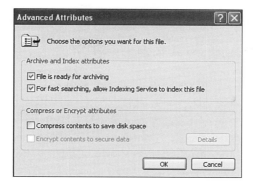

CAUTION

You should keep in mind some disk space requirements when using compression. If you try to compress a volume that's running extremely low on free space, you might see this error message:

```
Compression Error
File Manager/Explorer cannot change compress attributes for:
"path\filename"
```

These error messages indicate that the system needs additional free space to perform compression. The system is not designed to manipulate the data in place on the disk. Additional space is needed to buffer the user data and to possibly hold additional file-system metadata (information about the files, typically for use by Windows). The amount of additional free space required depends on the cluster size, file size, and available space on the volume. Clear up some space on the drive volume and try again.

INDEXING

Windows XP comes with a file, folder, and text-search system called the Indexing Service. This system scans files and folders on your hard disk and builds a database of the words it finds in them. This database helps speed up the Search for Files and Directories option when you're looking for words within files or keywords in file descriptions. It also helps the Internet Information Services (IIS) Web server perform Web site searches. In addition, you can query the index directly. True, Windows has for some time had a Search function for files (from the Start button), but it's laborious and slow, particularly on large hard drives, because it doesn't pre-index your files. Each time you conduct a search, it starts from the square one and pores over all your files, one folder at a time. XP's Indexing service builds a quick-lookup database and maintains it in the background. You still conduct your searches in the same way, but with indexing turned on searches complete much faster, even down to the words within the files (not just filenames).

26

NOTE

Right off the bat, I should reassure you that the Indexing Service pays attention to file privileges when it displays results of searches. It never reports a match for a file the person searching doesn't have permission to view.

MANAGING THE INDEXING SERVICE

To view the Indexing Service Manager, open Computer Management from Administrative Tools (open the Control Panel and choose Performance and Maintenance), expand Services and Applications, then select Indexing Service (as shown in Figure 26.8). Under Indexing Service, the manager displays any *catalogs* defined on your system. A catalog is a self-contained index for a folder or group of folders. By default, a System catalog is defined for use by Search for Files and Folders. If you've installed Internet Information Services, you also have a Web index, which can be used by scripts to let visitors to your Web site search its pages.

Figure 26.8
The Indexing Service Manager displays all defined index catalogs.

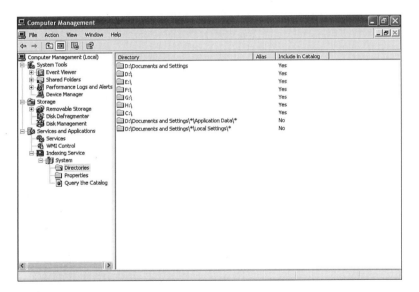

26

If you want to use the Indexing Service, select Indexing Service in the left pane, and choose Action, Start from the menu. Answer Yes to Do You Want the Indexing Service to Start whenever You Boot Your Computer.

There is a simpler way to turn on the Indexing Service. Open the Search tool (Start, Search), and then click the Change preferences link. Click With Indexing Service (for faster local searches), select the Yes, Enable Indexing Service radio button, and then click OK. This setting is a simple toggle to enable the Indexing Service (you can disable it with the same keystrokes, just select Without Indexing Service, and then No). It will start each time the system is booted. However, you still must go through the Indexing Service Manager to configure what is indexed.

Choosing Yes starts the service, which immediately begins its job of cataloging files on your hard drive. It does its job of scanning files periodically from now on, as long as the computer is turned on.

NOTE

Indexing happens in the background, and you probably won't even notice that it's happening, except for your hard drives being accessed occasionally when you didn't request it. However, if you are doing highly data-intensive work and need all the computing horsepower you can get, you might want to leave the Indexing Service turned off.

INDEXING SERVICE PROPERTIES

You can right-click the Indexing Service entry in Computer Management to adjust the service's global properties. The Generation tab has some useful settings, as shown in Table 26.1.

TABLE 26.1 GENERATION TAB OPTIONS	
Index Files with Unknown Extensions	If this option is checked, the Indexing Service includes all files in the index, regardless of file type. If it is unchecked, only registered file types are indexed. It's probably best to leave the box checked.
Generate Abstracts	If this option is checked, for each indexed file, the Indexing Service extracts and stores the first few sentences of each matching file and displays them on the search results. Check this box with caution because it can consume an enormous amount of disk space. I recommend that you leave it unchecked on the Service's Properties sheet.
Maximum Size	This option sets the maximum length in characters of abstracts. If you choose to generate abstracts, keep them short. I suggest going no higher than the default 320 characters.

26

The Tracking tab of the Indexing Service Properties dialog box boasts a single check boxed control: Add Network Share Alias Automatically. This setting determines whether the aliases for shared network drives are added or removed from the index. Leaving this enabled is typically the best option.

CATALOG PROPERTIES

By default, the Indexing Service Properties settings apply to each catalog managed by the Indexing Service. However, you can select the Properties sheet for each individual catalog by right-clicking the catalog name in the left pane and selecting Properties (in Figure 26.8, the catalog is named "System"). Then you can uncheck Inherit Above Settings from Service on the Generation tab and customize them on a catalog-by-catalog basis.

A good use of this capability would be to enable abstracts for the Web index if you have installed Internet Information Services and use searching on your Web site.

NOTE

> Under each catalog is an entry named Properties, but it is a display page only. To change the catalog's properties, you have to right-click its name in the left pane.

CATALOG DIRECTORIES

You can control which directories (drives and folders) are included in and excluded from a catalog by using the Directories folder. Under any catalog name in the left pane, select the Directories entry, and view the cataloged folders in the right pane.

Here, you can add any additional drives to include in your index and add any folders you want to exclude from the index. To add an Include or Exclude entry, right-click in the right pane, and select New, Directory.

In the resulting dialog, enter the full path to the folder to be indexed, or use $X:\backslash$ to add the entire drive $X:$. Check Yes or No under Include in Index. If you want to add a directory on a remote computer, enter its full *UNC* network name, for example, `\\machine\sharename\folder`, and a username and password to be used to access the shared folder.

CONTROLLING INDEXING OF INDIVIDUAL FILES

You also can remove files or folders from all catalogs by using the files' or folders' Properties sheets.

To exclude a file from any catalogs, right-click the file or folder, and select Properties, Advanced. Under Archive and Index attributes on the resulting dialog, you can uncheck For Fast Searching, Allow Indexing Service to Index This File or Folder. Unchecking this box prevents the Indexing Service from ever scanning the file. However, just checking the box is not enough to put the file into an index; the folder must be listed in the catalog's Directories list or in a subfolder of a listed folder.

USING THE INDEXING SERVICE

The System catalog is used automatically by the Start button's Search for Files or Folders item, and it's especially handy when you're searching for a keyword or specific file type. The index is used to hasten the search of any cataloged folder.

You can also search any catalog directly from the Indexing Service Manager. Select Query the Catalog in the left pane, and a search form appears in the right. Enter any desired keywords, and click Search to begin a query. I was surprised to find that my system's temporary

Internet files are included in the catalog, as test queries returned matches based on words in Web pages I had recently visited.

DISK CLEANUP UTILITY

In the course of daily use, Windows XP generates thousands of temporary files to aid in system operation. These files are critical to the operation of the programs that use them when the programs are being used. As most people are all too well aware, though, temporary files have a habit of being much more persistent than their name implies. And over the course of time, these files add up in a hurry and consume large amounts of valuable disk space. The Disk Cleanup utility provides you with a safe and reliable way to delete these temporary files from all their various hiding spots and thus free up disk space on your hard drive.

To access this utility, do the following:

1. Choose Start, All Programs, Accessories, System Tools, Disk Cleanup. In the resulting dialog, choose the drive to analyze. Alternatively, you can right-click a drive in the Explorer, and then choose Properties, General, Disk Cleanup.

2. The program then searches this drive for files that can be safely deleted or compressed. The details of this analysis are then displayed in a dialog similar to the one shown in Figure 26.9.

Figure 26.9
Report of a disk cleanup analysis allows you to choose which category of files to delete off the selected drive.

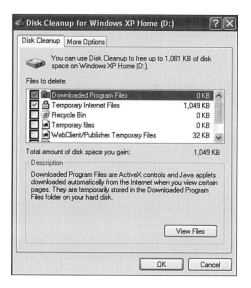

Near the top of the dialog is the total amount of disk space you can free on this drive by accepting the selected recommendations listed below. You can exclude or include file groups from the cleanup process by placing a check mark in front of the types listed. When you select an entry, you see a description of which files that group contains and what their purpose is. By selecting a group and then the View Files button, you can see exactly which files are slated for death in the resulting folder window. Use this option if you have any doubts about a group of files, where they reside, or what they do.

The following file groupings might be listed:

- **Downloaded Program Files**—These files are ActiveX controls and Java applets used by Web pages you have visited. If you delete them, they are simply reloaded the next time you visit the pages.

- **Temporary Internet Files**—This one is a biggie. Every time you access a Web page, your browser stores or caches the various elements of that page on the hard disk. When you revisit a page, any elements that have not changed since your last visit are reloaded from the hard disk rather than the site itself to speed the rendering process. Deleting these temporary Internet files frees the largest amount of disk space of any of the group lists. If you use a modem to access the Internet, however, you will notice longer rendering times the next time you return to one of your favorite sites.

NOTE

> Agreeing to delete temporary Internet files does not delete your *cookies* (personalized settings for Web sites), so don't worry about having to reenter user ID information or other such information for sites you visit a lot. Cookies are stored in x:\Documents and Settings\<*username*>\Cookies. Temporary Internet files are stored by default in x:\Documents and Settings\<*username*>\Local Settings\Temporary Internet Files (where x: is the volume on which the system is installed).

- **Recycle Bin**—Clearing this folder is the same as manually clearing your Recycle Bin. It is a good idea to have a quick look at the files stored there before choosing this option. Select this option, and click the View Files button under the group description; a folder window then opens, listing the contents.

- **Temporary Files and WebClient/Publisher Temporary Files**—Similar to cached Web pages, when you connect to a network location, access a read-only file, or when needed by an application, a temporary copy is sometimes stored on your hard drive. Clearing these temporary copies does not erase the files you explicitly marked as available for offline use, so this is a safe choice.

- **Compress Old Files**—Windows can compress files not accessed within a specified period. To configure this period, select this group and click the More Options button.

- **Catalog File for the Content Indexer**—The Windows Indexing Service (see the description earlier in this chapter) speeds file searches by building and maintaining indexes on your hard disk. Selecting this option removes any old index files not in use but does not delete any current indexes.

On the Disk Cleanup dialog, also notice the second tab marked More Options. The Windows Components option provides a quick access shortcut to the Windows Components Wizard. From this wizard, you can select major system components (such as IIS and Indexing Services) to add or remove. Also on this tab is a shortcut to Add/Remove

Programs under the section labeled Installed Programs. The System Restore Clean up button is used to delete all but the most recent restore points. This may free up a significant amount of drive space, but it will eliminate your ability to rollback to previous states of the system. (See Chapter 30, "Troubleshooting and Repairing Windows XP," for information about System Restore).

TIP

> Running Disk Cleanup weekly does wonders to improve a system's performance. The first time you run it, the program might take quite awhile to run, but with regular exercise, this program speeds up because the disk stays cleaner. Once a month—after you check the contents of the individual folder groups carefully—you should empty all folders of all temporary files. Then follow up by running a defragmentation utility.

USING INTERNET EXPLORER'S CACHE CLEANUP

If you would prefer not to use the Disk Cleanup utility, you can choose a second option for clearing out those disk-hogging cached Internet files.

To access it, open the Control Panel, select Network and Internet Connections, and click the Internet Options icon. On the Internet Properties dialog, you will find a section titled Temporary Internet Files. The Delete Files button works exactly as advertised. The Settings button allows you to configure options for how often cached files are checked against their original counterparts, how much disk space these cached files are allowed to take up, and which folder they are stored in.

When the disk space setting is exceeded, files are removed on a "First In, First Out" basis; that is, the oldest files are deleted to create space for newer ones.

The Move Folder option lets you specify a location where these temporary files will be stored. I think it's a great idea to change this path to a temporary folder or a drive with lots of free space. I usually redirect Internet Explorer to deposit its temporary Internet files into a \temp folder I create on one of my drives. If you do a lot of Web surfing, you'll want to map this temp location to a fast volume that is not on the same hard drive as your main Windows partition.

BACKUP TOOLS AND STRATEGIES

Nobody plans to lose or corrupt an important file. But then again, no one I know gets up in the morning and plans to crash his car either. Things happen, though, and for all the same reasons you buy car insurance, you should also be taking all the necessary steps to safeguard all those bits and bytes that reside on your system's hard drive.

WINDOWS BACKUP PROGRAM

Windows XP Home does not install a backup utility by default, but it is present on the distribution CD. To install it, just double-click on the NTBACKUP.MSI file in the

\ValueAdd\MSFT\NTBACKUP folder on the CD. When the wizard completes the installation, click Finish.

TIP

> If you don't have the CD because your computer came with XP already installed and a CD sometimes isn't supplied, you might still be in luck. If the computer is a Hewlett-Packard, it has the capability to make a restore/recovery CD. That might put the Value Added folder on the CD. Some HPs and Compaqs have a "hidden" partition on the hard drive that might contain the folder you need. Open My Computer; go to Tools, Folder Options, View tab; check Show Hidden Files and Folder; and uncheck Hide Protected Operating System Files; and click OK. See whether that partition shows in My Computer or Windows Explorer. If so, poke around on it for the ValueAdd folder. If your computer is another brand, such as Dell, try calling the manufacturer and asking them to send you an XP CD.

The Windows backup utility should meet the needs of most individual users. With it, you can back up folders or files—both local and remote—either to a Windows recognized tape device, to a removable storage device (Jaz drive, MO drive, Zip drive, and so on), or to a file on a local or remote drive. If Windows XP can read the file (FAT16, FAT32, or NTFS natively), it can be backed up.

The first time backup is launched (Start, All Programs, Accessories, System Tools, Backup), the Backup or Restore Wizard is launched. The first page of this wizard has a check box that controls whether the wizard is launched every time. The wizard can be used to back up or restore files. These wizards offer few options; they mainly ask whether you want to back up or restore, what types of documents to manage (My Documents and settings only, everyone's documents and settings, or all data), and where to put the backup. If that's all you need then you don't need me.

However, there is a lot more to explore in the Backup utility if you switch to Advanced Mode. You can do so by clicking on the link. Plus, you can choose to always open Backup in Advanced Mode by deselecting the Always Start in Wizard Mode check box.

When you reach Advanced Mode, you'll actually be seeing the Backup utility proper (see Figure 26.10). From the Welcome tab of the Backup utility, you can launch more advanced wizards that offer a broader range of activities and settings. There is a wizard for backing up, restoring, and Automated System Recovery (ASR).

Although you can see the option to run ASR, it does not function properly in Windows XP Home Edition. The ASR Wizard appears to run, but will fail because XP Home Edition does not come with all the files it needs to create the boot disk.

In addition to the Welcome tab's wizards, there are three other tabs of control. The Backup tab is used to manually configure a backup operation. The Restore and Manage Media tab is used to manually configure a restore operation and perform basic media management tasks. The Schedule Jobs tab is used to view and alter scheduled backup jobs.

Figure 26.10
The Welcome tab of
the Backup program.

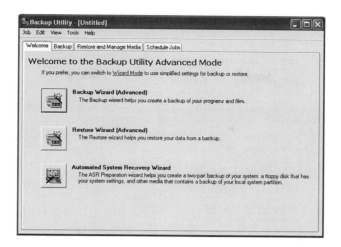

If you are completely new to backing up, use either the default wizard or the advanced wizard to walk you through the process. You'll get the hang of it very quickly. If you are a backup veteran, I don't even need to tell you how to perform a backup.

The Backup tab's interface is very straightforward. Just mark the check box beside each item you want to include in the backup. Keep in mind that marking a parent box will automatically include all subfolders and file contents. And don't forget to mark the System State check box to protect your Registry and system configuration.

Backups can be stored to tapes or files. The tape option is available only if you have a tape device installed locally. Otherwise, all other storage locations are accessible through the File option. Through the File option, you can define the destination path to a file on a local hard drive, on a Zip disk, on floppies, or even across the network to a network share.

TIP

Selecting the option to back up to a file actually is a blessing in disguise. Because many people don't have traditional backup devices such as DAT tapes or DLT drives, backing up to a file facilitates backup to other common removable media, such as CD-Rs. Backing up your data in this manner is preferable to simply writing files to a CD-R. Normally, if you simply back up files and directories to your CD-R drive, you lose your permissions as well as make all the files read-only by virtue of the fact that they are backed up to read-only media. By backing up to a single file from Backup, you retain these settings and can restore with all of them intact. You can even compress this file before you write it to your CD-R by using your favorite zip program.

After you make your file selections and define the destination, click the Start Backup button. This reveals the Backup Job Information dialog box (see Figure 26.11). From this dialog box, the following items can be configured:

26

- Description
- Append or overwrite/replace media
- Allow only the owner and administrator access to the backup
- Schedule the backup (using the Schedule button)

Figure 26.11
The Backup Job
Information
dialog box.

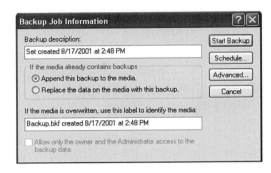

- Set Advanced options (using the Advanced button)
- Cancel backup (using the Cancel button)
- Start backup (using the Start Backup button)

Scheduling a backup is not difficult; just follow the prompts. You'll need to save your backup selections, and then provide the username and password under which you want the backup job to execute. When you are presented with the Scheduled Job Options dialog box, be sure to click the Properties button to define the schedule you need. A thorough discussion of the scheduling options is included later in this chapter.

The Advanced options include

- Backup data in Remote Storage

NOTE

Remote Storage is an optimization mechanism where unused or infrequently accessed files are moved off to a remote storage location, such as a network share or a tape device. If the user requests a migrated file, it is automatically retrieved and returned to its original location invisible to the user. Remote Storage is supported by Windows XP through NTFS. However, no details are included in Windows XP's Help system on how to configure it. Please consult the Windows XP Resource Kit for details.

- Verify data after backup
- Compress data to save space
- Include System Protected Files with System State
- Disable volume snapshot

NOTE

> A volume snapshot allows most open and locked files to be included in the backup. If this feature is disabled, open and locked files probably will not be included in the backup.

- Set backup type

Five types of backup are supported by Windows XP's Backup utility. It is a good idea to consider the different types of backups available before initiating your backup. As you probably know, the operating system provides a means for keeping track of which files have been changed since the last backup—the archive bit. Based on whether a file's archive bit is turned on or off, the backup program either backs it up or skips over it. Your job is to set the correct options so the Backup program is relative to this bit. You can find these options through the Advanced button as discussed or by opening the Tools, Options dialog box and selecting the Backup Type tab. Here, you can set how your files are backed up to your media with the following options:

- **Normal**—The Normal backup does a backup of every file you've selected while also clearing, or turning off, the archive bit on each file. This type of backup sets each file's attribute to signify that it does not need to be backed up again until it has changed.

- **Copy**—The Copy type of backup simply copies the files to your backup media and leaves the archive bit alone. Using this option, you can have several backups happening on the same files without each of them stepping on each other's toes. In other words, if you use the Copy backup option, using the Normal option still backs up every file because the archive bit is still set on them.

- **Differential**—This option backs up only the files that have changed since the last normal or incremental backup, while leaving the archive bit set for each file. With this option, any file backed up looks as though it has not been backed up.

- **Incremental**—The Incremental option is the same as the Differential option, with the exception that it does, in fact, clear the archive bit on files that it backs up.

- **Daily**—The Daily option backs up all files that have been modified only on the day that the backup is performed. Be careful with this one because you could end up not backing up everything you want if you do not run nightly backups.

26

Differential Versus Incremental Backups

Let me give you a bit more explanation of the differences between *differential* and *incremental* backups. You can use the differential and incremental options to save time and tapes when backing up frequently. Keep in mind that full backups can take a lot of time and can fill more than one tape or disk.

If you do a full backup and then successive differential backups, each differential backup includes any files changed or added since the full backup. The successive backups grow in size, but not by much, and you need only two backup sets to fully restore a system: the full backup and the most recent differential.

With incremental backups, only files changed since the last full or incremental backup are saved. With incremental, the individual backup sets are indeed smaller, but you would need to restore the full and all subsequent incremental backups, in date order, to fully recover all your files. This situation is rather dangerous, in my opinion. I can hardly find my own head some days, let alone a dozen backup tapes.

For a LAN server or business computer, I recommend that you do a full backup weekly and a differential backup daily. For a home computer, you might try a monthly full backup and weekly differential backups.

All the backup options have their places in certain situations. I personally leave the backup type at Normal so that all my files are always backed up, no matter what. You might find that another option suits you better, so feel free to experiment with all these options to find the best one for you.

RESTORING DATA FROM A BACKUP

"The best laid plans of mice and men oft gang a'glay," as the saying goes. When you've lost data and had enough foresight to have backed it up, you're in luck. Or you hope you are, at least. Backing up is the first half of recovering your data. With any luck, you'll be able to get it back the way it was before whatever bolt of lightning hit your PC. The Restore tab of the Backup dialog box comes in at this point. Restoring from a backup is a very simple process, which you can execute in three essential steps:

1. Run the Backup program by choosing Start, All Programs, Accessories, System Tools, ~system restore
   Backup.

2. Use the Restore Wizard from the Welcome tab if you want a walkthrough. Alternatively, select the Restore tab, and adjust a few simple parameters.

3. Begin the restore, and insert media if and when prompted.

Of course, you might want to understand a few option and parameter details, for better control of your restorations. The following sections discuss them. You probably should read along before doing your first couple of data recoveries. After you have the theories under your belt, then you can proceed.

Notice the left pane of the Restore tab. Here, you can view all the available Backup media pools. You can expand these nodes to display all possible source media and pools. They're displayed in a familiar tree view of the directories and files backed up to each related medium. As with the process of Backup, you simply select the files or folders you want to restore. And, of course, by selecting a top node of the tree, you include everything beneath it.

Next, it's a good idea to look at the settings on the Restore tab of the Options dialog box (Tools menu, Options). Here, you can choose from options that dictate how files will be handled if you are restoring one that already exists in your restore destination. The safest bet here is to not replace any file with a restored version. This is generally the best bet unless you have a specific reason to do so. Reasons for overwriting existing files do crop up, though. For example, if know that you somehow trashed, misedited, or otherwise mangled the file you currently have on disk, you can revert to the last backed-up one. In that case, you need to enable replacement.

Other than the general restore options, the only real option for the restore portion of the Backup program is the option to specify the location in which you want to restore the files. You choose this option from the drop-down list at the bottom of the Restore tab. Three options are available:

- **Original Location**—This option restores the files to the exact place from which they were backed up. Be careful with this one; it could cause you problems with files that are open. You should be sure you're not trying to restore over a file that might be in use by another application or the system.

- **Alternate Location**—This option gives you the opportunity to restore the files to a destination of your choosing. If this option is selected, you are prompted for the location to which you want to restore through an entry box beneath the location options. From there, you can use the Browse button to find your restore destination. If you use this option, the directory structure of your backed-up files will be retained in the new destination.

- **Single Folder**—Selecting this option dumps all the files from your backup to a single folder. Be aware that using this option does not preserve the directory structure of your backed-up data. It simply ignores the structure and restores all the files to the directory you choose.

After you've selected your restore destination, you can click the Start Restore button to begin. If you selected Alternate Location or Single Folder, you're given the option to configure Restore options using the Advanced button on the Confirm Restore dialog box. The options in the Advanced Restore Options dialog are as follows:

- **Restore Security**—This option enables you to restore the same permissions for the files and folders you're restoring to their original settings. In most cases, choosing this option is best because you don't want to have to set them one-by-one after the restore has finished.

- **Restore Junction Points, and Restore File and Folder Data Under Junction Points to the Original Location**—Turn on this check box if you've created junction points using the `linkd` command, and you're trying to restore the junction points and the data to which the junction points point. If you don't, only the pointers are restored, not the data. You also should turn on this box if you are restoring a mounted drive's data.

- **When Restoring Replicated Data Sets, Mark the Restored Data as the Primary Data for All Replicas**—This option is relevant only to Windows Server 2003 and should be grayed out on any machine running Windows XP Professional or Home.

- **Restore the Cluster Registry to the quorum disk and all other nodes**—This option is relevant only to Windows Server 2003 and should be grayed out on any machine running Windows XP Professional or Home.

26

■ **Preserve Existing Volume Mount Points**—This option most often applies when you're restoring the data for an entire drive, such as when you're replacing a drive. Typically, you put in a formatted drive, re-create the mount points, and then restore the data. You don't want to overwrite the mount points, so you turn on this option. If you have not re-created the mount points, and you want to restore the entire data and mount points as stored in the backup set, uncheck this box.

Finally, after selecting the OK button, you can then select OK on the Confirm Restore dialog box to start the restore.

SCHEDULING JOBS

Finally, we come to my personal favorite, the Schedule Jobs tab of the Backup dialog box. This feature is a great addition to an already very capable backup program. There should really be no reason for most people to not have a reasonably current backup of their system at any given time if they use this tool.

Strategies for scheduling backups vary from person to person or machine to machine. Some people, myself included, are extremely paranoid and go for the "back up every single night" method. As you can guess, backing up this frequently saves a great deal of heartache in the event of a total system meltdown. I can't tell you how many times backing up has saved my neck. On the other hand, say you have a machine at your home or business that rarely gets used or is just acting as a proxy server. This kind of machine really only needs backups at much longer intervals than your personal workstation. In this case, it's usually safe to back up a system like this only every week or so. In the end, it's up to you how you feel you need to schedule your backups. Just remember, your system will probably go down at some point. Being prepared is the best insurance around for this nasty inevitability.

To use the scheduling features of backup, you simply double-click any date using the provided calendar or click the Add Job button. This gives you a chance to use the Backup Wizard. The options for it are very straightforward. In fact, if you read the previous section on backing up, you should have no problem whatsoever using this wizard.

NOTE

You will be prompted to set the account information for the backup because it might end up running when another logged-in user doesn't have the rights to initiate the backup. When you're prompted, you can specify a "Run As" user and password.

The Schedule Job dialog box actually is the same one used when scheduling any common task using Scheduled Tasks, a system tool covered in Chapter 24. You might want to refer to that chapter for some more details on the options.

The Settings tab on the Schedule Job dialog box offers somewhat lower-priority options. You should take a gander at them, though, if you intend to get serious about automated backups. Among the settings are those that affect idle time and power management. You should consider power settings if you're doing a backup from a laptop running on batteries.

The Idle Time options could be useful if there is a possibility that someone will be using the computer when backup begins. If good responsiveness of the computer is important, you can ensure the backup process stops if someone sits down at the keyboard and begins work. Check the Stop the Task If the Computer Ceases to Be Idle check box.

Making Inaccessible Devices Accessible

The backup strategy described here, at first glance, looks a bit convoluted, but if you apply a little thought and creativity, you will be amazed at the range of possibilities that unfold from it.

Every power user has at least one device in his or her computer stable that won't play nice with another. In my case, it happens to be my USB Zip drive. The device works flawlessly on my IBM ThinkPad, but the USB port on my main working machine will not work under Windows XP until Epox comes out with a BIOS update. (Another example might be that you have a CD-RW on one machine across the LAN, but not on the one where you want to do your backups.)

This kind of minor irritation would have remained minor had I not developed such a high regard for my trusty little Zip drive. It is fast, convenient, and flexible. It addition, it is a perfect place to copy chapter versions and backups as they evolve. In short, I wanted the same backup flexibility I had on my notebook available to me on my main machine. And being the doggedly persistent person I am, I finally found a way.

A crossover cable, which is a $2-7 cable that lets you connect the LAN cards of two computers together into a mini-network without hubs or any other hardware, connects my desktop system (Janus) to my laptop (Penelope). Because Janus (A) can see Penelope (B) and Penelope can see and utilize the Zip drive (Janus cannot), is there a way I can give A access to C? Yes.

Here's how to make it so:

- On computer B, select the device from Windows Explorer and share it (select the device, right-click, and select Share from the pop-up menu displayed). Give it a share name to reflect its function or purpose.
- Now go back to computer A and map a drive to that device (via Windows Explorer, Tools, Map Network Drive). In the folder box, you have to specify both the computer name and the device's share name. In my case, it is \\penelope\zip.

I created a shortcut on my desktop for this drive mapping and added it to my Send To menu. Now I can quickly back up a file from Windows Explorer with a single right-click. You can apply the same type of philosophy to multiple devices you use at home.

26

Guarding Your Profile

Windows XP stores your user profile in the folder \Documents and Settings\ <*yourusername*>. The subfolders contained here contain all the tweaks, configurations, and data files that make up what you see and access while working under Windows XP. Guard this folder tree with your life! With a little manipulation, this information can be copied to a safe haven and slipped back into place should the unforeseen occur, and you have to reinstall your operating system.

The following are some of the invaluable goodies contained on the profile tree:

- Your Favorites folder
- Your History folder

- All the configuration settings and program templates for Office
- Your Desktop settings
- The default folder for data files (My Documents)
- Your most recently accessed files list
- The folder your cookies are stored in
- Your SendTo folder
- Your Start menu configuration
- Your section of the Windows Registry
- A bevy of application settings, temp files, and IE history files, in a folder called Local Settings

If you can't see all of these items, then your Folder Options are set to hide them. If you want to see them, open the Folder Options applet (through Control Panel or the Tools menu of Windows Explorer/My Computer). Select the View tab, and then select the Show Hidden Files and Folders option, and deselect Hide Extensions for Known File Types and Hide Protected Operating System Files (Recommended).

As you can see, all this stuff is very good, and it's tailored specifically to your computing experience under Windows XP.

The root folder of your profile (in my case, C:\Documents and Settings\Bob) contains two key files: NTUSER.DAT and a backup of this file, NTUSER. They are your user Registry settings and are locked by the operating system in such a way as to forbid any other program from accessing them directly. Therefore, you cannot copy either of these files while logged on as *yourusername* (even if you have administrative rights under *yourusername)*. An attempted copy operation will fail. The problem is that the rest of the tree structure is useless without these key files because they tell the operating system (and indirectly, the programs that use them) which files can be found where.

Ah, Grasshopper, but this problem is not insurmountable. The following steps illustrate how you can wrest a copy of your profile away from the arms of Windows XP.

> **NOTE**
>
> The following example uses a network drive as a copy point for simplicity. Realistically, the place you copy your profile is dependent on the resources at hand. The key here is to get it off the computer that uses it and put it somewhere safe. This location can be a Zip drive (if it will fit), a CD-RW drive, or at the very least, a separate partition. Personally, I keep my profile backed up to both another partition on my main system and a backup partition on my notebook. I tend to be a bit protective of my data, and for good reason, as you will read shortly.

1. Log off from *yourusername* and log on as Administrator. This is a key step; as noted previously, you cannot properly copy your profile tree while logged on as yourself.

2. In Windows Explorer, create a folder on a network drive you have access to, and name it—for example, `Profile Backup`.

3. Go to your user profile (in my case, C:\Documents and Settings\Bob), select the highest folder in your profile tree (Bob), and drop it on the network folder you just created (Profile Backup). Go have a cup of coffee; this process could take a while if you have several data files stored here.

4. Last but not least, be sure you keep this backup profile updated on a routine basis. Most users can generally afford to lose a day or so of work; losing some work is unpleasant, but it is tolerable. But if you're like me, by the end of a busy week, I've probably added 10 or more "gems" to my Favorites list, messed with my NORMAL.DOT template three or four times, and shuffled my Start menu at least once. You could use the Files and Settings Transfer Wizard to protect these items (see Chapter 25, "Managing Users").

The preceding routine is not about protecting your data; that is a separate routine which should be done on a level that reflects the value you place on the data you create every day. What it is about is protecting the configuration settings that represent your daily working environment under Windows XP.

So, you follow this sage advice and dutifully copy your profile somewhere safe on a routine basis. How is this effort going to reward you? Well, should you need to reinstall your operating system, your efforts are going to reward you by allowing you to re-create your desktop, its shortcuts, and most of your program configurations quickly and painlessly. Here is the process you'll need to follow:

1. Reinstall Windows XP Home.

2. Create a user account where your settings will be restored into. Call this account NEWME.

3. Create a second account which is a Computer Administrator. Call this account ADMIN.

4. Log in with NEWME. Then log out.

5. Log in with ADMIN.

6. Copy your backup user profile into the \Documents and Settings\NEWME\ folder. This may take a while.

7. Log out.

8. Log in with NEWME.

This process will restore most of your desktop environment. However, there are a few caveats. First, this restore process should be combined with a software reinstallation plan. The restored Start menu will only be useful if you've reinstalled all of your preexisting software back into their exact same locations. Second, be sure that the drive letters of your partitions have not changed. Any changes to drive letters or paths statements will render parts of your restored profile useless.

You probably noticed that the profile restore process not only requires that you log in then log out before restoring the profile, but requires that another user account be employed to perform the copy operation. Windows XP will create the user profile directory only after a user account logs on to the system. Otherwise, if a user profile directory already exists using the same name it wants to create, it will create a new directory by appending .000 to the username. So, letting the system create the user profile first eliminates that problem. A significant portion of a user profile is comprised of Registry settings. These settings are stored in a file which is locked while that user is logged on. A second user account must be used in order to overwrite all files within the profile.

Trust Me, It Happens to Everyone

What follows is a personal experience I had right in the midst of writing this very chapter.

Some hard drives run for 10 years; some die an untimely death when they are only a month old—hence the term *Mean* Time Between Failure (MTBF), which is an average estimate of how long the drive manufacturer expects its product to run before it fails. Unfortunately, I ended up on the low end of the bell curve the other day when my three-month old hard drive died a prompt and dramatic death. Luckily, I had made a profile backup the night before onto a partition on my notebook reserved solely for machine-to-machine backups.

I borrowed a spare hard drive from a friend, partitioned it in two (*always, always* make a data partition on your drive), installed Windows XP on the boot partition, and installed the base productivity programs I use every day (Office 2000 and a smattering of "can't live without" utilities). This last step is an important one. To slide an alternative profile into an existing installation, you must restore your system to a point that closely mirrors when you backed up your earlier profile. In my case, this necessitates installing Office. You do not have to configure or tweak anything; just install it to ensure the Windows XP Registry knows it exists.

With all key applications installed, I connected my trusty crossover cable to my notebook, logged off as Bob, and logged back on as Administrator. I connected to the notebook's backup partition and copied my saved profile to my main system. I logged off as Administrator, logged on as Bob, and presto-pocus: My desktop returned, Word found all my tweaked document templates, my Favorites were right where I left them, and Outlook knew exactly where to find my data files. I often find myself cursing as I watch a progress bar tick away at 3 a.m. as I store my day's profile onto my notebook for safekeeping, but when I'm going the other way and fixing a disaster, that progress bar is a lovely sight indeed.

ZIPPING FILES

If you've been on the Internet for any length of time, you've run into zipped files (*filename*.zip). Zipping files is a way to combine multiple files and even a directory structure into one single file that is compressed. Zipped files makes the transfer of data files and a programs not just simpler but faster too. PKZip 2.04g was a command line utility that was used to create zip files. As zipping became popular, many third-parties created utilities to perform zipping operations through GUI interfaces. Windows 98 (when the Plus! pack is installed) and Windows Me integrated zip file management right into the OS, calling them Compressed Folders. My favorite utility of these is WinZip. But with Windows XP, I may never use it again, since XP does the same.

Windows XP includes built in zipping capabilities—viewing, creating, and extracting. Viewing zip files is easy. Windows XP treats .zip files as a compressed folder, no matter what utility was used to create them. They appear as folders with a zipper. You can view and access the contents just as if they were stored in any typical folder on the filesystem.

Zip files are created by issuing the New, Compressed (zipped) Folder command from either the File menu or the right-click menu from Windows Explorer or My Computer. After naming the folder (be sure to retain the .zip extension), you can drag and drop files or folder structures into it. Once your files are inside the "compressed folder," the .zip file can be manipulated like any other file, including attaching to emails or uploaded via FTP. Very convenient.

Extracting files from a .zip file via Windows XP is no different than moving or copying files from normal folders, just drag and drop. Or, while viewing the contents of a .zip file, issue the Extract command. This launches the Compressed (zipped) Folders Extraction Wizard, which walks you through the process of locating a destination for the contents and initiating the extraction.

It has taken a bit of getting used to. I'm so in the habit of viewing and extracting the contents of zip files through WinZip that I can't seem to remember that Windows XP will perform the tasks for me. I've had to uninstall WinZip, but now that it's gone I don't miss it.

THIRD-PARTY MANAGEMENT TOOLS

Table 26.2 provides a list of tools that you should not be without if you are serious about hard disk tweaking, backup, and recovery. By searching on the Web, you can find any of these programs easily because they are so popular.

TABLE 26.2   THIRD-PARTY TOOLS

Type of Program	Vendor	Product Name
Defragmentation	Executive Software	Diskeeper
	Symantec	Norton Utilities (part of SystemWorks)
Undelete	Executive Software	Undelete
	Symantec	Norton Utilities (part of SystemWorks)
Disk Management	Symantec	Drive Image
	Symantec	Norton Ghost
	Symantec	Partition Magic
	V Communications	System Commander
Compression	PowerArchiver	Conexware
	Nico Mak Computing	WinZip
	PKWare	PKZip

continues

TABLE 26.2	CONTINUED	
Type of Program	**Vendor**	**Product Name**
	Pacific Gold Coast	TurboZIP Corp.
	Info-Zip	Info-Zip
	Winrar	Rarsoft

MOVE VERSUS COPY

There is an important convention you need to be aware of when working with any Microsoft OS product. I usually call it the container rule, but you also can call it move versus copy. As you know, files are stored within folders. Folders (that is, child folders) can be stored within other folders (that is, parent folders). It is possible to change the settings on a parent folder, which then propagate down to all child folders and even contained files. However, it is possible to select a child folder or a contained file and individually alter its settings (such as permissions, auditing, ownership, compression, and so on) so they are different from other files and any parent folders.

When a new file is created, it is always created within a parent folder. Even when a file is created within the root directory of a drive, that is considered a parent folder. A new file always inherits the settings of its parent container. This is the container rule. Now, apply that rule to the operations of move and copy. There are two types of moves and two types of copies. One type is within the same volume; the other is from one volume to another. A copy within the same volume or a copy from one volume to another always creates a new file at the destination. That new file always inherits the settings of its new container (parent folder). A move within the same volume simply changes the directory listing of the file. This causes the file to retain its original settings even though it now appears in a new parent folder. A move from one volume to another is actually a two-step process. The first step is to copy the file; the second step is to delete the original file. Because a new file is created, it will inherit the settings of its new parent container.

These rules apply when the default copy or move functions of Windows are used. But, there is an exception. That is when the Shared Documents folder is involved. This folder is used to quickly and easily share files with other workgroup members. When files are transferred into this folder, the system will automatically set its parameters so they can be read by everyone. The only exception to this exception is when you use the command line to move the files. In that case, the original rule of move within a volume applies (that is, the files retain their original settings).

CD BURNING

Windows XP includes native CD burning capabilities. You must have a CD-R or CD-RW properly installed and a writable CD in the CD recorder drive. To burn a CD, just follow these general directions:

1. Copy files and folders to the CD recording drive using Windows Explorer or My Computer.
2. Double-click on the CD-R or CR-RW drive icon. A dialog box displaying the files to be written to the CD are displayed.
3. Click Write These Files to CD to initiate the burn.
4. After the files are written, you are given the option to burn a second CD with the same file/folder collection.

Windows XP can be used to duplicate CDs, copy audio CDs, and more. Just search on "writable CD" and/or "burn" in the Help and Support Center for details.

HARD DISK TROUBLESHOOTING

Eventually, if you work with computers for long enough, you are going to face some form of hard disk problem. It's not a matter of *if*; it's a matter of *when*. The laws of statistics apply to everyone and everything—and that includes hard drives. In the following sections, when I speak of hard drive problems, I'm not referring to a software program that is acting petulantly or a DLL that has been overwritten by a poorly designed installation routine. I'm talking about the inability to access a critical file, a hard drive that will not boot, or one of those cryptic `Fatal Error - Cannot access hard disk` messages that cause the blood to drain from the face of even the hardiest administrator.

These sections are not meant to be comprehensive. Full books have been written on solving hardware problems, and thousands of individual chapters on hard drives and the multitude of problems they can exhibit. What these sections will do, however, is give you some tried-and-true directions to head in if your hard drive starts to give you grief.

Hard drive problems range from filesystem structures that have been twisted out of shape to catastrophic, dead-in-the-water hard drive failures. And as any seasoned administrator will tell you, the catastrophic failures are the easy ones to diagnose and fix. More often than not, the inconsistent "what the heck?" problems are the real head-scratchers.

To keep it simple, let's begin with the most important factor in troubleshooting problems of all shapes and sizes—be it a car that will not start or a computer that will not boot. And that is....

TAKE THE MENTAL APPROACH FIRST

I come from a long line of tradesmen who made a living getting their hands dirty and solving mechanical problems. As a writer and computer consultant, I rarely get my hands dirty

26

anymore, but I have discovered that the principles of problem solving I learned when I was young are the same across all fields. You need to be methodical, and if you are going to make assumptions, they had better be good ones; otherwise, you just might steer yourself down the wrong garden path.

The very first step to take when you have a disk access problem is to stop, sit down, and think. Although this advice might seem obvious, it is seldom realized in practice. People experience what they conclude is a hard drive problem, open their case, and start ripping out components when, in fact, they have a filesystem problem that could have been easily resolved by running ScanDisk on their drive. Similarly, others start reinstalling operating systems when the problem is not software at all, but a failing CMOS battery that is causing the motherboard to lose sight of the hard drive.

None of this exposition is meant to imply that I'm smarter or better at diagnosing problems than the next guy, and in the end, I might come to the same conclusion as the person who leapt in and started ripping his or her case apart. What separates us, in my humble opinion, is that the steps I use to solve a problem today will apply equally well to a completely different problem I encounter a week from now.

So, when you have a hard drive problem—or what you think is a hard drive problem—before you pick up a CD-ROM or a screwdriver, get yourself a cup of coffee, and take a few minutes to get a clear picture of the nature of the problem in front of you. The following are some questions you might want to ask yourself:

- When did the problem start?
- What was I doing when I first noticed the problem?
- Is the problem consistent? If so, how? If not, what is missing from the puzzle?

This last point bears some elaboration. Computers, as a whole, are extraordinarily consistent devices. Input goes in here; output comes out over there. In the case of hard drives, you lay out structures on them, and the operating system uses these structures to tell programs where their data is located. When you have inconsistencies at work, one of two forces is at work:

1. You are not seeing or you're overlooking something.
2. You could have more than one problem on your hands.

The key of this forced reflection is to have a plan before you react. And the cornerstone of that plan must be to do no further harm and to figure out what the problem is without complicating matters further.

So, the next highly recommended tools to pick up, after you've pondered and had a cup of coffee, are a notepad and a pencil. Begin by jotting down some notes on what happened, what you think the problem is, and what might be a good course of action to solve that problem. Use your notepad to reason out the problem; more often than not, eliminating a piece of flawed logic with an eraser is easier than restoring all the programs to your hard drive.

PROBLEMS AND SOLUTIONS

Hard drive problems fall into two general categories:

- Hardware
- File structure

Hardware-related problems involve the hard drive itself, cabling, power, connections, and the motherboard.

File structure problems involve the tracks and partitions on the hard disk, the boot records, and the files the operating system uses to initialize itself.

If you power up your computer, and the BIOS cannot find the attached hard drive, chances are you have a hardware problem. On the other hand, if the BIOS finds and recognizes your hard drive but fails to boot, you likely have a file structure problem. Note the *chances are* and *likely* qualifiers. Bear in mind, as you read through the following scenarios, the complications that can be brought on by compounded problems. In other words, file structure problems and hardware problems can, at times, overlap. For example, a damaged master boot record (MBR) may be the result of a failing hard drive; repairing the MBR might fix a consequence of the problem but not the problem itself.

SCSI Disk Boot Problems

A boot problem can sometimes be caused by SCSI settings that have changed since you installed Windows XP. The state of the SCSI BIOS at the time you installed Windows XP becomes part of the setup of the operating system and is stored in the BOOT.INI file. If you subsequently make a change in the SCSI BIOS after NT is installed, that alone can contradict the stored BOOT.INI file settings and can prevent the operating system from finding the system files and booting up. Don't change the SCSI BIOS settings after you install Windows XP, or if you do, you should edit BOOT.INI in a text editor (carefully!) to reflect the changes. The BOOT.INI file uses the following syntax:

```
scsi(A)disk(B)rdiskpartition\<winnt_dir>
```

Here are the specifics for the parameters in the ARC path when you use the `scsi()` syntax on an X86 computer:

- A is the ordinal number for the adapter linked to the Ntbootdd.sys driver.
- B is the SCSI ID for the target disk.
- C is always 0 when SCSI drives are used.
- D is the partition.

When an IDE ATA drive is in use, this line will have multi(A) as its front item. Then, B remains 0 and C indicates the drive used.

Take note that A, B, and C are all ordinal numbers, that means they start with zero. So, the second drive is 1, the third is 2, and so on. But, D is a cardinal number, so the first partition is 1, the second is 2, and so on.

SYSTEM STARTS BUT CANNOT FIND THE HARD DRIVE

If the computer fires up (the BIOS information appears and the floppy drive is accessed but nothing more), you have some sleuthing to do. Just follow these steps:

1. Turn off the computer, open it, and check the cables. Are the power and data cables attached to the drive? Is the wide, flat data cable flipped over backward on end? Check to see that pin #1 on the motherboard connects to pin #1 on the drive.

2. Check the settings on the drive to make sure they are correct. If you have a SCSI drive, check the ID number and termination as per the instruction manual for the drive. If you have an IDE drive, check the master/slave settings and channel assignment. If you have two devices on the same IDE channel, both set to master or both set to slave, there will be a conflict. You can have only one master and one slave per IDE channel. You typically change the setting by using a little jumper on the back of the hard drive next to the data and power connectors (ditto for IDE-based CD-ROM drives).

3. Check the BIOS settings by pressing the appropriate key during POST (Power-On Self Test) and having the computer autodetect the drive type. Make sure the drive is listed and/or recognized.

4. If your computer has a voltage monitoring program (many motherboards come with such things), check to see if the voltages are within spec. Sometimes a power supply that is on the verge of dying could be low on a particular voltage (+5, -5, +12, -12). If you've just added a new CD-RW or additional hard drive, and your power supply isn't hefty enough, that could do it. Try popping in a new power supply and see if your hard drive now works.

> **TIP**
>
> Most modern PCs and BIOSes autodetect the hard drive that's connected to the data cable after the drive gets power. You no longer have to enter all the explicit information about the drive, such as number of heads, sectors, the landing zone, and so on. Just set the BIOS to Autodetect.

HARD DRIVE INITIALIZES BUT WILL NOT BOOT

Windows XP offers several features that allow you to repair a system that will not start or will not load Windows XP. These features are useful if some of your system files become corrupted or are accidentally erased, or if you have installed software or device drivers that cause your system to not work properly. However, these features are used more to restore a system with a damaged Registry or destroyed system files rather than hard drive specific problems. If you've already tried the actions listed in this section to no avail, flip over to Chapter 30 for details on numerous other recovery techniques that may benefit you. Be sure to check out Safe Mode, Recovery Console, and parallel installations.

TIPS FROM THE WINDOWS PROS: QUIETING A NOISY SYSTEM

Hard drives vary in the noise output they produce. Sometimes the stepper motors are annoyingly loud. Other drives have loud spindle motors. When a drive is coupled to the body of the computer housing, motor noises can be effectively amplified, increasing the aggravation you experience using a system. If your computer sounds like a garbage disposal from time to time, chances are good that the stepper is not a quiet one, and as the head dances around on the platters, the drive shakes just enough to get the computer chassis rattling a bit, too. It's a bit like the relationship between the strings and the body of a violin.

Spindle motors (the motor that turns the platters at high speed) often start out life quietly, only to get noisy over time as the bearings wear in (or out). This noise is particularly annoying in laptop computers if you happen to use them in a quiet place, such as a library or in a home office. I actually replaced my 8GB IBM 3.5-inch drive once this year (Dell laptop, free of charge thanks to Dell), only to find that within a few months it developed the same annoying whine again, so I gave up and accepted it.

Some environments, such as recording studios, require that a computer be seen and not heard. For desktop systems, there are a couple of solutions. One is to make up some long wires for the keyboard monitor, and so on and relegate the computer to a closet. A more practical approach is to buy an after-market kit that quiets your PC's power supply and hard disk. Check the Web for information about such kits. Here's what my quick check as of this writing found:

www.directron.com/silencer275.html

fredrik.hubbe.net/watercool.html

www.quietpc.com/

One solution we have successfully used in our Brainsville video studio is to use a laptop computer for video editing and capturing. Laptops tend to be very quiet. The laptop has an internal 30GB drive, but we use external Maxtor 80GB FireWire hard drive which has no fan in it and is thus also very quiet. This is the system we used for capturing digital video straight from our DV camera, for creating the video lessons included with this book. At this point, we have six such drives, totaling 480GB of storage online at one time, and it's still very quiet!

The bottom line here is to check out the specs on drive noise if you care about that. Or you can listen for a quiet computer, find out what kind of drive it has, and then order that brand and model the next time you're shopping.

In the case of serious noise (you turn on the computer, and it really does sound like a garbage disposal), well, you're in trouble. This noise is the sign of your hard disk after crashing (the heads are actually rubbing on the surface of the platters) or in the process of crashing. Get out while the getting is good. Back up your data or whole drive, and replace it as soon as possible. Then restore the data.

26

In some cases, the noise you hear is not from your hard drive, but from the fans on the case or the power supply. These plastic fan blades collect dust. The dustier your environment and the higher your average humidity, the faster these fans become caked with crud. In many cases you can use a can of compressed air to clean off the fans. But when that doesn't work, you can attempt to remove the fan's protective screen and wipe the blades clean with a slightly moist paper towel. Don't spray or drip any liquids into the system.

If you find that you are cleaning off your fan every month or so, you should consider getting a room filter to clean your air or attach part of an A/C filter over the air intake holes on your system. Just be sure that the airflow is not restricted or you'll end up overheating the system. Keep in mind your CPU and hard drives are air cooled, that's why there are fans in the case. If you restrict the airflow too much, the heat will build up and cause problems. If you hear a beeping sound much like that of European police cars, that's the warning sign that the CPU is too hot.

CHAPTER 27

INSTALLING AND REPLACING HARDWARE

In this chapter

Upgrading Your Hardware

Some of us are content to use our computer as it comes out of the box, and are happy enough if it just turns on and manages to boot up. Others are like hot-rod enthusiasts and fuss over each component in our machines, replacing one part after another in an obsession to have the fastest, the slickest, and the most impressive technology. And all of us eventually realize that our once amazingly fast computer is starting to feel kind of clunky next to the ones we see our friends and coworkers using. Whatever your obsession level, you'll want to read this chapter for advice on making hardware changes—large or small—to get the most work and useful life out of your computer. We'll discuss how to upgrade and install hardware, how to add a second monitor, how to connect new and old hard drives, and how to add memory.

The single most helpful thing you can do to make your Windows XP computer run at peak speed is give it enough memory (or *RAM*, short for Random Access Memory). Just as a reminder, there are two types of memory in your computer: hard disk space and RAM. RAM is used to hold Windows and the programs you're actually using at the moment, and Windows XP wants *lots* more than any previous version of Windows. As we discussed in the early chapters of this book, XP is said to be capable of running with as little as 64MB of RAM, but it will run *very* slowly and you'll find the experience unpleasant. Memory is *very* inexpensive these days, and boosting your RAM up to at least 256MB will make a huge difference. I'll discuss adding RAM later in this chapter.

Now, if you're already running Windows XP Home Edition on a full-bore, state-of-the-art system such as a 3 Gigahertz-plus Pentium 4 or AMD Athlon system, and your computer has a fast video accelerator, a SCSI drive, and a gigabyte or more of memory, you don't have much more to do in the way of actual hardware optimizing. You might just adjust the page-file sizes, or convert as many partitions to NTFS as you can. Some of the settings you can make are discussed in Chapter 22, "Configuration via Control Panel Applets," and Chapter 23, "Maintaining and Optimizing System Performance" and the remainder are discussed in Chapter 24, "System Utilities."

By the same token, if you're doing common, everyday tasks such as word processing and Internet browsing over a dial-up connection, and you're already satisfied with the performance of your computer as a whole, you probably don't need to worry about performance boosters anyway. Your system is probably running just fine, and the time you'd spend trying to fine-tune it might be better spent doing whatever it is you use your computer for (like earning a living).

If you're anywhere between these two extremes however, you might want to look at the tune-ups and hardware upgrades we'll discuss in this chapter.

TIP

> This chapter just scratches the surface of the ins and outs of hardware installation and updates. If you want all the details, and I mean *all* the details, you should get a copy of the best-selling book *Upgrading and Repairing PC's, 16th Edition*, by Scott Mueller, published by Que.

BIOS Settings

Windows XP depends upon proper BIOS settings to enable it to detect and use hardware correctly. At a minimum, your drives should be properly configured in the system BIOS, and your CPU type and speed should be properly set (either in the BIOS or on the motherboard, depending upon the system). Windows XP boots much faster than other recent flavors of Windows, but you can improve boot speed even more with these tips:

- Set up your BIOS boot order to start with drive C: so that you can skip the floppy stepper motor test.
- Disable the floppy drive seek.
- Enable BIOS and video shadowing.

If, after tinkering with your BIOS settings, you find that your computer will no longer boot up, see "Altered BIOS Settings Prevent Computer from Booting" in the "Troubleshooting" section at the end of this chapter. Remember, too, that if you're looking at BIOS settings, most systems give you the option of exiting the BIOS without saving the settings. If you think you made a mistake, exit without saving, and try again.

Upgrading Your Hard Disk

One of the most effective improvements you can make to a system is to get a faster or larger hard drive, or add another drive. SCSI hard disks used to seriously one-up IDE drives, but the new breed of UDMA EIDE drives (which I call Old Macdonald Disks—EIEIO!) and Serial ATA (SATA) drives are quite speedy and a whole lot cheaper than SCSI. An EIDE bus supports four drives (two each on the primary and secondary channels) and is almost always built into your motherboard. Adding a CD-ROM (or CD-RW or DVD-ROM) drive claims one, leaving you with a maximum of three EIDE hard drives unless you install separate add-on EIDE host adapter or have a motherboard with RAID support. SATA supports one drive per channel, but the latest SATA II connection system can reach top transfer speeds of 300MBps.

TIP

Many recent motherboards feature on-board IDE RAID, which can perform either mirroring (which makes an immediate backup copy of one drive to another) or striping (which treats both drives as part of a single drive for speed). Although the RAID features on these motherboards don't support RAID 5, the safest (and most expensive!) form of RAID, they work well and are much less expensive than any SCSI form of RAID. Just remember that mirroring gives you extra reliability at the expense of speed, because everything has to be written twice, and striping with only two disks gives you extra speed at the expense of reliability—if one hard disk fails you lose everything.

27

The following are some essential considerations for upgrading your hard disk system:

- Don't put a hard drive and a CD-ROM drive on the same channel unless necessary (put the hard drive on the primary IDE1 channel and the CD-ROM on the secondary IDE2 channel). On some computers, the IDE channel negotiates down to the slowest device on a channel, slowing down the hard disk's effective transfer rate. Make sure the hard drive containing Windows is designated as the Primary Master drive.

- Defragment the hard disk with the Defragmenter utility, which you can reach through Start, Control Panel, Performance and Maintenance, Rearrange Items on your Hard Disk. You can also purchase third-party defragmenting programs that do a more thorough job. For more about defragmenting, see Chapter 26, "Managing the Hard Disk."

- Upgrade the disk controller (more properly called a *host adapter*). If you're using an Ultra Wide SCSI or later hard disk, for example, be sure you have a controller that takes maximum advantage of it. If you're using IDE, your host adapter is most likely built into the motherboard on any Pentium-class or better system. If your drives support UDMA/33 (Ultra DMA) or faster UDMA modes but your motherboard supports only the slower PIO modes, install a replacement UDMA host adapter or upgrade your motherboard. I should point out that most modern motherboards do support UDMA, so you're probably okay on this score.

- Get a faster disk drive: UDMA/66 or faster for IDE; Ultra2Wide or faster for SCSI (but remember, you need to match the drive to the SCSI host adapter you have or plan to buy). 7,200 RPM IDE drives are now common, and the faster spin rate compared to the previous 5,400 RPM standard makes most of them transfer data a bit quicker than their slower siblings. Some SCSI drives go up to 10,000rpm, making for even faster transfer and lower latency (rotational delay).

ADDING RAM

Perhaps the most cost-effective upgrade you can make to any Windows-based system is to add RAM. This one is a no-brainer: If your disk is pausing and thrashing each time you switch between running applications or documents, you need more RAM. Although Microsoft says Windows XP can run with as little as 64MB of RAM, we've found that this results in intolerably slow performance. XP only really runs at a (barely) acceptable speed with 128MB, and 256MB is far better. If you run memory-intensive applications, get even more.

Windows automatically recognizes newly added RAM and adapts internal settings, such as when to swap to disk, to take best advantage of any RAM you throw its way. Buy more if you can afford it, especially if your system uses the economical SDRAM or DDR SDRAM DIMM modules. Memory prices fluctuate constantly, but these days 256MB memory modules are selling for under $40. This is a very cost-effective upgrade indeed. But be sure to get the right memory for your motherboard. There is a huge variety of memory technologies out there. At the time this was written, common technologies included SDRAM, DDR and RDRAM (RAMBus). Memory speeds range from 100MHz (labeled PC100) to 4400MHz (labeled PC4400). And, on top of that, there are error correcting (ECC) and non-error-correcting varieties.

To find out what type of memory you need, you should check with your computer manufacturer or the manual that came with your computer or motherboard. You should get the fastest compatible memory that your CPU can use and that your motherboard supports. You can get RAM that's rated faster than you currently need, motherboard can go, but you won't gain any speed advantage—just a greater likelihood of being able to reuse the memory if you later upgrade your motherboard.

TIP

> If you run very disk and memory-intensive applications such as high-resolution scanning, image processing, video editing, or databases, consider adding memory well beyond 128MB. Windows XP Home Edition isn't crippled by the 512MB limit found in Windows 9x and Me, and many systems on the market today can use as much as 1.5GB of RAM. For most serious computer users, 512MB or 1GB should do the trick.

ADDING HARDWARE

One of the tasks that is most common for anyone responsible for configuring and maintaining PCs is adding and removing hardware. The Control Panel contains an applet designed for that purpose; it's called the Add Hardware applet. You can use it in cases in which the operating system doesn't automatically recognize that you've swiped something or added something new, whether it's a peripheral such as a printer or an internal device such as a DVD-ROM, additional hard disk, or whatever.

If you're a hardware maven, you'll be visiting this applet a lot, especially if you're working with non–Plug and Play hardware. Plug and Play hardware installation is often completely effortless, because Windows XP Home Edition is good at detection and should install items fairly automatically, along with any necessary device drivers that tell Windows how to access the new hardware.

TIP

> You use the System applet or the Computer Management "Device Manager" Console, not Add Hardware, for fine-tuning device settings, such as IRQ and port, updating devices and drivers, and removing hardware. You use Add Hardware only for adding or trouble-shooting hardware.
>
> A quick way to get to either utility is to click Start and right-click My Computer. Select Properties, and then select the Hardware tab. From there you can open the Device Manager.

If you've purchased a board or other hardware add-in, you should first read the supplied manual for details about installation procedures. Installation tips and an install program may be supplied with the hardware.

NOTE

> *Always* check the installation instructions before you install the new hardware. In some cases, the instructions tell you to install some software *before* you install the new hardware. If they do, follow this advice!

27

However, if no instructions are included, you can physically install the hardware and keep reading.

If you're installing an internal device, you have to shut down your computer before you open the case. You should also unplug it because most modern PCs actually keep part of the system powered up even when they appear to be off.

TIP

> You might be tempted to move some of the adapter cards that are plugged into your motherboard from one slot to another, but don't do this unless you really have to. To Windows, it looks like you've added an entirely new device. In some cases you have to reinsert the driver disks for the device you moved, and you might have to reconfigure its software settings.

When the device is installed, power your PC back up and log on with a Computer Administrator account; then wait a minute or so. In most cases the New Hardware Wizard automatically detects and sets up the new device.

If you're adding a USB or FireWire device, you don't need to shut down before plugging the new device in, but you should close any programs you have running, just in case the installation process hangs the computer. Windows XP doesn't hang very often in NT-based Windows, but it can happen. Save your work, and close your applications.

For non-Plug and Play hardware, or for Plug and Play stuff that isn't detected or doesn't install automatically for some reason, you need to run the Add Hardware applet from the Control Panel while logged on as a Computer Administrator user. The wizard starts by searching for new Plug and Play hardware. If nothing is found, Windows asks whether the device is installed already. If you select "Yes, I have already connected the hardware," Windows assumes you're having some trouble with a device or need to install it manually (see Figure 27.1). Your currently installed devices are listed with an option to troubleshoot or to add something new. For veterans, the combination option of adding new hardware or troubleshooting installed hardware seems a bit weird until you get used to it. I guess Microsoft wanted the wizard to perform double-duty. If you select "No, I have not added the hardware yet" the wizard closes.

Next, you're asked whether you want the wizard to attempt to detect and install the hardware automatically or specify the item yourself. (Legacy hardware interrogation is a science all its own, and I'm always amazed when some old job like a sound card is detected properly.) If you select Search, you'll see a "gas gauge" apprising you of the progress for each category and the overall progress, and you'll hear lots of hard disk activity.

If a new device is found that doesn't require any user configuration, a help balloon appears on-screen near the system tray, supplying the details of what was located (see Figure 27.2). Windows displays the device at the end of the search process.

27

Figure 27.1
When a new Plug and Play device isn't found, you see this dialog box. Scroll down and choose add a new hardware device.

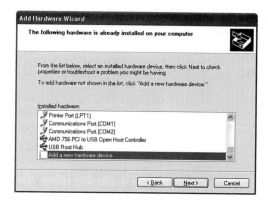

Figure 27.2
During the search process, any new hardware located is displayed near the system tray/clock.

In case the item isn't detected properly, click Next and a list of common hardware types is displayed (see Figure 27.3). If you don't see a category that matches your hardware, select "Show All Devices." Just choose the applicable category, and click Next.

Figure 27.3
Common hardware types are listed in alphabetical order. Select the type, or Show All Devices to install your device manually.

27

Be sure you choose the precise brand name and model number/name of the item you're installing. You might be prompted to insert your Windows XP CD-ROM so that the appropriate driver file(s) can be loaded. If your hardware came with a driver disk, use the Have Disk button to directly install the driver from the manufacturer's driver disk or downloaded file.

Early in the wizard's steps, you have the option of specifying the hardware yourself and skipping the legacy scan. Choosing this option can save you time and, in some cases, is the surer path to installing new hardware. It also lets you physically install the hardware later, should you want to. The wizard doesn't bother to authenticate the existence of the hardware; it simply installs the new driver.

If the device plugs into an external serial, parallel, or SCSI port, you might want to connect it, turn it on, and restart your system to install it. Some of these devices can't be installed via the Add Hardware wizard if they're not present when the system is started.

TIP

In some cases, you are given the option of adjusting settings after the hardware is installed and possibly adjusting your hardware to match. (Some legacy cards have switches or software adjustments that can be made to them to control the I/O port, DMA address, and so forth.) You may be told which settings to use to avoid conflicts with other hardware in the system.

If, for some reason, you don't want to use the settings that the wizard suggests, you can use your own settings and manually configure them. You can do so from the Add Hardware Wizard or via the Device Manager (from the System applet). See "The Device Manager" later in this chapter.

CAUTION

In general, be cautious about configuring resource settings manually. When you change settings manually, the settings become fixed, and Windows XP's built-in device contention resolution is less likely to work. Also, if you install too many devices with manually configured settings, you might not be able to install new Plug and Play devices because none will be available. In the worst-case scenario, the system might not even boot if conflicts occur with primary hardware devices such as hard disk controllers or video cards. If you decide to use manual configuration, make sure you know what you're doing, and have the specs for the hardware in question at hand.

In cases in which the wizard detects a conflict, you are alerted when you finish walking through the wizard steps. You then have the option of bailing out or continuing despite the conflict. You can also back up and choose a different model of hardware, such as one you think is compatible with what you're attempting to install. Figure 27.4 shows a typical message when a conflict is detected.

You now have the choice of setting the hardware resources for this device manually. Click View or change resources for this hardware (Advanced) to change the settings. On the next screen, click Set Configuration Manually. You'll see something similar to the dialog box in Figure 27.5, displaying the conflicting setting and the other device that uses the same setting.

Figure 27.4
When a hardware conflict is detected, it's reported by the wizard at the end of the installation process.

Figure 27.5
Use caution when manually changing resources for a device. You may end up choosing an unavailable resource. In this dialog box, the I/O range is not available because of a conflict with another COM port.

Click Change Setting to change the settings; if the system displays an error message, use the Setting Based On scroll box to try a different Basic configuration, or change the manual settings you made to alternate values. Keep trying configurations until the conflicting device listing is clear. Then, click OK and restart your computer if prompted.

If you're unable to select a nonconflicting setting with the device you're installing, change the settings for the conflicting device with the Device Manager as discussed later in this chapter. In some cases, particularly with ISA cards, you might not be able to resolve a conflict and will need to remove one of the cards or disable the conflicting device on one of the cards with the Device Manager. PCI and AGP cards can share IRQ settings and fully support Windows XP's Plug and Play feature, making them a much better choice for installation in today's crowded systems.

27

PROVIDING DRIVERS FOR HARDWARE NOT IN THE LIST

When the hardware you're attempting to install isn't on the device list, the problem is one of the following:

- The hardware is newer than Windows XP
- The hardware is really old and Microsoft decided not to include support for it
- The hardware must be configured with a special setup program, as with some removable-media drives such as the Iomega Zip drive

In these cases, you need to obtain the driver from the manufacturer's website (or Microsoft's; check both) and get it ready on floppy disk, CD-ROM, or on the hard disk (either locally or across an available network). If the manufacturer supplies a setup disk, forget my advice, and follow the manufacturer's instructions. However, if the manufacturer supplies a driver disk and no instructions, follow along with these steps:

1. Run the Add Hardware applet and click Next.
2. Select Yes, I Have Already Connected the Hardware and click Next.
3. Scroll to the bottom of the list and select Add a New Hardware Device. Click Next.
4. Select Install the Hardware that I Manually Select From a List and click Next.
5. Select the appropriate device category and click Next.
6. Click the Have Disk button. Enter the location of the driver (you can enter any path, such as a directory on the hard disk or network path). Typically, you insert a disk in your floppy or CD-ROM drive. If you downloaded the driver software from a Web site, locate it on your hard drive. In either case you can use the Browse button if you don't know the exact path or drive. If you do use the Browse option, look for a directory where an .INF file appears in the dialog box.
7. Assuming the wizard finds a suitable driver file, choose the correct hardware item from the resulting dialog box, and follow the onscreen directions.

> **TIP**
>
> If you're not sure which ports and interrupts your other boards are using, you can use the Device Manager to locate available and used IRQs, ports, DMA, and so on.

 If you've added some hardware and it doesn't work, see "New Hardware Doesn't Work" in the "Troubleshooting" section at the end of this chapter.

REMOVING HARDWARE

Before unplugging a USB, FireWire, or PCMCIA device, tell Windows XP to stop using it. This prevents data loss caused by unplugging the device before XP has finished saving all your data. You can stop these devices by clicking the PC Card icon in the system tray. Unplug the device or card only after Windows informs you that it is safe to do so.

For the most part, other hardware can be removed simply by turning off your computer, unplugging it, and removing the unwanted hardware. When Windows restarts, it recognizes that the device is missing and carries on without problems.

If you want to completely delete the driver for an unneeded device, use the Device Manager computer management application. Delete the drivers *before* uninstalling the hardware; otherwise, the device won't appear in the Device Manager's list. For details, see "The Device Manager," later in this chapter.

> **TIP**
>
> You can stop PC Cards (PCMCIA cards) by clicking the PC Card icon in the system tray, which has the same effect as disabling the item from this applet. You can remove the PC Card after you stop it.

MAINTAINING AND UPDATING DEVICE DRIVERS

One of the tools you're more than likely to rely on frequently for management of the computer's hardware is the Control Panel's System applet. Although there are a few others we'll mention here and in other chapters, the System applet's Hardware tab is most likely to be of use to you when managing hardware. To open the System applet, click Start, right-click the My Computer icon and choose Properties. You can also choose the Performance and Maintenance option in the Control Panel and click the System button.

The General tab tells you which version of the operating system is running, the number of the last service pack applied, the registered user's name, the type and speed of the processor, and the amount of RAM. Checking this tab is a relatively quick way to find out the amount of RAM Windows is detecting—which is particularly useful if you've just added some and you're wondering whether you installed it correctly. Also, if you're considering adding more RAM and don't recall how well the computer is currently endowed this is the place to look.

The other tabs and settings in this applet deal more with network and system repair issues and are discussed in other chapters. So, let's start with the Hardware tab. Figure 27.6 shows the Hardware tab of the Control Panel's System applet.

The Hardware tab's first option is the Add Hardware Wizard button. This button runs the same Add Hardware Wizard covered earlier in this chapter.

> **TIP**
>
> You can't install new hardware or drivers if you're logged in as a user with limited privileges. You must have a Computer Administrator account to work with hardware.

27

After your hardware is installed, the other buttons on the Hardware tab (Driver Signing, Device Manager, and Hardware Profiles) are used to manage hardware and resolve problems.

Figure 27.6
The Hardware tab of the System applet is a control center for examining and modifying hardware.

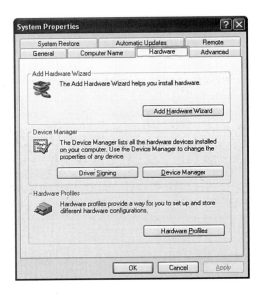

The two buttons we're going to focus in the next two sections are the Driver Signing and Device Manager buttons. The fact that these two buttons are grouped together on the Hardware tab is no accident. Drivers make hardware work with Windows, and Microsoft has gone to great lengths to make sure that Windows XP Home Edition users have reliable drivers for their hardware.

Although you work with hardware and its drivers through the Device Manager, how well your hardware works with Windows depends upon the settings in Driver Signing.

DRIVER SIGNING

Driver Signing is a safety feature first developed by Microsoft for Windows 2000 and Windows Me. *Signed* drivers are drivers which have passed testing standards established by the Windows Hardware Quality Labs (WHQL), and are the preferred drivers for use with Windows XP. All drivers supplied on the Windows XP CD-ROM and provided through Windows Update bear a *digital signature* indicating they've passed WHQL testing. You can use non-signed (non-WHQL approved) drivers with Windows XP, but the default Driver Signing setting will warn you if you do. Generally, you should use signed drivers for your hardware; use unsigned drivers only if signed drivers are unavailable or you need to fix an urgent hardware problem with a driver that hasn't had time to go through WHQL testing.

If you go to the hardware manufacturer's Web site for drivers, you might see both signed and unsigned drivers. If you want to block the use of any unsigned drivers, or turn off the warning that an attempt to install unsigned drivers will display, click the Driver Signing button and select the option you want to use.

The Device Manager

The Device Manager provides a one-stop solution for checking device settings, reinstalling and updating drivers for existing drivers, and removing devices.

You can get to the Device Manager in two main ways:

- Choose Start, Control Panel, Printers and Other Hardware, System, Hardware, Device Manager.

- Choose Start, Control Panel, Performance and Maintenance, Administrative Tools, and then double-click Computer Management. Open the System Tools branch, and then click Device Manager. While more tedious to get to, you do get quicker access to the other administrative tools from this view (see Figure 27.7).

In the Device Manager listing, you can click a + (plus) sign to expand a device category to investigate the installed components in the category. Note that problematic items are marked with a yellow exclamation mark. You can check on any item's status by right-clicking it and choosing Properties.

Choosing this option opens a Properties dialog box, like the one shown in Figure 27.8. You can do some serious device tweaking from this dialog box.

Choices on the dialog box vary from device to device, but almost all devices use the General, Driver, and Resources tabs as shown in Figure 27.8. The most important items are discussed in Table 27.1.

Figure 27.7
The Device Manager through the eyes of the Computer Management Console.

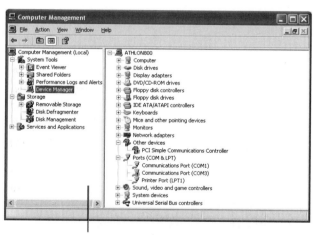

When you choose Device Manager from the Hardware tab of the System applet, you don't see this list of administrative tools.

27

Figure 27.8
A Properties dialog box for a malfunctioning piece of hardware.

This doubles as a troubleshooting button as necessary.

TABLE 27.1 PROPERTIES DIALOG BOX TABS

Tab	Options and Notes
General	Device Status: Displays whether the device is reported as working properly or indicates device problems.
	Troubleshoot: If the device is not working, you can click the troubleshooter to walk through a wizard. Reinstall Driver: Click this button to reinstall the driver for the device.
	Device Usage: You can check the hardware configurations that are available on your computer. You also can disable a device in a hardware configuration by selecting Disable from this scroll box.
Settings	The options on this tab vary with the device.
Driver	Driver Details: This section of the Driver tab displays the author of the driver, version, and location on the hard disk. It's worth checking. Most of the drivers will be from Microsoft, unless you installed one from another manufacturer.
	Update Driver: This button runs the Upgrade Device Driver Wizard, which walks you through the process of adding a driver. Refer to the "Adding and Removing Hardware" section earlier in the chapter if you have questions about the process of changing a driver.
	Roll Back Driver: Restores the previously-installed driver. Very useful if a new driver causes the system to fail.

27

Tab	Options and Notes
	Uninstall: You can use this tab to remove the device drivers for this device. Removing the drivers effectively kills the device. You might have to reboot afterward, but in many cases, it's not required. You can add the device manually later if you change your mind. Sometimes removing and reinstalling a device can clear up problems you were having with it.
Resources	Set Configuration Manually: If you suspect that the device is conflicting with other devices and this is why it's not working, you may be allowed to configure it manually.

In the following sections we'll take a closer look at some of the functions found on the various tabs described in the preceding table.

USING THE TROUBLESHOOTER

The Windows XP troubleshooters have been mentioned several times in this book, beginning in Chapter 1, "Introducing Windows XP Home Edition." Nine hardware troubleshooters are supplied with Windows XP Home Edition. Although they won't always solve your problems, they'll at least walk you through a logical train of investigation for your malady, possibly leading you to a conclusion or avenue of thought you hadn't previously tried.

You can start troubleshooters from various points within Windows, such as Display properties and Device Manager, but you can access most of them through the Help and Support Center:

1. Choose Start, Help and Support.
2. Type Troubleshooter into the search box and click the arrow to start the search.
3. You then see a list of troubleshooter wizards.
4. Run the troubleshooter that applies. You may be asked some questions that require running the Device Manager to determine the status of your hardware.

TIP

> If a USB controller doesn't install properly, especially if the controller doesn't show up in the Device Manager, the problem might be in your system BIOS. Most BIOSes have a setting that can enable or disable the USB ports. Shut down and restart. Do whatever your computer requires for you to check the BIOS settings during system startup (usually hitting the Del or Esc keys on the initial boot screen). Then enter the BIOS setup and enable USB support.
>
> When that is done, if the USB controller still doesn't appear in the Device Manager, it's possible that the computer's BIOS might be outdated. Check with the computer's or motherboard's manufacturer for a possible update to support USB under Windows XP Home Edition.

27

Note that you can attempt to troubleshoot a specific installed device by running the Add Hardware applet from the Control Panel and highlighting the afflicted item. Also, the properties sheet for some devices offers a troubleshooter as well.

UPDATING DEVICE DRIVERS

At some point, you'll need to get the latest driver for a device. You might have to do this if you encounter problems with the device—for example, if printing glitches have occurred or Windows crashes with the famous Blue Screen of Death. If you encounter this sort of problem, you might find that the support pages on the manufacturer's Web site direct you to download and install an updated driver. They should give you clear instructions, but here is some additional advice.

Before you download and install the new driver, use this checklist:

1. Do you have permission to upgrade drivers? Your Windows login account needs Administrator privileges, which are the default for new users in Windows XP Home Edition.

2. Is it really the latest driver? Check the manufacturer's site and the Microsoft site to see what you can find. The following sites are good places to start:

   ```
   www.microsoft.com/hcl
   www.windrivers.com
   www.windowsmarketplace.com
   ```

   NOTE

   > You might want to try running Start, All Programs, Windows Update, choosing Product Updates, and then choosing Device Drivers. Microsoft may have listed updated device drivers for your system.

3. Does the "new" driver work with Windows XP Home Edition? In a pinch, you might be able to use Windows 2000 drivers. Windows 95, 98, and Me drivers are not acceptable.

After you've downloaded the new driver, open the Device Manager using either of the methods described earlier, in the section, "The Device Manager." You can install your new driver using these steps:

1. Open the Device Manager (if you're using the Computer Management approach, choose Device Manager in the left pane).

2. Click the device in question, and open its Properties dialog box.

3. In the Properties dialog box, select the Driver tab, and click Details if you want to see what version of the driver you are currently using, or just click Update Driver to proceed with updating the driver.

4. When the Update Wizard starts running, select Install From a List and click Next.

5. On the second page, choose the second option, Don't Search, and click Next.

6. Click Have Disk. Browse to the location of the driver. If the driver isn't found on the disk, you're in trouble. The .INF file on the disk and the accompanying driver files must meet the requirements of Windows XP to be deemed acceptable for installation. Return to the manufacturer's Web site and look for another driver.

> **TIP**
>
> Downloadable drivers are usually stored in compressed form on the manufacturer's Web site. If the file is an .EXE (executable) file, you will need to open it in Windows Explorer before you can use its contents; opening it might also install the driver for you. If the driver is in a .ZIP archive file, you will need to uncompress it. Fortunately, Windows Explorer in Windows XP Home Edition can uncompress .ZIP files for you. You won't need to download a separate unzipping utility.

DEVICE DRIVER ROLLBACK

Device driver rollback allows you to "roll back the clock" and use the previous driver you installed for a device if the newly installed driver doesn't work. When Windows XP installs a new driver for a device, it backs up the old driver, rather than simply replacing it as with previous versions of Windows.

To start the process, click the Roll Back Driver button on the Driver tab discussed in the previous section. If there are no previous driver versions, you are given the opportunity to run the Troubleshooter instead to help solve problems with your device.

If a previous driver version is available, click Yes to roll back to that driver. The Driver display changes to show the driver release date and information for the previous driver. Restart the computer if prompted.

THE RESOURCES TAB

If you decide to change the resources for a device using the Resource tab that appears when you view a device's properties in Device Manager, be cautious. Manually setting a device's resource assignment can result in conflicts with other installed devices, and doing so imposes restrictions on the Plug and Play system's capability to dynamically allocate resources in the future.

To reassign a resource, click the resource in question on the Resources tab, and choose Change Setting. In an attempt to prevent folks from inadvertently doing damage, the manual resource assignment dialog box keeps an eye on what you're doing. If you attempt to reassign to a resource that is already in use, you'll be warned about the conflict as you saw in Figure 27.4 earlier in this chapter.

Some drivers don't have resources that can be reassigned. Others have an option button called Reinstall Driver that's useful if the system thinks that would solve a nonfunctioning-device problem. Most PCI cards don't permit their resources to be reassigned, because they obtain their resource settings from Windows or from the system BIOS. Some systems allocate resources depending upon which slot you use for a particular card.

27

CAUTION

Notice the Setting Based On drop-down list on the Resources tab. It lists the hardware configurations in which the currently selected device is enabled. If you choose a hardware configuration other than the default, and you change any resource settings, resource conflicts may occur when you use the default hardware configuration. Resource conflicts can disable your hardware and cause your computer to malfunction or to be inoperable.

If you have multiple hardware configurations (see later in this chapter), the moral of the story is to try to keep the same configurations for hardware between them. It's okay to totally *turn off* specific pieces of hardware for a given saved hardware configuration, but when you start changing the resource allocations for each one, you could end up with a mess.

UNDERSTANDING AND RESOLVING HARDWARE CONFLICTS

Windows, together with its Plug and Play technology, has grown far better at detecting and preventing hardware conflicts over the past few years. Still, system conflicts do arise, especially when you're using old ISA cards and other legacy hardware. (We suspect that there is little of this equipment still in use and look forward to the day that we can delete this section from some future edition of this book. Until that day comes, we're stuck with it.)

More often than not, configuration and installation problems are due to incorrect settings on an ISA network, I/O, sound, modem, and SCSI cards. The result is cards that conflict with one another for the same IRQ (interrupt request line), base I/O port address, DMA, or base memory address. Usually, these settings are made by changing jumpers or DIP switches on the board.

NOTE

Some legacy cards can be configured via software settings rather than DIP switches and jumpers. For example, 3Com's popular 3C509B Ethernet adapter card uses its own utility program to set the IRQ and port address. You might have to run such a configuration program (typically using a DOS command prompt) to set up the card before it will run correctly under Windows XP.

Some ISA cards can also be switched into a true Plug-and-Play mode by flipping a switch or moving a jumper block on the actual card or running a software configuration program.

27

As I mentioned earlier, you can force Windows XP to use manually selected system resources, such as IRQ, for a given piece of gear. In the Device Manager, choose the item, open its Properties dialog box, click the Resources tab, turn off Use Automatic Settings, and enter the resource or resources you want to assign. If the card uses manual configuration, you will need to set the board to the settings you select in the Device Manager.

CAUTION

> Don't manually assign resources unless you know what you're doing. The result can be an operating system that won't boot or a bunch of other components in your system that no longer work.

There are four major resources that hardware uses:

- IRQ
- DMA
- I/O Port Addresses
- DMA channel

If you install Plug and Play cards (which configure themselves automatically), you seldom need to be concerned about these settings, especially if the cards use the PCI expansion slot (virtually any current card does). If your system originally ran Windows 98 or newer versions, it probably supports a feature called IRQ steering or IRQ sharing, which eliminates the major cause for hardware conflicts when you use PCI cards.

However, if your system uses ISA cards, or you still use legacy ports such as serial (COM), parallel (LPT), and PS/2 mouse ports, IRQ and other resource conflicts can still be a problem. To learn more about these resources, see the following section.

HARDWARE RESOURCES AND WINDOWS XP

Windows XP's Device Manager can help you determine the resources used by your hardware, and Windows XP normally can manage Plug and Play hardware installation with little or no help from you. However, ISA cards and conflicts between built-in ISA ports (serial, parallel, and PS/2 mouse) and PCI cards can cause your system to malfunction. Use the information in this section to understand the potential causes of conflicts and how to avoid them.

IRQs

PC architecture includes a means for a piece of hardware to quickly gain the attention of the CPU through a message called an *interrupt request*, or *IRQ*. Interrupts are sent over one of the 15 IRQ wires on the computer's bus. Such a request is a direct line to the CPU, which then services the request accordingly. A common example occurs when data comes into your system's modem or LAN card. The modem or LAN card triggers the predetermined interrupt line (IRQ), and the CPU then begins to execute the program code that is appropriate for handling that interrupt. In fact, a part of the operating system called the *interrupt handler* is responsible for making it so.

Table 27.2 lists the common IRQs in an Intel-based computer. This information, in conjunction with the IRQ and the Conflicts/Sharing nodes of the Computer Management

27

application, might help you assign boards effectively. But remember, it's always best to let Windows make hardware assignments unless you are really stuck and something important just won't work. Also, remember that if hardware isn't on the Hardware Compatibility List (HCL), you're better off just going shopping than wasting a day tinkering with settings.

TABLE 27.2   TYPICAL IRQ ASSIGNMENTS IN 80286-BASED OR LATER X86 SYSTEMS

IRQ	Typical Assignment
0	System Timer (used by system; not available)
1	Keyboard (used by system; not available)
2	Redirected to IRQ 9; not available
3	COM2:, COM4: (can be shared *only* if COM 2/COM 4 are *not* used at the same time)
4	COM1:, COM3: (can be shared *only* if COM 1/COM 3 are *not* used at the same time)
5	LPT2: or Sound Blaster/compatible sound card
6	Floppy disk controller (used by system; never available)
7	LPT1: (printer port) can be shared only if used on a PCI card; the built-in parallel port's IRQ can't be shared
8	System clock (used by system; never available)
9	Old EGA/VGA cards or available
10	Often available
11	Often available
12	PS/2 mouse (available only on systems that don't have a PS/2-style mouse or have the port disabled)
13	Math coprocessor (not available; all modern CPUs have a built-in math coprocessor)
14	IDE hard disk controller (never available)
15	Secondary IDE hard disk controller (never available on 1995 or later systems)

(Modern PCI cards may use interrupt numbers higher than 15.)

Common add-on devices that use an IRQ include

- Modern PCI and AGP video cards
- SCSI host adapter cards
- IDE host adapter cards
- Fax/modem cards
- Network interface cards

27

With only IRQ 9, 10, and 11 to choose from on many systems, it would be impossible to install all of these cards unless

- An existing device is disabled
- IRQ sharing is possible

If two ISA devices (or an ISA and a PCI device) try to share an IRQ, a system lockup usually will take place, or at best, neither device will work. A common cause of this a few years ago was when a serial mouse was attached to COM 1 and a fax/modem was assigned to COM 3. As you can see from the IRQ table, both of these ports use IRQ 4. The system worked until the user tried to operate the modem; then, the system locked up.

MS-DOS and old versions of Windows didn't always use the printer (LPT) ports' IRQs, enabling IRQ 7 (LPT1) and IRQ 5 (LPT2) to be used by other devices. However, Windows XP uses the IRQs assigned to a device, so sharing can take place only under these circumstances:

- Both devices using the IRQ are PCI devices. On most recent systems, this enables the PCI cards and any built-in PCI devices to share IRQs.
- When two ISA cards or an ISA and a PCI card are set to the same IRQ, Windows XP shifts to a "polling" mode, wherein the CPU regularly checks for and services I/O requests rather than waits for IRQ lines to be activated. Obviously, this process can slow down overall system performance because it creates another software loop that the operating system has to service.

IRQ steering is enabled automatically by Windows XP when the system supports it. In some cases, however, some motherboards might not permit IRQs to be shared, even by PCI devices.

If you find yourself short on IRQs or if you have two devices attempting to use the same IRQ and creating a conflict, you can try these possible solutions:

- One solution with PCI cards causing conflicts is to try moving the PCI card to another slot. On some machines, each PCI slot's PCI Interrupt (A through D) is mapped to an ISA-type IRQ. By simply moving a card to a neighboring slot, you might be able to get your hardware working.
- Another solution for IRQ cram is to set up multiple hardware profiles. You might not get all items to work under one profile, but you can have a couple of profiles and at least not have to throw anything away. Just reboot in another profile when you need access to a specific piece of gear.
- Another workaround is to use USB, IEEE-1394, and SCSI devices. As you probably know, all of these port types support multiple devices on the same wire. No IRQs are required other than for the controller, which typically takes only one, and most recent systems already have USB ports onboard and enabled. Yet, USB supports up to 127 devices, IEEE-1394 up to 63 devices, and SCSI typically 7 (or 15 if your card supports

27

Wide SCSI). If you're struggling with where to put a scanner, printer, digital camera, or additional external hard drive, consider these buses. Although you can daisy-chain devices from the parallel port, it's difficult to get more than two devices (printer and another one) working correctly. And, even the "high-speed" EPP and ECP parallel port modes are scarcely faster than USB, and are considerably slower than any form of SCSI or IEEE-1394.

DMA CHANNELS

A typical PC has eight DMA channels, labeled 0 to 7. DMA channels are used for rapidly transferring data between memory and peripherals without the help of the CPU. Some cards even use several of these channels at once. (For example, the SoundBlaster 16 WaveEffects sound card uses two DMA channels.) Typical users of DMA channels are

- Memory access controllers
- ECP printer ports
- Floppy disk controllers
- ISA Network cards
- ISA Scanner cards
- ISA SCSI host adapters
- ISA sound cards

Although recent EIDE hard drives use a variation of DMA called Ultra DMA (UDMA) for fast data transfer, DMA transfers performed by PCI-based devices don't use specific DMA channels. The only time a PCI device ever needs to use a DMA channel is if it's emulating an ISA device that uses one, such as a PCI-based sound card emulating an ISA-based sound card.

Sharing DMA channels is even worse than sharing IRQs. Because DMA channels are used to transfer data, not simply to activate devices, you should *never* share DMA channels used by network cards, scanners, or SCSI host adapters, because a DMA conflict could result in data loss. Fortunately, with relatively few devices requiring DMA channels today, it's normally quite easy to avoid sharing a DMA channel.

Table 27.3 shows the typical assignments.

TABLE 27.3   TYPICAL DMA CONTROLLER ASSIGNMENTS

Channel	Typical Assignment
0	Generally used for DMA refresh
1	Available; can be used by ISA sound cards or by PCI sound cards emulating ISA sound cards
2	Floppy disk controller

Channel	Typical Assignment
3	ECP printer ports; some can use DMA 1 instead
4	DMA controller; used by system and not available
5	Available; can be used by ISA sound cards or by PCI sound cards emulating ISA sound cards
6	Available
7	Available

TIP

Some devices are hidden from view in the Device Manager. Hidden devices include non-Plug and Play devices (devices with earlier Windows 2000 device drivers) and devices that have been physically removed from the computer but have not had their drivers uninstalled. To see hidden devices in the Device Manager list, choose View, Show Hidden Devices. A check mark should appear on the menu, indicating that hidden devices are showing. Click it again to hide them.

I/O Port Assignments

Using DMA is the fastest way to transfer data between components in the PC. However, an older technology called *memory-mapped I/O* is still in use today. (*I/O* means *input/output*.) In PC architecture, I/O ports are mapped into system memory and therefore are accessed by the CPU using memory addresses. As you might expect, each device that uses an I/O port must have a different port address, or data intended for one device will end up at another.

Check out the I/O folder off the Hardware Resources node in Computer Management to see a sample list of I/O addresses and assignments. This folder contains quite a few assignments. Note that the addresses are in standard memory-mapping parlance—hexadecimal.

NOTE

A common source of I/O contention occurs among video cards, SCSI devices, and network cards. However, most devices can use a choice of several I/O port address ranges to avoid conflicts.

27

Memory Addresses

Similar to the I/O port address, the base memory address is the beginning memory address that some cards or motherboard hardware use to communicate with the CPU. Sometimes this setting is called the *RAM starting address* (or *start address*).

Some older cards (you'll notice this often with network adapters or SCSI cards that have an onboard BIOS) must have their base memory address set by a jumper or software. Then the device driver for that component needs its software setting to match the jumper. A typical base memory address reads like this: 0xA0000 or just A0000. Sometimes the last digit is dropped, like this: A000.

If you open Computer Management and go to System Information, Hardware Resources, Memory, you'll see memory addresses such as the following:

```
0xA0000-0xBFFFF    PCI bus
```

This address means the memory area between A0000 and BFFFF is assigned to the PCI bus. (The 0x indicates that it is a hexadecimal address.) So, when setting memory addressing, you need to consider not only the base addresses, but also the amount of RAM space the addresses will occupy. Some cards use 16KB of space, and others use 32KB or more. Check the card's manual for options. Using more memory can, in some cases, improve the operation of the card, but it decreases your system's memory availability because that space will be occupied. The end result depends on the type of card.

When you specify a memory address for a card, the operating system reserves that memory area for it. Regular RAM in that area is not used by the CPU, to prevent conflicts that could result from trying to write data or program code into system RAM at that address. Instead, the reserved area is used only by the device driver for your piece of hardware.

Most older ISA cards use an upper memory address that falls somewhere between a000 and FFFF. However, many VL-Bus, PCI, and some ISA cards can use address space above 1MB, or even above 16MB in the case of 32-bit cards. If your card can use a high address, it's better to do so because it minimizes the chances of conflicting with the operating system.

INSTALLING AND USING MULTIPLE MONITORS

Windows XP Home Edition supports multiple monitors, a great feature first developed for Windows 98. You can run up to ten monitors with Windows XP, but most commonly, you will probably run just two or three. By using multiple monitors, you can place a large amount of information on your screens at once. Use one screen for working on video editing, Web design, or graphics and the other for toolbars. Leave a Web or email display on at all times while you use the other monitor for work or play. Display huge spreadsheets across both screens.

The following are some rules and tips to know about using multiple monitors:

- Some laptops support attaching an external monitor and can display different view on the internal LCD screen and on the external monitor. This is called DualView, and if your laptop supports it, your user's manual will show you how to enable the feature. You can ignore this section's instructions on installing a device adapter and just follow the instructions for setting the Display properties to use the second monitor.

- Because most computers don't have more than one or two PCI slots open, if you want to max out your video system, look into the new breed of multimonitor video cards available from Matrox, ATI, and various other vendors. In a single slot, you can drive two or four monitors with these cards. With only two slots, you can drive four to eight monitors. Multimonitor video cards are available for either AGP or PCI slots.

- Many multimonitor situations consist of two cards: either two PCIs or a mix of one PCI and one AGP.

- If you mix AGP and PCI, older BIOSes sometimes have a strange habit of forcing one or the other to become the "primary" display. This is the display that Windows first boots on and the one you use for logging on. You might be annoyed if your better monitor or better card isn't the primary display because most programs are initially displayed on the primary monitor when you launch them. Therefore, you might want to flash-upgrade your BIOS if the maker of your computer or motherboard indicates that such an upgrade will advance the multiple-monitor support for your computer by letting you choose which monitor or card you want to make the primary display.

- If you're unhappy with your system's choice of the primary display, you can adjust it with Display properties once both displays are running.

 If you aren't having luck assigning the primary display, and your secondary card is taking over the role of primary display, see "Can't Select the Primary Display" in the "Troubleshooting" section at the end of this chapter.

- The operating system always needs a VGA device, which becomes the primary display. The BIOS detects the VGA device based on slot order, unless the BIOS offers an option for choosing which device is to be treated as the VGA device. Check your BIOS settings to see whether any special settings might affect multimonitor display, such as whether the AGP or PCI card will default to primary display, or the PCI slot order. Slot 1 is typically the slot nearest the power supply connector.

- The design of the card itself is what makes it capable of operating on multiple monitors with Windows XP, not the driver. Don't expect any vendors to be able to add multiple monitor support simply by implementing a driver update. Either the card can support multimonitoring, or it can't. Some cards should technically be able to do so but are not stable enough to handle the capability at this time.

- Some motherboard with on-board I/O such as sound, modem, and LAN may have difficulties with multiple monitor configurations, especially if the devices share an IRQ with a particular PCI slot. You might want to disable any on-board devices you're not using to free up resources that can be used for additional video cards.

- Just because a set of cards supports multimonitoring under Windows 98 doesn't mean it can under Windows XP. These two operating systems have completely different video architectures.

27

TIP

Microsoft doesn't provide much specific information on which video cards/chipsets work in multimonitor mode, perhaps because BIOS and motherboard issues can affect the results different users will have with the same video cards. The RealTimeSoft Web site contains a searchable database of thousands of working combinations as well as links to other multiple monitor resources, including RealTimeSoft's own UltraMon multi-monitor utility. Check it out at

    www.realtimesoft.com

Follow these steps to install a secondary display adapter for use with multiple monitors:

1. Boot up your system into Windows XP, and right-click a blank area of your desktop. From the resulting pop-up menu, select Properties.

2. Go to the Settings tab. Confirm that your primary display adapter is listed correctly (that is, if you have an ATI Rage Pro, then ATI Rage Pro should be listed under Display). Your display adapter *should not* be listed as plain-old "VGA", or multimonitoring will not work. If this is the case, you need to find and install correct Windows XP drivers, or consult your display manufacturer's Web site.

3. Be sure you are using at least Medium (16-bit) colors quality. Then click OK, and when prompted, select Apply Without Restarting.

4. After you've confirmed that you have drivers loaded for your display adapter and that you are in a compatible color depth, shut down and then power off your system.

5. Disconnect the power cable leading to the back of your system, and remove the case cover. Confirm that you have an available PCI slot. Before inserting your secondary display adapter, disable its VGA mode if possible by adjusting a jumper block or DIP switch on the card. Newer cards use the software driver or BIOS settings to enable or disable VGA mode.

 If you have problems setting up your monitor, see "Can't Select the Primary Display" in the "Troubleshooting" section at the end of this chapter.

6. Insert your secondary display adapter, secure it properly with a screw, reassemble your system, and reconnect the power. Next, connect a second monitor to the secondary display adapter.

7. Turn on both the monitors, and power up the system. Allow the system to boot into Windows XP.

8. After you log in, Windows XP detects your new display adapter and brings up the Hardware Wizard. Confirm that it detects the correct display adapter and, when prompted, tell Windows XP to search for a suitable driver. Then click Next.

9. Windows XP then finds information on the display adapter. When you are prompted, insert your Windows XP installation CD or the driver disk that came with your adapter, and click OK.

10. Windows XP then copies files. When the process is completed, click Finish. Windows XP then also detects your secondary monitor (if it is a PnP monitor). When you are prompted, click Finish again.

11. Now that all appropriate drivers are installed, right-click a blank portion of your desktop, and select Properties again. Next, go to the Settings tab. You will notice that two Monitor icons now appear in the center window of the display applet representing your two monitors (look ahead to Figure 27.9). Left-click the Monitor icon labeled 2, and it is highlighted in blue.

12. Under Display, your secondary adapter should be displayed. In the lower-left corner below the Colors section, check the box labeled Extend My Windows Desktop into This Monitor.

13. When Windows XP gives you a warning concerning compatibility, click Yes.

14. While the Monitor icon labeled 2 is highlighted, adjust the color depth and resolution for the new monitor.

15. You might want to change the way your monitors are positioned by left-clicking and holding down the mouse button while you drag the Monitor icons. (Note that the displays must touch along one edge.) When you find a desirable position, just release the mouse button, and the Monitor icon is aligned adjacent to the first Monitor icon. Also note that wherever the two displays meet is the location your mouse will be able to pass from one display to the next, so a horizontal alignment is preferred for a standard desktop monitor arrangement (see Figure 27.9).

16. Click OK. Windows XP then asks whether you want to restart or apply your changes. Select Restart to allow Windows XP to reboot your system.

17. After the system is rebooted and you log on to your system, multimonitoring should be functional, and you should have an extended desktop displayed on your second monitor. You also should be able to move your mouse into this extended desktop.

Figure 27.9
A system running dual monitors. The relative size of monitors 1 and 2 reflects the resolution (monitor 1 has a higher resolution than monitor 2).

NOTE

You can set up Windows XP with more than one secondary display adapter, up to a maximum of nine additional displays. To do so, just select another supported secondary display adapter with VGA disabled, and repeat the preceding steps with another monitor attached to the additional secondary adapter.

27

After you finish these steps, you can drag items across your screen onto alternative monitors. Better yet, you can resize a window to stretch it across more than one monitor. Things get a little weird at the gap, though. You have to get used to the idea of the mouse cursor jumping from one screen into the next, too.

NOTE

> If you're not sure which monitor is which, click the Identify button shown in Figure 27.9 to display a large number across each monitor for a few seconds.

 If you're having trouble getting your multimonitor setup to work, see "Can't Select the Primary Display" in the "Troubleshooting" section at the end of this chapter.

TIP

> If you don't have enough open slots to install the extra adapter(s) needed for multiple monitors, you can buy a single multiheaded video adapter card that supports two or four monitors.

INSTALLING A UPS

Blackouts and power outages (and the data loss they can cause) can happen anywhere. While Windows XP Home Edition contains a backup utility that can be used to protect your data, you should also be concerned about keeping power going to your PC between those weekly (or monthly, or whenever . . .) backup sessions that I know you *never* forget to make.

A battery backup unit (also called a *UPS*, which is short for *Uninterruptible Power Supply)* can provide battery power to your system for as much as ten to fifteen minutes, which is long enough for you to save your data and shut down your system. The UPS plugs into the wall (and can act as a surge suppressor) and your computer and monitor plug into outlets on the rear of the UPS.

Electronic circuitry in the UPS continually monitors the AC line voltages, and should the voltage rise above or dip below predefined limits or fail entirely, the UPS takes over, powering the computer and cutting off the computer from the AC wall outlet. An intelligent UPS can also connect to the computer's data inputs (typically through a serial port) to send a data message to the computer's operating system, alerting it of the nature of the power problem. The computer's software can then decide what evasive maneuvers to take.

As you might imagine, to prevent data loss, the system's response time has to be very fast. As soon as the AC power gets flaky, the UPS has to take over within a few milliseconds, at most. Many (but not all) UPS models feature a serial (COM) or USB cable, which attaches to the appropriate port on your system. The cable sends signals to your computer to inform it when the battery backup has taken over and to start the shutdown process; some units also broadcast a warning message over the network to other computers. UPS units with this feature are often called *intelligent UPS* units.

TIP

> If the UPS you purchase (or already own) doesn't come with Windows XP-specific drivers for the shutdown and warning features, contact the vendor of the UPS for a software update.

27

You can find the Power Options applet in Control Panel by clicking Start, Control Panel, Performance and Maintenance, Power Options. Figure 27.10 shows the UPS tab that enables you to select the model of UPS that's connected to your system, set up signaling for models that support automatic shutdown, and inform you of the battery's condition and how long you can expect the system to work from battery (a factor often called the *UPS runtime*).

Figure 27.10
The UPS tab in Power Options after a UPS model has been selected, but before the UPS has been connected.

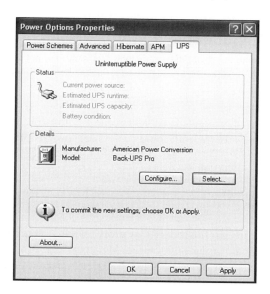

If your UPS doesn't have provisions for automatic shutdown, its alarm will notify you when the power has failed. Shut down the computer yourself after saving any open files, grab a flashlight, and relax until the power comes back on.

USING HARDWARE PROFILES

Windows has a feature called Hardware Profiles that lets you boot up Windows with different sets of hardware devices enabled. Profiles grew out of the need for docking laptops to be able to boot with a different set of driver settings based on whether the laptop was on the road or connected to a docking station with its own external monitor, additional CD-ROM drive, and so on. Profiles have become more capable with Plug and Play, sensing when the computer is hot-docked and kicking in the appropriate profile when needed. Also, for complex arrangements such as on a desktop computer stuffed to the gills with devices, it is sometimes necessary to disable some devices so that others can have access to certain limited resources, such as interrupt requests (IRQs). I should add that hot-dockable ports such as USB, IEEE-1394, and PC Cards have reduced the need for hardware profiles somewhat, because their hardware can be attached and removed on-the-fly without rebooting.

27

In addition to allowing different combinations of hardware, Hardware Profiles allow the same hardware to be configured with different resource settings. In essence, you can have almost a different computer with each hardware profile.

Hardware profiles are set up on the System applet, which you can view by clicking Start, right-clicking My Computer, and selecting Properties. View the Hardware tab and click the Hardware Profiles to bring up the Hardware Profile manager.

NOTE

> Windows enables or disables devices simply by installing or not installing their drivers at boot time.

Windows XP creates one hardware profile called Profile 1 automatically whenever it's installed on any type of computer. As additional devices are installed, they're automatically added to Profile 1.

To create an additional hardware profile, open the System properties sheet, click the Hardware tab, click Hardware Profiles, and copy Profile 1 to another profile (see Figure 27.11).

To change the hardware in any profile, select that profile when you reboot, and disable or change the settings for devices through the Device Manager. The Properties button on the Hardware Profiles screen lets you adjust profiles for portable computer use and select whether the profile is displayed as a startup option.

Figure 27.11
User Profiles on a system with two profiles available.

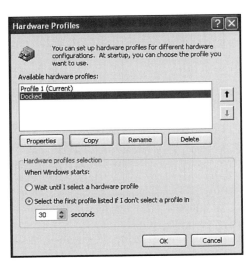

To switch between hardware profiles, reboot your computer and select the hardware profile you want to use at boot time. You can also specify whether the system should wait for you to select a profile, or run the first profile listed if you don't make a selection within a specified time period (30 seconds is the default. I prefer to set this to 10 seconds to save time).

TROUBLESHOOTING

CAN'T SELECT THE PRIMARY DISPLAY

I can't get my multimonitor system to choose the primary display properly.

As discussed in the section about multimonitor arrangements earlier in the chapter, it can be tricky to force Windows XP to use a particular video display card as the secondary display. If a display card isn't disabled from running in VGA mode, the computer runs the card's Power-On Self Test (POST). When that happens, Windows XP assigns it primary display status; if the other card's VGA mode can't be disabled, you will not be able to use the secondary card. Most users will want to keep their first video card as the primary display, so they need to know how to prevent the POST from happening.

Generally, dual-display works best when one video card is AGP and one is PCI. However, this doesn't guarantee that the faster AGP video card will wind up being your primary display. You may need to set the system BIOS option for default video to PCI to enable an AGP+PCI dual display to work properly.

If your video card has a jumper block or switch that can be used to disable VGA mode, this option will make it easier to use the card as a secondary card, since only the primary card needs VGA mode. VGA mode is used for the system's power-on self-test (POST) and to display startup options before the Windows GUI is initialized.

Many systems with on-board video automatically disable the on-board video when you install a PCI or AGP video card, making it necessary to install two video cards (or a multimonitor video card) if you want multiple monitor support.

Generally, you can't tell if a secondary card will work until after you boot Windows XP with the secondary card in place, the system detects it and installs the drivers, and the system tries to initialize the card. If the card is initialized successfully, you should see the Windows desktop on both screens. If the secondary monitor's screen stays black, check the Device Manager listing for the video card. If the card is listed with a yellow exclamation mark, it's not working properly. A Code 10 error on the card's properties sheet's General tab indicates the card was unable to start. Restart the system and change the default display setting in the BIOS and retry it. If necessary, try a different slot for the card.

ALTERED BIOS SETTINGS PREVENT COMPUTER FROM BOOTING

I've altered my BIOS settings, and now the computer won't start.

Today's computer BIOSes have *so* many arcane settings that it's quite possible to alter one that will prevent proper booting. Before you futz with the advanced CMOS settings (not just the simple stuff like time, date, boot order, power settings, ports, and such), read the manual that came with the computer or motherboard. If you decide to change something, write down the old value before doing so. When in doubt, don't alter advanced CMOS settings that affect how the chip set works, whether and where the BIOS and video shadowing is done, and so on. The default settings are designed by the motherboard maker to work under most situations and operating systems. Because Windows is the most popular operating system, you can bet it was already tested and configured for Windows 9x, NT, 2000 or XP (unless you have a very old motherboard).

That said, what do you do if you've changed something in the CMOS and now the computer won't boot? You can try the computer's or motherboard's manual or Web site for information about settings for Windows XP. If you find nothing, then you should wind back the settings to the factory defaults. Most CMOS setups have a "Set to Default" or similar command you can issue. This should get you out of most any jam.

The Set to Default option also might be a good course to take if you make CMOS settings that prevent your computer from booting and you can't remember how to undo the changes. The Default settings are usually conservative enough to work under most circumstances.

If what you've done has changed the hard disk "Type," or if you manually entered the number of sectors, tracks, platters, and so on, and now it won't boot, use the Auto Detect Hard Disk BIOS setting to discover and enter those numbers automatically (this is known as *drive autotyping*).

NEW HARDWARE DOESN'T WORK

I've added some hardware, but it doesn't work.

Try these steps, in this order:

1. Try the troubleshooters included in the Help system, assuming the hardware fits into one of the neatly packaged categories. Open them through the Help and Support page as described above.
2. Try rebooting Windows XP.
3. Use the Computer Management Console and the Device Manager to check resources assigned to the hardware to be sure that it's not conflicting. Check the hardware's manual to determine whether you should be setting some DIP switches or jumpers on it to avoid conflicts if the device isn't a Plug and Play device.
4. Open the Device Manager, locate the device's entry, and press the Delete key to remove the entry. Then, power down, remove the device, and restart Windows.
5. Power down again, add the hardware again (running the Add Hardware applet if the hardware isn't detected at bootup), and configure as necessary.
6. Check Google; search to see whether anyone else has written about the problem and its solution.
7. Check the manufacturer's Web site. If it has a Knowledge Base feature, search that.

8. If you purchased the hardware from a local store, contact them for assistance.

9. Contact the manufacturer via email or phone.

TIPS FROM THE WINDOWS PROS: UPGRADING AND OPTIMIZING YOUR COMPUTER

Following are several tips I've learned over the years that will help save you hours of headaches.

MAKE THE MOVE TO PCI CARDS

Even if your system still has one or more ISA slots and you have cards to match, it's time to retire this 1984-vintage technology and switch to PCI cards. Here are a few of the reasons why:

- Most recent systems support PCI IRQ steering, which enables multiple PCI devices to share a single IRQ without conflicts. However, if an ISA card uses an IRQ, it usually can't be shared with any other card, ISA or PCI. A single ISA sound card, for example, might use two IRQs, preventing any other device from using those IRQs. The ISA cards in your system could literally prevent you from installing other cards, no matter how many free slots you have.

- ISA cards are much slower than PCI cards, and require much more CPU attention. The result? Your system is a lot slower than it needs to be.

- ISA cards don't support recent technologies that are now common with PCI cards. Here are just a couple of examples: If you want Fast Ethernet's 100Mbps network speed, you can't achieve it with an ISA card. Want Dolby Digital 5.1 sound for your DVD movies? Forget that old ISA sound card; only some top-of-the-line PCI sound cards support it.

Use the Device Manager to uninstall your old card, shut down your machine, and remove it before you install a PCI card to replace it. If you're changing motherboards, keep in mind that many recent motherboards have on-board sound and many also have a built-in modem, Ethernet, FireWire, and USB ports as well.

KEEP YOUR EYES ON THE HARDWARE COMPATIBILITY LIST

If you've been accustomed to thumbing your nose at Microsoft's Hardware Compatibility Listing because you've been using Windows 9x, it's time to reform your behavior. In a pinch, Windows 9x could use older Windows drivers and could even load MS-DOS device drivers to make older hardware work correctly. Windows XP, like other NT-based versions of Windows, has done away with AUTOEXEC.BAT and CONFIG.SYS, so you can't use DOS-based drivers anymore. And, while Windows XP can use some Windows 2000 drivers in an emergency, you're much better off with drivers made especially for Windows XP.

You can view the online version of the HCL by setting your browser to

www.microsoft.com/hcl

The HCL also offers links to let you download drivers from either Microsoft or the manufacturer's Web site.

NOTE

There is a difference between the Windows Catalog and Windows Hardware Compatibility List. Check the Hardware Compatibility List first, as it contains just unbiased, straightforward lists of compatible hardware—"just the facts, ma'am." Yes, it only lists compatibility with Windows 2000, but if a device works with Windows 2000, it works with XP. Unfortunately, Windows Catalog adds sales pitches and "featured products," whose manufacturers have paid for them to be listed. The URL windowsmarketplace. com says it all—it's more of a sales channel than an objective reference source.

TIP

Hardware failures, power failures, and human errors can prevent Windows XP from starting successfully. Recovery is easier if you know the configuration of each computer and its history and if you back up critical system files when making changes to your Windows XP configuration.

A good hedge against this problem is to create a technical reference library for all your hardware and software documentation. Your reference library should include the history of software changes and upgrades for each machine, as well as hardware settings such as those described here.

Lest this all sound too dire, remember that Windows XP has been the personal computer industry's mainstream operating system for more than two years now, so virtually all newly manufactured hardware has XP support. It might not have been tested and approved by Microsoft, but at least the motivation to make it work is there.

CHAPTER 281

MULTIBOOTING WINDOWS XP WITH OTHER OPERATING SYSTEMS

In this chapter

WHY MULTIBOOT?

In today's world of advanced operating systems and low hard disk prices, it certainly is not uncommon for many users to want to experiment with different operating systems. The world of consumer computing is ripe with many options. With the proliferation of the Internet and its accompanying high-bandwidth needs, whole operating systems are available for free download, in particular numerous versions of the Unix and Linux operating systems.

Along with just plain curiosity and experimentation, here are some other good reasons for wanting to switch between operating systems:

- Many users use two or more operating systems because of application compatibility issues. Hardware support issues arise too: Windows 98 might have drivers for old hardware that Windows XP doesn't support. And I know people who still have to use some old and esoteric hardware devices that work only under MS-DOS.

- Some users want to run specific applications or games in the optimal environment.

- A developer might swap between Windows XP and Windows 9x or NT 4.0 to test application compatibility.

- Web site developers need to use different OS versions to see how their pages look with the corresponding different Web browser versions.

- As an author, I need several operating systems functioning on a single computer to meet my testing and writing needs.

Other than buying multiple computers, there are two ways of accommodating these needs. You can multiboot—that is, select your desired operating system at bootup time. Or you can run another operating system in a "virtual" computer—that is, in a special application program that lets the alternative OS think it's running on a PC of its own. The virtual approach is very useful, and we'll cover it later in the chapter.

NOTE

> You should read, or at least skim, this entire chapter before beginning to implement a complex multiboot arrangement. We have not reiterated some considerations under each scenario. Pay particular attention to the issues of file formats, as well as applications and data sharing between operating systems. Then, be sure to see "Tips from the Windows Pros: Living with More Than One OS" at the end of the chapter, which covers third-party multiboot solutions.
>
> And although this chapter provides some solid fundamentals, an in-depth discussion of the topic could—and, in fact, does—fill an entire book. For additional details on setting up multiboot scenarios, we recommend you pick up a copy of *The Multi-Boot Configuration Handbook*, published by Que.

28

Windows XP Home Edition directly supports multibooting with the following operating systems:

- Windows XP Professional and Windows 2000 Professional
- Windows NT 3.51 or Windows NT 4.0
- Windows 95 and Windows 98
- Windows 3.1 or Windows for Workgroups 3.11
- MS-DOS
- OS/2

Multibooting with Unix and Linux is also possible, although it takes some extra effort.

PREPARATION

As discussed in Chapter 2, "Getting Your Hardware and Software Ready for Windows XP" and Chapter 3, "Installing Windows XP Home," it is certainly possible, with a bit of work, to run multiple operating systems on your Windows XP Home Edition computer. Whatever the operating system on your machine at the moment, you've no doubt spent hours and hours fine-tuning it and learning all the little quirks, and you probably have all the settings, applications, and data files arranged to your liking. Well, take heart—you can probably make it live harmoniously with Windows XP.

CAUTION

> Installing a new operating system is not always a smooth procedure, as you probably know. I strongly recommend that you create a backup before you install another operating system on your computer. That way, you can revert to it in case of catastrophe.

Depending on your current or planned system, running multiple operating systems can be as simple as installing your new copy of Windows XP alongside your current operating system. But if you're like me, that will not be the perfect choice. Either way, I'll try to cover all the common methods so you can make the choice that's right for you. After all, if you were the type who settles for things the way they were, you would skip this chapter because a single operating system would be all you need.

FILE SYSTEM SPECIFICS

Your goal in creating a multiboot system is to have all the operating systems coexist in such a manner that they will be capable of sharing files with each other. Nothing is more frustrating than realizing that you must reboot to retrieve a file, copy it to a floppy, and reboot again to copy it into your other operating system. A little bit of knowledge about file systems can save you many headaches down the road.

Not all operating systems use hard disks in the same manner. Several different *file system* formats are available, which determine how file space is allocated, where directory information is stored, and so on. The problem is that each operating system has its own list of

28

support file system types. Table 28.1 lists the various file systems supported by the operating systems discussed in this chapter. Note that in the table, RO stands for read-only, RW stands for read/write, and NS stands for not supported. Be sure to read the footnotes for any operating system you want to use.

TABLE 28.1   RELATIONSHIPS BETWEEN FILE SYSTEMS AND OPERATING SYSTEMS

	FAT16	FAT32	NTFS4	NTFS5	Extended2
MS-DOS 6.22	RW	—	—	—	—
Windows 95	RW	NS	RO[1]	RO[1]	RO[2]
Windows 95b	RW	RW	RO[1]	RO[1]	RO[2]
Windows 98	RW	RW	RO[1]	RO[1]	RO[2]
Windows NT 4.0	RW	NS[3]	RW[4]	RW[4]	RO[6]
Windows 2000	RW	RW	RW[7]	RW	RO[6]
Windows XP	RW[5]	RW	RW[7]	RW	RO[6]
Linux	RW	RW	RO[8]	RW	

1. *Windows Me/9x can read the NTFS file system via a free utility called NTFS For Windows 98. Although NTFSFW98 is read-only, it works very well and is highly recommended. A version with limited write capability can be purchased. You can obtain these products from* `http://www.sysinternals.com`.
2. *Windows Me/9x can gain read-only access to Linux's extended2 file system by using the free utility FSDEXT2. This utility can be found at* `http://www.yipton.demon.co.uk`.
3. *You can use the FAT32 utility for Windows NT 4.0 to read and write to FAT32 file systems from Windows NT 4.0. This utility can be obtained from* `http://www.sysinternals.com`. *This utility is not free.*
4. *If an NTFS partition is to be shared with Windows 2000 or XP, you must use Windows NT 4.0 Service Pack 4 or later.*
5. *You can't format a new partition with FAT16 during XP's installation process or disk manager. Another OS must create it.*
6. *Windows NT 4.0 and Windows 2000 can read extended file systems by using the free utility Explore2FS. This utility can be found at* `http://uranus.it.swin.edu.au/~jn/linux/explore2fs.htm`.
7. *Windows 2000 and XP automatically convert NTFS version 4 volumes to NTFS version 5.*
8. *Although the Linux kernel from 2.2.x on up provide a read/write driver for NTFS, you should use the driver only in read-only mode. The write portion of the NTFS driver is still in the very early stages of development and is safe to use only under very limited circumstances (see* `linux-ntfs.sourceforge.net`).

Understanding the interplay between these various file systems is key in creating an efficient multiboot system. To the extent possible, you should choose a format that's compatible with all the operating systems you'll want to use, on at least one disk partition. This will provide a place to store files that can be read no matter which OS you're using.

When you have the choice of several candidate file systems, you must decide which is best, based on your hardware and the application for which you are creating your multiboot system. The following sections quickly recap file system descriptions, with an eye toward multibooting issues.

FAT16

FAT16 is the oldest file system mentioned in this chapter. It was originally intended for file systems based on the DOS operating system. As such, it is quite antiquated and not often used today. FAT16 might be your only choice in some situations due to its two major advantages:

- FAT16 is supported by almost all operating systems, including all versions of Windows, OS/2, MS-DOS, and Linux. FAT16 is the only format supported by MS-DOS 6.22 and earlier.
- The structure of the FAT16 file system is much simpler than the others, giving it much less software overhead. This gives FAT16 increased speed on volumes less than 1GB in size.

One big limitation of FAT16 is the fact that it cannot be installed in partitions greater than 2GB in size. Also, the larger the partition, the less efficient FAT16 is in allocating space to small files, so more disk space is wasted. As explained later in the chapter, this limitation has been overcome by FAT16's new brother, FAT32.

> **NOTE**
>
> If you are using the first edition of Windows 95, you can use only the FAT16 file system. Versions of Windows 95 prior to Windows 95 OSR2 cannot use FAT32 partitions. A prompt upgrade to Windows 98 is recommended for this, as well as for many other reasons.
>
> Also, keep in mind that Microsoft frequently uses the term *FAT* to refer to both FAT16 and FAT32 file systems. The Disk Management program, in particular, formats hard drive partitions only with FAT32, not FAT16.

FAT32

The FAT32 file system was introduced with Windows 95 OSR2. FAT32 was essentially the answer to most of the shortcomings of FAT16. The following are among FAT32's strengths:

- FAT32 supports partitions up to 2TB in size (that's 2,048GB to you and me).
- FAT32 increased the number of clusters (decreasing the cluster size) on the hard disk, making the storage of small files take up less room than it did previously with FAT16.
- The structure of FAT32 remains very small, providing a notable speed increase over FAT16.

28

Of course, with all change comes pain and compatibility issues. To this day, Windows NT 4.0 does not natively support FAT32. The addition of FAT32 file support into Windows 2000 and XP is a welcome one, especially for multibooting users. However, neither FAT versions support the advanced security and reliability features of NTFS, as explained in the following section.

The versions of MS-DOS that runs underneath Windows 95 OSR2, 98, and Me can read and write FAT32 partitions, so you can use the Command Line mode of these operating systems if you need MS-DOS access to FAT32 partitions. The standalone versions of MS-DOS up to and including Version 6.22 cannot use FAT32 partitions.

NTFS

The New Technology File System, or NTFS, brought with it many welcome additions to the world of Microsoft computing, including the following:

- **Permissions**—NTFS brought with it a concept used in the Novell and Unix worlds for quite some time. Permissions enable you to configure files and folders to be accessible only by specific people, groups of people, or both. This is imperative for networked multiuser operating systems.

- **Compression**—You can transparently compress folders or files on an NTFS volume.

- **Reliability**—NTFS is much more reliable, and as such is suited to a server environment. Disk repair applications seldom need to be run on an NTFS file system.

- **Quicker access of large volumes with NTFS**—Although FAT still rules the below-1GB world, NTFS excels at accessing files and folders in very large disk partitions.

A disadvantage of NTFS is that it can't be read directly by DOS, OS/2, Unix, or Windows Me/9x. You can download a free utility to read NTFS disks from http://www. sysinternals.com, and can purchase a program with limited writing capability. Still, this isn't as straightforward as having support built into the operating system. Likewise, Linux has only limited support for NTFS—reading works but writing is dangerous. So, NTFS is not a generally useful format for a *shared* partition on multiboot systems.

> **NOTE**
>
> By the way, there now are two versions of NTFS: versions 4 and 5. Version 4 was used by Windows NT version 4.0. The updated version 5 is used by Windows 2000 and XP and supports additional capabilities, such as encrypted files and dynamic disk partitions that can be rearranged while Windows is running. These capabilities aren't directly accessible with XP Home Edition, but Home Edition still uses the newer disk format.
>
> The version difference will affect you only if you share an NTFS-formatted disk volume between Windows NT 4.0 and Windows XP or 2000. The newer OSes will update your NTFS partitions to version 5, so you must update Windows NT 4.0 to service pack 4 or later so that it can read the new format.

28

APPLICATION CONSIDERATIONS

Along with all the file system considerations of a multiboot system, application installation problems also can arise unless you install each operating system and its applications in a separate partition. This is particularly true of the Microsoft operating systems because some of them share some of the same fixed directory names ("Program Files" is a notable example). Because of these potential problems, the following list of precautions is particularly useful:

- It's good practice to isolate operating systems whenever possible to minimize the impact of any catastrophic events, such as system crashes, crunched file allocation tables, or applications that run amok. In other words, good disk partitioning is one way to increase protection for all the operating systems you run.

- Putting different OSes on separate partitions minimizes the chances that applications running on the different platforms will dump on one another's settings in unexpected ways.

- Many applications install files in the Windows or other common folders, and you must reinstall these applications under each OS to ensure that all files are copied where necessary. If you can tolerate the trouble, it's best to install the application into a different folder (on a different partition) each time. A common "Program Files" folder shared by multiple OSes brings the chance that OS-specific settings might give you trouble with other OSes.

NOTE

> That last bit of advice is a contentious one. Even your authors disagree. Bob thinks it's usually safe to use a single folder for an application's common files, and that it saves disk space, whereas Brian thinks that disk space is cheap, and having to chase down installation conflicts is an expensive waste of time. You might have to decide on a case-by-case basis after some experimentation.

If you find that an application acts erratically when installed into the same folder on several different OSes, reinstall it into a separate directory from each operating system. That is, install it onto the separate OS-specific partitions, or create a special application folder for each operating system (for example, \program files\win98\badapp and \program files\winXP\badapp, and so on) and install the problem applications there.

THE WINDOWS XP BOOT LOADER

As mentioned earlier in this chapter, one of the great advantages of the approaches we're advocating in this chapter is that we're using the Windows XP boot loader. It gives you a menuing system that lets you choose which OS to start every time you boot up your computer. The following sections explain the functioning of the boot loader.

28

The Master Boot Record

The *master boot record (MBR)* is the portion of the disk that tells your computer where to find the partition boot sector. All operating systems must be started up by some type of master boot record, whether this contains the system's native code or a multiboot utility. When your system is booted, a chain of events ensues, based on your currently installed operating systems. The following is a simplified version of this chain of events for a single-operating system setup containing only Windows XP:

1. After POST (power on self test), the system BIOS reads the master boot record.

2. Control is passed to the master boot record, which then looks for the partition listed as the "active partition" in the partition table of the startup disk, as defined in your BIOS.

3. After the active partition is found, the master boot record loads sector 0, the partition's boot sector, into memory and executes it.

4. The partition boot sector points to NTLDR (NT loader) in the root of the partition and executes that.

5. NTLDR reads the contents of BOOT.INI, located in the partition's root folder. BOOT.INI lists the locations and names of the computer's bootable operating system(s). If more than one OS is listed, NTLDR displays a menu of OS choices. If only one is listed, which is the usual case, NTLDR fires it up directly.

At this point, the user can select the operating system to boot up. Windows 2000 and NT use this same system. In the next few sections, we'll explain how to set up multiple operating systems so they all end up as choices in BOOT.INI.

 If you are having problems with the Windows boot loader, see "Boot Menu Isn't Displayed" in the "Troubleshooting" section at the end of this chapter.

 If you want to remove the Windows boot loader, see "Removing the Windows 2000 Boot Loader" in the "Troubleshooting" section at the end of this chapter.

The BOOT.INI Settings File

BOOT.INI handles many options for booting your system. For now, you can see your current BOOT.INI by selecting Start, Run and entering **notepad C:\boot.ini**.

> **NOTE**
>
> BOOT.INI is marked as a Hidden, Read-Only System file. If you need to change this, see "Installing Windows XP Home Edition into the Second Partition," later in this chapter.

The BOOT.INI file has two sections.

THE [boot loader] SECTION

This section defines two specific settings:

- **Timeout**—This setting defines how long the system will wait until it boots into the default operating system. This value is in seconds. A value of –1 makes the system wait indefinitely until you make a manual selection. A value of 0 makes the system immediately boot into the default operating system.
- **Default**—This is the default operating system that will boot up, unless there is user intervention. The value of the Default entry must match the *location* part of one of the operating systems entries, which are described in the next section.

THE [operating systems] SECTION

This section contains a list of operating systems installed on your computer. You can see the option for Windows XP in your BOOT.INI file if you've successfully completed an installation.

Each entry in this section is of the form

location="OS Name" */options*

where `location` specifies the drive and folder on which the operating system is stored, "OS Name" is a text description of the OS, and *options* is an optional list of operating system load modifiers. For Windows NT, 2000, XP Home Edition and Windows XP Professional, an entry might look like this:

```
multi(0)disk(0)rdisk(0)partition(1)\WINDOWS="Windows XP Home Edition"
```

(This strange format is a throwback from the days when Windows NT ran on the Alpha and MIPS processors. The format for Windows XP 64-bit Edition is different, and equally obtuse.) In most setups, the rdisk number indicates the physical hard drive (0 = first), and `partition` indicates the partition number on the drive (1 = first). The entry is followed by a folder name.

TIP

> For a listing of the /options permitted in BOOT.INI, check out http://labmice.
> techtarget.com/windows2000/install/bootini.htm and http://
> appdeploy.com/tips/bootiniswitches.shtml.

Non–NT-based operating systems are loaded through files that contain images of the master boot record that the OS is usually loaded by. For example, if you install Windows XP over MS-DOS, the original MS-DOS boot sector will be saved in a file, and the resulting BOOT.INI entry is

```
C:\ ="MS-DOS"
```

28

MULTIBOOT SCENARIOS

The possibilities for multibooting are nearly endless when you consider that a system can have multiple drives, each drive can have multiple partitions, and each partition can have an operating system on it. However, the scenarios discussed next represent the most common and usable configurations. When you understand the scenarios offered here, you should be able to effectively conquer any multiboot setup.

We recommend that you at least read through the first scenario fully, regardless of your own designs. This will give you a better understanding of the overall process. We'll also refer to that scenario so we can reduce repetition. All these configurations assume that you already have a working computer with at least a CD-ROM drive and hard disk.

NOTE

Always be careful to consider file-system compatibility between all these operating systems. Use Table 28.1 as a reference before forging ahead with your installations. This will save you many of the common problems associated with setting up a multiboot system.

TIP

All the following scenarios work on the assumption that you are able to boot from your CD-ROM drive. Most modern computers have this capability. A little-known fact is that some of the older operating systems in these examples are capable of booting from their respective CD-ROM installation discs. Windows NT 4.0, 2000, and XP can and will boot from your CD-ROM drive, as will OEM versions of Windows 98 and most modern versions of Linux. This method is much quicker and less error-prone than the traditional method of booting from a floppy disk.

Booting from the CD-ROM is usually enabled simply by changing the boot sequence from within your system's BIOS so that it checks the CD for an operating system before checking the hard drive. Consult your computer's operating manual for the proper method to enable this feature for your specific system BIOS. Chapter 3 has more ideas on how to boot from a CD-ROM in case you're having trouble in this department. Look for the troubleshooting tip at the end of the chapter titled "DOS Won't Recognize the CD-ROM Drive."

DUAL-BOOTING WINDOWS XP HOME EDITION AND WINDOWS ME/9X

Many people want or need to run Windows XP and Windows Me, 95, or 98 in the same computer. Because the Windows 95, 98, and Me behave almost identically in this situation, for the remainder of this section, I'll use 9x to refer to all three of these older versions.

The following sections discuss two ways of dual booting:

- In the same partition
- In separate partitions

PUTTING WINDOWS XP HOME EDITION AND WINDOWS 9X IN THE SAME PARTITION

If you already have a Windows 95/98 installation, you can install Windows XP beside it for a dual-boot arrangement from the same partition. I don't recommend this setup, however. Because this arrangement will mix Windows XP and Windows 9x programs in one \Program Files folder, you could end up with serious software version conflicts, such as

- Dual-booting Windows XP and Windows 9x from the same partition is ill-advised. In this configuration, for example, both operating systems use the same Program Files folder, which can result in version conflicts.

- Be aware, also, that Registry settings for an application on Windows 9x do not follow you into the Registry of Windows XP, and vice versa. You might have to reinstall some applications for them to function correctly in both operating systems. In some instances, you might even have to purchase separate Windows 9x- or Windows XP-specific versions of some applications. Finding out which ones you need to do this with is simply a matter of experimenting with each respective operating system.

TIP

> Don't worry about the Registries from the two OSes stepping on each other. Windows 9x stores user Registry information in \Windows or \windows\profiles, whereas Windows XP stores user Registry data in \Documents and Settings\<username>.

Despite this, if it's absolutely necessary, you can follow these steps to install both Windows XP and 9x on the same partition:

1. Assuming you have successfully installed Windows 98 or 95 on your system, begin the Windows XP installation wizard by inserting the CD-ROM.

2. If the wizard does not autorun, you can initialize it by choosing Start, Run and then typing `D:\i386\winnt32`, where D: is the letter of your CD-ROM drive.

3. After Windows Setup has launched, select New Installation as the Installation Type. This installs Windows XP into a new system folder called \WINNT. From here, simply continue the Windows XP installation as usual.

4. When asked if you want to update your hard drive to use the NTFS format, choose No (leave the partition alone). If you upgraded to NTFS, Windows 9x would not be able to read the disk.

5. When the Windows XP installation has concluded, you should be able to successfully boot into either Windows XP or Windows 9x using the Windows XP boot menu presented at system startup.

28

PUTTING WINDOWS XP HOME EDITION AND WINDOWS 9X IN SEPARATE PARTITIONS

As you have no doubt gathered by now, the preferred approach uses separate partitions. This arrangement is more flexible and foolproof in the long run.

First, you must plan the installation from a file system standpoint. This gives you a better foundation from which to proceed:

- The Windows 9x partition should be a FAT32 file system with `C:\WINDOWS` (the system directory), along with `C:\Program Files` contained in it.
- Windows XP will reside on the second partition, containing the Windows XP `%SystemRoot%` directory (typically `D:\WINNT`), along with `D:\Program Files`. You can format this partition with NTFS or FAT32.
- You might want to reserve a third and final FAT32 partition solely for sharing data between the two operating systems. You can use drive C for this, too, of course.

> **NOTE**
>
> Wherever I suggest that you might want multiple partitions, remember they don't all need to be placed on the same drive. You can add more hard drives and install partitions there. The setup procedure remains the same, however. Just select the additional drive when you're choosing a partition to set up, format, or install.

If you format the Windows XP partition with NTFS during installation, remember that it will not be visible to Windows 9x. Any FAT16 or FAT32 partitions located after the NTFS partition will be visible to Win9x. This can have the odd effect of making these extra partitions appear with different drive letters in the different operating systems, as each OS assigns letters to the partitions it recognizes, in order. I'll give you a concrete example of this later in the chapter under "Avoiding Drive Letter Madness."

USING FDISK TO DEFINE PARTITIONS

Chapter 3 covers the fact that Setup enables you to use unpartitioned free space to create a second partition (either NTFS or not) for installing Windows XP. You also learned about using a third-party program, such as PartitionMagic, to more flexibly help in that process, especially if you don't have any "free" (meaning unpartitioned) space on your hard disk, which is likely the case. If you already have a free partition or two for installing Windows XP after Windows 9x/Me, you can skip ahead to the section titled "Installing Windows XP Home Edition into the Second Partition." If you need to define partitions before starting the Windows XP setup process (for example, to set up versions of Windows 9x or other operating systems), this section will give you an overview of the FDISK partitioning program that comes with DOS and Windows 9x.

> Using the FDISK editor is a permanent process. If you have any disk partitions currently defined on your system, be sure to have a backup of all your important data because it might be damaged in this process. Unless you are partitioning your disk for the first time, you might find PartitionMagic more suited to the task of configuring your disk partitions. PartitionMagic also has the added advantage of being capable of actually resizing your existing partitions for a maximum amount of flexibility. More information on PartitionMagic can be found at this address:
>
> http://www.symantec.com/partitionmagic

If you need to set up partitions on a new disk, in lieu of using PartitionMagic (for whatever reason), you can opt to use the trusty old Microsoft-supplied FDISK program to do the job. It works okay in a pinch (especially on an unpopulated drive or one you're going to wipe), and a knowledge of FDISK can sometimes come in handy.

The following discussion shows how to start with a blank hard disk, use FDISK to create the partitions, and then install Windows 9x and Windows XP. The following explains how to define partitions for each operating system:

1. First, boot from the Windows 9x CD-ROM and select the second option, Boot from CD-ROM. If you are booting from a floppy disk, just proceed to step 2.

2. Select Start Computer with CD-ROM Support.

3. After finally booting into DOS, run the FDISK program, which will give you the opportunity to partition your disk so that each operating system can occupy a different partition. This is simply done by typing **fdisk** at the prompt:

   A:>fdisk

4. When FDISK is loaded, you are asked whether you want to enable large disk support. Select Yes, which enables you to later format the disk with the FAT32 file system. (If you selected No here, you would only be able to create a partition of 2048MB or less using the FAT16 file system.)

5. Next, you are presented with a menu of options for partitioning your hard disk, as shown in Figure 28.1. For the purposes of this installation, select option 1—Create DOS Partition or Logical DOS Drive. This option enables you to create the first partition for installing Windows 9x.

6. Select Create Primary DOS Partition to create a bootable primary partition.

NOTE

> All Microsoft operating systems must boot from the first primary partition on the primary IDE bus. The only exclusion to this is a SCSI-based system, which must be bootable from the first primary partition of the SCSI controller-assigned boot disk. This does not mean the system and other files must be installed here; it only means that the Windows boot information must be installed in the MBR of this partition.

28

Figure 28.1
The FDISK main menu screen.

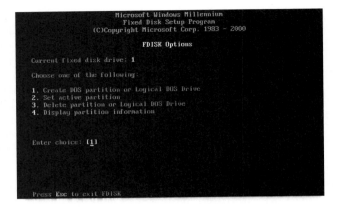

```
                    Microsoft Windows Millennium
                       Fixed Disk Setup Program
              (C)Copyright Microsoft Corp. 1983 - 2000

                            FDISK Options

   Current fixed disk drive: 1

   Choose one of the following:

   1. Create DOS partition or Logical DOS Drive
   2. Set active partition
   3. Delete partition or Logical DOS Drive
   4. Display partition information


   Enter choice: [1]



   Press Esc to exit FDISK
```

7. When asked whether you want to use the maximum available size for this partition, select No. You will need additional space to be left on the disk for the other two partitions that will house the Windows XP system and the shared data partition.

8. Next you are asked for the size of the first partition. This particular setting varies depending on the operating systems involved and the amount of disk space available.

   Table 28.2 (immediately following this set of steps) shows the minimum and recommended sizes for each operating system. You can make the partition larger than the recommended size, if you have the space.

9. Use the backspace key to erase the size that FDISK has filled in. Using the information in Table 28.2, enter the desired size for your first primary partition, in MB. For a 2GB partition, enter **2000**.

10. Next, you must define the first partition as being the *active partition* so that the computer knows from which partition it should try to boot. Press Esc to return to the main FDISK menu. Select the option 2—Set Active Partition—to pick the first partition and set it as active.

11. If you want to create the XP and data sharing partitions during the XP install procedure, you can leave the remainder of the disk unpartitioned and skip ahead to step 15.

    Otherwise, you now can create the logical partitions to house your remaining two file systems. This can be done by selecting option 1 (Create a DOS Partition or Logical DOS Drive) and then selecting option 2 (Create Extended DOS Partition).

12. FDISK adds all addition FAT partition entries inside what it calls an *extended DOS partition*. Therefore, you should allocate enough space for the extended DOS partition to hold your Windows XP volume *and* your shared data volume. If you need no other partitions, you can allocate all remaining space to the extended partition. Select a size, press Enter, and then press Esc.

13. FDISK will prompt you for the size of the first FAT partition to create inside the extended partition—FDISK calls this a *logical DOS drive*. Select a size in MB for the Windows XP partition, press Enter, and then press Esc.

28

14. FDISK will prompt you for the size of the next logical DOS drive. Allocate the remaining space to your data drive, and press Enter.

15. Press Esc to exit FDISK. Finally, press Ctrl+Alt+Delete to restart the computer.

TABLE 28.2   RECOMMENDED HARD DRIVE CAPACITY FOR EACH OPERATING SYSTEM

Operating System	Minimum Size	Recommended Size
MS-DOS 6.22	1MB	40MB
Windows 98	205MB–400MB	2000MB
Windows NT 4.0	124MB	1000MB
Windows 2000 Professional	650MB	2000MB
Windows XP Home Edition	1500MB	2000MB
Windows XP Professional	1500MB	2000MB
	135MB–1.8GB*	2000MB

Disk space requirement depends on installation options selected. Choosing both the Gnome and KDE desktop environments requires at least 1.8GB. Installing source code pushes the space requirement up quite a bit more.

INSTALLING WINDOWS 9X INTO THE FIRST PARTITION

After you've defined at least two partitions, you are ready to install Windows 9x into the first one. After that, we'll install Windows XP in the second one:

1. If you are installing Windows 9x (and you have a bootable version of the installation CD), you can install it by booting from its installation CD-ROM. Select Start Windows 9x Setup from CD-ROM.

> **NOTE**
>
> If you're having trouble accessing the CD-ROM drive, check the BIOS settings, or as a good little trick, many systems will boot up from a Windows 9x emergency startup disk with CD-ROM support (even one made on another machine). You can boot into DOS this way, with CD-ROM drivers loaded. Then, run the Setup program located on the CD.

2. When you're in the Windows 9x installation program, you will be given the option to format drive C: and continue with the installation. Setup also might require that you format partition D:. It's okay to do this.

3. Continue with the Windows 9x installation, making sure that Windows is placed in the \WINDOWS folder on the C: partition by accepting the default.

28

CAUTION

> If you've been booting from your CD-ROM installation disk, be sure to change the boot sequence in your BIOS so that your hard disk boots before your CD-ROM. This is essential for a successful installation.

TIP

> Windows 9x is installed first for a very important reason: Windows 9x always writes its own master boot record to make the system boot into it after an installation. You'll want to ensure that Windows XP has the last say in what gets installed at the master boot level so you can take advantage of its versatile boot loader.

INSTALLING WINDOWS XP HOME EDITION INTO THE SECOND PARTITION

Continue your multiboot pursuit with the installation of Windows XP. Per Microsoft's recommendations, you should run the Windows XP installation program from within Windows 9x:

1. Insert the Windows XP disc. The Windows XP Installer should autorun. If it doesn't, select Start, Run, and type **D:SETUP**, where D: is your CD-ROM drive letter.

2. Select Install Windows XP. When asked what type of installation you want to perform, select New Installation (Advanced) and click Next, as shown in Figure 28.2.

Figure 28.2
Select New Installation here to install XP into a separate partition.

3. Proceed through the License Agreement and Product Key pages to the Setup Options page. Click Advanced Options, and check I Want to Choose the Install Drive Letter and Partition During Setup. This gives you the opportunity to select the D: partition as well as convert it to the NTFS file system later in the setup. Click OK, and then click Next.

4. After the Windows Setup Wizard copies some files to your hard disk, it reboots your system and continues the installation from a text-based setup. From this setup, you have the option to select where you want to install your Windows XP system, as shown

28

in Figure 28.3. If you didn't create the XP and data partitions earlier, you can use this menu to create new partitions by pressing C. Finally, select the second partition as the Windows XP install procedure and press Enter.

Figure 28.3
Selecting the location of the \WINDOWS install directory from within the text-mode Windows XP Setup. Windows 2000 and NT Setup offer a similar choice.

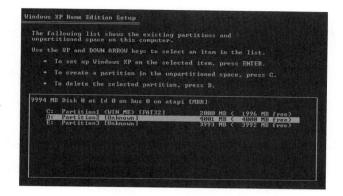

5. Next, you are given the option to select the type of file system to use. You can keep your already formatted partition intact, or you can select a new file system format, as shown in Figure 28.4.

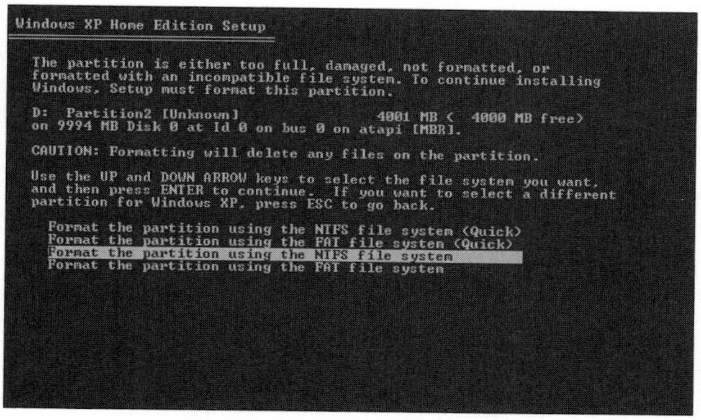

Figure 28.4
Here, you can choose to leave the original file system intact or select a different file system for the Windows XP partition.

The "Quick" versions of these choices do not test the drive as it formats. Testing takes some time, but it's worthwhile, so I recommend that you not use the Quick format options.

TIP

> Remember, you can convert a FAT partition to NTFS at any later time using a Windows command-line utility. Windows can't convert NTFS back to FAT, however. Also, remember that Windows 9x can't read NTFS partitions. If in doubt, use FAT for now.

28

6. After making your choice, Setup proceeds to do its thing and installs Windows XP. During setup one or two restarts will occur, and you'll see the Multiboot menu. Ignore it, and let the default Windows XP Setup choice start up. This choice disappears when Setup has completed successfully.

7. When you subsequently restart your computer, you should see the options shown in Figure 28.5.

Figure 28.5
The final result—The Windows XP boot loader now shows both operating systems at boot time.

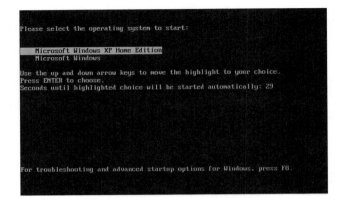

Renaming Boot Selection Choices

Wouldn't it be nice to change the boring name of your Windows 9x boot selection from Microsoft Windows to something a bit more apropos? This can be done as easily as opening the file `C:\boot.ini` from either operating system and editing the selection's name found in double quotation marks under the operating systems section.

You can do this most easily in Windows XP by opening the System control panel applet (which can be selected after selecting Performance and Maintenance from the Control Panel). Select the Advanced tab, and click Setup under Startup and Recovery. Click Edit, and you'll get BOOT.INI in a Notepad window.

If you want to edit BOOT.INI with any other editor or OS, you must first turn off the read-only attribute by right-clicking the file, selecting Properties, and unchecking the Read-Only check box. After editing this file, be sure to turn the read-only attribute back on.

To edit it from an MS-DOS command prompt, you must first type

```
attrib -s -h -r
```

to clear the read-only, system, and hidden attributes. Then, you can edit it as desired.

I would be negligent, however, if I didn't warn you that improperly editing this file can leave your system in an unbootable state. You might want to make a copy of it first, just in case. You can call it `BOOT.BAK` or something similar. Another good approach is to print a hard copy before you edit it.

FORMATTING THE DATA-SHARING PARTITION

On some of our machines, we're quite content with two partitions only, with data placed either on the Windows 9x partition or the Windows XP partition. However, I recommend using a third partition to give you a place to store files you want to keep while installing and uninstalling operating systems on the other two. I used such a partition while writing this book to hold my screen-capture program and notes; the main OS partitions needed to be erased and reinstalled dozens of times.

If you did create an extra data partition as I described in the previous section, the final installation step is to format this remaining partition. This can be done by using the Windows XP Disk Administration program or the FORMAT command from a command prompt window in either OS.

→ **See** Chapter 26, "Managing the Hard Disk," **p. 901**, for more about formatting partitions with Disk Management.

AVOIDING DRIVE LETTER MADNESS

As I mentioned earlier, when you use file formats that are not compatible among all the operating systems you're using, logical drive letters will likely shift around based on which operating system you're booting.

The reason for this is that on bootup, Windows scans your disk controllers in the following order:

1. Primary IDE Controller, Master Drive
2. Primary IDE Controller, Slave Drive
3. Secondary IDE Controller, Master Drive
4. Secondary IDE Controller, Slave Drive
5. SCSI Controllers, in SCSI ID order
6. Additional controllers (for example, USB, IEEE-1394 drives)

When it scans these, it's looking for fixed or removable hard disks. (If your computer boots from a SCSI drive, the SCSI drives are scanned first.) Only the compatible partitions on these drives are scanned, and they're assigned drive letters in the order in which they're found. Windows 9x skips over NTFS partitions and will thus assign different drive letters to any subsequent FAT partitions than Windows XP/2000/NT.

For example, if I had one hard drive with three partitions, defined as follows:

1. FAT32, Windows 98 Boot partition
2. NTFS, Windows XP Boot partition
3. FAT32, Data only

and a CD-ROM drive, Windows 98 and Windows XP would assign the default drive letters shown in Table 28.3.

28

		TABLE 28.3 LOGICAL DRIVE LETTER ASSIGNMENTS	
Drive	**Partition**	**Drive Letter Assigned by Windows 98**	**Drive Letter Assigned by Windows XP**
Hard drive	#1, FAT32	C:	C:
	#2, NTFS	(none)	D:
	#3, FAT32	D:	E:
CD-ROM	CDFS	E:	F:

Notice that under Windows 98 the data partition is D:, whereas under Windows XP it is E:. This is not a problem if you store only data on the drive. However, it becomes more complicated if your applications expect to find support files on a given drive under any OS.

You might have already thought about using Windows XP Disk Management to reassign the drive letters while Windows XP is running. Although it is true that Disk Management can set drive letters in any way you please, you can't change the boot drive's letter. In our example, this means that we can't reverse the D and E drives letters to match Windows 98.

However, there is another way. Retail copies of PartitionMagic include a program called DriveMapper that can remap the drive letters under Windows 98. You can run PartitionMagic in Windows 98, use the DriveMapper option, and reassign the data drive to E:, skipping D: altogether when you're running Windows 98. Then, you can make your CD-ROM drive F:. Now, you can have the same logical drive assignment in both operating systems.

CAUTION

> If possible, reassign letters before you install applications; otherwise, Registry settings, shortcuts, and support files can point to the wrong drive. Consult the PartitionMagic user's guide or Help file for more about considerations when reassigning drive letters.

WINDOWS XP AND MS-DOS

Hard as it is to believe, sometimes it makes sense to run plain old MS-DOS. Games are usually not the reason—most games that were designed back in the DOS days can't cope with the blazing speed of today's processors. However, some people still need to use specialized hardware that works only under DOS, such as industrial control and hardware programming systems. The software for these devices often don't work when run from an XP Command Prompt window because Windows doesn't give it the direct access to hardware it needs. So, for occasional use, you might want to run MS-DOS to perform specialized tasks.

This section discusses ways to boot your computer under DOS, so that Windows isn't running at all. You might be able to run your MS-DOS program in an *emulator*—a program that mimics a PC running DOS. This might let you run games and old DOS software without going to the trouble of booting up DOS itself, but it probably won't help you with old hardware issues, unless you can extend the emulator (the open-source DOSBOX emulator could be a candidate for extension). For a discussion of emulators, see the end of this chapter.

If your computer is set up to multiboot to Windows 95 or 98, getting to plain MS-DOS is easy. You can press F8 while one of these versions is booting and select the Command Prompt mode. Alternatively, with Windows 95 or 98 running, you can click Start, Shutdown, Exit to MS-DOS.

If Windows 95 or 98 isn't available, you have to install a version of DOS on your computer. The procedure you need to follow depends on which version of DOS you want to install. If you have a boot disk from a version of Windows 95 or 98, its version of DOS supports FAT32 partitions. In this case, you can install it on a new partition or an existing FAT32 partition, even if it's the partition from which XP boots. Use either of the two procedures that follow this section.

NOTE

You must install DOS in a partition on the first physical drive (Drive 0) in your system. It must be installed in a Primary (not logical) partition.

If you have only DOS 5–6.22, you need to install it on a FAT16 partition because these older DOS versions can't read the FAT32 format. It's best if this is a small partition set up expressly for this purpose. You can't install Windows XP on a FAT16 partition. Other OSs will be able to see this partition and copy files to and from it, so the partition needs to be only big enough to hold DOS, the DOS applications you need, and the data files. 40MB is probably enough, although your application might need more, and remember that DOS can't handle partitions larger than 2048MB. Use only the first of the two installation procedures that follow this section.

CAUTION

Windows XP can't format a FAT16 partition. To format the partition, you need to use the FORMAT program that comes with DOS. If you create the partition with the DOS FDISK program, be very careful not to delete any existing partitions. In particular, if you've already installed XP, be extremely careful if you use MS-DOS Setup disks to install DOS. The Setup program overwrites the partition information for the first drive it finds and could blow your Windows XP partition out of the water. Your best bet is to use the setup program's Install to Floppy Disk option and then copy the program and system files to the hard drive later.

28

Create a bootable DOS disk partition by performing one of the two following procedures. The procedure depends on whether the partition is the one from which Windows boots.

INSTALLING MS-DOS ON A NONBOOT PARTITION

To set up a FAT16 partition (for any version of DOS) or a FAT32 partition (for the Win95/98 versions of DOS) that no other operating system boots from, follow this procedure:

1. Shut down Windows, and boot up from a bootable DOS floppy disk.

2. Find out which drive letters are available, from C: on up, by typing **dir c:**, **dir d:** and so on. If you're installing into a new partition, the response you're looking for is `Invalid media type reading drive X`; that's your new, unformatted partition. If you're installing DOS onto an existing formatted partition, check the drives' contents to determine which drives they correspond to in Windows, and determine which is the one to use for the DOS installation. It should not be the boot drive for any other operating system.

   If no hard drive letters are defined, you need to use FDISK to allocate a partition. This procedure is beyond the scope of this book. Be very careful not to delete your XP partition. After creating the partition, reboot and repeat this step.

   NOTE

   Remember, the DOS boot partition must be on the first physical drive—drive 0—in your computer.

3. To format and install the DOS boot files on a new partition, type the command **FORMAT X: /S**, where *X* is the drive letter you chose to use for DOS. To install the DOS boot files on an existing formatted partition, just type the command **SYS X:**.

4. Copy all the files from the DOS floppy to *X*:\DOS.

5. Reboot Windows and log on as a Computer Administrator.

6. Determine the drive letter onto which the DOS files were installed. This might not be the same drive letter as under MS-DOS because DOS couldn't see your FAT32 and NTFS partitions.

7. Use Notepad to type the following text into a new file:

```
L 100 n 0 1
N C:\BOOTSECT.DOS
R BX
0
R CX
200
W
Q
```

However, in the first line, instead of *n* type the number corresponding to the drive letter you found for the DOS partition. Use 2 for C:, 3 for D:, and so on. For example, if the DOS partition is D:, the line should be `L 100 3 0 1`. (The number is entered in hexadecimal, so drive J: is 9, K: is 0A, L: is 0B, and so on.)

8. Save the file with the name **bootblock.txt**. Then, start an NT command prompt window, change directories to the location of this text file, and type the following command

```
debug <bootblock.txt
```

9. Right-click My Computer, select Properties, and select the Advanced tab. Under Startup and Recovery click Settings, and click Edit.

10. Add this line to the end of `boot.ini`:

```
C:\BOOTSECT.DOS=MS-DOS
```

11. Save *boot.ini*. Set Time to Display List of Operating Systems to a reasonable number, such as 10.

You should now be able to restart your computer and select MS-DOS. Once it's running, set up an `autoexec.bat` file and a `config.sys` file. The `config.sys` file should have at least the following:

```
device=X:\DOS\himem.sys
device=X:\DOS\emm386.exe
files=99
```

with additional commands to load a CD-ROM device driver, if necessary.

`autoexec.bat` should have at least the following:

```
@echo off
path X:\DOS
prompt $p$g
smartdrv
```

with additional commands to load a mouse driver and the CD-ROM extensions `mscdex.exe`, if necessary.

INSTALLING MS-DOS ON THE WINDOWS XP BOOT PARTITION

If your only option is to install MS-DOS on a FAT32 partition from which Windows XP boots, be sure you have a Windows XP installation CD and that you can successfully boot from it. You must use the DOS version from Windows 95 OSR2 or 98. Follow these steps:

1. Perform steps 1–4 in the procedure in the previous section. In this case, though, you'll be copying DOS to the partition from which Windows boots. The `sys` command overwrites the Windows master boot record (and the boot manager) with the MS-DOS boot program.

2. Reboot your computer from the Windows XP Setup CD-ROM.

3. Select the Repair option and then the Manual repair option. You want to perform only the Verify Boot Files step; there is no need to have the repair process inspect other files or the Windows boot environment. This reinstalls the Windows XP boot manager.

28

4. Reboot Windows and log on as a Computer Administrator.

5. Perform steps 9 through the end of the procedure in the previous section.

Windows XP Home Edition and Windows XP Professional

Installing both the Home Edition and Professional versions of Windows XP on the same system is popular for many people who need to test applications in both environments.

Because both operating system use the same boot loader and compatible file systems, installation and setup are simple. However, you must ensure that the two versions are installed on different partitions or hard drives.

To set up dual-booting of Windows XP Home Edition and XP Professional, simply install them both one after the other, taking care to click the Advanced Options button on the Special Options page during setup. Check I Want to Choose the Install Drive Letter and Partition During Setup; then click OK. This will let you select the partition on which each version gets installed.

Windows XP and Linux

Using both Windows XP and Linux on the same system is a very rewarding multiboot scenario. This gives you two very powerful operating systems that can work in harmony on the same system. Linux can be booted from any type of partition on any installed disk, be it primary or logical. This enables you to create a Linux partition anywhere you have enough space to put it.

One of the great advantages of this configuration is Linux's capability to read, and sometimes write, nearly every file system under the sun. You'll be able to share files between your two systems with a minimal amount of hassle. Be sure to refer to Table 28.1 (earlier in this chapter) to properly plan for file sharing between both operating systems.

NOTE

> Linux can read NTFS partitions quite well. But with the current level of NTFS support, when Linux writes to an NTFS partition, it causes some repairable damage to the file system that Windows XP has to fix the next time it boots. This makes me nervous, so I'd suggest that you avoid the need to have Linux write to an NTFS disk. Install Windows XP in a FAT32 partition, or use a third FAT16 or FAT32 partition to store common files.

28

LILO, the Linux Loader

Just as Windows XP uses the Windows loader to select an operating system and boot up, Linux uses a boot loader as well. Linux users have several to choose from: the LInux

LOader (LILO), GNU GRUB, SYSLINUX, and LOADLIN. This chapter discusses just LILO.

However, configuring LILO is beyond the scope of this book. I'll discuss a multibooting setup that uses the Windows loader, so if you're following these instructions it's important that whatever process you use to set up your system, you end up with the Windows loader on your primary disk's MBR, rather than LILO.

Here are the two ways to make sure this happens:

- If you install Linux first, and then Windows XP, the XP loader replaces LILO. Then, you can use the procedure described later in this section to create a Linux boot file for the Windows loader.

- If you install XP first, then Linux, you'll have to take care to tell the Linux installation system not to put LILO on your computer's MBR. If it does, the XP loader will be overwritten. How you specify this differs from one Linux distribution to another, and it might even differ between versions of the same distribution. In the instructions later in this section, I'll describe how to do this for Red Hat Linux version 7.1, but the procedure might be different for your copy of Linux. If the XP boot loader does get overwritten, you'll find out quickly: You won't get a boot choice menu. You'll have to follow the procedure under "Boot Menu Isn't Displayed" in the "Troubleshooting" section at the end of this chapter.

Clearly, it's easiest and safest if you can install Linux first. If you can't, please read your Linux distribution's installation instructions carefully, and select an installation mode that does not automatically put LILO on the MBR.

 If you do accidentally overwrite the Windows Loader with LILO, see "Boot Menu Isn't Displayed" in the "Troubleshooting" section at the end of this chapter.

INSTALLING LINUX

This section deals with the task of installing Linux in a multiboot situation with Windows XP. Although a complete tutorial on the installation of Linux is out of the scope of this chapter, we will try to cover the essential points needed to make your system multibootable.

The procedures in this chapter assume that you are using Red Hat Linux version 7.1, but they should be similar for more recent versions and for other Linux distributions. For the purposes of this example, you will be installing Linux onto a separate partition on the same disk as your Windows XP installation. Refer to Table 28.2 to be sure you have enough free space to install both Windows XP and Linux.

TIP

> If you do not have enough space in your hard drive, consider adding a second disk or using the PartitionMagic program to shrink an existing partition.

28

NOTE

Although the following information provides the basics for dual-booting Windows XP with Linux, you'll find much more detailed coverage in *The Multi-Boot Configuration Handbook*, published by Que. You should also search the Web for information about multibooting your particular version of Linux.

You can install Linux and Windows XP in either order. Just be sure to read the previous section, "LILO, the Linux Loader." If you want to use NTFS for Windows XP, be sure to leave additional room for a FAT32 partition on which to store files you want to share between the two operating systems. Refer to Table 28.2 to find the minimum amounts of space needed. If you can, allow 3 or more GB for each partition.

Then, follow your Linux version's installation procedure. When asked to choose a boot loader, select LILO and enable the option to create a boot disk (floppy).

Write down the name of the partition that contains LILO. It will be named something similar to /dev/hda1. You need to know this later when I discuss locating the Linux boot sector.

GETTING THE LINUX BOOT SECTOR

After you install Linux, you'll need to create an image or file dump of the Linux boot sector. You need this to configure the Windows XP boot loader to boot into Linux. Here's how to get it:

1. Get a blank, formatted 1.44MB floppy disk
2. Shut down and reboot your computer with the Linux boot disk discussed in the previous section.
3. When Linux has finished booting, log in as root using the password you supplied during installation. All the following steps must be performed as root.
4. Remove the boot disk, insert the formatted MS-DOS floppy into your disk drive, and type the following command:

   `mount -t msdos /dev/fd0 /mnt/floppy`

   This makes the disk available to you by mounting it in the directory /mnt/floppy.

TIP

If you need to format the floppy from within Linux, you can do so by typing the following command from the prompt:

    fdformat /dev/fd0; /sbin/mkfs -t msdos

This command gives you a freshly formatted MS-DOS disk in Linux. From there, you can simply mount the disk to get access to it.

5. The next step is to write the Linux boot sector to the disk. The most important part of this step is to be sure you take the boot sector from the correct partition. This partition

is the one that was installed in LILO during the Linux installation. If you're unsure which partition contains the Linux boot sector, issue the following command:

```
more /etc/lilo.conf
```

This gives you output similar to the following:

```
boot=/dev/hda1
map=/boot/map
install=/boot/boot.b
prompt
timeout=50
image=/boot/vmlinuz-2.4.2-2
    label=linux
    root=/dev/hda1
    read-only
```

6. The `boot=` entry at the top of the file tells you that LILO is installed in `/dev/hda1`. Using the dd program, issue the following command:

```
/bin/dd if=/dev/hda1 of=/mnt/floppy/bootsect.lnx bs=512 count=1
```

This command copies the Linux boot sector at `/dev/hda1` to a file called `bootsect.lnx` on your disk.

7. Next, unmount the floppy disk using the following command:

```
umount /dev/fd0
```

8. Finally, remove the floppy disk from your computer and reboot the system:

```
/sbin/reboot
```

If you haven't already installed Windows XP, do this now. If you created an extra partition to use for shared file storage, you can create it now, as well.

ADDING LINUX TO THE WINDOWS XP BOOT LOADER

After both Linux and Windows XP are installed, you can add Linux to the Windows XP boot loader from any version of Windows you have installed. The steps are exactly the same and are not operating system-dependent:

1. First, boot up Windows. Copy the `bootsect.lnx` file, which you created in the previous section, from your floppy disk to the root of your C: drive. This can be done from a command prompt or from the Windows Explorer. This file must be located in the root folder.

2. Modify the `BOOT.INI` file to add an entry for Linux. The easiest way is to open the System control panel applet, view the Advanced tab, select Settings under Startup and Recovery, and click Edit.

3. Next, add the following line at the end of the `BOOT.INI` file:

```
C:\bootsect.lnx="Red Hat Linux Version xxx"
```

Of course, you must substitute the appropriate Linux distribution name and version number.

28

4. You can now save BOOT.INI, reboot, and select Red Hat Linux as one of your boot menu options.

It's a long and complex procedure, but that's one of the reasons we love Linux!

Mounting Windows Disks Within Linux

Next, you'll want Linux to mount your Windows disks so that you can share files between both operating systems. This will enable you to copy files back and forth without using external media, such as floppy disks. All the following steps must be performed as root because they are system-sensitive procedures:

1. First, create the directories within which you will mount the Windows file systems. The normal Linux convention is to create these directories in the /mnt tree.

2. Issue commands to create the directories for your Windows FAT16 or FAT32 partitions:
   ```
   mkdir /mnt/windisk1
   mkdir /mnt/windisk2
   ```

   NOTE

   > These directory names are a matter of taste. You can use whatever name you feel comfortable with at this point. As long as these directories exist, your Windows partitions should mount easily.

3. To test the first mount point, attempt to mount the first FAT32 partition using this command:
   ```
   mnt -t vfat /dev/hda1 /mnt/windisk1
   ```

4. You can examine the contents of this partition by simply executing this command:
   ```
   ls /mnt/windisk1
   ```

5. If the mount was successful, you will see a familiar list of files and directories found on your first Windows partition.

6. Likewise, you can mount an NTFS partition with the following command:
   ```
   mount -t ntfs /dev/hda2 /mnt/windisk2
   ```

   You must use the correct hard drive number, of course.

   NOTE

   > By default, the NTFS file system driver is not enabled most versions of Linux. You must consult your documentation to enable this driver—that is, to have it built in to the kernel or loaded at boot time. As stated previously, if you use this driver, it is recommended that you use the read-only version.

28

Enabling these file systems to automatically mount in Linux involves a procedure that is out of the scope of this discussion. Although it is possible, only experienced Linux users should attempt to modify the system's boot time mount parameters. Typically, the changes needed to automount foreign file systems are made in /etc/fstab. Red Hat Linux includes a GUI utility, called linuxconf, that makes this task much simpler. Consult the documentation that came with your Linux distribution.

THE VIRTUAL MACHINE APPROACH

If you need access to multiple operating systems primarily for testing purposes, rather than for long periods of work, you can enjoy the use of multiple operating systems without any of the hassle of multiboot setups. In fact, you can even use multiple operating systems simultaneously on the same computer. It's done with a setup called a *virtual machine*. It's an old concept—IBM used it on its mainframes since the 1970s—making a big comeback thanks to today's fast processors and huge hard disks.

A virtual machine program emulates (simulates) in software all the hardware functions of a PC. It lets an entire operating system (called a *guest* operating system) run as an ordinary application program on a *host* operating system, such as Windows XP. Because all the hardware functions are emulated, the guest OS doesn't "know" it's not in complete control of a computer. When it attempts to physically access a hard disk, display card, network adapter, or serial port, the virtual machine program calls on the host operating system to actually carry out the operation.

Even though the software might need to execute several hundred instructions to emulate one hardware operation, the speed penalty is only 5%–10%. And, if a guest OS crashes, it doesn't take down your system. You can simply click a Reset menu choice and "reboot" the virtual machine. Check out Figure 28.6, where I have DOS, Linux, and Windows Me running in separate virtual machines.

Another advantage of the virtual machine programs currently on the market is that they don't allow the guest OS unfettered access to your real disk drives. Instead, you create a *virtual disk*, a single large file on your host operating system that contains the contents of what the virtual machine sees as a hard drive. With today's large hard drives, it's no big deal to create a 1GB or 2GB file to serve as a virtual hard drive to host Windows 95 and create another for Windows NT, and another for Linux…you get the picture.

If you make a backup copy of the file after installing a guest operating system on one of these virtual disk drives, you can return the guest OS to its original, pristine state just by copying the backup over the virtual disk file. You can even boot up a guest OS, start a bunch of applications, and save the virtual machine in this exact state. When you want to use it again, you can just fire up the whole system starting right from this point. If you're a tester or an experimenter, a virtual computer can save you hours of time installing, reinstalling, and rebooting.

28

Figure 28.6
Virtual PC running Windows Me, Linux, and DOS on three virtual machines hosted by Windows 2000.

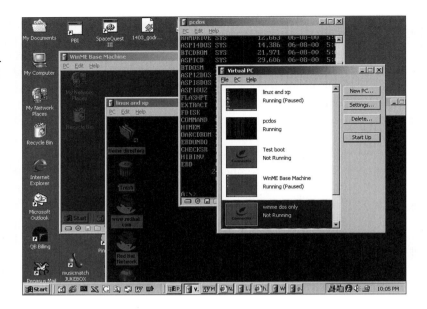

Of course, you need still separate licenses for all the extra operating systems you install, but the virtual machine can let you run as many OSes—and as many configurations of these OSes—as you like, separately or simultaneously. And all of this comes without the need to hassle with BOOT.INI or worry about partitions.

NOTE

> Have you wondered how operating system book authors get screen pictures of the bootup and installation process? In the old days, we had to use film cameras or video recorders. Now, we just use virtual PC programs and use screen capture software to get images of our desktops. It's a walk in the proverbial park.

If this sounds interesting, here are two products you should check into:

- **VMWare**—Sold by VMWare. Check out www.vmware.com. VMWare was the first commercial system to emulate a PC on a PC. (Previous PC emulators ran on other computing platforms.) It's the most industrial-strength PC emulator available.

- **Microsoft Virtual PC**—Microsoft bought this program from Connectix Corporation. Versions are available for Windows and for the Mac. Check out www.microsoft.com/virtualpc. The Windows version comes for free as part of some Microsoft Developers Network subscriptions. Unfortunately, Microsoft has, shall we say, degraded Virtual PC somewhat. The original developers are still involved with and proud of the product, and they directly communicate with users via the microsoft.public.virtualpc newsgroup, but I think marketing decisions have negatively impacted the product. In my experience, it is now slower, is buggier, and doesn't support alternative operating systems such as Linux as well as it used to (no big surprise there). And, for some unfathomable reason, Microsoft does not support using Virtual PC on Windows XP Home Edition. It does work, but if you run into trouble, you're on your own.

Both vendors have trial versions you can download and test before buying. Both also support networking, device and file sharing, and cut-and-paste capability between the host OS and several selected guest OSes.

Finally, if DOS compatibility is all you're after and the MS-DOS subsystem built in to Windows XP doesn't do an adequate job for you, check out DOSBOX, a free, open-source program available at `dosbox.sourceforge.net`. It's another "work-in-progress" program developed by a group of volunteers. DOSBOX lets you install a copy of DOS and run old games and DOS programs in an emulated environment. Because the source code for DOSBOX is freely available, there's even the potential to add support for specialized hardware devices so old DOS programs could continue to use them or use their modern replacements.

MACINTOSH AND WINDOWS

A few years ago there were several cross-platform emulation systems that let you run Windows on a Macintosh computer and several that let you run the MacOS on Windows. The pickings have gotten pretty slim in both categories, but you still have some options.

First, Microsoft Virtual PC for Macintosh lets you run Intel-based operating systems on the Mac, pretty credibly. That means your Mac can run MS-DOS, Windows XP, and Linux. Because Mac OS-X makes it is a snap to copy files to Windows-formatted floppies and to share files over a Windows network, you don't need an emulator just for file transfer anymore. But, an emulator can be a workable alternative to having two computers on your desk or giving up your Mac.

In the other direction, emulation of Macs on Windows machines is much less workable, and Apple has put great effort into making it difficult or impossible, in an effort to protect its market from knock-offs. For one thing, Macs have a large chunk of the operating system in read-only memory (ROM) chips inside each of their computers, and it's illegal to distribute this code.

One solution to this problem is to develop a from-scratch replacement for the licensed ROM code. This is the approach used by Executor, a Mac emulator produced by ARDI. Executor is a virtual Macintosh machine program for reading and writing Macintosh-formatted media and running Macintosh programs.

ARDI has implemented the core of the Macintosh operating system independently from Apple Computer, Inc. As such, Executor requires no software (or ROM chip) from Apple, which makes it the only solution for many customers who need to run Macintosh programs who don't already have a Macintosh. (Some of the other emulators require you to have an Apple ROM chip from one of their computers.)

Executor runs as a native Windows application, either in full-screen mode or in a window (see Figure 28.7). You can print from Executor to any printer your system can talk to (local printers, remote printers, faxes if you have the right software, and so on). You can cut and paste text and graphics between Executor and other applications. You also can create shortcuts for a Macintosh application so that Executor will start up and run that application.

Figure 28.7
Executor runs many Mac programs on the PC under Windows 9x, NT, 2000, and XP.

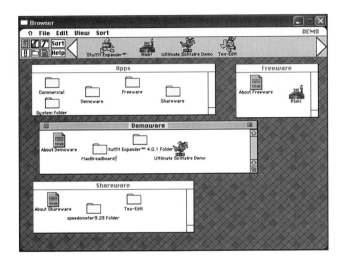

Unfortunately, Executor will not support applications that are "PowerPC-only," which is an increasing proportion. Additionally, although ARDI supports most core operating system services, INITs, CDEVs, and services added after System 7.0 are not supported. ARDI has a compatibility database on its Web site at http://www.ardi.com, which you should check if you're interested in running a particular program.

Another Mac emulator is SoftMac, from www.emulators.com/softmac.htm. It, too, emulates the Motorola 68000 processor series, so it can't run modern PowerPC-only applications, nor any MacOS version from 8.5 onward. SoftMac achieves better emulation than Executor by relying on the programs in Apple's proprietary ROM chips. If you don't have a working Mac, you can purchase a set of these chips or pull a set out of a broken Mac. You can also copy the programs out of a functioning Mac, although this is a legally dubious procedure.

Finally, you should check out PearPC, a free, open-source Power PC Mac emulator available at pearpc.sourceforge.net. PearPC is a work-in-progress, but it can reportedly run Mac OS X 10.3 (for which you must have a license, of course) with networking support on a Windows host. Be warned: this is not a commercial product, so installation and maintenance are going to be a bit on the hairy side. However, it has an enthusiastic community of users and developers, and it's constantly being improved and extended.

EMULATING OTHER COMPUTERS

Although emulation of today's Apple Macintosh computers is a shaky business at best, emulation of machines that are no longer manufactured or are no longer commercially viable is a bustling arena. Why? One word: *games*. Well, actually there are two reasons: games and historical interest.

Games are an obvious reason to emulate older computers. Many people have fond memories of computer games that ran on their old Ataris, Amigas, Apple IIs, game consoles, and other fun old machines. Today's powerful computers have no problem simulating the hardware and software behavior of these old boxes. Emulator programs like Bochs, MAME, and others re-create the early days of PCs and video games. The software for these old machines often took less disk space than one graphics-intensive email does today. So, it's no problem having the software for hundreds of games, including old operating systems, on your own disk.

The historical arena is also pretty busy. Today, you can download and run operating systems for the famous computers of the early days of computing, and you can experience what it was like to interact with groundbreaking machines like the Eniac, the IBM-360, the PDP-11, and even the Altair-8800—the first "personal" microcomputer. In fact, I wrote an emulator myself for the IBM 1130, the first computer that I ever got to program. (You just don't know how much to appreciate a Windows workstation unless you've spent some time working with punched cards.)

The operating systems and compilers of many early computer were open source—that is, they were publicly available and can legally be copied. And, many manufacturers have made early operating systems available, either through free licensing options or as public domain releases. There is also the large grey area of *abandonware*, ancient software whose manufacturers and copyright holders have completely disappeared.

For some links to interesting emulation Web sites, check out these three sites:

- `http://directory.google.com/Top/Computers/Emulators`
- `simh.trailing-edge.com`
- `www.ibm1130.org`

TROUBLESHOOTING

BOOT MENU ISN'T DISPLAYED

When I start up my PC, I don't get a choice of operating systems. Instead, an operating system boots up directly.

What has happened is that an installation program overwrote the normal XP boot loader (for example, Linux may have installed the Linux Loader LILO. The MS-DOS sys command can also do this). To restore the Windows loader, boot your computer from your

Windows XP installation CD and follow the instructions to repair a damaged Windows XP installation. The only repair options you need to select at this point are the options to repair the startup environment and the boot sector.

REMOVING THE WINDOWS XP BOOT LOADER

I want to remove the Windows XP Boot Loader. How do I do this?

This might be necessary if you have incorrectly installed an operating system and want to remove it to start over. The same process of removing the Windows XP boot loader is applicable to the Windows 2000 and NT 4.0 boot loader. If you choose to perform this step, however, you must ensure that you have an operating system to boot into. For this example, assume you have Windows 98/95 installed and want to return to a state in which it is the only operating system available.

First, while you are booted into Windows 98/95, you must create a bootable system disk. This can be accomplished by selecting the Add/Remove Programs control panel. Then, select the Startup Disk tab.

After creating a startup disk, reboot your system using the new disk. After you have fully booted into MS-DOS, simply enter the following command from the command prompt:

```
sys C:
```

This installs the Windows 98 startup boot sector onto drive C: and removes the Windows XP boot loader. Now that you're able to boot back into Windows 9x, simply remove the Windows XP directories.

You can optionally remove the following files to clean up the rest of the Windows XP boot loader files:

```
C:\boot.ini
C:\ntldr
C:\ntdetect.com
```

TIPS FROM THE WINDOWS PROS: LIVING WITH MORE THAN ONE OS

Even with all the advice in this chapter, managing more than one operating system on the same machine at the same time can be a daunting task. Fortunately, some special tools can save you in your darkest moments. (You never expected to find purple prose in a computer book, did you?)

The Windows XP multiboot loader is capable of supporting a large number of multiboot situations—probably more than will fit on the screen in a list. Still, editing the BOOT.INI file is an intimidating process, and you must remember quirky rules about the order of operating system installation.

If you're interested in loading up a killer system with three or more operating systems, we recommend using a program designed specifically for the job. I'll describe a couple of them for your consideration.

Once again, the PowerQuest people come to the rescue with its offering, called BootMagic, which is bundled with PartitionMagic and is now owned by Symantec. This program uses a graphical interface to help you set up and run multiple operating systems in the same machine, with a minimum of compatibility problems. You can run the setup interface from DOS, Windows 9x, or Windows NT/2000/XP. The program supports Windows XP/2000, Windows 95/Windows 98, Windows NT 4.0 (server and workstation), Windows NT 3.51 (server and workstation), Windows 3.x (must be installed with DOS 5 or later), MS-DOS 5.0 or later, PC-DOS 6.1 or later, Open DOS, OS/2 3.0 or later, Linux, BeOS, and most other versions of DOS and PC-compatible OSes. Check its site at www.symantec.com/partitionmagic for more information. (The Symantec purchase is worrisome because its customer support is at the abysmal end of the spectrum, but we'll see how the product fares.)

Another similar program is System Commander, from V Communications. This product has received rave reviews from some magazines. System Commander enables you to install and run any combination of PC-compatible operating systems, including Windows 95/98, Windows 3.x, Windows NT, DOS, OS/2, and all the PC-compatible Unixes including Linux. Similar to BootMagic, this program also has a graphical user interface. In addition, it does partition management such as resizing, creation, and deletion. It's available from V Communications, Inc. (check its site at www.v-com.com).

CHAPTER **29**

THE REGISTRY

In this chapter

29

WHAT IS THE REGISTRY?

The *Registry* is a database in which Windows and application programs store startup information, hardware settings, user preferences, file locations, license and registration information, last-viewed file lists, and so on. In addition, the Registry stores the *associations* between file types and the applications that use them. For example, the Registry holds the information that tells Windows to use Media Player when you click on an MPG movie file. In the early days of DOS and Windows, programs stored this kind of information in a random collection of hundreds of files scattered all over your hard disk. (Remember CONFIG.SYS?) Thankfully, those days are now only a dim memory.

Most of the time, you can get by without giving the Registry a second thought, because almost every useful Registry entry is set from a Control Panel applet, an application's preference dialog, or Windows Setup. From time to time, though, you might have to roll up your sleeves to find the location of an errant device driver, you might need to remove an unwanted startup program, or you might just be curious what kind of information Microsoft Office keeps on file about you. This chapter tells you how to go on these kinds of missions.

Two Different Views

One of the advantages of having two authors for this book is that you get two viewpoints. I (Brian) must confess I am a card-carrying Registryphobe; I think Registry tweaking is dangerous and minimally useful. As far as I'm concerned, the Registry is best left alone. I make my living programming with my computer, and the less fancy and more stable it is, the better. "Stock" is the way for me.

For my co-author Bob, who also makes his living with his computer, the Registry is a tweaker's paradise of undocumented adjustments and fascinating Windows trivia. He can change file locations, tune up networking performance, and generally adjust his computer to be "just so." To each his own! We'll both have our say here in telling you how to be careful with the Registry and in showing you how to work with it effectively.

HOW THE REGISTRY IS ORGANIZED

The Windows XP Registry leaves the plain text files of AUTOEXEC.BAT and WIN.INI far, far behind. It is a specialized database organized a lot like the files and folders on a hard disk. In fact, the Registry Editor navigates through the Registry using the same expandable list display that Windows Explorer uses to display a disk.

Just as a hard disk contains partitions, the Registry contains separate sections called *hives*. (The reason Microsoft chose the word *hive* is unclear. It had something to do with busy bees, but more than that, the folks there won't say.) In each hive is a list of named *keys* that correspond to the folders on a hard disk. Just as a file folder can contain files and yet more folders, a Registry key can contain *values*, which hold information such as numbers or text strings, and yet more keys. Even the naming of file folders and keys are similar: A folder might be named \Documents and Settings\brian\chapter29, and a Registry key might be named \HKEY_CURRENT_USER\Software\Microsoft. Let's look at the Registry, starting with its top-level keys.

The two main "top-level" keys are as follows:

- **HKEY_LOCAL_MACHINE**—Contains all the hardware and machine-specific setup information for your computer. For example, it lists every device driver to load and all your hardware's interrupt settings. It also holds software setup information that is common to all users.

- **HKEY_USERS**—Has a subkey for each user of the computer. Under each user's key, Windows stores user-specific information, such as color preferences, sounds, and the location of email files.

The Registry Editor also presents three other sections that look like separate top-level keys:

- **HKEY_CURRENT_USER**—The subsection of HKEY_USERS corresponding to the logged-on user. It holds preferences and software setup information specific to the current user, such the choice of screen saver and Office's default language.

- **HKEY_CURRENT_CONFIG**—A shortcut to HKEY_LOCAL_MACHINE\System\CurrentControlSet\Hardware Profiles\Current, contains the hardware settings specific to the hardware profile chosen when Windows was started.

- **HKEY_CLASSES_ROOT**—This Registry section stores file associations, linking file types to applications. It's a combined view of two other Registry sections: HKEY_LOCAL_MACHINE\Software\Classes, which holds settings for all users, with the addition of HKEY_CURRENT_USER\Software\Classes, which holds any personal settings stored for the current user. If the same value is defined in both HKEY_CURRENT_USER\...and HKEY_LOCAL_MACHINE, the HKEY_CURRENT_USER value is used.

In reality, these keys are views into subkeys of the first two, as illustrated in Figure 29.1.

These three "virtual" top-level keys are there for convenience—it's easier to look in HKEY_CURRENT_USER than to try to remember where to find user entries under the ugly numbered keys inside HKEY_USERS.

Within each of the top-level keys, there are several subkeys holding related information. HKEY_CURRENT_CONFIG, for example, contains two keys: Software and System. Software in turn contains two keys: Fonts and Microsoft. (By the way: with keys, just as with folders, you can spell out the full path—HKEY_CURRENT_CONFIG\Display\Settings— or just refer to Settings, if you know you're discussing HKEY_CURRENT_CONFIG\Display).

All this might seem a little daunting, but remember that the purpose of the Registry keys is to organize setup information sensibly. Instead of having this information in many mysteriously named and randomly located files, it's all here, filed away in the Registry.

Figure 29.1
The Registry is composed of two true top-level keys and three "virtual" top-level keys.

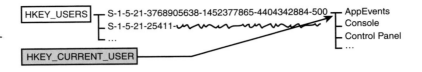

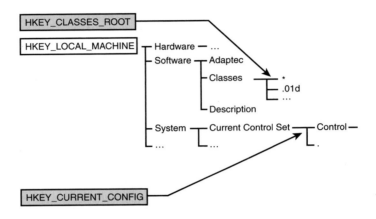

The Registry database itself is stored in several separate files, called *hives*, which I mentioned earlier. HKEY_LOCAL_MACHINE is stored in the folder \windows\system32\config, in several hive files: SAM, SECURITY, SOFTWARE, and SYSTEM. HKEY_USERS is stored with each user's subkey in a separate hive file. These are kept in each user's profile folder (\Documents and Settings*username*) as a file named NTUSER.DAT, except the "Default User" key, which is in \windows\system32\config\DEFAULT. Finally, each user has a list of keys used to add to or override HKEY_CLASSES_ROOT, which is stored in \Documents and Settings*username*\Local Settings\Application Data\Microsoft\Windows\UsrClass.dat. (If you're interested, you can see that even the information about which file supports which section is maintained in the Registry, under the key HKEY_LOCAL_MACHINE\SYSTEM\ControlSet001\Control\hivelist. Just don't try to change these values!)

You generally can't examine or modify these files directly while Windows is running because Windows maintains exclusive control of them. Backup software uses special Windows program functions to get access to back up or restore them. The exception, though, is that the NTUSER.DAT files for users not currently logged in are not locked, so they can be copied and backed up as normal files.

REGISTRY CONTENTS

What's in the Registry, anyway? There's a lot to it; many entire books have been written about it. If you want a full-blown guide to the Windows XP Registry, you might look for Microsoft's *Windows XP Resource Kit*, or check your local bookstore for other weighty tomes. Short of that (way short) I can still do a quick overview of the Registry to give you some idea of its organization and contents.

You just learned about the five main sections of the Registry. Let's go through them one by one now, and hit on some of each section's highlights.

HKEY_LOCAL_MACHINE

As you might expect, HKEY_LOCAL_MACHINE contains information specific to your computer, settings that aren't user-specific. They include hardware settings and software information that is global for all users.

The main keys in HKEY_LOCAL_MACHINE are shown in Table 29.1.

TABLE 29.1 MAIN KEYS IN HKEY_LOCAL_MACHINE

Key	Description
HARDWARE	Contains information about the computer's hardware platform and Plug and Play devices, discovered afresh each time the system is booted. No configurable settings are located here.
SAM and SECURITY	Contain the Windows Security Account Manager databases. These keys always appear to be empty because only Windows itself is allowed to read or edit the information.
SOFTWARE	Contains system-wide software settings for applications and Windows itself. The Classes subkey is special and is given its own virtual view as HKEY_CLASSES_ROOT. The other entries are generally named after software manufacturers. I'll describe some of the more interesting keys in a moment.
SYSTEM	Contains a series of numbered ControlSet entries, each of which contain the settings for hardware and system services. One of them is chosen as the CurrentControlSet subkey. As you install or remove hardware, Windows rotates through the ControlSet entries, using one as the "current control set." This way, it can keep previous versions to use as a backup.

The fun bits are in the SOFTWARE keys under HKEY_LOCAL_MACHINE. Under SOFTWARE is the special Classes subkey, which I'll describe in the HKEY_CLASSES_ROOT section of this chapter. Also, there are subkeys named after software manufacturers that contain system wide settings for these companies' various programs.

29

Under Microsoft, naturally, is a slew of subkeys for the software systems provided with Windows and for any add-ons you've purchased, such as Office. You'll have more than 100 subkeys in HKEY_LOCAL_MACHINE\Software\Microsoft just after installation and more when you start adding your own software.

Most of the juicy settings that control Windows itself are found in HKEY_LOCAL_MACHINE\Software\Microsoft\Windows\CurrentVersion.

I'll discuss just one of these juicy keys. When you log in to your computer, you know that Windows can start up some programs automatically. You can actually set a program to be started up at login in any of five ways:

- A shortcut in the Startup folder of your Start menu (in \Documents and Settings\ *yourloginname*\Start Menu\Programs\Startup)

- A shortcut in \Documents and Settings\All Users\Start Menu\Programs\Startup

- A key named Run, RunOnce, or RunOnceEx in \HKEY_LOCAL_MACHINE\ Software\Microsoft\Windows\CurrentVersion

- A key named Run, RunOnce, or RunOnceEx in \HKEY_CURRENT_USER\ Software\Microsoft\Windows\CurrentVersion

- A `run=` or `load=` entry in WIN.INI in the Windows directory (usually \windows or \winnt).

> **NOTE**
>
> To maintain compatibility with older 16-bit Windows software (and even some new software that should know better), the original Windows SYSTEM.INI and WIN.INI files still exist, and Windows XP keeps a few of their entries up-to-date with information copied from the Registry. This lets older software that really depends on the old INI file system still function. It's too bad that this old stuff is still around, but compatibility has turned out to be more important than neatness.

The Run keys are often set by software manufacturers who want their software to run automatically when you log on. Sometimes this is a good thing—as when Windows uses it to start the taskbar program. But this technique is sometimes used to install annoying programs you really don't want to run. If the programs don't have configuration or preference settings that will disable the run-on-logon behavior, you can delete their value entries under these keys.

The RunOnce and RunOnceEx keys are used mostly by installation programs that need to complete their work after you restart your computer. Windows normally deletes these entries after you've logged in once and these programs have run, but they are sometimes not properly removed.

If you're plagued by unwanted or buggy programs when you log in, see "Tracking Down Errant Startup Programs" in the "Troubleshooting" section at the end of this chapter.

HKEY_CURRENT_CONFIG

HKEY_CURRENT_CONFIG is a virtual top-level key containing information Windows uses to initialize during its bootup phase, and very little else. Despite its important-sounding name, you'll find virtually nothing of interest to humans in here. The information is all set up automatically when you create Hardware Profiles.

By *virtual*, I mean that the keys in HKEY_CURRENT_CONFIG are really contained in other parts of the Registry, and using HKEY_CURRENT_CONFIG is just a convenient way to get at them. A curious feature of this one is that its subkeys come from several different parts of the Registry. Its System\CurrentControlSet subkey comes from one of the HKEY_LOCAL_MACHINE\SYSTEM\ControlSet### keys, and various parts of its Software subkey come from other parts of HKEY_LOCAL_MACHINE. The Registry presents the information from these various keys again under HKEY_CURRENT_CONFIG as a matter of convenience.

HKEY_CLASSES_ROOT

HKEY_CLASSES_ROOT is another of these "virtual" keys, provided to give programmers quick access to information from other places in the Registry. What you see under HKEY_CLASSES_ROOT is the contents of HKEY_LOCAL_MACHINE\Software\ Classes, plus any additional user-specific settings stored under HKEY_CURRENT_USER\ Software\Classes, whose entries add to or override the HKEY_LOCAL_MACHINE entries.

A large part of the Classes section is devoted to the associations the Explorer makes between file types (or filename extensions, like .doc) and the programs that are used to open, display, or edit them. This is the information you're editing when you change associations in the Explorer by choosing Tools, Folder Options, File Types, as discussed in Chapter 21, "Tweaking the GUI."

These entries contain the nitty-gritty linkage information that Windows uses to locate software components based on ActiveX Controls, OLE, and the COM+ interprocess communication system. These entries are confusing, complex, and best left completely alone.

Table 29.2 gives an overview of the structure of HKEY_CLASSES_ROOT.

TABLE 29.2   THE STRUCTURE OF HKEY_CLASSES_ROOT

Entry	Description
`*.*` through `.zip`	For each listed file extension, the default value assigns a name to the file type. Each of these file type names appears later as a subkey of its own.
	File types that have OLE handlers have a subkey PersistentHandler, which gives a Class ID (a string of numbers like {098f2570-b…-03f3}). They are listed under the CLSID subkey, where the program file for the handler is named.

continues

29

TABLE 29.2 CONTINUED

Entry	Description
	Files that have associated programs to edit or display them also have `shell` or `shellx` subkeys, which contain the commands Explorer uses when you attempt to open a file using a double-click. This file type/application association can also be stored under a OpenWithList key, which I'll describe under HKEY_CURRENT_USER.
filetype	Each named file type (for example, VBScript) contains the CLSID number of the associated handler for the file type. Windows looks up this information through the CLSID subkey to find the associated program. File type name keys can also have `shell` or `shellx` subkeys, listing the commands used to open, edit, or print this type of file.
CLSID	Contains a subkey for each registered Active-(*something*) handler; the sub keys and values name the handler and point to the file containing its program code.

HKEY_USERS

HKEY_USERS contains a subkey for each authorized user of the computer and an entry named .DEFAULT. The .DEFAULT section contains just that—the basic settings given to each new user added to the computer.

The user subkeys of HKEY_USERS have long numeric names. These names are the GUID or Globally Unique User Identification numbers generated by Windows as a computer-friendly representation of the user's name. It's by these numbers that Windows tracks users, whether local or domain-based.

Nothing else is in HKEY_USERS besides these per-user subkeys. They appear as the contents of HKEY_CURRENT_USER and HKEY_CLASSES_ROOT when the associated user is logged in.

HKEY_CURRENT_USER

HKEY_CURRENT_USER contains settings, preferences, and other information specific to the currently logged-in user. This whole "section" is actually a subkey of HKEY_USERS, as discussed previously, but is provided this way as an easy way to get to the information.

The Software keys in HKEY_CURRENT_USER are similar to the Software subkeys in HKEY_LOCAL_MACHINE. They're grouped by software manufacturer, and Windows entries are stored in HKEY_CURRENT_USER\Software\Microsoft\Windows\CurrentVersion.

Windows has several ways to associate filename extensions with applications. Besides the .xxx and filetype keys under `HKEY_CLASSES_ROOT`, Explorer also uses `HKEY_CURRENT_USER\Software\Microsoft\Windows\CurrentVersion\Explorer\FileExts`. This Registry key holds the application associations you see when you right-click a file and see the Open with choices. Have you ever noticed that Windows remembers which application you last used to open a given file type?

Take a look under this key and you'll see subkeys of the form .xxx, listing many file extensions. Under these are subkeys named OpenWithList and OpenWithProgids. OpenWithList has values named with the letters a, b, c, and so on, each of which has as its value the path to an application program that could be used to open the file type. The value MRUList lists the letters of the applications in the order in which they were most recently used. This is why Explorer remembers which application to offer first in the list of possible choices.

BACKING UP AND RESTORING THE REGISTRY

Because the Registry is now the *one* place where all the Windows hardware and software settings are stored, it's also the one thing that Windows absolutely needs to run. You will hear dire warnings from Microsoft, other computer books, installation manuals, and now me: It's very important to back up the Registry before you edit it. If a critical entry is lost or changed incorrectly (for example, one that holds the name of a driver file for your graphics display adapter), Windows may not be able to start at all.

 If you have a Registry problem, before attempting any drastic measures, see "Recovering from a Suspected Registry Problem" in the "Troubleshooting" section at the end of this chapter.

Make it a habit to back up the Registry every time you back up your hard disk and before you install new hardware or software. I can tell you from personal experience that without a Registry backup, something as common as a bad graphics card installation program can cost you a whole day of trying to get your system to boot again! Windows XP has some built-in protection to help avoid this type of disaster, but you should still take your own precautions.

BACKING UP THE REGISTRY

You can back up the Registry in Windows XP in two main ways: You can back it up as part of a regular disk backup, or you can use the Registry Editor to save a key to a disk file. I suggest that you set your favorite disk backup program to back up the Registry files every time you back up your hard disk. Before you install a piece of new hardware or a significant software package, do a full disk backup, including the Registry. Before you manually edit the Registry for some purpose, use the Registry Editor backup technique.

In the next several sections, I'll list ways to back up the Registry before you begin making changes.

BACKING UP WITH WINDOWS BACKUP

A Backup utility is included with Windows XP Home Edition, but it isn't installed by default. I strongly recommend that you do install it if you haven't already—it's on your Windows XP Home Edition CD-ROM in the \VALUEADD\MSFT\NTBACKUP folder.

→ For more information about installing and using Windows Backup, **see** "Windows Backup Program," **p. 923**.

If you have installed Windows Backup, you can use it to back up the Registry prior to making changes. Here are the steps.

1. Open the Start menu and choose All Programs, Accessories, System Tools, Backup.

2. Click Advanced mode, and select the Backup tab.

3. Check System State as shown in Figure 29.2. If you want to back up more than just the Registry, select any other drives and/or folders you wish to back up.

4. Select a destination for the Registry backup. You can save to a tape drive, network drive, Zip disk, or to a file on your hard drive (for example, you could enter **C:\regback.bkf**). Select the desired backup destination (for example, File), and enter the desired location under Backup media or file name. Click Start Backup.

5. Click Advanced and uncheck Automatically back up System Protected Files with the System State. (This will cut the backup from more than 1GB of data down to around 10MB.) Click OK.

6. Check Replace the data on the media with this backup, and then click Start Backup.

Figure 29.2
Check System State to add the Registry to your backup set.

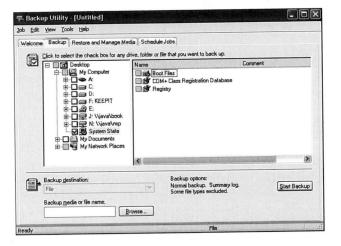

Now, with this backup on hand, if Registry problems occur after your installation, you can use the Backup utility again to restore the Registry to its previous state.

Although it's best to perform a full backup to tape, disk, or other high-capacity storage media, you can perform a quick System State backup to a local disk file in preparation for adding new hardware or software.

→ To learn more about Backup, **see** "Windows Backup Program," **p. 923**.

NOTE

> With Backup, you cannot save the System State of a remote computer, only the local computer. For remote or centralized backup services—to back up the Registries of all the computers on your network—you need to buy a third-party backup program.

BACKING UP WITH THIRD-PARTY REGISTRY BACKUP SOFTWARE

There are third-party programs specifically designed to back up and restore the Registry and other critical Windows files. For example, SuperWin's WinRescue program (www.superwin.com) cannot only back up and restore the Registry, but can defragment the Registry's files and work magic to revive a non-bootable Windows system. If you're a Registry hacker, it would be worth buying such a Registry backup tool.

These programs come with their own extensive instructions on backing up, restoring, repairing and maintaining the Registry.

You can and should also specify that the Registry is to be backed up if you use a tape backup system, or use a backup program to make backups onto another hard drive.

BACKING UP WITH REGEDIT

The Registry Editor, called Regedit, has a mechanism to export a set of Registry keys and values to a text file. If you can't or won't use a more comprehensive backup system before you manually edit the Registry, at least use this editor to select and back up the key that contains all the subkeys and values you plan to modify. This way, you can back up all the sections you plan to edit in one backup.

That way, if it's necessary later, you can restore these exported files, recovering any changed or deleted keys and values. Remember, though, that Regedit cannot remove entries you added that were not in the Registry before the backup! So, if an entry you add causes problems, the Registry Editor backup will not help you recover.

To back up a key and its subkeys and values, follow these steps:

1. To run Regedit, choose Start, Run. Type **regedit** and click OK.
2. Select the key you plan to modify, or a key containing all the keys you plan to modify, in the left pane.
3. Select File, Export (see Figure 29.3).
4. Choose a location and filename to use to store the Registry keys. I usually use the Desktop for temporary files like this, so I'll see them and delete them later.

Figure 29.3
You can save a Registry key and any keys and values it contains with Regedit.

TIP

> I recommend *not* using the default extension .REG when you're creating a Registry backup. This extension is associated with Registry entries in the Windows Explorer, and selecting a REG file in Explorer instantly and silently restores it to the Registry. This operation is far too serious to have happen with just a mouse click or two.
>
> I do use the .REG extension for files that I use to contain specific, always-wanted Registry entries. For example, in the tip described at the end of the chapter, I put a single Registry entry in a .REG file so that it can be installed easily.

5. Select All Files from the Save As Type list, and enter a name with an extension other than .reg—for example, c:\before.sav.

6. Click Save. The chosen key or keys are then saved as a text file.

TIP

> You can use this technique to copy a set of keys and values from one section of the Registry to another. First, export the desired key and values to a file. Edit the file with Notepad, and use the Edit/Replace feature to change all of the key names to the desired new location. Then import the file back into the Registry. I have used this method to copy a group of Registry entries under HKEY_CURRENT_USER to HKEY_USERS\.Default, for example, so that all newly created user accounts will have the desired setting.

RESTORING THE REGISTRY

If you've made Registry changes that cause problems, you can try to remember each and every change you made, re-enter the original information, delete any keys you added, and thus undo the changes manually. Good luck! If you were diligent and made a backup before you started, however, you can simply restore the backup and have confidence that the recovery is complete and accurate.

 If you think you have Registry problems, see "Signs of Registry Problems" in the "Troubleshooting" section at the end of this chapter.

To restore a Registry backup you made, follow the steps described in the following sections.

RESTORING THE REGISTRY WITH DRIVER ROLLBACK

If you encounter problems immediately after installing or updating a device driver, you might be lucky enough not to need to manually restore the Registry. Windows XP may be able to help you automatically. Use the Device Manager's "Roll Back Driver" feature to see if this fixes your problem.

→ To see detailed instructions on updating device drivers, **see** "Updating Device Drivers," **p. 958**.

RESTORING THE REGISTRY FROM WINDOWS BACKUP

If you installed and used the Windows Backup utility, its Restore feature lets you replace Registry and other System files saved before a failed installation or change. This step is fairly drastic, so be sure you've exhausted the less invasive procedures before you resort to this method. If you did a full backup, you're fairly safe because all program files will be restored along with the Registry. If you backed up only the Registry itself, there's a chance that the old Registry entries won't solve any problems created by replaced system programs.

Follow these steps to restore the backup:

1. Click Start, All Programs, Accessories, System Tools, Backup (or choose Backup if it's on your Start menu).

2. Click Advanced Mode, and select the Restore and Manage Media tab.

3. Select Tools, Options. Choose Always Replace the File on My Computer. (You must choose this option because you're replacing files that exist but contain the wrong information.) Then click OK.

4. Expand the list of cataloged backups (see Figure 29.4). Then locate the backup you want to restore, and check System State. If you want to restore other files and/or volumes backed up at the same time, check them as well.

5. Select Start Restore. A dialog box then warns you that System State is always restored to the current location. Click OK.

6. When a dialog box offers you Advanced options, just click OK to proceed.

7. A dialog box appears to let you enter the name of the backup set file you're restoring. Enter the name you used when you made the backup—for example, c:\before.bkf. Correct the name if necessary, and click OK.

Figure 29.4
You can restore the
Registry by restoring a
System State backup.

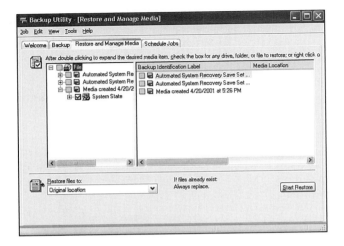

8. When the backup is complete, Backup asks you to restart the system. You really must reboot now because the Registry files have not actually been restored. The recovered Registry data has been set aside and will only be installed the next time Windows starts. If you make any other Registry changes before restarting, they will be lost when the restored files are installed.

Restoring the Registry from Regedit

If a Registry editing session has gone awry, and you need to restore the Registry from a Regedit backup, follow these steps:

1. In Regedit, select File, Import.
2. Select All Files from the Files of Type list.
3. Locate the file you used to back up the Registry key or keys—for example, `c:\before.sav`.
4. Select Open.

The saved Registry keys are then imported, replacing any changes or deletions. However, any keys or values you've added to the Registry will not be removed. If they are the cause of the problem, this restore will *not* help.

If the Registry problems persist, you can try a rather drastic measure: You can use Regedit to delete the key or keys that were changed and then import the backup file again. This time, any added keys or values are removed. I suggest you try this approach only with keys related to add-on software, *not* for any of the Microsoft software or hardware keys.

TIP

> My final word on Registry repair: If you encounter problems with the Registry entries for hardware or for Windows itself, and restoring the Registry doesn't help, you are probably better off reinstalling Windows or using the Emergency Recovery procedure than trying any further desperate measures to fix the Registry.
>
> If you encounter what you think are Registry problems with add-on software, your best bet is to uninstall the software, if possible, and reinstall it before attempting *any* Registry restores or repairs.

USING REGEDIT

You might never need to edit the Registry by hand. Most Registry keys are set by the software that uses them. For example, Microsoft Office sets its own preference values, and the Control Panel applets set the appropriate Display, Sound, and Networking Registry entries. In a way, the Control Panel is mostly just a Registry Editor in disguise.

You might need to edit the Registry by hand if directed by a technical support person who's helping you fix a problem, or when you're following a published procedure to make an adjustment for which there is no Control Panel setting.

In the latter case, before going any further, I need to say this one last time, to make it absolutely clear: Few circumstances really require you to edit the Registry by hand. Be sure you really need to before you do and, if so, back up the Registry, or at least the section you want to change, before making any changes.

Before getting into Registry exploration techniques and some tips and tricks, I'll cover the basics of the Registry Editor.

VIEWING THE REGISTRY

The Registry Editor doesn't have a Start menu item. You must run it from the Start, Run dialog. Enter regedit and click OK.

Regedit displays a two-pane display much like Explorer, as shown in Figure 29.5. The top-level keys, which are listed below My Computer, can be expanded just like drives and folders in the Explorer. In the right-hand pane are the values for each key. The name of the current selected key is shown in the status bar.

Values have names, just as the files in a folder do, and it's here that configuration information is finally stored. Each key has a (Default) value, which is the value of the key itself, and any number of named values. For example, in Figure 29.5, key HKEY_CURRENT_USER\ Desktop is shown. The value of HKEY_CURRENT_USER\Desktop itself is undefined (blank), and the value HKEY_CURRENT_USER\Control Panel\Desktop\CoolSwitch is 1.

Registry values have a data type, which is usually one of the types shown in Table 29.3.

Figure 29.5
The Regedit screen shows keys on the left and values on the right.

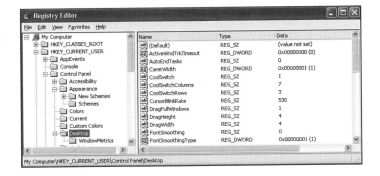

TABLE 29.3	DATA TYPES SUPPORTED BY REGEDIT
Data Type	**Description**
REG_SZ	Textual information, a simple string of letters
REG_DWORD	A single number displayed in hexadecimal or decimal
REG_BINARY	Binary data, displayed as an arbitrary number of hexadecimal digits
REG_MULTI_SZ	A string that can contain more than one line of text
REG_EXPAND_SZ	Text that can contain environment variables (such as %TEMP%)

Other data types such as REG_DWORD_BIG_ENDIAN and REG_FULL_RESOURCE_ DESCRIPTOR exist, but they are obscure, rare, and can't be edited with Regedit.

SEARCHING IN THE REGISTRY

You can search for a Registry entry by key name, value name, or the contents of a value string. First, select a starting point for the search in the left pane. You can select My Computer to select the entire Registry, or you can limit your search to one of the top-level keys or any subordinate key. Next, select Find from the menu, and enter a search string into the Find dialog. The Find feature is not case sensitive, so upper- and lowercase don't matter. You can check any of the Look At boxes, as shown in Figure 29.6, to designate where in the Registry you expect to find the desired text: in the name of a key, in the name of a value, or in the data, the value itself.

Figure 29.6
In the Find dialog box, you can select whether to search key names, value names, or value data.

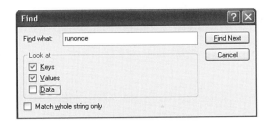

Check Match Whole String Only to search only for items whose whole name or value is the desired string.

Select Find Next to start the search. The Regedit display indicates the first match to your string, and by pressing F3, you can repeat the search to look for other instances.

TIP

The search function has two limitations:

1. You can't enter a backslash (\) in the search string when looking for a key or value name; Regedit won't complain, but it won't find anything either.

2. You can't search for the initial HKEY_*xxx* part of a key name. That's not actually part of the name; it's just the section of the Registry in which the key resides.

So, to find a key named, for example, HKEY_CLASSES_ROOT\MIDFile\shell\Play\ Command, you can't type all that in and have Find jump right to the key. If you already know the full pathname of a key, use the left pane of Regedit to browse for the key directly.

EDITING KEYS AND VALUES

Regedit has no Save or Undo menu items. Changes to the Registry happen *immediately* and *permanently*. Additions, deletions, and changes are for real. This is the reason for all the warnings to back up before you poke into the Registry.

ADDING A VALUE

To add a value to a key, select the key in the left pane, and choose Edit, New. Select the type of value to add; you can select any of the supported Registry data types: String, Binary, DWORD, Multi-String, or Expandable String. (The instructions you're following will indicate which type of value to add.) A new value entry then appears in the right pane, as shown in Figure 29.7.

Figure 29.7
New value adds an entry in "Rename" mode.

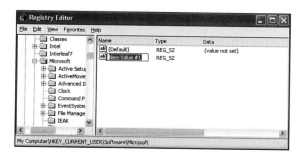

Enter the new value's name, and press Enter to edit the value.

- For string values, enter the text of the desired string.
- For DWORD values, choose Decimal or Hexadecimal, and enter the desired value in the chosen format (see Figure 29.8).
- For binary values, enter pairs of hexadecimal characters as instructed. (You'll never be asked to do this, I promise.)

Figure 29.8
You can choose to enter a DWORD value in either decimal or hexadecimal notation.

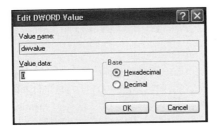

CHANGING A VALUE

If you want to change a value, double-click it in the right-hand pane to bring up the Edit Value dialog. Alternatively, you can select it and choose Edit, Modify from the menu, or right-click and select Modify from the context menu. Then make the desired change, and click OK.

That is all you will likely ever need to do with Regedit. However, in the extremely unlikely case that you would want to delete a value or add or remove a key, the following sections can help see you through these processes.

DELETING A VALUE

If you've added a Registry value in the hope of fixing some problem and found that the change wasn't needed, or if you're instructed to delete a value by a Microsoft Knowledge Base article or other special procedure, you can delete the entry by viewing its key and locating the value on the right-hand pane.

Select the value and choose Edit, Delete from the menu, or right-click and select Delete from the context menu. Confirm by clicking OK.

CAUTION

There is no Undo command in the Registry Editor—when you delete a value, it's gone for good. Be sure you've made a Registry backup before editing or deleting Registry keys and values.

ADDING OR DELETING A KEY

Keys must be added as subkeys to existing keys; you can't add a top-level key. To add a key, select an existing key in the left pane, and select Edit, New, Key from the menu.

Alternatively, right-click the existing key, and select New, Key from the context menu. A new key appears in the left pane, where you can edit its name, as shown in Figure 29.9. Press Enter after you enter the name.

Figure 29.9
A new key appears in "Rename" mode.

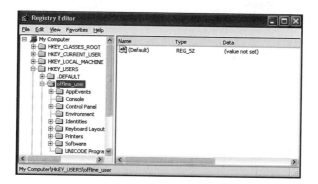

You can delete a key by selecting it in the left pane and choosing Edit, Delete from the drop-down menu, or by right-clicking it and selecting Delete from the context menu. Click OK to confirm that you do intend to delete the key. Deleting a key deletes its values and all its subkeys as well, so without the protection of Undo (or a Registry Recycling Bin), this action is serious.

RENAMING A KEY

As you have probably guessed, the pattern for renaming a key follows the Explorer exactly: Choose the key in the left pane and select Edit, Rename, or right-click the key and select Rename. Finally, enter a new name, and press Enter.

CAUTION

> Don't attempt to rename keys without a *very good* reason, such as you mistyped the name of the key you were adding. If Windows can't find specific Registry keys it needs, it might not boot or operate correctly.

USING COPY KEY NAME

As you have probably noticed by now, Registry keys can be pretty long, tortuous things to type. The Registry Editor offers a bit of help to finger-fatigued Registry editors (and authors): Choosing Edit, Copy Key Name puts the name of the currently selected key into the Clipboard, so you can paste it elsewhere, should the need arise. For example, when you've found a neat Registry trick, you might want to email your friends about it. To type the key name into your message, issue the paste command (it's Ctrl+V in most programs).

Editing Registry Entries for Another User

If you open a Registry Editor and look under HKEY_USERS, you will find that the only available subkeys are .DEFAULT, four entries for system services, and your own subkey, which is also accessible as HKEY_CURRENT_USER. As I mentioned earlier, Windows stores various parts of the Registry in data files called hives, and loads the hive containing your part of HKEY_USER only when you are currently logged on. When you log out, your subkey is unloaded from the Registry, and the hive file is left in your user profile folder.

As a Computer Administrator, you might find it necessary to edit Registry HKEY_USER entries for another user. For example, a startup program in HKEY_CURRENT_USER\ Software\Windows\CurrentVersion\Run might be causing such trouble that the user can't log on. (Can you tell this is a pet peeve of mine?) If you can't log on as that user, you can edit his or her HKEY_CURRENT_USER Registry keys in another way:

1. Log on as Administrator and run Regedit.
2. Select the HKEY_USERS window.
3. Highlight the top-level key HKEY_USERS.
4. Select File, Load Hive.
5. Browse to the profile folder for the desired user. It is in \Documents and Settings\ *username* for a local machine user, although the name of this folder might have the computer name. For example, on one computer my profile folder name is `bknittel.java`. This happens when an account is deleted and another account of the same name is created.
6. Type the filename `NTUSER.DAT`. (The file does not appear in the browse dialog because it's "super hidden": a hidden system file). Then click Open.
7. A dialog then appears, asking you to enter a name for the hive. While HKEY_USERS normally loads user hives with a long numeric name, I suggest that you type the user's logon name. Click OK. The user's Registry data is then loaded and can be edited, as shown in Figure 29.10.

Figure 29.10
An offline user's Registry hive is now loaded and can be edited.

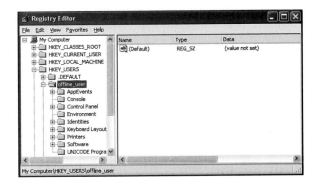

8. When you're finished editing, unload the hive. Select the key you added under HKEY_USERS (for example, the `offline user` key in Figure 29.10), and select File, Unload Hive. Confirm by clicking Yes on the warning dialog.

EDITING REGISTRY ENTRIES FOR ANOTHER WINDOWS INSTALLATION

If you need to retrieve Registry entries from an installation of Windows 2000 or XP on another hard disk or partition, you can load any of that installation's hive files for editing or exporting. This might happen when you

- Install a new hard disk and install Windows XP on the new disk.
- Have a severe Registry error that prevents Windows from booting at all. If you can't use the Emergency Recovery procedure to fix the problem, you can install Windows onto another drive, partition, or folder on your computer. When you boot up that copy of Windows, you can load the original installation's Registry files for editing. Then you can try to boot up the original installation.

To edit the other installation's Registry, you will need to locate its hive files. They are usually found in the locations shown in Table 29.4.

TABLE 29.4   USUAL LOCATION OF HIVE FILES

Key	Hive File
HKEY_LOCAL_MACHINE\SAM	\winnt\system32\config\sam
HKEY_LOCAL_MACHINE\Security	\winnt\system32\config\security
HKEY_LOCAL_MACHINE\Software	\winnt\system32\config\software
HKEY_LOCAL_MACHINE\System	\winnt\system32\config\system
HKEY_USERS\.Default	\winnt\system32\config\default

To edit another Windows installation's Registry, use the technique I described under "Editing Registry Entries for Another User." But instead of locating a user's NTUSER.DAT file, locate the desired hive file on the other hard drive or partition. Unload it after you've exported or corrected the desired information.

OTHER REGISTRY TOOLS

I've said that, although most Windows functions are controlled by Registry entries, most of these settings are made using Control Panel applets, Computer Management tools, and application preferences menus. There are some settings, however, that can't be made using any standard Windows program.

29

Making these changes used to require you to directly edit the Registry. Now, however, you'll find a raft of third-party add-on tools to make these changes more safely via a nice graphical user interface. Let's go through a couple of the more popular utilities.

TWEAKUI

Microsoft produced a tool called TweakUI. If you don't geek-speak, its name means "adjust the user interface in cool and arcane ways." You can download TweakUI from Microsoft's Web site at www.microsoft.com; search for "Windows XP Powertoys". Windows XP PowerToys. TweakUI is definitely worth having.

Using TweakUI, you can adjust mouse sensitivity, window movement, animation effects, the appearance of icons in the Explorer views, the visibility of desktop icons such as Internet Explorer, the visibility of local and network drives in the Explorer, and some security features such as hiding the name of the last-logged-on user.

Tweak UI is covered in more detail in Chapter 21.

X-SETUP

X-Setup Pro, by Xteq, is like TweakUI on steroids. This shareware program presents nearly 1,700 Registry-only settings and tweaks using a slick graphical Explorer-like interface. It includes wizards for some of the more complex tasks like mapping file types to Explorer icons. One of its niftiest features is its ability to record a series of changes to a log file that it can then play back on other computers Its pricing structure was undergoing change at press time, but the cost should be somewhere between free and $7. You can download it from www.x-setup.net.

REGISTRY TOOLKIT

Registry Toolkit is a shareware Registry Editor made by Funduc software with a nifty search-and-replace system. You can scan the Registry, changing all occurrences of one string to another, which is great for some nasty jobs. It also keeps a log of changes made so that edits can be undone. Its user interface isn't very comfortable or slick, but if you need to manage a lot of identical changes in the Registry, this is one tool to check out. It's free to try; $25 to register, at www.funduc.com.

RESPLENDENT REGISTRAR

Resplendent Registrar is a powerful Registry editing tool produced by Resplendence Software Projects (www.resplendence.com) with a drag and drop interface. Other features include a Registry defragmentation tool, a Registry compare tool, support for volatile Registry keys, and the option to edit Registry hive files on disk, allowing power users and administrators to edit Registry images of broken Windows installations. It's also shareware ($44.95), and there's a free "lite" version.

TWEAK-XP PRO

Tweak-XP Pro, available from www.totalidea.com, combines tweaking tools with additional enhancements and optimizing tools such as a RAM-disk, pop-up ad blocker, RAM reorganizer, file shredder, and so on. The cost is $39.95 for one computer, with multiple-license discounts available.

TROUBLESHOOTING

SIGNS OF REGISTRY PROBLEMS

How can I determine whether Windows problems are caused by the Registry?

Registry corruption can take two forms: either the Registry's database files can be damaged by an errant disk operation, or information can be entered incorrectly, by hand or by a buggy program. No matter what the cause, the result can be a system that won't run. (I have encountered this problem myself. A bad display driver entry caused Windows to reboot over and over.)

Other signs of Registry corruption or errors could be as follows:

- Drivers aren't loaded, or they give errors while Windows is booting.
- Software complains about components that aren't registered or cannot be located.
- Undesirable programs attempt to run when you log in.
- Windows does not boot, or it starts up only in Safe mode.

RECOVERING FROM A SUSPECTED REGISTRY PROBLEM

How do I recover from a Registry problem?

If any of the signs of a Registry problem occur just after you install new software or hardware, after you've edited the Registry manually, or after an unexpected and unprotected power loss to the computer, then you might have a Registry problem. Try these fixes in turn, checking after each step to see whether the problem is resolved:

1. If the problem occurred right after you installed new software, see whether the software manufacturer has released any updates for the software. If an update is available, install the updated software before proceeding. In any case, try reinstalling the software. If that doesn't fix the problem, *uninstall* it and then reinstall it again.

2. If the problem occurred right after installing a new piece of hardware or updating a device driver, try updating the device driver or using the Driver Rollback feature.

→ For information on the Device Rollback, **see** "Device Driver Rollback," **p. 959**.

3. Restart Windows, and just before Windows startup screen would appear, or when the "Please select the operating system to start" appears, press the F8 key. Select Last Known Good Configuration. Last Known Good uses the previous boot's version of HKEY_LOCAL_CONFIG, so good hardware settings might be preserved there.

4. If you get to this point, get professional technical help if it is available. If that's not an option, continue to step 5.

5. Use System Restore to try to return to an earlier saved system configuration.

→ For information on the System Restore, **see** "System Restore," **p. 1049**.

6. If none of these fixes solve the problem, or if you can't get Windows started, try starting Windows in Safe mode. Starting this way circumvents many display driver setup problems. If you suspect the problem is caused by the display driver, set Windows to use the Standard VGA driver and restart. Then reinstall your normal graphics adapter (using the most recent updated driver).

7. If you have a backup containing the Registry (System State), restore it. This fix should return you to a state where you had a working system.

8. Reinstall Windows in Repair mode.

→ For more information about reinstalling Windows, **see** "Recovery Console," **p. 1043**.

9. Reinstall Windows in Clean Install mode. This will require you to reinstall all of your applications and reconfigure users, so it's an absolute last resort.

TRACKING DOWN ERRANT STARTUP PROGRAMS

How do I track down and eliminate startup programs that don't appear in the Start menu but start anyway when I launch Windows?

When you log on, Windows examines the Startup folder in your personal Start Menu\Programs folder as well as in the corresponding folder under \Documents and Settings\All Users.

Windows also looks in the Registry for values in the following keys:

> HKEY_LOCAL_MACHINE\Software\Microsoft\Windows\CurrentVersion\Run
>
> HKEY_LOCAL_MACHINE\Software\Microsoft\Windows\CurrentVersion\RunOnce
>
> HKEY_CURRENT_USER\Software\Microsoft\Windows\CurrentVersion\Run
>
> HKEY_CURRENT_USER\Software\Microsoft\Windows\CurrentVersion\RunOnce

The LOCAL_MACHINE entries are run for all users, and the CURRENT_USER entries are, of course, specific to each individual user.

And, as I mentioned earlier in the chapter, because some older software depended on Windows to start it as Windows started, Windows XP still examines SYSTEM.INI for run and load entries in the [boot] section that these older programs might make.

If you're trying to eliminate a Startup program and can't find it in your own Startup folder, look in the following places:

1. Look for a shortcut or program in the folder \Documents and Settings\All Users\ Start Menu\Programs\Startup.

2. Examine SYSTEM.INI in the %systemroot% folder (for example, C:\windows). Look for `load=` or `run=` lines in the `[boot]` section. The program might be run from here.

3. Examine the Startup folders under Programs in both your Start Menu folder and in the All Users\Start Menu folder. Right-click your Start button, and select Explore to examine these folders. Note: If your disk uses the NTFS format, you must have Computer Administrator privileges to delete an entry from the All Users folder.

4. Run Regedit, and browse to key HKEY_CURRENT_USER\Software\Microsoft\ Windows\CurrentVersion. Look for subkeys named Run, RunOnce, and RunOnceEx. Check their values for entries that are starting the undesired program. The RunOnce entries are often set by installer programs to complete an installation process after rebooting and are sometimes not eliminated properly.

5. Repeat the same process with HKEY_LOCAL_MACHINE\Software\Microsoft\ Windows\CurrentVersion, again looking for Run, RunOnce, and RunOnceEx keys.

NOTE

> If you can't log in as the affected user, and you suspect that the startup program is run from the HKEY_CURRENT_USER Registry entry, see "Editing Registry Entries for Another User" earlier in this chapter.

TIPS FROM THE WINDOWS PROS: REGISTRY TIPS ON THE WEB

As I've said repeatedly in this chapter, I don't much like the idea of fooling with the Registry. Although I like to set up my desktop with a familiar set of icons, I don't like to customize things much beyond that because I want a computer to behave the way the documentation says it will. (And if something doesn't work, I like to be able to just blame Microsoft and not worry that I might have caused the problem.)

But that's just me. Many people are interested in knowing what you can alter through Registry settings, and whole Web sites have sprung up to share Windows Registry tips and tricks. If you're interested, you might check out these two:

```
www.winguides/registry
www.jsiinc.com/reghack.htm
```

To be honest, I don't find many of the listed tips to be helpful, and the TweakUI program I discussed earlier provides an easy way to do the same things.

All that said, there's a better tool at your disposal for Registry information: Google. As for so many things, when it comes to demystifying the Registry, Google is your best friend. If you're looking for the purpose and valid settings of a particular Registry key, search Google for the full key name. It's easy: Right-click the key name in the Registry editor, select Copy Key Name, and paste the name into the Google.com search field. If you don't get an answer, pare the name down section by section, starting at the left side:

name1\name2\name3\name4

then

name2\name3\name4

then

name3\name4

finally

name4

You can also try searching the microsoft.com Web site using Microsoft's search function, but frankly, Google does a much better job of indexing Microsoft's site than Microsoft does.

TROUBLESHOOTING AND REPAIRING WINDOWS XP

In this chapter

TROUBLESHOOTING 101

Inevitably, the only time you'll ever have a problem with your computer system is the exact moment when it's not convenient. Or more specifically, the moment when any delay would be severely detrimental to the continuation of your job or life. Fortunately, Windows XP has benefited from the failures of its preceding OSes and as a result is more stable than any other Microsoft OS.

That is not to say that Windows XP will never experience a failure. However, the frequency of such failures is greatly reduced and in many cases Windows XP can self-heal.

In this chapter, I discuss many of the fault-tolerant features of Windows XP, along with specific tools you can employ to resolve problems.

With the information in this chapter, and the other parts of this book, you should be adequately equipped to resolve most problems you may experience as a home or small-office user. However, don't be afraid to ask for help if you need it. Microsoft offers online and over-the-phone-for-a-fee tech support (support.microsoft.com), or you can always consult with a local computer store or repair shop.

Windows XP is chock full of helpful troubleshooting information. In many locations throughout the user experience, you'll see a button labeled Troubleshooter. This button is most common when viewing the Properties dialog box of a device. This button launches a troubleshooting wizard that walks you through common resolution techniques for the problems you are encountering. You also can locate troubleshooting links within the Help and Support Center. Just search on a topic and look for the link to launch the Troubleshooting Wizard.

Although I'm discussing device Properties dialog boxes, I should also mention that you can gain access to these through the Device Manager (among a few others, such as Computer Management for drives and Phone and Modem options for modems). Within the Device Manager you can look for devices with problems by looking for the yellow exclamation point or the red stop sign over the device's icon. See the section titled "System: Device Manager" in Chapter 22,"Configuration via Control Panel Applets," for details.

BOOT OPTIONS

Windows XP offers several alternate boot methods which can be used to bypass a problem or boot into a reduced environment so you can solve the problem. For example, if you've recently installed a new device driver that caused a system failure, a boot option can be used to boot without that driver (Last Known Good Configuration to be exact).

The boot options of Windows XP are accessed during the early stages of system startup. If you have more than one OS on your system, the boot menu will be displayed. You'll have until the counter reaches zero to press F8. If you have only Windows XP Home on your computer, you'll see a message about pressing F8 after the computer's own power-on self-test and the display of the graphical booting screen. You'll have only a few seconds, so keep your finger over the F8 button and press it when the message appears. Pressing F8 at the correct moment reveals the Advanced Options menu, which contains several boot options. These options are listed in Table 30.1.

TABLE 30.1   SAFE MODE STARTUP OPTIONS

Option	Description
Safe Mode	Starts Windows XP using only basic files and drivers (mouse, except serial mouse devices; monitor; keyboard; mass storage; basic video; default system services; and no network connections).
Safe Mode with Configuration via Control Panel Applets	Starts Windows XP using only basic files Configuration via Control Panel Applets and drivers, plus network connections.
Safe Mode with Command Prompt	Starts Windows XP using only basic files and drivers. After you log on, the command prompt is displayed instead of the Windows desktop.
Enable Boot Logging	Starts Windows XP while logging all the drivers and services that were loaded (or not loaded) by the system to a file. This file, called ntbtlog.txt, is located in the %windir% directory. Safe Mode, Safe Mode with Networking, and Safe Mode with Command Prompt add to the boot log a list of all the drivers and services that are loaded. The boot log is useful in determining the exact cause of system startup problems.
Enable VGA Mode	Starts Windows XP using the basic VGA driver. This mode is useful when you have installed a new driver for your video card that is causing Windows XP to hang or start and lock up half-way into the initialization process. The basic video driver is always used when you start Windows XP in Safe mode (Safe Mode, Safe Mode with Networking, or Safe Mode with Command Prompt).
Last Known Good Configuration	Starts Windows XP using the Registry information that Windows saved at the last shutdown. Use this option only in cases in which you strongly suspect a program has written incorrect or damaging information to the Registry. The last known good configuration does not solve problems caused by corrupted or missing drivers or files. Also, any changes made since the last successful startup are lost.
Directory Services Restore Mode	This option is only valid for domain controllers.
Debugging Mode	Starts Windows XP while sending debug information through a serial cable to another computer.

continues

30

TABLE 30.1 CONTINUED	
Option	**Description**
Start Windows Normally	This option boots the system without altering the normal boot operation. Use this selection to return to normal booting after you've made any other selection from the advanced menu. Selecting this option causes the normal boot to occur immediately; you will not be returned to the boot menu.
Reboot	This command reboots the system immediately, without first booting into Windows XP or even returning to the boot menu.
Return to OS Choices Menu	This command returns to the boot menu without making an alternate boot selection.

After you've made a selection from the Advanced Options Menu, you are returned to the boot menu. Notice your selected option is listed in blue at the bottom of the screen. From this point, you can select an OS from the list and continue with booting based on your selections.

> **TIP**
>
> If a symptom does not reappear when you start in Safe mode, you can eliminate the default settings and minimum device drivers as possible causes.

Using Safe mode, you can start your system with a minimal set of device drivers and services. For example, if newly installed device drivers or software is preventing your computer from starting, you might be able to start your computer in Safe mode and then remove the software or device drivers from your system. Safe mode does not work in all circumstances, especially if your system files are corrupted or missing, or your hard disk is damaged or has failed.

In general, if you've just performed some operation that caused a system failure, the best first reboot action is to use the Last Known Good Configuration. If that fails to resolve the issue, use Safe Mode. If the problem is specific to the video drivers (or suspect that it is), you might want to use Enable VGA Mode instead of Safe Mode. If you've just recently changed video drivers or the video card itself, you may want to use the Enable VGA mode if things don't act normally during the reboot.

When you are able to access the system through Safe Mode, you need to resolve the issue causing the boot problem. In most cases, this will require you to reverse your last system alteration, application install, driver update, etc. If your system stops booting properly and you did not make any changes, then you should probably call Microsoft tech support. They may be able to help track down the culprit and get things back on track.

If none of these boot options results in a repaired system or offers you the ability to repair the system, you'll need to move on to the Recovery Console.

RECOVERY CONSOLE

The Recovery Console feature provides you with a command-line interface that enables you to repair system problems via a limited set of commands. For example, you could use the Recovery Console to enable and disable services, repair a corrupted master boot record, or copy system files from a floppy disk or a CD-ROM. The Recovery Console gives you complete control over the repair process but can be dangerous if not used with caution. If you're not an advanced user, you should stay away from this set of commands. If you do plan to pursue use of the Recovery Console, I highly recommend consulting the Windows XP Resource Kit.

The Recovery Console can be used in two ways. It can be installed so that it always appears on the boot menu as an alternate OS. Or, you can use it by initiating a repair via the setup routine. Both of these methods are discussed in this section.

TIP

The following procedure assumes you have boot floppies or the original XP CD. If you don't have them (typically because your computer came with XP already installed and many branded computers don't comes with an XP CD), you might still be in luck. If the computer is a Hewlett-Packard, it has the capability to make a restore/recovery CD using files in a special maintenance partition on the hard disk that essentially contains everything the XP installation CD does. Check the computer's user's manual or phone tech support and ask them how to install the Recovery Console.

To run the Recovery Console on a system that will not start, do the following:

1. Insert the Windows XP Setup Disk into your floppy drive or, if you have a bootable CD-ROM drive, insert the Windows XP CD into your CD-ROM drive.

2. Restart your computer.

3. Follow the directions on the screen. If you're using the Setup disks, you are prompted to insert the other Setup disks into the disk drive. Loading files might take several minutes. Choose the options to repair your Windows XP installation when prompted (press R for repair instead of Enter to install) and finally to start the Recovery Console when prompted.

NOTE

To see the commands available on the Recovery Console, type `help` at its command prompt.

To install the Recovery Console on your computer so that it is always available, you must be logged on to Windows XP as a user with a Computer Administrator account type to be able to complete this procedure:

NOTE

The Recovery Console must be installed before you install SP2. If you have already installed SP2, you cannot install the Recovery Console on your computer. However, you can use the previous procedure to run the Recovery Console from the Windows XP product CD.

1. Log on to Windows as a Computer Administrator user.

2. With Windows running, insert the Windows XP CD into your CD-ROM drive.

3. If you're prompted to upgrade to Windows XP, choose No. Or, if you're already running XP, you have to click Exit from the Welcome (What Do You Want to Do?) screen.

4. At the command prompt (Start, All Programs, Accessories, Command Prompt), switch to your CD-ROM drive, and then type the following:

   `\i386\winnt32.exe /cmdcons`

5. A dialog box appears, explaining what the Recovery Console is for, telling you it requires about 7MB of hard disk space, and asking whether you want to proceed. Click Yes.

6. A wizard starts and copies the files onto your hard disk. That's it.

Now that the Recovery Console is installed, it is listed as a selection on the boot menu—not on the Advanced Options Menu.

The following are some notes on installing the Recovery Console:

- To run the Recovery Console after it has been installed, you must restart your computer and select the Recovery Console option from the boot menu.

- You must be logged on as a Computer Administrator user to be able to install the Recovery Console. If your computer is connected to a network, network policy settings may also prevent you from completing this procedure.

- To see the commands available on the Recovery Console, type `help` at the command prompt.

- You can allow a user to run the Recovery Console without logging on by enabling the Auto Admin Logon attribute in the Security Configuration Editor. The AutoAdminLogin attribute is located in the Console tree under Local Computer Policy/Computer Configuration/Windows Settings/Security Settings/Local Policies/Security Options. Otherwise, once the Recovery Console is started, you'll be prompted for the Computer Administrator user account's password.

- If your computer does not start, you can run the Recovery Console from the Windows XP CD (if you have a bootable CD-ROM drive) or the Setup disks.

In many cases, the Recovery Console offers you enough reach to repair most problems. However, in the event that the Recovery Console fails to support necessary system alterations, you'll need to attempt a parallel installation.

PARALLEL COPIES OF WINDOWS XP

Before you resort to doing a fresh installation over the top of a dead system, or wiping out the disk and starting over, you might want to try one other approach. This trick can sometimes get you up and running again, assuming you have enough disk space—and some patience. The following procedure creates a back door into a broken installation so that you can remove or change offending drivers, disable some offending services, tweak the Registry, and so on in hopes of getting it back up again. If nothing else, you can do a clean installation and pull in your settings from the old installation.

The basic idea is that you do a clean installation of Windows XP into a fresh directory. Then you can use Regedt32 either to alter the Registry of the dead system or pull what you can out of it (such as user settings) into the new one so that you can trash the old installation.

Here are the basic steps:

1. Install Windows XP into a fresh directory (a clean installation). For example, if your Windows directory is C:\Windows, you might use C:\Windows2 for this new installation.

2. Boot up Windows using the newly installed system. This should occur by default.

3. Try to repair the old copy by deleting or replacing defective driver files in the original Windows installation directory structure.

If you suspect that a system service is crashing on bootup and that's what's crashing your computer, you can try editing the old system's Registry to disable the service. Here's how:

1. Run Regedt32.exe from the newly installed version of Windows XP and select the following key:

HKEY_LOCAL_MACHINE

> **N O T E**
>
> If you need help running Regedt32, see Chapter 29, "The Registry." Don't tinker with the Registry unless you know what you're doing. Improper editing of the Registry can result in a dead computer.

2. Click Load Hive on the File menu, and open the following Registry file on the original Windows XP installation folder:

\oldwindowsfolder\System32\Config\System

where oldwindowsfolder is the name of the folder of your original Windows installation.

3. Assign this hive a name such as OldSystem. This key contains the old HKEY_LOCAL_MACHINE\System data from your old setup.

30

4. Browse into the subkey CurrentControlSet if it's displayed. If it's not, look in key Select at Value Current. It will be a number such as 1, 2, or 3. Back in OldSystem, open key ControlSet00*x*, where *x* is the number you found under Current.

5. Browse into the Services key, and look for the likely offending service. Under each service's key is a value named Start, with one of the following values:

   1. Starts in the first phase of bootup (these services are usually used to access file systems)

   2. Starts automatically, just after booting

   3. Starts manually

   4. Disabled

   Services with a Start value of 1 are used to boot Windows, and you shouldn't touch them. Services with a Start value of 2 are started just about the same time as the Login dialog appears in Windows. If your Windows system boots and then promptly crashes without your help, try setting the Start value of any suspected service(s) to 3 or 4. Be sure to write down the names of the services and their original Start values before you change anything!

6. Select the OldSystem key, and select the File menu, Unload Hive.

7. Use Notepad to view the file C:\BOOT.INI. You should see two entries for Windows XP, one using the original directory and one using the new directory. Note the order in which they're listed.

8. Shut down Windows and reboot. You have to select a Windows installation from the two Windows XP entries listed. Refer to your notes made in step 7 to determine which entry is which. Select the old (original) installation to boot.

You might need to repeat this process a few times, disabling a different service or two each time. If you can manage to reboot the old system with some system services disabled, uninstall and reinstall those services to recover your installation.

This procedure is a little bit like performing brain surgery with a shovel, but it has resurrected systems for me before.

AS A LAST RESORT

You can reinstall Windows XP over a damaged Windows XP system. Doing so might be time-consuming, but reinstalling is useful if other repair attempts do not solve your problem. You should attempt an upgrade install first. If this works, you will have repaired your OS and retained your installed applications and most system configuration settings. If upgrading fails, you must perform a fresh install, which means you'll have to re-install all of your applications and remake all your setting changes. Unless you format the drive, your data files will remain unaffected by the upgrade or fresh install process.

> **TIP**
>
> If you do a fresh install, you don't have to worry that your documents and settings will get wiped out. They won't. During a re-install, Windows XP setup checks to see whether there are preexisting Documents and Settings for each user account you create, and uses a modification of that name to create the new account settings. For example, my account name is Bob. So, under D:\Documents and Settings, there is a subfolder called D:\Documents and Settings\Bob. When I did a fresh reinstallation on the same drive and set up my user account again (using the name Bob once again), XP did not overwrite the existing Bob folder. Instead, it created a new folder called D:\Documents and Settings\Bob.HP-Laptop. XP appended the name of my computer onto my user name. Now all I had to do was fish around in files and folders under Bob (such as Desktop, Favorites, Cookies, Application Data, and so on) and copy those over to the new Bob.HP-Laptop folder. Then I was back in business.

However, it is always a good idea to back up your data. Go back and check out the "Backup Tools and Strategies" section in this chapter for ideas on performing that activity. Keep in mind that if your system fails to boot, you can't get access to the Windows backup tool to create a backup. So, you must be proactive by backing up your important files on a regular basis. You might get lucky and be able to use the Safe Mode command prompt or the Recovery Console to access a command prompt where you can copy files to a floppy, removable media, or other drives. But relying on this is not smart.

> **TIP**
>
> If data recovery is what you're after, there are ways to reclaim your data from the hard drive. These techniques assume that the files or folders you want to reclaim did not use NTFS encryption. Because encryption is not an option in XP Home, it's not likely. There are several approaches you could consider. First, if you have a dual-boot system, look for the Documents and Settings folder on the XP boot drive. Drill down until you find the files you want. This assumes the OS into which you boot can read the file system under which your user files are stored, of course. Second, you can try connecting the drive to another computer that boots an OS capable of reading the volumes and folders in question. Then, go looking for the files. Find them, and copy them where you'd like.

PREVENTING PROBLEMS

I have never believed that having to re-install and re-configure an OS is a true recovery method. It's more of a start-over-from-scratch method. There are some system failures which require such far reaching procedures, but in many cases you can prevent them. The most successful preventative measure is backing up. In fact, the only insurance you have from one moment to the next that your system and your data will even be accessible is a backup. Backups should be performed automatically and frequently. But just backing up is not enough; you must also verify that your backups are working properly and periodically walk through the process of restoring your system in the event of a failure.

Backups are the key to a long life of your data. In fact, most of the repair capabilities of Windows XP are based around backups. Many repair functions don't correct problems directly; instead they restore saved functioning files over problematic ones. This includes the Last Known Good Configuration, many functions within Recovery Console, and the System Restore capability (discussed later in this chapter). But all of these restore or repair functions focus on the OS, not on your data. Only a backup you configure and execute will protect your data.

Flip back to Chapter 26, "Managing the Hard Disk," for more details about backups.

Backups are not the only preventative measures you should take. You should also regularly check your system's performance. This process was discussed in Chapter 23, "Maintaining and Optimizing System Performance."

It is also a good idea to use a UPS (Uninterruptible Power Supply). A UPS conditions the power being fed to the computer and can provide several minutes of power in the event of a blackout. A UPS will prolong the life of your computer by protecting its sensitive components from electric fluctuations.

Regularly check the Event Viewer for device, driver, and service problems. Problems of this nature usually appear in the System log. They are usually indicated by a yellow triangle or a red stop sign as the event detail's icon. If you see problems related to key components of the system, you need to investigate the situation and resolve the problem. Unfortunately, the event details do not always provide enough information. You'll need to use the Help and Support Center, the Microsoft online knowledge base (support.microsoft.com), or contact Microsoft technical support over the phone to decipher what cryptic information is presented. In many cases, the Windows XP troubleshooter will provide a workable solution. Otherwise, you should consult the vendor's Web site for updated drivers and troubleshooting instructions.

NOTE

> The Event Viewer is discussed in Chapter 24, "System Utilities." The hardware troubleshooter (both through the Add Hardware applet and the Device Manager) is discussed in Chapter 22 "Configuration via Control Panel Applets."

You should also endeavor to regularly perform drive maintenance on your system. Maintaining healthy drives reduces the number of drive and file system related problems. Drive maintenance involves the following:

- Manually removing old data files, either via deletion or backup
- Use Disk Cleanup to remove unnecessary files
- Use Error-checking to verify the volume is supporting its file system properly
- Use Defragmenter to consolidate files and aggregate free space

NOTE

> These drive tools are discussed in Chapter 26.

SYSTEM RESTORE

System Restore is a fabulous mechanism that first appeared with Windows Me. Now Windows XP incorporates it, too. System Restore enables you to restore the computer to a previously saved state. So, you can roll back your computer to the way it was working before your dog jumped on the keyboard, or before you installed that stupid program or device driver that lunched your system. Here's how it works.

Performing a system restore does not affect personal files, such as documents, Internet favorites, or email. It simply reverses system configuration changes and removes installed files to return the system to a stored state. System Restore automatically monitors your system for changes. Periodically easily identifiable restoration points are created. Plus, you can create your own restoration points manually.

It should be obvious, but I'll state it anyway: System Restore is only accessible if you can boot Windows XP. If your system does not boot, you must use one of the previously mentioned system recovery techniques.

There are two control interfaces for System Restore. One is on the System Restore tab of the System applet. The other is the System Restore utility itself accessed through Start, All Programs, Accessories, System Tools, System Restore.

The System Restore tab (see Figure 30.1) of the System applet is where System Restore is enabled or disabled for all drives in the computer. It is enabled by default.

Figure 30.1
The System Restore tab of the System applet.

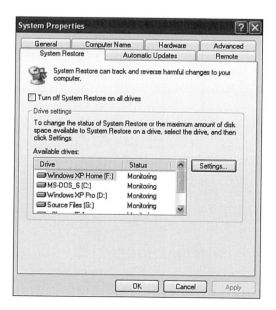

While enabled, you can define on a drive-by-drive basis how much space can be consumed by System Restore to maintain restoration points. You can choose to turn off System Restore for individual drives or set the percentage of the drive usable by System Restore. Each drive has either 20% or 12% of its total size set as the default and maximum allowed usage levels (see Figure 30.2). (It seems that if the 20% level results in a value over 400MB, then the 12% level is used.) Keep in mind that if you disable System Restore on a drive, no changes to that drive are retained in restore points.

Figure 30.2
Drive settings dialog box for System Restore.

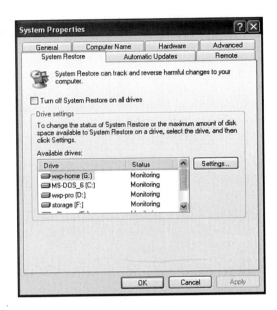

The number of restore points retained by System Restore will depend on the amount of allowed drive space usage as well as the rate and significance of changes to the system.

Restore points are created by Windows XP automatically whenever any one of several specific events occurs:

- On first boot after installation
- Every 24 hours of calendar time or every 24 hours of computer uptime
- When a program is installed using InstallShield or Windows Installer
- Automatic updates via Windows Update
- Any restore operation
- Installation of unsigned device drivers
- At any restore operation using Backup

Keep in mind that not all program installations use InstallShield or Windows Installer. Thus, you should always manually create a restore point before installing applications.

The creation of a restore point at any restore operation allows you to reverse a restoration. Thus, if after a successful restoration you are not pleased with the outcome, you can reverse the restoration. The system automatically removes any failed or incomplete restoration operations.

System Restore does not replace the uninstallation process for removing an application. System Restore only monitors and protects against changes to the OS. It does not track the addition of new files to the system. Use the Add or Remove Programs utility or a vendor provided uninstall routine to remove applications.

The System Restore tool (see Figure 30.3) is actually a wizard accessed by clicking its icon in the Start menu under All Programs, Accessories, System Tools. This wizard walks you through the process of restoring the system to a previous saved state or to manually create a restore point. Just make a radio button selection and then click Next.

When restoring a system, the list of available restoration points is displayed along with a calendar to help in time-lining and identifying. Once you've selected a restore point, you'll be asked to confirm your wish to restore the system to the saved state and informed that the system will reboot to perform the action. Once the restore is complete, a new third radio button option for Undo My Last Restoration will appear on the first page of the System Restore Wizard.

Creating a restore point is even simpler. All you need to do is provide a name for the restore point and click Create. The system state data will be saved.

Figure 30.3
The System Restore tool.

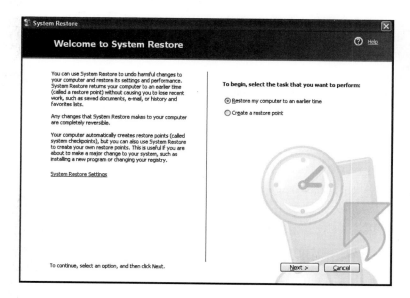

30

BLACK MAGIC OF TROUBLESHOOTING

It often seems like many professional technophiles have some sort of black magic they use when resolving problems. If you blink, you miss whatever it is they do to get the system back in working order. It's often as if you are working with a techno-mage.

Yes, it is true that some of our skills at resolving problems do seem like hocus pocus. But in reality, it's a mixture of experience and knowledge. Both of which you can gain with time and effort.

In my experience, I've found that most computer problems are physical in nature. Meaning some component is not connected properly or has become damaged. Of the remaining 5%, more than 4.99% is caused directly by the user—whether through deliberate or accidental activity. User caused problems are typically configuration changes, installation of new drivers, or deletion of important files and folders.

When I troubleshoot a problem on my own systems, I try to mentally walk backwards through whatever I've done to the system over the last few days or weeks. In many cases, I'll remember installing some downloaded application or changing some Control Panel setting that I meant to uninstall or reverse, but never got around to do it. If the brainstorming fails to highlight any suspects, I check for physical issues. Is everything powered on? Are cooling fans still spinning? Are all the right cables still firmly connected?

If I don't discover anything obvious physically, I try a power-off reboot. The power-off reboot will reset all hardware devices, and in many cases resolve the problem (if it was device related). If possible, shut down the system gracefully. Then keep the power off for about 10 seconds before switching the system back on. You'll be amazed at how often this works.

My next steps always include a walk through the Event Viewer and any other types of log files I can find. Let the problem guide you in this process. For example, if the video system is failing, you probably don't need to look through the modem logs.

For me, every problem is unique, often requiring a different resolution than any other problem I've tackled in the past. However, there are some general rules or guidelines I try to follow:

- Try only one change at a time
- Reboot twice after each change
- Test each change for success
- Try the least invasive first
- Keep a log of your changes; you may need to undo them to produce a result, or you may need the resolution process again in the future
- Consult vendor Web sites for possible solutions, if the problem seems to be specific to one device or software component
- Be patient and take your time

- After a few attempts at possible solutions, step back and re-evaluate before continuing
- If you get frustrated, take a break. Anger and frustration are counter-productive when you need to be thinking clearly
- Try to undo any recent changes to the system, including new hardware or software patches
- Review areas of the system which have caused problems in the past
- Try to repeat the failure; knowing where, how, or why the failure occurs can lead to a solution

Troubleshooting is both an art and a science. You'll need organized patience and outrageous ingenuity. Plus, knowing where to look stuff up never hurts. Keep in mind that the entire Internet is waiting at your fingertips and mouse clicks. Search groups.google.com as well the regular Web. You'll be amazed at what you find there. It's so easy to search all the popular newsgroups at once. Be precise in your search techniques to help find the exact messages you need to read. The MS knowledge base is extremely helpful, too. Plus, lots of helpful information is included within the Help and Support system of Windows XP as well as the Windows XP Resource Kit. If all else fails, contact Microsoft technical support over the phone (see support.Microsoft.com for contact numbers). In most cases, if the troubleshooting techniques in this book don't resolve the issue, it usually is beyond the end user to correct.

SCATTER-GUN TROUBLESHOOTING

Not all of the troubleshooting techniques applicable to Windows XP are contained within this one chapter. If you've noticed, we've been discussing troubleshooting within every chapter. That organizational decision was intended to group recovery information with the discussion of the related technologies, deployment, usage, and management. So, before you throw your hands up in frustration that your questions are not answered or your problem is not resolved in this chapter, go check out the chapter dedicated to the specific subject earlier in this book.

APPENDIXES

Installing Service Pack 2

In this appendix

ABOUT SERVICE PACKS

Windows XP is part of Microsoft's New Technology (NT) family of operating systems, along with Windows NT, Windows 2000 Professional, and the various flavors of Windows 2000 Server and Windows Server 2003. These operating systems were designed from the ground up for stability, reliability, and security, and to keep them in tip-top shape, Microsoft releases a constant stream of software updates called critical updates, recommended updates, and hotfixes:

- **Critical updates**—These are fixes for bugs that are so severe or involve such serious security risks that you really *have* to install them. As you know, XP can automatically download and install these, or at least offer to install them, so you don't miss out. You can also find a list of critical updates by visiting the Windows update Web site.

- **Recommended updates**—These are not security fixes but updates to accessory programs such as Messenger and Media Player, new desktop themes, and the like. Recommended updates are also listed on the Windows update Web site.

- **Hotfixes**—These are bug fixes that affect a small enough group of users that Microsoft doesn't send them out to everyone. Instead, you have to hunt for them by researching the Knowledge Base at support.microsoft.com or hear about them from Microsoft's Tech Support department. They're not widely advertised because (a) if you're running into a serious enough problem, you'll go looking for the solution and (b) hotfixes tend to be released in a hurry without extensive testing, so they sometimes cause new problems of their own. Hotfix users tend to be corporate IT people whose job it is to stay on top of these things.

Periodically—it's supposed to be every 12 months but in practice it's less often—Microsoft gathers all the critical updates, recommended updates, and hotfixes; tests them extensively; and releases them as a service pack (SP). Service packs, then, represent a complete, cumulative set of fixes and additions made since the initial release of an operating system. Service packs can be obtained on CD-ROM media or downloaded from Microsoft's Web site.

If you're used to Windows 95, 98, and Me, where you are basically left twisting slowly in the wind when it comes to bug fixes, this is a big deal. You have a real operating system and are now getting the kind of support you should have been receiving all along.

Service Pack 2 (SP2) contains not only fixes for hundreds of bugs and security issues, but also many new features mostly centered on improving security (see Appendix B, "New Features in Service Pack 2," for the details). Don't let the "hundreds of bugs" worry you—in a collection of programs as large as XP, there are bound to be thousands of bugs. (*That* should worry you.) Luckily, most of them are extremely obscure and affect only a few users with specific hardware and software combinations.

NOTE

> At this writing, SP2 is not available for Windows XP 64-bit Edition.
>
> However, if you are running one of the 32-bit versions of Windows XP (Home Edition, Professional, Tablet, and Media Center) on an AMD 64-bit (Opteron) processor, you can install SP2. Be sure to read the notes on the new NX option in Appendix B.

You might wonder whether you really need to install service packs because you probably install the critical updates XP downloads and informs you of from time to time. The answer is emphatically *yes*, for two reasons. First, service packs fix those annoying but minor bugs you might not even realize are there—that odd crash every other week or that weird sound Media Player makes once in a while. Second, application programs will eventually appear that require a certain service pack level to run correctly. Windows evolves, so you need to keep up. These two reasons alone are enough to warrant installing any service pack, but SP2 is extraordinarily important because of the many Internet-related security issues it addresses.

The following are some other things you should know about service packs:

- They're cumulative. For example, SP2 includes all the changes in Service Pack 1. If you skipped a previous service pack, you can still install a newer one without missing anything.

- If you use Add/Remove Programs to install optional Windows components after installing a service pack, you don't have to install the service pack again, as you did with Windows NT and 2000. Windows Setup might still ask you to insert the service pack media or it might need to download updated files, but it won't mess you up by installing out-of-date components.

- Starting about the same time Microsoft releases a service pack to the public, new computers purchased from major vendors should come with the service pack preinstalled. (At least, it should be an option. If you're buying a new computer, ask for the latest version.) To check the current service pack level of your Windows XP computer, open Windows Explorer and select Help, About Windows. You can also type `winver` at the command prompt. Compare what you find to the current service pack level listed at `windowsupdate.microsoft.com`.

- Although this appendix describes the procedure for obtaining and installing SP2,the procedure will likely be similar for subsequent service packs as well.

Now, let's talk about how to install a service pack on your computer.

INSTALLATION OPTIONS

Windows XP SP2 comes in four flavors. The following list summarizes the four ways of installing SP2, and the rest of this appendix explains them in detail:

- **Automatic updates**—If your computer is set up to automatically download critical updates from Microsoft and you spend enough time connected to the Internet, SP2 automatically downloads. All the required service pack files will already be downloaded by the time you get the notification to install them. I'll discuss the installation procedure shortly.

■ **Windows Update**—If the automatic updates feature is not enabled, you can install SP2 from the standard Windows Update Web page. Windows Update downloads from Microsoft just those service pack components needed for your computer, saving some download time over the standalone method. However, if you have more than one or two computers to update, you'll save time by using the standalone version.

■ **Standalone**—The standalone version is the traditional service pack format. It's a compressed file that, for SP2, weighs in at nearly 275MB and contains all the updated files needed to add SP2 to any version of Windows XP. If you have two or more computers to update, the standalone method is the one to use. It's bulky and contains updated components your particular computers might not need, but it's still faster to download this one large file than to have several computers download the Windows Update version independently. You can download the SP2 setup file from www.microsoft.com/technet. If you have a slow Internet connection, you can order the standalone version on a free setup CD from Microsoft at www.microsoft.com/windowsxp/sp2, or you can likely obtain one at a computer store or from a friend.

> **TIP**
>
> If you download the standalone service pack file, its default name will be something like WindowsXP-KB835935-SP2-ENU.exe. I recommend that you save it with a more presentable name, such as XPSP2.exe, unless you have to keep track of several service pack versions in different languages. Save the file in a shared network folder or burn it onto a CD.

You can either expand the service pack onto a shared network folder for faster, easier installation onto several computers or carry the service pack CD from one computer to another.

■ **Integrated**—The integrated version is a full, fresh installation version of Windows XP that has SP2 already included into its code. Installing an integrated version performs a full, clean installation of Windows XP SP2 without the need to subsequently install the service pack. However, it can't be used to upgrade an existing XP setup.

BEFORE INSTALLING THE SERVICE PACK

Regardless of which update method you choose, you should first perform the following steps:

■ If you use Fast User Switching, be sure all users are logged off. Then log on as a Computer Administrator and close any applications that are running.

■ We recommend that you perform a full backup of the files you keep on your computer.

→ To learn more about the Windows Backup utility, **see** "Backup Tools and Strategies," **p. 923**.

- Check the Web sites of the manufacturers of your computer, application software, and antivirus and antispyware packages for updates or special instructions regarding SP2. Some programs might need to be updated to work with SP2.

- If you suspect that your computer has viruses, spyware, adware, or other pestilential software, take steps to remove it *before* installing SP2. These programs can cause serious networking and Internet connection problems after installing SP2, and without a functioning Internet connection, you might not be able to download the necessary cleanup tools.

- Disable any real-time virus scanners because they can slow down and possibly interfere with the installation. You should disconnect from the Internet first. (And be sure to reenable the virus scanners after you install SP2.)

- You need 1100MB of free space on your hard drive if you're installing preexpanded files from a network folder and 1600MB of free space if you're installing directly from a CD-ROM or downloaded file. (Microsoft Knowledge Base article 837783 gives a detailed description of the disk space requirements.)

Then, use one of the update procedures described in the next several sections.

INSTALLING VIA AUTOMATIC UPDATES

If your computer is set up to receive automatic updates, Windows automatically downloads the service pack files while you're connected to the Internet. However, even if you've configured automatic updates to automatically install the updates it receives, it never installs a full service pack without your permission.

After performing the preparation steps in the previous section, follow these steps:

1. Log on as a Computer Administrator and close any running applications.

2. When the Express Updates icon appears in the Notification Area on the task bar, double-click it and ask to view the update details. If SP2 is listed, the files are already downloaded. Follow the screen's instructions to tell Windows to perform the installation.

3. The Windows XP SP2 Setup Wizard appears, reminding you to perform a backup. Click Next to continue.

4. On the License Agreement page, click I Agree; then click Next to continue. The wizard works awhile as it inspects your Windows installation.

5. On the Select Options page (see Figure A.1), you are asked where to store the system files SP2 is replacing so you can uninstall the SP2 upgrade at a later time if necessary. You can leave this set to the default folder \WINDOWS\$NTServicePackUninstall$, or you can select another location to hold the archive folder. For example, if disk space is tight, you can put it on a drive with more space. (You can delete the 300Mb of archived files later, using the procedure at the end of this appendix.) After making your selection, click Next to continue.

Figure A.1
Windows saves a copy of the files being replaced by the service pack so you can uninstall it if problems arise.

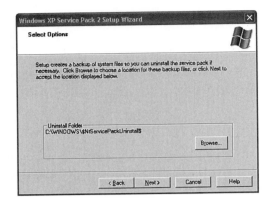

6. The Updating Your System page appears. During this phase of the upgrade, Windows inspects your current Windows XP files, archives your current Windows files, and installs the SP2 files. This phase can take a long time.

7. After some time, you are presented with a summary page informing you that the installation of SP2 is complete. Restart your computer to finish the installation of SP2. Skip ahead to the section titled "After Installing Service Pack 2" in this appendix.

INSTALLING VIA WINDOWS UPDATE

If you have a single computer to update, you can use Windows Update. The procedure is as follows:

1. Log on as a Computer Administrator and close any running applications.

2. Check to see whether the Express Updates icon appears in the Notification Area on the task bar. If it does, double-click it and ask to view the update details. If SP2 is listed, the files are already downloaded and all you have to do is let Windows complete the installation by following the procedure in the previous section.

3. Open Internet Explorer and visit `windowsupdate.microsoft.com`. You might be asked to install the latest version of the Windows update software. If a pop-up appears asking you to do this, click Yes.

4. Select a custom install. From the list of available critical updates, select Service Pack 2 Express Install. Windows downloads the service pack installer and components.

From this point, follow steps 3–7 in the previous section, "Installing via Automatic Updates."

INSTALLING VIA THE STANDALONE PACKAGE

As mentioned previously, if you have only one or two computers to update, the automatic updates or Windows Update saves you time by downloading only the necessary files. However, if you have a slow Internet connection or many computers to update, it's worth getting the standalone update package on a CD or via download.

The standalone upgrade is the most robust of the three versions of SP2. You can use the standalone SP2 package in two ways:

- To upgrade a copy of Windows XP by running the service pack program directly
- To upgrade a copy of Windows XP using preexpanded files stored in a shared network folder

The following two sections describe the procedures.

INSTALLING SERVICE PACK 2 LOCALLY

Most home and small office users want to install SP2 locally. You can use either a CD-ROM–based installation kit or a service pack .exe file downloaded from Microsoft. The procedure is identical after you've determined the location of the service pack setup file. Proceed as outlined here:

1. Log on as a Computer Administrator and close any running applications.
2. If you are using a Microsoft-supplied CD, insert the CD and the setup program should automatically start up. If it doesn't or you are using a downloaded service pack file, locate and double-click the service pack's .exe file in Windows Explorer or start the installation program from the command line.

From this point, you can follow steps 3–7 in the section titled "Installing via Automatic Updates," earlier in this appendix.

INSTALLING SERVICE PACK 2 FROM THE NETWORK

Installing SP2 from a network file share is the best option when you have several computers to upgrade—you save a lot of time by expanding the service pack files just once. This option works equally well at home, in a small office, or in a corporate domain network environment. Here is the procedure to prepare the installation file set:

1. Choose a file server or computer to host the service pack setup files. On that computer, create and share a folder to hold the installation files. Name the shared folder **xpsp2**. Make a note of the full path to this folder.
2. Locate the service pack's .exe file, and make a note of the full path and name of this file. This could be something like d:\xpsp2.exe if you are using a Microsoft-supplied CD-ROM or c:\downloads\WindowsXP-KB835935-SP2-ENU.exe if you downloaded the file from Microsoft's Web site.

3. Open a command prompt window. Type the full pathname followed by /x, as in this example:

```
d:\xpsp2.exe /x
```

You are prompted to specify the location to store the extracted files in, as illustrated in Figure A.2. Enter the local or network path of the shared folder that you created in step 1 and click OK.

Figure A.2
Extracting the SP2 files.

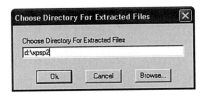

4. Ensure that the network folder has NTFS or share permissions that let network users read but not modify the files.

Now, at each computer you want to update with the service pack, including the one that is hosting the files, browse to the shared network folder you created in the previous steps and run the program i386\update\update.exe. You can do this from Windows Explorer or the command line. The command line command would be something like this:

```
\\servername\xpsp2\i386\update\update
```

with the actual name of the computer that is sharing the xpsp2 folder in place of servername.

The rest of the procedure is identical to steps 3–7 in "Installing via Automatic Updates," earlier in this appendix.

MODIFYING INSTALLATION BEHAVIOR OF SERVICE PACK 2 FROM THE COMMAND LINE

As with all service packs, Windows XP SP2 can be installed from the command line, using switches to modify the behavior of the setup process. The full list of command-line options is

```
xpsp2.exe /f /l /n /q /integrate:folder /u /z /norestart /forcerestart
```

or for the already-expanded version, it's

```
update.exe /f /l /n /q /integrate:folder /u /z /norestart /forcerestart
```

These options are described in Table A.1.

TABLE A.1   COMMAND-LINE OPTIONS FOR SERVICE PACK INSTALLATION

Switch	Description
/f	Forces all open applications to close before the computer is restarted following the installation of the service pack. It cannot be used with /s, /l, or /z.
/l	Lists all hotfixes currently installed on the computer. Does not install anything.
/n	Installs the SP but does not enable support for uninstalling it later. It cannot be used with /l or /s.
/q	Installs the SP in quiet mode, suppressing all user interface screens.
/integrate:*folder*	Installs the SP and Windows XP from source files in the specified folder.
/u	Installs the SP in unattended mode. Although the prompts appear, the installation proceeds without waiting for user input. Neither the progress bar nor any errors that might occur appear during the installation. Only critical error prompts are displayed.
/z	Installs the SP but does not automatically restart the computer upon the completion of the installation. Cannot be used with /l or /s.
/norestart	Same as /z.
/forcerestart	Forces the computer to restart after installing the SP.

NOTE

The switches described in Table A.1 work with either the XPSP2.exe self-extracting archive (which expands the service pack files) or the update.exe file (which actually performs the service pack installation).

You can precede the switches in Table A.1 with either a slash (/) or a dash (-); it makes no difference to the setup routine. Additionally, the switches are not case sensitive.

In addition to the switches listed in Table A.1, two more switches can be used only with the XPSP2.exe program. These are listed in Table A.2.

TABLE A.2   ADDITIONAL XPSP2.exe SWITCHES

Switch	Description
/x	Extracts service pack files without starting update.exe
/u /x:*folder*	Extracts service pack files and places them in the specified folder without prompting or starting update.exe

INTEGRATED INSTALLATION

The process to install from an integrated setup CD-ROM is the same as installing Windows XP from the CD-ROM, as discussed in Chapter 3, "Installing Windows XP Home." This procedure can be used on an existing Windows XP computer, as well as a new computer with a blank hard drive. However, this is a clean install, with only the default user accounts and no installed applications. It's not a way to upgrade an existing XP installation.

NOTE

> Reinstalling XP over an old installation using the integrated version of the service pack does not require a new product key. If you are prompted for a product key, use the one with which the machine was originally activated.

AFTER INSTALLING SERVICE PACK 2

When you restart Windows after installing the service pack, you are shown two new screens. The first appears before the logon screen and encourages you to enable automatic updates (see Figure A.3). You should enable automatic downloading of critical updates.

Figure A.3
After installing Service Pack 2, Windows asks you to enable automatic updates.

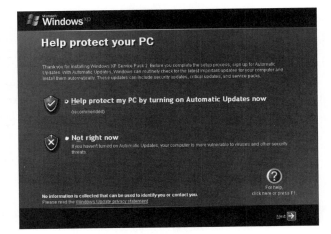

The choice of whether to have them automatically install after downloading is up to you:

- If you leave your computer on all the time, you can leave the default settings in place and Windows installs the updates automatically at 3 a.m. This ensures that updates are always installed as soon as they are available, reducing the window of opportunity for hackers to exploit whatever new bugs have been found. (By the way, Windows never automatically installs a full service pack. You always are given the opportunity to permit or defer the service pack upgrade.)

- If you don't usually leave your computer on all night, tell Windows to download but not install the updates. You have to remember to log on as a Computer Administrator periodically—at least once a week—so Windows can notify you when new updates are ready to install.

To change the automatic installation time or to disable automatic installation, you need to change the default settings.

→ To learn how to make changes to the automatic updates settings, **see** "Setting Automatic Updates," **p. 843**.

The first time you log on after installing SP2, log on as a Computer Administrator. Windows displays the new Security Center screen (see Figure A.4). This screen shows, at a glance, whether automatic updates are enabled; whether the Windows Firewall is enabled (and it should be enabled at this point, just after installing the service pack); and whether you have antivirus software that is installed, enabled, and up-to-date.

Figure A.4
The new Security Center screen summarizes your computer's hacker-repellent status.

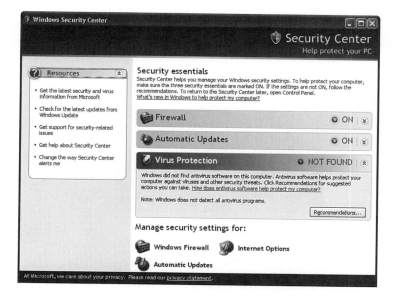

If you have antivirus software you disabled before installing the service pack, reenable it now. If the Security Center still indicates that it is disabled, your virus software needs to be updated to work with SP2. Visit the manufacturer's Web site for an update.

If you don't have antivirus software, Windows pesters you with a pop-up balloon at least once a day until you get some or until you disable the warning. We recommend that you do get a good antivirus program and that you configure it to update itself at frequent intervals—out-of-date antivirus software is as bad as none at all.

NOTE

> If you don't have antivirus software and you are absolutely sure you don't want to get it, here's how to disable the annoying daily pop-up warning: Open the Windows Security Center (get there through the Control Panel if it's not already open) and under Resources, click Change the Way Security Center Alerts Me. Uncheck Virus Protection; then click OK.
>
> If you later do install an antivirus package, be sure to re-check this box, so Windows can periodically check to ensure your antivirus package is up-to-date.
>
> If you choose to disable Windows Firewall or Automatic Updates, you will get frequent warnings about it; you can use this same technique to disable those warnings.

The service pack installation procedure is now complete. At this point, you might want to make another full backup (onto a different tape or disk file!). Also, read Appendix B for a discussion of the changes in SP2.

You might still have to deal with some issues with network software.

NETWORK AND FIREWALL ISSUES

SP2 differs from all previous Windows service packs in that it changes network security settings to very restrictive values. The new Windows Firewall is automatically enabled, for starters. You might see the effects of this immediately if you have automatic startup programs that want to receive network connections from other computers. AOL Instant Messenger and Windows Messenger are such programs. A pop-up dialog box similar to the one shown in Figure A.5 might appear.

Figure A.5
Windows Firewall might pop up a warning that a program wants to receive network connections.

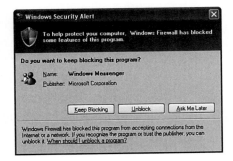

If this happens, check the name and publisher of the program *very carefully*. This kind of warning can come from legitimate software such as Windows Messenger, in which case you should click Unblock to let the program do its job. However, the warnings could also come as a result of a Trojan horse (virus) program that infected your computer prior to installing the service pack. In this case, click Keep Blocking and find out what the program is.

NOTE

> You have to be logged on as a Computer Administrator to unblock programs.

→ To learn more about Windows Firewall, **see** "Configuring Windows Firewall," **p. 681**.

For the most part, this kind of pop-up warning does not appear if a system service wants to receive network connections. If you had a service like a mail server or a Web server installed before installing SP2, these services are no longer accessible to other users on your network or the Internet. If you had a Web server or other network services installed, you must manually make entries to open the firewall so other users can reach the services.

→ To learn more about opening the firewall for network services, **see** "Making Services Available," **p. 648**.

Some services, such as Remote Assistance, automatically add themselves to the firewall list, so you should not need to make entries for these programs. Finally, many corporate enterprise applications based on DCOM or COM+ networking service for Windows might stop working after SP2 is installed due to tightened network security. If you have this sort of software, your vendor might need to update it or reconfigure your computer. Microsoft's TechNet Web site (www.microsoft.com/technet) contains extensive information on this issue. It's written for software developers and network managers rather than end users.

NOTE

> If you run into problems after installing the service pack, you might want to check this nice index of Microsoft Knowledge Base articles pertaining to SP2:
> http://bink.nu/files/sp2kbs.htm.

REMOVING SERVICE PACK 2

Should SP2 not be to your liking or if serious and irresolvable problems arise after installing it, you can easily uninstall SP2 from the Add or Remove Programs applet of the Control Panel. To remove SP2, proceed as follows:

1. Open the Add or Remove Programs applet by clicking Start, Settings, Control Panel, Add or Remove Programs.

2. Highlight the Windows XP Service Pack 2 entry and click Remove.

3. When Windows asks you to confirm that you want to remove the service pack, click Yes. Follow the remaining prompts to finish the process. You might see a dialog box displaying a list of applications you have installed since installing SP2. These applications might not function properly after the removal of SP2 and thus might require reinstallation.

REMOVING THE REMOVE OPTION

If, after testing SP2, you don't want to keep the option of uninstalling it, you can recover about 300MB of disk space by deleting the archived files.

To do this, follow these steps:

1. Log on as a Computer Administrator.

2. Open Windows Explorer. Click Tools, Folder Options and select the View tab. Under Advanced settings, be sure that Show Hidden Files and Folders is selected. If it isn't, select it. Click OK to close the dialog box.

3. Click View, Details.

4. Browse to the Windows folder, usually `C:\WINDOWS`. You should see a folder named `$NtServicePackUninstall$`. Right-click it and select Delete.

5. Open the Control Panel, and open Add or Remove Programs. Highlight Windows XP Service Pack 2 and click Remove.

   If Windows asks whether you really want to remove the service pack, click No! Bad news: The uninstall folder is still present. You might have deleted the folder from an inactive Windows folder; find and delete the correct uninstall folder before proceeding.

   You want to see the message `An error occurred while trying to remove Windows XP Service Pack 2`. Click Yes to remove the entry from the Add or Remove Programs list.

6. Empty the Recycle Bin to recover the disk space.

New Features in Service Pack 2

In this appendix

WHAT'S NEW?

Service Pack 2 (SP2) for Windows XP fixes many bugs, but most importantly, it includes significant changes to Windows networking and Internet security. The major features of SP2 include

Windows Firewall—The original Internet Connection Firewall has been replaced with a more sophisticated firewall service called Windows Firewall that provides much more fine-grained protection against hackers and viruses. On a corporate domain network, Windows Firewall can be configured with different security profiles depending on whether a computer is plugged into the network, taken into the field, or taken home. The new and improved firewall also protects your computer during XP's bootup process, which, amazingly, the old firewall didn't.

→ To learn more about the new firewall, **see** "Configuring Windows Firewall," **p. 681**.

Windows Security Center—A new control panel window displays the status of the three main lines of defense against Internet attacks: Automatic Updates, Windows Firewall, and antivirus protection. The settings and status of these three systems can be seen at a glance. Windows pops up annoying reminder balloons if your computer doesn't have an up-to-date third-party antivirus program installed.

→ To learn more about the security center, **see** "Security Center," **p. 773**.

Improved Windows Update and Automatic Updates—SP2 delivers new versions of Windows Update and the Automatic Updates system. The new systems perform more intelligent downloading of update files (for example, interrupted downloads are resumed where they left off), a boon for people with dial-up Internet connections. The intention of these changes is that no Windows computer should ever miss a critical security fix, even if the owner neglects his or her computer. Windows Update now lets you select any assortment of updates, even those that must be installed separately.

→ To learn how to configure Automatic Updates, **see** "Setting Automatic Updates," **p. 843**.

Wireless Networking enhancements—SP2 includes a replacement for the Wireless Network configuration dialogs, for people who use 802.11a, b, or g Wireless networking. The new dialogs are more streamlined. SP2 also adds support for Wireless Protection and Authentication (WPA), an advanced encryption scheme that is supplanting WEP.

→ For details on the new Wireless Networking setup dialogs, **see** "Installing a Wireless Network," **p. 501**.

Bluetooth—Service Pack 2 integrates support for Bluetooth short-range network devices like cell phones and printers, if an XP-compatible Bluetooth networking adapter is installed.

Security improvements for Internet Explorer—Microsoft has *finally* given IE a means of blocking pop-up and pop-under ads, those annoying advertising windows that appear when you visit many commercial websites. IE no longer lets websites hide the URL field a new window is opened, has improved detection of dangerous file downloads, and provides a tool to let you see and manage IE plug-ins.

→ For a description of the new Internet Explorer security features, **see** Chapter 9, "Browsing the World Wide Web with Internet Explorer."

Security improvements for Outlook Express—Again, finally, after several years of Microsoft foot-dragging, Outlook express will no longer automatically display images linked-to by HTML-formatted email. This stops it from automatically notifying spam senders that they have found a valid email address—yours. OE also has improved detection of dangerous attachments and can be set to block execution of all HTML code because it can cause harm.

→ For a description of the new Outlook Express security features, **see** Chapter 10.

Security improvements at the System level—The Windows XP system kernel and many system components have been updated to provide better protection against programs whose bugs were previously exploited by hackers to run malicious code. SP2 provides better management and protection of internal memory and includes support for "No Execute" (NX) mode. NX mode, available only on modern processors such as the AMD Opteron, lets Windows prevent programs from executing instructions out of memory that has been designated for holding data only. This may prevent some programs that use "Just-In-Time" compilation from working (Java, for instance), but closes the door on a large category of bugs that have been exploited by hackers to take control of Windows systems.

→ To see how to enable NX protection on a compatible processor, **see** "Enabling Data Execution Prevention," **p. 794**.

Security improvements for RPC and DCOM—Microsoft's RPC and DCOM (COM+) components, which form the basis of many advanced networked application programs, have undergone extensive changes to minimize vulnerabilities from Internet hacking. These changes will break many corporate software applications but, for the increased security, Microsoft believed that the tradeoff made the changes worthwhile. Some network applications will have to be updated or reconfigured to work correctly after SP2 is installed.

New Scheduled Tasks option—The Scheduled Tasks window now has an option to run a scheduled task only if a specific user is logged on. In this mode a password is not stored with the task definition.

→ To see how to set up a scheduled task, **see** "Scheduled Tasks,", **p. 836**.

Windows Messenger Version 4.7—The new version of Windows Messenger includes improved audio and video compression for better sound and picture quality, improved response to network dropouts and congestion, and several security fixes. Internally, it has enhanced hooks that should make it easier for third-party developers to create and offer enhanced function plug-ins.

→ To learn how to use Windows Messenger, **see** Chapter 12.

Windows Media Player 9 Series—SP2 installs Windows Media Player version 9, although this was superceded by version 10 immediately after SP2's release. Media Player 9 includes a

B

new mini-player mode that includes a tiny control panel in the task bar when the player is minimized, cross-fade and automatic volume adjustment tools, pitch control, and a queue-it-up feature that lets you quickly add songs to the current playlist.

→ To learn how to use the new version of Windows Media Player, **see** "Windows Media Player," **p. 245**.

Service Pack 1 updates—SP2 includes all of the bug enhancements in Service Pack 1, including USB 2.0 support, IPv6 networking support and the "Set Program Activation and Defaults" control panel applet.

Hotfixes and security updates—SP2 includes a "roll-up" of all security patches and hot fixes that have been released for Windows XP since it was sent to manufacturing in 2001. Hot Fixes are security updates and bug fixes that are important enough to be released before and between service packs. While Windows Update delivers the most critical Hot Fixes, there are hundreds of others that are announced only in the Microsoft Knowledge base and must be downloaded manually. Service Packs like SP2 deliver *all* of collected Hot Fixes. To see a list of the bug fixes included in SP2, visit www.microsoft.com/technet and search the Knowledge Base for article number 811113, "List of fixes included in Windows XP Service Pack 2." The article lists 818 items, each described in detail in another Knowledge Base article. These were just the most significant fixes; there are likely many other small changes not documented.

GETTING MORE INFORMATION

Because SP2 has so many changes that impact Windows' networking functions, Microsoft has published an extensive array of articles describing SP2's features and implications. Check out some of these links:

■ For information about how SP2 impacts you as an end-user, visit www.microsoft.com/windowsxp/sp2.

■ For technical information appropriate for IT professionals, visit www.microsoft.com/windowsxp/sp2 and follow the link "Information for IT professionals on Microsoft TechNet."

■ Software developers can find information about DCOM changes and Windows Firewall technology by visiting www.microsoft.com/windowsxp/sp2 and following the link "Information for developers on MSDN."

B

H

help resources, 245
HighMAT technology, 243
image acquisition overview, 212-213
importing from digital cameras, 234
organizing clips, 234
playing
  online video, 300-304
  Windows Media Player, 247
  Windows Movie Maker, 235
rendering, 243-244
saving, 242
sound files, adding, 234
storyboarding clips, 235-236
trimming, 237

Video Capture Wizard, 232-233

View menu (Windows Explorer), 729-730

View Network Connections (My Network Places), 539

View tab
Folder options applet, 110
Folder Options dialog box, 731

View Workgroup Computers (My Network Places), 526, 540
troubleshooting, 529-530

viewing
add-ons (Internet Explorer), 311
applications running, 867-868
blocked pop-up windows, 320
digital pictures, 219-222
faxes, 206-207
file details, 127
fonts, 758

hidden files, 207
processes running, 869-870

views
folder view, 118-119
My Computer, 126-127
Windows Explorer views, 120

virtual
desktops, 728
disks, 1005
machines, 1005-1007
memory, optimizing file size, 790-793

Virtual DOS Machine. *See* **VDM**

Virtual PC, 65

Virtual Private Networking (VPN), 475

viruses, 348-349

visual effects, adjusting for improved system performance, 733, 788

VMWare, 1006

voice chat (Messenger), 413-417
hardware requirements, 400-401
hardware setup, 414
starting conversations, 415-417
stopping conversations, 417
troubleshooting, 427-428

voice recording, setting default hardware, 777

Volume Control, 159

volume levels, adjusting, 769, 774

Volume tab (Sounds and Audio Devices), 774

volumes, 903
compressing, 916-917
converting from FAT to NTFS, 915

Disk Management utility, 906-910
expanding, 904
grafting, 908-909
property sheets, 906
snapshots, 927

VPN (Virtual Private Networking), 475, 596-597
editing properties, 599-600
incoming connections, allowing, 601-602
  with ICS, 649-652
  with sharing routers, 652-655
setting up, 597-599
starting connections, 600
TCP/IP routing, 600-601
troubleshooting, 618

vsafe command, 825

W

wallpaper, 712-713

WANs (wide area networks), 459

warchalking, 595-596

wardriving, 595-596

WC3 (World Wide Web Consortium) PICS, 323

WDM (Windows Driver Model), 51

Web
audio, 300-303
  MP3 files, 305-306
  steaming, 303-304
background printing, 323
browsers. *See also* **Internet Explorer**
  alternatives to Internet Explorer, 326
  Mosaic, 290
  MSN Explorer, 326-328
  tabbed, 320

How can we make this index more useful? Email us at indexes@quepublishing.com

informIT

LICENSE AGREEMENT

By opening this package, you are agreeing to be bound by the following agreement:

You may not copy or redistribute the entire media as a whole. Copying and redistribution of individual software programs on the media is governed by terms set by individual copyright holders.

The installer and code from the authors are copyrighted by the publisher and authors. Individual programs and other items on the media are copyrighted by their various authors or other copyright holders. Some of the programs included with this product may be governed by an Open Source license, which allows redistribution; see the license information for each product for more information.

Other programs are included on the media by special permission from their authors.

This software is provided as is without warranty of any kind, either expressed or implied, including but not limited to the implied warranties of merchantability and fitness for a particular purpose. Neither the publisher nor its dealers or distributors assume any liability for any alleged or actual damages arising from the use of this program. (Some states do not allow for the exclusion of implied warranties, so the exclusion may not apply to you.)

set email address: Open Outlook Express <tools> <accounts>
<Mail Tab> double click <bend cable, icon>

RUNNING THE CD INCLUDED WITH THIS BOOK

This CD-ROM is optimized to run under Windows 95/98/Me/NT/2000/XP using the QuickTime Player version 5 (or greater), from Apple. This CD-ROM is not designed to run on a Mac. If you don't have the QuickTime Player installed, you must install it by downloading it from the Internet at http://www.quicktime.com. It's fine to use the free version of the QuickTime player. You don't need to purchase the full version.

RUNNING THE CD IN WINDOWS

Minimum Requirements:

- QuickTime 5 Player
- Pentium II P300 (or equivalent)
- 64MB of RAM
- 8X CD-ROM
- Windows 95, Windows 98, Windows 2000, Windows Me, or Windows NT 4.0 with at least Service Pack 4
- 16-bit sound card and speakers

This presentation can run directly from the CD (see below for running it from the hard drive for better performance if necessary) and should start automatically when you insert the CD in the drive. If the program does not start automatically, your system might not be set up to automatically detect CDs. To change this, you can do the following:

1. Choose Settings, Control Panel, and click the System icon.
2. Click the Device Manager tab in the System Properties dialog box.
3. Double-click the Disk drives icon and locate your CD-ROM drive.
4. Double-click the CD-ROM drive icon and then click the Settings tab in the CD-ROM Properties dialog box. Make sure that "Auto insert notification box" is checked. This specifies that Windows will be notified when you insert a compact disc into the drive.

If you don't care about the auto-start setting for your CD-ROM, and don't mind the manual approach, you can start the lessons manually, this way:

1. Insert the CD-ROM.
2. Double-click the My Computer icon on your Windows desktop.
3. Open the CD-ROM folder.
4. Double-click the startnow.exe icon in the folder.
5. Follow instructions on the screen to start.